West's Law School
Advisory Board

JESSE H. CHOPER
Professor of Law,
University of California, Berkeley

DAVID P. CURRIE
Professor of Law, University of Chicago

YALE KAMISAR
Professor of Law, University of San Diego
Professor of Law, University of Michigan

MARY KAY KANE
Chancellor, Dean and Distinguished Professor of Law,
University of California,
Hastings College of the Law

LARRY D. KRAMER
Dean and Professor of Law, Stanford Law School

WAYNE R. LaFAVE
Professor of Law, University of Illinois

ARTHUR R. MILLER
Professor of Law, Harvard University

GRANT S. NELSON
Professor of Law,
University of California, Los Angeles

JAMES J. WHITE
Professor of Law, University of Michigan

CIVIL PROCEDURE

A MODERN APPROACH

Fourth Edition

By

Richard L. Marcus

Horace O. Coil ('57) Chair in Litigation,
University of California
Hastings College of the Law

Martin H. Redish

Louis and Harriet Ancel Professor of Law and Public Policy,
Northwestern University School of Law

Edward F. Sherman

Moise S. Steeg, Jr., Professor of Law,
Tulane Law School

AMERICAN CASEBOOK SERIES®

Mat #40301042

Thomson/West have created this publication to provide you with accurate and authoritative information concerning the subject matter covered. However, this publication was not necessarily prepared by persons licensed to practice law in a particular jurisdiction. Thomson/West are not engaged in rendering legal or other professional advice, and this publication is not a substitute for the advice of an attorney. If you require legal or other expert advice, you should seek the services of a competent attorney or other professional.

American Casebook Series and West Group are trademarks
registered in the U.S. Patent and Trademark Office.

COPYRIGHT © 1989, 1995 WEST PUBLISHING CO.
© West, a Thomson business, 2000
© 2005 Thomson/West
      610 Opperman Drive
      P.O. Box 64526
      St. Paul, MN 55164–0526
      1–800–328–9352

Printed in the United States of America

ISBN 0–314–15613–5

TEXT IS PRINTED ON 10% POST CONSUMER RECYCLED PAPER

Preface

In this new edition, we have retained the framework of the past edition, which was well-received by its users. We include new materials to reflect the ever-changing face of this subject within the existing framework of the book. For example, we include treatment of recent rule amendments and legislation affecting class actions and the emerging issues regarding discovery of electronically stored information. In order to assure that the book will continue to have a manageable length, we have condensed the focus of the personal and subject matter jurisdiction chapters. All in all, we believe that the new edition provides an entirely up-to-date and comprehensive treatment of the subject.

An enduring reality for civil procedure teachers is the fact that many students perceive this to be the most difficult and least comprehensible course in their first-year curriculum. To a considerable extent, students' difficulty stems from the fact they have not encountered these issues before even though some of these issues have begun to arise in more general political discourse. Students have usually had some personal experience with the subject matter covered in torts, contracts, and even property courses, and most have some attitudes about criminal law and constitutional law (a subject in the first-year curriculum in many law schools). Few, however, have been personally involved with the intricacies of court rules and procedures. Although issues in substantive law courses relate to "real life" situations, issues of procedure may seem to involve only technical matters that students just beginning the study of law may find difficult to appreciate. For many, developing a taste for procedure is a gradual process; the reality that it will become second nature to many when they are in practice is likely to provide cold comfort at the outset.

This book is premised on the belief that a taste for civil procedure is worth cultivating and that students will find the study of civil procedure more challenging and rewarding than they might have expected. The procedure governing a trial or other dispute resolution process provides the ultimate context for enforcing substantive rights in society, and it is a commonplace that bears repeating that procedure is often critical to the outcome of a case. The initial impression of some law students that civil procedure is a rote-like study of precise rules should give way to an appreciation that procedure, no less than substantive law, is a complex subject that defies a simplistic approach. The perpetual tension between certainty and flexibility in the law is no less important in matters of procedure, and problems of generality and ambiguity are as inconsistent in procedure as they are in substantive law. Similarly, the impression that procedure does not go to the "heart" of what the law really is needs to be tempered with the realization that procedural rules reflect fundamental value judgments and social policies. The manner in which society chooses to resolve its disputes, and its notion of what constitutes procedural fairness, bear directly on social choices about the conduct we want to encourage or discourage and on the allocation and distribution of resources.

We have chosen the subtitle "A Modern Approach" in the belief that this casebook has a focus that puts a distinctive cast on the subject of civil procedure. Recent and ongoing developments have had a significant impact on the way we resolve disputes in this country. It is not so much that the basic procedural rules and mechanisms have been materially altered as that the way they are applied in dispute resolution processes has been affected. To mention only a few of the developments and their impacts on procedure:

• New and often more complex causes of action created by courts and legislatures demand more satisfactory ways to reach a resolution of the dispute;

• New causes of action and our strong societal impulse towards resolving disputes through litigation have resulted in serious court crowding and delay;

• For a generation, the high cost of legal services has prompted experiments with ways to cut costs and time in lawsuits through resort to alternative dispute resolution methods;

• Broader standards of legal responsibility and liability have enlarged the number of parties in suits and have complicated the procedural posture;

• The class action, in particular, has emerged as a prominent vehicle for "wholesale" redress and as the object of concerns about a variety of perceived abuses;

• The influence of such disciplines as economics, social science, and psychology has resulted in a more sophisticated approach to procedural issues involving questions of allocation of resources, fundamental fairness, and analysis of competing considerations in dispute resolution.

• Technological developments increasingly offer the possibility of very different methods of presenting evidence at trials and in the form of dispute resolution that could depart markedly from the traditional Anglo-American trial format.

This book attempts to reflect the impact of these kinds of contemporary developments without losing sight of the fact that much of civil procedure still concerns traditional rules and mechanisms and time-honored policies. Modern civil procedure has fortunately not been called upon to reinvent the wheel. In order to understand the contemporary "system" of civil procedure, students must still acquire a sense of its historical development, the traditional interrelationship of procedural devices, and the proper interaction of doctrine and policy. Thus history, doctrine, and key precedents remain important parts of this casebook.

The book also proceeds on the recognition that students cannot cover or absorb all the ramifications of recent developments in a first-year course. Thus the assumption is that there will be upper division offerings in complex litigation, federal courts, alternate dispute resolution, conflicts of law, and the like to reinforce and build on the teachings of the introductory course.

The book roughly follows the chronological order of a lawsuit—proceeding from the initial complaint and pleadings to appeal and the binding effect of a judgment. The first two chapters, however, deviate from the generally-chronological order of presentation, providing an overview of the policies and features of our adversary system (Chapter I) and of the remedies available in civil litigation (Chapter II). The chapters on jurisdiction and the choice between state and federal law (the *Erie* problem) follow the chapters on trial preparation and trial in the belief that students are better able to handle the conceptual complexities of these matters once they have an appreciation of the adjudication process.

We think this book offers some distinctive approaches that are not as comprehensively treated in other civil procedure casebooks. These include:

• A continuing reexamination of the policies and mechanisms of our American adversary system, including criticisms of the system and the procedural innovations (such as sanctions and early-decision devices) that attempt to remedy the shortcomings;

• A reflection, through choice of cases and descriptive material, of the impact that the development of public law and complex litigation has had on procedure;

• Treatment, both in an introductory chapter on remedies (Chapter II) and in a separate chapter on judicial supervision of pretrial and promotion of settlement (Chapter VII) of the developing processes and techniques of alternative dispute resolution;

• Examination of the new management techniques of trial courts, including the devices (such as docket and trial-preparation trial control, discovery, and use of surrogate judicial personnel) and the strengths and weaknesses of such responses;

• Use of interdisciplinary materials reflecting practices in other countries and various states to introduce the student to alternative ways of dealing with various procedural issues.

We hope that a student will come away from this course with a sense of the process called civil procedure, with an appreciation of both its strengths and weaknesses and the range of other solutions that are possible in particular solutions. We have put some emphasis on practice materials in the belief that one must be able to work effectively with the Federal Rules of Civil Procedure and the various doctrines to claim a mastery of civil procedure. But we also try to ensure that the practice materials force the student to think about the policies underlying the practice and to relate it to the general process themes of the book.

Finally, some comments on format: We have tried to make this text accessible to students by editing out unimportant materials and by minimizing the use of asterisks to indicate those omissions. Whenever we have deleted material from a case or other source, we have indicated that omission either by a bracketed summary of the omitted material or by asterisks. Where quoted material includes deletions by the court or other primary source, there is a conventional ellipse rather than asterisks. We have not indicated the deletion of case and source citations, and have made some effort to remove unimportant citations. We have omitted footnotes from cases and source materials unless they seemed to add something of use, but have retained their original numbering for footnotes we have not deleted.

Throughout the book, we have included substantial notes and questions because we believe they shed light on the principal cases and provide important backup information and citations for those who wish to pursue a matter further. The questions we have asked fall basically into three categories: (1) questions that ask the student to ascertain the answer from the applicable rule or statute; (2) questions, often leading questions, that challenge or provide new perspectives on the assertions made in the principal cases; and (3) questions that invite reflection on the underlying process issues we have tried to raise throughout the book. We hope students will quickly learn to identify the different types of questions and to appreciate the different mental activity called for by them.

We are indebted to many people for their help and guidance during the years we have been working on this book and the previous editions. Most of all, we want to thank our families for their understanding of the demands of the project, and particularly our spouses, Caren Redish, Andrea Saltzman, and Alice Sherman, for their advice, help, and patience. We also want to thank the research assistants who have helped out on this edition: Zhuanjia Gu of Hastings, and Katina Austin, Alexander Bilus, Nathan Larsen and Vanessa Zimmer of Northwestern.

Professor Laurens Walker of the University of Virginia Law School collaborated with Professor Sherman on an early version of portions of these materials. His contributions are gratefully acknowledged.

We are also indebted to the copyright holders identified below for permission to reprint excerpts from the following copyrighted materials (listed in the order they appear in the book):

L. Fuller, The Problems of Jurisprudence (1949), copyright © 1949, by Lon Fuller, reprinted by permission of Marjorie D. Fuller.

Zeidler, Evaluation of the Adversary System: As Comparison, Some Remarks on the Investigatory System of Procedure, 55 Australian L. J. 390 (1981), copyright © 1981, by The Law Book Company Ltd.

Frankel, The Search for Truth: An Umpireal View, 123 U.Pa.L.Rev. 1031 (1975), copyright © 1975, by Marvin E. Frankel.

Marcus, The Revival of Fact Pleading Under the Federal Rules of Civil Procedure, 86 Colum.L.Rev. 433 (1986), copyright © 1986, by the Columbia Law Review Association.

W. Glaser, Pretrial Discovery and the Adversary System (1968), copyright © 1968, by the Russell Sage Foundation.

Currie, Thoughts on Directed Verdicts and Summary Judgment, 45 U.Chi.L.Rev. 72 (1977), copyright © 1977, by the University of Chicago Law Review.

Sherman, The Impact of Litigation Strategy on Integrating Alternative Dispute Resolution Into the Pretrial Process, 168 F.R.D. 75 (1996), copyright © 1996, by West Group.

Ely, The Irrepressible Myth of Erie, 87 Harv.L.Rev. 693 (1974), copyright © 1974, by the Harvard Law Review Association.

RICHARD MARCUS
MARTIN REDISH
EDWARD SHERMAN

April, 2005

*

Summary of Contents

*

Table of Contents

Table of Cases

The principal cases are in bold type. Cases cited or discussed in the text are roman type. References are to pages. Cases cited in principal cases and within other quoted materials are not included.

Table of Secondary Authorities

CIVIL PROCEDURE

A MODERN APPROACH

Fourth Edition

*

Chapter I

CHOOSING A SYSTEM
OF PROCEDURE

Law can be conveniently divided into two categories, substance and procedure. Substantive law defines legal rights and duties in everyday conduct. Thus, it is a rule of substantive law that an individual will be liable in damages for injuring another person through negligence. Procedural law sets out the rules for enforcing substantive rights in the courts. It is a rule of procedure that a complaint filed in a federal court must contain "a short and plain statement of the claim showing that the pleader is entitled to relief" (Federal Rule of Civil Procedure 8(a)). The line between substance and procedure is sometimes difficult to draw, but the basic distinction is central to the theory of procedure.

A procedural system provides the mechanism for applying substantive law rules to concrete disputes. Without rules of procedure there would be no guidelines as to what information is received by the decision-maker (that is, the judge or jury in the American system), how the information is to be presented, or what standards of proof or scope of review apply. In short, without procedure there would be no standardized method of litigation, all cases would be decided *ad hoc,* and there would be no assurance that the same kinds of information and same standards of examination would be applied in similar cases.

The kind of procedural system with which we will be principally concerned in this course operates through formal courts. It contemplates ultimate resort to a trial, even though most suits filed in the United States end short of trial through negotiated settlements or other dispositions. In recent years alternate methods of dispute resolution (such as arbitration or summary presentation of the case to neutral observers) have sometimes been appended to the litigation model as nonbinding prerequisites to the right to a full trial. Thus in a very real sense litigation today is a wide-ranging process of dispute resolution rather than simply the preparation and trial of law suits.

The American legal system falls within the family of the "common law," that process, originating in England, by which many rules of law are derived from court cases arising out of disputes between adverse

1

parties. In terms of procedure, the "common law" is often referred to as an "adversary system," with the courts providing an impartial forum for resolution of private disputes in civil cases (and of prosecutions by the state in criminal cases). The moving party (called the plaintiff) is expected to take the initiative in filing a civil suit in the proper manner, and the parties (both plaintiff and defendant) are expected to prepare their cases and present them at trial with a minimum of judicial interference.

Of course, this is not the only plausible way for a court system to operate. In the European "civil law" system, for instance, the judge plays a much more active role in litigation. Indeed, many of the generalities once made about the common law adversary system are no longer invariably true. Law suits in the United States have changed in recent years—with an expansion of substantive law doctrines permitting judicial relief in a wider range of situations and a growth of procedural mechanisms allowing complicated multi-party suits termed "complex litigation." As a result, judges often exert greater control over litigation, and some of the traditional assumptions about the adversary conduct of lawyers are increasingly being challenged as inconsistent with the need for cooperation and coordination in modern litigation.

This chapter is entitled "Choosing a System of Procedure" to emphasize that rules of procedure reflect important policy values and that one must approach procedure with some appreciation of the objectives sought to be achieved through litigation.

Most people would list "truth" and "justice" as primary objectives of a good system of dispute resolution. If the only question were one of determining objective facts (as is usually the case in scientific inquiry), then "truth" would be the appropriate standard for decision-making. But the legal process is concerned, for the most part, with the resolution of conflicts of interests between competing parties. Although scientific inquiry may also involve disputes—as when there is disagreement over opposing theories—this is a purely "cognitive conflict," and once the true facts are determined, it is in the interest of all concerned to adopt the solution supported by the facts. Determining the facts, however, is often insufficient to resolve a law suit. A law suit is ordinarily a zero-sum game because it presents competing claims to rights or assets, and a decision that favors one party necessarily disfavors the other. It thus requires a determination of how rights, assets, or losses will be apportioned, and necessitates resort to policy values which we loosely attempt to describe by the term "justice." Inquiry into the "truth," of course, is a necessary aspect of the legal process, but much of what a court does is to go beyond the facts to decide which party has a "just" claim.

Apart from assuring that the outcome is consistent with the rules of substantive law, procedure has a function in making even an unsatisfactory outcome palatable to the parties by making them feel they have had their "day in court." We must recognize that the outcome of every case will not always be consistent with abstract substantive law rules, or with the outcomes in similar cases, and that at least one party is often unhappy with the outcome. Despite a variety of procedural mechanisms designed to prevent arbitrary results, there are too many vagaries in the dispute resolution process, not the least of which is the jury trial itself, to be able to guarantee absolute consistency. Nevertheless, there is reason to believe that litigants tend to judge the justness of dispute proceedings without reference to the outcome if they deem the process itself to have been fair.[1] Thus, procedure serves to validate the integrity of the legal system as a whole by providing a remedial process that replaces much more destructive motivations like self-help and personal retribution.

If truth, justice, and fair process are all objectives of a legal system, what system of procedure is best suited to accomplishing them? It has been suggested that the manner of distributing control over the process and the decision between the decision-maker and the parties is the most significant factor in characterizing a procedural system.[2] Since procedure largely governs what information will be provided to the decision-maker, the degree of control over the selection and presentation of information given to litigants is a critical feature of any procedural system. The role of attorneys is to exercise the control that is given to the parties. Although procedural systems exist which do not involve lawyers, attorneys play a vital role in our procedural system in ensuring that each party is able to take advantage of the degree of control accorded it. These themes will resurface later as we consider whether particular procedural rules should limit or enhance the control of various participants in particular situations.

It may now be useful to consider a concrete case in an attempt to discern the policies underlying our procedural system.

BAND'S REFUSE REMOVAL, INC.
v. BOROUGH OF FAIR LAWN

Superior Court of New Jersey, Appellate Division, 1960.
62 N.J.Super. 522, 163 A.2d 465.

GOLDMANN, S.J.A.D.

Defendants Capasso appeal from a Law Division judgment declaring void *ab initio* and setting aside their garbage removal contract with the Borough of Fair Lawn; declaring illegal and void *ab initio* all payments made to them under the contract; setting aside as illegal and void *ab initio* Fair Lawn ordinance No. 688, a supplement to the borough sanitary code; and awarding $303,052.62 in favor of the borough against them.

[In February 1957, the Borough of Fair Lawn advertised for bids for collection of garbage in town. After considering bids, the borough council

---

1. Walker, Lind & Thibaut, The Relation Between Procedural and Distributive Justice, 65 Va.L.Rev. 1401, 1412–1414 (1979).

2. Thibaut & Walker, A Theory of Procedure, 66 Calif.L.Rev. 541, 548–552 (1978).

unanimously voted to award the contract to the Capassos, the lowest qualifying bidder, at a base price of $18,260 per month. The contract was signed in May, the Capassos promptly began garbage collection, and they continued to do so in a satisfactory manner through the trial and ensuing appeal.

In August 1957, the borough adopted ordinance 688, which required a permit to collect garbage and provided that only a person who held a contract with the town could be granted a permit. In effect, this meant that only the Capassos could collect garbage in Fair Lawn. Plaintiff Band's Refuse then had a contract to collect garbage from the Western Electric plant in town, so it applied for a permit. The borough denied the application pursuant to the ordinance.

On November 25, 1957, Band's Refuse filed a complaint alleging that ordinance 688 was arbitrary, discriminatory, unconstitutional, and ultra vires. It asked the court to declare it void and order the borough to renew its previous permit or issue a new one. Plaintiff sued the borough and a number of its officials, and all these defendants filed an answer alleging their action was proper since the contract had been awarded to the Capassos under proper competitive bidding as required by state statute. On motion, the Capassos themselves were allowed to intervene in the suit as defendants and filed an answer that was identical with the borough's. They also filed a counterclaim asking that the borough be restrained from issuing a permit to plaintiff during the term of their contract, restraining plaintiff from collecting garbage in the town and adjudging ordinance 688 and the contract valid.

Meanwhile, a grand jury investigation into scavenger (garbage collection) contracts in the county disclosed allegations of improprieties in the bidding for the Fair Lawn contract and led to indictments of numerous Fair Lawn officials. On May 15, 1958, plaintiff was allowed (over defendants' objections) to file an amended complaint which added a third count alleging that the Fair Lawn–Capasso contract was not the result of open competitive bidding but of "secret agreements and understandings * * * which tainted the bidding with fraud." Both the municipal defendants and the Capassos filed answers denying fraud and claiming compliance with the bidding statutes.

At the same time the complaint was amended, the case was pretried by the trial judge who later presided at trial. Although the amendment expanded the issues involved, the pretrial order limited the fraud contentions to two discrete concerns. The trial was projected to take one day. In fact, it took 21 days.

Before turning to the Capassos' objections to the conduct of the trial, the appellate court held that ordinance 688 was valid and that Band's Refuse could not challenge the legality of the bidding procedure because it had not bid and was not a resident of Fair Lawn.][a]

---

a. Bracketed material was inserted by the editors to summarize portions of the opinion that were deleted. Asterisks indi-

The Capassos next contend that the judgment must be reversed because of the manner in which the trial judge conducted the proceedings. On the very first day of the trial, June 19, 1958, counsel for these defendants moved that the judge disqualify himself because his activities before trial demonstrated that he had prejudged the issues and exhibited a plan to use the litigation as a vehicle for a broad municipal investigation. Additionally, counsel during the trial objected repeatedly to the participation in the prosecution of the action by both the trial judge and the *amicus curiae* whom he had appointed. There were also several motions for mistrial because of the allegedly prejudicial actions of the court. All of these were overruled or denied.

The Capassos charge—and it is conceded by the trial judge and plaintiff's attorney, Mr. Zimel—that the judge communicated with Mr. Zimel before the trial began and discussed with him the production of various witnesses. It is also an admitted fact that when, during the course of a telephone conversation, Mr. Zimel informed the judge of the possibility of discontinuing the third count of the complaint, the judge said that if that were done he would immediately declare the contract void.[b] When this was subsequently revealed in the course of a colloquy shortly to be mentioned, the trial judge sought to justify what he said on the ground that this was his sole means of controlling the case, since a very important issue involving the public welfare would be eliminated. We find the justification without merit. What the trial court said suggests a possible prejudging of the issues before a single word of testimony had been adduced. Indeed, it foreshadows what later became manifest—an attitude on the part of the court that a complete exploration into everything that might possibly touch upon the contract was his personal responsibility.

In discharge of his duty, as he conceived it, the trial judge addressed letters to various counsel demanding the production of certain witnesses and records, thus reflecting a prior partisan analysis and preparation of the case normally considered the exclusive function and legitimate interest of counsel representing the respective parties.

* * *

Six days before the opening of the trial—on June 13, 1958—the trial judge requested counsel to appear before him. The attorney for the Capassos could not attend because he was engaged in another trial. Nevertheless, the court proceeded to question counsel for plaintiff and the borough, requesting that they produce and subpoena certain named witnesses. As to some of these, plaintiff's attorney said that he had had no intention of calling them. It was during this court appearance that mention was made of the telephone conversation between the trial judge and Mr. Zimel, in the course of which the possibility of discontinuing the third count of the amended complaint was discussed. Mr. Zimel told the

cate deletions of material by the editors.— Eds.

b. Presumably this refers to the contract between plaintiff and Western Electric.—Eds.

court on June 13 that he had amended the complaint because the grand jury had indicted Health Officer Begyn and made a presentment. He frankly admitted, "I have no information other than was contained in the indictment and in the newspapers ... I have no further proof on that than is contained in the presentment." He went on to explain that the reason he had mentioned dropping the third count when he spoke to the judge on the phone was that "In the recent trial of Mr. Begyn, that part of the indictment which involves him with Capasso Brothers was dismissed by the Court. Since that was dismissed by the Court and there was no ruling on it by any jury or otherwise, I felt that perhaps under those circumstances I might drop the third count and proceed on the illegality of the ordinance itself, feeling now very confident, in my mind anyway, that I would be successful on that point."

After further colloquy, the trial judge proceeded to read a statement obviously prepared in advance for public presentation at the June 13 court session. He reviewed the contents of the pleadings, their filing dates, and the similarity of the positions taken by the borough and the Capassos. He observed that "the fact that the Borough appears unwilling to inquire into the validity of the contract under the present circumstances is most unusual," and then went on to refer to such obviously extra-judicial and legally inadmissible materials as the grand jury investigation, its presentment, and the indictment of two Fair Lawn officials for an offense unrelated to the litigation. "These facts," he said, "together with the newspaper accounts of fraud connected with the collection of garbage under the contract involved in this suit, makes it imperative in the public interest that the matter be investigated...." He concluded this part of his statement with the remark that the apparent neglect of the borough to undertake and adequately protect the public interest and welfare involved in the suit "borders on criminal nonfeasance."

The trial judge then proceeded to appoint an *amicus curiae,* whose duty it would be "to present evidence, subpoena witnesses, examine all witnesses, and submit to the court briefs on the law and facts."

* * *

Even a casual reading of the record, covering some 2,000 pages of printed appendix, reveals an extraordinary participation by the judge in the trial of the cause. He obviously had devoted much time in preparing for the questioning of witnesses and the offering of exhibits. This preparation on the part of the court extended to the issuance of subpoenas by the court itself and by its *amicus curiae,* and the contacting of witnesses for their appearance. The trial judge secured files and documents from the prosecutor's office and sifted them in advance, in preparation of having such of them as he deemed relevant offered as exhibits.

At the hearings the judge called witnesses on his own motion or had the *amicus* do so, and examined and cross-examined them at length. He offered exhibits he had called for. He ruled upon the propriety of his own questions and upon the admissibility of his own exhibits. On occasion he attacked the credibility of witnesses called by him.

In all, there were 32 witnesses who took the stand during the 21 trial days. Of these, the parties produced five; the trial judge, by his own subpoena, direction or arrangement, called 27. Of the latter, 24 were permitted to testify upon questioning by the court or *amicus curiae,* and this over the objection of counsel for the Capassos that their names had not been supplied in answer to interrogatories.

* * *

Defendants Capasso do not question the right of a judge to interrogate a witness in order to qualify testimony or elicit additional information, or his right under special circumstances to summon a witness on his own initiative. Generally, a court's interrogation of witnesses, where not excessive, has been sustained. As was pointed out by our Supreme Court, the power to take an active part in the trial of a case must be exercised by the judge with the greatest restraint. "There is a point at which the judge may cross that fine line that separates advocacy from impartiality. When that occurs there may be substantial prejudice to the rights of one of the litigants."

The motivation of the trial judge may be found in what he said in his opinion in justification of his appointment of *amicus curiae*; he felt that the court was "faced with a grave situation testing its ability and will to use its powers, if necessary, to prevent fraud, preserve justice, and protect the public interest." He also observed that he had the power to investigate as auxiliary to his power to decide, and "the power to investigate implies necessarily the power to summon and to question witnesses."

What is called for here is a balancing of judicial power against the interests of a litigant. On the one hand, there is the recognized power of a trial judge to call witnesses. Balanced against this power of a trial judge must be the necessity of judicial self-restraint and the maintenance of an atmosphere of impartiality. Courts must not only be impartial; they must give the appearance of impartiality.

The power of a trial judge to call and examine witnesses is not unlimited. His conduct of a trial contrary to traditional rules and concepts which have been established for the protection of private rights constitutes a denial of due process. The limitations upon the activities and remarks of a trial judge have usually been considered within the frame of reference of a jury trial. However, the necessity of judicial self-restraint is no less important where the judge sits alone; if he participates to an unreasonable degree in the conduct of the trial, even to the point of assuming the role of an advocate, what he does may be just as prejudicial to a defendant's rights as if the case were tried to a jury.
* * *

It is our conclusion that the trial judge overstepped the permissible bounds of judicial inquiry in this case. In effect, he took on the role of advocate, his activities extending from investigation and preparation to the actual presentation of testimony and exhibits at the trial. He converted the action into what amounted to a municipal investigation. Cf. Canons of Judicial Ethics, Canon 15, dealing with a judge's interference in the conduct of a trial.

We agree with defendants Capasso that the trial court committed prejudicial error by producing a large number of witnesses and admitting their testimony in evidence.

Defendants Capasso served supplemental interrogatories upon plaintiff on May 20, 1958 requesting the names and addresses of all witnesses to the facts alleged in the third count of the amended complaint. The answer [contained the names of only seven witnesses]. This answer was not supplemented or amended before trial.

The court, as noted, produced 27 witnesses on its own motion; 24 had not been named in the answer to interrogatories. Counsel for the Capassos had no advance notice of the identity of these witnesses and no opportunity to conduct adequate pretrial investigation. He made proper objection as each witness was called, but to no avail. The testimony they gave, as a reading of the trial judge's lengthy opinion and supplemental opinion will demonstrate, played an important part in the factual conclusions he reached.

Under R.R. 4:23–12 of our interrogatory rules, the penalty for failure to name a witness in answer to interrogatories is the exclusion of the testimony of that witness at the trial. * * *

It would seem anomalous to give a party protection from surprise witnesses when they are called by the opposition, but not when called by the court itself. The potential for harm is identical in either case. In addition, the testimony of the witnesses here called by the court brought entirely new issues into the case which were in no wise comprehended by the pretrial order. These issues found their way into the court's opinions and will be mentioned hereinafter.

* * *

Prejudicial error also resulted from the creation of new issues by the court—issues never mentioned or suggested in the pretrial order.

On September 10, 1958, the eleventh day of the trial and four months after the pretrial conference was held, the trial judge on his own motion, and without prior notice, stated that he was adding new issues, and this over the most strenuous objection of counsel for the Capassos. [The new issues alleged noncompliance with the bidding process required by various state statutes.]

The five added issues provided a substantial foundation for the court's conclusion that the Capasso contract was invalid. Although the trial judge in his original opinion made the bare statement that "There was no justifiable reason to allege surprise on any new issue raised during the trial," we cannot agree. The issues were injected into the case without notice or warning. There was no reason for the Capassos or their counsel to anticipate that these questions were issues to be tried until the judge, against a background of testimony he was largely responsible for adducing, brought them into the trial picture.

As in the case of the judge's other activities before and during trial, so here—he apparently considered it his duty to introduce new issues because of the public character of the case, in disregard of those which had been defined by the parties, and in disregard of the rules and precedents applicable in civil cases.

The function of a trial judge is to serve litigants by determining their disputes and the issues implicated therein in accordance with applicable rules and law. Established procedures lie at the heart of due process and are as important to the attainment of ultimate justice as the factual merits of a cause. A judge may not initiate or inspire litigation and, by the same token, he may not expand a case before him by adding new issues which come to mind during the trial, without giving the parties affected a full and fair opportunity to meet those issues.

* * *

On September 11, 1958, the twelfth day of the trial, the recently substituted counsel for the borough and its officials applied for permission to change the position theretofore taken by them, as set forth in their original answer and amended answer and as repeated on a number of occasions during the preceding trial days. Up to that moment the borough and its officials had insisted that the ordinance and the contract were valid. These defendants were now allowed to file a second amended answer alleging fraud and the invalidity of the contract, and a cross-claim seeking recovery against the Capassos of all monies paid them under the contract. This change of position was permitted over the vigorous and extended objection of the Capassos' attorney. Counsel's request for adequate time to protect the interests of his client by investigation and discovery proceedings was promptly denied.

The Capassos insist that this sudden shift came as a shock and a surprise and amounted to a substantial deprivation of their fundamental rights. They quote from Grobart v. Society for Establishing Useful Manufactures, 2 N.J. 136, 149, 65 A.2d 833 (1949), where former Chief Justice Vanderbilt said:

> "... It is not a mere matter of formal logic that leads the courts to insist that litigants shall not shift their position in *successive* pleadings.
>
> ... [S]hifting causes of action in successive pleading will completely block the purpose of all pleading, i.e., getting to an issue or issues where one party asserts the affirmative and the other the negative on a question or questions of law or of fact."

It seems inappropriate to extend the *Grobart* rule in the present case. When the original answer was filed by the borough and borough officials—and so with the amended answer to plaintiff's amended complaint—the officials apparently had the honest belief that the Capasso contract was in all respects valid. What came out in the course of the trial, mostly through witnesses and exhibits brought into the case by the court and its *amicus curiae*, must have changed their minds. It is also possible that they had a second thought in the light of the impact of the grand jury's action upon the public and the newspapers, and the impending legislative investigation into the scavenger business.

If the Capasso contract was not in fact the result of *bona fide* competitive bidding, it was important and proper from the point of view of the paramount public right and interest to allow the amended answer. However, fairness to defendants dictated that they be allowed a reasonable time for discovery and investigation, in order that the facts in support of their claim that the contract was valid might be developed and presented. They had up to that moment been dealing with a situation where the borough and its officials had stoutly affirmed the validity of the contract. The municipality had taken no steps to rescind the agreement, but had accepted scavenger service and made monthly payments thereunder even during the period of the hearings. Its position had been affirmed and reaffirmed, in its pleadings, in the pretrial order, and during the trial. Fundamental fairness required that the court allow the Capassos sufficient time to meet the radically new situation facing them. The denial of that opportunity was the denial of due process.

* * *

The judgment is reversed and the matter remanded for a full trial to determine the validity of the scavenger contract. Substituted pleadings should be filed, reasonable discovery allowed and a new pretrial conference held, in order that the exact position of the several parties will be manifest, their respective contentions clearly defined, and the issues sharply drawn. In view of the fact that the borough, mayor and council, and borough manager now challenge the validity of the Capasso contract, there would appear to be no need for the services of an *amicus curiae*. The parties can be relied upon to develop fully what are patently the issues of the case, including such questions as compliance with the bidding, appropriation and prequalification statutes, and the charges of collusion and connivance among the bidders and between the Capassos and the borough officials.

Notes and Questions

1.   This suit, filed in a New Jersey trial court, was subject to the New Jersey rules of civil procedure, rather than the Federal Rules of Civil Procedure that apply in federal courts. Today many states' rules of civil procedure are directly modelled on the Federal Rules. The New Jersey rules applicable at the time of this case had a number of significant variations from the Federal Rules, but many of the basic steps in the litigation chronology are the same. Note the various pretrial procedural steps followed in this case (with the analogous Federal Rule shown in parentheses):

—complaint filed by plaintiff Band's Refuse Removal, Inc. (Fed.R.Civ.P. 8(a));

—answer filed by defendant Borough of Fair Lawn, containing five separate defenses (Fed.R.Civ.P. 8(b)–(d));

—motion of the Capassos to intervene as defendants granted (Fed. R.Civ.P. 24);

—answer and counterclaims filed by defendants Capasso (Fed.R.Civ.P. 8, 13);

—plaintiff permitted to file an amended complaint after Grand Jury issued indictments (Fed.R.Civ.P. 15);

—discovery conducted by the parties, including interrogatories requesting identity of witnesses (cf. Fed.R.Civ.P. 26, 33);

—judge held pre-trial hearing (cf. Fed.R.Civ.P. 16, 26(f));

—judge appointed *amicus curiae* to present evidence, subpoena and examine witnesses, and submit briefs (cf. Fed.R.Civ.P. 53);

—trial held (cf. Fed.R.Civ.P. 38–52);

—judgment entered (cf. Fed.R.Civ.P. 54(a); 58);

—appeal taken (cf. Fed.R.App.P. 3; 4).

2. If the trial judge had reason to believe that the Capassos had influence over the borough, was he powerless to do anything about it? Cf. Haitian Refugee Ctr. v. Civiletti, 503 F.Supp. 442, 461 (S.D.Fla.1980) ("Federal Courts are not roving engines of justice careening about the land in search of wrongs to right.") Does his claim that the public welfare was at stake justify a more activist role? If so, how did he err in carrying out that role? Does the fact that the borough eventually switched sides show that the trial judge was right to do as he did? If it had not switched sides, what would the appellate court have done with the case?

3. *Band's Refuse* says a trial judge can call witnesses in civil cases "under limited circumstances." What are those circumstances? Consider the following views regarding the judge's questioning of witnesses: "A trial judge may not advocate on behalf of a plaintiff or a defendant, nor may he betray even a hint of favoritism toward either side. This scrupulous impartiality is not inconsistent with asking a question of a witness in an effort to make the testimony crystal clear for the jury. The trial judge need not sit on the bench like a mummy when his intervention would serve to clarify an issue for the jurors." Ross v. Black & Decker, Inc., 977 F.2d 1178, 1187 (7th Cir.1992). How could the trial judge in *Band's Refuse* have exercised that power properly?

4. In a case involving alleged pollution of Lake Superior by Reserve Mining Co., a federal appellate court assigned a new judge upon a mandamus petition alleging improper conduct and bias by District Judge Miles Lord, who had exercised jurisdiction over the case over a lengthy period. Reserve Mining Co. v. Lord, 529 F.2d 181 (8th Cir.1976). After the appellate court's affirmance of his determination that Reserve Mining Co.'s discharges posed a public health hazard and must be abated, Judge Lord called a series of hearings on the question of remedy at which he expressed the view that, in

9½ months of trial, "in every instance Reserve Mining Company hid the evidence, misrepresented, delayed and frustrated the ultimate conclusions" and called witnesses in whom he did not have "any faith." The Eighth Circuit found, *inter alia:*

> Judge Lord seems to have shed the robe of the judge and to have assumed the mantle of the advocate. The court thus becomes lawyer, witness and judge in the same proceeding, and abandons the greatest virtue of a fair and conscientious judge—impartiality.
>
> A judge best serves the administration of justice by remaining detached from the conflict between the parties.

Should Judge Lord have held his tongue even though he believed there had been a studied course of misrepresentation and bad faith by Reserve Mining Co.? Was it proper for him to raise Reserve's past misdeeds if he believed them relevant to its on-going conduct in relation to the remedial phase of the suit that was before him? If so, how could these matters have been properly raised without demonstrating partiality on the judge's part? For a lively account of the controversial career of Judge Lord, see S. Engelmayer & R. Wagman, Lord's Justice (1985).

In *Band's Refuse*, should it matter whether the judge concluded that further information was needed based on presentations by the parties in court? In general, judges are disqualified on grounds of bias only where that attitude results from an "extrajudicial source," rather than from the evidence and other proceedings in the case. Liteky v. United States, 510 U.S. 540, 114 S.Ct. 1147, 127 L.Ed.2d 474 (1994). Should the reaction of the judge to the evidence presented in the case ever require disqualification?

5.   With these issues in mind, let us reflect on whether the American adversary model is inevitable, or even desirable.

LON FULLER, THE PROBLEMS OF JURISPRUDENCE
706–07 (1949).

Adjudication involves a complex of factors that may appear in various combinations and that may be present in varying degrees. We may, however, say that the moral force of a judgment or decision will be at a maximum when the following conditions are satisfied: 1) The judge does not act on his own initiative, but on the application of one or both of the disputants. 2) The judge has no direct or indirect interest (even emotional) in the outcome of the case. 3) The judge confines his decision to the controversy before him and attempts no regulation of the parties' relations going beyond that controversy. 4) The case presented to the judge involves an existing controversy, and not merely the prospect of some future disagreement. 5) The judge decides the case solely on the basis of the evidence and arguments presented to him by the parties. 6) Each disputant is given ample opportunity to present his case.

It is seldom that all of these conditions can be realized in practice, and it is not here asserted that it is always wise to observe all of them. What is asserted is merely that adjudication as a principle of order achieves its maximum force when all of these conditions are satisfied. Some of this moral or persuasive force may wisely be sacrificed when other considerations dictate a departure from the conditions enumerated above, and where the tribunal, as an agent of legitimated power, has the capacity to compel respect for its decision.

The connection between the conditions enumerated above and the moral force of the judgment rendered is not something irrational and fortuitous. The key to it is found in the fact that men instinctively seek to surround the process of adjudication with those conditions that will tend to insure that the decision rendered is the closest possible approximation of the common need. This obviously explains the conditions of disinterestedness on the part of the judge and the opportunity for a full hearing of both sides, that is, conditions 2 and 6 in the enumeration above. Underlying the other four conditions is a single insight, namely, that men's interests and desires form a complex network, and that to discover the most effective and least disruptive pattern of order within this network requires an intimate acquaintance with the network itself and the interests and desires of which it is composed. In other words, these conditions are designed to obviate an evil that may be broadly called "absentee management." The judge must stick to the case before him (condition 3), because if he ventures beyond it he may attempt to regulate affairs on which he is inadequately informed. The judge must work within the framework of the parties' arguments and proof (condition 5), because if he goes beyond these he will lack the guidance given him by the parties and may not understand the interests that are affected by a decision rendered outside that framework. The case must involve a present controversy (condition 4), because neither the parties nor the judge can be sure that they fully understand the implications of a possible, future controversy or the precise interests that may be affected by it when it arises. The first condition (that the judge should act on the application of the parties) is perhaps the most difficult to justify. It arises from the fact that the judge who calls the parties in and himself sets the framework of the hearing lays himself open to the suspicion of planning a general regulation in which the controversy on which he hears evidence and arguments appears as a mere detail. Thus a violation of condition 1 tends to carry with it a strong suspicion that condition 3 is being violated.

W. ZEIDLER, EVALUATION OF THE ADVERSARY SYSTEM: AS COMPARISON, SOME REMARKS ON THE INVESTIGATORY SYSTEM OF PROCEDURE

55 Australian L.J. 390, 394–97 (1981).

While the English judge is an umpire sitting at the sidelines watching the lawyers fight it out and afterwards declaring one of them the winner, the German judge is the director of an improvised play, the outcome of which is not known to him at first but depends heavily on his mode of directing.

Thus to our English colleague the German judge will seem highly vocal and dominant whereas counsel will appear to act with somewhat subdued adversary zeal. * * *

It is the task of the Continental lawyers to determine through the facts which they introduce and by the applications which they make what the specific question in issue in the litigation is. The parties, therefore, do draw the perimeters of the dispute and within these the court must determine the issues raised by the parties. But most of the rest is, it is true, then up to the judge. It is he who advances the course of the proceedings and conducts the hearings at the trial. He has the duty of finding out the law including the foreign law and to some extent even the facts of the case. To allow the examination of the witnesses and experts to be placed in the hands of the attorneys has always been thought to be incompatible with the most important rule, namely that it is the chief function of a court of law to find out the truth and not merely to decide which party has adduced better evidence. * * *

As a result, the judge interrogates the witnesses and experts, while the attorneys only put supplementary questions. * * *

The German judge is not * * * limited only to consideration of the probative value of the material put forward by the parties. The judge can, for example, appoint ex officio an independent expert even if neither of the parties requested this to be done. The judge may of his own motion make an order that a view be taken of a locus quo such as the scene of a traffic accident, and he may also request public authorities to transmit documents or to furnish official information. He may also order a litigant to produce any documents to which he has referred as a means of proof and which are in his possession. In the words of Kaplan, von Mehren and Schaefer: "Always examining the case as it progresses with understanding of the probably applicable norms, the court puts questions intended to mark out areas of agreement and disagreement, to elucidate allegations and proof offers and the meaning of matters elicited in proof-takings. In this way the court enlightens itself about the issues, and at the same time broadens the understanding of counsel and the parties. The court leads the parties by suggestion to strengthen their respective positions, to improve upon, change, and amplify their allegations and proof offers and to take other steps." [See Kaplan, von Mehren and Schaefer, Phases of German Civil Procedure, 71 Harv.L.Rev. 1193, 1225 (1958)].

The leading part played by the court both in deciding on the nature of the evidence to be examined and in taking it explains why the lawyers are generally not allowed to examine the witnesses privately before this is done by the court. It is feared that this could unduly influence their testimony. * * * It is the court who asks for the witness' name, age, occupation and residence and who warns him that he must tell the truth. The witness is then invited by the judge to tell in narrative form and without undue interruption what he knows about the matter. After he has told his story it is the court which asks questions designed to test, clarify and amplify it. When the lawyers' and the parties' turn comes to formulate pertinent questions, very little use is normally made of this opportunity, at least by English standards, perhaps because extensive questioning by them might appear to be critical of the court itself.

MARVIN FRANKEL,* THE SEARCH FOR TRUTH: AN UMPIREAL VIEW

123 U.Pa.L.Rev. 1031, 1042–43 (1975).

The fact is that our system does not allow much room for effective or just intervention by the trial judge in the adversary fight about the facts. The judge views the case from a peak of Olympian ignorance. His intrusions will in too many cases result from partial or skewed insights. He may expose the secrets one side chooses to keep while never becoming aware of the other's. He runs a good chance of pursuing inspirations that better informed counsel have considered, explored, and abandoned after fuller study. He risks at a minimum the supplying of more confusion than guidance by his sporadic intrusions.

principal

The ignorance and unpreparedness of the judge are intended axioms of the system. The "facts" are to be found and asserted by the contestants. The judge is not to have investigated or explored the evidence before trial. No one is to have done it for him. The judicial counterpart in civil law countries, with the file of the investigating magistrate before him, is a deeply "alien" conception. * * * Without an investigative file, the American trial judge is a blind and blundering intruder, acting in spasms as sudden flashes of seeming light may lead or mislead him at odd times.

The ignorant and unprepared judge is, ideally, the properly bland figurehead in the adversary scheme of things. Because the parties and counsel control the gathering and presentation of evidence, we have made no fixed, routine, expected place for the judge's contributions. It is not a regular thing for the trial judge to present or meaningfully to "comment upon" the evidence. As a result, his interruptions are just that—interruptions; occasional, unexpected, sporadic, unprogrammed, and unduly dramatic because they are dissonant and out of character. The result—to focus upon the jury trial, the model for our system including, of course, its rules of evidence—is that the judge's participation, whether in the form of questions or of comments, is likely to have a disproportionate and distorting impact. The jury is likely to discern hints, a point of view, a suggested direction, even if none is intended and quite without regard to the judge's efforts to modulate and minimize his role. Whether the jury follows the seeming lead or recoils from it is not critical. The point is that there has been a deviant influence, justified neither in adversary principles nor in the rational competence of the trial judge to exert it.

* At the time he wrote this article, Mar-   Eds.
vin Frankel was a federal district judge.—

We should be candid, moreover, in recognizing that juries are probably correct most of the time if they glean a point of view from the judge's interpolations. Introspecting, I think I have usually put my penetrating questions to witnesses I thought were lying, exaggerating, or obscuring the facts. Less frequently, I have intruded to rescue a witness from questions that seemed unfairly to put the testimony in a bad light or to confuse its import. Similar things appear in the reported decisions. The trial judge who takes over cross-examination seems to be hot on the scent after truth. Even the cold page conveys notes not wholly austere or detached. This would all be agreeable for a rational system of justice if there were grounds to suppose that the judge was always, or nearly always, on the right track. But there are not such grounds. The apparatus is organized to equip the judge poorly for the position of attempted leadership. Within the confines of the adversary framework, the trial judge probably serves best as relatively passive moderator.

Notes and Questions

1. Professor Fuller speaks in rather general terms of the attributes of adjudication. Do both the American and the Continental models embody the characteristics he endorses? Has he emphasized the wrong things?

2. There are aspects of the American system that resemble the Continental approach. Zeidler points to the judge's power to appoint an independent expert as though this is thoroughly alien to the Anglo–American approach. But Rule 706 of the Federal Rules of Evidence authorizes an American federal judge to do exactly that. See also Fed.R.Civ.P. 53 (authorizing the appointment of Special Masters to conduct hearings or investigate issues).

3. Some have argued that the American approach should be revised more radically to resemble the Continental model. Professor Langbein, for example, contends that it would be possible to preserve the adversary nature of adjudication while leaving fact development to the judge. See Langbein, The German Advantage in Civil Procedure, 52 U.Chi.L.Rev. 823 (1985). Does this argument disregard important differences between the two systems? For example, in the American system much of the law is derived from previous cases, while the Continental approach, influenced by the Napoleonic Code, relies more heavily on statutes. More significantly, the American commitment to the jury trial seems incompatible with the Continental emphasis on fact development by an investigating magistrate.

It becomes more difficult to insist on a specific model when litigation involves parties from different countries. Efforts have begun to "harmonize" the procedures of different countries, at least for some cases, when the disputants are from different nations. After several years of work, the American Law Institute and the International Institute for the Unification of Private Law have produced proposed Principles and Rules of Transnational Civil Procedure (proposed final draft, March 9, 2004). By their terms, these provisions are only for commercial disputes and not for personal-injury or wrongful-death actions because they do not include jury trial. This is a tentative first effort, dependent on the decision by various countries to participate and on the parties' willingness to proceed under this procedural

predict

regime. But it may augur more extensive blending of procedures in the future.

4. The role of the judge in the American system could be modified under 28 U.S.C.A. § 1915(e)(2) (formerly § 1915(d)), which authorizes a court to refuse in forma pauperis treatment (which frees an indigent party of having to pay filing fees) to a "frivolous" action. In Gentile v. Missouri Dept. of Corrections, 986 F.2d 214, 217–19 (8th Cir.1993), however, the court rejected the idea: "Personal investigation of a case is beyond the scope of the magistrate judge's function. The fact that one of the parties is indigent within the meaning of section 1915 does not mean that the participants at trial are to perform different duties from those they would perform if the plaintiff had been able to pay his filing fee." The appellate court objected that the judge acted on the basis of a "virtually formless" hearing and "appeared to be acting as a kind of ombudsman. * * * What happened here seems more akin to a civil-law proceeding, in which the judge takes the initiative to determine the truth. This inquisitorial method may have something to commend it, but it is not our system." Cf. Cobell v. Norton, 334 F.3d 1128 (D.C.Cir.2003) (criticizing the district court's appointment of a "monitor" who "was charged with an investigative quasi-inquisitorial, quasi-prosecutorial role that is unknown to our adversarial legal system").

5. What impact would shifting toward the Continental model have on the parties' willingness to accept the outcome? Would litigants be reluctant to turn over factual investigation to judges? How would plaintiffs suing the government be likely to view such a process?

6. The emergence in the last several decades of what has been termed "public law litigation"—such as school desegregation, employment discrimination, antitrust, securities fraud, corporate reorganizations, union governance, consumer fraud, and environmental management—has prompted some rethinking about the traditional passive view of a judge's role. These cases usually involve multiple parties, a sprawling and amorphous structure, the need for discovery of large amounts of information, lengthy pre-trial preparation, and complex forms of relief. In this context, Professor Abram Chayes argued, the judge becomes "the dominant figure in organizing and guiding" the case, drawing "for support not only on the parties and their counsel, but on a wide range of outsiders—masters, experts, and oversight personnel." The judge must act as "the creator and manager of complex forms of ongoing relief, which have widespread effects on persons not before the court and require the judge's continuing involvement in administration and implementation." Chayes, The Role of the Judge in Public Law Litigation, 89 Harv.L.Rev. 1281, 1284 (1976). Would the suit in *Band's Refuse* be considered a public law case, given the municipality's and public's interest in it? Was the judge's conduct there nevertheless inappropriate?

7. The traditional passive view of the judge's role has also been altered by expanded use of pretrial conferences pursuant to amendments to the Federal Rules. Fed.R.Civ.P. 16 now provides for two kinds of pretrial conferences—"scheduling and planning" and "final." A judge must hold a "scheduling and planning" conference, or at least enter a "scheduling order," within 120 days after the complaint is served. A "final" conference should be held "as close to the time of trial as reasonable" and result in a

pretrial order that "control[s] the subsequent course of the action." Some see a shift in the role of judges: "Judges began to see themselves less as neutral adjudicators—deciding what the parties brought to them for decision and proceeding at a pace to be determined by the parties—and more as managers of a costly and complicated process." Shapiro, Federal Rule 16: A Look at the Theory and Practice of Rulemaking, 137 U.Pa.L.Rev. 1969, 1983 (1989); see also Marcus, Reining in the American Lawyer: The New Role of American Judges, 27 Hast. Int'l & Compar. L. Rev. 3 (2003).

Consider the comments of Judge William Schwarzer, a federal district judge in California, that "to be effective, judges must roll up their sleeves, dig into the case and work diligently and patiently with the lawyers." He sees the judge's role as a facilitator "to strip the case to its essentials, and focus the lawyers' attention and effort on the issues on which the decision should turn, thereby increasing the effectiveness of advocacy and enhancing the working of the adversary process." W. Schwarzer, Managing Antitrust and Other Complex Litigation: A Handbook for Lawyers and Judges 9, 12 (1982).

Judicial management has been criticized as making judges meddling, bureaucratic administrators who lose their basic sense of judging. See Resnik, Managerial Judges, 96 Harv.L.Rev. 374, 445 (1982) ("Seduced by controlled calendars, disposition statistics, and other trappings of the efficiency era and the high-tech age, managerial judges are changing the nature of their work.") But the case management movement has nevertheless spread to other common law countries, and England has shifted toward similar techniques pursuant to the reforms sparked by Lord Woolf. See Marcus, "Deja Vu All Over Again"? An American Reaction to the Woolf Report, in Reform of Civil Procedure 219 (A. Zuckerman & R. Cranston, eds. 1995).

KOTHE v. SMITH

United States Court of Appeals, Second Circuit, 1985.
771 F.2d 667.

Before LUMBARD, VAN GRAAFEILAND and PIERCE, CIRCUIT JUDGES.

VAN GRAAFEILAND, CIRCUIT JUDGE:

Dr. James Smith appeals from a judgment of the United States District Court for the Southern District of New York (Sweet, J.), which directed him to pay $1,000 to plaintiff-appellee's attorney, $1,000 to plaintiff-appellee's medical witness, and $480 to the Clerk of the Court. For the reasons hereinafter discussed, we direct the judgment be vacated.

Patricia Kothe brought this suit for medical malpractice against four defendants, Dr. Smith, Dr. Andrew Kerr, Dr. Kerr's professional corporation, and Doctors Hospital, seeking $2 million in damages. She discontinued her action against the hospital four months prior to trial. She discontinued against Dr. Kerr and his corporation on the opening day of the trial.

Three weeks prior thereto, Judge Sweet held a pretrial conference, during which he directed counsel for the parties to conduct settlement negotiations. Although it is not clear from the record, it appears that Judge Sweet recommended that the case be settled for between $20,000 and $30,000. He also warned the parties that, if they settled for a comparable figure after trial had begun, he would impose sanctions against the dilatory party. Smith, whose defense has been conducted throughout this litigation by his malpractice insurer, offered $5,000 on the day before trial, but it was rejected.

Although Kothe's attorney had indicated to Judge Sweet that his client would settle for $20,000, he had requested that the figure not be disclosed to Smith. Kothe's counsel conceded at oral argument that the lowest pretrial settlement demand communicated to Smith was $50,000. Nevertheless, when the case was settled for $20,000 after one day of trial, the district court proceeded to penalize Smith alone. In imposing the penalty, the court stated that it was "determined to get the attention of the carrier" and that "the carriers are going to have to wake up when a judge tells them that they want to settle a case and they don't want to settle it." Under the circumstances of this case, we believe that the district court's imposition of a penalty against Smith was an abuse of the sanction power given it by Fed.R.Civ.P. 16(f).

Although the law favors the voluntary settlement of civil suits, it does not sanction efforts by trial judges to effect settlements through coercion. Del Rio v. Northern Blower Co., 574 F.2d 23, 26 (1st Cir.1978) (citing Wolff v. Laverne, Inc., 17 A.D.2d 213, 233 N.Y.S.2d 555 (1962)). In the *Wolff* case, cited with approval in *Del Rio,* supra, the Court said:

> We view with disfavor all pressure tactics whether directly or obliquely, to coerce settlement by litigants and their counsel. Failure to concur in what the Justice presiding may consider an adequate settlement should not result in an imposition upon a litigant or his counsel, who reject it, of any retributive sanction not specifically authorized by law.

In short, pressure tactics to coerce settlement simply are not permissible. "The judge must not compel agreement by arbitrary use of his power and the attorney must not meekly submit to a judge's suggestion, though it be strongly urged." Brooks v. Great Atlantic & Pacific Tea Co., 92 F.2d 794, 796 (9th Cir.1937).

Rule 16 of the Fed.R.Civ.P. was not designed as a means for clubbing the parties—or one of them—into an involuntary compromise. Although subsection (c)([9]) of Rule 16, added in the 1983 amendments of the Rule, was designed to encourage pretrial settlement discussion, it was not its purpose to "impose settlement negotiations on unwilling litigants." See Advisory Committee Note, 1983, 97 F.R.D. 205, 210.

We find the coercion in the instant case especially troublesome because the district court imposed sanctions on Smith alone. Offers to settle a claim are not made in a vacuum. They are part of a more complex process which includes "conferences, informal discussions, offers, countermands, more discussions, more haggling, and finally, in the great majority of cases, a compromise." J. & D. Sindell, Let's Talk Settlement 300 (1963). In other words, the process of settlement is a two-way street and a defendant should not be expected to bid against himself. In the instant case, Smith never received a demand of less than $50,000. Having received no indication from Kothe that an offer somewhere in the vicinity of $20,000 would at least be given careful consideration, Smith should not have been required to make an offer in this amount simply because the court wanted him to.

Smith's attorney should not be condemned for changing his evaluation of the case after listening to Kothe's testimony during the first day of the trial. As every experienced trial lawyer knows, the personalities of the parties and their witnesses play an important role in litigation. It is one thing to have a valid claim; it is quite another to convince a jury of this fact. It is not at all unusual, therefore, for a defendant to change his perception of a case based on the plaintiff's performance on the witness stand. We see nothing about that occurrence in the instant case that warranted the imposition of sanctions against the defendant alone.

Although we commend Judge Sweet for his efforts to encourage settlement negotiations, his excessive zeal leaves us no recourse but to remand the matter with instructions to vacate the judgment.

Notes and Questions

1. If the plaintiff's offer to settle for $20,000 had been communicated to the defendant, would sanctions still not have been appropriate? Given the court's comment that an attorney should not be condemned for changing her evaluation of the case after hearing the evidence, would it ever be fair to impose sanctions on one who thought that the case was stronger than it actually appeared at trial? Does the court's comment that the law does not support efforts "to effect settlements through coercion" mean that a judge can never sanction a party for refusal to settle? A district judge with a large number of asbestos personal injury cases set a time limit for settling cases set for trial, and the appellate court held that this was permissible under Rule 16: "[I]mposing sanctions for unjustified failure to comply with the court's schedule for settlement is entirely consistent with the spirit of Rule 16. The purpose of Rule 16 is to maximize the efficiency of the court system by insisting that attorneys and clients cooperate with the court and abandon practices which unreasonably interfere with the expeditious management of cases." Newton v. A.C. & S., 918 F.2d 1121 (3d Cir.1990).

2. Note that the judge in *Kothe* ordered the parties to conduct settlement negotiations, and that Rule 16 authorizes settlement conferences with the judge. For some time, there was a debate about whether Rule 16 permitted judges to require parties represented by counsel to attend settlement conferences. (This is discussed fully in G. Heileman Brewing Co. v. Joseph Oat Corp., infra p. 470.) In 1993 this rule was amended to permit the judge to "require that a party or its representative be present or reasonably available by telephone in order to consider possible settlement of the dispute." How should judges use this authority? Consider In re Stone, 986 F.2d 898 (5th Cir.1993), which held that a district judge should not have

required the federal government to send a representative with "full settlement authority" since some cases could only be settled by action of officials in Washington. Noting the "unique position" of the government, the appellate court insisted that the judge consider "less drastic steps" such as requiring availability by telephone. However, a decision by the same circuit, In re United States, 149 F.3d 332 (5th Cir.1998), found the trial court had not abused its discretion in ordering the government to send a person with full settlement authority to a mediation. A concurring opinion distinguished *Stone* on the ground that this was an exceptional case rather than routine litigation, and that the government had agreed to the court-ordered mediation.

In Nueces County v. De Penn, 953 S.W.2d 835 (Tex.App.1997), the appellate court found that the county executive did not have to attend under an order requiring the attendance of the person with settlement authority because he could only settle with the concurrence of the commissioner's court. Should all the members of the commissioner's court be required to attend? Is there any alternative to this unmanageable situation? Compare United States v. City of Garland, 124 F.Supp.2d 442 (N.D.Tex.2000) (mayor and city council member could be required to attend mediation session).

An additional complicating factor is the role of insurance companies in settlement. In *Kothe* the judge said he wanted to "get the attention" of insurance companies. Should the judge be allowed to compel their attendance? The reality is that insurers may play a critical role in controlling settlements. See Syverud, The Duty to Settle, 76 Va.L.Rev. 1113, 1115–17 (1990). Nevertheless, there is doubt about whether courts can require their participation in settlement conferences. Compare In re Novak, 932 F.2d 1397 (11th Cir.1991) (court may not compel attendance by representative of insurer) with Lockhart v. Patel, 115 F.R.D. 44 (E.D.Ky.1987) (court sanctioned defendant because his insurer did not send representative with authority to settle rather than "some flunky who has no authority to negotiate").

3. If a judge can require parties and counsel to attend a settlement conference, what can they be required to do there? In G. Heileman Brewing Co. v. Joseph Oat Corp., 871 F.2d 648 (7th Cir.1989) (reproduced in full, infra p. 470), the court upheld the power of a district court to order a corporate party represented by counsel to send a "corporate representative with authority to settle" to a settlement conference. The court found that this did not require attendance by a person "willing to settle on someone else's terms," but only a person with authority to speak definitively and to commit the corporation in the litigation. What does "authority to settle" mean? If the defendant's representative only has authority to settle the case for $100 "nuisance value," does that satisfy the court's requirement of coming with authority to settle? Does it suffice if the representative has been instructed "not to pay one cent" because the company believes the suit is without merit? Court orders to mediate sometimes require that the parties "participate in good faith." Is it possible to have a "good faith participation" standard that does not improperly interfere with the parties' right not to yield or settle? For discussion, see Sherman, Court–Mandated Alternative Dispute Resolution, 46 S.M.U.L.Rev. 2079, 2089–94 (1993).

In Shedden v. Wal–Mart Stores, Inc., 196 F.R.D. 484 (E.D. Mich. 2000), Wal–Mart sent one of its store managers to the final pretrial settlement conference, but the store manager reiterated Wal–Mart's policy that it would not settle suits brought by customers. According to Wal–Mart, there was accordingly nothing more to say. The judge reacted as follows (id. at 486):

> Because Wal–Mart's asserted "no settlement" litigation policy will require the Court to expend substantial judicial time and resources in a trial which might have been avoided if Wal–Mart had been willing to engage in meaningful settlement negotiations, the Court finds that it would be just to require the attendance at trial of Wal–Mart's general counsel or some other Wal–Mart corporate officer with litigation policy authority.

> The Court recognizes that a party has the right to refuse to offer any money for settlement in a given case and the court cannot require a party to make a monetary settlement offer in any given case. (Indeed, one might find it refreshing for a party to take a "principled stand" against settlement in a given case.) However, in the Court's view, an across-the-board policy of refusing to negotiate frustrates both the letter and spirit of both the Federal Rules of Civil Procedure and this Court's Local Rules, which encourage good faith settlement efforts in order to preserve scarce judicial resources. Here, the Court is, in fact, not even requiring Wal–Mart to engage in settlement negotiations. It is simply requiring Wal–Mart's General Counsel, or other responsible corporate officer, to be present for trial, as the Court believes that requiring the attendance of such a Wal–Mart official during trial could have a salutary effect in that the responsible officer would have an opportunity to observe first-hand the effect of the company's policy both on the Court in general and in a particular case. Certainly, if this policy is important enough for Wal–Mart to persist in, then it is not asking too much for a responsible corporate officer to be present for trial.

4. Whatever the judicial role, the reality is that most lawsuits are settled, not tried. In different jurisdictions, the rate of trial varies, but it is everywhere a small and declining percentage of civil filings. See Galanter, The Vanishing Trial: An Examination of Trials and Related Matters in State and Federal Courts, 1 J. Empir. Legal Stud. 439 (2004) (finding a large decline in trials between 1962 and 2002); compare Hadfield, Where Have All the Trials Gone?, 1 J. Empir. Legal Stud. 705 (2004) (suggesting that the decline has not been so large). Indeed, most grievances in our society never enter the litigation system at all. A survey of 5,000 households showed that in only 71.8% of grievances was there an informal complaint to the allegedly offending party, that a dispute arose in only 45% of these situations, and that only 5% of these disputes resulted in the filing of a lawsuit. Id. at 86. (See further discussion infra p. 108.) Trubek, Sarat, Felsteiner, Kritzer & Grossman, The Costs of Ordinary Litigation, 31 U.C.L.A.L. Rev. 72, 87 (1983). Do these figures argue in favor of promoting settlement of suits that would not settle without such pressure?

5. How should an American judge approach the question of settlement amount? One possibility is to try to find an amount both parties will accept. In *Kothe,* for example, the judge seems to have selected a figure this way.

Should the judge instead try to identify a figure that is "right"? What would make a figure "right"? Would a Continental judge who is more familiar with the evidence be in a better position to identify such a figure? Would that approach be more likely to prompt parties to settle cases? Alternatively, should a judge avoid giving any indication of the amount of settlement he considers fair?

At least in some cases, American judges do become deeply involved. For example, consider the much-celebrated settlement achieved by District Judge Weinstein in the Agent Orange class action brought against several chemical companies on behalf of Vietnam veterans who were exposed to the herbicide in Southeast Asia and claimed that it caused a variety of illnesses, including cancer. See P. Schuck, Agent Orange on Trial: Mass Toxic Disasters in the Courts (1986). Throughout the pretrial preparation of the case after he took it over from Judge Pratt, Judge Weinstein involved himself intensely in the details of the dispute about whether Agent Orange actually caused the types of harms plaintiffs claimed. Throughout, he also pressed for a settlement.

Over the weekend before trial was to begin, the lawyers for both sides were directed to report to the courthouse for around-the-clock settlement negotiations supervised by David Shapiro, an experienced lawyer whom the judge had appointed as a special settlement master (see Rule 53). Shapiro concluded at one point that the defendants would be willing to agree to plaintiffs' pending demand of $200 million. Believing he had a deal, he reported to the judge and received a rude shock: The judge refused to allow a settlement that high because he felt the veterans' case was extremely shaky and that he had an obligation to the legal system not to encourage groundless mass toxic tort litigation by allowing a settlement that would signal that the case was stronger than it actually was. When later informed of this, one of the lawyers for defendant Dow Chemical Co. said that the judge was "too much of an idealist." In any event, eventually a settlement at the judge's preferred figure of $180 million was reached at three o'clock on the morning that trial was to begin.

How does Judge Weinstein's role in Agent Orange compare with the behavior of the judges in *Band's Refuse* and *Kothe*? Consider Marcus, Apocalypse Now? (Book Review), 85 Mich.L.Rev. 1267, 1293–94 (1987):

> Is this judging? It is far from the classical view of the judge as an inactive figure who decides according to announced rules of law. Yet that vision has long since given way to a more flexible view of the judicial function, and promoting settlement is now an accepted part of the picture. It is surely troubling to picture judges as unprincipled settlement promoters who only care about achieving settlement, and not about the terms, particularly when they are armed with the variety of persuasive tools Judge Weinstein employed in the Agent Orange litigation. Better, perhaps, that they should be idealists whose settlement posture is informed by a vision of what is right. Indeed, that may make them superior in the settlement arena as well.

> The Agent Orange case illustrates this point. A primary impediment to settlement, from defendants' perspective, was allocation of any global settlement figure among defendants. Despite long efforts to resolve the problem among themselves, defendants failed. The defendants' solution?

"Let's let the judge do it; he's fair." And so Judge Weinstein devised a formula that "brought squeals of pain and shrieks of delight from the [defendants'] lawyers," but which even the unhappy accepted. Similarly, when the ability of one of the small defendants to pay threatened to derail the settlement later, the judge was again recruited to decide the issue. In each instance, "the settlement hinged on the lawyers' perception that Weinstein was scrupulously fair and their willingness to be guided by his decision when internal negotiations reached an impasse." An unscrupulous pursuer of a deal, any deal, would probably not be able to perform this function.

But is this judging? What standards did Judge Weinstein use in fashioning the critical allocation formula? Were they "legal"? In a sense, these episodes suggest a model of judging that depends more on the personality of the judge than on his position in the institutional hierarchy. Judge Weinstein could do it but Judge Pratt [who had presided over the case earlier in the litigation], perhaps, could not. It is nice to have charismatic judges, but this is hardly a trend to be embraced; as Max Weber observed long ago, in a complex society it is necessary to shift authority from a charismatic to an institutionalized leadership. Of all governmental officials, this should be most true of judges, and our system therefore resolutely opposes judge shopping while permitting forum shopping. Although *Agent Orange* thus affords an intriguing glimpse into the Brave New World of judging, the judge's resolution of defendants' internal disputes is institutionally troubling.

The judge's settlement figure, however, is more problematical. At least the defense lawyers submitted their internal disputes to the judge for his disposition with their eyes open. The [plaintiffs' lawyers] did not, so far as we are told. To the contrary, after he failed to persuade the judge to press for a $200 million settlement Special Master Shapiro told the [plaintiffs' lawyers] that "they would never get the *defendants* to go above $180 million" even though he had by then concluded that defendants could easily be convinced to pay more. No doubt the [plaintiffs'] lawyers did not, like Dow's lawyer, call the judge an "idealist" when they found out what really happened.

6.   Is the kind of intervention performed by Judge Weinstein an appropriate role for a judge in the American system? In any system? In Against Settlement, 93 Yale L.J. 1073 (1984), Professor Owen Fiss argues that "[t]o be against settlement is only to suggest that when the parties settle, society gets less than what appears, and for a price it does not know it is paying. Parties might settle while leaving justice undone." He explains:

I do not believe that settlement as a generic practice is preferable to judgment or should be institutionalized on a wholesale and indiscriminate basis. It should be treated instead as a highly problematic technique for streamlining dockets. Settlement is for me the civil analogue of plea bargaining. * * * Like plea bargaining, settlement is a capitulation to the conditions of a mass society and should be neither encouraged nor praised.

How persuasive are these arguments? So long as settlements accurately reflect forecasts about likely outcomes at trial, why should they not be favored and promoted by judges? Cf. McCoy & Mirra, Plea Bargaining as Due Process in Determining Guilt, 32 Stan.L.Rev. 887, 921–22 (1980) (arguing that the only due process concern with plea bargaining is that the innocent will plead guilty). Is justice advanced by judicial promotion of settlements?

7. We will return to issues raised by increasing enthusiasm for settlement at the end of Chapter II and in Chapter VII. Since settlement is the outcome of more litigated cases than judicial resolution, you should have the question of the relation between formal litigation and settlement in the back of your mind throughout the course.

PROCEDURAL COMPLICATIONS OF OUR FEDERAL SYSTEM

In the chapters that follow, we will focus on adjudication in the federal courts, deferring until later detailed consideration of the complications that can arise because this is a large country with many state court systems and a somewhat parallel federal court system. For background purposes, however, it is helpful to describe in a general fashion the rules that govern these problems.

Subject matter jurisdiction: One of the cases we have read in this chapter was decided in state court and the other was decided in federal court. Federal courts are courts of "limited jurisdiction" because they can decide only certain types of claims. In civil cases, there are basically two situations in which federal courts have such jurisdiction. First, there are cases in which there is a *federal question* (see 28 U.S.C.A. § 1331), which usually means that the plaintiff is asserting a claim created by federal law. Examples include claims for violation of civil rights, the federal antitrust laws, or federal rules against securities fraud. Second, federal courts have jurisdiction of cases in which all plaintiffs come from different states than the defendants, and *diversity of citizenship* therefore exists (see 28 U.S.C.A. § 1332). In Kothe v. Smith, for example, the ground for jurisdiction in federal court was diversity of citizenship because the malpractice action did not involve any federal question. Where a case cannot be brought in federal court, there will be a state court of "general jurisdiction" in which it can be brought, as was done in Band's Refuse v. Borough of Fair Lawn. We examine the rules governing these problems in Chapter X.

Personal jurisdiction: Defending a lawsuit is a burdensome undertaking. It can become much more burdensome if the suit is filed in a court a great distance from the defendant's residence. Accordingly, entirely separate from the question of subject matter jurisdiction is the question whether the defendant can be compelled to travel to the geographical location chosen by the plaintiff for the suit. The limitations on plaintiff's power to make defendant travel a great distance to defend the suit usually apply whether the case is in federal court or state court. The Supreme Court has held that the due process clause of the Constitution forbids assertion of personal jurisdiction unless the defendant has voluntarily established a contact with the state in which the court sits so that it is fair to require a defense there. We explore these problems in Chapter IX.

Federal v. state law: When cases like Kothe v. Smith are in federal court on grounds of diversity of citizenship, the judge must usually look to state law to decide them because they do not involve federal claims. Thus, you will find that in many of the cases that are covered in the coming chapters federal judges will be applying state substantive law to determine whether plaintiff has a valid claim against defendant. In general terms, federal judges in such cases are to apply state substantive law, but they should also apply federal procedural law. Thus, you will find that in such cases the federal judges apply the Federal Rules of Civil Procedure. We will examine the complexities of this subject (often called the *Erie* problem after a famous case) in Chapter XI.

Chapter II

THE REWARDS AND COSTS OF LITIGATION—OF REMEDIES AND RELATED MATTERS

Before they file lawsuits, people should stop and think about what they can obtain from the courts in order to decide whether litigation is worth the trouble. The relief that a court could grant may not be sufficient to warrant the investment involved in getting it; in any event, some other method may be a better way of seeking redress. Litigation is society's preferred substitute for private self-help; for that purpose the remedies it offers (using the assistance of the government) need to be sufficiently attractive to induce citizens to forgo other (possibly even more primitive) means.

The law of remedies exists uneasily in the area between "substantive" rules and "procedural" rules. Our interest in beginning with consideration of remedies is to explore the interaction between substance and procedure with a view to developing a thesis about when (and how) a court should mete out judicial relief. In your other courses (particularly torts and contracts, and later remedies) you should be able to explore remedial issues in more detail.

A. PREJUDGMENT SEIZURE

A party cannot expect, of course, to obtain the relief it seeks until the case is tried on the merits. However, there are a number of procedural devices which permit some form of interim relief before the case goes to trial. Their purpose is generally to preserve the status quo so that any relief obtained after a trial is really meaningful. Temporary restraining orders and preliminary injunctions (which we will consider in connection with Carey v. Piphus, infra p. 68) particularly serve this purpose by allowing the court to order the parties to do certain acts (or refrain from certain acts) that would change the status quo. Prejudgment seizure of the defendant's property is a means of ensuring that property will be available for execution in case the plaintiff prevails. We consider this device here to examine some considerations that infuse the subject of remedies, and to reflect further on the policies underlying procedure.

At common law, plaintiff usually had to wait until the end of the case to get judicial relief, although sometimes it was possible to have property of the defendant seized before trial to coerce the defendant to appear at the trial. In Chapter IX, we will examine the continuing validity of this method of securing jurisdiction over a defendant. See Shaffer v. Heitner, infra p. 791.

Over time, pretrial seizure of defendant's property came to serve another function—assuring plaintiff that there would be sufficient assets available to satisfy any judgment that might later be entered. This device could be especially important where the dispute was about possession of the very property that was seized at the beginning of the lawsuit. All states developed statutory procedures for some prejudgment seizure of assets under a variety of names—replevin, garnishment, attachment and sequestration. Although there were differences between states and among different types of prejudgment relief, there were many common features. Ordinarily the remedy was available only for certain kinds of claims, most often commercial obligations or claims to certain specific property. But once plaintiff asserted a claim of the correct type, it could easily have the sheriff or a similar officer seize the property either physically, or symbolically by serving an order on the custodian directing certain disposition of the property.

For our purposes, the principal concern is the procedure that attends use of these prejudgment remedies. Initially, these procedures were extremely casual. Arguably as a result, there were abuses. As one Congressman put it with regard to garnishment of wages: "What we know from our study of this problem is that in a vast number of cases the debt is a fraudulent one, saddled on a poor ignorant person who is trapped in an easy credit nightmare, in which he is charged double for something he could not pay for even if the proper price was called for, and then hounded into giving up his pound of flesh, and being fired besides." Remarks of Rep. Sullivan, Chairman of House Subcommittee on Consumer Affairs, 114 Cong.Rec. 1832. These preliminary remedies could, therefore, become the only remedies.

In Sniadach v. Family Finance Corp., 395 U.S. 337, 89 S.Ct. 1820, 23 L.Ed.2d 349 (1969), the Court held that the due process clause of the 14th Amendment* requires some procedural protections in connection with such remedies. In that case, a lender sued claiming that defendant had failed to pay $420 she owed on a promissory note and, without notice to her, obtained an order of garnishment directed at her employer. Under the order, the employer retained half of defendant's salary for disposition after trial according to the outcome, and paid her only the other half. Evidently there was no way for defendant to release the

---

* "[N]or shall any State deprive any person of life, liberty, or property, without due process of law * * *."

garnishment until the end of the trial. Stressing the "tremendous hardship" that seizure of this "special type of property" presented, the Court held that the state attachment law was unconstitutional for failure to provide notice and an opportunity to be heard before garnishment was issued.

The following cases try to work out the due process requirements for such immediate remedies. As you analyze their holdings reflect on the considerations identified in Chapter I. If due process sets an absolute minimum for procedure, is it being sensibly applied?

FUENTES v. SHEVIN

Supreme Court of the United States, 1972.
407 U.S. 67, 92 S.Ct. 1983, 32 L.Ed.2d 556.

JUSTICE STEWART delivered the opinion of the Court.

We here review the decisions of two three-judge federal District Courts* that upheld the constitutionality of Florida and Pennsylvania laws authorizing the summary seizure of goods or chattels in a person's possession under a writ of replevin. Both statutes provide for the issuance of writs ordering state agents to seize a person's possessions, simply upon the ex parte application of any other person who claims a right to them and posts a security bond. Neither statute provides for notice to be given to the possessor of the property, and neither statute gives the possessor an opportunity to challenge the seizure at any kind of prior hearing. The question is whether these statutory procedures violate the Fourteenth Amendment's guarantee that no State shall deprive any person of property without due process of law.

I

The appellant in No. 5039, Margarita Fuentes, is a resident of Florida. She purchased a gas stove and service policy from the Firestone Tire and Rubber Co. (Firestone) under a conditional sales contract calling for monthly payments over a period of time. A few months later, she purchased a stereophonic phonograph from the same company under the same sort of contract. The total cost of the stove and stereo was about $500, plus an additional financing charge of over $100. Under the contracts, Firestone retained title to the merchandise, but Mrs. Fuentes was entitled to possession unless and until she should default on her installment payments.

For more than a year, Mrs. Fuentes made her installment payments. But then, with only about $200 remaining to be paid, a dispute developed between her and Firestone over the servicing of the stove. Firestone instituted an action in a small-claims court for repossession of both the stove and the stereo, claiming that Mrs. Fuentes had refused to

---

* A three-judge federal court was a special device used in cases involving constitutional challenges to state statutes. For a variety of reasons the practice was largely abandoned in 1976.—Eds.

make her remaining payments. Simultaneously with the filing of that action and before Mrs. Fuentes had even received a summons to answer its complaint, Firestone obtained a writ of replevin ordering a sheriff to seize the disputed goods at once.

In conformance with Florida procedure, Firestone had only to fill in the blanks on the appropriate form documents and submit them to the clerk of the small-claims court. The clerk signed and stamped the documents and issued a writ of replevin. Later the same day, a local deputy sheriff and an agent of Firestone went to Mrs. Fuentes' home and seized the stove and stereo.

Shortly thereafter, Mrs. Fuentes instituted the present action in a federal district court, challenging the constitutionality of the Florida prejudgment replevin procedures under the Due Process Clause of the Fourteenth Amendment. She sought declaratory and injunctive relief against continued enforcement of the procedural provisions of the state statutes that authorize prejudgment replevin.

The appellants in No. 5138 filed a very similar action in a federal district court in Pennsylvania, challenging the constitutionality of that State's prejudgment replevin process. Like Mrs. Fuentes, they had had possessions seized under writs of replevin. Three of the appellants had purchased personal property—a bed, a table, and other household goods—under installment sales contracts like the one signed by Mrs. Fuentes; and the sellers of the property had obtained and executed summary writs of replevin, claiming that the appellants had fallen behind in their installment payments. The experience of the fourth appellant, Rosa Washington, had been more bizarre. She had been divorced from a local deputy sheriff and was engaged in a dispute with him over the custody of their son. Her former husband, being familiar with the routine forms used in the replevin process, had obtained a writ that ordered the seizure of the boy's clothes, furniture, and toys.[4]

In both No. 5039 and No. 5138, three-judge District Courts were convened to consider the appellants' challenges to the constitutional validity of the Florida and Pennsylvania statutes. The courts in both cases upheld the constitutionality of the statutes. We noted probable jurisdiction of both appeals.

II

Under the Florida statute challenged here, "[a]ny person whose goods or chattels are wrongfully detained by any other person ... may have a writ of replevin to recover them...." There is no requirement that the applicant make a convincing showing before the seizure that the goods are, in fact, "wrongfully detained." Rather, Florida law automatically relies on the bare assertion of the party seeking the writ that he is entitled to one and allows a court clerk to issue the writ summarily. It requires only that the applicant file a complaint, initiating a court action

---

4. Unlike Mrs. Fuentes in No. 5039, none of the appellants in No. 5138 was ever sued in any court by the party who initiated seizure of the property.

for repossession and reciting in conclusory fashion that he is "lawfully entitled to the possession" of the property, and that he file a security bond

> "in at least double the value of the property to be replevied conditioned that plaintiff will prosecute his action to effect and without delay and that if defendant recovers judgment against him in the action, he will return the property, if return thereof is adjudged, and will pay defendant all sums of money recovered against plaintiff by defendant in the action."

On the sole basis of the complaint and bond, a writ is issued "command[ing] the officer to whom it may be directed to replevy the goods and chattels in possession of defendant ... and to summon the defendant to answer the complaint." If the goods are "in any dwelling house or other building or enclosure," the officer is required to demand their delivery; but if they are not delivered, "he shall cause such house, building or enclosure to be broken open and shall make replevin according to the writ. . . ."

Thus, at the same moment that the defendant receives the complaint seeking repossession of property through court action, the property is seized from him. He is provided no prior notice and allowed no opportunity whatever to challenge the issuance of the writ. After the property has been seized, he will eventually have an opportunity for a hearing, as the defendant in the trial of the court action for repossession, which the plaintiff is required to pursue. And he is also not wholly without recourse in the meantime. For under the Florida statute, the officer who seizes the property must keep it for three days, and during that period the defendant may reclaim possession of the property by posting his own security bond in double its value. But if he does not post such a bond, the property is transferred to the party who sought the writ, pending a final judgment in the underlying action for repossession.

The Pennsylvania law differs, though not in its essential nature, from that of Florida. * * * Unlike the Florida statute, however, the Pennsylvania law does not require that there ever be opportunity for a hearing on the merits of the conflicting claims to possession of the replevied property. The party seeking the writ is not obliged to initiate a court action for repossession. Indeed, he need not even formally allege that he is lawfully entitled to the property. The most that is required is that he file an "affidavit of the value of the property to be replevied." If the party who loses property through replevin seizure is to get even a post-seizure hearing, he must initiate a lawsuit himself.[9] He may also, as under Florida law, post his own counterbond within three days after the seizure to regain possession.

III

* * *

---

9. None of the appellants in No. 70—5138 attempted to initiate the process to require the filing of a post-seizure complaint * * *.

Prejudgment replevin statutes like those of Florida and Pennsylvania are most commonly used by creditors to seize goods allegedly wrongfully detained—not wrongfully taken—by debtors. At common law, if a creditor wished to invoke state power to recover goods wrongfully detained, he had to proceed through the action of debt or detinue. These actions, however, did not provide for a return of property before final judgment.[12] And, more importantly, on the occasions when the common law did allow prejudgment seizure by state power, it provided some kind of notice and opportunity to be heard to the party then in possession of the property, and a state official made at least a summary determination of the relative rights of the disputing parties before stepping into the dispute and taking goods from one of them.

IV

For more than a century the central meaning of procedural due process has been clear: "Parties whose rights are to be affected are entitled to be heard; and in order that they may enjoy that right they must first be notified." It is equally fundamental that the right to notice and an opportunity to be heard "must be granted at a meaningful time and in a meaningful manner."

* * *

The constitutional right to be heard is a basic aspect of the duty of government to follow a fair process of decisionmaking when it acts to deprive a person of his possessions. The purpose of this requirement is not only to ensure abstract fair play to the individual. Its purpose, more particularly, is to protect his use and possession of property from arbitrary encroachment—to minimize substantively unfair or mistaken deprivations of property, a danger that is especially great when the State seizes goods simply upon the application of and for the benefit of a private party. So viewed the prohibition against the deprivation of property without due process of law reflects the high value, embedded in our constitutional and political history, that we place on a person's right to enjoy what is his, free of government interference.

The requirement of notice and an opportunity to be heard raises no impenetrable barrier to the taking of a person's possessions. But the fair process of decisionmaking that it guarantees works, by itself, to protect against arbitrary deprivation of property. For when a person has an opportunity to speak up in his own defense, and when the State must listen to what he has to say, substantively unfair and simply mistaken deprivations of property interests can be prevented.

* * *

If the right to notice and a hearing is to serve its full purpose, then, it is clear that it must be granted at a time when the deprivation can still be prevented. At a later hearing, an individual's possessions can be

---

12. The creditor could, of course, proceed without the use of state power, through self-help, by "distraining" the property before a judgment.

returned to him if they were unfairly or mistakenly taken in the first place. Damages may even be awarded to him for the wrongful deprivation. But no later hearing and no damage award can undo the fact that the arbitrary taking that was subject to the right of procedural due process has already occurred. "This Court has not … embraced the general proposition that a wrong may be done if it can be undone." Stanley v. Illinois, 405 U.S. 645, 647, 92 S.Ct. 1208, 1210, 31 L.Ed.2d 551.

* * *

The Florida and Pennsylvania prejudgment replevin statutes fly in the face of this principle. To be sure, the requirements that a party seeking a writ must first post a bond, allege conclusorily that he is entitled to specific goods, and open himself to possible liability in damages if he is wrong, serve to deter wholly unfounded applications for a writ. But those requirements are hardly a substitute for a prior hearing, for they test no more than the strength of the applicant's own belief in his rights.[13] Since his private gain is at stake, the danger is all too great that his confidence in his cause will be misplaced. Lawyers and judges are familiar with the phenomenon of a party mistakenly but firmly convinced that his view of the facts and law will prevail, and therefore quite willing to risk the costs of litigation. Because of the understandable, self-interested fallibility of litigants, a court does not decide a dispute until it has had an opportunity to hear both sides—and does not generally take even tentative action until it has itself examined the support for the plaintiff's position. The Florida and Pennsylvania statutes do not even require the official issuing a writ of replevin to do that much.

The minimal deterrent effect of a bond requirement is, in a practical sense, no substitute for an informed evaluation by a neutral official. More specifically, as a matter of constitutional principle, it is no replacement for the right to a prior hearing that is the only truly effective safeguard against arbitrary deprivation of property. While the existence of these other, less effective, safeguards may be among the considerations that affect the form of hearing demanded by due process, they are far from enough by themselves to obviate the right to a prior hearing of some kind.

V

The right to a prior hearing, of course, attaches only to the deprivation of an interest encompassed within the Fourteenth Amendment's protection. In the present cases, the Florida and Pennsylvania statutes were applied to replevy chattels in the appellants' possession. The replevin was not cast as a final judgment; most, if not all, of the

---

13. They may not even test that much. For if an applicant for the writ knows that he is dealing with an uneducated, uninformed consumer with little access to legal help and little familiarity with legal procedures, there may be a substantial possibility that a summary seizure of property—however unwarranted—may go unchallenged, and the applicant may feel that he can act with impunity.

appellants lacked full title to the chattels; and their claim even to continued possession was a matter in dispute. Moreover, the chattels at stake were nothing more than an assortment of household goods. Nonetheless, it is clear that the appellants were deprived of possessory interests in those chattels that were within the protection of the Fourteenth Amendment.

A

A deprivation of a person's possessions under a prejudgment writ of replevin, at least in theory, may be only temporary. The Florida and Pennsylvania statutes do not require a person to wait until a post-seizure hearing and final judgment to recover what has been replevied. Within three days after the seizure, the statutes allow him to recover the goods if he, in return, surrenders other property—a payment necessary to secure a bond in double the value of the goods seized from him.[14] But it is now well settled that a temporary, nonfinal deprivation of property is nonetheless a "deprivation" in the terms of the Fourteenth Amendment. Sniadach v. Family Finance Corp., 395 U.S. 337, 89 S.Ct. 1820, 23 L.Ed.2d 349 (1969).

* * *

The Fourteenth Amendment draws no bright lines around three-day, 10–day or 50–day deprivations of property. Any significant taking of property by the State is within the purview of the Due Process Clause. While the length and consequent severity of a deprivation may be another factor to weigh in determining the appropriate form of hearing, it is not decisive of the basic right to a prior hearing of some kind.

B

The appellants who signed conditional sales contracts lacked full legal title to the replevied goods. The Fourteenth Amendment's protection of "property," however, has never been interpreted to safeguard only the rights of undisputed ownership. Rather, it has been read broadly to extend protection to "any significant property interest," including statutory entitlements. See Goldberg v. Kelly, 397 U.S., at 262, 90 S.Ct., at 1017.

The appellants were deprived of such an interest in the replevied goods—the interest in continued possession and use of the goods. They had acquired this interest under the conditional sales contracts that entitled them to possession and use of the chattels before transfer of title. In exchange for immediate possession, the appellants had agreed to

---

14. The appellants argue that this opportunity for quick recovery exists only in theory. They allege that very few people in their position are able to obtain a recovery bond, even if they know of the possibility. Appellant Fuentes says that in her case she was never told that she could recover the stove and stereo and that the deputy sheriff seizing them gave them at once to the Firestone agent, rather than holding them for three days. She further asserts that of 442 cases of prejudgment replevin in small-claims courts in Dade County, Florida, in 1969, there was not one case in which the defendant took advantage of the recovery provision.

pay a major financing charge beyond the basic price of the merchandise. Moreover, by the time the goods were summarily repossessed, they had made substantial installment payments. Clearly, their possessory interest in the goods, dearly bought and protected by contract, was sufficient to invoke the protection of the Due Process Clause.

Their ultimate right to continued possession was, of course, in dispute. If it were shown at a hearing that the appellants had defaulted on their contractual obligations, it might well be that the sellers of the goods would be entitled to repossession. But even assuming that the appellants had fallen behind in their installment payments, and that they had no other valid defenses,[17] that is immaterial here. The right to be heard does not depend upon an advance showing that one will surely prevail at the hearing. "To one who protests against the taking of his property without due process of law, it is no answer to say that in his particular case due process of law would have led to the same result because he had no adequate defense upon the merits." Coe v. Armour Fertilizer Works, 237 U.S. 413, 424, 35 S.Ct. 625, 59 L.Ed. 1027. It is enough to invoke the procedural safeguards of the Fourteenth Amendment that a significant property interest is at stake, whatever the ultimate outcome of a hearing on the contractual right to continued possession and use of the goods.[18]

C

Nevertheless, the District Courts rejected the appellants' constitutional claim on the ground that the goods seized from them—a stove, a stereo, a table, a bed, and so forth—were not deserving of due process protection, since they were not absolute necessities of life. * * *

No doubt, there may be many gradations in the "importance" or "necessity" of various consumer goods. Stoves could be compared to television sets, or beds could be compared to tables. But if the root principle of procedural due process is to be applied with objectivity, it cannot rest on such distinctions. The Fourteenth Amendment speaks of "property" generally. And, under our free-enterprise system, an individual's choices in the marketplace are respected, however unwise they may seem to someone else. It is not the business of a court adjudicating due process rights to make its own critical evaluation of those choices and protect only the ones that, by its own lights, are "necessary."[21]

---

17. Mrs. Fuentes argues that Florida law allows her to defend on the ground that Firestone breached its obligations under the sales contract by failing to repair serious defects in the stove it sold her. We need not consider this issue here. It is enough that the right to continued possession of the goods was open to some dispute at a hearing since the sellers of the goods had to show, at the least, that the appellants had defaulted in their payments.

18. The issues decisive of the ultimate right to continued possession, of course,

may be quite simple. The simplicity of the issues might be relevant to the formality or scheduling of a prior hearing. But it certainly cannot undercut the right to a prior hearing of some kind.

21. The relative weight of liberty or property interests is relevant, of course, to the form of notice and hearing required by due process. But some form of notice and hearing—formal or informal—is required before deprivation of a property interest that "cannot be characterized as *de minimis.*" Sniadach v. Family Finance Corp., su-

VI

There are "extraordinary situations" that justify postponing notice and opportunity for a hearing. Boddie v. Connecticut, 401 U.S., at 379, 91 S.Ct., at 786. These situations, however, must be truly unusual.[22] Only in a few limited situations has this Court allowed outright seizure[23] without opportunity for a prior hearing. First, in each case, the seizure has been directly necessary to secure an important governmental or general public interest. Second, there has been a special need for very prompt action. Third, the State has kept strict control over its monopoly of legitimate force; the person initiating the seizure has been a government official responsible for determining, under the standards of a narrowly drawn statute, that it was necessary and justified in the particular instance. Thus, the Court has allowed summary seizure of property to collect the internal revenue of the United States,[24] to meet the needs of a national war effort, to protect against the economic disaster of a bank failure, and to protect the public from misbranded drugs and contaminated food.

The Florida and Pennsylvania prejudgment replevin statutes serve no such important governmental or general public interest. They allow summary seizure of a person's possessions when no more than private gain is directly at stake.[29] The replevin of chattels, as in the present

pra, 395 U.S., at 342, 89 S.Ct., at 1823 (Harlan, J., concurring).

22. A prior hearing always imposes some costs in time, effort, and expense, and it is often more efficient to dispense with the opportunity for such a hearing. But these rather ordinary costs cannot outweigh the constitutional right. Procedural due process is not intended to promote efficiency or accommodate all possible interests: it is intended to protect the particular interests of the person whose possessions are about to be taken. "The establishment of prompt efficacious procedures to achieve legitimate state ends is a proper state interest worthy of cognizance in constitutional adjudication. But the Constitution recognizes higher values than speed and efficiency. Indeed, one might fairly say of the Bill of Rights in general, and the Due Process Clause in particular, that they were designed to protect the fragile values of a vulnerable citizenry from the overbearing concern for efficiency and efficacy that may characterize praiseworthy government officials no less, and perhaps more, than mediocre ones." Stanley v. Illinois, 405 U.S. 645, 656, 92 S.Ct. 1208, 1215, 31 L.Ed.2d 551.

23. In three cases, the Court has allowed the attachment of property without a prior hearing. In one, the attachment was necessary to protect the public against the same sort of immediate harm involved in the seizure cases—a bank failure. Coffin

Bros. & Co. v. Bennett, 277 U.S. 29, 48 S.Ct. 422, 72 L.Ed. 768. Another case involved attachment necessary to secure jurisdiction in state court—clearly a most basic and important public interest. Ownbey v. Morgan, 256 U.S. 94, 41 S.Ct. 433, 65 L.Ed. 837. * * * Seizure under a search warrant is quite a different matter, see n. 30, infra.

24. Phillips v. Commissioner of Internal Revenue, 283 U.S. 589, 51 S.Ct. 608, 75 L.Ed. 1289. The Court stated that "[d]elay in the judicial determination of property rights is not uncommon where it is *essential* that governmental needs be *immediately* satisfied." (emphasis supplied). The Court, then relied on "the need of the government promptly to secure its revenues."

29. By allowing repossession without an opportunity for a prior hearing, the Florida and Pennsylvania statutes may be intended specifically to reduce the costs for the private party seeking to seize goods in another party's possession. Even if the private gain at stake in repossession actions were equal to the great public interests recognized in this Court's past decisions, the Court has made clear that the avoidance of the ordinary costs imposed by the opportunity for a hearing is not sufficient to override the constitutional right. See n. 22, supra. The appellees argue that the cost of holding hearings may be especially onerous in the context of the creditor-debtor relationship.

cases, may satisfy a debt or settle a score. But state intervention in a private dispute hardly compares to state action furthering a war effort or protecting the public health.

Nor do the broadly drawn Florida and Pennsylvania statutes limit the summary seizure of goods to special situations demanding prompt action. There may be cases in which a creditor could make a showing of immediate danger that a debtor will destroy or conceal disputed goods. But the statutes before us are not "narrowly drawn to meet any such unusual condition." Sniadach v. Family Finance Corp., supra, 395 U.S. at 339, 89 S.Ct. at 1821. And no such unusual situation is presented by the facts of these cases.

The statutes, moreover, abdicate effective state control over state power. Private parties, serving their own private advantage, may unilaterally invoke state power to replevy goods from another. No state official participates in the decision to seek a writ; no state official reviews the basis for the claim to repossession; and no state official evaluates the need for immediate seizure. There is not even a requirement that the plaintiff provide any information to the court on these matters. The State acts largely in the dark.[30]

[The Court held that appellants had not waived their right to a hearing by signing form contracts authorizing repossession.]

* * *

VIII

We hold that the Florida and Pennsylvania prejudgment replevin provisions work a deprivation of property without due process of law insofar as they deny the right to a prior opportunity to be heard before chattels are taken from their possessor. Our holding, however, is a narrow one. We do not question the power of a State to seize goods

But the Court's holding in Sniadach v. Family Finance Corp., supra, indisputably demonstrates that ordinary hearing costs are no more able to override due process rights in the creditor-debtor context than in other contexts.

In any event, the aggregate cost of an *opportunity* to be heard before repossession should not be exaggerated. For we deal here only with the right to an opportunity to be heard. Since the issues and facts decisive of rights in repossession suits may very often be quite simple, there is a likelihood that many defendants would forgo their opportunity, sensing the futility of the exercise in the particular case. And, of course, no hearing need be held unless the defendant, having received notice of his opportunity, takes advantage of it.

30. The seizure of possessions under a writ of replevin is entirely different from the seizure of possessions under a search warrant. First, a search warrant is generally issued to serve a highly important governmental need—e.g., the apprehension and conviction of criminals—rather than the mere private advantage of a private party in an economic transaction. Second, a search warrant is generally issued in situations demanding prompt action. The danger is all too obvious that a criminal will destroy or hide evidence or fruits of his crime if given any prior notice. Third, the Fourth Amendment guarantees that the State will not issue search warrants merely upon the conclusory application of a private party. It guarantees that the State will not abdicate control over the issuance of warrants and that no warrant will be issued without a prior showing of probable cause. Thus, our decision today in no way implies that there must be opportunity for an adversary hearing before a search warrant is issued.

before a final judgment in order to protect the security interests of creditors so long as those creditors have tested their claim to the goods through the process of a fair prior hearing. The nature and form of such prior hearings, moreover, are legitimately open to many potential variations and are a subject, at this point, for legislation—not adjudication. Since the essential reason for the requirement of a prior hearing is to prevent unfair and mistaken deprivations of property, however, it is axiomatic that the hearing must provide a real test. "[D]ue process is afforded only by the kinds of 'notice' and 'hearing' that are aimed at establishing the validity, or at least the probable validity, of the underlying claim against the alleged debtor before he can be deprived of his property...." Sniadach v. Family Finance Corp., supra, 395 U.S. at 343, 89 S.Ct. at 1823 (Harlan, J., concurring).

For the foregoing reasons, the judgments of the District Courts are vacated and these cases are remanded for further proceedings consistent with this opinion.

It is so ordered.

Vacated and remanded.

JUSTICE POWELL and JUSTICE REHNQUIST did not participate in the consideration or decision of these cases.

JUSTICE WHITE, with whom THE CHIEF JUSTICE and JUSTICE BLACKMUN join, dissenting.

Because the Court's opinion and judgment improvidently, in my view, call into question important aspects of the statutes of almost all the States governing secured transactions and the procedure for repossessing personal property, I must dissent for the reasons that follow.

* * *

It goes without saying that in the typical installment sale of personal property both seller and buyer have interests in the property until the purchase price is fully paid, the seller early in the transaction often having more at stake than the buyer. Nor is it disputed that the buyer's right to possession is conditioned upon his making the stipulated payments and that upon default the seller is entitled to possession. Finally, there is no question in these cases that if default is disputed by the buyer he has the opportunity for a full hearing, and that if he prevails he may have the property or its full value as damages.

The narrow issue, as the Court notes, is whether it comports with due process to permit the seller, pending final judgment, to take possession of the property through a writ of replevin served by the sheriff without affording the buyer opportunity to insist that the seller establish at a hearing that there is reasonable basis for his claim of default. The interests of the buyer and seller are obviously antagonistic during this interim period: the buyer wants the use of the property pending final judgment; the seller's interest is to prevent further use and deterioration of his security. By the Florida and Pennsylvania laws the property is to all intents and purposes placed in custody and immobilized during this time. The buyer loses use of the property temporarily but is protected against loss; the seller is protected against deterioration of the property but must undertake by bond to make the buyer whole in the event the latter prevails.

In considering whether this resolution of conflicting interests is unconstitutional, much depends on one's perceptions of the practical considerations involved. The Court holds it constitutionally essential to afford opportunity for a probable-cause hearing prior to repossession. Its stated purpose is "to prevent unfair and mistaken deprivations of property." But in these typical situations, the buyer-debtor has either defaulted or he has not. If there is a default, it would seem not only "fair," but essential, that the creditor be allowed to repossess; and I cannot say that the likelihood of a mistaken claim of default is sufficiently real or recurring to justify a broad constitutional requirement that a creditor do more than the typical state law requires and permits him to do. Sellers are normally in the business of selling and collecting the price for their merchandise. I could be quite wrong, but it would not seem in the creditor's interest for a default occasioning repossession to occur; as a practical matter it would much better serve his interests if the transaction goes forward and is completed as planned. Dollar-and-cents considerations weigh heavily against false claims of default as well as against precipitate action that would allow no opportunity for mistakes to surface and be corrected. Nor does it seem to me that creditors would lightly undertake the expense of instituting replevin actions and putting up bonds.

The Court's rhetoric is seductive, but in end analysis, the result it reaches will have little impact and represents no more than ideological tinkering with state law. It would appear that creditors could withstand attack under today's opinion simply by making clear in the controlling credit instruments that they may retake possession without a hearing, or, for that matter, without resort to judicial process at all. Alternatively, they need only give a few days' notice of a hearing, take possession if hearing is waived or if there is default; and if hearing is necessary merely establish probable cause for asserting that default has occurred. It is very doubtful in my mind that such a hearing would in fact result in protections for the debtor substantially different from those the present laws provide. On the contrary, the availability of credit may well be diminished or, in any event, the expense of securing it increased.

None of this seems worth the candle to me.

Notes and Questions

1. In the Court's view, what is the purpose for holding the hearing? If the creditor establishes at the hearing that a prejudgment remedy is appropriate, does that mean that the hearing was a waste of time?

2. The Court downplays the costs associated with the hearing requirement. Has it properly appreciated those costs? What proportion of people

subjected to replevin have, like Ms. Fuentes, potential defenses or other grounds for retaining the goods? What will lenders and merchants do in response to this added wrinkle in the debt remedies procedure? See White, The Abolition of Self–Help Repossession: The Poor Pay More, 1973 Wis. L.Rev. 503, estimating that only 6 out of 1,000 people whose cars are repossessed have defenses on the merits and that interfering with this self-help alternative to judicial relief would significantly increase the cost of auto purchases, at least for the poor. On the basis of these estimates, Professor White concluded that "Fuentes v. Shevin is probably an undesirable outcome, and that the application of the same doctrine to self-help repossession would constitute due process gone berserk." Would the added costs be equally significant where plaintiffs resort to judicial prejudgment remedies instead of self-help? Do added procedures always lead to added costs? How do we decide if the costs are justified?

3.   To what extent will imposition of more procedures drive people to employ self-help? In *Fuentes,* what would have happened if the creditors had simply hired thugs to seize the property involved? Acting independently, people do not have the assistance of the sheriff or another state officer, and they may be prosecuted for a breach of the peace or something more significant if they try to do the same kinds of things themselves. Moreover, certain remedies, such as garnishment, probably do not have a self-help analogue. Hence many people will still use the judicial procedure even if it is costly and cumbersome.

For those who have workable self-help alternatives, the Court seemed to have removed any due process obstacles in their path in Flagg Brothers, Inc. v. Brooks, 436 U.S. 149, 98 S.Ct. 1729, 56 L.Ed.2d 185 (1978). Brooks was evicted by the city marshall who arranged to store her belongings in Flagg Brother's warehouse. Two months later, when Brooks refused to pay the storage charges because she disputed them, Flagg Brothers threatened to sell her goods to satisfy the debt, as permitted by the Uniform Commercial Code. Brooks sued in federal court to prevent the sale on the ground that due process forbade this self-help without a prior hearing to decide the dispute about the storage charges.

Despite the initial role of the city marshall in evicting Brooks and arranging to store the goods with Flagg Brothers, the Supreme Court upheld dismissal of the suit on the ground that there was no "state action" (a requirement of the 14th Amendment) involved in the sale. As Justice Rehnquist explained, "[t]his total absence of overt official involvement plainly distinguishes this case from earlier decisions imposing procedural restrictions on creditors' remedies." The complex application of the "state action" concept must await fuller development in courses on constitutional law. For our purposes, the basic focus is on the effect of this limitation of due process on the incentives confronting claimants. *Flagg Brothers* appears to eliminate Professor White's worry about "due process gone berserk" with regard to auto repossession. Are you comfortable with the result? If not, what different result might be prescribed? What costs might that generate?

4.   Besides cost, does the creditor have other interests that are threatened by requiring a hearing before seizure? Note that the Court acknowledges in *Fuentes* that in "extraordinary" situations pre-seizure notice and

hearing are not required. In Calero–Toledo v. Pearson Yacht Leasing Co., 416 U.S. 663, 94 S.Ct. 2080, 40 L.Ed.2d 452 (1974), the Court provided a further explanation of this concept. Plaintiff's yacht, which it had leased to two Puerto Rican residents, was seized by Puerto Rico when found to contain marijuana, and it was later forfeited to the government. The Court rejected plaintiff's claim that the seizure was invalid because there was no prior notice to them and hearing:

> First, seizure under the Puerto Rican statutes serves significant governmental purposes: Seizure permits Puerto Rico to assert *in rem* jurisdiction over the property in order to conduct forfeiture proceedings, thereby fostering the public interest in preventing continued illicit use of the property and in enforcing criminal sanctions. Second, preseizure notice and hearing might frustrate the interests served by the statutes, since the property seized—as here, a yacht—will often be of a sort that could be removed to another jurisdiction, destroyed, or concealed, if advance warning of confiscation were given. And finally, unlike the situation in *Fuentes,* seizure is not initiated by self-interested private parties; rather, Commonwealth officials determine whether seizure is appropriate under the provisions of the Puerto Rican statutes. In these circumstances, we hold that this case presents an "extraordinary" situation in which postponement of notice and hearing until after seizure did not deny due process.

5. What is the probable effect of the hearing requirement on the bargaining strength of the parties? Will the creditor be more likely to give the debtor "one more chance" to avoid the delay and trouble of the hearing? If the creditor goes through the hearing and obtains the seizure order, will the effort involved be likely to affect his willingness to "make a deal" then?

6. *Fuentes* is quite vague about the procedure for the actual hearing itself. Some insight on this subject can be gleaned from Goldberg v. Kelly, 397 U.S. 254, 90 S.Ct. 1011, 25 L.Ed.2d 287 (1970), in which the Court held that before welfare payments could be cut off the recipient was entitled to notice and a hearing. It went on to explain that the agency's practice of deciding questions about eligibility on written submissions was inadequate, at least where there were factual disputes:

> It is not enough that a welfare recipient may present his position to the decision maker in writing or secondhand through his caseworker. Written submissions are an unrealistic option for most recipients, who lack the educational attainment to write effectively and who cannot obtain professional assistance. Moreover, written submissions do not afford the flexibility of oral presentations; they do not permit the recipient to mold his argument to the issues the decision maker appears to regard as important. Particularly where credibility and veracity are at issue, as they must be in many termination proceedings, written submissions are a wholly unsatisfactory basis for decision. * * * Informal procedures will suffice; in this context due process does not require a particular order of proof or mode of offering evidence.
>
> In almost every setting where important decisions turn on questions of fact, due process requires an opportunity to confront and cross-examine adverse witnesses. What we said in Greene v. McElroy, 360

U.S. 474, 79 S.Ct. 1400, 3 L.Ed.2d 1377 (1959), is particularly pertinent here:

> Certain principles have remained relatively immutable in our juris-
> prudence. One of these is that where governmental action seriously
> injures an individual, and the reasonableness of the action depends
> on fact findings, the evidence used to prove the Government's case
> must be disclosed to the individual so that he has an opportunity to
> show that it is untrue. While this is important in the case of
> documentary evidence, it is even more important where the evi-
> dence consists of the testimony of individuals whose memory might
> be faulty or who, in fact, might be perjurers or persons motivated by
> malice, vindictiveness, intolerance, prejudice, or jealousy. * * *

Welfare recipients must therefore be given an opportunity to confront
and cross-examine the witnesses relied on by the department.

"The right to be heard would be, in many cases, of little avail if it
did not comprehend the right to be heard by counsel." We do not say
that counsel must be provided at the pre-termination hearing, but only
that the recipient must be allowed to retain an attorney if he so desires.
Counsel can help delineate the issues, present the factual contentions in
an orderly manner, conduct cross-examination, and generally safeguard
the interests of the recipient. We do not anticipate that this assistance
will unduly encumber the hearing. Finally, the decisionmaker's conclusion as to a recipient's eligibility must rest solely on the legal rules and
evidence adduced at the hearing. To demonstrate compliance with this
elementary requirement, the decision maker should state the reasons for
his determination and indicate the evidence he relied on, though his
statement need not amount to a full opinion or even formal findings of
fact and conclusions of law. And, of course, an impartial decision maker
is essential. We agree with the District Court that a prior involvement in
some aspects of a case will not necessarily bar a welfare official from
acting as a decision maker. He should not, however, have participated in
the determination under review.

MITCHELL v. W. T. GRANT CO., 416 U.S. 600, 94 S.Ct. 1895, 40
L.Ed.2d 406 (1974):

Justice White delivered the opinion of the Court.

[Grant sold a refrigerator, range, stereo and washing machine to
Mitchell on credit and later filed suit in Louisiana state court claiming
some $574 was overdue and unpaid. Louisiana statutes provided for
sequestration where "one claims the ownership or right to possession of
property * * * if it is within the power of the defendant to conceal,
dispose of, or waste the property or the revenues therefrom, or remove
the property from the parish, during the pendency of the action." Grant
submitted the affidavit of its credit manager, which attested to the debt
and added that Grant "had reason to believe" Mitchell would encumber,
alienate or otherwise dispose of the merchandise described in the forego-

ing petition during the pendency of these proceedings. Under Louisiana law, the vendor's lien would expire if the buyer transferred possession. Based on the affidavit, without notice to Mitchell, a judge then signed an order of sequestration, directing a constable to take possession of the items after Grant posted $1,125 bond.

The Supreme Court held that the procedure was constitutional. It stressed that "[t]he question is not whether a debtor's property may be seized by his creditors, pendente lite, where they hold no present interest in the property sought to be seized. The reality is that both seller and buyer had current, real interests in the property." Finding that resolution of the due process challenge must therefore take account of the interests of the buyer and the seller in the property, the Court concluded further that "*Fuentes* was decided against a factual and legal background sufficiently different from that now before us and that it does not require the invalidation of the Louisiana sequestration statute."]

The Louisiana sequestration statute followed in this case mandates a considerably different procedure [from that in *Fuentes*]. A writ of sequestration is available to a mortgage or lien holder to forestall waste or alienation of the property, but, different from the Florida and Pennsylvania systems, bare conclusory claims of ownership or lien will not suffice under the Louisiana statute. Article 3501 authorizes the writ "only when the nature of the claim and the amount thereof, if any, and the grounds relied upon for the issuance of the writ clearly appear from specific facts" shown by verified petition or affidavit. Moreover, in the parish where this case arose, the requisite showing must be made to a judge, and judicial authorization obtained. Mitchell was not at the unsupervised mercy of the creditor and court functionaries. The Louisiana law provides for judicial control of the process from the beginning to the end.[12] This control is one of the measures adopted by the State to minimize the risk that the *ex parte* procedure will lead to a wrongful taking. It is buttressed by the provision that should the writ be dissolved there are "damages for the wrongful issuance of a writ" and for attorney's fees "whether the writ is dissolved on motion or after trial on the merits."

The risk of wrongful use of the procedure must also be judged in the context of the issues which are to be determined at that proceeding. In Florida and Pennsylvania [whose statutes were invalidated in *Fuentes*] property was only to be replevied in accord with state policy if it had been "wrongfully detained." This broad "fault" standard is inherently subject to factual determination and adversarial input. * * * In Louisiana, on the other hand, the facts relevant to obtaining a writ of sequestration are narrowly confined. As we have indicated, documentary proof is particularly suited for questions of the existence of a vendor's

---

12. The approval of a writ of sequestration is not, as petitioner contends, a mere ministerial act. "Since a writ of sequestration issues without a hearing, specific facts as to the grounds relied upon for issuance must be contained in the verified petition in order that the issuing judge can properly evaluate the grounds." Wright v. Hughes, 254 So.2d 293, 296–297 (La.Ct.App.1971) (on rehearing).

lien and the issue of default. There is thus far less danger here that the seizure will be mistaken and a corresponding decrease in the utility of an adversary hearing which will be immediately available in any event.

Of course, as in *Fuentes,* consideration of the impact on the debtor remains. Under Louisiana procedure, however, the debtor, Mitchell, was not left in limbo to await a hearing that might or might not "eventually" occur, as the debtors were under the statutory schemes before the Court in *Fuentes.* Louisiana law expressly provides for an immediate hearing and dissolution of the writ [upon defendant's filing a "contradictory motion"] "unless the plaintiff proves the grounds upon which the writ was issued."

To summarize, the Louisiana system seeks to minimize the risk of error of a wrongful interim possession by the creditor. The system protects the debtor's interest in every conceivable way, except allowing him to have the property to start with, and this is done in pursuit of what we deem an acceptable arrangement *pendente lite* to put the property in the possession of the party who furnishes protection against loss or damage to the other pending trial on the merits.

JUSTICE POWELL, concurring.

In sweeping language, Fuentes v. Shevin, 407 U.S. 67, 92 S.Ct. 1983, 32 L.Ed.2d 556 (1972), enunciated the principle that the constitutional guarantee of procedural due process requires an adversary hearing before an individual may be temporarily deprived of any possessory interest in tangible personal property, however brief the dispossession and however slight his monetary interest in the property. The Court's decision today withdraws significantly from the full reach of that principle, and to this extent I think it fair to say that the *Fuentes* opinion is overruled.

I could have agreed that the Florida and Pennsylvania statutes in *Fuentes* were violative of due process because of their arbitrary and unreasonable provisions. It seems to me, however, that it was unnecessary for the *Fuentes* opinion to have adopted so broad and inflexible a rule, especially one that considerably altered settled law with respect to commercial transactions and basic creditor-debtor understandings. Narrower grounds existed for invalidating the replevin statutes in that case.

[JUSTICE STEWART dissented, joined by JUSTICES DOUGLAS and MARSHALL. He accused the majority of overruling *Fuentes* without admitting it, concluding that "this case is constitutionally indistinguishable from Fuentes v. Shevin, and the Court today has simply rejected the reasoning of that case and adopted instead the analysis of the *Fuentes* dissent." JUSTICE BRENNAN wrote separately that he agreed *Fuentes* required invalidation of the Louisiana procedure.]

———

NORTH GEORGIA FINISHING, INC. v. DI–CHEM, INC., 419 U.S. 601, 95 S.Ct. 719, 42 L.Ed.2d 751 (1975):

JUSTICE WHITE delivered the opinion of the Court.

[Plaintiff sued defendant in a Georgia state court alleging that defendant owed over $51,000 for goods it bought from plaintiff. Georgia statutes authorized a writ of garnishment if plaintiff or its attorney submitted an affidavit "stating the amount claimed to be due" and asserting "that he has reason to apprehend the loss of the same or some part thereof unless process of garnishment shall issue." Plaintiff therefore filed an affidavit of its president (seemingly on a printed form) asserting the defendant owed over $51,000 and that plaintiff "has reason to apprehend the loss of said sum or some part thereof unless process of Garnishment issues." The clerk of the court issued a summons of garnishment to defendant's bank, in effect freezing defendant's bank account. The Georgia courts rejected defendant's constitutional objections to the procedure.

The Supreme Court held that the Georgia courts had failed to take account of *Fuentes*. Justice White explained the import of *Fuentes* as follows: "Because the official seizures [in *Fuentes*] had been carried out without notice and without opportunity for a hearing or other safeguard against mistaken repossession they were held to be in violation of the Fourteenth Amendment."]

The Georgia statute is vulnerable for the same reasons [as the statutes in *Fuentes*]. Here, a bank account, surely a form of property, was impounded and, absent a bond, put totally beyond use during the pendency of the litigation on the alleged debt, all by a writ of garnishment issued by a court clerk without notice or opportunity for an early hearing and without participation by a judicial officer.

Nor is the statute saved by the more recent decision in Mitchell v. W.T. Grant Co., 416 U.S. 600, 94 S.Ct. 1895, 40 L.Ed.2d 406 (1974). That case upheld the Louisiana sequestration statute which permitted the seller-creditor holding a vendor's lien to secure a writ of sequestration and, having filed a bond, to cause the sheriff to take possession of the property at issue. The writ, however, was issuable only by a judge upon the filing of an affidavit going beyond mere conclusory allegations and clearly setting out the facts entitling the creditor to sequestration. The Louisiana law also expressly entitled the debtor to an immediate hearing after seizure and to dissolution of the writ absent proof by the creditor of the grounds on which the writ was issued.

The Georgia garnishment statute has none of the saving characteristics of the Louisiana statute. The writ of garnishment is issuable on the affidavit of the creditor or his attorney, and the latter need not have personal knowledge of the facts. The affidavit, like the one filed in this case, need contain only conclusory allegations. The writ is issuable, as this one was, by the court clerk, without participation by a judge. Upon service of the writ, the debtor is deprived of the use of the property in the hands of the garnishee. Here a sizable bank account was frozen and the only method discernable on the face of the statute to dissolve the garnishment was to file a bond to protect the plaintiff creditor. There is no provision for an early hearing at which the creditor would be required to demonstrate at least probable cause for the garnishment. Indeed, it would appear that without the filing of a bond the defendant debtor's challenge to the garnishment will not be entertained, whatever the grounds may be.

JUSTICE STEWART, concurring.

It is gratifying to note that my report of the demise of Fuentes v. Shevin, see Mitchell v. W.T. Grant Co., 416 U.S. 600, 629–36, 94 S.Ct. 1895, 1910, 40 L.Ed.2d 406 (1974) (dissenting opinion) seems to have been greatly exaggerated. Cf. S. Clemens, cable from Europe to the Associated Press, quoted in 2 A. Paine, Mark Twain, A Biography 1039 (1912).

JUSTICE POWELL, concurring in the judgment.

* * * The Court's opinion in this case, relying substantially on *Fuentes,* suggests that decision will again be read as calling into question much of the previously settled law governing commercial transactions. I continue to doubt whether *Fuentes* strikes a proper balance, especially in cases where the creditor's interest in the property may be as significant or even greater than that of the debtor. Nor do I find it necessary to relegate *Mitchell* to its narrow factual setting in order to determine that the Georgia garnishment statutes fail to satisfy the requirements of procedural due process.

* * *

In my view, procedural due process would be satisfied where state law requires that the garnishment be preceded by the garnishor's provision of adequate security and by his establishment before a neutral officer[3] of a factual basis of the need to resort to the remedy as a means of preventing removal or dissipation of assets required to satisfy the claim. Due process further requires that the State afford an opportunity for a prompt postgarnishment judicial hearing in which the garnishor has the burden of showing probable cause to believe there is a need to continue the garnishment for a sufficient period of time to allow proof and satisfaction of the alleged debt. Since the garnished assets may bear no relation to the controversy giving rise to the alleged debt, the State also should provide the debtor with an opportunity to free those assets by posting adequate security in their place.

The Georgia provisions fall short of these requirements. Garnishment may issue on the basis of a simple and conclusory affidavit that the garnishor has reason to apprehend the loss of money already owed. As

---

3. I am not in accord with the Court's suggestion that the Due Process Clause might require that a *judicial* officer issue the writ of garnishment. The basic protec- tion required for the debtor is the assur- ance of a prompt postgarnishment hearing before a judge.

shown by the affidavit filed in this case, an unrevealing assertion of apprehension of loss suffices to invoke the issuance of garnishment. This is insufficient to enable a neutral officer to make even the most superficial preliminary assessment of the creditor's asserted need.

The most compelling deficiency in the Georgia procedure is its failure to provide a prompt and adequate postgarnishment hearing. * * * [T]he Georgia statute contains no provision enabling the debtor to obtain prompt dissolution of the garnishment upon a showing of fact, nor any indication that the garnishor bears the burden of proving entitlement to the garnishment.

JUSTICE BLACKMUN, with whom JUSTICE REHNQUIST joins, dissenting.

* * *

Fuentes, a constitutional decision, obviously should not have been brought down and decided by a 4–3 vote when there were two vacancies on the court at the time of argument. It particularly should not have been decided by a 4–3 vote when Justices filling the vacant seats had qualified and were on hand and available to participate on reargument.[1]

* * *

[T]he Court now has embarked on a case-by-case analysis (weighted heavily in favor of *Fuentes* and with little hope under *Mitchell*) of the respective state statutes in this area. That road is a long and unrewarding one, and provides no satisfactory answers to issues of constitutional magnitude.

[CHIEF JUSTICE BURGER also dissented.]

Notes and Questions

1. Did *Mitchell* overrule *Fuentes,* as Justice Stewart contended? What would you emphasize in support of the argument that *Fuentes* was overruled? Does Justice White's characterization of *Fuentes'* rule in *Di–Chem* accurately reflect the decision in *Fuentes?* Recall that *Fuentes* noted that "[t]here may be cases in which a creditor could make a showing of immediate danger that a debtor will destroy or conceal disputed goods." See supra p. 37. Does that observation invite a reconciliation of the two cases?

2. Note Justice White's efforts to distinguish *Fuentes* in *Mitchell:*

(a) *Mitchell* stresses Louisiana's emphasis on specificity instead of "conclusory claims." What is the value of specificity? What should the plaintiff be specific about? Are more specific claims inherently more trustworthy? Keep these issues in mind for the discussion of pleading in Chapter III.

(b) *Mitchell* also says that the basis for obtaining a writ under the Louisiana procedure—with the nature and amount of the claim and grounds relied upon appearing from specific facts—is significantly different from the "broad fault" standard involved in *Fuentes.* Would the Louisiana standard

---

1. *Fuentes* was decided June 12, 1972. Mr. Justice Powell and Mr. Justice Rehnquist had taken their respective seats as Members of the Court five months before, on January 7. *Fuentes* had been argued November 9, 1971.

require consideration of contentions like those made by Ms. Fuentes about Firestone's failure to perform its servicing obligations? Would it be fair to require plaintiffs to identify and provide specifics about the debtor's possible defenses?

(c) *Mitchell* stresses the involvement of the judge in issuance of the writ. Why are judges to be preferred to other state employees? Is the need for the judge related to the specificity requirement? Recall the interventionist behavior of the judge in *Band's Refuse,* supra p. 3. Is a more activist approach what the *Mitchell* Court has in mind? Compare the role of the judge in issuing a search warrant (see n. 30 in *Fuentes*): "It is almost as if the *Mitchell* Court is carrying into the due process clause the very special requirements of the fourth amendment [for a search warrant]." Catz & Robinson, Due Process and Creditor's Remedies, 28 Rutgers L.Rev. 541, 559–60 (1975).

(d) Finally, *Mitchell* relies on Louisiana's provision of a post-seizure hearing at which plaintiff has the burden of proving grounds for issuance of the writ. Would this alternative suffice under *Fuentes*? Does *Mitchell* place as much emphasis as does *Fuentes* on participation by the defendant to assure an accurate decision?

3. Is *Mitchell* of continuing importance after *Di–Chem*? Courts have continued to rely upon it in some circumstances. See McLaughlin v. Weathers, 170 F.3d 577, 581 (6th Cir.1999) ("Under the *Mitchell* rationale, we deem the Tennessee prejudgment statute not to be facially invalid as lacking due process.").

4. In *Di–Chem,* Justice Blackmun protests that *Fuentes* should not have been decided by a Court with positions unfilled. After *Di–Chem,* does *Fuentes* have any lasting importance? Is Justice White's position in *Di–Chem* consistent with his position in *Fuentes?*

5. What was the "rule" regarding the need for preseizure notice after *Di–Chem*? Leading constitutional scholars opined that a statute authorizing seizure without a hearing "must have the following features: (1) the creditor must post a bond to safeguard the interest of the debtor; (2) the creditor or someone with personal knowledge of the facts must file an affidavit which sets out a prima facie claim for prejudgment attachment of the property; (3) a neutral magistrate must determine that the affidavit is sufficient before issuing the writ of attachment or replevin; (4) there must be a provision for a reasonably prompt post-attachment hearing for the debtor." J. Nowak, R. Rotunda & J. Young, Constitutional Law § 13.9 at 504 (1986). Based on your reading of the cases, would you add considerations to this list? Why should provision of these factors make a hearing unnecessary? Note that in *Di–Chem* Justice White says that *Fuentes* required either a hearing "or other safeguard against mistaken repossession."

6. In his *Fuentes* dissent, Justice White concluded that requiring preseizure notice and hearing was not worth the candle. Given the elaborateness of the ex parte procedure mandated by *Di–Chem*, could the same be said of efforts to relieve the creditor of the need to give notice before seizure? Assuming most debtors would not appear and contest, wouldn't it make sense for creditors to rely on hearings unless they were genuinely afraid the

debtors would make off with the goods before the sheriff arrived? Consider whether Justice White's views changed as you read the next case.

7. *Mathews v. Eldridge*: The Court's procedural due process analysis was further clarified in Mathews v. Eldridge, 424 U.S. 319, 96 S.Ct. 893, 47 L.Ed.2d 18 (1976), which cut back on the 1970 holding in Goldberg v. Kelly (supra p. 41 n.6) that a trial-type evidentiary hearing was always required before termination of welfare benefits. In *Mathews* the question was whether Social Security disability benefits could be terminated based on an administrative finding that the disability had ceased. The Social Security administrative process afforded what the Court called "elaborate" opportunities for claimants to contest the conclusion that their disability had ended, but allowed a full evidentiary hearing only after actual cessation of benefits. Noting that due process is a flexible concept in the administrative arena, the Court explained that the due process decision calls for consideration of three factors:

> First, the private interest that will be affected by the official action; second, the risk of an erroneous deprivation of such interest through the procedures used, and the probable value, if any, of additional or substitute procedural safeguards; and finally, the Government's interest, including the function involved and the fiscal and administrative burdens that additional or substitute procedural requirement would entail.

Examining the Social Security disability situation, the Court found that a pre-termination hearing should not be required. Since disability benefits are not based on financial need, the likelihood of serious loss due to an erroneous termination is less than in the welfare situation. Because the question of disability ordinarily turns on review of routine medical reports, the potential value of an evidentiary hearing is less than with the question of welfare eligibility. Finally, considerable burdens would result from a requirement for a pre-termination evidentiary hearing because continuance of benefits will prompt many who might not otherwise demand such a hearing to ask for one, and there will be few opportunities for the Government to recoup the additional payments if the initial decision is found correct.

This approach can be challenged. Mashaw, The Supreme Court's Due Process Calculus for Administrative Adjudication in Mathews v. Eldridge: Three Factors in Search of a Theory of Value, 44 U. Chi. L. Rev. 28 (1976), asserts that the Court's embrace of utilitarianism fails to credit "process values" that might be served by oral hearings, and that it tends to undermine individual dignity by denying a right to be heard before the sensitive judgment whether the person is entitled to continued support is made. See also R. Dworkin, Principle, Policy, Procedure, in A Matter of Principle (1985) at 72, 102 (the "psychological fact that people generally mind an adverse decision more if it is taken facelessly, without their participation, * * * is the sort of harm that figures in any decent utilitarian calculation"). Moreover, it has been said that, "by including the recipient's substantive interests in the balance, the Court signalled just how tenuous the distinction between procedure and substance really was," and that *Mathews* suggested "that adversary process was not always optimal." Bone, The Process of Making Process: Court Rulemaking, Democratic Legitimacy, and Procedural Efficacy, 87 Geo.L.J. 887, 902 (1999).

Mathews did not directly address procedure in formal courts, however. We turn now to its implications for prejudgment remedies.

CONNECTICUT v. DOEHR

Supreme Court of the United States, 1991.
501 U.S. 1, 111 S.Ct. 2105, 115 L.Ed.2d 1.

JUSTICE WHITE delivered an opinion, Parts I, II, and III of which are the opinion of the Court.*

This case requires us to determine whether a state statute that authorizes prejudgment attachment of real estate without prior notice or hearing, without a showing of extraordinary circumstances, and without a requirement that the person seeking the attachment post a bond, satisfies the Due Process Clause of the Fourteenth Amendment. We hold that, as applied to this case, it does not.

I

On March 15, 1988, Petitioner John F. DiGiovanni submitted an application to the Connecticut Superior Court for an attachment in the amount of $75,000 on respondent Brian K. Doehr's home in Meridan, Connecticut. DiGiovanni took this step in conjunction with a civil action for assault and battery that he was seeking to institute against Doehr in the same court. The suit did not involve Doehr's real estate nor did DiGiovanni have any pre-existing interest either in Doehr's home or any of his other property.

Connecticut law authorizes prejudgment attachment of real estate without affording prior notice or the opportunity for a prior hearing to the individual whose property is subject to the attachment. The State's prejudgment remedy statute provides, in relevant part:

> "The court or a judge of the court may allow the prejudgment remedy to be issued by an attorney without hearing as provided in sections 52–278c and 52–278d upon verification by oath of the plaintiff or of some competent affiant, that there is probable cause to sustain the validity of the plaintiff's claims and (1) that the prejudgment remedy requested is for an attachment of real property...." Conn.Gen.Stat. § 52–278e (1991).

The statute does not require the plaintiff to post a bond to insure the payment of damages that the defendant may suffer should the attachment prove wrongfully issued or the claim prove unsuccessful.

As required, DiGiovanni submitted an affidavit in support of his application. In five one-sentence paragraphs, DiGiovanni stated that the facts set forth in his previously submitted complaint were true; that "I was willfully, wantonly and maliciously assaulted by the defendant, Brian K. Doehr"; that "said assault and battery broke my left wrist and further caused an ecchymosis to my right eye, as well as other injuries";

---

* The Chief Justice, Justice Blackmun, Justice Kennedy, and Justice Souter join   Parts I, II, and III of this opinion, and Justice Scalia joins Parts I and III.

and that "I have further expended sums of money for medical care and treatment." The affidavit concluded with the statement, "In my opinion, the foregoing facts are sufficient to show that there is probable cause that judgment will be rendered for the plaintiff."

On the strength of these submissions the Superior Court judge, by an order dated March 17, found "probable cause to sustain the validity of the plaintiff's claim" and ordered the attachment on Doehr's home "to the value of $75,000." The sheriff attached the property four days later, on March 21. Only after this did Doehr receive notice of the attachment. He also had yet to be served with the complaint, which is ordinarily necessary for an action to commence in Connecticut. As the statute further required, the attachment notice informed Doehr that he had the right to a hearing: (1) to claim that no probable cause existed to sustain the claim; (2) to request that the attachment be vacated, modified, or that a bond be substituted; or (3) to claim that some portion of the property was exempt from execution. Conn.Gen.Stat. § 52–278e(b) (1991).

Rather than pursue these options, Doehr filed suit against DiGiovanni in Federal District Court, claiming that § 52–278e(a)(1) was unconstitutional under the Due Process Clause of the Fourteenth Amendment. The District Court upheld the statute and granted summary judgment in favor of DiGiovanni. Pinsky v. Duncan, 716 F.Supp. 58 (D.Conn.1989). On appeal, a divided panel of the United States Court of Appeals for the Second Circuit reversed. Pinsky v. Duncan, 898 F.2d 852 (1990).[3] Judge Pratt, who wrote the opinion for the court, concluded that the Connecticut statute violated due process in permitting ex parte attachment absent a showing of extraordinary circumstances. "The rule to be derived from *Sniadach* and its progeny, therefore, is not that post attachment hearings are generally acceptable provided that the plaintiff files a factual affidavit and that a judicial officer supervises the process, but that a prior hearing may be postponed where exceptional circumstances justify such a delay, and where sufficient additional safeguards are present." This conclusion was deemed to be consistent with our decision in Mitchell v. W.T. Grant Co., 416 U.S. 600 (1974), because the absence of a preattachment hearing was approved in that case based on the presence of extraordinary circumstances.

A further reason to invalidate the statute, the court ruled, was the highly factual nature of the issues in this case. In *Mitchell*, there were "uncomplicated matters that lent themselves to documentary proof" and "the nature of the issues at stake minimized the risk that the writ [would] be wrongfully issued by a judge." Similarly, in Mathews v. Eldridge, 424 U.S. 319, 343–344 (1976), where an evidentiary hearing was not required prior to the termination of disability benefits, the determination of disability was "sharply focused and easily documented." Judge Pratt observed that in contrast the present case involved the

---

3. The Court of Appeals invited Connecticut to intervene pursuant to 28 U.S.C. § 2403(b) after oral argument. The State elected to intervene in the appeal, and has fully participated in the proceedings before this Court.

fact-specific event of a fist fight and the issue of assault. He doubted that the judge could reliably determine probable cause when presented with only the plaintiff's version of the altercation. "Because the risk of a wrongful attachment is considerable under these circumstances, we conclude that dispensing with notice and opportunity for a hearing until after the attachment, without a showing of extraordinary circumstances, violates the requirements of due process." Judge Pratt went on to conclude that in his view, the statute was also constitutionally infirm for its failure to require the plaintiff to post a bond for the protection of the defendant in the event the attachment was ultimately found to have been improvident.

Judge Mahoney was also of the opinion that the statutory provision for attaching real property in civil actions, without a prior hearing and in the absence of extraordinary circumstances, was unconstitutional. He disagreed with Judge Pratt's opinion that a bond was constitutionally required. Judge Newman dissented from the holding that a hearing prior to attachment was constitutionally required and, like Judge Mahoney, disagreed with Judge Pratt on the necessity for a bond.

The dissent's conclusion accorded with the views of the Connecticut Supreme Court, which had previously upheld § 52–278e(b) in Fermont Division, Dynamics Corp. of America v. Smith, 178 Conn. 393, 423 A.2d 80 (1979). We granted certiorari to resolve the conflict of authority.

II

With this case we return to the question of what process must be afforded by a state statute enabling an individual to enlist the aid of the State to deprive another of his or her property by means of the prejudgment attachment or similar procedure. Our cases reflect the numerous variations this type of remedy can entail. In Sniadach v. Family Finance Corp. of Bay View, 395 U.S. 337 (1969), the Court struck down a Wisconsin statute that permitted a creditor to effect prejudgment garnishment of wages without notice and prior hearing to the wage earner. In Fuentes v. Shevin, 407 U.S. 67 (1972), the Court likewise found a Due Process violation in state replevin provisions that permitted vendors to have goods seized through an ex parte application to a court clerk and the posting of a bond. Conversely, the Court upheld a Louisiana ex parte procedure allowing a lienholder to have disputed goods sequestered in Mitchell v. W.T. Grant Co., 416 U.S. 600 (1974). *Mitchell,* however, carefully noted that *Fuentes* was decided against "a factual and legal background sufficiently different . . . that it does not require the invalidation of the Louisiana sequestration statute." Those differences included Louisiana's provision of an immediate postdeprivation hearing along with the option of damages; the requirement that a judge rather than a clerk determine that there is a clear showing of entitlement to the writ; the necessity for a detailed affidavit; and an emphasis on the lienholder's interest in preventing waste or alienation of the encumbered property. In North Georgia Finishing, Inc. v. Di–Chem, Inc., 419 U.S. 601 (1975), the Court again invalidated an ex parte garnishment statute that not only failed to provide for notice and prior hearing but that also failed to require a bond, a detailed affidavit setting out the claim, the determination of a neutral magistrate, or a prompt postdeprivation hearing.

These cases "underscore the truism that 'due process unlike some legal rules, is not a technical conception with a fixed content unrelated to time, place and circumstances.'" Mathews v. Eldridge, supra, [424 U.S.] at 334. In *Mathews,* we drew upon our prejudgment remedy decisions to determine what process is due when the government itself seeks to effect a deprivation on its own initiative. That analysis resulted in the now familiar threefold inquiry requiring consideration of "the private interest that will be affected by the official action"; "the risk of an erroneous deprivation of such interest through the procedures used, and the probable value, if any, of additional or substitute safeguards"; and lastly "the Government's interest, including the function involved and the fiscal and administrative burdens that the additional or substitute procedural requirement would entail."

Here the inquiry is similar but the focus is different. Prejudgment remedy statutes ordinarily apply to disputes between private parties rather than between an individual and the government. Such enactments are designed to enable one of the parties to "make use of state procedures with the overt, significant assistance of state officials," and they undoubtedly involve state action "substantial enough to implicate the Due Process Clause." Tulsa Professional Collection Services, Inc. v. Pope, 485 U.S. 478, 486 (1988). Nonetheless, any burden that increasing procedural safeguards entails primarily affects not the government, but the party seeking control of the other's property. See Fuentes v. Shevin, supra, at 99–101 (White, J., dissenting). For this type of case, therefore, the relevant inquiry requires, as in *Mathews,* first, consideration of the private interest that will be affected by the prejudgment measure; second, an examination of the risk of erroneous deprivation through the procedures under attack and the probable value of additional or alternative safeguards; and third, in contrast to *Mathews,* principal attention to the interest of the party seeking the prejudgment remedy, with, nonetheless, due regard for any ancillary interest the government may have in providing the procedure or forgoing the added burden of providing greater protections.

We now consider the *Mathews* factors in determining the adequacy of the procedures before us, first with regard to the safeguards of notice and a prior hearing, and then in relation to the protection of a bond.

III

We agree with the Court of Appeals that the property interests that attachment affects are significant. For a property owner like Doehr, attachment ordinarily clouds title; impairs the ability to sell or otherwise alienate the property; taints any credit rating; reduces the chance of obtaining a home equity loan or additional mortgage; and can even place an existing mortgage in technical default where there is an insecurity clause. Nor does Connecticut deny that any of these consequences occurs.

Instead, the State correctly points out that these effects do not amount to a complete, physical, or permanent deprivation of real property; their impact is less than the perhaps temporary total deprivation of household goods or wages. But the Court has never held that only such extreme deprivations trigger due process concern. To the contrary, our cases show that even the temporary or partial impairments to property rights that attachments, liens, and similar encumbrances entail are sufficient to merit due process protection. Without doubt, state procedures for creating and enforcing attachments, as with liens, "are subject to the strictures of due process."[4]

We also agree with the Court of Appeals that the risk of erroneous deprivation that the State permits here is substantial. By definition, attachment statutes premise a deprivation of property on one ultimate factual contingency—the award of damages to the plaintiff which the defendant may not be able to satisfy. For attachments before judgment, Connecticut mandates that this determination be made by means of a procedural inquiry that asks whether "there is probable cause to sustain the validity of the plaintiff's claim." Conn.Gen.Stat. § 52–278e(a). The statute elsewhere defines the validity of the claim in terms of the likelihood "that judgment will be rendered in the matter in favor of the plaintiff." Conn.Gen.Stat. § 52–278c(a)(2) (1991). What probable cause means in this context, however, remains obscure. The State initially took the position, as did the dissent below, that the statute requires a plaintiff to show the objective likelihood of the suit's success. DiGiovanni, citing ambiguous state cases, reads the provision as requiring no more than that a plaintiff demonstrate a subjective good faith belief that the suit will succeed. At oral argument, the State shifted its position to argue that the statute requires something akin to the plaintiff stating a claim with sufficient facts to survive a motion to dismiss.

We need not resolve this confusion since the statute presents too great a risk of erroneous deprivation under any of these interpretations. If the statute demands inquiry into the sufficiency of the complaint, or, still less, the plaintiff's good-faith belief that the complaint is sufficient, requirement of a complaint and a factual affidavit would permit a court to make these minimal determinations. But neither inquiry adequately reduces the risk of erroneous deprivation. Permitting a court to author-

---

4. Our summary affirmance in Spiel-man–Fond, Inc. v. Hanson's Inc., 417 U.S. 901 (1974), does not control. In *Spielman–Fond,* the District Court held that the filing of a mechanic's lien did not amount to the taking of a significant property interest. 379 F.Supp. 997, 999 (Ariz.1973) (three-judge court) (per curiam). A summary disposition does not enjoy the full precedential value of a case argued on the merits and disposed of by a written opinion. The facts of *Spielman–Fond* presented an alternative basis for affirmance in any event. Unlike the case before us, the mechanic's lien statute in *Spielman–Fond* required the creditor to have a pre-existing interest in the property at issue. As we explain below, a heightened plaintiff interest in certain circumstances can provide a ground for upholding procedures that are otherwise suspect.

ize attachment merely because the plaintiff believes the defendant is liable, or because the plaintiff can make out a facially valid complaint, would permit the deprivation of the defendant's property when the claim would fail to convince a jury, when it rested on factual allegations that were sufficient to state a cause of action but which the defendant would dispute, or in the case of a mere good-faith standard, even when the complaint failed to state a claim upon which relief could be granted. The potential for unwarranted attachment in these situations is self-evident and too great to satisfy the requirements of due process absent any countervailing consideration.

Even if the provision requires the plaintiff to demonstrate, and the judge to find, probable cause to believe that judgment will be rendered in favor of the plaintiff, the risk of error was substantial in this case. As the record shows, and as the State concedes, only a skeletal affidavit need be and was filed. The State urges that the reviewing judge normally reviews the complaint as well, but concedes that the complaint may also be conclusory. It is self-evident that the judge could make no realistic assessment concerning the likelihood of an action's success based upon these one-sided, self-serving, and conclusory submissions. And as the Court of Appeals said, in a case like this involving an alleged assault, even a detailed affidavit would give only the plaintiff's version of the confrontation. Unlike determining the existence of a debt or delinquent payments, the issue does not concern "ordinarily uncomplicated matters that lend themselves to documentary proof." *Mitchell,* 416 U.S., at 609. The likelihood of error that results illustrates that "fairness can rarely be obtained by secret, one-sided determination of facts decisive of rights.... [And no] better instrument has been devised for arriving at truth than to give a person in jeopardy of serious loss notice of the case against him and an opportunity to meet it." Joint Anti–Fascist Refugee Committee v. McGrath, 341 U.S. 123, 170–172 (1951) (Frankfurter, J., concurring).

What safeguards the State does afford do not adequately reduce this risk. Connecticut points out that the statute also provides an "expeditious" postattachment adversary hearing, § 52–278e(c);[5] notice for such a hearing, § 52–278e(b); judicial review of an adverse decision, § 52–278*l*(a); and a double damages action if the original suit is commenced without probable cause, § 52–568(a)(1). Similar considerations were present in *Mitchell* where we upheld Louisiana's sequestration statute despite the lack of predeprivation notice and hearing. But in *Mitchell,* the plaintiff had a vendor's lien to protect, the risk of error was minimal because the likelihood of recovery involved uncomplicated matters that

---

5. The parties vigorously dispute whether a defendant can in fact receive a prompt hearing. Doehr contends that the State's rules of practice prevent the filing of any motion—including a motion for the mandated post attachment hearing—until the return date on the complaint, which in this case was 30 days after service. Under state law at least 12 days must elapse between service on the defendant and the return date. The State counters that the postattachment hearing is available upon request. Even on this assumption, the State's procedures fail to provide adequate safeguards against the erroneous deprivation of the property interest at stake.

lent themselves to documentary proof, and plaintiff was required to put up a bond. None of these factors diminishing the need for a predeprivation hearing is present in this case. It is true that a later hearing might negate the presence of probable cause, but this would not cure the temporary deprivation that an earlier hearing might have prevented. "The Fourteenth Amendment draws no bright lines around three-day, 10–day or 50–day deprivations of property. Any significant taking of property by the State is within the purview of the Due Process Clause." *Fuentes,* 407 U.S., at 86.

Finally, we conclude that the interests in favor of an ex parte attachment, particularly the interests of the plaintiff, are too minimal to supply such a consideration here. Plaintiff had no existing interest in Doehr's real estate when he sought the attachment. His only interest in attaching the property was to ensure the availability of assets to satisfy his judgment if he prevailed on the merits of his action. Yet there was no allegation that Doehr was about to transfer or encumber his real estate or take any other action during the pendency of the action that would render his real estate unavailable to satisfy a judgment. Our cases have recognized such a properly supported claim would be an exigent circumstance permitting postponing any notice or hearing until after the attachment is effected. See *Mitchell,* supra, at 609; *Fuentes,* supra, at 90– 92; *Sniadach,* 395 U.S., at 339. Absent such allegations, however, the plaintiff's interest in attaching the property does not justify the burdening of Doehr's ownership rights without a hearing to determine the likelihood of recovery.

No interest the government may have affects the analysis. The State's substantive interest in protecting any rights of the plaintiff cannot be any more weighty than those rights themselves. Here the plaintiff's interest is de minimis. Moreover, the State cannot seriously plead additional financial or administrative burdens involving predeprivation hearings when it already claims to provide an immediate post deprivation hearing.

Historical and contemporary practice support our analysis. Prejudgment attachment is a remedy unknown at common law. Instead, "it traces its origin to the Custom of London, under which a creditor might attach money or goods of the defendant either in the plaintiff's own hands or in the custody of a third person, by proceedings in the mayor's court or in the sheriff's court." Ownbey [v. Morgan], 256 U.S., at 104. Generally speaking, attachment measures in both England and this country had several limitations that reduced the risk of erroneous deprivation which Connecticut permits. Although attachments ordinarily did not require prior notice or a hearing, they were usually authorized only where the defendant had taken or threatened to take some action that would place the satisfaction of the plaintiff's potential award in jeopardy. Attachments, moreover, were generally confined to claims by creditors. As we and the Court of Appeals have noted, disputes between debtors and creditors more readily lend themselves to accurate ex parte assessments of the merits. Tort actions, like the assault and battery claim at issue here, do not. Finally, as we will discuss below, attachment statutes historically required that the plaintiff post a bond.

Connecticut's statute appears even more suspect in light of current practice. A survey of state attachment provisions reveals that nearly every State requires either a preattachment hearing, a showing of some exigent circumstance, or both, before permitting an attachment to take place. Twenty-seven States, as well as the District of Columbia, permit attachments only when some extraordinary circumstance is present. In such cases, preattachment hearings are not required but postattachment hearings are provided. Ten States permit attachment without the presence of such factors but require prewrit hearings unless one of those factors is shown. Six States limit attachments to extraordinary circumstance cases but the writ will not issue prior to a hearing unless there is a showing of some even more compelling condition. Three States always require a preattachment hearing. Only Washington, Connecticut, and Rhode Island authorize attachments without a prior hearing in situations that do not involve any purportedly heightened threat to the plaintiff's interests. Even those States permit ex parte deprivations only in certain types of cases: Rhode Island does so only when the claim is equitable; Connecticut and Washington do so only when real estate is to be attached, and even Washington requires a bond. Conversely, the States for the most part no longer confine attachments to creditor claims. This development, however, only increases the importance of the other limitations.

We do not mean to imply that any given exigency requirement protects an attachment from constitutional attack. Nor do we suggest that the statutory measures we have surveyed are necessarily free of due process problems or other constitutional infirmities in general. We do believe, however, that the procedures of almost all the States confirm our view that the Connecticut provision before us, by failing to provide a preattachment hearing without at least requiring a showing of some exigent circumstance, clearly falls short of the demands of due process.

IV

A

Although a majority of the Court does not reach the issue, Justices Marshall, Stevens, O'Connor, and I deem it appropriate to consider whether due process also requires the plaintiff to post a bond or other security in addition to requiring a hearing or showing of some exigency.

As noted, the impairments to property rights that attachments affect merit due process protection. Several consequences can be severe, such as the default of a homeowner's mortgage. In the present context, it need only be added that we have repeatedly recognized the utility of a bond in protecting property rights affected by the mistaken award of prejudgment remedies. *Di–Chem,* 419 U.S., at 610, 611 (Powell, J., concurring in judgment); id., at 619 (Blackmun, J., dissenting); *Mitchell,* 416 U.S., at 606, n. 8.

Without a bond, at the time of attachment, the danger that these property rights may be wrongfully deprived remains unacceptably high even with such safeguards as a hearing or exigency requirement. The need for a bond is especially apparent where extraordinary circumstances justify an attachment with no more than the plaintiff's ex parte assertion of a claim. We have already discussed how due process tolerates, and the States generally permit, the otherwise impermissible chance of erroneously depriving the defendant in such situations in light of the heightened interest of the plaintiff. Until a postattachment hearing, however, a defendant has no protection against damages sustained where no extraordinary circumstance in fact existed or the plaintiff's likelihood of recovery was nil. Such protection is what a bond can supply. Both the Court and its individual members have repeatedly found the requirement of a bond to play an essential role in reducing what would have been too great a degree of risk in precisely this type of circumstance. *Mitchell,* supra, at 610, 619; *Di–Chem,* supra, at 613 (Powell, J., concurring in judgment); id., at 619 (Blackmun, J., dissenting); *Fuentes,* 407 U.S., at 101 (White, J., dissenting).

But the need for a bond does not end here. A defendant's property rights remain at undue risk even when there has been an adversarial hearing to determine the plaintiff's likelihood of recovery. At best, a court's initial assessment of each party's case cannot produce more than an educated prediction as to who will win. This is especially true when, as here, the nature of the claim makes any accurate prediction elusive. In consequence, even a full hearing under a proper probable-cause standard would not prevent many defendants from having title to their homes impaired during the pendency of suits that never result in the contingency that ultimately justifies such impairment, namely, an award to the plaintiff. Attachment measures currently on the books reflect this concern. All but a handful of States require a plaintiff's bond despite also affording a hearing either before, or (for the vast majority, only under extraordinary circumstances) soon after, an attachment takes place. Bonds have been a similarly common feature of other prejudgment remedy procedures that we have considered, whether or not these procedures also included a hearing.

The State stresses its double damages remedy for suits that are commenced without probable cause. Conn.Gen.Stat. § 52–568(a)(1).[8] This remedy, however, fails to make up for the lack of a bond. As an initial matter, the meaning of "probable cause" in this provision is no more clear here than it was in the attachment provision itself. Should the term mean the plaintiff's good faith or the facial adequacy of the complaint, the remedy is clearly insufficient. A defendant who was

---

8. Section 52–568(a)(1) provides:
"Any person who commences and prosecutes any civil action or complaint against another, in his own name, or the name of others, or asserts a defense to any civil action or complaint commenced and prosecuted by another (1) without probable cause, shall pay such other person double damages, or (2) without probable cause, and with a malicious intent unjustly to vex and trouble such other person, shall pay him treble damages."

deprived where there was little or no likelihood that the plaintiff would obtain a judgment could nonetheless recover only by proving some type of fraud or malice or by showing that the plaintiff had failed to state a claim. Problems persist even if the plaintiff's ultimate failure permits recovery. At best a defendant must await a decision on the merits of the plaintiff's complaint, even assuming that a § 52–568(a)(1) action may be brought as a counterclaim. Settlement, under Connecticut law, precludes seeking the damages remedy, a fact that encourages the use of attachments as a tactical device to pressure an opponent to capitulate. An attorney's advice that there is probable cause to commence an action constitutes a complete defense, even if the advice was unsound or erroneous. Finally, there is no guarantee that the original plaintiff will have adequate assets to satisfy an award that the defendant may win.

Nor is there any appreciable interest against a bond requirement. Section 52–278e(a)(1) does not require a plaintiff to show exigent circumstances nor any pre-existing interest in the property facing attachment. A party must show more than the mere existence of a claim before subjecting an opponent to prejudgment proceedings that carry a significant risk of erroneous deprivation.

B

Our foregoing discussion compels the four of us to consider whether a bond excuses the need for a hearing or other safeguards altogether. If a bond is needed to augment the protections afforded by preattachment and postattachment hearings, it arguably follows that a bond renders these safeguards unnecessary. That conclusion is unconvincing, however, for it ignores certain harms that bonds could not undo but that hearings would prevent. The law concerning attachments has rarely, if ever, required defendants to suffer an encumbered title until the case is concluded without any prior opportunity to show that the attachment was unwarranted. Our cases have repeatedly emphasized the importance of providing a prompt postdeprivation hearing at the very least. Every State but one, moreover, expressly requires a preattachment or postattachment hearing to determine the propriety of an attachment.

The necessity for at least a prompt postattachment hearing is self-evident because the right to be compensated at the end of the case, if the plaintiff loses, for all provable injuries caused by the attachment is inadequate to redress the harm inflicted, harm that could have been avoided had an early hearing been held. An individual with an immediate need or opportunity to sell a property can neither do so, nor otherwise satisfy that need or recreate the opportunity. The same applies to a parent in need of a home equity loan for a child's education, an entrepreneur seeking to start a business on the strength of an otherwise strong credit rating, or simply a homeowner who might face the disruption of having a mortgage placed in technical default. The extent of these harms, moreover, grows with the length of the suit. Here, oral argument indicated that civil suits in Connecticut commonly take up to four to seven years for completion. Many state attachment statutes require that the amount of a bond be anywhere from the equivalent to twice the amount the plaintiff seeks. These amounts bear no relation to the harm the defendant might suffer even assuming that money damages can make up for the foregoing disruptions. It should be clear, however, that such an assumption is fundamentally flawed. Reliance on a bond does not sufficiently account for the harms that flow from an erroneous attachment to excuse a State from reducing that risk by means of a timely hearing.

If a bond cannot serve to dispense with a hearing immediately after attachment, neither is it sufficient basis for not providing a preattachment hearing in the absence of exigent circumstances even if in any event a hearing would be provided a few days later. The reasons are the same: a wrongful attachment can inflict injury that will not fully be redressed by recovery on the bond after a prompt postattachment hearing determines that the attachment was invalid.

Once more, history and contemporary practice support our conclusion. Historically, attachments would not issue without a showing of extraordinary circumstances even though a plaintiff bond was almost invariably required in addition. Likewise, all but eight States currently require the posting of a bond. Out of this 42 State majority, all but one requires a preattachment hearing, a showing of some exigency, or both, and all but one expressly require a postattachment hearing when an attachment has been issued ex parte. This testimony underscores the point that neither a hearing nor an extraordinary circumstance limitation eliminates the need for a bond, no more than a bond allows waiver of these other protections. To reconcile the interests of the defendant and the plaintiff accurately, due process generally requires all of the above.

V

Because Connecticut's prejudgment remedy provision, Conn.Gen. Stat. § 52–278e(a)(1), violates the requirements of due process by authorizing prejudgment attachment without prior notice or a hearing, the judgment of the Court of Appeals is affirmed, and the case is remanded to that court for further proceedings consistent with this opinion.

CHIEF JUSTICE REHNQUIST with whom JUSTICE BLACKMUN joins, concurring.

I agree with the Court that the Connecticut attachment statute, "as applied in this case," fails to satisfy the Due Process Clause of the Fourteenth Amendment. I therefore join Parts I, II and III of its opinion. Unfortunately, the remainder of the Court's opinion does not confine itself to the facts of this case, but enters upon a lengthy disquisition as to what combination of safeguards are required to satisfy Due Process in hypothetical cases not before the Court. I therefore do not join Part IV.

As the Court's opinion points out, the Connecticut statute allows attachment not merely for a creditor's claim, but for a tort claim of assault and battery; it affords no opportunity for a pre-deprivation hearing; it contains no requirement that there be "exigent circumstances," such as an effort on the part of the defendant to conceal assets; no bond is required from the plaintiff; and the property attached is one in which the plaintiff has no pre-existing interest. The Court's opinion is, in my view, ultimately correct when it bases its holding of unconstitutionality of the Connecticut statute as applied here on our cases of Sniadach v. Family Finance Corp., 395 U.S. 337 (1969); Fuentes v. Shevin, 407 U.S. 67 (1972), Mitchell v. W.T. Grant Co., 416 U.S. 600 (1974), and North Georgia Finishing v. Di–Chem, Inc., 419 U.S. 601 (1975). But I do not believe that the result follows so inexorably as the Court's opinion suggests. All of the cited cases dealt with personalty— bank deposits or chattels—and each involved the physical seizure of the property itself, so that the defendant was deprived of its use. These cases, which represented something of a revolution in the jurisprudence of procedural due process, placed substantial limits on the methods by which creditors could obtain a lien on the assets of a debtor prior to judgment. But in all of them the debtor was deprived of the use and possession of the property. In the present case, on the other hand, Connecticut's pre-judgment attachment on real property statute, which secures an incipient lien for the plaintiff, does not deprive the defendant of the use or possession of the property.

The Court's opinion therefore breaks new ground, and I would point out, more emphatically than the Court does, the limits of today's holding. In Spielman–Fond, Inc. v. Hanson's, Inc., 379 F.Supp. 997, 999 (D.Ariz.1973), the District Court held that the filing of a mechanics' lien did not cause the deprivation of a significant property interest of the owner. We summarily affirmed that decision. 417 U.S. 901 (1974). Other courts have read this summary affirmance to mean that the mere imposition of a lien on real property, which does not disturb the owner's use or enjoyment of the property, is not a deprivation of property calling for procedural due process safeguards. I agree with the Court, however, that upon analysis the deprivation here is a significant one, even though the owner remains in undisturbed possession. "For a property owner like Doehr, attachment ordinarily clouds title; impairs the ability to sell or otherwise alienate the property; taints any credit rating; reduces the chance of obtaining a home equity loan or additional mortgage; and can even place an existing mortgage in technical default when there is an insecurity clause." Given the elaborate system of title records relating to real property which prevails in all of our states, a lienor need not obtain possession or use of real property belonging to a debtor in order to significantly impair its value to him.

But in *Spielman–Fond, Inc.,* supra, there was, as the Court points out in fn. 4, ante, an alternate basis available to this Court for affirmance of that decision. Arizona recognized a pre-existing lien in favor of unpaid mechanics and materialmen who had contributed labor or supplies which were incorporated in improvements to real property. The existence of such a lien upon the very property ultimately posted or noticed distinguishes those cases from the present one, where the plaintiff had no pre-existing interest in the real property which he sought to attach. Materialman's and mechanic's lien statutes award an interest in real property to workers who have contributed their labor, and to suppliers who have furnished material, for the improvement of the real property. Since neither the labor nor the material can be reclaimed once it has become a part of the realty, this is the only method by which workmen or small businessmen who have contributed to the improvement of the property may be given a remedy against a property owner who has defaulted on his promise to pay for the labor and the materials. To require any sort of a contested court hearing or bond before the notice of lien takes effect would largely defeat the purpose of these statutes.

Petitioner in its brief relies in part on our summary affirmance in Bartlett v. Williams, 464 U.S. 801 (1983). That case involved a lis pendens, in which the question presented to this Court was whether such a procedure could be valid when the only protection afforded to the owner of land affected by the lis pendens was a post-sequestration hearing. A notice of lis pendens is a well established traditional remedy whereby a plaintiff (usually a judgment creditor) who brings an action to enforce an interest in property to which the defendant has title gives notice of the pendency of such action to third parties; the notice causes the interest which he establishes, if successful, to relate back to the date of the filing of the lis pendens. The filing of such notice will have an effect upon the defendant's ability to alienate the property, or to obtain additional security on the basis of title to the property, but the effect of the lis pendens is simply to give notice to the world of the remedy being sought in the lawsuit itself. The lis pendens itself creates no additional right in the property on the part of the plaintiff, but simply allows third parties to know that a lawsuit is pending in which the plaintiff is seeking to establish such a right. Here, too, the fact that the plaintiff already claims an interest in the property which he seeks to enforce by a lawsuit distinguishes this class of cases from the Connecticut attachment employed in the present case.

Today's holding is a significant development in the law * * *. The change is dramatically reflected when we compare today's decision with the almost casual statement of Justice Holmes, writing for a unanimous Court in Coffin Brothers v. Bennett, 277 U.S. 29, 31 (1928):

> "Nothing is more common than to allow parties alleging themselves to be creditors to establish in advance by attachment a lien dependent for its effect upon the result of the suit."

The only protection accorded to the debtor in that case was the right to contest his liability in a post-deprivation proceeding.

It is both unwise and unnecessary, I believe, for the Court to proceed, as it does in Part IV, from its decision of the case before it to discuss abstract and hypothetical situations not before it. This is especially so where we are dealing with the Due Process Clause which, as the Court recognizes, "unlike some legal rules, is not a technical conception with a fixed content unrelated to time, place and circumstances," and it is even more true in a case involving constitutional limits on the methods by which the states may transfer or create interests in real property; in other areas of the law, dicta may do little damage, but those who insure titles or write title opinions often do not enjoy the luxury of distinguishing between dicta and holding.

The two elements of due process with which the Court concerns itself in Part IV—the requirement of a bond, and of "exigent circumstances"—prove to be upon analysis so vague that the discussion is not only unnecessary, but not particularly useful. Unless one knows what the terms and conditions of a bond are to be, the requirement of a "bond" in the abstract means little. The amount to be secured by the bond and the conditions of the bond are left unaddressed—is there to be liability on the part of a plaintiff if he is ultimately unsuccessful in the underlying lawsuit, or is it instead to be conditioned on some sort of good faith test? The "exigent circumstances" referred to by the Court are admittedly equally vague; non-residency appears to be enough in some states, an attempt to conceal assets is required in others, an effort to flee the jurisdiction in still others. We should await concrete cases which present questions involving bonds and exigent circumstances before we attempt to decide when and if the Due Process Clause of the Fourteenth Amendment requires them as prerequisites for a lawful attachment.

Justice Scalia, concurring in part and concurring in the judgment.

Since the manner of attachment here was not a recognized procedure at common law, I agree that its validity under the Due Process Clause should be determined by applying the test we set forth in Mathews v. Eldridge, 424 U.S. 319 (1976); and I agree that it fails that test. I join Parts I and III of the Court's opinion, and concur in the judgment of the Court.

Notes and Questions

1. *Postscript*: Eventually, a jury awarded DiGiovanni $5,600 in damages in his state-court suit against Doehr. In the federal case, the district court rendered summary judgment in Doehr's favor on the constitutional deprivation issue, but found that no damages should be awarded against DiGiovanni. See Pinsky v. Duncan, 79 F.3d 306 (2d Cir.1996). For further details, see Bone, The Story of Connecticut v. Doehr: Balancing Costs and Benefits in Defining Procedural Rights, in Civil Procedure Stories (2004), at 153.

2. *Doehr* was the Supreme Court's first major decision regarding prejudgment remedies after *Di–Chem*. Is it consistent with *Fuentes*? Is Justice White's position consistent with his position in *Fuentes*?

In United States v. James Daniel Good Real Property, 510 U.S. 43, 114 S.Ct. 492, 126 L.Ed.2d 490 (1993), the Court held, 5–4, that seizure of Good's house without notice and a prior hearing pursuant to drug trafficking forfeiture laws violated Fifth Amendment due process under *Fuentes* and

Doehr. Good had pleaded guilty to "promoting a harmful drug" after 89 pounds of marijuana were seized at his Hawaii home in a search pursuant to a search warrant. More than four years later, the United States obtained an ex parte writ of arrest in rem from a Magistrate Judge on the basis that it had made a prima facie showing that the house was subject to forfeiture under 21 U.S.C.A. § 881(a) because it had been used in drug trafficking. The government did not dispossess Good's tenants, but ordered them to pay their rent to it rather than to Good.

Writing for the Court, Justice Kennedy first rejected the government's argument that since the procedures employed would suffice for a search warrant under the Fourth Amendment they were perforce sufficient for Fifth Amendment due process as well because the seizure was not to preserve evidence of wrongdoing but to assert ownership. He found Good's case distinguishable from the seizure of a yacht in Calero–Toledo v. Pearson Yacht Leasing Co. (supra pp. 40–41 n. 4) because real property like Good's house "can be neither moved nor concealed." Invoking *Fuentes* for the proposition that "[w]e tolerate some exceptions to the general rules requiring predeprivation notice and hearing, but only in 'extraordinary situations where some valid governmental interest is at stake,' " the Court concluded that the governmental interest at stake was not "some general interest in forfeiting property but the specific interest in seizing real property before the forfeiture hearing," noting that lesser measures such as a lis pendens would protect the government's interest in that interregnum. The Court also found that there was an unacceptable risk of error because the statute allows a defense of innocent ownership but the government is not required to put on evidence on that subject. The Court stated that its decision applied to all real property.

Chief Justice Rehnquist rejected the majority's "expansive readings" of *Fuentes* and *Doehr,* noting that *Fuentes* appeared to approve summary seizure of property to collect taxes, which he considered analogous to the seizure of Good's house, and argued that "the seizure of respondent Good's real estate serves important governmental purposes in combatting illegal drugs." Justice O'Connor, also dissenting, added that "it is difficult to see what advantage a preseizure hearing would have had in this case. There was already an ex parte hearing before a magistrate to determine whether there was proper cause to believe that Good's property had been used in connection with a drug trafficking offense."

3.   Note that the Court in *Doehr* says at the outset that the Connecticut statute violates due process "as applied in this case." What implication should that have for future cases? In Shaumyan v. O'Neill, 987 F.2d 122 (2d Cir.1993), the court held that attachment under the same statute was constitutional because the facts were different. Shaumyan, a Yale professor, had contracted for painting and repairs on his house in New Haven but refused to pay when the work was not done to his satisfaction. The contractor sued in a Connecticut state court and obtained an attachment on the home without a hearing or a bond, and Shaumyan responded with a class action in federal court on due process grounds.

The Second Circuit upheld summary judgment for defendants, distinguishing *Doehr* as an intentional tort case and limiting its attention to whether the statute was unconstitutional as applied to Shaumyan. Although the same property interests were involved, the court found that the risk of an erroneous deprivation was not high. The contractor had submitted an affidavit detailing the contract and plaintiff's failure to pay the amount due. The Second Circuit found the facts "easily documented" regarding liability in a sum certain and concluded that the safeguards of the statute were similar to those upheld in Mitchell v. W.T. Grant Co. (supra p. 42). In addition, unlike plaintiff in *Doehr,* the contractor had a preexisting interest in the property that the attachment protected. The court also rejected the claim that a bond should be required on the ground that there was no significant risk of an erroneous attachment.

Despite the possibility that its statute could still be constitutionally applied, Connecticut amended its § 52–278e(a) in 1991 and 1993 to require the plaintiff to file an affidavit setting forth facts sufficient to show probable cause that a judgment would be rendered in its favor and showing exigent circumstances including defendant's likely removal of property from the state or fraudulent hiding or disposition of property that would be available to satisfy a judgment. Defendant may request that a bond be posted. See § 52–278e(b).

4. In *Doehr,* the Court applies the three-part analysis of Mathews v. Eldridge to prejudgment remedies. Is this preferable to the approach adopted in the Court's earlier cases? Consider the following endorsement of this approach by the leading proponent of law and economics analysis:

> Of course, * * * it is rarely possible (or at least efforts are not made) to quantify the terms. But the formula is valuable even when used qualitatively rather than quantitatively. Suppose, for example, that the issue is whether the owner of an apparently abandoned car should be notified, and given an opportunity for a hearing, before the car is towed away and sold for scrap. The chance that the car wasn't really abandoned, but broke down or was stolen, is not trivial, and the cost of a hearing is modest relative to the value of the car; so maybe, as most courts have held, the owner should be entitled to the hearing. But suppose we are speaking not of abandoned but of illegally parked cars. Since the cars are not about to be destroyed, the deprivation is much less than in the case of the abandoned car. The probability of error is also much lower, because ordinarily the determination of whether a car is illegally parked is cut and dried. And the cost of a predeprivation hearing is very high; if the owner has to be notified before the car is towed, he'll remove it and the deterrent effect will be eliminated. So courts hold that due process does not require a predeprivation hearing in the case of illegally parked cars.

R. Posner, Economic Analysis of Law 600 (5th ed. 1998); compare Propert v. District of Columbia, 948 F.2d 1327 (D.C.Cir.1991) (due process violated by towing and destruction without a hearing of plaintiff's 1969 Volkswagen Karmann Ghia, which was parked near his house, removed on basis of determination of officer that due to its physical appearance it was "junk") with Patterson v. Cronin, 650 P.2d 531 (Colo.1982) (due process not violated by application of Denver boot to plaintiff's car without prior hearing for failure to pay seven outstanding parking tickets).

In City of Los Angeles v. David, 538 U.S. 715, 123 S.Ct. 1895, 155 L.Ed.2d 946 (2003), the Court faced a similar question. Plaintiff's car was towed from a no parking zone, but plaintiff claimed that the no parking sign was obscured by trees and insisted on a hearing to contest the $134.50 he had to pay to recover the car. The hearing was held 30 days later, and after he lost at the hearing plaintiff sued in federal court insisting that due process entitled him to a hearing within five days. The Supreme Court rejected his arguments, using the Mathews v. Eldredge three-part test. First, the private interest was merely a monetary interest, which could be compensated by an interest payment. Second, concern for accuracy does not require a hearing within five days because a delay of less than 30 days is unlikely to affect the accuracy of the decision. "[T]he straightforward nature of the issue—whether the car was illegally parked—indicates that initial towing errors, while they may occur, are unlikely." Finally, the governmental interest argues strongly for allowing the city more time, because scheduling hearings that quickly would pose severe administrative burdens on the city. See also Krimstock v. Kelly, 306 F.3d 40 (2d Cir.2002) (time lag of one or two months in initiating proceedings to forfeit a seized vehicle, during which owner could not challenge seizure, did not violate due process, particularly in light of the government's direct interest in the vehicle it claimed was subject to forfeiture).

5. Are the *Mathews* factors correctly applied in *Doehr*?

(a) Regarding the deprivation suffered by Doehr, note that the issue seems to be the effect of an attachment during the delay until a hearing is held. Given the depressed state of the Connecticut housing market in 1988, how likely is it that a lender would take any action against Doehr during that time due to the attachment if he had been making his mortgage payments on time? Wouldn't Doehr's only real deprivation during that interim occur if he were in the process of selling or refinancing his house? In fact, Doehr was in the process of putting his house on the market. Bone, supra note 1, at 156.

(b) Regarding the risk of error found by the Court, consider whether it was due to the type of issue presented in this tort suit or to the fact that there was no adversary proceeding.

(c) Regarding the plaintiff's interest, does the Court hold that attachment without notice is only permitted when the plaintiff has a preexisting interest in the property? Recall the suggestion above that the only significant deprivation Doehr would be likely to suffer would occur if he were about to sell or refinance his house. How would those circumstances bear on the question whether exigent circumstances warranting immediate action were present?

6. Recall the factors emphasized in the Court's decisions in *Mitchell* (supra p. 42) and *Di–Chem* (supra p. 45) such as (1) that there be a showing under oath by the plaintiff of a prima facie right to relief (2) presented to a judge, who should (3) require posting of a bond if attachment issues and afford defendant (4) an opportunity for a prompt post-deprivation hearing, and perhaps that (5) plaintiff have a pre-existing interest in the property such as a vendor's lien and/or (6) show exigent circumstances and/or (7) assert a claim readily resolved on documentary evidence. Which of the

Mathews factors do these various considerations address? In *Doehr* the Court discussed the expeditious postattachment hearing as an element of the risk of error. Does that seem to be the proper factor under *Mathews* for analysis of this consideration?

7. Prior to *Doehr,* it appeared that due process would invariably be satisfied by providing notice and a right to a hearing. Is that true after *Doehr?* Four Justices address the need for a bond after a hearing, and the Court examines various possible standards of proof that could be applied to the showing made at such a hearing by plaintiffs. Does due process now place limitations on these topics with regard to post-hearing attachments? Note also that four Justices say that "even when there has been an adversarial hearing to determine the plaintiff's likelihood of recovery * * * a court's initial assessment of each party's case cannot produce more than an educated guess as to who will win. This is especially true when, as here, the nature of the claim makes any accurate prediction elusive." Under those circumstances, should attachment be allowed at all in the absence of some exigent circumstances?

8. The Court emphasizes the current practice of other states in evaluating the constitutionality of Connecticut's prejudgment seizure statute. In some instances, the Court treats the prevalence of a practice among the states as important evidence that the practice satisfies due process. See Burnham v. Superior Court, infra p. 809 (upholding constitutionality of basing personal jurisdiction solely on personal service in state). But the practices condemned in *Fuentes* were widespread. Ironically, the current strictness exhibited by many states toward prejudgment seizure and relied upon by the Court in *Doehr* can be traced to the decision in *Fuentes,* which made it necessary for states to revise their attachment statutes. Connecticut itself had revised its attachment statutes based on *Mitchell.* See Bone, supra note 1, at 159.

B. POST JUDGMENT REMEDIES

The centerpiece of a law suit—indeed, the very reason it was filed— is the remedy sought by the claimant. A remedy, in the form of a judgment, may be awarded after a full trial, or, in certain circumstances, after a final determination short of trial (such as default judgment or summary judgment). The usual remedy in our legal system is money damages. "Actual damages are the bottom line in most lawsuits." Frey & Orr, Litigating Damages: Actual and Punitive, 29 Litigation 33, 33 (Winter 2003). However, other remedies such as equitable relief (for example, an injunction or specific performance) or declaratory relief (a court order declaring the respective rights of the parties) may be available. We will consider here certain aspects of the remedies of damages and injunctive relief in an attempt to give you an early insight into the nature of the judicial remedies that are the ultimate objective of the litigation process.

1. *Damages*

CAREY v. PIPHUS

Supreme Court of the United States, 1978.
435 U.S. 247, 98 S.Ct. 1042, 55 L.Ed.2d 252.

JUSTICE POWELL delivered the opinion of the Court.

In this case, brought under 42 U.S.C. § 1983, we consider the elements and prerequisites for recovery of damages by students who were suspended from public elementary and secondary schools without procedural due process. The Court of Appeals for the Seventh Circuit held that the students are entitled to recover substantial nonpunitive damages even if their suspensions were justified, and even if they do not prove that any other actual injury was caused by the denial of procedural due process. We disagree, and hold that in the absence of proof of actual injury, the students are entitled to recover only nominal damages.

I

Respondent Jarius Piphus was a freshman at Chicago Vocational High School during the 1973–1974 school year. On January 23, 1974, during school hours, the school principal saw Piphus and another student standing outdoors on school property passing back and forth what the principal described as an irregularly shaped cigarette. The principal approached the students unnoticed and smelled what he believed was the strong odor of burning marijuana. He also saw Piphus try to pass a packet of cigarette papers to the other student. When the students became aware of the principal's presence, they threw the cigarette into a nearby hedge.

The principal took the students to the school's disciplinary office and directed the assistant principal to impose the "usual" 20–day suspension for violation of the school rule against the use of drugs. The students protested that they had not been smoking marijuana, but to no avail. Piphus was allowed to remain at school, although not in class, for the remainder of the school day while the assistant principal tried, without success, to reach his mother.

A suspension notice was sent to Piphus' mother, and a few days later two meetings were arranged among Piphus, his mother, his sister, school officials, and representatives from a legal aid clinic. The purpose of the meetings was not to determine whether Piphus had been smoking marijuana, but rather to explain the reasons for the suspension. Following an unfruitful exchange of views, Piphus and his mother, as guardian ad litem, filed suit against petitioners in Federal District Court under 42 U.S.C. § 1983 and its jurisdictional counterpart, 28 U.S.C. § 1343, charging that Piphus had been suspended without due process of law in violation of the Fourteenth Amendment. The complaint sought declaratory and injunctive relief, together with actual and punitive damages in the amount of $3,000. Piphus was readmitted to school under a temporary restraining order after eight days of his suspension.

Respondent Silas Brisco was in the sixth grade at Clara Barton Elementary School in Chicago during the 1973–1974 school year. On September 11, 1973, Brisco came to school wearing one small earring. The previous school year the school principal had issued a rule against the wearing of earrings by male students because he believed that this practice denoted membership in certain street gangs and increased the likelihood that gang members would terrorize other students. Brisco was reminded of this rule, but he refused to remove the earring, asserting that it was a symbol of black pride, not of gang membership.

The assistant principal talked to Brisco's mother, advising her that her son would be suspended for 20 days if he did not remove the earring. Brisco's mother supported her son's position, and a 20–day suspension was imposed. Brisco and his mother, as guardian ad litem, filed suit in Federal District Court under 42 U.S.C. § 1983 and 28 U.S.C. § 1343, charging that Brisco had been suspended without due process of law in violation of the Fourteenth Amendment. The complaint sought declaratory and injunctive relief, together with actual and punitive damages in the amount of $5,000. Brisco was readmitted to school during the pendency of proceedings for a preliminary injunction after 17 days of his suspension.

Piphus' and Brisco's cases were consolidated for trial and submitted on stipulated records. The District Court held that both students had been suspended without procedural due process.[5] * * * Despite these holdings, the District Court declined to award damages because:

> "Plaintiffs put no evidence in the record to quantify their damages, and the record is completely devoid of any evidence which could even form the basis of a speculative inference measuring the extent of their injuries. Plaintiffs' claims for damages therefore fail for complete lack of proof."

The court also stated that the students were entitled to declaratory relief and to deletion of the suspensions from their school records, but for reasons that are not apparent the court failed to enter an order to that effect. Instead, it simply dismissed the complaints. No finding was made as to whether respondents would have been suspended if they had received procedural due process.

On respondents' appeal, the Court of Appeals reversed and remanded. It first held that the District Court erred in not granting declaratory and injunctive relief. It also held that the District Court should have considered evidence submitted by respondents after judgment that tended to prove the pecuniary value of each day of school that they missed while suspended. The court said, however, that respondents would not be entitled to recover damages representing the value of missed school

---

5. The District Court read Goss v. Lopez, [419 U.S. 565, 95 S.Ct. 729, 42 L.Ed.2d 725 (1975)], as requiring "more formal procedures" for suspensions of more than 10 days than for suspensions of less than 10 days, and it set forth a detailed list of procedural requirements. Petitioners have not challenged either the holding that respondents were denied procedural due process, or the listing of rights that must be granted.

time if petitioners showed on remand "that there was just cause for the suspension[s] and that therefore [respondents] would have been suspended even if a proper hearing had been held."

Finally, the Court of Appeals held that even if the District Court found on remand that respondents' suspensions were justified, they would be entitled to recover substantial "nonpunitive" damages simply because they had been denied procedural due process. Relying on its earlier decision in Hostrop v. Board of Junior College Dist. No. 515, 523 F.2d 569 (C.A.7 1975), cert. denied, 425 U.S. 963, 96 S.Ct. 1748, 48 L.Ed.2d 208 (1976), the court stated that such damages should be awarded "even if, as in the case at bar, there is no proof of individualized injury to the plaintiff, such as mental distress. . . ." We granted certiorari to consider whether, in an action under § 1983 for the deprivation of procedural due process, a plaintiff must prove that he actually was injured by the deprivation before he may recover substantial "nonpunitive" damages.

II

Title 42 U.S.C. § 1983, derived from § 1 of the Civil Rights Act of 1871, provides:

> "Every person who, under color of any statute, ordinance, regulation, custom, or usage, of any State or Territory, subjects, or causes to be subjected, any citizen of the United States or other person within the jurisdiction thereof to the deprivation of any rights, privileges, or immunities secured by the Constitution and laws, shall be liable to the party injured in an action at law, suit in equity, or other proper proceeding for redress."

The legislative history of § 1983, elsewhere detailed, demonstrates that it was intended to "[create] a species of tort liability" in favor of persons who are deprived of "rights, privileges, or immunities secured" to them by the Constitution.

Petitioners contend that the elements and prerequisites for recovery of damages under this "species of tort liability" should parallel those for recovery of damages under the common law of torts. In particular, they urge that the purpose of an award of damages under § 1983 should be to compensate persons for injuries that are caused by the deprivation of constitutional rights; and, further, that plaintiffs should be required to prove not only that their rights were violated, but also that injury was caused by the violation, in order to recover substantial damages. Unless respondents prove that they actually were injured by the deprivation of procedural due process, petitioners argue, they are entitled at most to nominal damages.

Respondents seem to make two different arguments in support of the holding below. First, they contend that substantial damages should be awarded under § 1983 for the deprivation of a constitutional right *whether* or *not* any injury was caused by the deprivation. This, they say, is appropriate both because constitutional rights are valuable in and of themselves, and because of the need to deter violations of constitutional rights. Respondents believe that this view reflects accurately that of the Congress that enacted § 1983. Second, respondents argue that even if the purpose of a § 1983 damages award is, as petitioners contend, primarily to compensate persons for injuries that are caused by the deprivation of constitutional rights, every deprivation of procedural due process may be presumed to cause some injury. This presumption, they say, should relieve them from the necessity of proving that injury actually was caused.

A

Insofar as petitioners contend that the basic purpose of a § 1983 damages award should be to compensate persons for injuries caused by the deprivation of constitutional rights, they have the better of the argument. Rights, constitutional and otherwise, do not exist in a vacuum. Their purpose is to protect persons from injuries to particular interests, and their contours are shaped by the interests they protect.

Our legal system's concept of damages reflects this view of legal rights. "The cardinal principle of damages in Anglo–American law is that of *compensation* for the injury caused to plaintiff by defendant's breach of duty." 2 F. Harper & F. James, Law of Torts § 25.1, p. 1299 (1956) (emphasis in original). The Court implicitly has recognized the applicability of this principle to actions under § 1983 by stating that damages are available under that section for actions "found ... to have been violative of ... constitutional rights *and to have caused compensable injury....*" Wood v. Strickland, 420 U.S., at 319, 95 S.Ct., at 999 (emphasis supplied). The lower federal courts appear generally to agree that damages awards under § 1983 should be determined by the compensation principle.

The Members of the Congress that enacted § 1983 did not address directly the question of damages, but the principle that damages are designed to compensate persons for injuries caused by the deprivation of rights hardly could have been foreign to the many lawyers in Congress in 1871. Two other sections of the Civil Rights Act of 1871 appear to incorporate this principle, and no reason suggests itself for reading § 1983 differently. To the extent that Congress intended that awards under § 1983 should deter the deprivation of constitutional rights, there is no evidence that it meant to establish a deterrent more formidable than that inherent in the award of compensatory damages.[11]

11. This is not to say that exemplary or punitive damages might not be awarded in a proper case under § 1983 with the specific purpose of deterring or punishing violations of constitutional rights. [The Court cited several lower court decisions upholding punitive awards in § 1983 cases.] Although we imply no approval or disapproval of any of these cases, we note that there is no basis for such an award in this case. The District Court specifically found that petitioners did not act with malicious intention to deprive respondents of their rights or to do them other injury, and the Court of Appeals approved only the award of "nonpunitive" damages.

We also note that the potential liability of § 1983 defendants for attorney's fees, see Civil Rights Attorney's Fees Awards Act of 1976, 42 U.S.C. § 1988, provides addition-

B

It is less difficult to conclude that damages awards under § 1983 should be governed by the principle of compensation than it is to apply this principle to concrete cases. But over the centuries the common law of torts has developed a set of rules to implement the principle that a person should be compensated fairly for injuries caused by the violation of his legal rights. These rules, defining the elements of damages and the prerequisites for their recovery, provide the appropriate starting point for the inquiry under § 1983 as well.

It is not clear, however, that common-law tort rules of damages will provide a complete solution to the damages issue in every § 1983 case. In some cases, the interests protected by a particular branch of the common law of torts may parallel closely the interests protected by a particular constitutional right. In such cases, it may be appropriate to apply the tort rules of damages directly to the § 1983 action. In other cases, the interests protected by a particular constitutional right may not also be protected by an analogous branch of the common law of torts. In those cases, the task will be the more difficult one of adapting common-law rules of damages to provide fair compensation for injuries caused by the deprivation of a constitutional right.

Although this task of adaptation will be one of some delicacy—as this case demonstrates—it must be undertaken. The purpose of § 1983 would be defeated if injuries caused by the deprivation of constitutional rights went uncompensated simply because the common law does not recognize an analogous cause of action. In order to further the purpose of § 1983, the rules governing compensation for injuries caused by the deprivation of constitutional rights should be tailored to the interests protected by the particular right in question—just as the common-law rules of damages themselves were defined by the interests protected in the various branches of tort law. We agree with Mr. Justice Harlan that "the experience of judges in dealing with private [tort] claims supports the conclusion that courts of law are capable of making the types of judgment concerning causation and magnitude of injury necessary to accord meaningful compensation for invasion of [constitutional] rights." With these principles in mind, we now turn to the problem of compensation in the case at hand.

C

The Due Process Clause of the Fourteenth Amendment provides:

> "[N]or shall any State deprive any person of life, liberty, or property, without due process of law...."

This Clause "raises no impenetrable barrier to the taking of a person's possessions," or liberty, or life. Fuentes v. Shevin, 407 U.S. 67, 81, 92 S.Ct. 1983, 1994, 32 L.Ed.2d 556 (1972). Procedural due process

al—and by no means inconsequential—as-   deliberately ignore due process rights.
surance that agents of the State will not

rules are meant to protect persons not from the deprivation, but from the mistaken or unjustified deprivation of life, liberty, or property. Thus, in deciding what process constitutionally is due in various contexts, the Court repeatedly has emphasized that "procedural due process rules are shaped by the risk of error inherent in the truth-finding process...." Mathews v. Eldridge, 424 U.S. 319, 344, 96 S.Ct. 893, 907, 47 L.Ed.2d 18 (1976). Such rules "minimize substantively unfair or mistaken deprivations of" life, liberty, or property by enabling persons to contest the basis upon which a State proposes to deprive them of protected interests. Fuentes v. Shevin, supra, 407 U.S., at 81, 92 S.Ct., at 1994.

In this case, the Court of Appeals held that if petitioners can prove on remand that "[respondents] would have been suspended even if a proper hearing had been held," then respondents will not be entitled to recover damages to compensate them for injuries caused by the suspensions. The court thought that in such a case, the failure to accord procedural due process could not properly be viewed as the cause of the suspensions. The court suggested that in such circumstances, an award of damages for injuries caused by the suspensions would constitute a windfall, rather than compensation, to respondents. We do not understand the parties to disagree with this conclusion. Nor do we.

The parties do disagree as to the further holding of the Court of Appeals that respondents are entitled to recover substantial—although unspecified—damages to compensate them for "the injury which is 'inherent in the nature of the wrong,'" even if their suspensions were justified and even if they fail to prove that the denial of procedural due process actually caused them some real, if intangible, injury. Respondents, elaborating on this theme, submit that the holding is correct because injury fairly may be "presumed" to flow from every denial of procedural due process. Their argument is that in addition to protecting against unjustified deprivations, the Due Process Clause also guarantees the "feeling of just treatment" by the government. They contend that the deprivation of protected interests without procedural due process, even where the premise for the deprivation is not erroneous, inevitably arouses strong feelings of mental and emotional distress in the individual who is denied this "feeling of just treatment." They analogize their case to that of defamation *per se,* in which "the plaintiff is relieved from the necessity of producing any proof whatsoever that he has been injured" in order to recover substantial compensatory damages.[16]

16. Respondents also contend that injury should be presumed because, even if they were guilty of the conduct charged, they were deprived of the chance to present facts or arguments in mitigation to the initial decisionmaker. They claim that "[i]t can never be known ... what, if anything, the exercise of such an opportunity to plead one's cause on judgmental or discretionary grounds would have availed." But, as previously indicated, the Court of Appeals held that respondents cannot recover damages for injuries caused by their suspensions if the District Court determines that "[respondents] would have been suspended even if a proper hearing had been held." This holding, which respondents do not challenge, necessarily assumes that the District Court can determine what the outcome would have been if respondents had received their hearing. We presume that this determination will include consideration of the likelihood that any mitigating circumstances to which respondents can point

Petitioners do not deny that a purpose of procedural due process is to convey to the individual a feeling that the government has dealt with him fairly, as well as to minimize the risk of mistaken deprivations of protected interests. They go so far as to concede that, in a proper case, persons in respondents' position might well recover damages for mental and emotional distress caused by the denial of procedural due process. Petitioners' argument is the more limited one that such injury cannot be presumed to occur, and that plaintiffs at least should be put to their proof on the issue, as plaintiffs are in most tort actions.

We agree with petitioners in this respect. As we have observed in another context, the doctrine of presumed damages in the common law of defamation *per se* "is an oddity of tort law, for it allows recovery of purportedly compensatory damages without evidence of actual loss." Gertz v. Robert Welch, Inc., 418 U.S. 323, 349, 94 S.Ct. 2997, 3011–3012, 41 L.Ed.2d 789 (1974). The doctrine has been defended on the grounds that those forms of defamation that are actionable per se are virtually certain to cause serious injury to reputation, and that this kind of injury is extremely difficult to prove. Moreover, statements that are defamatory *per se* by their very nature are likely to cause mental and emotional distress, as well as injury to reputation, so there arguably is little reason to require proof of this kind of injury either.[18] But these considerations do not support respondents' contention that damages should be presumed to flow from every deprivation of procedural due process.

First, it is not reasonable to assume that every departure from procedural due process, no matter what the circumstances or how minor, inherently is as likely to cause distress as the publication of defamation *per se* is to cause injury to reputation and distress. Where the deprivation of a protected interest is substantively justified but procedures are deficient in some respect, there may well be those who suffer no distress over the procedural irregularities. Indeed, in contrast to the immediately distressing effect of defamation *per se,* a person may not even know that procedures were deficient until he enlists the aid of counsel to challenge a perceived substantive deprivation.

Moreover, where a deprivation is justified but procedures are deficient, whatever distress a person feels may be attributable to the justified deprivation rather than to deficiencies in procedure. But as the Court of Appeals held, the injury caused by a justified deprivation, including distress, is not properly compensable under § 1983.[19] This ambiguity in causation, which is absent in the case of defamation *per se,*

would have swayed the initial decisionmakers.

18. The essence of libel *per se* is the publication in writing of false statements that tend to injure a person's reputation. The essence of slander *per se* is the publication by spoken words of false statements imputing to a person a criminal offense; a loathsome disease; matter affecting adversely a person's fitness for trade, business, or profession; or serious sexual misconduct.

19. In this case, for example, respondents denied the allegations against them. They may well have been distressed that their denials were not believed. They might have been equally distressed if they had been disbelieved only after a full-dress hearing, but in that instance they would have no cause of action against petitioners.

provides additional need for requiring the plaintiff to convince the trier of fact that he actually suffered distress because of the denial of procedural due process itself.

Finally, we foresee no particular difficulty in producing evidence that mental and emotional distress actually was caused by the denial of procedural due process itself. Distress is a personal injury familiar to the law, customarily proved by showing the nature and circumstances of the wrong and its effect on the plaintiff.[20] In sum, then, although mental and emotional distress caused by the denial of procedural due process itself is compensable under § 1983, we hold that neither the likelihood of such injury nor the difficulty of proving it is so great as to justify awarding compensatory damages without proof that such injury actually was caused.

D

The Court of Appeals believed, and respondents urge, that cases dealing with awards of damages for racial discrimination, the denial of voting rights and the denial of Fourth Amendment rights, support a presumption of damages where procedural due process is denied. Many of the cases relied upon do not help respondents because they held or implied that some actual, if intangible, injury must be proved before compensatory damages may be recovered. Others simply did not address the issue.[22] More importantly, the elements and prerequisites for recov-

20. We use the term "distress" to include mental suffering or emotional anguish. Although essentially subjective, genuine injury in this respect may be evidenced by one's conduct and observed by others. Juries must be guided by appropriate instructions, and an award of damages must be supported by competent evidence concerning the injury.

22. In Jeanty v. McKey & Poague, Inc., 496 F.2d 1119 (C.A.7 1974), and Seaton v. Sky Realty Co., 491 F.2d 634 (C.A.7 1974), the court held that damages may be awarded for humiliation and distress caused by discriminatory refusals to lease housing to plaintiffs. The court's comment in *Seaton* that "[h]umiliation can be inferred from the circumstances as well as established by the testimony," suggests that the court considered the question of actual injury to be one of fact.

In Basista v. Weir, 340 F.2d 74 (C.A.3 1965); Sexton v. Gibbs, 327 F.Supp. 134 (N.D.Tex.1970), aff'd, 446 F.2d 904 (C.A.5 1971), cert. denied, 404 U.S. 1062, 92 S.Ct. 733, 30 L.Ed.2d 751 (1972); and Rhoads v. Horvat, 270 F.Supp. 307 (Colo.1967), the courts indicated that damages may be awarded for humiliation and distress caused by unlawful arrests, searches, and seizures. In Basista v. Weir, the court held that nom-

inal damages could be awarded for an illegal arrest even if compensatory damages were waived; and that such nominal damages would, in an appropriate case, support an award of punitive damages. Because it was unclear whether the plaintiff had waived his claim for compensatory damages, that issue was left open upon remand. In Sexton v. Gibbs, where the court found "that Plaintiff suffered humiliation, embarrassment and discomfort," substantial compensatory damages were awarded. In Rhoads v. Horvat, the court allowed a jury award of $5,000 in compensatory damages for an illegal arrest to stand, stating that it did "not doubt that the plaintiff was outraged by the arrest."

Wayne v. Venable, 260 F. 64 (C.A.8 1919), and Ashby v. White, 1 Bro.P.C. 62, 1 Eng. Rep. 417 (H.L.1703), rev'd 2 Ld.Raym. 938, 92 Eng.Rep. 126 (K.B.1703), do appear to support the award of substantial damages simply upon a showing that a plaintiff was wrongfully deprived of the right to vote. Citing Ashby v. White, this Court has held that actions for damages may be maintained for wrongful deprivations of the right to vote, but it has not considered the prerequisites for recovery. Nixon v. Herndon, 273 U.S. 536, 540, 47 S.Ct. 446, 71 L.Ed. 759 (1927). The common-law rule of

ery of damages appropriate to compensate injuries caused by the deprivation of one constitutional right are not necessarily appropriate to compensate injuries caused by the deprivation of another. As we have said, these issues must be considered with reference to the nature of the interests protected by the particular constitutional right in question. For this reason, and without intimating an opinion as to their merits, we do not deem the cases relied upon to be controlling.

III

Even if respondents' suspensions were justified, and even if they did not suffer any other actual injury, the fact remains that they were deprived of their right to procedural due process. "It is enough to invoke the procedural safeguards of the Fourteenth Amendment that a significant property interest is at stake, whatever the ultimate outcome of a hearing...." Fuentes v. Shevin, 407 U.S., at 87, 92 S.Ct., at 1997.

Common-law courts traditionally have vindicated deprivations of certain "absolute" rights that are not shown to have caused actual injury through the award of a nominal sum of money. By making the deprivation of such rights actionable for nominal damages without proof of actual injury, the law recognizes the importance to organized society that those rights be scrupulously observed; but at the same time, it remains true to the principle that substantial damages should be awarded only to compensate actual injury or, in the case of exemplary or punitive damages, to deter or punish malicious deprivations of rights.

Because the right to procedural due process is "absolute" in the sense that it does not depend upon the merits of a claimant's substantive assertions, and because of the importance to organized society that procedural due process be observed, we believe that the denial of procedural due process should be actionable for nominal damages without proof of actual injury. We therefore hold that if, upon remand, the District Court determines that respondents' suspensions were justified, respondents nevertheless will be entitled to recover nominal damages not to exceed one dollar from petitioners.[25]

The judgment of the Court of Appeals is reversed, and the case is remanded for further proceedings consistent with this opinion.

It is so ordered.

JUSTICE MARSHALL concurs in the result.

damages for wrongful deprivations of voting rights embodied in Ashby v. White would, of course, be quite relevant to the analogous question under § 1983.

25. Respondents contend that the Court of Appeals' holding could be affirmed on the ground that the District Court held them to too high a standard of proof of the amount of damages appropriate to compensate intangible injuries that are proved to have been suffered. It is true that plaintiffs ordinarily are not required to prove with exactitude the amount of damages that should be awarded to compensate intangible injury. But, as the Court of Appeals said, "in the case at bar, there is no proof of individualized injury to [respondents], such as mental distress...." With the case in this posture, there is no occasion to consider the quantum of proof required to support a particular damages award where actual injury is proved.

JUSTICE BLACKMUN took no part in the consideration or decision of this case.

Notes and Questions

1. *Preliminary injunction*: Note that Piphus was readmitted after eight days of suspension pursuant to a temporary restraining order. This operates like an injunction by directing a party to do, or cease doing, something. Is this sort of remedy more useful in due process cases? See Whitman, Constitutional Torts, 79 Mich.L.Rev. 5 (1980) (arguing that injunctive relief, not damages, should be the preferred remedy in such cases). The procedures for issuing a temporary restraining order (TRO) and a preliminary injunction are found in Rule 65. The primary difference between them is that a TRO may be granted without notice to the adverse party but cannot remain in effect for more than ten days while a preliminary injunction can be issued only after notice (and opportunity to be heard) to the adverse party and can last indefinitely. See Four Seasons Hotels & Resorts, B.V. v. Consorcio Barr, S.A., 320 F.3d 1205 (11th Cir.2003) (two days' notice provided insufficient time to respond to preliminary injunction motion).

In general, it is said that courts should grant such relief only where plaintiff has shown (a) a strong likelihood of success on the merits, (b) irreparable harm should preliminary relief be denied; (c) that the balance of hardships strongly favors plaintiff; and (d) that issuing the injunction will advance the public interest. How should this analysis have been done in Carey v. Piphus?

The decision whether to grant a preliminary injunction lies within the discretion of the trial court, weighing the above factors. Judge Posner once urged that courts use a "simple formula":

> [G]rant the preliminary injunction if but only if $P \times H_p > (1{-}P) \times H_d$, or, in words, only if the harm to the plaintiff if the injunction is denied, multiplied by the probability that the denial would be error (that the plaintiff, in other words, will win at trial), exceeds the harm to the defendant if the injunction is granted, multiplied by the probability that granting the injunction would be an error.

American Hospital Supply Corp. v. Hospital Products Ltd., 780 F.2d 589, 593–94 (7th Cir.1986). Shortly thereafter, however, another panel of the same court raised a caution about this approach:

> A mathematical formula can create a false impression that the elements of the formula, the magnitudes and probabilities, can be accurately quantified and that through a specified type of mental calculus the singularly "correct" result can be arrived at with some exactitude. The obvious problem with this is that the impression is false; a figure representing the probability of success can be arrived at only through a subjective estimate by the court and the magnitudes of harm are rarely susceptible to quantification because of the subjective values, externalities, and effects on the public interest that may be involved in an injunction case. * * * [T]hus, the equation relies on the same type of subjective, impressionistic weighing that has been part of the traditional preliminary injunction determination.

Lawson Products, Inc. v. Avnet, Inc., 782 F.2d 1429, 1434–35 (7th Cir.1986); see also Mullenix, Burying (With Kindness) the Felicific Calculus of Civil Procedure, 40 Vand. L. Rev. 541, 543 (1987) (asserting that Judge Posner's formula approach is "an abomination in theory and practice"). Do you find this criticism of the formula persuasive? Compare the due process analysis adopted in Connecticut v. Doehr, supra p. 50.

2. Does *Carey* provide further insights into the purpose of procedural due process? Is the sole concern accuracy of outcome? Plaintiffs argued that, whatever the ultimate outcome, they were denied the opportunity to participate in the decisionmaking process. Does the Court conclude that concern is unimportant? Would it matter if the decision turned not only on resolution of a factual dispute but also on a discretionary evaluation of the facts found to be true?

3. What sort of hearing would suffice? In Goss v. Lopez, 419 U.S. 565, 95 S.Ct. 729, 42 L.Ed.2d 725 (1975), the Court spelled out what it had in mind for a student faced with suspension: "There need be no delay between the time 'notice' is given and the time of the hearing. In the great majority of cases the disciplinarian may informally discuss the alleged misconduct with the student minutes after it has occurred. We hold only that, in being given an opportunity to explain his version of the facts at this discussion, the student first be told what he is accused of doing and what the basis of the accusation is." What would be the value of even so abbreviated a "hearing" in the case of plaintiff Brisco? Isn't his real objection to the rule that forbids earrings? See the Court's footnote 16.

4. In *Carey,* the Court draws on the general law of tort remedies to handle a constitutional tort. The basic idea of tort remedies is that money damages should be sufficient to make up to plaintiff for what he or she wrongfully lost due to defendant's actions. See generally D. Dobbs, Remedies §§ 3.1; 3.2 (2d ed. 1993). How should that approach be applied here?

(a) Lost time at school: If it is determined that the plaintiffs would not have been suspended if they had been given a hearing, they may be compensated for the days of schooling lost due to their suspension without a hearing. How much is a day of schooling in the Chicago Public Schools worth? Should the court look to the tuition costs of private schools? Should the court try to value the extent to which schooling increases the future earning power of the plaintiffs? If so, how can it determine the shrinkage in earning power due to loss of a few weeks of high school?

(b) Lost procedural right: Whether or not they would have avoided suspension had they been granted hearings, plaintiffs are entitled to prove that they suffered damages because they were denied procedural due process, but such damages may not be presumed. What sort of showing should suffice to justify such damages? See Laje v. R. E. Thomason General Hosp., 665 F.2d 724 (5th Cir.1982) ("Dr. Laje and his wife both testified specifically that the summary proceedings surrounding his dismissal caused severe anxiety and distress, and that these feelings were not relieved until after the full hearing on his discharge.").

Note that in defamation cases plaintiffs need not put on such specific proof to recover "general" damages for mental distress. Should the denial of procedural due process be treated differently? In terms of plaintiffs' showing regarding distress, would it matter if the court concluded that they would not have been suspended had they been afforded a hearing? Would it be natural to assume that temporary exclusion from school (like defamation) would cause substantial mental distress?

Should the fact that we are dealing with the denial of basic constitutional rights affect the measure of damages? In Memphis Community School Dist. v. Stachura, 477 U.S. 299, 106 S.Ct. 2537, 91 L.Ed.2d 249 (1986), the Court found that *Carey* represents a "straightforward" application of compensatory principles, and therefore held invalid a jury instruction that allowed the jury to consider, in computing damages in a case involving denial of a constitutional right, "the importance of the right in our system of government."

5. In personal injury cases, a similar damages analysis prevails. See generally D. Dobbs, Remedies § 8.1 (1973). Thus, plaintiffs who are injured can recover for medical costs and lost earning capacity (including lost wages) by proving with reasonable certainty the amount of these losses. In addition, under the heading of "pain and suffering," plaintiffs can recover money to compensate them for the discomfort they have endured and (where applicable) for the discomfort they will endure in the future. How easily do these damages fit under the compensation idea described in *Carey?* "It is sometimes suggested that these damages can be used by an injured plaintiff to purchase distractions, but it is clear that the price of distractions is not the measure of these damages and it is equally clear that no plaintiff's attorney has ever argued to the jury that he only wanted $500 to buy a new TV set. * * * Because pain and suffering damages are not compensatory, at least in the ordinary sense, there is no clear method of measuring them; indeed, there is almost no method at all." Dobbs, supra, at 550; 545; see also Niemeyer, Awards for Pain & Suffering: The Irrational Centerpiece of Our Tort System, 90 Va.L.Rev. 1401 (2004). Nonetheless, personal injury plaintiffs are routinely allowed to recover for pain and suffering without making a specific showing of the extent of these damages. Should that type of damages be treated differently from the damages sought in *Carey?*

Should more "objective" methods of measuring damages be employed? In Geressy v. Digital Equip. Corp., 980 F.Supp. 640 (E.D.N.Y.1997), the court suggested a statistical analysis of verdicts in similar cases to establish outside limits for pain and suffering awards in suits for repetitive stress injuries. This was done pursuant to C.P.L.R. 5501(c), which is also involved in Gasperini v. Center for Humanities, infra p. 975. The statute directs a court to set aside a jury verdict that "deviates materially from what would be reasonable compensation." Even with pain and suffering awards, the judge concluded in *Geressy* that such an inquiry could be given meaning.

The judge's approach involved three steps. See id. at 657–60. First, both parties could present expert evidence to identify comparable cases resolved by juries. This effort would require that cases be sifted to ensure that the plaintiffs had similar injuries. In an Appendix (id. at 664–74), the judge provided details on about 90 cases he so considered. Second, the judge can use statistics to determine how far to permit deviation from the resulting norm, for which he used the median rather than the mean. Although the data he had available were skewed, the judge selected two standard deviations as the suitable measure. (It could be argued that all values within this deviation constitute reasonable compensation, but the judge seemed to treat the test as establishing the outside limit of those which deviate materially.) Third, the court needs to exercise its independent assessment; "[s]tatistical analysis can never be controlling." Id. at 660. Does this seem to be an improvement?

For further discussion of pain and suffering, see McCaffery, Kahneman & Spitzer, Framing the Jury: Cognitive Perspectives on Pain and Suffering Awards, 81 Va.L.Rev. 1341 (1995); Geistfeld, Placing a Price on Pain and Suffering: A Method for Helping Juries Determine Tort Damages for Nonmonetary Injuries, 83 Calif. L. Rev. 773 (1995).

6. It would seem that the task of measuring damages should be straightforward when the plaintiff's loss consists of items obtainable in the marketplace, but even there problems may arise. Consider the venerable case of Wall v. Platt, 48 N.E. 270 (Mass. 1897), in which a railroad started a fire that destroyed plaintiff's house and the contents of the house. The problem was that although the house would cost $5,250 to rebuild, rebuilding it would only add $3,250 to the value of the lot without the house. The trial court adopted the higher figure, and the appellate court affirmed on the ground that it reflected the "real value" of the buildings destroyed by the fire. Similarly, although defendant attempted to prove regarding the contents of the house that second-hand items could be obtained very cheaply, the court upheld a significantly higher amount as proper for the "intrinsic value of the articles," looking to the cost of new replacement articles and then determining their "worth to the owner" in light of their condition at the time of the fire.

Do you see any problems with the court's measure of damages? The court explained that the objective was "to restore [the plaintiff] to as good a position as he was in before the fire occurred." Should that include paying more than it would cost to replace the used clothing and furniture in the house with other furniture? Although the damages for loss of the house reflected the cost of rebuilding, plaintiff need not rebuild to receive that amount. Will this result in a windfall for plaintiff? The court did say that it was "excluding any fanciful or sentimental considerations." Should it do so? Compare Mieske v. Bartell Drug Co., 593 P.2d 1308 (Wash. 1979), in which plaintiffs recovered $7,500 for loss of their home movies, which included their wedding, honeymoon, vacations and their children growing up. The jury was instructed not to compensate for sentimental value, but did it really follow its instructions? Should it be so instructed?

7. The Court also mentioned punitive damages, but found them inapplicable. These damages are not designed to compensate, but to deter wrongful conduct or vindicate an important right that was violated. In a later case, the Court held that they could be recovered in a civil rights action "when the defendant's conduct is motivated by evil motive or intent, or when it involves reckless or callous indifference to the federally protected rights of others." Smith v. Wade, 461 U.S. 30, 103 S.Ct. 1625, 75 L.Ed.2d 632 (1983).

Traditionally, the measure of punitive damages has taken account of the outrageousness of defendant's conduct and also focused on defendant's wealth (so that the award is large enough to prompt a change in behavior).

This analysis has sometimes lead to remarkable punitive damage jury awards. See, e.g., Liggett Group, Inc. v. Engle, 853 So.2d 434 (Fla.Ct.App. 2003) ($145 billion in punitive damages in class action on behalf of 700,000 smokers overturned). Although such awards are controversial (and often overturned) they may be very rare: "Contrary to public belief, juries rarely award such damages, and award them especially rarely in products liability and medical malpractice cases. Rather, juries tend to award punitive damages in intentional misconduct cases. When juries do award punitive damages, they do so in ways that relate strongly to compensatory awards." Eisenberg, LaFountain, Ostrom, Rottman & Wells, Juries, Judges, and Punitive Damages, 87 Cornell L. Rev. 743, 745 (2002); compare Hersch & Viscusi, Punitive Damages: How Judges and Juries Perform, 33 J. Legal Stud. 1 (2004) (reporting that juries award punitive damages more frequently than judges, and that jury awards correlate less with compensatory damages).

The Supreme Court has emphasized that there are Due Process limits on punitive damages awards, and that appellate courts should not defer to district court decisions in reviewing those awards. Cooper Industries, Inc. v. Leatherman Tool Group, Inc., 532 U.S. 424, 121 S.Ct. 1678, 149 L.Ed.2d 674 (2001). In State Farm Mut. Auto Ins. Co. v. Campbell, 538 U.S. 408, 123 S.Ct. 1513, 155 L.Ed.2d 585 (2003), it held unconstitutional a $145 million punitive damages award in a case in which plaintiffs had won $1 million in compensatory damages for emotional distress, looking to three factors. First, the reprehensibility of defendant's conduct did not support the award because plaintiffs had been allowed to put in evidence of entirely unrelated types of misconduct by defendant, although they should have been limited to the one incident on which they sued. Second, the ratio of punitive damages to compensatory damages was too high. Although a high ratio may be allowed when particularly egregious conduct leads to small harm, "[w]hen compensatory damages are substantial, then a lesser ratio, perhaps equal to compensatory damages, can reach the outermost limit of the due process guarantee." The Court also said that compensatory damages for emotional distress "already contain this punitive element" and cast doubt on using defendant's wealth as a justification for a high punitive award: "The wealth of a defendant cannot justify an otherwise unconstitutional punitive damages award." Third, the award should be compared to civil penalties authorized in comparable cases; in this case the most comparable was a $10,000 fine.

Punitive awards that do not violate due process may nonetheless be windfalls for the plaintiffs who obtain them. In some states, statutes provide that plaintiffs should get only part of the punitive award. See, e.g., Mo. Ann. Stat. § 537.675; Ga. Code Ann. § 51–12–5.1. In Dardinger v. Anthem Blue Cross & Blue Shield, 781 N.E.2d 121 (Ohio S. Ct. 2002), the court itself ordered that two thirds of a $30 million punitive award not be paid to the plaintiff but instead "go to a place that will achieve a societal good, a good that can rationally offset the harm done by the defendants in this case." It explained (id. at 145–46):

> Ohio's courts have a central role to play in the distribution of punitive damages. Punitive damages should not be subject to bright-line division but instead should be considered on a case-by-case basis, with those

awards making the most significant societal statements being the most likely candidates for alternative distribution.

Should punitive damages be employed for such purposes? See Redish & Mathews, Why Punitive Damages are Unconstitutional, 53 Emory L.J. 1 (2004) (arguing that allowing private plaintiffs to seek punitive damages is "the legal version of vigilantism and blood feuds," and that "the power to do no more than punish is a power that is reserved exclusively to the state"). Compare Sharkey, Punitive Damages as Societal Damages, 113 Yale L.J. 347 (2003) (arguing that punitive damages should be understood and justified as compensating society, which would legitimate diverting a portion to social purposes).

8. In *Carey* the Court holds that plaintiffs can recover nominal damages of a dollar for the deprivation of procedural due process. Does this recovery have any real value to them? See Farrar v. Hobby, 506 U.S. 103, 113 S.Ct. 566, 121 L.Ed.2d 494 (1992) (party who obtains only nominal damages ordinarily may not recover attorneys' fees even if covered by a fee-shifting statute). But see Lucas v. Guyton, 901 F.Supp. 1047 (D.S.C.1995) (fees of $30,000 awarded where verdict of ten cents returned in suit by prisoner because counsel had a difficult time overcoming antipathy toward the prisoner and showing that he too had constitutional rights).

9. By now you should realize that the measurement of damages is often a difficult task, and that there are situations in which the amount a plaintiff can recover will not be nearly as substantial as hoped. We cannot canvas the whole law of remedies here, but you should keep this reality in mind as we examine other issues.

ENFORCING MONEY JUDGMENTS

Obtaining a money judgment may not end a case but merely move it into another stage of the litigation process. Although detailed examination of the problems of enforcing money judgments must await a course on creditors' remedies, it is worthwhile to pause now to sketch the available devices.

A money judgment "is not an *order* to the defendant; it is an *adjudication* of his rights or liabilities. No one may be held in contempt for failing to pay some debt as adjudicated by the law court." D. Dobbs, Remedies 94 (1973). See Baxter State Bank v. Bernhardt, 186 F.R.D. 621 (D.Kan.1999) (judgment creditor could not obtain court order requiring judgment debtor to satisfy judgment). Before judgment is entered, state law may authorize attachment of defendant's assets, but if it does not a federal court may not issue an injunction against defendant's dissipation of its assets. Grupo Mexicano de Desarrollo, S.A. v. Alliance Bond Fund, Inc., 527 U.S. 308, 119 S.Ct. 1961, 144 L.Ed.2d 319 (1999). So even successful suits for money damages may be fraught with peril.

Of course, defendant may pay promptly anyhow. If not, plaintiff, now known as the judgment creditor, must take further action to enforce the judgment against defendant, now known as the judgment debtor. Some actions may be rather simple. Thus, by recording the judgment plaintiff may obtain a lien (called a judgment lien) against all defendant's real property. Most states allow a similar filing procedure to give the judgment creditor a lien on personal property of the judgment debtor that is subject to other security interests filed with the state pursuant to the Uniform Commercial Code. But these liens are not worth a great deal unless the judgment debtor wants to sell the property.

Before we turn to methods of forcing sale of property, it is important to note another problem. Ordinarily, judgments can be enforced against assets, as opposed to income. Garnishment, which we examined in the first section of this chapter, affords a limited opportunity to reach the judgment debtor's earnings. See Sniadach v. Family Fin. Corp., supra p. 28. To enforce a money judgment, the plaintiff may often have to find other assets. Many people have few assets of significant value, and most people are reluctant to turn their assets over to people who have sued them. Accordingly, judgment creditors are afforded discovery to compel judgment debtors to reveal where their assets are located. Debtors are naturally reluctant to answer these questions, but courts can sometimes apply substantial pressure to force them to do so. You should reconsider the difficulties that might attend this process when you reach the discovery materials in Chapter V.

Once the judgment creditor has located the assets, she can obtain a writ of execution from the court directing the sheriff or similar officer to "levy" on the asset. This may take the form of physical seizure of the asset, or service of an order on a debtor of the judgment debtor (such as the judgment debtor's bank or employer) directing it to pay the money over to the court. If the physical seizure of the asset is accomplished, the sheriff may thereafter sell it at auction and (after deducting the costs of the sale) pay the balance over to the judgment creditor up to the amount of the judgment. But there may be other persons with an interest in the asset. The debtor's car, for example, may be subject to a lien in favor of the bank that loaned him the money to buy it. Those "secured" creditors, like the sheriff, stand in front of the judgment creditor seeking to collect. That special status, indeed, explains much of the concern about limiting the prejudgment remedies available to secured creditors under *Fuentes*.

Yet another problem for the judgment creditor is that all states exempt certain assets from execution. Thus, even if there are unencumbered assets, the judgment creditor may be unable to realize against them because the debtor has a right to keep them and, in essence, disregard the debt to plaintiff. These rules vary from state to state, but commonly include clothing, furniture and other household possessions, food, fuel, automobiles and tools of the debtor's trade. In addition, if the debtor owns a house, there may be a "homestead" exemption that protects it against execution.

Finally, the judgment creditor must worry about bankruptcy. A judgment debtor who cannot pay one bill may be unable to pay other bills. Such persons often seek protection against their creditors under the Bankruptcy Act, which automatically interdicts enforcement of existing judgments and pursuit of others. Then the debtor's non-exempt property is pooled by the court, and all the creditors are allowed to make claims against that property (which may be worth far less than the total of the claims). Meanwhile, the debtor may obtain a "discharge" from his prior debts, precluding his creditors from pursuing him.

This paints an overly pessimistic picture of the prospects for plaintiffs. In the first place, there are important policy reasons for affording judgment debtors protection against being completely impoverished to pay judgment creditors. We are not likely to revive debtor's prison soon. Moreover, the prospects of enforcing a money judgment against many defendants are very good. Large businesses are usually easy targets for collection, which may explain in part why they are such frequent targets for suits. Insurance companies will pay judgments, so plaintiff can recover if the defendant is insured. Nonetheless, this brief review shows why careful lawyers worry before they sue not only about the damages theory they will employ but also the defendant's ability to pay a judgment if they obtain one.

2. Equitable Remedies

Until now, we have focused on suits for money damages, and one might well conclude that this remedy is sometimes not sufficient to protect the plaintiff's rights. Money damages were the traditional remedy in England "at law." Alongside remedies at law, there developed "equitable" remedies that directly ordered defendant to take or cease certain specified action. To appreciate some of the limitations on equitable relief, it is important to provide a brief canvas for the gradual development of the English system of adjudication because that history had a profound impact on the way in which adjudication was organized in this country. Unfortunately, the English organization resulted as much from coincidence and politics as from rational examination of the sensible handling of disputes.

Courts as we know them now began to develop in England over a millennium ago as dispute resolution devices. Local disputes in those feudal times could be resolved by the local lord; when he "held court" this was one of the things he would do. Resolving other disputes required royal intervention. Royal authority was invoked by a "writ," which a complaining subject could obtain at the office of the Lord Chancellor. The writ empowered the King's courts at Westminster to decide the dispute. Unfortunately, some complainants had disputes that didn't fit into the traditional writs. At first, the Chancellor felt free to invent new writs to fit new situations. The nobles, however, feared royal intrusion into areas where they had traditionally held sway. As a result, in 1258 the Chancellor was forbidden to invent new writs, but this was softened by the Statute of Westminster in 1285, which authorized the Chancellor to adapt existing writs to new situations that were similar (*in consimili casu*).

Over the centuries, the established writs gradually evolved into what were known as the "forms of action." As their requirements were clarified, they gave birth to legal rules which we have come to call the common law. Thus, much of the legal doctrine that you will study in your substantive courses has its roots in the common law forms of action: trespass, debt, detinue, replevin, covenant, account, trespass on the case, trover, assumpsit and ejectment. Because this history bears on current practice only distantly, we will not try to master the special requirements of these different forms of action, but they will never be entirely forgotten. (For further discussion, see infra pp. 122-23.)

For present purposes, the point is that even though the writs could be adapted there still arose cases in which they did not suffice either because the common law offered no relief to a certain claimant, or because the relief that the common law courts would accord such a litigant was insufficient for some reason. In such cases, the Chancellor might intercede personally. For political reasons (if not a desire to limit his own workload), the Chancellor would not do so except where necessary because of some deficiency in the relief available to the claimant at law. (Common law judges, like local lords, could be jealous of their power.) This is the source of the current idea that equitable remedies are only available when plaintiff is faced with "irreparable" harm, i.e., when money damages would not be a sufficient remedy. When the Chancellor did intervene, however, he did more than issue the sort of judgment that the common law judges offered. Rather than making plaintiff pursue defendant's assets, the Chancellor would act "in personam" by issuing a personal order directing or forbidding specified action by defendant.

There thus developed two parallel systems of adjudication in England. The law courts administered the gradually evolving forms of action. Equity, as the Chancellor's court came to be called, had jurisdiction of cases falling generally into three categories: (1) cases in which the common law did not prescribe the legal rules, most notably the administration of trusts, so that equity's jurisdiction in such cases was "exclusive," (2) cases in which jurisdiction was "concurrent" in that the "substantive" legal rules governing plaintiff's right to relief were based on common law but equity would also entertain the suit because of some deficiency in the relief afforded at law, and (3) cases in which the equity action was "ancillary" to an action at law, most notably an action at equity for a bill of discovery which might be useful for a suit for damages in the law courts.

As the third type of equitable jurisdiction suggests, the two systems had different procedures. Four types of differences will concern us in this book. First, the rules surrounding the way in which plaintiff and defendant had to state their positions—pleading—were very strict at law, with the result that the outcome often turned not on the merits but on who won a stylized pleading contest. The Chancellor was much less interested in the formalities of pleading, so that petitions in equity tended to be more straightforward descriptions of the facts on which the plaintiff's claim was based. We shall examine the contemporary handling of these problems in Chapter III. Second, the common law courts severely limited a plaintiff's opportunity to combine claims or parties in one action. He could not combine claims under different writs in a single action, and he could very rarely sue more than one defendant at a time. The rules concerning joinder are examined in Chapter IV. Third, equity afforded assistance to parties in collecting information, while law did not; hence the "ancillary" action at equity for a bill of discovery. In Chapter V we shall see how discovery is currently handled. Finally, the manner of trial was markedly different. At law, factual disputes were resolved by a jury trial. At equity, however, there was no jury, and in some senses there was no trial. Instead, the decision was based on the material developed through the discovery process without a single presentation of evidence in a courtroom. For better or worse, this difference was written into the Seventh Amendment of our Constitution, which "preserves" the right to jury trial in "suits at common law." We shall deal with these problems in Chapter VIII.

The reason these ancient problems are still with us today is that the American Colonies modeled their legal system (like so much else) on the English system. But over time the system was changed. The English tinkered with their judicial system for much of the nineteenth century, eventually abandoning the forms of action in the Judicature Acts of the 1870s and merging the law and equity courts. Similar efforts were afoot in this country, and in the Field Code, adopted in New York in 1848, the forms of action were abandoned and the two systems merged. The federal courts had law and equity "sides" from 1789, when they were created, until 1938, when the federal rules were adopted. See Fed. R.Civ.P. 2 ("There shall be one form of action to be known as 'civil action.'") Most states have similarly changed their systems, although some still have separate equity courts. Procedure, meanwhile, has been modelled on the more flexible practices of equity rather than the rigid procedures of the common law, a choice that involves tradeoffs in simplicity and predictability of outcomes. See Subrin, How Equity Conquered Common Law: The Federal Rules of Civil Procedure in Historical Perspective, 135 U.Pa.L.Rev. 909 (1987). For purposes of this chapter, however, this historical background is a necessary introduction to the handling of equitable remedies.

SMITH v. WESTERN ELECTRIC CO.

Missouri Court of Appeals, 1982.
643 S.W.2d 10.

DOWD, PRESIDING JUDGE.

Plaintiff appeals from an order dismissing his petition on the ground that it fails to state a claim upon which relief can be granted.

The petition seeks an injunction to prevent plaintiff's employer from exposing him to tobacco smoke in the workplace and from affecting his pay or employment conditions because of his medical reaction to tobacco smoke. The petition alleges that by allowing smoking in the work area, defendant permits its employees to be exposed to a health hazard and thereby breaches its duty to provide a safe place in which to work.

The petition includes the following allegations. Plaintiff has been employed by defendant since 1950 and has worked in defendant's Missouri branch since 1967. He is a nonsmoker sharing an open office area with other employees, many of whom smoke tobacco products as they work. In 1975 plaintiff began to experience serious respiratory tract discomfort as a result of inhaling tobacco smoke in the workplace. A subsequent medical evaluation determined that plaintiff suffers a severe adverse reaction to tobacco smoke. His symptoms include sore throat, nausea, dizziness, headache, blackouts, loss of memory, difficulty in concentration, aches and pains in joints, sensitivity to noise and light, cold sweat, gagging, choking sensations, and lightheadedness. After a sufficient period of non-exposure to smoke, plaintiff's symptoms abate somewhat. The symptoms have become increasingly severe over the years, however. Doctors evaluating and treating plaintiff have advised him to avoid contact with tobacco smoke whenever possible.

The petition further alleges that plaintiff first complained to defendant about the tobacco smoke in the workplace in 1975. Defendant thereafter moved plaintiff to different locations within the plant, but no improvement resulted because each location contained significant amounts of tobacco smoke. In 1978 plaintiff was informed that he should no longer submit complaints about the smoke through defendant's anonymous complaint procedure since defendant would not process them. In response to recommendations of the National Institute for Occupational Safety and Health,[1] defendant adopted a smoking policy in April 1980. The declared policy was to protect the rights of both smokers and nonsmokers by providing accommodations for both groups and by making a reasonable effort to separate the groups in work areas. Because defendant has failed to implement its policy by making such a reasonable effort, improvement of the air in the workplace has not resulted.

According to the petition, in August 1980 plaintiff filed with defendant a Handicapped Declaration Statement that he was handicapped by his susceptibility to tobacco smoke. Refusing to segregate smokers or to limit smoking to non-work areas, defendant informed plaintiff he could either continue to work in the same location and wear a respirator or apply for a job in the computer room (where smoking is prohibited). The latter option would entail a pay decrease of about $500 per month. Defendant thereafter provided plaintiff with a respirator that has proven ineffective in protecting plaintiff from tobacco smoke.

The petition states that plaintiff has exhausted all avenues of relief through defendant; he has no adequate remedy at law; he is suffering and will continue to suffer irreparable physical injuries and financial

---

1. The Occupational Safety and Health Act of 1970, 29 U.S.C. §§ 651–678, established the National Institute for Occupa- tional Safety and Health, § 671, to develop safety standards and implement sections 669 and 670 of the Act.

losses unless defendant improves working conditions. The petition alleges that defendant is breaching its common law duty as an employer to provide plaintiff a safe place to work, and that defendant has available reasonable alternatives to avoid the continuing breach of duty, as demonstrated by defendant's ability to protect its computer equipment from tobacco smoke. The petition further states that, although "second-hand smoke" is harmful to the health of all employees, defendant is permitting them to be exposed in the workplace to this health hazard which is neither related to nor a necessary by-product of defendant's business.

Construing these allegations favorably to plaintiff, we must determine whether they invoke principles of law entitling him to relief.

It is well-settled in Missouri that an employer owes a duty to the employee to use all reasonable care to provide a reasonably safe workplace, and to protect the employee from avoidable perils. Whether the employer has fulfilled its duty depends upon the facts of each case. For example, in McDaniel v. Kerr, 258 S.W.2d 629 (Mo.1953), the employer had failed to provide a safe workplace where the employee's inhalation of dust on the job caused damage requiring removal of his lung. In DeMarco v. United States, 204 F.Supp. 290 (E.D.N.Y.1962), the court found a negligent failure to provide a safe working environment where the plaintiff was injured when he fainted and fell after complaining about gasoline fumes in an unventilated work area.

The allegations of the instant case, taken as true, show that the tobacco smoke of co-workers smoking in the work area is hazardous to the health of employees in general and plaintiff in particular. The allegations also show that defendant knows the tobacco smoke is harmful to plaintiff's health and that defendant has the authority, ability, and reasonable means to control smoking in areas requiring a smoke-free environment. Therefore, by failing to exercise its control and assume its responsibility to eliminate the hazardous condition caused by tobacco smoke, defendant has breached and is breaching its duty to provide a reasonably safe workplace. As stated in Thompson v. Kroeger, 380 S.W.2d 339, 343–44 (Mo.1964):

> the exercise of due care requires precautions which a reasonably prudent employer would have taken in given circumstances, even though other employers may not have taken such commensurate precautions. What usually is done may be evidence of what ought to be done, but what ought to be done is fixed by a standard of reasonable prudence, whether it usually is complied with or not.

If plaintiff's petition establishes defendant's failure to provide a safe place for plaintiff to work, we must next consider whether injunctive relief would be an appropriate remedy. An injunction may issue "to prevent the doing of any legal wrong whatever, whenever in the opinion of the court an adequate remedy cannot be afforded by an action for damages." § 526.030 RSMo 1978. Injunctive relief is unavailable unless irreparable harm is otherwise likely to result, and plaintiff has no adequate remedy at law.

The petition alleges that plaintiff's continuing exposure to smoke in the workplace is increasingly deleterious to his health and is causing irreparable harm. Assuming the allegations and reasonable inferences therefrom to be true, we think it is fair to characterize deterioration of plaintiff's health as "irreparable" and as a harm for which money damages cannot adequately compensate. This is particularly true where the harm has not yet resulted in full-blown disease or injury. Money damages, even though inadequate, are the best possible remedy once physical damage is done, but they are certainly inadequate to compensate permanent injury which could have been prevented. Plaintiff should not be required to await the harm's fruition before he is entitled to seek an inadequate remedy. Moreover, the nature of plaintiff's unsafe work environment represents a recurrent risk of harm that would necessitate a multiplicity of lawsuits. Finally, the petition states that plaintiff has no adequate remedy at law and alleges facts indicating that prior to this action plaintiff unsuccessfully pursued relief, both through his employer's in-house channels and through administrative agencies. Viewing the petition favorably, as we must to determine its sufficiency, we find that injunction would be an appropriate remedy.

Defendant contends the trial court lacks jurisdiction to provide relief, and therefore the petition fails to state a claim upon which relief can be granted, because the subject matter of this case is preempted by the Occupational Safety and Health Act (OSHA), 29 U.S.C. §§ 651–678 (1970). The Act specifically states, however, that it does not affect the common law regarding "injuries, diseases, or death of employees arising out of . . . employment." § 653(b)(4). The Act also declares that it does not prevent a state court from asserting jurisdiction over an occupational safety or health issue for which no OSHA standard is in effect. § 667(a). We are unpersuaded by defendant's argument that § 653(b)(4) refers only to the common law pertaining to workers' compensation laws. In addition, defendant has not directed our attention to any OSHA standard which would appear to cover tobacco smoke. No such standard figured in the opinions of other courts considering OSHA and tobacco smoke. Furthermore, defendant conceded in oral argument that a court may retain jurisdiction in the absence of an OSHA standard.

We conclude that plaintiff has stated a claim upon which relief can be granted and that the trial court therefore erred in dismissing the petition. Plaintiff should be allowed the opportunity to prove his allegations.

Notes and Questions

1. Note that the court does not hold that plaintiff is entitled to an injunction, but only that he may be. What will plaintiff have to prove to obtain one? On remand, there was a three-day trial after which the judge ruled that plaintiff had not proved that second-hand smoke was dangerous, resulting in judgment for defendant.

The criteria for granting a permanent injunction resemble those for granting a preliminary injunction. Thus, the court is to ask (1) whether plaintiff has actually succeeded on the merits, (2) whether he has an adequate remedy at law, (3) whether he risks imminent irreparable harm, (4) whether the balance of hardships weighs against issuance of an injunction, (5) whether an injunction would serve the public interest, and (6) whether the court can, as a practical matter, administer the injunction. As might be expected, it is easier for a plaintiff who has won to obtain final injunctive relief than for a plaintiff who only hopes to win to obtain preliminary injunctive relief. At the same time, it is important to appreciate that courts are often reluctant to issue permanent injunctions. Does *Smith* suggest reasons why this reluctance makes sense?

The second and third criteria above state what has become known as the irreparable injury rule, derived in part from the historical unwillingness of the English Chancellor to intervene in a dispute unless the complainant showed that there was something wrong with the relief afforded by the law courts. Laycock, The Death of the Irreparable Injury Rule, 103 Harv. L. Rev. 688 (1990), argues on the basis of a review of over 1,400 cases that there really is no such rule, and that "our law embodies a preference for specific relief if plaintiff wants it. The principal doctrinal expression for this preference is the rule that damages are inadequate unless they can be used to replace the specific thing that plaintiff lost." Id. at 691. He adds that "[d]amages are the standard remedy for personal injury only because personal injuries can rarely be anticipated in time to prevent them by injunction." Id. at 709. He concludes, however, that the rule continues to be important in cases involving preliminary injunctions (id. at 732):

> The irreparable injury rule has teeth at the preliminary injunction stage because it still serves a purpose there. At the preliminary injunction stage, the merits are unresolved, plaintiff may be undeserving, and it is still possible that plaintiff will not get any remedy at all. Defendant has a legitimate interest in a full hearing and in freedom to act in ways not yet shown to be unlawful. These interests coincide with the court's interest in avoiding error and being fair to both sides.

It is usually said that the court has substantial discretion to refuse a request for an injunction after considering the above factors. As you review the further questions below, consider whether you might hesitate to grant Smith's request if you were the judge in this case.

2. Is plaintiff's legal remedy inadequate in *Smith* because damages are an inadequate substitute for health? The court emphasizes that the exposure "has not yet resulted in full-blown disease or injury." Should courts be receptive to injunctive suits by plaintiffs whose damages claims are not ripe? Ordinarily our legal system limits remedies to those who have actually suffered harm. In Helling v. McKinney, 509 U.S. 25, 113 S.Ct. 2475, 125 L.Ed.2d 22 (1993), a prisoner who shared a cell with a smoker sued the warden for inflicting cruel and unusual punishment. The Court rejected defendant's argument that plaintiff had no claim because he had not yet suffered any demonstrable harm, but held that to prevail on his Eighth Amendment claim plaintiff had to show that the level of smoke in the cell "is such that his future health is unreasonably endangered," and also prove that "it is contrary to current standards of decency for anyone to be so exposed against his will and that prison officials are deliberately indifferent to his

plight." Eventually plaintiff settled the case for the Department of Prisons' agreement to try to house him with a nonsmoking inmate. Compare Metro–North Commuter R.R. Co. v. Buckley, 521 U.S. 424, 117 S.Ct. 2113, 138 L.Ed.2d 560 (1997) (worker heavily exposed to asbestos in the workplace could not sue for damages for emotional distress because he had not developed any disease).

3.   If plaintiff in *Smith* is now entitled to injunctive relief, how much sooner could he have sought it? Presumably smoking in the workplace was as much a hazard to workers in 1950 as it is now. Could plaintiff have obtained an injunction in 1950 (assuming that the health hazards of smoking could have been shown at that time)? Could he have obtained one in 1975, when he first suffered symptoms? In 1980, when the defendant refused to segregate smokers and non-smokers? Generally, courts refuse to issue injunctions unless the plaintiff's claim is "ripe" because irreparable harm is imminent. When did plaintiff reach that point?

4.   Obviously few would favor subjecting people to personal injuries that could be avoided. Should that fact prompt courts to favor preventive injunctive relief over compensatory relief? How about an injunction ordering a taxicab company not to allow its drivers to drive negligently? Would it be better to enjoin individual cab drivers from driving hazardously? Are injunctions a good way to deal with the problem of injuries inflicted by cabs? Are they better suited to a case like *Smith?*

5.   If the court is going to try to make the workplace at Western Electric safe, should it limit its attention to cigarette smoke? Should it instead investigate the possibility that there are other hazards in the workplace and, if it finds those, enjoin those hazards as well? Are there any problems with the court using the case as a vehicle to clean up defendant's plant?

Suppose there is racial harassment at the plant. Can the court enjoin that? In Aguilar v. Avis Rent A Car System, Inc., 980 P.2d 846 (Cal.1999), Hispanic employees of Avis won damages in a jury trial for demeaning comments directed at them by their supervisor. Based on that jury verdict and his own conclusion that there was a substantial likelihood that the supervisor would continue this harassment, the trial judge enjoined the supervisor from using "any derogatory racial or ethnic epithets directed at * * * Hispanic employees." Defendants appealed on First Amendment free speech grounds, arguing that this injunction was an illegal prior restraint on speech, but the California Supreme Court upheld it by a 4–3 vote because it was based on a jury finding of harassment.

6.   What injunction should the court issue to solve plaintiff's smoke exposure problem? The court cites two cases in support of the idea that noxious fumes can make the workplace unsafe within the meaning of the common law employer's duty on which it relies. But McDaniel v. Kerr and DeMarco v. United States were both suits for damages by workers who claimed compensable injuries, and in measuring relief those courts could refer to traditional remedial guidelines for personal injury cases. What guidelines should the court use in fashioning a decree for plaintiff in *Smith?* Would it be sufficient to order defendant not to expose plaintiff to smoke, or should it adopt a more specific decree? See Rule 65(d) (stating that the

decree "shall be specific in terms" and "describe in reasonable detail * * * the act or acts sought to be restrained"). If it should be more specific, where does it look for the specifics that it will use? Should it begin to monitor the conditions at defendant's plant on a regular basis? Are regulatory agencies like the National Institute for Occupational Safety and Health better equipped for this task? Courts trying to desegregate schools or improve conditions in prisons are regularly faced with such problems of designing appropriate injunctions. See Chayes, The Role of the Judge in Public Law Litigation, 89 Harv.L.Rev. 1281, 1298–1302 (1976). Does Smith's claim justify a similar effort by the court? Wouldn't an injunction have been easier to fashion in Carey v. Piphus, supra p. 68?

7.   If the court is going to design an injunction, should the smokers in defendant's workforce have a say about the terms of the decree? See Nowaczyk v. Shaheen, 49 Fed.R.Serv.3d 107 (D.N.H. 2001) (rejecting prisoners' claim that prison's tobacco-free policy violated the constitutional rights of prisoners who smoke). We will deal with problems of necessary parties in Chapter IV, but it is important to note now that injunctive relief may widen the circle of affected parties greatly. Is that a reason for favoring monetary relief? Would the smokers at the Western Electric plant be similarly affected by a judgment for money damages?

8.   Should the cost of complying with the court's decree matter? In Boomer v. Atlantic Cement Co., 26 N.Y.2d 219, 309 N.Y.S.2d 312, 257 N.E.2d 870 (1970), the trial court found that defendant's cement plant was a nuisance because it was so noisy and made so much dust that it interfered with the dairy farms operated by plaintiffs (seven farmers whose land abutted defendant's factory). Noting that no existing technology would eliminate either the noise or the dust, however, the trial court refused to order defendant to stop operating its $45 million plant, thereby putting defendant's 300 employees out of work, instead awarding plaintiffs $185,000 for the diminution in value of their farms. Should similar cost considerations bear on plaintiff's request for injunctive relief against Western Electric?

9.   Limitations on smoking in the workplace have proven an explosive political issue in a number of communities. Putting aside questions of expertise in solving such problems, should courts get involved in such controversies? Obviously courts have taken on controversial issues in such cases as school desegregation. Is Smith's problem of equal moment?

10.   Injunctions are not the only equitable remedies. Courts also use their equitable powers when they order parties to perform their contractual commitments (specific performance), appoint receivers to take control of businesses or other institutions and run them, or intervene in other ways in out-of-court activities.

11.   Yet another possibility in many cases is to seek a declaratory judgment. 28 U.S.C.A. § 2201(a) authorizes federal courts, where there is an "actual controversy," to "declare the rights and other legal relations of any interested party seeking such declaration, whether or not further relief is or could be sought." Section 2202 empowers the court to enforce a declaratory judgment with "[f]urther necessary and proper relief," which may include an injunction. Would a declaratory judgment be an attractive remedy in Smith v. Western Electric Co.? In Carey v. Piphus, supra p. 68?

JUSTICIABILITY

The declaratory judgment possibility suggests that remedies problems might sometimes be avoided by simply having courts declare the law as an abstract matter. That is not the way our judicial system works, and it is therefore appropriate to mention a number of doctrines together known as problems of "justiciability". Careful consideration of these problems is extremely challenging and beyond the scope of this book. Nevertheless, it is important that you have some appreciation of these issues because they bear on a number of procedural matters we will consider. For an overview, see C. Wright & M. Kane, Law of Federal Courts §§ 12; 13 (6th ed. 2002).

In the federal judicial system, the source of the doctrine is Art. III § 2 of the Constitution, which authorizes federal courts to decide only "cases" or "controversies." In upholding the federal declaratory judgment act, the Supreme Court explained that "[a] 'controversy' in this sense must be one that is appropriate for judicial determination. A justiciable controversy is thus distinguished from a dispute of a hypothetical character; from one that is academic or moot. The controversy must be definite and concrete, touching the legal relations of parties having adverse legal interests. It must be a real and substantial controversy admitting of specific relief through a decree of a conclusive character, as distinguished from an opinion advising what the law would be upon a hypothetical state of facts." Aetna Life Ins. Co. v. Haworth, 300 U.S. 227, 239, 57 S.Ct. 461, 463, 81 L.Ed. 617 (1937). Justiciability problems arise most often in suits challenging governmental action, but they can occur in litigation between private parties. In *Haworth,* for example, the issue was whether four insurance policies had lapsed for nonpayment, and the Court held that the suit was proper even though no claims had yet been made on the policies.

Justiciability has been broken down into a number of doctrines that deserve separate mention:

Ripeness: It is not enough that a controversy might one day erupt; plaintiff must show that it has already done so, thereby presenting a legal issue in a concrete context. For example, in United Public Workers v. Mitchell, 330 U.S. 75, 67 S.Ct. 556, 91 L.Ed. 754 (1947), federal employees challenged the provision of the Hatch Act that forbade them from participating in political activities. The court held that their suit was not ripe because "[w]e can only speculate as to the kinds of political activity the appellants desire to engage in" and that this would be ripe only "when definite rights appear on one side and definite prejudicial interferences upon the other." This limitation has been relaxed more recently years. See Doe v. Bolton, 410 U.S. 179, 93 S.Ct. 739, 35 L.Ed.2d 201 (1973) (doctors may challenge constitutionality of anti-abortion law because they confront a real threat of prosecution).

Standing to sue: Not only must there be a ripe controversy, but plaintiff must also demonstrate that he is "himself among the injured, for it is this requirement that gives a litigant a direct stake in the case or controversy and prevents the judicial process from becoming no more than a vehicle for the vindication of the value interests of concerned bystanders." United States v. SCRAP, 412 U.S. 669, 93 S.Ct. 2405, 37 L.Ed.2d 254 (1973). This inquiry is said to look to whether the plaintiff has suffered an "injury in fact" and has a "personal stake" in the outcome that differentiates him from the public at large. In *SCRAP,* the Court upheld standing for a group of law students who challenged federal approval of railroad freight rate increases they said would reduce recycling of refuse that had to be transported by rail to recycling plants, thereby causing more littering in parks and interfering with their use of the parks. Compare Simon v. Eastern Kentucky Welfare Rights Organization, 426 U.S. 26, 96 S.Ct. 1917, 48 L.Ed.2d 450 (1976), in which the Court held that welfare recipients lacked standing to challenge IRS approval of charitable tax treatment for hospitals that did not provide free health care for the poor because it was "purely speculative" whether plaintiffs would be denied such services due to IRS approval or other reasons. For an examination of the confusion in the area, see Chayes, Foreword: Public Law Litigation and the Burger Court, 96 Harv.L.Rev. 4, 8–26 (1982); Nichol, Rethinking Standing, 72 Calif.L.Rev. 68 (1984).

Mootness: Mootness is "the doctrine of standing set in a time frame: The requisite personal interest that must exist at the commencement of the litigation (standing) must continue throughout its existence (mootness)." Monaghan, Constitutional Adjudication: The Who and When, 82 Yale L.J. 1363, 1384 (1973). In a sense, this is an amalgam of ripeness and standing—the suit may be pursued only if there is an actual controversy in which plaintiff still has a personal stake. Where the controversy would unavoidably expire before adjudication, however, the mootness problem may be disregarded if the problem is "capable of repetition, but evading review."

Feigned or collusive cases: Not only must plaintiff have a personal stake in a ripe controversy, he must actively desire to assert his interest. Thus, where a landlord persuaded one of his tenants to serve as nominal plaintiff in a suit claiming the landlord was charging rents that exceeded federal regulations in order to get a ruling on the validity of the regulations, the Court invalidated the resulting judgment. It reasoned that "such a suit is collusive because it is not in any real sense adversary. It does not assume the 'honest and actual antagonistic assertion of rights' to be adjudicated—a safeguard essential to the integrity of the judicial process." United States v. Johnson, 319 U.S. 302, 63 S.Ct. 1075, 87 L.Ed. 1413 (1943).

Notes and Questions

1. Up to this point, we have treated the adversary process principally as a way of assuring the parties' personal participation in litigation. Adversariness is central to the justiciability doctrines as well. Does it serve the same ends here? For an overview, see Brilmayer, The Jurisprudence of Article III: Perspectives on the "Case or Controversy" Requirement, 93 Harv.L.Rev. 297 (1979).

2. Sometimes plaintiff may have standing to seek one remedy but not another. In City of Los Angeles v. Lyons, 461 U.S. 95, 103 S.Ct. 1660, 75 L.Ed.2d 675 (1983), plaintiff was injured when a police officer subdued him with a choke hold. He sued for damages and an injunction against future use of the choke hold, alleging that the police had a practice of using it on unresisting people. The Court held that the allegation of routine use of the hold provided no reason for believing that plaintiff would himself again be subjected to it, and that he therefore lacked standing to sue for an injunction even though he could sue for damages. In the alternative, it reasoned that "the equitable remedy is unavailable absent a showing of irreparable injury, a requirement that cannot be met where there is no showing of any real or immediate threat that the plaintiff will be wronged again. * * * Lyons is no more entitled to an injunction than any other citizen of Los Angeles; and a federal court may not entertain a claim by any or all citizens who no more than assert that certain practices of law enforcement officers are unconstitutional." Does this make sense? For a criticism, see Fallon, Of Justiciability, Remedies, and Public Law Litigation: Notes on the Jurisprudence of Lyons, 59 N.Y.U.L. Rev. 1 (1984).

3. Reconsider the questions after Smith v. Western Electric Co., supra p. 86. Would justiciability concerns bear on the resolution of any of them?

ENFORCING EQUITABLE DECREES—CONTEMPT

Unlike money judgments, equitable decrees such as injunctions often order defendant to take some action. Because the court itself has ordered defendant to act, it cannot accept defendant's failure to do so with the kind of indifference that may attend defendant's failure to pay plaintiff the amount of a money judgment. Instead, defendant may be cited for contempt, which has been described as a "civil-criminal hodgepodge." United States v. United Mine Workers, 330 U.S. 258, 364, 67 S.Ct. 677, 91 L.Ed. 884 (1947) (Rutledge, J., dissenting). See generally Dobbs, Contempt of Court: A Survey, 56 Cornell L.Q. 183 (1971). Basically, the hodgepodge falls into three categories:

Criminal Contempt: Violation of a court's order can be prosecuted as a crime. Usually, the initiator in such a prosecution is the plaintiff, but the plaintiff does not control the case and cannot "settle" for a payment of money in return for dropping the prosecution. The distinguishing feature of criminal contempt is that the penalty imposed is not designed either to compensate the plaintiff or to prompt compliance in the future. Because it is a criminal case, the prosecution must prove guilt beyond a reasonable doubt. In addition, defendant has a right to a jury trial unless the contempt is a "petty offense," one involving imprisonment for less than six months. If a fine is involved, the outside limit of petty offenses is less clear, but it is generally felt to be $500 with individuals.

Compensatory Civil Contempt: The court may direct defendant to pay plaintiff an amount that will compensate plaintiff for the harm caused by violation of the decree. This resolution of the problem is rather odd, however, in that the court presumably determined that money damages were an inadequate remedy when it decided to issue the injunction in the first place. Nevertheless, an inadequate monetary payment is better for plaintiff than no relief at all. See generally Rendleman, Compensatory Contempt: Plaintiff's Remedy When a Defendant Violates an Injunction, 1980 U.Ill.L.F. 971.

Coercive Civil Contempt: This approach is a genuine addition to the criminal law features of criminal contempt and the civil damages features of compensatory civil contempt. Using this type of contempt, the court may impose a penalty on defendant in order to prompt future compliance with the decree (rather than punishing defendant for past violations). In general, the penalty must be contingent in that it applies only if defendant does not obey the order. If that is so, defendants "carry the keys to their prison in their own pockets." In re Nevitt, 117 Fed. 448, 461 (8th Cir.1902). But the penalty may be quite severe, including imprisonment for an indefinite period or rather hefty fines. See, e.g., Chadwick v. Janecka, 312 F.3d 597 (3d Cir.2002) (former husband who had refused to reveal where he had hidden marital assets continued in custody after seven years); International Business Mach. Corp. v. United States, 493 F.2d 112 (2d Cir.1973), cert. denied, 416 U.S. 995, 94 S.Ct. 2409, 40 L.Ed.2d 774 (1974) (IBM fined $150,000 per day until it turned over documents).

Notes and Questions

1. If the court in Smith v. Western Electric Co., supra p. 86, enjoined defendant to provide smoke-free areas for nonsmoking workers and the company failed to do so, which type of contempt should plaintiff seek? How should the court fashion an appropriate contempt sanction?

2. Whatever its utility in litigation between private parties, contempt may prove to be a blunt instrument against public officers. For example, assume that in Carey v. Piphus, supra p. 68, the court had ordered defendant not to suspend students without a hearing, but that defendant continued suspending them on the spot as before. How should the court use contempt to enforce its decree? By putting the school officials in jail? By fining the school system? Judges trying to enforce "structural injunctions" to desegregate schools or improve prisons have faced such problems, and some of them have ordered elected officials to jail. At least one judge in a prison overcrowding case decided instead to order the release of specific inmates when state officials failed to correct the overcrowding problem. See Newman v. State of Alabama, 683 F.2d 1312 (11th Cir.1982) (reversing the order after some 277 inmates had been released). Should judges be leery of issuing such injunctions for fear of having their own orders disobeyed with impunity by local officials?

Contempt sanctions against elected officials can present great difficulties. For example, in Spallone v. United States, 493 U.S. 265, 110 S.Ct. 625, 107 L.Ed.2d 644 (1990), the city council of Yonkers, New York, voted 4–3 not to comply with an injunction requiring the city to build low-cost housing to remedy years of racial discrimination in the location of such housing. Besides imposing escalating and substantial fines on the city, the district court also imposed fines on the four recalcitrant members of the city council. The Supreme Court held that this was improper under "traditional equitable principles" because the court should limit its use of the contempt power to "the least power adequate to the end proposed." The large fines against the city should have sufficed, and the individual fines against members of the city council risked "a much greater perversion of the normal legislative process" by influencing councilmembers' votes on personal grounds.

3. Fed. R. Civ. P. 65(d) provides that an injunction "is binding only upon the parties to the action, their officers, agents, servants, employees, and attorneys, and upon those persons in active concert or participation with them who receive actual notice of the order by personal service or otherwise." These limitations become important when someone who is not obviously a party is cited for contempt. Should Rule 65(d) be interpreted broadly? Could a fellow employee of plaintiff Smith be held in contempt for smoking at the Western Electric plant? Could the court put the employee in jail until he kicks the smoking habit? See United States v. Hall, 472 F.2d 261 (5th Cir.1972) (nonparty held in contempt of order from court supervising integration of school that forbade anyone except teachers and students to go on school grounds); Note, Binding Nonparties to Injunctive Decrees, 49 Minn.L.Rev. 719 (1965).

4. *The collateral bar rule*: As should be apparent by now, contempt shows how serious courts are about enforcing injunctions. This resolve is further emphasized by the collateral bar rule, which precludes the defendant from challenging the validity of the injunction in the "collateral" contempt proceeding. See United States v. United Mine Workers, 330 U.S. 258, 67 S.Ct. 677, 91 L.Ed. 884 (1947); Cox, The Void Order and the Duty to Obey, 16 U.Chi.L.Rev. 86 (1948). Perhaps the most controversial application of this rule was in Walker v. City of Birmingham, 388 U.S. 307, 87 S.Ct. 1824, 18 L.Ed.2d 1210 (1967), in which Rev. Martin Luther King, Jr., and a group of local Birmingham, Alabama, ministers planned a parade to protest racial segregation during the Easter holidays. The protesters attempted unsuccessfully to obtain a permit to march, as required by a local ordinance. Local authorities obtained an ex parte temporary restraining order in state court against the demonstrations, and Dr. King and others marched anyway and were held in contempt.

The Supreme Court upheld the contempt convictions despite very serious questions about the constitutional validity of the ordinance. (Indeed, the Court held this very ordinance unconstitutional two years later.) But the possible invalidity of the ordinance was irrelevant, said the Court, because "in the fair administration of justice no man can be judge in his own case." Instead, the validity of a court order should be challenged through the appeals process even though this particular order was obtained ex parte only a week before the scheduled march. The Court did suggest that a different result might obtain if the injunction were "transparently invalid" or "had only a frivolous pretense to validity."

Curiously, the same principle is *not* used when a person is prosecuted for violating a statute she claims is unconstitutional. Indeed, that is how the Birmingham ordinance was eventually held invalid. See Shuttlesworth v. City of Birmingham, 394 U.S. 147, 89 S.Ct. 935, 22 L.Ed.2d 162 (1969) (reversing conviction for marching without a permit on ground that permit requirement was unconstitutional). Should court orders receive greater respect than statutes? Consider the arguments of Chief Justice Warren, dissenting in Walker v. City of Birmingham, 388 U.S. at 327, 87 S.Ct. at 1835:

> It has never been thought that violation of a statute indicated such a disrespect for the legislature that the violator always must be punished even if the statute was unconstitutional. On the contrary, some cases have required that persons seeking to challenge the constitutionality of a statute first violate it to establish their standing to sue. Indeed, it shows no disrespect for law to violate a statute on the ground that it is unconstitutional and then to submit one's case to the courts with the willingness to accept the penalty if the statute is held constitutional.

Is the collateral bar doctrine necessary to orderly operation of the courts? What would happen if parties routinely disregarded orders they believed to be invalid even though the judge has rejected their arguments? If the doctrine is generally justified, should it apply to a case like *Walker* where the injunction was obtained ex parte and the defendants had no opportunity to be heard before it was entered? Note that the Court in *Walker* suggested that there might be an exception to the doctrine if the order was "transparently invalid." Could that idea subvert the doctrine? For a discussion of the collateral bar rule, see M. Redish, Freedom of Expression: A Critical Analysis 164–70 (1984).

Whatever your reaction to the collateral bar doctrine, it is worthwhile noting the consequence of its operation in Birmingham, as chronicled in Oppenheimer, Martin Luther King, Walker v. City of Birmingham, and the Letter From the Birmingham Jail, 26 U.C. Davis L.Rev. 791 (1993). Dr. King had earlier seen an effort to fight segregation in Albany, Ga., fail because of a similar injunction that was reversed on appeal, but only after resistance to segregation in the city had withered under the effect of the injunction. Moreover, by the time he decided to march in Birmingham, Dr. King knew that if he were arrested for violating the injunction there would not be funds to bail him out. But rather than see another challenge to segregation die during the appeals process, Dr. King marched, was arrested and jailed. While in the jail he wrote the *Letter From the Birmingham Jail*, which "has come to be widely recognized as the most important single document of the civil rights era." Id. at 816. King eventually spent eight days in jail before being bailed out by singer Harry Belafonte.

C. COST OF LITIGATION

VENEGAS v. MITCHELL

Supreme Court of the United States, 1990.
495 U.S. 82, 110 S.Ct. 1679, 109 L.Ed.2d 74.

JUSTICE WHITE delivered the opinion of the Court.

Under 42 U.S.C. § 1988, a court may award a reasonable attorney's fee to the prevailing party in civil rights cases. We granted certiorari to resolve a conflict among the Courts of Appeals as to whether § 1988 invalidates contingent-fee contracts that would require a prevailing civil rights plaintiff to pay his attorney more than the statutory award against the defendant.

I

This dispute arises out of an action brought by petitioner Venegas under 42 U.S.C. § 1983 in the United States District Court for the Central District of California, alleging that police officers of the city of Long Beach, California, falsely arrested Venegas and conspired to deny him a fair trial through the knowing presentation of perjured testimony. After an order of the District Court dismissing Venegas' complaint as barred by the statute of limitations was reversed by the Court of Appeals, Venegas retained respondent Mitchell as his attorney. Venegas and Mitchell signed a contingent-fee contract providing that Mitchell would represent Venegas at trial for a fee of 40% of the gross amount of any recovery. The contract gave Mitchell "the right to apply for and collect any attorney fee award made by a court," prohibited Venegas from waiving Mitchell's right to court-awarded attorney's fees, and allowed Mitchell's intervention to protect his interest in the fee award. The contract also provided that any fee awarded by the court would be applied, dollar for dollar, to offset the contingent fee. The contract obligated Mitchell to provide his services for one trial only and stated that "[i]n the event there is a mistrial or an appeal, the parties may mutually agree upon terms and conditions of [Mitchell's] employment, but are not obligated to do so." Venegas subsequently consented to the association of co-counsel with the understanding that co-counsel would share any contingent fee equally with Mitchell.

Venegas obtained a judgment in his favor of $2.08 million. Mitchell then moved for attorney's fees under § 1988, and on August 15, 1986, the District Court entered an order awarding Venegas $117,000 in attorney's fees, of which $75,000 was attributable to work done by Mitchell. The District Court calculated the award for Mitchell's work by multiplying a reasonable hourly rate by the number of hours Mitchell expended on the case, and then doubling this lodestar figure to reflect Mitchell's competent performance. Negotiations between attorney and client about the possibility of Mitchell's representing Venegas on appeal broke down, and on September 14, 1986, Mitchell signed a stipulation withdrawing as counsel of record. Venegas obtained different counsel for the appeal.

[Mitchell then asserted a $406,000 attorney's lien against the judgment proceeds, representing his half of the 40% fee. Venegas objected that the fee was excessive, arguing that Mitchell should be limited to the $75,000 found to be reasonable on the motion for attorney's fees. The district court refused to disallow or reduce the fee, finding it reasonable and not a windfall for Mitchell. The court of appeals affirmed the district court with regard to the fee dispute. Venegas v. Mitchell, 867 F.2d 527 (9th Cir.1989).]

II

Section 1988 states in pertinent part that "[i]n any action or proceeding to enforce a provision of sections 1981, 1982, 1983, 1985, and

1986 of this title, . . . the court, in its discretion, may allow the prevailing party, other than the United States, a reasonable attorney's fee as part of the costs." The section by its terms authorized the trial court in this case to order the defendants to pay to Venegas, the prevailing party, a reasonable attorney's fee. The aim of the section, as our cases have explained, is to enable civil rights plaintiffs to employ reasonably competent lawyers without cost to themselves if they prevail. It is likely that in many, if not most, cases a lawyer will undertake a civil rights case on the express or implied promise of the plaintiff to pay the lawyer the statutory award, i.e., a reasonable fee, if the case is won. But there is nothing in the section to regulate what plaintiffs may or may not promise to pay their attorneys if they lose or if they win. Certainly § 1988 does not on its face prevent the plaintiff from promising an attorney a percentage of any money judgment that may be recovered. Nor has Venegas pointed to anything in the legislative history that persuades us that Congress intended § 1988 to limit civil rights plaintiffs' freedom to contract with their attorneys.

It is true that in construing § 1988, we have generally turned away from the contingent-fee model to the lodestar model of hours reasonably expended compensated at reasonable rates. See Blanchard v. Bergeron, 489 U.S. 87, 94, 109 S.Ct. 939, 945, 103 L.Ed.2d 67 (1989); Riverside v. Rivera, 477 U.S. 561, 574, 106 S.Ct. 2686, 2694, 91 L.Ed.2d 466 (1986) (plurality opinion); Blum v. Stenson, 465 U.S. 886, 897, 104 S.Ct. 1541, 1548, 79 L.Ed.2d 891 (1984). We may also assume for the purposes of deciding this case that § 1988 would not have authorized the District Court to enhance the statutory award upward from the lodestar figure based on the contingency of nonrecovery in this particular litigation. But it is a mighty leap from these propositions to the conclusion that § 1988 also requires the District Court to invalidate a contingent-fee agreement arrived at privately between attorney and client. We have never held that § 1988 constrains the freedom of the civil rights plaintiff to become contractually and personally bound to pay an attorney a percentage of the recovery, if any, even though such a fee is larger than the statutory fee that the defendant must pay to the plaintiff.

Indeed, our cases look the other way. Section 1988 makes the prevailing party eligible for a discretionary award of attorney's fees. Evans v. Jeff D., 475 U.S. 717, 730, 106 S.Ct. 1531, 1538, 89 L.Ed.2d 747 (1986). Because it is the party, rather than the lawyer, who is so eligible, we have consistently maintained that fees may be awarded under § 1988 even to those plaintiffs who did not need them to maintain their litigation, either because they were fortunate enough to be able to retain counsel on a fee-paying basis, Blanchard v. Bergeron, supra, at 94–95, 109 S.Ct., at 944–945, or because they were represented free of charge by nonprofit legal aid organizations, Blum v. Stenson, supra, 465 U.S., at 894–895, 104 S.Ct., at 1546–1547. We have therefore accepted, at least implicitly, that statutory awards of fees can coexist with private fee arrangements. And just as we have recognized that it is the party's entitlement to receive the fees in the appropriate case, so have we recognized that as far as § 1988 is concerned, it is the party's right to waive, settle, or negotiate that eligibility. See Evans v. Jeff D., supra, 475 U.S., at 730–731, 106 S.Ct., at 3089–3090.

Much the same is true of the substance of a money judgment recovered under § 1983 (exclusive of fees awarded under § 1988), of which the contingent fee in this case is a part. A cause of action under § 1983 belongs "to the injured individua[l]," Newton v. Rumery, 480 U.S. 386, 395, 107 S.Ct. 1187, 1193, 94 L.Ed.2d 405 (1987) (plurality opinion), and in at least some circumstances that individual's voluntary waiver of a § 1983 cause of action may be valid. If § 1983 plaintiffs may waive their causes of action entirely, there is little reason to believe that they may not assign part of their recovery to an attorney if they believe that the contingency arrangement will increase their likelihood of recovery. A contrary decision would place § 1983 plaintiffs in the peculiar position of being freer to negotiate with their adversaries than with their own attorneys.

Relying heavily on Blanchard v. Bergeron, supra, Venegas argues that if a contingent-fee agreement does not impose a ceiling on the amount of a "court awarded fee which would go to the attorney" (as he understands the holding of *Blanchard*), such a fee agreement should also be ignored for the benefit of the client so that he need pay only the statutory award. There are two difficulties with this argument. First, *Blanchard* did not address contractual obligations of plaintiffs to their attorneys; it dealt only with what the losing defendant must pay the plaintiff, whatever might be the substance of the contract between the plaintiff and the attorney. Second, we have already rejected the argument that the entitlement to a § 1988 award belongs to the attorney rather than the plaintiff. See Evans v. Jeff D., supra, 475 U.S., at 731–732, 106 S.Ct., at 1539–1540.

Venegas also argues that because Congress provided for a reasonable fee to be paid by the defendant so that "a plaintiff's recovery will not be reduced by what he must pay his counsel," *Blanchard*, supra, 489 U.S., at 94, 109 S.Ct., at 944, the plaintiff should be protected from paying the attorney any more than the reasonable fee awarded by the trial court. Otherwise, Venegas contends, paying the contingent fee in full would greatly reduce his recovery and would impose a cost on him for enforcing the civil rights laws, a cost that the defendant should pay. This argument, too, is wide of the mark. *Blanchard* also noted that "[p]laintiffs who can afford to hire their own lawyers, as well as impecunious litigants, may take advantage" of § 1988. Civil rights plaintiffs, if they prevail, will be entitled to an attorney's fee that Congress anticipated would enable them to secure reasonably competent counsel. If they take advantage of the system as Congress established it, they will avoid having their recovery reduced by contingent-fee agreements. But neither *Blanchard* nor any other of our cases has indicated that § 1988, by its own force, protects plaintiffs from having to pay what they have contracted to pay, even though their contractual liability is greater than the statutory award that they may collect from losing opponents. Indeed, depriving plaintiffs of the option of promising to pay more than the statutory fee if that is necessary to secure counsel of their choice would not further § 1988's general purpose of enabling such plaintiffs in civil rights cases to secure competent counsel.

* * *

Venegas also argues that even if contingent fees exceeding statutory awards are not prohibited per se by § 1988, nonetheless the contingent fee in this case is unreasonable under federal and state law. Venegas made this contention to both lower courts, and both courts rejected it. We find no reason in the record or briefs to disturb their conclusion on this issue. We therefore have no occasion to address the extent of the federal courts' authority to supervise contingent fees.

Notes and Questions

1. As almost everyone seems to recognize, litigation is expensive. See Hadfield, The Price of Law, 98 Mich.L.Rev. 953 (2000) (reporting that the average hourly fees for lawyers in the U.S. were $180, and that larger firm partners averaged $250). From the perspective of the litigants, that expense ordinarily needs to be factored into the determination whether to litigate. At least some of the expense ordinarily is recoverable. Thus, Fed. R. Civ. P. 54(d)(1) provides that the prevailing party usually can recover its costs of suit. But these costs are ordinarily limited to the items listed in 28 U.S.C. § 1920—filing fees and certain out-of-pocket expenditures. In most cases these costs are much smaller than attorneys' fees, but they can be considerable. See Depasquale v. International Business Mach. Corp., 40 Fed.R.Serv.3d 425 (E.D.Pa.1998) (in product liability action, defendant sought to recover over $50,000 in costs from plaintiff). How should a court approach its discretion whether to award costs to the prevailing party? In Cherry v. Champion Int'l Corp., 186 F.3d 442 (4th Cir.1999), the appellate court held that the district court in an employment discrimination action abused its discretion when it refused to impose the prevailing defendant's costs on the plaintiff because plaintiff was unemployed and defendant was a large corporation. See also In re Paoli R.R. Yard PCB Litigation, 221 F.3d 449 (3d Cir.2000) (holding that the relative wealth of the parties is not a ground for denying a cost award).

From an early date, however, American courts refused to make the loser pay the winner's attorneys' fees. See Arcambel v. Wiseman, 3 U.S. 306, 3 Dall. 306 (1796) (attorneys' fees could not be recovered as a part of costs because "[t]he general practice of the United States is in opposition to it."). The requirement that each party bear its own attorneys' fees has become known as the "American rule." This will be considered further in Chapter VII. Should the American rule be changed? A damage recovery that is depleted by attorneys' fees would seem incomplete. A defendant who is exonerated arguably should not be impoverished by the cost of the successful defense. That seems to be the idea behind routine shifting of ordinary costs. Beyond the compensation rationale, routine fee-shifting might have desirable effects on behavior of litigants. Intuitively, allowing the winner to recover fees would seem likely to deter the assertion of groundless claims and defenses because those would increase the cost of litigation without improving the chance of winning. For reasons like these, almost all other countries allow recovery of some attorneys' fees, and some urge that this country should follow suit. Proposals to modify the rule have been presented in Congress.

How would bilateral fee shifting really work in practice? Would plaintiffs with good claims but moderate means be willing to sue large organizations and risk liability for the defendant's attorneys' fees? How sure would plaintiff have to feel about success before filing suit? Would the risk of liability for plaintiff's added fees really deter defendants from asserting groundless defenses? For an examination of these problems, see Rowe, Predicting the Effects of Attorney Fee Shifting, 47 Law & Contemp.Probs. 139 (Winter 1984) (noting that "[t]hinking about the effects of attorney fee shifting is surprisingly complex").

In terms of incentives, shifting away from the American rule might have harmful effects on the parties' attitudes toward the proper expenditure on litigation. If the parties must pay their own lawyers, win or lose, it makes sense for them to be frugal. If they can collect from their opponents if they win, they may be willing to spend more lavishly. Consider the following description of the consequences of the English full indemnity rule:

> [O]nce it is clear that a dispute is destined to go all the way to trial, the indemnity principle tends to erode resistance to costs. * * * Indeed, a point may come where the parties would have reason to persist with investment in litigation, not so much for the sake of a favorable judgment on the merits as for the purpose of recovering the money already expended in the dispute, which may well outstrip the value of the subject matter in issue.

Zuckerman, Lord Woolf's Access to Justice: Plus Ca Change ..., 59 Mod. L.Rev. 773, 778 (1996). Similarly, the American rule may prompt settlement of cases because the prospect of paying attorneys' fees sometimes causes even the confident to compromise. Even in countries that do routinely allow recovery of fees, the winner may be required to absorb a portion of the fees to "serve as a brake against dilatory tactics, harassment, or other abusive litigation practices." Tomkins & Willging, Taxation of Attorneys' Fees: Practices in English, Alaskan and Federal Courts 7–8 (1986).

2. Whatever your reaction to the policy debate about the American rule, the reality in this country is that fees are recoverable only if there is an exception to that rule. Various exceptions exist. One is that when a lawyer's or litigant's activities create a "common fund" for the benefit of others, the resulting fund can be "taxed" for the fair value of the lawyer's work to avoid unjustly enriching the beneficiaries. See Dawson, Lawyers and Involuntary Clients: Attorney Fees From Funds, 87 Harv.L.Rev. 1597 (1974). Another is that parties may by contract provide that in the event of a dispute the prevailing party is entitled to recover attorneys' fees. See Cal.Civ.Code § 1717 (directing that if a contract provides fee-shifting for one party it shall automatically provide fee-shifting for the other party as well). Yet another, recognized in some states, is the "private attorney general" concept. In California, for example, a statute provides that attorneys' fees can be awarded to a party whose action has "resulted in the enforcement of an

important right affecting the public interest" if a significant benefit has been conferred on the general public. Cal.Code Civ.Proc. § 1021.5.

In Alyeska Pipeline Serv. Co. v. Wilderness Society, 421 U.S. 240, 95 S.Ct. 1612, 44 L.Ed.2d 141 (1975), the Court held that Congress had not "extended any roving authority to the Judiciary to allow counsel fees as costs or otherwise whenever the courts might deem them warranted." In response, Congress amended 42 U.S.C.A. § 1988 the following year to add the fee-shifting provisions involved in Venegas v. Mitchell. Although it appears bilateral, this provision has been interpreted in the same way as Title VII of the 1964 Civil Rights Act. Title VII has been held to authorize recovery of fees by defendants only when plaintiff's suit is "frivolous, unreasonable, or without foundation." Christiansburg Garment Co. v. EEOC, 434 U.S. 412, 98 S.Ct. 694, 54 L.Ed.2d 648 (1978). But when civil rights plaintiffs prevail, defendants must usually pay their fees whether or not the defenses were groundless. Newman v. Piggie Park Enter., Inc., 390 U.S. 400, 88 S.Ct. 964, 19 L.Ed.2d 1263 (1968). Compare Fogerty v. Fantasy, Inc., 510 U.S. 517, 114 S.Ct. 1023, 127 L.Ed.2d 455 (1994) (refusing to read a similar pro-plaintiff intention into the fee-shifting provisions of the Copyright Act, 17 U.S.C.A. § 505 even though it is "virtually identical" to § 1988 because "in the civil rights context, impecunious 'private attorney general' plaintiffs can ill afford to litigate their claims against defendants with more resources. Congress sought to redress this balance in part, and to provide incentives for the bringing of meritorious lawsuits, by treating successful plaintiffs more favorably than successful defendants.").

Besides § 1988 and the copyright act, there are more than 100 other federal statutes that provide for fee shifting. See Marek v. Chesny, 473 U.S. 1, 44–51, 105 S.Ct. 3012, 3034–38, 87 L.Ed.2d 1 (1985) (Brennan, J., dissenting, listing statutes). See further discussion in Chapter VII.

3.   Ordinarily, as in § 1988, fee-shifting statutes authorize the award of a "reasonable" fee. In Venegas v. Mitchell, this fee award is calculated by what is called the "lodestar" method—multiplying the hours worked by the lawyer times the lawyer's hourly rate. In deciding whether the fee award is reasonable, the court may disallow hours that were spent on unsuccessful claims or inefficiently used. Regarding billing rate, ordinarily the court will use the attorney's customary rate for paying clients. But where the attorney does not have a customary rate, the court may look to "comparable" lawyers. In Blum v. Stenson, 465 U.S. 886, 104 S.Ct. 1541, 79 L.Ed.2d 891 (1984), involving lawyers who worked for a nonprofit legal aid organization, the Court held that "prevailing market rates in the relevant community" should still be allowed.

Note that in *Venegas*, the court doubled the fee award because Mitchell performed "competently." For some time, courts using the lodestar would increase awards to reflect the quality of representation or the risk of nonpayment. In Blum v. Stenson, supra, the Court held that, because the hourly rate should reflect the quality of the lawyer, a multiplier based on quality would be double counting. In City of Burlington v. Dague, 505 U.S. 557, 112 S.Ct. 2638, 120 L.Ed.2d 449 (1992), it held that fee enhancement for contingency should not be allowed either. Thus, it is likely that under current law Mitchell's work would result in a fee award half the size approved by the district court—$37,500.

4. In Blanchard v. Bergeron, 489 U.S. 87, 109 S.Ct. 939, 103 L.Ed.2d 67 (1989), plaintiff had a contract with his attorney providing that the lawyer would accept 40% of the award as payment, but the district court awarded more using the lodestar method. Defendant argued that the contract should set a ceiling for the fee award, but the Court disagreed, holding that the lodestar approach is "the centerpiece of attorney's fee awards" and that fees so calculated "by definition will represent the reasonable worth of the services rendered in vindication of a plaintiff's civil rights claim." It found this result consistent with the purpose of Congress that "a plaintiff's recovery will not be reduced by what he must pay his counsel."

If under the lodestar Mitchell's fee of $37,500 was by definition reasonable in *Venegas*, how could a fee of 20% of the recovery, over ten times that large, also be reasonable? See Model Rules of Professional Conduct 1.5(a) ("A lawyer's fee shall be reasonable."). Note that there is an inherent tension between the lawyer and the client in the negotiation of a fee. At some point a court may disallow a fee as too high. Do you think that it should have been trimmed in this case?

Some additional facts revealed in the lower courts' decisions and the oral arguments may shed light on this question. Mitchell was hired three months before the trial of Venegas' suit, after the bulk of discovery had been done. A state court suit by Venegas had already resulted in a $1,000,000 verdict that was overturned on grounds not applicable to the federal claim. Mitchell insisted on a $10,000 nonrefundable retainer and took the case to trial. After trial, defendants moved to have the judgment set aside and, when those motions were denied, appealed. Mitchell then offered to handle the appeal for an additional 10% of the recovery ($200,000 more, as things turned out). The appellate court affirmed in all respects. See Venegas v. Wagner, 831 F.2d 1514 (9th Cir.1987); Venegas v. Mitchell, 867 F.2d 527 (9th Cir.1989). Should Mitchell have offered Venegas the alternative of paying by the hour? Can you think of a reason why Venegas might not have taken this option?

5. An increasing number of courts in "common fund" class action situations have rejected the lodestar method of computing attorney's fees that was used in *Venegas*, using instead a percentage of the total award received. See Manual for Complex Litigation (4th) § 14.121 (2004) ("the vast majority of courts of appeals now permit or direct district courts to use the percentage method in common-fund cases"). A Task Force has described the lodestar method as a "cumbersome, enervating and often surrealistic process of preparing and evaluating fee petitions that now plagues the Bench and Bar." Court Awarded Attorney Fees, Report of the Third Circuit Task Force, 108 F.R.D. 237, 255 (1986). It said that the lodestar method consumed enormous judicial resources by requiring courts to review attorney billing information, gave attorneys little incentive to settle early, and "rewards plodding mediocrity and penalizes expedient success." Judge Posner, writing in In re Continental Illinois Securities Lit., 962 F.2d 566, 568 (7th Cir.1992), argued that "it is not the function of judges in fee litigation to determine the equivalent of the medieval just price. It is to determine what the lawyer

would receive if he were selling his services in the market rather than being paid by court order." Courts using the percentage method have typically awarded fees in the 25–35% range, but have reduced the percentage when the amount of the recovery is very large.

6.   Percentage contingent fees are a uniquely American invention. They are particularly common in the personal injury area, where it is said that they "unlock the door to the courthouse" by making it possible for a plaintiff who cannot afford to pay a lawyer by the hour to obtain representation. See generally F. MacKinnon, Contingent Fees for Legal Services (1964). The 40% charged by Mitchell was within the range commonplace in personal injury litigation. Should that be a model for civil rights suits? One court has concluded that "the risks plaintiffs face in § 1983 litigation are greater and the rewards are smaller" than in ordinary personal injury litigation because the standard for liability and possible immunity of the defendant make recovery more difficult. Kirchoff v. Flynn, 786 F.2d 320, 323–24 (7th Cir. 1986).

Are percentage fees unfair to the client? Some have objected that in personal injury cases percentage fees often result in excessive compensation for lawyers where there is in reality no significant risk of loss. See Brickman, Contingent Fees Without Contingencies: *Hamlet* without the Prince of Denmark, 37 U.C.L.A.L.Rev. 29 (1989). Note that with a 40% fee the client by definition is barely half compensated. Note also that the lawyer is in a sense subsidizing her unsuccessful cases with the charges to successful clients. What impact will this have on her selection of clients? See Kritzer, Seven Dogged Myths Concerning Contingency Fees, 80 Wash.U.L.Rev. 739 (2002) (reporting that contingency fee lawyers actively screen cases and, as a result, run only a small risk of nonrecovery). Once she has taken a case, will the fee arrangement affect her interest in settling? For an argument favoring blending the hourly and percentage fee approaches to harmonize the lawyers' incentives and those of the clients, see Clermont & Currivan, Improving on the Contingent Fee, 63 Cornell L. Rev. 529 (1978).

7.   If fees are not to be a percentage of the recovery, must they at least bear some relationship to the recovery? In Riverside v. Rivera, 477 U.S. 561, 106 S.Ct. 2686, 91 L.Ed.2d 466 (1986), plaintiffs sued a variety of police officers for illegal arrest and ultimately obtained judgments against some of them totalling $33,000. The district court awarded $245,000 in fees, noting that the police misconduct "had to be stopped and * * * nothing short of having a lawsuit like this would have stopped it." Justice Rehnquist argued that "billing judgment" should have prevented the lawyers from seeking such a fee, but the Court affirmed the award because Justice Powell decided the findings regarding the larger public importance of the suit were not clearly erroneous. Justice Brennan, writing for a plurality, asserted that "[w]e reject the notion that a civil rights action for damages constitutes nothing more than a private tort suit benefitting only the individual plaintiffs whose rights were violated. Unlike most private tort litigants, a civil rights plaintiff seeks to vindicate important civil and constitutional rights that cannot be valued solely in monetary terms." Should this mean that in civil rights cases the size of the claim is no constraint on the amount of lawyer time invested in the case?

8. Note that Mitchell's contract with Venegas forbade Venegas from waiving court-awarded attorneys' fees. In Evans v. Jeff D., 475 U.S. 717, 106 S.Ct. 1531, 89 L.Ed.2d 747 (1986), defendants in a class action brought on behalf of handicapped children regarding health-care treatment offered plaintiffs "virtually all the injunctive relief" they had sought provided that plaintiffs would waive attorneys' fees. The Court rejected the argument that this was improper:

> Although respondents contend that Johnson, as counsel for the class, was faced with an "ethical dilemma" when petitioners offered him relief greater than that which he could reasonably have expected to obtain for his clients at trial (if only he would stipulate to a waiver of the statutory fee award), * * * we do not believe that the "dilemma" was an "ethical" one in the sense that Johnson had to choose between conflicting duties under the prevailing norms of professional conduct. Plainly Johnson had no *ethical* obligation to seek a statutory fee award. His ethical duty was to serve his clients loyally and competently. Since the proposal to settle the merits was more favorable than the probable outcome of the trial, Johnson's decision to recommend acceptance was consistent with the highest standards of our profession.

Given that defendants in *Jeff D.* seem almost to have conceded that they violated plaintiffs' rights, does this decision unduly erode the value of the fee-shifting statute? Will the risk that defendants may insist on a fee waiver in return for favorable relief on the merits affect the willingness of attorneys to accept such cases? Does a provision like the one used by Mitchell solve that problem? Does it raise an ethical problem?

9. *Publicly subsidized attorneys*: Some countries have tried to assure legal representation for all by subsidizing lawyers for the poor, but many such programs have been cut back. See A. Zuckerman, Civil Procedure 949–51 (2003) (describing "radical reform" to cut the costs of of English scheme for government to pay for privately-retained lawyers). In the 1960s, the federal government in this country created a network of legal services offices in this country that provided lawyers on the government payroll for eligible poor people. In the 1980s, however, funding for this program was cut.

10. *Tax consequences:* In Commissioner v. Banks, ___ U.S. ___, 125 S.Ct. 826 (2005), the Court held that "when a litigant's recovery constitutes income, the litigant's income includes the portion of the recovery paid to the attorney as a contingent fee." Many lower courts had held that, in situations in which the plaintiff had a percentage contingency arrangement with the attorney, the attorney's share was not taxable income to the plaintiff. Plaintiffs in the cases before the Court had sued their former employers for violating their rights. Both had substantial recoveries and owed their attorneys substantial amounts (in one case over $3.8 million). Although the cost of obtaining those recoveries could be listed as itemized deductions, tax would still be due under the Alternative Minimum Tax. Personal injury compensation was already exempt from taxation, and during the pendency of this case Congress amended the tax code to add 26 U.S.C.A. § 62(a)(19) permitting deduction of attorney fees involved in litigating a claim for unlawful employment discrimination, which would cover cases like the plaintiffs' in the future. In addition, the Court did not address the question

whether a fee award made under a fee-shifting statute and calculated on a lodestar basis should be treated as income to the plaintiff. Tax consequences may continue to be important in much litigation not covered by Congress' amendment of the tax code, however.

11. *Filing fees*: Besides paying lawyers, litigants must initially pay filing fees and the like even if they are ultimately able to recoup them. Federal courts will excuse payment of those fees by people eligible to file in forma pauperis, 28 U.S.C.A. § 1915, but that option is not always available. The Supreme Court has sometimes found the imposition of these fees to violate due process when a "fundamental right" is involved and a litigant cannot afford the fees. See Boddie v. Connecticut, 401 U.S. 371, 91 S.Ct. 780, 28 L.Ed.2d 113 (1971) (holding that state could not impose a filing fee for obtaining a divorce); compare United States v. Kras, 409 U.S. 434, 93 S.Ct. 631, 34 L.Ed.2d 626 (1973) ($50 filing fee for bankruptcy petition could be imposed because bankruptcy discharge is not a fundamental right like dissolving a marriage); Ortwein v. Schwab, 410 U.S. 656, 93 S.Ct. 1172, 35 L.Ed.2d 572 (1973) (upholding $25 fee for court review of reduction of welfare allowance for the aged on ground that no fundamental right was involved). See also M.L.B. v. S.L.J., 519 U.S. 102, 117 S.Ct. 555, 136 L.Ed.2d 473 (1996) (due process violated by state requirement that party seeking to appeal termination of parental rights post over $2,300 to cover the cost of preparing a transcript of the proceedings from which the appeal was taken).

D. PRIVATE ORDERING THROUGH ALTERNATIVES TO LITIGATION

Now that we have examined some of the difficulties in fashioning judicial remedies for disputes, and before we turn to the litigation process itself, it is useful to consider alternative means of resolving disputes. Until fairly recently, discussion of alternative processes would not be found in a first-year civil procedure casebook. But developments since the 1980s have contributed to a new awareness of the close interrelationship between litigation and other means of resolving disputes. First, the movement referred to as "Alternative Dispute Resolution" or "ADR" has generated both a new philosophy and new processes for resolving disputes short of trial. Second, courts have embraced settlement as a principal objective in every case, shaping settlement conferences and other devices for use in case administration. We have already encountered this phenomenon in Kothe v. Smith, supra p. 18. Third, creative experimentation by both dispute resolution professionals and judges has resulted in a cornucopia of new methods for aiding disputants to find solutions to their disputes. We will address many of these developments in much greater detail in Chapter VII entitled Judicial Supervision of Pretrial and Promotion of Settlement.

For our purposes here of providing an overview of the remedies offered by our court system, it is useful to consider three of the principal alternatives to a full trial—negotiation and settlement promotion; third-party intervention; and arbitration. Adjudication in a court involves an ultimate decision on the rights of the parties by a public officer, the judge, or by a jury sworn to uphold the law and instructed in the applicable legal principles by the judge. The decision is made after a public trial at which the parties have the right to present evidence they have obtained through pretrial efforts assisted by the court (as in allowing discovery, see Chapter V). The decision of the case is supposed to conform to legal rules of substantive law, and can therefore be scrutinized by another group of public officials, judges of an appellate court, who determine whether it was correct under that law.

A central difference between adjudication and the three alternatives is that they are conducted privately and extrajudicially (although, under newly developing procedures, they may be "court-annexed" and thus serve as a step in the litigation process, as will be discussed more fully in Chapter VII). Thus, these alternatives can be viewed as a form of "private ordering" of disputes. Legal standards still provide a guide for resolution of the dispute under these alternatives, but there is greater latitude than in litigation to reach a solution that does not mirror the rights and remedies that would be applied in a court.

Another difference is in the degree of formality. The alternative processes vary in formality, from negotiation, which is an essentially unstructured process, through mediation and other forms of third-party intervention which involve certain formalities, to arbitration which follows formal procedures for the presentation of the case. But they are not bound by court procedures nor strict standards of evidence, and they lack the stuffiness (or majesty, depending on your point of view) of the courtroom with its robed judge and ritual. These differences may be viewed as either advantages or disadvantages depending on one's philosophy of dispute resolution.

NEGOTIATION AND SETTLEMENT PROMOTION

Negotiation is as old as social interaction. It occurs when one person attempts to persuade another to agree to his or her terms. Consciously or not, each of us has engaged in negotiation, often over such insignificant details as selecting a movie to see, or a restaurant to go to. Some may have negotiated in more "official" circumstances as, for example, trying to persuade a police officer not to issue a speeding ticket.

Negotiation is a common first reaction to a dispute. If a neighbor is playing loud music, negotiation may lead to a reduction in the noise level. The potential value of negotiation may explain why such a small percentage of disputes actually lead to litigation, although calculating that percentage with precision is difficult. Researchers who tried to measure the winnowing effect of pre-litigation factors on pursuit of disputes found that, among people who had grievances, negotiated agreements before litigation were much more frequent than actual commencement of litigation.[1]

---

1. See Miller & Sarat, Grievances, Claims and Disputes: Assessing the Adversary Culture, 15 Law & Soc'y Rev. 525, 537 (1981); see generally Galanter, Reading the Landscape of Disputes: What We Know and Don't Know (and Think We Know) About Our Allegedly Contentious and Litigious Society, 31 U.C.L.A.L.Rev. 4, 11–18 (1983)

Once lawyers do get involved, the negotiation process usually continues, often both before and after formal litigation is commenced. This reality is confirmed by the fact that many more lawsuits that are filed are settled rather than decided by a court or jury. Indeed, some suggest that the process might better be called "litigotiation" than litigation.[2] At this point, however, the negotiation is usually done by the lawyers, and not by the parties themselves.

Negotiation is a tool of the trade for lawyers, but sometimes outside assistance is needed to encourage them to employ it effectively. Wariness over appearing too anxious to settle or over making the first offer can be overcome by court promotion of settlement. Rule 16 includes "facilitating settlement" and consideration of "the use of extrajudicial procedures to resolve the dispute" as objectives for a settlement conference. Settlement conferences can be held with or without the judge being present. The judge's active involvement can sometimes be effective but also runs the risk of coercion, as was seen in the *Kothe* case, (supra at p. 18). Suffice it to say that today judges are very much involved in the promotion of settlement, whether through informal jaw-boning, mandated conferences, or more formal ADR devices.

THIRD–PARTY INTERVENTION

Settlement negotiations can often be assisted by the intervention of a third party, as suggested by the common role of judges in promoting settlement. The role of the third party can vary considerably, ranging from facilitating discussion and generating options (in the traditional "mediation") to providing an evaluation of the strengths of the parties' cases on the law or facts (found in "neutral evaluation" programs that have been adopted by some federal courts), to more formal "trial runs" in which the third party or parties give a nonbinding opinion after hearing the parties summarize their cases (for example, in a "summary jury trial" before a representative jury, a "court-annexed arbitration" before volunteer attorneys, or a "mini-trial" before the decision-makers of the parties). We will consider these methods in more detail in Chapter VII, but something more might be said here about the most frequently used form of third-party intervention, mediation.

Mediation is a step away from negotiation because the parties turn to a third person to help them make a deal to end their dispute. Like negotiation, it has existed since humans began to develop social organization because people seem to have a natural instinct to seek the guidance of others in settling their differences. Mediation is widely used in the United States in divorce and related family law cases and is increasingly being used in labor law employee grievances, low-level disputes taken to neighborhood dispute resolution centers, public law

(examining the attrition rate among potential disputes before a third party—such as a lawyer—is called upon).

2. See Galanter, Worlds of Deals: Using Negotiation to Teach About Legal Process, 34 J.Legal Ed. 268, 269 (1984).

disputes such as civil rights and environmental cases, and personal injury and commercial suits.

The function of the mediator is quite different from that of a judge. Rather than applying legal rules to the parties' behavior, the mediator lacks any authority to decide who is right. Furthermore, the parties are not bound by legal rules about behavior. "[I]n mediation—as distinguished from adjudication and, usually, arbitration—the ultimate authority resides with the disputants. The conflict is seen as unique and therefore less subject to solution by application of some general principle. The case is neither to be governed by a precedent nor to set one. Thus, all sorts of facts, needs, and interests that would be excluded from consideration in an adversary, rule-oriented proceeding become relevant in a mediation. Indeed, whatever a party deems relevant is relevant."[3]

Although without power to enforce rules, the mediator can perform important tasks. One is to reduce the level of antagonism between the parties to persuade them to trust each other. "The adversary process—the engine of the adjudicatory system—operates on a theory of fundamental distrust: Never put faith in the adversary. Litigation thus becomes formal, tricky, divisive, time-consuming, and distorting. * * * In contrast, the creation of trust is central to the design of many ADR processes."[4] To avoid these disruptive effects of litigation, mediators have sometimes insisted that the parties leave their lawyers (if they have any) behind and handle the mediation sessions alone. However, as mediation is increasingly used as a pretrial settlement device, lawyers generally participate, contributing legal expertise and advice.

Another task for the mediator is creativity. The parties may have turned to the mediator not only because of mistrust but also because they are at loggerheads. Here again, the absence of legal limitations on the mediator's actions can prove helpful because "participants in ADR are free to go beyond the legal definition of the scope of their dispute. They can search for creative solutions to the problem that gave rise to the dispute, and those solutions may be far more novel than any remedy a court has the power to provide."[5] Thus, "the mediator employs two fundamental principles of effective mediation: creating doubt in the minds of the parties as to the validity of their positions on issues; and suggesting alternative approaches which may facilitate agreement. These are two functions which parties to a dispute are very often unable to perform by themselves. To carry out these functions, the mediator has the parties separately 'brainstorm' to produce alternatives or options; discusses the workability of each option; encourages the parties by noting the probability of success, where appropriate; suggests alternatives not raised by the parties and then repeats the three previous

---

3. Riskin, Mediation and Lawyers, 43 Ohio St.L.J. 29, 34 (1982).

4. Lieberman & Henry, Lessons From the Alternative Dispute Resolution Movement, 53 U.Chi.L.Rev. 424, 427 (1986).

5. Id. at 429.

steps."[6] The most used form of mediation is often called "non-directive" or "facilitative," in which the mediator seeks to facilitate communication but not to impose her values or solutions on the parties. However, there is a variety of other approaches, depending on the mediator, such as a "therapeutic" approach (more often taken in family law cases) in which the mediator plays a more active role in helping the parties resolve their differences and an "evaluative" approach (more often used by former judges) in which the mediator is more inclined to give her opinion as to how the case might be resolved in the courts.[7] There has also been considerable discussion of a "transformative" approach in which the mediator seeks to engender "moral growth" in the parties through "empowerment" and "recognition."[8]

The goal is that the parties ultimately agree voluntarily to a specific solution to their dispute. Once they do, the mediator will ordinarily put the agreement in writing and have the parties sign the agreement. Mediation agreements are legally binding, if they satisfy the requirements of contract law. It is said that they are actually followed more often than decrees by judges: "The internal and interactional dynamics of consensual settlement processes combine to create pressures toward compliance that are largely lacking in adjudication. * * * Consent, unlike command, brings with it an assumption of responsibility for the settlement and for its implementation. This sense of responsibility, along with general normative pressures to live up to commitments, can weigh heavily on disputants, even those who may regret having given consent in the heat of negotiation or mediation. The more explicit these pressures, the more effective they are. Our data suggest that the personal and immediate commitments generated by consensual processes bind people more strongly to compliance than the relatively distant, impersonal obligations imposed by authorities."[9]

Since the 1980s mediation has become "court-annexed" in many jurisdictions. Statutes and court rules now often either encourage or require the parties to a law suit to mediate as an integral part of the litigation process.[10]

---

6. Cooley, Arbitration vs. Mediation— Explaining the Differences, 69 Judicature 263, 267 (1986).

7. See Riskin, Mediator Orientations, Strategies, and Techniques, 12 Alternatives 111 (1994).

8. See R. Bush & J. Folger, The Promise of Mediation: Responding to Conflict Through Empowerment and Recognition (1994). The U.S. Postal Service adopted an ambitious dispute resolution program called "Redress" that uses a "transformative" approach to mediation of employee grievance and disciplinary disputes. See Advanced Mediation Skills for Postal Service Mediators: Practice Within A Transformative Framework (A Course Prepared for the U.S. Postal Service by Robert A. Baruch

Bush, Joseph P. Folger, Dorothy J. Della Noce, & Sally Ganong Pope, 2000).

9. McEwen & Maiman, Mediation in Small Claims Court: Achieving Compliance Through Consent, 18 Law & Soc'y Rev. 11, 42, 44–45 (1984).

10. See Sherman, Court–Mandated Alternative Dispute Resolution: What Form of Participation Should be Required?, 46 S.M.U.L.Rev. 2079 (1993); Plapinger & Stienstra, ADR and Settlement in the Federal District Courts: A Sourcebook for Judges and Lawyers (2000); Welsh, Making Deals in Court–Connected Mediation: What's Justice Got to Do With It?, 79 Wash.U.L.Q. 787 (2001) (observing that bargaining in court-ordered mediation is similar to that in private mediation).

ARBITRATION

Arbitration has long been an alternative to litigation. One of the purposes behind the creation of the Chambers of Commerce in the colonial period was to arbitrate disputes among their members.[11] George Washington himself put an arbitration clause in his will to resolve any disputes among his heirs.

Arbitration resembles adjudication more closely than mediation because the third person, the arbitrator, has the authority to *decide* the dispute, not merely to try to get the parties to agree on a decision. This power is conferred on the arbitrator by the parties' agreement to submit their dispute to arbitration. Although arbitration produces a decision, it is still an example of private ordering. An agreement to arbitrate can occur after the dispute arises, but ordinarily it is part of an agreement on some other subject between the parties that is made before there was any dispute (as was the clause inserted in George Washington's will and as in many contracts today). Clauses requiring arbitration of any dispute are commonplace today in collective bargaining agreements and commercial contracts (particularly those of certain industries such as construction, or those involving parties from different countries).

To initiate the arbitration process, one of the parties demands arbitration of a specified dispute. If the other party refuses, it is usually possible to get a court order to arbitrate pursuant to the agreement. See Federal Arbitration Act, 9 U.S.C.A. § 4. The first step is selection of the arbitrator or arbitrators. Sometimes an organization like the American Arbitration Association (AAA) is delegated the task of selecting an arbitrator after consultation with the parties, but more often they must agree themselves or, as is the case in certain types of disputes, each party gets to appoint one arbitrator and these two select a third, making a panel of three. If the parties cannot agree on an arbitrator, it is often possible to have a court appoint one for them. See 9 U.S.C.A. § 5.

Beyond selecting the arbitrator, the parties may have specified the process to be used in advance, providing for such things as evidence-gathering (discovery), the right to call witnesses, the timing and place of the hearings, etc. Subject to such an agreement, the arbitrator(s) can fashion a procedure. Usually this will be more limited than full-blown litigation. The AAA and other administering organizations also provide procedures that may be agreed to either in advance or ad hoc for a particular arbitration.

After a hearing at which the parties present their cases (usually through lawyers), the arbitrator(s) render a decision, called an award, which, in American practice, usually does not contain the reasons for the result (labor arbitration is an exception). Often a judgment can be obtained in court on the basis of this award. See 9 U.S.C.A. § 9. Once arbitration is over, the award is regarded as conclusive of the claims that were arbitrated, and it can be set aside by a court only if obtained by

11. Mentschikoff, Commercial Arbitration, 61 Colum.L.Rev. 846, 854–55 (1961).

corruption, if there was evident partiality, or if the arbitrator was guilty of serious misconduct. See 9 U.S.C.A. § 10.

One of the most significant developments in the field of dispute resolution in recent years is the explosive growth of contractual arbitration, which the Federal Arbitration Act makes enforceable in contracts "evidencing a transaction involving commerce." The effect of an arbitration clause is to deny the customer the right to a jury trial as to any dispute arising out of the contract. Arbitration has been embraced by various institutions for numerous reasons—perceived quicker and less costly resolution than litigation, finality because of limited review, resort to a decision-maker with more experience and expertise in the subject matter than the average jury member, and avoidance of high damage awards associated with jury trials.

There are many legal issues attending this growth of contractual arbitration. The FAA, passed in 1925, provides that federal courts will order compliance with arbitration agreements and, if a party files suit, will stay such proceedings pending arbitration. The Supreme Court has applied the FAA broadly, holding that it "declared a national policy favoring arbitration and withdrew the power of the states to require a judicial forum for the resolution of claims which the contracting parties agreed to resolve by arbitration."[12] Supreme Court decisions have found that a variety of state laws imposing restrictions on arbitrations are preempted by the FAA.[13] In recent years, the Court has also rejected exceptions for claims brought under certain federal statutes that had been previously thought to require a trial by jury.[14]

In the wake of expanded resort to arbitration clauses in adhesion contracts, courts often scrutinize the circumstances to ensure that there was knowing waiver of the right to sue, and that it does not involve fundamental unfairness. For example, in Kummetz v. Tech Mold, Inc., 152 F.3d 1153 (9th Cir.1998), the court found that an employee's signed acknowledgement that he was covered by the company's Employment Information Booklet (that contained an arbitration provision) did not bar him from suing under the ADEA because the acknowledgement did not specifically notify him that arbitration was required.

Although the FAA preempts state laws considered to disadvantage the enforcement of arbitration, it must be applied against the backdrop

---

12. Southland Corp. v. Keating, 465 U.S. 1, 10 (1984).

13. See Southland Corp. v. Keating, 465 U.S. 1 (1984) (state statute prohibiting arbitration in franchise agreements); Allied–Bruce Terminix Cos., Inc. v. Dobson, 513 U.S. 265, 115 S.Ct. 834, 130 L.Ed.2d 753 (1995) (state statute invalidating pre-dispute arbitration agreements).

14. See Gilmer v. Interstate/Johnson Lane corp., 500 U.S. 20, 111 S.Ct. 1647, 114 L.Ed.2d 26 (1991); Rodriguez de Quijas v. Shearson/American Express, Inc., 490 U.S. 477, 109 S.Ct. 1917, 104 L.Ed.2d 526 (1989); Mitsubishi Motors Corp. v. Soler Chrysler–Plymouth, Inc., 473 U.S. 614, 105 S.Ct. 3346, 87 L.Ed.2d 444 (1985) (antitrust). Compare Alford v. Dean Witter Reynolds, Inc., 905 F.2d 104 (5th Cir.1990) (Title VII employment discrimination claim subject to arbitration) with Duffield v. Robertson Stephens & Co., 144 F.3d 1182 (9th Cir.1998) (arbitration clause does not bar Title VII suit).

of state contract law.[15] Thus all of the usual defenses under state law to a breach of contract suit—such as failure of meeting of the minds, lack of consideration, mistake, duress and coercion, fraud, and unconscionability—may be raised in challenging the enforcement of an arbitration clause.[16] Unconscionability[17] has become a principal ground for challenging arbitration clauses in adhesion contracts as banks, credit card issuers, service industries, product manufacturers, employers, and the health care industry have increasingly added such clauses to their contracts. The California Supreme Court, for example, has held that to overcome a challenge of unconscionability, an arbitration clause must: 1) allow all remedies available in court 2) provide for adequate discovery 3) require a written arbitration award and judicial review, and 4) not require the claimant to pay the arbitration costs.[18] Other courts differ as to the exact standards necessary to avoid unconscionability, and, as a result, there is a wide variety in court outcomes.

One of the most controversial issues concerning arbitration is the rapidly growing inclusion in arbitration clauses of a prohibition on class actions or class treatment in consumer contracts. Some courts have found such a ban is unconscionable in preventing consumers who have small dollar claims from seeking a class action in order to obtain a lawyer and prosecute their claims effectively.[19] A number of federal courts, on the other hand, have held that unless the arbitration clause specifically provided for classwide arbitration, a court had no authority to certify class arbitration and arbitration.[20] Other courts have found a waiver of class arbitration to be enforceable.[21]

Green Tree Financial Corp. v. Bazzle[22] was expected to produce an answer by the Supreme Court whether prohibition of class treatment in

15. The Federal Arbitration Act, 9 U.S.C.A. § 2, provides that "arbitration agreements shall be valid, irrevocable, and enforceable, save upon such grounds as exist at law or in equity for the revocation of any contract."

16. See Rau, Sherman, & Peppet, Processes of Dispute Resolution: The Role of Lawyers 695–712 (3d ed. 2002).

17. Unconscionability includes both substantive and procedural elements. Procedural unconscionability addresses the manner in which agreement to the disputed term was sought or obtained, such as unequal bargaining power between the parties and hidden terms included in contracts of adhesion. Substantive unconscionability addresses the impact of the term itself, such as whether the provision is so harsh or oppressive that it should not be enforced. Szetela v. Discover Bank, 118 Cal.Rptr.2d 862 (Ct. App. 2002), cert. denied, 537 U.S. 1226 (2003).

18. Armendariz v. Foundation Health Psychcare Services, Inc., 6 P.3d 669 (Cal. 2000).

19. See Szetela v. Discover Bank, 118 Cal.Rptr.2d 862 (Ct. App. 2002), cert. denied, 537 U.S. 1226, 123 S.Ct. 1258 (2003) (class action waiver is substantively unconscionable, thus granting motion to certify a class in arbitration); Ting v. AT & T, 319 F.3d 1126 (9th Cir.2003); Powertel, Inc. v. Bexley, 743 So.2d 570 (Fla. Dist. Ct. App. 1st Dist. 1999); Dickler v. Shearson Lehman Hutton, Inc., 596 A.2d 860 (Pa. Super. Ct. 1991). See Sternlight & Jensen, Using Arbitration to Eliminate Consumer Class Actions: Efficient Business Practice or Unconscionable Abuse?, 67 Law & Contemp. Probs. 75 (2004).

20. Champ v. Siegel Trading Co., Inc., 55 F.3d 269 (7th Cir.1995); Deiulemar Compagnia di Navigazione S.p.A. v. M/V Allegra, 198 F.3d 473 (4th Cir.1999); Furgason v. McKenzie Check Advance of Indiana, Inc., 2001 WL 238129 (S.D. Ind. 2001).

21. See Zawikowski v. Beneficial Nat. Bank, 1999 WL 35304, at *1 (N.D. Ill. 1999) ("nothing prevents the Plaintiffs from contracting away their right to a class action").

22. 539 U.S. 444, 123 S.Ct. 2402, 156 L.Ed.2d 414 (2003).

an arbitration clause is enforceable. In that case the arbitration clause in the defendant's standard loan agreements was silent as to class treatment. When the plaintiffs filed a class action in state court, the court referred the case to the arbitrator who treated it as a classwide arbitration, awarding the class members $9.2 million for violations of consumer protection laws. The Supreme Court ruled that the question of "arbitrability" was for the arbitrator rather than the court, and, on remand, the arbitrator reaffirmed the class treatment and the award. But many companies have now rewritten their arbitration clauses to expressly forbid class treatment,[23] and a case challenging such clauses for unconscionability will undoubtedly have to be decided by the Supreme Court in the future.

Following the decision in *Bazzle*, the American Arbitration Association announced that it would not administer class arbitrations unless both parties agreed or the court so directed. However, it also issued "Supplementary Rules for Class Arbitrations" (Oct. 8, 2003), see http://www.adr.org/index, which contain many features of the federal class action rule (Rule 23). Classwide arbitrations have long been conducted by direction of courts in California.[24]

The spectacular growth in the use of arbitration in recent years has led to calls for revising the Federal Arbitration Act and the various state arbitration acts. A revised Uniform Arbitration Act, adopted in ten states by the end of 2004, made changes in such procedures as the availability of discovery (making arbitration more like litigation), remedies such as attorneys' fees and punitive damages, and disclosure requirements by arbitrators.

It appears that binding arbitration is becoming a primary mode of dispute resolution for many contractual disputes in our society. Lawyers are likely to find in the future that a larger part of their litigation practices involves arbitration, requiring them to adapt to different procedures and decision-makers than in a jury trial. At the same time, there seems to be some adaptation of both trial and arbitration procedures that bring them closer together. Arbitrators are increasingly ordering discovery and holding pre-arbitration hearings to resolve case management issues. On the litigation side, judges are increasingly limiting the

---

23. See, e.g., the clause in the Cingular Wireless contract with customers: "Cingular and you ... agree to arbitrate all disputes and claims (including ones that already are the subject of litigation) arising out of or relating to this Agreement, or to any prior oral or written agreement, for Equipment or services between Cingular and you. Notwithstanding the foregoing, either party may bring an individual action in small claims court.... You agree that, by entering into this Agreement, you and Cingular are waiving the right to a trial by jury.... YOU AND CINGULAR MAY BRING CLAIMS AGAINST THE OTHER ONLY IN YOUR OR ITS INDIVIDUAL CAPACITY, and not as a plaintiff or class member in any purported class or representative proceeding. Further, you agree that the arbitrator may not consolidate proceedings or more than one person's claims, and may not otherwise preside over any form of a representative or class proceeding...."

24. See Blue Cross of California v. Superior Court, 78 Cal.Rptr.2d 779 (Cal. Ct. App. 1998).

scope of oral testimony and requiring expert testimony to be presented in affidavit form which is closer to arbitration practice. Significant differences, however, remain in the respective remedies provided by litigation and arbitration. A court, whether acting on its own in a bench trial or instructing the jury in a jury trial, is limited by what the law of remedies provides and may be reversed if it strays from those standards. An arbitrator possesses greater flexibility of remedy to achieve the essential purposes of the contract and can only be overturned under the limited court review for gross misconduct.[25] This has its good side (in allowing greater flexibility to achieve raw justice) and its bad side (in the often-made charge that arbitrators tend to "split the difference" in violation of the contract terms).

Notes and Questions

1.   There has been a long-standing debate over the virtues of adjudication versus settlement. Concerns have been expressed that judicial encouragement of settlement could deny parties the protection of courts, which are best suited to preserving constitutional and public law rights, and could undermine the rights-oriented litigation process which provides binding precedents applicable to others similarly situated. Although these criticisms are generally leveled at mediation, they may also apply to arbitration since arbitrator awards in non-labor cases are generally without an opinion which provides a precedent.

Professor Owen Fiss, in his article Against Settlement, 93 Yale L.J. 1073, 1085 (1984), argued that "[a]djudication uses public resources, and employs [public officials whose] job is not to maximize the ends of private parties, nor simply to secure the peace, but to explicate and give force to the values embodied in authoritative texts such as the Constitution and statutes: to interpret those values and to bring reality into accord with them."

Judge Harry Edwards added: "one essential function of law is to reflect the public resolution of such irreconcilable differences; lawmakers are forced to choose among these differing visions of the public good. A potential danger of ADR is that disputants who seek only understanding and reconciliation may treat as irrelevant the choices made by our lawmakers and may, as a result, ignore public values reflected in rules of law. We must also be concerned lest ADR becomes a tool for diminishing the judicial development of legal rights for the disadvantaged. * * * Inexpensive, expeditious, and informal adjudication is not always synonymous with fair and just adjudication." Edwards, Alternative Dispute Resolution: Panacea or Anathema, 99 Harv. L. Rev. 668, 676–77 (1986).

Professor Edward Brunet observed that "the output of conventional litigation should be viewed as a public good": "Litigation guides third parties. Litigation results in written opinions that apply necessarily vague positive law to concrete fact situations." Private ordering devices and ADR erode the guidance function of law, he argued: "In the worst case scenario, widespread ADR independent of substantive law could increase disputes since third parties would lack the incentive to perform in accordance with

25. See Federal Arbitration Act, 9 U.S.C.A. § 10 (1925).

custom crafted legal norms. For example, a rational polluter would be foolish to comply with a published regulation permitting a low amount of emissions when it could probably pollute at a substantially greater amount through environmental mediation." Brunet, Questioning The Quality of Alternate Dispute Resolution, 62 Tulane L.Rev. 1, 19–20 (1987).

Is there a response to these concerns of the ADR critics? There is a risk of overstating the case. Professor Fiss has challenged the idea that courts should be concerned with dispute resolution at all: "To my mind courts exist to give meaning to our public values, not to resolve disputes." As to disputes that do not involve public values, he suggests that having courts resolve them is "an extravagant use of public resources, and thus it seems quite appropriate for those disputes to be handled not by courts, but by arbitrators." Fiss, Foreword: The Forms of Justice, 93 Harv.L.Rev. 1, 29–30 (1979). Although it must be noted that Fiss defines "public value" broadly, doesn't this attitude underestimate the importance of courts as devices for resolving a whole range of disputes?

2.   For many clients the greater flexibility represented by private ordering devices and ADR approaches may be more important than litigation opportunities. Lawyers are not social workers, but they should be alert to the possibility that creative compromises may be more useful to their clients in many instances than insisting on litigation to the end. Where the parties to the dispute expect to have a long-term relationship with one another, there may be particular reasons to think seriously about something short of full adjudication. At the same time, it is important to realize that the anti-litigation sentiment prevalent in some quarters is not universally shared, and that the grounds for it are subject to serious question. The existence of a litigation "boom," for example, is highly debated. Those who claim it has occurred point to dramatic increases in court filings. Others, however, look closely at the statistics and report that the increase is not so dramatic as is claimed. See Galanter, Reading the Landscape of Disputes: What We Know And Don't Know (And Think We Know) About Our Allegedly Contentious and Litigious Society, 31 U.C.L.A.L.Rev. 4 (1983) (arguing that the patterns in litigation relate to other changes in society). Galanter, The Vanishing Trial: An Examination of Trials and Related Matters in Federal and State Courts, 1 J. Empir. Studies 459 (2004).

3.   A prevalent attitude in the ADR movement has been that litigation is bad. One ADR organization, for example, asks its members to sign a pledge: "In the event of a business dispute between our company and another which has made or shall make a similar statement, we are prepared to explore with that other party resolution of the dispute through negotiation or ADR techniques before pursuing full-scale litigation." Center For Public Resources, Corporate Policy Statement: Alternative Dispute Resolution. Except for considerations of cost and delay, are there reasons to shun litigation in this way?

4.   Another common ADR theme is that lawyers and litigation are too adversary. In place of what is perceived as a cult of adversariness, ADR advocates cooperative solutions in which parties are not riveted on notions of their "rights." This is reflected in the idea that ADR produces better outcomes than litigation.

Some advocates of ADR consider it a "self-empowering process." The argument is that because the parties participate voluntarily, the less powerful party is able to confront the other with commonly-accepted standards and thus to achieve basic fairness that might not be possible in a formal legal proceeding. Critics, however, doubt the efficacy of mediation, any more than litigation, in getting disputing parties to recognize and accept higher values not in their immediate self interest. ADR advocates respond that mediation is better able to make them appreciate that those values are in their ultimate self interest.

Critics also argue that, without an advocate in mediation, the less powerful party is more likely to surrender rights that would be protected in a court. This disagreement recalls our discussion in Chapter I of the adversary versus other forms of justice. The amophorphous, informal procedures of ADR have been faulted for putting the less powerful party at risk. ADR has been especially criticized as disadvantaging women, poor people, and minorities. Grillo, The Mediation Alternative: Process Dangers for Women, 100 Yale L.J. 1545 (1991); Delgado, et al., Fairness and Formality: Minimizing the Risks of Prejudice in Alternative Dispute Resolution, 1985 Wis. L. Rev. 1359.

In family law disputes, it has been argued that mediation enables the spouse with greater social and financial power (often the man) to dominate the other. "The claim that people have common interests can be a way of misleading the less powerful into collaborating with more powerful in schemes that mainly benefit the latter." J. Mansbridge, Beyond Adversarial Democracy 5 (1983). But does litigation effectively protect against the effects of such imbalance? Note that the American courts usually do not appoint counsel for litigants who cannot afford to hire their own lawyers. Could a careful mediator be more likely to equalize power imbalances? At least in theory, the mediator is to pursue a fair outcome, and thereby to keep one disputant from taking advantage of the other by virtue of greater power. A process referred to as "collaborative divorce" involves an agreement among the parties and counsel not to seek contested hearings or discovery, to make full disclosure of all relevant financial information, and to refrain from acting in a manner detrimental to the future relationship of the parties. Herman, Collaborative Divorce: A Short Overview, 4 Divorce Litig. 68 (April 2001). Does this assuage concerns over gender-based power disparities?

5. A serious question exists about whether the substantive law would continue to exert influence on out-of-court deals to the same degree if ADR methods, particularly mediation, were to become the norm. Family law provides an informative context for examining this question because ADR techniques have become mandatory in some places in certain family law matters. See, e.g., Cal. Family Code § 3170 (whenever custody or visitation of a minor child is in issue, mediation is mandatory). Making mediation mandatory seems inconsistent with the ADR emphasis on private ordering and the importance of voluntariness for making ADR effective. It is justified by the "better results" argument, in general by the "helping professions" (mainly social workers) who criticize the adversariness of litigated outcomes. Often there is antagonism to the substantive law itself:

Divorce mediation rejects the idea that legal rules should be used as weapons to improve one party's position at the expense of the other.

Similarly, it rejects the idea that these legal rules and principles embody any necessary wisdom or logic. In fact, it views them as being arbitrary principles, having little to do with the realities of a couple's life and not superior to the judgments that the couple could make on their own. What relevance do these rules and principles have in mediation, then, and why is it necessary to know them?

Whether laws are fair or unfair, parties believe them to be significant and this shapes their expectations. This is just a fact. If the law says that when title to a couple's home is in the husband's name alone, that the wife will not have an interest in it, then the husband does not expect to have to give her any portion of it—this is so whether the wife feels this to be fair or unfair. This is a reality with which a mediator must deal. However, unlike the lawyer in an adversarial setting, he is not bound by it. He does not believe that these rules embody any necessary logic, let alone guarantee any necessary justice. They may be limiting factors, but they are not absolutes. In fact, from his standpoint, the problem is that the expectations created by these rules and principles will produce an agreement between the parties that is not fair. In this instance, therefore, the law is an obstacle to a fair agreement. The mediator's job is to effect a fairer agreement than the law would provide, despite the expectations that the husband (in this case) has based on the law.

Marlow, The Rule of Law in Divorce Mediation, 9 Mediation Q. 5, 5–6 (1985).

6. The contentious issue of whether arbitration clauses that forbid class treatment (either in court or in a classwide arbitration) are unconscionable reflects how procedure might affect outcome and substance. See Sternlight & Jensen, Using Arbitration to Eliminate Consumer Class Actions: Efficient Business Practice or Unconscionable Abuse?, 67 Law & Contempt. Probs. 101 (Winter/Spring 2004): "The court decisions striking class action prohibitions have all emphasized that many small-dollar claims are simply not feasible if brought individually. * * * At the same time, these courts have emphasized that a company that has perpetrated small-dollar illegal acts against numerous consumers should not be permitted to escape liability simply because it would be irrational or impossible for any single individual to bring the claim. Such an enforcement gap would lead to unjust enrichment and the failure to deter illegal conduct." Is this an example of improper private ordering?

Chapter III

DESCRIBING AND DEFINING
THE DISPUTE

A central function of a system of civil procedure is to describe and define the dispute between the parties. It is preferable if this can be accomplished early in the litigation because the nature of the dispute affects both the substantive law that will be applied to the facts and the procedural course to be taken. It is not always possible, however, to define a dispute comprehensively from the start. All the facts may not yet be known, and the exact structure of the suit may not take shape until various moves are made by each side. Thus the objective of assuring certainty through early definition of disputes, and perhaps of deciding disputes early in the litigation, can clash with the objective of allowing flexibility to take account of unforeseen developments. We will examine in this chapter the procedural devices that seek to achieve early definition of disputes and to weed out groundless claims, while attempting to retain flexibility and fairness.

A. THE HISTORICAL EVOLUTION OF PLEADING

Under English common law, the issues in a suit were defined by pleadings. The word *pleading* derives from the practice that developed after the Norman Conquest (1066) by which persons filed *pleas* in the emerging royal courts for a remedy against one who had wronged them. The pleas were originally addressed only to violations of the king's peace, but in course of time, as the historian Maitland has written, "the king's peace devours all other peaces."[1] The royal courts thus came to accept a wide range of disputes between private individuals that did not directly affect the monarch. The courts responded by issuing a *writ*—an order to the sheriff to bring the person complained of before the judge on a certain day to answer the allegations. These writs gradually became standardized as it became established that courts would hear particular kinds of complaints.[2]

1. F. Maitland, The Constitutional History of England 107 (1908).

2. By the 14th century, the royal courts included the *King's (Queen's) Bench* for criminal cases, *Common Pleas* for civil

1. The Forms of Action

The standardization of writs resulted in the development of *forms of action* as each writ came to embody an action which included both the substantive theory of recovery and the procedures for obtaining a remedy. A suit had to be cast in terms of the "procedural pigeon-hole" of one of the forms of action which a court would recognize.[3] The forms of action had different procedures as to such matters as the form of bond required to avoid arrest or seizure of goods and the type of trial. The allegations that had to be made for each form were stylized and sometimes fictional. For example, the writ of ejectment could only be used by a freeholder to recover land wrongfully withheld by alleging the fiction that the plaintiff had demised the land to a fictional John Doe, who was ejected, and then bringing the action in John Doe's name. The writ of trover, a means of recovering goods which had been lost, could be used for any conversion of property by alleging the fiction that the property had been lost and that the defendant had found it but refused to return it.[4]

Over the years, the number and complexity of the forms of action grew. By the early 19th century, there were 60 forms of action just dealing with real property and dozens more for personal actions. The forms of action had also leaped the ocean and were firmly ensconced in pleading practices in many American states. Among the commonly used forms of personal actions (the names of which we sometimes still find in American common law and statutes) were:

Trespass—An action for damages for unlawful injury to plaintiff's person, property, or rights. It was necessary that the act be done with force and that the injury be immediate as opposed to consequential. The modern notion of trespass as an unlawful entry upon the plaintiff's land was only one of a number of applications of this form of action.

Trespass on the Case (or simply *Case*)—An action that developed for the situation in which the injury did not result from direct or immediate force, but as an indirect consequence of defendant's act. It is hard for us today, used to the notion of "negligence," to fully appreciate the conceptual development that was required for common law courts to move from allowing recovery for injuries resulting from direct force under *trespass* (as in hitting someone with a stick) to allowing recovery for the injuries resulting from indirect action under *case* (as in leaving a log on the highway where a passer-by is injured by driving over it).

Covenant—An action for damages for breach of a contract under seal. Other contract-remedy forms of action obviously had to develop to cover the much more common situation of contracts not under seal.

cases, *Exchequer* for matters involving royal revenues, and *Chancery* for equitable actions.

3. F. Maitland, The Forms of Action at Common Law 3 (1909, reprinted 1971). See also Milsom, Historical Foundations of the Common Law 28–40 (1969).

4. Cooper v. Chitty, 97 Eng.Rep. 166, 172 (K.B. 1756) ("in form it is a fiction"). For a demonstration of the useful role that fictions can serve in the law, see L. Fuller, Legal Fictions (1967).

Debt—An action to recover a specific sum of money, or a claim that could be reduced to a certainty, due under an express agreement. Debt, however, carried with it various unattractive procedural features (such as the right to invoke "wager of law"[5]). This form has only a vague relationship to what we today loosely refer to as a "debt."

Assumpsit—An action for damages for non-performance of a parol contract not under seal. It was based on the premise that the defendant had undertaken to do something and had injured the plaintiff in his person or goods by failing to perform. *Special Assumpsit* ultimately developed as a remedy for breach of promise even if the breach had no element of misfeasance but was simply a failure to perform. Pleaders developed "common counts" as simplified forms for various situations (see Forms 4 through 8 in the Appendix to the Federal Rules of Civil Procedure). *General Assumpsit,* which did not arise until the 18th century, was based on the sophisticated concept that an implied promise arises from unjust enrichment. It allowed recovery on contracts implied in fact even though all the elements of a contract claim could not be satisfied.

Detinue—An action to recover personal chattels *in specie* from one who acquired them lawfully, but retained them without right (for example, a bailment). An ancient writ, it had procedural disadvantages (such as trial by wager of law) that led to the development of other actions for recovery of property.

Replevin—An action to recover possession of goods unlawfully taken. The remedy was recovery of the goods *in specie,* and thus if the goods had been injured or destroyed, a different action that provided damages would be necessary. Cf. Fuentes v. Shevin, supra p. 29.

Trover—An action, originally a sub-category of *case,* for damages against a defendant who had found another's goods and wrongfully converted them. It was broadened to provide a remedy for any wrongful interference with or detention of another's goods by fictionalizing the allegation that the goods had been lost and then found.

2. Common Law Pleading

The plaintiff initiated suit and caused a writ to issue by invoking an appropriate form of action in a *declaration*. This was the beginning of a complicated process of pleading designed to reduce the dispute to a single issue. The defendant had three choices in responding (called *pleas*). Defendant could file a *plea in bar* that either denied one or more of the essential allegations (a *traverse*) or admitted them, but stated that some legal right, such as being a minor, justified the conduct (*confession and avoidance*). Second, defendant could file a *dilatory plea* challenging the

---

5. Wager of law was an ancient procedure whereby the defendant could disprove a claim by taking an oath in open court that he did not owe the debt and bring with him eleven neighbors (called "compurgators") who would swear that they believed he told the truth. It is considered by some to be a forerunner of the jury trial.

jurisdiction of the court (*plea to jurisdiction*) or alleging some procedural defect in the structure of the suit, such as improper joinder of parties or lack of capacity (*plea in abatement*). Third, defendant could file a *demurrer*, which claimed that even if the facts were as stated by the plaintiff, they did not state a claim for which the law provided a remedy (*general demurrer*) or that there were defects in the form of the pleading (*special demurrer*).

The defendant's pleas did not generally end the pleading process at common law. The plaintiff could file a *replication* designed to join issue with the defendant's pleas, for example, by either traversing the defendant's confession and avoidance or further confessing and avoiding it. Then the defendant could file a *rejoinder*, joining issue with any issues raised by the replication which had not been specifically responded to. Further pleadings, termed *surrejoinder, rebutter,* and *surrebutter,* were available to insure that issue was joined as to all matters.

All this made for an arduous process which, by the 19th century, had taken on an extraordinary degree of complexity in the belief that precision could be achieved in an almost scientific manner. The result was that pleading was the central focus of law suits, and cases were often won or lost on the pleading skills of the attorneys. "Half the labor of the bar," wrote a commentator about the persistence of common law pleading practices in the U.S. in the 19th century, "was bestowed upon questions of pleading, and the lawyer who mistook his form of action sometimes lost his case from that cause alone. The merits of the case were often wholly lost sight of and never brought to trial."[6]

This frustration of the merits resulted in large measure from two features of the system. First, the single issue idea mentioned above meant that once the parties were "at issue" the court might decide the case in favor of the winner on that issue. If defendant filed a general demurrer, for example, that might put the case at issue; if the demurrer were not sustained plaintiff could win the case because the defendant chose the wrong point to fight. Second, the pigeon-hole strictness of the forms of action could prevent relief for a plaintiff clearly entitled to relief who had chosen the wrong writ due to uncertainty about what the evidence would show. For example, if plaintiff chose to proceed under *case*, defendant's evidence that the injury was inflicted on purpose (and therefore that the proper form of action was *trespass*) could defeat the action on the case. Plaintiff would then have to start over in trespass (if the statute of limitations had not run); there was no opportunity to switch writs in a given proceeding or to combine them in one proceeding.

The forms of action and rules of pleading just described applied to law, as opposed to equity, courts. A grievance was brought to a court of equity by filing a *bill* which contained a narrative section describing the

---

6. Eastman, Chief Justice Charles Doe, 9 Green Bag 245, 246 (1897). Charles Doe (not to be confused with the fictitious John Doe) was an ardent reformer of procedures on pragmatic grounds who served on the New Hampshire Supreme Court in the 19th century.

complaint, a charging section that rebutted anticipated defenses, and an interrogative section designed to demonstrate that relief was equitable and fair. Recall the discussion of the emergence of equity in Chapter II, supra pp. 84–86. The defendant had to file a detailed reply, but further pleadings were unnecessary. One of the procedures available at equity was the *bill of discovery* which is the forerunner of our modern discovery procedures. Equity pleading procedures were far less technical than those at law, but over the years they took on their own refinements and complexities.

3.   *The American Reform Experience*

Reform and simplification of common-law pleading began in England in the 1820's and were largely completed by 1873 with the passage of the Judicature Act. The American colonies, and then the states, varied in the degree of acceptance of the English model. Over the years, conflicting movements—democratic impulses directed at diminishing the role of lawyers and legalisms versus attempts to impose more professionalism and procedural regularity on courts—had their impact on American pleading rules.

By the 1830's the reforms taking place in England had spread to the United States as the utilitarian jurisprudence of Jeremy Bentham "cast a long shadow."[7] The most important American attack on the common-law pleading system was the development of "code pleading" with the passage of the Code of Civil Procedure in New York in 1848. Often referred to as the "Field Code" for David Dudley Field (1805–94), the renowned New York practitioner who spearheaded the reform effort, it abolished the existing forms of action and mandated that there be "but one form of action." The complaint only had to contain "a statement of the facts constituting the cause of action, in ordinary and concise language, without repetition, and in such a manner as to enable a person of common understanding to know what is intended." The answer should contain "a specific denial of each material allegation of the complaint controverted by the defendant" and "a plain and concise statement of any new matter constituting a defense or set-off without unnecessary repetition." Pleadings were limited to complaint, answer, reply, and demurrers.

The Field Code ultimately served as the model for some half of the states, primarily in the west, and its impact on the Federal Rules of Civil Procedure was considerable. Today some states, notably New York and California, still retain features of code pleading. The code played an important role in accustoming courts and attorneys to non-technical "fact pleading." But pleading problems remained. In part this was because human institutions have a way of developing beyond the intentions of their creators, but it also reflected some intractable difficulties

7. L. Friedman, A History of American Law 123 (1979).

with refining pleading practice that have not disappeared under the Federal Rules. Hence we begin with a code pleading case.

GILLISPIE v. GOODYEAR SERVICE STORES

Supreme Court of North Carolina, 1963.
258 N.C. 487, 128 S.E.2d 762.

BOBBITT, J.

The hearing below was on demurrers to the complaint.

Plaintiff alleges she and each of the four individual defendants are citizens and residents of Alamance County, North Carolina; that defendant Goodyear Tire & Rubber Company is a corporation doing business in North Carolina and having a place of business and store in Burlington, North Carolina; and that Goodyear Service Stores is a division of defendant Goodyear Tire & Rubber Company.

The remaining allegations of the complaint and the prayer for relief are as follows:

"4. On or about May 5, 1959, and May 6, 1959, the defendants, without cause or just excuse and maliciously came upon and trespassed upon the premises occupied by the plaintiff as a residence, and by the use of harsh and threatening language and physical force directed against the plaintiff assaulted the plaintiff and placed her in great fear, and humiliated and embarrassed her by subjecting her to public scorn and ridicule, and caused her to be seized and exhibited to the public as a prisoner, and to be confined in a public jail, all to her great humiliation, embarrassment and harm.

"5. By reason of the defendants' malicious and intentional assault against and humiliation of the plaintiff, the plaintiff was and has been damaged and injured in the amount of $25,000.00.

"6. The acts of the defendants as aforesaid were deliberate, malicious, and with the deliberate intention of harming the plaintiff, and the plaintiff is entitled to recover her actual damages as well as punitive damages from the defendants and each of them.

"THEREFORE, the plaintiff prays that she have and recover of the defendants the sum of $25,000.00 as damages and $10,000.00 in addition thereto as punitive damages, and that she have such other and further relief as may be just and proper."

[The trial court sustained defendants' demurrers. Plaintiff appealed.]

* * *

The judgments now under consideration do not specify the ground on which the demurrers were sustained. However, the fact the court did not dismiss the action but granted plaintiff leave to file an amended complaint indicates the court sustained the demurrers on the ground the

complaint did not state facts sufficient to constitute a cause of action.
* * *

Does the complaint state *facts* sufficient to constitute *any* cause of action?

A complaint must contain "(a) plain and concise statement of the facts constituting a cause of action...." G.S. § 1–122. "The cardinal requirement of this statute ... is that the facts constituting a cause of action, rather than the conclusions of the pleader, must be set out in the complaint, so as to disclose the issuable facts determinative of the plaintiff's right to relief." Shives v. Sample, 238 N.C. 724, 79 S.E.2d 193. The cause of action consists of the facts alleged. The statutory requirement is that a complaint must allege the material, essential and ultimate facts upon which plaintiff's right of action is based. "The law is presumed to be known, but the facts to which the law is to be applied are not known until properly presented by the pleading and established by evidence." McIntosh, North Carolina Practice and Procedure, § 379.

The facts alleged, but not the pleader's legal conclusions, are deemed admitted when the sufficiency of the complaint is tested by demurrer. "Where the complaint merely alleges conclusions and not facts, it fails to state a cause of action and is demurrable. G.S. § 1–127(6)." However, it is well settled that a complaint must be fatally defective before it will be rejected as insufficient, and "if in any portion of it or to any extent it presents *facts* sufficient to constitute a cause of action the pleading will stand."

When a complaint alleges defendant is indebted to plaintiff in a certain amount and such debt is due, but does not allege in what manner or for what cause defendant became indebted to plaintiff, it is demurrable for failure to state facts sufficient to constitute a cause of action.

"The liability for tort grows out of the violation of some legal duty by the defendant, not arising out of contract, and the complaint should state facts sufficient to show such legal duty and its violation, resulting in injury to the plaintiff. What these facts are must depend upon the elements which go to make up the particular tort complained of, under the substantive law." McIntosh, North Carolina Practice and Procedure, § 388.

"In an action or defense based upon negligence, it is not sufficient to allege the mere happening of an event of an injurious nature and call it negligence on the part of the party sought to be charged. This is necessarily so because negligence is not a fact in itself, but is the legal result of certain facts. Therefore, the facts which constitute the negligence charged and also the facts which establish such negligence as the proximate cause, or as one of the proximate causes, of the injury must be alleged." Shives v. Sample, supra.

* * *

As stated by Barnhill, J., in Parker v. White, 237 N.C. 607, 610, 75 S.E.2d 615, 617: "The competency of evidence, the form of the issues, and the charge of the court are all controlled in very large measure by the nature of the cause of action alleged by plaintiff. Hence, the trial judge, as well as the defendant, must know the exact right plaintiff seeks to assert or the legal wrong for which he seeks redress before there can be any intelligent trial under the rules of procedure which govern our system of jurisprudence."

Plaintiff alleges, in a single sentence, that defendant, "without cause or just excuse and maliciously," trespassed upon premises occupied by her as a residence, assaulted her and caused her to be seized and confined as a prisoner. The complaint states no facts upon which these legal conclusions may be predicated. Plaintiff's allegations do not disclose *what* occurred, *when* it occurred, *where* it occurred, *who* did *what*, the relationships between defendants and plaintiff or of defendants *inter se*, or any other factual data that might identify the occasion or describe the circumstances of the alleged wrongful conduct of defendants.

A plaintiff must make out his case *secundum allegata*. There can be no recovery except on the case made by his pleadings. Here, there is no factual basis to which the court could apply the law. When considered in the light most favorable to plaintiff, this complaint, in our opinion, falls short of minimum requirements.

In Stivers v. Baker,, 10 Ky.L.Rptr. 523, 87 Ky. 508, 9 S.W. 491, it was held that a petition alleging the defendant unlawfully assaulted the plaintiff, thereby putting him in great fear, but not stating how the assault was made, stated a mere conclusion of law and was demurrable as not stating facts constituting a cause of action as required by the Kentucky statute. The court, in opinion by Holt, J., points out that a statement of the facts constituting a cause of action "is not only necessary to enable the opposite party to form an issue, and to inform him of what his adversary intends to prove, but to enable the court to declare the law upon the facts stated. It cannot do so if a mere legal conclusion is stated. The term 'assault' has a legal meaning; as much so as the word 'trespass.' " In Shapiro v. Michelson, 19 Tex.Civ.App. 615, 47 S.W. 746, the Court of Civil Appeals of Texas, in opinion by Fisher, C.J., said: "The use of the expression 'assaulted' is not the averment of a fact, but is simply a statement which expresses the conclusion of the pleader."

The judgments sustaining the demurrers are affirmed on the ground the complaint does not state facts sufficient to constitute any cause of action. It would seem appropriate that plaintiff, in accordance with leave granted in the judgments from which she appealed, now file an amended complaint and therein allege the facts upon which she bases her right to recover.

Notes and Questions

1.   Besides giving plaintiff's lawyer a lesson in pleading, why should the court be concerned with the content of the complaint? One can discern at least three general purposes for pleading requirements:

(a) Notice to defendant: It seems intuitively fair that defendant be given notice of what plaintiff is upset about since the suit is likely to impose noncompensable litigation costs on defendant. But why insist that this be in the complaint? Shouldn't there be better ways for defendant to find out what plaintiff claims occurred? (Reconsider this concern in connection with discovery in Chapter V.) Does defendant need to know the details of plaintiff's claim at the outset? (Reconsider this concern in connection with the materials later in this chapter regarding the answer.)

(b) Notice to the court: A related objective is giving the court guidelines for determining whether discovery sought, or evidence offered at trial, is relevant to the case. Should we depend on the pleadings to accomplish this objective?

(c) Deciding the merits: As the court suggests in *Gillispie,* the complaint may supply the "factual basis to which the court could apply the law." That legal analysis may sometimes show that plaintiff has no right to relief against defendant, even on the complaint's version of the facts, permitting the termination of the suit at this early stage. Would encouraging early merits decisions be consistent with the objections that the framers of the Codes had to the common-law pleading system?

2. With regard to the third objective of pleadings, the court will ask whether the plaintiff has adequately pled the elements of the claim, which are defined by the substantive law. For purposes of assessing plaintiff's complaint in *Gillispie,* you may wish to refer to the following summaries of the elements of various possible claims from the Restatement (Second) of Torts:

Assault: "An actor is subject to liability to another for assault if (a) he acts intending to cause a harmful or offensive contact with the person of the other or a third person, or an imminent apprehension of such a contact, and (b) the other is thereby put in such imminent apprehension." (Restatement § 21(1).)

False arrest or imprisonment: "An actor is subject to liability to another for false imprisonment if (a) he acts intending to confine the other or a third person within boundaries fixed by the actor, and (b) his act directly or indirectly results in such a confinement of the other, and (c) the other is conscious of the confinement or is harmed by it." (Restatement § 35(1).)

Intentional infliction of emotional distress: "One who by extreme and outrageous conduct intentionally or recklessly causes severe emotional distress to another is subject to liability for such emotional distress." (Restatement § 46(1).)

Trespass to land: "One is subject to liability to another for trespass, irrespective of whether he thereby causes harm to any legally protected interest of the other, if he intentionally (a) enters land in the possession of the other, or (b) remains on the land." (Restatement § 158.)

In *Gillispie,* the court states that the complaint should stand if it presents facts sufficient to constitute any cause of action. Assuming that the law of North Carolina was the same as the Restatement of Torts provisions above, are there facts in the complaint sufficient to constitute any of those causes of action? Is plaintiff's problem one of the substance or the form of her allegations? Cf. Fed.R.Civ.P. 10(b). Using the allegations given, could you redraft the complaint to state a claim on one of the grounds enumerated above?

3. The court criticizes the complaint for relying on conclusions rather than facts. What is wrong with conclusions? The court suggests, for example, that it would not be sufficient for a plaintiff merely to allege that defendant is indebted to him in a certain amount. Why not? Does the same reasoning apply to plaintiff's complaint in *Gillispie?*

4. In general, code pleading states came to insist, as does the court in *Gillispie,* on "ultimate facts." These ultimate facts were derived from the elements of the substantive claim and were distinguished from unacceptable allegations characterized as "conclusions," on the one hand, and "mere evidence," on the other. See Cal. Code Civ. Proc. § 431.10(a) (requiring allegations "that are essential to the claim"). How precisely can these categories be applied? For example, was it too conclusory for plaintiff in *Gillispie* to allege that defendants used "harsh and threatening language and physical force"? Should she have repeated the exact words they used and described in detail each physical action taken by defendants? Would it be sufficient for her to allege that one defendant "walked angrily toward plaintiff"? For an argument that the distinctions relied upon by code pleading are ultimately meaningless, see Cook, Statements of Fact in Pleading Under the Codes, 21 Colum.L.Rev. 416 (1921).

5. Note that the court uses as an example of unduly conclusory allegations a complaint for personal injuries that merely labels defendant's actions negligent because "negligence is not a fact in itself, but is the legal result of certain facts." In an auto collision case, what more should plaintiff have to allege? Would it be sufficient to say that defendant "failed to keep a proper lookout"? Should this specification foreclose inquiry during discovery into whether defendant properly maintained the brakes on his car? If so, would plaintiff be allowed to pursue discovery on maintenance of the car by alleging as well that defendant "failed to maintain his automobile in proper condition"? How is plaintiff to determine which line to pursue before discovery? Do the suggested specifications serve any of the purposes of pleading mentioned in note 1 any better than a simple allegation that defendant negligently injured plaintiff? Compare Form 9 to the Federal Rules of Civil Procedure; see Thornburg, Detailed Fact Pleading: The Lessons of Scottish Civil Procedure, 36 Int'l Lawyer 1185, 1194 (2002) ("A pleading that a [defendant] was negligent in driving at an excessive rate of speed provides far more significant limits on evidence than does a pleading that a [defendant] drove negligently.").

6. *Leave to amend:* Even if the complaint is deficient, courts will usually grant the plaintiff an opportunity to file an amended complaint before dismissing the suit. In the federal system, it is sometimes said that courts must provide such a chance to replead. E.g., Mitchell v. Archibald & Kendall, Inc., infra p. 156 (if a complaint is dismissed, plaintiff has an "absolute right" to file an amended complaint embodying a new theory); Dubicz v. Commonwealth Edison Co., 377 F.3d 787 (7th Cir.2004) (district court improperly denied leave to amend); compare Bradley v. Val–Mejias, 379 F.3d 892 (10th Cir.2004) (it is proper to deny leave to amend if the

amendment would be futile because it would be subject to dismissal). This liberal rule means that the courts will usually treat dismissal on the pleadings as a decision on the merits for purposes of res judicata. See Rinehart v. Locke, infra p. 1121.

7. What if one of the defendants in *Gillispie* had been in jail on the dates of the incidents referred to in plaintiff's complaint, and that he was therefore demonstrably innocent of plaintiff's charges? Could he base a demurrer on that ground? Could he submit the jailer's affidavit attesting that he was in custody? Ordinarily a defendant was said to admit plaintiff's well-pleaded allegations by demurring, and the court would not consider anything beyond the face of the complaint. On that point, see the last sentence in Fed.R.Civ.P. 12(b). But these rules can be relaxed on occasion:

> When ruling on a Rule 12(b)(6) motion to dismiss, if a district court considers evidence outside the pleadings, it must normally convert the 12(b)(6) motion into a Rule 56 motion for summary judgment, and it must give the nonmoving party an opportunity to respond. A court may, however, consider certain materials—documents attached to the complaint, documents incorporated by reference in the complaint, or matters of judicial notice—without converting the motion to dismiss into a motion for summary judgment. * * *

> Certain written instruments attached to pleadings may be considered part of the pleading. See Fed.R.Civ.P. 10(c). Even if a document is not attached to a complaint, it may be incorporated by reference into a complaint if the plaintiff refers extensively to the document or the document forms the basis of the plaintiff's claim. The defendant may offer such a document, and the district court may treat such a document as part of the complaint, and thus assume that its contents are true for purposes of a motion to dismiss under Rule 12(b)(6). The doctrine of incorporation by reference may apply, for example, when a plaintiff's claim about insurance coverage is based on the contents of a coverage plan, or when a plaintiff's claim about stock fraud is based on the contents of SEC filings.

U.S. v. Ritchie, 342 F.3d 903, 907–08 (9th Cir.2003); compare Sira v. Morton, 380 F.3d 57 (2d Cir.2004) (defendant's submission of hearing transcripts that were neither expressly cited nor integral to the claims in the complaint required conversion to summary judgment). See also Cal.Code Civ. Proc. § 430.70 (allowing consideration of materials of which the court can take judicial notice in connection with demurrer); consider Greene v. Brown & Williamson Tobacco Corp., 72 F.Supp.2d 882 (W.D.Tenn.1999) (court takes judicial notice on Rule 12(b)(6) motion that consumers were aware that cigarette smoking posed health risks, and rejected plaintiffs' product liability claim based on the "consumer expectations" test).

B. DESCRIBING AND TESTING THE PLAINTIFF'S CLAIM

The Federal Rules of Civil Procedure were drafted by a committee headed by Charles Clark, then Dean of Yale Law School. They installed what has been described as the "liberal ethos," in which the preferred disposition of cases is on the merits, by jury trial, after full disclosure through discovery. See Marcus, The Revival of Fact Pleading Under the

Federal Rules of Civil Procedure, 86 Colum.L.Rev. 433, 439 (1986). A central ingredient to this shift in focus was reliance on generalized pleading.

To get away from the charged terms "facts" and "cause of action," therefore, Rule 8(a)(2) requires only that the plaintiff provide "a short and plain statement of the claim showing that the pleader is entitled to relief." Moreover, Clark at first favored eliminating pleading motions altogether, but eventually they were retained in Rule 12, including the Rule 12(b)(6) motion to dismiss for "failure to state a claim upon which relief can be granted." Other pleading motions are authorized by Rules 12(c) (motion for judgment on the pleadings), 12(e) (motion for a more definite statement), and 12(f) (motion to strike).

Changing the rules did not change the habits of lawyers and judges, and the old Code pleading attitudes persisted for some time after the rules were adopted in 1938. Clark himself (appointed to the Second Circuit Court of Appeals in 1939) continued to view the Rule 12(b)(6) motion as "a mere formal motion, directed only to the face of the complaint" which too often led to "judicial haste which in the long run makes waste." Dioguardi v. Durning, 139 F.2d 774 (2d Cir.1944). In *Dioguardi*, the court reversed dismissal of an "obviously home drawn" complaint against the Collector of Customs for mishandling imported merchandise because, "however inarticulately they may be stated, the plaintiff has disclosed his claims" and "we do not see how the plaintiff may properly be deprived of his day in court to show what he obviously so firmly believes."

The Supreme Court, meanwhile, observed in 1947 that the Federal Rules "restrict the pleadings to the task of general notice-giving." Hickman v. Taylor, 329 U.S. 495, 501, 67 S.Ct. 385, 388, 91 L.Ed. 451 (1947). In Conley v. Gibson, 355 U.S. 41, 78 S.Ct. 99, 2 L.Ed.2d 80 (1957), it applied this principle to overturn a dismissal on the pleadings. In that case, African–American union members accused their union of racial discrimination. Though the complaint contained no specific, direct factual allegation indicating conscious discrimination by the union, it did allege that in May 1954, the railroad had purported to abolish 45 jobs held by African–Americans and that despite repeated pleas "the Union, acting according to plan, did nothing to protect them against these discriminatory discharges and refused to give them protection comparable to that given white employees." 355 U.S. at 43, 78 S.Ct. at 100. The Court upheld the sufficiency of their complaint on the basis of an extremely broad standard for Rule 12(b)(6) motions: "[A] complaint should not be dismissed for failure to state a claim unless it appears beyond doubt that the plaintiff can prove no set of facts in support of his claim that would entitle him to relief." In response to the argument "that the complaint failed to set forth specific facts to support its general allegations of discrimination and that its dismissal is therefore proper," the Court stated: "The decisive answer to this is that the Federal Rules of Civil Procedure do not require a claimant to set out in detail the facts upon which he bases his claim. To the contrary, all the Rules require is 'a short and plain statement of the claim' that will give the defendant fair notice of what the plaintiff's claim is and the grounds upon which it rests." Some took this to signal the arrival of "notice pleading." Professor Moore, for example, concluded that pleadings "need do little more than indicate generally the type of litigation that is involved." 2A Moore's Federal Practice ¶ 8.03 at 8–10 (2d ed. 1985). But note that Rule 8(a)(2) also says that the complaint should "show that the pleader is entitled to relief." It has been asserted that "Conley v. Gibson turned Rule 8 on its head by holding that a claim is insufficient only if the insufficiency appears from the pleading itself." Hazard, From Whom No Secrets Are Hid, 76 Texas L. Rev. 1665, 1685 (1998).

Some federal courts have resisted the minimal pleading requirements sometimes associated with "notice pleading." Consider the views of Judge Posner, affirming a Rule 12(b)(6) dismissal in Sutliff, Inc. v. Donovan Companies, Inc., 727 F.2d 648, 654 (7th Cir.1984):

> Although the exceedingly forgiving attitude toward pleading deficiencies that was expressed by Justice Black for the Supreme Court in Conley v. Gibson * * * continues to be quoted with approval, it has never been taken literally. Professors Wright and Miller treat as authoritative the statement in an earlier case that the pleader must "set out sufficient factual matter to outline the elements of his cause of action or claim, proof of which is essential to his recovery," and add in their own words that "the complaint must contain either direct allegations on every material point necessary to sustain a recovery on any legal theory, even though it may not be the theory suggested or intended by the pleader, or contain allegations from which an inference fairly may be drawn that evidence of these material points will be introduced at trial." 5 Federal Practice and Procedure § 1216 at pp. 121–23 (1969). The heavy costs of modern federal litigation, especially antitrust litigation, and the mounting caseload pressures on the federal courts, counsel against launching the parties into pretrial discovery if there is no reasonable prospect that the plaintiff can make out a cause of action from the events narrated in the complaint.

See also DM Research v. College of American Pathologists, 170 F.3d 53, 55 (1st Cir.1999) ("The price of entry, even to discovery, is for plaintiff to allege a *factual* predicate concrete enough to warrant further proceedings, which may be costly and burdensome. Conclusory allegations in a complaint, if they stand alone, are a danger sign that plaintiff is engaging in a fishing expedition.").

Even Judge Charles Clark, reporter for the committee that drafted the original Federal Rules of Civil Procedure and the individual generally considered the creator of the "notice pleading" concept, did not believe in a total abandonment of the requirement of allegations of specific fact in pleadings. See Smith, Judge Charles E. Clark and The Federal Rules of Civil Procedure, 85 Yale L.J. 914, 917–18 (1976): "Clark insisted that there were limits to the generality of pleading allowed under the Federal Rules. A bare allegation that the defendant had injured the plaintiff through negligence, he said, would not suffice." Thus, it was probably incorrect to characterize the adoption of notice pleading as the signal that wholly unsupported, conclusory factual allegations would render a pleading sufficient to withstand a motion to dismiss. Nonetheless, compared to reported practice before 1938, it seems clear that cases were ended much less frequently by pleading decisions under the Federal Rules. A study in 1962 showed that pleadings motions led to final terminations in only about 2% of all cases, and others suggested a dismissal rate of 3% to 6% in the 1970s and 1980s. See Marcus, The Puzzling Persistence of Pleading Practice, 76 Texas L. Rev. 1749, 1754 (1998). To put these figures in context, however, one should remember that fewer than 5% of civil cases in federal court are terminated by a trial.

Against this background, we turn to contemporary pleading and related issues. Before doing so, read Rules 7 through 12.

1. *The Problem of Specificity*

UNITED STATES v. BOARD OF HARBOR COMMISSIONERS

United States District Court, District of Delaware, 1977.
73 F.R.D. 460.

LATCHUM, CHIEF JUDGE.

Defendants The SICO Company ("SICO") and North American Smelting Company ("NASCO") have moved pursuant to Rule 12(e), F.R.Civ.P., for a more definite statement on the ground that the complaint filed against them by the government is so vague and ambiguous that they are unable to frame a responsive pleading as required by Rule 7, F.R.Civ.P. * * *

The complaint, filed by the government on November 23, 1976, alleges in paragraph 11 that

> "The defendants, and each of them, own and operate onshore facilities located on or near Wilmington Marine Terminal from which oil was discharged into the Delaware River during the period June 25 through November 27, 1973, or the defendants, and each of them, took actions which caused such oil to be discharged."

The discharge of oil into navigable waters of the United States is expressly prohibited by the [Federal Water Pollution Control Act], 33 U.S.C. § 1321(b)(3),[a] and the owner or operator of a facility responsible for the discharge of oil in or upon any navigable waterway can be held liable to the United States in the amount of any actual costs incurred for the removal of such oil. 33 U.S.C. § 1321(f)(2).[b]

---

a. "The discharge of oil or hazardous substances into or upon the navigable waters of the United States * * * is prohibited * * *."—Eds.

b. "Except where an owner or operator of an onshore facility can prove that a dis-

Defendants SICO and NASCO contend that paragraph 11 is deceptively vague because it fails to specify (1) which defendants are responsible for the alleged discharge of oil, (2) the amount of oil discharged and the removal costs incurred, and (3) the "actions" which are alleged to have caused the discharge. Therefore, before filing a responsive pleading, SICO and NASCO want the government to clarify paragraph 11 by including the foregoing details.

A motion for a more definite statement under Rule 12(e) is ordinarily restricted to situations where a pleading suffers from "unintelligibility rather than the want of detail." 2A Moore's Federal Practice ¶ 12.18[1] at 2389 (2nd ed. 1975). If the requirements of Rule 8 are satisfied and the opposing party is fairly notified of the nature of the claim, a Rule 12(e) motion is inappropriate. Id.; 5 Wright & Miller, Federal Practice & Procedure: Civil § 1376.

In this case, the complaint on its face can be fairly read to charge each of the defendants with owning or operating on-shore facilities which discharged oil into the Delaware River, or that each of the defendants took actions causing such oil to be discharged. This allegation, together with the other averments in the complaint, fairly notifies defendants of the nature of the claim against them. Defendants' motion for a more definite statement is really an effort to "flesh out" the government's case;[2] as such it is a misuse of Rule 12(e). The evidentiary information they seek is more properly the subject of discovery under Rules 26 through 36. Accordingly, the SICO and NASCO motions for a more definite statement will be denied.

Notes and Questions

1. Are the allegations in *Board of Harbor Commissioners* sufficient to state a claim for relief? What are the elements that must be pleaded? Examine the statutory sections quoted in footnotes a and b. Should paragraph 11 be considered sufficient? In what way does it show that defendants are liable to plaintiff?

2. Why shouldn't the plaintiff have been required to be more specific about *which* defendants discharged the oil, *what amounts* were discharged, and *what caused* the discharge? Is it because it couldn't reasonably have known these details until it obtained information from the defendants through discovery? Or is it because, even if it knew these details, it need not

charge was caused solely by (A) an act of God, (B) an act of war, (C) negligence on the part of the United States Government, or (D) an act or omission of a third party without regard to whether any such act or omission was or was not negligent, or any combination of the foregoing causes, such owner or operator of any such facility from which oil or a hazardous substance is discharged in violation of subsection (b)(3) of this section shall be liable to the United States Government for the actual costs in-

curred * * * for the removal of such oil or substance by the United States in an amount not to exceed $50,000,000 * * *."— Eds.

2. Defendants' 12(e) motion might also be viewed as preparatory to a motion to dismiss. The majority of cases, however, have held this to be an improper use of Rule 12(e), which is designed to enable a litigant to answer, not to move for dismissal. See, e.g., 5 Wright & Miller, Federal Practice & Procedure: Civil § 1376 at 746.

"flesh out" the essential allegations of the complaint? How do we differentiate between essential allegations and unnecessary fleshing out? In this regard, contrast the analysis in *Board of Harbor Commissioners* with that in *Gillispie,* supra p. 126. Though *Gillispie* was decided under a considerably more stringent pleading standard, might a persuasive argument be made that the complaint in *Gillispie* lacked sufficient detail, even under a "notice pleading" standard? Is it reasonable, under a notice-pleading standard, to expect greater detail in the *Gillispie* complaint than in cases like *Board of Harbor Commissioners* and Conley v. Gibson, supra pp. 132–33? Should the degree of specificity required depend on whether the plaintiff has access to necessary sources of information?

Can we say that the defendants are really "on notice" of what they will have to defend against? They haven't been told which of them is supposed to have discharged the oil or when the discharges were supposed to have occurred within the five-month period. The court says they have been informed that they are each charged with operating a facility which discharged oil *or* that each caused oil to be discharged. Is that sufficient to inform them as to the acts they are charged with in this suit?

3. Can a complaint be too long, prolix, or detailed so as to run afoul of the "short and plain statement of the claim" requirement of Rule 8(a) or the "simple, concise, and direct" requirement as to averments in Rule 8(e)(1)? In Mendez v. Draham, 182 F.Supp.2d 430 (D.N.J.2002), the complaint had 1020 numbered paragraphs in 392 pages. Calling this "the longest, most needlessly repetitive pleading I have ever seen," the judge granted defendants' motion to strike it. He explained why this problem matters (id. at 433):

> It is this very prolixity that makes the Complaint unclear and incomprehensible. Only through superhuman patience, effort, and insight, could any attorney review the allegations of the Complaint and make paragraph-by-paragraph responses. * * * [I]f [defendants' attorneys] fail to notice that one or two words have been varied, with meaningful import, in one of the Complaint's thousand-odd paragraphs, and inadvertently admit that allegation, they face the risk of malpractice.

See also Decker v. Massey–Ferguson, Ltd., 681 F.2d 111, 114–15 (2d Cir. 1982) (finding complaint to be "an 'everything but the kitchen sink' type of pleading which would give plaintiff's attorneys carte blanche in the area of liberal federal discovery"); Gordon v. Green, 602 F.2d 743 (5th Cir.1979) (complaint and amendments totaled over 4,000 pages and occupied 18 volumes, "requiring a hand truck or cart to move").

4. The court says that a motion for a more definite statement should not be used to prepare for a motion to dismiss, citing Wright & Miller. Consider the views expressed in the current edition in the same section (5C C. Wright & A. Miller, Federal Practice and Procedure § 1376 at 335–36 (3d ed. 2004)):

> [S]ome cases state that it always is improper to use a Rule 12(e) motion to obtain admissions from the claimant in the hopes of clearing the way for a later Rule 12(b)(6) motion to dismiss. Although judicial statements of this type arguably are consistent with the wording of Rule 12(e), they probably go too far in limiting the availability of the motion. The courts

need not completely refrain from using Rule 12(e) as an aid in achieving the summary adjudication of certain cases; it merely is necessary to act with caution to keep its use within proper bounds.

Consequently, there should be a bias against use of the Rule 12(e) motion as a precursor to a Rule 12(b)(6) motion or as a method for seeking out a threshold defense. * * * A request for a more definite statement for either of these purposes should not be granted unless the movant shows that there actually is a substantial threshold question that may be dispositive, such as a critical date. In the absence of some restraint, the motions undoubtedly will be used by litigants as a vehicle for a fishing expedition at the pleading stage.

5.   Could the court in *Board of Harbor Commissioners* have required more details pursuant to Rule 16? In Acuna v. Brown & Root, Inc., 200 F.3d 335 (5th Cir.2000), approximately 1,600 plaintiffs sued over 100 defendants in related cases before the district court, alleging injuries due to defendants' uranium mining activities. Before allowing discovery, the district ordered plaintiffs to submit affidavits specifying the injuries or illnesses they suffered due to alleged uranium exposure and the materials or substances causing the injury, and identifying the facility thought to be the source of the uranium materials in question and dates of exposure. After plaintiffs responded with a form affidavit from a single expert that generally identified a series of maladies that can be caused by exposure to uranium and asserted that the expert had reviewed plaintiffs' medical data and come to the conclusion that each of them had received clinically significant doses of radiation, the district court dismissed, and the appellate court affirmed, relying on the authority of the court to manage the cases under Rule 16 (id. at 340):

> The scheduling orders issued below essentially required that information which plaintiffs should have had before filing their claims pursuant to Fed. R. Civ. P. 11(b)(3) [be supplied]. Each plaintiff should have had at least some information regarding the nature of his injuries, the circumstances under which he could have been exposed to harmful substances, and the basis for believing that the named defendants were responsible for his injuries.

6.   Most other countries insist on much more detailed and focused pleadings than American courts. For example, consider the following requirements specified in a set of proposed rules for commercial disputes involving litigants form different countries: "The plaintiff must state the facts on which the claim is based, describe the evidence to support those statements, and refer to the legal grounds that support the claim, including foreign law, if applicable." Rule 12.1, ALI/UNIDROIT Transnational Rules of Civil Procedure (Proposed Final Draft, March 9, 2004). The Comment to this rule explains that it "calls for particularity of statement, such as that required in most civil-law and most common-law jurisdictions. In contrast, some American systems, notably those employing 'notice pleading' as under the Federal Rules of Civil Procedure, permit very general allegations." Should American rules move toward the approach of other countries? Consider Thornburg, Detailed Fact Pleading: The Lessons of Scottish Civil Procedure, 36 Int'l Lawyer 1185, 1186 (2002):

Scotland's pleading requirements serve as the enforcers of an underlying requirement that a plaintiff must have pre-suit access to detailed facts and evidence sufficient to prove a claim or that claim should not be filed. This predictably skews the procedural system in favor of repeat institutional defendants and against individual plaintiffs in ways that can both prevent suits from being filed and prevent persons with legitimate claims from winning at trial.

7. Rule 12(f) authorizes a motion to strike portions of a pleading that are "redundant, immaterial, impertinent, or scandalous." How often might that be useful? See Atraqchi v. Williams, 220 F.R.D. 1 (D.D.C.2004) (court strikes complaint "that contains the wildly immaterial, delusional, and quite possibly pathological allegations that these [pro se] plaintiffs have made about a world-wide religious inquisition, illegal wire-tapping by the U.S. Government and others to 'homosexualize them and convert them to this cult,' and conspiracy against them by Black people"). A motion to strike can also be used to attack an insufficient defense, or a part of a prayer for relief that is not justified by the law (such as a request for punitive damages in a breach of contract case).

8. *The Making of a Motion*: It seems useful to say a few words about how lawyers make motions, which applies not only to the motions covered by Chapter III, but all the others addressed in this book. Ordinarily the moving party files a notice of motion supported by a memorandum of points and authorities with written legal argument in favor of the motion. If there are factual assertions in the motion, they usually must be supported by affidavits under oath. The opposing party then is allowed to file an opposing memorandum (and possibly affidavits), and in some places the moving party can then file a reply. After the moving papers are submitted, the court usually holds a hearing during which the judge can ask questions and the lawyers can make any clarifying points that seem useful. Sometimes the judge issues a tentative decision before the hearing. The motion will either be decided at the end of the hearing or taken under submission for later decision.

2. Consistency and Honesty in Pleading

a. Inconsistent Allegations

McCORMICK v. KOPMANN

Appellate Court of Illinois, Third District, 1959.
23 Ill.App.2d 189, 161 N.E.2d 720.

REYNOLDS, PRESIDING JUSTICE.

[Lewis McCormick was killed when a truck operated by defendant Kopmann collided with his automobile. McCormick's widow sued Kopmann and the Huls, owners of a tavern where McCormick had drunk beer before the accident. Count I, for damages under the Illinois Wrongful Death Act, alleged that Kopmann negligently drove his truck across the center line and collided with McCormick's automobile and that "the said decedent was in the exercise of ordinary care for his own safety and that of his property." Count IV, brought "in the alternative to Count I," sought damages under the Illinois Dram Shop Act. It alleged that the Huls sold alcoholic beverages to McCormick which rendered him intoxicated and that "as a result of such intoxication" he drove his automobile "in such a manner as to cause a collision" with Kopmann's truck.

Before trial, Kopmann moved to dismiss the complaint on the theory that the contradictions between Count I and Count IV were fatal. The trial court denied his motion. There was conflicting testimony at trial concerning whether McCormick or Kopmann had driven over the center line. There was also testimony that McCormick had drunk several beers at the Huls' tavern. Defendants' motions for directed verdict were denied, and the jury returned a verdict against Kopmann for $15,500 under Count I and for the Huls under Count IV.]

* * *

Kopmann has appealed. His first contention is that the trial court erred in denying his pre-trial motion to dismiss the complaint. Kopmann is correct in asserting that the complaint contains inconsistent allegations. The allegation of Count I that McCormick was free from contributory negligence, cannot be reconciled with the allegation of Count IV that McCormick's intoxication was the proximate cause of his death. Freedom from contributory negligence is a prerequisite to recovery under the Wrongful Death Act. If the jury had found that McCormick was intoxicated and that his intoxication caused the accident, it could not at the same time have found that McCormick was not contributorily negligent. The Illinois Supreme Court has held that "voluntary intoxication will not excuse a person from exercising such care as may reasonably be expected from one who is sober." Keeshan v. Elgin A. & S. Traction Co., 229 Ill. 533, 537, 82 N.E. 360, 362.

In addition to this factual inconsistency, it has been held that compensation awarded under the Wrongful Death Act includes reparation for the loss of support compensable under the Dram Shop Act.

Counts I and IV, therefore, are mutually exclusive; plaintiff may not recover upon both counts. It does not follow, however, that these counts may not be pleaded together.

* * *

[The Illinois Civil Practice Act contains provisions, similar to F.R.Civ.Pro. 8(e)(2), that claims may be made in the alternative "regardless of consistency." Urnest v. Sabre Metal Products, Inc., 22 Ill.App.2d 172, 159 N.E.2d 512 (1959), stated:]

The theory is that on the trial the proof will determine on which set of facts, if any, the plaintiff is entitled to recover. Where the pleading is in the alternative in different counts, each count stands alone and the inconsistent statements contained in a count cannot be used to contradict statements in another count. The intent of the cited section of the Practice Act is that counts can be pleaded in the alternative regardless of inconsistency.

* * *

Sound policy weighs in favor of alternative pleading, so that controversies may be settled and complete justice accomplished in a single action. If the right is abused, as where the pleader has knowledge of the true facts (viz., he knows that the facts belie the alternative), pleading in the alternative is not justified. Thus in Church v. Adler, 350 Ill.App. 471 at page 483, 113 N.E.2d 327 at page 332, we said:

"... alternative pleading is not permitted when in the nature of things the pleader must know which of the inconsistent averments is true and which is false. Plaintiff must know whether she will be sick, sore, lame and disordered for the rest of her life or whether on the contrary she has regained her health, as alleged in Count II. She must make up her mind which is the fact, and strike the inconsistent allegation from her pleading on remand."

There is nothing in the record before us to indicate that plaintiff knew in advance of the trial that the averments of Count I, and not Count IV, were true. In fact, at the trial, Kopmann attempted to establish the truth of the allegations of Count IV that McCormick was intoxicated at the time of the collision and that his intoxication caused his death. He can hardly be heard now to say that before the trial, plaintiff should have known that these were not the facts. Where, as in the Church case, the injured party is still living and able to recollect the events surrounding the accident, pleading in the alternative may not be justified, but where, as in the case at bar, the key witness is deceased, pleading alternative sets of facts is often the only feasible way to proceed.

We hold that, in the absence of a severance, plaintiff had the right to go to trial on both Counts I and IV, and to adduce all the proof she had under both Count I and Count IV.

* * *

Here, either of two defendants may be liable to plaintiff, depending upon what the jury finds the facts to be. It has been aptly said that "truth cannot be stated until known, and, for purposes of judicial administration, cannot be known until the trier of facts decides the fact issues." Plaintiff need not choose between the alternative counts. Such a requirement would, to a large extent, nullify the salutary purposes of alternative pleading. Since she could bring actions against the defendants seriatim, or at the same time in separate suits, she is entitled to join them in a single action, introduce all her proof, and submit the entire case to the jury under appropriate instructions.

Notes and Questions

1. Could plaintiff have solved the inconsistent allegations problem by filing two lawsuits, one against the truck driver and the other against the

bar owners? Is it important that the truck driver might win the suit against him by blaming the bar owners, while the bar owners might similarly escape liability by blaming the truck driver in the suit against them? As we will see when we deal with joinder of parties, modern rules permit plaintiffs to sue numerous defendants in order to avoid this possibility. Recall United States v. Board of Harbor Comm'rs, supra p. 134. This combination avoids the risk of inconsistent results in the two cases and saves the court the effort of trying the same matters twice (since a trial against either the truck driver or the bar owners would be likely to involve examination into the events at the bar and the circumstances surrounding the accident).

2. The court speaks of whether plaintiff knew the "truth" of her claim against the truck driver before trial. In what sense are we talking about the truth? If there is a risk of inconsistent results in separate suits against the truck driver and the bar owners, does that suggest that there is a difference between litigation outcomes and the truth? Are we bringing litigation outcomes closer to the "truth" by allowing the combination of the claims?

3. Besides avoiding inconsistent outcomes, plaintiff may derive other tactical advantages from suing the truck driver and the bar owners in the same case because there is a substantial likelihood that each defendant will help the plaintiff make out a case against the other. For example, the truck driver attempted at trial to prove plaintiff's claim against the bar owners. Does this effect of combined treatment make it unfair to allow a single trial as to both defendants? Is there any way that a jury could consistently deny plaintiff's claim against both the truck driver and the bar owners? Is that likelihood reduced if the cases are combined?

4. How can plaintiff make any allegations against either the truck driver or the bar owners, assuming that she was not in the bar or the car on the night of the accident? Under Code practice, it was often required that pleadings be "verified," which compels the party to swear under oath that the allegations in the pleading are true. How can somebody who lacks personal knowledge do that? The answer has been to make allegations on "information and belief," asserting that the pleader is not claiming personal knowledge as to these matters although they are believed to be true. The Federal Rules generally do not require verification, but rely instead on the lawyer's signature on a complaint to show that it is justified. The only exception is Rule 23.1, dealing with stockholders' derivative actions. Are these suits especially subject to abuse?

In Surowitz v. Hilton Hotels Corp., 383 U.S. 363, 86 S.Ct. 845, 15 L.Ed.2d 807 (1966), the Court examined the verification requirement in Rule 23.1. Plaintiff, a Hilton shareholder, charged that the officers and directors of the company had defrauded it of several million dollars. As directed by the Rules, plaintiff verified that she knew some of the allegations were true and that on information and belief she thought that all the other allegations were true. The trial court allowed defendants to take plaintiff's deposition before filing their answer. That showed that plaintiff, a Polish immigrant with limited command of English, did not understand the complaint or know what the lawsuit was about. Instead, she had relied on her son-in-law, Irving Brilliant, an investment advisor who had graduated from Harvard Law School, whose investigation had uncovered the alleged fraud. The trial court dismissed the complaint as a "sham pleading." The Supreme Court reversed because the record (including affidavits detailing the investigation by Irving Brilliant) showed the charges "to be based on reasonable beliefs growing out of careful investigation. The basic purpose of the Federal Rules is to administer justice through fair trials, not through summary dismissals as necessary as they may be on occasion. These rules were designed in large part to get away from some of the old procedural booby traps which common-law pleaders could set to prevent unsophisticated litigants from ever having their day in court."

5. How much uncertainty is necessary to justify alternative allegations? Had plaintiff's husband survived the accident could he have sued the truck driver and the bar owners in the alternative? Would he be foreclosed from doing so if he genuinely believed he could hold his liquor?

6. Consider the views of one court on the scope of permissible alternative pleading:

> Courts allow a pleading of the sort "I never borrowed the lawn mower, it was broken when I borrowed it, and I returned it in perfect condition" because pleadings precede discovery and trial. Until the last minute it may be hard to tell what the evidence will show, and inconsistent pleadings allow a party to preserve its options.

Astor Chauffeured Limousine Co. v. Runnfeldt Invest. Corp., 910 F.2d 1540, 1548 (7th Cir.1990). Is this latitude too great? Would it be consistent with the view in many other countries that pleadings should set forth claims and defenses (and evidence) with specificity? See supra p. 137 n.6.

In Smith v. Cashland, Inc., 193 F.3d 1158 (10th Cir.1999), the court held that defendant (plaintiff's former employer) could attempt to prove not only that plaintiff was not terminated (as she claimed), but also that firing her would have been justified due to her poor performance. Although the employer claimed there never had been a decision to terminate, it should have been allowed to try to prove that a hypothetical decision to terminate was based on a legitimate, nondiscriminatory motive. See also Henry v. Daytop Village, Inc., 42 F.3d 89 (2d Cir.1994) (plaintiff who claimed she was fired for discriminatory reasons and was not guilty of misconduct charged against her could also argue that, even if she were guilty of the alleged misconduct, white employees who engaged in similar misconduct had not been fired).

7. Alternative pleading can be extremely important in many product liability suits. Consider, for example, the possibility that the accident in McCormick v. Kopmann resulted from the failure of the brakes on the truck. Plaintiff might sue the truck driver, the manufacturer, the dealer who sold the truck, the current owner and every prior owner of the truck, and every truck-service mechanic who had ever worked on the truck. Plaintiff would do so because she could not tell who was responsible for the defective condition of the brakes, and she would therefore allege alternatively, on information and belief, that each was in some way responsible. Should the law look with favor on such complexities? Should the plaintiff be allowed to file a suit that assumes that most of the defendants are not liable?

b. Certification by Signing—Rule 11

ZUK v. EASTERN PENNSYLVANIA PSYCHIATRIC INSTITUTE OF THE MEDICAL COLLEGE OF PENNSYLVANIA

United States Court of Appeals, Third Circuit, 1996.
103 F.3d 294.

Before SLOVITER CHIEF JUDGE, MCKEE and ROSENN, CIRCUIT JUDGES.

ROSENN, CIRCUIT JUDGE.

This appeal brings into focus difficult questions relating to the evolving uses and purposes of Federal Rules of Civil Procedure Rule 11 sanctions, the more narrow statutory function of sanctions permitted under 28 U.S.C.A. § 1927, and differences between the two. The sanctions here stem from a suit filed in the United States District Court for the Eastern District of Pennsylvania by Benjamin Lipman, the appellant, in behalf of Dr. Gerald Zuk for copyright infringement against the Eastern Pennsylvania Psychiatric Institute (EPPI). The district court dismissed the action on a Rule 12(b)(6) motion filed by the defendant, and appellant and his client thereafter were subjected to joint and several liability in the sum of $15,000 for sanctions and defendant's counsel fees. Dr. Zuk settled his liability and Lipman appealed. We affirm in part and vacate in part.

I.

Dr. Zuk, a psychologist on the faculty [of] EPPI, early in the 1970s had an EPPI technician film two of Dr. Zuk's family therapy sessions. As academic demand for the films developed, Zuk had EPPI duplicate the films and make them available for rental through [its] library. Zuk subsequently wrote a book which, among other things, contained transcripts of the therapy sessions. He registered the book in 1975 with the United States Copyright Office.

In 1980, upon a change in its ownership, EPPI furloughed Zuk. He thereupon requested that all copies of the films be returned to him; EPPI ignored the request. It would appear that EPPI continued to rent out the films for at least some time thereafter. For reasons which have not been made clear, after a long hiatus, Zuk renewed his attempts to recover the films in 1994. In 1995, appellant filed a suit in Zuk's behalf, alleging that EPPI was renting out the films and thereby infringed his copyright.

On June 19, 1995, EPPI moved for dismissal under Rule 12(b), and appellant filed a memorandum in opposition. While the motion was pending, EPPI mailed to Lipman a notice of its intention to move for sanctions under Rule 11(c)(1)(A) on the grounds essentially that appellant had failed to conduct an inquiry into the facts reasonable under the circumstances and into the law. The district court entered an order granting the motion to dismiss. The court found that the copyright of the book afforded no protection to the films, that EPPI owned the copies of the films in its possession and that their use was not an infringement, and that in any event, Zuk's claims were barred by the statute of limitations.

On August 16, EPPI filed a motion for attorney's fees pursuant to 17 U.S.C.A. § 505 which appellant opposed by a memorandum in opposition on August 31. On September 15, EPPI also filed a Rule 11 motion for sanctions, and appellant filed a memorandum in opposition. On November 1, the court entered an order to "show cause why Rule 11 sanctions should not be imposed for (a) filing the complaint, and failing to withdraw it; and (b) signing and filing each and every document presented." Appellant responded on December 1 with a declaration reiterating the facts of the case as he viewed them.

On February 1, 1996, the court, upon consideration of defendant's motion for attorney's fees and sanctions, ordered: "That plaintiff, Gerald Zuk, Ph.D., and plaintiff's counsel, Benjamin G. Lipman, Esq. are jointly and severally liable to the defendant for counsel fees in the sum of $15,000." We must ascertain the underpinnings for the Order. It appears that Dr. Zuk subsequently settled his liability with EPPI in the amount of $6,250, leaving appellant liable for $8,750. Appellant timely appealed.

II.

[The Copyright Act provides that the court may award a reasonable attorney's fee to the prevailing party. Fee awards are at the discretion of the district court, and do not depend on a showing of bad faith by the losing party. The district court recognized that the award should not be automatic in this case, but believed that an award was justified. A fee award on this ground can only be entered against a party, however, and the fee-shifting provisions provided no basis for an award against the lawyer. That would have to be justified under 28 U.S.C.A. § 1927 or Rule 11.]

We turn first to the propriety of the district court's imposition of sanctions under 28 U.S.C.A. § 1927. We review a district court's decision to impose sanctions for abuse of discretion. Cooter & Gell v. Hartmarx Corp., 496 U.S. 384, 385, 110 S.Ct. 2447, 2450, 110 L.Ed.2d 359 (1990).

Section 1927 provides in pertinent part: "Any attorney or person admitted to conduct cases who so multiplies the proceedings in any case unreasonably and vexatiously may be required by the court to satisfy personally the excess costs, expenses and attorney's fees reasonably incurred because of such conduct." Although a trial court has broad discretion in managing litigation before it, the principal purpose of imposing sanctions under 28 U.S.C.A. § 1927 is "the deterrence of intentional and unnecessary delay in the proceedings." In this case, the trial court imposed sanctions on plaintiff and his counsel, not because of any multiplicity of the proceedings or delaying tactics, but for failure to make a reasonably adequate inquiry into the facts and law before filing the lawsuit. Thus, the statute does not apply to the set of facts before us.

Furthermore, the statute is designed to discipline counsel only and does not authorize imposition of sanctions on the attorney's client.

Finally, this court has stated that "before a court can order the imposition of attorneys' fees under § 1927, it must find wilful bad faith on the part of the offending attorney." Although the court need not "make an express finding of bad faith in so many words," there must at least be statements on the record which this court can construe as an implicit finding of bad faith.

At oral argument before us, counsel for EPPI conceded that the district court had made no express finding of bad faith. Our review of the record, which in relevant part consists only of a two-page Memorandum and Order, reveals no statements which we can interpret as an implicit finding of willful bad faith. At most, the court's statements might be interpreted to indicate a finding of negligence on appellant's part.

[The appellate court concluded that the sanctions order against the attorney had to be vacated because the district court did not subdivide the sanctions between the supposed § 1927 violation and Rule 11.]

IV.

Because the order imposing sanctions on appellant must be vacated and the matter remanded, we conclude that certain issues will probably arise on the remand and should, in the interest of justice, be addressed. We refer here specifically to the question of the proper type and amount of sanctions to be imposed pursuant to Rule 11 under the particular circumstances of this case.

A.

We note at the outset that we find no error in the district court's decision to impose sanctions pursuant to Fed.R.Civ.P. 11.[3] As noted above, we review a district court's decision to impose sanctions for abuse of discretion. An abuse of discretion in this context would occur if the court "based its ruling on an erroneous view of the law or a clearly erroneous assessment of the evidence."

Prior to a significant amendment in 1983, Rule 11 stated that an attorney might be subjected to disciplinary action only for a "wilful" violation of the rule. The Advisory Committee Notes to the 1983 amendment make clear that the wilfulness prerequisite has been deleted. Rather, the amended rule imposes a duty on counsel to make an inquiry

---

3. Appellant contended that he was not given the benefit of Rule 11's 21–day safe harbor, because the court dismissed the action before he had had the full opportunity to withdraw it. He thus claimed that sanctions were improper under Rule 11(c)(1)(A) (upon motion by other party). EPPI maintained that the sanctions actually were imposed under Rule 11(c)(1)(B) (on the court's initiative), which has no safe harbor provision. The court issued an order to show cause, which is required only under 11(c)(1)(B), but stated that it was "in consideration of defendant's motion for sanctions." In its accompanying memorandum, the district court did not address this apparent inconsistency. At oral argument before this court, appellant acknowledged that he would not have withdrawn the complaint even if he had been given the full 21–day safe harbor. Thus, we need not address this contention.

into both the facts and the law which is "reasonable under the circumstances." This is a more stringent standard than the original good-faith formula, and it was expected that a greater range of circumstances would trigger its violation. The district court did not abuse its discretion in determining that appellant had not sufficiently investigated the facts of the case nor had he educated himself well enough as to copyright law. We therefore see no error in the court's decision to impose sanctions.

1.   THE INQUIRY INTO THE FACTS

In dismissing the complaint, the court found that "[i]t ... seems highly probable that plaintiff's claims are barred by the three-year statute of limitations." Later, in the Memorandum and Order imposing sanctions, the court noted that the "obvious" statute of limitations issue would have been resolved and no lawsuit filed, had appellant conducted an adequate investigation.

Dr. Zuk left EPPI in 1980, and it is undisputed that EPPI continued to rent out the films in question for some time thereafter. Appellant, however, had no evidence whatsoever, other than conjecture, to prove that the films were being rented in the three years preceding the commencement of this action. The Advisory Committee Notes to the 1993 amendments to Rule 11 explain:

> "Tolerance of factual contentions in initial pleadings ... when specifically identified as made on information and belief does not relieve litigants from the obligation to conduct an appropriate investigation into the facts that is reasonable under the circumstances; it is not a license to ... make claims ... without any factual basis or justification."

Appellant's assertions in ¶¶ 36 and 37 of the complaint (in regard to EPPI's ongoing use of the films) are based purely upon Dr. Zuk's beliefs.[4] What little investigation appellant actually conducted did not reveal any information that the films were being rented out during the relevant period. Indeed, certain pre-filing correspondence with EPPI indicated that, pursuant to Dr. Zuk's earlier instructions, the library staff was cautioned not to rent any of Dr. Zuk's films. Nor are we persuaded by appellant's contention that further information would have been obtained during discovery. The [Advisory Committee] Note cited above observes that discovery is not intended as a fishing expedition permitting the speculative pleading of a case first and then pursuing discovery to support it; the plaintiff must have some basis in fact for the action. The need for a reasonable investigation with respect to distribution of the film during the three-year period prior to the filing of the lawsuit is evident because of the long period allegedly spanned by the distribution.

---

4. EPPI emphasizes that while ¶¶ 36 and 37 should have been pleaded on information and belief, they were instead phrased as "Dr. Zuk believes, and therefore avers, ..." In light of liberal federal pleading practice, we do not find this to be an important distinction.

2. The Inquiry into the Law

Rule 11(b)(2) requires that all "claims, defenses, and other legal contentions [be] warranted by existing law or by a nonfrivolous argument for the extension, modification, or reversal of existing law or the establishment of new law." Appellant does not contend that any of the latter justifications apply, and so we must ascertain whether his legal arguments are "warranted by existing law." For reasons that follow, we conclude that they are not, and that sanctions therefore were within the sound discretion of the district court.

Appellant's legal research was faulty primarily in two particular areas: copyright law (pertaining to what the parties call the "registration issue") and the law of personal property (the "ownership issue"). Turning to the registration issue, appellant states that this was the first copyright case which he had handled, and points out that a practitioner has to begin somewhere. While we are sympathetic to this argument, its thrust is more toward the nature of the sanctions to be imposed rather than to the initial decision whether sanctions should be imposed. Regrettably, the reality of appellant's weak grasp of copyright law is that it caused him to pursue a course of conduct which was not warranted by existing law and compelled the defendant to expend time and money in needless litigation.

Appellant's primary contention is that by registering a copyright in his book, Dr. Zuk had somehow also protected the films reproduced in them. The logical progression is that because the book contained transcripts of the films, the words spoken in the films were protected, and thus so were the films. Although perhaps logical, this argument runs contrary to copyright law. "The copyright in [a derivative] work ... does not affect or enlarge the scope, duration, ownership, or subsistence of, any copyright protection in the preexisting material." 17 U.S.C.A. § 103(b).

In all fairness to appellant, we should note that the cases and commentary interpreting this provision focus on derivative works which incorporate the preexisting work of a different author. Had appellant presented his argument as a matter of first impression, and argued for a new interpretation of the statute where the same individual authored both works, he might have stood upon a more solid footing. Instead, appellant's brief evidences what strikes us as a cursory reading of the copyright laws, and a strained analysis of what appears to be an inapposite case.

We now focus on the ownership issue. The parties agree that if EPPI owns the copies of the film in its possession, then 17 U.S.C.A. § 109[5] permits EPPI to rent out the films. Appellant maintains, however, that EPPI does not own the copies, because they were made specifically for Dr. Zuk at his behest, and as a perquisite of his faculty position at EPPI.

5. This section states in pertinent part that a nonprofit library (such as that operated by EPPI) is free to rent, lease, or lend copywritten material without authority of the copyright owner, so long as the library owns a lawfully made copy of such material.

This question raises reasonable issues as to the rights of an employer in the work product of an employee, and its resolution is not so clear as to itself warrant the sanctioning of appellant for advancing this claim.

EPPI contends, however, that it is too late in the day to raise this argument. The Pennsylvania statute of limitations on replevin is two years. Dr. Zuk demanded the return of the copies in 1980, and EPPI refused to comply, based upon a claim of ownership. EPPI's possession thereafter was open, notorious, and under claim of right, and yet Dr. Zuk did not institute an action to replevy. It would therefore appear that EPPI now holds superior title, and that an inquiry into Pennsylvania personal property law would have revealed that appellant's claim was far too stale. However, EPPI raises its argument too late in this proceeding. It did not rely upon, or even mention, the adverse possession theory before the district court. Because the court could not have relied upon this aspect of the ownership issue in imposing sanctions, it is inappropriate for us to consider it at this time.

B.

Having concluded that there is no error in the district court's decision to impose sanctions upon appellant under Rule 11, we turn now to the type and amount of sanctions imposed. We review the appropriateness of the sanctions imposed for abuse of discretion. As the courts have undergone experience with the application of Rule 11 sanctions, its scope has broadened and the emphasis of the Rule has changed.

According to Wright & Miller:

> The 1993 revision ... makes clear that the main purpose of Rule 11 is to deter, not to compensate. Accordingly, it changes the emphasis in the types of sanctions to be ordered. It envisions as the norm public interest remedies such as fines and reprimands, as opposed to the prior emphasis on private interest remedies. Thus, the Advisory Committee Notes state that any monetary penalty "should ordinarily be paid into the court" except "under unusual circumstances" when they should be given to the opposing party. Any sanction imposed should be calibrated to the least severe level necessary to serve the deterrent purpose of the Rule. In addition, the new Rule 11 contemplates greater use of nonmonetary sanctions, including reprimands, orders to undergo continuing education, and referrals to disciplinary authorities.

5A Charles Alan Wright & Arthur R. Miller, Federal Practice & Procedure § 1336 (2d ed. Supp.1996).

This court has instructed the district courts that "[f]ee-shifting is but one of several methods of achieving the various goals of Rule 11," that they should "consider a wide range of alternative possible sanctions for violation of the rule," and that the "district court's choice of deterrent is appropriate when it is the minimum that will serve to adequately deter the undesirable behavior." Doering v. Union County Bd. of Chosen Freeholders, 857 F.2d 191, 194 (3d Cir.1988).

Thus, the district courts have been encouraged to consider mitigating factors in fashioning sanctions, most particularly the sanctioned party's ability to pay. Courts were also given examples of other factors they might consider, including whether the attorney has a history of this sort of behavior, the defendant's need for compensation, the degree of frivolousness, and the "willfulness" of the violation.

In *Doering*, a $25,000 sanction was imposed on a sole practitioner with less than $40,000 gross income per annum. We affirmed the district court's decision to impose sanctions, but vacated and remanded as to the amount. We noted that "in order for the district court to exercise properly its discretion in setting the amount of fees to be assessed against counsel, further evidence must be developed upon the issue of his ability to pay."

Although money sanctions are not encouraged under Rule 11, they are not forbidden. Under the circumstances of this case, we see no error in the district court's imposition of fee sanctions upon the appellant, although the amount may be contrary to the current spirit of Rule 11. The present case differs from *Doering* in that appellant did not request that the district court mitigate the sanctions. Appellant also faces a lesser financial burden in that he is liable for only $8,750, his client having paid the difference. Nonetheless, when we look to the list of mitigating factors, and consider the non-punitive purpose of Rule 11, we conclude that it was error to invoke without comment a very severe penalty. On remand, the district court should apply the principles announced by this court in *Doering*.

Notes and Questions

1. As the court notes in *Zuk*, Rule 11 was extensively amended in 1993 to change features of a previous amendment in 1983 that strengthened the rule's provisions. Many objected that the 1983 version of the rule resulted in too much sanctions activity, and actually deterred litigants from dropping weak contentions for fear that they would be sanctioned for doing so. In particular, many objected that the rule impeded the assertion of civil rights claims. Among the concerns were the mandatory nature of sanctions under the 1983 version of the rule, and the inclination of some courts to use the rule as a fee-shifting device to compensate victims of violations. The 1993 amendments made the imposition of sanctions discretionary, introduced the "safe harbor" in Rule 11(c)(1), and reoriented the choice of sanction toward deterrence and away from compensation. Some opposed these changes in the rule, and there have been proposals to restore the 1983 provisions. See, e.g., the proposed Lawsuit Abuse Reduction Act of 2004, H.R. 4571, passed by the House of Representatives in mid–2004, which would make sanctions mandatory again and provide in the rule that compensation for attorneys' fees is a proper sanction.

Are sanctions, particularly against lawyers, a suitable way for dealing with perceived problems of lawsuit abuse? Consider the views of the court in In re Pennie & Edmonds LLP, 323 F.3d 86, 90–91 (2d Cir.2003):

Any regime of sanctions for a lawyer's role in the course of representing a client inevitably has implications for the functioning of the adversary process. If the sanction regime is too severe, lawyers will sometimes be deterred from making legitimate submissions on behalf of clients out of apprehension that their conduct will erroneously be deemed improper. On the other hand, if the sanction regime is too lenient, lawyers will sometimes be emboldened to make improper submissions on behalf of clients, confident that their misconduct will either be undetected or dealt with too leniently to matter.

2. Initially, defendant in *Zuk* moved to dismiss the complaint under Rule 12(b)(6). Was this a proper motion? Can the question whether plaintiff's copyright was violated by defendant's lending practices properly be determined on a motion to dismiss? Should the statute of limitations be a proper ground for such a motion? Note that it is classified as an affirmative defense under Rule 8(c). See note 4(b) below for further discussion. Should every granted motion to dismiss for failure to state a claim be followed by imposition of Rule 11 sanctions?

3. 28 U.S.C.A. § 1927 authorizes sanctions for willful "multiplication" of proceedings. What does this mean? Why should it be wrong for lawyers to do that? Why should sanctions be warranted only when the lawyer acted in bad faith? According to commentators, the limitations on Rule 11 adopted in 1993 have prompted some litigants and courts and to resort more frequently to § 1927 as a ground for sanctions "to circumvent the procedural requirements of Rule 11." Hart, And the Chill Goes On—Federal Civil Rights Plaintiffs Beware: Rule 11 Vis-a-Vis 28 U.S.C. § 1927 and the Court's Inherent Power, 37 Loyola L.Rev. 645, 656–47 (2004). It has also been reported that the federal courts of appeals are split on whether § 1927 requires a showing of subjective bad faith or only recklessness. See id. at 653.

4. The district court ordered plaintiff and his lawyer to justify filing the suit, failing to withdraw it, and signing and filing each subsequent document they submitted in the case. Review Rule 11 and consider how it operates:

(a) *Signature requirement*: The rule applies to the person who signs the document submitted to the court, ordinarily a lawyer, and authorizes sanctions against the lawyer's firm. Except for discovery, Rule 11 applies to all papers filed in court, so you should keep it in mind in connection with the other matters covered in this course.

(b) *Factual inquiry*: By signing and submitting a document, the lawyer represents that there has been a reasonable inquiry, and that the claim has evidentiary support. This calls for an "objective" inquiry; "[a]n empty head but a pure heart is no defense." Thornton v. Wahl, 787 F.2d 1151, 1154 (7th Cir.1986). Recall Fuentes v. Shevin, supra p. 29: "Lawyers and judges are familiar with the phenomenon of a party mistakenly but firmly convinced that his view of the facts and law will prevail and therefore quite willing to risk the costs of litigation."

Is the requirement that plaintiff have an evidentiary basis for the suit consistent with the notice pleading orientation of Rule 8, which appears to contemplate the availability of discovery to obtain information after suit is filed? The 1983 version was criticized on this ground:

> Applying rule 11 to pleading in order to forestall opportunities for discovery abuse or to pressure litigants into refraining from filing claims contingent on discovery alters the Federal Rules' approach to exploring and articulating factual grounds. To the degree that rule 11 is interpreted to force early formulation of legal theories and to discourage experimental claims, it operates according to a different model than does the liberal pleading regime. Liberal pleading favors decisions on the merits only after the particular circumstances of a claim have been revealed.

Note, Plausible Pleadings: Developing Standards for Rule 11 Sanctions, 100 Harv.L.Rev. 630, 636–37 (1987).

If the lawyer does no investigation at all before filing, but the claim is borne out by later developments, has Rule 11(b) been violated? If not, does the rule exempt those with good intuition? Compare Lichtenstein v. Consolidated Serv. Group, Inc., 173 F.3d 17 (1st Cir.1999) ("a party who brings a suit without conducting a reasonable inquiry * * * and who through sheer fortuity is rewarded for his carelessness, is liable for sanctions"); Garr v. United States Healthcare, Inc., 22 F.3d 1274 (3d Cir.1994) (attorney who did an inadequate prefiling inquiry should not be shielded due to "the stroke of luck that the document happened to be justified"), with Moore v. Keegan Manag. Co., 78 F.3d 431 (9th Cir.1996) (counsel cannot be sanctioned if there is evidence supporting the claim even though there was no reasonable inquiry before suit was filed).

What more should the plaintiff's lawyer have done in *Zuk*? After filing suit, wouldn't it be easier to find out about the defendant's lending practices? What if defendant refused to answer any questions about its practices before suit was filed? See Q–Pharma, Inc. v. Andrew Jergens Co., 360 F.3d 1295 (Fed.Cir.2004) (even after suit was filed, defendant refused to provide information about the contents of its hand lotion that would have permitted plaintiff to determine that its patent was not infringed; sanctions were therefore denied even though plaintiff could have conducted its own chemical analysis of defendant's product before filing suit). Note that the *Zuk* court says that the plaintiff may not embark on a "fishing expedition" by using "speculative pleading" and then pursuing discovery to support it. Since it seems to be conceded that defendant continued to rent out the films for some time, how much more was the lawyer required to obtain before filing suit? Before filing a motion to dismiss on statute of limitations grounds, should the defendant's lawyer have investigated to see if the films had been rented out recently? If she found there had been recent rentals, would it be a violation of Rule 11 to file the motion to dismiss?

Lawyers frequently must decide whether to file when there is factual uncertainty, and Rule 11 may mean they must act at their peril. For example, consider Albright v. Upjohn Co., 788 F.2d 1217 (6th Cir.1986), a case decided under the 1983 version of Rule 11. Plaintiff there claimed she had been injured because of treatment she received as a girl with tetracycline-based drugs. Her lawyers investigated and found medical records from two doctors who had treated her but, as the statute of limitations was running out, were unable to find records about the treatment she received from another doctor who had since died. So the lawyers sued not only the pharmaceutical companies whose tetracycline products had been prescribed by the two doctors whose records had been found, but also Upjohn (a major producer of tetracycline drugs) even though they had as yet no evidence that the deceased doctor had used Upjohn products. The appellate court held that the lawyers should be sanctioned for suing Upjohn because there was no likelihood that additional medical records would be located. Should the lawyers have had to run the risk that more records would be unearthed, but that it would then be too late to sue Upjohn?

Compare Uy v. Bronx Municipal Hospital Center, 182 F.3d 152 (2d Cir.1999), a suit charging discriminatory discharge based on national origin in which plaintiff claimed he was told he could be fired because he was a foreigner. After defendant's witnesses contradicted that assertion, the district court found plaintiff's lawyer guilty of violating Rule 11, but the Court of Appeals reversed: "[The attorney] had no way of ascertaining before he entered into the representation whether the defendants' witnesses would corroborate or contradict the plaintiff's assertion. The defendant's employees are unlikely to make themselves available to be interviewed by an attorney who is contemplating representing the plaintiff. As a practical matter, in the usual case, the only way the attorney can discover what adverse witnesses will say is by taking their deposition, and that cannot be done until the attorney assumes the representation."

Can the lawyer usually rely on the client, or must she make her own investigation? An experienced judge cautions that "attorneys can be conned by devious clients." He adds: "Clients come to them with stories that are, at the very least, slanted and, at the very worst, outright lies. Often clients convince themselves of the truth of their story—they fervently believe things that simply are not true. That is the difficult circumstance in which trial attorneys operate. It is the nature of our adversary system of justice. Clients feel that they have to color their story to win their case." Ward, Lawyer Beware, Calif. Lawyer, Feb., 2005, at 80. In In re Pennie & Edmonds, 323 F.3d 86 (2d Cir.2003), new counsel for defendant came into the case after defendant's evidence that he had been using a label that allegedly infringed plaintiff's trademark before plaintiff first marketed its product had been proven false during a hearing on plaintiff's application for a preliminary injunction. Defendant told his new lawyers that he had made a mistake in supplying this evidence, explaining how the mistake occurred, but there were questions about the explanation. Nevertheless, persuaded that the client was telling the truth, the lawyers submitted the client's affidavit with the explanations to the judge in opposition to plaintiff's motion for summary judgment. In his order granting plaintiff's summary judgment motion, the district judge sua sponte ordered the lawyers to show why they should not be sanctioned for submitting the affidavit, which the judge concluded was false. The appellate court did not decide whether there had been a violation because it held that the sanction was not proper under the safe harbor provision (discussed below) because the judge accepted the lawyers' assertion that they were acting in good faith. See also Jimenez v. Madison Area Technical College, 321 F.3d 652 (7th Cir.2003) (upholding sanctions on plaintiff's lawyer, who told the court that it was his "standing position" to side with the client whenever a credibility call is presented). When the lawyer properly relies on the client, the client can be sanctioned even if the lawyer committed no violation of the rule. See Business Guides, Inc. v. Chromatic Communications Ent., Inc., 498 U.S. 533, 111 S.Ct. 922, 112 L.Ed.2d 1140 (1991) ("The Magistrate did not recommend that [the law firm] be sanctioned for the initial application [for a temporary restraining order], however, as the firm had been led to believe that there was an urgent need to act quickly and thus relied on the information supplied by its sophisticated corporate client.").

Note also that Rule 8(c) says that the statute of limitations is an affirmative defense, which only applies if defendant raises it. Should this have a bearing on whether plaintiff's lawyer is required to investigate whether it applies? Consider Kane, The Lawyer as Litigator in the 1980's, 14 No.Ky.L.Rev. 311, 330–31 (1988):

> [D]ifficult questions are presented for plaintiff's counsel when the facts as revealed indicate a clear defense, but the defense is waivable. Is it consistent with the obligations of Rule 11 to file the pleading knowing it can be destroyed? Some courts have said yes, some no. The problem is an important one. Insofar as courts imposing sanctions in these circumstances do so because the plaintiff's lawyer did not even inquire as to whether the statute of limitations had run or jurisdiction was proper, those rulings are consistent with the purpose of the rule and serve as a needed reminder to counsel to prepare adequately before filing suit.

> But the notion that some matters constitute defenses, easily waived, at least traditionally has meant that the plaintiff has no obligation to raise the matter. Consistent with that view, then, Rule 11 requirements would mean only that plaintiff had an obligation to desist from objecting if the defendant raised the defense because any resistance would be frivolous. Yet some courts now seem to be suggesting that when the plaintiff files an action knowing there is an ironclad defense, that constitutes the filing of an objectively frivolous pleading. * * * [T]he impact of this interpretation is far-reaching because it effectively transforms a defense into an element of plaintiff's case.

(c) *Legal inquiry*: The court in *Zuk* holds that the lawyer did not do a sufficient legal inquiry even though this was the first copyright case he had filed. Does this mean that a lawyer can be sanctioned for failing to recognize what an expert in copyright law would recognize? The court does acknowledge that the question whether 17 U.S.C.A. § 103(b) should apply if the preexisting work was by the same author raises issues that one could debate. Why isn't that sufficient to satisfy Rule 11(b)(2)? Compare Thornton v. Wahl, 787 F.2d 1151 (7th Cir.1986) (failure to clarify that argument was not based on existing law can be sanctioned) with Golden Eagle Distrib. Corp. v. Burroughs Corp., 801 F.2d 1531 (9th Cir.1986) (no need to explain that argument is for an extension of law rather than based on existing law). What arguments could be made for the Ninth Circuit approach? The Advisory Committee did not explicitly resolve this question in the 1993 amendments, but noted that "[a]lthough arguments for a change of law are not required to be so identified, a contention that is so identified should be viewed with greater tolerance under the rule." 146 F.R.D. at 53.

(d) *Harassment*: Sanctions are also warranted for actions that harass or needlessly increase the cost of litigation. What does this add to 28 U.S.C.A.

§ 1927? Could filing a valid claim violate this portion of the rule? Consider National Association of Government Employees, Inc. v. National Fed. of Federal Employees, 844 F.2d 216, 223 (5th Cir.1988): "We do not condone litigation instituted for ulterior purposes rather than to secure judgment on a well-grounded complaint the plaintiff sincerely believes. Yet the Rule 11 injunction against harassment does not exact of those who file pleadings an undiluted desire for just deserts. * * * [I]f an initial complaint passes the test of non-frivolousness, its filing does not constitute harassment for the purposes of Rule 11." See also Sussman v. Bank of Israel, 56 F.3d 450 (2d Cir.), cert. denied, 516 U.S. 916, 116 S.Ct. 305, 133 L.Ed.2d 210 (1995) (suit designed to generate adverse publicity about defendant cannot be sanctioned unless frivolous). If this is correct, what is left of the prohibition against harassment as an independent Rule 11 consideration? Compare Whitehead v. Food Max of Mississippi, Inc., 332 F.3d 796 (5th Cir.2003) (divided court holds that flamboyant tactics to enforce judgment could be sanctioned as harassing for trying to embarrass defendant).

(e) *Later advocating*: Before the 1993 amendment, courts were divided on whether sanctions could be imposed where a party had a legitimate basis for a filing when it was made, but later learned it was unjustified. Rule 11(b) now provides that a sanction may be imposed on a lawyer for "later advocating" a position taken in a paper even though no violation occurred when that paper was filed. For example, in Phonometrics, Inc. v. Economy Inns of America, 349 F.3d 1356 (Fed.Cir.2003), plaintiff sued for patent infringement in 1997, and the district court stayed proceedings pending a decision by the Federal Circuit (which hears appeals in patent infringement cases from across the country) on the construction of the patent in issue. After the Federal Circuit construed the patent in a way that undermined the claims, plaintiff's counsel told the district court it would continue to pursue the claims. Defendants served a Rule 11 motion demanding dismissal, and counsel responded that the appellate court's decision was "mistaken." The appellate court affirmed the imposition of sanctions on counsel for persisting in the litigation. In *Zuk*, how should this "later advocating" provision be applied? Should it matter that during the argument on the appeal plaintiff's lawyer said that he would not have withdrawn the complaint?

(f) *Safe harbor*: Even if there has been a violation, the court may impose sanctions on motion only if the violator has been warned and invited to desist. See Rule 11(c)(1)(A). Is this a good idea? Justice Scalia thought it was not and dissented from the 1993 amendment: "The Rules should be solicitous of the abused (the courts and the opposing party), and not of the abuser. Under the revised Rule, parties will be able to file thoughtless, reckless, and harassing pleadings, secure in the knowledge that they have nothing to lose: If objection is raised, they can retreat without penalty." 146 F.R.D. at 508 (Scalia, J., dissenting from amendments).

How should the safe harbor provision be applied in *Zuk*? The appellate court declines to address the question because counsel said he would not have withdrawn the complaint anyway. Is this a sensible application of the rule? The safe harbor provision was added in part to respond to reports that under the 1983 version parties routinely requested Rule 11 sanctions in conjunction with other motions, so that now sanctions must be sought by a separate motion. In addition, the provision was prompted by reports that parties facing Rule 11 requests were reluctant to withdraw positions for fear of strengthening the sanctions motion. Are safe harbor protections available only to one who volunteers to abandon a position? If so, why would a moving party ever give the required notice rather than coupling its substantive motion with a companion Rule 11 motion? Then the other side would be presented with the choice of admitting the substantive motion or waiving the safe harbor protections. But see Giganti v. Gen–X Strategies, Inc., 222 F.R.D. 299, 307 (E.D.Va.2004) (safe harbor not available because plaintiffs never had any intention of withdrawing their claims).

In *Zuk*, isn't Rule 11(c)(1)(B) the applicable provision? The Advisory Committee Notes say that "[t]he power of the court to act on its own initiative is retained, but with the condition that this be done through a show cause order. * * * Since show cause orders will ordinarily be issued only in situations akin to a contempt of court, the rule does not provide a 'safe harbor.'" 146 F.R.D. at 591–92. In In re Pennie & Edmonds LLP, 323 F.3d 86 (2d Cir.2003), the court held that a district judge may impose sanctions sua sponte without an opportunity to withdraw the claim only if it finds that the lawyer acted in bad faith. There was a vigorous dissent asserting that the district judge should not be thus hamstrung. See also Radcliffe v. Rainbow Const. Co., 254 F.3d 772 (9th Cir.2001) ("It would render Rule 11(c)(1)(A)'s 'safe harbor' provisions meaningless to permit a party's noncompliant motion to be converted automatically into a court-initiated motion"); Methode Electronics, Inc. v. Adam Technologies, Inc., 371 F.3d 923 (7th Cir.2004) (when court acts sua sponte, it may not impose attorney's fees).

The courts have generally been vigorous in applying the safe harbor requirement. For example, in Ridder v. City of Springfield, 109 F.3d 288 (6th Cir.1997), the district court granted summary judgment to defendants when plaintiff could not come up with any evidence supporting his allegations the city had engaged in an illegal custom or practice in a case that required such proof. A month after that motion was granted, the city moved for Rule 11 sanctions. Treating the safe harbor provision as an "absolute requirement," the appellate court held that the city had lost the opportunity to move for sanctions by waiting until after summary judgment was granted to serve its motion because plaintiff's counsel might have withdrawn the claims if warned of the sanctions possibility. "A party seeking sanctions must leave sufficient opportunity for the opposing party to choose whether to withdraw or cure the offense voluntarily before the court disposes of the challenged contention." See also Barber v. Miller, 146 F.3d 707 (9th Cir.1998) (after defendant's motion to dismiss was granted, it was too late for defendant to serve a sanctions motion because counsel could not then withdraw the claim).

5. How should the court decide whether to impose a sanction if there has been an unremedied violation of the rule? The decision whether to sanction is up to the district judge, and subject to reversal only for abuse of discretion. Would it have been an abuse of discretion not to impose Rule 11 sanctions in *Zuk*? Cf. Chicago Truck Drivers, Helpers & Warehouse Workers Union Pension Fund v. Brotherhood Labor Leasing, 166 F.3d 1269 (8th Cir.1999) (court remands with directions for district judge to provide adequate reasons for denying request for Rule 11 sanctions).

6. If the court does decide to sanction, Rule 11(c)(2) provides directions on what the sanction should be. Sanctions need not be monetary. See In re Pennie & Edmonds LLP, 323 F.3d 86 (2d Cir.2003) (sanctioned firm required to send copies of the court's sanction opinion to every lawyer in the firm). Could the sanction imposed in *Zuk* be justified under these provisions?

7. *Other grounds for sanctions*: Besides Rule 11 and 28 U.S.C.A. § 1927, the Supreme Court held in Chambers v. NASCO, Inc., 501 U.S. 32, 111 S.Ct. 2123, 115 L.Ed.2d 27 (1991), that federal courts have "inherent power" to sanction a litigant for bad-faith conduct that has not been displaced by the more specific provisions of Rule 11 and § 1927, but said that this power should be used rarely. "The imposition of sanctions using inherent powers must be accompanied by a specific finding of bad faith." Goldin v. Bartholow, 166 F.3d 710, 722 (5th Cir.1999).

8. Another possibility is that the victim of litigation misconduct of the sort that may justify Rule 11 sanctions may file a separate lawsuit against the lawyer for this misconduct. For examples, see General Refractories Co. v. Fireman's Fund Ins. Co., 337 F.3d 297 (3d Cir.2003) (holding that using legal process primarily to harass an adversary could constitute "perversion" of that process actionable as abuse of process under Pennsylvania law); Zamos v. Stroud, 1 Cal. Rptr. 3d 484 (Cal. Ct. App. 2003) (holding that a lawyer could be sued for malicious prosecution if he continued to pursue a suit after learning that it was groundless).

3.   *Scrutinizing the Legal Sufficiency of Plaintiff's Claim*

MITCHELL v. ARCHIBALD & KENDALL, INC.

United States Court of Appeals, Seventh Circuit, 1978.
573 F.2d 429.

Before FAIRCHILD, CHIEF JUDGE, PELL and WOOD, CIRCUIT JUDGES.

PELL, CIRCUIT JUDGE.

Plaintiffs-appellants Lawrence and Algerie Mitchell appeal from the judgment of the district court in dismissing their cause against Archibald & Kendall, Inc. (A & K) for failure to state a claim for which relief can be granted. The major legal question presented in this diversity case is whether the owner or occupier of land has a duty of reasonably guarding an invitee against criminal attacks that take place beyond the boundaries of his premises and on a public thoroughfare.[1]

---

1. In his memorandum opinion, the district court judge stated that Mitchell was parked in his truck near defendant's place of business. After citing cases holding that the liability of a landowner to an invitee for criminal acts is generally limited to criminal acts occurring *on the premises* and still other cases recognizing an occupier's duty to protect invitees *beyond* the boundaries of the premises by providing means of ingress and egress reasonably free from hazardous physical conditions, the district court judge asserted:

"Plaintiff Mitchell's injury neither occurred on an ingress or egress to defendant's premises nor resulted from hazardous physical conditions. Further, the criminal act in question did not occur on defendant's premises but on a public street. This Court is of the opinion that defendant's duty as a landowner should not be extended to such a degree."

The complaint sets forth the following facts. Lawrence Mitchell, accompanied by his wife and two grandchildren, drove a truckload of A & K's products from New Jersey to Chicago and tendered the cargo for delivery to A & K's employees at its warehouse on Fulton Street at 9:30 a. m. on November 12, 1973. At the time when the Mitchells arrived, A & K's employees were already loading a truck in the receiving area. Because A & K's receiving dock area allowed only one truck to be unloaded at a time, A & K's employees directed and ordered Lawrence Mitchell to remain in his truck and to park it on the area of Fulton Street immediately opposite A & K's warehouse and adjacent to its driveway until they could unload it.

The complaint alleged that it was A & K's practice, custom and habit over a period of several years openly and visibly to use the area directly in front of and immediately surrounding the receiving area of its warehouse as an extension of the receiving dock area and a parking area for trucks waiting to unload deliveries to and for A & K at its place of business. After Mitchell parked his tractor-trailer on Fulton Street as ordered by A & K's employees and while [he was] sitting in the cab with his family, two unknown males approached him and demanded his money. When Mitchell refused this unlawful demand, one of the men produced a 12–gauge shotgun and, from a distance of approximately three feet, fired it directly into Mitchell's face. The shotgun blast caused permanent injuries to Mitchell.

A & K's employees had experience on repeated occasions prior to November 12, 1973, of various criminal acts on and about A & K's premises. The complaint alleges that A & K knew or should have known of the high risk of drivers being subjected to a criminal attack and assault while waiting in the cab of a truck parked in the area. A & K allegedly knew that some three weeks earlier an armed robbery was perpetrated against another truck driver "while parked on defendant's premises waiting to make a delivery at said private warehouse dock." The Mitchells had no knowledge or means of becoming aware of the inherent risk, dangers and probabilities of a criminal assault associated with attempting to make deliveries at A & K's warehouse or in parking on the area of Fulton Street as directed by A & K's employees.

The complaint set forth five duties which A & K assertedly breached. According to the complaint, it was A & K's duty to exercise ordinary care to maintain its premises and the adjacent areas in a reasonably safe condition so as to avoid leading Mitchell into a dangerous and perilous risk of injury by the criminal conduct of third persons of which A & K was aware. A & K further owed Mitchell the duty to exercise reasonable care to provide a reasonably safe means of ingress and egress, both within the confines of the premises owned and controlled by A & K and beyond the precise boundaries of such premises. A & K owed the Mitchells the duty to exercise reasonable care to protect them from

Accordingly, because plaintiffs have not shown any existing duty of defendant, defendant's motion to dismiss the complaint is granted."

criminal acts of third persons while on A & K's premises and beyond the precise boundaries of such premises and to provide a reasonably sufficient number of servants or employees to afford reasonable protection to invitees. A & K owed Mitchell the duty to give adequate and timely notice and warning of latent or concealed perils which were known to A & K but not to the Mitchells. Finally, according to the complaint, it was A & K's duty towards the Mitchells to keep its premises and the immediate adjacent area reasonably well policed and to exercise reasonable care to see that its invitees were protected from injury from criminal acts of third persons and to take reasonable steps to prevent injury to invitees.

I. CLAIMED ERROR IN DISTRICT COURT'S USE OF RULE 12(b)(6)

An initial issue in the present appeal is whether dismissal under Rule 12(b)(6), Fed.R.Civ.P., was procedurally proper. The plaintiffs-appellants contend that the district court found that plaintiff Mitchell's injuries occurred neither on an ingress nor an egress to A & K's premises and that the criminal act occurred on a public street instead of on A & K's premises. They assert that the issues decided by the district court's opinion involved one of a material fact, i.e., did the attack on Mitchell take place on A & K's premises? The plaintiffs-appellants assert that their complaint alleges extensive and sufficient facts to support the allegation that the area of Fulton Street is a part of A & K's premises, noting that under Illinois law the word "premises" does not have one precise and fixed meaning in law and that its definition is dependent on the underlying factual circumstances and the context in which the term arises. They insist that through the habit and practices of A & K, the public way in question has become an integral adjunct of A & K's business at its Fulton Street address and that a jury might determine that the accident occurred on A & K's premises. The plaintiffs-appellants thus read the district court's memorandum opinion as suggesting that an affirmative answer to the question whether the attack occurred on A & K's "premises" would require denial of the motion to dismiss. They argue that the district court erred in granting A & K's motion because factual disputes cannot be resolved by a motion under Rule 12(b)(6).

Where the pleadings raise a contested issue of material fact, a Rule 12(b)(6) motion must be denied. In reviewing the grant of a motion to dismiss a complaint for failure to state a claim, it is elementary that all material facts well pleaded in the complaint must be taken as true. However, the court is required to accept only well-pleaded facts as true in deciding whether the motion to dismiss was properly granted and is not required to accept legal conclusions that may be alleged or that may be drawn from the pleaded facts.

We think that the district court properly relied upon Rule 12(b)(6) in disposing of the present case. The plaintiffs-appellants' complaint itself distinguished carefully between A & K's "premises" and the adjacent area on Fulton Street which A & K assertedly used as a warehouse parking area. Their present argument that a jury could find that the street area was a part of A & K's "premises" sets forth a new theory of liability. The allegations actually incorporated into the drafted complaint were not sculpted in such a fashion as to articulate that theory. The district court judge in dismissing the cause was in effect ruling that the complaint as drafted was legally insufficient.

The specious character of the plaintiffs-appellants' argument of procedural irregularity is highlighted by their filing of a notice of appeal. In this litigation originally the court's order merely dismissed the complaint and no final judgment was entered. As noted in the margin this case is presently before us for the second time. When the order dismissing the complaint was entered in the district court, under Rule 15(a), Fed.R.Civ.P., as construed by this court, the plaintiffs would have had an absolute right to file an amended complaint embodying the claimed theory that a public street was part of the defendant's premises. By appealing, the plaintiffs-appellants elected to stand on their original complaint and thereby relinquished the legal theory they now assert. It is clear that the district court completely determined that the plaintiffs-appellants had no right of action for a criminal attack in a public street. That was the issue framed by the pleadings, and the court's summary of the allegations of the complaint was not a determination of fact but merely a narrative recital of the pleaded facts bearing upon the issue of A & K's duty.

Finally, and in any event, it appears to us that despite the flexibility which has been accorded by the cases to the term "premises," the proper view is that surrounding streets and sidewalks are beyond the meaning of the term. The underlying rationale appears to lie in the fact that there is no right of control over the public thoroughfare.

II. DUTY TO PROTECT AGAINST CRIMINAL ACTS
OF THIRD PERSONS ON A PUBLIC STREET

Under Illinois law, a complaint must allege the breach of a duty owed by the defendant to the plaintiff in order to state a cause of action for negligence. The existence of a duty is a question of law to be determined by the court. Our answer to the question posed by the complaint must be based on Illinois state law. Inasmuch as both parties agree that there are no Illinois cases "on all fours" with the present case, we must decide the case as we believe the Illinois courts would. And we must give some deference to a district judge's interpretation of the law of the state where he sits unless his legal determination is clearly wrong or unreasonable.

Our task in the instant case is precise and clear. A & K concedes that under Neering v. Illinois Central R. R. Co., 383 Ill. 366, 50 N.E.2d 497 (1943), an owner or occupier of land in Illinois owes a duty to invitees *on his premises* reasonably to guard against criminal acts of third parties when knowledge of previous incidents or circumstances charges him with knowledge of this danger. Similarly, the Mitchells rely upon *Neering* and its progeny as supporting the proposition that the

Illinois cases clearly establish that where the defendant-invitor has knowledge of previous criminal acts, the defendant becomes charged with the responsibility to protect its invitees from other illegal acts. Accordingly, we must begin with this leading Illinois case regarding a landowner's duty to protect against the criminal acts of third parties and trace the subsequent Illinois reading of its underlying rationale. If A & K had no duty under the circumstances disclosed in the complaint, the district court's order must be affirmed. If A & K was under a duty to the Mitchells, the court's order must be reversed.

[The court examined the Illinois decisions in the *Neering* line and concluded that later decisions had limited liability in accordance with the principles set out by the American Law Institute in its Restatement (Second) of Torts.]

In this appeal, A & K's basic contention is that under Illinois law it owed no duty to the plaintiffs-appellants under the facts stated in the complaint. The Mitchells contend that A & K had certain duties because the Illinois courts have recognized the views stated in the Restatement (Second) of Torts. For purposes of this appeal, it is conceded that Lawrence Mitchell was an invitee. * * * Thus, the Illinois courts would presumably determine that Restatement (Second) of Torts § 344 controls.[10]

That formulation of the liability rule clearly precludes any possibility of A & K's legal responsibility. A possessor of land is subject to liability to business invitees "while they are upon the land." In the present case, the Mitchells were parked upon a public thoroughfare. It is true that A & K would not have endured much inconvenience by warning the Mitchells that there was the possibility of an armed robbery in that area of Fulton Street. Our task, however, is not to measure the moral blame or worth of A & K. The Illinois cases have retreated from the broad view of tort liability espoused in *Neering* by accepting the liability rules formulated by the American Law Institute. Because the clear wording of the appropriate section denies the business proprietor's liability, we fulfill our adjudicative function by adhering to its formulation.

[The court concluded that "it is clear that A & K had no duty to the Mitchells," and affirmed the dismissal.]

---

10. Restatement (Second) of Torts § 344 provides:

Business Premises Open to Public: Acts of Third Persons or Animals

A possessor of land who holds it open to the public for entry for his business purposes is subject to liability to members of the public *while they are upon the land* for such a purpose, for physical harm caused by the accidental, negligent, or intentionally harmful acts of third persons or animals, and by the failure of the possessor to exercise reasonable care to

(a) discover that such acts are being done or are likely to be done, or

(b) give a warning adequate to enable the visitors to avoid the harm, or otherwise to protect them against it. [Emphasis supplied.]

FAIRCHILD, CHIEF JUDGE, dissenting.

The crucial question involved in this case is whether, under Illinois law, and accepting the averments of the complaint as true, defendant owed plaintiff any duty which was breached. I have no quarrel with the general proposition adopted by the majority that no duty is owed to protect against criminal acts of third persons on a public street. However, I do not believe this proposition fits the facts of this case. Plaintiff alleged that defendant ordered him to remain in his truck and park it on a street when defendant knew or should have known that plaintiff would be in danger of criminal attack. Plaintiff followed defendant's instructions and was subsequently shot in the face. In my view, this affirmative conduct of defendant greatly increased the risk of harm to plaintiff, thus creating a duty on defendant to warn plaintiff of the danger or to direct plaintiff to a place of safety until the delivery could be made.

The principle that affirmative conduct by an actor can create a duty to exercise reasonable care is recognized in the Restatement (Second) of Torts, § 302B, Comment e, which provides in relevant part:

> There are, however, situations in which the actor, as a reasonable man, is required to anticipate and guard against the intentional, or even criminal, misconduct of others. In general, these situations arise where the actor is under a special responsibility toward the one who suffers the harm, which includes the duty to protect him against such intentional misconduct; *or where the actor's own affirmative act has created or exposed the other to a recognizable high degree of risk of harm through such misconduct, which a reasonable man would take into account.* (Emphasis added.)

I conclude that Illinois courts would follow the position of the Restatement and find a duty owed by defendant to plaintiff under the facts of this case.

Notes and Questions

1. Would plaintiff's complaint have been subject to dismissal if it had merely alleged that plaintiff was "on the premises" at the time the incident occurred?

(a) Could plaintiff's lawyer have made such an allegation in compliance with Rule 11 after learning where plaintiff was actually parked? In view of the flexible interpretation of the term "premises" under Illinois law, would the lawyer have had a valid argument for the extension of existing law? If so, would the lawyer's failure to include the specifics in the complaint reflect on his *bona fides* in making the argument? See supra p. 153 n. 4(c).

Suppose plaintiff had visited another lawyer who refused to take the case because plaintiff was not parked in the driveway. If plaintiff told the second lawyer that he was parked in the driveway, should that lawyer have investigated further before filing suit? Consider Schuchman, Relations Between Lawyers, in Ethics and Advocacy 79 (1978): "I have no compunctions in requiring more investigation when a large business firm or governmental agency is the client and an ordinary individual or small business firm is the other party. Such clients should have a greater burden to justify the lawyer's belief in the truth of the factual allegations of the complaint or answer."

(b) Assuming plaintiff could stave off dismissal in good faith by alleging merely that he was "on the premises," why would he want to do so? Might he be hopeful that his claim for an extension of the law will be more attractive once he has obtained added facts through discovery? Might it be that he hopes by prolonging the litigation to prompt a "nuisance settlement" from defendants?

(c) If plaintiff merely alleged that he was "on the premises," could defendant support its Rule 12(b)(6) motion with an affidavit establishing where plaintiff was actually parked? See the last sentence of Rule 12(b). Could defendant move for a more definite statement requiring plaintiff to specify where he claims he was parked at the time of the attack?

2. Note that plaintiff was granted leave to amend but, as the appellate court notes, chose to "stand on his complaint." Ordinarily, federal courts will, in granting a motion to dismiss for failure to state a claim, also grant plaintiff leave to amend at least once to try to cure the defect that prompted the dismissal. By this means, the court also tries to assure itself that it will not, as Conley v. Gibson, supra pp. 132–33, forbids, dismiss cases where plaintiff could prove facts that support relief.

3. Is the dismissal in Mitchell v. Archibald & Kendall consistent with Conley v. Gibson? Could the substantive law be accurately applied on the basis of the allegations of the complaint? Is the application of the law similarly possible where the fact pattern is more complicated?

4. If judges allow bare-bones pleading, won't plaintiffs always avoid specificity? If the lawyers include more details, they may risk dismissal; some courts are puzzled that they do anyway. See Jackson v. Marion County, 66 F.3d 151, 154 (7th Cir.1995) ("If plaintiff's lawyers want to live dangerously—or want to find out sooner rather than later whether they have a claim— they can."). Could plaintiffs ever choose this course on purpose? Consider the following ideas:

> The willingness to "live dangerously" may, however, demonstrate counsel's rationality. At least some plaintiffs' attorneys will not wish to fly blind into massive discovery without knowing whether the court would sustain a claim on their version of events. * * * [I]n a number of instances the prospective cost of discovery might prompt counsel to prefer an early ruling on whether their legal theory will satisfy the judge. Recent data indicating the discovery often costs plaintiffs (or their lawyers) as much as it costs defendants suggest a reason for counsel to want an early resolution of the threshold question in a number of cases. Coupled with the possible value in advancing their own cases through precise pleading, this urge could explain why plaintiffs in some cases set forth detail even if they are not required to do so.

Marcus, The Puzzling Persistence of Pleading Practice, 76 Texas L. Rev. 1749, 1769 (1998).

4. *Heightened Requirements for Specificity*

ROSS v. A. H. ROBINS COMPANY

United States Court of Appeals, Second Circuit, 1979.
607 F.2d 545, cert. denied, 446 U.S. 946, 100 S.Ct. 2175, 64 L.Ed.2d 802 (1980).

Before MANSFIELD and GURFEIN, CIRCUIT JUDGES, and MISHLER, DISTRICT JUDGE.

MISHLER, DISTRICT JUDGE.

This is an appeal from an order of the United States District Court for the Southern District of New York, Pierce, J., dismissing plaintiffs' proposed class action. Plaintiffs, Kalman and Anita Ross, allege that on July 23, 1973 they purchased 100 shares of common stock of the defendant company, A. H. Robins Company, Inc., ("Robins"), a manufacturer and distributor of pharmaceutical products. They instituted this action pursuant to § 10(b) of the Securities Exchange Act of 1934, 15 U.S.C. § 78j,[a] Rule 10b–5, promulgated thereunder, 17 C.F.R. § 240.10b–5[b] and common law principles, on behalf of all persons who purchased such stock "from April 1972 through in or about July, 1974 . . . and who still owned shares of Robins at the end of said period and who have suffered damages as a result thereof." In addition to Robins, also named as defendants are seven individuals who are identified as directors and/or officers of Robins.

* * *

The gist of plaintiffs' claim is contained in paragraph 13:

> Since sometime in or about April 1972 and continuing in or about July, 1974, Robins and the individual defendants herein have engaged in a scheme and plan and continuous course of conduct to deceive the investing public, including plaintiffs, as to the true financial condition and prospects of Robins, particularly with respect to matters concerning the Dalkon Shield, and to conceal from the

a. 10(b) provides:

It shall be unlawful for any person, directly or indirectly, by the use of any means or instrumentality of interstate commerce or of the mails, or of any facility of any national securities exchange
* * *

(b) To use or employ, in connection with the purchase or sale of any security registered on a national securities exchange or any security not so registered, any manipulative or deceptive device or contrivance in contravention of such rules and regulations as the Commission may prescribe as necessary or appropriate in the public interest or for the protection of investors.—Eds.

b. Rule 10b–5 provides:

It shall be unlawful for any person, directly or indirectly, by the use of any means or instrumentality of interstate commerce, or of the mails or of any facility of any national securities exchange,

(a) To employ any device, scheme or artifice to defraud,

(b) To make any untrue statement of a material fact or to omit to state a material fact necessary in order to make the statements made, in the light of the circumstances under which they were made, not misleading, or

(c) To engage in any act, practice or course of business which operates or would operate as a fraud or deceit upon any person, in connection with the purchase or sale of any security.—Eds.

investing public, including plaintiffs, facts, among other things, concerning the safety and efficiency of the Dalkon Shield and the effect of such upon Robins' operating and financial condition.

According to paragraph 14:

Prior to the commencement of the class period, Robins with approval of its Board of Directors which consisted of defendant Robins, Robins, Jr., Roberts, Saltzman and Shumate, prepared, issued and disseminated statements to the investing public high-lighting developments with regard to the Dalkon Shield and publicizing its significant impact upon the business affairs of Robins. Said statements also stressed the safety, reliability and efficiency of the Dalkon Shield, particularly with regard to Robins' testing procedures and practices.

These statements are quoted at length and identified as appearing in Robins' 1970 Annual Report, 1971 Annual Report and a prospectus issued in or about March 1972.

Paragraph 18 is of crucial importance. It charges that

[d]uring the class period, Robins and the individual defendants knew or recklessly disregarded the fact that there were serious questions as to the safety and efficiency of the Dalkon Shield....

Specifically, it alleges that "among other things" the "defendants knew or recklessly disregarded," *inter alia,* the "facts" that the pregnancy rate from use of the shield "was significantly higher than the low pregnancy rate Robins had indicated in [its] 1970 Annual Report ...," and that "the rate of medical removals of the shield required by manifestations of pain, bleeding and infection was significantly higher than ... indicated in the 1970 Annual Report...." These facts were evidenced by data "found in an updated April 1972 unpublished study on the Shield by Mary Gabrielson...." Paragraph 18 further states the defendants knew or recklessly disregarded the fact that: their conclusions about the shield's safety and effectiveness were based on insufficient data; that in 1972 and 1973 there was an "alarming increase" in the rate of septic abortions and deaths resulting from the shield; and that other "significant health hazards" existed.

Paragraph 20 states that the defendants "failed to make proper and timely disclosure" of these facts and the fact that "Robins was incurring substantial risks to its reputation ... and substantial risks of substantial liability for injuries from use of the Dalkon Shield."

The complaint also charges that "during the class period" further misleading statements "were made and issued with the knowledge, approval and/or acquiescence of Robins' Board of Directors which consisted at all relevant times of the individual defendants." These statements, language of which is quoted, were allegedly contained in: Robins' 10–K forms for the fiscal years ending December 1972 and December 1973; a press release issued April 19, 1973; press releases dated July 18, 1973, January 31, 1974 and April 18, 1974; and Robins' 1973 Annual

Report issued in March 1974. In plaintiffs' view, these statements were misleading in that they continued to speak glowingly of the company and of continued expectations of success and did not disclose the serious problems concerning Robins' continued sale and distribution of the Dalkon Shield.

The named plaintiffs and members of the putative class allegedly "made their purchases of Robins' common stock at prices that were inflated by [these] misleading public reports and press releases and the representations contained therein and by defendants' failure to disclose ... adverse matter...."

Sometime beginning in or about the middle of May 1974, information about the serious medical problems which were resulting from use of the Dalkon Shield began to be disclosed to the public. As a consequence of this, of resulting investigations by the Food and Drug Administration, and the Department of Health, Education and Welfare, and the institution of over 500 product liability suits, "Robins' reputation and position in its industry have been jeopardized and its business prospects adversely affected." The value of its common stock "dropped from approximately $19 to $13 per share on the New York Stock Exchange."

The defendants' conduct is alleged to have violated § 10(b) and Rule 10b–5.[7] Specifically, it is stated that the "defendants had a duty to disclose [adverse] information [about the Dalkon Shield] in order to correct the false and misleading impression created by [their earlier] statements...."

[The district court granted defendants' motion to dismiss on the ground that the complaint did not comply with Fed.R.Civ.P. 9(b).]

Rule 9 (b)

* * *

[Rule 9(b)] "is a special pleading requirement and contrary to the general approach of simplified pleading adopted by the federal rules," 5 Wright & Miller, Federal Practice and Procedure: Civil § 1297 at 405, [which] generally serves two important purposes. First, it assures the defendant of " 'fair notice of what the plaintiff's claim is and the grounds upon which it rests.' " Denny v. Barber, 576 F.2d 465, 469 (2d Cir.1978). Secondly, the specificity requirement grows out of "the desire to protect defendants from the harm that comes to their reputations or to their goodwill when they are charged with serious wrongdoing...." Segal v. Gordon, 467 F.2d 602, 607 (2d Cir.1972). In the context of securities litigation Rule 9(b) serves an additional important purpose. It operates to diminish the possibility that " 'a plaintiff with a largely

---

7. Plaintiffs charge, in language almost identical to that of Rule 10b–5, that the defendants:

    (a) employed devices, schemes and artifices to defraud, (b) made untrue statements of material facts or omitted to state material facts necessary in order to make statements made, in light of the circumstances under which they were made, not misleading, or (c) engaged in acts, practices and a course of business that operated as a fraud or deceit upon plaintiffs and others similarly situated in connection with their purchases of Robins stock.

groundless claim [will be able] to simply take up the time of a number of other people [by extensive discovery], with the right to do so representing an *in terrorem* increment of the settlement value, rather than a reasonably founded hope that the process will reveal relevant evidence....' " Denny v. Barber, supra, 576 F.2d at 470 (quoting Blue Chip Stamps v. Manor Drug Stores, 421 U.S. 723, 741, 95 S.Ct. 1917, 1928, 44 L.Ed.2d 539 (1975)).[20]

* * *

[A] plaintiff alleging fraud in connection with a securities transaction must specifically allege the acts or omissions upon which his claim rests. It will not do merely to track the language of Rule 10b–5 and rely on such meaningless phrases as "scheme and conspiracy" or "plan and scheme and course of conduct to deceive." A defendant is entitled to a reasonable opportunity to answer the complaint and must be given adequate information to frame a response.

There is no question that the plaintiffs in this instance adequately identified the alleged "misrepresentations." They point to the following specific documents: 1970 Annual Report; 1971 Annual Report; prospectus issued in or about March 1972; press release issued on or about April 19, 1973; press release issued July 18, 1973; press release dated January 31, 1974; 1973 Annual Report; and finally a press release dated April 18, 1974. However, we believe that the pleading is deficient in other important respects.

The complaint alleges only in a most sketchy fashion circumstances which would give rise to an inference of fraud. The complaint sets forth numerous facts which, it is alleged, indicate that "there were serious questions as to the safety and efficiency of the Dalkon Shield...." Some, but not all, of these facts are alleged to have been contained in a 1972 unpublished report on the Dalkon Shield prepared by a Mary Gabrielson. It is not indicated what relationship, if any, exists between Mary Gabrielson and Robins, or whether plaintiffs have any reason to believe that the defendants were even aware of the report's existence. Plaintiffs also indicate that the defendants' knowledge of the facts contained in paragraph 18 is evidenced by "among other things" the 1972 unpublished report. Plaintiffs should indicate whether they are relying solely on the study or have other reasons to believe that the defendants had knowledge of facts raising serious questions about the efficiency of the Dalkon Shield. Additionally, knowledge of many of the facts alleged in paragraph 18, e.g., the number of deaths, septic abortions and other

---

20. Of course, Rule 9(b) cannot be viewed in vacuo.

The requirement of particularity does not abrogate Rule 8, and it should be harmonized with the general directives ... of Rule 8 that the pleadings should contain a "short and plain" statement of the claim or defense and with each averment should be "simple, concise and direct." Rule 9(b) does not require nor make legitimate the pleading of detailed evidentiary matter. The Second Circuit has very recently expressed this same view that "F.R.Civ.P. 9(b) must be reconciled with F. R. Civ. P. 8(a)(2)...."

Denny v. Barber, supra, 576 F.2d at 467.

complications resulting from the Dalkon Shield in 1972–1973, is in no way attributed to the defendants.

Plaintiffs have also failed to indicate when the defendants allegedly came into possession of this crucial information. No one disputes that the defendants eventually became aware of major safety problems involving their product. The facts alleged in paragraph 34—that by letter dated May 8, 1974 Robins informed approximately 120,000 physicians nationwide that severe complications including death had resulted in instances where the Dalkon Shield remained in place during pregnancy—do give rise to the inference that by 1974 officials at Robins were aware that major medical problems existed. However, it is only if the defendants' knowledge of various problems with the Dalkon Shield coalesced into a duty to disclose prior to July 1973 (the time when the named plaintiffs bought stock in Robins) that the action can be prosecuted as a class action by these named plaintiffs. We believe that it is proper to require the plaintiffs, even at the pleading stage, to fix more definitively the time at which these crucial events in the complaint occurred.

As indicated above, although Rule 9(b) requires that "circumstances constituting fraud ... shall be stated with particularity" it provides that "[m]alice, intent, *knowledge,* and other condition of mind of a person may be averred generally." (emphasis added). Of course, defendants' awareness of the facts alleged by the plaintiffs in paragraph 18 indicating that there were serious questions about the safety and efficacy of the Dalkon Shield is central to plaintiffs' Rule 10b–5 claim. However, at this stage of the litigation, we cannot realistically expect plaintiffs to be able to plead defendants' actual knowledge. On the other hand, plaintiffs can be required to supply a factual basis for their conclusory allegations regarding that knowledge. It is reasonable to require that the plaintiffs specifically plead those events which they assert give rise to a strong inference that the defendants had knowledge of the facts contained in paragraph 18 of the complaint or recklessly disregarded their existence. And, of course, plaintiffs must fix the time when these particular events occurred.

* * *

However, notwithstanding the deficiencies which exist in the pleading, we believe, as we indicated at the outset, that plaintiffs should be given a final chance to replead.

Notes and Questions

1. Why are there special pleading requirements for cases involving mistake and fraud? Judge Charles Clark viewed the rule as reflecting judges' habits, explaining that it "probably states only what courts would do anyhow." Clark, Simplified Pleading, 2 F.R.D. 456, 463 (1942). In *Ross,* the court offers three justifications:

(a) Notice: Certainly some fraud cases may involve more complicated transactions and numerous parties so that more detail could be important in providing notice. Is that not true of other kinds of cases? Recall United

States v. Board of Harbor Comm'rs, supra p. 134. Have plaintiffs in *Ross* provided sufficient detail for this purpose?

(b) Injury to reputation: Is fraud especially threatening to reputations? Consider the views of Judge Cardamone, dissenting from dismissal of claims brought under the Racketeer Influenced Corrupt Organizations statute (RICO):

> Today, defendants in civil suits are labelled as violators of environmental laws when pumping coal byproducts into the atmosphere, despoilers of our rivers when emptying oil from their tankers' bilges, adulterers in state divorce actions, and killers in vehicular wrongful death actions. The allegations of the civil complaint do not make these citizens criminals, although their conduct may well subject them to criminal prosecutions. Why the outcry over RICO?

Sedima, S.P.R.L. v. Imrex Co., Inc., 741 F.2d 482, 508 (2d Cir.1984). In reversing the dismissal of the case, the Supreme Court noted that "[a]s for stigma, a civil RICO proceeding leaves no greater stain than do a number of other civil proceedings." Sedima, S.P.R.L. v. Imrex Co., Inc., 473 U.S. 479, 105 S.Ct. 3275, 3283, 87 L.Ed.2d 346 (1985).

(c) Limiting *in terrorem* value of suit: In Blue Chip Stamps v. Manor Drug Stores, 421 U.S. 723, 95 S.Ct. 1917, 44 L.Ed.2d 539 (1975), the Court (dealing with an unrelated issue) warned that "in this type of litigation * * * the mere existence of an unresolved lawsuit has settlement value to the plaintiff not only because of the possibility that he may prevail on the merits, an entirely legitimate component of settlement value, but because of the threat of extensive discovery and disruption of normal business activities which may accompany a lawsuit which is groundless in any event, but cannot be proved so before trial." Are securities fraud lawsuits really different in this respect? See Ackerman v. Northwestern Mut. Life Ins. Co., 172 F.3d 467, 469 (7th Cir.1999) ("charges of fraud (and also mistake, the other charge that Rule 9(b) requires to be pleaded with particularity) frequently ask courts in effect to rewrite the parties' contract or otherwise disrupt established relationships"). In what ways are they different from the personal injury suits brought against Robins by women claiming injury due to the Dalkon Shield?

Research by Professor Alexander suggests that in securities fraud suits the merits appear to have no substantial bearing on the amount of settlements. She found that these cases are routinely settled for a relatively small consistent percentage of the prospective damages, seemingly without any emphasis on the strength of the case. She explains that a number of factors combine to cause this result—risk aversion among defendants when cases threaten a substantial portion of the company's assets or personal ruin, availability of insurance to fund settlements, and unwillingness of plaintiffs' lawyers to risk a trial (which might lead to a loss and no payment for them as opposed to a settlement) in order to assure that they will be paid for their efforts in the case. Another factor is the impossibility of obtaining a judicial decision before trial: "With adjudication before trial unavailable as a practical matter and adjudication at trial a virtually unthinkable alternative, settlement becomes a foregone conclusion." Alexander, Do the Merits Matter? A Study of Settlements in Securities Class Actions, 43 Stan.L.Rev. 497,

567 (1991); compare Seligman, The Merits Do Matter, 108 Harv.L.Rev. 438 (1994) (questioning Alexander's conclusions).

2.   How should Rule 9(b) be applied to achieve these purposes? In *Ross* the court says the complaint should identify the sources plaintiffs rely upon in concluding that defendants knew of the problems of the Dalkon Shield by 1973. Indeed, it says that this showing must provide a "strong inference" to support plaintiffs' claim that defendants knew. Compare Tomera v. Galt, 511 F.2d 504 (7th Cir.1975) (Rule 9(b) requires only "slightly more" detail than Rule 8(a)(2)); Rodi v. Southern New England School of Law, 389 F.3d 5, 15 (1st Cir.2004) (intent and knowledge may be averred in general terms). Is this the sort of detail that we have been discussing in the earlier cases in this chapter? Is the court asking plaintiffs to show that they have enough evidence to prevail at trial? Can you fashion an argument using the facts alleged that supports the required inference of fraudulent intent?

3.   How can the court's insistence on detail be squared with the second sentence of Rule 9(b)? Why was that included in the rule? Will the detail the court requires in *Ross* assist defendants in drafting their answer? Note that cases like *Ross* are now governed by the Private Securities Litigation Reform Act. See Requirements of the Private Securities Litigation Reform Act, infra p. 170.

4.   One gets the impression that the court hopes that requiring detail will be helpful in screening out lawsuits that will fail at an early point. Recall Mitchell v. W. T. Grant Co., supra p. 42, where the Court emphasized the importance of the Louisiana procedure requiring "specific facts" rather than "conclusory allegations." Will such specifics help the court make an accurate assessment of the validity of the claim? Consider what the Seventh Circuit said in another context: "Even the most specific allegations do not establish probable cause unless they are reliable. We are, to say the least, perplexed as to how a court might undertake such evaluations of reliability in deciding a motion to dismiss under Rule 12." Haroco, Inc. v. American Nat. Bank and Trust Co., 747 F.2d 384, 404 (7th Cir.1984), affirmed on other grounds, 473 U.S. 606, 105 S.Ct. 3291, 87 L.Ed.2d 437 (1985).

5.   If the basic goal is to ensure that plaintiff has done an investigation and has a legitimate basis for the charges, why doesn't Rule 11 adequately serve that purpose? In the Private Securities Litigation Reform Act (PSLRA) (see infra pp. 170–73), Congress indicated that it was not satisfied with that reassurance and also sought to undo some of the changes to Rule 11 effected by the 1993 amendments to the rule. Accordingly, the PSLRA requires the court to make findings about compliance with Rule 11(b) in every case and to impose sanctions on any party or attorney found to have violated the rule. 15 U.S.C.A. § 78u–4(c). This change "eliminates the [Rule 11 (c)(1)] safe harbor for federal securities litigation." Smith v. Smith, 184 F.R.D. 420, 422 (S.D.Fla.1998).

6.   Could the insistence on detail undermine the substantive law by impeding prosecution of meritorious claims? Consider Friedenthal, A Divided Supreme Court Adopts Discovery Amendments to the Federal Rules of Civil Procedure, 69 Calif.L.Rev. 806, 815–16 (1981): "It is always to a defendant's advantage to require the plaintiff to pinpoint its case specifically and in detail. First, if the case is based primarily on speculation, the plaintiff may be unable to allege sufficient facts to sustain the complaint and the action

can be dismissed immediately. Second, even if the complaint is sufficient, it necessarily narrows the range of facts that the plaintiff will be allowed to discover and to prove at trial. If plaintiff's attorney has erred at the pleading stage as to the specific facts by which a valid case for his client could be established, defendant can thwart successful prosecution of the action by keeping out vital facts on the ground that they were not pleaded and, hence, are not relevant."

7. The appellate court in *Ross* remands to give plaintiffs another try at pleading a claim. Evidently they did, since the case was still pending several years later. See Ross v. A.H. Robins, [1982–83 Transfer Binder] Fed.Sec. L.Rep. (CCH) ¶ 99,095 (S.D.N.Y.1983). Does this indicate that the motion proceedings in *Ross* were an example of what Charles Clark called "judicial haste which in the long run makes waste"? Dioguardi v. Durning, supra p. 132.

8. As a further postscript to *Ross:* It should be noted that in 1984 Robins filed for protection under Chapter 11 of the federal Bankruptcy Act. In addition, it has been reported that during the period in question in the suit Robins used information from Mary Gabrielson in publicity designed to assuage doubts about the safety of the Dalkon Shield. See S. Engelmayer & R. Wagman, Lord's Justice 48–50 (1985).

9. For arguments that Rule 9(b) should be abandoned, see Fairman, An Invitation to the Rule-Makers—Strike Rule 9(b), 38 U.C. Davis L.Rev., 281 (2004); Richman, Lively & Mell, The Pleading of Fraud: Rhymes Without Reason, 60 So.Cal.L.Rev. 959 (1987).

REQUIREMENTS OF THE PRIVATE SECURITIES LITIGATION REFORM ACT (PSLRA)

In 1995 Congress passed the Private Securities Litigation Reform Act. The Act did not change Rule 9(b), but did prescribe pleading requirements for federal securities fraud actions like Ross v. A.H. Robins Co., supra p. 163. 15 U.S.C.A. § 78u–4(b) now provides:

(1) Misleading statements and omissions

In any private action arising under this chapter in which the plaintiff alleges that the defendant—

(A) made an untrue statement of a material fact; or

(B) omitted to state a material fact necessary in order to make the statements made, in the light of the circumstances in which they were made, not misleading;

the complaint shall specify each statement alleged to have been misleading, the reason or reasons why the statement is misleading, and, if an allegation regarding the statement or omission is made on information and belief, the complaint shall state with particularity all facts on which that belief is formed.

(2) Required state of mind

In any private action arising under this chapter in which the plaintiff may recover money damages only on proof that the defendant acted with a particular state of mind, the complaint shall, with respect to each act or omission alleged to violate this chapter, state with particularity facts giving rise to a strong inference that the defendant acted with the required state of mind.

In addition, the Act imposes a stay of discovery pending the court's ruling on a motion to dismiss under the foregoing pleading standard: "[A]ll discovery and other proceedings shall be stayed during the pendency of any motion to dismiss, unless the court finds upon the motion of any party that particularized discovery is necessary to preserve evidence or to prevent undue prejudice to that party." 15 U.S.C.A. § 78u–4(b)(3)(B). In 1998, Congress added authority for federal courts to stay discovery proceedings in state court cases where that discovery might "circumvent" the discovery stay in federal court. 15 U.S.C.A. § 78u–4(b)(3)(D). The lower courts have generally applied this discovery stay vigorously. See, e.g., SG Cowen Securities Corp. v. U.S. Dist. Ct., 189 F.3d 909 (9th Cir.1999) (district court may not permit discovery that will enable plaintiffs to uncover facts sufficient to satisfy the Act's pleading requirements); Medhekar v. U.S. District Court, 99 F.3d 325 (9th Cir.1996) (discovery stay applies to initial disclosure under Fed. R.Civ.P. 26(a)(1) as well as to formal discovery). In some instances, however, lower courts have allowed limited discovery before ruling on motions to dismiss. See, e.g., In re WorldCom, Inc. Securities Litigation, 234 F.Supp.2d 301 (S.D.N.Y.2002) (plaintiffs could obtain copies of documents previously provided to public agencies in related proceedings); de la Fuente v. DCI Telecommunications, Inc., 206 F.R.D. 369 (S.D.N.Y.2002) (plaintiffs could have discovery to respond to defendants' motion for summary judgment even though the stay had applied to defendants' motion to dismiss).

As you can see, the Act's pleading standard—relying on a "strong inference" of knowledge—resembles the Second Circuit's standard in *Ross*. That resemblance is no accident; the Act was at least partly modeled on the Second Circuit standard. But in applying the Act's pleading requirements "[c]ourts have split sharply over precisely what the 'strong inference' portion of the standard requires. Some courts have suggested that the PSLRA does nothing more than codify the pre-PSLRA Second Circuit standard." Perino, Did the Private Securities Litigation Reform Act Work?, 2003 U. Ill. L. Rev. 913, 926. The Second Circuit has concluded that the Act adopted its standard, and that its caselaw therefore continues to apply. See, e.g., Novak v. Kasaks, 216 F.3d 300 (2d Cir.2000). But the Ninth Circuit, while recognizing that the "strong inference" language is "taken directly" from the Second Circuit cases, had held that the Act requires more detailed pleading. In re Silicon Graphics, Inc. Securities Litigation, 183 F.3d 970 (9th Cir.1999). A particular bone of contention is whether anonymous sources must be named in the complaint; the Second Circuit says no and the Ninth Circuit says yes. For a detailed examination of the caselaw on the application of the Act's pleading requirements, see 2 H. Bloomenthal,

Securities Law Handbook § 29 (2004 ed.) (providing over 140 pages of analysis of the interpretation of the Act's pleading standards).

Detailed analysis of the PSLRA pleading standards, which depends in part on application of substantive provisions elsewhere in the Act, is beyond the scope of this book. But you should be aware that the Act is an additional feature in the landscape of securities fraud cases like Ross v. A.H. Robins.

Notes and Questions

1. Recall the arguments for more stringent pleading that the court reviewed in *Ross*, discussed supra p. 167 n.1. Does the PSLRA seem to be an effective way of dealing with those issues?

2. Filing a motion to dismiss produces an automatic discovery stay. Would that be likely to prompt defendants to move to dismiss?

3. Is the PSLRA overkill in relation to the problems that prompted calls for stricter pleading? Consider Sale, Heightened Pleading an Discovery Stays; An Analysis of the Effect of the PSLRA's Internal–Information Standard on '33 and '34 Act Claims, 76 Wash. U. L. Rev. 537, 564 (1998):

> [T]he Reform Act is likely to allow only the more flagrant and obvious cases of securities fraud to proceed past a motion to dismiss, while being overinclusive in its elimination of cases where it is more difficult to identify, and therefore to plead, fraud. Presumably, the SEC, with its limited resources, pursues the flagrant and obvious cases of securities fraud. Arguably, however, the more difficult to identify frauds are precisely the ones that the plaintiffs, who function as private attorneys general, pursue. Indeed, the Commissioner of the SEC has stressed that private mechanisms are important to the enforcement of the Acts. Because the plaintiffs lack access to the information the Reform Act requires them to plead at the motion-to-dismiss stage, however, the strict application of the heightened-pleading standard is likely to result in unredressed fraud.

In Lipton v. Pathogenesis Corp., 284 F.3d 1027 (9th Cir.2002), plaintiffs sued on behalf of a class of purchasers of defendant's stock during a two-month period after company officials had announced that they foresaw growth in sales of a new product. These announcements followed an upsurge in sales of this product after the company announced a price increase that wholesalers could avoid by placing orders immediately, prompting a substantial increase in orders before the price increase. Plaintiffs alleged that defendant knew by the time the positive statements were made that retail demand for this new product had reached a plateau, and that it had nonetheless touted the misleading results from the period when orders were placed to avoid the price increase. In addition, plaintiffs alleged that defendant's CEO had, for the first time, begun selling his stock, suggesting that he realized the stock was overvalued. Finally, plaintiffs claimed that defendant wanted to impress lenders with reports of strong sales to obtain financial backing. The court of appeals affirmed dismissal of the complaint. Plaintiffs did not provide specifics on the internal reports they claimed showed that sales were leveling off, and the CEO's sales of stock totalled only 1.4% of his overall holdings. The allegation that the company wanted to obtain favorable financing did not suffice either, since that was a routine business objective that could not, standing alone, serve as a motivation for fraud.

Contrast Nursing Home Pension Fund v. Oracle Corp., 380 F.3d 1226 (9th Cir.2004), which reversed a dismissal. Plaintiffs alleged that Oracle continued to make positive statements about sales of a new computer program even though it knew of problems with application of the program and the general slowdown of the economy. Two months after these statements, Oracle announced reduced revenues and earnings for the period, and the stock price fell. The court noted that "[t]he most direct way to show * * * that the party making the statement knew that it was false is via contemporaneous reports of data, available to the party, which contradict the statement." Because Oracle officials had claimed that they could instantaneously determine sales levels, the court found the allegation that defendants knew of the reduced sales persuasive. Defendant Larry Ellison, the CEO of Oracle, had said at the time that the company could instantly determine how much it had sold. In addition, Ellison, who had sold none of his own stock for the previous five years, sold $900 million worth before the announcement of the unfavorable results, and another high official sold $30 million worth. Even though Ellison's sale represented only 2.7% of his holdings, the court treated it as significant. Finally, the court credited plaintiffs' allegations that Oracle had used improper accounting procedures during the period that tended to inflate its apparent earnings because the complaint identified the witnesses with sufficient particularity to show that they were in a position to know Oracle's accounting practices. Although plaintiffs' allegations did not, taken separately, create a strong inference of scienter, "the totality of the allegations does create a strong inference that Oracle acted with scienter."

4. Could the Act increase the settlement value of some securities fraud suits? Consider Cox, Making Securities Fraud Class Actions Virtuous, 39 Ariz. L. Rev. 497, 520 (1997):

> Though lax pleading requirements made the nuisance value of a suit much more difficult to address through pretrial motions, it must also be understood that the Reform Act's heightened pleading standard credentials suits that survive pretrial motions so that [they] will have a greater settlement value than such suits had on average before the Reform Act. * * * [C]ounsel should feel more confident in the case after satisfying the new pleading requirements than the counsel who had previously had to know less and plead less to withstand a challenge to the pleadings.

CASH ENERGY, INC. v. WEINER

United States District Court, District of Massachusetts, 1991.
768 F.Supp. 892.

KEETON, DISTRICT JUDGE.

This case concerns the alleged environmental contamination of a property in North Andover, Massachusetts, owned and developed by plaintiffs. Over a period of years, defendant corporations engaged in the storage and/or transfer of chemical solvents on a site adjacent to plaintiffs' property.

[Plaintiffs sought to recover cleanup costs, which can be very substantial, under the Comprehensive Environmental Response, Compensation, and Liability Act, 42 U.S.C. § 9607 (CERCLA) from the defendant corporations. Plaintiffs also sued four individuals who were officers of these corporations, alleging in a single paragraph of the complaint that "at all relevant times" these four "actually participated in and exercised control over the affairs of one or more" of the corporate defendants. The individual defendants moved to dismiss for failure to state a claim, arguing that these allegations were insufficient to state claims against them.

Noting that ordinarily corporate officers are not personally liable for acts of their corporate employers, the judge concluded that in order to prevail against the individual defendants plaintiffs must show "not simply active participation in the 'affairs' of the corporations, but that each participated in the relevant tortious affair (release of toxic material), and that the conduct of each constituted a 'legal cause' of the harm of which plaintiffs are complaining."]

[M]ost fundamentally, plaintiffs' complaint rests heavily on "bald assertion." Plaintiffs fail utterly to state or outline the facts beneath their allegations that individual defendants participated in and exerted control over the contamination of the North Andover site. In response to defendants' criticism that the complaint rests on bald assertion, plaintiffs point to the modest pleading requirements of the Federal Rules. This response touches on a basic tension among federal pleading rules—a tension that bears further examination.

Breaking sharply from the earlier practice of fact pleading, the Federal Rules of Civil Procedure, effective in 1938, embody a principle of summary pleading. The "short and plain statement of facts" prescribed in Rule 8(a) has been interpreted to require only "that the plaintiffs give the defendant[s] fair notice of what the plaintiff[s'] claim is and the grounds upon which it rests." Conley v. Gibson, 355 U.S. 41, 47, 78 S.Ct. 99, 103, 2 L.Ed.2d 80 (1957). And the generous policy of amendment mandated by Rule 15 further promotes the aim that disputes be decided on the merits.

Even within the Federal Rules, however, the seeds of a countervailing tendency are sown. First, Rule 9(b) explicitly recognizes an exception for allegations of fraud and mistake, where a higher standard of particularity is required. Second, Rule 8(f), stating that all pleadings shall be construed so as to do "substantial justice," may be read as requiring judges to exercise some degree of discretion rather than invariably applying the general rule of notice pleading. Third, the Rules provide for a "motion for more definite statement" as a formal method of challenging a pleading that is "so vague or ambiguous that a party cannot reasonably be required to frame a responsive pleading." Fed.R.Civ.P. 12(e). This Rule authorizes the court, upon failure to obey its order for a more definite statement, to "strike the pleading to which the motion was directed or make such order as it deems just." This Rule has been invoked infrequently. More often, a court concluding that a complaint fails particularity requirements either enters an interlocutory order dismissing the complaint, but allowing leave to amend within a specified time, or allows leave to amend and defers ruling on the motion to dismiss. Either type of order has an effect closely analogous to that of an order pursuant to Rule 12(e) that unless a more definite statement is filed within a specific time a further appropriate order will be entered. If a complaint were stricken because of noncompliance with an order for more definite statement, dismissal would be an obvious possibility.

Rule 9(b) requires more than the statement of a mere conclusion that the plaintiff has satisfied the elements of a given claim. Beneath the higher particularity requirement, here as elsewhere, rests a concern about abusive use of legal processes. The rule "operates to diminish the possibility that 'a plaintiff with a largely groundless claim [will be able] to simply take up the time of a number of other people [by extensive discovery], with the right to do so representing an in terrorem increment of the settlement value, rather than a reasonably founded hope that the process will reveal relevant evidence. . . .' " Ross v. A.H. Robins Co., 607 F.2d 545 (2d Cir.1979) (quoting Blue Chip Stamps v. Manor Drug Stores, 421 U.S. 723, 741, 95 S.Ct. 1917, 1928, 44 L.Ed.2d 539 (1975)).

Over time, the exception for fraud has been extended to a number of analogous areas involving statutory causes of action, where the original concern about opportunities for abuse inherent in the freedom to plead conclusions rather than facts applies with like force. * * * But it was in the area of civil rights that courts first systematically developed requirements for particularity, or "specificity," a term also used with no apparent suggestion of different meaning.

Apart from the fraud exception prescribed in Rule 9(b), the most frequently occurring context in which specificity of pleading requirements are imposed remains civil rights litigation. This development was well under way before courts or commentators paid much, if any, attention to the tension between Rule 8 and the specificity requirements that precedents were developing in civil rights cases. Though Rule 8(f)'s call for construing pleading rules to achieve "substantial justice" and Rule 12(e)'s provisions regarding motions for more definite statement might have been thought to support these decisions, opinions were not reasoned on this ground.

As claims under 42 U.S.C. § 1983 began to be presented in significant volume, increasingly distinctive requirements of specificity of pleading appeared in circuit court opinions. This development may be understood as the response of the court system to the large percentage of wholly unfounded claims that came into the system as excess baggage along with claims that were meritorious, and claims that were genuinely disputable and thus appropriate for full adjudication.

The trend toward the requirement of higher standards of particularity has accelerated in recent years. Two reasons are apparent. First, the rising cost of litigation has made threats of false claims on the one hand,

and false defenses on the other, more powerful weapons of intimidation. This tendency increases both the temptation for parties and their attorneys to wield the weapon and the resulting harm to other parties when the temptation proves irresistible. Second, given the worsening caseload crisis in the federal courts, every additional frivolous claim or defense impairs the quality of justice in the system as a whole.

The most widely accepted extension of the Rule 9(b) exception by analogy is to areas of securities law other than those regulated by Rule 9(b) itself.

It is but a short leap from securities litigation to claims under the Racketeer Influenced and Corrupt Organizations Act ("RICO"), where mail and wire fraud may constitute predicate acts. Moreover, the opportunity for abusive pleading may be even greater in RICO cases, because of the severity of the remedies provided. Not surprisingly, a specificity standard appears to be developing. It should be noted, however, that some courts have allowed further discovery before dismissal where the complaint at least does allege facts sufficient to support a reasoned inference that most of the relevant evidence is uniquely within the control of the defendants.

* * *

In several areas that do not involve fraud, or even analogies to fraud by any stretch of the imagination, courts have nonetheless developed higher standards of particularity in pleading. In each of these areas, increased specificity may be seen to promote "substantial justice."

Some of these areas have been identified as appropriate for a strict standard of particularity of pleading because of a heightened "concern for due process which arises by reason of the 'drastic nature' of the remedies" sought. United States v. Pole No. 3172, 852 F.2d 636, 638 (1st Cir.1988) (forfeiture of property bought with proceeds from drug trafficking).

The drastic nature of the remedy invoked may have been a reason underlying the development of a specificity standard in antitrust cases, which (like RICO cases) offer the prospect of treble damages. Another cause for concern has been the unusually high cost of antitrust litigation.
* * *

Policy concerns underlying the development of specificity standards in particular areas of the law have influenced, as well, the amendment of rules of procedure bearing upon attorney and party responsibility for representations made in pleadings and in discovery demands and responses. Amendments of Rule 11 of the Federal Rules of Civil Procedure illustrate the point. They are also relevant to the appropriate disposition of the present matter, because any amendment alleging a factual basis for a claim must, of course, be certified by the signature of a party or attorney pursuant to Rule 11.

In summary, by the fiftieth anniversary of the Federal Rules of Civil Procedure in 1988, the rules of pleading had become less generous and forgiving than they were in 1938. The trend continues. Particularity is more often demanded. Discovery is less often allowed before the pleader is required to allege at least an outline or summary of facts sufficient under the applicable substantive law to support a claim on which relief can be granted, or a defense on which judgment can be entered. * * *

Is CERCLA yet another area where a high standard of particularity will be required? Although an analogy to fraud is strained, CERCLA involves many of the circumstances that have led courts to invoke higher standards of specificity in other contexts. The consequences of individual liability for an environmental violation may be severe. Even more relevant to the present issue is the fact that defending against a non-meritorious claim—even one that upon reasonable inquiry could be determined to be patently non-meritorious—can be very expensive. The cost of establishing that a claim lacks merit is more likely to be subject to reasonable controls if some standard of specificity of pleading is enforced. I conclude that it is a reasonable prediction that higher courts, including the First Circuit, will extend specificity of pleading require-ments to CERCLA cases * * *. Unless and until guidance to the con-trary appears in legislation or precedent, I will so rule.

* * *

The claims against individual defendants * * * will be dismissed unless * * * plaintiffs file an amended complaint that pleads at least an outline or summary of the factual basis for the claims rather than mere conclusions.

SWIERKIEWICZ v. SOREMA, N.A.

Supreme Court of the United States, 2002.
534 U.S. 506, 122 S.Ct. 992, 152 L.Ed.2d 1.

Justice THOMAS delivered the opinion of the Court.

This case presents the question whether a complaint in an employ-ment discrimination lawsuit must contain specific facts establishing a prima facie case of discrimination under the framework set forth by this Court in *McDonnell Douglas Corp. v. Green,* 411 U.S. 792, 93 S.Ct. 1817, 36 L.Ed.2d 668 (1973). We hold that an employment discrimination complaint need not include such facts and instead must contain only "a short and plain statement of the claim showing that the pleader is entitled to relief." Fed. Rule Civ. Proc. 8(a)(2).

I

Petitioner Akos Swierkiewicz is a native of Hungary, who at the time of his complaint was 53 years old.[1] In April 1989, petitioner began working for respondent Sorema N. A., a reinsurance company headquar-tered in New York and principally owned and controlled by a French

---

1. Because we review here a decision granting respondent's motion to dismiss, we must accept as true all of the factual allegations contained in the complaint.

parent corporation. Petitioner was initially employed in the position of senior vice president and chief underwriting officer (CUO). Nearly six years later, François M. Chavel, respondent's Chief Executive Officer, demoted petitioner to a marketing and services position and transferred the bulk of his underwriting responsibilities to Nicholas Papadopoulo, a 32–year-old who, like Mr. Chavel, is a French national. About a year later, Mr. Chavel stated that he wanted to "energize" the underwriting department and appointed Mr. Papadopoulo as CUO. Petitioner claims that Mr. Papadopoulo had only one year of underwriting experience at the time he was promoted, and therefore was less experienced and less qualified to be CUO than he, since at that point he had 26 years of experience in the insurance industry.

Following his demotion, petitioner contends that he "was isolated by Mr. Chavel ... excluded from business decisions and meetings and denied the opportunity to reach his true potential at SOREMA." Petitioner unsuccessfully attempted to meet with Mr. Chavel to discuss his discontent. Finally, in April 1997, petitioner sent a memo to Mr. Chavel outlining his grievances and requesting a severance package. Two weeks later, respondent's general counsel presented petitioner with two options: He could either resign without a severance package or be dismissed. Mr. Chavel fired petitioner after he refused to resign.

Petitioner filed a lawsuit alleging that he had been terminated on account of his national origin in violation of Title VII of the Civil Rights Act of 1964, 42 U.S.C. § 2000e *et seq.*, and on account of his age in violation of the Age Discrimination in Employment Act of 1967 (ADEA), 29 U.S.C. § 621 *et seq.* The United States District Court for the Southern District of New York dismissed petitioner's complaint because it found that he "ha[d] not adequately alleged a prima facie case, in that he ha[d] not adequately alleged circumstances that support an inference of discrimination." The United States Court of Appeals for the Second Circuit affirmed the dismissal, relying on its settled precedent, which requires a plaintiff in an employment discrimination complaint to allege facts constituting a prima facie case of discrimination under the framework set forth by this Court in *McDonnell Douglas, supra,* at 802, 93 S.Ct. 1817. The Court of Appeals held that petitioner had failed to meet his burden because his allegations were "insufficient as a matter of law to raise an inference of discrimination." 5 Fed.Appx. 63, 65 (C.A.2 2001). We granted certiorari to resolve a split among the Courts of Appeals concerning the proper pleading standard for employment discrimination cases, and now reverse.

II

Applying Circuit precedent, the Court of Appeals required petitioner to plead a prima facie case of discrimination in order to survive respondent's motion to dismiss. In the Court of Appeals' view, petitioner was thus required to allege in his complaint: (1) membership in a protected group; (2) qualification for the job in question; (3) an adverse employment action; and (4) circumstances that support an inference of discrimination.

The prima facie case under *McDonnell Douglas*, however, is an evidentiary standard, not a pleading requirement. In *McDonnell Douglas*, this Court made clear that "[t]he critical issue before us concern[ed] the order and allocation *of proof* in a private, non-class action challenging employment discrimination." In subsequent cases, this Court has reiterated that the prima facie case relates to the employee's burden of presenting evidence that raises an inference of discrimination.

This Court has never indicated that the requirements for establishing a prima facie case under *McDonnell Douglas* also apply to the pleading standard that plaintiffs must satisfy in order to survive a motion to dismiss. For instance, we have rejected the argument that a Title VII complaint requires greater "particularity," because this would "too narrowly constric[t] the role of the pleadings." *McDonald v. Santa Fe Trail Transp. Co.*, 427 U.S. 273, 283, n. 11, 96 S.Ct. 2574, 49 L.Ed.2d 493 (1976). Consequently, the ordinary rules for assessing the sufficiency of a complaint apply.

In addition, under a notice pleading system, it is not appropriate to require a plaintiff to plead facts establishing a prima facie case because the *McDonnell Douglas* framework does not apply in every employment discrimination case. For instance, if a plaintiff is able to produce direct evidence of discrimination, he may prevail without proving all the elements of a prima facie case. See *Trans World Airlines, Inc. v. Thurston*, 469 U.S. 111, 121, 105 S.Ct. 613, 83 L.Ed.2d 523 (1985) ("[T]he *McDonnell Douglas* test is inapplicable where the plaintiff presents direct evidence of discrimination"). Under the Second Circuit's heightened pleading standard, a plaintiff without direct evidence of discrimination at the time of his complaint must plead a prima facie case of discrimination, even though discovery might uncover such direct evidence. It thus seems incongruous to require a plaintiff, in order to survive a motion to dismiss, to plead more facts than he may ultimately need to prove to succeed on the merits if direct evidence of discrimination is discovered.

Moreover, the precise requirements of a prima facie case can vary depending on the context and were "never intended to be rigid, mechanized, or ritualistic." Before discovery has unearthed relevant facts and evidence, it may be difficult to define the precise formulation of the required prima facie case in a particular case. Given that the prima facie case operates as a flexible evidentiary standard, it should not be transposed into a rigid pleading standard for discrimination cases.

Furthermore, imposing the Court of Appeals' heightened pleading standard in employment discrimination cases conflicts with Federal Rule of Civil Procedure 8(a)(2), which provides that a complaint must include only "a short and plain statement of the claim showing that the pleader is entitled to relief." Such a statement must simply "give the defendant fair notice of what the plaintiff's claim is and the grounds upon which it rests." *Conley v. Gibson,* 355 U.S. 41, 47, 78 S.Ct. 99, 2 L.Ed.2d 80 (1957). This simplified notice pleading standard relies on liberal discovery rules and summary judgment motions to define disputed facts and issues and to dispose of unmeritorious claims. See *id.,* at 47–48, 78 S.Ct. 99; *Leatherman v. Tarrant County Narcotics Intelligence and Coordination Unit,* 507 U.S. 163, 168–169, 113 S.Ct. 1160, 122 L.Ed.2d 517 (1993). "The provisions for discovery are so flexible and the provisions for pretrial procedure and summary judgment so effective, that attempted surprise in federal practice is aborted very easily, synthetic issues detected, and the gravamen of the dispute brought frankly into the open for the inspection of the court." 5 C. Wright & A. Miller, Federal Practice and Procedure § 1202, p. 76 (2d ed. 1990).

Rule 8(a)'s simplified pleading standard applies to all civil actions, with limited exceptions. Rule 9(b), for example, provides for greater particularity in all averments of fraud or mistake. This Court, however, has declined to extend such exceptions to other contexts. In *Leatherman* we stated: "[T]he Federal Rules do address in Rule 9(b) the question of the need for greater particularity in pleading certain actions, but do not include among the enumerated actions any reference to complaints alleging municipal liability under § 1983. *Expressio unius est exclusio alterius.*" Just as Rule 9(b) makes no mention of municipal liability under 1979, 42 U.S.C. § 1983, neither does it refer to employment discrimination. Thus, complaints in these cases, as in most others, must satisfy only the simple requirements of Rule 8(a).[4]

Other provisions of the Federal Rules of Civil Procedure are inextricably linked to Rule 8(a)'s simplified notice pleading standard. Rule 8(e)(1) states that "[n]o technical forms of pleading or motions are required," and Rule 8(f) provides that "[a]ll pleadings shall be so construed as to do substantial justice." Given the Federal Rules' simplified standard for pleading, "[a] court may dismiss a complaint only if it is clear that no relief could be granted under any set of facts that could be proved consistent with the allegations." If a pleading fails to specify the allegations in a manner that provides sufficient notice, a defendant can move for a more definite statement under Rule 12(e) before responding. Moreover, claims lacking merit may be dealt with through summary judgment under Rule 56. The liberal notice pleading of Rule 8(a) is the starting point of a simplified pleading system, which was adopted to focus litigation on the merits of a claim.

Applying the relevant standard, petitioner's complaint easily satisfies the requirements of Rule 8(a) because it gives respondent fair notice of the basis for petitioner's claims. Petitioner alleged that he had been

---

4. These requirements are exemplified by the Federal Rules of Civil Procedure Forms, which "are sufficient under the rules and are intended to indicate the simplicity and brevity of statement which the rules contemplate." Fed. Rule Civ. Proc. 84. For example, Form 9 sets forth a complaint for negligence in which plaintiff simply states in relevant part: "On June 1, 1936, in a public highway called Boylston Street in Boston, Massachusetts, defendant negligently drove a motor vehicle against plaintiff who was then crossing said highway."

terminated on account of his national origin in violation of Title VII and on account of his age in violation of the ADEA. His complaint detailed the events leading to his termination, provided relevant dates, and included the ages and nationalities of at least some of the relevant persons involved with his termination. These allegations give respondent fair notice of what petitioner's claims are and the grounds upon which they rest. In addition, they state claims upon which relief could be granted under Title VII and the ADEA.

Respondent argues that allowing lawsuits based on conclusory allegations of discrimination to go forward will burden the courts and encourage disgruntled employees to bring unsubstantiated suits. Whatever the practical merits of this argument, the Federal Rules do not contain a heightened pleading standard for employment discrimination suits. A requirement of greater specificity for particular claims is a result that "must be obtained by the process of amending the Federal Rules, and not by judicial interpretation." *Leatherman, supra,* at 168, 113 S.Ct. 1160. Furthermore, Rule 8(a) establishes a pleading standard without regard to whether a claim will succeed on the merits. "Indeed it may appear on the face of the pleadings that a recovery is very remote and unlikely but that is not the test."

For the foregoing reasons, we hold that an employment discrimination plaintiff need not plead a prima facie case of discrimination and that petitioner's complaint is sufficient to survive respondent's motion to dismiss. Accordingly, the judgment of the Court of Appeals is reversed, and the case is remanded for further proceedings consistent with this opinion.

Notes and Questions

1. In Leatherman v. Tarrant County Narcotics and Coordination Unit, 507 U.S. 163, 113 S.Ct. 1160, 122 L.Ed.2d 517 (1993), plaintiffs sued under 42 U.S.C.A. § 1983, claiming that local law enforcement officers had violated their constitutional rights. Because they were suing a county and two municipal corporations that employed the officers who took the actions leading to the suit, prevailing law required that they prove that the incidents resulted from official policy, custom, or practice. But plaintiffs did not allege that there had been multiple incidents of the sort of which they complained, undermining their claim that there was such a policy or practice. The Fifth Circuit upheld dismissal under its "heightened pleading standard" for such claims.

The Supreme Court held that dismissal was wrong because the rules provided no ground for heightened pleading requirements. The Court acknowledged defendants' arguments that "the degree of factual specificity required of a complaint by the Federal Rules of Civil Procedure varies according to the complexity of the underlying substantive law." But it found that the lower court's requirement that plaintiffs "state with factual detail and particularity the basis for the claim" could not be squared with the "liberal system of 'notice pleading' set up by the Federal Rules." It noted that Rule 9(b) requires greater particularity in pleading of certain claims, but that rule did not apply to this case. It concluded: "Perhaps if Rules 8 and 9 were rewritten today, claims against municipalities under § 1983 might be subjected to the added specificity requirement of Rule 9(b). But that is a result which must be obtained by the process of amending the Federal Rules, and not by judicial interpretation. In the absence of such an amendment, federal courts and litigants must rely on summary judgment and control of discovery to weed out unmeritorious claims sooner rather than later."

2. Judge Keeton reasoned in Cash Energy v. Weiner that the Federal Rules are "less generous and forgiving than they were in 1938." Do *Swierkiewicz* and *Leatherman* show that he was wrong? Other courts have so concluded in CERCLA cases. See Canadyne–Georgia Corp. v. NationsBank, 183 F.3d 1269 (11th Cir.1999) ("There is no heightened pleading in CERCLA cases"). But other comments by the Supreme Court have also indicated that there is latitude for demanding more specificity in certain cases. In Crawford–El v. Britton, 523 U.S. 574, 118 S.Ct. 1584, 140 L.Ed.2d 759 (1998), the Court emphasized that the district court "must exercise its discretion so that officials are not subjected to unnecessary and burdensome discovery or trial proceedings." It explained that there are "two primary options" available to accomplish this objective at the pleading stage:

> [T]he court may order a reply to the defendant's or a third party's answer under Federal Rule of Civil Procedure 7(a), or grant the defendant's motion for a more definite statement under Rule 12(e). Thus, the court may insist that the plaintiff "put forward specific, nonconclusory factual allegations" that establish improper motive causing cognizable injury in order to survive a prediscovery motion for dismissal or summary judgment. Siegert v. Gilley, 500 U.S. 226, 236 (1991) (Kennedy, J., concurring).

See also Associated General Contractors, Inc. v. California State Council of Carpenters, 459 U.S. 519, 528 n.17 (1983) ("Certainly in a case of this magnitude, a district court must retain the power to insist upon some specificity in pleading before allowing a potentially massive factual controversy to proceed.").

Fairman, The Myth of Notice Pleading, 45 Az. L. Rev. 987 (2003), finds that "notice pleading as a universal standard is a myth," and that "the reality of federal court practice—using all manner of fact-based particularity requirements—is shocking." Id. at 989; 997. For examples, consider Goad v. Mitchell, 297 F.3d 497, 504 (6th Cir.2002) (permitting district courts "to require plaintiffs to produce specific, nonconclusory factual allegations of improper motive before discovery in cases in which the plaintiff must prove wrongful motive"); Browning v. Clinton, 292 F.3d 235, 242 (D.C.Cir.2002) ("we accept neither inferences drawn by plaintiffs if such inferences are unsupported by the facts set out in the complaint, nor legal conclusions cast in the form of factual allegations"). Is there any justification for the lower courts' persistence in demanding details? Regarding civil rights suits, for example, it has been argued that "these situations present particularly difficult problems involving the potential abuse of litigation because they often involve outwardly innocent or admitted behavior that can, depending on the defendant's state of mind, result in very substantial liability." Marcus, The Revival of Fact Pleading Under the Federal Rules of Civil

Procedure, 86 Colum. L. Rev. 433, 450 (1986). Consider, for example, a plaintiff who sues in federal court claiming that she has received a number of parking citations over the past year because of her religious beliefs. Religious discrimination would violate plaintiff's constitutional rights, but should the court be required to credit her claim that this is why she received the tickets without an indication of the basis for this conclusion?

3. In *Swierkiewicz*, the Court notes that plaintiff "detailed the events leading up to his termination." The Second Circuit had found plaintiff's allegations insufficient: "With respect to national origin, the only circumstances Swierkiewicz pled are that he is Hungarian, others at Sorema are French, and the conclusory allegation that his termination was motivated by national origin discrimination. * * * [Regarding age discrimination,] [t]he only circumstance that Swierkiewicz alleges gives rise to an inference of age discrimination is Chavel's comment in 1995 that Chavel wanted to 'energize' the underwriting department." Swierkiewicz v. Sorema, N.A., 5 Fed.Appx. 63, 64–65 (2d Cir.2001). Do you agree that plaintiff did not do enough to support his conclusion that he was discriminated against? What more would he have to do—allege "direct" statements on behalf of defendant that he was terminated due to his age or national origin? How often would employers that discriminate make such statements?

At trial, under Title VII, plaintiff has the burden of proof. We will examine this concept in detail in Chapter VI (see infra pp. 425–27), but a foretaste of that discussion is helpful at this point. Ordinarily a plaintiff has the burden of proving all the elements of the claim; to do so requires evidence sufficient to establish each of those elements. See Fed. R. Civ. P. 50(a) (the court may grant defendant judgment as a matter of law if "there is no legally sufficient evidentiary basis for a reasonable jury to find for" plaintiff). Plaintiff in *Swierkiewicz* relied on "circumstantial" evidence rather than a direct statement by defendant that he was being terminated due to his age or national origin. Should proof of the allegations of his complaint suffice to satisfy his burden of proof at trial?

McDonnell Douglas Corp. v. Green, 411 U.S. 792, 93 S.Ct. 1817, 36 L.Ed.2d 668 (1973), addressed the specific requirements of Title VII for plaintiffs relying on circumstantial proof. Plaintiff there had worked for defendant for eight years as a mechanic when he was laid off as part of a general reduction in workforce. Plaintiff protested that his discharge and the defendant's general hiring practices were racially motivated. A long-time activist in civil rights causes, plaintiff participated in a "stall-in" at defendant's plant in an effort to block traffic during the morning rush hour, and was arrested and pleaded guilty to a charge of obstructing traffic. He was also implicated in a "lock-in" at defendant's plant which involved chaining the front door to prevent ingress and egress. Shortly after these events, defendant advertised that it was hiring mechanics, and plaintiff applied for a job but was rejected. Plaintiff claimed that defendant discriminated against him in refusing to rehire him. Defendant countered that it had rejected him because of his involvement in the stall-in and the lock-in. The Court held that plaintiff had adequately supported his prima facie case by proving the points identified in *Swierkiewicz*, so that he was entitled to a retrial for the jury to determine whether defendant had discriminated against him. If defendant could show that its decision was based on plaintiff's illegal activities, however, it would prevail.

4. The Court cites Form 9 of the Federal Rules of Civil Procedure and emphasizes that discovery is the appropriate method of developing the evidentiary basis for a claim. Does that mean that Swierkiewicz need not have included the detail that he provided in his complaint? One lower court has opined that all an employment discrimination plaintiff need allege is "I was turned down for a job because of my race." Bennett v. Schmidt, 153 F.3d 516, 518 (7th Cir.1998). Does *Swierkiewicz* show that this view is correct?

5. The Court also emphasizes the importance of discovery. It says, for example, that requiring that a complaint specify a prima facie circumstantial case would be improper because discovery might unearth direct evidence of discrimination. Should there be any limit on plaintiff's ability to do discovery without first specifying a ground for suspecting discrimination? In McDonald Douglas Corp. v. Green, for example, the Supreme Court noted that evidence that white employees involved in acts similar to plaintiff's participation in the stall-in were nonetheless rehired or retained would be "[e]specially relevant," and added that evidence regarding defendant's "general policy and practice with regard to minority employment" would also be relevant. Would it have been proper for plaintiff in *McDonnell Douglas* to demand discovery regarding all white employees subjected to discipline, and detailed information on all defendant's hiring practices? Would that be equally proper if plaintiff had alleged nothing more than the conclusion that he was a victim of racial discrimination?

6. Judge Keeton, the author of *Cash Energy*, seemingly has continued to favor specificity, but instead of relying on a synthesis of the Federal Rules has insisted on it as a feature of case management under Rule 16. Thus, in Feliciano v. DuBois, 846 F.Supp. 1033 (D.Mass.1994), a pro se prison conditions civil rights suit, the judge noted that after *Leatherman* (supra note 1) "[t]he federal law regarding particularity of complaint requirements is currently quite unsettled," but that at least such requirements could be imposed "in ways other than dismissing a civil action." Accordingly, he entered a case management order requiring on pain of dismissal that plaintiffs file a "written submission * * * stating with particularity at least an outline or summary of the facts and the legal grounds of each claim." How different is this technique from demanding specificity at the pleading stage? Is this consistent with the directive of Rule 8(a)?

7. What should be the role of a motion for more definite statement in policing complaints? In McHenry v. Renne, 84 F.3d 1172 (9th Cir.1996), the court upheld dismissal of a complaint that did set forth a claim because plaintiff refused to obey the district judge's order that he abandon the "novelized form" he had adopted, which "reads like a magazine story" and "seems designed to provide quotations for newspaper stories." Although plaintiff tried to justify this pleading technique as necessary to satisfy heightened pleading requirements applicable to constitutional tort claims, the appellate court rejected this argument. "The propriety of dismissal for failure to comply with Rule 8 does not depend on whether the complaint is wholly without merit. The magistrate was able to identify a few possible

claims which were not, on their face, subject to being dismissed under Rule 12(b)(6). Rule 8(e), requiring each averment of a pleading to be 'simple, concise and direct,' applies to good claims as well as bad, and is a basis for dismissal independent of Rule 12(b)(6)." Compare Davis v. Ruby Foods, Inc., 269 F.3d 818 (7th Cir.2001) (rejecting dismissal of cluttered complaint, and holding that the most that could be done would be to strike the surplusage).

8.   If specificity may only be required in cases covered by Rule 9(b), will courts be tempted to take an expansive view of that rule? Consider Chiron Corp. v. Abbott Laboratories, 156 F.R.D. 219 (N.D.Cal.1994), a patent infringement action in which defendant raised the affirmative defense of inequitable conduct by plaintiff in obtaining the patent. Plaintiff moved to strike the defense as insufficient under Rule 9(b). Although this defense is broader than common-law fraud, the court found that Rule 9(b) should apply because of "public policy considerations" such as the cost of litigating such claims, the ease with which they can be used as a delaying tactic and the temptation to use them to launch a fishing expedition. Id. at 221. Do these justifications affect the scope of Rule 9(b)? Aren't they the same as those invoked by Judge Keeton in *Cash Energy*? See Hrick, Wrong About Everything: The Application by the District Courts of Rule 9(b) to Inequitable Conduct, 86 Marq.L.Rev. 894 (2003) (arguing against application of Rule 9(b)). In Pelman v. McDonald's Corp., 396 F.3d 508 (2d Cir.2005), the court reversed dismissal of a suit claiming that McDonald's had violated the New York Consumer Protection Act by creating a false impression that its products were part of a healthy lifestyle if consumed daily, resulting in obesity and other health problems of plaintiffs and the class of customers they sought to represent. Because the pertinent New York law did not require proof of actual reliance, and "extends beyond common-law fraud to cover a broad range of deceptive practices," this claim is "not subject to the pleading-with-particularity requirements of Rule 9(b), but need only meet the bare-bones notice-pleading requirements of Rule 8(a)."

9.   If plaintiff seeks to avoid paying the filing fee to sue, under 28 U.S.C.A. § 1915(e) the court may dismiss the suit as "frivolous." The Supreme Court has recognized that a suit in forma pauperis may be dismissed even where a complaint on which the filing fee was paid would not be subject to dismissal, Denton v. Hernandez, 504 U.S. 25, 112 S.Ct. 1728, 118 L.Ed.2d 340 (1992). It explained that, unlike Rule 12(b)(6), this statute gives judges "the unusual power to pierce the veil of the complaint's factual allegations and dismiss those claims whose factual contentions are clearly baseless." Neitzke v. Williams, 490 U.S. 319, 327, 109 S.Ct. 1827, 1833, 104 L.Ed.2d 338 (1989).

10.   *The Rules Amendment Process*: *Swierkiewicz* and *Leatherman* both emphasized that changes to the pleading rules should be sought through the rule-amendment process; it seems appropriate to provide some background on that process. Pursuant to the Rules Enabling Act of 1934, the entire set of Federal Rules was drafted by a blue ribbon committee in about a year and a half in the 1930s. In recent years, however, the amendment process has become quite public and takes much more time. Initially, rule proposals are generated by Advisory Committees, whose meetings must be public. See 28 U.S.C.A. § 2073(c). Any proposals to change the rules must be published for public comment and hearings. Based on the public input, the Advisory

Committee considers modifications, and then approved proposals are forwarded to the Judicial Conference and, if further approved, to the Supreme Court. If the Court adopts them, they are submitted to Congress, which has seven months to act before proposals take effect. Altogether, it normally takes about three years for a rule change to become effective. For an overview, see Marcus, Reform Through Rulemaking?, 80 Wash.U.L.Rev. 901 (2002). The process has become more political that it was in the 1930s. "Participatory democracy now is emerging in the rulemaking process." Mullenix, Hope Over Experience: Mandatory Informal Discovery and the Politics of Rulemaking, 69 N.C.L.Rev. 795, 800 (1991).

Who should design court procedures? Congress can do so by statute, as it did in the Private Securities Litigation Act. See Requirements of the Private Securities Litigation Act, supra p. 170; Burbank, Procedure, Politics and Power: The Role of Congress, 79 Notre Dame L. Rev. 1677 (2004). But the idea behind the Rules Enabling Act is that the rules committee should have primary authority for devising procedural changes. The rules process is dominated by judges, however, and some predict that they would try to further their self interests in drafting rules. See Macey, Judicial Preferences, Public Choice, and the Rules of Procedure, 33 J. Legal Stud. 627 (1994); compare Alexander, Judges' Self-interest and Procedural Rules, 33 J. Legal Stud. 647 (1994) (questioning assertion that judges will significantly favor their self interests in rulemaking). Both rulemaking and action by Congress remain possible with regard to any controversial topic.

5. *The Future of Pleading Practice*

RICHARD MARCUS, THE REVIVAL OF FACT PLEADING UNDER THE FEDERAL RULES OF CIVIL PROCEDURE, 86 Colum.L.Rev. 433, 454–58, 493–94 (1986):

Most cases are never resolved by a court, on the merits or otherwise, because they are settled. Recently this statistic has kindled a debate between the proponents of the "dispute resolution" model of litigation and the advocates of the "public interest" model. Imported into the pleading practice area, the debate identifies the underlying issues.

Proponents of the public interest model oppose viewing the court system primarily as a lever or facilitator for essentially private dispute resolution. To some, this means that any resolution of a lawsuit except by judicial decision represents a failure of the judicial system. * * * Although the proponents of the public interest view seem generally to have in mind a decision after a full dress trial, the reasoning appears to apply equally to pretrial judicial decisions, including pleading dispositions. Indeed, given the impossibility of actually trying all civil cases, logic seems to favor pretrial disposition.

The dispute resolution advocates, on the other hand, mistrust judicial resolution. Even judges openly question the desirability of complete resolution after trial as the generally preferred outcome. As one experienced federal judge put it in a seminar for new judges, "[o]ptimal justice is usually found somewhere between the polar positions of the litigants.

Trial is likely to produce a polar solution, and often the jury or the judge has no choice except all or nothing. Settlement is usually the avenue that allows a more just result than trial." This view evinces great skepticism about the liberal ethos and its preference for judicial resolution on the merits. Instead, a settlement may be preferable, whatever the ultimate merits of the claim,[130] so long as the plaintiff "firmly believes" he has a legitimate grievance against defendant.[131] Arguably, then, dismissal on the pleadings would not be a desirable alternative.

Thus, the two schools pose the core problem: Are pleadings decisions or settlements better? Denial of a motion to dismiss often means only that a defendant who will ultimately prevail must litigate longer. Even the confident defendant may decide to settle, however. To the extent that decision is made "in the shadow of the law" because it reflects a prediction of the substantive merits of the case, it accomplishes the objectives of the substantive law, albeit in a modified form because a settlement is not an "all or nothing" result. Freed of the burden of deciding the settled case, the court system is able to turn its attention to other cases, and there apply the substantive law.

The settlement model breaks down, however, when the defendant's payment to the plaintiff is based mainly on factors other than the substantive merits of the suit. This is the spectre which haunts the liberal ethos. The financial burden of litigation is obviously an important factor, but it is not the only one. The pendency of a lawsuit imposes other costs that settlement can avert, whether or not the claim is well founded. In derivative suits, for example, the defendants' desire to avoid publicity and to reduce the time drain of litigation may incline them toward settlement. In antitrust cases, the unavailability of contribution may make the risk of litigation so great that settlement seems essential. Moreover, the value of a decision by a court deserves some deference; without a body of such decisions the law may not cast a discernible shadow for those who seek to rely on the law in fashioning settlements. Accordingly, pleadings decisions on the merits seem justified when they can be made reliably.

The pressure to encourage pleadings decisions is far from overwhelming, however, and there is much dispute about the extent to which nuisance settlements are in fact extracted. For example, although the class action procedure has been blamed for breeding vexatious litigation, existing empirical data do not show that the problem is severe. Litigation cost, the most-cited villain, has an ambivalent effect. When the cost of litigating a meritorious claim is greater than the expected recovery, a suit filed in hopes of an early settlement may be characterized as a

---

130. Cf. Marek v. Chesny, 473 U.S. 1, 105 S.Ct. 3012, 3018, 87 L.Ed.2d 1 (1985) [infra p. 505] ("Rule 68's policy of encouraging settlements is neutral, favoring neither plaintiffs nor defendants; it expresses a clear policy of favoring settlements of all lawsuits.").

131. The phrase comes from Clark's famous opinion reversing a dismissal in Dioguardi v. Durning, 139 F.2d 774, 775 (2d Cir.1944) [supra p. 132].

nuisance suit even though the claim has merit. Moreover, defendants can limit their costs. Accordingly, there is no compelling impetus toward radical change, and care is in order before concluding that a particular case can be reliably decided on the pleadings.

* * *

The circumstances in which such merits decisions are possible on the pleadings, however, are distressingly limited. * * * [S]uch situations fall generally into two categories, those in which more detail will reveal a fatal defect and those in which sufficient detail will show that the defendant has not violated the plaintiff's rights. * * * [But] it is often difficult to identify elements of a claim that plaintiffs should be forced to establish. Even more troubling is the risk that courts will indulge in weighing of evidence in the process of trying to decide on the basis of the pleadings whether the defendant's conduct violated the plaintiff's rights. Outside these limited areas, more stringent pleading practices cannot be justified as appropriate for "suspicious" cases or as part of the trial court's discretion in handling litigation.

Instead, more flexible use of summary judgment, in tandem with case management, seems the more promising course. This approach reduces the disquieting possibility that a plaintiff will be unable to satisfy the court's demand for proof of the defendant's misconduct because he has been denied discovery. It is also comforting to have merits decisions based on evidence rather than allegations. Moreover, selective cost-shifting, coupled with active case management, should diminish some concerns about litigation abuse. This course is neither easy nor foolproof, however. Case management is time-consuming and vexing, and Rule 56(f) requests for postponements [of summary judgment motions to permit discovery] will often require particularly difficult determinations about the utility of further discovery. Evaluating evidence in the summary judgment context is not easy, but it should be more reliable than scrutinizing factual conclusions in the pleadings. Thus, the suggestion is simply a better course, not a panacea.

Notes and Questions

1. Does your review of the cases in this chapter suggest that the above article is too pessimistic about effective pleadings scrutiny of the merits of claims? Would reformulation of the pleading rules lead to better outcomes? Should pleadings decisions simply be eliminated, as Charles Clark originally wanted?

A 1998 review of pleading practice found that courts can continue to adhere to the notion that "our task is, in the first instance, one of deciding what the claim is; what is short and plain has no universal meaning independent of the nature of the claim. It does no violence to notice pleading to suggest that the adequacy of a pleading is case specific." Elliott v. Perez, 751 F.2d 1472, 1483 (5th Cir.1985) (Higginbotham, J., concurring); see also Schultea v. Wood, 47 F.3d 1427, 1430 (5th Cir.1995) ("insistence on greater pleading detail ought to rest on the reality that what is short and plain is inseparable from the legal and factual complexity of the case at issue"):

> What remains, then, involves a kind of common-law activity in which judges develop standards for assessing the complaints in different kinds of cases. Much as this process might be attacked as inconsistent with the transsubstantive orientation of the rules, it actually comports with the relatively loose wording of the rules. Even the official forms, spare though they are, vary in detail depending on the type of claims asserted. Perhaps it would be profitable to promote some additional attention to the adequacy of pleadings by upgrading Rule 12(e) to say that the motion for a more definite statement can properly serve the function the commentators view as appropriate [of paving the way for a Rule 12(b)(6) motion], but that endorsement will not provide a guide to determining when requiring further specifics is warranted. As with the decision whether the case can be reliably resolved on the pleadings, that determination necessarily turns on some assessment of the individual case.

Marcus, The Puzzling Persistence of Pleading Practice, 76 Texas L. Rev. 1749, 1778 (1998).

2. The "case management" referred to is a process of active control of the suit from its inception that has gained increasing popularity among judges. One such judge urges that "judicial management must be directed from the beginning of the litigation first at identifying and clarifying and then at narrowing and limiting the issues" and that "issue identification and limitation and discovery control must proceed hand in hand." W. Schwarzer, Managing Antitrust and Other Complex Litigation: A Handbook for Lawyers and Judges 18–19 (1982). For examples, see supra p. 137 n. 5 and p. 184 n. 6. Is this attitude consistent with Conley v. Gibson? To the extent you are uneasy about the stricter pleading requirements some courts have developed for some kinds of cases, would extension of this sort of activity to all cases seem an even worse idea?

3. We shall examine summary judgment in Chapter VI. At that time, reflect on whether it seems to be a more effective device for weeding out groundless claims than pleadings decisions.

C. DEFENDANT'S RESPONSE

1. *Pre-answer Motions Under Rule 12*

We have already considered the Rule 12(b)(6) motion in some detail and compared it to the Rule 12(e) motion for a more definite statement. In addition, there is a Rule 12(f) motion to strike "redundant, immaterial, impertinent, or scandalous matter" or "any insufficient defense." Before we turn to the usual method of asserting defenses—the answer— we need to reflect a bit longer on some of the practical concerns surrounding Rule 12 motions.

The seven defenses set out in Rule 12(b), except for failure to state a claim, are all objections of a procedural nature—that the court is not empowered to exercise jurisdiction over the subject matter of the suit

(Rule 12(b)(1)); that the court lacks personal jurisdiction over the defendant (Rule 12(b)(2)); that this particular court is not the proper location (venue) for the suit (Rule 12(b)(3)); that the circumstances or method for serving process were incorrect (Rule 12(b)(4) & (5)); or that the suit shouldn't go forward without a necessary party (Rule 12(b)(7)). The one exception is Rule 12(b)(6)—failure to state a claim upon which relief can be granted—which challenges the legal sufficiency of the allegations in the complaint.

The filing of a pre-answer motion under Rule 12 affects the time periods for filing responsive pleadings. If the defendant files a pre-answer motion within the 20–day period following service of the summons and complaint, the deadline for filing an answer is extended. Rule 12(a)(1). If the court *denies* the motion or postpones its disposition, the defendant has until 10 days after notice of the court's action to file an answer. If the court *grants* the motion, plaintiff will usually be granted leave to amend (which starts the process again) or the suit will be dismissed; however, if a motion for a more definite statement is granted, the defendant has until 10 days after service of an amended complaint containing a more definite statement in which to file his answer.

Rules 12(g) and (h) set out consolidation and waiver provisions concerning the Rule 12 motions. Their purpose is to prevent the pleader from using multiple pre-answer motions for different defenses and from omitting certain defenses from motions or answers. Rule 12(g) provides that if a party makes a pre-answer motion, but omits one of the Rule 12 defenses then available, it cannot make any further pre-answer motions. Rule 12(h)(1) provides that four *disfavored defenses*—lack of jurisdiction over the person, improper venue, insufficiency of process, or insufficiency of service of process—will be waived forever if omitted from a pre-answer motion or, if no motion is made, from the answer. Rule 12(h)(2) provides that three *favored defenses*—failure to state a claim upon which relief can be granted, failure to join an indispensable party, and failure to state a legal defense to a claim—can be made in any pleading, or by motion for judgment on the pleadings, or at trial on the merits. Finally Rule 12(h)(3) states that the *most favored defense*—lack of jurisdiction of the subject matter—may be made at any time.

Notes and Questions

1. Why would a defendant want to raise one of the Rule 12(b) defenses in a *pre-answer motion* instead of just including it in the *answer*? The fact that a pre-answer motion extends the time for filing an answer should provide a hint as to one of the reasons. What advantages might a defendant obtain by putting off having to answer immediately?

2. Might there be tactical advantages that could prompt a defendant to raise defenses by answer rather than by motion?

(a) Would the plaintiff ever prefer to have the issues resolved at the outset of the case? Cf. Rule 12(d) (providing that any party can insist on determination before trial of any defenses specified in Rule 12(b), even if they are only raised in the answer). Why might a plaintiff want to force pretrial resolution of such defenses?

(b) With the defense of failure to state a claim, would there be any advantage for a defendant not to move to dismiss when plaintiff has omitted allegations regarding an essential element of his case? What does that omission suggest about whether plaintiff has paid attention to that aspect of his case? Does plaintiff's inattention create an opportunity for defendant?

3.   Consider the following problems:

(a) Within 20 days after service of the complaint and summons, defendant files a pre-answer motion alleging the defense of *insufficiency of service of process*. 15 days later, when the court has not yet ruled on the motion and no answer has yet been filed, defendant realizes that (1) *venue was improper* and (2) there has been a *failure to join an indispensable party*. Can these defenses be made in another pre-answer motion? Can they be made in the answer when it is filed? Would it matter whether, at the time of the filing of the pre-answer motion, the defendant was aware of the facts on which it would base the additional defenses of improper venue and indispensable party?

(b) Defendant filed a pre-answer motion alleging the defense of *improper venue* and, when it was denied, filed an answer responding on the merits. Six months later, defendant's counsel realizes that there is a defense of *lack of jurisdiction over the subject matter*. Can this defense be raised as the basis for a motion to dismiss? Can it be raised for the first time on appeal after judgment for the plaintiff?

(c) Defendant did not file a pre-answer motion, but timely filed an answer responding on the merits to the allegations of the complaint. Four weeks after filing the answer, he realizes that there is a defense of *insufficiency of service of process* and of *failure to state a claim upon which relief can be granted*. Can he raise these defenses? If so, in what manner?

2. *Failure to Answer—Default*

SHEPARD CLAIMS SERVICE, INC. v. WILLIAM DARRAH & ASSOCIATES

United States Court of Appeals, Sixth Circuit, 1986.
796 F.2d 190.

Before LIVELY, CHIEF JUDGE; WELLFORD and NELSON, CIRCUIT JUDGES.

LIVELY, CHIEF JUDGE.

On August 21, 1984, Shepard Claims Services, Inc. (Shepard) filed this contract action in the district court against William Darrah & Associates (Darrah), with jurisdiction based on diversity of citizenship. The complaint alleged essentially that Darrah, a South Carolina-based insurance broker, failed to pay Shepard, a Michigan independent claims adjuster, for services rendered. Following some difficulty in service by mail, service in person was carried out on February 7, 1985.

On February 22, 1985 Darrah's attorney's secretary secured by telephone an extension of time for filing an answer. A confirmation letter from defense counsel, drafted and signed by the secretary with the vacationing counsel's permission, stated:

> This letter will confirm my secretary's conversation with your secretary of February 22, 1985, to the effect that you have granted my office *45 days from February 22, 1985,* to answer the Complaint in the above captioned cause of action against my client, Will Darrah.

(Emphasis added). By April 10 defendant had filed no answer, so plaintiff Shepard requested that the clerk enter Darrah's default. On April 19 Darrah filed a "Notice of Retention," following on April 26 with an answer and then on April 29 with a notice of affirmative defenses, a counterclaim, interrogatories and a request for production of documents. On May 1 defendant filed a response to plaintiff's motion for default judgment (which had not been filed as of that time) and a motion to set aside entry of default pursuant to Rule 55(c), Fed.R.Civ.P. On May 8 plaintiff filed its motion for default judgment and response to defendant's motion to set aside entry of default. Along with the motion to set aside entry of default defendant filed two affidavits, from defense counsel and his secretary, in which they stated their understanding of the extension to run 45 days in addition to the normal period of 30 days under Rule 4(e), Fed.R.Civ.P.,* rather than from February 22. Under this interpretation the answer would have been due on April 23. The confirming letter, according to the secretary, "contained a misstatement" of what she believed was the arrangement and what she informed her employer. Defense counsel did not review the confirming letter upon his return and apparently did not examine the file until the day he filed his "appearance." Defense counsel insists that he did not learn of the April 10 entry of default until April 29, by letter from opposing counsel.

The district court held a hearing on pending motions on May 28, after which the court denied defendant's motion to set aside entry of default. In its order the district court found that defendant's attorney engaged in culpable conduct when he permitted his secretary to make arrangements for the extension and then failed to review the secretary's letter upon returning from vacation.

The district court denied the defendant's motion for reconsideration and certified the case for an interlocutory appeal pursuant to 28 U.S.C. § 1292(b) upon finding that "a substantial basis exists for a difference of opinion on the question of setting aside the default in this matter, and that an immediate appeal may materially advance the termination of this litigation."

In United Coin Meter Co. v. Seaboard Coastline R.R., 705 F.2d 839 (6th Cir.1983), this court considered a set of circumstances quite similar to those recorded in the present case. After the parties were unable to go forward with a scheduled hearing on the defendant's motion to dismiss, opposing counsel agreed to a 20–day period for the defendant to file an

---

* Now a defendant has 20 days to answer.
See Rule 12(a)(1)(A).—Eds.

answer. Plaintiff's counsel construed the agreement as running from April 28, while defendant's counsel believed the time ran from May 5. When no answer was filed by April 28, plaintiff's counsel caused a default to be entered by the clerk. The only matter in dispute was the date from which the 20–day period was to run.

Following a hearing the district court found no "excusable neglect" on the part of the defendant. The court also concluded that the affidavits of the defendant failed to establish the existence of a meritorious defense. The district court refused to set aside the default and entered a default judgment for the full amount sought in the complaint. A hearing was held on the defendant's motion for reconsideration. The district court denied reconsideration, finding that there was no "good cause" for setting aside entry of default or the default judgment.

This court reversed the district court in *United Coin*, finding that the criteria controlling the court's decision on a Rule 55(c) motion had not been satisfied. In agreement with other courts, we concluded that three factors determine the outcome of such a motion:

    1.   Whether the plaintiff will be prejudiced;

    2.   Whether the defendant has a meritorious defense; and

    3.   Whether culpable conduct of the defendant led to the default.

In *United Coin* the plaintiff did not claim prejudice and this court found that the defendant had established a meritorious defense, one "good at law" without reference to the likelihood of success. The decisive issue was whether the default resulted from the defendant's "culpable conduct." In determining that the third requirement had not been met, we repeatedly stated that the defendant's conduct had not been "willful."

The present case differs from *United Coin* in at least one material respect. In *United Coin,* a default judgment was entered, whereas this interlocutory appeal was taken before entry of judgment. If the only issue relates to entry of default, Rule 55(c), Fed.R.Civ.P., provides the standard—"good cause shown." After entry of a default judgment, the court may set the judgment aside "in accordance with Rule 60(b)," which lists several grounds for relief from judgment. Despite this difference the district court and the parties in the present case recognized *United Coin* as the controlling decision. However, the district court found the *United Coin* opinion "ambiguous as to the precise definition of culpable conduct." On appeal Darrah argues that *United Coin* is not ambiguous, that it clearly adopted the "willful conduct" definition by citing with approval cases from other circuits that equated culpable conduct with willfulness. The sole reference to negligence in the *United Coin* opinion is contained in a discussion of the standards applicable to a Rule 60(b) motion, under which "excusable neglect" is a ground for relief. Darrah asserts that nothing in the opinion indicates that the "good cause" standard of Rule 55(c) is satisfied by a showing of counsel's negligence.

militate — to have a substantial effect, weigh heavily

Shepard contends that the district court correctly found that counsel for the defendant was the "designer" of the agreement for additional time to plead, and that his failure to comply with the agreed limitations was "culpable negligence." Shepard argues that the failure of Darrah and its counsel to abide by the time limits they "designed" could properly be found willful, and therefore culpable, conduct.

Rule 55(c) leaves to the discretion of the trial judge the decision whether to set aside an entry of default. However, a strong preference for trials on the merits in federal courts has led to the adoption of a somewhat modified standard of review where defaults are involved. * * *

Since entry of default is just the first procedural step on the road to obtaining a default judgment, the same policy of favoring trials on the merits applies whether considering a motion under Rule 55(c) or Rule 60(b). In practice a somewhat more lenient standard is applied to Rule 55(c) motions where there has only been an entry of default than to Rule 60(b) motions where judgment has been entered. * * * The distinction between the two standards was discussed in Jackson v. Beech, 636 F.2d 831, 835 (D.C.Cir.1980):

> * * * Once a defendant fails to file a responsive answer, he is in default, and an entry of default may be made by either the clerk or the judge. A default judgment can be entered by a clerk only if a claim is liquidated or, if a claim is unliquidated, by the judge after a hearing on damages. A default can be set aside under rule 55(c) for "good cause shown," but a default that has become final as a judgment can be set aside only under the stricter rule 60(b) standards for setting aside final, appealable orders.

In a different setting the district judge's orders in the present case might not constitute an abuse of discretion. However, we must consider the fact that the plaintiff suffered no prejudice by reason of the tardy pleadings and the defendant did present a meritorious defense in its answer. These findings of the district court are clearly supported by the record. All three factors must be considered in ruling on a motion to set aside entry of default. However, when the first two factors militate in favor of setting aside the entry, it is an abuse of discretion for a district court to deny a Rule 55(c) motion in the absence of a willful failure of the moving party to appear and plead.

The conduct of Darrah's counsel, Mark Shreve, was careless and inexcusable. Nevertheless, it is not necessary that conduct be excusable to qualify for relief under the "good cause" standard of Rule 55(c). * * *

The district court stated that defense counsel's conduct, "if not intentional, is certainly 'culpable conduct.'" In making this finding the district court apparently relied on the negligence of the defendant's lawyer in not reviewing the work of his secretary.

To be treated as culpable, the conduct of a defendant must display either an intent to thwart judicial proceedings or a reckless disregard for

How condition 3 is met

the effect of its conduct on those proceedings. As in *United Coin,* the delay in the present case resulted from a dispute over the date from which an agreed extension was to run. Darrah's attorney filed an entry of appearance and an answer shortly after learning that default had been entered on the basis of Shepard's interpretation of the agreement. The delay was not lengthy and there was no pattern of disregard for court orders or rules. Under these circumstances the strong policy in favor of deciding cases on their merits outweighs any inconvenience to the court or Shepard resulting from the relatively short delay in answering. We agree with the summary of court holdings in 6 Moore's Federal Practice ¶ 55.01[2] at 55–61, 62 (1985 ed.):

> Where the defaulting party and counsel have not shown disrespect for the court, or have given evidence of respect for the court's process by their haste in acting to set aside the default, the courts have been inclined towards leniency.... Clearly, however, the court may refuse to set aside a default, where the defaulting party has no meritorious defense, where the default is due to willfulness or bad faith, or where the defendant offers no excuse at all for the default.

We do not believe it appropriate to attempt a precise definition of "culpable conduct." Where the party in default satisfies the first two requirements for relief and moves promptly to set aside the default before a judgment is entered, the district court should grant the motion if the party offers a credible explanation for the delay that does not exhibit disregard for the judicial proceedings.

A default judgment deprives the client of his day in court, and should not be used as a vehicle for disciplining attorneys. Although Shepard has made unverified claims that Darrah encouraged its attorney's conduct, there is no basis in the record for finding that the present case involved a deliberate attempt by Darrah to delay the proceedings. Although a party who chooses an attorney takes the risk of suffering from the attorney's incompetence, we do not believe that this record exhibits circumstances in which a client should suffer the ultimate sanction of losing his case without any consideration of the merits because of his attorney's neglect and inattention.

We can understand and sympathize with the reaction of the district court to Shreve's conduct and his explanations or excuses. The "Notice of Retention" indicated that someone in Shreve's office recognized that the time for pleading might be near, or past. Yet another week went by before Shreve filed his answer. The secretary's affidavit ascribed the misunderstanding to a "misstatement" in the letter that the affiant herself wrote. The misunderstanding could have been cured if Shreve had examined the correspondence upon his return from vacation and contacted Shepard's attorney for confirmation. Despite this evidence of inattention and disarray in defense counsel's office, the fact remains that Shepard suffered no prejudice and Darrah would be deprived of an opportunity to present its defense at a trial if the default were not set aside.

Our disposition of the case does not preclude the district court from assessing or determining some appropriate penalty or sanction against the defendant or his counsel for the delay occasioned by the careless and inexcusable conduct of defendant's counsel herein discussed.

The judgment of the district court is reversed, and the cause is remanded for further proceedings. No costs are allowed.

Notes and Questions

1. The idea behind default derives from the premises of the adversary system; if one side does not want to contest the other side's case, the court is not obliged to inquire further. "New York does not require civil litigants to show up in court only to fall on their swords. If a defendant does not contest his liability as set out in the complaint, he need not appear in the action." Connecticut Bank of Commerce v. Republic of Congo, 309 F.3d 240, 251 (5th Cir.2002).

2. Rule 55(b)(1) sets out the only situation in which the clerk, rather than the judge, may enter a default judgment. It provides that if a defendant has been defaulted for failure to appear (and isn't an infant or incompetent), the clerk, upon plaintiff's request and filing an affidavit as to the amount due, shall enter judgment if the claim is "for a sum certain or for a sum which can by computation be made certain." A claim for damages for a liquidated amount meets this requirement, but not a generalized statement of the amount due. See United States v. Melichar, 56 F.R.D. 49 (E.D.Wis. 1972) (claim for conversion of cows and heifers without specifying their value is not for a sum certain). Plaintiff must also show that the sum certain is reasonable under the circumstances. United States v. Miller, 9 F.R.D. 506 (M.D.Pa.1949). The defendant must have completely failed to appear, and not merely have defaulted after an initial appearance, for the clerk to be allowed to enter judgment.

3. The entry of default, on the other hand, may be fairly routine; unless defendant has filed an answer, the clerk may enter default when the time to answer expires. At that point, the defendant is entitled to notice of further hearings only if it has entered an "appearance." In cases like *Shepard,* should the defendant's request for additional time to respond be treated as an appearance? See Rogers v. Hartford Life & Accident Ins. Co., 167 F.3d 933 (5th Cir.1999) (waiver of service was not an appearance despite prior informal contacts between parties about the dispute); Wilson v. Moore & Associates, Inc., 564 F.2d 366 (9th Cir.1977) (declining to find that informal contacts between defendant and plaintiff's lawyer constituted appearance where defendant failed to answer after threat of default); compare H.F. Livermore Corp. v. Aktiengesellschaft Gebruder Loepfe, 432 F.2d 689 (D.C.Cir.1970) (informal settlement negotiations sufficient to constitute appearance where defendant indicated intent to defend on merits). Why should the law ever dispense with notice? Is this result consistent with the Supreme Court's handling of due process requirements for prejudgment remedies?

4. A more basic problem yet is to determine what should be treated as an answer. Consider Wheat v. Eakin, 491 So.2d 523 (Miss.1986). Acting *pro se,* defendant responded to the complaint with a handwritten document addressed to the clerk that stated in its entirety: "Not only do I deny all the

allegations in the above styled suit, I contend, with all due respect, that the plaintiff must be suffering from a condition of brown eyeballs since he is full of so much bullshit." Id. at 527 (reproducing handwritten document). The appellate court held that it was error to enter default: "While the form and language of the appellant's response are less than desirable and more frank than customary, the appellant did state in short and plain terms his general denial of appellees' claims. A motion to strike the answer would have been appropriate, but none was filed." Is there a reason for taking such a lenient view of the requisites for an answer in the default context?

5. Once default is properly entered, what impact should that action have on the court's evaluation of the merits of the case? At a minimum, it appears that the court may refuse to grant a judgment for plaintiff if the complaint fails to state a claim for relief. See Productora e Importadora de Papel, S.A. v. Fleming, 376 Mass. 826, 383 N.E.2d 1129, 1135 (1978). Beyond that, the court may insist that plaintiff make some showing of factual support for his allegations. See 10A Wright, Miller & Kane, Federal Practice & Procedure § 2688. And the question of the amount of damages remains open for full scale litigation. Why should defendant's right to have the court probe the merits of plaintiff's case be curtailed by entry of default?

Troublesome questions may emerge where plaintiff seeks equitable relief rather than money damages. For example, in United States v. Di Mucci, 879 F.2d 1488 (7th Cir.1989), defendants were charged with discriminating against black applicants for apartments in their apartment complexes, in violation of the Fair Housing Act. After their default was entered for failure to comply with discovery, the government requested an injunction directing them to undertake a variety of curative measures, which the district court granted after a hearing.

On appeal, defendants argued that the government had to prove a continuing pattern and practice of discrimination to support an injunction even though they were in default. The appellate court upheld the injunction, noting that ordinarily no showing of violation need be made at the remedy stage. In a default case, however, proper practice would be different:

> As a general rule, a default judgment establishes, as a matter of law, that defendants are liable to plaintiff as to each cause of action alleged in the complaint. Thus, entry of the default judgment established that defendant violated the Fair Housing Act.

> In this case, however, the fact that the government generally does not have to introduce evidence of a pattern or practice of discrimination at the relief stage of a case such as this is of little moment. Because the DiMuccis' liability was established by default, the law in this circuit indicates that in a case such as this an evidentiary hearing may be required to establish what type of relief is necessary. Although upon default, the well-pleaded allegations of a complaint relating to liability are taken as true, allegations of a complaint relating to the amount of damages suffered ordinarily are not. * * * A judgment by default may not be entered without a hearing on damages unless the amount claimed is liquidated or capable of ascertainment from definite figures contained in the documentary evidence or in detailed affidavits.

The magistrate treated this case as if it were a case presenting unliquidated damages required to be determined by hearing. She noted, however, that unlike an unliquidated damages case, where the issue of damages is separate from the facts decided by the default, the facts establishing the necessity for affirmative injunctive relief are not likely to be different from the facts already legally determined by the entry of the default judgment. In any event, it was proper for the magistrate first to determine whether an injunction was necessary, and if so, what that decree should provide. Thus, it was necessary, in effect, for the government to show in this case that defendants engaged in a pattern or practice of discrimination.

Id. at 1497–98. The court then found that the government had made the required showing; in cases seeking injunctions, plaintiff may, in effect, have to prove the case on the merits even though there has been a default.

6. In order to have a properly entered default set aside, defendant must make a motion and show a meritorious defense. In *Shepard*, the court suggests that, to support a motion to set aside a default, defendant need only show that its defense is "good at law," and not that it is likely to succeed. But couldn't defendant always do that by indicating its intention to deny some of plaintiff's allegations? How can the court disregard such denials? In general, courts tend to say they want more than conclusory statements about defenses in support of motions to set aside defaults, insisting instead on some factual showing of a basis for defense. See Gomes v. Williams, 420 F.2d 1364, 1366 (10th Cir.1970). Could this approach be adapted to all cases to permit judges to scrutinize defenses on the pleadings? Cf. Ross v. A.H. Robins, supra p. 163.

In at least one instance, the good defense requirement cannot be imposed on a defendant moving to set aside a default. In Peralta v. Heights Medical Center, Inc., 485 U.S. 80, 108 S.Ct. 896, 99 L.Ed.2d 75 (1988), the Court held that, where defendant has not been served, the resulting default must be set aside even though defendant cannot cite a good defense. Although defendant's inability to identify a valid defense may mean that plaintiff will win the suit, the Court reasoned that "it is no answer to say that in his particular case due process of law would have led to the same result because he had no adequate defense upon the merits."

7. The court in *Shepard* also says that plaintiff must show some prejudice to preserve the default. How could plaintiff do that?

8. Should it matter in *Shepard* that the mistake was made by the lawyer, not the client? Some courts say that difference is critical to the assessment of the culpable conduct issue: "The focus on the source of the default represents an equitable balance between our preference for trials on the merits and the judicial system's need for finality and efficiency in litigation. When the party is blameless and the attorney is at fault, the former interests control and a default judgment should ordinarily be set aside. When the party is at fault, the latter interests dominate and the party must adequately defend its conduct in order to show excusable neglect." Augusta Fiberglass Coatings, Inc. v. Fodor Contracting Corp., 843 F.2d 808 (4th Cir.1988).

9. Default causes additional difficulties in cases involving numerous defendants whom plaintiff claims are jointly liable. In Frow v. De La Vega, 82 U.S. (15 Wall.) 552, 21 L.Ed. 60 (1872), plaintiff sued eight defendants for conspiring to defraud him of title to a tract of land. Seven answered, but one defaulted. At trial, the seven who answered prevailed, and the Supreme Court held that this success foreclosed entry of judgment on the default of the eighth because it would be "incongruous and illegal." Rule 54(b) reinforces the *Frow* doctrine by restricting a court's power to enter final judgment for less than all the parties. A court may do so only "upon an express determination that there is no just reason for delay and upon an express direction for the entry of judgment." See Chapter XII for further discussion of this rule regarding appealability.

In re Uranium Antitrust Litigation, 617 F.2d 1248 (7th Cir.1980), distinguished *Frow* where the defendants were alleged to be severally, as opposed to jointly, liable. There twenty-nine defendants were alleged to have participated in a price-fixing conspiracy in violation of the antitrust laws. They were alleged to be jointly and severally liable (that is, if found to have acted together they could be held jointly liable or each could be held severally liable for his own conduct). The Seventh Circuit interpreted *Frow* as limited to cases of multiple defendants charged with joint liability or charged with liability as to a single res in controversy. Since here the defendants could be held individually liable, it found that entry of judgment against the defaulting defendants would not undermine the *Frow* "desire to avoid logically inconsistent adjudications as to liability." "Different results as to different parties," it said, "are not logically inconsistent or contradictory" when several liability is available.

10. Filing an answer is not absolute protection against being held in default; a defendant who fails to participate in the lawsuit after filing the answer may find his answer stricken and his default entered. Cf. Rule 37(b)(2)(C). Should the court approach a motion to set aside such a default with a similarly lenient attitude?

3.   *The Answer*

a.   *Admitting or Denying the Averments*

Rule 8(b) requires a defendant, in the answer, to "admit or deny the averments upon which the adverse party relies." This is usually done by going down each paragraph in the complaint and stating that it is either admitted or denied. However, a paragraph, and even a sentence, may contain a number of different allegations (although ideally this should be avoided, see Rule 10(b)). If so, the answer should indicate which portions are admitted and which denied, if they cannot be admitted or denied *in toto.*

At common law it was permissible to make a *general denial*, which was a way of saying to the plaintiff: "I don't admit anything. You prove it." This is still permissible in a number of states. Note the limited circumstances under which a general denial may be made under Rule 8(b).

If the defendant is "without knowledge or information sufficient to form a belief as to the truth of an averment, the party shall so state and this has the effect of a denial." (Rule 8(b)).

DAVID v. CROMPTON & KNOWLES CORP.

United States District Court, Eastern District of Pennsylvania, 1973.
58 F.R.D. 444.

HUYETT, DISTRICT JUDGE.

The present case is a products liability action involving a serious personal injury. Defendant, Crompton & Knowles Corporation (Crompton), seeks to amend its answer to Paragraph 5 of the complaint which alleges that Crompton designed, manufactured and sold a shredding machine, 600 AAZ Series 11, to Crown Products Corporation (Crown) [plaintiff's employer]. In its answer to the complaint Crompton averred that it was without sufficient knowledge or information to admit or deny the allegation and demanded proof. It now seeks to deny that it designed, manufactured and sold the machine in question.

Crompton bases its proffered denial upon information which it claims it discovered during 1972. It alleges that the machine was designed, manufactured and sold by James Hunter Corporation (Hunter) prior to its purchase of Hunter, and that it did not assume liabilities for the negligent design, manufacture or sale of machines by Hunter prior to its purchase of Hunter's assets in 1961.

An answer to an averment in a complaint which states that the party lacks sufficient information or knowledge to admit or deny the averments is permitted by Fed.R.Civ.P. 8(b) and it has the effect of a denial. A party, however, may not deny sufficient information or knowledge with impunity, but is subject to the requirements of honesty in pleading. An averment will be deemed admitted when the matter is obviously one as to which defendant has knowledge or information. Mesirow v. Duggan, 240 F.2d 751 (8 Cir.1957), cert. denied sub nom. Duggan v. Green, 355 U.S. 864, 78 S.Ct. 93, 2 L.Ed.2d 70 (1957). Crompton claims that it only recently discovered the information which it now uses as a basis to deny the allegations of Paragraph 5. Plaintiff contends that Crompton's denial of knowledge or information was patently false and should be treated as an admission.

The request for leave to amend assumes significance if Crompton's original answer to Paragraph 5 is deemed an admission. If it is considered an admission, then it is necessary to decide whether an amendment which might greatly affect plaintiff's right to recovery should be allowed, but if it is not deemed admitted and is considered denied in the original answer then the amendment will only serve as a clarification.

The machine which was involved in the accident was designed, manufactured and sold by Hunter to Crown in 1961.[2] Crompton admits

_____

2. The shredding machine denominated in the complaint is not the correct machine.

that it was aware that the machine was a Hunter product at the time it answered the complaint or very shortly thereafter.[3] Nevertheless, in answers to interrogatories and in a third-party complaint Crompton indicated that it was responsible for the design, manufacture and sale of the machine which was made prior to its purchase of Hunter. Crompton relies entirely on its claim that it has only recently discovered that the contract by which it purchased Hunter did not make it responsible for liabilities of this kind.

In Mesirow v. Duggan, supra, the court held that if the matter alleged in the averment was a matter of record peculiarly within the control and knowledge of the defendant, an answer that defendant was without knowledge or information sufficient to form a belief did not constitute a denial under Fed.R.Civ.P. 8(b). In the present case Crompton admits knowledge of Hunter's role in the design, manufacture and sale of the machine. Its assertion of lack of knowledge or information, therefore, must have been in relation to responsibility which it assumed for such a claim. Any responsibility, of course, arises from the agreement of sale between Crompton and Hunter. The terms of this agreement are certainly peculiarly within the control and knowledge of Crompton, one of the parties to the agreement. It does not seem too burdensome to hold Crompton to knowledge of the terms of its purchase agreement and their effect on its rights and liabilities more than nine years after the sale of Hunter was completed. The averment of lack of knowledge or information sufficient to admit or deny the allegations of Paragraph 5 is not proper under these circumstances and plaintiff's allegation should be deemed admitted.

[The portion of the opinion discussing the question whether Crompton will be allowed to amend its answer appears infra at p. 215].

Notes and Questions

1. The starting point in assessing rules governing denials is the effect of an admission. When defendant admits an allegation of the complaint, that allegation is taken as true for purposes of the litigation whether or not it is accurate in fact. Why should courts thus confine the pursuit for objective truth? Is such acquiescence in the parties' willingness to treat fiction as fact inherent in the adversary system? Given the effect of an admission, why should the law pressure a defendant into admitting anything?

2. What should a defendant do if it is not absolutely certain as to the truth of a fact alleged in the complaint? *Crompton* indicates that pleading lack of knowledge may be taken as an admission when the matter is one as to which the defendant has knowledge or information. Rule 11(b)(4), as amended in 1993, explicitly addresses the legitimate grounds for denials. See Profile Pub. & Manag. Corp. v. Musicmaker.com, Inc., 242 F.Supp.2d 363

The proper machine was a Model F–4000 Garnett machine which Crompton referred to in answers to interrogatories filed October 1, 1971. This machine was sold by Hunter to Crown as was the shredding machine mentioned in the complaint.

3. In answers to interrogatories Crompton asserted that it learned of the action from Hunter, which is now a division of Crompton.

(S.D.N.Y.2003) (defendant sanctioned after refusing to withdraw defenses). In connection with allegations about which a party is ignorant, the Advisory Committee Notes explain that "a denial is permissible because, after an appropriate investigation, a party has no information concerning the matter or, indeed, has a reasonable basis for doubting the credibility of the only evidence relevant to the matter. A party should not deny an allegation it knows to be true; but it is not required, simply because it lacks contradictory evidence, to admit an allegation that it believes is not true. * * * If, after further investigation or discovery, a denial is no longer warranted, the defendant should not continue to insist on that denial." 146 F.R.D. at 586. Does this help? As shown by the remainder of the case, infra p. 215, defendant appeared to acknowledge responsibility during discovery. Should that bear on whether the answer was sufficient? Do statements in discovery supersede pleadings?

3. In *Crompton*, the court stresses that the pertinent information was "peculiarly within the control and knowledge of Crompton." How should courts approach the duty to make admissions where this is not true? Consider the well-known case of Zielinski v. Philadelphia Piers, Inc., 139 F.Supp. 408 (E.D.Pa.1956), which points up a risk in making a denial of a multi-faceted allegation. Plaintiff sued defendant (PPI) for personal injuries he alleged he sustained in an accident on Pier 96 in Philadelphia. In paragraph 5 of his complaint, plaintiff alleged that, on the date of the accident, "a forklift or chisel, owned, operated and controlled by the defendant, its agents, servants and employees, was so carelessly managed . . . that the same . . . did come into contact with the plaintiff causing him to sustain the injuries more fully hereinafter set forth." The answer stated that "Defendant . . . denies the averments of paragraph 5." The problem was that PPI, which had once operated the pier involved, had transferred this operation to Carload Carriers, Inc. (CCI) before the date of plaintiff's alleged injury. Moreover, this fact did not surface until it was too late for plaintiff to substitute CCI as defendant because the statute of limitations had run, a problem that would probably not exist today under the revised provisions of Rule 15(c) (see infra pp. 218–27).

Under the circumstances, the court held that PPI would be estopped to deny that it had operated Pier 96 on the date of plaintiff's accident. In part, this ruling was based on PPI's discovery responses, which failed to alert plaintiff to the problem. But the court also held that PPI had failed to comply with Rule 8(b)'s direction that "[w]hen a pleader intends in good faith to deny only a part or a qualification of an averment, the pleader shall specify so much of it as is true and material and shall deny only the remainder." The court reasoned that PPI had not complied with the rule because it was aware of a report stating that there had been an accident in which plaintiff had been injured. Accordingly, "[a] specific denial of parts of this paragraph and specific admission of other parts would have warned plaintiff that he had sued the wrong defendant." The court declined, however, to find that PPI had been guilty of any bad faith in answering as it did.

Given the binding nature of admissions, should defendants be required to rely on reports they receive from others in answering allegations about matters discussed in those reports? Given that PPI did not in fact operate

Pier 96, was there anything in paragraph 5 of the complaint that it could not have denied in good faith? If it were acting in good faith, however, wouldn't it have volunteered that plaintiff had sued the wrong party?

4.   Should defendant's obligation to admit parts of a paragraph of the complaint pursuant to Rule 8(b) be relaxed where the complaint itself is ambiguously or confusingly drafted? See Rule 10(b). Some courts have said that the existence of a poorly drawn complaint gives defendant no excuse unless defendant has objected to the complaint under Rule 12. See Winslow v. National Elec. Products Corp., 5 F.R.D. 126, 129 (W.D.Pa.1946). Is this fair to defendants? Could the complaint in *Zielinski* (note 3 above) have been drafted in a more precise way that would have isolated the problem that later arose when it was revealed that PPI no longer operated the pier?

5.   Is there any legitimate reason why plaintiffs may incline toward vague allegations? Consider Willinger v. Mercy Catholic Medical Center, 241 Pa.Super. 456, 362 A.2d 280 (1976), in which plaintiffs' healthy five year old son checked into the hospital on June 2, 1969, for a tonsillectomy and died shortly after the operation. Plaintiffs alleged as follows in paragraph 3 of their complaint:

> 3.   On or about June 3, 1969, defendant through its agents, ser-vants and employees, acting within the course and scope of their employment, did so carelessly and negligently treat said Leonard Wil-linger . . . that he developed a serious and permanent injury resulting in his death.

Assume that the hospital denied all allegations of this paragraph. Should it later be allowed to contend that while it admits the operation was negligent-ly done, it claims that the persons responsible for the negligence were not its agents, servants or employees? Is there anything in paragraph 3 that the hospital should have admitted? Can you see any reason why plaintiff was so vague?

Assuming that defendant generally may not excuse defects in the answer by relying on defects in the complaint, should an exception be made in *Crompton*, where it appears that plaintiff's complaint identified the wrong machine?

6.   *Negative pregnant:* Sometimes even today one will encounter men-tion of the negative pregnant, one of the rules of construction under the old common-law pleading practice. Suppose, for example, that in response to paragraph 5 of the complaint in *Crompton,* defendant had asserted that it "denies that it designed, manufactured and sold a shredding machine . . . to Crown." Because of the conjunctive nature of this response, some courts would find that its negative was "pregnant with admission." Thus, it may be that defendant did manufacture and sell the machine, but did not design it, etc. Courts might find this tactic misleading and treat it as ineffective. The easy solution, of course, is simply to deny each and every allegation, as defendant did in *Zielinski,* without adding anything more. Hence, the problems of the negative pregnant are largely behind us; Professors Wright and Miller report that there has been only one reported federal case involving the issue since the rules were adopted in 1938. 5 C. Wright & A. Miller, Federal Practice & Procedure § 1267 at 554 (3d ed. 2004).

b. Affirmative Defenses

As we have seen, a responsive pleading must admit or deny each averment upon which the adverse party relies (Rule 8(b)). However, there are times when affirming or denying is inadequate: for example, a responding party may be willing to admit a factual allegation but still contend that she had a justifiable reason for her action. At common law, this was called pleading in "confession and avoidance." It was a way of saying that even if the allegation is proven, there is an excuse that is recognized under the law. It is different from a denial because it does not seek to deny an element of the opposing party's case, but rather sets out affirmatively a new issue that goes beyond disproving that element.

Affirmative defenses are the modern equivalent of the common-law plea in confession and avoidance, and Rule 8(c) requires them to be "set forth affirmatively." Nineteen affirmative defenses are listed in Rule 8(c), but this is not a comprehensive list, and any other "matter constituting an avoidance or affirmative defense" must also be pleaded affirmatively.

It is not always easy to determine whether a matter is an affirmative defense that must be pleaded by the responding party or simply relates to an element of the claim. Statutory language can sometimes determine who has pleading responsibility. Recall, for example, United States v. Board of Harbor Commissioners, supra p. 134. There a federal statute provided that the owner or operator of a facility from which a hazardous substance is discharged is liable to the U.S. government, *except* when the owner or operator can prove the discharge was caused solely by an act of God, act of war, negligence of the U.S., or act of a third party. The "except" language indicates that the owner of the facility has the burden of pleading and proving one of the four circumstances that will negative liability, and thus that they are affirmative defenses.

Another example is Gomez v. Toledo, 446 U.S. 635, 100 S.Ct. 1920, 64 L.Ed.2d 572 (1980). Plaintiff there was a former police officer who sued the Superintendent of Police for firing him without a hearing (based on the officer's alleged use of illegal wiretapping). The district court dismissed the case on the ground that the defendant superintendent was entitled to qualified immunity for acts done in good faith within the scope of his official duties and that the plaintiff had failed to plead as part of his claim for relief that defendant was motivated by bad faith.

The suit was brought under 42 U.S.C.A. § 1983, which provides a cause of action for "the deprivation of any rights, privileges, or immunities secured by the Constitution and laws" by any person acting "under color of any statute, ordinance, regulation, custom, or usage, of any State or Territory." The Supreme Court read § 1983 as only requiring two allegations—that the defendant deprived plaintiff of a federal right and that this was done under color of law. "Since qualified immunity is a defense," the court said, "the burden of pleading it rests with the defendant." It went on to note that whether the defendant had acted in good faith "depends on facts peculiarly within the knowledge of the defendant" and that "[t]here may be no way for a plaintiff to know in advance whether the official has such a belief or, indeed, whether he will even claim that he does." For that reason, it makes sense that defendant have the burden of raising the issue affirmatively.

Policies affecting burden allocation: As indicated in *Gomez*, statutory language may be helpful or even determinative as to whether a matter is an affirmative defense, but there are also policies that help to allocate pleading burdens when the language is not so clear. In a leading article, Professor Cleary found three types of concerns in the decisions although he also observed that none affords a complete working rule. Cleary, Presuming and Pleading: An Essay on Judicial Immaturity, 12 Stan. L.Rev. 5, 11–13 (1959):

(1) *Policy*. As Judge Clark remarks, "One who must bear the risk of getting the matter properly set before the court, if it is to be considered at all, has to that extent the dice loaded against him." While policy more obviously predominates at the stage of determining what elements are material, its influence may nevertheless extend into the stage of allocating those elements by way of favoring one or the other party to a particular kind of litigation. Thus a court which is willing to permit a recovery for negligence may still choose to exercise restraints by imposing on plaintiff the burden of freedom from contributory negligence, as a theoretical, though perhaps not a practical, handicap. Or the bringing of actions for defamation may in some measure be discouraged by allocating untruth to plaintiff as an element of his prima facie case, rather than by treating truth as an affirmative defense. * * *

(2) *Fairness*. The nature of a particular element may indicate that evidence relating to it lies more within the control of one party, which suggests the fairness of allocating that element to him. Examples are payment, discharge in bankruptcy, and license, all of which are commonly treated as affirmative defenses. However, caution in making any extensive generalization is indicated by the classification of contributory negligence, illegality, and failure of consideration also as affirmative defenses, despite the fact that knowledge more probably lies with plaintiff. Certainly in the usual tort cases, knowledge of his own wrongdoing rests more intimately in defendant, though the accepted general pattern imposes this burden on plaintiff.

(3) *Probability*. A further factor which seems to enter into many decisions as to allocation is a judicial, i.e., wholly nonstatistical, estimate of the probabilities of the situation, with the burden being put on the party who will be benefited by a departure from the supposed norm.

The probabilities may relate to the type of situation out of which the litigation arises or they may relate to the type of litigation itself. The standards are quite different and may produce differences in result. To illustrate: If it be assumed that most people pay their bills, the probabilities are that any bill selected at random has been paid; therefore, a plaintiff suing to collect a bill would be responsible for nonpayment as an element of his prima facie case. If, however, attention is limited to bills upon which suit is brought, a contrary conclusion is reached. Plaintiffs are not prone to sue for paid bills, and the probabilities are that the bill is unpaid. Hence payment would be an affirmative defense.

Note that the burden of proving an affirmative defense at trial usually follows the burden of pleading, but that this result does not always follow. In his concurring opinion in *Gomez*, for example, Justice Rehnquist stated that he left open the question whether the defendant superintendent would have the burden of proving qualified immunity at trial. (Burden of proof at trial will be considered in Chapter VI.)

Effect of failure to plead an affirmative defense: If an affirmative defense is not pleaded, the issue is not in the case, and evidence relating to it is not admissible at trial (unless such evidence is independently relevant to an essential element of the case). Because there usually need not be a reply to an answer even if it contains affirmative defenses, the allegations supporting them are taken as denied by the opposing party. If an affirmative defense is not pleaded, the defendant may not rely upon it. See Harris v. Secretary, U.S. Department of Veterans Affairs, 126 F.3d 339 (D.C.Cir.1997) (holding it was improper to grant defendant's motion for summary judgement on the ground plaintiff delayed too long in filing suit even though the district court could grant defendant leave to amend the answer to add that affirmative defense); compare Lafreniere Park Foundation v. Broussard, 221 F.3d 804 (5th Cir.2000) (defendant could raise res judicata by summary judgment motion even though it was not asserted in the answer). In any event, this is not the same as the waiver effected by Rule 12(h)(1), which is designed to force parties to raise certain kinds of objections early or lose them. An amendment to add an omitted affirmative defense would be governed by Rule 15(a), which states that leave to amend "shall be freely granted when justice so requires."

Relation to motion for judgment on the pleadings: From the perspective of the defendant, a Rule 12(c) motion for a judgment on the pleadings is essentially the same as a Rule 12(b)(6) motion to dismiss. Johnson v. Johnson, 385 F.3d 503, 529 (5th Cir.2004). But for the plaintiff, the contents of the answer may make such a motion possible. If defendant has admitted the essential allegations or plaintiff's case and has not pleaded an affirmative defense, plaintiff could file a motion for judgment on the pleadings, which tests the legal sufficiency of all the pleadings (just as a Rule 12(b)(6) motion tests the legal sufficiency of the complaint). But what if the defendant has pleaded an affirmative defense? Assume, for example, that the complaint alleges that the defendant assaulted and battered the plaintiff, and the answer admits the acts but raises the affirmative defense that the defendant was a policeman. The plaintiff, by making a motion for judgment on the pleadings, asks the court to determine that the complaint makes out a prima facie case of assault, that the defendant has admitted the essential facts, and that the defendant's purported affirmative defense is legally insufficient. Should the defense that the defendant is a policeman be legally sufficient? If the court determines that the defense is not legally sufficient, it may strike it (Rule 12(f)) and, with the defense gone, grant the plaintiff judgment on the pleadings. If matters outside the pleadings are presented, the court may treat the motion as one for summary judgment.

The statute of limitations: The statute of limitations, one of the nineteen affirmative defenses enumerated in Rule 8(c), poses special problems. Should a defendant have to file an answer to raise an affirmative defense that, as shown on the face of the complaint, the claim is barred by the statute of limitations? Could defendant move to dismiss under Rule 12(b)(6) instead? Recall Zuk v. Eastern Pennsylvania Psychiatric Inst., supra p. 143. Many courts would entertain a Rule 12(b)(6) motion on the theory that the defense is "built into" plaintiff's complaint because it appears on the face of the complaint. Must plaintiff volunteer such detail as to dates in his complaint? Cf. Rule 9(f); Sidney S. Arst Co. v. Pipefitters Welfare Educ. Fund, 25 F.3d 417, 421 n. 6 (7th Cir.1994) ("Given the liberty of notice pleading, dismissal for failure to state a claim is likely only when the complaint shows some bar to relief on its face, or when the complaint's allegations indicate the existence of an affirmative defense."). Other courts require the statute of limitations to be raised by an affirmative defense in the answer so that any factual disputes (such as plaintiff's rejoinder that the statute was tolled due to defendant's fraudulent concealment) can be dealt with by summary judgment procedures. See Richards v. Mileski, 662 F.2d 65, 73 (D.C.Cir. 1981); Marcus, Fraudulent Concealment in Federal Court: Toward a More Disparate Standard?, 71 Geo.L.J. 829, 902–04 (1983).

    c.   *Counterclaims*

WIGGLESWORTH v. TEAMSTERS LOCAL UNION NO. 592

United States District Court, Eastern District of Virginia, 1975.
68 F.R.D. 609.

WARRINER, DISTRICT JUDGE.

Plaintiff Welford Wigglesworth, Jr., a member of Teamsters Local Union No. 592, has filed a complaint under the Labor Management Reporting Disclosures Act, "Act," 29 U.S.C. § 401 et seq., alleging that the union and its president have violated certain of his rights as protected by the Act. Specifically, the complaint avers that during meetings of defendant Local No. 592 held on 8 September 1974 and 13 October 1974, plaintiff was prevented from exercising his right to freedom of speech, and was denied his request to have the union membership informed of their rights as required by the Act.

In addition to denying generally the allegations in the complaint, defendants asserted a counterclaim alleging the following: On 3 Decem-

ancillary - helping subordinate

ber 1974, the day on which the complaint was filed, plaintiff called a press conference at which he accused the union of being dominated by the "Mafia" and that a certain past local union election had been "fixed." Defendants claim that these remarks constituted libel and slander. The counterclaim further alleges that plaintiff maliciously misused and abused the processes of law by maintaining the instant lawsuit for wholly vindictive and wrongful purposes.

The matter is now before the Court on plaintiff's motion to dismiss the counterclaim, inter alia, for lack of subject matter jurisdiction. There is no diversity of citizenship between the parties, and jurisdiction is founded solely on 29 U.S.C. § 412.

Defendants' initial contention is that the motion to dismiss for lack of subject matter jurisdiction is untimely and should therefore be denied. However, Rule 12(h)(3), Fed.R.Civ.P., plainly states that challenges to the Court's subject matter jurisdiction may be raised at any time, and the cases have consistently so held. Therefore, the defendants' claim of untimeliness is without merit.

Defendants' counterclaim was filed pursuant to Rule 13, Fed. R.Civ.P. which distinguishes between "compulsory" and "permissive" counterclaims. If the defendants' claim arises out of the transaction or occurrence that is the subject matter of the opposing party's claim, then, if certain other requisites not here pertinent are met, it is compulsory. By definition, compulsory claims are "ancillary to the claim asserted in the complaint and [sic] no independent basis of [f]ederal jurisdiction is required." Alternatively, if the counterclaim is unconnected with the transaction out of which the primary claim arose, it is permissive, and independent jurisdictional grounds are required.

The threshold question to be decided is whether defendants' counterclaims arise out of the same transaction or occurrence that is the subject matter of the plaintiff's claim. If so, then the counterclaims are compulsory, and are properly before the Court. Thus, the definition of "transaction or occurrence" is critical to this determination.

There is a substantial body of law which liberally defines the test of compulsoriness as requiring that there be not so much "an absolute identity of factual backgrounds for the two claims, but only a logical relationship between them." United Artists Corp. v. Masterpiece Productions, 221 F.2d 213, 216 (2d Cir.1955). In Moore v. New York Cotton Exchange, 270 U.S. 593, 610, 46 S.Ct. 367, 371, 70 L.Ed. 750 (1926), the Supreme Court explained that " '[t]ransaction' is a word of flexible meaning. It may comprehend a series of many occurrences, depending not so much upon the immediateness of their connection as upon their logical relationship."

Defendants maintain that under this liberal test, their counterclaims meet the criteria set forth for compulsoriness, and therefore are properly within the Court's ancillary jurisdiction. We must disagree.

The gravamen of plaintiff's claim is that he was denied his right to free speech and expression at certain past union meetings. Thus, the claim arises solely from the alleged wrongful conduct on the part of the union at the specific union meetings in question. Determination of the validity of that claim is limited to ascertaining whether the challenged union meetings were conducted in conformity with the mandates of the Act. However, defendants' counterclaim for libel and slander is predicated on events which are in no wise part of the transactions or occurrences which gave rise to plaintiff's claim. This aspect of the counterclaim is grounded on words allegedly spoken by plaintiff many months after the union meetings in question. There is no indication that the alleged remarks at the press conference on 3 December 1974 had any relationship, logical or otherwise, to the events which transpired at certain past union meetings.

On issues of law almost identical to those presented here, the Court in Bose Corp. v. Consumers Union of the United States, Inc., 384 F.Supp. 600 (D.C.Mass.1974),* found defendant's counterclaims to be permissive. In *Bose,* the complaint alleged unfair competition and violations of the Lanham Act. The defendant filed a counterclaim for malicious abuse of process and for defamation arising out of the filing of the complaint and the issuance of a press release on the same day. Although the issue to be decided was whether the counterclaims were barred by the statute of limitations, the resolution necessarily turned on whether the claims were compulsory or permissive. After an extensive analysis of the various standards which have been employed to ascertain the nature of a counterclaim, the Court based its determination on whether the same evidence would support or refute the opposing claims. If the same evidence would substantially dispose of the issues raised by the opposing claims, then the counterclaims were compulsory; if not, then they were permissive.

After observing that the issues of law and fact raised by the opposing claims were significantly dissimilar, the Court in *Bose* determined that application of the "same evidence" standard revealed that the counterclaims for libel and malicious abuse of process were permissive.

Applying the *Bose* standard to the facts of this case, a like conclusion seems inescapable. The evidence necessary for the union to prevail on its libel and slander claims is not relevant to plaintiff's case. Alternatively, the proof of violations by the union under the L.M.R.D.A. varies substantially from that necessary to recover for libel and slander. Similarly, proof of plaintiff's willful abuse of process with resulting damage to the union is quite distinct from that necessary to establish an infringement of plaintiff's rights under the federal statute.

There being no connection between the events giving rise to the counterclaims asserted by defendants, and the transaction or occurrence upon which plaintiff's claim is based, the Court holds that the counter-

---

* A different decision in the same *Bose* case is reproduced infra p. 1078.—Eds.

claims are permissive. Noting that such claims are between non-diverse parties, and are grounded solely in state law, the Court observed that they are without independent jurisdictional support, and must therefore be dismissed unless falling within an exception to the jurisdictional requirement.

* * *

Accordingly, plaintiff's motion to dismiss the counterclaims will be granted.

Notes and Questions

1. This is the first case we have seen involving the question of the number of events that can properly be grouped together as part of a common "transaction or occurrence" or "series of transactions or occurrences" in a given litigation. For purposes of reference at the outset, various situations dealing with this general question are:

—Compulsory counterclaims (Rule 13(a))

—Relation back of amendments (Rule 15(c))

—Permissive joinder of parties (Rule 20) (see Chapter IV)

—Supplemental jurisdiction (see Chapter X)

—Res judicata (see Chapter XIII)

For a review of interpretations of the various contexts in which the "transaction" is important, see Kane, Original Sin and the Transaction in Federal Civil Procedure, 76 Texas L. Rev. 1723 (1998).

2. What test does the court in *Wigglesworth* adopt to determine whether the counterclaim is compulsory? Professors Wright, Miller and Kane distill the following four tests from the cases, while noting that "the courts have refrained from making any serious attempt to define the transaction or occurrence concept in a highly explicit fashion":

   (a) Are the issues of fact and law raised by the claim and counterclaim largely the same?

   (b) Would res judicata bar a subsequent suit on defendant's claim absent the compulsory counterclaim rule?

   (c) Will substantially the same evidence support or refute plaintiff's claim as well as defendant's counterclaim?

   (d) Is there any logical relation between the claim and the counterclaim?

6 Federal Practice & Procedure § 1410. Do these tests (except (b), which we address in Chapter XIII) lead to the same result in *Wigglesworth*?

3. *Ancillary (now supplemental) jurisdiction*: Why was it necessary for the court in *Wigglesworth* to determine whether the counterclaim for libel and abuse of process was compulsory or permissive? The answer has to do with subject matter jurisdiction. Note that this was a suit based on a federal statute, 29 U.S.C.A. § 412. In general, a plaintiff asserting a federal claim invokes "federal question" jurisdiction under 28 U.S.C.A. § 1331. But the counterclaim for libel and abuse of process arose under state law and would

not independently satisfy federal jurisdictional requirements. This is where what was called ancillary jurisdiction (now called supplemental jurisdiction) comes in. Because it seems unfair to make a defendant respond to suit in a federal court without allowing it to counterclaim as to matters arising out of the same transaction or occurrence, the courts have jurisdiction over compulsory counterclaims. As with Rule 13(a), the question whether ancillary jurisdiction existed depended on the connection between the grounds for plaintiff's claim and the grounds for defendant's counterclaim. The application of these jurisdictional principles is considered in detail in Chapter X.

4. How does the counterclaim in *Wigglesworth* differ from a defense that plaintiff's claims lack merit? Didn't plaintiff's decision to call a press conference suggest that he viewed the claims in the lawsuit to be related to the charges made at the press conference? Compare Great Lakes Rubber Corp. v. Herbert Cooper Co., 286 F.2d 631 (3d Cir.1961), in which plaintiff's initial complaint for theft of trade secrets was dismissed for lack of federal subject matter jurisdiction, but only after defendant Cooper asserted a counterclaim alleging that the plaintiff's suit was groundless and part of an effort to prevent competition by Cooper, thereby violating the antitrust laws. Great Lakes then repackaged its original claims as a compulsory counterclaim to Cooper's counterclaim, and the appellate court held that this was proper:

> Cooper alleges that the claims originally asserted in Great Lakes' amended complaint, reiterated in substance in its counterclaim, are "unjustified" and were brought in "bad faith and without color of right with the sole object of harassing and preventing defendant [Cooper] from competing in the manufacture and sale of flexible hose." These are the only allegations set out in Cooper's counterclaim which demonstrate a relationship within the purview of Rule 13(a) to Great Lakes' amended complaint or counterclaim. But that they do demonstrate a relationship is unquestionable. It is clear that a determination that Cooper's claims that the claims asserted in Great Lakes' amended complaint and reiterated in substance in its counterclaim are harassing will entail an extensive airing of the facts and the law relating to Great Lakes' counterclaim.

Is this case distinguishable from *Wigglesworth?*

5. Rule 13(a) says that counterclaims arising out of the same transaction or occurrence are "compulsory." Should the court refuse to let the defendant defend the case unless it asserts such counterclaims? It does not do so, and, in reality, the effect of the rule is only to forbid a later suit on the claim that should have been asserted as a counterclaim. Is it likely that defendants are often reluctant to assert claims against those who sue them? Cf. Rule 13(b). Why might a defendant decline to assert a claim against a plaintiff that it had a right to assert? Note that the rule does not make compulsory any claims that are already the subject of pending litigation. Why should these be exempted?

6. Rule 13(g) permits a party to state a cross-claim against a co-party (i.e., one defendant may assert a claim against another defendant) if it arises out of the same transaction or occurrence. But such claims are never compulsory. Should they be compulsory in the same way as claims against an

opposing party? Are there stronger reasons for giving co-defendants the option not to sue one another?

D. VOLUNTARY DISMISSAL

Plaintiffs sometimes want to dismiss a suit they have brought. This can occur when a plaintiff realizes that it does not have a winning suit and wants to end it without further expenditure of time and money. But a plaintiff may also want only to end the particular suit in the particular court, with the freedom to file it again, or to file it in a modified form, in another court. This may happen if the plaintiff is persuaded that it can get a more favorable result in another forum. Examples include cases in which defendant has pleaded a statute of limitations defense that seems likely to be upheld in the court in which the suit is pending but might not be in another forum, or cases in which preliminary rulings of the judge lead the plaintiff to believe that the judge is unfavorable to the claim.

At common law, a plaintiff's right to a voluntary dismissal or "nonsuit" without prejudice was absolute at any time before judgment. Ex parte Skinner & Eddy Corp., 265 U.S. 86, 44 S.Ct. 446, 68 L.Ed. 912 (1924). "State practices permitted a plaintiff to dismiss the action up to various points in the proceeding ranging from before the issue had been joined, just before the trial began, before the case was submitted to the jury, to before the verdict was returned." 9 C. Wright & A. Miller, Fed. Prac. & Pro. § 2363, at 253.

Today, however, we recognize that a liberal voluntary dismissal rule can cause needless expenditure of judicial resources and impose burdens on the defendant in defending against a suit that is ultimately withdrawn. Although some states still accord plaintiffs a broad right to dismiss or nonsuit, in federal court Rule 41(a)(1) reflects a policy that voluntary dismissal should be limited to the early stages of the litigation. A plaintiff is allowed to dismiss without order of the court by filing (i) a notice of dismissal at any time before service of an answer or of a motion for summary judgment, whichever first occurs, or (ii) a stipulation of dismissal signed by all parties. Unless otherwise stated in the notice, a dismissal is without prejudice, except when filed by a plaintiff who has once dismissed an action based on or including the same claim. Rule 41(a)(2) contemplates the exercise of judicial discretion in all other situations, providing that an action shall not be dismissed without prejudice "save upon order of the court and upon such terms and conditions as the court deems proper." For an analysis of the policy issues involved, see Solomine & Lippert, Deregualting Voluntary Dismissals, 36 U.Mich.J. of Law Ref. 367 (2003).

Rule 41(a)(1)(i) provides a very specific time period for allowing a voluntary dismissal without court order—it must be filed before service of an answer or motion for summary judgment. However, even when voluntary dismissal is sought before an answer or motion for summary judgment, some courts have been unwilling to allow it if the merits of the case have already been addressed. In Harvey Aluminum, Inc. v. American Cyanamid Co., 203 F.2d 105 (2d Cir.), cert. denied, 345 U.S. 964, 73 S.Ct. 949, 97 L.Ed. 1383 (1953), a notice of dismissal was filed after a hearing was held on plaintiff's request for a preliminary injunction, but before an answer or motion for summary judgment had been filed. The appellate court vacated the dismissal, noting that the preliminary injunction had been denied because "the plaintiffs' chances of success on the ultimate trial were 'remote, if not completely nil,' " and the defendants had been put to considerable research and preparation. How can this be squared with the language of Rule 41(a)(1)(i)? Is the decision reading into Rule 41(a)(1)(i) an additional requirement for voluntary dismissal—that the merits have not been addressed? Can this be justified by a concern that voluntary dismissal not be used as a vehicle for forum shopping?

A later case, D.C. Electronics, Inc. v. Nartron Corp., 511 F.2d 294 (6th Cir.1975), questioned whether *Harvey* was still good law, noting that "the drafters employed precise language to define an 'early stage' of a proceeding." Upon filing suit, plaintiff in that case sought and obtained a temporary restraining order (TRO) and scheduled a hearing for a preliminary injunction. After the TRO was dissolved, plaintiff withdrew its request for a preliminary injunction and thereafter gave notice of voluntary dismissal. Although neither an answer nor a motion for summary judgment had been filed, the district court held that "the case has progressed too far to allow dismissal," and ordered the notice of voluntary dismissal vacated. The appellate court reversed, noting that "Rule 41(a)(1)(i) is clear and unambiguous on its face and admits of no exceptions that call for the exercise of judicial discretion by any court." It also noted that, even under the *Harvey* test, the merits were not reached because only a TRO had been issued and the hearing on the motion for a preliminary injunction had been aborted. Does a TRO, as opposed to a preliminary injunction, not involve the merits? The court also rejected the policy argument that if a plaintiff could always dismiss so long as an answer or motion for summary judgment had not been filed, the defendant would be rendered "defenseless against the whim and caprice of the plaintiff." "The defendant can protect himself," it said, "by merely filing an answer or motion for summary judgment."

Might there sometimes be a question about whether defendant has filed a motion for summary judgment? Recall that the last sentence of Rule 12(b) says that if defendant supports a Rule 12(b)(6) motion with matters outside the pleading the court shall be treated as one for summary judgment unless the court excludes these outside matters. If the defendant files a 12(b)(b) motion, should plaintiff be allowed to dismiss under Rule 41(a)(1)(i)?

Once plaintiff has filed a notice of dismissal, it may not unilaterally withdraw or amend the notice. However, it may move to vacate it under Rule 60(b) (see infra pp. 653–57) for mistake, surprise, inadvertence, or excusable neglect, or on a showing of good cause. See Noland v. Flohr Metal Fabricators, 104 F.R.D. 83, 87 (D.Alaska.1984) (permitting amendment to limit dismissal to one defendant, and not the entire action, where plaintiff's mistake had been inadvertent).

Once defendant's answer or motion for summary judgment has been filed, the plaintiff can dismiss only upon stipulation of all the parties or by order of court upon such terms and conditions as it deems proper. Courts usually allow dismissal without imposing conditions unless the defendant has suffered prejudice. See Moore's Federal Prac. ¶ 41.10 (3d ed.1999). The mere prospect of having to defend against a suit in another forum is not prejudice. D'Alto v. Dahon Cal., Inc., 100 F.3d 281, 283 (2d Cir.1996) (fact that plaintiff could refile the suit is not "legal prejudice"). Compare Paulucci v. City of Duluth, 826 F.2d 780 (8th Cir.1987) (refusing dismissal where continuing uncertainty as to title to land would prejudice defendant). Court-imposed conditions on dismissal can reduce the likelihood of prejudice. For example, requiring plaintiff to pay the opposing party's costs in defending the case might be such a condition. But would that be appropriate in light of the American rule that a winning defendant cannot usually recover its attorneys' fees? See supra p. 102 n.1. See Marlow v. Winston & Strawn, 19 F.3d 300, 306 (7th Cir.1994) ("Typically, a court imposes as a term and condition of dismissal that plaintiff pay the defendant the expenses he has incurred in defending the suit, which usually includes reasonable attorneys' fees").

If the court has the power to condition a dismissal, can it make the dismissal with prejudice? See Gravatt v. Columbia University, 845 F.2d 54 (2d Cir.1988) (dismissal without prejudice can be converted into dismissal with prejudice). If the plaintiff does not like the conditions imposed, can it change its mind about dismissing? See GAF Corp. v. Transamerica Ins. Co., 665 F.2d 364, 367–68 (D.C.Cir.1981) ("a plaintiff has the choice between accepting the conditions and obtaining dismissal and, if he feels that the conditions are too burdensome, withdrawing his dismissal motion and proceeding with the case on the merits"). If the plaintiff moves to dismiss with prejudice, can the court refuse to grant dismissal because defendant wants to obtain vindication at trial? See Smoot v. Fox, 340 F.2d 301 (6th Cir.1964) (plaintiff has absolute right to obtain dismissal with prejudice).

A plaintiff may want a voluntary dismissal to attempt to avoid Rule 11 sanctions (see supra pp. 143–55). Cooter & Gell v. Hartmarx Corp., 496 U.S. 384, 110 S.Ct. 2447, 110 L.Ed.2d 359 (1990), held that a voluntary dismissal did not deprive the court of jurisdiction to consider Rule 11 sanctions. The 1993 amendments to Rule 11 preclude sanctions, however, if the complaint is dismissed within 21 days after service of a motion for sanctions. See Rule 11(c)(1)(A).

E. AMENDMENTS TO PLEADINGS

Attorneys are often rushed for time in filing pleadings. The plaintiff's attorney might only be brought into the case a short time before the statute of limitations runs and, absent an extension of time, the defendant's attorney has only 20 days after service of the complaint to file an answer. Depending on the complexity of the case and difficulty of access to information, pleadings sometimes have to be filed when very little is known about the events. It would, therefore, be contrary to the interests of justice not to permit amendments to pleadings as the case is investigated and prepared for trial. This liberal approach to amendments is reflected in Rule 15.

A liberal approach to amendments, however, has its own costs. Parties may rely on the pleadings of their opponents, believing that they are facing only the claims alleged and therefore may forgo investigation into matters that are not pleaded. Thus, even a liberal pleading rule like Rule 15 must contain some limitations.

1. Permission to Amend

DAVID v. CROMPTON & KNOWLES CORP.

United States District Court, Eastern District of Pennsylvania, 1973.
58 F.R.D. 444.

[The facts and the first portion of this opinion appear supra p. 200. The court there decided that defendant Crompton's denial, on grounds of lack of knowledge, of plaintiff's allegation that it designed, manufactured and sold the machine that injured plaintiff was ineffective, and constituted an admission.]

The next question is whether Crompton should now be permitted to amend its answer to deny the allegation in Paragraph 5. Crompton relies upon Fed.R.Civ.P. 15(a) which provides that leave to amend an answer should be freely given when justice requires. The Federal Rules clearly favor a liberal attitude towards amendments. The purpose of a permissive attitude is to encourage decision of the case on the merits by allowing parties to present the real issues of the case.

A court may deny a request to amend if it bases such denial upon a valid ground. Among the reasons commonly cited for denying permission to amend are that the amendment will result in undue prejudice to the other party, or that it has been unduly delayed. Plaintiff claims that Crompton should be denied leave to amend because of undue delay by defendant and prejudice to plaintiff if Crompton's motion is granted.

Crompton, as indicated above, knew the basic facts surrounding the manufacture and delivery of the machine no later than October 1, 1971 when it filed answers to interrogatories. It almost certainly knew the essential facts much earlier. Crompton had examined the machinery in question by June, 1971. It had received information concerning the machine from plaintiff's counsel in March, 1971. The proffered reason for this delay, Crompton's recent discovery that it was not liable for such liabilities of Hunter, cannot be considered good cause for the reasons discussed above.

The effect of this delay could be highly prejudicial to the plaintiff. The action arose on November 27, 1969. The two-year statute of limitation expired on November 27, 1971. Plaintiff is now barred from instituting this action against another party. The running of the statute is the serious type of prejudice which may justify a denial of defendant's motion to amend his answer.

In the present case the action was filed more than 11 months prior to the running of the statute. In its answer to interrogatories and in its third-party complaint Crompton gave a clear indication that it had assumed Hunter's liabilities in cases such as this. It referred to Hunter's agent as "defendant's sales representative" and averred that the machine "was received from defendant". Plaintiff cannot be considered negligent for not discovering Crompton's alleged defense. Crompton never gave any indication prior to June, 1972 that it was asserting such a defense. If plaintiff had received timely notice of this alleged defense he would have had sufficient time to investigate the relationship between Crompton and Hunter and determine which is the proper party. That possibility was denied to him by defendant's long delay.

Crompton cites Jacobs v. McCloskey & Co., 40 F.R.D. 486 (E.D.Pa. 1966) to support its motion to amend. In that case the district court permitted a defendant to amend its answer to deny ownership of a building which belonged to its wholly owned subsidiary. The effect of the amendment was to deny recovery from one defendant since the statute had run. The action, however, had been filed only nine days prior to the expiration of the statute and the answer was not filed until after the statute had run. In granting leave to amend the court stated:

> Had the Defendant answered within the nine day period remaining before the expiration of the statute, thus lulling Plaintiff into believing that his action had been properly brought, this Court would be more sympathetic to the Plaintiff's appeal. However, the Defendant was entitled to forbear responding for the twenty day period specified in the summons. Moreover, it is questionable whether the plaintiff suffered any prejudice by virtue of the erroneous admission after the statute had expired. The Defendant could have denied ownership at that time, and the Plaintiff's amended complaint against First Penco Realty, Inc., would still have been subject to the defense of the statute of limitations.

Plaintiff in the present case was certainly lulled by defendant during the period between the filing of the complaint and the running of the statute, and it is unquestionable that he has been prejudiced by the delay.

Under the circumstances of this case defendant's motion to amend will be denied. This may be burdensome to defendant and may deny to it an otherwise valid defense, but that is a situation of its own making. To allow the amendment would be to penalize the plaintiff who is without fault and leave him without a possible remedy for very severe injuries.

Notes and Questions

1. *Crompton* found prejudice justifying denial of the right to amend where the defendant's incorrect answer gave the plaintiff no reason to

believe that it had sued the wrong defendant, and therefore that it needed to bring in the right defendant before the statute of limitations had run. What other situations would demonstrate prejudice? What if a party waits until the eve of trial to amend, adding a new claim or defense to which the opponent is not prepared to respond? Would the possibility of a continuance remove the prejudice? Would the opponent have to show that evidence or witnesses were no longer available, so that even if he were granted a continuance he would still be prejudiced? If it could not do so, would the expense and delay inherent in a continuance be enough to demonstrate prejudice? Would conditioning a continuance on the amending party's paying the opponent's expenses resulting from the continuance remove the prejudice?

2.   The effect of the *Jacobs* case, cited in *Crompton*, is to allow a defendant to amend where the plaintiff filed just before the statute of limitations had run even though the statute of limitations has run and plaintiff cannot join the right party. Would it make a difference whether the defendant knew (or should have known) at the time it filed its answer that its failure to deny that it designed the machine was incorrect?

3.   In ruling on a motion to amend, should the judge consider judicial efficiency and economy? For example, is it relevant whether the amendment will take the preparation and trial in a new direction or whether the discovery and preparation already done would be sufficient?

4.   If a party seeks to amend only after it is clear it has no cause of action under the existing pleading, should a judge be less willing to grant the amendment?

5.   *The role of discretion:* Review of decisions whether to allow amendments is governed by an abuse of discretion standard; an appellate court will reverse only if the trial court's decision is outside the bounds of reasonable decisions. Thus, there will be many cases in which the judge could, without risking reversal, decide to allow or deny amendment. Would it have been an abuse of discretion for the court in *Crompton* to allow the amendment? The abuse of discretion standard lends itself to decisions tailored to the unique facts of the given case. It also may reward good lawyering, for the judge's reaction often depends on counsel's ability to emphasize certain facts and make others seem unimportant. For an analysis, see Marcus, Slouching Toward Discretion, 78 Notre Dame L. Rev. 1561 (2003).

AMENDMENTS AT TRIAL

Rule 15(b) provides for an automatic amendment of the pleadings "when issues not raised by the pleadings are tried by express or implied consent of the parties." Thus, once evidence is admitted without objection as to a claim not pleaded in the complaint, that claim will be treated as though it were raised in the complaint. What if evidence could reasonably relate to both an issue that is pleaded and one that is not? What degree of awareness should a party have in order to be considered to consent to the trial of an issue by failing to object?

Rule 15(b) also provides that amendment of the pleadings may be made to conform them to the evidence, but "failure so to amend does not affect the result of the trial of these issues." Why would a party seek a formal amendment?

Note that even if the opposing party objects, Rule 15(b) directs that the court should allow amendments "freely when the presentation of the merits of the action will be subserved thereby and the objecting party fails to satisfy the court that the admission of such evidence would prejudice the party in maintaining the party's action or defense." How does this standard compare to the standard in Rule 15(a) for pretrial amendments? Should the court be more amenable to amendments at trial than before trial?

Contrast the provisions of Rule 16(e) relating to amendment of final pretrial orders. Such orders are to be entered after the final pretrial conference (see Rule 16(d)) and may be amended "only to prevent manifest injustice." When would amendments be necessary to subserve the merits of the action but not to prevent manifest injustice?

Probably the actual behavior of courts is to become more restrictive about amendments as the trial date draws near, at least where the proposed change may disrupt preparation for, or conduct of, the trial. In the same vein, the court in *Crompton* seemed to stress the position defendant had taken in discovery in denying leave to amend. Should judges be less willing to permit parties to change positions they take later in litigation, when they presumably know more about the case?

SUPPLEMENTAL PLEADINGS

What if events relevant to a claim or defense arise after the pleading is filed? Rule 15(d) provides for "supplemental pleadings" for after-occurring transactions, occurrences, or events. An obvious use of supplemental pleadings would be for injuries that become manifest after filing the complaint. Would the same be true as to issues that become apparent only after discovery? Note that supplemental pleadings have been interpreted as intended to be in aid of the claim already made and not to allege a new claim. See Giglio v. Konold, 214 N.E.2d 806, 808 (Ohio App.1965) (new action, rather than supplemental pleading, should be used to allege defendant's refusal to obey court order pending appeal). Should parties be encouraged to add new disputes to existing lawsuits?

2. *Relation Back of Amendments*

SWARTZ v. GOLD DUST CASINO, INC.

United States District Court, District of Nevada, 1981.
91 F.R.D. 543.

Edward C. Reed, Jr., District Judge.

Defendant Cavanaugh Properties has moved for judgment on the pleadings, pursuant to Fed.R.Civ.P. 12(c), on the ground of the two-year Nevada statute of limitations applicable to personal injuries caused by negligence. * * * [T]he Court has treated it as a Rule 56(b) motion for summary judgment. * * *

Plaintiff Doris M. Swartz was injured on May 4, 1979, in a fall on a staircase in the Gold Dust Casino. A complaint alleging diversity jurisdiction was filed in this U.S. District Court on April 30, 1980. The defendants therein listed were Gold Dust Casino, Inc., and Does I through V. The pleading alleged that the true names and identities of the Doe defendants were not known or ascertainable, but that they were liable to the plaintiffs for damages " ... by reason of the fact that each of said Defendants is an owner or has some interest in the real property and/or corporation herein described." No other contentions concerning the Doe defendants were made in the original complaint. As to defendant Gold Dust Casino, Inc., it was alleged that said defendant had negligently permitted the staircase to become tread bare, worn and slippery. The answer of that defendant denied the material allegations of the complaint.

In answers to interrogatories served and filed August 21, 1980, Gold Dust Casino, Inc., disclosed that it leased the casino premises from Cavanaugh Properties.

The plaintiffs, in supplemental answers to interrogatories filed December 9, 1980, disclosed that they had employed engineering consultant Stephen I. Rosen. A letter report from him to the plaintiffs' attorney, dated September 23, 1980, was attached to the supplemental answers. It stated, among other things, that the local building code had been violated by the stairway upon which Mrs. Swartz had fallen. The riser heights exceeded code by half an inch and the treads were one inch narrower than permitted by the code. Mr. Rosen concluded that the staircase was dangerous as a result.

In points and authorities filed February 19, 1981, in support of a motion to extend discovery, the plaintiffs stated that they had discovered the true name of defendant Doe I was Cavanaugh Properties, which was the owner and lessor of the Gold Dust Casino premises. They prayed for leave to amend their complaint by substituting Cavanaugh Properties for Doe I.

United States District Judge Bruce R. Thompson, to whom the case was then assigned, denied Gold Dust Casino, Inc.'s motion for a summary judgment by Order filed April 1, 1981. That Order included the following:

> "The record as of now does not support a claim of defective maintenance as contrasted with defective construction. The complaint alleges only negligent maintenance."

On April 9, 1981, the plaintiffs filed a motion for leave to amend their complaint by adding additional claims for relief and by adding Cavanaugh Properties as a party defendant. A copy of the proposed amended complaint was attached to the motion. It alleged, inter alia, that Cavanaugh Properties was responsible for the design and installation of the stairway. Further, the riser height and tread width violations of the building code were alleged to have caused Mrs. Swartz's injuries.

The motion for leave to amend the complaint and add Cavanaugh Properties was granted by Judge Thompson on May 7, 1981. The amended complaint was filed May 8, 1981, which was more than two years after the May 4, 1979, accident. Cavanaugh Properties is a partnership. The amended complaint was served on John Cavanaugh, a general partner, on May 8, 1981. Mr. Cavanaugh, at all times herein material, has also been the president of defendant Gold Dust Casino, Inc.

Cavanaugh Properties raised the two-year statute of limitations as an affirmative defense in its answer to the amended complaint. At the same time it filed the instant motion for judgment on the pleadings, based on the fact that the amended complaint (in which it was first made a party) was not filed within the time allowed by the statute of limitations. It emphasizes that it was added as a party in the amended complaint.

In their opposition to the motion, the plaintiffs rely on the relation back provisions of Fed.R.Civ.P. 15. * * *

The plaintiffs point out that Mr. John Cavanaugh wears two hats; namely, as a general partner of defendant Cavanaugh Properties and as president of defendant Gold Dust Casino, Inc. In addition, in his latter capacity Mr. Cavanaugh received, through his attorney, a copy of the plaintiffs' motion to amend the complaint before the statute of limitations had expired. Attached to the motion was a copy of the proposed amended complaint, which was identical to the one eventually filed.

In reply, defendant Cavanaugh Properties argues:

(1) The amended complaint does not simply set forth a different theory of law but, on the contrary, it sets forth a new and different cause of action that won't relate back to the date of filing of the original complaint. The distinction is between the claim of negligent maintenance of the stairway by defendant Gold Dust Casino, Inc., in the original complaint, and negligence in the design and installation of the stairway by Cavanaugh Properties in the amended complaint. In other words different wrongful conduct is claimed in the two pleadings.

(2) The adding of Cavanaugh Properties as a defendant in the amended complaint does not comply with the prerequisites to relation back specified by Rule 15(c). It is not as though there had been a mistake concerning the identity of the proper party. Gold Dust Casino, Inc., remains a defendant in the amended complaint, based on its allegedly negligent maintenance of the stairway. If Cavanaugh Properties had reviewed the original complaint prior to the expiration of the statute of limitations, it would not have known that, but for a mistake in identity, the action would have been brought against it. Gold Dust Casino, Inc., had acknowledged, in the course of discovery, that the responsibility for maintaining the stairway rested with it. Substitution of the correct party for the one mistakenly named in the original pleading is contemplated by the Rule, not the addition of a new party to defend against a new cause of action.

(3) The filing of the motion to amend the complaint, prior to the expiration of the statute of limitations, did not toll the running of the statute. It is the filing date of the amended complaint after leave to amend has been granted that is determinative. Even the granting of leave within the statutory period (which did not happen here) will not toll the statute.

As a general rule, the use of a fictitious name to identify a defendant is not favored in the Ninth Circuit; however, it is permissible where the identity of the alleged defendant is not known at the time of the filing of the complaint. In such circumstances, the plaintiffs should be given an opportunity through discovery to identify the unknown defendant. Thus, the substitution of defendant Cavanaugh Properties for Doe I was proper herein. Doe I had been described in the original complaint as owner of the casino premises. Discovery was utilized to ascertain the true identity of the owner. Now that such identification has been made, the plaintiffs should drop Does II through V as defendants in order to preserve the diversity jurisdiction of this Court.

> "Rule 15(c) of the Federal Rules of Civil Procedure was amended in 1966 for the express purpose of solving statutes of limitations problems when new parties are added after the limitation period has expired. It should be liberally interpreted to achieve the end sought. There are three requirements, (1) the claim asserted in the amended pleading must have arisen from the conduct, transaction or occurrence set forth in the original pleading; (2) the new defendant must have received notice of the action within the limitations period; and (3) the new defendant should have known that but for a mistake concerning the identity of the proper party, the action would have been brought against him." Williams v. Avis Transport of Canada, Ltd., 57 F.R.D. 53, 55 (D.Nev.1972).

The claims asserted in the amended complaint herein arose from the same occurrence set forth in the original complaint, namely the fall of Mrs. Swartz on the staircase. In the case of Blair v. Durham, 134 F.2d 729 (6th Cir.1943), the plaintiff was an office worker who had been struck by a piece of timber falling from a scaffold erected in the office. Her original complaint had alleged negligence by the contractor and its employees in handling timbers on and about the scaffolding. Subsequently she amended her complaint to allege that the negligence had been in erecting the scaffold in such a manner that persons required to work thereunder were not properly protected. Relation back to avoid a statute of limitations bar to the amended complaint was approved. On page 731, the Court held:

> "The original complaint which alleged that appellee's injuries were due to the negligence of appellant's employees in the use of the scaffold states no different cause of action as respects limitation than the amended complaint which stated that her injuries were due to the negligent manner in which the scaffold was constructed, because the two acts alleged were but different invasions of appel-

lee's primary right and different breaches of the same duty. There was but one injury and it is immaterial whether it resulted from the negligence of the users of the scaffold or from its construction, since in either case it was a violation of the same obligation."

The same principle applies here. Whether Mrs. Swartz's injuries resulted from negligence in the design or the installation or the maintenance of the stairway does not change the fact that all the claims in both pleadings arose from her fall.

The notice of the institution of the lawsuit required by Rule 15(c) need not be formal. If a person who receives notice of the legal action within the limitations period should know from the information received that he may be liable to the plaintiff by reason of the claim for relief asserted against another, he has received the notice required by the Rule. In the instant case, Mr. John Cavanaugh received a copy of the proposed amended complaint within the statutory period. In addition, the dual capacities of Mr. Cavanaugh as president of the corporate defendant and as a general partner of the partnership defendant supports the premise that the partnership had such notice of the lawsuit within the limitations period as should have induced it to commence investigations and other preparations to defend itself.

As to Rule 15(c)'s requirement that the new defendant should have known that but for a mistake concerning identity the action would have been brought against him, such a mistake " . . . exists whenever a party who may be liable for the actionable conduct alleged in the Complaint was omitted as a party defendant." Williams v. Avis Transport of Canada, Ltd., 57 F.R.D. 53, 55 (D.Nev.1972).

Finally, the question of whether Cavanaugh Properties would be prejudiced if required to defend against the amended complaint is relevant.

A lack of diligence on the part of the plaintiffs' counsel after receiving the information as to the true identity of the property owner is insufficient to prevent him from seeking to amend, in the absence of purposeful delay or bad faith. The unavailability of the statute of limitations as a defense does not by itself constitute prejudice. Undue difficulty in defending the lawsuit by reason of the passage of time would be prejudicial. Specific prejudice must be shown. No such showing has been made herein.

IT IS, THEREFORE, HEREBY ORDERED that defendant Cavanaugh Properties' motion, treated herein as a motion for summary judgment, be, and the same hereby is, DENIED.

Notes and Questions

1. *Swartz* takes a liberal view of relation back—particularly regarding adding parties (explored in the notes below). Before turning to that, reflect on the "same transaction" requirement of Rule 15(c)(2). The original complaint in *Swartz* alleged *defective maintenance*—that Gold Dust Casino had negligently permitted the staircase to become tread bare, worn and slippery.

The amended complaint alleged *defective construction*—that Gold Dust Casino and Cavanaugh Properties were responsible for the design and installation of the stairway in violation of the building code as to the riser height and tread width. How can the defective maintenance and defective construction claims be said to arise out of the same conduct, transaction, or occurrence? Aren't they different events occurring at different times, involving different acts or omissions, and done by different parties? Note that plaintiff would have needed to rely on Rule 15(c) relation back *even if* she had not also sought to add a new defendant (Cavanaugh Properties) because she sought to amend the allegation of negligence.

Would the same evidence be used to prove the original allegation of defective maintenance and the amended allegation of defective construction? It would not seem so since the witnesses who know about the maintenance might be different from those who know about or were involved in the original construction. Although Rule 13(a)'s same "transaction or occurrence" test for a compulsory counter claim was interpreted in *Wigglesworth*, supra p. 207, as requiring the "same evidence," that is not the way the same "conduct, transaction, or occurrence" language in Rule 15(c)(2) is read for allowing relation back. Why the difference?

Blair v. Durham, cited in *Swartz*, found that the amended complaint stated the same "cause of action." Why is that a relevant inquiry when Rule 15(c) does not use the term "same cause of action"? Indeed, the Federal Rules nowhere use the term "cause of action," rejecting it for the term "claim." Note that state statutes of limitations usually provide that a suit must be commenced within a certain time "after the cause of action accrued." Does this give you a clue? If the function of Rule 15(c) is to avoid the application of the state statute of limitations, should the same "conduct, transaction, or occurrence" standard used in Rule 15(c) be read as prohibiting an amendment when the policies of the statute of limitations would be undercut? What policies does the statute of limitations serve? Would allowance of the amendment in *Swartz* undermine those policies?

2. *Amendment to add a party*–Plaintiff's motion to add Cavanaugh Properties as a party raises more difficult issues than the motion to add only a new claim. Rule 15(c)(3) allows relation back if "the amendment changes the party or the naming of the party against whom a claim is asserted." Rule 15(c)(2) requires that the amended claim or defense "arose out of the same transaction or occurrence as set forth in the original pleading." Since the court in *Swartz* concluded that the injurious fall (and not the *defective maintenance* or *defective construction*) was the transaction or occurrence sued upon, the amended claim against Cavanaugh Properties would also arise out of that transaction or occurrence.

There are, however, two additional requirements for relation back of an amendment to add a party. Rule 15(c) adds the requirement that the new party (A) "received such notice of the institution of the action that it will not be prejudiced" and (B) "knew or should have known that, but for a mistake concerning the identity of the proper party, the action would have been brought against the party." A policy-oriented application of the "same transaction or occurrence" test might actually have considered such matters in order to ensure that relation back under Rule 15 would not undermine the notice and repose interests protected by the Statute of Limitations. But Rule 15(c)(3) expressly spells out these requirements as to new parties. *Swartz* found that, because John Cavanaugh was both a general partner in Cavanaugh Properties and president of the defendant casino, and had received a copy of the motion to amend before the Statute of Limitations ran, Cavanaugh Properties had adequate notice and should have known that but for a mistake it would have been sued.

Other cases support *Swartz*'s statement that the notice need not be formal. See Loveall v. Employer Health Servs., Inc., 196 F.R.D. 399, 403 (D. Kan. 2000) (letter from corporation named as defendant to the company that had sold the allegedly defective product advising that, in the view of its attorneys, the other company would likely be drawn into the action was sufficient notice). However, some courts have stated that "only service constitutes notice," Williams v. Army & Air Force Exchange Serv., 830 F.2d 27, 30 n. 2 (3d Cir.1987), and others have required more than mere awareness of the suit. See Gardner v. Gartman, 880 F.2d 797, 799 (4th Cir.1989) (suits against the U.S. and certain officials did not constitute notice to the head of the U.S. department where plaintiff worked); Bell v. Veterans Administration Hospital, 826 F.2d 357 (5th Cir.1987) (relation back not allowed even though administrative hearings put the party to be joined on notice of the suit). However, the better practice seems to be otherwise. See 6A C. Wright, A. Miller & M. Kane, Fed. Prac. & Pro. § 1498, at 129–30. "The conclusion of a growing number of courts and commentators is that sufficient notice may be deemed to have occurred where a party who has some reason to expect his potential involvement as a defendant hears of the commencement of the litigation through some informal means." Kinnally v. Bell of Pennsylvania, 748 F.Supp. 1136, 1141 (E.D.Pa.1990). Notice to the party sued may be imputed to the party sought to be added by amendment if there is an "identity of interests" between them. Hernandez Jimenez v. Calero Toledo, 604 F.2d 99 (1st Cir.1979); but see Columbus Board of Education v. Armstrong World Indus., Inc., 627 N.E.2d 1033, 1040 (Ohio App. 1993) (service on parent constituted notice to wholly owned subsidiary, but the third requirement of Rule 15(c)(3)(B) was not met because there was no showing that the subsidiary knew or should have known that, but for the mistake in identity, the action would have brought against it).

3.   On a more fundamental question as to what is meant in Rule 15(c) by "a mistake concerning the identity of the proper party," a number of federal courts disagree with *Swartz* that an amendment can relate back when there is lack of knowledge as to *identify* as opposed to a *misnomer* or *misidentification. Swartz* cited Williams v. Avis Transport of Canada, Ltd., 57 F.R.D. 53, 55 (D. Nev. 1972), for the broad position that a mistake exists "whenever a party who may be liable for the actionable conduct alleged in the Complaint was omitted as a party defendant." But see Barrow v. Wethersfield Police Dep't, 66 F.3d 466, 469 (2d Cir.1995) ("the rule is meant to allow an amendment changing the name of a party to relate back to the original complaint only if the change is the result of an error, such as misnomer or misidentification."). In *Barrow*, an amendment identifying police officers who had been referred to in the complaint as "unknown police officers" was found ineligible for relation back because it was simply due to lack of knowledge as to their identities and not a mistake in their names. In

Schieszler v. Ferrum College, 233 F. Supp. 2d 796 (C.D.Va. 2002), an amendment to add a counseling service used by a college which was sued concerning a student's suicide did not relate back because the new defendant was not a substitute for the existing defendant nor was the failure to sue it in the original complaint a mistake.

There are several factors that seem to be significant in these cases. First, there is a reluctance to allow "John Doe" or other general descriptions of defendants to be later amended when the identities are discovered. See Butler v. Robar Enterprises, Inc., 208 F.R.D. 621 (C.D.Cal. 2002) (amendment to substitute employer's CEO for a "John Doe" defendant in employment discrimination suit did not relate back because the employee made no mistake in identifying the correct defendant in the original complaint; "the courts of appeal that have confronted the issue are in near-unanimity that lack of knowledge is not a 'mistake.'"); Henry v. FDIC, 168 F.R.D. 55, 59 (D.Kan. 1996) ("By naming John Doe as the second defendant, plaintiffs did not make a mistake in identification. They accurately identified the second defendant, as unknown. Because plaintiffs' failure to name John Doe stemmed from lack of knowledge rather than mistake in identification, the plain language of Rule 15(c)(3) does not permit relation back.").

One would think that inability to identify certain defendants until discovery becomes available on filing suit would be a paradigm for relation back under Rule 15(c), especially since it also has to be shown that the added defendants had notice and should have known they would have been sued. However, the strict interpretation of the relation back rule may reflect the concern of some federal courts with sometimes spurious civil rights suits against governments that join individual officials without naming them. Some courts, both federal and state, are more tolerant of John Doe practice (as will be seen in SMU Association of Women Law Students v. Wynne & Jaffe, infra p. 230). California's Code of Civil Procedure permits a plaintiff to name Doe defendants if ignorant of their identity, and relation back of amendments substituting their names is allowed (California, however, does not require a newly named defendant to have notice of the suit within the Statute of Limitations period). See Cal. Code Civ. Proc. § 474; Hogan, California's Unique Doe Defendant Practice: A Fiction Stranger Than Truth, 30 Stan.L.Rev. 51 (1977). For discussion of Doe defendant practice in federal court, see Rice, Meet John Doe: Is it Time for Federal Civil Procedure to Recognize John Doe Parties?, 57 U.Pitt.L.Rev. 883 (1996).

Second, some of the cases applying a strict definition of "mistake" to deny relation back emphasize that the plaintiff could with due diligence have discovered the names or involvement of the parties who are later sought to be added. See Bass v. World Wrestling Federation Entertainment, Inc., 129 F.Supp.2d 491 (E.D.N.Y. 2001) (when plaintiff knew of employee's involvement when she filed her complaint, but did not attempt to excuse her failure to name him as a defendant, not a case of mistaken identity); Hedvat v. Rothschild, 175 F.R.D. 183 (E.D.N.Y. 1997) (amendment to add partners of brokerage firm sued in original complaint would not relate back since failure to join them was a deliberate strategic choice and not the result of any mistake as to who was intended to be sued). It has been suggested that this issue is only relevant to whether an amendment should be permitted at all rather than whether there was a mistake under Rule 15(c). See 6A Wright,

Miller, & Kane, Federal Practice & Procedure § 1498, at 142–43 (2d ed. 1990) ("A few cases tend to suggest that if plaintiff's own inexcusable neglect was responsible for the failure to name the correct party, an amendment substituting the proper party will not be allowed, notwithstanding adequate notice to the new party. Although this factor is germane to the question of permitting an amendment, it is more closely related to the trial court's exercise of discretion under Rule 15(a) whether to allow the change than it is to the satisfaction of the notice requirements of Rule 15(c).").

Other courts have taken a broader view of "mistake," more consistent with the outcome in *Swartz.* In Leonard v. Parry, 219 F.3d 25 (1st Cir.2000), the plaintiff moved, after the Statute of Limitations had run, to substitute the correct driver of the car with whom he had an accident for the named defendant who had been mistakenly believed to be the driver. The First Circuit stated that "[v]irtually by definition, every mistake involves an element of negligence, carelessness, or fault—and the language of Rule 15(c) does not distinguish among types of mistakes concerning identity. Properly construed, the rule encompasses both mistakes that were easily avoidable and those that were serendipitous." The court also refused to find that the fact that the defense attorney had notified plaintiff's lawyer of the mistake before the statute ran would prevent relation back. It found that "what the plaintiff knew (or thought he knew) at the time of the original pleading generally is the relevant datum in respect to the question of whether a mistake concerning identity actually took place," and that what plaintiff learned later is not relevant. The court did note that it was suggested that plaintiff had intentionally sued the person who turned out not to be the driver (but who was the insurance policy holder) on a theory of negligent entrustment, but that this theory was not supported by the facts. Accord, Centuori v. Experian Information Solutions, Inc., 329 F. Supp. 2d 1133 (D. Ariz. 2004) (failure to name in original complaint a credit agency that had furnished reports to the defendant that was sued for violating the Fair Credit Reporting Act was result of a "mistake" since plaintiff had not known at the time of filing suit of the agency's involvement; plaintiff and his counsel "might have been negligent, careless, or even arguably at fault" for not naming the agency, but the facts do not show that such failure was a strategic decision); Lacedra v. Donald W. Wyatt Detention Facility, 334 F.Supp.2d 114 (D. R.I. 2004) (although plaintiff knew the party ultimately sought to be added owned the detention building in a suit alleging unconstitutional exposure to second-hand smoke, he did not make "a deliberate decision not to sue a party whose identity the plaintiff knew from the outset" and the amendment could relate back). Could "deliberate choice" and "strategic decision" considerations be a way to reconcile the conflicting lines of cases?

4. Before 1991, Rule 15(c) required that where a new defendant is to be added by amendment the amended claims only relate back if the new defendant was on notice of certain matters "within the period provided by law for commencing the action." Curiously, a party properly named has no right actually to receive notice within the limitations period. If the suit is filed within the limitations period, the summons and complaint may usually be served after the period expires. See Rule 4(m) (providing that summons and complaint must be served within 120 days after suit filed). Should an additional party be entitled to earlier notice than one properly named in the

complaint? In Schiavone v. Fortune, 477 U.S. 21, 106 S.Ct. 2379, 91 L.Ed.2d 18 (1986), the Court held that Rule 15(c) meant that the additional party must be notified *before* the expiration of the limitations period even though there is no corresponding requirement for the properly named defendant. For criticism of this decision, see Brussack, Outrageous *Fortune*: The Case For Amending Rule 15(c) Again, 61 So.Cal.L.Rev. 671 (1988); see also Lewis, The Excessive History of Federal Rule 15(c) and Its Lessons for Civil Rules Revision, 85 Mich.L.Rev. 1507 (1987).

In 1991, Rule 15(c) was amended to provide that the new defendant must be on notice "within the period provided by Rule 4(m) for service of the summons and complaint." The Advisory Committee Notes state that the intention is "to change the result in Schiavone v. Fortune." Note that, in cases where suit is filed more than 120 days before the expiration of the limitations period, such as *Swartz*, the amendment actually requires that notice be received earlier than formerly was necessary.

5.   Defendant in *Swartz* filed a motion for judgment on the pleadings, but the court chose to treat the motion under Rule 56, dealing with summary judgment. Why would the court do that? See the last sentence in Rule 12(b).

Chapter IV

ESTABLISHING THE STRUCTURE
AND SIZE OF THE DISPUTE

When the Federal Rules were adopted, a suit by a single plaintiff against a single defendant was a fairly representative model of litigation in American courts. But that has changed dramatically with more complex business and social arrangements and new theories of liability. Today the multi-party suit is the usual form of litigation. This development has required an evolution of court procedures to accommodate the demand for resolution of disputes involving many parties and for disposition of grievances in the aggregate. This evolution was not easily accomplished. Common-law procedures developed in a very different legal landscape, and a certain amount of shaping and jettisoning of traditional forms has been required to satisfy modern needs. Because these procedural reforms have been largely accomplished through incremental changes, some review of the old forms and their history is necessary to an understanding of the modern devices for establishing the structure and size of disputes.

A. PROPER PARTIES TO A SUIT

A proper party to a suit should have a sufficient relationship to the dispute that it may appropriately be brought into the litigation. Today we normally look to substantive law, as found, for example, in state statutes, or to the principles of "standing" (discussed in Chapter II, supra p. 93, to determine whether a particular person or entity is a proper party. However, there are some distinctive federal procedural applications involving proper parties that will be explored in this section.

1. Real Party in Interest (Rule 17(a))

Rule 17(a) provides that "[e]very action shall be prosecuted in the name of the real party in interest." The reason for this rule is essentially historical. At common law, an action had to be brought in the name of the person who had legal title to the right being asserted. Thus persons who had only an equitable interest, such as assignees, could not sue in their own name. Such equitable-interest owners would be dependent upon the willingness of the person with the legal interest to bring suit for their use. Courts of equity, however, allowed persons with equitable interests to sue in their own name (with the owner of the legal interest typically joined so as to bind him by the decree).

The Field Code, in merging law and equity, rejected the common-law rule and, in language later borrowed for Rule 17(a), provided that actions should be prosecuted in the name of the real party in interest. The purpose was to alter the common-law requirement that suit must be brought by the party who, under substantive law, possessed the right sought to be enforced, and who was not necessarily the person who would ultimately benefit from the recovery. Rule 17(a) adds further language that "an executor, administrator, guardian, bailee, trustee of an express trust, a party with whom or in whose name a contract has been made for the benefit of another, or a party authorized by statute may sue in that person's own name without joining with him the party for whose benefit the action is brought." This makes explicit the fact that the real party in interest need not have a beneficial interest in order to sue so long as it has sufficient interest in the outcome.

One objective of Rule 17(a) is to protect the legitimate interests of the defendant. "Rule 17 now serves primarily a negative function. It is to enable the defendant to present defenses he has against the real party in interest, to protect the defendant against a subsequent action by the party actually entitled to relief, and to ensure that the judgment will have proper res judicata effect." Virginia Elec. & Power Co. v. Westinghouse Elec. Corp., 485 F.2d 78 (4th Cir.1973). These objectives are also served by Rule 19 joinder (see infra pp. 242–58) and the doctrine of res judicata (considered in Chapter XIII), leading some commentators to consider the rule unnecessary. See Entman, More Reasons For Abolishing Federal Rule of Civil Procedure 17(a): The Problem of the Proper Plaintiff and Insurance Subrogation, 68 N.C.L.Rev. 893, 920–22 (1990); Kennedy, Federal Rule 17(a): Will the Real Party in Interest Please Stand?, 51 Minn.L.Rev. 675, 724 (1967).

The real party in interest rule is relevant to subrogation. Subrogation involves the substitution of one person (or entity) in the place of another with the substituted person succeeding to the rights of the other. It includes the situation in which one person pays the debt of another and is substituted to the other's rights, and the debt is treated in equity as existing for the substitute person's benefit.

Subrogation often takes place in the context of insurance whereby an insurer's payment to the insured for a harm inflicted by a third party subrogates the insurer to the insured's rights against the third party. If the insurer pays all the insured's losses, the insured no longer has a pecuniary interest in the case, and only the insurer is the real party in interest in a suit to recover against the third party. However, partial subrogation can occur when, because the loss exceeds the coverage, the insured is only paid the amount of the coverage, or when an insurance policy had a deductible that the insurer subtracted from its payment to the insured. Then both the insured subrogor and the insurer subrogee are real parties in interest and may sue in their own names. United States v. Aetna Cas. & Sur. Co., 338 U.S. 366, 70 S.Ct. 207, 94 L.Ed. 171 (1949). If either sues alone, the other may intervene to protect its interest. If the other does not intervene, the defendant may protect itself from multiple suits by having the missing party joined. See 6A C. Wright, A. Miller & M. Kane, Fed. Prac. & Pro. § 1546 at 363.

Whether there has been a subrogation is not always clear. For example, insurers sometimes enter into a "loan receipt" arrangement whereby they lend the insured the amount due on the policy and the insured is only required to pay it back to the extent that it recovers from the defendant. Some courts have treated this as a loan that does not result in subrogation, and thus the insured is still the real party in interest who must bring the suit. R.J. Enstrom Corp. v. Interceptor Corp., 520 F.2d 1217 (10th Cir.1975). Other courts have viewed it as a sham loan that actually constitutes payment, thus resulting in subrogation that makes the insurer the real party in interest. City Stores Co. v. Lerner Shops of District of Columbia, Inc., 410 F.2d 1010 (D.C.Cir.1969). Why might an insurer want to have the insured named as the only party in a suit against a third person to recover for injuries for which the insured has been compensated by the insurer? Cf. Fed. R. Evid. 411 (evidence that defendant was insured is not admissible on the issue whether defendant was negligent).

A liberal definition of "real party in interest" raises the possibility that the named plaintiff may be chosen solely to satisfy the requirements of federal court diversity jurisdiction. Thus a person from a state different from the defendants may be assigned a claim, or may be appointed as a fiduciary (such as an executor, administrator, trustee, or guardian) in order to be named as the plaintiff and invoke diversity jurisdiction to get into federal court. The limitations on such jurisdiction-motivated assignment will be considered in Chapter X.

2. *Fictitious Names*

SOUTHERN METHODIST UNIVERSITY AS-SOCIATION OF WOMEN LAW STU-DENTS v. WYNNE AND JAFFE

United State Court of Appeals, Fifth Circuit, 1979.
599 F.2d 707.

Before AINSWORTH and VANCE, CIRCUIT JUDGES, and BOTTLE, DISTRICT JUDGE.

AINSWORTH, CIRCUIT JUDGE.

In these companion Title VII [42 U.S.C. §§ 2000e–2000e–17] sex discrimination suits, the Southern Methodist University (SMU) Association of Women Law Students (Association) and Lawyers A, B, C and D (A–D), four female lawyers seeking to proceed anonymously, allege that defendants, two Dallas law firms, discriminated against women in hiring summer law clerks and associates and request injunctive relief. Plaintiffs appeal from various pretrial orders of the district court requiring the Association to reveal by proper pleadings the true identities of lawyers A–D.

[Defendants served interrogatories asking the true identities of plaintiffs A–D. Plaintiffs objected to disclosure, proposing that if some disclosure were required it be available only to defendants' attorney. The trial court directed that the identities of these plaintiffs be disclosed "for all further purposes."]

Plaintiffs have not cited, nor have we found, any prior decisions which recognize or even discuss the right of Title VII plaintiffs to proceed anonymously. Neither the Federal Rules of Civil Procedure nor Title VII itself make provision for anonymous plaintiffs. The rules require that "[i]n the complaint the title of the action shall include the names of all the parties." Fed.R.Civ.P. 10(a), and the language of Title VII establishes no exception to the general principle that "the identity of the parties to a lawsuit should not be concealed." Doe v. Deschamps, D. Montana, 1974, 64 F.R.D. 652, 653.

Under certain special circumstances, however, courts have allowed plaintiffs to use fictitious names. "[W]here the issues involved are matters of a sensitive and highly personal nature," such as birth control, abortion, homosexuality or the welfare rights of illegitimate children or abandoned families, the normal practice of disclosing the parties' identities yields "to a policy of protecting privacy in a very private matter." Id. However, the cases affording plaintiffs anonymity all share several characteristics missing here. The plaintiffs in those actions, at the least, divulged personal information of the utmost intimacy; many also had to admit that they either had violated state laws or government regulations or wished to engage in prohibited conduct. Here, by contrast, to prove their case A–D need not reveal facts of a highly personal nature or express a desire to participate in proscribed activities. Furthermore, all of the plaintiffs previously allowed in other cases to proceed anonymously were challenging the constitutional, statutory or regulatory validity of government activity. While such suits involve no injury to the Government's "reputation," the mere filing of a civil action against other private parties may cause damage to their good names and reputation and may also result in economic harm. Defendant law firms stand publicly accused of serious violations of federal law. Basic fairness dictates that those among the defendants' accusers who wish to participate in this suit as individual party plaintiffs must do so under their real names.

Plaintiffs argue that disclosure of A–D's identities will leave them vulnerable to retaliation from their current employers, prospective future employers and an organized bar that does "not like lawyers who sue lawyers." In our view, A–D face no greater threat of retaliation than the typical plaintiff alleging Title VII violations, including the other women who, under their real names and not anonymously, have filed sex discrimination suits against large law firms.

Because we find neither an express congressional grant of the right to proceed anonymously nor a compelling need to "protect privacy in a very private matter," Doe v. Deschamps, supra, 64 F.R.D. at 653, we hold that these Title VII plaintiffs may not sue under fictitious names and therefore affirm the district court's order requiring disclosure of A–D's identities by proper pleadings.

Notes and Questions

1.   Why shouldn't the plaintiffs' concern in *SMU*—that they would be stigmatized in the legal community if they were identified as suing law firms—be given the same protection of anonymity accorded to plaintiffs in cases where facts of a highly personal nature would be revealed? In Doe v. City of New York, 201 F.R.D. 100 (S.D.N.Y.2001), a lawyer suing two police officers for violating her constitutional rights sought to proceed anonymously because otherwise a computer search of court records would turn up her name. The judge agreed that, due to computer searches of court records, "the privacy that litigants once enjoyed as a practical matter has been diminished greatly," but declined plaintiff's request. See also Doe v. Merten, 219 F.R.D. 387 (E.D.Va.2004) (plaintiff challenging policy of various colleges to deny admission to illegal immigrants would not be allowed to proceed anonymously); Doe v. Federal Bureau of Investigation, 218 F.R.D. 256 (D. Colo.2003) (state-court judge would not be allowed to proceed anonymously in Freedom of Information Act suit against the FBI). But see EW v. New York Blood Center, 213 F.R.D. 108 (E.D.N.Y.2003) (plaintiff allowed to proceed anonymously to avoid revealing that she suffered from Hepatitis B); Doe v. Barrow County, 219 F.R.D. 189 (N.D.Ga.2003) (plaintiff challenging the display of the Ten Commandments could proceed anonymously; opponents to the suit had even tried to intimidate the district court). In Carhart v. Ashcroft, 300 F.Supp.2d 921 (D.Neb.2004), the court allowed an expert witness to act anonymously in a suit to enjoin enforcement of the Partial–Birth Abortion Ban Act of 2003. The witness was a doctor who had performed the forbidden procedure, and the judge was persuaded that the witness's life would be in danger otherwise: "In 17 years of dealing with questions like this in both criminal and civil cases, I have never seen a more compelling showing for the need to protect the identity of a witness."

2.   Should "John Doe (or Roe, Coe, etc.)" or "Jane Doe" pleading ever be used against a private defendant given the *SMU* court's rationale that fairness dictates that the accusers use their real names? Even in suits challenging governmental activity, isn't there a potential injury to officials' good names and reputations akin to the effect on private defendants? Fairness concerns may also arise if a defendant has reason to doubt the capacity or standing of the plaintiff, but cannot investigate it because the identity is not known. If the identity is never known, it may also be difficult to apply the standards of res judicata to know who is bound by the judgment. See discussion in Note, Anonymity in Civil Litigation: The Doe Plaintiff, 57 Notre Dame Lawyer 580 (1982). Should the identities at least be made available to the court and opposing parties through sealed pleadings?

3. *SMU* makes the point that the plaintiffs face no greater threat of retaliation than the typical plaintiff alleging Title VII violations. But just because Title VII does not accord anonymity for sex discrimination complaints, should there be no such right in a court suit? Some regulatory schemes do recognize the need for anonymity by allowing the agency to sue on behalf of unnamed persons. See Gomez v. Buckeye Sugars, 60 F.R.D. 106 (N.D.Ohio 1973) (allowing migrant farm workers to use fictitious names in suing employers for wage and hour violations, noting that the Fair Labor Standards Act allows the Secretary of Labor to bring such suits for unnamed persons).

4. In Doe v. Shakur, 164 F.R.D. 359 (S.D.N.Y. 1996), a prominent rapper, who had been convicted of sexual abuse, was sued for damages by the victim who sought to remain anonymous. The court noted that courts have considered the following factors: (1) whether the plaintiff is challenging governmental activity; (2) whether the plaintiff would be required to disclose information of the utmost intimacy; (3) whether the plaintiff would be compelled to admit his or her intention to engage in illegal conduct, thereby risking criminal prosecution; (4) whether the plaintiff would risk suffering injury if identified; and (5) whether the party defending against a suit brought under a pseudonym would be prejudiced. See Doe v. Frank, 951 F.2d 320, 323 (11th Cir.1992). The court found plaintiff's fear of being "publicly humiliated and embarrassed" insufficient to overcome the fact that "this is a private suit for damages, where plaintiff is seeking to vindicate primarily her own interests," defendant would be "at a serious disadvantage in being required to defend himself publicly while plaintiff could make her accusations from behind a cloak of anonymity," and "the public has a right of access to the courts." The court noted that the plaintiff's allegation of death threats would provide a legitimate basis, but said she had provided no details to support this claim and that if she had been threatened, her identity must already be known to those who would do her harm. Compare Javier H. v. Garcia–Botello, 211 F.R.D. 194 (W.D.N.Y. 2002) (finding, in a suit for wages by migrant farm worker, that although "fairness usually requires that a plaintiff stand behind its charges publicly" in a civil suit, threats of violence to plaintiff had been substantiated by previous indictments of defendants).

5. Fictitious names are sometimes used for defendants when plaintiffs do not know their names. Recall Swartz v. Gold Dust Casino, Inc., supra p. 218. This arises often in cases against police officers or governmental officials whose identities are unknown, resulting in suits against "Police Officer John Doe 1," "Jailer John Doe 2," "Detective Mary Doe," etc. This practice has been tacitly approved by the Supreme Court. Bivens v. Six Unknown Named Agents of the Federal Bureau of Narcotics, 403 U.S. 388, 91 S.Ct. 1999, 29 L.Ed.2d 619 (1971). But, as reflected in cases that disagree with the *Swartz* court's allowing relation back of a substitution of a party due to a mistake (see supra, note 3, p. 224), an amendment to add the correct names after the Statute of Limitations has run may not relate back, and thus the "Doe" designation would fail to preserve the claim.

6. Note that the named plaintiff in the *SMU* suit is an association. How can it file a suit for sex discrimination? While the matter is not always clear, associations are often allowed to sue to assert the rights of members.

Thus, dealing with problems of standing, the Supreme Court has said that "the association may assert the rights of its members, at least so long as the challenged infractions adversely affect its members' associational ties." Warth v. Seldin, 422 U.S. 490, 511, 95 S.Ct. 2197, 2211, 45 L.Ed.2d 343 (1975).

Related to the standing question is the problem of capacity to sue, which is covered by Rule 17(b). The association would have capacity in this case because it sued to enforce a substantive right under the laws of the United States. More generally, concern with capacity is designed to ensure that the party litigating has a sufficient legal right to litigate so that the outcome will be binding, a concern reflected in Rule 17(c) (dealing with incompetent persons) as well.

7. For further discussion, see Rice, Meet John Doe: Is it Time for Federal Civil Procedure to Recognize John Doe Parties?, 57 U. Pitt. L. Rev. 883 (1996); Steinman, Public Trial, Pseudonymous Parties: When Should Litigants be Permitted to Keep Their Identities Confidential?, 37 Hast. L.J. 1 (1985).

B. JOINDER OF CLAIMS (RULE 18(a))

At common law, a plaintiff was usually prohibited from joining two different claims against the same defendant unless both claims involved the same form of action. Thus a plaintiff could not join claims for breach of contract and tort even though they arose out of the same transaction, but could join two unrelated assaults because they did arise out of the same form of action. This was a good example of the formalism of the common law that viewed the rigid forms of action as the organizing principle for a law suit. Even equity was somewhat restrictive, generally limiting joinder to claims that involved common issues or the same transaction.

Rule 18(a), in contrast, is completely permissive as to joinder of claims against the same party in a single suit. It allows a party to join "as many claims, legal, equitable, or maritime, as the party has against an opposing party." The claims need not even be related, the theory being that there is no point in requiring multiple law suits once parties are in court against each other. This liberal rule of joinder of claims does not, however, mean that unrelated claims will necessarily be tried together. Rule 18(a) is only a pleading rule, and the Advisory Committee Notes observe that "a claim properly joined as a matter of pleading need not be proceeded with together with the other claims if fairness or convenience justifies separate treatment." Under Rule 42(b), a court may sever unrelated claims and order separate trials when it would be "in furtherance of convenience or to avoid prejudice, or when separate trials would be conducive to expedition and economy."

C. PERMISSIVE JOINDER OF PARTIES (RULE 20)

At common law, joinder of parties was extremely difficult. Multiple plaintiffs could join in one suit only if they had a "joint" interest. This was found where they were joint promisees on the same obligation or instrument, partners at the time of a contract, or joint owners of property that was allegedly injured by defendant. In such situations, joinder of plaintiffs was not only permitted but required. With regard to joinder of defendants, things were a bit more complicated. "Joint obligors" had to be joined, and joinder was not permitted if defendants were "several obligors," but plaintiff had the choice whether to join where defendants were joint and several obligors.

In general, the focus on the nature of the rights or obligations being asserted has less importance in modern procedure. Joinder of parties is more restricted under the Federal Rules than joinder of claims. The rules distinguish between permissive joinder (Rule 20) and mandatory joinder (Rule 19), with rather different standards and policies applying to each.

Rule 20(a) allows joinder of multiple persons as parties if they assert any right to relief jointly, severally, or in the alternative (or such a right is asserted against them) "in respect of or arising out of the same transaction, occurrence, or series of transactions or occurrences" and "if any question of law or fact common to all these persons will arise in the action." This rule originated in English practice and spread to this country in the 1820s. Similar rules have now been adopted by most states.

KEDRA v. CITY OF PHILADELPHIA

United States District Court, Eastern District of Pennsylvania, 1978.
454 F.Supp. 652.

LUONGO, DISTRICT JUDGE.

This civil rights action arises out of an alleged series of brutal acts committed by Philadelphia policemen against the plaintiffs. The events set forth in the complaint span one and one-half years, from December 1975 to February or March 1977.

[The plaintiffs are Delores Kedra and her eight children, three of them minors, and a son-in-law. The defendants are the City of Philadelphia, the Police Commissioner, and various police officials and officers. The complaint alleges that two of the Kedra children and the husband of another were arrested without probable cause on December 22, 1975 and beaten and illegally interrogated at the police station. Seven days later, other police officers conducted an unlawful search of the Kedra home, unlawfully detained members of the family in the house, and took certain of them to the police station where they were beaten. Thereafter it is alleged that the police engaged "in a systematic pattern of harassment, threats and coercion" of the Kedra family. As part of this pattern, one Kedra son was arrested in June 1976 and beaten, and another son was "harassed and threatened without cause" by police in February or March 1977. Suit was filed under civil rights statutes, 42 U.S.C. §§ 1983, 1985, 1986, for deprivation of constitutional rights, seeking compensatory and punitive damages.]

Defendants contend that there has been an improper joinder of parties under Federal Rule of Civil Procedure 20(a). * * * Defendants argue that plaintiffs' claims against them do not "aris[e] out of the same transaction, occurrence, or series of transactions or occurrences" because they stem from events spanning a fourteen or fifteen month period.[6]

The joinder provisions of the Federal Rules are very liberal. As the Supreme Court noted in United Mine Workers v. Gibbs, 383 U.S. 715, 86 S.Ct. 1130, 16 L.Ed.2d 218 (1966),

> "Under the Rules, the impulse is toward entertaining the broadest possible scope of action consistent with fairness to the parties: joinder of claims, parties and remedies is strongly encouraged."

The reason for the liberality is that unification of claims in a single action is more convenient and less expensive and time-consuming for the parties and the court. Mosley v. General Motors Corp., 497 F.2d 1330, 1332 (8th Cir.1974). In recognition of this attitude, the "transaction or occurrence" language of Rule 20 has been interpreted to "permit all reasonably related claims for relief by or against different parties to be tried in a single proceeding. Absolute identity of all events is unnecessary." Id. at 1333.

Although the events giving rise to plaintiffs' claims in this case occurred over a lengthy time period, they all are "reasonably related." The complaint sets forth a series of alleged unlawful detentions, searches, beatings and similar occurrences and charges defendants with "engag[ing] in a systematic pattern of harassment, threats and coercion with the intention of ... depriving plaintiffs of [their] rights"; each of the incidents set forth is encompassed within the "systematic pattern." There is no logical reason why the systematic conduct alleged could not extend over a lengthy time period and, on the face of these allegations, there is nothing about the extended time span that attenuates the factual relationship among all of these events. The claims against the defendants "aris[e] out of the same transaction, occurrence, or series of transactions or occurrences" for purposes of Rule 20(a), and therefore joinder of defendants in this case is proper.

Apart from the procedural propriety of the joinder under Rule 20(a), however, there is a question whether a single trial of all claims against all defendants will prejudice some of the defendants. Some of the defendants were involved in only one of the several incidents alleged, and lumping them together with other defendants who were involved in

---

6. The Federal Rules permit unlimited joinder of claims against an opposing party (Fed.R.Civ.P. 18(a)), but in multiparty cases joinder is limited by the requirement of Rule 20(a) that plaintiffs or defendants may not be joined in the same case unless some of the claims by or against each party arise out of common events and contain common factual or legal questions. Defendants have not argued that common factual and legal questions are not present in this case; the similarity of the claims against each defendant makes it abundantly clear that there are common issues. Once parties are joined under Rule 20(a), Rule 18(a)'s allowance of unlimited joinder of claims against those parties is fully applicable.

more than one incident may be unfair. This problem is of particular concern with respect to the December 29, 1975 incident, which, apart from the allegations of direction, supervision, and control, appears to involve different actors than the other incidents alleged. Federal Rule 20(b) provides the court with power to remedy this situation:

> "The court may make such orders as will prevent a party from being embarrassed, delayed, or put to expense by the inclusion of a party against whom he asserts no claim and who asserts no claim against him and may order separate trials or make other orders to prevent delay or prejudice."

At oral argument, counsel for both sides recognized the potential prejudicial effect of the joinder in this case and suggested formulation of a stipulation which would attempt to remedy the problem. It appears, however, that it will be better to deal with the problem after discovery has been completed and the case is ready for trial. At that time, the degree of involvement of each of the defendants will be more clear and potential prejudice will be easier to assess. I therefore shall defer decision of this aspect of the case. I shall retain flexibility to sever portions of it or to take other remedial actions, if necessary, once the prejudice issue is more clearly focused.

INSOLIA v. PHILIP MORRIS, INC.

United States District Court, Eastern District of Wisconsin, 1999.
186 F.R.D. 547.

CRABB, District Judge.

This is a civil action for money damages brought by three former smokers and their spouses against the country's major cigarette manufacturers and two tobacco industry trade organizations. In an order dated December 17, 1998, I denied plaintiffs' motion for class certification. [Insolia v. Philip Morris Inc., 186 F.R.D. 535 (E.D.Wis.1998)] The case is back before the court on defendants' motion to sever the claims of the three sets of plaintiffs into three separate actions pursuant to Fed.R.Civ.P. 21. According to defendants, these claims have been joined improperly under Rule 20 because they do not arise from the same transaction or series of transactions and because they do not share a common question of fact or law. Plaintiffs contend that their claims arise from an industry-wide conspiracy to deceive consumers about the addictive, deadly characteristics of cigarettes. * * * Even under the less stringent requirements of Rule 20, plaintiffs' claims are not sufficiently similar to warrant joining them in a single proceeding.

Complaint

[The complaint alleged claims for fraud and civil conspiracy to commit fraud. To prevail, the plaintiffs would have to prove that false statements were made by defendants on which the plaintiffs had relied. The three plaintiffs, who were recently diagnosed as suffering from lung cancer, had each smoked a pack a day for many years. Insolia began smoking at the age of 12 in 1934, but quit in 1974. Mays and Lovejoy each began smoking at 16 in 1953 and quit about 42 years later.

Evidence presented by the plaintiffs in support of a class action showed that the tobacco companies had worked together for many years to counteract emerging scientific evidence that smoking was harmful and tobacco was addictive. See 186 F.R.D. at 539–41. In 1958, the companies formed a trade association, the defendant Tobacco Institute, whose strategy was, among other things, to create doubt about the health effects of smoking through advertising, research reports, and lobbying. Although a tobacco industry researcher commented in 1953 that "It's fortunate for us that cigarettes are a habit they can't break," the industry actively promoted the view over the next forty years that smoking was not addictive.

The plaintiffs' motion to certify a class of all Wisconsin residents who had smoked for 20 years and had been diagnosed with lung cancer was denied by the court on the ground that common questions did not "predominate" as is required by Rule 23(b)(3). Class actions are considered in the last section of this chapter.]

I conclude that plaintiffs' claims do not arise from the same transaction or series of transactions, as they must in order to satisfy Rule 20. On an abstract level, dissimilarities in the claims brought by plaintiffs suggest that these claims are not related logically to one another. Plaintiffs began smoking at different ages; they bought different brands throughout their years as smokers; and they quit for different reasons and under different circumstances. As already mentioned, the only thread holding these disparate factual scenarios together is the allegation of an industry-wide conspiracy but this theory does not hold up on its terms much less under the weight of the individual issues associated with each plaintiff. * * * Plaintiffs' depositions revealed that tobacco industry propaganda regarding the health effects of smoking reached them, if at all, through a variety of different channels and with varying degrees of success. Complicating matters further, defendants allegedly unleashed the stream of misrepresentations in furtherance of the conspiracy over the course of a 30–year period. As emphasized by defendants, plaintiff Vincent Insola began smoking almost two decades before the industry hatched its scheme and has not smoked for more than a quarter of a century. By contrast, plaintiffs Billy Mays and Maureen Lovejoy took up the habit in the early '50s and continued to smoke well into [the] '90s. Even if the conspiracy charged held together, serious questions exist regarding medical causation. * * * For example, medical evidence suggests that the cancer contracted by Mays may be attributable to a work-related accident, not smoking, and that Insola's risk of developing lung cancer returned to that of a nonsmoker ten years after he quit. With this motion, defendants have submitted the report of a pathologist that casts into doubt whether plaintiff Maureen Lovejoy ever had cancer. In the face of this evidence, plaintiffs' argument that causation and other medical issues can be resolved without engaging in highly individualized inquiries is even less persuasive here than it was in their briefs in support of class certification.

The practical implications of allowing these claims to go forward suggest that joinder would not serve the policies underlying rule 20. Plaintiffs disagree, maintaining that joinder would promote efficiency. In doing so, plaintiffs rely heavily on * * * Hohlbein v. Heritage Mutual Ins. Co., 106 F.R.D. 73 (E.D.Wis.1985). * * * *Hohlbein* arose out of a series of fraudulent statements and omissions made by a defendant to more than one plaintiff—in this case, during the recruitment and employment of four executives by an insurance company. The district court acknowledged that some factual dissimilarities existed between these claims but held that they satisfied Rule 20 because each sprung "from a consistent pattern or practice of employment behavior on the part of a single defendant ..." Specifically, the circumstances under which the company hired, employed and fired each plaintiff bore sufficient similarity to one another, even if they were not identical; the company engaged in all of the fraudulent conduct within a discrete two and one-half year time period; at least one material aspect of this conduct applied uniformly to all of the plaintiffs; and the plaintiffs had sustained similar damages. Taken together, these considerations persuaded the court that the additional burden imposed upon the defendant and the risk of jury confusion would be "far outweighed by the practical benefits likely to accrue to all players in the conservation of judicial, prosecutorial, and defensive resources."

* * *

In contrast to the misrepresentations at issue in *Hohlbein*, the life span of the alleged conspiracy perpetrated by defendants is measured in decades, not years. Many of the facts needed to prove the existence of the conspiracy and its effect on plaintiffs Lovejoy and Mays would be irrelevant to the smoking history of plaintiff Insolia, who reached the age of majority before defendants launched the plan and who quit long before it petered out. Rather than the single employer implicated in *Hohlbein*, this case involves five tobacco companies who have manufactured hundreds of brands of cigarettes. It is unlikely that a jury could keep track of which plaintiff smoked which brand and for how long while also retaining a coherent grasp of the minutiae associated with addiction, medical causation and legal causation. But this is not simply a matter of jury confusion. Judicial resources are wasted, not conserved, when a jury is subjected to a welter of evidence relevant to some parties but not others. Confusion can lead to prejudice when there are inadequate assurances that evidence will be weighed against the appropriate party and in the proper context. Defendants are correct that the trial plan proposed by plaintiffs not only fails to address this concern effectively but may actually compound it. Under the plan, a jury would be allowed to decide whether a conspiracy existed, whether cigarettes are unreasonably dangerous and whether defendants intentionally disregarded the rights of plaintiffs—all without regard to reliance, contributory negligence, assumption of risk, addiction and medical causation. These issues, which are normally linked inextricably with a final determination on liability, would be litigated in a subsequent phase. I share defendants' concern that partitioning the trial in such an unorthodox manner would prejudice their ability to protect their rights effectively.

Notes and Questions

1.   We have encountered the "same transaction or occurrence" language in other federal rules: Rule 13(a) uses that standard to determine when a counterclaim is compulsory [see Wigglesworth v. Teamsters Local Union No. 592, supra p. 207], as does Rule 15(c) to determine when an amended pleading relates back for purposes of the statute of limitations [see Swartz v. Gold Dust Casino, Inc., supra p. 218]. The test for applying the standard differs in those two rules according to the policy they serve: Rule 13(a) looks to whether the matters would make a convenient trial package, while Rule 15(c) looks to whether there was adequate notice at the time of filing so that the defendant can be said to have been aware that the suit included the amended matters. Which of these policies is closest to the Rule 20 standard?

2.   Why were the actions of different police officers, occurring at different places and under different circumstances over a one and a half-year period, considered in *Kedra* to arise out of the same transaction or occurrence (or series thereof), while the actions of the tobacco defendants' collaborative propaganda activities in *Insolia* were not? Is it because a pattern of harassment was alleged in *Kedra*? Why wouldn't the allegation of conspiracy have had the same effect in *Insolia*?

3.   In Poleon v. General Motors Corp., 1999 WL 1289473 (D.Virgin Islands), five police officers who were injured in three different accidents involving different police vehicles sued the common manufacturer of their vehicles, alleging that the Antilocking Brake System and air bags malfunctioned. The court rejected defendant's claim that these were three different transactions, stating that "the controlling consideration is the extent of any product defects, and absolute identity of all events is not necessary."

4.   *Kedra* states that "unification of claims in a single action is more convenient and less expensive and time-consuming for the parties and court." The judge in *Insolia* concludes that convenience and economy would not be served by joinder, citing differing individual experiences of the various plaintiffs. Is the Rule 20 "same transaction or occurrence" test essentially one of efficiency and economy? The plaintiffs in *Kedra* also had very different experiences in relation to defendants. Would a joint trial in *Kedra* be more efficient than in *Insolia*?

5.   In *Insolia*, plaintiffs proposed a trial plan by which common issues (whether there was a conspiracy, whether cigarettes were unreasonably dangerous, and whether defendants intentionally disregarded plaintiffs' rights) would be tried to a jury, and then individual issues (such as reliance, contributory negligence, assumption of risk, addiction, and medical causation) would be "litigated in a subsequent phase." Why would the latter issues require individual, as opposed to common, evidence? Such "phased trials" will be discussed further regarding class actions at pp. 322–24 nn. 5–6

(discussing Castano v. American Tobacco Co.). Why does the court say this trial sequence would prejudice the defendants' ability "to protect their rights effectively?" In *Kedra*, the judge reserved ruling on whether, even though joinder was appropriate, there would be a joint trial. Would "phased trials" be appropriate there?

6. Mosley v. General Motors Corp., 497 F.2d 1330 (8th Cir.1974), cited in *Kedra*, upheld the joinder of race discrimination claims by ten employees from two different divisions of General Motors because of their "logical relationship." The court emphasized the plaintiffs' allegations of a company-wide policy of discrimination. United States v. Mississippi, 380 U.S. 128, 85 S.Ct. 808, 13 L.Ed.2d 717 (1965) similarly permitted joinder of claims against six county registrars who were alleged to have acted "as part of a state-wide system" designed to discriminate on the basis of race in voter registration.

The claims in *Mosley* and U.S. v. Mississippi made a convenient, efficient, and economical trial package because the same evidence could be used to show a common discriminatory policy. But if there were no such common policy—and thus the claims of discrimination would have to be proven with individual evidence as to each of the employees in *Mosley* or as to each of the county registrars in U.S. v. Mississippi—would joinder under Rule 20 have been proper? How does a court determine what the evidence will be when it must rule on a motion for misjoinder before discovery is even undertaken? Should the court rely entirely on the plaintiffs' allegations or should it go beyond them to assess whether, in fact, it is likely that the different claims will involve similar evidence? Is an evidentiary hearing necessary or can a misjoinder motion be decided on briefs?

7. Notice that the remedy for misjoinder under Rule 21 is not to dismiss the action, but to drop or add parties by order of the court or to sever and proceed with claims separately.

8. Would joinder be proper under Rule 20 in the following cases:

a. Fifty home owners from the neighborhood join in the same suit against a large restaurant and night club for damages resulting from its customers taking up all available parking on the streets and blocking their driveways. What if the suit were for an injunction to abate a nuisance?

b. Twenty purchasers of vacuum cleaners purchased from different door-to-door salesmen of the same manufacturer join in the same suit against the manufacturer for fraudulent misrepresentations as to the product. What if the suit were for breach of contract or strict liability due to various design and manufacturing defects?

c. A bank that has five hundred notes on which payments are overdue sues the five hundred makers of the notes in a single suit. Compare Tele-Media Co. v. Antidormi, 179 F.R.D. 75 (D.Conn.1998) (cable television company could not bring single action against 104 individuals, alleging that each had used an altered converter to obtain programming without paying).

9. Even if joinder is permissible under Rule 20, it could create problems with federal-court jurisdiction when jurisdiction is based on "diversity of citizenship." If a party who is a citizen of the same state as an opposing party is joined, there would be no diversity of citizenship. 28 U.S.C.A. § 1367

(examined in Chp. X, infra p. 890) accords "supplemental jurisdiction" over the claim of a non-diverse party that is "so related to claims in the action within such original jurisdiction that they form part of the same case or controversy under Article III of the United States Constitution." The Supreme Court granted certiorari to resolve a split among the lower courts about whether supplemental jurisdiction applies in such a case. See Rosario Ortega v. Star–Kist Foods, Inc., infra p. 892. Supplemental jurisdiction will also be discussed in the next section on compulsory joinder.

D. COMPULSORY JOINDER OF PARTIES (RULE 19)

Compulsory joinder of parties raises the issue whether certain persons not joined as parties have sufficient interests in the suit that they must be joined and whether, if they cannot be joined, the suit will be allowed to proceed without them or must be dismissed. The history of the legal rules governing compulsory joinder of parties is complicated, indeed one might even say byzantine, in nature. Concerns over joinder of missing parties were addressed by equity courts in the seventeenth and eighteenth centuries, resulting at that time in what Professor Hazard has referred to as "fairly workable necessary party rules":

1. All persons who are interested in a controversy are necessary parties to a suit involving that controversy, so that a complete disposition of the dispute may be made.

2. Joinder of necessary parties is excused when it is impossible, impractical, or involves undue complications.

3. A person who is not a party, unless represented by one who is a party, is not bound by a decree.

Hazard, Indispensable Party: The Historical Origin of a Procedural Phantom, 61 Colum.L.Rev. 1254, 1255 (1961).

It was after these developments that what has come to be known as the "indispensable party" rule was invented. That rule was based on the premise that a court should do "complete justice or none at all" and that if a party found to be necessary could not be joined, the suit had to be dismissed. This doctrine contained the fallacy, as pointed out by Professor Reed, that because a court does not have jurisdiction over the absentee, it cannot act with respect to others that are properly before it. Reed, Compulsory Joinder of Parties in Civil Actions, 55 Mich.L.Rev. 327, 330 (1957). The Supreme Court's decision in Shields v. Barrow, 58 U.S. (17 How.) 130, 15 L.Ed. 158 (1854), had embedded this fallacy in American procedural law by categorizing parties as "necessary" and "indispensable" according to the nature of their rights ("common," "joint," or "united in interest") and applying them in a rigid and nonfunctional manner.

"The sonorous generalities of Shields v. Barrow," Professors Wright and Kane wrote, "led, perhaps inevitably, to a jurisprudence of labels" that became "treacherous and misleading [when] applied as a substitute for reasoning." C. Wright & M. Kane, Law of Federal Courts 498 (6th ed. 2002). The *Shields* approach, dominant as it had been for almost a century, was continued in the new Federal Rules in 1938. Rule 19 made the possession of a "joint interest" the dividing line between permissive and compulsory joinder and, without providing guidelines, went on to state that an action could not proceed if persons with "joint interests" were not joined unless they were not "indispensable." That approach was altered in 1966 amendments to Rule 19, and you are fortunate in being spared the necessity of studying the tortured precedents under the former rule that tried to make the term "joint interest" into a workable distinction and to define the hazy line between "necessary" and "indispensable" parties.

Rule 19, as amended in 1966, describes, in subsection (a), those persons who are needed for just adjudication and provides that they will be joined if feasible. Sometimes, however, an absentee found to satisfy the criteria in subsection (a) cannot be joined. The usual reasons in a federal court are that the absentee comes from the same state as an opposing party and his joinder would therefore destroy diversity jurisdiction; the absentee has insufficient contacts with the forum to permit personal jurisdiction; or venue would be improper. In that case, subsection (b) requires an analysis of four factors to determine whether "equity and good conscience" permit the action to proceed without the absent party.

Under Rule 19 the terms "necessary" and "indispensable" are sometimes loosely employed to refer to the parties identified in subsection (a) ("necessary") and subsection (b) ("indispensable"), but they are inexact terms and do not convey the meanings they carried under the old rules. Rule 19 uses functional and pragmatic tests for determining who falls under (a) and (b). This means that whole categories of missing parties can no longer be said in the abstract to fall within a certain category (for example, joint obligors, subrogees, or co-owners), and a case-by-case analysis must often be made to determine the requirements of compulsory joinder.

JANNEY MONTGOMERY SCOTT, INC. v. SHEPARD NILES, INC.

United States Court of Appeals, Third Circuit, 1993.
11 F.3d 399.

Before STAPLETON, HUTCHINSON and ROTH, Circuit Judges.

HUTCHINSON, Circuit Judge.

Appellant, Janney Montgomery Scott, Inc. ("Janney"), appeals an order of the United States District Court for the Eastern District of Pennsylvania granting appellee, Shepard Niles, Inc.'s ("Shepard Niles") motion for judgment on the pleadings under Federal Rule of Civil Procedure 12(c) for failure to join an indispensable party in Janney's breach of contract action. The person whose non-joinder resulted in dismissal is Shepard Niles' parent corporation, The Underwood Group, Ltd. ("Underwood"), a citizen of Pennsylvania. In doing so, the district court had to make an initial determination that Underwood, Shepard

Niles' parent, was a necessary party under Rule 19(a) before it could hold that Underwood was an indispensable party under Rule 19(b) whose non-joinder required dismissal because joinder would deprive the district court of diversity jurisdiction. Initially, the district court had subject matter jurisdiction in diversity because Janney is a citizen of Pennsylvania and Shepard Niles is a citizen of New York.

In Shepard Niles' motion to dismiss for failure to join Underwood, it stated that Underwood, its parent and the sole signatory to the contract Janney sued on, was both necessary and indispensable to Janney's action under Rule 19. The question before us is whether the district court could give complete relief to the parties before it without prejudice to them or the absent person, Underwood, in a breach of contract action against only one of the two co-obligors that might be liable to Janney, the obligee on the contract. If the relief Janney requests does not prejudice the absent co-obligor, Underwood, or subject either Janney or Shepard Niles to a threat of duplicative or inconsistent judgments, Underwood is not a necessary party under Rule 19(a). If Underwood is not a necessary party under Rule 19(a), we need not reach the question whether it is indispensable under Rule 19(b). In this case, we have concluded that Underwood will not be prejudiced and neither Janney nor Shepard Niles will be subjected to duplicative or inconsistent judgments. Therefore, we hold that Underwood is not a necessary party under Rule 19(a). Accordingly, we will reverse the district court's order granting Shepard Niles' motion to dismiss without reaching the question whether Underwood is indispensable under Rule 19(b).

I. FACTUAL & PROCEDURAL HISTORY

Janney is an investment banking corporation organized under Pennsylvania law with its principal place of business in Philadelphia, Pennsylvania. Underwood is a closely-held Pennsylvania corporation with its principal place of business in Pennsylvania; Shepard Niles is incorporated under New York law, with its principal place of business in New York.

On January 12, 1990, Janney and Underwood executed an Investment Banking Agreement ("Agreement"). In it, Janney agreed to serve as an advisor to Underwood and its subsidiaries, including Shepard Niles, and to assist them in obtaining private placement financing to refinance Shepard Niles' debt obligations.

In February 1990, when Janney's efforts had yet to show concrete results, Underwood entered into negotiations with Unibank PLC and its parent corporation Unibank A/S (collectively "Unibank") to provide private placement financing that its subsidiary, Shepard Niles, needed. By the fall of 1990, Unibank and Ampco–Pittsburgh Corporation ("Ampco") had given Shepard Niles the financing it needed. Janney did not introduce either of these two companies to Underwood and its subsidiaries, but Janney does allege that it provided substantial advice and support to Underwood and Shepard Niles throughout the negotiations. It contends that under the Agreement this advice and support entitle it to a contingent fee which it seeks to recover from Shepard Niles in this action and from Underwood in the related state action that Janney filed in the Philadelphia Court of Common Pleas on October 4, 1990, against Underwood, Shepard Niles, and Underwood's two other subsidiaries. In addition, on October 23, 1991, after some discovery in the state action, Janney filed an action in the district court against Unibank for tortious interference with contract.

On February 7, 1992, in the federal action against Unibank for tortious interference with contract, Janney filed a motion to amend its complaint to add Shepard Niles as a defendant. The district court denied it. Thereafter, on March 17, 1992, Janney filed the present breach of contract action against Shepard Niles. Shepard Niles responded with a Federal Rule of Civil Procedure 12(b)(6) motion to dismiss or, in the alternative, to stay the federal action while Janney's case was pending in common pleas. The district court denied this motion. After the pleadings in the district court had closed and discovery was nearly completed, Shepard Niles filed its Rule 12(c) motion for judgment on the pleadings for failure to join Underwood as an indispensable party. On January 4, 1993, the district court granted Shepard Niles' Rule 12(c) motion. In the meantime, Janney had filed a motion to consolidate its breach of contract action against Shepard Niles with its tort action against Unibank, but the district court's order dismissing the action against Shepard Niles mooted Janney's motion to consolidate. Janney has timely appealed the order granting Shepard Niles' Rule 12(c) motion for judgment on the pleadings and dismissing of the breach of contract action for non-joinder.

[While Rule 19 decisions are usually reviewed under an abuse of discretion standard, the appellate court found a de novo review should be employed because the district court's decision was based on the legal conclusion that its decision in this case would have collateral estoppel effect against Shepard Niles, or become a precedent against Underwood, in the pending state court action. "To the extent that a district court's Rule 19(a) determination is premised on a conclusion of law, * * * our scope of review is plenary."]

III.   Rule 19 Analysis

Federal Rule of Civil Procedure 19 determines when joinder of a particular party is compulsory. A court must first determine whether a party should be joined if "feasible" under Rule 19(a). If the party should be joined but joinder is not feasible because it would destroy diversity, the court must then determine whether the absent party is "indispensable" under Rule 19(b). If the party is indispensable, the action therefore cannot go forward. * * *

Rule 19(a) defines the parties who are "necessary" in the sense that their joinder is compulsory "if feasible." It states, in pertinent part:

A person … shall be joined as a party in the action if (1) in the person's absence complete relief cannot be accorded among those already parties, or (2) the person claims an interest relating to the subject of the action and is so situated that the disposition of the action in the person's absence may (i) as a practical matter impair or impede the person's ability to protect that interest or (ii) leave any of the persons already parties subject to a substantial risk of incurring double, multiple, or otherwise inconsistent obligations by reason of the claimed interest.

Fed.R.Civ.P. 19(a). Clauses (1) and (2) of Rule 19(a) are phrased in the disjunctive and should be so treated. Thus, any party whose absence results in any of the problems identified in either subsections (a)(1) or (a)(2) is a party whose joinder is compulsory if feasible. In other words, a holding that joinder is compulsory under Rule 19(a) is a necessary predicate to a district court's discretionary determination under Rule 19(b) that the case must be dismissed because joinder of the party is not feasible and the party is indispensable to the just resolution of the controversy.

A. Rule 19(a)(1)

Under Rule 19(a), we ask first whether complete relief can be accorded to the parties to the action in the absence of the unjoined party. A Rule 19(a)(1) inquiry is limited to whether the district court can grant complete relief to the persons already parties to the action. The effect a decision may have on the absent party is not material. Here, the district court concluded that complete relief could be afforded Janney and Shepard Niles in the absence of Underwood. Shepard Niles does not seriously dispute this conclusion. For the following reasons, we agree with the district court on this point.

In applying Rule 19(a)(1) to this case, the specific question before us is whether a court can grant complete relief in a breach of contract action to the parties before it when only one of two co-obligors has been joined as a defendant.[5] The answer to this specific question depends on the law of contracts concerning the joint and several liability of persons who are co-promisors or co-obligors on one agreement. Two general authorities on the subject have identified a strong trend in favor of a principle that co-signers or co-obligors on a contract are jointly and severally liable for its performance. See 2 Samuel Williston, Williston on Contracts §§ 320, 336, at 649–657, 697–706 (3d ed. 1959); Restatement (Second) of Contracts § 289, at 410–11 (1981). In Pennsylvania,[6] whether liability on a contract is joint or joint and several seems to be treated as a question of construction or interpretation, not as a rule of law.

---

5. The parties' emphasis on the effect of the parent-subsidiary relationship between Underwood and Shepard Niles only obscures this issue. Janney does not argue that Shepard Niles is an agent or alter ego of Underwood. Thus, this case must be considered as a simple breach of contract action brought against one of two co-obligors to a contract.

6. The district court indicated that Pennsylvania law applied to the question of contract formation. No choice of law problem has been raised. Therefore, we conclude that Pennsylvania provides the law which governs this contract's interpretation.

If the Agreement in question can be construed or interpreted as a contract imposing joint and several liability on its co-obligors, Shepard Niles and Underwood, complete relief may be granted in a suit against only one of them. Though the record before us does not show that the Agreement signed by Underwood and said to include Shepard Niles as a co-obligor imposes joint and several liability, it does not rule out such a construction. In deciding Shepard Niles' Rule 12(c) motion for judgment on the pleadings, the district court had to review the facts and inferences to be drawn from the pleadings in the light most favorable to the nonmoving party, Janney. Therefore, because the Agreement can be construed to impose joint and several liability, Underwood is not a necessary party under subsection (a)(1), and we must affirm the district court's holding that complete relief could be granted between Shepard Niles and Janney without Underwood's presence.

B. Rule 19(a)(2)

Though Underwood was not a party that had to be joined under Rule 19(a)(1) because complete relief could be granted the parties already present, the district court concluded Underwood's joinder was compulsory under both Rule 19(a)(2)(i) and 19(a)(2)(ii). Unlike subsection (a)(1), subsection (a)(2) requires a court to take into consideration the effect that resolution of the dispute among the parties before it may have on an absent party.

1. Rule 19(a)(2)(i)

Subsection (a)(2)(i) requires a court to decide whether determination of the rights of the parties before it would impair or impede an absent party's ability to protect its interest in the subject matter of the litigation. Shepard Niles argues that the district court correctly held Underwood is a necessary party because any decision in the federal action in Janney's favor would be a persuasive precedent against Underwood in the ongoing state action.[7] The district court agreed and held that "as a practical matter, the disposition of this action in Underwood's absence [would] impair or impede Underwood's ability to protect its interest."

According to the district court, it was likely that any decision reached in the federal action would affect the pending state court action "either as collateral estoppel against Shepard Niles,[8] or as persuasive

---

7. Shepard Niles' argument that an adjudication against it in federal court would create a persuasive precedent against Underwood in the corresponding state action involves a kind of sleight of hand. If Shepard Niles is found not liable, its precedential effect would harm Janney, not Underwood. On the other hand, if Shepard Niles is found liable, it is unlikely that Janney would need to continue the state action against Underwood. See Goldberg v. Altman, 190 Pa.Super. 495, 154 A.2d 279,

282 (1959) ("Even though [the plaintiff] has two judgments, he can only have one satisfaction.").

8. Rule 19(a)(2)(i) only directs the court to determine whether the continuation of the action will impair or impede the absent party's ability to protect its interest. As such, the court's indication that any decision it rendered might have a collateral estoppel affect on Shepard Niles is not relevant to its 19(a)(2)(i) determination. Any adverse effect on Shepard Niles will be con-

precedent against Underwood." We disagree with the district court's conclusion that a decision against Shepard Niles in the pending action could have such a potential effect on a future state action that it would make Underwood's joinder compulsory under Rule 19(a)(2)(i).[9]

We are not sure what the district court means by the phrase "persuasive precedent." To the extent it involves the doctrine of stare decisis, we are not inclined to hold that any potential effect the doctrine may have on an absent party's rights makes the absent party's joinder compulsory under Rule 19(a) whenever "feasible." Such a holding would greatly expand the class of "necessary" or compulsory parties Rule 19(a) creates. Moreover, to whatever extent the rule's phrase "as a practical matter impair or impede" has broader meaning than that given by principles of issue preclusion, we think the effect of the federal decision must be more direct and immediate than the effect a judgment in Shepard Niles' favor would have on Underwood here. They are, after all, separate corporate entities. In any event, we do not believe any possibility of a "persuasive precedent" requires joinder under subsection 19(a)(2)(i).

Shepard Niles relies primarily on two cases, Marra v. Burgdorf Realtors, Inc., 726 F.Supp. 1000 (E.D.Pa.1989) and Acton Co. v. Bachman Foods, Inc., 668 F.2d 76 (1st Cir.1982), to support its argument. Both are distinguishable. *Marra* involved an action by a putative owner of real estate against a real estate agent and brokerage firm over the real estate agent's sales of some of the putative owner's property. Record title to the property sold was in the name of the putative owner's son. The complaint alleged violations of a number of Pennsylvania statutes regulating the sale of real estate, as well as a common law action for fraud and misrepresentation. The brokerage firm moved to dismiss for failure to join an indispensable party. The *Marra* court granted the brokerage firm's motion. It held that the record title holder was a "necessary party" under Rule 19(a)(2)(i) to the litigation because claims asserting misrepresentation as to ownership of property against the real estate agent applied only if the putative owner had valid title to the properties in question. Therefore, the litigation was likely to determine title to the property. That holding is unremarkable.

Shepard Niles says *Marra* stands for the principle that any potentially persuasive effect a federal judgment may have on the rights of an absent party makes the absent party one whose joinder is compulsory under Rule 19(a)(2)(i), if feasible. We do not read *Marra* so broadly. There, determination of title to the real estate in which the absent party had an interest appeared inevitable if the dispute between the parties present in the federal court was to be resolved. In those circumstances, it

sidered under the court's 19(a)(2)(ii) analysis.

9. We note that if Shepard Niles is not liable to Janney, an attempt by Shepard Niles to invoke the district court's final judgment in its favor as a collateral estop-pel in an action against it by Underwood for contribution or indemnification would be unavailing because Underwood is most likely not a party whose interests are the same as Shepard Niles.

is clear that the absent party should be joined if feasible. In the case before us, the persuasive effect of a district court decision on Underwood's rights is speculative. We are unable to say with any assurance that a decision in Janney's action against Shepard Niles will be likely to impair or impede Underwood's ability to defend itself in the state action or to obtain indemnity or contribution from Shepard Niles. Accordingly, the "precedential" effect of a decision by the district court does not, in this case, justify a holding that Underwood is a "necessary" party under Rule 19(a)(2)(i). Accord, Drankwater v. Miller, 830 F.Supp. 188, 193 (S.D.N.Y.1993) ("[W]hile it may be true that a court in a later litigation may consider an earlier finding, it is plain that a prior finding would not be binding upon [the absent party] since [it] was not a party to the instant action. Thus, the Court finds the 'negative precedent' argument unpersuasive and insufficient alone to support a finding that [the absent party] should be joined if feasible."). The rationale of *Marra* is not applicable here.

Shepard Niles also relies heavily on the Court of Appeals for the First Circuit's decision in *Acton*. *Acton*, too, is distinguishable from the case at hand. There, a parent corporation, the Acton Corp. ("Acton") and its subsidiary, Acton Co., Inc. of Massachusetts ("ACIM") entered into an asset purchase agreement with the defendant, Bachman Foods, Inc. ("Bachman"). Both Acton and ACIM were signatories to the contract. Acton refused to complete performance, claiming that Bachman had not only breached the agreement but had also made material misrepresentations which induced Acton to enter into the contract. Bachman filed a breach of contract action against both Acton and ACIM in a New York state court. ACIM then filed, in district court under diversity jurisdiction, damage claims for fraud and misrepresentation along with a claim seeking a declaratory judgment that no enforceable agreement existed between Bachman and ACIM. ACIM did not join Acton in its federal action against Bachman because Acton's presence would have destroyed complete diversity and deprived the district court of subject matter jurisdiction under 28 U.S.C.A. § 1332. The district court dismissed the action because of failure to join Acton as an indispensable party.

The United States Court of Appeals for the First Circuit affirmed the district court's dismissal of the action for failure to join an indispensable party. The court of appeals initially held that Acton's non-joinder raised a substantial question as to whether complete relief could be granted in Acton's absence under Rule 19(a)(1). In that respect, its concern centered on the ability of Acton, there a *co-obligee* on the agreement, to bring a separate action of its own against Bachman that could subject Bachman to double liability on the same claim that ACIM was making in the federal action. Therefore, it held Acton's presence was necessary for the grant of complete relief. No such concern is present here. Shepard Niles argues that Underwood is a necessary and indispensable defendant because it is potentially a co-obligor with Shepard

Niles, not a potential co-obligee, as in *Acton*. As one commentator has noted:

> Today the joinder of obligors is left to plaintiff's discretion by many courts and he may select defendants without being concerned about dismissal because of nonjoinder. Joint obligors thus are treated as Rule 19(a) parties, but are not deemed indispensable under Rule 19(b).... Joint obligees, on the other hand, usually have been held indispensable parties and their nonjoinder has led to a dismissal of the action.

7 Charles A. Wright et al., Federal Practice and Procedure § 1613 at 182–85 (1986).

Here, Shepard Niles cites *Acton* to support its argument that the potentially persuasive effect of the federal action on any related litigation justifies the district court's conclusion that the absent party's joinder is compulsory under Rule 19(a)(2)(i). That argument ignores the United States Court of Appeals for the First Circuit's refusal to adopt a persuasive precedent standard for a Rule 19(a) determination that all tortfeasors who could be jointly and severally liable should be joined if feasible. See Pujol v. Shearson/American Express, Inc., 877 F.2d 132, 136 (1st Cir.1989) ("The mere fact, however, that Party A, in a suit against Party B, intends to introduce evidence that will indicate that a non-party, C, behaved improperly does not, by itself, make C a necessary party."). Though we recognize that the *Pujol* court distinguished joint tortfeasors from joint obligors and stated that *Acton* was still good law as applied to contract liability, we see no logical distinction that would justify treating contract actions differently than tort actions for purposes of compulsory joinder. * * * [W]e hold instead that Underwood, a co-obligor, is not a party whose joinder Rule 19(a)(2)(i) requires because continuation of the federal litigation in Underwood's absence will not create a precedent that might persuade another court to rule against Underwood on principles of stare decisis, or some other unidentified basis not encompassed by the rules of collateral estoppel or issue preclusion.

We do not ignore the *Acton* court's suggestion that joinder of an absent party is compulsory under Rule 19(a)(2)(i) if the federal litigation would have a preclusive effect against the absent party in subsequent state litigation. Indeed, we agree. If issue preclusion or collateral estoppel could be invoked against Underwood in other litigation, continuation of the federal action could "as a practical matter impair or impede" Underwood's interests and so Rule 19(a)(2)(i) would require its joinder if joinder were feasible. In the case before us, however, this argument lacks force. Mere presentation of an argument that issue preclusion is possible is not enough to trigger Rule 19(a)(2)(i). Rather, it must be shown that some outcome of the federal case that is reasonably likely can preclude the absent party with respect to an issue material to the absent party's rights or duties under standard principles governing the effect of prior judgments.[12] If impairment of the absent party's interest is not shown in that sense, the adequacy of Shepard Niles' representation of Underwood's interest is not material.[13] Shepard Niles' assumption that any potential for issue preclusion compels a holding that a party is necessary under Rule 19(a)(2)(i) cannot be accepted.

The district court itself acknowledges that subsection (a)(2)(i) does not make Underwood's joinder compulsory, if feasible, because of any effect issue preclusion may have on Underwood. While noting that a final judgment in this action would be inadequate and result in piecemeal litigation and would still leave Shepard Niles subject to inconsistent or double liability, it specifically stated, in the course of its Rule 19(b) analysis, that "the judgment would be binding as to Shepard Niles *only*." In this respect, the district court is correct. Its conclusion that Underwood would not be bound is a corollary of the general rule that issue preclusion applies only to persons who were either parties to the prior action or shared the same interest as the parties who were present in the prior action. Underwood does not share Shepard Niles' interest. Indeed, its interests are adverse to those of Shepard Niles with respect to any right of contribution or indemnity that may arise out of either's potential liability to Janney.

For issue preclusion to apply against Underwood, the state court would thus have to find Underwood in privity with Shepard Niles because Underwood controlled or directed the previous litigation or Shepard Niles was sued in a representative capacity. This inquiry made for collateral estoppel purposes is similar to that made in a Rule 19(a)(2)(i) determination: if the court finds that an absent party's interest will be impaired and impeded if it is not joined as a party to the present action it implicitly indicates that the absent party's interests are not sufficiently protected in its absence. Conversely, if another court is later to invoke issue preclusion on the basis of privity, it will have to determine that the absent party's interest was adequately protected by a party to the previous litigation. We will not theorize in determining necessary party status about the potential preclusive effect of this action on a later lawsuit as this would be premature. See Johnson & Johnson v. Coopervision, Inc., 720 F.Supp. 1116, 1124 (D.Del.1989) (holding it would be premature for court in Rule 19(b) indispensable party analysis to decide whether the absent party is in privity for purpose of determin-

---

12. In Pennsylvania, a party may be precluded from relitigating an issue if: (1) the issue decided in the prior adjudication was identical with the one presented in the later action; (2) there was a final judgment on the merits; (3) the party against whom the plea is asserted was a party or in privity with a party to the prior adjudication; and (4) the party against whom it is asserted has had a full and fair opportunity to litigate the issue in question in a prior action. Sanders v. Sanders, 384 Pa.Super. 311, 558 A.2d 556, 560 (1989) (citation omitted), ap-

peal denied, 525 Pa. 635, 578 A.2d 930 (1990).

13. We need not consider Janney's argument that Shepard Niles will adequately represent Underwood's interest and therefore Underwood's joinder is not necessary to meet the requirement of Rule 19(a)(2)(i). Adequacy of representation is the fourth subject of inquiry under Pennsylvania law on collateral estoppel or issue preclusion. It is not reached unless the first three requirements are met.

ing preclusive effect of lawsuit given highly factual nature of privity analysis). Underwood could have sought leave to intervene in this action under Rule 24(b)(2) if it wished to insure that its right of contribution is not adversely affected by a judgment in the Janney–Shepard Niles litigation, but intervention is not necessary to protect its right of contribution or indemnity against collateral estoppel. In addition, Underwood can always bring its own action against Shepard Niles for contribution or indemnification.

The case law and commentary that supports the proposition that one co-obligor may be sued without joinder of its co-obligors implicitly supports the proposition that issue preclusion for or against an absent co-obligor is not a consequence of any final decision for or against the co-obligor who is present as a party in a contract action. Thus, the United States Supreme Court has stated:

> [T]he plaintiff, by his judgment against one of his joint debtors, gets the relief he is entitled to. . . . The absent joint obligors are not injured, because *their rights are in no sense affected*, and they remain liable to contribution to their co-obligor who may pay the judgment by suit, as they would have been had he paid it without suit.

Barney v. Baltimore City, 73 U.S. (6 Wall) 280, 287, 18 L.Ed. 825 (1867) (emphasis in original).

The district court erred in holding that the mere possibility that its decision in the present action would be a "persuasive precedent" in any subsequent state action against Underwood could, as a practical matter, impair or impede Underwood's interest under Rule 19(a)(2)(i). Accordingly, we hold Underwood is not an absent party whose joinder is compulsory, if feasible, under Rule 19(a)(2)(i).

2. Rule 19(a)(2)(ii)

We have yet to consider the effect of Rule 19(a)(2)(ii) on the non-joinder of Underwood. It requires us to decide whether continuation of this action in the absence of Underwood would expose Shepard Niles to the "substantial risk of incurring double, multiple, or otherwise inconsistent obligations by reason of the claimed interest." The district court decided that "the continuation of this action in Underwood's absence may expose Shepard Niles to a substantial risk of incurring double or inconsistent obligations" because Shepard Niles may be found liable under the Agreement in the federal action while Underwood may be found not liable in the state court action.

Janney argues that the district court erred in concluding that continuation of the federal action had the potential of subjecting Shepard Niles to double liability. Janney states, "[r]egardless of who wins in federal court, the outcome of the case will be res judicata or collateral estoppel as between Janney and Shepard Niles ... resolv[ing] the dispute between Janney and Shepard Niles *once and for all*." We agree. If Shepard Niles is held not liable in the federal action, it cannot be liable under principles of issue and claim preclusion in the state court action. But if Shepard Niles is held liable, the result will bind it only in its dispute with Janney, and it will remain free to claim contribution or indemnity from Underwood.

It is, of course, possible, as the district court concluded, that if Shepard Niles is held liable in the federal action, it "may ultimately be responsible for the entire claim if Underwood is found not liable in the State Court Action." This is not, however, the double liability that Rule 19(a)(2)(ii) refers to. Thus, the district court erred in concluding that continuation of this action exposed Shepard Niles to a risk of double liability within the meaning of Rule 19(a)(2)(ii). Beneath the district court's conclusion lies an unstated premise—if Shepard Niles is liable on the agreement, Underwood, the signer, must be liable too. That might be so in "the best of all possible worlds," as Dr. Pangloss would say, but Dr. Pangloss does not rule the legal system and in it judges and juries, not Candide, are the arbiters of lawsuits. Thus, in this imperfect world, the district court's premise is contradicted by the law's refusal to consider the real possibility that one court could find Shepard Niles liable while another was finding Underwood not liable in separate proceedings to which the rules of claim or issue preclusion do not apply.[14]

A holding that Shepard Niles is liable to Janney does not legally imply that Underwood is also liable. See Mamalis [v. Atlas Van Lines, Inc.], 528 A.2d at 202 [(Pa.Super.Ct.1987)] ("Each obligor under a contract has independently consented to the obligation.... [A] contract cause of action against an individual obligor does not depend on the status of a separate claim."). Underwood's liability as Shepard Niles' co-obligor is not a condition precedent to Shepard Niles' liability under the agreement.

The possibility that Shepard Niles may bear the whole loss if it is found liable is not the equivalent of double liability. It is instead a common result of joint and several liability and should not be equated with prejudice. Inherent in the concept of joint and several liability is the right of a plaintiff to satisfy its whole judgment by execution against any one of the multiple defendants who are liable to him, thereby forcing the debtor who has paid the whole debt to protect itself by an action for contribution against the other joint obligors.

An outcome adverse to Shepard Niles in Janney's present action against it does not have any legal effect on whatever right of contribution or indemnification Shepard Niles may have against Underwood. Though federal civil practice, in common with other modern Anglo–American procedural systems, permits a party defendant who claims a right of contribution or indemnity from third persons to protect itself from potentially inconsistent verdicts by impleading the absent party under Federal Rule of Civil Procedure 14, it is not required to do so; and,

14. We recognize, of course, that if Janney should obtain full recovery from Shepard Niles in federal court, it could not seek to double that recovery by maintaining the state court action against Underwood.

if it does not, its right to bring a separate action for contribution or indemnity is unaffected.[15] Thus, in Bank of America National Trust and Savings Association [v. Hotel Rittenhouse Assoc.], 844 F.2d [1050,] at 1054 [(3d Cir.1988)], we stated, "[a] defendant's right to contribution or indemnity from an absent non-diverse party does not render that absentee indispensable pursuant to Rule 19." In Field [v. Volkswagenwerk AG, 626 F.2d 293 (3d Cir.1980)], this Court, in reviewing whether an absent non-diverse party was necessary and indispensable to a tort action, stated:

> [T]he possibility that [the defendant] may have a right of reimbursement, indemnity, or contribution against [the absent party] is not sufficient to make [the absent party] indispensable to the litigation. This is so because under Fed.R.Civ.P. 14(a) a defendant is authorized to bring into a lawsuit any person "not a party to the action who is or may be liable to him for all or part of the plaintiff's claim against him."

We concluded in *Field* that a defendant's potential loss of its right to contribution from an absent party did not subject it to multiple liability within the meaning of Rule 19. Although *Field* involved potential liability in tort from an auto accident, we think its reasoning is equally applicable to cases involving co-obligors who may be jointly and severally liable on a contract. Shepard Niles is free to implead Underwood, using Rule 14, to assert its claim for contribution or indemnity in the pending state action or to institute a separate action against Underwood for contribution or indemnity upon principles of restitution if it is ultimately held liable to Janney. The continuation of this case in the absence of Underwood does not subject Shepard Niles to double or inconsistent liabilities. Therefore, we hold that Underwood is not a necessary party under Rule 19(a)(2)(ii).

CONCLUSION

Underwood's joinder is not necessary under Rule 19(a)(1) because the district court can give complete relief to Janney and Shepard Niles in their action. Rule 19(a)(2)(i) is not triggered by the mere possibility that continuation of this federal case could have some effect on later litigation

---

15. Rule 14 provides, in pertinent part:
[A] defending party, as a third-party plaintiff, may cause a summons and complaint to be served upon a person not a party to the action who is or may be liable to the third-party plaintiff for all or part of the plaintiff's claim against the third-party plaintiff.

Fed.R.Civ.P. 14(a). This, of course, raises the issue of supplemental jurisdiction. The district court, however, would have jurisdiction over Shepard Niles' claim of contribution under 28 U.S.C.A. § 1367(a) (West Supp.1993). Janney, however, is explicitly precluded from amending its complaint to include Underwood and, thus, litigate Underwood's liability to it. See 28 U.S.C.A. § 1367(b) (West Supp.1993) ("In any civil action of which the district courts have original jurisdiction founded solely on section 1332 of this title, the district courts shall not have supplemental jurisdiction under subsection (a) over claims by *plaintiffs* against persons made parties under Rule 14 ... when exercising supplemental jurisdiction over such claims would be inconsistent with the jurisdictional requirements of section 1332.") (emphasis added). [Supplemental jurisdiction is discussed in detail in Chapter X. See infra pp. 890–910.—Eds.]

between Janney and Underwood. That possibility is too speculative to support a holding that Underwood's interests will, as a practical matter, be impaired or impeded by the continuation of this litigation in its absence. Nor will continuation of this action in Underwood's absence expose Shepard Niles to inconsistent obligations or double liability under Rule 19(a)(2)(ii). Therefore, we conclude that the district court erred when it held that Underwood was a party who had to be joined under Rule 19(a) if its joinder were feasible. That conclusion makes it unnecessary for us to decide whether the district court abused its discretion when it decided that Underwood was an indispensable party under Rule 19(b).

Notes and Questions

1. Recall that Fuentes v. Shevin (supra p. 29) said that the "central meaning" of procedural due process is that persons whose rights are to be affected are entitled to be heard. Consider the extent to which Rule 19 ensures that the due process rights of absentees are protected.

2. Does the Third Circuit's decision in *Janney* reflect a general rule that co-obligors in a contract suit are not necessary parties? Do *Marra* and *Acton* suggest there is no such general rule, or are they distinguishable on their facts? What particular circumstances in *Janney* weighed in favor of the circuit court's finding that the co-obligor, Underwood, was not a necessary party?

3. A decision in the federal court in *Janney* would not have a collateral estoppel (issue preclusive) effect on Underwood in the Pennsylvania court because Underwood was not a party or in privity with a party (preclusion doctrines will be considered in more detail in Chapter XIII, infra pp. 1164). Even so, why wasn't the lower court correct in finding that the federal-court decision could have a precedential effect in the state court that could "as a practical matter impair or impede [Underwood's] ability to protect [its] interest?" Rule 19(a)(2)(i). Although the federal-court decision would not be *stare decisis* in the state court, might it not have a persuasive effect on the state-court judge?

Some other courts have found that the persuasive effect of a ruling could adversely affect the absent party so as to make it a necessary party. In Pulitzer–Polster v. Pulitzer, 784 F.2d 1305 (5th Cir.1986), like *Janney*, similar suits were pending in state court (where all the interested parties were joined) and in federal court (where certain interested parties were left out because their presence would destroy diversity jurisdiction). The Fifth Circuit found that the absent parties (who were co-beneficiaries of a trust) were necessary parties in the federal-court suit brought by another trust beneficiary against the trustee for breach of fiduciary duty. There was a possible "negative precedent," the court said, because the same witnesses would testify on issues of credibility, making the state court more likely to respect credibility findings of the federal court.

Pulitzer involved similar, but not identical suits, which made the precedential effect more problematical. A stronger case for finding a possible adverse precedent is Read v. Phillips Petroleum Co., 441 F.Supp. 1184 (E.D.La.1977), in which absent siblings, in a suit brought by their brother asserting drilling rights in land co-owned by all of them, were found necessary because although "the plaintiff's unsuccessful assertion of his rights in this suit would not be binding on other family members," it "could have at least precedential effect in a subsequent suit by his brothers and sisters."

Is *Janney* distinguishable from these cases on the issue of a possible precedential effect? It appears that the pending suits in state and federal court in *Janney* are similar if not identical, the primary difference being that Underwood and two subsidiaries are parties in the state suit but not the federal. Should the Third Circuit have given greater attention to determining the extent of similarity and the likelihood that findings in the federal court would in fact be persuasive in the state court? What is the support for the court's conclusion that the possibility of "some effect" on later state litigation "is too speculative to support a holding that Underwood's interests will, as a practical matter, be impaired or impeded by the continuation of this litigation in its absence"?

4. Note that the risk under Rule 19(a)(2)(i) is that "as a practical matter" disposition of the action in the nonparty's absence would impair or impede the nonparty's ability to protect its interest. That term is used to indicate that even where the absent party is not bound by a judgment under preclusion law, the judgment may still have the practical effect of impeding its ability. Take the example of a case in which the plaintiff seeks relief other than damages. A judgment awarding an injunction or specific performance could have an immediate impact on the interests of the absent parties. See Ford Motor Co. v. Bisanz Brothers, 249 F.2d 22 (8th Cir.1957), where Ford, a non-party, would have been affected as a practical matter by a suit by adjoining property owners to enjoin the defendant railroad from using a spur to the Ford plant. Judgment for the plaintiffs would have prevented the railroad from using the spur and would have resulted in Ford's loss of the railroad's services. Another example involves a plaintiff's claim of entitlement to a limited fund held by defendant to which the absent parties also have a claim. The absent parties would not be bound by the judgment under res judicata, but the fund might be spent by the plaintiff before they could establish their rights to it in another suit.

5. A Rule 19 motion to dismiss for failure to join a necessary party is invoked by a defendant, not the absent party. Should consideration of the interests of the absent party have to depend on the defendant? See Freer, Rethinking Compulsory Joinder: A Proposal to Restructure Federal Rule 19, 60 N.Y.U.L.Rev. 1061, 1085–86 (1985) (arguing that relying on defendant gives the absentee "sporadic, limited protection"). Note that Rule 19(c) directs the pleader to identify necessary parties. How often would plaintiffs be likely to do so?

An absent party is not before the court and has no status to object to a suit in which it is not joined. However, two joinder devices might be available for it to become a party by its own initiative—intervention and interpleader (which will be examined later in this chapter). Would it be appropriate for a court to assume that the absent party's interests will not be impaired if it has not sought to join the suit by intervention or interpleader? The Notes of the Advisory Committee on the 1966 Amendments to Rule

19 observe that an absent party may be able to take measures to avoid prejudice, such as using defensive interpleader, voluntarily appearing, or intervening on an ancillary basis. They state: "The court should consider whether this, in turn, would impose undue hardship on the absentee."

6. Why wasn't the defendant Shepard Niles found to be subject to a "substantial risk of incurring double, multiple, or otherwise inconsistent obligations by reason of [Janney's] claimed interest?" What if the jury in the federal-court suit found Shepard Niles liable to Janney on the contract, while the jury in the state-court suit found no contractual liability to Janney by any of the parties? Shepard Niles would then have to pay the federal-court judgment but would not be entitled to contribution from Underwood because of the contrary state-court judgment that there was no liability. Why does the Third Circuit not find this to constitute double liability? How does the fact that under Pennsylvania state law Shepard Niles and Underwood are jointly and severally liable bear on this issue?

Janney's conclusion that the fact that "Shepard Niles may bear the whole loss if it is found liable is not the equivalent of double liability," but simply "a common result of joint and several liability," resembles the reasoning in Helzberg's Diamond Shops, Inc. v. Valley West Des Moines Shopping Center, Inc., 564 F.2d 816 (8th Cir.1977). Plaintiff Helzberg, which had leased a store from defendant Valley West for its jewelry business, sued for breach of a provision in the lease that other premises in the shopping center would not be leased for additional jewelry stores. Plaintiff sought an injunction against defendant's complying with a new lease it had made with Lord's, another jewelry business. Defendant moved to dismiss on the ground that Lord's, which was not subject to personal jurisdiction, was indispensable. Defendant claimed that if it were enjoined from complying with the lease with Lord's, it would still be bound by that lease agreement, but would not be able to comply because of the injunction. The court agreed that Lord's was a necessary party, but did not find it indispensable, stating: "It is true that the obligations of Valley West to Helzberg, as determined in these proceedings, may be inconsistent with Valley West's obligations to Lord's. However, we are of the opinion that any inconsistency in those obligations will result from Valley West's voluntary execution of two Lease Agreements which impose inconsistent obligations rather than from Lord's absence from the present proceedings."

7. Should a defendant be required to invoke available joinder devices to bring an absent party into the suit or lose its right to object to the party's absence on the ground that it is threatened with inconsistent obligations? The court in *Janney* observes that Shepard Niles is free to implead Underwood, using Rule 14, which will be discussed infra p. 260. Why wouldn't this also run afoul of the complete diversity rule that prevented Janney (a Pennsylvania resident) from joining Underwood (also a Pennsylvania resident) as a defendant? The answer can be found in "supplemental jurisdiction" (see footnote 15) which acts as an exception to the complete diversity rule (this will be considered in more detail in Chapter X). If supplemental jurisdiction would be accorded to impleading a third-party defendant (which, as will be discussed in the next section, is not always so), why shouldn't Shepard Niles be required to implead Underwood? In Pasco International (London) v. Stenograph Corp., 637 F.2d 496, 505 (7th Cir.1980), plaintiff sued another corporation for conspiring with plaintiff's chief engineer to

interfere with plaintiff's business relations. Defendant claimed the engineer, whose joinder would destroy diversity, was indispensable. The court rejected this claim of prejudice since defendant could implead the engineer under Rule 14 and invoke supplemental jurisdiction. But see Acton Co., Inc. of Massachusetts v. Bachman Foods, Inc., 668 F.2d 76 (1st Cir.1982) (the "complete diversity" rule could not be avoided by requiring defendant to assert a counterclaim against the plaintiff and the absent party, which defendant had chosen not to do).

8. Due to the 1966 amendments to Rule 19, putting a label on an absent party does not necessarily determine whether it is a party to be joined if feasible as a case-by-case analysis is required. But labels are still sometimes found attractive by courts; for example, it is still often said that joint tort-feasors and potential indemnitors are not required to be joined if feasible. Consider cases involving the following categories of absent parties: *subsidiaries and third-party beneficiaries*, WMX Technologies, Inc. v. Jackson, 168 F.R.D. 64 (M.D.Ala. 1996) (not necessary parties); *limited partners*, Schmidt v. E.N. Maisel and Associates, 105 F.R.D. 157 (N.D. Ill. 1985) (found to be indispensable parties); Northrop Corp. v. McDonnell Douglas Corp., 705 F.2d 1030 (9th Cir.1983) (not necessary parties); *joint obligees*, 7 Wright, Miller & Kane, Federal Practice & Procedure: Civil § 1613, ftn 12, 13 (2004 Pocket Part) (generally treated as indispensable parties); *joint obligors*, id., ftn 8 (generally treated as necessary, but not indispensable, parties). Treatment under Rule 19 will often turn on the particular circumstances. See Spiller v. Tennessee Trailers, Inc., 97 F.R.D. 347 (N.D.Ga. 1982) (since the applicable state law requires privity of contract for a breach of warranty claim, retailer is a necessary party in a suit against the manufacturer, and where, as here, there was an issue as to what role each played in the events precipitating the injury, both were required for complete relief; retailer also found to be indispensable).

9. As the interpretation of Rule 20 indicates, there is a strong preference for efficient use of the courts through joinder of all parties involved in a given claim. Should this bear on the interpretation of Rule 19? The Supreme Court has noted that one of the factors to be considered under Rule 19(b) when a necessary party cannot be joined is "the interest of the courts and the public in complete, consistent, and efficient settlement of controversies." Provident Tradesmens Bank & Trust Co. v. Patterson, 390 U.S. 102, 111, 88 S.Ct. 733, 739, 19 L.Ed.2d 936 (1968). However, in Temple v. Synthes Corporation, Ltd., 498 U.S. 5, 111 S.Ct. 315, 112 L.Ed.2d 263 (1990), the Court resisted an effort to extend such considerations to identifying necessary parties under Rule 19(a): "It has long been the rule that it is not necessary for all joint tortfeasors to be named as defendants in a single lawsuit. Nothing in the 1966 amendment to Rule 19 changed that principle."

THE RULE 19(b) DETERMINATION WHETHER TO PROCEED OR DISMISS

The appellate court in *Janney* found it unnecessary to make a determination under Rule 19(b) whether the suit should proceed in the absence of necessary parties because it found that Underwood was not a party to be joined if feasible under Rule 19(a). If Underwood had been found a necessary party, the court would have had to make the further Rule 19(b) determination because Underwood could not have been joined as a defendant as this would have destroyed federal diversity jurisdiction. Thus Rule 19(b) is a "second best" determination—given that necessary parties can not be joined due to the limitations of *subject matter jurisdiction* (here diversity) or *venue*, or due to lack of *personal jurisdiction* over the absent party, should the court proceed with the suit in its piecemeal form, or instead dismiss it in the expectation that there is some other forum where joinder of necessary parties can be better achieved?

It should be apparent that the four factors listed in Rule 19(b) are not totally exclusive of the factors in Rule 19(a) and that there is some overlap. For example, had the court determined under Rule 19(a) that Underwood's interests could be impaired, or that Shepard Niles could be subjected to inconsistent obligations, this would indicate the presence of the first factor under Rule 19(b)—that "a judgment in the person's absence might be prejudicial to that person or to those already parties." Other factors under Rule 19(b) focus on whether prejudice can be lessened, the judgment will be adequate, and there is an adequate remedy in another court if this suit is dismissed.

The second factor under Rule 19(b) directs attention to "the extent to which, by protective provisions in the judgment, by the shaping of relief, or other measures, the prejudice can be lessened or avoided." An example of shaping the judgment to avoid prejudice is found in Provident Tradesmens Bank & Trust Co. v. Patterson, 390 U.S. 102, 88 S.Ct. 733, 19 L.Ed.2d 936 (1968). There prejudice was claimed to an absent potential defendant, the driver in an auto accident, by virtue of the possibility that the suit would exhaust the amount of an insurance liability policy and leave him, as a practical matter, without an opportunity to assert his interest in it as a defendant in other cases. The Supreme Court noted, in not finding him indispensable, that the lower court could have refused to order immediate payment on the judgments pending completion of suits against the driver and litigation (if that became necessary) by him. Cf. State Farm Fire & Cas. Co. v. Tashire, *infra* p. 268. This possibility was enhanced by the voluntary agreement of plaintiffs that they would limit their claims arising out of the accident to the amount of the insurance policy.

The fourth factor under Rule 19(b) requires a court to consider whether the plaintiff will have an adequate remedy if this suit is dismissed. The most obvious possibility would be to sue in another court that would allow joinder of all necessary parties. There is usually a state-court forum available (since state courts do not premise subject-matter jurisdiction on diversity of citizenship) so long as personal jurisdiction over the defendant can be obtained. In *Janney* the plaintiff had already filed in the state court in which it joined all the interested parties. Thus if the federal court had found that Underwood was a necessary party, this factor might have weighed heavily in favor of a federal-court dismissal.

What characteristics must a possible alternative forum have to offer an adequate remedy? Whyham v. Piper Aircraft Corp., 96 F.R.D. 557 (M.D.Pa.1982), involved an airplane crash in Scotland. The plaintiff, the representative of the deceased Scottish pilot, sued the manufacturer, a Pennsylvania corporation, in federal court in Pennsylvania. The defendant contended that two Scottish companies that had owned and serviced the plane for seven years were responsible for the crash and that, since jurisdiction could not be obtained over them in an American court, they should be found indispensable and the suit dismissed. The plaintiff's only alternative forum would be in Scotland where strict products liability is not recognized. The court found Scotland to be an adequate alternative forum and, finding the absent parties indispensable, dismissed the suit. Was this correctly decided? See also Piper Aircraft Co. v. Reyno, 454 U.S. 235, 102 S.Ct. 252, 70 L.Ed.2d 419 (1981) (infra p. 847), where a similar suit filed in a federal court was dismissed under the doctrine of *forum non conveniens*. Is that a more satisfactory way to deal with cases in doubtful fora where there appears to have been forum-shopping than by dismissing under Rule 19(b)?

E.   IMPLEADER (RULE 14)

"Impleader" has its roots in the "vouching to warranty" practice at common law where a person whose title to land was challenged could vouch in the grantor of the land who had warranted the title. The term "implead," however, has taken on a much broader meaning as it is used today in Rule 14. It refers to the right of a defendant to bring in a new party who may be liable for plaintiff's claim against it, under what we now call "third party practice."

CLARK v. ASSOCIATES COMMERCIAL CORP.

United States District Court, District of Kansas, 1993.
149 F.R.D. 629.

BELOT, DISTRICT JUDGE.

[Plaintiff sued Associates Commercial for damages to his property and person (including a broken leg) arising out of Associates' agents' repossession by force of a tractor that was collateral for a loan that Associates had made to plaintiff. The complaint alleged causes of action in tort and contract (by negative implication in the security agreement prohibiting the secured party from proceeding contrary to plaintiff's rights under the Uniform Commercial Code). Defendant Associates then filed a third-party complaint seeking indemnity from its employee (Howard) and two parties who assisted him in the repossession (Clark, who is no relation to plaintiff, and Lett). The third-party defendants moved to dismiss the third-party complaint, and plaintiff moved to strike the third-party complaint or, in the alternative, for a separate trial of the issues it raised.]

Defendant Associates Commercial Corp. ("Associates") alleges in its third-party complaint that it hired Bob Howard, who—without the knowledge of Associates—subcontracted with Clark Investigation & Recovery ("Clark") to repossess plaintiff's tractor-trailer unit. Associates further alleges that Randall Lett and an unknown second person were employees of Clark, and that these employees conducted the actual repossession of the collateral. Plaintiff alleges that the repossession was effected through a breach of peace, and that Clark and its employees were agents of Associates. Associates brings an indemnity claim against third-party defendants Howard, Clark, and Lett for any amount that Associates may be found liable to plaintiff.

* * *

Third-party defendants allege that Associates' claim is based upon "implied indemnity" under the rubric of the "active/passive" dichotomy, which is no longer recognized in Kansas. Third-party defendants note that under the Kansas comparative fault statute, each defendant is liable only in proportion to his relative fault. Thus, because impleader is proper only if the party has a right to relief under the governing substantive law, third-party defendants contend that Associates has no valid claim for indemnity against them.

This argument is meritless. The basis for Associates' indemnity claim against third-party defendants is an agency theory, whereby Associates seeks to hold its alleged agents liable for any amounts that Associates is found liable to plaintiff. Although third-party defendants correctly note that Kansas no longer recognizes implied indemnity based upon the "active" wrong of another,[1] no Kansas case has questioned the viability of implied indemnity based upon agency principles. Indeed, Kansas continues to recognize the right of an employer to seek indemnity against his employee for liability resulting from the employee's tortious acts. Thus, because Associates has sued each third-party defendant as a person "who is or may be liable to the third-party plaintiff for all or part of the plaintiff's claim against the third-party plaintiff," Fed.R.Civ.P. 14(a), Associates has properly impleaded third-party defendants.

The third-party complaint is also opposed by plaintiff.[3] Plaintiff argues that his claims against Associates are based upon duties imposed

---

1. The court notes, however, that the Kansas comparative fault statute only applies to negligent tortious conduct, and that joint and several liability remains the law as to intentional tortfeasors. Moreover, the Kansas Supreme Court has expressly held that an employer who negligently hires an intentional tortfeasor may not proportionately reduce his liability to a plaintiff injured by that employee. Regardless of whether Associates becomes liable to plaintiff vicariously under respondeat superior, or directly under plaintiff's claim of negligent retention, the Kansas comparative fault statute would not allow Associates to reduce its liability for the intentional torts

of its agents. Thus, not only do third-party defendants fail to recognize that Associates' indemnity claim is properly based on agency principles, third-party defendants have also proceeded from the erroneous legal premise that Associates may not be found jointly and severally liable for plaintiff's injuries

3. The court will consider plaintiff's substantive objections to Associates' claims against third-party defendants, for Fed. R.Civ.P. 14(a) expressly provides that "[a]ny party may move to strike the third-party claim, or for its severance or separate trial." (emphasis added).

under the Uniform Commercial Code and by contract, and thus, that third-party defendants have "no duty" under the contract between plaintiff and Associates. A proper third-party complaint, however, does not depend upon the existence of a duty on the part of the third-party defendant toward the plaintiff. To the contrary, impleader is proper *only* if the third-party defendant "is or may be liable *to the third-party plaintiff* for all or part of the plaintiff's claim against the third-party plaintiff. . . ." Fed.R.Civ.P. 14(a). Although plaintiff correctly quotes the rule that "a defendant has no right under Rule 14(a) to implead a non-party who is only liable to plaintiff," plaintiff fails to appreciate that this very rule defeats his argument.

Moreover, contrary to plaintiff's belief, a third-party defendant need not be "necessarily liable over" to the third-party plaintiff in the event the third-party plaintiff is found liable toward the plaintiff. A third-party defendant must be "liable over" to the defendant only in the sense that the third-party claim is derivative of, and dependent upon, the success of the plaintiff's claim. Although Rule 14 does not allow a defendant to assert an independent claim for relief from a liability that does not arise out of the plaintiff's claim against the defendant, Rule 14(a) expressly allows impleader of a person who "is or *may be* liable to the third-party plaintiff for all or part of the plaintiff's claim against the third-party plaintiff." (emphasis added). Thus, "[t]he third-party claim need not be based on the same theory as the main claim," and "impleader is proper even though the third-party defendant's liability is not automatically established once the third-party plaintiff's liability to the original plaintiff has been determined." 6 C. Wright, A. Miller, & M. Kane, Federal Practice and Procedure § 1446, at 372 & 373 (2d ed. 1990).

Nor does the court find any relevance to plaintiff's observation that it is "inconsistent" for Associates to deny the existence of an agency relationship between it and third-party defendants, while at the same time Associates claims indemnity based upon this relationship. In essence, plaintiff argues that Associates is not entitled to plead alternative or inconsistent claims and defenses, contrary to the permissibility of this practice under Fed.R.Civ.P. 8(a) and (e)(2).

The court finds that Associates has stated a valid claim for indemnity against third-party defendants.

Plaintiff also opposes impleader on the ground that the inclusion of Associates' indemnity claims against third-party defendants will unduly complicate the original suit.

Whether to allow a defendant to prosecute a third-party proceeding under Rule 14 rests within the sounds discretion of the trial court. In exercising its discretion, the court is mindful that the purpose of Rule 14 is

> to accomplish in one proceeding the adjudication of the rights of all persons concerned in the controversy and to prevent the necessity of trying several related claims in different lawsuits. The rule should be liberally construed to effectuate its intended purposes.

United States v. Acord, 209 F.2d 709, 712 (10th Cir.), cert. denied, 347 U.S. 975, 74 S.Ct. 786, 98 L.Ed. 1115 (1954). Thus, the court should generally allow impleader of a proper third-party action unless it will result in some prejudice to the other parties.

The court finds no merit to plaintiff's fear of confusing the issues. Indeed, many of the issues are so closely related that resolution of plaintiff's claims might well collaterally estop Associates from relitigating these issues in a separate proceeding—to the significant prejudice of Associates. For example, the primary basis on which plaintiff seeks to hold Associates liable for the acts of its agents is respondeat superior, which, if meritorious, would then allow Associates to recover against its agents.

The court finds that the practical and equitable considerations overwhelmingly favor trial of all claims herein to a single jury. The motion to strike the third-party complaint or separate trial will therefore be denied.

* * *

[The third-party defendants also moved to dismiss defendant Associates' claims against them for indemnity for any punitive damages awarded to plaintiff against defendant. The court found that, under the applicable state law, punitive damages could be awarded against a principal for acts of its agents.]

Because plaintiff has stated a viable claim for punitive damages against Associates, and because Associates has stated an indemnity claim against third-party defendants for any amounts for which Associates is held vicariously liable to plaintiff, the court rejects the substantive arguments of third-party defendants.

Notes and Questions

1. Why do you think the plaintiff objected to the third-party complaint? Must he have standing to do so? See footnote 3. Does the plaintiff have different reasons for objecting to the third-party complaint than do the third-party defendants?

2. Must the third-party defendants be "necessarily liable over" to the defendant to permit impleader under Rule 14? Note that Rule 14 only requires that the third-party defendant "is or may be liable to the third-party plaintiff for all or part of the plaintiff's claim against the third-party plaintiff," and such liability need not be automatically established by a finding that the third-party plaintiff is liable to the plaintiff. Is the question and amount of indemnity from the third-party defendant determined in the same suit? How is that done?

3. It is inconsistent for the defendant Associates to deny (in reference to the claims of the plaintiff) that the third-party defendants were acting as its agents while asserting (in reference to its third-party complaint claims for indemnity) that there was an agency relationship. Why is this permitted? Recall McCormick v. Kopmann, supra p. 138. Is it relevant that there is efficiency in not having to redetermine in another lawsuit whether there was

an agency relationship that would support an indemnity claim against the third-party defendants?

4. Note that the substantive law of Kansas governs whether the defendant has a right to indemnity. Once having determined that there is a right to indemnity under state law, the court then found that the third-party complaint satisfied the requirements of Rule 14 by impleading persons who may be derivatively liable for the plaintiff's claim against the defendant.

5. Rule 13(h) allows joinder of additional parties by a party "to a counterclaim or cross-claim in accordance with the provisions of Rules 19 and 20." There is no requirement that the claim against such additional parties must be derivative, as opposed to simply arising out of the same transaction. Why is joinder more limited under Rule 14?

6. In Augenti v. Cappellini v. Holy Spirit Association for the Unification of World Christianity, 30 Fed.R.Serv.2d 382 (M.D.Pa.1980), the plaintiff sued a "deprogrammer" who had been hired by plaintiff's parents to hold him against his will for five weeks and make him give up his association with the Unification Church. He alleged that defendant had violated his constitutional rights. Defendant filed a third-party complaint seeking compensatory and punitive damages against the Unification Church, its President, and its attorney, with the following counts:

a. Champerty and maintenance based on a contract between the Church and plaintiff whereby it agreed to pay the costs of bringing this action and plaintiff agreed to reimburse it out of any recovery.

b. Conspiracy between plaintiff and the Church to deprive defendant of his constitutional rights of freedom of speech and association with former members of the Unification Church in violation of a federal civil rights statute.

c. Intentional infliction of emotional distress through harassment of defendant by surveillance of his home, trespass, and instigation of frivolous law suits.

d. Libel and defamation against the attorney who filed the original complaint.

On motion of the third-party defendants, the court struck the third party complaint, reasoning as follows (30 Fed.Rules Serv.2d at 385–86):

This concept of derivative liability is central to the application of Rule 14. The typical fact pattern in which federal courts have permitted third-party practice is where one event gives rise to double liability, defendant to plaintiff and third-party defendant to defendant. Since Rule 14 relies on the discretion of the court in its application, the Rule had been broadly interpreted. However, there is still a requirement of some causal connection between the original action and the action brought in the third-party suit.

The proposed third-party complaint in this action, though related to the original action, does not bear this causal connection to the main action. The original action arose out of the events which occurred in December 1977 and January through February of 1978, when defendant Cappellini and others sought to persuade Frank Augenti to abandon his membership in the Unification Church through the deprogramming process. All of the counts in the original action are concerned with this discrete set of events—the issuance of the original guardianship order and Frank's subsequent deprogramming.

The proposed third-party action arose out of the filing of the main lawsuit and events which occurred afterward—the signing of the contract between Frank Augenti and the Unification Church, and the alleged harassment and alleged injuries to the third-party plaintiff as an individual. If the church were found liable to him on these claims it would not be as a direct result of the determination of the main claim. These third-party claims are independent.

* * *

Allowing the joinder of the third-party claim here would serve to complicate the case. It would broaden the scope of the evidence to be presented from Frank Augenti's personal involvement with the Unification Church and whether any of his Constitutionally protected rights were violated, or whether there was any tortious conduct engaged in by his family and the "de-programmers," to include testimony about the church in general and the methods it uses to protect its members. This expansion of the issues would not further the purposes of Rule 14 to avoid circuitry of action, but would further complicate what has already become a complex lawsuit. Presentation to the jury of so many claims related in such a tenuous way to those initially brought by the original plaintiff may prove to be unduly prejudicial to the original plaintiff.

Is the concept of derivative liability well suited to avoid the kind of complication of the case that the court feared? Couldn't such concerns be solved by an order under Rule 42 that the parts of the case be handled separately?

7. In Klotz v. Superior Electric Products Corp. v. Butz, 498 F.Supp. 1099 (E.D.Pa.1980), plaintiff sued Superior, alleging that she had contracted trichinosis after eating a pork sausage cooked on a "Super-electric Super Twin–Burger" cooker manufactured and sold by Superior. She alleged that she had followed cooking directions supplied by Superior but that, due to a defect in the cooker, the sausage was not properly cooked. Superior then impleaded Wilkes College, alleging that the plaintiff's trichinosis resulted from her ingesting pork in the college cafeteria on July 8, and not from the July 9 incident involving the cooker. Wilkes College moved to dismiss the third-party complaint against it as improper under Rule 14(a) because the liability asserted against it was not derivative. How should the court rule? Would the complication factors cited in *Augenti* (in note 6 above) be present here?

F.   COUNTERCLAIMS AND CROSS–CLAIMS (RULE 13)

Counterclaims and cross-claims are not primarily devices for bringing in additional parties, but they permit expansion of the issues in the suit and may bring in additional parties as well. They serve the important interest of fairness by allowing a party to make claims against one who has made claims against him and the interest of economy and efficiency in permitting claims between existing parties in the same suit.

Rule 13(a) is a sort of rule-mandated res judicata. It has the effect of barring a party from recovering on a claim "which at the time of serving the pleading the pleader has against any opposing party, if it arises out of the transaction or occurrence that is the subject matter of the opposing party's claim." It has been considered in Chapter III. See supra p. 207.

Rule 13(b) sets out a liberal permissive counterclaim rule, allowing a party to bring as a counterclaim any claim it has against the opposing party. A permissive counterclaim is, by definition, one that does not arise out of the same transaction or occurrence. It has the potential for permitting a number of different claims that would not constitute a convenient trial package. But it is consistent with Rule 18(a)'s allowance of joinder of claims in pleading without a requirement that they be related. The solution to badly-matched claims is severance and separate trial. See Rule 42(b).

A cross-claim, authorized under Rule 13(g), allows a claim against a co-party (i.e., co-plaintiffs, co-defendants, or co-third-party defendants). It is limited to claims "arising out of the transaction or occurrence that is the subject matter either of the original action or of a counterclaim therein or relating to any property that is the subject matter of the original action."

Under Rule 13(h), the addition of claims can result in addition of parties if they can be sued as additional parties to the counterclaim or cross-claim "in accordance with the provisions of Rules 19 and 20." This means that so long as a current party to the litigation can assert a counterclaim or cross-claim under Rule 13, it can add parties to that claim provided that its claim against the added parties arises from the same transaction or series thereof within the meaning of Rule 20.

Notes and Questions

1. Why must cross-claims arise out of the same transaction or occurrence as the original claim, while permissive counterclaims need not?

2. Why are cross-claims permissive, thus allowing a party to hold them back and sue in another suit? Note, however, that res judicata or collateral estoppel may affect the right of a party to sue later.

3. Consider the following situation in terms of the availability of claims between the parties:

A, B, and C were involved in a three-way auto accident. Each of them received serious personal injuries, and all three cars that they were driving were badly damaged. There is reason to believe that the negligence of each of them in driving may have caused or contributed to the accident.

A's car had been repaired the day before the accident by D, an auto dealer. There is reason to believe that D's negligent failure to fix the brakes may have caused or contributed to the accident.

The car B was driving was owned by O. O lent his car to B knowing that B had received several citations for reckless driving. The law of the state makes the owner of a car liable for the conduct of a person to whom he has negligently entrusted it if he knew that the entrustee was a reckless driver. It also treats the borrower of a car as an agent of the owner, allowing the owner to recover from the agent for liability imposed on the owner as a result of the agent's negligence to which the owner did not contribute.

C's car was manufactured by M, an auto manufacturer. There is reason to believe that the car had a design defect in the steering mechanism that caused or contributed to the accident.

Assume that A sues B in federal court. What claims should B assert in reply? In turn, what claims should be made in reply to the claims asserted by B, and by any other parties brought into the action. You will find it helpful to use a diagram.

4. For an analysis of the complications that can arise due to the varying treatment of co-party and third-party claims, see Greenbaum, Jacks or Better to Open: Procedural Limitations on Co–Party and Third–Party Claims, 74 Minn.L.Rev. 507 (1990).

G. INTERPLEADER (RULE 22 AND 28 U.S.C.A. § 1335)

Interpleader has ancient origins in common law, but it was equity that developed it into a suitable device for permitting a person faced with conflicting claims to a limited fund or property (referred to as the "stake") to bring all the claimants into a single proceeding. In this manner, the stakeholder could avoid the unfairness of inconsistent judgments or multiple liability that might result if the claimants were to sue individually. Interpleader allowed the stakeholder, fearing separate suits by individual claimants, to institute its own action in which all the claimants would be required to litigate their claims simultaneously.

Classically, the "strict" bill of interpleader was said to be limited by four technical requirements, the meaning and purpose of which were never altogether clear:

(1) The same thing, debt, or duty must be claimed by both or all the parties against whom the relief is demanded; (2) All their adverse titles or claims must be dependent on or be derived from a common source; (3) The person asking the relief—the plaintiff—must not have or claim any interest in the subject matter; (4) He must have incurred no independent liability to either of the claimants; that is, he must stand perfectly indifferent between them, in the position merely of a stakeholder.

4 J. Pomeroy, Equity Jurisprudence § 1322 (5th ed. 1941).

According to one group of commentators, "[i]f the court demanded literal adherence to these requirements, the range of situations in which equitable interpleader could be used was very limited and applied to only a few of the instances in which plaintiff might be exposed to double vexation. It is not surprising, therefore, that many courts honored these strictures in name only." 7 C. Wright, A. Miller & M. Kane, Federal

Practice and Procedure: Civil 2d § 1701 (1986). In any event, the historical accuracy of these requirements has been questioned. See Hazard & Moskovitz, An Historical and Critical Analysis of Interpleader, 52 Calif.L.Rev. 706 (1964). Early on, equity courts developed a method of circumventing the requirement that the stakeholder must claim no interest in the stake by developing the bill "in the nature of interpleader," which allowed a stakeholder to claim all or part of the stake itself. However, this device could be employed only if some independent basis of equity jurisdiction existed. Today, all four of the classical limitations have, for all practical purposes, been abandoned, either explicitly or implicitly. See C. Wright & M. Kane, Law of Federal Courts § 74 (6th ed. 2002).

The availability of interpleader was restricted by the Supreme Court's decision in New York Life Insurance Co. v. Dunlevy, 241 U.S. 518, 36 S.Ct. 613, 60 L.Ed. 1140 (1916), which held that personal jurisdiction could not be obtained unless all the claimants were personally served within the territorial limits of the forum state. This meant that businesses and insurance companies engaged in interstate commerce, which were often confronted with conflicting claims to a fund or property by persons from different states, could not use a single interpleader suit and were often forced to defend multiple suits in different states.

This situation prompted Congress to overrule *Dunlevy* by a federal interpleader statute passed in 1917. It was considerably revised in 1936, essentially into the form now found in 28 U.S.C.A. § 1335 (referred to as "statutory interpleader"). A question still remained, after the passage of the interpleader statutes, as to whether federal courts retained their traditional equity jurisdiction over interpleader actions. This was resolved with the adoption in 1938 of the Federal Rules containing Rule 22 which provided for an interpleader action based on general federal court jurisdiction (federal question or diversity). Called "rule interpleader," Rule 22 also considerably expanded the scope of traditional equitable interpleader.

Thus, today we have two sources of interpleader—*statutory* and *rule*. They have been applied very similarly as to the scope of the interpleader remedy, but, as will be seen, they have quite different provisions as to jurisdiction and venue. They are both available, but because of the differences in jurisdictional and venue requirements a party that can use one in a particular situation may not be able to use the other.

STATE FARM FIRE & CASUALTY CO. v. TASHIRE

Supreme Court of the United States, 1967.
386 U.S. 523, 87 S.Ct. 1199, 18 L.Ed.2d 270.

JUSTICE FORTAS delivered the opinion of the Court.

Early one September morning in 1964, a Greyhound bus proceeding northward through Shasta County, California, collided with a southbound pickup truck. Two of the passengers aboard the bus were killed. Thirty-three others were injured, as were the bus driver, the driver of the truck and its lone passenger. One of the dead and 10 of the injured passengers were Canadians; the rest of the individuals involved were citizens of five American States. The ensuing litigation led to the present case, which raises important questions concerning administration of the interpleader remedy in the federal courts.

The litigation began when four of the injured passengers filed suit in California state courts, seeking damages in excess of $1,000,000. Named as defendants were Greyhound Lines, Inc., a California corporation; Theron Nauta, the bus driver; Ellis Clark, who drove the truck; and Kenneth Glasgow, the passenger in the truck who was apparently its owner as well. Each of the individual defendants was a citizen and resident of Oregon. Before these cases could come to trial and before other suits were filed in California or elsewhere, petitioner State Farm Fire & Casualty Company, an Illinois corporation, brought this action in the nature of interpleader in the United States District Court for the District of Oregon.

In its complaint State Farm asserted that at the time of the Shasta County collision it had in force an insurance policy with respect to Ellis Clark, driver of the truck, providing for bodily injury liability up to $10,000 per person and $20,000 per occurrence and for legal representation of Clark in actions covered by the policy. It asserted that actions already filed in California and others which it anticipated would be filed far exceeded in aggregate damages sought the amount of its maximum liability under the policy. Accordingly, it paid into court the sum of $20,000 and asked the court (1) to require all claimants to establish their claims against Clark and his insurer in this single proceeding and in no other, and (2) to discharge State Farm from all further obligations under its policy—including its duty to defend Clark in lawsuits arising from the accident. Alternatively, State Farm expressed its conviction that the policy issued to Clark excluded from coverage accidents resulting from his operation of a truck which belonged to another and was being used in the business of another. The complaint, therefore, requested that the court decree that the insurer owed no duty to Clark and was not liable on the policy, and it asked the court to refund the $20,000 deposit.

Joined as defendants were Clark, Glasgow, Nauta, Greyhound Lines, and each of the prospective claimants. Jurisdiction was predicated upon 28 U.S.C. § 1335, the federal interpleader statute,[1] and upon general diversity of citizenship, there being diversity between two or more of the

---

1. 28 U.S.C. § 1335(a) provides: "The district courts shall have original jurisdiction of any civil action of interpleader or in the nature of interpleader filed by any person, firm, or corporation, association, or society having in his or its custody or possession money or property of the value of $500 or more, or having issued a . . . policy of insurance . . . of value or amount of $500 or more . . . if

"(1) Two or more adverse claimants, of diverse citizenship as defined in section 1332 of this title, are claiming or may claim to be entitled to such money or property, or to any one or more of the benefits arising by virtue of any . . . policy . . .; and if (2) the plaintiff has . . . paid . . . the amount due under such obligation into the registry of the court, there to abide the judgment of the court. . . ."

claimants to the fund and between State Farm and all of the named defendants.

An order issued, requiring the defendants to show cause why they should not be restrained from filing or prosecuting "any proceeding in any state or United States Court affecting the property or obligation involved in this interpleader action, and specifically against the plaintiff and the defendant Ellis D. Clark." Personal service was effected on each of the American defendants, and registered mail was employed to reach the 11 Canadian claimants. Defendants Nauta, Greyhound, and several of the injured passengers responded, contending that the policy did cover this accident and advancing various arguments for the position that interpleader was either impermissible or inappropriate in the present circumstances. Greyhound, however, soon switched sides and moved that the court broaden any injunction to include Nauta and Greyhound among those who could not be sued except within the confines of the interpleader proceeding.

When a temporary injunction along the lines sought by State Farm was issued by the United States District Court for the District of Oregon, the present respondents moved to dismiss the action and, in the alternative, for a change of venue—to the Northern District of California, in which district the collision had occurred. After a hearing, the court declined to dissolve the temporary injunction, but continued the motion for a change of venue. The injunction was later broadened to include the protection sought by Greyhound, but modified to permit the filing— although not the prosecution—of suits. The injunction, therefore, provided that all suits against Clark, State Farm, Greyhound, and Nauta be prosecuted in the interpleader proceeding.

On interlocutory appeal, the Court of Appeals for the Ninth Circuit reversed. The court found it unnecessary to reach respondents' contentions relating to service of process and the scope of the injunction, for it concluded that interpleader was not available in the circumstances of this case. It held that in States like Oregon which do not permit "direct action" suits against insurance companies until judgments are obtained against the insured, the insurance companies may not invoke federal interpleader until the claims against the insured, the alleged tortfeasor, have been reduced to judgment. Until that is done, said the court, claimants with unliquidated tort claims are not "claimants" within the meaning of § 1335, nor are they "persons having claims against the plaintiff" within the meaning of Rule 22 of the Federal Rules of Civil Procedure.[3] In accord with that view, it directed dissolution of the

3. We need not pass upon the Court of Appeals' conclusions with respect to the interpretation of interpleader under Rule 22, which provides that "(1) Persons having claims against the plaintiff may be joined as defendants and required to interplead when their claims are such that the plaintiff is or may be exposed to double or multiple liabil- ity...." First, as we indicate today, this action was properly brought under § 1335. Second, State Farm did not purport to invoke Rule 22. Third, State Farm could not have invoked it in light of venue and service of process limitations. Whereas statutory interpleader may be brought in the district where any claimant resides (28 U.S.C.

temporary injunction and dismissal of the action. Because the Court of Appeals' decision on this point conflicts with those of other federal courts, and concerns a matter of significance to the administration of federal interpleader, we granted certiorari. Although we reverse the decision of the Court of Appeals upon the jurisdictional question, we direct a substantial modification of the District Court's injunction for reasons which will appear.

I

Before considering the issues presented by the petition for certiorari, we find it necessary to dispose of a question neither raised by the parties nor passed upon by the courts below. Since the matter concerns our jurisdiction, we raise it on our own motion. The interpleader statute, 28 U.S.C. § 1335, applies where there are "Two or more adverse claimants, of diverse citizenship...." This provision has been uniformly construed to require only "minimal diversity," that is, diversity of citizenship between two or more claimants, without regard to the circumstance that other rival claimants may be co-citizens. The language of the statute, the legislative purpose broadly to remedy the problems posed by multiple claimants to a single fund, and the consistent judicial interpretation tacitly accepted by Congress, persuade us that the statute requires no more. There remains, however, the question whether such a statutory construction is consistent with Article III of our Constitution, which extends the federal judicial power to "Controversies ... between citizens of different States ... and between a State, or the Citizens thereof, and foreign States, Citizens or Subjects." In Strawbridge v. Curtiss, 3 Cranch 267, 2 L.Ed. 435 (1806), this Court held that the diversity of citizenship statute required "complete diversity": where co-citizens appeared on both sides of a dispute, jurisdiction was lost. But Chief Justice Marshall there purported to construe only "The words of the act of congress," not the Constitution itself. And in a variety of contexts this Court and the lower courts have concluded that Article III poses no obstacle to the legislative extension of federal jurisdiction, founded on diversity, so long as any two adverse parties are not co-citizens. Accordingly, we conclude that the present case is properly in the federal courts.

II

We do not agree with the Court of Appeals that, in the absence of a state law or contractual provision for "direct action" suits against the insurance company, the company must wait until persons asserting claims against its insured have reduced those claims to judgment before

§ 1397), Rule interpleader based upon diversity of citizenship may be brought only in the district where all plaintiffs or all defendants reside (28 U.S.C. § 1391(a)). [After 1993 amendments, this statute provides that venue is permissible where all defendants reside, where a substantial part of the events occurred (or property that is the subject of the action is located), or where defendants are subject to personal jurisdiction if there is no other district where the action can be brought.—Eds.] And whereas statutory interpleader enables a plaintiff to employ nationwide service of process (28 U.S.C. § 2361), service of process under Rule 22 is confined to that provided in Rule 4.

seeking to invoke the benefits of federal interpleader. That may have been a tenable position under the 1926 and 1936 interpleader statutes. These statutes did not carry forward the language in the 1917 Act authorizing interpleader where adverse claimants "may claim" benefits as well as where they "are claiming" them. In 1948, however, in the revision of the Judicial Code, the "may claim" language was restored. Until the decision below, every court confronted by the question has concluded that the 1948 revision removed whatever requirement there might previously have been that the insurance company wait until at least two claimants reduced their claims to judgments. The commentators are in accord.

Considerations of judicial administration demonstrate the soundness of this view which, in any event, seems compelled by the language of the present statute, which is remedial and to be liberally construed. Were an insurance company required to await reduction of claims to judgment, the first claimant to obtain such a judgment or to negotiate a settlement might appropriate all or a disproportionate slice of the fund before his fellow claimants were able to establish their claims. The difficulties such a race to judgment pose for the insurer, and the unfairness which may result to some claimants, were among the principal evils the interpleader device was intended to remedy.

III

The fact that State Farm had properly invoked the interpleader jurisdiction under § 1335 did not, however, entitle it to an order both enjoining prosecution of suits against it outside the confines of the interpleader proceeding and also extending such protection to its insured, the alleged tortfeasor. Still less was Greyhound Lines entitled to have that order expanded so as to protect itself and its driver, also alleged to be tortfeasors, from suits brought by its passengers in various state or federal courts. Here, the scope of the litigation, in terms of parties and claims, was vastly more extensive than the confines of the "fund," the deposited proceeds of the insurance policy. In these circumstances, the mere existence of such a fund cannot, by use of interpleader, be employed to accomplish purposes that exceed the needs of orderly contest with respect to the fund.

There are situations, of a type not present here, where the effect of interpleader is to confine the total litigation to a single forum and proceeding. One such case is where a stakeholder, faced with rival claims to the fund itself, acknowledges—or denies—his liability to one or the other of the claimants. In this situation, the fund itself is the target of the claimants. It marks the outer limits of the controversy. It is, therefore, reasonable and sensible that interpleader, in discharge of its office to protect the fund, should also protect the stakeholder from vexatious and multiple litigation. In this context, the suits sought to be enjoined are squarely within the language of 28 U.S.C. § 2361, which provides in part:

"In any civil action of interpleader or in the nature of inter-pleader under section 1335 of this title, a district court may issue its process for all claimants and enter its order restraining them from instituting or prosecuting *any proceeding* in any State or United States court *affecting the property, instrument or obligation involved in the interpleader action . . . .*" (Emphasis added.)

But the present case is another matter. Here, an accident has happened. Thirty-five passengers or their representatives have claims which they wish to press against a variety of defendants: the bus company, its driver, the owner of the truck, and the truck driver. The circumstance that one of the prospective defendants happens to have an insurance policy is a fortuitous event which should not of itself shape the nature of the ensuing litigation. For example, a resident of California, injured in California aboard a bus owned by a California corporation should not be forced to sue that corporation anywhere but in California simply because another prospective defendant carried an insurance poli-cy. And an insurance company whose maximum interest in the case cannot exceed $20,000 and who in fact asserts that it has no interest at all, should not be allowed to determine that dozens of tort plaintiffs must be compelled to press their claims—even those claims which are not against the insured and which in no event could be satisfied out of the meager insurance fund—in a single forum of the insurance compa-ny's choosing. There is nothing in the statutory scheme, and very little in the judicial and academic commentary upon that scheme, which requires that the tail be allowed to wag the dog in this fashion.

State Farm's interest in this case, which is the fulcrum of the interpleader procedure, is confined to its $20,000 fund. That interest receives full vindication when the court restrains claimants from seeking to enforce against the insurance company any judgment obtained against its insured, except in the interpleader proceeding itself. To the extent that the District Court sought to control claimants' lawsuits against the insured and other alleged tortfeasors, it exceeded the powers granted to it by the statutory scheme.

We recognize, of course, that our view of interpleader means that it cannot be used to solve all the vexing problems of multiparty litigation arising out of a mass tort. But interpleader was never intended to perform such a function, to be an all-purpose "bill of peace." Had it been so intended, careful provision would necessarily have been made to insure that a party with little or no interest in the outcome of a complex controversy should not strip truly interested parties of substantial rights—such as the right to choose the forum in which to establish their claims, subject to generally applicable rules of jurisdiction, venue, service of process, removal, and change of venue. None of the legislative and academic sponsors of a modern federal interpleader device viewed their accomplishment as a "bill of peace," capable of sweeping dozens of lawsuits out of the various state and federal courts in which they were brought and into a single interpleader proceeding. * * *

In light of the evidence that federal interpleader was not intended to serve the function of a "bill of peace" in the context of multiparty litigation arising out of a mass tort, of the anomalous power which such a construction of the statute would give the stakeholder, and of the thrust of the statute and the purpose it was intended to serve, we hold that the interpleader statute did not authorize the injunction entered in the present case. Upon remand, the injunction is to be modified consistently with this opinion.

[Dissenting opinion of Justice Douglas omitted.]

Notes and Questions

1. The Court of Appeals in *Tashire* ruled that State Farm could not invoke interpleader until the claimants had reduced their claims to judgment (in the absence of a state "direct action" statute that allowed the claimants to sue the insurance company directly). The Supreme Court rejected that position, pointing out that § 1335 allows interpleader by claimants who are claiming or "may claim" to be entitled to money or property. Rule 22(1), referring to situations where a plaintiff is "or may be" exposed to multiple liability, also allows an insurance company to sue in interpleader without there first being a judgment against its insured. Notice that although suit had been filed by the claimants in *Tashire* before State Farm filed its interpleader action, a prior suit (or even a formal demand for payment) is not necessary to allow a stakeholder with a genuine anticipation of double exposure to invoke interpleader.

2. Why wasn't State Farm allowed to invoke interpleader to prevent prosecution of the suits against its insured (Clark), Greyhound, and Greyhound's driver? Why wasn't the liability insurance policy "fund" which State Farm held as stakeholder sufficient to force all of the suits arising out of the same accident to be tried in the interpleader action?

3. Could the defendant Greyhound have filed its own interpleader action on the ground that it was exposed to the possibility of multiple and inconsistent suits? Notice that, unlike State Farm, whose liability was limited to the amount of the liability insurance policy, Greyhound's liability was unlimited. For interpleader, there must be an identifiable limited fund ("the stake"). Although it will usually be money or an insurance obligation, it may be any protectable property interest. 7 C. Wright, A. Miller, & M. Kane, Federal Practice and Procedure § 1704, at 505 (1986). Interpleader has been allowed as to conflicting claims to an El Greco painting, United States v. Herce, 334 F.Supp. 111 (S.D.N.Y.1971), and rights to use (as opposed to ownership, which was not disputed) an original print of the silent film "Birth of a Nation." United States v. American Film Institute, 79 F.R.D. 374 (D.D.C.1978).

4. As a result of the Court's denial in *Tashire* of interpleader protection against the prosecution of separate suits against the defendants, there will be multiple litigation, including (1) this federal interpleader action limited to the conflicting claims to the amount of State Farm's liability policy, (2) the four pending California suits, and (3) whatever suits are filed by or on behalf of the other thirty-one passengers. Multiple litigation has a number of drawbacks. It wastes judicial time and resources, can result in

inconsistent judgments that are an embarrassment to a legal system that adheres to the principle of "like treatment for like cases," and creates enormous problems in determining the preclusive effects of the judgments on other similar cases. But the Supreme Court was unwilling to view interpleader as a grand mechanism for unitary disposition of related disputes (as in the "bill of peace," the forerunner of the class action), and ruled that the right to the plaintiffs' choice of forum could not be denied.

5. Interpleader is not limited to the *Tashire* situation in which the stakeholder sues the claimants in an original interpleader action. Defensive interpleader is available to a stakeholder who is sued by one of the claimants, allowing the stakeholder to interplead the other claimants by way of a third-party claim, cross-claim, or counterclaim. The language of Rule 22(1) expressly authorizes interpleader by cross-claim and counterclaim, and precedents have also extended it to third-party claims and intervention. Although § 1335 does not expressly refer to defensive interpleader, it has been held to permit it by counterclaim. 7 C. Wright, A. Miller, & M. Kane, Federal Practice and Procedure § 1708 (1986). A defendant stakeholder should not be able to claim that absent claimants are indispensable under Rule 19 where it has the power to bring them in through defensive interpleader. See Advisory Committee Notes on the 1966 Amendments to Rule 19.

6. In contrast to the practice at common law, today a party invoking interpleader is not required to admit liability to any of the claimants. The stakeholder may plead in the alternative that it is not liable, as when an insurance company, exposed to multiple claims on a policy, contends that the terms of the policy have not been satisfied.

7. An interpleader action has two stages—the first concerns whether the stakeholder has a genuine fear of exposure to multiple liability upon the same obligation, and the second concerns the merits of the claims of the claimants. A court should base its ruling on a request for interpleader solely on a determination of the first stage, which is satisfied by proof of good faith fear of multiple exposure. The merits of the claims should be reserved for the second stage of the proceeding.

8. As footnote 3 of *Tashire* suggests, the primary differences between statutory and rule interpleader are found in the requirements for diversity, service of process, and venue. Actions brought under rule interpleader are governed by the general statutes and rules governing diversity subject matter jurisdiction (28 U.S.C.A. § 1332), service of process (Rule 4), and venue (28 U.S.C.A. § 1391). Thus Rule 22(1) actions require complete diversity between the stakeholders, on one side, and the claimants, on the other, as well as $50,000 in controversy. However, statutory interpleader contains special provisions for these matters: diversity is only required as between the claimants, and only $500 is required for the amount in controversy (28 U.S.C.A. § 1335); there is nationwide service of process (28 U.S.C.A. § 2361); and venue lies in the district of the residence of one or more claimants (28 U.S.C.A. § 1397). The following chart shows these differences:

	Diversity	Venue	Service
Rule Interpleader	Between stake-holder & all claimants (complete diversity)	Residence of all defendants, or where events occurred or property located (§ 1391(a))	As under Rule 4
Statutory Interpleader	Between two or more claimants (minimal diversity)	Residence of one or more claimants	Nationwide

9. There is also a difference between rule and statutory interpleader as to the authority of the court to enjoin other suits by the claimants. In rule interpleader, the "Anti–Injunction Act," 28 U.S.C.A. § 2283, provides the only exception that could conceivably allow a federal court to enjoin ongoing state proceedings, that is, "where necessary in aid of its jurisdiction," a provision which has received an extremely narrow construction. However, the Act also provides an exception when "expressly authorized by Act of Congress," and statutory interpleader under 28 U.S.C.A. § 2361 expressly allows an order restraining claimants "from instituting or prosecuting any proceeding in any State or United States court affecting the property, instrument or obligation involved in the interpleader action until further order of the court."

H. INTERVENTION (RULE 24)

Intervention, unlike most of the other joinder devices already discussed, does not have a long history in Anglo–American jurisprudence. It arose in statutes after the adoption of code pleading, and is peculiarly the product of the twentieth century.

Intervention is a device for an outsider who has an interest in a lawsuit to voluntarily join it as a party. Sometimes an intervenor has an obvious interest in a suit. The intervenor might, for example, be someone who should have been joined but was not due to insufficient contacts with the forum state to support personal jurisdiction. Indeed, very similar language to that used in Rule 19(a) to describe parties who should be joined if feasible is used in Rule 24(a) to describe intervention of right. If such a person wants voluntarily to enter the suit, Rule 24(a) should allow that. Sometimes, however, a person seeking intervention has a much less obvious interest in the suit, as, for example, someone or some organization that is concerned about governmental action or policy. Rule 24(b) recognizes that intervention may be useful to the court even if a party lacks the compelling interest of an intervenor of right. Permissive intervention, however, is left to the discretion of the court.

NATURAL RESOURCES DEFENSE COUNCIL, INC. v. UNITED STATES NUCLEAR REGULATORY COMMISSION

United States Court of Appeals, Tenth Circuit, 1978.
578 F.2d 1341.

Before DOYLE and LOGAN, CIRCUIT JUDGES, and STANLEY, SENIOR DISTRICT JUDGE.

WILLIAM E. DOYLE, CIRCUIT JUDGE.

The American Mining Congress and Kerr–McGee Nuclear Corporation seek review of the order of the United States District Court for the District of New Mexico denying their motions to intervene as a matter of right or on a permissive basis, pursuant to Rule 24(a)(2) and (b), Fed.R.Civil Proc.

The underlying action in which the movants requested intervention was instituted by the Natural Resources Defense Council, Inc., and others. In the action, declaratory and injunctive relief is directed to the United States Nuclear Regulatory Commission (NRC) and the New Mexico Environmental Improvement Agency (NMEIA), prohibiting those agencies from issuing licenses for the operation of uranium mills in New Mexico without first preparing environmental impact statements. Kerr–McGee and United Nuclear are potential recipients of the licenses.

Congress, in the Atomic Energy Act of 1954, 42 U.S.C. §§ 2011–2296, has authorized the NRC to issue such licenses. NMEIA is involved because under § 274(b) of the Act, 42 U.S.C. § 2021(b) (1970), the NRC is authorized to enter into agreements with the states allowing the states to issue licenses. Such agreements have been made with about 25 states including New Mexico. Thus, the action below in effect seeks to prevent the use of § 274(b) of the Act so as to avoid the requirement of an impact statement for which provision is made in the National Environmental Policy Act.

42 U.S.C. § 4332(2)(C) (1970) requires that a detailed environmental impact statement must be prepared by all federal agencies "in every recommendation or report on proposals for legislation and other major Federal actions significantly affecting the quality of the human environment." The complaint cites this requirement and alleges that an environmental impact statement would ordinarily be required here as a prerequisite to the issuance of licenses for the operation of uranium mills were it not for the arrangement which gives jurisdiction to the state. It further alleges that such statements are now prepared by the NRC in states that have not entered into agreements with the NRC, but that the NRC does not prepare such statements where there is an agreement with a state such as New Mexico. Plaintiff contends that the granting of licenses by state agencies predicated on delegation of authority from the NRC causes the NRC to consider the aspect of "major federal action" to be thereby eliminated. The New Mexico agency, NMEIA, which grants

the license, does not prepare environmental impact statements since it is not a federal agency and is not required either by its agreement with NRC or by state law to prepare such a statement.

The relief sought by the plaintiffs' complaint is, *first,* that NRC's involvement in the licensing procedure in New Mexico is, notwithstanding the delegation to the state, sufficient to constitute major federal action, whereby the impact statement requirement is not eliminated. *Second,* that if an impact statement is not required in connection with the granting of licenses, the New Mexico program is in conflict with § 274(d)(2) of the Atomic Energy Act of 1954, 42 U.S.C. § 2021(d)(2) (1970).

The motion of United Nuclear Corporation to intervene is not opposed by the parties and was granted. On May 3, 1977, the date that the complaint herein was filed, NMEIA granted a license to United Nuclear to operate a uranium mill at Church Rock, New Mexico. The complaint seeks to enjoin the issuance of the license thus granted.

It was after that that Kerr–McGee Nuclear Corporation, Anaconda Company, Gulf Oil Corporation, Phillips Petroleum Company, and the American Mining Congress filed motions to intervene. These motions, insofar as they sought intervention as of right, were denied on the ground that the interests of the parties or movants would be adequately represented by United Nuclear. Permissive intervention was also denied.

* * *

The district court's order denying intervention by the several corporations focused on whether the interest of the party seeking to intervene was adequately represented by a fellow member of the industry. * * * The court decided that the interests of the movants were adequately protected by United Nuclear, which possessed the necessary experience and knowledge in a complex area of business, whereby the representative's capability was competent to meet the demands. The court thought that to allow the intervention would engender delay and produce unwieldy procedure; and that the movants' requirements were met by allowing the filing of *amicus curiae* briefs.

Our conclusion is that the interests of movants in the subject matter [are] sufficient to satisfy the requirements of Rule 24 and that the threat of loss of their interest and inability to participate is of such magnitude as to impair their ability to advance their interest.

I.

The position adopted by the trial court that Kerr–McGee was adequately represented dispensed with the need for the court to consider the question whether Kerr–McGee had an interest in the litigation before the court. Plaintiffs-appellees maintain that the appellants do not have the requisite interest because they are not directly involved; that the controversy centers on the effort of Natural Resources Defense Council, Inc. to prevent the issuance of a license to United Nuclear unless and until an environmental impact statement is issued. The question then is whether the contention made is a correct concept of interest. Strictly to require that the movant in intervention have a *direct* interest in the outcome of the lawsuit strikes us as being too narrow a construction of Rule 24(a)(2). Kerr–McGee argues that the meaning of interest is one which, if they do not prevail in the intervention, threatens them with a disposition of the action which may, as a practical matter, impair or impede their efforts to protect the interest. Thus, we are asked to interpret interest in relationship to the second criterion in Rule 24(a)(2), impairment or impeding ability to protect the interest.

The Supreme Court has said that the interest must be a significantly protectable interest. See Donaldson v. United States, 400 U.S. 517, 91 S.Ct. 534, 27 L.Ed.2d 580 (1971). The Supreme Court held that a taxpayer did not have a right to intervene in a judicial enforcement proceeding seeking issuance of an Internal Revenue summons ordering production of business records of his employer. The narrowness of the *summons proceeding* was noted, and it was said that an objection of the taxpayer could be raised at the proper time in a subsequent trial.

Cascade Natural Gas Corp. v. El Paso Natural Gas Co., 386 U.S. 129, 135–36, 87 S.Ct. 932, 17 L.Ed.2d 814 (1967), held that the interest claimed by the applicant in intervention did not have to be a direct interest in the property or transaction at issue provided that it was an interest that would be impaired by the outcome. There Cascade's source of supply would have been a new company created by an antitrust divestiture, a significant change. In view of this consequence of the litigation, it was held that Cascade had a sufficient interest. See also Allard v. Frizzell, 536 F.2d 1332, 1334 n. 1 (10th Cir.1976). In *Allard* it was ruled that the applicant in intervention did not have a sufficient interest. Movant's interest there was general and somewhat abstract.

In our case the matter of immediate interest is, of course, the issuance and delivery of the license sought by United Nuclear. However, the consequence of the litigation could well be the imposition of the requirement that an environmental impact statement be prepared before granting any uranium mill license in New Mexico, or, secondly, it could result in an injunction terminating or suspending the agreement between NRC and NMEIA. Either consequence would be felt by United Nuclear and to some degree, of course, by Kerr–McGee, which is said to be one of the largest holders of uranium properties in New Mexico. It operates a uranium mill in Grants, New Mexico, pursuant to an NMEIA license, which application for renewal is pending. A decision in favor of the plaintiffs, which is not unlikely, could have a profound effect upon Kerr–McGee. Hence, it does have an interest within the meaning of Rule 24(a)(2). This interest of Kerr–McGee is in sharp contrast to the minimal interest which was present in *Allard*, wherein it was an interest of environmental groups in the protection of living birds. This was considered insufficient to justify intervention in a case involving feathers which are part of Indian artifacts. Their interest was said to be limited to a general interest in the public. The interest asserted on behalf of Kerr–

McGee and the American Mining Congress is one which is a genuine threat to Kerr–McGee and the members of the American Mining Congress to a substantial degree.

We do not suggest that Kerr–McGee could expect better treatment from state authorities than federal. We do recognize that a change in procedure would produce impairing complications.

II.

The next question is whether, assuming the existence of an interest, the chance of impairment is sufficient to fulfill the requirement of Rule 24(a)(2).

As already noted, the question of impairment is not separate from the question of existence of an interest. The appellants both claim an interest in licenses that are now before NMEIA or will be in the future. If the relief sought by the plaintiffs is granted, there can be little question but that the interests of the American Mining Congress and of Kerr–McGee would be affected. Plaintiffs contend, however, that appellants would not be bound by such a result if they are not participants. Kerr–McGee points out that even though it may not be res judicata, still it would have a stare decisis effect. Moreover, with NRC and NMEIA as parties, the result might be more profound than stare decisis.

It should be pointed out that the Rule refers to impairment "as a practical matter." Thus, the court is not limited to consequences of a strictly legal nature. The court may consider any significant legal effect in the applicant's interest and it is not restricted to a rigid res judicata test. Hence, the stare decisis effect might be sufficient to satisfy the requirement. It is said that where, as here, the case is of first impression, the stare decisis effect would be important.

Finally, the considerations for requiring an environmental impact statement will be relatively the same in respect to the issuance of a uranium mining license in every instance. Hence, to say that it can be repeatedly litigated is not an answer, for the chance of getting a contrary result in a case which is substantially similar on its facts to one previously adjudicated seems remote.

We are of the opinion, therefore, that appellants have satisfied the impairment criterion.

III.

The final question is whether the trial court was correct in its conclusion that United Nuclear would adequately represent Kerr–McGee and the American Mining Congress.

The finding and conclusion was that the representation would be adequate because United Nuclear, a fellow member of the industry, has interests which were the same as those of the appellants and possessed the same level of knowledge and experience with the ability and willingness to pursue the matter and could adequately represent Kerr–McGee and the members of the American Mining Congress.

We have held in accordance with Trbovich v. UMW, 404 U.S. 528, 538 n. 10, 92 S.Ct. 630, 30 L.Ed.2d 686 (1972), that the burden continues to be on the petitioner or movant in intervention to show that the representation by parties may be inadequate. We have also recognized the holding in *Trbovich* that the burden is minimal; that it is enough to show that the representation "may be" inadequate.

United Nuclear is situated somewhat differently in this case than are the other members of the industry since it has been granted its license. From this it is urged by Kerr–McGee that United Nuclear may be ready to compromise the case by obtaining a mere declaration that while environmental impact statements should be issued, this requirement need be prospective only, whereby it would not affect them. While we see this as a remote possibility, we gravely doubt that United Nuclear would opt for such a result. It is true, however, that United Nuclear has a defense of laches that is not available to Kerr–McGee or the others.

7A C. Wright & A. Miller, Federal Practice & Procedure, § 1909, at 524 (1972), says:

> [I]f [an applicant's] interest is similar to, but not identical with, that of one of the parties, a discriminating judgment is required on the circumstances of the particular case, but he ordinarily should be allowed to intervene unless it is clear that the party will provide adequate representation for the absentee.

While the interest of the two applicants may appear similar, there is no way to say that there is no possibility that they will not be different and the possibility of divergence of interest need not be great in order to satisfy the burden of the applicants.

There are other reasons for allowing intervention. There is some value in having the parties before the court so that they will be bound by the result. American Mining Congress represents a number of companies having a wide variety of interests. This can, therefore, provide a useful supplement to the defense of the case. The same can be said of Kerr–McGee.

The trial court was concerned that the addition of these movants would make the litigation unwieldy. If the intervenors are limited to this group, unwieldiness does not become a problem which the trial court cannot control. It does not appear that there would be a need for additional parties in view of the presence of the American Mining Congress. While we do not express an opinion on the possibilities of further additions, we wish to make clear that the present holdings that the two applicants should be allowed to intervene does not say that others should be added. The two appellants here have satisfied their burden of the three requirements of Rule 24(a)(2). Consequently, they should be and they are hereby allowed to intervene. Accordingly, we need not determine whether the district court erred in denying permissive intervention under Rule 24(b).

The order of the district court is reversed and the cause is remanded with instructions to the trial court to grant the appellants, Kerr–McGee's and American Mining Congress', motions to intervene.

Notes and Questions

1. We first saw intervention in Band's Refuse Removal, Inc. v. Borough of Fair Lawn, supra p. 3, where the Capassos intervened in the suit. Was intervention there proper under the standards of Rule 24?

2. Compare Rule 19(a)(2) with Rule 24(a)(2). Does their similarity mean that, whenever an intervenor qualifies under Rule 24(a)(2), all others who have the same characteristics should also be treated as necessary parties under Rule 19(a)? Is one rule narrower in scope than the other? If so, why is it permissible to deny intervention to parties who qualify under Rule 24(a)(2) if they are adequately represented? Note that there is no similar provision in Rule 19, except to the extent that it is somehow implicit in Rule 19(b).

3. The definition of interest under Rule 24(a) is discussed in some detail below. Assuming the intervenor claims the right kind of interest, intervention of right is proper only if that interest will be impaired should intervention be denied. The court suggests that the stare decisis effect should be sufficient. Consider Olympus Corp. v. United States, 627 F.Supp. 911 (E.D.N.Y.1985), in which the exclusive U.S. distributor of Olympus-brand optical products sued customs officials challenging regulations that allowed importation of "gray market" Olympus products—products imported by persons other than the manufacturer's authorized representative. 47th Street Photo, which imported a substantial quantity of Olympus "gray market" products, and K–Mart Corporation, which purchased other "gray market" goods and said it was a "potential customer" of Olympus "gray market" products, moved to intervene. The court found that 47th Street Photo possessed an adequate interest to intervene as of right, but not K–Mart. Why? How could 47th Street Photo's interest be impaired by the action? The court stated: "Although apprehension concerning the force of *stare decisis* will not support intervention in all cases, its effect under the circumstances presented here, presenting a significant case of apparent first impression, suffices." Who could intervene as of right in a case in which plaintiff seeks to persuade a court in a state that presently treats contributory negligence as a complete defense to switch to a comparative negligence regime?

4. Once the intervenor can show prospective impairment of the right kind of interest, intervention is to be denied only if the intervenor's interests are adequately represented by the present parties. The intervenor need only show that "representation of his interest 'may be' inadequate; and the burden of making that showing should be treated as minimal." Trbovich v. United Mine Workers, 404 U.S. 528, 538 n. 10, 92 S.Ct. 630, 636, 30 L.Ed.2d 686 (1972). However, "[w]hen the party seeking intervention has the same ultimate objective as a party to the suit, a presumption arises that its interests are adequately represented, against which the petitioner must

demonstrate adversity of interest, collusion, or nonfeasance." International Tank Terminals, Ltd. v. M/V Acadia Forest, 579 F.2d 964, 967 (5th Cir. 1978). See also Supreme Beef Processors, Inc. v. U.S. Dept. of Agriculture, 2000 WL 127281 (N.D.Tex) (in suit by beef processor challenging Department of Agriculture regulations governing processing of meat and poultry, intervention by trade association of packers, processors, and distributors denied, finding claim of a broader interest was not sufficient where the same objective and relief were sought). Why weren't Kerr–McGee and the American Mining Congress adequately represented by United Nuclear? Would others interested in the business be deemed adequately represented by Kerr–McGee and the American Mining Congress should they try to intervene?

5.   Consider the application of these intervention criteria in Grutter v. Bollinger, 188 F.3d 394 (6th Cir.1999). Plaintiffs were white students rejected for admission by the University of Michigan. They claimed that the university illegally considered race in making admissions decisions, and sought an injunction against future consideration of race. Seventeen African–American and Hispanic individuals who intended to apply to the university and non-profit organizations dedicated to preserving higher educational opportunities for minority students sought to intervene on the side of the defendant university. The district court denied intervention.

The court of appeals reversed. Noting that the Sixth Circuit takes an expansive view of the interest sufficient to justify intervention of right, the court found that requirement satisfied because "[t]he proposed intervenors have enunciated a specific interest in the subject matter of this case, namely their interest in gaining admission to the University." There was "little room for doubt" that access to the university would be impaired for such applicants if the university were precluded from considering race as a factor in admissions, the court added, citing recent experiences in California and Texas as evidence. The university was not an adequate representative for the intervenors, moreover, because it was subject to internal and external institutional pressures that might prevent it from asserting some defenses of affirmative action, and because it had less to lose then the intervenors did. On this last point, one judge dissented, asserting that the university had "zealously defend[ed] its voluntarily-adopted admissions policies." Is the court's reasoning persuasive?

6.   Intervention must be "timely." Rule 24(a)(2). In United Airlines, Inc. v. McDonald, 432 U.S. 385, 97 S.Ct. 2464, 53 L.Ed.2d 423 (1977), an application for intervention, made only after the intervenor learned that the plaintiffs in this sex discrimination case would not appeal the denial of class certification, was found to have been made "as soon as it became clear" that her interests were no longer protected by the class representatives. Stallworth v. Monsanto Co., 558 F.2d 257 (5th Cir.1977), listed four factors for assessing timeliness: 1) when the intervenor knew or should have known of his interest in the case, 2) whether there was prejudice to existing parties from the delay in seeking intervention, 3) whether there would be prejudice to the intervenor if intervention were denied, and 4) any unusual circumstances.

7.   To what extent is an intervenor bound by rulings made by the court before its intervention? See Hall County Historical Society, Inc. v. Georgia

Dept. of Transp., 447 F.Supp. 741, 746 n. 1 (N.D.Ga.1978) ("Although an intervenor as of right is entitled to fully litigate the merits by pleading and setting forth additional claims and defenses where they arise from the same transaction(s) as the main claim(s) or are ancillary thereto, it is also well settled that an intervenor in equitable proceedings is bound by all prior orders and decrees as though he had been a party from the inception of the suit.").

8. Under Rule 24(a) intervention is "of right." What rights does that mean the intervenor has? One of the concerns of the district court in denying intervention to Kerr–McGee and the American Mining Congress was that their presence would unduly complicate the case. What could it do to minimize those problems? In Stringfellow v. Concerned Neighbors in Action, 480 U.S. 370, 107 S.Ct. 1177, 94 L.Ed.2d 389 (1987), the neighbors' association was allowed to intervene in an action brought by the United States and the State of California concerning the Stringfellow Acid Pits, an abandoned hazardous waste disposal site. The trial court limited the intervenors in three ways: (1) Intervenors could not assert a claim for relief that was not already raised because that would "expand an already complex litigation, and could jeopardize the possibility of settlement"; (2) Intervenors could not seek a share of the government's recovery of clean-up costs; (3) Intervenors could not file motions or initiate discovery without first conferring with all the litigants and obtaining permission from at least one of the others. The Supreme Court rejected arguments that these limitations amounted to a complete denial of intervention. Justice Brennan, concurring, noted that "restrictions on participation may also be placed on an intervenor of right and on an original party." For another example, see United States v. Reserve Mining Co., 56 F.R.D. 408 (D.Minn.1972) (requiring intervenors to make uniform presentations and agree on witnesses to be called).

9. Had there been an applicable fee-shifting statute in the *Natural Resources Defense Council* case, would the intervenors have run the risk of liability for part of plaintiffs' fees if plaintiffs were ultimately successful? In Independent Federation of Flight Attendants v. Zipes, 491 U.S. 754, 109 S.Ct. 2732, 105 L.Ed.2d 639 (1989), a sex discrimination action, other employees were allowed to intervene to challenge a settlement between plaintiffs and the employer. When plaintiffs prevailed against the intervenors, the district court then awarded plaintiffs some $180,000 under the applicable fee-shifting statute for the fees incurred during this litigation against intervenors.

The Supreme Court reversed, interpreting the employment discrimination fee-shifting statute as allowing such an award against intervenors under the same standard as govern an award against an unsuccessful plaintiff (see supra p. 104 n. 2)—where intervenor's assertions were "frivolous, unreasonable, or without foundation." The Court reasoned that "losing intervenors * * * have not been found to have violated anyone's civil rights" and that intervention by "employees innocent of any wrongdoing" would be "particularly welcome" in assessing prospective remedies in employment discrimination cases.

10. Can a government intervene in a private suit involving the interpretation of a statute or regulation if it feels that the suit may create a bad

precedent that will affect its enforcement responsibilities? See Blake v. Pallan, 554 F.2d 947 (9th Cir.1977), where a state Commissioner of Corporations was not allowed to intervene in a private securities fraud suit based on federal securities statutes on which the California securities statutes were modeled.

11. *Intervention for a limited purpose*: The constraints on intervention may be viewed differently when a party seeks to intervene for a limited purpose and not to litigate the validity of the claim asserted by plaintiff. For example, in Sackman v. Liggett Group, 167 F.R.D. 6 (E.D.N.Y.1996), nonparty tobacco companies were allowed to intervene as of right in a smoker's personal injury action against a cigarette manufacturer for the limited purpose of contesting an order permitting plaintiff to discover certain documents that allegedly showed improper conduct by the companies.

THE DEFINITION OF "INTEREST" IN RULE 24(a)(2)

Rule 24(a)(2) applies "when the applicant claims an interest relating to the property or transaction which is the subject of the action." What sort of interest is sufficient to invoke Rule 24(a)(2)? *Natural Resources Defense Council* cites Donaldson v. United States, 400 U.S. 517, 91 S.Ct. 534, 27 L.Ed.2d 580 (1971), as establishing that the interest must be a "significantly protectable interest." This is in contrast to the requirement at an earlier time that the interest must be a "legal interest," that is, that an intervenor must actually have a legally-protectable interest, such as a property right, in the matter being sued on. But just exactly what the "significantly protectable interest" test requires is a matter of continuing debate because *Donaldson* was one of three cases decided by the Supreme Court between 1967 and 1972 that are not entirely consistent. All three of these cases are cited in the *Natural Resources Defense Council* decision and in many other intervention cases.

The earliest of the three cases was Cascade Natural Gas Corp. v. El Paso Natural Gas Co., 386 U.S. 129, 87 S.Ct. 932, 17 L.Ed.2d 814 (1967). After El Paso's acquisition of the Pacific Northwest Pipeline Corp. was found to violate the antitrust laws, the court undertook proceedings to consider the remedy of divestiture. Intervention was sought by *California*, the market for most of El Paso's gas, which wanted to assure that Pacific Northwest "would be restored as an effective competitor in California;" *South California Edison*, "a large industrial user of natural gas purchasing from El Paso sources and desirous of retaining competition in California;" and *Cascade*, a natural gas utility that had used Pacific Northwest as its sole supplier and would use its successor after the divestiture. The Court found that intervention as of right should have been granted, because the intervenors were so situated as to be adversely affected "by a merger that reduces the competitive factor in natural gas available to Californians." This decision was widely taken to represent a broad interpretation of the "interest" required for Rule 24(a)(2), including non-legally protected interests, such as economic concerns.

In *Donaldson,* the Court implied a narrower concept of "interest." There, in furtherance of an investigation of petitioner's tax returns, the Internal Revenue Service issued summonses to petitioner's putative former employer, Acme, for production of its records of petitioner's employment and compensation during the years under investigation. Petitioner sought to intervene in the enforcement proceeding. In rejecting intervention as of right, the Court reasoned:

> The material sought * * * consists only of Acme's routine business records in which the taxpayer has no proprietary interest of any kind * * *. Donaldson's only interest—and of course it looms large in his eyes—lies in the fact that those records presumably contain details of Acme-to-Donaldson payments possessing significance for federal income tax purposes.

> This asserted interest, however, is nothing more than a desire by Donaldson to counter and overcome * * * Acme's willingness, under summons, to comply and to produce records.

> * * * This interest cannot be the kind contemplated by Rule 24(a)(2) * * *. What is obviously meant there is a significantly protectable interest. And the taxpayer, to the extent that he has such a protectable interest, as, for example, by way of privilege, or to the extent he may claim abuse of process, may always assert that interest or that claim in due course at its proper place in any subsequent trial.

Thus, while the Court in *Cascade* seemed to focus upon pragmatic or economic factors in defining "interest," in *Donaldson* the Court refused intervention, despite an admittedly strong *practical* interest on the part of the intervenor, because no "significantly protectable interest" was asserted. Is what the Court meant that the intervenor was asserting no *legally-protected* interest in Acme's production of his employment records?

In the third case, Trbovich v. United Mine Workers, 404 U.S. 528, 92 S.Ct. 630, 30 L.Ed.2d 686 (1972), a union member sought to intervene in an action by the Secretary of Labor to set aside a union election for violating the Labor–Management Reporting and Disclosure Act. Only the Secretary was authorized to file suits under the Act, and union members were prohibited from filing private suits. The Supreme Court upheld the intervention even though he had no right to file suit himself and made no mention of *Donaldson.*

A subsequent Fifth Circuit opinion, New Orleans Public Service, Inc. (*NOPSI*) v. United Gas Pipe Line Co., 732 F.2d 452 (5th Cir.1984), was unwilling to read *Trbovich* as retreating from the requirement of a "significantly protectable interest." It saw the substantive right being litigated in *Trbovich* as the right to have elections conducted in conformity with the Act and concluded that the union member's interest in having elections so conducted "was within the zone of interests protected by the [Act's] substantive provision regulating such elections." Being within the zone of interests intended to be protected by a statute would thus satisfy the "significantly protectable interest" test.

In contrast to *Trbovich*, the interest in *NOPSI* was found insufficient to allow intervention. The City of New Orleans sought to intervene on its own behalf and on behalf of rate-paying customers in a suit brought by the local utility against its natural gas supplier challenging a rate increase as violating their supply contract. Since this was simply a breach of contract suit between two private companies to which the city was not a party, the city had no "significantly protectable interest.": "What is required is that the interest be one which the substantive law recognizes as belonging to or being owned by the applicant. The real party in interest requirement of Rule 17(a) applies to intervenors as well as plaintiffs, as does the rule that a party has no standing to assert a right if it is not his own." The court noted that this was not a case of the city seeking to assert its regulatory rights in a public law suit, and that "the only 'interest' asserted as a basis for intervention is a purely economic interest" that "alone is insufficient, as a legally protectable interest."

The court in *Natural Resources Defense Council* found that the interest of Kerr–McGee was "in sharp contrast to the minimal interest which was present in *Allard*, wherein it was an interest of environmental groups in the protection of living birds." There environmental groups sought to intervene in a suit by sellers of Indian artifacts challenging the constitutionality of a federal act that forbade use of the feathers of protected birds. The interest in *Allard*, the court said, was "general and somewhat abstract" and was "limited to a general interest in the public." Why is this an insufficient interest? Is it that if an interest is too general and shared by too many members of the public, there will be no easy way to limit intervenors (for example, general interests in protecting the environment or aesthetics, or reflecting philosophical, political, or religious views)? Is an individual financial, or "pocket-book" interest, required to assure that an interest is not too general or abstract? Is this consistent with the comment in NOPSI that a "purely economic interest" interest is insufficient?

Sometimes intervenors with strongly-held religious, social, or political views seek to intervene in cases involving issues central to those views. Should those interests suffice? In Planned Parenthood v. Citizens for Community Action, 558 F.2d 861 (8th Cir.1977), a citizens group opposed to abortion sought to intervene in a suit by a family planning clinic challenging an ordinance imposing a moratorium on construction of abortion facilities. The court held that the intervenors had a significantly protectable interest in protecting property values because some lived in the vicinity and a real estate expert opined that presence of an abortion clinic would lower their property values. Should anti-abortion views alone suffice? Contrast Keith v. Daley, 764 F.2d 1265 (7th Cir. 1985), upholding denial of intervention by the Illinois Pro–Life Coalition (IPC) in an action seeking to enjoin enforcement of an anti-abortion law:

In an America whose freedom is secured by its ever vigilant guard on the openness of its marketplace of ideas, IPC is encouraged to thrive, and to speak, lobby, promote, and persuade, so that its principles may become, if it is the will of the majority, the law of the land. Such a priceless right to free expression, however, does not also suggest that IPC has a right to intervene in every lawsuit involving abortion rights, or to forever defend statutes it helped to enact. Rule 24(a) precludes a conception of lawsuits, even public lawsuits, as necessary forums for such public policy debates.

Standing: The question whether intervenors must satisfy standing requirements remains open. In Diamond v. Charles, 476 U.S. 54, 106 S.Ct. 1697, 90 L.Ed.2d 48 (1986), the Court did not decide the question. A doctor who opposed abortion was allowed to intervene on the defense side in an action against Illinois officials challenging the state's abortion law. After the lower courts held the law unconstitutional, the state officials declined to seek Supreme Court review, but the intervenor did. The Court dismissed the appeal: "Diamond's status as an intervenor below, whether permissive or as of right, does not confer standing sufficient to keep the case alive in the absence of the State on this appeal. Although intervenors are considered parties entitled, among other things, to seek review by this Court, an intervenor's right to continue a suit in the absence of the party on whose side intervention was permitted is contingent on a showing by the intervenor that he fulfills the requirements of Article III." For lower court treatment of the question, compare Ruiz v. Estelle, 161 F.3d 814 (5th Cir.1998) (intervenors need not possess standing) with Mova Pharmaceutical Corp. v. Shalala, 140 F.3d 1060 (D.C.Cir.1998) (party that seeks to intervene as of right must demonstrate standing).

I. CLASS ACTIONS (RULE 23)

"The class action was an invention of equity ... mothered by the practical necessity of providing a procedural device so that mere numbers would not disable large groups of individuals, united in interest, from enforcing their equitable rights nor grant them immunity from their equitable wrongs." Montgomery Ward & Co. v. Langer, 168 F.2d 182, 187 (8th Cir.1948). The modern class action is one of the most versatile and powerful joinder devices, offering enormous savings of judicial resources but also providing a significant potential for abuse.

The class action provided in equity was confined to the limited situation when joint rights or rights against a specific property were asserted. An example is the 1921 case Supreme Tribe of Ben–Hur v. Cauble, 255 U.S. 356, 41 S.Ct. 338, 65 L.Ed. 673 (1921). Several members of the fraternal organization were allowed to sue on behalf of all 70,000 members to overturn a reorganization that had unfavorably reclassified their insurance certificates. The class members all had a joint property interest that was threatened by the same conduct of the defendant. However, suits involving such a close identity of interests are not common, and thus class actions at this time were still rare.

The great change came in 1966 when the federal class action rule, Rule 23, was amended. The new Federal Rules in 1938 had divided class actions into three categories based on "jural relationships"—called true, hybrid, and spurious. The distinctions among these categories were difficult to maintain, and students should be happy to know that the 1966 amendments did away with them. The 1966 amendments created three new categories of class actions—referred to as (b)(1), (b)(2), and (b)(3) class actions. The limited situations like *Ben Hur* where there is a close identity of interests and compelling reasons to avoid individual litigation were essentially preserved as *(b)(1)(A)* and *(b)(1)(B)* class actions. These categories involve situations like those calling for compulsory joinder under Rule 19. The two new categories—*(b)(2)* and *(b)(3)*—would bring about great changes in class action practice.

The *(b)(2) class action* is a suit for injunctive or declaratory relief against a party who had acted or refused to act on grounds generally applicable to the class. The paradigms are the "civil rights" suits of the 1960s and 1970s that brought an end to segregation and enforced the civil rights acts, and the "institutional reform" suits of the 1970s and 1980s that applied constitutional and statutory standards to institutions like police departments, prisons, mental hospitals, and welfare agencies. The principal defendants were often either governmental bodies or companies charged with unfair employment practices, and although there were complaints of abusive class actions, many class actions were successful, and significant reforms were sometimes achieved.

The second new category (the *(b)(3) class action*) was more problematic. It is required that "questions of law or fact common to the members of the class predominate" and that a class action is "superior" to other available methods for the adjudication of the controversy. Unlike the other categories, a (b)(3) class action can be for monetary damages, and so there was now money to be had, providing new entrepreneurial incentives for the plaintiffs' bar.

For the first couple of decades after 1966, most (b)(3) class actions were based on federal statutes such as antitrust, securities fraud, and civil rights. However, by the 1980s, class action suits were being filed for a broad spectrum of product liability, mass tort, commercial, and consumer claims. Class actions for mass torts arising from an accident, product defect, or exposure to a harmful substance became highly controversial. Since mass torts often involve individualized circumstances as to a class member's exposure to an environmental or other condition or use of a product, and as to damages, and class certification is still hard to come by in such cases. See, e.g., Southwestern Ref. Co. v. Bernal, 22 S.W.3d 425 (Tex.2000) (denying certification of a class of persons exposed to toxic substances as a result of an explosion).

1. The Problem of Representation

The class action is a representative suit by which the class representative or representatives sue on behalf of class members similarly situated:

The class representatives are self-appointed, having talked with a lawyer and decided that they want to sue on behalf of the class. This may be done for a variety of reasons. The person suing may genuinely feel that the defendant whose conduct harmed him should also have to answer to other persons similarly harmed. Or, on talking with a lawyer, he may have learned that his possible recovery in an individual suit is too small to justify the expense of the litigation, and he can only get a lawyer to take the case if the lawyer can obtain his fees and litigation expenses out of the benefits to a class as a whole. Many class actions are primarily the creation of a lawyer or law firm that recruit the representative plaintiffs and finance the costs of the suit. Indeed, "entrepreneurial litigation," in which the class attorneys are the primary interested parties in the suit, is the subject of much debate in the American class action scene.

* * *

By allowing individuals to sue not only for themselves, but also on behalf of others similarly situated, the class action "empowers plaintiffs to bring cases that otherwise either would not be possible or would only be possible in a very different form." Business critics see this in consumer suits as enabling "lawyers [to] seek out opportunities to bring these large-scale suits in the expectation that they will receive large fees, whether or not the suit has underlying merit and whether or not the individuals on whose behalf the suit is brought benefit significantly from its resolution." Consumer advocates, on the other hand, see it as providing "a means of bringing a legal action on behalf of a large number of consumers who may be harmed when corporations engage in wrongful behavior" that can "succeed in eliminating inappropriate business practices that would otherwise impose unwarranted costs on individuals."

Sherman, "American Class Actions: Significant Features and Developing Alternatives in Foreign Legal Systems," 215 F.R.D.130, 139 (2003); Sherman, Consumer Class Actions: Who Are the Real Winners?, 56 Maine L. Rev. 223 (2004).

The class representative(s) and class counsel have the authority to act on behalf of the class and thus have fiduciary responsibilities to the class. If they are not successful and lose the class action suit, the class members will be bound by the judgment. The prerequisites for a class action (which will be taken up in the next section) require that the claims of the class representative(s) must be "typical" of the claims of the class members and that there is "adequacy of representation" by both the class representative(s) and attorney(s).

In a landmark case predating the 1966 amendments to the class action rule, Hansberry v. Lee, the Supreme Court made it clear that there are constitutional due process limitations on the preclusive effect of a class action judgment.

HANSBERRY v. LEE

Supreme Court of the United States, 1940.
311 U.S. 32, 61 S.Ct. 115, 85 L.Ed. 22.

JUSTICE STONE delivered the opinion of the Court.

The question is whether the Supreme Court of Illinois, by its adjudication that petitioners in this case are bound by a judgment rendered in an earlier litigation to which they were not parties, has deprived them of the due process of law guaranteed by the Fourteenth Amendment.

[The Hansberrys, who were African American, bought and moved into a home in Chicago in an area covered by a racially restrictive covenant. The area was bounded by 60th and 63rd streets and Cottage Grove and South Park (now Martin Luther King Memorial Drive) and included about 500 homes. In reaction, owners of neighboring homes *plaintiff* sued in an Illinois state court to void the sale to the Hansberrys. The *defense* Hansberrys defended on the ground that the covenant never became effective because it wasn't signed by 95% of the homeowners in the area, as required by its terms. The trial court found that only 54% of the landowners had signed the agreement.

The trial court nevertheless voided the sale to the Hansberrys and ordered them to move out because it found that they were bound by a decision that the covenant was valid in Burke v. Kleiman, an earlier suit to enforce the covenant in an Illinois state court. That suit was filed at the instance of the Woodlawn Property Owners Association, a neighborhood association, against Kleiman, a white property owner who rented to an African American, and Hall, his African–American tenant. It was brought "on behalf of" all landowners in the area and alleged that the covenant had been signed by the required 95% of the owners. Defendants in the *Burke* case stipulated that the requisite number of signatures had been obtained and defended on the ground that the covenant should no longer be enforceable due to changed conditions. The court in *Burke* rejected that defense and held the agreement enforceable.

In *Hansberry*, the trial court found that it could not reopen the issue because *Burke* had been a class action that was binding on the Hansberrys' grantor (who, as a property owner, was a member of the class), and *Burke* had decided that there were enough signatures. The Illinois Supreme Court, noting that "[i]t cannot be seriously contended that [the *Burke* case] was not properly a representative suit," affirmed. It concluded that the stipulation in *Burke* that 95% had signed, while factually inaccurate, had not been collusive or fraudulent.]

State courts are free to attach such descriptive labels to litigations before them as they may choose and to attribute to them such consequences as they think appropriate under state constitutions and laws, subject only to the requirements of the Constitution of the United States. But when the judgment of a state court, ascribing to the judgment of another court the binding force and effect of res judicata, is challenged for want of due process it becomes the duty of this Court to examine the course of procedure in both litigations to ascertain whether the litigant whose rights have thus been adjudicated has been afforded such notice and opportunity to be heard as are requisite to the due process which the Constitution prescribes.

It is a principle of general application in Anglo–American jurisprudence that one is not bound by a judgment in personam in a litigation in which he is not designated as a party or to which he has not been made a party by service of process. Pennoyer v. Neff, 95 U.S. 714, 24 L.Ed. 565. A judgment rendered in such circumstances is not entitled to the full faith and credit which the Constitution and statute of the United States prescribe,* and judicial action enforcing it against the person or property of the absent party is not that due process which the Fifth and Fourteenth Amendments require.

To these general rules there is a recognized exception that, to an extent not precisely defined by judicial opinion, the judgment in a "class" or "representative" suit, to which some members of the class are parties, may bind members of the class or those represented who were not made parties to it.

The class suit was an invention of equity to enable it to proceed to a decree in suits where the number of those interested in the subject of the litigation is so great that their joinder as parties in conformity to the usual rules of procedure is impracticable. Courts are not infrequently called upon to proceed with causes in which the number of those interested in the litigation is so great as to make difficult or impossible the joinder of all because some are not within the jurisdiction or because their whereabouts is unknown or where if all were made parties to the suit its continued abatement by the death of some would prevent or unduly delay a decree. In such cases where the interests of those not joined are of the same class as the interests of those who are, and where it is considered that the latter fairly represent the former in the prosecution of the litigation of the issues in which all have a common interest, the court will proceed to a decree.

It is evident that the considerations which may induce a court thus to proceed, despite a technical defect of parties, may differ from those which must be taken into account in determining whether the absent parties are bound by the decree or, if it is adjudged that they are, in ascertaining whether such an adjudication satisfies the requirements of due process and of full faith and credit. Nevertheless there is scope within the framework of the Constitution for holding in appropriate cases that a judgment rendered in a class suit is res judicata as to members of the class who are not formal parties to the suit. Here, as elsewhere, the Fourteenth Amendment does not compel state courts or legislatures to adopt any particular rule for establishing the conclusiveness of judgments in class suits; nor does it compel the adoption of the

* See U.S.Const. Art. IV, § 1; 28 U.S.C. § 1738—Eds.

particular rules thought by this court to be appropriate for the federal courts. With a proper regard for divergent local institutions and interests, this Court is justified in saying that there has been a failure of due process only in those cases where it cannot be said that the procedure adopted, fairly insures the protection of the interests of absent parties who are to be bound by it.

It is familiar doctrine of the federal courts that members of a class not present as parties to the litigation may be bound by the judgment where they are in fact adequately represented by parties who are present, or where they actually participate in the conduct of the litigation in which members of the class are present as parties, or where the interest of the members of the class, some of whom are present as parties, is joint, or where for any other reason the relationship between the parties present and those who are absent is such as legally to entitle the former to stand in judgment for the latter.

In all such cases, so far as it can be said that the members of the class who are present are, by generally recognized rules of law, entitled to stand in judgment for those who are not, we may assume for present purposes that such procedure affords a protection to the parties who are represented though absent, which would satisfy the requirements of due process and full faith and credit. * * * We decide only that the procedure and the course of litigation sustained here by the plea of res judicata do not satisfy these requirements.

The restrictive agreement did not purport to create a joint obligation or liability. If valid and effective its promises were the several obligations of the signers and those claiming under them. The promises ran severally to every other signer. It is plain that in such circumstances all those alleged to be bound by the agreement would not constitute a single class in any litigation brought to enforce it. Those who sought to secure its benefits by enforcing it could not be said to be in the same class with or represent those whose interest was in resisting performance, for the agreement by its terms imposes obligations and confers rights on the owner of each plot of land who signs it. If those who thus seek to secure the benefits of the agreement were rightly regarded by the state Supreme Court as constituting a class, it is evident that those signers or their successors who are interested in challenging the validity of the agreement and resisting its performance are not of the same class in the sense that their interests are identical so that any group who had elected to enforce rights conferred by the agreement could be said to be acting in the interest of any others who were free to deny its obligation.

Because of the dual and potentially conflicting interests of those who are putative parties to the agreement in compelling or resisting its performance, it is impossible to say, solely because they are parties to it, that any two of them are of the same class. Nor without more, and with the due regard for the protection of the rights of absent parties which due process exacts, can some be permitted to stand in judgment for all.

It is one thing to say that some members of a class may represent other members in a litigation where the sole and common interest of the class in the litigation, is either to assert a common right or to challenge an asserted obligation. It is quite another to hold that all those who are free alternatively either to assert rights or to challenge them are of a single class, so that any group merely because it is of the class so constituted, may be deemed adequately to represent any others of the class in litigating their interests in either alternative. Such a selection of representatives for purposes of litigation, whose substantial interests are not necessarily or even probably the same as those whom they are deemed to represent, does not afford that protection to absent parties which due process requires. The doctrine of representation of absent parties in a class suit has not hitherto been thought to go so far. Apart from the opportunities it would afford for the fraudulent and collusive sacrifice of the rights of absent parties, we think that the representation in this case no more satisfies the requirements of due process than a trial by a judicial officer who is in such situation that he may have an interest in the outcome of the litigation in conflict with that of the litigants.

The plaintiffs in the *Burke* case sought to compel performance of the agreement in behalf of themselves and all others similarly situated. They did not designate the defendants in the suit as a class or seek any injunction or other relief against others than the named defendants, and the decree which was entered did not purport to bind others. In seeking to enforce the agreement the plaintiffs in that suit were not representing the petitioners here whose substantial interest is in resisting performance. The defendants in the first suit were not treated by the pleadings or decree as representing others or as foreclosing by their defense the rights of others, and even though nominal defendants, it does not appear that their interest in defeating the contract outweighed their interest in establishing its validity. For a court in this situation to ascribe to either the plaintiffs or defendants the performance of such functions on behalf of petitioners here, is to attribute to them a power that it cannot be said that they had assumed to exercise, and a responsibility which, in view of their dual interests it does not appear that they could rightly discharge.

JUSTICE MCREYNOLDS, JUSTICE ROBERTS and JUSTICE REED concur in the result.

Notes and Questions

1. *Postscript*: Some time after the Supreme Court decided this case, the Hansberrys, reportedly disgusted with racism in this country, moved to Mexico. In 1950 their daughter Lorraine, who had been seven years old when they moved into the house involved in the suit, moved to New York to pursue a career as a writer. In 1958 she published a play entitled "A Raisin in the Sun," in which a central event is the effort of a black family on the South Side of Chicago to move into an all-white area over the objections of the local neighborhood association. The play won the New York Drama Critics Circle Award for 1958–59. Ms. Hansberry died of cancer in 1965, at

the age of 34. For more background on the case, see Tidmarsh, the Story of Hansberry: The Foundation for Modern Class Actions, in Civil Procedure Stories 193 (2004); Kamp, The History Behind Hansberry v. Lee, 20 U.C. Davis L.Rev. 481 (1987). In 1948, the Supreme Court held that the Fourteenth Amendment forbade states from enforcing racially restrictive covenants. Shelley v. Kraemer, 334 U.S. 1, 68 S.Ct. 836, 92 L.Ed. 1161 (1948).

2. Why should the law ever deputize one person to represent another in litigation? In some instances this is done because a person is incompetent. Cf. Rule 17(c). In general, however, we insist that a person represent her own interest, as Rule 17 emphasizes. The original justification for representative litigation in class actions was, as the Court points out in *Hansberry,* simple necessity. Where those interested in the suit were too numerous to be joined, the court would disregard this "mere technical defect of parties" and proceed with the case. If the requirement that "those interested in the suit" are too numerous to be joined is treated as a "mere technical defect," the way is open to require only, as does the present Rule 23(a)(1), that "the class" is too numerous to be joined—whether or not the potential class members are currently "interested in the suit" or not. What then is the justification for a class action?

3. What is a "class"? The Court says that persons sought to be bound by the agreement would not constitute a single class since some would support enforcement of the covenant and others would oppose it. Should it matter whether the class members conceive themselves to be linked together? Professor Yeazell has traced the origin of the modern class action to medieval group litigation, in which suits by or against groups such as the tenants of a certain village were common. But in medieval cases the group was really that—a functioning social entity—and group litigation merely recognized this social reality. Moreover, there was substantial effort to ensure that the group had actually deputized the person who purported to represent it. See S. Yeazell, From Medieval Group Litigation to the Modern Class Action (1987). Other countries experimenting with some form of "representative" or "group" actions tend to require a closer tie between the class members, for example, members of a consumer association or an environmental organization. Gidi, Class Actions in Brazil—A Model for Civil Law Countries, 51 Am. J. Comp. L. 311 (2003); Sherman, Group Litigation Under Foreign Legal Systems: Variations and Alternatives to American Class Actions, 52 DePaul L. Rev. 401, 418–424 (2002). The modern class action, by way of contrast, usually agglomerates people who otherwise have no ties to one another. Does this suggest special reasons for worry about the problem of representation?

4. The Court points out that plaintiffs in *Burke* did not take the precaution of designating the defendants in that case as representatives of a defendant class of homeowners opposed to the enforcement of the covenant. Had they done so, would defendants there have been proper representatives for the Hansberrys? Could the white landlord there have adequately represented the interest of African Americans like the Hansberrys? Would the African–American tenant in that case have been an adequate representative for others, like the Hansberrys, who wanted to buy homes in the area?

Consider how much more difficult it is to identify an adequate representative for a defendant class. "[N]amed defendants almost never choose their role as class champion—it is a potentially onerous one thrust upon them by their opponents. * * * But courts must not readily accede to the wishes of named defendants in this area, for to permit them to abdicate so easily would utterly vitiate the effectiveness of the defendant class action as an instrument of correcting widespread illegality." Marcera v. Chinlund, 595 F.2d 1231, 1239 (2d Cir.), vacated on other grounds, 442 U.S. 915, 99 S.Ct. 2833, 61 L.Ed.2d 281 (1979).

5. Defendants in the *Burke* case stipulated that the 95% signature requirement had been satisfied. Assuming that this was not collusive, but merely an honest mistake, would it show that they were inadequate representatives? Wouldn't a later plaintiff always have some criticism of the unsuccessful prosecution of the earlier case?

6. The problem of representation results from the courts' insistence that the class action proceed much like an individual lawsuit, with the class representative controlling the case and standing in judgment for the members of the class; hence the focus on the congruence between the class representative's interests and those of the class members. Would it make more sense for the court itself to take control of class actions in order to protect the interests of the class? In some ways, it does. See Rule 23(e) (class action can be settled only with approval of the court). Would it be proper to expand the court's role to make it responsible for the entire development and prosecution of the suit? Cf. Band's Refuse Removal, Inc. v. Borough of Fair Lawn, supra p. 3.

Criticisms of securities fraud class actions led to congressional action in the 1995 Private Securities Litigation Reform Act (PSLRA), 15 U.S.C.A. § 78u–4(a)(3)(B)(i). Recall the discussion of the PSLRA in Chapter III, supra p. 170. It directs the initial plaintiff to provide detailed notice about the claims to other investors, inviting them to express an interest in serving as "lead plaintiff." The court will then appoint as lead plaintiff the person "most capable of adequately representing the interests of class members." The court must presume that "the person or group of persons ... that has the largest financial interest in the relief sought by the class" is best qualified, although the presumption can be rebutted. The lead plaintiff then chooses the class counsel who need not be the attorney(s) who filed the class action. Should this serve as a model for other class actions? What might be the disadvantages in, for example, a consumer or mass tort class action?

7. Adequacy of representation concerns have generally focused on the adequacy of class counsel and ensuring that the named class representatives will protect the interests of the other members of the class. Rule 23(g), added in 2003, requires the court to appoint class counsel only after scrutinizing her for adequacy, and specifies that class counsel's duty is to "represent the interests of the class." What if those interests diverge from the interests of the class representative? Who should determine what those interests are in cases like *Hansberry*? Sometimes, as in school desegregation litigation, members of the excluded group may favor improvement of their existing facilities over integration into those traditionally used by whites. For discussion of these sorts of problems, see Bell, Serving Two Masters: Integration

Ideals and Client Interests in School Desegregation Litigation, 85 Yale L.J. 470 (1976) (describing tension between the goal of integration and parental desires to place more emphasis on educational quality); cf. Rubenstein, Divided We Litigate: Addressing Disputes Among Group Members and Lawyers in Civil Rights Campaigns, 106 Yale L.J. 1623 (1997) (discussing the tension between individualism and group interests).

8. In Stephenson v. Dow Chemical Co., 273 F.3d 249 (2d Cir.2001), aff'd per curiam, 539 U.S. 111, 123 S.Ct. 2161, 156 L.Ed.2d 106 (2003), the Supreme Court affirmed a Second Circuit opinion that allowed two Vietnam War veterans to collaterally attack a class action judgment for inadequate representation. They had been members of a class of service members exposed to Agent Orange in Vietnam. The class action had been settled almost twenty years before, see supra pp. 23–24, but the settlement did not provide for any recovery by persons who, like the plaintiffs, manifested disease after the trust fund had been closed in 1994. Invoking the due process clause, the court found they had not been adequately represented. Does this undermine the finality of class action judgments? This case is considered in more detail, in Chapter XIII, infra p. 1188.

2. The Standards for Certification

In addition to creating the three categories of class actions set out in subsection (b) (see supra p. 289), the 1966 amendments to Rule 23 established four general prerequisites for class certification—numerosity, commonality, typicality, and adequacy of representation. See Rule 23(a). Every class action must satisfy all four of these prerequisites as well as meeting the criteria for one of the (b)(1), (2), or (3) categories of class action.

WALTERS v. RENO

United States Court of Appeals, Ninth Circuit, 1998.
145 F.3d 1032.

Before: GOODWIN, and REINHARDT, Circuit Judges, and KING, Senior District Judge.

REINHARDT, Circuit Judge:

* * *

The plaintiffs brought suit against the government on behalf of themselves and similarly situated noncitizens, seeking declaratory and injunctive relief on the ground that the administrative procedures used by the INS to obtain final orders under the document fraud provisions of the Immigration and Naturalization Act of 1990 ("INA" or "the Act") violated their rights to procedural due process. Under § 274C of the Act, 8 U.S.C. § 1324c, the INS may issue an unappealable final order against an alien who has been accused of document fraud if the alien does not request a hearing in writing within 60 days of receiving the notice of intent to fine ("the fine notice") and the notice of rights/waiver ("the rights/waiver notice") forms. Such an order renders the alien deportable and permanently excludable. Deportation is automatic, except in narrowly limited circumstances. If the alien signs a statement waiving his rights with respect to the document fraud charges, including his right to a hearing, the INS will immediately issue an unappealable final order assessing a fine and requiring the alien to cease and desist from his wrongful conduct, but the ultimate result that ordinarily will follow soon thereafter will be the issuance of an order of deportation.

In their complaint, the plaintiffs contend that despite the dramatic immigration consequences for those charged with violating the document fraud provisions of the INA, the forms served on aliens in connection with these charges are dense and written in complex, legal language. The plaintiffs allege that on account of the confusing nature of the forms, aliens in document fraud proceedings are not adequately informed of the steps they must take in order to contest the charges brought against them and thus do not learn how to obtain a hearing on them. Moreover, they allege, they do not learn the true consequences of failing to request that hearing. They also challenge the general procedures by which the forms are presented to them. The plaintiffs moved to certify a class of approximately 4,000 aliens who had been or were subject to final orders, and moved for the entry of a preliminary injunction, summary judgment, a permanent injunction, and an order requiring the INS to reopen each plaintiff's document fraud case and provide hearings if necessary.

In March 1996, Judge Coughenour certified the plaintiffs as a class with the following characteristics:

> All non-citizens who have or will become subject to a final order under § 274C of the Immigration and Naturalization Act because they received notice forms that did not adequately advise them of their rights, of the consequences of waiving their rights or of the consequences of failing to request a hearing.

Under the district court's order, an individual alien can establish his status as a class member by attesting that he did not understand either his rights in the document fraud proceedings or the consequences of waiving his rights. In the same order, Judge Coughenour ruled on summary judgment that the procedures and forms used by the INS in document fraud cases are unconstitutional because they deny aliens their rights to due process of law. The court also granted permanent injunctive relief; the terms of the injunction were to be decided after the parties submitted proposals to the court.

In October 1996, Judge Coughenour entered final judgment in favor of the plaintiffs and granted a permanent injunction requiring the INS to take a variety of actions to remedy the constitutional violations. According to the terms of the injunction, the INS must: (1) revise the two misleading forms (the fine notice and the rights/waiver notice); (2) send notice to possible class members at their last known addresses, and, through a publicity campaign that must include specific attempts to contact all class members inside and outside of the country, publicize the opportunity for class members to reopen their document fraud proceedings; (3) refrain from deporting noncitizens on the basis of § 274C final orders that were entered without a hearing until class members have the opportunity to pursue reopening procedures; (4) reopen § 274C proceedings for each class member who was subject to a § 274C final order, unless the government can show that alien received adequate notice; (5) parole or make other arrangements for class members outside the United States to pursue reopened proceedings; and (6) recharge any alien charged with deficient forms who failed to request a hearing but has not yet been subjected to a final order, unless the government can show that the alien received adequate notice.

* * *

Although there is no question that the United States has extraordinarily broad powers in the area of immigration and border control, it is also well established that aliens facing deportation from this country are entitled to due process rights under the Fifth Amendment. As the Supreme Court has explained on a number of occasions, "once [an] alien gains admission to our country and begins to develop the ties that go with permanent residence his constitutional status changes accordingly." *Landon v. Plasencia,* 459 U.S. 21, 32, 103 S.Ct. 321, 74 L.Ed.2d 21 (1982). Thus, the government is not free to deport an alien from the United States unless it has first accorded him the most basic procedural protections—notice and a hearing at a meaningful time and in a meaningful manner.[2] The plaintiffs assert that the INS regularly violates these constitutional precepts in the context of document fraud proceedings.

At the heart of this case is the plaintiffs' allegation that the procedures by which INS agents procured waivers of the right to a hearing in document fraud proceedings were constitutionally deficient because the forms used in connection with these proceedings did not adequately inform aliens of their right to a hearing or of the drastic immigration consequences that would ensue if the alien failed to request a hearing. As a result, the aliens' waivers were not made knowingly and voluntarily. These procedures, the plaintiffs contend, have been employed nationwide by the INS in virtually every case in which the government has charged an alien with committing document fraud.

* * *

[A]n alien charged with civil document fraud receives three forms advising him of two hearings. One hearing, he is told—the hearing on the document fraud charges, the consequence for which is stated to be a fine and a cease and desist order—will be held only if the alien submits a written request. The other hearing, the alien is advised—the hearing on the far graver issue whether he will be deported—will be held automati-

---

2. A waiver of either of these basic rights is valid only if the government demonstrates that the alien intentionally relinquished a known right or privilege.

cally, without the need for him to do anything. He is also told that at *that* hearing he will be able to respond to the allegations that constitute the basis for the threatened deportation. None of the forms advises the alien that if he fails to request a *separate* hearing on the document fraud charges, the deportation hearing he receives will ordinarily be meaningless, that he will be found deportable and excludable on the ground of document fraud without any further opportunity to challenge that determination, and that his deportation will in most instances be virtually automatic.

Summary Judgment

As a threshold matter, we must determine whether the district court's grant of summary judgment was proper. * * *

The district court concluded that the plaintiffs were entitled to summary judgment because the INS procedures for securing waivers of a hearing on document fraud charges create an unacceptable risk of confusion likely to result in erroneous deportation.

* * *

Given the essential facts that determine the outcome in this case— the complexity and ineptness of the forms and the fact that they are designed to provide essential information of constitutional significance to persons of foreign birth—we conclude that the district court properly found that no issues of material fact precluded summary judgment.

Due Process Analysis

According to the government, the district court's legal conclusions regarding the constitutionality of the INS forms are erroneous, and it advances the following arguments in support of this position: (1) the contents of the forms adequately apprise the alien of his rights and the direct consequences of waiving those rights, and due process does not require that forms, such as the waiver of rights form, be in any language other than English; (2) in applying *Mathews v. Eldridge,* 424 U.S. 319, 96 S.Ct. 893, 47 L.Ed.2d 18 (1976), the district court erred in calculating the various interests at stake and, as a consequence, misapplied the balancing test; and (3) even if there was a constitutional violation, the plaintiffs failed to demonstrate that any prejudice flowed therefrom.

[The court concludes that the forms "are not only confusing, they are affirmatively misleading."]

The government maintains that the district court erred in evaluating the relevant interests under the calculus established in *Mathews v. Eldridge.* As the *Mathews* balancing test makes clear, whether a particular procedure is sufficient to satisfy due process depends on the circumstances. Thus,

[i]n evaluating the procedures in any case, the courts must consider the interest at stake for the individual, the risk of an erroneous deprivation of the interest through the procedures used as well as

[handwritten margin note top:] plaintiff interest - to stay and work in USO

[handwritten margin note:] government interest - administration of immigration law + preventing document fraud

the probable value of additional or different procedural safeguards, and the interest of the government in using the current procedures rather than additional or different procedures.

Id. at 34, 96 S.Ct. 893 (citing *Mathews,* 424 U.S. at 319, 96 S.Ct. 893). We agree with the district court that the relevant factors weigh in favor of altering the document fraud forms.

It is clear that the plaintiffs' interests in this case are significant. *See Plasencia,* 459 U.S. at 34, 103 S.Ct. 321 (noting that the alien's interest in deportation proceedings "is, without question, a weighty one" because "[s]he stands to lose the right 'to stay and live and work in this land of freedom.'") (quoting *Bridges v. Wixon,* 326 U.S. 135, 154, 65 S.Ct. 1443, 89 L.Ed. 2103 (1945)). The government's interests in the administration of its immigration laws and in preventing document fraud are likewise considerable. Striking the proper balance between these interests can be achieved by adopting procedures that reduce the risk of erroneous deprivation without imposing an undue burden on the government.

[handwritten margin note:] only minor changes to forms to make them constitutional

Requiring the government to alter slightly its procedures in document fraud proceedings will achieve the desired effect—additional safeguards—without visiting upon it any inordinate hardship. Specifically, it is possible to reduce the risk of erroneous deprivation (*i.e.,* erroneous deportation) by ensuring that aliens facing charges of document fraud are adequately notified that they *must* request a separate hearing to contest those charges and that their failure to do so will ordinarily foreclose their ability to challenge their status as deportable aliens. Providing constitutionally adequate notice requires only minor changes in the content of the forms themselves and equally slight adaptations in the INS's method of presenting the forms. Requiring the INS to ensure that there are no significant inconsistencies in the written language of forms that affect whether or not an alien will be rendered deportable and permanently excludable, and requiring minor modifications to the written content of the forms will not be unduly burdensome, particularly in light of the benefits of such safeguards.

PREJUDICE *[handwritten note:] - aliens have to show that forms affected outcome of proceedings*

* * *

When it is necessary to demonstrate prejudice as a result of a constitutional violation, the alien must show that the inadequate procedures occurred "in a manner so as potentially to affect the outcome of the proceedings." *Hartooni v. INS,* 21 F.3d 336, 340 (9th Cir.1994); *see also United States v. Jimenez-Marmolejo,* 104 F.3d 1083, 1086 (9th Cir.1996) (holding that in order to show prejudice, an alien need not prove that he would not have been deported, just that he had "plausible grounds for relief"). Ordinarily, there must be plausible scenarios in which the outcome of the proceedings would have been different, absent the constitutional violation.

Here, the district court determined that at least two class plaintiffs had demonstrated that the lack of adequate notice as to their document fraud proceedings potentially affected the outcome of their document fraud proceedings. In the cases of Ninfa Guerrero de Adames and Antonio Santana–Alvarez, the district court found that each had a viable legal defense to the charges that had been brought against them. With respect to Adames, the district court found that she could have made a persuasive argument that the document fraud charges, as applied to her, violated the prohibition against ex post facto laws. In Santana–Alvarez's case, the district court found that he had a strong legal argument that his conduct did not constitute a violation of the document fraud laws. There is no evidence to suggest that these findings are erroneous. The district court determined that if Adames and Santana–Alvarez had not waived their right to a hearing, they might have been able to defend against the charges successfully. Accordingly, the district court concluded that the lack of notice regarding the right to a hearing potentially affected the outcome of the proceedings.

We agree with the district court that Adames and Santana–Alvarez are not precluded from showing prejudice simply because they admitted, while testifying under grants of immunity, that they had used fraudulent immigration documents. It is sufficient for purposes of showing prejudice that the plaintiffs have demonstrated *plausible* grounds for relief. The potential legal defenses identified by the district court satisfy this standard.

CLASS CERTIFICATION

Rule 23(a) provides that a court should certify a class only if the following prerequisites are met: (1) the class is too numerous, making joinder of the parties impracticable; (2) common questions of law or fact exist among the class members; (3) the claims of the class representatives are typical of the claims of the class; and (4) the class representatives will adequately represent the interest of the class. In addition to satisfying the mandatory prerequisites in Rule 23(a), the potential class members must also demonstrate that they meet at least one of the alternative requirements under Rule 23(b). In this case, the government disputes the existence of two of these requirements—commonality and adequacy of representation. Additionally, the government challenges the district court's certification of the class under Rule 23(b)(2).

A. COMMONALITY

Requiring there to be common questions of law or fact prior to certifying a class serves chiefly two purposes: (1) ensuring that absentee members are fairly and adequately represented; and (2) ensuring practical and efficient case management. In this case, each class member raises the same constitutional question: whether the nationwide procedures used by INS in document fraud proceedings sufficiently apprise aliens of their constitutional right to a hearing, thereby satisfying the notice component of due process.

[handwritten top margin: commonality is lacking b/c]

The government maintains that the commonality requirement is lacking because the actual experiences of the class members are not sufficiently similar. Some individual INS agents and branch offices, for example, have consistently disregarded the Agency's official policy regarding the use of forms in § 274C proceedings and have instituted supplemental explanations of the potential immigration consequences. Therefore, some aliens who were subject to document fraud charges may have received adequate notice in spite of the constitutionally deficient official procedures.

[handwritten right margin: government argues no commonality b/c actual experiences of class members are not similar]

To support its contention that the class members' claims lack commonality, the government points to terms of the injunction that provide for individualized proceedings. Specifically, it relies on the portions of the injunction providing the government with the opportunity to demonstrate that an individual class member "received constitutionally adequate notice despite having received the section 274C notice forms that the Court has found defective." According to the government, these proceedings demonstrate that there is no common factual or legal basis for the class claims; if commonality existed, there would be no need for such individualized procedures.

[handwritten right margin: terms of injunction are individual proceedings]

We think the government misses the point. There is nothing wrong with the district court's presumption that the INS actually employed its constitutionally deficient policies and procedures. The government made no showing in the district court that its procedures were modified by more than just a few agents and branch offices. Thus, it is reasonable to presume that class members involved in document fraud proceedings did not receive due process because of the inadequate forms. Moreover, as the district court observed, it would be "a twisted result" to permit an administrative agency to avoid nationwide litigation that challenges the constitutionality of its general practices simply by pointing to minor variations in procedure among branch offices and individual INS agents, particularly because the variations were designed to avoid the precise constitutional inadequacies identified by the plaintiffs in this action.

The government further argues that commonality is nonexistent on account of factual distinctions in the class members' underlying claims. Differences among the class members with respect to the merits of their actual document fraud cases, however, are simply insufficient to defeat the propriety of class certification. What makes the plaintiffs' claims suitable for a class action is the common allegation that the INS's procedures provide insufficient notice. *See Forbush v. J.C. Penney Co., Inc.,* 994 F.2d 1101, 1106 (5th Cir.1993) (noting that the need for subsequent individual proceedings, even complex ones, "does not supply a basis for concluding that [the named plaintiff] has not met the commonality requirement").

[handwritten right margin: common allegation that INS procedure provided insufficient notice]

ADEQUACY OF REPRESENTATION

Requiring the claims of the class representatives to be adequately representative of the class as a whole ensures that the interests of absent class members are adequately protected. *Hansberry v. Lee,* 311 U.S. 32, 42, 61 S.Ct. 115, 85 L.Ed. 22 (1940). Whether the class representatives satisfy the adequacy requirement depends on "the qualifications of counsel for the representatives, an absence of antagonism, a sharing of interests between representatives and absentees, and the unlikelihood that the suit is collusive." Here, the district court specifically found that the attorneys for the class representatives were well qualified and that the class representatives themselves were adequate because they were not antagonistic to the interests of the class and were "interested and involved in obtaining relief."

In challenging the adequacy of the class representatives, the government primarily relies on the fact that some of the named plaintiffs have admitted under grants of immunity that they committed document fraud. According to the government, these admissions preclude the possibility that these representative class members would have prevailed at a hearing on their document fraud charges, and because some of the class representatives cannot demonstrate prejudice—which, as we noted above, the parties assume to be a prerequisite to a finding of a due process violation—the class representatives are hindered in their ability to represent the class before the district court.

We find no merit in the government's position. Once again, the government erroneously emphasizes factual differences in the merits of the underlying document fraud charges. Such differences have no bearing on the class representatives' abilities to pursue the class claims vigorously and represent the interests of the absentee class members. Moreover, we note that the government's argument is particularly weak in light of the fact that the class representatives have been so successful in their efforts to obtain relief for the entire class.

RULE 23(b)(2) CERTIFICATION

Related to the commonality issue is the government's challenge to the district court's finding that the class was properly certified pursuant to Rule 23(b)(2). Certification under Rule 23(b)(2) is appropriate in cases in which

> the party opposing the class has acted or refused to act on grounds generally applicable to the class, thereby making appropriate final injunctive relief or corresponding declaratory relief with respect to the class as a whole.

Fed.R.Civ.P. 23(b)(2). Here, the district court found certification proper because the plaintiffs claimed that the INS's practices in document fraud proceedings were violative of due process. The forms and procedures in question were used by the INS in document fraud cases on a nationwide basis. Further, the plaintiffs sought injunctive, not monetary relief.

With respect to certification under Rule 23(b)(2), the government's primary objection appears to be that certifying this class does not further the purposes of Rule 23. Again, the government points to the individual proceedings that will result from the district court's injunction as evidence that judicial efficiency will actually be undermined by the class action. While the government correctly observes that numerous individual administrative proceedings may flow from the district court's decision, it fails to acknowledge that the district court's decision eliminates the need for individual litigation regarding the constitutionality of INS's official forms and procedures. Absent a class action decision, individual aliens across the country could file complaints against the INS in federal court, each of them raising precisely the same legal challenge to the constitutionality of the § 274C forms. Contrary to the government's assertion, therefore, class certification in this case is entirely proper in light of the general purposes of Rule 23, avoiding duplicative litigation.

We note that with respect to 23(b)(2) in particular, the government's dogged focus on the factual differences among the class members appears to demonstrate a fundamental misunderstanding of the rule. Although common issues must predominate for class certification under Rule 23(b)(3), no such requirement exists under 23(b)(2). It is sufficient if class members complain of a pattern or practice that is generally applicable to the class as a whole. Even if some class members have not been injured by the challenged practice, a class may nevertheless be appropriate. *See* 7A Charles Alan Wright, Arthur R. Miller & Mary Kay Kane, *Federal Practice & Procedure* § 1775 (2d ed. 1986) ("All the class members need not be aggrieved by or desire to challenge the defendant's conduct in order for some of them to seek relief under Rule 23(b)(2)."); *see also Adamson v. Bowen*, 855 F.2d 668, 676 (10th Cir.1988) (emphasizing that although "the claims of individual class members may differ factually," certification under Rule 23(b)(2) is a proper vehicle for challenging "a common policy").

Moreover, the claims raised by the plaintiffs in this action are precisely the sorts of claims that Rule 23(b)(2) was designed to facilitate. As the Advisory Committee Notes explain, 23(b)(2) was adopted in order to permit the prosecution of civil rights actions.

this case was what 23(b)(2) was created for

THE INJUNCTION

According to the government, even if we uphold the district court's rulings with respect to the constitutional claims and class certification, we should nonetheless find that the district court erred in granting permanent injunctive relief.

[The court finds that injunctive relief is appropriate as it had determined that the forms were constitutionally defective (satisfying the "likelihood of success" requirement), monetary or other legal remedies were inadequate, and plaintiffs would suffer irreparable injury if the procedures were continued.]

Once a class has been certified and a constitutional violation has been ascertained, the district court retains broad discretion in fashioning a remedy. We review the terms of the district court's injunction for abuse of discretion. Here, the injunction serves a narrow purpose and is carefully tailored to achieve that goal. The order is designed to allow the members of the class to reopen their document fraud and deportation proceedings, thereby remedying the lack of adequate notice.

At the outset of its attack on the terms of the injunction, the government objects to the district court's issuing an injunction that provides classwide relief. Citing *Lewis v. Casey,* 518 U.S. 343, 116 S.Ct. 2174, 135 L.Ed.2d 606 (1996), the government maintains that the systemwide relief mandated by the injunction is unwarranted because the plaintiffs only demonstrated that the constitutional violation prejudiced a few individuals. In *Lewis,* the Supreme Court reversed as overly broad an injunction that essentially called for an overhaul of law libraries in the Arizona prison system pursuant to *Bounds v. Smith,* 430 U.S. 817, 97 S.Ct. 1491, 52 L.Ed.2d 72 (1977). Because there were only two instances in which prisoners were hindered from pursuing their legal claims due to the inadequacy of the prison law libraries, the Supreme Court held that systemwide relief was inappropriate.

In *Lewis,* the constitutional violation was not the violation of the right to adequate law libraries in prisons, but was instead the deprivation of the right of meaningful access to the courts. There was no showing that more than two prisoners suffered deprivation of that constitutional right and thus there was no showing of the need for systemwide relief. By contrast, the constitutional violation in this case is the inadequate notice itself. Thus, once the district court determined that the constitutionally insufficient forms and procedures were employed by the INS on a *systemwide* basis, the court had also determined systemwide injury. Every alien who received the fine notice and the rights/waiver notice forms suffered an injury because he did not receive the notice to which he was constitutionally entitled. Moreover, the lack of notice directly resulted in the failure of the class members to obtain constitutionally required hearings—a further constitutional injury.

* * *

[W]e uphold the district court's grant of summary judgment and, with one minor exception, the terms of its injunction. We remand so that the district court may modify its order granting permanent injunctive relief in accordance with this opinion and may take whatever other action it may deem appropriate.

Notes and Questions

1. *Walters v. Reno* was a (b)(2) class action based on the claim that "the party opposing the class has acted or refused to act on grounds generally applicable to the class," making injunctive or declaratory relief for the class as a whole appropriate. We call it a "mandatory class action" because the class members are not permitted to opt out.

A *Rule 23(b)(1) class action* is also mandatory, based on the necessity for a class action to avert unfairness that could result from multiple individual suits. In a (b)(1)(A) class, the unfairness is to the party opposing the class who may be subjected to "inconsistent or varying adjudications" resulting in "incompatible standards" if there were individual suits by class members.

This refers to the opposing party's uncertainty as to what standards it must follow in its future conduct, as in the risk of being subjected to incompatible affirmative relief (for example, a defendant corporation being subjected to differing injunctions as to how it must treat various classes of stockholders). But this does not encompass the risk that individual suits by class members might result in different adjudications as to *damages*, see Alexander Grant & Co. v. McAlister, 116 F.R.D. 583 (S.D.Ohio 1987), and so, for example, it would not justify a mandatory class of bus passengers suing the bus company for injuries from the same accident.

A *(b)(1)(B) class action*, which is also mandatory without a right to opt out, is based on unfairness to missing class members if there were individual suits by class members. It applies if "as a practical matter" adjudications by individual class members would be dispositive of the interests of missing class members that would "substantially impair or impede their ability to protect their interests." The paradigm is where individual suits could exhaust a "limited fund" to which all class members have a claim, and thus, as a practical matter, would impair the missing class members' rights. Cf. State Farm Fire & Casualty Co. v. Tashire, supra p. 268 (insurance proceeds insufficient to pay all accident victims).

2. The denial of a right to opt out in (b)(1) and (2) class actions where monetary relief is also sought, raises possible constitutional problems. Phillips Petroleum Co. v. Shutts, 472 U.S. 797, 105 S.Ct. 2965, 86 L.Ed.2d 628 (1985), suggested that due process may require that "an absent plaintiff be provided with an opportunity to remove himself from the class by executing and returning an 'opt out' or 'request for exclusion' form to the court," if monetary claims are involved. However, a footnote stated: "Our holding today is limited to those class actions which seek to bind known plaintiffs concerning claims wholly or predominantly for money judgments. We intimate no view concerning other types of class action lawsuits, such as those seeking equitable relief." Id. at 811 n. 3.

A Ninth Circuit case, Brown v. Ticor Title Ins. Co., 982 F.2d 386 (9th Cir.1992), held, concerning a (b)(1) and (b)(2) class, that class members were not barred from bringing individual suits for damages even though the claims had been settled as part of a mandatory class. It reasoned that due process requires notice and a right to opt out in order to settle monetary claims. The Supreme Court granted certiorari, but later dismissed the appeal and has not since resolved the issue. In light of the possible due process problems, some courts have permitted opt-outs in (b)(1) and (b)(2) actions where damages are also sought. Others have certified "hybrid" classes—a mandatory class for non-monetary claims and an opt-out class for monetary claims. The 2003 amendments to Rule 23 allow but do not require the court to direct notice in (b)(1) and (b)(2) class actions. See Rule 23(c)(2)(A).

3. Walters v. Reno was a (b)(2) class action seeking only injunctive relief. The Advisory Committee notes recognized that cases might be brought for injunctive or declaratory relief in which damages would also be recoverable, stating that (b)(2) "does not extend to cases in which the appropriate final relief relates exclusively or predominantly to money damages." An example would be an employment discrimination suit brought under Title VII of the 1964 Civil Rights Act that sought injunctive relief such as reinstatement or promotion but which also sought back pay. Employment discrimination cases were especially appropriate for (b)(2) because Congress,

in passing Title VII of the Civil Rights Act of 1964, only authorized recovery of money in the form of "back pay," which was considered an equitable remedy rather than damages, and which did not entitle the parties to a right to jury trial (which the bill's sponsors wanted to avoid, given the largely white juries that prevailed at that time in the South).

However, in 1991, Congress amended Title VII to allow punitive and compensatory damages for intentional discrimination and a right to jury trial. 42 U.S.C. § 1981a(a)(1)(2000). The purpose was to provide "additional remedies under Federal law * * * needed to deter * * * intentional discrimination in the workplace." Ironically, this change was used by the Fifth Circuit in its decision in Allison v. Citgo Petroleum Corp., 151 F. 3d 402 (5th Cir. 1998), to find that a (b)(2) class was not available because damages now available were not merely "incidental" to the declaratory and injunctive relief sought. "Monetary relief predominates in (b)(2) class actions," the court stated, "unless it is incidental to requested injunctive or declaratory relief," that is, "damages that flow directly from liability to the class as a whole on the claims forming the basis of the injunctive or declaratory relief. Ideally, incidental damages should be only those to which class members automatically would be entitled once liability to the class (or subclass) as a whole is established."

The Second Circuit in Robinson v. Metro–North Commuter R.R. Co., 267 F.3d 147 (2d Cir. 2001, rejected *Allison*'s interpretation of the "incidental damages" requirement, saying it should be left to the discretion of the district court, applying an "ad hoc" test, to evaluate the significance of the injunctive relief to the plaintiffs in determining whether a reasonable plaintiff would seek it if the money damages were not available.

In a subsequent opinion in In re Monumental Life Insurance Co., 365 F.3d 408 (5th Cir. 2004). the Fifth Circuit modified the strictness of the Allison opinion, at least in a classic race discrimination case. A class action was filed against three life insurance companies on behalf of black policy owners alleging that, for decades, they were discriminated against in the premiums and benefits provided in low value life insurance policies. The suit sought injunctive relief requiring the insurance companies to reform existing policies and restitution of the value of overcharges over the years. The district court denied (b)(2) certification on the ground that many class members whose policies had lapsed, had been voluntarily adjusted or had been paid on death would not benefit from injunctive relief. It concluded that "this is a case in which individuality overrides any bland group-think, and money becomes the prime goal . . . not injunctive relief."

The Fifth Circuit reversed, stating that *Allison* had not held that the predomination of monetary relief depends on the intentions of the class representatives and counsel, an approach closer to *Robinson* which it rejected. "Certification under rule 23(b)(2) is appropriate," it said, "only if members of the proposed class would benefit from the injunctive relief request." However, noting that the expert witnesses had estimated that millions of the policies were still in force, the court said, "the proportion is sufficient, absent contrary evidence from defendants, that the class as a whole is deemed properly to be seeking injunctive relief." The court went on to find that "equitable monetary relief is compatible with a rule 23(b)(2) class," and "such damages flow from liability in much the same manner that an award of backpay results from a finding of employment discrimination."

Why is it important to determine whether a claim for damages is inconsistent with a (b)(2) class? Why shouldn't plaintiffs in such cases simply seek a (b)(3) class, which was created for seeking damages? The reason is that there are two additional requirements for a (b)(3) class–that common questions *"predominate"* and that class treatment is *"superior"* to other methods of resolving the dispute (these will be considered in connection with the next case). Note the comment in Walters v. Reno that there is no "predominance" requirement for a (b)(2) class. As courts in recent years have often applied these requirements to refuse to certify a class under (b)(3), plaintiffs' attorneys have tried to fit their cases under (b)(2), and sometimes they seek certification jointly or alternatively under either (b)(2) or (b)(3). This was unsuccessful in *Allison* as the court denied certification under both categories—(b)(3) because common issues would not predominate and (b)(2) because the damages were not incidental. Other courts have allowed certification of "hybrid" class actions–a (b)(2) class for injunctive relief, then a (b)(3) class for damages which might require severing off certain individual issues for individual trials. *Allison* also rejected such "hybrid" classes.

With the Fifth and Second circuits divided on the standards for determining when a (b)(2) class is available because the damages sought are incidental, it may take a Supreme Court decision to decide the issue. If the Allison approach is followed, employment discrimination class actions will be severely affected, see Hart, Will Employment Discrimination Class Actions Survive?, 37 Akron L. Rev. 811 (2004), and strategic shaping of a class action primarily for injunctive relief (despite seeking substantial damages) will not generally permit plaintiffs to avoid the additional requirements of (b)(3).

IN THE MATTER OF RHONE–POULENC RORER, INC.

United States Court of Appeals, Seventh Circuit, 1995.
51 F.3d 1293.

Before POSNER, Chief Judge, and BAUER and ROVNER, Circuit Judges.
POSNER, Chief Judge.

Drug companies that manufacture blood solids are the defendants in a nationwide class action brought on behalf of hemophiliacs infected by the AIDS virus as a consequence of using the defendants' products. The defendants have filed with us a petition for mandamus, asking us to direct the district judge to rescind his order certifying the case as a class action. [Although mandamus is very rarely available to allow appellate review before final judgment, the court found it appropriate because the case was "quite extraordinary," and because the writ was sought to protect the right to jury trial. The timing of appellate review is examined in Chapter XII.]

The suit to which the petition for mandamus relates, Wadleigh v. Rhone–Poulenc Rorer Inc., 157 F.R.D. 410 [N.D.Ill.1994], arises out of the infection of a substantial fraction of the hemophiliac population of this country by the AIDS virus because the blood supply was contaminated by the virus before the nature of the disease was well understood or adequate methods of screening the blood supply existed. The AIDS virus (HIV—human immunodeficiency virus) is transmitted by the exchange of bodily fluids, primarily semen and blood. Hemophiliacs depend on blood solids that contain the clotting factors whose absence defines their disease. These blood solids are concentrated from blood obtained from many donors. If just one of the donors is infected with the AIDS virus the probability that the blood solids manufactured in part from his blood will be infected is very high unless the blood is treated with heat to kill the virus.

First identified in 1981, AIDS was diagnosed in hemophiliacs beginning in 1982, and by 1984 the medical community agreed that the virus was transmitted by blood as well as by semen. That year it was demonstrated that treatment with heat could kill the virus in the blood supply and in the following year a reliable test for the presence of the virus in blood was developed. By this time, however, a large number of hemophiliacs had become infected. Since 1984 physicians have been advised to place hemophiliacs on heat-treated blood solids, and since 1985 all blood donated for the manufacture of blood solids has been screened and supplies discovered to be HIV-positive have been discarded. Supplies that test negative still are heat-treated, because the test is not infallible and in particular may fail to detect the virus in persons who became infected within six months before taking the test.

The plaintiffs have presented evidence that 2,000 hemophiliacs have died of AIDS and that half or more of the remaining U.S. hemophiliac population of 20,000 may be HIV-positive. Unless there are dramatic breakthroughs in the treatment of HIV or AIDS, all infected persons will die from the disease. The reason so many are infected even though the supply of blood for the manufacture of blood solids (as for transfusions) has been safe since the mid–80s is that the disease has a very long incubation period; the median period for hemophiliacs may be as long as 11 years. Probably most of the hemophiliacs who are now HIV-positive, or have AIDS, or have died of AIDS were infected in the early 1980s, when the blood supply was contaminated.

Some 300 lawsuits, involving some 400 plaintiffs, have been filed, 60 percent of them in state courts, 40 percent in federal district courts under the diversity jurisdiction, seeking to impose tort liability on the defendants for the transmission of HIV to hemophiliacs in blood solids manufactured by the defendants. Obviously these 400 plaintiffs represent only a small fraction of the hemophiliacs (or their next of kin, in cases in which the hemophiliac has died) who are infected by HIV or have died of AIDS. One of the 300 cases is *Wadleigh,* filed in September 1993, the case that the district judge certified as a class action. Thirteen other cases have been tried already in various courts around the country, and the defendants have won twelve of them. All the cases brought in federal court (like *Wadleigh*)—cases brought under the diversity jurisdiction—have been consolidated for pretrial discovery in the Northern District of Illinois by the panel on multidistrict litigation.

The plaintiffs advance two principal theories of liability. The first is that before anyone had heard of AIDS or HIV, it was known that Hepatitis B, a lethal disease though less so than HIV–AIDS, could be transmitted either through blood transfusions or through injection of blood solids. The plaintiffs argue that due care with respect to the risk of infection with Hepatitis B required the defendants to take measures to purge that virus from their blood solids, whether by treating the blood they bought or by screening the donors—perhaps by refusing to deal with paid donors, known to be a class at high risk of being infected with Hepatitis B. The defendants' failure to take effective measures was, the plaintiffs claim, negligent. Had the defendants not been negligent, the plaintiffs further argue, hemophiliacs would have been protected not only against Hepatitis B but also, albeit fortuitously or as the plaintiffs put it "serendipitously," against HIV.

The plaintiffs' second theory of liability is more conventional. It is that the defendants, again negligently, dragged their heels in screening donors and taking other measures to prevent contamination of blood solids by HIV when they learned about the disease in the early 1980s. The plaintiffs have other theories of liability as well, including strict products liability, but it is not necessary for us to get into them.

The district judge did not think it feasible to certify *Wadleigh* as a class action for the adjudication of the entire controversy between the plaintiffs and the defendants. Fed.R.Civ.P. 23(b)(3). The differences in the date of infection alone of the thousands of potential class members would make such a procedure infeasible. Hemophiliacs infected before anyone knew about the contamination of blood solids by HIV could not rely on the second theory of liability, while hemophiliacs infected after the blood supply became safe (not perfectly safe, but nearly so) probably were not infected by any of the defendants' products. Instead the judge certified the suit "as a class action with respect to particular issues" only. Fed.R.Civ.P. 23(c)(4)(A). He explained this decision in an opinion which implied that he did not envisage the entry of a final judgment but rather the rendition by a jury of a special verdict that would answer a number of questions bearing, perhaps decisively, on whether the defendants are negligent under either of the theories sketched above. If the special verdict found no negligence under either theory, that presumably would be the end of all the cases unless other theories of liability proved viable. If the special verdict found negligence, individual members of the class would then file individual tort suits in state and federal district courts around the nation and would use the special verdict, in conjunction with the doctrine of collateral estoppel, to block relitigation of the issue of negligence.

With all due respect for the district judge's commendable desire to experiment with an innovative procedure for streamlining the adjudication of this "mass tort," we believe that his plan so far exceeds the permissible bounds of discretion in the management of federal litigation as to compel us to intervene and order decertification. The plaintiffs' able counsel argues that we need not intervene now, that it will be time enough to intervene if and when a special verdict adverse to the defendants is entered and an appeal taken to us. But of course a verdict as such is not an appealable order. Only when a final judgment is entered, determining liability and assessing damages, will the case, including interim rulings such as the certification of certain issues in the case for determination in a class action, be appealable to us. Since without a final judgment the special verdict would not (with an exception noted later in this opinion) even have collateral estoppel effect, the district judge may have intended that the special verdict would be followed by a trial on any remaining liability issues, and on damages, limited to Wadleigh and the other named plaintiffs in the *Wadleigh* case. That trial would culminate in a final judgment, which would both be appealable to us and impart collateral estoppel effect to the special verdict. The members of the class, other than the named plaintiffs, would take the special verdict back to their home districts and use it to limit the scope of the individual trials that would be necessary—for remember that the district judge has refused to certify the case as a class action for a final adjudication of the controversy between the class and the defendants—to determine each class member's actual entitlement to damages and in what amount.

* * *

[W]e shall assume * * * that eventually there will be a final judgment to review. Only it will come too late to provide effective relief to the defendants; and this is an important consideration in relation to the first condition for mandamus, that the challenged ruling of the district court have inflicted irreparable harm, which is to say harm that cannot be rectified by an appeal from the final judgment in the lawsuit. The reason that an appeal will come too late to provide effective relief for these defendants is the sheer magnitude of the risk to which the class action, in contrast to the individual actions pending or likely, exposes them. Consider the situation that would obtain if the class had not been certified. The defendants would be facing 300 suits. More might be filed, but probably only a few more, because the statutes of limitations in the various states are rapidly expiring for potential plaintiffs. The blood supply has been safe since 1985. That is ten years ago. The risk to hemophiliacs of having become infected with HIV has been widely publicized; it is unlikely that many hemophiliacs are unaware of it. Under the usual discovery statute of limitations, they would have to have taken steps years ago to determine their infection status, and having found out file suit within the limitations period running from the date of discovery, in order to preserve their rights.

Three hundred is not a trivial number of lawsuits. The potential damages in each one are great. But the defendants have won twelve of the first thirteen, and, if this is a representative sample, they are likely to win most of the remaining ones as well. Perhaps in the end, if class-action treatment is denied (it has been denied in all the other hemophiliac HIV suits in which class certification has been sought), they will be compelled to pay damages in only 25 cases, involving a potential liability of perhaps no more than $125 million altogether. These are guesses, of course, but they are at once conservative and usable for the limited purpose of comparing the situation that will face the defendants if the class certification stands. All of a sudden they will face thousands of plaintiffs. Many may already be barred by the statute of limitations, as we have suggested, though its further running was tolled by the filing of *Wadleigh* as a class action.

Suppose that 5,000 of the potential class members are not yet barred by the statute of limitations. And suppose the named plaintiffs in *Wadleigh* win the class portion of this case to the extent of establishing the defendants' liability under either of the two negligence theories. It is true that this would only be prima facie liability, that the defendants would have various defenses. But they could not be confident that the defenses would prevail. They might, therefore, easily be facing $25 billion in potential liability (conceivably more), and with it bankruptcy. They may not wish to roll these dice. That is putting it mildly. They will be under intense pressure to settle.

* * *

We do not want to be misunderstood as saying that class actions are bad because they place pressure on defendants to settle. That pressure is a reality, but it must be balanced against the undoubted benefits of the class action that have made it an authorized procedure for employment by federal courts. We have yet to consider the balance. All that our discussion to this point has shown is that the first condition for the grant of mandamus—that the challenged ruling not be effectively reviewable at the end of the case—is fulfilled. The ruling will inflict irreparable harm; the next question is whether the ruling can fairly be described as usurpative. We have formulated this second condition as narrowly, as stringently, as can be, but even so formulated we think it is fulfilled. We do not mean to suggest that the district judge is engaged in a deliberate power-grab. We have no reason to suppose that he wants to preside over an unwieldy class action. We believe that he was responding imaginatively and in the best of faith to the challenge that mass torts, graphically illustrated by the avalanche of asbestos litigation, pose for the federal courts. But the plan that he has devised for the HIV-hemophilia litigation exceeds the bounds of allowable judicial discretion. Three concerns, none of them necessarily sufficient in itself but cumulatively compelling, persuade us to this conclusion.

The first is a concern with forcing these defendants to stake their companies on the outcome of a single jury trial, or be forced by fear of the risk of bankruptcy to settle even if they have no legal liability, when it is entirely feasible to allow a final, authoritative determination of their liability for the colossal misfortune that has befallen the hemophiliac population to emerge from a decentralized process of multiple trials, involving different juries, and different standards of liability, in different jurisdictions; and when, in addition, the preliminary indications are that the defendants are not liable for the grievous harm that has befallen the members of the class. These qualifications are important. In most class actions—and those the ones in which the rationale for the procedure is most compelling—individual suits are infeasible because the claim of each class member is tiny relative to the expense of litigation. That plainly is not the situation here. A notable feature of this case, and one that has not been remarked upon or encountered, so far as we are aware, in previous cases, is the demonstrated great likelihood that the plaintiffs' claims, despite their human appeal, lack legal merit. This is the inference from the defendants' having won 92.3 percent (12/13) of the cases to have gone to judgment. Granted, thirteen is a small sample and further trials, if they are held, may alter the pattern that the sample reveals. But whether they do or not, the result will be robust if these further trials are permitted to go forward, because the pattern that results will reflect a consensus, or at least a pooling of judgment, of many different tribunals.

For this consensus or maturing of judgment the district judge proposes to substitute a single trial before a single jury instructed in accordance with no actual law of any jurisdiction—a jury that will receive a kind of Esperanto instruction, merging the negligence standards of the 50 states and the District of Columbia. One jury, consisting of six persons (the standard federal civil jury nowadays consists of six regular jurors and two alternates), will hold the fate of an industry in the palm of its hand. This jury, jury number fourteen, may disagree with twelve of the previous thirteen juries—and hurl the industry into bankruptcy. That kind of thing can happen in our system of civil justice (it is not likely to happen, because the industry is likely to settle—whether or not it really is liable) without violating anyone's legal rights. But it need not be tolerated when the alternative exists of submitting an issue to multiple juries constituting in the aggregate a much larger and more diverse sample of decision-makers. That would not be a feasible option if the stakes to each class member were too slight to repay the cost of suit, even though the aggregate stakes were very large and would repay the costs of a consolidated proceeding. But this is not the case with regard to the HIV-hemophilia litigation. Each plaintiff if successful is apt to receive a judgment in the millions. With the aggregate stakes in the tens or hundreds of millions of dollars, or even in the billions, it is not a waste of judicial resources to conduct more than one trial, before more than six jurors, to determine whether a major segment of the international pharmaceutical industry is to follow the asbestos manufacturers into Chapter 11.

We have hinted at the second reason for concern that the district judge exceeded the bounds of permissible judicial discretion. He proposes to have a jury determine the negligence of the defendants under a legal standard that does not actually exist anywhere in the world. One is put in mind of the concept of "general" common law that prevailed in the era of Swift v. Tyson. The assumption is that the common law of the 50 states and the District of Columbia, at least so far as bears on a claim of negligence against drug companies, is basically uniform and can be abstracted in a single instruction. It is no doubt true that at some level of generality the law of negligence is one, not only nationwide but worldwide. Negligence is a failure to take due care, and due care a function of the probability and magnitude of an accident and the costs of avoiding it. A jury can be asked whether the defendants took due care. And in many cases such differences as there are among the tort rules of the different states would not affect the outcome. The Second Circuit was willing to assume dubitante that this was true of the issues certified for class determination in the Agent Orange litigation. In re Diamond Shamrock Chemicals Co., 725 F.2d 858, 861 (2d Cir.1984).

We doubt that it is true in general, and we greatly doubt that it is true in a case such as this in which one of the theories pressed by the plaintiffs, the "serendipity" theory, is novel. If one instruction on negligence will serve to instruct the jury on the legal standard of every state of the United States applicable to a novel claim, implying that the claim despite its controversiality would be decided identically in all 50 states and the District of Columbia, one wonders what the Supreme Court thought it was doing in the *Erie* case when it held that it was unconstitutional for federal courts in diversity cases to apply general common law rather than the common law of the state whose law would apply if the case were being tried in state rather than federal court. Erie R.R. v. Tompkins, 304 U.S. 64, 78–80, 58 S.Ct. 817, 822, 82 L.Ed. 1188 (1938).* The law of negligence, including subsidiary concepts such as duty of care, foreseeability, and proximate cause, may as the plaintiffs have argued forcefully to us differ among the states only in nuance, though we think not, for a reason discussed later. But nuance can be important, and its significance is suggested by a comparison of differing state pattern instructions on negligence and differing judicial formulations of the meaning of negligence and the subordinate concepts. [Judge Posner cited decisions from state courts across the country.] "The common law is not a brooding omnipresence in the sky, but the articulate voice of some sovereign or quasi sovereign that can be identified." Southern Pacific Co. v. Jensen, 244 U.S. 205, 222, 37 S.Ct. 524, 531, 61 L.Ed. 1086 (1917) (Holmes, J., dissenting). The voices of the quasi-sovereigns that are the states of the United States sing negligence with a different pitch.

The "serendipity" theory advanced by the plaintiffs in Wadleigh is that if the defendants did not do enough to protect hemophiliacs from the risk of Hepatitis B, they are liable to hemophiliacs for any consequences—including infection by the more dangerous and at the time completely unknown AIDS virus—that proper measures against Hepatitis B would, all unexpectedly, have averted. This theory of liability,

---

* *Erie* requires federal courts to apply state law to issues not governed by federal   law. It will be examined in detail in Chapter XI.—Eds.

which draws support from Judge Friendly's opinion in Petition of Kinsman Transit Co., supra, 338 F.2d [708] at 725 [(2d Cir.1964)], dispenses, rightly or wrongly from the standpoint of the Platonic Form of negligence, with proof of foreseeability, even though a number of states, in formulating their tests for negligence, incorporate the foreseeability of the risk into the test. These states follow Judge Cardozo's famous opinion in Palsgraf v. Long Island R.R., 248 N.Y. 339, 162 N.E. 99 (1928), under which the HIV plaintiffs might (we do not say would— we express no view on the substantive issues in this litigation) be barred from recovery on the ground that they were unforeseeable victims of the alleged failure of the defendants to take adequate precautions against infecting hemophiliacs with Hepatitis B and that therefore the drug companies had not violated any duty of care to them.

The plaintiffs' second theory focuses on the questions when the defendants should have learned about the danger of HIV in the blood supply and when, having learned about it, they should have taken steps to eliminate the danger or at least warn hemophiliacs or their physicians of it. These questions also may be sensitive to the precise way in which a state formulates its standard of negligence. If not, one begins to wonder why this country bothers with different state legal systems.

Both theories, incidentally, may be affected by differing state views on the role of industry practice or custom in determining the existence of negligence. In some states, the standard of care for a physician, hospital, or other provider of medical services, including blood banks, is a professional standard, that is, the standard fixed by the relevant profession. In others, it is the standard of ordinary care, which may, depending on judge or jury, exceed the professional standard. Which approach a state follows, and whether in those states that follow the professional-standard approach manufacturers of blood solids would be assimilated to blood banks as providers of medical services entitled to shelter under the professional standard, could make a big difference in the liability of these manufacturers. We note that persons infected by HIV through blood transfusions appear to have had little better luck suing blood banks than HIV-positive hemophiliacs have had suing the manufacturers of blood solids.

* * * [U]nder the district judge's plan the thousands of members of the plaintiff class will have their rights determined, and the four defendant manufacturers will have their duties determined, under a law that is merely an amalgam, an averaging, of the nonidentical negligence laws of 51 jurisdictions. No one doubts that Congress could constitutionally prescribe a uniform standard of liability for manufacturers of blood solids. It might we suppose promulgate pertinent provisions of the Restatement (Second) of Torts. The point of *Erie* is that Article III of the Constitution does not empower the federal courts to create such a regime for diversity cases.

If in the course of individual litigations by HIV-positive hemophiliacs juries render special verdicts that contain findings which do not depend on the differing state standards of negligence—for example a finding concerning the date at which one or more of the defendants learned of the danger of HIV contamination of the blood supply—these findings may be given collateral estoppel effect in other lawsuits, at least in states that allow "offensive" use of collateral estoppel. In that way the essential purpose of the class action crafted by Judge Grady will be accomplished. If there are relevant differences in state law, findings in one suit will not be given collateral estoppel effect in others, and that is as it should be.

The plaintiffs argue that an equally important purpose of the class certification is to overcome the shyness or shame that many people feel at acknowledging that they have AIDS or are HIV-positive even when the source of infection is not a stigmatized act. That, the plaintiffs tell us, is why so few HIV-positive hemophiliacs have sued. We do not see how a class action limited to a handful of supposedly common issues can alleviate that problem. Any class member who wants a share in any judgment for damages or in any settlement will have to step forward at some point and identify himself as having AIDS or being HIV-positive. He will have to offer jury findings as collateral estoppel, overcome the defendants' defenses to liability (including possible efforts to show that the class member became infected with HIV through a source other than the defendants' product), and establish his damages. If the privacy of these class members in these follow-on proceedings to the class action is sought to be protected by denominating them "John Does," that is something that can equally well be done in individual lawsuits. The "John Doe" device—and with it the issue of privacy—is independent of class certification.

The third respect in which we believe that the district judge has exceeded his authority concerns the point at which his plan of action proposes to divide the trial of the issues that he has certified for class-action treatment from the other issues involved in the thousands of actual and potential claims of the representatives and members of the class. Bifurcation and even finer divisions of lawsuits into separate trials are authorized in federal district courts. Fed.R.Civ.P. 42(b). And a decision to employ the procedure is reviewed deferentially. However, as we have been at pains to stress recently, the district judge must carve at the joint. Of particular relevance here, the judge must not divide issues between separate trials in such a way that the same issue is reexamined by different juries. The problem is not inherent in bifurcation. It does not arise when the same jury is to try the successive phases of the litigation. But most of the separate "cases" that compose this class action will be tried, after the initial trial in the Northern District of Illinois, in different courts, scattered throughout the country. The right to a jury trial in federal civil cases, conferred by the Seventh Amendment, is a right to have juriable issues determined by the first jury impaneled to hear them (provided there are no errors warranting a new trial), and not reexamined by another finder of fact. This would be obvious if the second finder of fact were a judge. But it is equally true if it is another jury. * * *

The plan of the district judge in this case is inconsistent with the principle that the findings of one jury are not to be reexamined by a second, or third, or nth jury. The first jury will not determine liability. It will determine merely whether one or more of the defendants was negligent under one of the two theories. The first jury may go on to decide the additional issues with regard to the named plaintiffs. But it will not decide them with regard to the other class members. Unless the defendants settle, a second (and third, and fourth, and hundredth, and conceivably thousandth) jury will have to decide, in individual follow-on litigation by class members not named as plaintiffs in the *Wadleigh* case, such issues as comparative negligence—did any class members knowingly continue to use unsafe blood solids after they learned or should have learned of the risk of contamination with HIV?—and proximate causation. Both issues overlap the issue of the defendants' negligence. Comparative negligence entails, as the name implies, a comparison of the degree of negligence of plaintiff and defendant. Proximate causation is found by determining whether the harm to the plaintiff followed in some sense naturally, uninterruptedly, and with reasonable probability from the negligent act of the defendant. It overlaps the issue of the defendants' negligence even when the state's law does not (as many states do) make the foreseeability of the risk to which the defendant subjected the plaintiff an explicit ingredient of negligence. A second or subsequent jury might find that the defendants' failure to take precautions against infection with Hepatitis B could not be thought the proximate cause of the plaintiffs' infection with HIV, a different and unknown blood-borne virus. How the resulting inconsistency between juries could be prevented escapes us.

* * *

We know that an approach similar to that proposed by Judge Grady has been approved for asbestos litigation. See in particular Jenkins v. Raymark Industries, Inc., 782 F.2d 468 (5th Cir.1986); In re School Asbestos Litigation, 789 F.2d 996 (3d Cir.1986). Most federal courts, however, refuse to permit the use of the class-action device in mass-tort cases, even asbestos cases. Those courts that have permitted it have been criticized, and alternatives have been suggested which recognize that a sample of trials makes more sense than entrusting the fate of an industry to a single jury. The number of asbestos cases was so great as to exert a well-nigh irresistible pressure to bend the normal rules. No comparable pressure is exerted by the HIV-hemophilia litigation. That litigation can be handled in the normal way without undue inconvenience to the parties or to the state or federal courts.

The defendants have pointed out other serious problems with the district judge's plan, but it is unnecessary to discuss them. The petition for a writ of mandamus is granted, and the district judge is directed to decertify the plaintiff class.

① prompt a settlement

ILANA DIAMOND ROVNER, Circuit Judge, dissenting.

The majority today takes the extraordinary step of granting defendants' petition for a writ of mandamus and directing the district court to rescind its order certifying the plaintiff class. Although certification orders like this one are not immediately appealable, the majority seizes upon our mandamus powers to effectively circumvent that rule. Because, in my view, our consideration of Judge Grady's decision to certify an issue class under Fed.R.Civ.P. 23(c)(4) should await an appeal from the final judgment in Wadleigh, I would deny the writ.

* * *

[I] cannot agree with the majority's premise that Judge Grady's order in fact will prompt a settlement. Contrary to the clear implication of the majority's opinion, the class portion of the anticipated trial in this case would not go so far as to establish defendants' liability to a class of plaintiffs; it would instead resolve only the question of whether defendants were negligent in distributing tainted clotting factor at any particular point in time. Even if defendants were faced with an adverse class verdict, then, a plaintiff still would be required to clear a number of hurdles before he would be entitled to a judgment. For example, defendants no doubt would contest at that stage whether a particular plaintiff could establish proximate causation or whether his or her claim is in any event barred by the statute of limitations. Thus, contrary to the majority's implication, a class verdict in favor of plaintiffs would not automatically entitle each member of the class to a seven-figure judgment. The defendants will thus have ample opportunity to settle should they lose the class trial. And that would seem to me an advisable strategy in light of the success they have had in earlier cases. That factor distinguishes this case from a more standard class action, where a non-bifurcated trial would resolve all relevant issues and conclusively establish liability to the class. Perhaps that explains why defendants' own arguments in support of their petition are based on the assumption that a class trial would ensue, rather than on the proposition that a settlement would follow inevitably from Judge Grady's order.

Finally, although the availability of review on direct appeal after final judgment makes it unnecessary for me to discuss the merits of the certification order, the majority's arguments addressed to the propriety of forcing "defendants to stake their companies on the outcome of a single jury trial" or of allowing a single jury to "hold the fate of an industry in the palm of its hand" seem to me at odds with Fed.R.Civ.P. 23 itself. That rule expressly permits class treatment of such claims when its requirements are met, regardless of the magnitude of potential liability. And I see nothing in Rule 23, or in any of the relevant cases, that would make likelihood of success on the merits a prerequisite for class certification. The majority's preference for avoiding a class trial and for submitting the negligence issue "to multiple juries constituting in the aggregate a much larger and more diverse sample of decision-makers" is a rationale for amending the rule, not for avoiding its application in a specific case.

I must concede that I too have doubts about whether the class trial proposed by Judge Grady will succeed, and I sympathize with many of the apprehensions of my brothers. But in my view, the law requires that Judge Grady's plan be given the opportunity to succeed. Class certification orders are, after all, conditional orders subject to modification or revocation as the circumstances warrant. If the problems envisioned by the majority were to materialize at a class trial, Judge Grady could always modify his earlier ruling or even abandon it altogether, and his response in that regard would be reviewable by this court on direct appeal, once the actual ramifications of the certification order were evident.

Notes and Questions

1. The numerosity of the class was not challenged in *Rhone-Poulenc* (the estimated number of class members being more than 20,000). The test for numerosity is whether "the class is so numerous that joinder of all members is impracticable." Because there is no mystical number at which the numerosity requirement is established, courts have found this element satisfied when the putative class consists of as few as 30 to 40 class members. See Markham v. White, 171 F.R.D. 217, 221 (N.D.Ill.1997) (35–40 class members); Hendricks–Robinson v. Excel Corp., 164 F.R.D. 667, 671 (C.D.Ill.1996) (38 class members); Riordan v. Smith Barney, 113 F.R.D. 60, 62 (N.D.Ill.1986) (29 class members). Numerosity was found lacking in State of Utah v. American Pipe & Const. Co., 49 F.R.D. 17 (C.D.Cal.1969), where there were 350 potential class numbers. Courts look to such factors as the relative difficulties of joinder versus class treatment, whether individual joinder might still be accompanied by representation by a single attorney and identical pleadings, and the geographical location of the potential plaintiffs.

2. Some courts have found a lack of numerosity when there is no showing of "interest" in filing suit by a sufficient number of class members who have a sizable economic stake. In Block v. First Blood Associates, 743 F.Supp. 194 (S.D.N.Y.1990), 763 F.Supp. 746 (S.D.N.Y.1991), aff'd, 988 F.2d 344 (2d Cir.1993), a securities fraud class action was sought on behalf of purchasers of units in a limited partnership that owned the film "Rambo–First Blood." The court denied class certification with leave to renew within 90 days if plaintiffs "can establish that a meaningful number of limited partners have expressed an identity of interest" in the case. It noted that only 24 of the 57 investors (with investments ranging from $50,000 to $400,000) had expressed interest in the suit and that "the putative class members . . . are easily identifiable and have the financial resources and stake in the partnership which would make joinder practicable." This decision has been criticized as amounting to an "opt in" requirement: "That most did not express an 'interest' in joining suggests joinder impracticability, not the opposite. And as in all opt-in situations, the 'response' of the class members likely would have been far more positive had there already been a class recovery on their behalf." 16 Class Action Reports 173 (1993).

3. The Advisory Committee Note accompanying the 1966 amendment to Rule 23 warned that "a 'mass accident' resulting in injuries to numerous persons is ordinarily not appropriate for a class action" because it "would degenerate in practice into multiple lawsuits separately tried." However, as the volume of product liability and toxic exposure litigation rose, the class action became more attractive in such cases. Judge Jack Weinstein observed regarding the Advisory Committee Note: "As authority for this warning against attempts to use class actions in torts, the note cites an article [I] wrote as a law professor. As a judge [I have] been forced to ignore this indiscretion when faced with the practicalities of mass tort litigation. In the earlier 1960's we did not fully understand the implications of mass tort demands on our legal system." Weinstein & Hershenov, The Effects of Equity on Mass Torts, 1991 U.Ill.L.Rev. 269, 288.

4. Mass torts vary in their suitability for class action treatment. Those most amenable are mass accident cases, like a train wreck, plane crash, or collapse of a bridge or building. "In such cases, the focus of a common trial will generally be on the single event and the conduct of the defendant in bringing it about. Liability and causation issues are generally common, and defensive issues involving the conduct of the plaintiffs are minimal." Sherman, Complex Litigation: Aggregating Related Cases for Unitary Disposition, 30 Chuo Univ. Comp. L. Rev. 57, 68 (Tokyo 1996). The more difficult cases are those involving exposure to environmental conditions, medicines, or products. "Cases involving exposure of many persons to toxic substances at different times and places could still be suitable for aggregate treatment if the focus of the suit will be on the single course of conduct or condition at a single site without likelihood of individualized defensive or causation issues. * * * Tending towards the side disfavoring aggregation would be mass toxic tort suits in which large numbers of persons claim exposure under very differing conditions to a product or substance which is only harmful under certain circumstances relating to individual characteristics and in which the conduct of each class member may give rise to differing defenses to which the defendant is entitled under substantive law." Id. at 69. Where would *Rhone-Poulenc* fit on this continuum?

5. After many refusals of courts to certify class actions in product liability suits against manufacturers of asbestos, the Fifth Circuit in Jenkins v. Raymark Indus., Inc., 782 F.2d 468 (5th Cir.1986), upheld the class certification for some 5,000 pending asbestos cases to resolve the "state of the art" defense raised in every case. It agreed with the district judge's conclusion that "[c]onsiderable savings, both for the litigants and for the court, could be gained by resolving this and other defense and defense-related questions, including product identification, product defectiveness, gross negligence and punitive damages, in one class trial." Over the following decade, a number of courts, both federal and state, certified mass tort class actions. E.g., Sterling v. Velsicol Chemical Corp., 855 F.2d 1188 (6th Cir.1988) (class action for leakage of toxics from landfill). *Rhone-Poulenc* was one of the first of a number of federal appellate opinions that took a more critical view of what some considered an abusive use of class actions.

Shortly after the *Rhone-Poulenc* decision, the Fifth Circuit dealt with what was termed the largest class action in history. Castano v. American Tobacco Co., 84 F.3d 734 (5th Cir.1996), was a class action brought on behalf of all "nicotine-addicted" smokers (estimated at 50 million people) for damages for mental and emotional suffering. In reversing class certification, the court expressed doubt that the trial of the common issues (such as the tobacco companies' conduct and the addictive nature of tobacco) would lead to the efficient termination of the litigation because significant issues still had to be resolved individually (such as the nicotine addiction of each class member). Like *Rhone-Poulenc*, it also found that the case could not be brought as a nationwide class action because of the differences in state substantive laws.

The same year, a decision of the Sixth Circuit in In re American Medical Systems, Inc., 75 F.3d 1069 (6th Cir.1996), overturned class certification of a nationwide class of people who suffered damages from implants of allegedly defective penile prostheses manufactured by defendant. The appellate court did not reject mass tort class actions out of hand, but found that individualized issues would predominate, making a class trial unmanageable. It noted that class members had used at least ten different models of the prosthesis and that the legal claims would "differ depending upon the model and the year it was issued." It also found that there would be individualized evidence as to such issues as "surgical error, improper use of the device, anatomical incompatibility, infection, device malfunction, or psychological problems," as well as what statements, oral or written, were made to class members and whether they relied on them.

Class certification of mass torts now depends very much on the circumstances of each case. See, for example, Valentino v. Carter–Wallace, Inc., 97 F.3d 1227 (9th Cir.1996), a class action on behalf of users of an epilepsy drug, claiming the manufacturer had not warned of serious side effects. Because the case involved only one manufacturer, one product, and a single marketing program over a relatively short period of time, the appellate court thought that the case was likely to be more manageable, although it held that the district court's certification was not justified on the record before it due to the requirements of predominance and superiority.

The difficulties presented by mass tort class actions may prompt re-examination of the attitude the courts sometimes utilize in scrutinizing these cases. Would it be more appropriate to emphasize the class itself as an entity, thereby downplaying individual concerns? For a reflection on these questions, see Shapiro, Class Actions: The Class as Party and Client, 73 Notre Dame L.Rev. 913 (1998).

6. Jenkins v. Raymark Indus., Inc. (supra note 5) approved an asbestos class action even though there were many individualized issues (for example, whether each class member had been exposed to the defendant's product, affirmative defenses like the statute of limitations, and measurement of damages). Its solution was the use of "phased trials." First there would be a classwide trial of the common issues (e.g., defectiveness of the product and knowledge of the defendant about the defect), and then the individual issues would be resolved in mini-trials of seven to ten plaintiffs. This use of phased trials is also called "bifurcation" or "polyfurcation" (when there are more than two phases). One attractive feature of such a plan is that once the common issues are decided, the parties may be more inclined to settle, making further individualized phases unnecessary.

Phased or bifurcated trials are conducted pursuant to the authority provided in Rule 23(c)(4) that "when appropriate an action may be brought or maintained as a class action with respect to particular issues." Professor Laura Hines examined the drafting history and concluded that "[i]n light of the complete absence of evidence that the Committee ever conceived of (c)(4)(a) as anything other than a 'usable detail,'" "issue" certification should not be permitted to circumvent the predominance requirement of Rule 23(b)(3). Hines, Challenging the Issue Class Action End–Run, 52 Emory L.J. 758 (2003). "Issue" certifications, however, are still commonplace, particularly in state courts.

If individual trials are necessary in a later phase, there is still a question whether any efficiency has really been obtained by certifying a class action only for the common issues. When a later phase requires individualized trials of such issues as reliance, causation, and damages, some of the same evidence necessary for the common trial may have to be presented again, raising a question as to whether there has been any economy in certifying the class in the first place. On the other hand, issues that normally require individualized evidence can sometimes be made susceptible to common proof. For example, in an asbestos case involving claims of exposure at a single facility (such as an oil refinery or ship), proof of class members' exposure to defendant's asbestos (which is critical to causation) could be presented by common evidence that the asbestos was present in certain rooms and locations during certain periods of time. Then each class member's exposure could be determined administratively by referring to employment records indicating where and when each class member worked, without having to present individualized evidence at the trial. Damages are always an individualized issue, but courts have now generally accepted that damages can be severed from liability and tried separately in individual or mini-trials after a class trial on liability.

A creative attempt to avoid individualized evidence in an asbestos class action as to such individual issues and causation and damages was adopted in Cimino v. Raymark Industries, Inc., 751 F.Supp. 649 (E.D. Tex. 1990). After a phase I common trial on such classwide issues as the defectiveness of the product, the judge held individual trials of 160 plaintiffs randomly selected from the five categories of asbestos diseases and extrapolated an average damage award for each class member. However, on appeal the Fifth Circuit ruled that this violated the 7th Amendment rights of the defendants to a jury determination of causation and damages as to each class member. 151 F.3d 297 (5th Cir.1998).

7. How important to the holding in *Rhone-Poulenc* is the concern that class certification creates insurmountable pressure on defendants to settle? One federal district judge has taken issue with the importance given this concern by Judge Posner's "economic theories and distrust of juries." In re Telectronics Pacing Systems, Inc., 172 F.R.D. 271 (S.D.Ohio 1997). Class treatment certainly increases the stakes for defendants, but it is also an opportunity for defendants to resolve all the claims at one time and to reduce the transaction costs of multiple litigation. Keep these issues in mind in connection with settlement classes, note 12 below.

8. The charge of judicial blackmail referred to in *Rhone-Poulenc* took on added weight in *Castano* where the court found that the "nicotine addiction" claims were "novel" legal issues that had not had the benefit of prior litigation. The opinion noted that with such "immature torts" there is no learning curve and thus a greater likelihood of error. Consistent with *Castano's* demand for a "track record" of trials from which to draw the information necessary to make the predominance and superiority determinations, one court ordered three bellwether trials (the first involving five plaintiffs) "to familiarize itself and the parties with the contours of this litigation." In re Norplant Contraceptive Prods. Liabil. Litig., MDL No. 1039, order of May 17, 1996 (E.D. Tex.), 955 F.Supp. 700 (E.D.Tex.1997).

9. Both the Seventh Circuit in *Rhone-Poulenc* and the Fifth Circuit in *Castano* expressed concern over how a unitary trial could be conducted in a nationwide class action where there are variations in the elements of the causes of action under different state laws. Since *Rhone-Poulenc* and *Castano*, courts have frequently refused to certify nationwide class actions for failure of plaintiffs to do a comparison of the governing state laws to indicate a class action trial is manageable. See Spence v. Glock, 227 F.3d 308 (5th Cir.2000) (in nationwide class action against Georgia gun manufacturer for design defect, there was insufficient comparative analysis of the laws of Georgia and other states to support a finding, under the forum state's choice of law rules, that Georgia law would apply); In re Bridgestone/Firestone, Inc., 288 F.3d 1012 (7th Cir.2002) (in product defect class action, the forum state's choice of law rules would call for application of the laws of the fifty states where the injury occurred rather than the principal place of business of the defendants).

Plaintiffs may argue that, under the forum's choice of law doctrine, the law of one state will apply. See Farmers Ins. Exchange v. Leonard, 125 S.W.3d 55 (Tex. App.—Austin 2003), rev. denied (Tex. 2004) (in multi-state class action on behalf of insurance agents alleging failure to comply with bonus promises, the law of California, the state where the bonus brochures and administration took place, applied); Ysbrand v. DaimlerChrysler Corp., 81 P.3d 618 (Okla. 2003) (in nationwide class action alleging breach of warranty under UCC, the law of Michigan, defendant's principal place of business, would apply). Plaintiffs may also be able to show that the laws of all the relevant states are sufficiently similar, or fall into a small number of categories, that a jury trial would be manageable. See In re Prudential Ins. Co. Sales Practices, 962 F.Supp. 450 (D.N.J. 1997) (approving a settlement class action on behalf of a nationwide class of purchasers of insurance, based on charts showing state laws would fall into a small number of similar groupings). But see Compaq Computer Corp. v. Lapray, 135 S.W.3d 657 (Tex. 2004) (state laws vary in significant ways); In re Telectronics Pacing Systems, Inc., 172 F.R.D. 271 (S.D.Ohio 1997) (compilation of state laws done by court personnel show very different standards for medical monitoring).

10. It has always been a tenet of class action procedure that courts should not consider the merits of the case in determining whether it should be certified. However, the *Castano* opinion criticized the lower court for believing that "it could not go past the pleadings for the certification decision." It said "a court must understand the claims, defenses, relevant

facts, and applicable substantive law in order to make a meaningful determination of the certification issues." If the defendants have a strong defense, or plaintiffs have a weak element in their cause of action, could a court determine that class treatment is not "superior" (see Rule 23(b)(3)) because of the likelihood that after invoking the expensive and cumbersome class action procedure, the case would still be lost?

11. Mass tort class actions were not the only class action growth industry of the 1990s. Consumer, commercial, securities, and employment class action cases, often involving claims of fraud or misrepresentation, have been common against banks, insurance companies, telephone and communications enterprises, service industries, retailers, and employers. When the same misrepresentations have been made to all class members, as in a stock prospectus or advertisement, evidence of the wrongful conduct can often be presented on a classwide basis, and common questions may predominate. Even when misrepresentations to class members are not uniform, a common policy or course of fraudulent conduct may still satisfy commonality. See Adams v. Reagan, 791 S.W.2d 284, 291 (Tex. Ct. App. 1990) ("where the defendant is alleged to have engaged in a common course of conduct, the commonality requirement is met," and "despite the fact that one of a variety of devices for deceit may have been used upon differing claimants, nevertheless a common thread of deceit runs through all alleged claims."). However, the Eleventh Circuit, in Andrews v. American Tel. & Tel. Co., 95 F.3d 1014, 1023 (11th Cir.1996), found a common policy (failure to monitor fraudulent use of an 800 number) insufficient to establish predominance of common issues because "as a practical matter, the resolution of this overarching common issue breaks down into an unmanageable variety of individual legal and factual issues."

State-law causes of action for fraud and misrepresentation generally require the plaintiff to prove reliance. Recall Insolia v. Philip Morris, Inc., supra p. 237. Even if common misrepresentations were made to the class members, proof of reliance normally requires individualized evidence which could predominate over evidence as to common issues. In federal securities fraud cases, the Supreme Court adopted a "fraud on the market" theory that "where materially misleading statements have been disseminated into an impersonal, well-developed market for securities, the reliance of individual plaintiffs on the integrity of the market may be presumed." Basic Inc. v. Levinson, 485 U.S. 224, 248, 108 S.Ct. 978, 992, 99 L.Ed.2d 194 (1988). Some courts have been willing to presume reliance in situations other than where there is a regulated market like the stock exchange. See Shores v. Sklar, 647 F.2d 462 (5th Cir.1981) (reliance is presumed where the misrepresentations at issue arise from "material" omissions); cf. Affiliated Ute Citizens v. United States, 406 U.S. 128, 92 S.Ct. 1456, 31 L.Ed.2d 741 (1972) (when an omission is involved, individualized proof of reliance is not required if the omission is material). However, individual proof of reliance is still required in many states in common-law fraud cases, raising the question whether common issues can predominate so as to allow class certification.

12. In Amchem Products, Inc. v. Windsor, 521 U.S. 591, 117 S.Ct. 2231, 138 L.Ed.2d 689 (1997), the Supreme Court addressed a settlement class action. Before the suit was even filed, twenty asbestos manufacturers

had reached an agreement with leading asbestos plaintiffs lawyers for settlement of a class action on behalf of all people in the U.S. who had been exposed occupationally to defendants' asbestos products but had not yet filed suit for personal injuries, and on behalf of the members of the exposed workers' families. The settlement included instances in which no disease had yet manifested itself ("future claims") as well as those in which the class member had suffered a medical consequence but had not yet sued. The Supreme Court agreed that "settlement is relevant to a class certification" but was cautious about this technique:

> Confronted with a request for settlement-only class certification, a district court need not inquire whether the case, if tried, would present intractable management problems, see Fed. Rule Civ. Proc. 23(b)(3)(D), for the proposal is that there be no trial. But other specifications of the rule—those designed to protect absentees by blocking unwarranted or overbroad class definitions—demand undiluted, even heightened attention in the settlement context.

The Court found that in *Amchem* the attempt to lump all future claimants together in a single class action was inappropriate and overturned the class certification. Among other things, the conflicts of interest between those with presently manifested disease and future claimants could not be ignored. The Court urged that there must be a "structural assurance of fair and adequate representation," seemingly calling for creation of appropriate subclasses, each with its own attorney.

13. *Coupon settlements*: Numerous class action settlements awarded class members coupons that can be reclaimed for services or products of the defendant rather than cash. Is this an attractive option? Consider that in many cases the class has alleged that the defendant's goods or services are defective or harmful. There is considerable concern that such a deal may provide an excuse of a large fee award to class counsel while giving the class members little of value. For example, in In re General Motors Corp. Pickup Truck Fuel Tank Prod. Liabil. Litig., 55 F.3d 768 (3d Cir.1995), the class alleged that pickup trucks sold by defendant were defective because they had side-mounted gas tanks that might burst into flame in a crash. The district court approved a settlement giving class members a nontransferable $1,000 discount certificate that could be used within 15 months to buy a new G.M. truck or van, or exchanged for a $500 discount certificate that could be transferred to somebody who wanted to buy such a G.M. product. Class counsel were to be paid $9.5 million by G.M. for achieving this result. Objectors challenged the settlement as inadequate and argued that it should not be approved under Rule 23(e).

The court of appeals agreed with the objectors, finding the settlement to be "a sophisticated GM marketing program." There was reason to doubt that many class members would want to use the certificate within the allowed 15–month period. The option of selling a coupon was hamstrung by the delay involved in exchanging the original $1,000 certificate for the $500 transferrable one, and there was no indication that there would be a market for the $500 certificate either. The court found G.M.'s willingness to pay such substantial attorneys' fees an indication that it valued the claims being released at some substantial multiple of the fee award even though the certificates did not appear to have such a value

Should "coupon settlements" be banned? Consider Miller & Singer, Nonpecuniary Class Action Settlements, 60 Law & Contemp. Probs. 97 (1997) (arguing that such settlements are sometimes desirable). Sometimes a defendant might be driven into bankruptcy if substantial cash damages are awarded, while coupons can provide class members with some benefit. "There are cases where the recovery for each class member would be small and a discount or coupon for future purchases is worth more to the class member than it costs to the defendant. This can be fair where class members will have to continue buying the defendant's service—as in a suit for overcharges by a utility—or where the suit is likely to remedy the defect in the product or service." Sherman, Consumer Class Actions: Who Are the Real Winners?, 56 Maine L. Rev. 223, 229 (2004). The Class Action Fairness Act of 2005 added § 1712 to Title 28 to deal with coupon settlements of class actions in federal court. It permits coupon settlements only after a hearing and a court finding that the settlement is "fair, reasonable and adequate for class members." 28 U.S.C.A. § 1712(e). In addition, it provides that "the portion of an attorney's fee award to class counsel that is attributable to the award of coupons shall be based on the value to class members of the coupons that are redeemed." Id., § 1712(a). A Texas statute passed in 2003 goes further, providing that "if any portion of the benefits recovered for the class are in the form of coupons or other noncash common benefits, the attorney's fees awarded in the action must be in cash and noncash amounts in the same proportion as the recovery for the class." Tex. Civ. Prac. & Rem. Code Ann. § 26.003(b) (2003).

14. Consumer class actions are often criticized for resulting in only small recoveries for class members and large fees for the attorneys. A Washington Post editorial objected that class members often only "get token payments while the lawyers receive enormous fees." Making Justice Work, Wash. Post, Nov. 25, 2002, at A14. Defenders of the class action reply that the objective of class actions is not only compensation, but also deterrence and disgorgement of wrongful profits. Most "negative value" cases, where the expected recovery is less than the cost of litigation, would not be litigated if there were no class actions, and thus wrongdoers might never have to answer for their conduct. However, such deterrence is obtained at the cost of providing handsome incentives to lawyers to finance and litigate class actions. "For good or for bad, American have rejected the kind of broad governmental regulation of business that is often found in European countries. The American preference for market approaches results in an opportunity for litigation fueled by entrepreneurial lawyers to enforce laws, regulations, and standards." Sherman, Consumer Class Actions: Who Are the Real Winners?, 56 Maine L. Rev. 223, 231–32 (2004). A Rand Corporation report on class actions commented:

> The key public policy question is whether the entrepreneurial behavior of private attorneys produces litigation that is socially beneficial. Whereas *public* attorneys general may be reluctant to bring meritorious suits because of financial or political constraints, *private* attorneys general may be too willing to bring nonmeritorious suits if these suits produce generous financial rewards for them.

D. Hensler, et al, Class Action Dilemmas: Pursuing Public Goals for Private Gain 72 (Rand Inst. for Civil Justice 2000).

15. Besides its provisions regulating coupon settlements (see supra note 11), the Class Action Fairness Act of 2005, ___ Stat. ___, also was designed to address concerns that some state courts had not been sufficiently careful in permitting consumer class actions, sometimes on the behalf of nationwide classes. It therefore expanded the ability of defendants to remove such cases to federal court, and also allows filing of such cases in federal court in the first instance. There is an exception to this federal-court jurisdiction for cases in which most of the class members come from the same state, if that state is also the residence of the "primary defendants." Whether this legislation will have a major impact on the frequency or extent of consumer class actions remains to be seen.

16. *"Limited fund" mass tort class actions*: Recall that interpleader is available when there are multiple claimants against a limited fund. See supra p. 267. In some mass tort cases, it has seemed that the claims made against defendants outstrip their assets and insurance, and efforts have been made to use this predicament as a ground for certification of a "mandatory" (no opt out) class action under Rule 23(b)(1)(B). There have long been questions about whether this practice was consistent with the rule. See Marcus, They Can't Do That, Can They? Tort Reform Via Rule 23, 80 Cornell L. Rev. 858, 877–81 (1995) (arguing that the rule does not work in such situations). In Ortiz v. Fibreboard Corp., 527 U.S. 815, 119 S.Ct. 2295, 144 L.Ed.2d 715 (1999), the Supreme Court overturned a limited fund class certification in an asbestos personal injury case but suggested that there might be situations in which this technique could be used. For an examination of the questions left unanswered by *Ortiz*, see Marcus, Benign Neglect Reconsidered, 148 U.Pa.L.Rev. 2009 (2000).

17. *Consolidation*: Some of the same issues that confront mass tort class actions have arisen in situations in which district courts use Rule 42 to consolidate large numbers of separate personal injury cases for combined trial, particularly in asbestos cases. For discussion, see Marcus, Confronting the Consolidation Conundrum, 1995 B.Y.U.L.Rev. 879.

3. Notice and Opt-out Rights

For a class to be certified under Rule 23(b)(3), "the court must direct to class members the best notice practicable under the circumstances, including individual notice to all members who can be identified through reasonable effort." Rule 23(c)(1)(A). As beefed up by the 2003 amendments to Rule 23, the rule requires that the notice must "concisely and clearly state in plain, easily understood language" certain specifics about the action, that "a class member may enter an appearance thought counsel" if desired, and that "the court will exclude from the class any member who requests exclusion, stating when and how members may elect to be excluded."

Eisen v. Carlisle & Jacquelin, 417 U.S. 156, 94 S.Ct. 2140, 40 L.Ed.2d 732 (1974), addressed the notice requirement. It was a class action brought on behalf of some six million purchasers of odd-lot shares of stock alleging improper charges. The district court found that only 2.25 million of the class members could be identified, but, because of the cost, ordered that individual notice would only be sent to those who had ten or more odd-lot trades and to 5,000 others to be selected at random. Plaintiff was also required to take out advertisements in the Wall Street Journal and New York and California papers.

The Supreme Court rejected this approach, noting that due process required that notice "reasonably calculated, under all the circumstances, to apprise interested parties of the pendency of the action and afford them an opportunity to present their objections." Mullane v. Central Hanover Bank & Trust Co., 339 U.S. 306, 70 S.Ct. 652, 94 L.Ed. 865 (1950). It therefore interpreted Rule 23(c)(2) as requiring individual notice to all the 2.25 million class members who were identifiable through reasonable notice. Furthermore, it ruled that the plaintiff had to bear the cost of the notice, reversing the district court's order that defendants pay 90% of the cost. A judge, it stated, has no authority to conduct a preliminary inquiry into the merits of a suit in order to determine whether it may be maintained as a class action, and therefore "a plaintiff must initially bear the cost of notice to the class" (except in situations where a fiduciary duty pre-existed between plaintiff and defendant, as in a shareholder derivative suit).

By imposing the cost of notice on plaintiffs, *Eisen* made class actions with a large number of class members difficult to finance. Class members could not generally be expected to pay for notice costs, and it is perhaps not surprising that most (b)(3) class actions would have to be financed by the attorneys, thus further encouraging the "entrepreneurial" nature of class action practice.

Another cost factor that plaintiffs must confront in many cases is the expense of identifying class members so that notice can be sent to them. In Oppenheimer Fund, Inc. v. Sanders, 437 U.S. 340, 98 S.Ct. 2380, 57 L.Ed.2d 253 (1978), involving a plaintiff class of securities purchasers, the Court held that defendant could not be required through discovery to compile a list of securities purchasers from its records where the effort would require computer operations costing over $16,000. The Court acknowledged that discovery could be used "to illuminate issues upon which a district court must pass in deciding whether a suit should proceed as a class action under Rule 23, such as numerosity, common questions and adequacy of representation," but concluded that the requested list did not serve this function.

In many consumer and product liability class actions where there are insufficient records of purchase, notice must be made through publication in newspapers, periodicals, radio, television, or the Internet, or through posting in places calculated to be seen by class members. Publication may sometimes be ordered as an extra precaution even when individual notice is given, in recognition of the fact that, in our mobile society, many notices sent to the last-known address will be returned or never reach the addressee. Since a high percentage of class actions are settled, the notice often comes when the parties have entered a settle-ment agreement and the court has approved it subject to notice, right to opt out, and opportunity to object by the class members.

The Class Action Fairness Act of 2005 adds a requirement that defendants provide state and federal officials with notice of any proposed settlement. See 28 U.S.C.A. § 1715.

Opt-Out Rights

The 1966 amendments abandoned the "opt-in" requirement that was contained in the old rule. In a (b)(3) suit for damages, the notice to the putative class members will tell them that they need not take any action if they want to be a member of the class, and that unless they mail in an "opt-out" form, they will be bound by the results of the litigation. One who "opts out" will be excluded as a member of the class and can pursue the claim on her own if she wishes. However, the percentage of "opt outs" in most class actions is small. This might be explained by the fact that many class members, particularly in consumer and product liability cases, are content to have the case brought on their behalf without any demands on them, or simply by the natural inclina-tion of people toward inaction in such situations. The RAND study of class actions commented:

> Most individuals are too preoccupied with daily life and too un-informed about the law to pay attention to whether they are being overcharged or otherwise inappropriately treated by those with whom they do business. Even if they believe that there is something inappropriate about a transaction, individuals are likely just to "lump it," rather than expend the time and energy necessary to remedy a perceived wrong.

D. Hensler, Class Action Dilemmas: Pursuing Public Goals for Private Gain 68 (2000).

On the other hand, the low rate of opt-outs could indicate the disinterest of class members in the suit and put into question the fairness of allowing self-appointed class representatives and attorneys to leverage their case through disinterested absent class members. Business interests have urged a change in the rule to require an affirmative act to "opt in."

Consider the following argument:

> By establishing membership in the class through the inherently passive procedure of opt-out, Rule 23 creates a framework for litigation that undermines the essential premises of the private compensatory model of adjudication. * * *

> At its start, the inherent passivity brought about by the use of opt-out sets the groundwork for an entirely comatose class of plain-tiffs, who have never chosen to enforce their private rights and are even unaware that a suit has been brought on their behalf. At its close, even a successful class action may fail to vindicate class members' private rights by providing meaningful compensation—a

result easily predictable at the outset of the suit, because of the inherent impossibility of translating a class-based award into concrete, individualized damage awards to class members. In one sense or another, both of the bookends contribute to the ultimate transformation of the class action from an aggregative private compensatory action into what amounts to a pure bounty hunter action.

Redish, Class Actions and the Democratic Difficulty: Rethinking the Intersection of Private Litigation and Public Goals, 2003 U. Chi. Legal Forum 71, 94.

Notice in (b)(1) and (b)(2) Classes

Rule 23(b)(1) and (b)(2) class actions are mandatory, that is, there is no requirement that the class members receive notice or have a right to opt out. It was assumed that the interests of the class members were so cohesive (as in a (b)(2) suit for injunctive relief that would benefit the whole class) or that the necessity for class treatment was so great (as in a (b)(1) action where individual suits would prejudice the individual class members) that class members should not be allowed to split off and bring suits individually. However, under an amendment to Rule 23(c) in 2003, the judge may order that notice be given to the individual class members, although it is still to be seen if this option is much used. The Advisory Committee Notes state that the judge's discretion to order notice "should be exercised with care." They also comment that notice in (b)(1) and (b)(2) class actions is generally less important because opt-outs are not permitted and the costs may "cripple actions that do not seek damages." Informal methods, such as "[a] simple posting in a place visited by many class members, directing attention to a source of more detailed information, may suffice."

Chapter V

OBTAINING INFORMATION FOR TRIAL

The common law pleading system, with its insistence on formulation of a single issue, left the parties relatively focused on the subjects that would be addressed at trial. But the common law provided no further assistance to the parties in obtaining information to prepare for trial. Instead (except for a "bill of discovery" in equity) the trial was a realm for surprise and dramatic maneuver.

As procedure evolved away from the common law approach to pleadings, it also shifted toward a regime of increased pre-trial disclosure of evidence. Building on the discovery practices at equity (which in turn had been based partly on practices at canon law), the reformers provided for compelled revelation of information. The Federal Rules of Civil Procedure completed this development; Rule 26(a) mandates certain disclosures, and Rule 26(b)(1) provides a broad scope of discovery. Rules 27 through 35 provide a number of tools the parties may use to obtain this information. Altogether, these rules effected a "revolution" in discovery practice. The federal rules "included every type of discovery that was known in the United States and probably England up to that time. * * * If one adds up all the types of discovery permitted in individual state courts, one finds some precursors to what later became discovery under the Federal Rules but * * * no one state allowed the total panoply of devices. Moreover, the Federal Rules, as they became law in 1938, eliminated features of discovery that in some states had curtailed the scope of discovery and the breadth of its use." Subrin, Fishing Expeditions Allowed: The Historical Background of the 1938 Federal Discovery Rules, 39 Bos. Col. L. Rev. 691, 718–19 (1998). After reading Rule 26, turn to the problems that attended the reforms.

A. THE PROMISE AND REALITY OF BROAD DISCOVERY

HICKMAN v. TAYLOR, 329 U.S. 495, 67 S.Ct. 385, 91 L.Ed. 451 (1947):

JUSTICE MURPHY delivered the opinion of the Court.

[This case established what is known as the work product immunity to discovery, and is reproduced at p. 380 infra. It was the Court's first major discovery decision after adoption of the Federal Rules of Civil Procedure, and the Court therefore explained its general attitude toward the purpose of discovery.]

The pre-trial deposition-discovery mechanism established by Rules 26 to 37 is one of the most significant innovations of the Federal Rules of Civil Procedure. Under the prior federal practice, the pre-trial functions of notice giving, issue-formulation and fact-revelation were performed primarily and inadequately by the pleadings. Inquiry into the issues and the facts before the trial was narrowly confined and often cumbersome in method. The new rules, however, restrict the pleadings to the task of general notice-giving and invest the deposition-discovery process with a vital role in the preparation for trial. The various instruments of discovery now serve (1) as a device, along with the pretrial hearing under Rule 16, to narrow and clarify the basic issues between the parties, and (2) as a device for ascertaining the facts, or information as to the existence of whereabouts of facts, relative to those issues. Thus civil trials in the federal courts no longer need be carried on in the dark. The way is now clear, consistent with recognized privileges for the parties to obtain the fullest possible knowledge of the issues and facts before the trial.

* * *

No longer can the time-honored cry of "fishing expedition" serve to preclude a party from inquiring into the facts underlying his opponent's case. Mutual knowledge of all the relevant facts gathered by both parties is essential to proper litigation. To that end, either party may compel the other to disgorge whatever facts he has in his possession. The deposition-discovery procedure simply advances the stage at which the disclosure can be compelled from the time of trial to the period preceding it, thus reducing the possibility of surprise.

———

WILLIAM GLASER, PRETRIAL DISCOVERY AND THE ADVERSARY SYSTEM 233–34 (1968):

The expansion of discovery is part of a historic trend relaxing the wholly adversarial and self-interested model of civil litigation under the common law. The judge has been given more authority in presenting evidence and in pushing the progress of the case. Procedures have been made less formal, so that one side can invoke fewer technicalities at the expense of the other. The scope of allowable information during trials and during pretrial preparation has been expanded, so that the litigants and the court have a better understanding of the case. Judicial systems are becoming more unified, better planned, and more organized.

Some advocates of the adversary system have feared that discovery could wreck it and that justice would suffer. Some critics of the system hoped that discovery would eliminate all its defects. But in practice discovery has been designed as a single part of a complex set of institutions and—like many reforms—its effects have been limited. Its achievements have been important, but it has been neither panacea nor cataclysm.

By means of discovery and other reforms of recent centuries, the adversary system has been altered but not transformed. Deeply rooted in tradition, in the rules, and in the interests of litigants, the adversarial method of conducting civil suits has determined how discovery has worked in practice. Basically, it is used by each side to strengthen its own case. * * * Most lawyers use it for the informational purposes anticipated by the rules and not for the tactical purposes condemned by the authorities. Most lawyers use discovery successfully, with gains in evidence, names of witnesses, awareness of new issues, and other information useful in settlement negotiations and at trial. Discovery enables each side to learn more about the other's position, but each is still motivated to conceal as much as possible, particularly evidence or witnesses that will have a dramatic effect at trial. Many lawyers continue to be surprised by their adversaries at trial, despite their own use of discovery.

POWELL, J., DISSENTING FROM AMENDMENTS TO FEDERAL RULES OF CIVIL PROCEDURE, 446 U.S. 997 (1980):

[In 1980, the Supreme Court adopted amendments to certain discovery rules designed to cure defects that had been revealed by experience. Justice Powell, joined by Justices Stewart and Rehnquist, dissented on the ground that more aggressive reforms were needed.]

When the Federal Rules first appeared in 1938, the discovery provisions properly were viewed as a constructive improvement. But experience under the discovery Rules demonstrates that "not infrequently [they have been] exploited to the disadvantage of justice." Properly limited and controlled discovery is necessary in most civil litigation. The present Rules, however, invite discovery of such scope and duration that district judges often cannot keep the practice within reasonable bounds. Even in a relatively simple case, discovery through depositions, interrogatories and demands for documents may take weeks. In complex litigation, discovery can continue for years. One must doubt whether empirical evidence would demonstrate that untrammeled discovery actually contributes to the just resolution of disputes. If there is disagreement about that, there is none whatever about the effect of discovery practices upon the average citizen's ability to afford legal remedies.

Delay and excessive expense now characterize a large percentage of all civil litigation. The problems arise in significant part, as every judge and litigator knows, from abuse of the discovery procedures available under the Rules. Indeed, the National Conference on the Causes of

Popular Dissatisfaction with the Administration of Justice, led by the Chief Justice, identified "abuse in the use of discovery [as] a major concern" within our legal system. Lawyers devote an enormous number of "chargeable hours" to the practice of discovery. We may assume that discovery usually is conducted in good faith. Yet all too often, discovery practices enable the party with greater financial resources to prevail by exhausting the resources of a weaker opponent.

Notes and Questions

1. The tocsin sounded by Justice Powell reflects the attitudes of many about the undesirable effects of untrammeled discovery, but others disagree. Labelling Justice Powell's dissent "political," Professor Friedenthal argued that "[i]t is not surprising to find that the battle over specificity has shifted from pleading to discovery. The relationship between the policy of pleading and that of discovery is obvious. The very purpose of permitting pleadings based upon good faith speculation must be to permit plaintiffs to employ the discovery provisions to determine whether a valid case in fact exists." Friedenthal, A Divided Supreme Court Adopts Discovery Amendments to the Federal Rules of Civil Procedure, 69 Calif.L.Rev. 806, 816 (1981).

Lower court judges, however, often rule that discovery may not be used to determine whether a claim exists. For example, in McLaughlin v. Copeland, 455 F.Supp. 749 (D.Del.1978), the court refused plaintiff discovery after rejecting his initial effort to state a claim: "Having failed to state a claim upon which relief can be granted, McLaughlin is not entitled to discovery merely to determine whether or not additional, unasserted claims might exist. While a plaintiff is entitled to a full opportunity to adduce evidence in support of the cognizable claims set out in his complaint, he is not entitled to discovery for the purpose of determining whether or not there may be a factual basis for a claim he has not made." Consistent with this view, the Committee Note to a 2000 amendment to Rule 26(b)(1) observed that the rule change "signals to the parties that they have not entitlement to discovery to develop new claims or defenses that are not already identified in the pleadings." Courts have thus held that, even where discovery may be necessary to comply with Rule 11, it is not available to one who has not asserted a cognizable claim. See, e.g., In re Petition of Ford, 170 F.R.D. 504 (M.D.Ala.1997); compare Petition of Alpha Industries, Inc., 159 F.R.D. 456 (S.D.N.Y.1995) (allowing discovery). Is this approach consistent with Professor Friedenthal's? Which view better accomplishes the goals of the Federal Rules of Civil Procedure? Why would judges resist allowing plaintiff discovery to find out whether there is a claim?

2. Arguably the relaxation on access to discovery has influenced the development of the substantive law as well. Thus, Professor Friedenthal observed that "over the years developments in areas such as products liability, employment discrimination, and consumer protection have been the result at least partly of broad-ranging discovery provisions. For example, lawyers would not have pushed in the courts and in the legislatures for expanded causes of action hinged on proof that defendants knew or should have known of a product's danger, if such proof were normally unavailable. The ability of plaintiff's attorneys to obtain a corporate defendant's records,

to depose corporate employees, and to send searching interrogatories has had a substantial impact on particular areas of law, and is one important factor in the dramatic increase in cases filed." Friedenthal, supra, 69 Calif.L.Rev. at 818. Did the framers of the Federal Rules foresee such a synergy between discovery and substantive law? Is there any argument that this synergy is a bad thing?

3. Justice Powell speaks of empirical evidence about the effects of discovery. Although many lawyers and judges have strong views on the desirability of broad discovery, there is little empirical basis for concluding that there are widespread problems with the operation of discovery. A Federal Judicial Center survey in 1997 found that the median discovery expense for a party was 3% of the amount at stake in the case, with discovery constituting about 50% of the total litigation cost in average cases. At the 95th percentile, however, discovery costs constituted 90% of litigation cost, and they were higher for plaintiffs than for defendants. See Willging, Stienstra, Shapard & Miletich, An Empirical Study of Discovery and Disclosure Practice Under the 1993 Federal Rule Amendments, 39 Bos. Col. L. Rev. 525 (1998). Similarly, a 1992 study of five state courts by the National Center for State Courts found that formal discovery was conducted less frequently in those courts than might be expected by some opponents of discovery, but that certain types of cases seemed to generate more discovery and that higher discovery volume is associated with greater discovery-related motion activity. Keilitz, Hanson & Daley, Is Civil Discovery in State Courts Out of Control?, 17 St.Ct.J. 8 (1993). Thus, discovery abuse does not seem acute in terms of numbers. On the other hand, a survey of Chicago litigators indicated that in at least 50% of the more complex cases, one party believes that it has avoided revealing something important despite discovery. Brazil, Views From the Front Lines: Observations by Chicago Lawyers About the System of Civil Discovery, 1980 A.B.F.Res.J. 217. In terms of its stated purpose, then, discovery is not universally successful.

4. Whatever the strength of the empirical case against broad discovery, since the mid 1970's there has been considerable pressure to restrain overbroad discovery, and the changes in the federal rules during that time generally cut back on the scope of discovery and emphasized the judge's responsibility to manage it. See Marcus, Discovery Containment Redux, 39 Bos. Col. L. Rev. 747 (1998). In 2000, the Supreme Court adopted further amendments that continued this trend toward constraint.

5. The rest of the world, however, approaches these questions differently; almost no other country has discovery on the scale of the U.S. See Subrin, Discovery in Global Perspective: Are We Nuts?, 52 DePaul L. Rev. 299 (2002). Some countries have even enacted "blocking" statutes designed to prevent compliance with American discovery within their borders. Some non-Americans argue that broader discovery should be adopted in the rest of the world, see K. Huang, Introducing Discovery Into Civil Law (2003), but that has not happened to any substantial degree. The modest narrowing of U.S. discovery in response to criticisms, meanwhile, has not done much to move the American approach toward the general practice in other countries. See Marcus, Retooling American Discovery for the Twenty–First Century: Toward a New World Order?, 7 Tulane L. Rev. 153 (1999). Broad discovery can be viewed as an integral feature of American litigation: "Broad discovery

is thus not a mere procedural rule. Rather, it has become, at least in our era, a procedural institution perhaps of virtually constitutional foundation." Hazard, From Whom No Secrets are Hid, 76 Tex. L. Rev. 1665, 1694 (1998).

IN RE CONVERGENT TECHNOLOGIES
SECURITIES LITIGATION

United States District Court, Northern District of California, 1985.
108 F.R.D. 328.

BRAZIL, U.S. MAGISTRATE.

The principal issue in this discovery dispute can be simply framed: *when* (at which juncture in the pretrial period) should plaintiffs answer "contention" interrogatories served by defendants. The parties do *not* disagree about *whether* the questions should be answered. The sole question is when.

Counsel already have spent upwards of $40,000 of their clients' money on this one discovery dispute.[3] That fact strikes this court as strong evidence that there has been in this case a major breakdown in what is supposed to be the self-executing system of pretrial discovery. The spirit of Rule 26,[4] as amended in 1983, has been violated. So has the

---

3. The $40,000 figure does not include money counsel spent drafting, serving and initially objecting to the interrogatories themselves.

4. The following provisions were added to Rule 26 in 1983. Subparagraph (b)(1) [now (b)(2)] was amended to include this paragraph:

The frequency or extent of use of the discovery methods set forth in subdivision (a) shall be limited by the court if it determines that: (i) the discovery sought is unreasonably cumulative or duplicative, or is obtainable from some other source that is more convenient, less burdensome, or less expensive; (ii) the party seeking discovery has had ample opportunity by discovery in the action to obtain the information sought; or (iii) the discovery is unduly burdensome or expensive, taking into account the needs of the case, the amount in controversy, limitations on the parties' resources, and the importance of the issues at stake in the litigation. The court may act upon its own initiative after reasonable notice or pursuant to a motion under subdivision (c). Fed.R.Civ.P. 26(b)(1).

In addition, a new subparagraph (g) was added:

Every request for discovery or response or objection thereto made by a party represented by an attorney shall be signed by at least one attorney of record in his individual name, whose address shall be

stated. A party who is not represented by an attorney shall sign the request, response, or objection and state his address. The signature of the attorney or party constitutes a certification that he has read the request, response, or objection, and that to the best of his knowledge, information, and belief formed after a reasonable inquiry it is: (1) consistent with these rules and warranted by existing law or a good faith argument for the extension, modification, or reversal of existing law; (2) not interposed for any improper purpose, such as to harass or to cause unnecessary delay or needless increase in the cost of litigation; and (3) not unreasonable or unduly burdensome or expensive, given the needs of the case, the discovery already had in the case, the amount in controversy, and the importance of the issues at stake in the litigation. If a request, response, or objection is not signed, it shall be stricken unless it is signed promptly after the omission is called to the attention of the party making the request, response, or objection and a party shall not be obligated to take any action with respect to it until it is signed.

If a certification is made in violation of the rule, the court, upon motion or upon its own initiative, shall impose upon the person who made the certification, the party on whose behalf the request, response, or objection is made, or both, an

spirit of Rule 1, which declares that the purpose of the Federal Rules of Civil Procedure is "to secure the just, speedy, and inexpensive determination of every action." The discovery system depends absolutely on good faith and common sense from counsel. The courts, sorely pressed by demands to try cases promptly and to rule thoughtfully on potentially case-dispositive motions, simply do not have the resources to police closely the operation of the discovery process. The whole system of civil adjudication would ground to a virtual halt if the courts were forced to intervene in even a modest percentage of discovery transactions. That fact should impose on counsel an acute sense of responsibility about how they handle discovery matters. They should strive to be cooperative, practical and sensible, and should turn to the courts (or take positions that force others to turn to the courts) only in extraordinary situations that implicate truly significant interests.

These are not simply the sentiments of an idealistic and frustrated magistrate. They are the law. They were clearly made so by the 1983 amendments to Rule 26. Those amendments formally interred any argument that discovery should be a free form exercise conducted in a free for all spirit. Discovery is not now and never was free. Discovery is expensive. The drafters of the 1983 amendments to sections (b) and (g) of Rule 26 formally recognized that fact by superimposing the concept of proportionality on all behavior in the discovery arena. It is no longer sufficient, as a precondition for conducting discovery, to show that the information sought "appears reasonably calculated to lead to the discovery of admissible evidence." After satisfying this threshold requirement counsel also *must* make a common sense determination, taking into account all the circumstances, that the information sought is of sufficient potential significance to justify the burden the discovery probe would impose, that the discovery tool selected is the most efficacious of the means that might be used to acquire the desired information (taking into account cost effectiveness and the nature of the information being sought), and that the timing of the probe is sensible, i.e., that there is no other juncture in the pretrial period when there would be a clearly happier balance between the benefit derived from and the burdens imposed by the particular discovery effort.

This articulation of the responsibilities counsel must assume in conducting or responding to discovery may make it appear that the 1983 amendments require counsel to conduct complex analyses each time they take action in the discovery arena. Not so. What the 1983 amendments require is, at heart, very simple: good faith and common sense. Counsel can satisfy these requirements by *not* using or responding to discovery for some ulterior purpose and by exercising straight forward judgment. The questions are simply stated: 1) what information am I really likely

appropriate sanction, which may include an order to pay the amount of the reasonable expenses incurred because of the violation, including a reasonable attorney's fee.

Fed.R.Civ.P. 26(g) (as amended Apr. 28, 1983, eff. Aug. 1, 1983).

to need and 2) what is the most cost effective way to get it. Tailoring probes and responses to the real issues in the case at hand, rather than relying on stock questions or knee jerk objections and evasive responses, is all that is required.

The problem, one senses, is not that the requirements the law imposes are too subtle. Rather, the problem is more likely to be that counsel are less interested in satisfying the law's requirements than in seeking tactical advantages. At least in cases involving big economic stakes, good faith and common sense hardly seem to be the dominant forces. Instead, it appears that the root evil in complex civil litigation continues to be the pervasiveness of gaming. Civil litigation is too often civil only on the surface. Underneath, it is obsession with pursuit of procedural or psychological edge. In adopting the 1983 amendments, the rulemakers have unequivocally condemned that obsession.

[The court then turned to the question of timing. Defendants had served more than 1,000 questions, many of them seeking to elicit the facts plaintiffs contended supported certain of their allegations about what defendants had done in violation of the securities laws. Noting that contention interrogatories "can be almost mindlessly generated," and that they are unlikely to produce useful information until discovery is completed if they focus on defendants' conduct, the court directed that plaintiffs be excused from responding to most of the interrogatories until they had completed a substantial amount of discovery, particularly document inspection.]

Notes and Questions

1. There has never been any question that efforts to falsify or hide evidence violate a lawyer's ethical duties. Is it also improper to turn discovery into a war of attrition either by fighting over everything, as in *Convergent Technologies,* or by deluging the opposition with more material than can realistically be digested? This sort of abuse also threatens to pervert the truth-seeking process. For a broad attack on such behavior, see Brazil, The Adversary Character of Civil Discovery: A Critique, 31 Vand. L. Rev. 1348 (1978) (written, while he was a law professor, by the magistrate judge who decided *Convergent Technologies).*

Who is at fault for this tendency? Responding to the charge that corporate parties "use discovery as a tactical weapon to cause delay, disrupt the other party's business, or even to induce settlements," Robert S. Banks, then General Counsel of Xerox Corporation, argued that "a well-managed firm would never behave in such a manner. First, cost-benefit principles deter such practice. Moreover, the greatest cost in litigation is the so-called 'lost opportunity cost' resulting from the distractions of litigation which take the businessman away from his day-to-day operations and which impede his decision-making. The delays resulting from discovery only exacerbate the problem." Annual Judicial Conference, Second Judicial Circuit of the United States, 101 F.R.D. 161, 192 (1983). How many clients are likely to be equally sophisticated in restraining their lawyers?

2. For the attorney, many suggest, "the quality of 'hired gun' is close to the heart and substance of the litigating lawyer's role." Frankel, The Search for Truth: An Umpireal View, 123 U.Pa.L.Rev. 1031 (1975). Indeed, a "tacticians' guide" for lawyers is entitled Guerilla Discovery. See A. Lipson, Guerilla Discovery (2003). Judge Frankel urged that "[w]e should consider whether the paramount commitment of counsel concerning matters of fact should be to the discovery of truth rather than to the advancement of the client's interest." What kinds of difficulties might such a commitment present for lawyers? Would clients want to pay lawyers engaged in this truth-seeking effort? Would lawyers who did not push discovery to the limit risk suits by their clients? See Barthold, Negligence in Discovery: No Paper Tiger, 6 Litigation 39 (Fall 1979).

Putting aside the killer instinct and the fear of malpractice suits, some discern an undesirable psychological shift toward discovery as an occupation. Consider Lundquist, Litigator or Trial Lawyer, 7 Litigation 3 (Summer 1981):

> It is a vicious circle. Broadened discovery has eroded trial skills; lessened trial skills have led to discovery abuse. Fewer and fewer lawyers today try cases, particularly complex cases involving considerable discovery. Fewer lawyers understand how to try cases because discovery has replaced trial as the ultimate adversary weapon. Since they do not know how to try a case, more and more lawyers overuse discovery.

* * *

> As a result, discovery has replaced trial as the mechanism for resolving disputes. Litigators march forth from law firms flanked by junior partners, associates and paralegals much as fifteenth century Italian armies ventured from warring city-states. These armies left home and lived well off the land as they proceeded to confront the enemy. They avoided direct combat at all costs. The process leading to it was too rewarding, while battle itself was too risky. Thus does litigation proceed today.

3. Why were defendants in *Convergent Technologies* willing to spend so much money on this discovery dispute? Were they seeking to do something more than sidetrack plaintiffs?

4. Instead of junking the adversary ideal, one might solve some of these problems by shifting the job of assembling evidence to judicial officers. Thus, Professor Langbein endorses the German system, which leaves fact investigation to the judge, and says that it co-exists with the adversary ideal:

> This all-or-nothing argument [that the investigative judge undermines the adversary system] overlooks the fundamental distinction between fact-gathering and the rest of civil litigation. Outside the realm of fact-gathering, German civil procedure is about as adversarial as our own. Both systems welcome the lawyerly contribution to identifying legal issues and sharpening legal analysis. German civil procedure is materially less adversarial than our own only in the fact-gathering function, where partisanship has such potential to pollute the sources of truth.

Accordingly, the proper question is not whether to have lawyers, but how to use them; not whether to have an adversarial component to civil procedure, but how to prevent adversarial excesses. If we were to incorporate the essential lesson of the German system in our own procedure, we would still have a strongly adversarial civil procedure. We would not, however, have coached witnesses and litigation-biased experts.

Langbein, The German Advantage in Civil Procedure, 52 U.Chi.L.Rev. 823, 842–43 (1985). Given the common law history of trial by surprise, is it true that shifting to judicial fact gathering would not involve dislocation in our system? Reconsider this question in connection with the work product doctrine, infra pp. 380–91.

5. Amendments to the Federal Rules of Civil Procedure have taken a less radical tack than Professor Langbein suggests, but they contemplate involving the judge much more closely in the discovery process. Thus, Rule 26(f) requires the parties to confer at the outset of the case to devise a discovery plan, and to submit this plan to the judge before entry of the Rule 16 scheduling order, so the judge can supervise discovery. How is a jurist who lacks the familiarity of an investigating magistrate to perform this task? Consider the reaction of one judge: "It's very difficult for a judge to ask, 'Well, you're spending too much time with John Jones, Sales Vice President of the Company. Why are you spending so much time with a salesman?' He can't know why you're spending so much time with him; he can't know that much about your case." Higginbotham, Discovery Management Considerations in Antitrust Cases, 51 Antitrust L.J. 231, 236 (1982). Instead of individualized treatment, aren't judges likely to employ standardized limitations on discovery such as rules that permit only specified numbers of interrogatories in certain kinds of cases?

6. The addition of the "proportionality" provisions of Rule 26(b)(2) was intended to accomplish "a 180 degree shift" in judges' orientation toward broad discovery. A. Miller, the August 1983 Amendments to the Federal Rules of Civil Procedure: Promoting Effective Case Management and Lawyer Responsibility 32–33 (1984). But "the amendment itself seems to have created only a ripple in the caselaw, although some courts now acknowledge that it is clearer than it was before that they should take responsibility for the amount of discovery in cases they manage." 8 C. Wright, A. Miller & R. Marcus, Federal Practice & Procedure § 2008.1 at 121.

Part of the reason the rule had only modest effect may be that it calls for a very difficult determination. Consider Sherman & Kinnard, Federal Court Discovery in the '80's—Making the Rules Work, 95 F.R.D. 245, 276 (1982):

The list of circumstances invokes cost-benefit principles which contemplate both achieving an optimal level of discovery beyond which additional discovery would not be cost-effective and restricting discovery when the dollar amount or values at stake are low. * * *

A potential difficulty with this approach is in finding principled criteria for differentiating between various types of cases. What values should be used in deciding whether, for example, the plaintiff in a

$10,000 personal injury case should be limited in the number of depositions he may take, or the plaintiff seeking reinstatement in an employment discrimination case should be prohibited from discovering documents only tangentially related to the claim, or the defendant in a $10,000,000 product liability case should be allowed to require answers to voluminous interrogatories involving the most searching details of the plaintiff's past life?

7. Additional changes to the rules since 1980 have included numerical limitations on interrogatories and depositions and a time limit for depositions. The scope of discovery has been moderately trimmed, and reminders about the limitations of Rule 26(b)(2) have been inserted elsewhere in the discovery rules. In addition, a requirement of automatic "initial disclosure" has been added in Rule 26(a)(1) to direct the early disclosure of certain "core information" that might otherwise remain under wraps until well into the discovery process. Thus, the general orientation has been to curtail, but preserve, the authority of the parties and their lawyers to control and direct discovery. We turn now to the devices available to them.

B. THE DISCOVERY DEVICES

If he would be a great lawyer, he must first consent to become a great drudge.

—Daniel Webster

Whether or not one must be a drudge to prepare a case properly, it is apparent that one must be discerning in using the tools of modern discovery. To a large extent, the lawyer's choice among the devices in a given case depends upon tactical considerations canvassed at the end of this section. There are also legal limitations on the use of the various discovery devices, most of which are spelled out in the Rules themselves. Read Rules 27–37. We will survey some practicalities of the more important discovery devices and raise some questions about the application of those legal limitations.

INITIAL DISCLOSURE

As demonstrated by In re Convergent Technologies, supra p. 337, discovery can use up a great deal of time and money. In order to reduce some of the cost and adversary maneuvering, in the 1980's courts began insisting that parties turn over "core materials" before formal discovery began. See Marcus, Of Babies and Bathwater: The Prospects for Procedural Progress, 59 Brooklyn L. Rev. 761, 805–12 (1993) (describing the evolution of this practice). In 1992, the state courts in Arizona adopted a rule making initial disclosure mandatory. See Symposium, Mandatory Disclosure and Limiting Discovery: The 1992 Amendments to Arizona's Rules of Civil Procedure and Comparable Federal Proposals, 25 Az.St. L.J. 1 (1992). Other states have adopted similar rules.

In the federal courts, initial disclosure was added in Rule 26(a)(1) in 1993. When adopted, it was extremely controversial because it seemed to compromise the loyalty a lawyer owed to the client by requiring in some instances that information harmful to the client be turned over. For example, Justice Scalia dissented from adoption of this requirement (146 F.R.D. at 511 (1993)):

> The proposed new regime does not fit comfortably within the American judicial system, which relies on adversarial litigation to develop the facts before a neutral decisionmaker. By placing upon lawyers the obligation to disclose information damaging to their clients—on their own initiative, and in a context where the lines between what must be disclosed and what need not be disclosed are not clear but require the exercise of considerable judgment—the new Rule would place intolerable strain upon lawyers' ethical duty to represent their clients and not to assist the opposing side. Requiring a lawyer to make a judgment as to what information is "relevant to disputed facts" plainly requires him to use his professional skills in the service of the adversary.

Despite opposition on this ground, lawyers and judges found the disclosure provisions useful. See Willging, Stienstra, Shapard & Miletich, An Empirical Study of Discovery and Disclosure Practice Under the 1993 Federal Rules Amendments, 39 Bos. Col. L. Rev. 525, 562–64 (1998). In 2000, the rule was changed to direct that a party disclose witnesses and documents it "may use to support its claims or defenses." There is thus no current directive to turn over harmful information, which neutralizes the objection mentioned above, and the burden on responding parties seems modest. See, e.g., PAS Communications, Inc. v. Sprint Corp., 139 F.Supp.2d 1149 (D.Kan.2001) (the disclosure obligation did not apply because the complaint was too vague to notify defendants what they must disclose).

One might ask why any requirement was needed at all to prompt parties to reveal the strengths of their cases to their opponents. Indeed, there have long been reports that litigants do so in the absence of a rule requirement during negotiation with the other side. Moreover, Rule 11's safe harbor provisions (see supra p. 154) may also prompt parties to do so in an attempt to persuade the other side to drop a claim or defense. Besides these incentives and the fact that Rule 26(a)(1) now requires it, initial disclosure is enforced by Rule 37(c)(1), which forbids use of materials that should have been disclosed but were not. This means that if a party tries to present evidence that should have been disclosed, the opposing party can argue that it should not be allowed to do so. That argument can be made at trial, and also with regard to pretrial motions such as summary judgment motions. So a party has an incentive to disclose materials that it may want to use at trial or to support or oppose a motion for summary judgment. The Committee Note accompanying Rule 26(a)(1) makes clear that trying to use a document in discovery is also subject to Rule 37(c)(1). Accordingly, if a party tries to question a witness during a deposition about a document that was not disclosed, the opposing party may object that this use of the document is not allowed. To some extent, then, the possibility of surprise during a deposition has been eroded. Although Rule 37(c)(1) says that the court may permit the materials to be used even if they were not disclosed, there can be considerable risk for a party that tries to use something it has not disclosed.

Some hoped that disclosure would supplant formal discovery in many cases, but that does not seem to have happened. One reason is that disclosure does not include information harmful to the disclosing party's position; only discovery exists to elicit that sort of information. Another is that, given the American adversarial litigation background, it would seem against the grain to insist that a party trust its adversary to make full disclosure. For the present and the foreseeable future, then, formal discovery is likely to follow initial disclosure in most cases. But at the same time, parties must be thorough in deciding what to disclose for fear that failure to do so may deprive them of important evidence later in the case.

DOCUMENT INSPECTION

Rule 34 permits parties to demand an opportunity to inspect and copy documents and other tangible things possessed by other parties. This opportunity can be critical to effective development of a case. Technological advances like the photocopier and the computer have greatly increased the number of documents in existence in most organizations. Note the breadth of the term "document," as defined in the Rule. Proposals have been made to add explicit authority for discovery of "electronically stored information" to Rule 34. As presently written, the rule applies to electronically stored information, although it may be preferable to ask specifically for that. See McPeek v. Ashcroft, infra. p. 368. Documents don't forget, as witnesses are wont to do, so that they provide not only evidence but a starting place for examining witnesses in deposition and preparing witnesses for deposition.

The procedure for using this discovery tool is simple. If plaintiff wants to inspect defendant's documents, plaintiff's lawyer sends a request for production of documents to defendant's lawyer. The request should describe the documents with "reasonable particularity." While parties sometimes specify the precise items they desire (e.g., "the letter to plaintiff dated January 1, 2002"), they often rely on a categorical description (e.g., "all documents that relate or refer to the meeting between plaintiff and defendant on January 1, 2002"). Often that practice is due in large measure to the fact that the discovering party does not know much about what documents the other parties possess. Because Rule 26(a)(1)(B) calls for parties to disclose some pertinent information about documents before formal discovery begins or to provide a listing of them by category, parties may be able to identify and describe with specificity documents they wish to request under Rule 34.

The defendant serves a written response specifying the items that will be made available or objecting to some or all of the requests. As to those it agrees to produce, defendant should assemble the requested documents in its "possession, custody, or control." The "control" idea has been extended to require efforts to obtain documents from others, where the party responding to discovery is believed to have "influence" over the possessor of the documents. See Cooper Industries, Inc. v. British Aerospace, Inc., 102 F.R.D. 918 (S.D.N.Y.1984) (documents in possession of defendant's British affiliate were in defendant's custody or control for purposes of discovery); In re Folding Carton Antitrust Litigation, 76 F.R.D. 420 (N.D.Ill.1977) (defendants required to attempt to obtain documents from former employees if they receive compensation of any kind from defendant).

This "influence" test derives from the decision in Societe Internationale v. Rogers, 357 U.S. 197, 78 S.Ct. 1087, 2 L.Ed.2d 1255 (1958). The plaintiff, a Swiss holding company, sued the Attorney General pursuant to section 9(a) of the Trading with the Enemy Act, 50 U.S.C.A.App. § 9(a), to recover assets seized by the United States pursuant to other provisions of the Act. Section 9(a) authorized recovery of seized assets by "[a]ny person not an enemy or ally of an enemy." The government moved under Rule 34 for an order requiring plaintiff to make available certain banking records for inspection. Plaintiff failed to produce the records in the manner ordered, arguing that it lacked "control" of them because applicable Swiss penal law prohibited their production, and criminal sanctions might be imposed as a result of compliance with the production order. The Supreme Court held that plaintiff had "control" of the records for purposes of Rule 34, because plaintiff "is in a most advantageous position to plead with its own sovereign for relaxation of penal laws * * *." Does this "influence" test represent a wise construction of the "control" requirement of Rule 34? What are the competing considerations?

When the request seeks all documents falling within a category, the responding party usually has to search its files to collect responsive material. The documents are usually made available in the location where they are kept if they are numerous. See Mid–America Facilities, Inc. v. Argonaut Ins. Co., 78 F.R.D. 497 (E.D.Wis.1978) (plaintiffs required to inspect California defendant's documents in California). As noted above, Rule 34(b) requires that documents either be produced as they are kept by the producing party, or grouped according to the specifications of the request. Which option would you expect to be employed more often? The discovering party gets to look through the documents and copy some or all of them, usually by photocopier, microfilming, or other imaging technique. However the documents are organized, the process of reviewing them can be drudgery. Deriving useful information from a mass of material can be a great challenge as well, and litigators rely on computerized litigation support systems to assist them in analyzing the fruits of discovery, particularly documents, and in retrieving pertinent data. With electronically stored information, the usual objective is that the information be electronically searchable.

Rule 34 also authorizes entry onto property for purposes of testing or measuring. Should courts be more restrictive in ordering such entry? Consider Belcher v. Bassett Furniture Industries, Inc., 588 F.2d 904 (4th Cir.1978): "Since entry upon a party's premises may entail greater burdens and risks than mere production of documents, a greater inquiry into the necessity for inspection would seem warranted."

If a party wants to examine materials possessed by a nonparty, a similar procedure is used but a subpoena is required. Rule 45(a)(1)(C) authorizes a subpoena to command a nonparty to produce designated documents in its control or permit inspection of premises. Rule 45(c), however, requires a party to "take reasonable steps to avoid imposing undue burden or expense" on a person subject to a subpoena, and it may be that courts will be more solicitous of nonparties' objections to subpoenas than parties' objections to production of documents.

INTERROGATORIES

Rule 33 permits any party to send written questions to another party that must be answered under oath. Since the responding party is usually required to make reasonable efforts to obtain the information sought, this discovery tool may appear extremely valuable because it could allow a party to do much or all of its pretrial preparation fairly inexpensively. The reality, however, has been disappointing, and by 1970 it was recognized that interrogatories had spawned more discovery disputes than any other discovery device.

One problem has been that interrogatories are too susceptible to abuse. Questions that are simple to write may be very burdensome to answer. Consider the following question in an employment discrimination suit by a rejected job applicant: "Separately with respect to each person who applied for a job with defendant between 2002 and 2004, identify such person by name, address and race; describe in detail all qualifications such person had for the job sought, state whether such person was offered a job, and describe in detail all reasons for defendant's decision to offer or not to offer such person a job." Word processing gives litigants the ability to generate such questions in large numbers. See, e.g., In re U.S. Financial Securities Litigation, 74 F.R.D. 497 (S.D.Cal.1975) (381 pages of interrogatories containing almost 3,000 questions held unduly burdensome). Rule 33(a) now limits the number of interrogatories to 25 per party absent stipulation or court order.

Another problem is that interrogatory answers are almost invariably written by lawyers who wish to avoid disclosing harmful information. As a result, the answers tend to reveal very little even though they are long (for these lawyers have word processors also), and to indulge in generalities where the discovering party wants specifics. Would using a different discovery device solve such problems?

Perhaps the most basic difficulty with interrogatories is that they are ill suited to effective exploration of much information that is critical in litigation. Where a narrative answer is sought, for example, an interrogatory often fails to do the job. Consider, for example, the following interrogatory from the defendant in an auto accident case: "Describe in detail everything plaintiff observed during the period from ten minutes before the accident until ten minutes after the accident." As plaintiff's lawyer, would you find this question unfair? Would the information you might provide be of use to defendant? How might defendant better obtain the information it seeks?

Interrogatories can, however, be very useful for identifying witnesses and discovering the location of documents or other tangible evidence, although that task may be eased by Rule 26(a)(1) initial disclosure. They can also be used to obtain precise information (e.g., "State the number of widgets defendant sold in this state during each month in 2003."). Due to the responding party's duty to obtain information to respond, interrogatories can be particularly useful to a party confronted by a large organizational opponent.

Even restricted to these areas, however, interrogatories raise problems of drafting. Consider, for example, the following question posed by plaintiff to defendants in Roesberg v. Johns–Manville Corp., 85 F.R.D. 292 (E.D.Pa.1980), an action for injuries to plaintiff allegedly resulting from his exposure to asbestos produced by defendants: "When and by what manner were you first aware of the hazards relating to exposure to asbestos products?" What objections might defendants make to this question? Would it matter whether the defendants admitted asbestos products were hazardous?

One type of question deserves special note—the "contention" interrogatory. Rule 33(c) makes it clear that questions are not improper merely because they seek to elicit an opinion, even where they seek an opinion about the application of law to fact. In practice, contention interrogatories are an effective way of exploring the basis for an adversary's position, but the court may defer the duty to answer until discovery has been completed. Recall In re Convergent Technologies Securities Litigation, supra p. 337.

Despite the difficulties that interrogatories have presented over the years, they can serve important purposes. In particular, they may provide the predicate for a motion for summary judgment based on non-existence of evidence supporting a critical part of plaintiff's case. Keep these discovery problems in mind when you read Celotex Corp. v. Catrett, infra p. 435.

DEPOSITIONS

The deposition permits the questioner to compel the witness to answer questions fairly spontaneously and allows the interrogating party to follow up on the answers, particularly unexpected revelations, with further questions. The flexibility and importance of depositions mandate intense preparation on the part of both the interrogating party and the witness. Empirical data indicate that depositions are the most expensive form of discovery in terms of overall litigation expenditure. See Willging, Stienstra, Shapard & Miletich, An Empirical Study of Discovery and Disclosure Practice Under the 1993 Federal Rule Amendments, 39 Bos. Col. L. Rev. 525, 576–77 (1998).

Rule 30(b)(1) allows any party to schedule a deposition on "reasonable notice" in writing. Rule 30(a)(2)(A) imposes a numerical limit of ten depositions per side, and Rule 30(d)(2) limits each deposition to "one day of seven hours." The interrogating party can also ask the witness to bring documents along, but that invokes the time limits of Rule 34. See Rule 30(b)(5). If the witness is a party, nothing further need be done to compel the witness to attend, and Rule 37(b) sanctions can be applied when a party witness fails to appear. See Rule 37(d). Otherwise, the party seeking discovery must also serve a subpoena to ensure the attendance of the witness. See Rule 45.

Depositions usually do not occur in the courthouse unless the court itself is supervising the deposition in an effort to iron out conflicts between the lawyers (a rare thing). Ordinarily the interrogating lawyer will designate her own office as the place of the deposition. When the attendance of the witness must be compelled by subpoena, the geographical limitations applicable to a subpoena apply. With the deposition of a party, however, there are no explicit geographical limitations, and disputes about the location may arise if the witness is located at some distance from the interrogating lawyer. If the parties cannot resolve these disputes by themselves, they may ask the court to do so. Although the discretionary nature of such matters makes prediction uncertain, courts are more likely to require the plaintiff who has sued away from home to travel to the jurisdiction where the suit was filed than to require the distant defendant to come to the jurisdiction where the suit is pending for his deposition. But see Ocasek v. Hegglund, 116 F.R.D. 154 (D.Wyo.1987) (singer Bruce Springsteen not required to appear for deposition in Wyoming even though he is nominal plaintiff in suit filed there).

Before the deposition, the witness will usually consult with his attorney about the deposition process and the subjects that are likely to be covered, a process often called "woodshedding the witness." See D. Small, Preparing Witnesses—A Practical Guide for Lawyers and Their Clients (ABA 1998). With party witnesses, the woodshedding process can be very protracted. The witness's lawyer tries to alert the witness to the pitfalls she will confront and school the witness in revealing as little as possible. The preparation may sharpen the witness's testimony, and for this reason some attorneys choose not to try to refresh the witness's memory before the deposition. But many do so, in part because they are able to mold the testimony, which raises serious risks of impeding the truth-seeking process. Whether or not witnesses would testify more accurately and honestly without preparation, woodshedding is ingrained in our current adversary system to the extent that the lawyer who fails to prepare a witness may be charged with failing to satisfy his professional obligations.

Occurring as it usually does in a lawyer's office, the deposition itself appears informal in many ways; it looks more like a business meeting than a court hearing. Ordinarily, the interrogating attorney will sit at one side of the table facing the witness, with the court reporter between them. The witness's attorney will sit next to the witness, and lawyers for other parties will sit at other points in the room. Other observers may be present; unless there is a court order excluding them, the parties are allowed to attend. The participants may be quite relaxed about matters of personal deportment and dress. But in one regard the deposition is not informal—anything that is transcribed by the reporter ("on the record") may be available for use in the case as though it occurred in open court (to the extent it is admissible). Before the questioning begins, the witness is given the oath, and the interrogating attorney then starts asking questions and continues until she has no further questions to ask.

Although the main actors are the interrogating attorney and the witness, the witness's attorney is not inactive. Instead, she listens to the questions and can object when they are improper. On one level, the pressure to object is moderate since the only objections that are waived are objections on grounds that could be obviated if made at the deposition. Rule 32(d)(3)(A). Thus, where the objection is to the form of the question (that it is leading, or compound, or confusing) the question could be rephrased to avoid the difficulty. Indeed, Rule 30(c) states that if there are objections, "the examination shall proceed, with the testimony being taken subject to objections," so objections seem ineffective even to prevent improper inquires. Why, then, would the lawyer object?

The reality has been that too often objections were used to continue the woodshedding process mentioned above concerning deposition preparation, and instructions to the witness not to answer "improper" questions were actually used to suggest answers or interfere with the taking of the deposition. In Hall v. Clifton Precision, 150 F.R.D. 525 (E.D.Pa. 1993), the court reasoned that "[t]he witness comes to the deposition to testify, not to indulge in a parody of Charlie McCarthy, with lawyers coaching or bending the witness's words to mold a legally convenient record." It therefore ordered that there be no off-the-record consultation between lawyer and witness during the taking of the deposition, including during recesses, except to determine if a privilege applied. Rule 30(d) provides explicit constraints on the behavior of the lawyer for the witness. Rule 30(d)(1) directs that objections "shall be stated concisely and in a non-argumentative and non-suggestive manner." It adds that a lawyer may instruct a witness not to answer only to preserve a privilege, to enforce a limitation on discovery imposed by the judge in this case, or to permit a motion for a protective order. In addition, Rule 30(d) authorizes sanctions for "impediment, delay, or other conduct that has frustrated the fair examination of the deponent," and for other misconduct in a deposition.

Once all the other lawyers have finished their questioning, the witness's lawyer can also question the witness, but ordinarily she will not. Why not? Why would the lawyer decide to break from this norm and question her own witness at a deposition?

Traditionally, depositions have been recorded by court reporters who used special machines to take notes of the questions and answers. In the

1970's experiments with electronic recording of depositions began, and in 1993 Rule 30(b)(2) was amended to provide that a party noticing a deposition could select videotape or audiotape as well as the traditional method. Rule 30(b)(3) allows any other party to designate another method (at its own expense). Lawyers may prefer a videotaped deposition where the witness will not be available to testify at trial because reading aloud from the deposition transcript tends to be extremely boring. See Balabanian, Medium v. Tedium: Video Depositions Come of Age, 7 Litigation 25 (Fall 1980). Rule 32(c) accordingly expresses a preference for use at trial of a nonstenographic recording if one exists. Could a videotape discourage obstructive conduct by counsel during the deposition?

Although this description applies to most depositions, other procedures do exist. Rule 31, for example, authorizes depositions on written interrogatories, with the attorney preparing written questions which the reporter then reads to the witness, recording the answers. Although this is a cost-saving alternative, it is rarely employed. Why would lawyers be reluctant to handle depositions in this inexpensive way? Rule 27(a) also authorizes deposition before suit is filed to "perpetuate testimony" where the party anxious to take the deposition expects to be a party to a suit but is presently unable to bring it, and fears the witness may become unavailable by the time the case is filed. Notice should be given to all persons likely to be named parties so that they can attend and ask questions also.

PHYSICAL OR MENTAL EXAMINATION

Physical or mental examinations are the only discovery tools for which stipulation or advance court approval is necessary. Rule 35(a) provides that when the mental or physical condition of a party or a person under the legal control of a party is "in controversy" a court may order the person to submit to an examination by a "suitably licensed or certified examiner." This allows examination by a range of specialists, but "only on motion for good cause shown."

In Schlagenhauf v. Holder, 379 U.S. 104, 85 S.Ct. 234, 13 L.Ed.2d 152 (1964), the Supreme Court explained the proper application of Rule 35. The suit resulted from a rear-end collision between a tractor-trailer and a Greyhound bus, and Greyhound claimed that the tractor-trailer was not equipped with proper rear lights. The owners of the tractor-trailer asserted claims against both Greyhound and Schlagenhauf, the driver of the bus, alleging that the accident was Schlagenhauf's fault and that his eyes and vision were impaired at the time of the crash. They applied for an order requiring Schlagenhauf to submit to nine medical examinations by specialists in internal medicine, ophthalmology, neurology and psychiatry. They based the application on their allegation that Schlagenhauf had impaired eyes and vision, Schlagenhauf's deposition testimony that he had been involved in another rear-end crash, that he had seen the rear lights of the tractor-trailer for 10 to 15 seconds before the crash, and the fact that another witness said he had seen the rear lights from a distance of one-half to three quarters of a mile. Though the other parties had sought only one examination by a specialist in each area, they submitted the names of nine specialists from which the court could choose. Inexplicably, the district court ordered examinations by all nine specialists.

The Supreme Court held that the discovery order was improper because it was not supported by a sufficient showing. It emphasized Rule 35's requirement that the party's condition be "in controversy" as well as the good cause requirement. Together, these necessitate something more than "mere conclusory allegations of the pleadings" or "mere relevance to the case." There must be "an affirmative showing by the movant that each condition as to which examination is sought is really and genuinely in controversy." It acknowledged that things might well have been different if Schlagenhauf, like a personal injury plaintiff, had put his condition in issue, but found that the "general conclusory statement" in the pleadings was insufficient, even when coupled with Schlagenhauf's deposition testimony and the statements of the other witness. It remanded for more careful evaluation, leaving open the possibility of a vision examination. Was the Court correct in believing that only the vision examination might meet the "good cause" and "in controversy" requirements? On the basis of the record, is there any reason to believe that the accident was more likely caused by Schlagenhauf's vision than by his mental or physical condition? In his opinion, Justice Goldberg stated: "Obviously, what may be good cause for one type of examination may not be so for another." What does this mean? Might it explain why the Court believed that only a vision examination was permissible on the basis of the record?

In dissent, Justice Black denounced the majority's insistence on a further showing: "In a collision case like this one, evidence concerning very bad eyesight or impaired mental or physical health which may affect the ability to drive is obviously of the highest relevance. It is equally obvious, I think, that when a vehicle continues down an open road and smashes into a truck in front of it although the truck is in plain sight and there is ample time and room to avoid collision, the chances are good that the driver has some physical, mental or moral defect. When such a thing happens twice, one is even more likely to ask, 'What is the matter with that driver? Is he blind or crazy?'" Are these arguments persuasive? Should they justify medical examinations in all rear-end crash cases? For a general discussion of leave to examine parties, see 8 A C. Wright, A. Miller & R. Marcus, Federal Practice & Procedure § 2234.1.

When the examination is ordered, the court may specify the time and place. Ordinarily counsel for the party being examined is not permitted to attend. In McDaniel v. Toledo, Peoria and Western R. Co., 97 F.R.D. 525 (C.D.Ill.1983), for example, the court refused to permit plaintiff's lawyer to attend the medical examination, even though a state statute provided the lawyer could attend, because "the examination should be divested as far as possible of any adversary character" and because allowing the lawyer to attend might make him a witness and thereby require his withdrawal as counsel in the case. This sort of reasoning has been applied to court-ordered psychiatric examinations as well. See Edwards v. Superior Court, 549 P.2d 846 (Cal.1976) ("the presence and participation of counsel would hinder the establishment of the rapport that is so necessary"). Compare the deposition, where the witness's lawyer is not only present but allowed to interrupt the proceedings. Is it more likely counsel will disrupt a medical examination? Is the more pertinent difference the identity of the person asking questions? Compare United States v. Wade, 388 U.S. 218, 87 S.Ct. 1926, 18 L.Ed.2d 1149 (1967) (presence of defendant's counsel at pretrial lineup is constitutionally required to protect rights of defendant in criminal case). A number of state statutes provide a right to have counsel present. See, e.g., Ill. Rev. Stat. Ch. 735, § 1103(d). See generally 8A C. Wright, A. Miller & R. Marcus, supra, § 2236.

DISCOVERY SEQUENCE AND TACTICS

Now that you have some familiarity with the operation of the discovery devices, it is worthwhile to introduce some of the tactical considerations that bear on use of these devices.

The starting point is the pleading stage:

> Establish facts through the pleadings. The complaint is often the plaintiff's first discovery device. A carefully drafted complaint can streamline the discovery process by eliminating unnecessary time and expense. In order to do this, numbered individual paragraphs should generally contain only one central thought or factual allegation. Eliminate all unnecessary adjectives and adverbs. It is always tempting to use the complaint as a polemic, but it is almost always inappropriate and strategically wrong.

> A nonargumentative and simple paragraph within a complaint may very well elicit an admission in the answer, thereby conclusively establishing the facts alleged in that particular paragraph. An admission of a particular factual allegation in a complaint will not preclude further discovery on that factual issue, but it will establish some central facts early on that could greatly assist subsequent discovery motions or a defense against a motion to dismiss or a motion for summary judgment.

Fox, Planning and Conducting a Discovery Program, 7 Litigation 13, 14 (Summer 1981). Would this lead to good pleading? See Rule 10(b).

After the pleadings stage, initial disclosure usually will come next. For formal discovery, many lawyers have a routine sequence, such as interrogatories, followed by document requests based in part on the interrogatory answers, followed by depositions. Given the difficulties in using interrogatories, it is easy to see some problems with this strategy. Some other factors may argue for starting with a deposition:

> For example, if you expect that your adversary is not very well versed in the central claims or legal issues of the case, you might want to depose the defendant immediately to catch him and his counsel off guard. They may not understand what you are really getting at and may make some damaging admissions early on. Second, an early discovery deposition may clear up some unknowns about the case and the defendant so that you will be able to prepare a more precise and meaningful set of interrogatories.

Fox, supra, 7 Litigation at 15.

Depositions also have advantages for the litigant in a hurry, although the Rule 26(d) moratorium usually requires that formal discovery await the discovery conference under Rule 26(f). Consider how depositions could be used before Rule 26(d) was adopted:

> Use depositions to accelerate discovery. Depositions get a case moving better than any other discovery device. First, depositions can be scheduled thirty days after the filing of the complaint and, if leave of court can be obtained, can even be scheduled before the complaint is filed, F.R.C.P. 27, or before the thirty-day period has expired. F.R.C.P. 30(a). Second, there is no time lag between the time questions are asked and answers obtained.

> Third, refusals to answer deposition questions are rare both because the question can be immediately rephrased to eliminate any objectionable aspects, and because defending lawyers are reluctant to object when they know they will be confronted with an immediate motion to compel the witness to answer.

Fox, supra, 7 Litigation at 17. There can be drawbacks to speed, however, since one cannot compel the witness to bring documents without allowing the time for a document production, and there is a significant likelihood under Rule 30(a)(2)(B) that an early witness will not be subject to recall later in the discovery process when more information is available for questions.

Other sequence issues depend upon the way in which early discovery unfolds. One kind of discovery may be necessary to lay the groundwork for another kind. Thus, interrogatories may be necessary to locate documents and witnesses, requests for documents to obtain the materials needed to prepare for depositions, and depositions to lay the groundwork for a request for a medical examination. For example, in Schlagenhauf v. Holder, supra pp. 350–51, plaintiff used the deposition of the bus driver to support his application for a medical examination. Without the showing from the deposition, there would have been no basis for the medical examination. Similarly, it may often happen that judges actively managing discovery will entertain requests to expand discovery on the basis of a showing that useful information has been obtained through completed discovery that points up the need for more.

Not only must lawyers grapple with these sorts of tactical issues, they also confront tactical problems with ethical overtones. A common example is the maladroit discovery request. Suppose your opponent has made a request for production of documents that arguably covers certain damaging materials from your client's files, but only in a very indirect way. Can you make a good faith argument that the request does not actually ask for the damaging material, knowing all the while that your opponent would certainly want this material if aware of it? If you can make the argument in good faith, should you? If there is a substantial likelihood that the material will come out later in the case anyway, it might be best to turn it over now rather than highlighting its importance (and providing an occasion for allegations of concealing evidence) when the material surfaces later.

Notes and Questions

1. *Discovery from nonparties*: As suggested above, discovery from nonparties is more limited than discovery from parties. Note, for example, that there is no way to send interrogatories to nonparties, and nonparties are not subject to court-ordered physical examinations under Rule 35. Rule 45 allows discovery from nonparties comparable to party discovery under Rules 30 (depositions) and 34 (document requests) because it authorizes a party to use a subpoena to compel a nonparty to appear and testify at a deposition or to allow inspection of documents or premises. Consider the following hypothetical: You wish to obtain information about the eyesight of a nonparty witness to the accident that prompted the lawsuit. How can you do so under the current discovery rules? Cf. Harris v. Athol–Royalston Regional School Dist., 206 F.R.D. 30 (D.Mass.2002) (court orders handwriting exemplars and fingerprints from nonparty personnel of defendant).

Rule 45(c) also requires that parties avoid unfairly burdening nonparties and alert them in the subpoena itself to the right to seek a protective order. Among other things, the court may require the party seeking discovery to reimburse the nonparty for the costs of responding. This cost can be substantial. For example, in United States v. Columbia Broadcasting System, Inc., 666 F.2d 364 (9th Cir.1982), defendant television networks subpoenaed material from five producers of television programming. To comply with the document requests, the producers hired lawyers, had thousands of boxes of documents reviewed and eventually had 17 officers and employees deposed over a period of more than 80 days. They then asked for $2.3 million to compensate them for the cost of responding to this discovery, and the appellate court reversed the trial judge's refusal to award any compensation: "Although party witnesses must generally bear the burden of discovery costs, the rationale for the general rule is inapplicable where the discovery demands are made on nonparties. Nonparty witnesses are powerless to control the scope of litigation and discovery, and should not be forced to subsidize an unreasonable share of the costs of a litigation to which they were not a party." Are nonparties really in a position that is so different from defendants?

Given this difference in treatment between party and nonparty discovery, one solution to discovery problems is to name as parties all those from whom one will seek discovery. Is this solution ethical? Is it consistent with Rule 11?

2. *Discovery from corporate party:* Discovery against a corporate or other organizational party may be more difficult because both responsibility and knowledge are diffuse. Consider Judge Frank Theis's description of difficulties encountered by plaintiffs in Dalkon Shield cases: "The project manager for Dalkon Shield explains that a particular question should have gone to the medical department, the medical department representative explains that the question was really [in] the bailiwick of the quality control department. The quality control department representative explains that the project manager was the one with the authority to make a decision on that question. * * * [I]t is not at all unusual for the hard questions posed in Dalkon Shield cases to be unanswerable by anyone from Robins." Lord, The Dalkon Shield Litigation: Revised Annotated Reprimand by Chief Judge Miles W. Lord, 9 Hamline L. Rev. 7, 11 (1986).

One antidote for this merry-go-round problem is to use interrogatories to identify the persons within the organization who have knowledge about the matter at issue. Initial disclosure pursuant to Rule 26(a)(1)(A) of identities of people with pertinent information may be another. Rule 30(b)(6) provides yet another: It permits a party to notice a deposition of a corporation, partnership, or government agency, whether or not a party, with a description of the matters to be covered, and to require the organization to designate a person able to answer questions on that subject. See In re Vitamins Antitrust Litigation, 216 F.R.D. 168 (D.C.D.C.2003) (defendant and its lawyer would be sanctioned for failure to produce a knowledgeable witness to testify). It has also been held that the scope of examination of the representative extends to all relevant topics, not just the ones indicated in the notice, Overseas Private Investment Corp. v. Mandelbaum, 185 F.R.D. 67 (D.D.C.1999), and perhaps that the corporation is "bound" by the answers given. See Rainey v. American Forest and Paper Association, 26 F.Supp.2d 82 (D.D.C.1998). Are these results sensible? See generally Sinclair & Fendrich, Discovering Corporate Knowledge and Contentions: Rethinking Rule 30(b)(6) and Alternative Mechanisms, 50 Ala.L.Rev. 651 (1999).

3. *Requests for admissions:* Rule 36 authorizes what appears to be another discovery tool: It permits any party to send requests to any other party asking for an admission of the truth of any matter within the scope of Rule 26(b). The responding party is deemed to have admitted these matters unless he denies them, and denials are to be specific and "fairly meet the substance of the requested admission." Cf. Rule 8(b). Where a matter is admitted, it is deemed conclusively established for the purpose of the litigation at hand, but the admission cannot be used in any other litigation.

Technically requests for admission are not discovery devices but more analogous to pleadings. In reality, however, they can form a part of a discovery package, and parties often serve them coupled with interrogatories asking for specifics about any matters that are denied. Some courts have expressed concern that requests for admissions have been used too often and too early; parties should not be expected to be in a position to make admissions, they reason, until substantial discovery has been completed. Nevertheless, these requests are quite useful to establish the genuineness of documents and to verify basic facts that are within the knowledge of the party.

4. *Admissibility at trial:* Besides assisting parties in locating information, discovery can yield evidence that is admissible at trial. In general, the admissibility of such materials depends on the rules of evidence. Thus, documents obtained through discovery may not be admissible unless "authenticated" (see Fed.R.Evid. 901–02), perhaps by a request for admission of their genuineness. Since virtually all discovery produces evidence that is hearsay, the elaborate rules governing admissibility of hearsay (see Fed. R.Evid. 801–07) play a large role in admission of the fruits of discovery.

Rule 32(a) provides some specifics regarding depositions: Beyond uses allowed by the Federal Rules of Evidence, any deposition may be used for impeachment at trial, the deposition of a party (or a representative designated under Rule 30(b)(6)) may be used by an adverse party for any purpose, and the deposition of a witness may be used for any purpose if the witness is not present at trial and the witness's absence has not been procured by the party offering the deposition. This last provision has been interpreted to permit a plaintiff from California to offer her own deposition in evidence in a trial in New York rather than travel to New York to testify personally. See Richmond v. Brooks, 227 F.2d 490 (2d Cir.1955).

5. *Discovery disputes:* As should be apparent, discovery matters often cause disputes between the parties, and ultimately the party seeking discovery can ask the court to compel the desired response (see infra pp. 415–24). In part because these disputes often revolve around scheduling details and the like, judges became impatient with parties who squabbled and ran to court to resolve their differences. Consider the following judicial reaction: "If there is a hell to which disputatious, uncivil, vituperative lawyers go, let it be one in which the damned are eternally locked in discovery disputes with other lawyers of equally repugnant attributes." Dahl v. City of Huntington Beach, 84 F.3d 363 364 (9th Cir.1996). Rule 37 requires that a motion to compel be accompanied by "a certification that the movant has in good faith conferred or attempted to confer with the party not making the discovery in an effort to secure the information or material without court action." Rule 37(a)(2)(B); see also Rules 37(a)(2)(A); 37(d).

6. *Duty to supplement:* It often happens that a party acquires additional responsive information after responding to discovery. Rule 26(e) provides that whenever "the response is in some material respect incomplete or incorrect" the response must be supplemented. Rule 26(e) does not apply if the additional information has "otherwise been made known to the other parties during the discovery process or in writing." Failure to supplement is subject to sanctions. See Rule 37(c)(1).

7. *Preservation of evidence:* Nobody keeps everything forever, but failure to keep items sought through discovery can lead to sanctions for spoliation. The exact dimensions of the duty to preserve evidence and the exact time when that duty comes into play are sometimes uncertain. But failure to retain information under circumstances indicating a desire to suppress evidence can result in very severe sanctions, including criminal convictions. It may be that negligence is enough fault to justify serious sanctions. See Residential Funding Corp. v. DeGeorge Financial Corp., 306 F.3d 99 (2d Cir.2002). For discussion, see J. Gorelick, S. Marzen & L. Solum, Destruction of Evidence (1989). In Silvestri v. General Motors Corp., 271

F.3d 583 (4th Cir.2001), a plaintiff who claimed his serious injuries resulted from a malfunction of the air bag in somebody else's car suffered dismissal due to his failure to arrange for G.M. to have a chance to inspect the car before the owner sold it.

8. *Investigation*: Later in this chapter (see infra p. 412) we will examine the role of investigation. For the present, it is sufficient to mention that discovery is not the only, and sometimes not the best, way to obtain information for use in a lawsuit.

9. *Discovery abroad*: Increasingly, litigation in American courts involves litigants or witnesses who are in other countries. American courts can issue "letters rogatory" seeking assistance of foreign courts in obtaining discovery for use in American courts. See 28 U.S.C.A. § 1781. Recall, however, that foreign discovery is much more limited than American discovery. See supra p. 336 n.5. In addition, the Hague Convention on Taking Evidence Abroad has since 1972 provided procedures for judicial authorities in signatory countries to obtain discovery in other signatory countries. The Supreme Court has held that district courts may decide on a case-by-case basis whether to employ this Convention. Societe Nationale Industrielle Aerospatiale v. United States District Court, 482 U.S. 522, 107 S.Ct. 2542, 96 L.Ed.2d 461 (1987). But because they view American discovery as unduly intrusive, many countries have adopted "blocking" laws that forbid or limit compliance with discovery efforts within their borders. See G. Born, International Litigation in U.S. Courts 856–71 (3d ed. 1996). The U.S. also offers foreign litigants access to American discovery. A statute authorizes district courts to order discovery in this country for use in litigation pending in another country. See 28 U.S.C.A. § 1782; Intel Corp. v. Advanced Micro Devices, Inc., 542 U.S. 241, 124 S.Ct. 2466 (2004) (party seeking discovery in U.S. need not show that the information sought would be discoverable in the country in which the proceeding is pending).

C. MANAGING THE SCOPE AND BURDEN OF DISCOVERY

DAVIS v. ROSS

United States District Court, Southern District of New York, 1985.
107 F.R.D. 326.

ROBERT L. CARTER, DISTRICT JUDGE.

Plaintiff Gail Davis has instituted this defamation action, seeking one million dollars in compensatory damages and one million dollars in punitive damages, based on an October 11, 1983 letter written and disseminated by defendant Diana Ross. [Davis alleged in her complaint that, from January, 1982, until she voluntarily resigned in November, 1982, she was employed as executive assistant to Ross, a well-known recording artist. The October 11, 1983, letter stated in part:

To Whom it May Concern:

The following [seven] people are no longer in my employment:

Gail Davis

If I let an employee go, it's because either their work or their personal habits are not acceptable to me. I do not recommend these people. In fact, if you hear from these people, and they use my name as a reference I wish to be contacted.

Plaintiff sued, claiming that the letter was false in asserting that Ross fired her, that she was fired because of inadequate work or personal habits, and that her inadequacies warranted Ross' recommendation that she not be hired. The district court granted Ross' motion to dismiss on the ground that, as a matter of law, the text of the letter was not libelous but only expressed Ross' personal dissatisfaction rather than making a representation of fact about Davis's job performance. 602 F.Supp. 504 (S.D.N.Y.1984). The court of appeals reversed and remanded, reasoning that the letter was susceptible to several interpretations, at least one of which is defamatory. 754 F.2d 80 (2d Cir.1985).] * * * The case is currently before the court on the parties' cross-motions to compel discovery.

Davis seeks discovery of three sets of data. First, she wishes to obtain information concerning Ross' net worth and annual income. Davis argues that this material is discoverable because evidence of a defendant's wealth is relevant in an action for punitive damages. Rupert v. Sellers, 48 A.D.2d 265, 368 N.Y.S.2d 904 (4th Dep't 1975).

The New York courts have recognized, however, that a plaintiff's interest in proving the amount of the defendant's wealth must be balanced against the defendant's right to privacy and general desire not to divulge his or her financial status—especially since plausible claims for punitive damages can easily be made in many actions. Consequently, the rule in New York is that "evidence of defendant's wealth [can] not be brought out upon trial unless and until the jury [brings] in a special verdict that plaintiff is entitled to punitive damages against defendant." [Rupert v. Sellers, 48 A.D.2d] at 272, 368 N.Y.S.2d at 912. Discovery of defendant's net wealth will become necessary only in the event plaintiff obtains such a special verdict.

Davis argues that the rule of Rupert v. Sellers should not govern this case because she entered into a confidentiality order which, she says, should eliminate any concern for privacy on defendant's part. Defendant responds, quite rightly, that the existence of a confidentiality order does not undermine the rationale of Rupert v. Sellers. Ross should not be compelled to disclose private facts to anyone—even to someone who has agreed to keep the information confidential—until it is found that plaintiff is entitled to punitive damages. * * * The motion to compel discovery of Ross' wealth and income is denied.

Plaintiff's second discovery request is for documents reflecting billings by the law firm of Loeb & Loeb and/or John Frankenheimer (a partner in the firm) to Ross and to entities in which she has an interest, and for the records reflecting payment of such bills. Plaintiff argues that this material is discoverable because the defendant has stated that Frankenheimer will be an important witness; therefore, plaintiff asserts, the amount of fees Ross paid Frankenheimer would be relevant to the issue of Frankenheimer's bias and credibility.

Plaintiff is entitled to probe for bias by inquiring into the existence and nature of the relationship between Frankenheimer and Ross. Specifically, plaintiff may discover what, if any, fee arrangements and retainer agreements were entered into between the two. However, the amount of fees earned, without more, is not probative of a witness' bias. Even where a witness' entire livelihood derives from employment by the party for whom he testifies, courts have declined to infer bias from the mere fact of employment. In this case, the court is especially reluctant to pry into the details of the attorney-client relationship or to order burdensome discovery. Consequently, plaintiff's motion to compel discovery of legal fees is denied.

Plaintiff's third request is to discover the names of other employees who have complained about defendant, and the nature of their complaints. Plaintiff's argument for discoverability rests on the Second Circuit's interpretation of the allegedly libelous letter in question. In the letter, Ross stated that Davis no longer worked for her, and then wrote: "If I let an employee go, it is because their work or their personal habits are not acceptable to me. I do not recommend these people." According to the Court of Appeals, the statement, "I do not recommend these people," tends to objectify Ross' evaluation of Davis, and implies that others would also find Davis' work or personal habits unacceptable.

Plaintiff argues that the truth of this statement—that Davis' work or personal habits are objectively unacceptable—will be at issue. Consequently, plaintiff asserts, the material sought is discoverable because "[i]f in fact it was defendant's personality that was a problem and not plaintiff's the jury would be entitled to conclude that there was nothing objectionable about plaintiff's work or personal habits and that defendant is liable for defamation."

The logic of plaintiff's argument is tenuous. Whether Ross is a "good" or "bad" employer, popular or unpopular with employees, is not probative of whether Davis' personal or work habits were objectively satisfactory. Even if other employees have complained about Ross, that would not affect a jury's assessment of Davis' personal or work habits one way or the other. The issue in this case is whether Ross libeled Davis, and the material plaintiff seeks to discover does not bear on that.

Plaintiff also argues that the information is discoverable because it bears on Ross' credibility. The court simply does not see the connection between Ross' reputation as an employer and her capacity for truthtelling. In short, the information sought by plaintiff is irrelevant to any material issue, and is not calculated to lead to any admissible evidence. Consequently, plaintiff's motion is denied.

The court turns now to the motion to compel discovery brought by defendant. Ross seeks discovery of Davis' treatment by a psychiatrist during the period Davis worked for Ross, arguing that the material is relevant and that any physician-patient privilege has been waived.

When the mental or physical condition of the plaintiff is in issue, the physician-patient privilege is waived and cannot be invoked to foreclose discovery of relevant evidence. Defendant argues that plaintiff put her mental condition in issue when she sued to recover for "great mental pain and anguish" (Complaint ¶ 17).

It is generally true that "[w]here compensation is sought for personal injury, the health of the plaintiff before and after the accident may be inquired into. This principle would seem to have equal applicability to an emotional or mental injury when that is what a plaintiff seeks compensation for." Miller v. Colonial Refrigerated Transportation, Inc., 81 F.R.D. 741, 742 (M.D.Pa.1979). See also Mancinelli v. Texas Eastern Transmission Corp., 34 A.D.2d 535, 308 N.Y.S.2d 882 (1st Dep't 1970) (psychiatric treatment held relevant and discoverable when damages sought for mental injury); Awtry v. United States, 27 F.R.D. 399, 402 (S.D.N.Y. 1961) (plaintiff's medical and psychiatric history discoverable where plaintiff alleged mental anguish as result of the entry on his medical chart that he was a hypochondriac).

Plaintiff argues, however, that her mental condition is not in issue, notwithstanding her claim for mental pain and anguish, because her action is one for libel per se and in such actions under New York law, general damages are presumed and need not be specifically pleaded or proved. Under plaintiff's view of New York law, it is unnecessary for her to prove either the existence or amount of damages. Consequently, plaintiff argues, information relating to the existence or amount of mental pain and anguish is not relevant and therefore not discoverable.

Defendant contends that New York's rule permitting recovery for presumed damages in libel cases has been overruled by Gertz v. Robert Welch, Inc., 418 U.S. 323, 94 S.Ct. 2997, 41 L.Ed.2d 789 (1974), and that New York courts, in conformance with the Supreme Court's ruling, now require plaintiffs in cases of libel per se to prove they were damaged (in the absence of a showing of actual malice). [The court found that *Gertz* had been modified by a later Supreme Court decision, and that the New York courts might return to their former rule, as plaintiff urged.] * * *

[E]ven if plaintiff's view of the law prevails and presumed damages are reinstated, that does not mean that information relating to the existence or amount of damages is irrelevant or not discoverable. General damages may be presumed, but defendant must be permitted to rebut the presumption, to try to disprove the existence of damage. Moreover, the amount of damages will always be in issue; plaintiff seeks one million dollars in compensatory damages, and evidence must be introduced to demonstrate that the award should be more than nominal. See Wood v. Lee, 41 A.D.2d 730, 341 N.Y.S.2d 738 (1st Dep't 1973) (it is assumed that defamation causes some damage though it be nominal). Plaintiff may not sue to recover for mental pain and anguish, only to deny the defendant the evidence she needs to argue that there was no damage, or that the amount of compensation sought is excessive.[5]

---

5. Defendant also argues that the psychiatric material is relevant to the issue of

Accordingly, defendant's motion to compel discovery of plaintiff's treatment by a psychiatrist is granted.

Notes and Questions

1. The district judge had earlier dismissed plaintiff's suit on the ground that she had failed to state a claim. Here the court denies all plaintiff's discovery requests and grants defendant's discovery request. Could the court's view of the merits have affected its ruling on the discovery issues? Should it? See Rule 26(b)(2). Students should recognize that the judge's discovery rulings can be debated.

2. It should be apparent that the concept of relevance is critical to the scope of discovery. Relevance analysis has developed in evidence law; Fed. R.Evid. 402 declares that all relevant evidence is admissible, but the law has not developed a precise standard for determining what is relevant. Fed. R. Evid. 401 thus states that " '[r]elevant evidence' means evidence having any tendency to make the existence of any fact that is of consequence to the determination of the action more probable or less probable than it would be without the evidence." The Advisory Committee notes explain how the rule should be applied:

> Relevancy is not an inherent characteristic of any item of evidence but exists only as a relation between an item of evidence and a matter properly provable in the case. Does the item of evidence tend to prove the matter sought to be proved? Whether the relationship exists depends upon the principles evolved by experience or science, applied logically to the situation at hand. The rule summarizes this relationship as a "tendency to make the existence" of the fact to be proved "more probable or less probable." Compare Uniform Rule [of Evidence] 1 (2) which states the crux of relevancy as "a tendency in reason," thus perhaps emphasizing unduly the logical process and ignoring the need to draw upon experience or science to validate the general principle upon which relevancy in a particular situation depends.

* * *

> The rule uses the phrase "fact that is of consequence to the determination of the action" to describe the kind of fact of which proof may properly be directed. * * * The fact to be proved may be ultimate, intermediate, or evidentiary; it matters not, so long as it is of consequence to the determination of the action.

> The fact to which the evidence is directed need not be in dispute. While situations will arise which call for the exclusion of evidence offered to prove a point conceded by the opponent, the ruling should be made on the basis of such considerations as waste of time and undue prejudice rather than under any general requirement that evidence is admissible only if directed to matters in dispute. Evidence which is essentially background in nature can scarcely be said to involve disputed

whether the allegedly libelous statement was true—whether Davis' personal or work habits truly were objectively unacceptable. In light of the court's decision based on the relevance of the material to the issue of damages, it is unnecessary to reach defendant's other argument.

matter, yet it is universally offered and admitted as an aid to understanding.

How does this relevance reasoning apply to the types of information in dispute in Davis v. Ross? How does the court decide what is a "fact of consequence" in the case?

3. To be discoverable under Rule 26(b)(1), material has needed only to be "relevant to the subject matter involved in the pending action," sometimes a broader concept than relevance for purposes of admissibility under the evidence rules. In 2000, the Supreme Court amended Rule 26(b)(1) to limit party-controlled discovery to matters "relevant to the claim or defense of any party." Would the change alter the result on the discovery disputes in Davis v. Ross? The amended rule authorizes the court to extend discovery to the entire "subject matter" for good cause. Should the change make a difference in many cases? The Committee Note observes as follows:

> The Committee intends that the parties and the court focus on the actual claims and defenses involved in the action. The dividing line between information relevant to the claims and defenses and that relevant only to the subject matter of the action cannot be defined with precision. A variety of types of information not directly pertinent to the incident in suit could be relevant to the claims or defenses raised in a given action. For example, other incidents of the same type, or involving the same product, could be properly discoverable under the revised standard. information about organizational arrangements or filing systems of a party could be discoverable if likely to yield or lead to the discovery of admissible information. Similarly, information that could be used to impeach a likely witness, although not otherwise relevant to the claims or defenses, might be properly discoverable. In each instance, the determination whether such information is discoverable because it is relevant to the claims or defenses depends on the circumstances of the pending action.

The rule amendment has had a very modest effect on the scope of discovery. See, e.g., Sanyo Laser Products, Inc. v. Arista Records, Inc., 214 F.R.D. 496 (S.D.Ind.2003) (new scope of discovery is not dramatically different, and broad discovery remains the norm); Graham v. Casey's General Stores, 206 F.R.D. 251 (S.D.Ind.2002) ("Even after the recent amendment * * * courts employ a liberal discovery standard"); Thompson v. Department of Housing and Urban Devel., 199 F.R.D. 168 (D.Md.2001) (preoccupation with the difference between relevance to the subject matter and to the claims and defenses is "the juridical equivalent to debating the number of angels that can dance on the head of a pin"); Rowe, A Square Peg in a Round Hole? The 2000 Limitation on the Scope of Federal Civil Discovery, 69 Tenn. L. Rev. 12 (2001).

4. Why is information about Ross's financial condition relevant? Would it be relevant to determine whether Ross could pay a judgment? Note that Rule 26(a)(1)(D) now requires disclosure of insurance policies. When discovery of these was first authorized, the Advisory Committee explained this provision as follows:

> Disclosure of insurance coverage will enable counsel for both sides to make the same realistic appraisal of the case, so that settlement and

litigation strategy are based on knowledge and not speculation. It will conduce to settlement and avoid protracted litigation in some cases, though in others it may have the opposite effect. The [rule] is limited to insurance coverage, which should be distinguished from any other facts concerning defendant's financial status (1) because insurance is an asset created specifically to satisfy the claim; (2) because the insurance company ordinarily controls the litigation; (3) because information about coverage is available only from defendant or his insurer; and (4) because disclosure does not involve a significant invasion of privacy.

How persuasive is this reasoning? Should it apply more generally to information about the financial condition of a defendant?

With respect to the financial information sought by plaintiff in Davis v. Ross, the court relies on New York rules governing timing of admission of such material into evidence at trials. How can those rules have any bearing on whether discovery should be allowed? Should discovery regarding the extent of plaintiff's damages await a jury determination that defendant is liable for them? Compare Cal. Civ. Code § 3295(c) (precluding discovery by plaintiff regarding defendant's financial condition until plaintiff establishes a "substantial probability" of prevailing on punitive damages).

The court's principal concern seems to be protecting Ross' privacy. Should privacy concerns prompt courts to narrow discovery? A highly-respected former federal judge has noted that "[a] foreigner watching the discovery proceedings in a civil suit would never suspect that this country has a highly-prized tradition of privacy enshrined in the Fourth Amendment." Rifkind, Are We Asking Too Much of Our Courts?, 70 F.R.D. 96, 107 (1976). For an example of discovery intrusiveness, consider Zises v. Department of Social Services, 112 F.R.D. 223 (E.D.N.Y.1986). Plaintiff in a Title VII employment discrimination suit for sexual harassment revealed in her deposition that during the period in question she had kept an extensive "journal," writing 20 to 30 pages daily in a "stream of unconscious becoming conscious." Because plaintiff testified that she wrote about her experiences at work, the court ordered her to turn over the journal to defendant, and plaintiff decided to abandon her suit rather than turn over her journals. See also Simpson v. University of Colorado, 220 F.R.D. 354 (D.Colo.2004) (student suing university for sexual harassment had to turn over diary entries).

Courts have, however, shown some receptiveness to privacy and related concerns in disposing of discovery issues. See, e.g., Reproductive Services, Inc. v. Walker, 439 U.S. 1307, 99 S.Ct. 1, 58 L.Ed.2d 16 (1978) (Brennan, J., in chambers) (in malpractice action by patient who had abortion, discovery of identities of other abortion patients should be conditioned on protections for privacy of other patients); Britt v. Superior Court, 20 Cal.3d 844, 143 Cal.Rptr. 695, 574 P.2d 766 (1978) (order compelling disclosure of identity of persons protesting airport expansion infringed their First Amendment right of association).

5. Where privacy interests are involved, should the courts routinely issue protective orders to limit the disclosure of discovered material if discovery is ordered? Is there any limitation on what Ross does with the information she obtains through discovery about Davis' psychiatric treatment? "Generally speaking, when a party obtains documents or information

through the discovery process, he can 'use that information in any way which the law permits.' The discovery rules themselves place no limitations on what a party may do with the materials obtained in discovery." In re Halkin, 598 F.2d 176, 188 (D.C.Cir.1979). The court in In re Halkin reasoned that the First Amendment forbids limits on a litigant's use of materials obtained through discovery unless a very rigorous standard fashioned for "prior restraints" on speech is satisfied. In Seattle Times Co. v. Rhinehart, 467 U.S. 20, 104 S.Ct. 2199, 81 L.Ed.2d 17 (1984), however, the Supreme Court endorsed broad discretion for imposition of limitations on dissemination of discovered material where supported by "good cause." For an argument that more weight should be given to limiting use of discovered material to preparation for trial, see Marcus, Myth and Reality in Protective Order Litigation, 69 Cornell L.Rev. 1 (1983).

6.   Should confidentiality concerns other than privacy justify denial of discovery? Consider Coca–Cola Bottling Co. v. Coca–Cola Co., 107 F.R.D. 288 (D.Del.1985), in which plaintiffs sought to compel defendant to turn over "one of the best-kept trade secrets in the world," the formula for Coca–Cola. Only two people in the company knew the formula, which was kept in a bank vault in Atlanta, Georgia, that could only be opened upon a resolution by the Company's board of directors. Plaintiffs were independent bottlers who produced the drink by mixing syrup they bought from the company with carbonated water. In 1921, they had entered into contracts that specified the price they would have to pay for "Coca–Cola Bottling syrup." When Diet Coke was introduced in 1982, the company claimed that it was not covered by the contracts because Coca–Cola and diet Coke were different products. Plaintiffs sued to enforce their contractual right to buy diet Coke syrup at the contractual price and sought the formula because it bore on the question whether these were different products. Eventually the discovery dispute expanded to include old Coke ("Coca–Cola Classic"), new Coke and caffeine free Coke.

The court granted plaintiffs' motion:

> The issue squarely presented by plaintiffs' motion to compel is whether plaintiffs' need for the secret formula outweighs defendant's need for protection of its trade secrets. In considering this dispute, I am well aware of the fact that disclosure of trade secrets in litigation, even with the use of an appropriate protective order, could "become by indirection the means of ruining an honest and profitable enterprise." Moreover, I am also aware that an order compelling disclosure of the Company's secret formula could be a bludgeon in the hands of plaintiffs to force a favorable settlement. On the other hand, unless defendant is required to respond to plaintiffs' discovery, plaintiffs will be unable to learn whether defendant has done them a wrong. Except for a few privileged matters, nothing is sacred in civil litigation; even the legendary barriers erected by the Coca–Cola Company to keep its formulae from the world must fall if the formulae are needed to allow plaintiffs and the Court to determine the truth in these disputes.

* * *

As in most disputes over the discoverability of trade secrets, the necessity of the discovery for the complete formulae follows logically from the determination that the formulae are relevant. Plaintiffs need the complete formulae in order to address the product identity issue by comparing the ingredients of the various soft drinks involved. Plaintiffs cannot respond to the assertions of defendant's experts that diet Coke and Coca–Cola are two products unless plaintiffs' experts can analyze the complete formulae and explain why the products are the same. Merely using the publicly-disclosed ingredients is obviously insufficient, because they would present an incomplete picture, and because the secret ingredients are the key to the taste of Coca–Cola. The differences in the public ingredients, including sweeteners, cannot be understood unless they are put in context through disclosure of the similarities and differences in the secret ingredients. Without the complete formulae, plaintiffs will be foreclosed from presenting all the relevant evidence in support of their position.

In addition, plaintiffs need the complete formulae in order to explore on cross-examination the bases for the opinions of Company witnesses that Coca–Cola and diet Coke are two separate products. * * * It follows that discovery of the complete formulae is necessary.

* * *

The potential harm that would come from public disclosure of the formulae for old Coke, new Coke, diet Coke, and caffeine free Coke is great, but virtually all of that harm can be eliminated with stringent protective orders and other safeguards. Because plaintiffs are Coca–Cola bottlers, they will have an incentive to keep the formulae secret. The likelihood of harm is less than if defendant's trade secrets were disclosed in litigation to competitors. The potential for harm from protected disclosure of the formulae for old Coke, new Coke, diet Coke, and caffeine free Coke is outweighed by the plaintiffs' need for the information.

Is this information less confidential than financial information about Diana Ross? Is the need for the information greater? What protective order provision should the court use to protect the company? Couldn't a similar order be fashioned to protect Ross' privacy interest?

7. Should protective orders also be granted for business information that is not, like the formula for Coca–Cola, a trade secret? There has been much consternation about the possibility that information about allegedly dangerous products has been produced through discovery but has been kept from the general public under protective orders. See, e.g., Cipollone v. Liggett Group, Inc., 785 F.2d 1108 (3d Cir.1986), cert. denied, 484 U.S. 976, 108 S.Ct. 487, 98 L.Ed.2d 485 (1987) (protective order applied to all discovery in tobacco products liability litigation). Some states have imposed restrictions on protective orders in cases involving "public health hazards." See Florida "Sunshine in Litigation Act," Fla.Stats. § 69.081; Tex.R.Civ.P. 76a. Should discovery be used as a device to provide the public with information? For discussion see Marcus, The Discovery Confidentiality Controversy, 1991 U.Ill.L.Rev. 457; Miller, Confidentiality, Protective Orders, and Public Access to the Courts, 105 Harv.L.Rev. 427 (1991).

8. Should the court in Davis v. Ross have been solicitous of plaintiff's desire to keep confidential her treatment by a psychiatrist while she was working for Ross? Besides damages, would information about this treatment be relevant to the case? See the court's footnote 5. Yet this relevant evidence may be unavailable due to the psychotherapist-patient privilege. The court holds that plaintiff has waived this privilege by placing her mental condition at issue in her claim for mental pain and anguish. Is this fair?

9. Could defendant also require plaintiff to submit to a mental examination regarding her pain and suffering claim? In Vinson v. Superior Court, 740 P.2d 404 (Cal.1987), plaintiff sought damages for mental distress in her sexual harassment employment discrimination suit. The state supreme court refused to overturn an order that she undergo a psychological examination. It noted that "plaintiff haled defendants into court and accused them of causing her various mental and emotional ailments" and that her mental state was therefore in controversy. It added, however, that "[a] simple sexual harassment claim asking for compensation for having to endure an oppressive work environment or for wages lost following an unjust dismissal would not normally create a controversy regarding the plaintiff's mental state." Id. at 409; see also Robinson v. Jacksonville Shipyards, Inc., 118 F.R.D. 525, 531 (N.D.Fla.1988) ("ruling in favor of a mental examination * * * would endorse mental examinations in every Title VII hostile work environment sexual harassment case").

KOZLOWSKI v. SEARS, ROEBUCK & CO.

United States District Court, District of Massachusetts, 1976.
73 F.R.D. 73.

JULIAN, SENIOR DISTRICT JUDGE.

A brief statement of the prior events in this case suffices to explain the present posture of the defendant's motion to remove the default judgment. Plaintiff, a minor, was severely burned on November 11, 1970, in Royal Oak, Michigan, when a pair of pajamas allegedly manufactured and marketed by defendant was "caused to ignite." Plaintiff commenced this product liability action on April 9, 1975, asserting claims sounding in negligence, breach of warranty, and strict liability in tort.

On July 17, 1975, the plaintiff filed a "Request to Produce" pursuant to Rule 34, Federal Rules of Civil Procedure, seeking, among other items, a record of all complaints and communications concerning personal injuries or death allegedly caused by the burning of children's nightwear which had been manufactured or marketed by the defendant, Sears, Roebuck & Co. On August 8, 1975, the defendant filed a motion to quash. The plaintiff opposed the defendant's motion to quash and filed a motion to compel discovery pursuant to Rule 37, Federal Rules of Civil Procedure. On January 22, 1976, United States Magistrate Princi filed a "Memorandum and Order," after a hearing on the motions, overruling the defendant's objections and ordering production within thirty days of all thirty-one items.[2] Because the material was not forthcoming, the

---

2. The Magistrate's order modified the plaintiff's request to produce as to twenty-

plaintiff filed, on April 16, 1976, a motion for entry of judgment by default against the defendant, pursuant to Rule 37, Federal Rules of Civil Procedure. On July 14, 1976, this Court, finding that the defendant's failure to comply with a previous discovery order was "willful and deliberate," entered a judgment by default against the defendant on the issue of liability, but conditioned its removal upon the defendant's "full compliance" with the Court's discovery order on or before September 15, 1976. On September 14, 1976, the defendant filed the instant motion to remove the judgment by default. The Court held a hearing on the motion on October 20, 1976, and took it under advisement. On the basis of that hearing, the Court finds that the defendant has failed substantially to comply fully with the Court's July 14 Order, and thus has not fulfilled the condition for removal of the default judgment.

The Court now denies defendant's motion for reasons hereinafter stated.

In the instant case, information concerning accidents similar to the one alleged in the complaint is clearly relevant to the issues of whether the pajamas allegedly marketed by the defendant were an unreasonably dangerous product and whether the defendant knew, or in the exercise of due care should have known, of that danger. Furthermore, even though the records of similar suits might be inadmissible in evidence (Narring v. Sears, Roebuck & Co., 59 Mich.App. 717, 229 N.W.2d 901 (1975) (circumstances of prior accident were too dissimilar to accident alleged in complaint)), the records might contain facts which would lead to the discovery of admissible evidence. See Rule 26(b)(1). Accordingly, most courts have held that the existence and nature of other complaints in product liability cases is a proper subject for pretrial discovery.

Nevertheless, information of similar complaints has not been produced by the defendant. The defendant has contended throughout this litigation and reiterated at the October 20 hearing that because of its longstanding practice of indexing claims alphabetically by name of claimant, rather than by type of product, there is no practical way for anyone to determine whether there have been any complaints similar to those alleged in the complaint at bar, "other than [by] going through all of the ... claims ... in the Sears Index ... which is the equivalent of an impossible task." No evidence has been produced tending to establish the truth of this representation.

Under Rule 34, Fed.R.Civ.P., the party from whom discovery is sought has the burden of showing some sufficient reason why discovery should not be allowed, once it has been determined that the items sought are properly within the scope of Rule 26(b). Merely because compliance with a "Request for Production" would be costly or time-consuming is not ordinarily sufficient reason to grant a protective order where the requested material is relevant and necessary to the discovery of evidence.

five of the items by imposing a time limit on the materials requested of five years prior and three years subsequent to November 11, 1970.

In the instant case, the requested documents are clearly within the scope of Rule 26(b), Fed.R.Civ.P., the plaintiff has a demonstrable need for the documents, the defendant undisputedly has possession of them, and the plaintiff has no other access to them. Thus, the defendant has a duty pursuant to Rule 34, Fed.R.Civ.P., to produce its records of similar suits. The defendant seeks to absolve itself of this responsibility by alleging the herculean effort which would be necessary to locate the documents. The defendant may not excuse itself from compliance with Rule 34, Fed.R.Civ.P., by utilizing a system of record-keeping which conceals rather than discloses relevant records, or makes it unduly difficult to identify or locate them, thus rendering the production of the documents an excessively burdensome and costly expedition. To allow a defendant whose business generates massive records to frustrate discovery by creating an inadequate filing system, and then claiming undue burden, would defeat the purposes of the discovery rules.

* * *

Finally, the defendant makes a confusing offer to finance the transportation to Chicago, Illinois (where the records are kept), by the plaintiff's attorney so that he may either attempt to locate the desired documents among the defendant's massive files, or else verify for himself the impossibility of such a task. The defendant has in essence told the plaintiff that, if he wishes, he may hunt through all its documents and find the information for himself. "This amounts to nothing more than a gigantic 'do it yourself' kit." This Court will not shift the financial burden of discovery onto the discovering party, in this case an indigent plaintiff, where the costliness of the discovery procedure involved is entirely a product of the defendant's self-serving indexing scheme over which the plaintiff has no control.

McPEEK v. ASHCROFT

United States District Court, District of Columbia, 2001.
202 F.R.D. 31,

FACCIOLA, United States Magistrate Judge

Plaintiff, Steven McPeek, began working for the Bureau of Prisons ("BOP") on May 27, 1986. He insists that, upon his promotion to Assistant to the Director in 1990, then-Director of the BOP, J. Michael Quinlan ("Quinlan"), began to sexually harass him and did so for the next two years. Plaintiff then filed an informal complaint against Quinlan, with the Department of Justice ("DOJ") Equal Employment Opportunity Staff. The matter was investigated and culminated in a Settlement Agreement on September 30, 1992. The agreement required that McPeek's complaints about Quinlan be kept confidential by both sides and that McPeek be transferred to the Management and Planning Staff ("MPS"), Justice Management Division ("JMD"), of DOJ. By 1994, plaintiff was working for the Justice Performance Review ("JPR"), under the Office of Policy Development and would ultimately become the

Deputy Director of JPR, where he reported to Robert F. Diegelman ("Diegelman"), Director of MPS.

Plaintiff's complaint identifies two forms of retaliation. He first complains that, despite the confidentiality of the settlement agreement, his claims against Quinlan were known by the people with whom he worked and that he suffered humiliation and retaliation at their hands. He then complains that, after hiring counsel in July 1998 to pursue formal legal remedies beginning with EEO counseling, he suffered renewed retaliation efforts.

In responding to plaintiff's discovery, defendants have searched for electronic and paper documents. Since defendants have already searched for electronic records, they do not quarrel with their obligation to do so. During discovery, the producing party has an obligation to search available electronic systems for the information demanded. See Fed. R.Civ.P. 34(a) (document(s) include "data compilations from which information can be obtained"). Plaintiff, however, wants more. He wants to force DOJ to search its backup systems since they might yield, for example, data that was ultimately deleted by the user but was stored on the backup tape and remains there today.

Defendants protest that the remote possibility that such a search will yield relevant evidence cannot possibly justify the costs involved. In support of that claim, defendants submit the declaration of Billy Hoppis, Branch Chief within the JMD office responsible for technology services. Hoppis explains that for the period 1992–1998, the DOJ computer system was known as "Eagle." In 1998, DOJ computers were briefly connected to a system called "JCON1." From 1998 to the present, they have been connected to "JCON2."

There was never a system-wide backup policy for Eagle servers. Each DOJ building had a server and an administrator who had his or her own backup policies. DOJ never intended a system which perfectly preserved all data. The purpose of having a backup system and retaining the tapes was to permit recovery from a disaster, not archival preservation. As a result, there are backup tapes for some periods of time but not others. Additionally, Hoppis explains:

> These backup tapes record only a "snapshot" of the contents of a user's working directory and emails (in the inbox, outbox, and trash) as of the specific date and time the backup was run, and therefore do not necessarily contain all emails sent or from a user, or all documents. In addition, unless a user deletes emails or documents between backups, each backup tape might contain many duplicate emails and documents that were captured on previous backup tapes.

Finally, the backup tapes have to be "restored" or rendered readable by returning the files to a source (i.e., a disk or hard drive) from which they can be read by the application which originally created them. Then, someone would have to review the restored file, whether a word processing document or e-mail, and determine whether it falls within one of plaintiff's document requests. Hoppis estimates that using

JCON2, the present operating system, merely restoring the e-mail from a single backup tape would take eight hours at a cost of no less than $93 per hour.

Using traditional search methods to locate paper records in a digital world presents unique problems. In a traditional "paper" case, the producing party searches where she thinks appropriate for the documents requested under Fed.R.Civ.P. 34. She is aided by the fact that files are traditionally organized by subject or chronology ("chron" files), such as all the files of a particular person, independent of subject. Backup tapes are by their nature indiscriminate. They capture all information at a given time and from a given server but do not catalogue it by subject matter.

Unlike a labeled file cabinet or paper files organized under an index, the collection of data by the backup tapes in this case was random. It must be remembered that the DOJ's use of a backup "synch" software system was not for the purpose of creating a perfect mirror image of each user's hard drive. Instead, the system was designed to prevent disaster, i.e., the destruction of all the data being produced on a given day if the network system crashed. Once the day ended and the system had not crashed, the system administrator could breathe a sigh of relief. She may then have maintained that day's backup tapes for some period of time, but then eventually taped over them. This explains why the tapes that remain today, ones which I ordered preserved, are tapes for certain days or periods of time but not for others and therefore not in perfect (or for that matter imperfect) chronological order.

It is therefore impossible to know in advance what is on these backup tapes. There is a theoretical possibility that there may be something on the tapes that is relevant to a claim or defense, for example, a subsequently deleted e-mail that might be evidence of a retaliatory motive. That possibility exists because other information establishes that the persons plaintiff claims retaliated against him used their computers for word processing and e-mail, and the backup tapes may have captured what those persons have since deleted from their computer files.

DOJ has chosen not to search these backup tapes and therefore runs the risk that the trial judge may give the jury an instruction that this failure to search permits the inference that the unfound files would contain information detrimental to DOJ. Conversely, the trial judge may ultimately determine that an instruction should not be given, and therefore DOJ lacks any incentive to conduct a search. Given the potential costs involved, a defendant may be more than willing to decline to search the backup tapes and take the chance that either the court will not give such an instruction at trial, or that if such an instruction is given, defendant will still prevail. In any event, a substantial number of civil cases settle and discovery advances the prospects of settlement. Any potential advancement of settlement would be foregone if the defendant has the option of choosing not to do the search and there is good reason to think that information on the backup tapes might induce one party or the other to settle.

There is certainly no controlling authority for the proposition that restoring all backup tapes is necessary in every case. The Federal Rules of Civil Procedure do not require such a search, and the handful of cases are idiosyncratic and provide little guidance. The one judicial rationale that has emerged is that producing backup tapes is a cost of doing business in the computer age. *In re Brand Name Prescription Drugs,* 1995 WL 360526 at * 3 (N.D.Ill., June 15, 1995). But, that assumes an alternative. It is impossible to walk ten feet into the office of a private business or government agency without seeing a network computer, which is on a server, which, in turn, is being backed up on tape (or some other media) on a daily, weekly or monthly basis. What alternative is there? Quill pens?

Furthermore, making the producing party pay for all costs of restoration as a cost of its "choice" to use computers creates a disincentive for the requesting party to demand anything less than all of the tapes. American lawyers engaged in discovery have never been accused of asking for too little. To the contrary, like the Rolling Stones, they hope that if they ask for what they want, they will get what they need. They hardly need any more encouragement to demand as much as they can from their opponent.

The converse solution is to make the party seeking the restoration of the backup tapes pay for them, so that the requesting party literally gets what it pays for. Those who favor a "market" economic approach to the law would argue that charging the requesting party would guarantee that the requesting party would only demand what it needs. Under that rationale, shifting the cost of production solves the problem.

But, there are two problems with that analysis. First, a strict cost-based approach ignores the fact that a government agency is not a profit-producing entity and it cannot be said that paying costs in this case would yield the same "profit" that other foregone economic activity would yield. Additionally, the government, which has no fewer rights than anyone else, has to insist that its employees do the restoration lest confidential information be seen by someone not employed by the government who has no right to see it. The reality, therefore, is that a government employee will be diverted from his ordinary duties to search backup tapes. When employees are thus diverted from their ordinary duties, the function of the agency suffers to the detriment of the taxpayers. Moreover, if government agencies are consistently required to pay for the restoration of backup tapes, they may be sorely tempted not to have such systems. There lies disaster; one shudders to think what would happen if the computer system at the Social Security Administration crashed and there was no backup system. While the notion that government agencies and businesses will not have backup systems if they are forced to restore them whenever they are sued may seem fanciful, courts should not lead them into temptation.

Second, if it is reasonably certain that the backup tapes contain information that is relevant to a claim or defense, shifting all costs to the requesting party means that the requesting party will have to pay for the agency to search the backup tapes even though the requesting party would not have to pay for such a search of a "paper" depository.

A fairer approach borrows, by analogy, from the economic principle of "marginal utility." The more likely it is that the backup tape contains information that is relevant to a claim or defense, the fairer it is that the government agency search at its own expense. The less likely it is, the more unjust it would be to make the agency search at its own expense. The difference is "at the margin."

Finally, economic considerations have to be pertinent if the court is to remain faithful to its responsibility to prevent "undue burden or expense". Fed.R.Civ.P. 26(c). If the likelihood of finding something was the only criterion, there is a risk that someone will have to spend hundreds of thousands of dollars to produce a single e-mail. That is an awfully expensive needle to justify searching a haystack. It must be recalled that ordering the producing party to restore backup tapes upon a showing of likelihood that they will contain relevant information in every case gives the plaintiff a gigantic club with which to beat his opponent into settlement. No corporate president in her right mind would fail to settle a lawsuit for $100,000 if the restoration of backup tapes would cost $300,000. While that scenario might warm the cockles of certain lawyers' hearts, no one would accuse it of being just.

Given the complicated questions presented, the clash of policies and the lack of precedential guidance, I have decided to take small steps and perform, as it were, a test run. Accordingly, I will order DOJ to perform a backup restoration of the e-mails attributable to Diegelman's computer during the period of July 1, 1998 to July 1, 1999. I have chosen this period because a letter from plaintiff's counsel to DOJ, complaining of retaliation and threatening to file an administrative claim, is dated July 2, 1998, and it seems to me a convenient and rational starting point to search for evidence of retaliation. I have chosen e-mail because of its universal use and because I am hoping that the restoration will yield both the e-mails Diegelman sent and those he received.

The DOJ will have to carefully document the time and money spent in doing the search. It will then have to search in the restored e-mails for any document responsive to any of plaintiff's requests for production of documents. Upon the completion of this search, the DOJ will then file a comprehensive, sworn certification of the time and money spent and the results of the search. Once it does, I will permit the parties an opportunity to argue why the results and the expense do or do not justify any further search.

Notes and Questions

1. Discovery not only can intrude into private affairs, it also can be very costly for the responding party, particularly for requests under Rule 34.

In *Kozlowski*, the judge said that "[m]erely because compliance with a 'Request for Production' would be costly or time-consuming is not ordinarily sufficient reason to grant a protective order where the requested material is relevant and necessary to the discovery of evidence." Does the judge in *McPeek* have the same attitude? One reason for the attitude of the judge in *McPeek* is that discovery of electronically stored information presents distinctive challenges. See The Challenges of E–Discovery, infra p. 377.

In *Kozlowski*, the judge says that cost should not ordinarily be an excuse for refusing to provide discovery that is "relevant and necessary." How important was the material that plaintiff sought there? Would evidence of complaints involving the flammability of children's nightwear manufactured for Sears by companies other than Russell Mills be relevant to this case? Would evidence of complaints about blouses manufactured for Sears by Russell Mills be relevant? Are there reasons why courts might hesitate to admit such evidence? Would discovery about these products nevertheless be reasonably calculated to lead to the discovery of admissible evidence?

Would evidence about the experiences of nonparties be more important in other kinds of cases? Consider Hollander v. American Cyanamid Co., 895 F.2d 80 (2d Cir.1990), an Age Discrimination in Employment Act suit by a fired manager. The appellate court held that the district judge had improperly refused to require an answer to plaintiff's interrogatory about all other management personnel over 40 whom defendant had fired in the previous five years:

> Because employers rarely leave a paper trail—or "smoking gun"—attesting to discriminatory intent, disparate treatment plaintiffs often must build their cases from pieces of circumstantial evidence which cumulatively undercut the credibility of various explanations offered by the employer. * * * The district court's refusal to compel an answer from American Cyanamid deprived Hollander of evidence potentially helpful to his attempt to assemble such a quantum of circumstantial evidence supporting his argument of pretext.

Is the relevance argument equally strong in *Kozlowski*? Compare the information sought in *McPeek*. Isn't that information more important to the claims raised by plaintiff there than the information sought in *Kozlowski*?

2. After *Kozlowski* was decided, Rule 26(b)(2) was added, calling for the court to curtail discovery in some situations, and in 2000 an invocation of Rule 26(b)(2) was added to Rule 26(b)(1), the general provision on relevance. Should American courts adopt a "pay as you go" approach to discovery? Cooter & Rubinfeld, Reforming the New Discovery Rules, 84 Geo.L.J. 61 (1995), define any discovery request for which compliance costs exceed the expected value of the evidence to be produced in strengthening the case of the party seeking discovery as "abusive." Should such an approach be taken under Rule 26(b)(2)? Note the reference to "marginal utility" in *McPeek*. Compare Hay, Civil Discovery: Its Effects and Optimal Scope, 23 J. Legal Stud. 481 (1994) (arguing that, even in economic terms, the Cooter and Rubinfeld view would not prompt a socially desirable level of discovery). Should this attitude be taken toward discovery of electronically stored information?

In Zubulake v. UBS Warburg LLC, 217 F.R.D. 309 (S.D.N.Y.2003), the court carefully explored these questions (id. at 316; 317–18):

> The application of these various discovery rules is particularly complicated where electronic data is sought because otherwise discoverable evidence is often only available from expensive-to-restore backup media. That being so, courts have devised creative solutions for balancing the broad scope of discovery prescribed in Rule 26(b)(1) with the cost-consciousness of Rule 26(b)(2). By and large, the solution has been to consider cost-shifting: forcing the requesting party, rather than the answering party, to bear the cost of discovery.

> * * *

> The first question, however, is whether cost-shifting must be considered in every case involving the discovery of electronic data, which—in today's world—includes virtually all cases. In light of the accepted principle * * * that electronic evidence is no less discoverable than paper evidence, the answer is, "No." The Supreme Court has instructed that "the presumption is that the responding party must bear the expense of complying with discovery requests...." [Oppenheimer Fund, Inc. v. Sanders, 437 U.S. 340, 358, 98 S.Ct. 2380 (1978)] Any principled approach to electronic evidence must respect this presumption.

> Courts must remember that cost-shifting may effectively end discovery, especially when private parties are engaged in litigation with large corporations. As large companies increasingly move to entirely paper-free environments, the frequent use of cost-shifting will have the effect of crippling discovery in discrimination and retaliation cases. This will undermine the "strong public policy favor[ing] resolving disputes on their merits," and may ultimately deter the filing of potentially meritorious claims.

> Thus, cost shifting should be considered *only* when electronic discovery imposes an "undue burden or expense" on the responding party.
> * * *

> Many courts have automatically assumed that an undue burden or expense may arise simply because electronic evidence is involved. This makes no sense. Electronic evidence is frequently cheaper and easier to produce than paper evidence because it can be searched automatically, key words can be run for privilege checks, and the production can be made in electronic form obviating the need for mass photocopying.

Compare Toshiba America Electronic Components, Inc. v. Superior Court, 21 Cal.Rptr.3d 532 (Cal.Ct.App.2004), holding that a California statute requires the demanding party to pay the cost of conversion of backup tapes unless the trial court finds that the conversion of the tapes was not necessary, or that the cost was not reasonable. Cal. Civ. Pro. § 2031(g) says that "if necessary, the responding party at the reasonable expense of the demanding party shall, through detecting devices, translate any data compilations included in the demand into reasonably usable form." Toshiba said it had over 800 backup tapes, and that the cost of restoring them would be $1.5–1.9 million. The court recognized that the California provision "conflicts with the federal rule, but it appears that the Legislature intended it to be that way." Therefore it was not a matter of discretion for the trial court, and Toshiba had a right to be paid the reasonable cost of restoring the tapes.

3. In McPeek v. Ashcroft, 212 F.R.D. 33 (D.D.C.2003), after the restoration ordered in the decision reprinted above was completed, the court ruled that further searches of backup tapes were, for the most part, not justified because the unsearched tapes related to time periods when it was extremely unlikely or impossible that references to plaintiff's pertinent activities could be found. In Zubulake v. UBS Warburg LLC, supra note 2, another sexual harassment case, the judge followed the lead of the judge in *McPeek* and ordered restoration and review of a "sample" of five backup tapes in a similar workplace retaliation case. After restoration at a cost of approximately $11,500, some 600 e-mail messages that were responsive to plaintiff's document request were found on these five tapes. Plaintiff argued that some 68 of the emails were important. Taking these 68 as reasonably representative of what would be found on the unrestored tapes, the judge decided that the rest of the tapes should be restored, and that plaintiff should pay 25% of the $166,000 cost of restoration of those tapes. See Zubulake v. UBS Warburg LLC, 216 F.R.D. 280 (S.D.N.Y.2003).

The judge in *Zubulake* articulated a seven-factor test for deciding whether to shift the cost of discovery of electronically stored information: (1) the extent to which the request is specifically tailored to discover relevant information; (2) the availability of such information from other sources; (3) the total cost of production, compared to the amount in controversy; (4) the total cost of production, compared to the resources available to each party; (5) the relative ability of each party to control costs and its incentive to do so; (6) the importance of the issues at stake in the litigation; and (7) the relative benefits to the parties of obtaining the information.

In allocating the costs as she did, the judge in *Zubulake* noted that plaintiff's discovery request—for messages about her—was tailored as best it could be to focus on relevant materials, and that plaintiff had shown that without searching backup tapes defendant had not produced all relevant materials, indicating that searching backup tapes was important. Although plaintiff had received a salary of approximately $500,000 per year (plus bonuses) while working for defendant, she had not found a new job after being fired by defendant, and defendant had "exponentially more resources" than plaintiff, so the judge fixed on 25% as an appropriate share for plaintiff. Compare XPedior Creditor Trust v. Credit Suisse First Boston (USA), Inc., 309 F.Supp.2d 459 (S.D.N.Y.2003) (no costs would be shifted even though restoration of backup tapes would cost approximately $400,000 because plaintiff was a bankrupt corporation, defendant had net revenues during previous year of $5.7 billion, the documents were unavailable from any other source, and potential damages in the case were $68 million); OpenTV v. Liberate Technologies, 219 F.R.D. 474 (N.D.Cal.2003) (costs of extracting inaccessible electronically stored information would be split evenly because both parties were similarly situated corporations).

4. The court in *Kozlowski* intimates that Sears may have set up its records in a way that is designed to frustrate discovery. Is there any evidence to support this suspicion? Does Sears have a duty to keep its records in a way that assists discovery by people who sue it? Must it computerize its

records to streamline discovery? See Fautek v. Montgomery Ward & Co., 96 F.R.D. 141 (N.D.Ill.1982) (employment discrimination plaintiffs need access to computer readable information on defendant's employment practices). Is there reason to suspect improper file-management practices in *McPeek*?

5. Would interrogatories be a better way to inquire initially about other complaints? Rule 33(d) gives the responding party the option to produce business records where the answer can be derived from them and "the burden of deriving or ascertaining the answer is substantially the same for the party serving the interrogatory as for the party served." Could that be true in *Kozlowski?*

In Saddler v. Musicland–Pickwick International, Inc., 31 Fed.R.Serv.2d 760 (E.D.Tex.1980), plaintiff in an employment discrimination action sought detailed statistical information, and defendant invoked Rule 33(d). Plaintiff contended that it did not apply because defendant could find the information in its own records more easily than plaintiff could. The court disagreed, although it did require defendant to make a knowledgeable employee available to assist plaintiff in locating information:

> As defendant properly points out, mere familiarity with a set of records cannot be dispositive in weighing the comparative burdens upon plaintiff and defendant in eliciting relevant data from those records. The party which compiles and maintains its own records will invariably be more conversant upon them than its adversary in litigation. If a disparity in familiarity necessarily created an inequality in the ease of discovery, the procedure provided by Rule 33[d] would rarely, if ever, be utilized. But the applicability of the Rule depends, not upon familiarity with a set of records, but with the relative difficulty of analyzing those records to derive the information desired. If both parties will be required to carry out an identical series of steps to obtain the information sought, the burden upon both is substantially the same as required by the Rule.

* * *

> While the court is sympathetic to the plight of an individual litigant faced with the considerable time and expense required to review extensive documentary evidence in preparation for trial, it has no authority to shift that burden of trial preparation to the opposing party.

6. Rule 34 does not have a "look at my files" option similar to the provisions of Rule 33(d). Ordinarily, the responding party must locate and assemble the items requested at its own expense. That is what Sears was refusing to do, since plaintiff did not want all files on complaints, but only those regarding burning pajamas. If the requests are broad, however, culling important information from the mass of produced documents may impose a burden similar to that under Rule 33(d). Rule 34(b) does, however, give the producing party a choice between organizing the produced documents in accordance with the requests or as they are kept in the usual course of business. There is disagreement on whether the party doing discovery can insist that the producing party organize the material in accord with the requests. Compare Sherman & Kinnard, Federal Court Discovery in the 80's—Making the Rules Work, 95 F.R.D. 245, 256–57 (1982) (arguing that "[i]n a case like *Kozlowski*, the discovered party should only be allowed to

produce its documents as kept in the usual course of business if that method is shown to provide sufficient indexing so that relevant documents can be found") with 8A C. Wright, A. Miller & R. Marcus, Federal Practice & Procedure § 2213 (2d ed. 1994) (arguing that rearrangement of files is not required).

7.   Cases like *McPeek* can raise significant privacy issues as well as cost issues. Consider the range of personal matters that may be discussed in e-mail or otherwise be stored on a computer hard drive. See, e.g., Fraser v. Nationwide Mutual Ins. Co., 352 F.3d 107 (3d Cir.2003) (defendant employer did not violate plaintiff employee's privacy rights by reviewing plaintiff's e-mail because it was stored on defendant's system).

8.   E-mail can provide forceful evidence. "Employees say things in e-mail messages that would never be stated directly to a person or consciously memorialized in writing." Pooley & Shaw, Finding Out What's There: Technical and Legal Aspects of Discovery, 4 Tex. Intell. Prop. L.J. 57, 63 (1995). Some employers are training their employees to ask "How would I feel if this message appeared on the front page of a newspaper?" See Varchaver & Bonamici, The Perils of E-mail, Fortune, Feb. 17, 2003. Because many litigants may seek to follow the "e-mail trail," this form of discovery will continue to be important.

THE CHALLENGES OF E–DISCOVERY

As suggested by McPeek v. Ashcroft, supra p. 368, discovery of electronically stored information has presented challenges for lawyers and courts. See generally Redish, Electronic Discovery and the Litigation Matrix, 51 Duke L.J. 561, 588–92 (2001) (describing the special challenges of E-discovery); see also Kerr, Digital Evidence and the New Criminal Procedures, 105 Colum.L.Rev. 279 (2005) (describing the broad impact of electronic evidence on procedure in criminal cases). Particularly since the introduction of the personal computer and e-mail, this sort of discovery has assumed great importance. That importance is likely to grow, as more and more information is electronically stored and not available in other forms. For example, it is estimated that over 90% of all business information is created electronically and never printed out.

An early judicial reaction to this phenomenon is reflected in In re Brand Name Prescription Drugs, 1995 WL 360526 (N.D.Ill.1995), in which the court observed that "if a party chooses an electronic storage method, the necessity for a retrieval program or method is an ordinary and foreseeable risk." The court refused to make plaintiffs pay for restoration of e-mail information, citing Kozlowski v. Sears Roebuck & Co. (supra p. 366) for the proposition that "the costliness of the discovery procedure involved is * * * a product of the defendant's record-keeping scheme over which the [plaintiffs have] no control."

As *McPeek* shows, the judicial attitude that one who relies on computers may not resist discovery on the basis of the difficulty posed by extracting some sorts of information from them is passing from the scene. In its place has come a recognition that, in some ways, E-discovery is distinctive. Some put the differences quite strongly: "[T]he document production of 2003 bears little resemblance to that of the 1980s or 1990s. * * * [T]echnology has changed forever the way lawyers produce their client's documents." Horrigan, Producing Those Documents, Nat. L.J., March 17, 2003, at C3. "Within three years, I'm sure almost all evidence collected in discovery will be electronic-based." Byron, Computer Forensics Sleuths Help Find Fraud, Wall St.J., March 18, 2003, at B1. For examination of these developments, see Marcus, Only Yesterday: Reflections on Rulemaking Responses to E–Discovery, 73 Fordham L. Rev. 1 (2004); Marcus, Confronting the Future: Coping With Discovery of Electronic Material, 64 Law & Contemp. Probs. 253 (Spring/Summer 2001).

One distinctive feature of E-discovery is volume: "Some major cases now involve one terabyte of information, which, if printed to paper, would fill the Sears Tower four times." Krause, What a Concept!, ABA Journal, Aug. 2003, at 60. Another is that computerized information may be found in dynamic databases that "exist" only in the sense that they will provide responsive information when queried.

As a result of distinctive features of E-discovery, proposals to amend the Federal Rules of Civil Procedure have been made. See Preliminary Draft of Proposed Amendments to the Federal Rules of Bankruptcy, Civil and Criminal Procedure and the Federal Rules of Evidence (Jud. Conf. of U.S., Aug. 9, 2004). If adopted, these changes could become effective as soon as Dec. 1, 2006. Whether or not formal rule changes are adopted, the courts will have to address the issues raised by discovery of electronically stored information. The rule-amendment proposals may differ from the way some courts have resolved such issues:

Form of production: With hard copy materials, the form of production rarely raises issues (unless there is a concern about assuring access to originals). With electronically stored information, there is a range of possibilities. One is to print out the information and provide it in paper. But a paper printout would not include what is called "metadata," containing information about the development of the document, often including information about the date of each change to the document and the like. Paper also does not disclose what is called "embedded data," containing information about prior drafts of the document and, perhaps, electronic notations made on the document.

An electronic version of the document may possess metadata or embedded data, but not all electronic versions will contain this information. TIFF images and PDF files, for example, do not contain this information. What is sometimes called "native data" usually will, although it may require specialized software to make use of the files. Whether or not metadata and embedded data are provided, it is likely that parties seeking discovery will prefer electronically stored information that can be electronically searched. As a result, form of production can be a major concern.

Under the proposed amendment to Rule 34, a party seeking production of electronically stored information may have to say so explicitly in the request. A proposed amendment to Rule 34(b) would permit the party seeking discovery additionally to designate the form for production. See Super Film of America, Inc. v. UCB Films, Inc., 219 F.R.D. 649 (D.Kan.2004) (requiring production in electronic form). There is also a proposal to amend Rule 26(f) to direct that the conference for planning discovery include discussion of E-discovery if it is contemplated in the action; that may provide useful information for later designation of forms for production. If the request does not designate a form for production, the proposed amendment would permit the responding party to select any form in which it maintains the data, or an electronically searchable form. It would also provide that the responding party need only produce the information in one form. Compare Cornell Research Found., Inc. v. Hewlett Packard Co., 223 F.R.D. 55 (N.D.N.Y.2003) (fact electronically stored information was initially produced in hard copy does not excuse production in electronic form as well).

Inaccessible material: As *McPeek* demonstrates, the problem of accessing certain electronically stored information can present great difficulties. In Zubulake v. UBS Warburg LLC, 217 F.R.D. 309, 318–19 (S.D.N.Y.2003), the court discerned five categories of data: (1) Active, online data: These data are readily accessed in ordinary operations; (2) Near-line data: These data are quickly accessible, usually using robotic means of access; (3) Offline storage/archives: These data are stored on removable optical disks or magnetic tapes, and access usually takes hours, or perhaps days; (4) Backup tapes: These storage media contain data that usually require restoration before they can be used, and are not organized in a way that facilitates archival use of the medium; and (5) Erased, fragmented or damaged data: These data result when material is "deleted;" that does not physically remove the information from a hard drive or other storage medium, but it does free up the space for other uses, leading to possible overwriting of some or all the information at some point. The court in *Zubulake* explained the significance of these categories as follows (217 F.R.D. at 319–20):

> Of these, the first three categories are typically identified as accessible, and the latter two as inaccessible. The difference between the two classes is easy to appreciate. Information deemed "accessible" is stored in a readily usable format. Although the time it takes to actually access the data ranges from milliseconds to days, the data does not need to be restored or otherwise manipulated to be usable. "Inaccessible" data, on the other hand, is not readily usable. Backup data must be restored * * *, fragmented data must be de-fragmented, and erased data must be reconstructed, all before the data [are] usable. That makes such data inaccessible.

A proposed amendment to Rule 26(b)(2) would relieve a responding party of the obligation to provide discovery regarding electronically stored information that is not reasonably accessible. Should the other side move to compel production, the responding party has the burden to show that the information is not reasonably accessible. Even if that showing is made, the court can order production consistent with Rule

26(b)(2), and can condition production on some cost-bearing by the party seeking discovery.

Spoliation: As noted above (see supra p. 356 n. 7), evidence preservation has become increasingly important. Electronically stored information often presents distinctive preservation problems. "Deleting" a document does not really remove it from the hard drive, but only frees up the space until it is overwritten. So electronically stored information is, in some ways, singularly hardy. A hard copy document, on the other hand, is effectively gone soon after it is discarded. But electronically stored information is also easily altered. Merely turning on a computer can modify or destroy data, as can any use of an electronic file. Reviewing a hard copy document, on the other hand, does not alter it. Moreover, computers can be (and often are) programmed to delete information after the passage of a certain amount of time. Trying to halt all the processes by which data are changed or superseded could play havoc with a party's computer system.

The proposed amendments deal with these concerns in two ways. First, a change to Rule 26(f) would direct the parties to discuss preservation of evidence during their early conference. Second, a new Rule 37(f) would forbid sanctions against a party for loss of information caused by the routine operation of its electronic information system.

These issues are likely to percolate through the courts for some time, whether or not the proposed rule amendments are adopted. Technological change may ease or eliminate some of the concerns listed above, and it may also create other problems. For example, one difficulty encountered in some discovery is what is called "legacy data," data preserved on outdated systems that don't exist any more. Accessing such data can prove extremely challenging.

D. EXEMPTIONS FROM DISCOVERY

Even though relevant, "privileged" material is exempt from discovery. Probably the most important privilege from the perspective of lawyers is the attorney-client privilege, discussed in Upjohn Co. v. United States, infra p. 391. It protects confidential communications between lawyer and client in which the client seeks legal advice. The idea is to promote full disclosure by the client to the lawyer. At the time Hickman v. Taylor was decided, the rules contained no further provisions about exemptions from discovery; Rule 26(b)(3) (dealing with "trial preparation materials") and 26(a)(2) and 26(b)(4) (dealing with discovery from experts) were added later.

HICKMAN v. TAYLOR
Supreme Court of the United States, 1947.
329 U.S. 495, 67 S.Ct. 385, 91 L.Ed. 451.

Justice Murphy delivered the opinion of the Court.

This case presents an important problem under the Federal Rules of Civil Procedure as to the extent to which a party may inquire into oral and written statements of witnesses, or other information, secured by an adverse party's counsel in the course of preparation for possible litigation after a claim has arisen. Examination into a person's files and records, including those resulting from the professional activities of an attorney, must be judged with care. It is not without reason that various safeguards have been established to preclude unwarranted excursions into the privacy of a man's work. At the same time, public policy supports reasonable and necessary inquiries. Properly to balance these competing interests is a delicate and difficult task.

On February 7, 1943, the tug "J.M. Taylor" sank while engaged in helping to tow a car float of the Baltimore & Ohio Railroad across the Delaware River at Philadelphia. The accident was apparently unusual in nature, the cause of it still being unknown. Five of the nine crew members were drowned. Three days later the tug owners and the underwriters employed a law firm, of which respondent Fortenbaugh is a member, to defend them against potential suits by representatives of the deceased crew members and to sue the railroad for damages to the tug.

A public hearing was held on March 4, 1943, before the United States Steamboat Inspectors, at which the four survivors were examined. This testimony was recorded and made available to all interested parties. Shortly thereafter, Fortenbaugh privately interviewed the survivors and took statements from them with an eye toward the anticipated litigation; the survivors signed these statements on March 29. Fortenbaugh also interviewed other persons believed to have some information relating to the accident and in some cases he made memoranda of what they told him. At the time when Fortenbaugh secured the statements of the survivors, representatives of two of the deceased crew members had been in communication with him. Ultimately claims were presented by representatives of all five of the deceased; four of the claims, however, were settled without litigation. The fifth claimant, petitioner herein, brought suit in a federal court under the Jones Act on November 26, 1943, naming as defendants the two tug owners, individually and as partners, and the railroad.

One year later, petitioner filed 39 interrogatories directed to the tug owners. The 38th interrogatory read: "State whether any statements of the members of the crews of the Tugs 'J.M. Taylor' and 'Philadelphia' or of any other vessel were taken in connection with the towing of the car float and the sinking of the Tug 'John M. Taylor'. Attach hereto exact copies of all such statements if in writing, and if oral, set forth in detail the exact provisions of any such oral statements or reports."

Supplemental interrogatories asked whether any oral or written statements, records, reports or other memoranda had been made concerning any matter relative to the towing operation, the sinking of the tug, the salvaging and repair of the tug, and the death of the deceased. If the answer was in the affirmative, the tug owners were then requested to set forth the nature of all such records, reports, statements or other memoranda.

The tug owners, through Fortenbaugh, answered all of the interrogatories except No. 38 and the supplemental ones just described. While admitting that statements of the survivors had been taken, they declined to summarize or set forth the contents. They did so on the ground that such requests called "for privileged matter obtained in preparation for litigation" and constituted "an attempt to obtain indirectly counsel's private files." It was claimed that answering these requests "would involve practically turning over not only the complete files, but also the telephone records and, almost, the thoughts of counsel."

In connection with the hearing on these objections, Fortenbaugh made a written statement and gave an informal oral deposition explaining the circumstances under which he had taken the statements. But he was not expressly asked in the deposition to produce the statements. The District Court for the Eastern District of Pennsylvania, sitting en banc, held that the requested matters were not privileged. The court then decreed that the tug owners and Fortenbaugh, as counsel and agent for the tug owners forthwith "Answer Plaintiff's 38th interrogatory and supplemental interrogatories; produce all written statements of witnesses obtained by Mr. Fortenbaugh, as counsel and agent for Defendants; state in substance any fact concerning this case which Defendants learned through oral statements made by witnesses to Mr. Fortenbaugh whether or not included in his private memoranda and produce Mr. Fortenbaugh's memoranda containing statements of fact by witnesses or to submit these memoranda to the Court for determination of those portions which should be revealed to Plaintiff." Upon their refusal, the court adjudged them in contempt and ordered them imprisoned until they complied.

The Third Circuit Court of Appeals, also sitting en banc, reversed the judgment of the District Court. It held that the information here sought was part of the "work product of the lawyer" and hence privileged from discovery under the Federal Rules of Civil Procedure. The importance of the problem, which has engendered a great divergence of views among district courts, led us to grant certiorari.

[Before turning to the merits, the Court dealt with what it deemed a "procedural irregularity" regarding the discovery tools employed. Prior court approval was then required for production of documents under Rule 34, so that to the extent plaintiff was trying to obtain documents by using interrogatories, he had employed the wrong device. While "[a] party clearly cannot refuse to answer interrogatories on the ground the information sought is solely within the knowledge of his attorney," the Court saw plaintiff's interrogatories as tantamount to a document production request. Noting that "[t]he deposition-discovery rules create integrated procedural devices," however, the Court declined to decide the case on this ground. Instead, the Court emphasized the need for a liberal interpretation of the discovery rules, see supra p. 332, and turned to "the basic question at stake," which it described as "whether any of those devices may be used to inquire into materials collected by an adverse party's counsel in the course of preparation for possible litigation." It concluded that the materials sought were not covered by the attorney-client privilege because "the protective cloak of this privilege does not extend to information which an attorney secures from a witness while acting for his client in anticipation of litigation. Nor does this privilege concern the memoranda, briefs, communications and other writings prepared by counsel for his own use in prosecuting his client's case."]

* * *

But the impropriety of invoking that privilege does not provide an answer to the problem before us. Petitioner has made more than an ordinary request for relevant, non-privileged facts in the possession of his adversaries or their counsel. He has sought discovery as of right of oral and written statements of witnesses whose identity is well known and whose availability to petitioner appears unimpaired. He has sought production of these matters after making the most searching inquiries of his opponents as to the circumstances surrounding the fatal accident, which inquiries were sworn to have been answered to the best of their information and belief. Interrogatories were directed toward all the events prior to, during and subsequent to the sinking of the tug. Full and honest answers to such broad inquiries would necessarily have included all pertinent information gleaned by Fortenbaugh through his interviews with the witnesses. Petitioner makes no suggestion, and we cannot assume, that the tug owners or Fortenbaugh were incomplete or dishonest in the framing of their answers. In addition, petitioner was free to examine the public testimony of the witnesses taken before the United States Steamboat Inspectors. We are thus dealing with an attempt to secure the production of written statements and mental impressions contained in the files and the mind of the attorney Fortenbaugh without any showing of necessity or any indication or claim that denial of such production would unduly prejudice the preparation of petitioner's case or cause him any hardship or injustice. For aught that appears, the essence of what petitioner seeks either has been revealed to him already through the interrogatories or is readily available to him direct from the witnesses for the asking.

The District Court, after hearing objections to petitioner's request, commanded Fortenbaugh to produce all written statements of witnesses and to state in substance any facts learned through oral statements of witnesses to him. Fortenbaugh was to submit any memoranda he had made of the oral statements so that the court might determine what portions should be revealed to petitioner. All of this was ordered without any showing by petitioner, or any requirement that he make a proper showing, of the necessity for the production of any of this material or any demonstration that denial of production would cause hardship or injustice. The court simply ordered production on the theory that the facts sought were material and were not privileged as constituting attorney-client communications.

In our opinion, neither Rule 26 nor any other rule dealing with discovery contemplates production under such circumstances. That is not because the subject matter is privileged or irrelevant, as those concepts are used in these rules.[9] Here is simply an attempt, without purported necessity or justification, to secure written statements, private memoranda and personal recollections prepared or formed by an adverse party's counsel in the course of his legal duties. As such, it falls outside the arena of discovery and contravenes the public policy underlying the orderly prosecution and defense of legal claims. Not even the most liberal of discovery theories can justify unwarranted inquiries into the files and the mental impressions of an attorney.

Historically, a lawyer is an officer of the court and is bound to work for the advancement of justice while faithfully protecting the rightful interests of his clients. In performing his various duties, however, it is essential that a lawyer work with a certain degree of privacy, free from unnecessary intrusion by opposing parties and their counsel. Proper preparation of a client's case demands that he assemble information, sift what he considers to be the relevant from the irrelevant facts, prepare his legal theories and plan his strategy without undue and needless interference. That is the historical and the necessary way in which lawyers act within the framework of our system of jurisprudence to promote justice and to protect their clients' interests. This work is reflected, of course, in interviews, statements, memoranda, correspondence, briefs, mental impressions, personal beliefs, and countless other tangible and intangible ways—aptly though roughly termed by the Circuit Court of Appeals in this case as the "work product of the lawyer." Were such materials open to opposing counsel on mere demand, much of what is now put down in writing would remain unwritten. An attorney's thoughts, heretofore inviolate, would not be his own. Inefficiency, unfairness and sharp practices would inevitably develop in the giving of legal advice and in the preparation of cases for trial. The effect on the legal profession would be demoralizing. And the interests of the clients and the cause of justice would be poorly served.

We do not mean to say that all written materials obtained or prepared by an adversary's counsel with an eye toward litigation are necessarily free from discovery in all cases. Where relevant and non-privileged facts remain hidden in an attorney's file and where production

---

9. The English courts have developed the concept of privilege to include all documents prepared by or for counsel with a view to litigation. "All documents which are called into existence for the purpose—but not necessarily the sole purpose—of assisting the deponent or his legal advisers in any actual or anticipated litigation are privileged from production.... Thus all proofs, briefs, draft pleadings, etc., are privileged; but not counsel's endorsement on the outside of his brief ..., nor any deposition or notes of evidence given publicly in open Court.... So are all papers prepared by any agent of the party bona fide for the use of his solicitor for the purposes of the action, whether in fact so used or not.... Reports by a company's servant, if made in the ordinary course of routine, are not privileged, even though it is desirable that the solicitor should have them and they are subsequently sent to him; but if the solicitor has requested that such documents shall always be prepared for his use and this was one of the reasons why they were prepared, they need not be disclosed." Odgers on Pleading and Practice (12th ed., 1939), p. 264.

of those facts is essential to the preparation of one's case, discovery may properly be had. Such written statements and documents might, under certain circumstances, be admissible in evidence or give clues as to the existence or location of relevant facts. Or they might be useful for purposes of impeachment or corroboration. And production might be justified where the witnesses are no longer available or can be reached only with difficulty. Were production of written statements and documents to be precluded under such circumstances, the liberal ideals of the deposition-discovery portions of the Federal Rules of Civil Procedure would be stripped of much of their meaning. But the general policy against invading the privacy of an attorney's course of preparation is so well recognized and so essential to an orderly working of our system of legal procedure that a burden rests on the one who would invade that privacy to establish adequate reasons to justify production through a subpoena or court order. That burden, we believe, is necessarily implicit in the rules as now constituted.

Rule 30(b),* as presently written, gives the trial judge the requisite discretion to make a judgment as to whether discovery should be allowed as to written statements secured from witnesses. But in the instant case there was no room for that discretion to operate in favor of the petitioner. No attempt was made to establish any reason why Fortenbaugh should be forced to produce the written statements. There was only a naked, general demand for these materials as of right and a finding by the District Court that no recognizable privilege was involved. That was insufficient to justify discovery under these circumstances and the court should have sustained the refusal of the tug owners and Fortenbaugh to produce.

But as to oral statements made by witnesses to Fortenbaugh, whether presently in the form of his mental impressions or memoranda, we do not believe that any showing of necessity can be made under the circumstances of this case so as to justify production. Under ordinary conditions, forcing an attorney to repeat or write out all that witnesses have told him and to deliver the account to his adversary gives rise to grave dangers of inaccuracy and untrustworthiness. No legitimate purpose is served by such production. The practice forces the attorney to testify as to what he remembers or what he saw fit to write down regarding witnesses' remarks. Such testimony could not qualify as evidence; and to use it for impeachment or corroborative purposes would make the attorney much less an officer of the court and much more an ordinary witness. The standards of the profession would thereby suffer.

Denial of production of this nature does not mean that any material, non-privileged facts can be hidden from the petitioner in this case. He need not be unduly hindered in the preparation of his case, in the discovery of facts or in his anticipation of his opponents' position.

---

* Under the 1970 amendments, Rule 30(b) was moved to Rule 26, where it ap-   pears as Rule 26(c).—Eds.

Searching interrogatories directed to Fortenbaugh and the tug owners, production of written documents and statements upon a proper showing and direct interviews with the witnesses themselves all serve to reveal the facts in Fortenbaugh's possession to the fullest possible extent consistent with public policy. Petitioner's counsel frankly admits that he wants the oral statements only to help prepare himself to examine witnesses and to make sure that he has overlooked nothing. That is insufficient under the circumstances to permit him an exception to the policy underlying the privacy of Fortenbaugh's professional activities. If there should be a rare situation justifying production of these matters, petitioner's case is not of that type.

JUSTICE JACKSON, concurring.

* * *

The primary effect of the practice advocated here would be on the legal profession itself. But it too often is overlooked that the lawyer and the law office are indispensable parts of our administration of justice. Law-abiding people can go nowhere else to learn the ever changing and constantly multiplying rules by which they must behave and to obtain redress for their wrongs. The welfare and tone of the legal profession is therefore of prime consequence to society, which would feel the consequences of such a practice as petitioner urges secondarily but certainly.

Counsel for the petitioner candidly said on argument that he wanted this information to help prepare himself to examine witnesses, to make sure he overlooked nothing. He bases his claim to it in his brief on the view that the Rules were to do away with the old situation where a law suit developed into "a battle of wits between counsel." But a common law trial is and always should be an adversary proceeding. Discovery was hardly intended to enable a learned profession to perform its functions either without wits or on wits borrowed from the adversary.

The real purpose and the probable effect of the practice ordered by the district court would be to put trials on a level even lower than a "battle of wits." I can conceive of no practice more demoralizing to the Bar than to require a lawyer to write out and deliver to his adversary an account of what witnesses have told him. Even if his recollection were perfect, the statement would be his language permeated with his inferences. Every one who has tried it knows that it is almost impossible so fairly to record the expressions and emphasis of a witness that when he testifies in the environment of the court and under the influence of the leading question there will not be departures in some respects. Whenever the testimony of the witness would differ from the "exact" statement the lawyer had delivered, the lawyer's statement would be whipped out to impeach the witness. Counsel producing his adversary's "inexact" statement could lose nothing by saying, "Here is a contradiction, gentlemen of the jury. I do not know whether it is my adversary or his witness who is not telling the truth, but one is not." Of course, if this practice were adopted, that scene would be repeated over and over again. The lawyer who delivers such statements often would find himself branded a deceiver afraid to take the stand to support his own version of the witness's conversation with him, or else he will have to go on the stand to defend his own credibility—perhaps against that of his chief witness, or possibly even his client.

Every lawyer dislikes to take the witness stand and will do so only for grave reasons. This is partly because it is not his role; he is almost invariably a poor witness. But he steps out of professional character to do it. He regrets it; the profession discourages it. But the practice advocated here is one which would force him to be a witness, not as to what he has seen or done but as to other witnesses' stories, and not because he wants to do so but in self-defense.

And what is the lawyer to do who has interviewed one whom he believes to be a biased, lying or hostile witness to get his unfavorable statements and know what to meet? He must record and deliver such statements even though he would not vouch for the credibility of the witness by calling him. Perhaps the other side would not want to call him either, but the attorney is open to the charge of suppressing evidence at the trial if he fails to call such a hostile witness even though he never regarded him as reliable or truthful.

JUSTICE FRANKFURTER joins in this opinion.

Notes and Questions

1. Rule 26, as written in 1947, exempted only "privileged" information from discovery, but the Court in *Hickman* simultaneously declares that the material sought is not privileged and that it is not discoverable although relevant. Are the Court's reasons persuasive in view of its emphasis on the broad discovery authorized under the federal rules? Consider Professor Cooper's evaluation:

> Clearly no one would argue today that a court should be forced to determine a law suit on the basis of inadequate information in order to preserve for one party the advantages gained by luck, skill, or wealth. Discovery itself rests on the impatient rejection of any assertion of a proprietary privilege to prevail because of unilateral ignorance; if there is some "unfairness" in unbridled discovery, it must be sought in terms of interference with the just disposition of litigation.

> In searching for interference with the litigation process, the Court's stern reference to "inefficiency, unfairness and sharp practices," and its clarion cry against demoralizing the legal profession, make heady reading. Unfortunately, they add nothing but an obscuring color of rhetoric to the implicit proposition that the adversary system of litigation cannot function in an atmosphere of complete candor; if no one mourns the sporting theory of justice, still there must be an area of gamesmanship in which fear of the unknown enforces an honesty which mere ethics could not achieve. The fact that litigation has remained adversarial in form and an operational reality must be thought to be responsible for generating pressure toward winning representation, which could lead to dishonest tactics if there were no limits on discovery.

Lacking any basis in controllable or even measurable experience to test such a fear about the effects of discovery, it would be difficult to quarrel with it except by advancing an intuition that no such special protection is really needed. And intuition tugs at least as strongly toward the proposition that discovery can best serve the ultimate truth-finding purposes of the adversary system if its equalizing function is subject to some such limitations. As long as the attorney is charged with the duty of presenting the most favorable case possible for his client, there will be the temptations and impetus of advocacy to strain his ultimate obligation to justice as well as to victory. Perfect knowledge of every item of proof and argument, of the complete trial "strategy" of opposing counsel, would often result—unconsciously in most cases—in a development of position and response calculated to impede rather than advance the search for whatever truth ex post inquiry can obtain.

Cooper, Work Product of the Rulesmakers, 53 Minn.L.Rev. 1269, 1274–75 (1969); compare Wells, the Attorney Work Product Doctrine and Carry–Over Immunity: An Assessment of their Justifications, 47 U.Pitt.L.Rev. 675, 683 (1986) ("a closer look at the specific rationales [for the work product rule], however, suggests that the work product immunity is largely designed to protect lawyers from themselves and their own unprofessionalism, rather than from their adversaries.")

2. If the idea behind work product protection is to preserve some element of surprise for trial, similar concerns have surfaced in connection with certain types of impeachment evidence which might be rendered ineffective if the witness could find out about it before testifying. As one judge put it, "[a] certain amount of surprise is often a catalyst which precipitates the truth. * * * [T]here are facile witnesses whose interest in 'knowing the truth before trial' is prompted primarily by a desire to find the most plausible ways to defeat the truth." Margeson v. Boston & Maine R.R., 16 F.R.D. 200, 201 (D.Mass.1954). Accordingly, some judges have denied access to tools of impeachment such as films showing that the plaintiff is not as badly injured as he claims. Does such a procedure subject parties to unfair risks at trial? See Boldt v. Sanders, 261 Minn. 160, 111 N.W.2d 225 (1961) ("it is implicit in [defendant's] position that witnesses whose testimony is designed to impeach invariably have a monopoly on virtue and that evidence to which the attempted impeachment is directed is, without exception, fraudulent"). See Denham & Bales, The Discoverability of Surveillance Videotapes Under the Federal Rules, 52 Baylor L. Rev. 753 (2000).

3. The simple expedient of taking the deposition of the other side's lawyer might not have occurred to lawyers at the time *Hickman* was decided, but some see a change in that: "In recent years, the boundaries of discovery have steadily expanded, and it appears that the practice of taking the deposition of opposing counsel has become an increasingly popular vehicle of discovery. To be sure, the Federal Rules of Civil Procedure do not specifically prohibit the taking of opposing counsel's deposition. See Fed.R.Civ.P. 30(a) (a party may take the deposition of 'any person'). We view the increasing practice of taking opposing counsel's deposition as a negative development in the area of litigation, and one that should be employed only in limited circumstances." Shelton v. American Motors Corp., 805 F.2d 1323, 1327 (8th Cir.1986). If the work product doctrine is available to resist improper

questions, is the taking of the lawyer's deposition a significant threat to work product concerns?

4. The *Hickman* Court's refusal to call work product a privilege persists to this day among some. See Cohn, The Work–Product Doctrine: Protection, Not Privilege, 71 Geo.L.J. 917 (1983). But the only sense in which it is not a privilege is that it is not absolute, as the attorney-client privilege is supposed to be. The Court may have rejected the privilege designation in *Hickman* due to embarrassment: "the Court was once more trapped by an apparently felt necessity of saving face by refusing to admit that a contingency had arisen which the rules had not foreseen or had dealt with improvidently." Cleary, Hickman v. Jencks: Jurisprudence of the Adversary System, 14 Vand.L.Rev. 865, 866 (1961). Even the Court itself has since referred to it as "the work product privilege." F.T.C. v. Grolier Inc., 462 U.S. 19, 26, 103 S.Ct. 2209, 2213, 76 L.Ed.2d 387 (1983).

5. In 1970, the Court adopted Rule 26(b)(3), which formally incorporated protection for "trial preparation materials" into the rules. In what way is the protection afforded by Rule 26(b)(3) different from that provided in *Hickman?* See Marcus, The Story of Hickman: Preserving Adversarial Incentives While Embracing Broad Discovery, in Civil Procedure Stores (2004) at 307, 331–32 (comparing Rule 26(b)(3) and *Hickman*). For example, consider:

(a) Would *Hickman* have provided any protection had the statements in that case been taken by an insurance adjuster? How would these be handled under the rule?

(b) Would Rule 26(b)(3) provide Fortenbaugh any basis for refusing in his deposition to answer questions about what he recalled of his interviews with the witnesses?

6. Both *Hickman* and Rule 26(b)(3) direct that special protection be afforded the kind of material whose revelation Professor Cooper found most troubling—information about trial strategy. Are there any circumstances under which such materials should be turned over? In Duplan Corp. v. Moulinage et Retorderie de Chavanoz, 509 F.2d 730 (4th Cir.1974), cert. denied, 420 U.S. 997, 95 S.Ct. 1438, 43 L.Ed.2d 680 (1975), the court concluded that "no showing of relevance, substantial need or undue hardship should justify compelled disclosure of an attorney's mental impressions, conclusions, opinion or legal theories." See also Cal.Code Civ.Proc. § 2018.030(a) (effective July 1, 2005): "A writing that reflects an attorney's impressions, conclusions, opinions, or legal research or theories is not discoverable under any circumstances." In Holmgren v. State Farm Mut. Auto. Ins. Co., 976 F.2d 573 (9th Cir.1992), a bad faith action against an insurer, the court disagreed and upheld discovery of memoranda prepared by defendant's adjuster even though it was opinion work product. It found that the adjuster's opinions were "directly in issue" and concluded that Rule 26(b)(3) "permits discovery when mental impressions are the pivotal issue in the current litigation and the need for the material is compelling."

7. Work product protection is available only if material is produced in anticipation of litigation. Why is this consideration important to the policies furthered by the doctrine? How likely must litigation appear? Although four of the five possible claims in *Hickman* were settled, it is doubtful that a court would hold that in such a situation there was not a sufficient

likelihood of litigation, but the doctrine does not protect all attorney action, only that directed toward preparation for trial. Thus, in United States v. El Paso Co., 682 F.2d 530 (5th Cir.1982), cert. denied, 466 U.S. 944, 104 S.Ct. 1927, 80 L.Ed.2d 473 (1984), the court, noting that "determining whether a document is prepared in anticipation of litigation is a slippery task," held that El Paso's "tax pool analysis" of its potential exposure for underpayment of taxes was part of its ordinary accounting procedure and therefore not entitled to protection. Ordinarily, the anticipation of litigation test looks to the date a document came into existence, the date of attorney involvement, and the date on which suit was first filed or threatened. Customarily material generated in the ordinary course of business is not considered to have been developed in anticipation of litigation. See generally Note, Work Product Discovery: A Multifactor Approach to the Anticipation of Litigation Requirement in Federal Rule of Civil Procedure 26(b)(3), 66 Iowa L.Rev. 1277 (1981).

8. If litigation is too remote a prospect to afford protection to some attorney work, does the fact that the litigation for which the work was done has ended mean that the protection should be removed in a second, unrelated litigation? The lower courts have divided on this question, some ruling that the protection only endures in "related" litigation. In Federal Trade Com'n v. Grolier Inc., 462 U.S. 19, 103 S.Ct. 2209, 76 L.Ed.2d 387 (1983), the Court confronted the question whether work product generated in connection with terminated litigation could be withheld from a request under the Freedom of Information Act because it was still protected by the doctrine. The Court held that the material could be withheld, but did not hold that the same would be true in civil litigation.

Justice Brennan, concurring, urged that the protection should be permanent:

> [D]isclosure of work product connected to prior litigation can cause real harm to the interests of the attorney and his client even after the controversy in the prior litigation is resolved. Many government agencies, for example, deal with hundreds or thousands of essentially similar cases in which they must decide whether and how to conduct enforcement litigation. Few of these cases will be "related" to each other in the sense of involving the same private parties or arising out of the same set of historical facts; yet large classes of them may present recurring, parallel factual settings and identical legal and policy considerations. It would be of substantial benefit to an opposing party (and of corresponding detriment to an agency) if the party could obtain work product generated by the agency in connection with earlier, similar litigation against other persons. * * * Any litigants who face litigation of a commonly recurring type—liability insurers, manufacturers of consumer products or machinery, large-scale employers, securities brokers, regulated industries, civil rights or civil liberties organizations, and so on— have an accurate interest in keeping private the manner in which they conduct and settle their recurring legal disputes.

How persuasive are these arguments? Do they provide a basis for a blanket rule that work product protection can endure forever?

9.   The Court in *Hickman* emphasized the duty of the party to provide, in response to discovery, factual information learned by its attorney. Why won't this deter the lawyer from investigating? Can a litigant simply ask its opponent to describe in detail all investigation done by its attorney? See Massachusetts v. First National Supermarkets, Inc., 112 F.R.D. 149 (D.Mass. 1986), in which the court held that an interrogatory asking for the identity of every person interviewed by counsel invaded work product, adding that the questioner could ask for identities of all known witnesses. To the extent that the witnesses were unearthed by counsel, how meaningful is this distinction?

10.   Note the special treatment of witness statements in Rule 26(b)(3). Why should they be treated in a different way? Consider the ultimate fate of the statements in *Hickman* itself:

> After fighting for the right to secure the statements of the accident witnesses from Fortenbaugh's file all the way to the Supreme Court, Freedman [plaintiff's lawyer] objected to the admission of the very same material at Hickman's trial. His objection, moreover, was sustained. Freedman today explains his objection by claiming that the statements must have been all favorable to Fortenbaugh's client, or else he would not have taken them. "When my opponent takes a statement from a witness, I'm going to fight like hell to keep it out."

Coady, Dredging the Depths of Hickman v. Taylor, Harvard Law Record, May 6, 1977, at 7.

11.   What showing should be required to justify discovery of work product? Could plaintiff have made a showing in *Hickman?* See Coogan v. Cornet Transportation Co., 199 F.R.D. 166 (D.Md.2001) (plaintiffs would be allowed to obtain the statement prepared by one defendant at the scene of the accident because it captured defendant's immediate perceptions of the accident); compare Goodyear Tire & Rubber Co. v. Chiles Power Supply, Inc., 190 F.R.D. 532 (N.D.Ind.1999) (witness statements prepared by defendant's insurer need not be produced; although three years had passed, plaintiff offered no evidence to show that it was prevented from obtaining the information it desired). Would the fact that there was a record of the hearing before the U.S. Steamboat Inspectors affect the decision whether plaintiff in *Hickman* had made the showing?

UPJOHN CO. v. UNITED STATES

Supreme Court of the United States, 1981.
449 U.S. 383, 101 S.Ct. 677, 66 L.Ed.2d 584.

JUSTICE REHNQUIST delivered the opinion of the Court.

* * *

I

Petitioner Upjohn Co. manufactures and sells pharmaceuticals here and abroad. In January 1976 independent accountants conducting an audit of one of Upjohn's foreign subsidiaries discovered that the subsidiary made payments to or for the benefit of foreign government officials in order to secure government business. The accountants so informed petitioner Mr. Gerard Thomas, Upjohn's Vice President, Secretary, and General Counsel. Thomas is a member of the Michigan and New York Bars, and has been Upjohn's General Counsel for 20 years. He consulted with outside counsel and R.T. Parfet, Jr., Upjohn's Chairman of the Board. It was decided that the company would conduct an internal investigation of what were termed "questionable payments." As part of this investigation the attorneys prepared a letter containing a questionnaire which was sent to "All Foreign General and Area Managers" over the chairman's signature. The letter began by noting recent disclosures that several American companies made "possibly illegal" payments to foreign government officials and emphasized that the management needed full information concerning any such payments made by Upjohn. The letter indicated that the chairman had asked Thomas, identified as "the company's General Counsel," "to conduct an investigation for the purpose of determining the nature and magnitude of any payments made by the Upjohn Company or any of its subsidiaries to any employee or official of a foreign government." The questionnaire sought detailed information concerning such payments. Managers were instructed to treat the investigation as "highly confidential" and not to discuss it with anyone other than Upjohn employees who might be helpful in providing the requested information. Responses were to be sent directly to Thomas. Thomas and outside counsel also interviewed the recipients of the questionnaire and some 33 other Upjohn officers or employees as part of the investigation.

On March 26, 1976, the company voluntarily submitted a preliminary report to the Securities and Exchange Commission on Form 8–K disclosing certain questionable payments. A copy of the report was simultaneously submitted to the Internal Revenue Service, which immediately began an investigation to determine the tax consequences of the payments. Special agents conducting the investigation were given lists by Upjohn of all those interviewed and all who had responded to the questionnaire. On November 23, 1976, the Service issued a summons pursuant to 26 U.S.C. § 7602 demanding production of:

> "All files relative to the investigation conducted under the supervision of Gerard Thomas to identify payments to employees of foreign governments and any political contributions made by the Upjohn Company or any of its affiliates since January 1, 1971 and to determine whether any funds of the Upjohn Company had been improperly accounted for on the corporate books during the same period.

> "The records should include but not be limited to written questionnaires sent to managers of the Upjohn Company's foreign affiliates, and memorandums or notes of the interviews conducted in the United States and abroad with officers and employees of the Upjohn Company and its subsidiaries."

The company declined to produce the documents specified in the second paragraph on the grounds that they were protected from disclosure by the attorney-client privilege and constituted the work product of attorneys prepared in anticipation of litigation. On August 31, 1977, the United States filed a petition seeking enforcement of the summons under 26 U.S.C. §§ 7402(b) and 7604(a) in the United States District Court for the Western District of Michigan. That court adopted the recommendation of a Magistrate who concluded that the summons should be enforced. Petitioners appealed to the Court of Appeals for the Sixth Circuit which rejected the Magistrate's finding of a waiver of the attorney-client privilege, but agreed that the privilege did not apply "[t]o the extent that the communications were made by officers and agents not responsible for directing Upjohn's actions in response to legal advice . . . for the simple reason that the communications were not the 'client's.' " The court reasoned that accepting petitioners' claim for a broader application of the privilege would encourage upper-echelon management to ignore unpleasant facts and create too broad a "zone of silence." Noting that Upjohn's counsel had interviewed officials such as the Chairman and President, the Court of Appeals remanded to the District Court so that a determination of who was within the "control group" could be made. In a concluding footnote the court stated that the work-product doctrine "is not applicable to administrative summonses issued under 26 U.S.C. § 7602."

II

Federal Rule of Evidence 501 provides that "the privilege of a witness . . . shall be governed by the principles of the common law as they may be interpreted by the courts of the United States in light of reason and experience." The attorney-client privilege is the oldest of the privileges for confidential communications known to the common law. Its purpose is to encourage full and frank communication between attorneys and their clients and thereby promote broader public interests in the observance of law and administration of justice. The privilege recognizes that sound legal advice or advocacy serves public ends and that such advice or advocacy depends upon the lawyer's being fully informed by the client. As we stated last Term in Trammel v. United States, 445 U.S. 40, 51, 100 S.Ct. 906, 913, 63 L.Ed.2d 186 (1980): "The lawyer-client privilege rests on the need for the advocate and counselor to know all that relates to the client's reasons for seeking representation if the professional mission is to be carried out." And in Fisher v. United States, 425 U.S. 391, 403, 96 S.Ct. 1569, 1577, 48 L.Ed.2d 39 (1976), we recognized the purpose of the privilege to be "to encourage clients to make full disclosure to their attorneys." This rationale for the privilege has long been recognized by the Court. Admittedly complications in the application of the privilege arise when the client is a corporation, which in theory is an artificial creature of the law, and not an individual; but this Court has assumed that the privilege applies when the client is a corporation, and the Government does not contest the general proposition.

The Court of Appeals, however, considered the application of the privilege in the corporate context to present a "different problem," since the client was an inanimate entity and "only the senior management, guiding and integrating the several operations, . . . can be said to possess an identity analogous to the corporation as a whole." 600 F.2d at 1226. The first case to articulate the so-called "control group test" adopted by the court below, Philadelphia v. Westinghouse Electric Corp., 210 F.Supp. 483, 485 (E.D.Pa. 1962), reflected a similar conceptual approach:

> "Keeping in mind that the question is, Is it the corporation which is seeking the lawyer's advice when the asserted privileged communication is made? the most satisfactory solution, I think, is that if the employee making the communication, of whatever rank he may be, is in a position to control or even to take a substantial part in a decision about any action which the corporation may take upon the advice of the attorney, . . . then, in effect, *he is (or personifies) the corporation* when he makes his disclosure to the lawyer and the privilege would apply." (Emphasis supplied.)

Such a view, we think, overlooks the fact that the privilege exists to protect not only the giving of professional advice to those who can act on it but also the giving of information to the lawyer to enable him to give sound and informed advice. The first step in the resolution of any legal problem is ascertaining the factual background and sifting through the facts with an eye to the legally relevant. See ABA Code of Professional Responsibility, Ethical Consideration 4–1:

> "A lawyer should be fully informed of all the facts of the matter he is handling in order for his client to obtain the full advantage of our legal system. It is for the lawyer in the exercise of his independent professional judgment to separate the relevant and important from the irrelevant and unimportant. The observance of the ethical obligation of a lawyer to hold inviolate the confidences and secrets of his client not only facilitates the full development of facts essential to proper representation of the client but also encourages laymen to seek early legal assistance."

In the case of the individual client the provider of information and the person who acts on the lawyer's advice are one and the same. In the corporate context, however, it will frequently be employees beyond the control group as defined by the court below—"officers and agents . . . responsible for directing [the company's] actions in response to legal advice"—who will possess the information needed by the corporation's lawyers. Middle-level—and indeed lower-level—employees can, by actions within the scope of their employment, embroil the corporation in serious legal difficulties, and it is only natural that these employees would have the relevant information needed by corporate counsel if he is adequately to advise the client with respect to such actual or potential difficulties.

This fact was noted in Diversified Industries, Inc. v. Meredith, 572 F.2d 596 (C.A.8 1977) (en banc):

> "In a corporation, it may be necessary to glean information relevant to a legal problem from middle management or non-management personnel as well as from top executives. The attorney dealing with a complex legal problem 'is thus faced with a "Hobson's choice". If he interviews employees not having "the very highest authority," their communications to him will not be privileged. If, on the other hand, he interviews only those employees with the "very highest authority", he may find it extremely difficult, if not impossible, to determine what happened.' "

The control group test adopted by the court below thus frustrates the very purpose of the privilege by discouraging the communication of relevant information by employees of the client to attorneys seeking to render legal advice to the client corporation. The attorney's advice will also frequently be more significant to noncontrol group members than to those who officially sanction the advice, and the control group test makes it more difficult to convey full and frank legal advice to the employees who will put into effect the client corporation's policy.

The narrow scope given the attorney-client privilege by the court below not only makes it difficult for corporate attorneys to formulate sound advice when their client is faced with a specific legal problem but also threatens to limit the valuable efforts of corporate counsel to ensure their client's compliance with the law. In light of the vast and complicated array of regulatory legislation confronting the modern corporation, corporations, unlike most individuals, "constantly go to lawyers to find out how to obey the law," particularly since compliance with the law in this area is hardly an instinctive matter, see, e.g., United States v. United States Gypsum Co., 438 U.S. 422, 440–441, 98 S.Ct. 2864, 2875–2876, 57 L.Ed.2d 854 (1978) ("the behavior proscribed by the (Sherman) Act is often difficult to distinguish from the gray zone of socially acceptable and economically justifiable business conduct").[2] The test adopted by the court below is difficult to apply in practice, though no abstractly formulated and unvarying "test" will necessarily enable courts to decide questions such as this with mathematical precision. But if the purpose of the attorney-client privilege is to be served, the attorney and client must be able to predict with some degree of certainty whether particular discussions will be protected. An uncertain privilege, or one which purports to be certain but results in widely varying applications by the courts, is little better than no privilege at all. The very terms of the test adopted by the court below suggest the unpredicta-

---

2. The Government argues that the risk of civil or criminal liability suffices to ensure that corporations will seek legal advice in the absence of the protection of the privilege. This response ignores the fact that the depth and quality of any investigations to ensure compliance with the law would suffer, even were they undertaken. The response also proves too much, since it applies to all communications covered by the privilege: an individual trying to comply with the law or faced with a legal problem also has strong incentive to disclose information to his lawyer, yet the common law has recognized the value of the privilege in further facilitating communications.

bility of its application. The test restricts the availability of the privilege to those officers who play a "substantial role" in deciding and directing a corporation's legal response. Disparate decisions in cases applying this test illustrate its unpredictability. Compare, e.g., Hogan v. Zletz, 43 F.R.D. 308, 315–316 (N.D.Okl.1967), aff'd in part sub nom. Natta v. Hogan, 392 F.2d 686 (C.A.10 1968) (control group includes managers and assistant managers of patent division and research and development department), with Congoleum Industries, Inc. v. GAF Corp., 49 F.R.D. 82, 83–85 (E.D.Pa.1969), aff'd, 478 F.2d 1398 (C.A.3 1973) (control group includes only division and corporate vice presidents, and not two directors of research and vice president for production and research).

The communications at issue were made by Upjohn employees[3] to counsel for Upjohn acting as such, at the direction of corporate superiors in order to secure legal advice from counsel. As the Magistrate found, "Mr. Thomas consulted with the Chairman of the Board and outside counsel and thereafter conducted a factual investigation to determine the nature and extent of the questionable payments and to be in a position to give legal advice to the company with respect to the payments." Information, not available from upper-echelon management, was needed to supply a basis for legal advice concerning compliance with securities and tax laws, foreign laws, currency regulations, duties to shareholders, and potential litigation in each of these areas. The communications concerned matters within the scope of the employees' corporate duties, and the employees themselves were sufficiently aware that they were being questioned in order that the corporation could obtain legal advice. The questionnaire identified Thomas as "the company's General Counsel" and referred in its opening sentence to the possible illegality of payments such as the ones on which information was sought. A statement of policy accompanying the questionnaire clearly indicated the legal implications of the investigation. The policy statement was issued "in order that there be no uncertainty in the future as to the policy with respect to the practices which are the subject of this investigation." It began "Upjohn will comply with all laws and regulations," and stated that commissions or payments "will not be used as a subterfuge for bribes or illegal payments" and that all payments must be "proper and legal." Any future agreements with foreign distributors or agents were to be approved "by a company attorney" and any questions concerning the policy were to be referred "to the company's General Counsel." This statement was issued to Upjohn employees worldwide, so that even those interviewees not receiving a questionnaire were aware of the legal implications of the interviews. Pursuant to explicit instructions from the Chairman of the Board, the communications were considered "highly confidential" when made, and have been kept confidential by the compa-

3. Seven of the eighty-six employees interviewed by counsel had terminated their employment with Upjohn at the time of the interview. Petitioners argue that the privilege should nonetheless apply to communications by these former employees concerning activities during their period of employment. Neither the District Court nor the Court of Appeals had occasion to address this issue, and we decline to decide it without the benefit of treatment below.

ny. Consistent with the underlying purposes of the attorney-client privilege, these communications must be protected against compelled disclosure.

The Court of Appeals declined to extend the attorney-client privilege beyond the limits of the control group test for fear that doing so would entail severe burdens on discovery and create a broad "zone of silence" over corporate affairs. Application of the attorney-client privilege to communications such as those involved here, however, puts the adversary in no worse position than if the communications had never taken place. The privilege only protects disclosure of communications; it does not protect disclosure of the underlying facts by those who communicated with the attorney:

> "[T]he protection of the privilege extends only to communications and not to facts. A fact is one thing and a communication concerning that fact is an entirely different thing. The client cannot be compelled to answer the question, 'What did you say or write to the attorney?' but may not refuse to disclose any relevant fact within his knowledge merely because he incorporated a statement of such fact into his communication to his attorney." Philadelphia v. Westinghouse Electric Corp., 205 F.Supp. 830, 831 (E.D.Pa.1962).

See also State ex rel. Dudek v. Circuit Court, 34 Wis.2d 559, 580, 150 N.W.2d 387, 399 (1967) ("the courts have noted that a party cannot conceal a fact merely by revealing it to his lawyer"). Here the Government was free to question the employees who communicated with Thomas and outside counsel. Upjohn has provided the IRS with a list of such employees, and the IRS has already interviewed some 25 of them. While it would probably be more convenient for the Government to secure the results of petitioner's internal investigation by simply subpoenaing the questionnaires and notes taken by petitioner's attorneys, such considerations of convenience do not overcome the policies served by the attorney-client privilege. As Justice Jackson noted in his concurring opinion in Hickman v. Taylor, 329 U.S., at 516, 67 S.Ct., at 396: "Discovery was hardly intended to enable a learned profession to perform its functions ... on wits borrowed from the adversary."

* * *

III

Our decision that the communications by Upjohn employees to counsel are covered by the attorney-client privilege disposes of the case so far as the responses to the questionnaires and any notes reflecting responses to interview questions are concerned. The summons reaches further, however, and Thomas has testified that his notes and memoranda of interviews go beyond recording responses to his questions. To the extent that the material subject to the summons is not protected by the attorney-client privilege as disclosing communications between an employee and counsel, we must reach the ruling by the Court of Appeals that the work-product doctrine does not apply to summonses issued under 26 U.S.C. § 7602.[6]

* * *

While conceding the applicability of the work-product doctrine, the Government asserts that it has made a sufficient showing of necessity to overcome its protections. The Magistrate apparently so found. The Government relies on the following language in *Hickman:*

> "We do not mean to say that all written materials obtained or prepared by an adversary's counsel with an eye toward litigation are necessarily free from discovery in all cases. Where relevant and nonprivileged facts remain hidden in an attorney's file and where production of those facts is essential to the preparation of one's case, discovery may properly be had.... And production might be justified where the witnesses are no longer available or can be reached only with difficulty."

The Government stresses that interviewees are scattered across the globe and that Upjohn has forbidden its employees to answer questions it considers irrelevant. The above-quoted language from *Hickman,* however, did not apply to "oral statements made by witnesses ... whether presently in the form of [the attorney's] mental impressions or memoranda." As to such material the Court did "not believe that any showing of necessity can be made under the circumstances of this case so as to justify production.... If there should be a rare situation justifying production of these matters petitioner's case is not of that type." Forcing an attorney to disclose notes and memoranda of witnesses' oral statements is particularly disfavored because it tends to reveal the attorney's mental processes.[8]

Rule 26 accords special protection to work product revealing the attorney's mental processes. The Rule permits disclosure of documents and tangible things constituting attorney work product upon a showing of substantial need and inability to obtain the equivalent without undue hardship. This was the standard applied by the Magistrate. Rule 26 goes on, however, to state that "[i]n ordering discovery of such materials when the required showing has been made, the court shall protect against disclosure of the mental impressions, conclusions, opinions or legal theories of an attorney or other representative of a party concerning the litigation." Although this language does not specifically refer to memoranda based on oral statements of witnesses, the *Hickman* court stressed the danger that compelled disclosure of such memoranda would

---

6. The following discussion will also be relevant to counsel's notes and memoranda of interviews with the seven former employees should it be determined that the attorney-client privilege does not apply to them. See n. 3, supra.

8. Thomas described his notes of the interviews as containing "what I considered to be the important questions, the sub-

stance of the responses to them, my beliefs as to the importance of these, my beliefs as to how they related to the inquiry, my thoughts as to how they related to other questions. In some instances they might even suggest other questions that I would have to ask or things that I needed to find elsewhere."

reveal the attorney's mental processes. It is clear that this is the sort of material the draftsmen of the Rule had in mind as deserving special protection.

Based on the foregoing, some courts have concluded that no showing of necessity can overcome protection of work product which is based on oral statements from witnesses. Those courts declining to adopt an absolute rule have nonetheless recognized that such material is entitled to special protection. We do not decide the issue at this time. It is clear that the Magistrate applied the wrong standard when he concluded that the Government had made a sufficient showing of necessity to overcome the protections of the work-product doctrine. * * * While we are not prepared at this juncture to say that such material is always protected by the work-product rule, we think a far stronger showing of necessity and unavailability by other means than was made by the Government or applied by the Magistrate in this case would be necessary to compel disclosure.

[Opinion of Chief Justice Burger, concurring in part and concurring in the judgment, omitted.]

Notes and Questions

1. A person asserting the attorney-client privilege must satisfy a number of requirements to show that it applies. A widely-cited statement of the requirements lists eight: "(1) Where legal advice of any kind is sought (2) from a professional legal adviser in his capacity as such, (3) the communications relating to that purpose, (4) made in confidence (5) by the client, (6) are at his instance permanently protected (7) from disclosure by himself or by the legal adviser, (8) except the protection be waived." 8 Wigmore on Evidence § 2292 (McNaughton ed. 1961). Does the Court in *Upjohn* adhere to this traditional definition? For example, is item no. 5 essential in the Court's view?

2. Given the truth-seeking purposes for discovery, does the attorney-client privilege further interests that justify denying access to this highly-probative evidence? The Court in *Upjohn* articulates the traditional analysis, commonly referred to as the utilitarian analysis—that the objective is to promote full client disclosure to the attorney. But there has never been empirical evidence that the existence of the privilege promotes disclosure by clients. E.g., Louisell, Confidentiality, Conformity and Confusion: Privileges in Federal Court Today, 31 Tulane L.Rev. 101, 112 (1956) (disclosure promotion theory premised on "sheer speculation"). Although lawyers can emphasize the existence of the privilege to their clients, it is not at all clear that clients place great importance on the existence of the privilege in deciding what to tell their lawyers. Moreover, since the lawyer can also tell the client that full disclosure is essential to valid legal advice, the client considering withholding information from the lawyer confronts a Hobson's choice since the risk of keeping the lawyer in the dark may seem as great as the risk of disclosure. Since the lawyer can also inform the client that only she (the lawyer) can decide whether the information is harmful, there would seem to be substantial pressures toward full candor with the lawyer. Why, then, have the privilege? The Supreme Court continues to believe in the

importance of the privilege. See Swidler & Berlin v. United States, 524 U.S. 399, 118 S.Ct. 2081, 141 L.Ed.2d 379 (1998) (privilege should continue to apply after the client's death because otherwise clients might be reluctant to confide in lawyers).

3. Does the Court in *Upjohn* actually adopt a utilitarian rationale for the privilege? Why protect what the attorney tells the client? Why not limit the privilege to those client confidences that the client would not reveal to the lawyer absent the privilege? See Wiessenberger, Toward Precision in the Application of the Attorney–Client Privilege for Corporations, 65 Iowa L. Rev. 899, 918–19 (1980) (adoption of a but-for analysis under which privilege attaches only if statement would not have been made absent privilege). How easily could a court fragment a lawyer-client conversation, protecting some parts but not others?

4. Assuming that the privilege generally promotes full client disclosure, how does it do so with regard to the lower-level corporate employees excluded from coverage by the control group test? The corporation can use the information they reveal to its lawyer as a basis for firing or disciplining them. Moreover, unless there is a personal attorney-client relation between the employee and the lawyer, the corporation can unilaterally decide to turn the employee's revelations over to the authorities. Accordingly, it has long been recognized that the corporate employee may have interests adverse to the employer in an investigation, and that the best solution may be to provide separate representation for the employee. See O'Leary, Criminal Antitrust and the Corporate Executive: The Man in the Middle, 63 A.B.A.J. 1389 (1977). How then can the Court even suggest that the privilege may apply to communications with *former* employees?

Does *Upjohn* really focus on the motivations of the employees at all? Consider Professor Salzburg's views:

> In their search to expand the privilege beyond the narrow control group formulation, the courts seem to inquire whether, without a guarantee of confidentiality, a lawyer will be reluctant to talk with employees of a corporation who have information—i.e., witness employees. The courts arrive at an affirmative answer. In the process, the courts assume that if lawyers would be reluctant to talk with employees, employees would be equally reluctant to talk with lawyers. * * * [T]he employee who talks without being a client might suffer for his cooperation. Such an employee, who is actually willing to talk without protection of the privilege, is like any witness who is willing to talk. The lawyer's apprehensiveness about possibly finding out information that might turn out to be detrimental to the corporation would be no different when he seeks out an employee than when he seeks out any other witness. The correct question for courts to ask, therefore, is whether a witness insists upon establishment of an attorney-client relationship and, thus, the protection of a privilege, before speaking with the corporation's attorney. Only where the answer to this question is affirmative is the attorney-client privilege properly applicable.

Saltzburg, Corporate and Related Attorney–Client Privilege Claims: A Suggested Approach, 12 Hofstra L.Rev. 279, 302–03 (1984).

5. If the Court's real concern is with the lawyer's motivations, is the additional stimulus to investigate provided by the protection necessary? The lawyer has an ethical duty to investigate. Putting that aside, could the lawyer disregard potentially harmful evidence? As one experienced lawyer observed: "Even lawyers in jurisdictions which followed the severely limited 'control group' test had to pretty well ignore it because they could not otherwise serve their clients. It has never made any sense to remain deliberately ignorant of the facts because of a fear of adverse discovery." Panel Discussion, Antitrust Investigations After *Upjohn,* 51 Antitrust L.J. 127, 133 (1982). Moreover, federal-court interpretations of privilege are not binding on the state courts, so that material that is privileged in federal court might be subject to disclosure in state court where the control group test still prevails. See, e.g., Consolidation Coal Co. v. Bucyrus–Erie Co., 89 Ill.2d 103, 59 Ill.Dec. 666, 432 N.E.2d 250 (1982) (retaining control group test under Illinois law). Indeed, under Fed.R.Evid. 501, state rules of privilege apply in federal court where the issue involved is governed by state law.

6. Under *Upjohn* should the witness statements in *Hickman* that were obtained from crew members who were employed by the defendant partnership have been covered by the attorney-client privilege?

7. Note the Court's handling of the work product issue in *Upjohn.* Does discovery of the materials involved there endanger the policies the Court is seeking to further?

8. When the attorney-client privilege applies, it can easily be lost. As Davis v. Ross, supra p. 357, suggests, privileged materials may be discovered where the privilege holder has taken a litigation stance that puts them "at issue." This reasoning can be applied to the attorney-client privilege. See, e.g., Pitney–Bowes, Inc. v. Mestre, 86 F.R.D. 444 (S.D.Fla.1980) (By suing for reformation of contract on grounds of mutual mistake, plaintiff waived attorney-client privilege regarding communications concerning the meaning of agreement). Other grounds for waiver abound. Thus, any revelation of privileged material to the opponent or to someone else (however unintentional) usually operates as a waiver, as does the use of privileged material in witness preparation. While supposedly "absolute," then, the protection accorded by the privilege is also very fragile. Does this fact further undermine the utility of the privilege in promoting full client disclosure? Should the same waiver approach be applied to work product protection? For an argument that courts should find waivers only where warranted by the risk of unfair selective use of privileged material to distort the truth, see Marcus, The Perils of Privilege: Waiver and the Litigator, 84 Mich.L.Rev. 1605 (1986).

IN RE SHELL OIL REFINERY

United States District Court, Eastern District of Louisiana, 1990.
132 F.R.D. 437.

MENTZ, DISTRICT JUDGE.

The court addresses here the plaintiffs' request for discovery of the defendant's experts. The defense experts include some who are expected to testify at trial and some who are not expected to testify at trial. The court finds that while discovery of experts expected to testify at trial is premature, the plaintiffs are not entitled to any discovery of experts not expected to testify at trial.

On May 5, 1988, the catalytic cracking unit (CCU) at the Shell Oil Refinery, Norco, Louisiana, exploded. The first of several suits ultimately certified as a class action was filed that day. The day after the explosion, the parties entered an agreement giving the Plaintiff's Legal Committee (PLC) and its experts access to the CCU to inspect, measure, and photograph. Following their agreement, Shell Oil Company (Shell) preserved all materials tagged by the PLC, as well as additional materials Shell wanted preserved.

Later, Shell conducted at its research facility metallurgical and chemical tests on material removed from the explosion site. R.E. Nordstrom and Paul A. Nelson are two Shell employees who were present during the testing. The PLC's experts observed certain of these tests.

From the beginning of this case, both the PLC and Shell retained experts and actively investigated the cause of the explosion. Three months post-explosion, the court ordered: "Any expert who has visited the Norco plant and will be an expert witness at trial shall submit a preliminary report to the court on Friday, September 23, 1988." Shell submitted five reports: two from its in-house employees, R.E. Nordstrom and Paul A. Nelson; one from Failure Analysis Associates; one from Arthur D. Little, Inc.; and one from Hercules, Inc. The PLC submitted three expert reports: one from C H & A Engineering Group; one from Metallurgical & Materials Technologies, Inc.; and one from Perez Architects. The parties did not exchange the preliminary expert reports until later, in April, 1989.

During the course of this litigation, the PLC filed several motions seeking expert discovery, particularly the identity of Shell's experts and the results of the tests conducted by Shell on the CCU material. In each instance, the court ruled against allowing the discovery, unless Shell intended to use the expert or test result at trial.

Before the court is the PLC's Motion for Reconsideration of the Court's August 21, 1989, Ruling. Specifically, the PLC seeks the results of tests conducted by Shell on material from the CCU and leave of court to depose the authors of the preliminary expert reports. Shell states that it has not yet decided which test results and experts it intends to use at trial. Shell also states that it does not intend to call Nordstrom and Nelson at trial or to use either of their preliminary expert reports.

EXPERTS EXPECTED TO BE CALLED AT TRIAL

Although Fed.R.Civ.P. 26(b)(4)(A) allows for interrogatory discovery of experts expected to be called at trial,* the court has discretion in this

---

* After this case was decided, the Federal Rules regarding testifying experts were amended. Rule 26(a)(2) was added, requiring disclosure regarding such testimony,

complex class action to control the sequence of discovery. The Case Management Order (CMO), adopted by the court on August 13, 1990, governs the time frame for discovery of experts. Under the CMO, the parties need not disclose the identity of experts expected to be called at trial until March 1, 1991. The exchange of expert reports is May 1, 1991 and expert depositions start on June 15, 1991. At this time, Shell has no obligation to decide which experts it will call at trial or disclose information about any experts expected to be called at trial. As stated in the Advisory Committee Notes to Rule 26:

> The procedure established in subsection (b)(4)(A) holds the risk [that one side will benefit unduly from the other side's better preparation] to a minimum. Discovery is limited to trial witnesses, and may be obtained only at a time when the parties know who their expert will be. A party must as a practical matter prepare his own case in advance of that time, for he can hardly hope to build his case out of his opponent's expertise.

Those who will testify at trial often cannot be identified until the later stages of litigation. Therefore, the court finds that the PLC's attempt to obtain discovery from experts expected to be called at trial is premature.

Experts Not Expected to Be Called at Trial

Under Fed.R.Civ.P. 26(b)(4)(B), the facts known and opinions held by non-testifying experts who are retained or specially employed in anticipation of litigation or preparation for trial are subject to discovery only in exceptional circumstances. This Rule recognizes that with non-testifying experts, there is no need to obtain discovery for effective cross-examination. See Hoover v. United States Dep't of the Interior, 611 F.2d 1132, 1142 (5th Cir.1980) ("The primary purpose of [Rule 26(b)(4)(A)'s required disclosures about experts expected to be called at trial] is to permit the opposing party to prepare an effective cross-examination.") The Rule is also designed to prevent a party from building his case on the diligent preparation of his adversary. See Pielemeier, Discovery of Non–Testifying "In–House" Experts Under the Federal Rules of Civil Procedure, 58 Ind.L.J. 597, 607–08 (1984).

Shell has stated its intention not to call at trial its in-house experts, Nordstrom and Nelson. No one disputes that Nordstrom and Nelson are experts. Even though Shell submitted the reports of Nordstrom and Nelson as preliminary reports of experts it expected to call at trial, Shell's later decision not to call them at trial is permissible. Prior to the court-imposed deadline for exchange of witness lists, a party is free to make strategic decisions changing an anticipated witness to a non-witness. Thus, Nordstrom and Nelson are properly designated as non-testifying experts.

and Rule 26(b)(4)(A) was amended to permit the deposition of each testifying expert. See infra p. 407 n.3.—Eds.

PLC's claims

The PLC maintains that Nordstrom and Nelson should be treated as ordinary witnesses under Fed.R.Civ.P. 26(b)(1) because they are in-house experts who would have performed the tests in question as part of their regular duties regardless of litigation. Alternatively, the PLC maintains that if Nordstrom and Nelson are non-testifying experts retained or specially employed in anticipation of litigation, then under Fed.R.Civ.P. 26(b)(4)(B) their facts and opinions are discoverable because of exceptional circumstances requiring great expense to duplicate the tests performed by Shell.

Nordstrom is the Manager of Heat Transfer and Pressure Equipment for Shell. His duties consist of technical input on operations and on design and construction of new facilities. Nelson is a Research Manager whose duties consist of managing 11 research engineers and nine technicians for Shell. Their affidavits show that during the week following the explosion, Shell's legal department and outside counsel requested them to help the investigation team defend the lawsuits filed against Shell. Also, in September, 1988, James Blasek, outside counsel for Shell, requested Nordstrom and Nelson to prepare preliminary reports of their investigation and study of the explosion. Nordstrom and Nelson sent their preliminary reports to only Blasek. Although Nordstrom and Nelson have not been assigned to work exclusively on this litigation, they remain available to assist outside counsel on an as needed basis.

The affidavits show that there can be no serious dispute that Nordstrom and Nelson's investigation and study of the explosion was in anticipation of litigation. Whether they were "retained or specially employed" within the meaning of Fed.R.Civ.P. 26(b)(4)(B) is a closer question.

The courts and other legal authority are not in agreement on the question of whether an in-house expert can be "retained or specially employed".

26(b)(4)(B) protection; in-house experts not remove from

The court finds that the persuasive authority favors application of Rule 26(b)(4)(B) to non-testifying in-house experts. To rule otherwise would encourage economic waste by requiring an employer to hire independent experts to obtain the protection of Rule 26(b)(4). Protection of an in-house expert's opinion supports improved public safety and other social benefits of self-analysis. That the work of an in-house expert is used not only to defend a lawsuit but also to improve a company's operations or product design does not remove him from the parameters of Rule 26(b)(4)(B).

Not all in-house experts fall within the parameters of the retained or specially employed language of Rule 26(b)(4)(B). The Advisory Committee Notes exclude from the scope of Rule 26(b)(4)(B) "an expert who is simply a general employee of the party not specially employed on the case." Those in-house experts who are not retained or specially employed should be treated as ordinary witnesses under Rule 26(b)(1), and if their work was in anticipation of litigation or preparation of trial, then discovery must be analyzed under the work product doctrine, Rule 26(b)(3).

Neither the Rule nor the Notes explain when a general employee may become retained or specially employed. Some courts have found that the terms retained or specially employed mean "something more than simply the assignment of a current employee to a particular problem raised by current litigation." See Kansas–Nebraska Natural Gas Co., Inc. [v. Marathon Oil Co.], 109 F.R.D. at 16 [D.Neb.1983]. To the contrary, other authority suggests that "a regular employee may become specially employed when he is designated and assigned by a party to apply his expertise to a particular matter in anticipation of litigation or for trial." Pielemeier, supra, 58 Ind.L.J. at 605.

Whether an in-house expert is retained or specially employed must be decided case-by-case. In this case, the court finds that Nordstrom and Nelson were retained or specially employed by Shell in preparation for trial. Shell's attorneys engaged Nordstrom and Nelson to perform specific tasks to help them defend the lawsuit. At the direction of Shell's legal department and outside counsel, Nordstrom and Nelson investigated and studied the cause of the explosion, and prepared preliminary reports. Copies of the reports were sent only to Shell's outside counsel. Although Nordstrom and Nelson might have studied the cause of the explosion regardless of litigation, their usual duties do not include litigation assistance. That Nordstrom and Nelson were not paid additional compensation or assigned exclusively to the litigation is not conclusive. An in-house expert may be specially employed without additional compensation or an exclusive assignment.

Having found that Nordstrom and Nelson are experts retained or specially employed in preparation for trial, the court must determine whether exceptional circumstances exist to permit discovery. A party seeking to show exceptional circumstances under Rule 26(b)(4)(B) carries a heavy burden. The exceptional circumstances requirement has been interpreted by the courts to mean an inability to obtain equivalent information from other sources.

The plaintiffs offered the affidavit of Thomas Shelton, President of Metallurgical and Materials Technology, Inc., to show that this case meets the exceptional circumstances requirement. Mr. Shelton was present at certain of the tests conducted by Shell and estimates that the total cost to duplicate the investigation and testing performed by Shell would be in the range of $230,000 to $315,000. The plaintiffs cited Pearl Brewing Co. v. Jos. Schlitz Brewing Co., 415 F.Supp. 1122 (S.D.Tex. 1976), to show that expense can satisfy the exceptional circumstances requirement. In that antitrust case, the plaintiff's experts, who were not expected to be called at trial, created a complicated computer program for a beer marketing distribution model. The plaintiff's expert to be called at trial relied on this model in reaching his conclusions. The court found that the defendant's expert would be unable to understand the model without explanations of the undefined short-hand codes used in the computer program. For defendant's expert to attempt to unravel the short-hand codes alone would be unduly time consuming and expensive. The court granted discovery of the code explanations only. The court noted that the defendant was not trying to find support for his case out of the plaintiff's efforts, but only expediting analysis of the plaintiff's trial expert's conclusions. In other words, the defendant was not going to rely on the plaintiff's distribution model to support its defense, but needed to know the codes in order for its expert to analyze the plaintiff's trial expert's conclusions.

In contrast, the plaintiffs in the case at bar do not seek Shell's test results to understand how Shell's experts will substantiate their conclusions at trial. The plaintiffs want Shell's test results to avoid the expense of conducting their own tests. To allow discovery of Shell's test results under these circumstances would defeat the Rule's intended purposes of protecting trial strategy and preventing one party from having a free ride at the expense of the other party.

The plaintiffs can obtain the substantial equivalent by having their own experts conduct tests. As a result of the parties' consent agreements, the PLC had access to the CCU for a total of fifteen days beginning on May 7 through June 3, 1988. The plaintiffs also have access to the materials tested by Shell. Aside from having to pay for their own testing, the plaintiffs will suffer no loss. During the period set aside for expert discovery, the parties can discover the basis for each other's expert's conclusions, including information received from non-testifying experts. For these reasons, the plaintiffs have failed to show exceptional circumstances.

Notes and Questions

1. Discovery regarding experts is important because experts are important in litigation. In some cases, such as medical malpractice, the substantive law may require expert testimony. That imperative sometimes leads to pressures on prospective expert witnesses who are called upon to testify against their professional peers. See, e.g., DiPaola, Cohen & Roberts, Silence of the Experts, Trial, Oct. 2004, at 20 (reporting that peer review and ethics panels of medical doctors have increasingly focused on the conduct of doctors who testify for medical malpractice plaintiffs, sometimes urging that the medical licenses of these doctors be suspended or revoked due to their testimony). In Austin v. American Ass'n of Neurological Surgeons, 253 F.3d 967 (7th Cir.2001), a doctor who was suspended from a medical association for six months after giving "irresponsible" testimony against another member sued the association. The court upheld dismissal of the suit because membership in the association was not necessary to practice medicine.

More generally, even though it is not required by law in many kinds of cases, expert testimony is very common. A survey of 529 civil trials before juries in California in the mid 1980s showed that experts testified in 86% of those cases and that an average of 3.8 experts testified per case. Gross, Expert Evidence, 1991 Wis.L.Rev. 1113, 1119; see also Green, Expert Witnesses and Sufficiency of Evidence in Toxic Substances Litigation, 86 Nw.

U.L.Rev. 643, 669 (1992) (between 1974 and 1989, number of regularly-testifying experts in Cook County, Ill., increased 1500%, from 188 to 3100).

In *Shell Oil Refinery* the court states that all agree Nordstrom and Nelson are experts. Who else qualifies? In evidentiary terms, the consequence of being designated an expert is that a witness is allowed to express opinions (rather than only describing what she observed) while testifying. Fed.R.Evid. 702 authorizes such opinion testimony by "a witness qualified as an expert by knowledge, skill, experience, training, or education" where "scientific, technical, or other specialized knowledge will assist the trier of fact to understand the evidence or determine a fact at issue." Besides people with advanced training, this could include auto mechanics and others who have specialized knowledge beyond the customary ken.

Concerns have been raised about inappropriate use of unfounded "scientific" theories in litigation. For an attack on this supposed problem, see P. Huber, Galileo's Revenge: Junk Science in the Courtroom (1991). In Daubert v. Merrell Dow Pharmaceuticals, Inc., 509 U.S. 579, 113 S.Ct. 2786, 125 L.Ed.2d 469 (1993), the Court refined the proper approach to such problems, emphasizing that the court must preliminarily find that "in order to qualify as 'scientific knowledge,' an inference or assertion must be derived by the scientific method." Kumho Tire Co. v. Carmichael, 526 U.S. 137, 119 S.Ct. 1167, 143 L.Ed.2d 238 (1999), held that courts should undertake a similar screening effort with regard to engineers and other experts who are not scientists but who testify based on technical or other specialized knowledge. For an examination of the resulting issues, see D. Faigman, D. Kaye, M. Saks & J. Sanders, Modern Scientific Evidence (1997).

2. Why does Rule 26(b)(4) provide special protections for expert information? "[T]he expert, unlike an ordinary witness, has no unique knowledge. That is, the other side, at least in theory, can obtain the same information merely by engaging an expert of its own. Hence, it may be argued that a lawyer could want to obtain information from his adversary's expert only to avoid doing any preparation himself, and to save his client considerable expense. Ultimately this could lead to a deterioration in case presentation and lower the standards of the bar generally." Friedenthal, Discovery and Use of an Adverse Party's Expert Information, 14 Stan.L.Rev. 455, 482–83 (1962). Are these concerns applicable in the *Shell Oil Refinery* case?

3. Regarding those experts who will testify at trial, from 1970 until 1993 Rule 26(b)(4)(A) provided that the only discovery of right was by interrogatory, and that further discovery could be had only by agreement or court order. Note that in *Shell Oil Refinery* the court replaced this regime with an order calling for identification of experts and exchange of expert reports, followed by depositions. As amended in 1993, Rules 26(a)(2) and 26(b)(4)(A) provide by rule for similar handling of experts who will testify at trial. Read Rule 26(a)(2) with care, noting in particular the report it requires from expert witnesses and the timing for these disclosures. The Advisory Committee Notes suggest that the time specified may often be altered to provide that the party with the burden of proof make expert witness disclosure first. Rule 37(c)(1) provides that opinions that should have been disclosed but were not should be excluded at the trial, and courts have often

done so. See, e.g., Hoffman v. Caterpillar, Inc., 368 F.3d 709 (7th Cir.2004) (expert opinion excluded because disclosures were not amended to include a videotape viewed by the expert); Macaulay v. Anas, 321 F.3d 45 (1st Cir.2003) (expert precluded from testifying because supplemental report adding a new theory of liability was not submitted until more than a month after the deadline for submitting expert reports).

Rule 26(b)(4)(C) directs that the party seeking discovery pay the fee of an expert for responding to discovery. Sometimes courts blanch at the amounts requested. See, e.g., Fisher–Price, Inc. v. Safety 1st, Inc., 217 F.R.D. 329 (D.Del.2003) (expert not entitled to be paid $495 per hour for performing administrative tasks that could easily have been delegated to assistants); Frederick v. Columbia University, 212 F.R.D. 176 (S.D.N.Y.2003) (hourly fee of $975 demanded by plaintiff's expert was unreasonable); Jochims v. Isuzu Motors, Ltd., 141 F.R.D. 493, 497 (S.D.Iowa 1992) ("Continuing escalation of expert witness fees and the all too frequent attitude of experts that their fees should be set at the maximum-the-traffic-will-bear is of great concern."). Compare Scheinholtz v. Bridgestone/Firestone, Inc., 187 F.R.D. 221 (E.D.Pa. 1999) (court sets unusually high rate of $600 per hour for expert's time because defendants had agreed to pay that amount).

4. Rule 26(b)(4)(B) addresses discovery regarding experts specially retained to prepare for trial but not expected to be called as witnesses, like Nordstrom and Nelson. Why would such people be retained? If you were the lawyer for a party in *Shell Oil Refinery,* would you need an expert like Nordstrom or Nelson to assist you in preparing your case? Assuming the other parties have many other experts to choose among, are there special reasons for limiting discovery regarding the views and knowledge of these expert consultants? As the court explained in Rubel v. Eli Lilly & Co., 160 F.R.D. 458, 460 (S.D.N.Y.1995), "there is an important interest in allowing counsel to obtain the expert advice they need in order properly to evaluate and present their clients' positions without fear that every consultation with an expert may yield grist for the adversary's mill." See also In re Pizza Time Theatre Securities Litigation, 113 F.R.D. 94, 98 (N.D.Cal.1986): "[A] lawyer's decision about which experts to consult, but not to call as a witness, also is a matter that implicates values that the work product doctrine was designed to protect. * * * A lawyer's decisions about which people to use in confidence for which purposes in preparing a case for trial is as central to lawyering strategy as one can get."

5. Why doesn't Shell want to call Nordstrom and Nelson as witnesses at trial? Suppose one of the plaintiffs in *Shell Oil Refinery* needs expert medical testimony concerning the extent of injuries and therefore visits and is examined by doctors X, Y and Z on recommendation of her lawyer. If Dr. Z submits a report to the lawyer saying that the plaintiff is not really injured and the lawyer therefore decides to call Dr. X or Dr. Y, should Dr. Z's report be discoverable? In Coates v. AC & S, Inc., 133 F.R.D. 109 (E.D.La.1990), an action against an asbestos producer, after plaintiff died of lung cancer defendant sent tissue samples to several expert consultants. Plaintiff sought copies of the reports made by all the experts even though they would not all testify, and the court granted the motion "in an effort to curtail the 'shopping' of tissue samples," which it viewed as falling within the extraordinary circumstances limitation on discovery regarding nontestifying experts.

Contrast Eliasen v. Hamilton, 111 F.R.D. 396, 401 (N.D.Ill.1986): "Even if we assume that plaintiffs chose not to use Gruy because he did not tell them what they wanted to hear, this is not only perfectly permissible, but * * * the very purpose of the rule is to protect plaintiffs from having Gruy's testimony used by their opponent." See also Dominguez v. Syntex Laboratories, Inc., 149 F.R.D. 158, 163 (S.D.Ind.1993) ("Visiting two experts for the purposes of litigation can hardly be considered 'expert shopping.' * * * If an expert botches the evaluation or uses unaccepted methodology, a litigant should not be expected to live with only that evaluation and divulge the results for use by his opponent.").

If expert-shopping is not an extraordinary circumstance warranting discovery regarding retained but nontestifying experts, what would suffice? Suppose that only Shell's experts had examined the site in the days after the explosion. The reporter for the committee that drafted Rule 26(b)(4)(B) offered two illustrations of extraordinary circumstances in a program on those amendments:

> (a) Circumstances in which an expert employed by the party seeking discovery could not conduct important experiments and tests because an item of equipment, etc., needed for the tests had been destroyed or is otherwise not available. If the party from whom the discovery is sought had been able to have its experts test the item before its destruction or nonavailability, then information obtained from those tests might be discoverable.

> (b) Circumstances in which it might be impossible for a party to obtain its own expert. Such circumstances would occur when the number of experts in a field is small and their time is already fully retained by others.

Sacks, Seminar on Discovery, Atlanta, Ga., Sept. 26–27, 1970, quoted in Ager v. Jane C. Stormont Hospital & Training School, 622 F.2d 496, 503–04 n. 8 (10th Cir.1980).

In *Shell Oil Refinery*, the court treated the roughly $300,000 cost of duplicating the analysis performed by defendant as insufficient to constitute extraordinary circumstances. Compare Bank Brussels Lambert v. Chase Manhattan Bank, 175 F.R.D. 34 (S.D.N.Y.1997), in which plaintiff retained Arthur Andersen & Co. to analyze the financial condition of a failing company, and Andersen based its advice on 10,000 hours spent by its personnel reviewing the company's financial records before those files were put into storage when the company failed. Noting that it was likely that documents were rearranged and that some were lost over the two years before defendant was sued, the court held that extraordinary circumstances had been established for access to Andersen's work.

6. Should regular employees like Nordstrom and Nelson be covered by Rule 26(b)(4)(B)? "[R]ule 26(b)(4)(B) permits a party to engage in discovery with respect to information consultative experts acquired *prior* to being retained by an opposing party." Rocky Mountain Natural Gas Co. v. Cooper Industries, Inc., 166 F.R.D. 481, 482 (D.Colo.1996). In light of that right, consider the following observations:

There is a legitimate concern that a party may try to immunize its employees who are actors or viewers against proper discovery by designating them experts retained for work on the case. One of the tasks of an employee of a party often must perform is to assist the party's lawyers in work on the case. * * * Something more than this ordinary assistance to counsel ought ordinarily be required to establish that an expert who is a regular employee was "specially" retained to work on the litigation. Accordingly, courts should be exceedingly skeptical when employees who have otherwise discoverable information are designated "experts," and efforts must be made to preserve the opportunity for the opposing party to discover that information.

8 C. Wright, A. Miller & R. Marcus, Federal Practice & Procedure § 2033 (2d ed. 1994).

7. In *Shell Oil*, trial witnesses had not yet been designated. What if a party designates an expert and then retracts the designation? In Durflinger v. Artiles, 727 F.2d 888 (10th Cir.1984), where plaintiff decided not to call a certain doctor after listing him as a trial witness, the court upheld an order preventing defendant from calling the doctor at trial on the ground that defendant had "circumvented the discovery process and subverted the principle of fairness that underlies Rule 26(b)(4)(B)." Should the court instead have allowed defendant to call the doctor as a witness but forbidden reference to the fact the doctor was originally retained by plaintiff? The court found this protection sufficient in Granger v. Wisner, 656 P.2d 1238 (Az.1982), although it recognized the perils:

Jurors unfamiliar with the role of counsel in adversary proceedings might well assume that plaintiff's counsel had suppressed evidence which he had an obligation to offer. Such a reaction could destroy counsel's credibility in the eyes of the jury. * * *

If the plaintiff sought to attack the expert's qualifications or credentials, he might well have some concern that the defendant would attempt to rehabilitate the witness by showing that plaintiff's counsel had thought well enough of the witness to consult him on this very case. Arguably, that consultation might be an admission that plaintiff believed the witness to be qualified.

656 P.2d at 1242–43. See also Agron v. Columbia University, 176 F.R.D. 445 (S.D.N.Y.1997) (psychiatric expert previously retained by plaintiff could testify for defendant at trial providing that there was no mention that the witness had been retained originally by plaintiff); compare Healy v. Counts, 100 F.R.D. 493, 496 (D.Colo.1984) ("I do not agree that such a restriction on defense counsel could adequately protect the plaintiffs here.").

In Peterson v. Willie, 81 F.3d 1033 (11th Cir.1996), plaintiff designated a doctor to testify regarding damages based on the doctor's initial examination of plaintiff. The doctor then examined plaintiff again without permission from plaintiff's lawyer, and testified in his deposition that he had changed his opinion. Plaintiff withdrew the designation, and defendant called the doctor at trial, eliciting the fact that he had first been retained by plaintiff's lawyer. After the jury found that defendant was not liable, the appellate court ruled that it was wrong to permit the jury to learn that plaintiff had first retained the doctor, but held that the error was harmless because the jury found no liability and the doctor was testifying only about damages.

Arguably a different attitude is proper when that expert has examined the opposing party under Rule 35. Rule 35(b) allows the examined party to obtain a copy of the report. If the report is favorable, can that party then call the expert as a witness? In Crowe v. Nivison, 145 F.R.D. 657 (D.Md.1993), the court held that, having submitted to the examination by the opposing party's expert, the examined party was entitled to use the expert's opinion at trial. See also House v. Combined Ins. Co., 168 F.R.D. 236, 246 (N.D.Iowa 1996) ("designation [as an expert witness], and submission to a medical examination by the designated expert, create the kind of reliance" that justifies allowing the testimony); Easton, "Red Rover, Red Rover, Send That Expert Right Over": Clearing the Way for Parties to Introduce the Testimony of Their Opponents' Expert Witnesses, 55 S.M.U. L. Rev. 1427 (2002) (arguing for broadening the opportunity to call the opponent's expert).

8. Besides experts who are specially retained, a party or lawyer may informally consult others. For example, in USM Corp. v. American Aerosols, Inc., 631 F.2d 420 (6th Cir.1980), defendant's president wrote to an official of another company in the industry asking for his "unbiased and analytical evaluation" of how the technical problem giving rise to the suit occurred. Noting that this contact occurred after plaintiff threatened suit, and that the official received no payment, the court held that he had only been informally consulted. In such instances, no discovery is allowed, even on a showing of extraordinary circumstances.

9. Sometimes, however, there are experts with no affiliation at all to a party. Consider, for example, the possibility that Professor A is a leading expert on catalytic cracking units like the one that exploded and had authored a leading article on defects leading to explosions. Could a party happy with Professor A's views in the article subpoena her to testify at trial? Could a party expecting her article to be used in evidence against it subpoena her research data in an effort to discredit her conclusions? Remember that Rule 26(b)(4) only limits discovery of material prepared in anticipation of litigation. See Wright v. Jeep Corp., 547 F.Supp. 871, 874 (E.D.Mich. 1982) (professor who wrote report on Jeep turnovers ordered to submit to deposition); Application of American Tobacco Co., 880 F.2d 1520 (2d Cir. 1989) (medical researcher who had published studies on synergistic effect of exposure to asbestos and smoking required to supply tobacco companies with research data); see generally Marcus, Discovery Along the Litigation/Science Interface, 57 Brooklyn L.Rev. 381 (1991).

Since 1991, many of these problems have been directly addressed by Rule 45(c)(3)(B), which provides that a subpoena seeking disclosure of "an unretained expert's opinion or information not describing specific events or occurrences in dispute and resulting from the expert's study made not at the request of any party" may be quashed or modified unless the party serving the subpoena shows substantial need for the information and assures that the recipient of the subpoena will be reasonably compensated.

10. If an expert testifies but does a poor job, can she be held liable for that? In Marrogi v. Howard, 282 F.3d 854 (5th Cir.2002), plaintiff's expert was tripped up by mistakes in his deposition during a suit against plaintiff's

former employer, and the employer was able to obtain summary judgment. Plaintiff then sued the expert for malpractice. The district court dismissed the case based on the normal rule that witnesses are immune from suit for their testimony in litigation, but the court of appeals reversed based on an exception to the immunity rule for retained experts providing litigation services.

E. INVESTIGATION—FACT GATHERING WITHOUT JUDICIAL ASSISTANCE

CORLEY v. ROSEWOOD CARE CENTER, INC., 142 F.3d 1041 (7th Cir.1998):

Before CUMMINGS, RIPPLE, and ROVNER, Circuit Judges.

ILANA DIAMOND ROVNER, Circuit Judge.

[In this RICO action based on defendants' alleged bait and switch tactics in connection with nursing home services, plaintiff had been conducting interviews with non-party witnesses under oath and with a court reporter present. The witnesses evidently participated voluntarily in this activity. When defendant found out, it persuaded the district court to grant a protective order requiring plaintiff to give notice of these sessions as though they were depositions. The appellate court held that this order was wrong.]

The district court viewed Corley's investigative technique as tantamount to a deposition under the Federal Rules. * * * But we see nothing in the Federal Rules that would support such a restriction on counsel's private inquiry into the facts underlying his client's claim. * * * [A]lthough court reporters were present and witnesses presumably were questioned under oath, the interviews in fact were not depositions precisely because Corley had not complied with the requirements of Rule 30(b). The statements thus could not be used as depositions under Rule 32.

But the fact that the statements could not be used as depositions does not mean, as the district judge apparently assumed, that Corley was not entitled to take them. The Supreme Court has long recognized that as part of his investigation and trial preparation, counsel may choose to take sworn statements from individual having knowledge of the claims or defenses at issue. See Hickman v. Taylor. [The court also noted that Rule 26(b)(3)(B) explicitly contemplates that witness statements may include "a stenographic, mechanical, electrical, or other recording."] This portion of Rule 26 therefore assumes that the taking of a witness statement is entirely proper, even where the statement is recorded and transcribed by a court reporter, and the rule proceeds to address the circumstances under which the statement may be discoverable. In light of that, there would seem to be no basis for restricting Corley's chosen investigative method of taking sworn statements from potential non-party witnesses. The Federal Rules of Civil Procedure do not prohibit that technique; the rules instead are concerned only with whether the statements are discoverable and with the uses to which they may be put at trial.

Notes and Questions

1.　Although we have concentrated thus far in this chapter on the use of the power of the court to extract information, it is important to realize that a great deal of extremely useful information is available for the asking. Responsible lawyers will use investigation instead of formal discovery wherever possible both because it is extremely flexible and because it can be conducted without notice to other parties. Indeed, it may be that the opposing party cannot use the power of the court to find out what the investigating attorney was seeking from a witness. See Ford v. Philips Elec. Instr. Co., 82 F.R.D. 359, 360 (E.D.Pa.1979) ("Insofar as defendant's question [in a deposition] attempted to elicit from the witness the specific question that plaintiff's counsel posed to him [during an interview], or even the area of the case to which he directed the majority of his questions, it exceeds the permissible bounds of discovery and begins to infringe on plaintiff's counsel's evaluation of the case."). Moreover, Rule 11 requires prefiling investigation by an attorney before taking a position in litigation. Finally, particularly where recurring fact patterns make the same kind of evidence relevant in a number of cases, investigation can often lead to pooling of the fruits of fact-gathering (through investigation and formal discovery) in many cases. See, e.g., Kirsch, Evidence Sharing, California Lawyer, June 1985, at 19.

2.　Given the utility of informal interviews with willing witnesses, why would a lawyer ever choose to take the deposition of such a person? Cf. Rule 27. Consider the views of the court in International Business Machines Corporation v. Edelstein, 526 F.2d 37 (2d Cir.1975): "In contrast to the pretrial interview with prospective witnesses, a deposition serves an entirely different purpose, which is to perpetuate testimony, to have it available for use or confrontation at the trial, or to have the witness committed to a specific representation for such facts as he might present. A desire to depose formally would arise normally after preliminary interviews might have caused counsel to decide to take a deposition." The court also noted that "[i]t is the common experience of counsel at the trial bar that a potential witness, upon reflection, will often change, modify or expand upon his original statement and that a second or third interview will be productive of greater accuracy."

3.　The attorney's freedom to interview witnesses stops, however, with the opposing party because rules of professional responsibility forbid a lawyer to talk to an opposing party who is represented by counsel unless the party's lawyer consents. With corporate or other organizational parties, this rule becomes difficult to apply. In Niesig v. Team I, 76 N.Y.2d 363, 559 N.Y.S.2d 493, 558 N.E.2d 1030 (1990), the court held that counsel may not interview corporate employees whose acts or omissions in the matter under inquiry are binding on the corporation, or whose acts are imputed to the corporation for purposes of its liability. See also Cagguila v. Wyeth Laboratories, Inc., 127 F.R.D. 653, 654 (E.D.Pa.1989) ("In such an uncertain area of ethical conduct, we believe that a prudent attorney would have given notice to opposing counsel of the intent to take such a statement.").

In Mompoint v. Lotus Devel. Corp., 110 F.R.D. 414 (D.Mass.1986), the court refused to go this far. Plaintiff claimed that he had been fired because he was black and a Haitian. Defendant claimed it fired him because it had received complaints from female employees that plaintiff had pressured them for sexual favors. Defendant moved for a protective order against interviews with these women by plaintiff's counsel. The court found that the complaints related to matters within the scope of their employment, but that there was no good cause to forbid interviews, citing Professor Leubsdorf's arguments: "The public interest in obtaining testimony should not be frustrated by the massive embargo that a warned employer could impose." Leubsdorf, Communicating with Another Lawyer's Client: The Lawyer's Veto and the Client's Interests, 127 U.Pa.L.Rev. 683, 708 (1979). The court did, however, order that plaintiff himself should not be present during any of these interviews.

4. Should there be any other court-ordered limitations on evidence gathering outside the discovery process? Compare Nemir v. Mitsubishi Motors Corp. 381 F.3d 540 (6th Cir.2004) (overturning district court order forbidding plaintiff's lawyer from contacting defendant's consumers because there was no showing of pertinent harm to defendant) with Cordy v. Sherwin–Williams Co., 156 F.R.D. 575 (D.N.J.1994) (disqualifying defense counsel for contacting an expert who had a written agreement with plaintiff's counsel to work for plaintiff on the case).

5. On analogy to decisions suppressing evidence in criminal cases, civil litigants sometimes try to suppress evidence that is illegally seized. Thus, in State of Iowa v. Union Asphalt & Roadoils, Inc., 281 F.Supp. 391 (S.D.Iowa 1968), affirmed sub nom. Standard Oil Co. v. State of Iowa, 408 F.2d 1171 (8th Cir.1969), the state's attorney general had sent his assistants and police officers into the offices of certain defendants just before he filed suit, and these agents carted away "substantially all of the business records contained in the offices." Noting the quasi-criminal nature of antitrust suits, and the use of official powers to effect seizure, the court ordered the return of all the material but refused to forbid the state from using discovery to obtain that material again. Compare Suburban Sew 'N Sweep, Inc. v. Swiss–Bernina, Inc., 91 F.R.D. 254 (N.D.Ill.1981), in which plaintiff embarked on a pretrial campaign of searching through the trash dumpster outside defendant's offices and found a number of items that would be privileged under the attorney-client privilege. The court refused to order these materials returned despite their privileged character, reasoning that defendant had not made sufficient efforts to maintain the confidentiality of the material. See also Sackler v. Sackler, 15 N.Y.2d 40, 255 N.Y.S.2d 83, 203 N.E.2d 481 (1964) ("Any court is taking extreme measures when it refuses convincing evidence because of the way it was procured. Proof of guilt collected in raids by private detectives has been, pursuant to rules not heretofore questioned, the basis for thousands of divorce decrees in our State."). Compare Arnold v. Cargill, Inc., 2004 WL 2203410 (D.Minn.2004) (plaintiff's counsel disqualified for obtaining privileged documents from a former employee of defendant).

F. ENFORCING THE DISCOVERY RULES—SANCTIONS

CINE FORTY–SECOND STREET THEATRE CORP. v. ALLIED ARTISTS PICTURES CORP.

United States Court of Appeals, Second Circuit, 1979.
602 F.2d 1062.

Before KAUFMAN, CHIEF JUDGE, and OAKES and MESKILL, CIRCUIT JUDGES.

IRVING R. KAUFMAN, CHIEF JUDGE.

Appellee Cine Forty–Second Street Theatre Corp. ("Cine"), has operated a movie theater in New York City's Times Square area since July 1974. It alleges that those owning neighboring theaters on West Forty–Second Street (the "exhibitors") attempted through abuse of City agency processes to prevent the opening of its theater. When this tactic was unsuccessful, Cine contends, the exhibitors entered into a conspiracy with certain motion picture distributors to cut off its access to first-run, quality films. Bringing suit on August 1, 1975, Cine claimed $3,000,000 in treble damages under the antitrust laws, and sought an injunction against the defendants' alleged anticompetitive practices.

On November 6, 1975, the eleven defendants served plaintiff with a set of consolidated interrogatories. Cine thereupon secured its adversaries' consent to defer discovery on the crucial issue of damages until it could retain an expert to review the rival exhibitors' box office receipts. Not until four months after the deadline upon which the parties had agreed, however, did Cine file its first set of answers to the remaining interrogatories. Moreover, even casual scrutiny reveals the patent inadequacy of these responses. Many were bare, ambiguous cross-references to general answers elsewhere in the responses. Highly specific questions concerning the design of Cine's theater were answered with architectural drawings that did not even purport to show the dimensions requested.

Although Cine now complains bitterly that these interrogatories amounted to pure harassment, it never moved to strike them as irrelevant or as harassing. Rather, it filed supplemental answers, which were similarly deficient, and then failed to obey two subsequent orders from Magistrate Gershon compelling discovery. At a hearing in October of 1977, the magistrate found Cine's disobedience to have been willful, and assessed $500 in costs against it. Soon afterwards, she further warned plaintiff that any further noncompliance would result in dismissal.

By the summer of 1977, as this conflict was coming to a head, Cine had still not retained the expert it claimed was necessary to respond to the damages interrogatories. Magistrate Gershon quite reasonably and leniently ordered Cine merely to produce a plan to answer, but this yielded no result. The magistrate then directed Cine to answer the damages interrogatories, admonishing its counsel that future nonfeasance would be viewed in light of past derelictions. Cine did file two sets of answers, one over two months late and both seriously deficient.

The responses omitted, inter alia, any information concerning significant time periods for which Cine claimed injury. Moreover, they failed to provide any indication as to the method of calculating a major portion of the alleged damages. Thereupon, at an unrecorded hearing held on September 7, 1978, Magistrate Gershon once again held off the imposition of final sanctions in these already over-protracted discovery proceedings and ordered the defects cured, on pain of dismissal of the complaint. Cine stood mute, neither appealing from, objecting to, nor complying with the order. On September 20, the defendants moved before the magistrate for dismissal of the complaint, citing plaintiff's failure to obey the order requiring responses on damages.

At a formal hearing on October 19, 1978, Cine's attorney argued that several months earlier he and defense counsel had reached an "understanding," pursuant to which a deposition of Cine's principal officer, Clark, would replace the answers at issue. Cine has never introduced any written evidence or corroborative testimony demonstrating the existence of such an understanding. In any case, the magistrate's subsequent oral order compelling answers to the interrogatories would have superseded it.

Accordingly, Magistrate Gershon found that Cine had no basis for assuming that the answers were not due on the dates set in her orders. After noting plaintiff's history of disobedience in the face of her own repeated warnings, the magistrate concluded that Cine's present non-compliance was willful.[5] "[T]he plaintiff," she stated, "has decided when it will be cooperative and when it will not be cooperative, and that it does not have any right to do." She thereupon recommended to the district court that Cine be precluded from introducing evidence with respect to damages. This sanction was, of course, tantamount to a dismissal of Cine's damage claim, but left standing its claim for injunctive relief.

Judge Goettel, the district judge to whom Magistrate Gershon's order was submitted for approval, reacted to Cine's behavior as did Magistrate Gershon. He wrote, "[i]f there were ever a case in which drastic sanctions were justified, this is it." But Judge Goettel could not fully accept the magistrate's finding of willfulness. "[T]he actions of plaintiff's counsel," he concluded, "were either willful or a total dereliction of professional responsibility. No other conclusion is possible. However, in the absence of a written direction, it is virtually impossible to establish that the attorney's action was in fact willful, rather than grossly negligent.

5. In light of our holding, it is not necessary for us to consider Cine's contention that a written order is, as a matter of law, a necessary prerequisite to a finding of "willfulness" under Rule 37. We note, en passant, however, that in Independent Investors Protective League v. Touche Ross & Co., 25 F.R.Serv.2d 222, 224, and Henry v. Sneiders, 490 F.2d 315, 318 (9th Cir.), cert. denied, 419 U.S. 832, 95 S.Ct. 55, 42 L.Ed.2d 57 (1974), preclusion was upheld on the basis of orders announced in open court.

The district judge thus apparently believed it possible that Cine's counsel, confused as to the precise terms of Magistrate Gershon's oral orders, could have thought in good faith that the answers were not due. Action taken upon that baseless belief, however, was, at the very least, grossly negligent. The district court "regretfully" concluded that under Flaks v. Koegel, 504 F.2d 702 (2d Cir.1974), it lacked the power, absent a finding of willfulness, to impose the extreme sanction recommended by the magistrate. Instead, the court merely assessed costs in the amount of $1,000.[6] But, recognizing that he might have "misperceive[d] the controlling law of this circuit," Judge Goettel certified this interlocutory appeal on his own motion under 28 U.S.C. § 1292(b).

On reargument, Judge Goettel expressed some doubt regarding the correctness of his prior decision. In light of plaintiff's subsequent response to the damages interrogatories, however, the court adhered to its earlier view.

The question before us is whether a grossly negligent failure to obey an order compelling discovery may justify the severest disciplinary measures available under Fed.R.Civ.P. 37. This rule provides a spectrum of sanctions. The mildest is an order to reimburse the opposing party for expenses caused by the failure to cooperate. More stringent are orders striking out portions of the pleadings, prohibiting the introduction of evidence on particular points and deeming disputed issues determined adversely to the position of the disobedient party. Harshest of all are orders of dismissal and default judgment.

These sanctions serve a threefold purpose. Preclusionary orders ensure that a party will not be able to profit from its own failure to comply. Rule 37 strictures are also specific deterrents and, like civil contempt, they seek to secure compliance with the particular order at hand. Finally, although the most drastic sanctions may not be imposed as "mere penalties," Hammond Packing Co. v. Arkansas, 212 U.S. 322, 29 S.Ct. 370, 53 L.Ed. 530 (1909); see Hovey v. Elliott, 167 U.S. 409, 17 S.Ct. 841, 42 L.Ed. 215 (1897), courts are free to consider the general deterrent effect their orders may have on the instant case and on other litigation, provided that the party on whom they are imposed is, in some sense, at fault. National Hockey League v. Metropolitan Hockey Club, Inc., 427 U.S. 639, 96 S.Ct. 2778, 49 L.Ed.2d 747 (1976) (per curiam); Societe Internationale Pour Participations Industrielles et Commerciales v. Rogers, 357 U.S. 197, 78 S.Ct. 1087, 2 L.Ed.2d 1255 (1958).

Where the party makes good faith efforts to comply, and is thwarted by circumstances beyond his control, for example a foreign criminal statute prohibiting disclosure of the documents at issue, an order dismissing the complaint would deprive the party of a property interest without due process of law. See Societe Internationale, supra, 357 U.S. at 212, 78 S.Ct. 1087. It would, after all, be unfair and irrational to prevent

---

6. Defendants estimate that their actual costs in seeking to compel discovery total at least $50,000.

a party from being heard solely because of a nonculpable failure to meet the terms of a discovery order. Indeed, such measures would be gratuitous, for if the party is unable to obey there can be no effective deterrence, general or specific. Accordingly, "Rule 37 should not be construed to authorize dismissal of [a] complaint because of petitioner's noncompliance with a pretrial production order when it has been established that failure to comply has been due to inability, and not to willfulness, bad faith, or any fault of petitioner." Societe Internationale, supra, 357 U.S. at 212, 78 S.Ct. at 1096.

The lower court did not determine whether willfulness caused plaintiff's failure to respond. It was possible, Judge Goettel apparently believed, that Cine's counsel simply did not understand the exact requirements of the magistrate's unwritten order compelling discovery. If so, Cine's failure to answer the damages interrogatories might not rise to the level of "willfulness" or "bad faith" for both of these conditions imply a deliberate disregard of the lawful orders of the court. The question, then, is whether gross negligence amounting to a "total dereliction of professional responsibility," but not a conscious disregard of court orders, is properly embraced within the "fault" component of Societe Internationale's triple criterion. Fault, of course, is a broad and amorphous concept, and the Courts of Appeals have had considerable difficulty construing it in this context. Indeed, one court defined "fault" by the apparent oxymoron "intentional negligence." Thus, commentators have opined that an element of willfulness or conscious disregard of the court's orders is a prerequisite to the harsher categories of Rule 37 sanctions. But the appellate cases commonly cited for this proposition hold only that dismissal is an abuse of discretion where failure to comply was not the result of the fault of any party.

Unless we are to assume that the Court chose its words carelessly, we must accord the term "fault" a meaning of its own within the Societe Internationale triad. And plainly, if "fault" has any meaning not subsumed by "willfulness" and "bad faith," it must at least cover gross negligence of the type present in this case. * * *

In the final analysis, however, this question cannot turn solely upon a definition of terms. We believe that our view advances the basic purposes of Rule 37, while respecting the demands of due process. The principal objective of the general deterrent policy of *National Hockey* is strict adherence to the "responsibilities counsel owe to the Court and to their opponents," 427 U.S. at 640, 96 S.Ct. at 2780. Negligent, no less than intentional, wrongs are fit subjects for general deterrence. And gross professional incompetence no less than deliberate tactical intransigence may be responsible for the interminable delays and costs that plague modern complex lawsuits. An undertaking on the scale of the large contemporary suit brooks none of the dilation, posturing, and harassment once expected in litigation. The parties, and particularly their lawyers, must rise to the freedom granted by the Rules and cooperate in good faith both in question and response.

Considerations of fair play may dictate that courts eschew the harshest sanctions provided by Rule 37 where failure to comply is due to a mere oversight of counsel amounting to no more than simple negligence. But where gross professional negligence has been found—that is, where counsel clearly should have understood his duty to the court—the full range of sanctions may be marshalled. Indeed, in this day of burgeoning, costly and protracted litigation courts should not shrink from imposing harsh sanctions where, as in this case, they are clearly warranted.

A litigant chooses counsel at his peril, Link v. Wabash Railroad Co., 370 U.S. 626, 82 S.Ct. 1386, 8 L.Ed.2d 734 (1962), and here, as in countless other contexts, counsel's disregard of his professional responsibilities can lead to extinction of his client's claim.[10] See, e.g., Anderson v. Air West, Inc., 542 F.2d 522 (9th Cir.1976) (dismissal for failure to proceed with due diligence); RePass v. Vreeland, 357 F.2d 801 (3d Cir.1966) (negligent failure to file suit within statute of limitations); Universal Film Exchanges, Inc. v. Lust, 479 F.2d 573 (4th Cir.1973) (party not relieved under Fed.R.Civ.P. 60(b) from summary judgment where counsel's failure to proffer defenses was grossly, rather than excusably, negligent).

Plaintiff urges that because it has at last filed answers to the damage interrogatories, it should be permitted to prove its losses at trial. But it forgets that sanctions must be weighed in light of the full record in the case. Furthermore, "[i]f parties are allowed to flout their obligations, choosing to wait to make a response until a trial court has lost patience with them, the effect will be to embroil trial judges in day-to-day supervision of discovery, a result directly contrary to the overall scheme of the federal discovery rules." Moreover, as we have indicated, compulsion of performance in the particular case at hand is not the sole function of Rule 37 sanctions. Under the deterrence principle of *National Hockey,* plaintiff's hopelessly belated compliance should not be accorded great weight. Any other conclusion would encourage dilatory tactics, and compliance with discovery orders would come only when the backs of counsel and the litigants were against the wall.

In light of the fact that plaintiff, through its undeniable fault, has frozen this litigation in the discovery phase for nearly four years, we see no reason to burden the court below with extensive proceedings on remand. Judge Goettel's opinion makes it abundantly clear that but for his misinterpretation of the governing law in this circuit, he would have wholeheartedly adopted Magistrate Gershon's original recommendation.

---

10. The acts and omissions of counsel are normally wholly attributable to the client. This case does not present the extraordinary circumstance of complete disappearance or mental illness of counsel that justified relief in Vindigni v. Meyer, 441 F.2d 376 (2d Cir.1971) and United States v. Cirami, 563 F.2d 26 (2d Cir.1977). Indeed, by Magistrate Gershon's finding and counsel's own admission, Clark, Cine's principal officer, was aware of every aspect of discovery and intimately involved with the progress of the case.

Accordingly, the judge's order declining to adopt the magistrate's recommendation that proof of damages be precluded is reversed.

[Concurring opinion of Judge Oakes omitted.]

Notes and Questions

1. How would similar damages issues be handled now? See Rules 26(a)(1)(C); 37(c)(1). How easily could plaintiff comply with such a disclosure requirement?

2. Should sanctions be employed often? Until the 1970s, the sanctions provisions of Rule 37 were rarely employed. See Renfrew, Discovery Sanctions, A Judicial Perspective, 67 Calif.L.Rev. 264, 272 (1981) (describing "a kind of gentlemen's agreement" under which sanctions were not sought). Beginning in the late 1970s, sanctions became more frequent. See G–K Properties v. Redevelopment Agency of City of San Jose, 577 F.2d 645, 647 (9th Cir.1978). ("Here the court dismissed the plaintiff's action with prejudice. It acted properly in so doing. We encourage such orders."). In the 1980s, partly prompted by the Rule 11 experience (see supra p. 149, n.1), sanctions became more frequent, but some were not enthusiastic: "Although sanctions are a necessary part of any court system, we are concerned that the recent preoccupation with sanctions and the use of dismissal as a necessary 'weapon' in the trial court's 'arsenal' may be contributing to or effecting an atmosphere in which the meritorious claims or defenses of innocent parties are no longer the central issue. It does not further the goal of a court system, that of delivering evenhanded justice to litigants, to suggest, as did the district court here, that the plaintiffs would have a remedy by suing their counsel for malpractice, since this would only multiply rather than dispose of litigation." Poulis v. State Farm Fire and Cas. Co., 747 F.2d 863, 867 (3d Cir.1984). By the late 1990s, some were complaining that district judges were sometimes too quick to impose severe sanctions.

3. The need to base judgments on the merits of the case has constitutional stature. In Hovey v. Elliott, 167 U.S. 409, 17 S.Ct. 841, 42 L.Ed. 215 (1897), the Court held that due process precludes a court from entering judgment against a party as punishment for disobeying an order because a litigant has a right to have the case decided on the merits. In Hammond Packing Co. v. Arkansas, 212 U.S. 322, 29 S.Ct. 370, 53 L.Ed. 530 (1909), however, the Court upheld default as a sanction against a party that failed to produce documents. It distinguished *Hovey* on the ground that this disobedience went to the merits because it supported a presumption that the party withheld evidence that would show that its position in the litigation was groundless. Will all willful refusals to comply with discovery support such a presumption? In what ways was such a merits inference justified in *Cine Forty–Second Street*?

4. A related due process requirement discussed by the court in *Cine Forty–Second Street* is the insistence that fault be found before extreme discovery sanctions are used. This requirement flows from Societe Internationale v. Rogers, 357 U.S. 197, 78 S.Ct. 1087, 2 L.Ed.2d 1255 (1958) (discussed supra p. 345), in which the district court dismissed plaintiff's suit when plaintiff failed to produce documents on the ground that Swiss law

forbade disclosure of the documents. The Supreme Court reversed, finding that dismissal was not justified because the district court had concluded that plaintiff had tried to comply in good faith with the production order. Citing "serious constitutional questions," the Court said that Rule 37 "should not be construed to authorize dismissal of [a] complaint because of [a plaintiff's] noncompliance with a pretrial production order when it has been established that failure to comply has been due to inability, and not to willfulness, bad faith, or any fault of [plaintiff]." How does this standard apply in *Cine Forty–Second Street?*

5. How concerned should the court be that the attorney, not the client, is at fault? Cases in which clients are unaware of discovery orders do occur. See Tamari v. Bache & Co., 729 F.2d 469, 471 (7th Cir.1984) (dismissal vacated because plaintiffs' lawyer failed to inform them of deposition cut-off date); compare United Artists Corp. v. La Cage Aux Folles, Inc., 771 F.2d 1265, 1270 (9th Cir.1985) (dismissal justified by client's failure to stay in contact with his lawyer). Would concerns about the client's involvement be solved by having the court itself notify the client directly? See Shea v. Donohoe Const. Co., 795 F.2d 1071, 1078 (D.C.Cir.1986), in which the court advised district judges contemplating dismissal to notify clients directly "in clear and unequivocal terms" of the risk of dismissal because the court may then assume that, if the lawyer's misconduct persists, the client shares responsibility for it. What problems might this directive create? Why shouldn't the client's right to sue the lawyer for malpractice be sufficient protection?

6. Rather than imposing sanctions against clients where the relative responsibilities of client and counsel are unclear, should courts prefer sanctions against lawyers themselves? Would that have been preferable in *Cine Forty–Second Street?* Could imposition of sanctions on lawyers drive an inappropriate wedge between counsel and client? How is the lawyer to conduct settlement negotiations in which the sanction might be forgiven? Consider Appeal of Licht & Semonoff, 796 F.2d 564, 572–73 (1st Cir.1986): "[W]e do not think that the [law] firm's interest in challenging the sanction order against it will put it in an impossible ethical dilemma during settlement negotiations. The sanction can be left out of the settlement and appealed afterwards. The firm's self interest in making the sanction part of the settlement is not a matter about which we should speculate. The firm's ethical obligation is to its client's best interest. * * * Furthermore, it would be within the district court's discretion to revoke the sanction in order to secure a settlement of the litigation." How persuasive are these arguments? See Comment, The Settled Sanction: Post–Settlement Appeal and Vacatur of Attorney Sanctions Payable to an Opponent, 61 U.Chi.L.Rev. 1627 (1994) (arguing that attorney should be able to appeal despite settlement); cf. Cunningham v. Hamilton County, 527 U.S. 198, 119 S.Ct. 1915, 144 L.Ed.2d 184 (1999) (holding that discovery sanction against attorney is not immediately appealable).

7. Under *Cine Forty–Second Street,* what degree of fault is required for "ultimate" sanctions? Would ordinary negligence be sufficient? Why is that not "fault"? See Note, Defining a Feasible Culpability Threshold for the Imposition of Severe Discovery Sanctions, 65 Minn.L.Rev. 137, 148 (1980) (ordinary negligence threshold "may be the inevitable outgrowth of the

* * * *Cine* position"). Courts of appeals have developed various multifactor tests to guide this decision. See Computer Task Group, Inc. v. Brotby, 364 F.3d 1112, 1115 (9th Cir.2004), calling for consideration of the following factors:

> (1) the public's interest in expeditious resolution of litigation; (2) the court's need to manage its docket; (3) the risk of prejudice to the opposing party; (4) the public policy favoring disposition of cases on the merits; and (5) the availability of less drastic sanctions.

As a starting point, the appellate courts defer to the district judge's selection of a sanction. See, e.g., Good Stewardship Christian Center v. Empire Bank, 341 F.3d 794 (8th Cir.2003) (court of appeals gives district court substantial discretion in sanctioning misconduct before it).

8. Where the necessary quantum of fault is found, should the court automatically use the most stringent sanctions? Why does Rule 37(b)(2) provide such a variety of sanctions? Compare Heartland Bank v. Heartland Home Finance, Inc., 335 F.3d 810 (8th Cir.2003) (district court's exclusion of plaintiff's nine witnesses for misleading defendant was unduly severe; the court should have considered the possibility of lesser sanctions) with Angu-lo–Alvarez v. Aponte de la Torre, 170 F.3d 246 (1st Cir.1999) (district court did not abuse its discretion in dismissing without first considering less severe sanctions). Is a requirement that lesser sanctions be considered dictated by the due process requirement that sanctions be based on legitimate presumptions about the merits of the case? In *Cine Forty–Second Street,* for example, did plaintiff's failure to respond to discovery support any presumption about its belief in its case on liability, as opposed to damages? If not, would dismissal of plaintiff's entire case have been an abuse of discretion?

Would a requirement that lesser sanctions be considered be consistent with the Supreme Court's pronouncement that "the most severe in the spectrum of sanctions provided by statute or rule must be available to the district court in appropriate cases, not merely to penalize those whose conduct may be deemed to warrant such a sanction, but to deter those who might be tempted to such conduct in the absence of such a deterrent." National Hockey League v. Metropolitan Hockey Club, Inc., 427 U.S. 639, 96 S.Ct. 2778, 49 L.Ed.2d 747 (1976).

9. Lest it be thought that lower courts invariably impose maximum sanctions, consider Coca–Cola Bottling Co. v. Coca–Cola Co., 110 F.R.D. 363 (D.Del.1986), in which defendant refused to comply with the court's order that it produce the secret formula for Coca–Cola (See supra p. 364 n.6). Even though the decision to disobey the order was clearly the willful decision of the client, the court denied plaintiffs' motion for entry of default. It emphasized that the sanction must be "just" and relate to the issue to which the discovery in question was directed and that defendant had not otherwise been dilatory in discovery. It therefore crafted an elaborate order concerning assumptions of fact and limitations on defendant's evidence to assure that "plaintiffs are entitled to the advantage of every possible inference that fairly could be drawn from the formulae evidence sought." See 110 F.R.D. at 374–77. Should courts be required to fashion such elaborate orders to avoid ultimate sanctions against those who disobey their discovery orders?

10.   Instead of, or in addition to, other sanctions, courts may impose the costs resulting from discovery disobedience on the disobedient party. These costs can be substantial. See, e.g., Mosaid Techs., Inc. v. Samsung Elecs. Co., 224 F.R.D. 595 (D.N.J.2004) (plaintiff awarded sanctions exceeding $500,000 for attorney's fees resulting from its efforts to secure discovery and litigation of the sanctions motion).

Chapter VI

ADJUDICATION BEFORE TRIAL: SUMMARY JUDGMENT

The procedural device of summary judgment provides an opportunity for either party to win a case prior to trial by demonstrating, in the words of Rule 56(c) of the Federal Rules of Civil Procedure, "that there is no genuine issue as to any material fact and that the moving party is entitled to a judgment as a matter of law." The procedure is often employed "to identify claimants who lack evidence sufficient to reach the jury and who will therefore probably suffer a directed verdict or its equivalent at trial." Louis, Federal Summary Judgment Doctrine: A Critical Analysis, 83 Yale L.J. 745 (1974). For a discussion of the history and policies of summary judgment, see Miller, The Pretrial Rush to Judgment: Are the "Litigation Explosion", "Liability Crisis" and Efficiency Cliches Eroding Our Day In Court and Jury Trial Commitments?, 78 N.Y.U. L. Rev. 982 (2003).

What function does summary judgment serve that is not served by the motion to dismiss? One commentator states that "the motion for summary judgment has become the first real opportunity [in the course of a litigation] for identifying factually deficient claims or defenses." Louis, 83 Yale L.J. at 746. Why isn't this function already performed by the motion to dismiss? In this context, examine the last sentence of Rule 12(b). Does this sentence help reveal the different functions performed by the two procedural devices?

It has been argued that summary judgment assumes special importance in a "notice pleading" system, such as the one adopted by the Federal Rules of Civil Procedure. See, e.g., E. Brunet, M. Redish & M. Reiter, Summary Judgment: Federal Law and Practice 1–11 (2nd ed. 2000); Marcus, The Revival of Fact Pleading Under the Federal Rules of Civil Procedure, 86 Colum.L.Rev. 433, 484–94 (1986). Why do you think this is so?

In answering, consider the appropriate timing of a summary judgment motion. Note that under Rule 56(a), a motion for summary judgment may be made "at any time after the expiration of 20 days from the commencement of the action or after service of a motion for summary judgment by the adverse party." Recall the time required for discovery. Might it be deemed improper to grant summary judgment prior to the conduct of discovery? See Fed. R. Civ. P. 56 (f). If so, does the device really avoid the problems for defendants generally associated with notice pleading? For a discussion of the timing of a summary judgment motion, see Brunet, The Timing of Summary Judgment, 198 F.R.D. 679 (2001).

Summary judgment can play an important role in modern civil procedure. To understand the nature of that role, it is first necessary to comprehend the nature and requirements of the device itself. To that end, this Chapter is divided into two sections. The first describes the concept of "burden shifting", which essentially constitutes the mechanics of the summary judgment device. The second section considers the standard of proof employed in deciding whether a summary judgment motion is to be granted.

A. THE NATURE OF THE SUMMARY JUDGMENT DEVICE: THE CONCEPT OF BURDEN SHIFTING

AN INTRODUCTION TO THE CONCEPT OF BURDEN OF PROOF

In a certain sense, a summary judgment motion seeks to establish that the party against whom the motion is made lacks sufficient evidence to meet his "burden of proof." But that term is ambiguous; as Professor Fleming James has written, "[t]he term 'burden of proof' is used in our law to refer to two separate and quite different concepts. * * * The two distinct concepts may be referred to as (1) the risk of non-persuasion, or the burden of persuasion or simply persuasion burden; (2) the duty of producing evidence, the burden of going forward with the evidence, or simply the production burden or the burden of evidence." James, Burdens of Proof, 47 Va.L.Rev. 51 (1961). Fundamentally, the burden of persuasion concerns which party must convince the trier of fact at trial of the accuracy of his factual assertions, while the burden of production concerns whether a party has sufficient evidence to go to trial in the first place. The summary judgment device is concerned exclusively with the latter burden.

Professor James describes the burden of persuasion in this manner:

Wherever in human affairs a question of the existence or non-existence of a fact is to be decided by somebody, there is the possibility that the decider, or trier of the fact, may at the end of his deliberations be in doubt on the question submitted to him. On all the material before him, he may, for example, regard the existence or non-existence of the fact as equally likely—a matter in equipoise. * * * Where the parties to a civil action are in dispute over a material issue of fact, then that party who will lose if the trier's mind is in equipoise may be said to bear the risk that the trier will not be affirmatively persuaded or the risk of non-persuasion upon that issue.

* * *

Where an issue of fact is tried to a jury, it is the members of the jury whose minds may be in doubt or equipoise and the judge is not directly concerned in solving the problem. Under our system, however, the court does not leave this problem entirely to the jury, but attempts to formulate guides or tests for them in its charge. * * *

The usual formulation of the test in civil cases is that there must be a *preponderance of evidence* in favor of the party having the persuasion burden (the proponent) before he is entitled to a verdict. * * * The general statement is usually explained as referring not to the number of witnesses or quantity of evidence but to the convincing force of the evidence. [47 Va.L.Rev. at 52–53.]

While the concept of burden of persuasion is designed to guide the fact finder (often the jury), the burden of production concept serves as a means of controlling the jury: unless the party upon whom that burden has been placed presents sufficient evidence to justify a verdict in his favor, the judge will take the case out of the hands of the jury by granting a directed verdict, because a jury verdict in that party's favor would be irrational. In Professor James' words, "[t]he concept of the production burden is addressed to the court's function, not the jury's. It is simply a device whereby the court determines whether, if the trial were stopped at any given point, it would send the case to the jury. If not, the court decides the case and the jury has no role to play. If the case is sent to the jury, the production burden drops out of the case and has no role to play. The jury will be concerned only with the persuasion burden." 47 Va.L.Rev. at 57.

To be able to get his case to a jury, then, the party with the burden of production must present evidence sufficient to meet that burden—i.e. enough evidence that a reasonable finder of fact *could* find for him. It is, of course, no small task to determine in a particular case what evidence is sufficient to meet that standard. To a certain extent, that issue is examined in Section B of this chapter, and it is also discussed in Chapter VIII, concerning the motions for directed verdict and judgment notwithstanding the verdict.

One further idea should be mentioned: the concept of burden shifting. Once the court has placed the burden of persuasion on a party (usually the plaintiff, except as to proof of affirmative defenses), the burden generally remains on that party throughout the litigation. In contrast, the burden of production may shift from party to party. A party with a burden of production may conceivably do more than simply *meet* his burden (i.e. present enough evidence that a reasonable finder of fact *could* find for him). He may *shift* his burden, by presenting enough evidence that a reasonable finder of fact *must* find for him. At that point, the burden of production has shifted to the opposing party, who then must respond with evidence of his own, sufficient to *allow* a reasonable finder of fact to find for him. If he fails, the case will not go to the jury. If he succeeds in *meeting* his newly-imposed burden, the case will go to the jury. If, however, he responds with enough evidence of his own that, on the basis of that evidence, a reasonable finder of fact *must* find for him, he has effectively *shifted* the burden of production back onto the party who had it initially. In this manner, the burden of production can be shifted from one party to the other. If at some point the party with the burden of production *meets* but *does not shift* the burden, this means that the court has concluded that a fact finder could reasonably find for either party.

To understand exactly how the burden of production functions in the use of the summary judgment device, it is first necessary to understand the relationship between the motions for summary judgment and judgment as a matter of law.

SUMMARY JUDGMENT AND JUDGMENT AS A MATTER OF LAW CONTRASTED

Like a motion for summary judgment, a motion for judgment as a matter of law (previously referred to as "directed verdict" and "judgment n.o.v.") seeks to establish that the non-movant has failed to meet his burden of production. It has been suggested that because summary judgment comes at a relatively early stage in the litigation, courts should be more reluctant to grant summary judgment than to direct a verdict. However, the Supreme Court has held that the standard of proof to be applied is identified in both motions. Reeves v. Sanderson Plumbing Products, Inc., 530 U.S. 133, 120 S.Ct. 2097, 147 L.Ed.2d 105 (2000); Anderson v. Liberty Lobby, Inc., 477 U.S. 242, 106 S.Ct. 2505, 91 L.Ed.2d 202 (1986) (discussed infra p. 463). Compare Miller, The Pretrial Rush to Judgment: Are the "Litigation Explosion," "Liability Crisis," and Efficiency Cliches Eroding Our Day in Court and Jury Trial Commitments?, 78 N.Y.U. L. Rev. 982, 1061 (2003) (referring to "the radical difference in the timing and context of the two motions").

At trial, the party who does not have the burden of production may, at the close of his opponent's case, move for judgment as a matter of law without presenting any evidence of his own. At that point, the court will inquire whether the evidence presented by the non-movant meets his burden of production—whether a finder of fact could reasonably find for that party on the basis of the evidence presented. It is unclear, however, whether a party seeking summary judgment may, in the pre-trial stage, simply demand that the opposing party present his evidence to establish that the opponent has met its burden of production. This is so, even though the party moving for summary judgment would not have the burden of production at trial, and at that time could move for judgment as a matter of law—presenting the exact same issue raised on the summary judgment motion—without presenting any of its own evidence.

The following cases and commentary consider the showing that the party moving for summary judgment must make to invoke the court's review of the other side's ability to satisfy its burden of production before trial. One should be careful, however, to distinguish between the two concepts, and focus on the ways in which the moving party's initial showing compares to the burden of production.

ADICKES v. S.H. KRESS & CO.

Supreme Court of the United States, 1970.
398 U.S. 144, 90 S.Ct. 1598, 26 L.Ed.2d 142.

JUSTICE HARLAN delivered the opinion of the Court.

[Petitioner Sandra Adickes, a white New York schoolteacher, taught at a Mississippi "Freedom School" during the summer of 1964. One day, she went into the lunchroom of Kress's store in Hattiesburg, Miss., accompanied by six African American students at the school. The store refused to serve her, and she was arrested for vagrancy by two police officers shortly after she left the store. She sued Kress in federal court in New York under 42 U.S.C.A. § 1983, alleging that there was a conspiracy between Kress and the police to arrest her because she was in the company of African Americans.

After some discovery, Kress moved for summary judgment. It relied on the deposition of its employee Mr. Powell, the manager of the lunchroom, who stated that, due to the "explosive" situation in the store he used a prearranged signal to Ms. Baggett, one of the waitresses, that petitioner not be served. He stated further that he had no communication with the police about petitioner. In addition, Kress submitted the affidavits of the two arresting officers and the chief of police, all asserting that there had been no request from Powell that petitioner be arrested. Kress also pointed out that in her deposition petitioner admitted she had no knowledge of any communications between any Kress employee and the police. Petitioner relied in response on an unsworn statement from a Kress employee that one of the arresting officers had been in the store on the day she was arrested, and the hearsay statement of one of the six students, described in plaintiff's deposition, about seeing an officer in the store.

The district court granted summary judgment, ruling that petitioner had "failed to allege any facts from which a conspiracy might be inferred." The court of appeals affirmed. On appeal, the Supreme Court recognized that under section 1983 petitioner had to prove "state action" by showing "that Kress' employee, in the course of employment, and a Hattiesburg policeman somehow reached an understanding * * * to cause her subsequent arrest because she was a white person in the company of Negroes." It nevertheless reversed.]

In granting respondent's motion, the District Court simply stated that there was "no evidence in the complaint or in the affidavits and other papers from which a 'reasonably-minded person' might draw an inference of conspiracy." Our own scrutiny of the factual allegations of petitioner's complaint, as well as the material found in the affidavits and depositions presented by Kress to the District Court, however, convinces us that summary judgment was improper here, for we think respondent failed to carry its burden of showing the absence of any genuine issue of fact.

* * *

We think that on the basis of this record, it was error to grant summary judgment. As the moving party, respondent had the burden of showing the absence of a genuine issue as to any material fact, and for these purposes the material it lodged must be viewed in the light most favorable to the opposing party. Respondent here did not carry its burden because of its failure to foreclose the possibility that there was a policeman in the Kress store while petitioner was awaiting service, and that this policeman reached an understanding with some Kress employee that petitioner not be served.

It is true that Mr. Powell, the store manager, claimed in his deposition that he had not seen or communicated with a policeman prior to his tacit signal to Miss Baggett, the supervisor of the food counter. But respondent did not submit any affidavits from Miss Baggett, or from Miss Freeman, the waitress who actually refused petitioner service, either of whom might well have seen and communicated with a policeman in the store. Further, we find it particularly noteworthy that the two officers involved in the arrest each failed in his affidavit to foreclose the possibility (1) that he was in the store while petitioner was there; and (2) that, upon seeing petitioner with Negroes, he communicated his disapproval to a Kress employee, thereby influencing the decision not to serve petitioner.*

Given these unexplained gaps in the materials submitted by respondent, we conclude that respondent failed to fulfill its initial burden of demonstrating what is a critical element in this aspect of the case—that there was no policeman in the store. If a policeman were present, we think it would be open to a jury, in light of the sequence that followed, to infer from the circumstances that the policeman and a Kress employee had a "meeting of the minds" and thus reached an understanding that petitioner should be refused service. * * * [W]e think respondent's failure to show there was no policeman in the store requires reversal.

Pointing to Rule 56(e), as amended in 1963, respondent argues that it was incumbent on petitioner to come forward with an affidavit properly asserting the presence of the policeman in the store, if she were to rely on that fact to avoid summary judgment. Respondent notes in

---

* The affidavits of the officers each stated: "This arrest was made on the public streets of Hattiesburg, Mississippi, and was an officers' discretion arrest. I had not consulted with Mr. G.T. Powell, Manager of S.H. Kress and Company in Hattiesburg, and did not know his name until this date. No one at the Kress store asked that the arrest be made and I did not consult with anyone prior to the arrest."—Eds.

this regard that none of the materials upon which petitioner relied met the requirements of Rule 56(e).

This argument does not withstand scrutiny, however, for both the commentary on and background of the 1963 amendment conclusively show that it was not intended to modify the burden of the moving party under Rule 56(c) to show initially the absence of a genuine issue concerning any material fact. The Advisory Committee note on the amendment states that the changes were not designed to "affect the ordinary standards applicable to the summary judgment." And, in a comment directed specifically to a contention like respondent's, the Committee stated that "[w]here the evidentiary matter in support of the motion does not establish the absence of a genuine issue, summary judgment must be denied *even if no opposing evidentiary matter is presented.*" Because respondent did not meet its initial burden of establishing the absence of a policeman in the store, petitioner here was not required to come forward with suitable opposing affidavits.

If respondent had met its initial burden by, for example, submitting affidavits from the policemen denying their presence in the store at the time in question, Rule 56(e) would then have required petitioner to have done more than simply rely on the contrary allegation in her complaint. To have avoided conceding this fact for purposes of summary judgment, petitioner would have had to come forward with either (1) the affidavit of someone who saw the policeman in the store or (2) an affidavit under Rule 56(f) explaining why at that time it was impractical to do so.

[Justice Marshall took no part in the decision. Justice Black, in a separate opinion, concurred in the judgment, reasoning that "[t]he existence or nonexistence of a conspiracy is essentially a factual issue that the jury, not the trial judge, should decide. * * * The advantages of trial before a live jury with live witnesses, and all the possibilities of considering the human factors, should not be eliminated by substituting trial by affidavit and the sterile bareness of summary judgment." Justice Douglas dissented in part on other grounds, and Justice Brennan concurred in part and dissented in part, also on other grounds.]

DAVID CURRIE, THOUGHTS ON DIRECTED VERDICTS AND SUMMARY JUDGMENTS

45 U.Chi.L.Rev. 72, 76–79 (1977).

In Adickes v. S.H. Kress Co. the Supreme Court reversed a summary judgment for the defendant because the materials supporting the motion failed to disprove an alleged conspiracy to deny civil rights. The Court strongly suggested in dictum that an uncontroverted affidavit denying the conspiracy allegations would have required the opposite result. The holding confines the summary judgment procedure so narrowly as to impair its effectiveness, while the dictum expands it far enough to threaten the right to jury trial.

* * *[I]f a jury would be free to disbelieve an uncontradicted witness at trial, as is sometimes the case, to grant summary judgment for a

party having the burden of proof on the basis of an affidavit embodying such a witness's testimony would infringe the right to jury trial guaranteed by the seventh amendment, the Rules Enabling Act, and federal rules themselves. * * *

The actual holding of *Adickes,* however, leans too far in the opposite direction. The defendant's crucial omission, according to the Court, was its failure to deny that a policeman had been in the store; if a policeman had been present, a jury might reasonably have inferred that he had conspired with the clerk to refuse the plaintiff service. The inference itself appears strained enough, but the striking fact is that there was no evidence before the Court suggesting a policeman was in the store. At trial the plaintiff would have had the burden of production and persuasion on the conspiracy issue, so on the record she would have suffered a directed verdict. Yet summary judgment was held improper because, in contrast to the situation at trial, the burden was on the defendant to show the absence of a genuine issue of fact. Some courts and commentators have carried this idea to the extreme of treating the moving party in such a case as though he were being required to discharge the burden of production or even persuasion at trial.

This reasoning is based on the ambiguous requirement of rule 56(c) that the materials on file "show . . . that the moving party is entitled to a judgment" and the statement of the Advisory Committee that the movant's evidentiary materials must "establish the absence of a genuine issue." This statement does indeed suggest that even a party with the burden of proof may avoid a summary judgment without producing any evidence unless his opponent makes a strong evidentiary showing. This conclusion, however, undermines the purpose of the rule, which is to discover whether the parties have enough evidence to justify the time and expense of a trial. Professor Louis, while criticizing the more extreme manifestations of the movant's burden on this ground, insists that the moving party, if he would not have the burden of proof at trial, make a showing that would justify a jury verdict in his favor if he had: anything less would allow harassment of the opposing party. This fear seems unfounded, for discovery can require far more burdensome disclosure, and the evidence must in any event be prepared for trial. Thus the *Adickes* dictum that an uncontradicted affidavit asserting the policeman's absence would have justified summary judgment seems correct in policy but not, as the Court intimated, because such an affidavit would have foreclosed a jury finding that a policeman was in the store. Rather, although a jury might have been entitled to disbelieve the arguably interested testimony of a policeman or of a store employee, its doing so would nevertheless have left the plaintiff subject to a directed verdict for failure to satisfy her burden of proof.

The purpose of rule 56 requires that summary judgment be granted if and only if the evidence before the court would justify a directed verdict if presented at trial. Consequently, the rule should be amended to make clear that a motion for summary judgment, without more, puts an opposing party with the burden of proof to the task of producing evidence sufficient to sustain a favorable verdict.

Notes and Questions

1. Professor Currie's position on the showing a movant must make on a summary judgment motion before the non-movant will be required to respond should be contrasted with two other approaches suggested in the scholarly literature. The traditional approach, associated with Professor J. William Moore [6 J. Moore, Federal Practice & Procedure, ¶ 56.15[3] (2d ed.)], posited that a movant must effectively *shift* a burden of production onto the non-movant, even if the movant would not have the burden of production at trial. Professor Currie believes that the decision in *Adickes* adopts such an approach.

2. Would adoption of Professor Currie's approach give rise to either harassment or inefficiency? Consider the argument made in Friedenthal, Cases on Summary Judgment: Has There Been a Material Change in Standards?, 63 Notre Dame L. Rev. 770, 776 (1988):

> [T]here are many cases, undoubtedly the vast majority, in which the litigants are fully aware that the party with the burden of production (at trial) is able to call witnesses on its behalf who will carry its burden of producing evidence. Any "automatic" rule requiring all such parties to make a showing would be extremely wasteful. If one party could, merely by filing an unsupported motion, force an opponent to make a substantial showing, there would be a strong incentive to make such a filing, if for no other reason than to harass the other party and raise its costs of litigation.

Consider Professor Currie's response to the harassment concern: "This fear seems unfounded, for discovery can require far more burdensome disclosure, and the evidence must in any event be prepared for trial." Might the harassment concern turn more on the timing of the summary judgment motion? In this regard, examine Rule 56(f). Could effective use of Rule 56(f) avoid the harms feared by Professor Friedenthal? Would Rule 11 deter abuses?

Professor Melissa Nelken has argued that "[i]f defendants seek to avoid the delay and expense of trial, at a minimum they should shoulder the expense of doing sufficient discovery to show that the plaintiff does not have a case." Nelken, One Step Forward, Two Steps Back: Summary Judgment After *Celotex*, 40 Hastings L.J. 53, 66 (1988); see also Nissan Fire & Marine Ins. Co. v. Fritz Companies, 210 F.3d 1099, 1105 (9th Cir.2000) ("In a typical case, in order to carry its initial burden of production by pointing to the absence of evidence to support the nonmoving party's claim or defense, the moving party will have made reasonable efforts, using the normal tools of discovery, to discover whether the nonmoving party has enough evidence to carry its burden of persuasion at trial."). On the other hand, it has been argued that "[i]mposition of the burden upon the movant as suggested by Professor Nelken * * * appears to amount to little more than extracting a toll for the making of a summary judgment motion." E. Brunet, M. Redish & M. Reiter, Summary Judgment: Federal Law and Practice 60 (1994).

3. Several years prior to Professor Currie's article, Professor Martin Louis [Louis, Federal Summary Judgment Doctrine: A Critical Analysis, 83 Yale L.J. 745 (1974)] criticized the traditional approach, arguing that "[i]mposing such a requirement on the movant makes it extremely difficult for him to compel the opposing party to preview his proof, even though the latter will bear the production burden at trial and even though it appears doubtful that he could discharge it. Thus the opposing party could sometimes defeat a motion for summary judgment simply by withholding proof, the inadequacy of which, if disclosed, would probably lead to his defeat." Moreover, he noted that use of the traditional approach is inconsistent with the relaxed pleading requirement of the Federal Rules: "[A] conclusory, factually deficient pleading will usually survive a motion to dismiss. If the party moving for summary judgment must discharge a rigorous proof burden regardless of whether he would bear the burden of proof at trial, he could almost never compel the pleader to demonstrate that he can prove the essential elements which he was in the past required to allege in detail. As a result the movant could rarely intercept a factually deficient claim or defense. Given the severe congestion of most court dockets, such an interpretation of the Federal Rules of Civil Procedure is most unfortunate." He therefore argued, like Professor Currie, that the burden imposed on a movant who does not have the burden of production at trial should be relaxed.

Unlike Professor Currie, however, Professor Louis was unwilling to remove completely the burden on a movant who would not have the burden of production at trial:

> A movant who would not have the trial proof burden clearly must support his motion with some affidavits or other materials showing or at least suggesting the nonexistence of an essential element of the opposing party's case. A more lenient requirement would permit him to harass the opposing party too easily. * * * [I]f [the moving party] fails to discharge the burden, his motion fails, even though the opposing party makes no response. * * * [I]f he discharges this burden, he should be deemed to have established the nonexistence of the essential element in question unless the opposing party responds adequately. * * *

> There are essentially two methods by which the moving party can discharge his burden. First, through discovery he can obtain a preview of his opponent's evidence on an essential element and contend, in support of his motion, that the evidence is insufficient to discharge the opponent's production burden. If his contention is correct he discharges his own burden and shifts to the opposing party the onus of producing additional evidence or excusing his failure to do so under Rule 56(f). Second, by previewing his own proof, he can attempt to show the nonexistence of an essential element asserted by the opposing party. He can, of course, combine these two approaches.

> The first approach is necessary when direct proof is generally lacking and commends itself whenever the opposing party's witnesses are few and can be deposed without undue effort or expense. On the other hand, this approach is burdensome and costly when the opposing party will rely upon a large number of witnesses or documents. In such

a situation the second approach may be more attractive. Furthermore, under the first approach a defendant-movant would assume the onus of showing that the plaintiff lacks a prima facie case in order to compel him to respond at his peril, even though at trial the plaintiff must present a prima facie case before the defendant must decide whether and how to respond.

For the reasons mentioned above, the moving party will often attempt to discharge his burden through a preview of his own proof. If a movant who would not have the production burden at trial chooses Professor Louis' second method, Professor Louis would require that she present only evidence sufficient to *meet* a burden of production—i.e., enough evidence so that a reasonable factfinder *could* find for her. In this important sense, Professor Louis' approach imposes a more lenient burden on the movant than that imposed under the traditional approach invoked in *Adickes*, which required the movant to *shift* a burden onto the nonmovant (i.e., present enough evidence that a reasonable finder of fact must find for him), even when the movant would not have the burden of production at trial.

4. There are thus three basic approaches to the problem. Under the traditional approach, in order to require a nonmovant to respond a movant for summary judgment who would not have the burden of production at trial must *establish* the truth of his position, whether or not the movant would have the burden of production at trial. Under Professor Louis' approach, such a movant would have only to *meet* a burden of production, or to demonstrate the absence of proof of an essential element of the nonmovant's case. Professor Currie, in contrast, would treat summary judgment in the same manner as a directed verdict motion at trial, imposing no burden whatsoever on a movant who would not have the burden of production at trial, in order to require the nonmovant to come forward with her supporting evidence. Note, however, that under all three approaches, a movant for summary judgment who *would* have the burden of production at trial must *shift* the burden before the nonmovant will be required to respond. Why do the Louis and Currie approaches draw a distinction between a movant who would have the burden of production at trial and one who would not?

Which of the three approaches comports most closely with the approach employed in *Adickes*? How persuasive is Professor Currie's criticism of *Adickes*?

5. Recall that Professor Louis suggests that one way in which a moving party can satisfy his burden in moving for summary judgment is to present a preview of his own proof. What tactical considerations would affect a party's willingness to make such a presentation? Would his opponent be able through discovery to require him to do so?

6. The other avenue identified by Professor Louis is that the moving party can use discovery to obtain a preview of his opponent's evidence. Will he encounter work product obstacles at this point? Cf. Rule 26(b)(3) (regarding opinion work product). Does your answer to that question depend on who has the burden of pleading and proof with regard to the issue involved? What happens if the party to whom the discovery is directed says "I have not completed my investigation and discovery yet and therefore cannot respond"? Cf. Rule 56(f).

7.   To what extent should the trial judge be vested with discretion to deny summary judgment, even if the motion should be granted on the basis of the parties' submissions? Compare In re Franklin National Bank Securities Litigation, 478 F.Supp. 210, 223 (E.D.N.Y. 1979) ("the rule is not mandatory in operation; 'a motion for summary judgment is always addressed to the discretion of the court' ") with Religious Tech. Ctr. v. Netcom On–Line Comm. Servs., Inc., 907 F.Supp. 1361, 1366 (N.D. Cal. 1995) (entry of summary judgment is mandated against a party that fails to make a sufficient showing). For a discussion of the question, see Friedenthal & Gardner, Judicial Discretion to Deny Summary Judgment in the Era of Managerial Judging, 31 Hofstra L. Rev. 91 (2002).

8.   Under the Civil Rights Act of 1964, 42 U.S.C.A. § 2000a(b), Adickes would have had a claim for denial of service without having to prove state action, but the statute was not yet in force when she was arrested. Might the Court have been stretching summary judgment doctrine to overcome that chronological difficulty? Is that appropriate as a matter of procedural law? Of substantive law?

CELOTEX CORP. v. CATRETT

Supreme Court of the United States, 1986.
477 U.S. 317, 106 S.Ct. 2548, 91 L.Ed.2d 265.

JUSTICE REHNQUIST delivered the opinion of the Court.

The United States District Court for the District of Columbia granted the motion of petitioner Celotex Corporation for summary judgment against respondent Catrett because the latter was unable to produce evidence in support of her allegation in her wrongful death complaint that the decedent had been exposed to petitioner's asbestos products. A divided panel of the Court of Appeals for the District of Columbia Circuit reversed, however, holding that petitioner's failure to support its motion with evidence tending to negate such exposure precluded the entry of summary judgment in its favor. * * *

Respondent commenced this lawsuit in September 1980, alleging that the death in 1979 of her husband, Louis H. Catrett, resulted from his exposure to products containing asbestos manufactured or distributed by 15 named corporations. Respondent's complaint sounded in negligence, breach of warranty, and strict liability. Two of the defendants filed motions challenging the District Court's in personam jurisdiction, and the remaining 13, including petitioner, filed motions for summary judgment. Petitioner's motion, which was first filed in September 1981, argued that summary judgment was proper because respondent had "failed to produce evidence that any [Celotex] product ... was the proximate cause of the injuries alleged within the jurisdictional limits of [the District] Court." In particular, petitioner noted that respondent had failed to identify, in answering interrogatories specifically requesting such information, any witnesses who could testify about the decedent's exposure to petitioner's asbestos products. In response to petitioner's summary judgment motion, respondent then produced three documents which she claimed "demonstrate that there is a genuine material factual dispute" as to whether the decedent had ever been exposed to petitioner's asbestos products. The three documents included a transcript of a deposition of the decedent, a letter from an official of one of the decedent's former employers whom petitioner planned to call as a trial witness, and a letter from an insurance company to respondent's attorney, all tending to establish that the decedent had been exposed to petitioner's asbestos products in Chicago during 1970–1971. Petitioner, in turn, argued that the three documents were inadmissible hearsay and thus could not be considered in opposition to the summary judgment motion.

In July 1982, almost two years after the commencement of the lawsuit, the District Court granted all of the motions filed by the various defendants. The court explained that it was granting petitioner's summary judgment motion because "there [was] no showing that the plaintiff was exposed to the defendant Celotex's product in the District of Columbia [or elsewhere] within the statutory period." Respondent appealed only the grant of summary judgment in favor of petitioner, and a divided panel of the District of Columbia Circuit reversed. The majority of the Court of Appeals held that petitioner's summary judgment motion was rendered "fatally defective" by the fact that petitioner "made no effort to adduce any evidence, in the form of affidavits or otherwise, to support its motion." According to the majority, Rule 56(e) of the Federal Rules of Civil Procedure, and this Court's decision in Adickes v. S.H. Kress & Co., 398 U.S. 144, 159, 90 S.Ct. 1598, 1609, 26 L.Ed.2d 142 (1970), establish that "the party opposing the motion for summary judgment bears the burden of responding *only after* the moving party has met its burden of coming forward with proof of the absence of any genuine issues of material fact." The majority therefore declined to consider petitioner's argument that none of the evidence produced by respondent in opposition to the motion for summary judgment would have been admissible at trial. The dissenting judge argued that "[t]he majority errs in supposing that a party seeking summary judgment must always make an affirmative evidentiary showing, even in cases where there is not a triable, factual dispute." Id. at 167, 756 F.2d, at 188 (Bork, J., dissenting).

We think that the position taken by the majority of the Court of Appeals is inconsistent with the standard for summary judgment set forth in Rule 56(c) of the Federal Rules of Civil Procedure. Under Rule 56(c), summary judgment is proper "if the pleadings, depositions, answers to interrogatories, and admissions on file, together with the affidavits, if any, show that there is no genuine issue as to any material fact and that the moving party is entitled to a judgment as a matter of law." In our view, the plain language of Rule 56(c) mandates the entry of summary judgment, after adequate time for discovery and upon motion, against a party who fails to make a showing sufficient to establish the existence of an element essential to that party's case, and on which that party will bear the burden of proof at trial. In such a situation, there can be "no genuine issue as to any material fact," since a complete failure of proof concerning an essential element of the nonmoving party's case necessarily renders all other facts immaterial. The moving party is "entitled to judgment as a matter of law" because the nonmoving party has failed to make a sufficient showing on an essential element of her case with respect to which she has the burden of proof. "[T]h[e] standard [for granting summary judgment] mirrors the standard for a directed verdict under Federal Rule of Civil Procedure 50(a)." Anderson v. Liberty Lobby, Inc., 477 U.S. 242, 250, 106 S.Ct. 2505, 2511, 91 L.Ed.2d 202 (1986).

Of course, a party seeking summary judgment always bears the initial responsibility of informing the district court of the basis for its motion, and identifying those portions of "the pleadings, depositions, answers to interrogatories, and admissions on file, together with the affidavits, if any," which it believes demonstrate the absence of a genuine issue of material fact. But unlike the Court of Appeals, we find no express or implied requirement in Rule 56 that the moving party support its motion with affidavits or other similar materials *negating* the opponent's claim. On the contrary, Rule 56(c), which refers to "the affidavits, *if any*" (emphasis added), suggests the absence of such a requirement. And if there were any doubt about the meaning of Rule 56(c) in this regard, such doubt is clearly removed by Rules 56(a) and (b), which provide that claimants and defendants, respectively, may move for summary judgment *"with or without supporting affidavits"*(emphasis added). The import of these subsections is that, regardless of whether the moving party accompanies its summary judgment motion with affidavits, the motion may, and should, be granted so long as whatever is before the district court demonstrates that the standard for the entry of summary judgment, as set forth in Rule 56(c), is satisfied. One of the principal purposes of the summary judgment rule is to isolate and dispose of factually unsupported claims or defenses, and we think it should be interpreted in a way that allows it to accomplish this purpose.[5]

Respondent argues, however, that Rule 56(e), by its terms, places on the nonmoving party the burden of coming forward with rebuttal affidavits, or other specified kinds of materials, only in response to a motion for summary judgment "made and supported as provided in this rule." According to respondent's argument, since petitioner did not "support" its motion with affidavits, summary judgment was improper in this case. But as we have already explained, a motion for summary judgment may be made pursuant to Rule 56 "with or without supporting affidavits." In cases like the instant one, where the nonmoving party will bear the burden of proof at trial on a dispositive issue, a summary judgment motion may properly be made in reliance solely on the "pleadings, depositions, answers to interrogatories, and admissions on file." Such a

---

5. See Louis, Federal Summary Judgment Doctrine: A Critical Analysis, 83 Yale L.J. 745, 752 (1974); Currie, Thoughts on Directed Verdicts and Summary Judgments, 45 U.Chi.L.Rev. 72, 79 (1977).

motion, whether or not accompanied by affidavits, will be "made and supported as provided in this rule," and Rule 56(e) therefore requires the nonmoving party to go beyond the pleadings and by her own affidavits, or by the "depositions, answers to interrogatories, and admissions on file," designate "specific facts showing that there is a genuine issue for trial."

We do not mean that the nonmoving party must produce evidence in a form that would be admissible at trial in order to avoid summary judgment. Obviously, Rule 56 does not require the nonmoving party to depose her own witnesses. Rule 56(e) permits a proper summary judgment motion to be opposed by any of the kinds of evidentiary materials listed in Rule 56(c), except the mere pleadings themselves, and it is from this list that one would normally expect the nonmoving party to make the showing to which we have referred.

The Court of Appeals in this case felt itself constrained, however, by language in our decision in Adickes v. S.H. Kress & Co., 398 U.S. 144, 90 S.Ct. 1598, 26 L.Ed.2d 142 (1970). There we held that summary judgment had been improperly entered in favor of the defendant restaurant in an action brought under 42 U.S.C. § 1983. In the course of its opinion, the *Adickes* Court said that "both the commentary on and the background of the 1963 Amendment conclusively show that it was not intended to modify the burden of the moving party ... to show initially the absence of a genuine issue concerning any material fact." We think that this statement is accurate in a literal sense, since we fully agree with the *Adickes* Court that the 1963 Amendment to Rule 56(e) was not designed to modify the burden of making the showing generally required by Rule 56(c). It also appears to us that, on the basis of the showing before the Court in *Adickes,* the motion for summary judgment in that case should have been denied. But we do not think the *Adickes* language quoted above should be construed to mean that the burden is on the party moving for summary judgment to produce evidence showing the absence of a genuine issue of material fact, even with respect to an issue on which the nonmoving party bears the burden of proof. Instead, as we have explained, the burden on the moving party may be discharged by "showing"—that is, pointing out to the District Court—that there is an absence of evidence to support the nonmoving party's case.

The last two sentences of Rule 56(e) were added, as this Court indicated in *Adickes,* to disapprove a line of cases allowing a party opposing summary judgment to resist a properly made motion by reference only to its pleadings. While the *Adickes* Court was undoubtedly correct in concluding that these two sentences were not intended to *reduce* the burden of the moving party, it is also obvious that they were not adopted to *add to* that burden. Yet that is exactly the result which the reasoning of the Court of Appeals would produce; in effect, an amendment to Rule 56(e) designed to *facilitate* the granting of motions for summary judgment would be interpreted to make it *more difficult* to grant such motions. Nothing in the two sentences themselves requires this result, for the reasons we have previously indicated, and we now put to rest any inference that they do so.

Our conclusion is bolstered by the fact that district courts are widely acknowledged to possess the power to enter summary judgments *sua sponte,* so long as the losing party was on notice that she had to come forward with all of her evidence. * * * It would surely defy common sense to hold that the District Court could have entered summary judgment *sua sponte* in favor of petitioner in the instant case, but that petitioner's filing of a motion requesting such a disposition precluded the District Court from ordering it.

Respondent commenced this action in September 1980, and petitioner's motion was filed in September 1981. The parties had conducted discovery, and no serious claim can be made that respondent was in any sense "railroaded" by a premature motion for summary judgment. Any potential problem with such premature motions can be adequately dealt with under Rule 56(f), which allows a summary judgment motion to be denied, or the hearing on the motion to be continued, if the nonmoving party has not had an opportunity to make full discovery.

In this Court, respondent's brief and oral argument have been devoted as much to the proposition that an adequate showing of exposure to petitioner's asbestos products was made as to the proposition that no such showing should have been required. But the Court of Appeals declined to address either the adequacy of the showing made by respondent in opposition to petitioner's motion for summary judgment, or the question whether such a showing, if reduced to admissible evidence, would be sufficient to carry respondent's burden of proof at trial. We think the Court of Appeals with its superior knowledge of local law is better suited than we are to make these determinations in the first instance.

* * * Summary judgment procedure is properly regarded not as a disfavored procedural shortcut, but rather as an integral part of the Federal Rules as a whole, which are designed "to secure the just, speedy and inexpensive determination of every action." Fed.Rule Civ.Proc. 1; see Schwarzer, Summary Judgment Under the Federal Rules: Defining Genuine Issues of Material Fact, 99 F.R.D. 465, 467 (1984). Before the shift to "notice pleading" accomplished by the Federal Rules, motions to dismiss a complaint or to strike a defense were the principal tools by which factually insufficient claims or defenses could be isolated and prevented from going to trial with the attendant unwarranted consumption of public and private resources. But with the advent of "notice pleading," the motion to dismiss seldom fulfills this function any more, and its place has been taken by the motion for summary judgment. Rule 56 must be construed with due regard not only for the rights of persons asserting claims and defenses that are adequately based in fact to have those claims and defenses tried to a jury, but also for the rights of persons opposing such claims and defenses to demonstrate in the man-

ner provided by the Rule, prior to trial, that the claims and defenses have no factual basis.

The judgment of the Court of Appeals is accordingly reversed, and the case is remanded for further proceedings consistent with this opinion.

JUSTICE WHITE, concurring in the Court's opinion and judgment.

I agree that the Court of Appeals was wrong in holding that the moving defendant must always support his motion with evidence or affidavits showing the absence of a genuine dispute about a material fact. I also agree that the movant may rely on depositions, answers to interrogatories and the like to demonstrate that the plaintiff has no evidence to prove his case and hence that there can be no factual dispute. But the movant must discharge the burden the rules place upon him: It is not enough to move for summary judgment without supporting the motion in any way or with a conclusory assertion that the plaintiff has no evidence to prove his case.

A plaintiff need not initiate any discovery or reveal his witnesses or evidence unless required to do so under the discovery rules or by court order. Of course, he must respond if required to do so; but he need not also depose his witnesses or obtain their affidavits to defeat a summary judgment motion asserting only that he has failed to produce any support for his case. It is the defendant's task to negate, if he can, the claimed basis for the suit.

Petitioner Celotex does not dispute that if respondent has named a witness to support her claim, summary judgment should not be granted without Celotex somehow showing that the named witness' possible testimony raises no genuine issue of material fact. It asserts, however, that respondent has failed on request to produce any basis for her case. Respondent, on the other hand, does not contend that she was not obligated to reveal her witnesses and evidence but insists that she has revealed enough to defeat the motion for summary judgment. Because the Court of Appeals found it unnecessary to address this aspect of the case, I agree that the case should be remanded for further proceedings.

JUSTICE BRENNAN, with whom THE CHIEF JUSTICE and JUSTICE BLACKMUN join, dissenting.

This case requires the Court to determine whether Celotex satisfied its initial burden of production in moving for summary judgment on the ground that the plaintiff lacked evidence to establish an essential element of her case at trial. I do not disagree with the Court's legal analysis. The Court clearly rejects the ruling of the Court of Appeals that the defendant must provide affirmative evidence disproving the plaintiff's case. Beyond this, however, the Court has not clearly explained what is required of a moving party seeking summary judgment on the ground that the nonmoving party cannot prove its case.[1] This lack of

1. It is also unclear what the Court of Appeals is supposed to do in this case on

clarity is unfortunate: district courts must routinely decide summary judgment motions, and the Court's opinion will very likely create confusion. For this reason, even if I agreed with the Court's result, I would have written separately to explain more clearly the law in this area. However, because I believe that Celotex did not meet its burden of production under Federal Rule of Civil Procedure 56, I respectfully dissent from the Court's judgment.

Summary judgment is appropriate where the Court is satisfied "that there is no genuine issue as to any material fact and that the moving party is entitled to a judgment as a matter of law." Fed.Rule Civ.Proc. 56(c). The burden of establishing the nonexistence of a "genuine issue" is on the party moving for summary judgment. * * * This burden has two distinct components: an initial burden of production, which shifts to the nonmoving party if satisfied by the moving party; and an ultimate burden of persuasion, which always remains on the moving party. * * * The court need not decide whether the moving party has satisfied its ultimate burden of persuasion[2] unless and until the Court finds that the moving party has discharged its initial burden of production. * * *

The burden of production imposed by Rule 56 requires the moving party to make a prima facie showing that it is entitled to summary judgment. * * * The manner in which this showing can be made depends upon which party will bear the burden of persuasion on the challenged claim at trial. If the moving party will bear the burden of persuasion at trial, that party must support its motion with credible evidence—using any of the materials specified in Rule 56(c)—that would entitle it to a directed verdict if not controverted at trial. Such an affirmative showing shifts the burden of production to the party opposing the motion and requires that party either to produce evidentiary

remand. Justice White—who has provided the Court's fifth vote—plainly believes that the Court of Appeals should reevaluate whether the defendant met its initial burden of production. However, the decision to reverse rather than to vacate the judgment below implies that the Court of Appeals should assume that Celotex has met its initial burden of production and ask only whether the plaintiff responded adequately, and, if so, whether the defendant has met its ultimate burden of persuasion that no genuine issue exists for trial. Absent some clearer expression from the Court to the contrary, Justice White's understanding would seem to be controlling. Cf. Marks v. United States, 430 U.S. 188, 193, 97 S.Ct. 990, 993, 51 L.Ed.2d 260 (1977).

2. The burden of persuasion imposed on a moving party by Rule 56 is a stringent one. Summary judgment should not be granted unless it is clear that a trial is unnecessary, Anderson v. Liberty Lobby, Inc., 477 U.S. 242, 250, 106 S.Ct. 2505, 2511, 91 L.Ed.2d 202 (1986), and any doubt as to the existence of a genuine issue for trial should be resolved against the moving party, Adickes v. S.H. Kress & Co., 398 U.S. 144, 158–159, 90 S.Ct. 1598, 1608–09, 26 L.Ed.2d 142 (1970). In determining whether a moving party has met its burden of persuasion, the court is obliged to take account of the entire setting of the case and must consider all papers of record as well as any materials prepared for the motion. As explained by the Court of Appeals for the Third Circuit in In re Japanese Electronic Products Antitrust Litigation, 723 F.2d 238 (1983), rev'd on other grounds sub nom. Matsushita Electric Industrial Co. v. Zenith Radio Corp., 475 U.S. 574, 106 S.Ct. 1348, 89 L.Ed.2d 538 (1986), "[i]f ... there is any evidence in the record from any source from which a reasonable inference in the [nonmoving party's] favor may be drawn, the moving party simply cannot obtain a summary judgment...." 723 F.2d, at 258.

materials that demonstrate the existence of a "genuine issue" for trial or to submit an affidavit requesting additional time for discovery. * * *

If the burden of persuasion at trial would be on the nonmoving party, the party moving for summary judgment may satisfy Rule 56's burden of production in either of two ways. First, the moving party may submit affirmative evidence that negates an essential element of the nonmoving party's claim. Second, the moving party may demonstrate to the Court that the nonmoving party's evidence is insufficient to establish an essential element of the nonmoving party's claim. See 10A Wright, Miller & Kane § 2727, pp. 130–131; Louis, Federal Summary Judgment Doctrine: A Critical Analysis, 83 Yale L.J. 745, 750 (1974) (hereinafter Louis). If the nonmoving party cannot muster sufficient evidence to make out its claim, a trial would be useless and the moving party is entitled to summary judgment as a matter of law. Anderson v. Liberty Lobby, Inc., 477 U.S. 242, 250, 106 S.Ct. 2505, 2511, 91 L.Ed.2d 202 (1986).

Where the moving party adopts this second option and seeks summary judgment on the ground that the nonmoving party—who will bear the burden of persuasion at trial— has no evidence, the mechanics of discharging Rule 56's burden of production are somewhat trickier. Plainly, a conclusory assertion that the nonmoving party has no evidence is insufficient. * * * Such a "burden" of production is no burden at all and would simply permit summary judgment procedure to be converted into a tool for harassment. * * * Rather, as the Court confirms, a party who moves for summary judgment on the ground that the nonmoving party has no evidence must affirmatively show the absence of evidence in the record. This may require the moving party to depose the nonmoving party's witnesses or to establish the inadequacy of documentary evidence. If there is literally no evidence in the record, the moving party may demonstrate this by reviewing for the court the admissions, interrogatories and other exchanges between the parties that are in the record. Either way, however, the moving party must affirmatively demonstrate that there is no evidence in the record to support a judgment for the nonmoving party.

If the moving party has not fully discharged this initial burden of production, its motion for summary judgment must be denied, and the Court need not consider whether the moving party has met its ultimate burden of persuasion. Accordingly, the nonmoving party may defeat a motion for summary judgment that asserts that the nonmoving party has no evidence by calling the Court's attention to supporting evidence already in the record that was overlooked or ignored by the moving party. In that event, the moving party must respond by making an attempt to demonstrate the inadequacy of this evidence, for it is only by attacking all the record evidence allegedly supporting the nonmoving party that a party seeking summary judgment satisfies Rule 56's burden of production.[3] Thus, if the record disclosed that the moving party had

---

3. Once the moving party has attacked whatever record evidence—if any—the non-

overlooked a witness who would provide relevant testimony for the nonmoving party at trial, the Court could not find that the moving party had discharged its initial burden of production unless the moving party sought to demonstrate the inadequacy of this witness' testimony. Absent such a demonstration, summary judgment would have to be denied on the ground that the moving party had failed to meet its burden of production under Rule 56.

The result in Adickes v. S.H. Kress & Co., supra, is fully consistent with these principles. In that case, petitioner was refused service in respondent's lunchroom and then was arrested for vagrancy by a local policeman as she left. Petitioner brought an action under 42 U.S.C. § 1983 claiming that the refusal of service and subsequent arrest were the product of a conspiracy between respondent and the police; as proof of this conspiracy, petitioner's complaint alleged that the arresting officer was in respondent's store at the time service was refused. Respondent subsequently moved for summary judgment on the ground that there was no actual evidence in the record from which a jury could draw an inference of conspiracy. In response, petitioner pointed to a statement from her own deposition and an unsworn statement by a Kress employee, both already in the record and both ignored by respondent, that the policeman who arrested petitioner was in the store at the time she was refused service. We agreed that "[i]f a policeman were present, . . . it would be open to a jury, in light of the sequence that followed, to infer from the circumstances that the policeman and Kress employee had a 'meeting of the minds' and thus reached an understanding that petitioner should be refused service." Consequently, we held that it was error to grant summary judgment "on the basis of this record" because respondent had "failed to fulfill its initial burden" of demonstrating that there was no evidence that there was a policeman in the store.

The opinion of the Court in *Adickes* has sometimes been read to hold that summary judgment was inappropriate because the respondent had not submitted affirmative evidence to negate the possibility that there was a policeman in the store. The Court of Appeals apparently read *Adickes* this way and therefore required Celotex to submit evidence establishing that plaintiff's decedent had not been exposed to Celotex asbestos. I agree with the Court that this reading of *Adickes* was erroneous and that Celotex could seek summary judgment on the ground that plaintiff could not prove exposure to Celotex asbestos at trial. However, Celotex was still required to satisfy its initial burden of production.

moving party purports to rely upon, the burden of production shifts to the nonmoving party, who must either (1) rehabilitate the evidence attacked in the moving party's papers, (2) produce additional evidence showing the existence of a genuine issue for trial as provided in Rule 56(e), or (3) submit an affidavit explaining why further discovery is necessary as provided in Rule 56(f). Summary judgment should be granted if the nonmoving party fails to respond in one or more of these ways, or if, after the nonmoving party responds, the court determines that the moving party has met its ultimate burden of persuading the court that there is no genuine issue of material fact for trial. See, e.g., First National Bank of Arizona v. Cities Service Co., 391 U.S. 253, 289, 88 S.Ct. 1575, 1592, 20 L.Ed.2d 569 (1968).

I do not read the Court's opinion to say anything inconsistent with or different than the preceding discussion. My disagreement with the Court concerns the application of these principles to the facts of this case.

Defendant Celotex sought summary judgment on the ground that plaintiff had "failed to produce" any evidence that her decedent had ever been exposed to Celotex asbestos. Celotex supported this motion with a 2–page "Statement of Material Facts as to Which There is No Genuine Issue" and a 3–page "Memorandum of Points and Authorities" which asserted that the plaintiff had failed to identify any evidence in responding to two sets of interrogatories propounded by Celotex and that therefore the record was "totally devoid" of evidence to support plaintiff's claim.

Approximately three months earlier, Celotex had filed an essentially identical motion. Plaintiff responded to this earlier motion by producing three pieces of evidence which she claimed "[a]t the very least ... demonstrate that there is a genuine factual dispute for trial": (1) a letter from an insurance representative of another defendant describing asbestos products to which plaintiff's decedent had been exposed, (2) a letter from T.R. Hoff, a former supervisor of decedent, describing asbestos products to which decedent had been exposed; and (3) a copy of decedent's deposition from earlier workmen's compensation proceedings. Plaintiff also apparently indicated at that time that she intended to call Mr. Hoff as a witness at trial.

Celotex subsequently withdrew its first motion for summary judgment. However, as a result of this motion, when Celotex filed its second summary judgment motion, the record did contain evidence—including at least one witness—supporting plaintiff's claim. Indeed, counsel for Celotex admitted to this Court at oral argument that Celotex was aware of this evidence and of plaintiff's intention to call Mr. Hoff as a witness at trial when the second summary judgment motion was filed. Moreover, plaintiff's response to Celotex' second motion pointed to this evidence— noting that it had already been provided to counsel for Celotex in connection with the first motion—and argued that Celotex had failed to "meet its burden of proving that there is no genuine factual dispute for trial."

On these facts, there is simply no question that Celotex failed to discharge its initial burden of production. Having chosen to base its motion on the argument that there was no evidence in the record to support plaintiff's claim, Celotex was not free to ignore supporting evidence that the record clearly contained. Rather, Celotex was required, as an initial matter, to attack the adequacy of this evidence. Celotex' failure to fulfill this simple requirement constituted a failure to discharge its initial burden of production under Rule 56, and thereby rendered summary judgment improper.[6]

6. If the plaintiff had answered Celotex' second set of interrogatories with the evi-

This case is indistinguishable from *Adickes*. Here, as there, the defendant moved for summary judgment on the ground that the record contained no evidence to support an essential element of the plaintiff's claim. Here, as there, the plaintiff responded by drawing the court's attention to evidence that was already in the record and that had been ignored by the moving party. Consequently, here, as there, summary judgment should be denied on the ground that the moving party failed to satisfy its initial burden of production.

[The dissenting opinion of Justice Stevens is omitted.]

Notes and Questions

1. Does the decision in *Celotex* represent a major alteration in the *Adickes* approach? Do either the majority or dissent in *Celotex* believe that it does? Consider Nissan Fire & Marine Ins. Co. v. Fritz Companies, 210 F.3d 1099, 1103–04 (9th Cir.2000):

> We believe that the perceived tension between *Adickes* and *Celotex* may be explained by the fact that the cases focused on different questions. The central question in *Adickes* was whether the moving party had carried its initial burden of production by producing affirmative evidence negating an essential element of the nonmoving party's claim. The central question in *Celotex* was whether the moving party had carried its initial burden of production by showing that the nonmoving party did not have enough evidence to carry its ultimate burden of persuasion at trial. In other words, *Adickes* and *Celotex* dealt with two different methods by which a moving party can carry its initial burden of production.

Relying in large part on *Adickes,* the lower court in *Celotex* had stated (756 F.2d at 184–85):

> It is firmly established that the party opposing the motion for summary judgment bears the burden of responding *only after* the moving party has met its burden of coming forward with proof of the absence of any genuine issues of material fact.

> At trial, of course, Mrs. Catrett would have the burden of proving by admissible evidence that her husband's exposure to Celotex's products had proximately caused his death. If Mrs. Catrett failed to satisfy her burden, then her case would be vulnerable to a motion for a directed verdict. However, * * * the party moving for summary judgment carries the burden of proving the absence of a material issue of fact "even on issues where the other party would have the burden of proof at trial."

> In this case Celotex proffered nothing. It advanced only the naked allegation that the *plaintiff* had not come forward in discovery with evidence to support her allegations of decedent's exposure to the defen-

dence in her response to the first summary judgment motion, and Celotex had ignored those interrogatories and based its second summary judgment motion on the first set of interrogatories only, Celotex obviously could not claim to have discharged its Rule 56 burden of production. This result should not be different simply because the evidence plaintiff relied upon to support her claim was acquired by Celotex other than in plaintiff's answers to interrogatories.

dant's product.[12] Under settled rules, that barebones approach will not do. Mrs. Catrett was simply not required, given this state of the record, to offer any evidence in response.

Is this an accurate characterization of the standard of *Adickes?* Why did the Supreme Court reverse? On remand from the Supreme Court, the same panel of the court of appeals held that plaintiff's reliance on the letter from the official of Louis Catrett's former employer, coupled with plaintiff's indication that this official would be a witness at trial, sufficed to show a genuine issue as to whether Catrett was exposed to Celotex products. 826 F.2d 33 (D.C.Cir.1987). Again dissenting, Judge Bork argued that the letter was not admissible and that plaintiff had made no showing that the official had personal knowledge of such exposure.

2. To which scholarly approach is the standard adopted by Justice Rehnquist in *Celotex* closer, Professor Currie's or Professor Louis'? Is it identical to either one?

The majority of post-*Celotex* lower courts have read that decision not to impose a significant triggering burden on a movant who lacks the burden of production at trial. Indeed, many lower court decisions following *Celotex* have either reduced the burden dramatically or ignored it completely. See, e.g., Chao v. Hall Holding Co., Inc., 285 F.3d 415 (6th Cir. 2002), cert. denied, 537 U.S. 1168 (2003); Adler v. Wal–Mart Stores, Inc. 144 F.3d 664 (10th Cir. 1998); Elkins v. Richardson–Merrell, Inc., 8 F.3d 1068 (6th Cir.1993); Whetstine v. Gates Rubber Co., 895 F.2d 388 (7th Cir.1990); Kauffman v. Puerto Rico Telephone Co., 841 F.2d 1169 (1st Cir.1988). But see Clark v. Coats & Clark, Inc., 929 F.2d 604 (11th Cir.1991). In that case, the district court had granted defendant's summary judgment motion on the ground that plaintiffs would not be able to prove their case. The appellate court reversed on the ground that defendant had not satisfied its initial burden to justify summary judgment. It concluded "emphatically" that "*Celotex* did not overrule *Adickes*," and was an "exception" for an "uncommon situation"—"where neither party could prove either the affirmative or the negative of an essential element of the claim." This decision has been criticized as "contrary to the letter and spirit of *Celotex*" because it overlooked the Supreme Court's statement that summary judgment is "an integral part of the Federal Rules as a whole" and recalls the "wariness (if not downright hostility) toward summary judgment common prior to [*Celotex*]." Schwarzer & Hirsch, Summary Judgment After *Eastman Kodak*, 45 Hast. L.J. 1, 12–13 (1993). See also Russ v. International Paper Co., 943 F.2d 589, 591 (5th Cir.1991): "[T]he district court * * * cite[s] language from

---

12. That is not to say that Celotex was required to come forward with some specific form of submission. Indeed, Rule 56 is clear that there is no absolute requirement that the moving party furnish affidavits in support of its motion. But here, Celotex did not simply fail to submit affidavits or declarations in support of its motion; it came forward literally with nothing save for pointing to perceived shortfalls in the plaintiff's case.

It is in no wise unfair to Celotex to require it to support its case under Rule 56,

even under the circumstances here. * * * [I]f a party has failed to comply with discovery requests, such as interrogatories and requests for production of documents, the Federal Rules provide an elaborately drawn system of sanctions for failures to comply, including the ultimate sanction of dismissal of one's case. Thus, our ruling in no manner leaves a party such as Celotex remediless in the face of unsuccessful efforts to effect discovery of the opposing side's case.

* * * *Celotex* and other cases suggesting that summary judgment is appropriate anytime a party fails to establish the existence of an element essential to his case and on which he will bear the burden of proof at trial. * * * This is incorrect. * * * *Celotex* makes clear that before the non-moving party is required to produce evidence in opposition to the motion, the moving party must first satisfy its obligation of demonstrating that there are no factual issues warranting trial." Is this an accurate reading of *Celotex*? To a similar effect see Hunter v. Caliber Sys., 220 F.3d 702, 725–26 (6th Cir. 2000).

3. Recall the initial disclosure provisions of Rule 26(a)(1). Once the disclosure exchange is completed, would defendant be in a position to move for summary judgment on the ground that plaintiff has disclosed no evidence to support his or her claims?

4. In his dissent, Justice Brennan contends that the only difference between his opinion and that of the majority is in the application of an accepted general standard to the facts. Do you agree that the two opinions adopt the same general approach to the movant's burden?

In footnote 2 of his dissent, Justice Brennan refers to "[t]he burden of persuasion imposed on a moving party by Rule 56." Does the summary judgment procedure actually have anything to do with the "burden of persuasion," as that term is traditionally defined? See the discussion of Professor James' work, supra pp. 425–26. What do you suppose Justice Brennan means by his use of the term? In footnote 1, he refers to a movant's "ultimate burden of persuasion that no genuine issue exists for trial." Does this statement provide a clue as to his meaning?

5. Does Justice Brennan adopt Professor Louis' approach to the ways in which the moving party may generate the material needed to make the showing required to support summary judgment? Does he give proper weight to the difficulties the moving party may confront in fashioning discovery to obtain this information?

6. Given possible uncertainty about whether the moving party has satisfied its initial burden, how does the responding party decide what needs to be submitted in opposition to a motion for summary judgment? Should the court first appraise the movant's showing and then advise the other side on whether it need bother to submit responsive materials? Although no courts require that the judge make that sort of initial appraisal, some do require that pro se litigants be advised (either by the judge or the moving party) of the general requirements that Rule 56 imposes on a party responding to a motion for summary judgment. See, e.g., Irby v. New York City Transit Auth., 262 F.3d 412 (2d Cir. 2001) ("the moving party should routinely provide a pro se party with notice of the requirements of Rule 56"). How well does such a burden fit in with the adversary system? See Rand v. Rowland, 154 F.3d 952, 968 (9th Cir. 1998) (dissenting opinion) ("We are not supposed to be advocates for a class of litigants, and it is hard to help pro ses very much without being unfair to their adversaries.").

7. Does the Court in *Celotex* relieve plaintiff of the obligation (See Rule 56(c)) of coming forward with admissible evidence? Professor Nelken suggests that Justice Rehnquist's opinion "opened the door to evidence that was not already reduced to admissible form, but merely was reducible to such form":

In distinguishing two questions for the court of appeals on re-mand—the "adequacy" of Mrs. Catrett's showing and its "suffi-cien[cy]," *"if reduced to admissible evidence,"* to carry her burden of proof at trial—Justice Rehnquist implicitly reiterated the view that inadmissible evidence may be used to oppose summary judgment, as long as it is reducible to admissible evidence at trial. Accordingly, Hoff's letter, although unauthenticated hearsay, could be considered in opposi-tion to summary judgment, since Hoff was apparently available to and competent to testify at trial about Louis Catrett's exposure to asbestos (or, at least, to authenticate the business records on which his letter was based). On the other hand, the Catrett deposition could not be consid-ered in opposition to summary judgment. It was not reducible to admissible evidence at trial because Celotex did not have an opportunity to cross-examine Mr. Catrett at the deposition and he had since died.

Nelken, One Step Forward, Two Steps Back: Summary Judgment After *Celotex*, 40 Hast. L.J. 53, 71 n. 92 (1988). See also Ford v. Wilson, 90 F.3d 245 (7th Cir. 1996) (in response to summary judgement motion, plaintiff may rely on verified complaint, which is as good as an affidavit).

8. The Court in *Celotex* points out that plaintiff was not "railroaded" by a premature motion for summary judgment, suggesting that such prob-lems can be dealt with under Rule 56(f). Does that provision protect plaintiffs adequately against premature motions? Should the court permit discovery on issues not raised by the summary judgment motion? With regard to discovery directed toward the issue raised by the summary judg-ment motion, must plaintiff make a showing that the discovery is likely to produce material that will defeat the motion? Consider the Second Circuit's test for the sufficiency of a Rule 56(f) affidavit: "The affidavit must include the nature of the uncompleted discovery; how the facts sought are reason-ably expected to create a genuine issue of material fact; what efforts the affiant has made to obtain these facts; and why these efforts were unsuccess-ful." Paddington Partners v. Bouchard, 34 F.3d 1132, 1138 (2d Cir.1994).

9. It has been said that *Celotex* "worked a systemic sea change" in promoting summary judgment. See Shadur, Trials or Tribulations (Rule 56 Style), 29 Litigation 5 (Winter 2003); see also Gonzalez, Depositions in the Age of Summary Judgment, Trial, Aug. 2004, at 20. ("The most dramatic change in employment discrimination litigation over the past two decades is the federal judiciary's increased use of summary judgment.") If so, is that necessarily a bad result? For a criticism of the trend towards the greater availability of summary judgment thought to be manifested in decisions such as *Celotex*, see generally Stempel, A Distorted Mirror: The Supreme Court's Shimmering View of Summary Judgment, Directed Verdict, and the Adjudi-cation Process, 49 Ohio St. L.J. 95 (1988). See also Issacharoff & Lowenstein, Second Thoughts About Summary Judgments, 100 Yale L.J. 73 (1990) (arguing that expanded use of summary judgment after *Celotex* alters the balance of power in pretrial by raising costs and risks to plaintiffs and has a further adverse effect on settlement when a summary judgment motion has been denied). Should *Celotex* be viewed instead as a positive development? See Redish, Summary Judgment and the Vanishing Trial: Implications of the Litigation Matrix, 57 Stan. L. Rev. ___ (2005) (praising *Celotex*'s removal of

"external barriers" to a trial court's reaching the merits of a summary judgment motion).

States also changed their practices. California decisions, for example, instructed that summary judgment in California courts should generally conform to *Celotex*. See, e.g., Aguilar v. Atlantic Richfield Co., 24 P.3d 493 (Cal. S.Ct. 2001). The California Legislature, however, responded by amending the state's summary judgment statute to require 75 days notice of a summary judgment motion, and to extend the time further if the party seeking summary judgment has unreasonably failed to allow discovery. See Cal. Code Civ. Proc. § 437(c).

10.   Note that Justice Rehnquist relies in part on a trial court's ability to award summary judgment *sua sponte*. This means that the court may award summary judgment, even though neither party has formally moved for it. However, it is generally error for the district court to award summary judgment *sua sponte* without providing notice to the party against whom the award has been made. Bendet v. Sandoz Pharmaceuticals Corp., 308 F.3d 907, 911–12 (8th Cir. 2002). But see Geraghty and Miller, Inc. v. Conoco, Inc. 234 F.3d 917 (5th Cir. 2000) (district court's award of *sua sponte* summary judgment without notice was harmless error because the court had accepted and considered the losing party's brief and gave it an opportunity to be heard on all issues). According to one court, while granting summary judgment *sua sponte* "is permissible . . . it is a hazardous procedure which warrants special caution." Osler Institute, Inc. v. Forde, 333 F.3d 832, 836 (7th Cir. 2003), cert. denied, 540 U.S. 1177, 124 S.Ct. 1407, 158 L.Ed.2d 78 (2004).

B.   MEETING THE BURDEN OF PRODUCTION: DETERMINING THE APPROPRIATE STANDARD

In the previous section, we examined exactly what a party who moves for summary judgment must produce in order to trigger the need for a response from the non-movant. Once the response is triggered, it is necessary to determine what evidence the non-movant must produce in order to avoid summary judgment.

If the non-movant would have the burden of production at trial, it must respond with sufficient evidence that a reasonable finder of fact *could* find in its favor—i.e., it must meet its burden of production. If the non-movant would not have the burden of production at trial, however, everyone agrees that the only way that a movant may obtain summary judgment is by *shifting* the burden of production—i.e., by providing sufficient evidence that, absent a response from the non-movant, a reasonable fact finder would have to find for the movant because it would be unreasonable to do otherwise.

In this section, we consider what constitutes evidence sufficient to meet a party's burden of production—in other words, when has a party presented enough evidence that a reasonable jury could find for him?

ARNSTEIN v. PORTER

United States Court of Appeals, Second Circuit, 1946.
154 F.2d 464.

Before L. HAND, CLARK, and FRANK, CIRCUIT JUDGES.

FRANK, CIRCUIT JUDGE.

[Plaintiff Arnstein sued noted song writer Cole Porter for copyright infringement, alleging that numerous well-known songs by the defendant were actually taken from a number of songs copyrighted by plaintiff. Plaintiff claimed that defendant "had stooges right along to follow me, watch me, and live in the same apartment with me", and that plaintiff's room had been ransacked on several occasions. Asked in his deposition how he knew that defendant had anything to do with any of these break-ins, plaintiff responded, "I don't know that he had to do with it, but I only know that he could have." Defendant in his deposition denied that he had ever seen or heard any of plaintiff's compositions or had had any acquaintance with persons who might have stolen any of them. The trial court granted defendant's summary judgment motion, and plaintiff, appearing *pro se*, appealed. The Court of Appeals reversed.]

The principal question on this appeal is whether the lower court, under Rule 56, properly deprived plaintiff of a trial of his copyright infringement action. * * * [I]t is important to avoid confusing two separate elements essential to a plaintiff's case in such a suit: (a) that defendant copied from plaintiff's copyrighted work and (b) that the copying (assuming it to be proved) went so far as to constitute improper appropriation.

As to the first—copying—the evidence may consist (a) of defendant's admission that he copied or (b) circumstantial evidence—usually evidence of access—from which the trier of the facts may reasonably infer copying.

* * *

After listening * * * to the compositions as played in the phonograph recordings submitted by defendant, we find similarities [between plaintiff's and defendant's compositions]; but we hold that unquestionably, standing alone, they do not compel the conclusion, or permit the inference, that defendant copied. The similarities, however, are sufficient so that, if there is enough evidence of access to permit the case to go to the jury, the jury may properly infer that the similarities did not result from coincidence.

Summary judgment was, then, proper if indubitably defendant did not have access to plaintiff's compositions. Plainly that presents an issue of fact. On that issue, the district judge, who heard no oral testimony, had before him the depositions of plaintiff and defendant. The judge characterized plaintiff's story as "fantastic"; and, in the light of the references in his opinion to defendant's deposition, the judge obviously accepted defendant's denial of access and copying. Although part of plaintiff's testimony on deposition (as to "stooges" and the like) does seem "fantastic," yet plaintiff's credibility, even as to those improbabilities, should be left to the jury. If evidence is "of a kind that greatly taxes the credulity of the judge, he can say so, or, if he totally disbelieves it, he may announce that fact, leaving the jury free to believe it or not." If, said Winslow, J., "evidence is to be always disbelieved because the story told seems remarkable or impossible, then a party whose rights depend on the proof of some facts out of the usual course of events will always be denied justice simply because his story is improbable." [Marston v. Dresen, 85 Wis. 530, 535, 55 N.W. 896, 899 (1893).] We should not overlook the shrewd proverbial admonition that sometimes truth is stranger than fiction.

But even if we were to disregard the improbable aspect of plaintiff's story, there remain parts by no means "fantastic." On the record now before us, more than a million copies of one of his compositions were sold; copies of others were sold in smaller quantities or distributed to radio stations or band leaders or publishers, or the pieces were publicly performed. If, after hearing both parties testify, the jury disbelieves defendant's denials, it can, from such facts, reasonably infer access. It follows that, as credibility is unavoidably involved, a genuine issue of material fact presents itself. With credibility a vital factor, plaintiff is entitled to a trial where the jury can observe the witnesses while testifying. Plaintiff must not be deprived of the invaluable privilege of cross-examining the defendant—the "crucial test of credibility"—in the presence of the jury. Plaintiff, or a lawyer on his behalf, on such examination may elicit damaging admissions from defendant; more important, plaintiff may persuade the jury, observing defendant's manner when testifying, that the defendant is unworthy of belief.

CLARK, J.,* dissenting.

Under the procedure employed, the parties were entitled to require discovery of the case relied on by the other. This they did by each taking the deposition of the other, resulting in a categorical denial by defendant of having ever seen or heard plaintiff's compositions and no showing by plaintiff of any evidence of access worthy of submission to any trier of fact. * * * My brothers, in a trusting belief in the virtues of cross-examination, rely upon a trial to develop more. But cross-examination can hardly construct a whole case without some factual basis on which to start. * * *

Since the legal issue seems thus clear to me, I am loath to believe that my colleagues will uphold a final judgment of plagiarism on a record such as this. The present holding is therefore one of those procedural mountains which develop where it is thought that justice must be

---

* Judge Clark had served as reporter of the committee that drafted the Federal Rules of Civil Procedure, and he was reporter to the Advisory Committee on the Civil Rules when this case was decided. He had early favored summary judgment over pleadings motions as a way to decide the merits of cases. See Smith, Judge Charles E. Clark and the Federal Rules of Civil Procedure, 85 Yale L.J. 914, 918–19—Eds.

temporarily sacrificed, lest a mistaken precedent be set at large. The conclusion that the precedent would be mistaken appears to rest on two premises: a belief in the efficacy of the jury to settle issues of plagiarism, and a dislike of the rule established by the supreme court as to summary judgments. Now, as to the first, I am not one to condemn jury trials (cf. Frank, Law and the Modern Mind) since I think it has a place among other quite finite methods of fact-finding. * * * [But] surely we cannot now say that a verdict should not be directed. * * *

The second premise—dislike of the summary-judgment rule—I find difficult to appraise or understand. [Judge Clark found the majority's opinion to suggest a special limitation on summary judgment in copyright cases.] * * * since, however, the clear-cut provisions of f.r. 56 conspicuously do not contain either a restriction on the kinds of actions to which it is applicable (unlike most state summary procedures), or any presumption against its use, it is necessary to refashion the rule. * * * that is a novel method of amending rules of procedure. It subverts the plans and hopes of the profession for careful, informed study leading to the adoption and to the amendment of simple rules which shall be uniform throughout the country. * * *

In fact, however, cases, texts, and articles without dissent accept and approve the summary judgment as an integral and useful part of the procedural system envisaged by the rules. * * * It is, indeed, more necessary in the system of simple pleading now enforced in the federal courts; for under older procedures, useless and unnecessary trials could be avoided, in theory at least, by the then existing demurrer and motion practice. But that stresses pleading forms, rather than the merits, while summary judgment and its popular correlative, pre-trial procedure, f.r. 16, go directly to the merits. One unfortunate consequence of eliminating summary procedure is that it affords support for the plea of return to the old demurrer, which, however clumsily, did get rid of some of the cases which did not deserve a protracted and expensive trial. Of course it is error to deny trial when there is a genuine dispute of facts; but it is just as much error—perhaps more in cases of hardship, or where impetus is given to strike suits—to deny or postpone judgment where the ultimate legal result is clearly indicated.

DYER v. MacDOUGALL

United States Court of Appeals, Second Circuit, 1952.
201 F.2d 265.

Before SWAN, CHIEF JUDGE, and L. HAND and FRANK, CIRCUIT JUDGES.

L. HAND, CIRCUIT JUDGE.

This case comes up on appeal by the plaintiff from a judgment summarily dismissing the third and fourth counts of a complaint for libel and slander. * * * We may start with the amended complaint, which was filed on November 24, 1950. It was in four counts, of which the first alleged that the defendant, Albert E. MacDougall, had said of the plaintiff at a directors' meeting of the "Queensboro Corporation": "You are stabbing me in the back." The second count alleged that MacDougall had written a letter to one Dorothy Russell Hope, the plaintiff's wife's sister, containing the words: "He"—the plaintiff—"has made false statements to my clients in Philadelphia," and "He has presented bills for work he has not done." The third count alleged that MacDougall had said to a lawyer, named Almirall, that a letter sent out by the plaintiff to the shareholders of the "Queensboro Corporation" was "a blackmailing letter." The fourth count alleged that MacDougall's wife, as MacDougall's agent, had said to Mrs. Hope that the plaintiff had "written and sent out a blackmailing letter."

On December 26, 1950, the defendants, before answer, moved for judgment summarily dismissing the second, third and fourth counts, supporting their motion by affidavits of MacDougall, MacDougall's wife, and Almirall, and by a deposition of Mrs. Hope, which the plaintiff himself had already taken. Each of the defendants unequivocally denied the utterance of the slanders attributed to him or her; and Almirall and Mrs. Hope denied that he or she had heard the slanders uttered. On his part the plaintiff replied with several affidavits of his own, the contents of all of which would, however, be inadmissible as evidence at a trial upon the issue of utterance. On January 24, 1951, the defendants filed an unverified answer denying the defamatory utterances, and on the same day they brought on their motion for hearing before Judge Kennedy. He offered the plaintiff an opportunity to take depositions of Mr. and Mrs. MacDougall and of Almirall, and a second deposition of Mrs. Hope; and by consent the case was then adjourned to allow the plaintiff to take the depositions. However, towards the end of October 1951, he told the court that he did not wish to do so, and on December 28, 1951 * * * the judge decided the defendants' motion by summarily dismissing the third and fourth counts on the ground that upon the trial the plaintiff would have no evidence to offer in support of the slanders except the testimony of witnesses, all of whom would deny their utterance.

* * *

The question is whether, in view of the defendants' affidavits and Mrs. Hope's deposition, there was any "genuine issue" under Rule 56(c) as to the utterance of the slanders. The defendants had the burden of proving that there was no such issue; on the other hand, at a trial the plaintiff would have the burden of proving the utterances; and therefore, if the defendants on the motion succeeded in proving that the plaintiff would not have enough evidence to go to the jury on the issue, the judgment was right. As the plaintiff has refused to avail himself of the privilege under Rule 56(f) of examining by deposition the witnesses whom the defendants proposed to call at the trial, we must assume that what they said in their affidavits they would have repeated in their depositions; and that what they would have said in their depositions, they would say at a trial, with one possible exception, the consideration of which we will postpone for the time being. With that reserved we will therefore first discuss the judgment on the assumption that the record before us contains all the testimony that would appear at a trial in support of the slanders. * * *

[If] the cause went to trial, the plaintiff would have no witnesses by whom he could prove the slanders alleged in the third and fourth counts, except the two defendants, Almirall and Mrs. Hope; and they would all deny that the slanders had been uttered. On such a showing how could he escape a directed verdict? It is true that the carriage, behavior, bearing, manner and appearance of a witness—in short, his "demeanor"—is a part of the evidence. The words used are by no means all that we rely on in making up our minds about the truth of a question that arises in our ordinary affairs, and it is abundantly settled that a jury is as little confined to them as we are. They may, and indeed they should, take into consideration the whole nexus of sense impressions which they get from a witness. This we have again and again declared, and have rested our affirmance of findings of fact of a judge, or of a jury, on the hypothesis that this part of the evidence may have turned the scale.[7] Moreover, such evidence may satisfy the tribunal, not only that the witness' testimony is not true, but that the truth is the opposite of his story; for the denial of one, who has a motive to deny, may be uttered with such hesitation, discomfort, arrogance or defiance, as to give assurance that he is fabricating, and that, if he is, there is no alternative but to assume the truth of what he denies.

Nevertheless, although it is therefore true that in strict theory a party having the affirmative might succeed in convincing a jury of the truth of his allegations in spite of the fact that all the witnesses denied them, we think it plain that a verdict would nevertheless have to be directed against him. This is owing to the fact that otherwise in such cases there could not be an effective appeal from the judge's disposition of a motion for a directed verdict. He, who has seen and heard the "demeanor" evidence, may have been right or wrong in thinking that it gave rational support to a verdict; yet, since that evidence has disappeared, it will be impossible for an appellate court to say which he was. Thus, he would become the final arbiter in all cases where the evidence of witnesses present in court might be determinative. We need not say that in setting aside a verdict the judge has not a broader discretion than in directing one; for we have before us only the equivalent of a direction. It may be argued that such a ruling may deprive a party of a possibly rational verdict, and indeed that is theoretically true, although the occasions must be to the last degree rare in which the chance so denied is more than fanciful. Nevertheless we do not hesitate to set against the chance so lost, the protection of a review of the judge's decision.

There remains the second point which we reserved for separate discussion: i.e. whether by an examination in open court the plaintiff might extract from the four witnesses admissions which he would not have got on the depositions that he refused. Although this is also at best

---

7. Arnstein v. Porter, 2 Cir., 154 F.2d 464.

a tenuous possibility, we need not say that there could never be situations in which it might justify denying summary judgment. It might appear for example that upon a deposition a witness had been recalcitrant, or crafty, or defiant, or evasive, so that the immediate presence of a judge in a court-room was likely to make him tell more. That would be another matter; and it might be enough. But the plaintiff is in no position to invoke such a possibility for he has refused to try out these witnesses upon deposition, where he might discover whether there was any basis for supposing that awe of a judge was necessary to make them more amenable. A priori we will not assume that that is true. The course of procedural reform has all indeed been towards bringing witnesses before the tribunal when it is possible; but that is not so much because more testimony can be got out of them as because only so can the "demeanor" evidence be brought before the tribunal.

Judgment affirmed.

[Concurring opinion of JUDGE FRANK omitted.]

Notes and Questions

1. For a thorough discussion of both *Arnstein* and the Clark–Frank debate, see Wald, Summary Judgment at Sixty, 76 Tex. L. Rev. 1897, 1898–1904 (1998). According to Judge Wald, "the disagreement between Judges Frank and Clark offers a penetrating preview of the extreme version of the pro-and anti-summary judgment positions that we see among current judges." Id. at 1903. See also Hazard, From Whom No Secrets Are Hid, 76 Tex. L. Rev. 1665 (1998).

2. How persuasive is the court's reasoning in *Dyer*? In a separate concurring opinion, Judge Frank criticized the logic of Judge Hand's opinion:

> Judge Hand's opinion states that, if defendant and the other witnesses testified, the trial court, evaluating their credibility in the light of their demeanor as witnesses, could rationally find not only that defendant's denial was false, but that the opposite was true, i.e., that defendant had made the slanderous statement. Yet Judge Hand holds that a trial judge in a jury trial of such a case would be obliged not to let the jury reach a verdict for plaintiff on that rational basis. As I understand Judge Hand, he says that the result of holding otherwise would be that the trial judge's disposition of a motion for a directed verdict (or a verdict n.o.v.) could not be effectively reviewed on appeal. On that ground alone—i.e., the supposed obstacle, in a jury trial of such a case, to review of a directed verdict—Judge Hand's opinion affirms the summary judgment for defendant here.

> * * *

> Judge Hand argues from the alleged unreviewability of a directed verdict in a case like this, if demeanor were a factor. But this argument cuts too far. For, if Judge Hand is correct, the same difficulty will attend the review of any directed verdict in any case where any important evidence consists of oral testimony. In any such case, one could say, as

Judge Hand says here: If the jury (should the case go to the jury) could rely on "demeanor evidence," then necessarily the trial judge could do likewise, on a motion for a directed verdict; and if he could, no directed verdict would be reviewable when important testimony in oral. But this is exactly not the rule in the federal courts: The well-settled rule is that, in passing on a motion for a directed verdict the trial judge always must utterly disregard his own views of witnesses' credibility, and therefore of their demeanor; that he believes or disbelieves some of the testimony is irrelevant.

Demeanor evidence may usually be relied upon by the jury to disbelieve witnesses with impeccable credentials; as is often said, a scoundrel's testimony could be believed over the testimony of 40 bishops. Does the law give too much weight to demeanor evidence? In general, the mannerisms that people tend to associate with lying are characteristics of people who are simply nervous. Many witnesses are nervous about testifying, and it may be that some liars are not nervous about lying. This should make us a bit uneasy about the heavy emphasis placed on demeanor evidence. Moreover, some psychological research indicates that people are not effective at detecting lies from observing the speaker. See, e.g., Bond, Kahler & Paolicelli, The Miscommunication of Deception: An Adaptive Perspective, 21 J. Exper. Social Psych. 331 (1985) (subjects of experiment were not much better than chance in detecting liars, presumably because they placed reliance on factors such as gestures that do not invariably indicate lying); Zuckerman, Koestner & Driver, Beliefs About Cues Associated with Deception, 6 J. Nonverbal Behavior 105 (Winter 1981) (subjects who answered questionnaire revealed about 10% accuracy in identifying those cues actually associated with lying). One old study even concluded that people make *more* accurate decisions on the basis of written materials than observation of witnesses. Marston, Studies in Testimony, 15 J.Amer.Inst.Crim.Law & Criminology 5, 22–26 (1924). These studies do not provide conclusive evidence that the law's reliance on demeanor evidence is misplaced since they do not recreate the trial atmosphere accurately enough for such a conclusion, but they do provide a basis for caution in assuming that demeanor evidence is critical to accurate results.

3. While Judge Frank, the author of *Arnstein*, rejected Judge Hand's reasoning in *Dyer*, he ultimately concurred in the court's judgment. Can *Arnstein* and *Dyer* be reconciled? Judge Frank believed that the facts in *Dyer* were "most unusual: The plaintiff asserts that in his absence he was slandered by defendant in the presence of but two other persons. As this fact is denied by all three, only plaintiff's own suit serves to publicize the alleged slander. In these peculiar circumstances, the plaintiff should not have the chance at a trial to discharge his burden of proof by nothing except the trial court's disbelief in the oral testimony of witnesses all of whom will deny that the alleged slanderous statement was made." Is this suggested distinction between *Dyer* and *Arnstein* persuasive?

4. If the decisions are, in fact, irreconcilable, which position do you find more compelling? Does your answer depend on how important we deem the litigants' access to a jury? As Judge Clark noted in his *Arnstein* dissent, Judge Frank was one of the harshest critics of the use of the jury. See, e.g., J. Frank, Law and the Modern Mind 191–93 (Anchor ed. 1963):

Proclaiming that we have a government of laws, we have, in jury cases, created a government of often ignorant and prejudiced men. * * * [A]re jurors good fact-finders? * * * Is it likely that twelve men, summoned from all sorts of occupations, unaccustomed to the machinery of the law, unacquainted with their own mental workings and not known to one another, can, in the scant time allowed them for deliberation, do as good a job in weighing conflicting testimony as an experienced judge? Can they as well see through the story of the glib liar, or of the unconsciously biased but conscientious witness, or as ably allow for the stage fright which often makes the honest but cautious man speak falteringly on the witness stand? It is hard to conceive that any astute person can take seriously the stereotyped praise of the jury. * * *

Is Judge Frank's position on summary judgment in *Arnstein* inconsistent with his views on the value of the jury? See R. Glennon, The Iconoclast as Reformer 156–57 (1985) (describing Frank's view that summary judgment should be curtailed *because* juries act unpredictably, and perhaps irrationally).

5.   Whatever the wisdom of overriding a jury decision, appellate courts have not been reluctant to reverse district court decisions granting summary judgment, and the fact that the district judge has seen things one way ordinarily has no influence on the appellate court. In *Arnstein*, for example, the appellate judges substituted their reaction to the recordings of the songs involved for the district judge's. Was this proper? For a more recent example, consider Twentieth Century–Fox Film Corp. v. MCA, Inc., 715 F.2d 1327 (9th Cir.1983), in which the producer of the film "Star Wars" sued the maker of the television show "Battlestar: Galactica" for copyright infringement. The district court granted summary judgment, finding that defendant's television show was so dissimilar to plaintiff's movie that there was no genuine dispute about whether they were substantially similar. The appellate panel disagreed: "After viewing the Star Wars and Battlestar motion pictures, we conclude that the films do in fact raise genuine issues of material fact as to whether only the Star Wars idea or the expression of that idea was copied." Does this kind of second guessing on appeal provide an important protection for the right to jury trial?

6.   The Cole Porter songs involved in Arnstein v. Porter included "Begin the Beguine," "Night and Day" and "You'd Be So Nice To Come Home To." A contemporary historian of popular music called Arnstein's suit "one of the most absurd plagiarism suits on record." After the summary judgment was reversed, there was a lengthy jury trial, followed by a verdict for Porter that was summarily affirmed on appeal. See 10A Wright, Miller & Kane, Federal Practice & Procedure § 2727 at 174 n.62.

7.   In his opinion for the court in Doehler Metal Furniture Co. v. United States, 149 F.2d 130, 135 (2d Cir.1945), Judge Frank developed the so-called "slightest doubt" test for summary judgment: "We take this occasion to suggest that trial judges should exercise great care in granting motions for summary judgment. A litigant has a right to a trial where there is the slightest doubt as to the facts." To what extent does Judge Frank's opinion in *Arnstein* reflect this approach? The "slightest doubt" test for summary judgment is criticized in E. Brunet, M. Redish & M. Reiter,

Summary Judgment: Federal Law and Practice 102–03 (2d ed.2000): "[Judge Frank's] language [in *Doehler*] is remarkable both for its negative attitude toward the use of summary judgment and for its complete failure to provide a clear legal source for the 'slightest doubt' standard. * * * Judge Frank's *Doehler* opinion casts a negative light upon the summary judgment mechanism and, if widely accepted, would deter most judges from seriously thinking about granting a Rule 56 motion."

8. More recent decisions have generally rejected the approach of *Arnstein*. As the Second Circuit stated in Beal v. Lindsay, 468 F.2d 287, 291 (2d Cir.1972), "The rule of Arnstein v. Porter * * * that summary judgment may not be rendered when there is the 'slightest doubt' as to the facts no longer is good law." See also Heyman v. Commerce & Industry Insurance Co., 524 F.2d 1317, 1319 (2d Cir.1975).

Judge Jack Weinstein has argued that "the 'slightest doubt' test, if it is taken seriously, means that summary judgment is almost never to be used— a pity in this critical time of overstrained legal resources." Chubbs v. City of New York, 324 F.Supp. 1183, 1189 (E.D.N.Y.1971). Thus, although several decisions continue to speak in terms of the "slightest doubt" test, the majority of cases today demand a stronger evidentiary showing by a nonmovant who will bear the burden of production at trial.

9. A strong argument could be fashioned that the Supreme Court effectively put an end to the "slightest doubt" test in Matsushita Electric Industrial Co. v. Zenith Radio Corp., 475 U.S. 574, 106 S.Ct. 1348, 89 L.Ed.2d 538 (1986). The case involved a factually complex antitrust suit, brought by American television manufacturers, alleging a conspiracy by 21 firms—either Japanese manufacturers or American firms controlled by Japanese parent companies—"to raise, fix and maintain artificially *high* prices for television receivers sold by [defendants] in Japan and, at the same time, to fix and maintain *low* prices for television receivers exported to and sold in the United States." These "low prices" were allegedly set at levels that produced substantial losses for defendants. This conduct was claimed to violate, *inter alia,* section 1 of the Sherman Act, which prohibits combinations or conspiracies in restraint of trade.

After several years of discovery, defendants moved for summary judgment, and the district court granted the motion, finding no genuine issue of material fact as to the existence of the conspiracy. The Third Circuit Court of Appeals reversed, but the Supreme Court agreed with the district court that summary judgment was proper:

> When the moving party has carried its burden under Rule 56(c), its opponent must do more than simply show that there is some metaphysical doubt as to the material facts. * * *

> It follows from these settled principles that if the factual context renders respondent's claim implausible—if the claim is one that simply makes no economic sense—respondents must come forward with more persuasive evidence to support their claim than would otherwise be necessary.

* * *

To survive a motion for summary judgment or for directed verdict, a plaintiff seeking damages for violation of § 1 [of the Sherman Act] must present evidence "that tends to exclude the possibility" that the alleged conspirators acted independently. Respondents in this case, in other words, must show that the inference of conspiracy is reasonable in light of the competing inferences of independent action or collusive action that could not have harmed respondents.

* * * According to petitioners, the alleged conspiracy is one that is economically irrational and practically infeasible. * * * Petitioners argue that, in light of the absence of any apparent motive and ambiguous nature of evidence of conspiracy, no trier of fact reasonably could find that the conspiracy with which petitioners are charged actually existed.

* * *

[T]here is a consensus among commentators that predatory pricing schemes are rarely tried, and even more rarely successful.

* * *

Finally, if predatory pricing conspiracies are generally unlikely to occur, they are especially so where, as here, the prospects of attaining monopoly power seem slight. * * *

The alleged conspiracy's failure to achieve its ends in the two decades of its asserted operation is strong evidence that the conspiracy does not in fact exist.

* * *

[T]he absence of any plausible motive to engage in the conduct charged is highly relevant to whether a "genuine issue for trial" exists within the viewing of Rule 56(e). Lack of motive bears on the range of permissible conclusions that might be drawn from ambiguous evidence: if petitioners had no rational economic motive to conspire, and if their conduct is consistent with other, equally plausible explanations, the conduct does not give rise to an inference of conspiracy. * * * In sum, in light of the absence of any rational motive to conspire, neither petitioners' pricing practices, nor their conduct in the Japanese market, nor their agreements respecting prices and distribution in the American market, suffice to create a "genuine issue for trial."

Justice White, joined by Justices Brennan, Blackmun and Stevens, dissented:

If the Court intends to give every judge hearing a motion for summary judgment in an antitrust case the job of determining if the evidence makes the inference of conspiracy more probable than not, it is overturning settled law. If the Court does not intend such pronouncement, it should refrain from using unnecessarily broad and confusing language.

In a later decision, the Court may have cast doubt on exactly how far it had intended to go in *Matsushita*. In Eastman Kodak Co. v. Image Technical Services, 504 U.S. 451, 112 S.Ct. 2072, 119 L.Ed.2d 265 (1992), the Court affirmed a Ninth Circuit decision that had reversed a grant of summary judgment to a defendant who had been accused of antitrust violations. The defendant had relied on *Matsushita* in support of its summary judgment motion. In an opinion focusing primarily on substantive antitrust law, the Court rejected these arguments:

> The Court's requirement in *Matsushita* that the plaintiffs' claims make economic sense did not introduce a special burden on plaintiffs facing summary judgment in antitrust cases. The Court did not hold that if the moving party enunciates *any* economic theory supporting its behavior, regardless of its accuracy in reflecting the actual market, it is entitled to summary judgment. *Matsushita* demands only that the nonmoving party's inference be reasonable in order to reach the jury, a requirement that was not invented, but merely articulated, in that decision. If the plaintiff's theory is economically senseless, no reasonable jury could find in its favor, and summary judgment should be granted.

According to one group of commentators, however:

> [T]his language * * * should not be construed to undermine *Matsushita*. The *Kodak* Court was merely underscoring the nonmovant's need to present an evidentiary basis to support reasonable inferences that are not "economically senseless" in order to reach a jury and survive summary judgment. In *Kodak*, the Court was unwilling to take the leap necessary to characterize the plaintiff's theory as "economically senseless." This left the movant, Kodak, in the normal summary judgment position of having it demonstrate the nonexistence of a critical element of the nonmovant plaintiff's case * * *.

E. Brunet, M. Redish & M. Reiter, Summary Judgment: Federal Law and Practice 269 (2d ed. 2000).

More recent lower court decisions generally reject the slightest doubt test. See, e.g., Shah v. Racetrac Petroleum Co., 338 F.3d 557, 566 (6th Cir. 2003) (noting that "the 'mere possibility' of a factual dispute does not suffice to create a triable case"); Harriscom Svenska, AB v. Harris Corp., 3 F.3d 576, 580 (2d Cir. 1993) (nonmovant "must demonstrate more than 'some metaphysical doubt' as to the material facts").

10. Summary judgment problems become more difficult when issues of motive and intent are presented. See, for example, Poller v. Columbia Broadcasting System, Inc., 368 U.S. 464, 82 S.Ct. 486, 7 L.Ed.2d 458 (1962) (whether motivation for purchase of a television station was anticompetitive). In cases where the critical issue is defendant's state of mind or intent when he engaged in conduct he admittedly undertook, should it ever be possible to grant summary judgment in favor of defendant based on his affidavit or deposition testimony averring that he did not entertain the forbidden state of mind? Recall Adickes v. S.H. Kress & Co., supra p. 428. The general rule, not surprisingly, is that it should not because here, at least, the jury should be allowed to view the defendant's demeanor when he testifies. The *Poller* decision has on occasion been construed to hold that summary judgment is generally inappropriate in so-called "complex cases." See, e.g., Timberlane Lumber Co. v. Bank of America, 549 F.2d 597, 602 (9th Cir.1976). Consider the impact of *Matsushita* on a doctrine calling for special reluctance to employ summary judgment in complex cases. To the extent

Poller *was properly read to establish such a doctrine, does it survive* Matsushita?

11. The general rule that summary judgment is inappropriate in cases raising issues of state of mind could affect the substantive law. For example, public officials charged with violation of citizens' constitutional rights may raise an affirmative defense of qualified, or "good faith" immunity. Traditionally, this was said to depend on whether the official knew or should have known that the action would violate a plaintiff's constitutional rights, and immunity would be unavailable if the official acted with the malicious intention of depriving plaintiff of his rights. In Harlow v. Fitzgerald, 457 U.S. 800, 102 S.Ct. 2727, 73 L.Ed.2d 396 (1982), the Court reasoned that this approach was unsatisfactory because, under Rule 56, "an official's good faith has been considered to be a question of fact that some courts have regarded as inherently requiring resolution by a jury." To remedy this problem and facilitate summary judgment, the Court held that the immunity defense should be judged under an objective standard, looking to whether a reasonable official in defendant's position would have realized at the time of the action in question that it was forbidden. Moreover, this determination should, the Court held, be made on the basis of the state of the law, and without discovery. The Court concluded that "[b]y defining the limits of qualified immunity essentially in objective terms, we provide no license to lawless conduct." Do you agree? Does this approach provide a useful solution to the impediment to summary judgment ordinarily presented in a case where the defendant's state of mind has traditionally been said to be relevant? [For another discussion of *Harlow,* see p. 1046.]

Post-*Harlow* decisions have reaffirmed the Supreme Court's desire to employ summary judgment as a means of reducing the costs of civil rights litigation. For example, in Anderson v. Creighton, 483 U.S. 635, 107 S.Ct. 3034, 97 L.Ed.2d 523 (1987), the Court once again asserted summary judgment's significance in the disposition of civil rights claims on the basis of the qualified immunity defense. Justice Scalia, writing for the Court, mandated a fact-specific examination into the objective reasonableness test set forth initially in *Harlow*, rejecting the application of the "clearly established law" test at an abstract generalized level. Under *Anderson*, the constitutional rights alleged to have been violated must be " 'clearly established' in a more particularized, and hence more relevant, sense." 483 U.S. at 640. As in *Harlow*, the *Anderson* Court recognized the need "to protect public officials from the 'broad-ranging discovery' that can be 'peculiarly disruptive of effective government.' " Id. at 646 n. 6 (quoting *Harlow*). On the general subject, see McKenzie, The Doctrine of Qualified Immunity in Section 1983 Actions: Resolution of the Immunity Issue on Summary Judgment, 25 Suffolk L.Rev. 673 (1991).

12. In deciding whether a party has met its burden of production, what role is played by Rule 56(e)? In Lujan v. National Wildlife Federation, 497 U.S. 871, 110 S.Ct. 3177, 111 L.Ed.2d 695 (1990), the Supreme Court discussed the provision's relevance:

> In ruling upon a Rule 56 motion, "a District Court must resolve any factual issues of controversy in favor of the non-moving party" only in the sense that, where the facts specifically averred by that party

contradict facts specifically averred by the movant, the motion must be denied. That is a world apart from "assuming" that general averments embrace the "specific facts" needed to sustain the complaint. * * * The object of [Rule 56(e)] is not to replace conclusory allegations of the complaint or answer with conclusory allegations of an affidavit. Rather, the purpose of Rule 56 is to enable a party who believes there is no genuine dispute as to a specific fact essential to the other side's case to demand at least one sworn averment of the fact before the lengthy process of litigation continues.

Id. at 888, 110 S.Ct. at 3188–89. The Court proceeded to apply this analysis to the specific factual issue raised by the summary judgment motion in *Lujan*—"whether one of respondent's members has been, or is threatened to be, 'adversely affected or aggrieved' by Government action" (id. at 889, 110 S.Ct. at 3189):

Rule 56(e) is assuredly not satisfied by averments which state only that one of respondent's members uses unspecified portions of an immense tract of territory, on some portions of which mining activity has occurred or probably will occur by virtue of the governmental action. It will not do to "presume" the missing facts because without them the affidavits would not establish the injury that they generally allege. That converts the operation of Rule 56 to a circular promenade: plaintiff's complaint makes general allegation of injury; defendant contests through Rule 56 existence of specific facts to support injury; plaintiff responds with affidavit containing general allegation of injury, which must be deemed to constitute averment of requisite specific facts since otherwise allegation of injury would be unsupported (which is precisely what defendant claims it is).

13.   The above discussion deals with cases in which the party moving for summary judgment does not have the burden of production at trial. What standard should apply where the party seeking summary judgment does have the burden? Recall that it is possible to shift the burden of production by producing such compelling evidence that no reasonable finder of fact could decide against him. That same idea applies to the movant who has the burden of proof; his showing to obtain summary judgment must shift the burden of production to the opposing party, and unless that party produces evidence permitting a decision in his favor, summary judgment should be entered.

14.   If plaintiff will have to prove his case by more than a preponderance of evidence (the usual standard in civil cases), should that affect the summary judgment decision? Note the treatment of the problem in Anderson v. Liberty Lobby, Inc., 477 U.S. 242, 106 S.Ct. 2505, 91 L.Ed.2d 202 (1986), discussed in the material on summary judgment in defamation cases that follows.

15.   *"Sham" affidavits*: The court may not weigh evidence in deciding a summary judgment motion, but sometimes courts will disregard affidavits that appear to create an issue. "If a party who has been examined at length on deposition could raise an issue of fact simply by submitting an affidavit contradicting his own prior testimony, this would greatly diminish the utility of summary judgment as a procedure for screening out sham issues of fact."

Perma Research & Devel. Co. v. Singer Co., 410 F.2d 572, 578 (2d Cir. 1969); see also Burns v. Board of County Commissioners, 330 F.3d 1275 (10th Cir. 2003) (court disregards plaintiff's "corrections" to deposition answers on the ground that trying to vary deposition testimony using a "correction sheet" should not be different from using an affidavit). But if there is a viable explanation for the change, the affidavit may be credited. Cf. McCormick v. City of Fort Lauderdale, 333 F.3d 1234 (11th Cir. 2003) (court credits plaintiff's affidavit contradicting his own sworn initial statement to police because plaintiff offered a plausible explanation for the differences). How different is this practice from weighing evidence? See also Rule 56(g).

SUMMARY JUDGMENT IN DEFAMATION CASES

In New York Times Co. v. Sullivan, 376 U.S. 254, 84 S.Ct. 710, 11 L.Ed.2d 686 (1964), the Supreme Court held that the First Amendment right of free expression prohibited the imposition of damages for defamation of a public official, unless the defamation was published with "actual malice"—defined as knowledge of falsity or reckless disregard of truth or falsity. The Court has since extended this modified constitutional protection to defamation of public figures, as well as public officials.

A potential factual issue in such suits, then, is whether the defamatory statement was made with "actual malice." Because of the importance of the constitutional right involved, the Court has held that the plaintiff must prove the presence of actual malice by "clear and convincing evidence," a standard of proof more strict than the traditional "preponderance of the evidence" standard normally employed in civil cases.

The possible use of summary judgment in these cases raises the question whether the presence of the higher burden of proof on the plaintiff should dictate a more lenient standard for the granting of such a motion made by the defendant. The Court considered this issue in Anderson v. Liberty Lobby, Inc., 477 U.S. 242, 106 S.Ct. 2505, 91 L.Ed.2d 202 (1986). Justice White, speaking for six Justices, initially concluded that the inquiry on a summary judgment motion "mirrors the standard for a directed verdict * * * which is that the trial judge must direct a verdict if, under the governing law, there can be but one reasonable conclusion as to the verdict." The Court then concluded that on either motion, the ruling "necessarily implicates the substantive evidentiary standard of proof that would apply at the trial on the merits." Therefore "where the First Amendment mandates a 'clear and convincing' standard, the trial judge in disposing of a directed verdict motion should consider whether a reasonable factfinder could conclude, for example, that the plaintiff had shown actual malice with convincing clarity."

The Court emphasized that its holding "does not denigrate the role of the jury. It by no means authorizes trial on affidavits. Credibility determinations, the weighing of the evidence, and the drawing of legitimate inferences from the facts are jury functions, not those of a judge, whether he is ruling on a motion for summary judgment or for a directed verdict."

Finding "the Court's analysis * * * deeply flawed," Justice Brennan dissented. He contended that "the Court's opinion is * * * full of language which could surely be understood as an invitation—if not an instruction—to trial courts to assess and weigh evidence much as a juror would," and expressed the fear "that this new rule * * * will transform what is meant to provide an expedited 'summary' procedure into a full blown paper trial on the merits."

Justice Rehnquist, joined by Chief Justice Burger, also dissented, finding the Court's holding to be "a procedural requirement engrafted onto Rule 56," contrary to the Court's previous statements that no special procedural protections are to be granted to defendants in defamation actions "in addition to the constitutional protections embodied in the substantive laws." Calder v. Jones, 465 U.S. 783, 790–91, 104 S.Ct. 1482, 1487–88, 79 L.Ed.2d 804 (1984) (reprinted infra p. 745 on a different point).

Do you agree with Justice Rehnquist that the Court's approach extends special procedural protection to defamation defendants? Should the invocation of plaintiff's trial standard of proof be extended to other types of cases?

Chapter VII

JUDICIAL SUPERVISION OF PRE-TRIAL AND PROMOTION OF SETTLEMENT

We are now ready to turn to the formal pretrial procedures that seek to prepare a case for trial and, if possible, to accomplish its early settlement. Beginning in the 1970's, this phase of litigation came under increasing judicial supervision as federal courts in particular have embraced the "managerial judge" model.[1] The two basic principles of effective case management are said to be that judges must show commitment, leadership, and supervision from the earliest stages and that they must establish clear timetables for different phases of a case's progress.[2]

The primary tool for judicial supervision is Rule 16, although judges have also invoked inherent powers for their pretrial-management rulings. Rule 16, as adopted in 1938, conceived of the pretrial conference as the means of preparing a case for trial. It was to take place just before trial and served to finalize such matters as contested issues, lists of witnesses and documents, and stipulations. "But federal courts came to appreciate more fully the value of earlier pretrial planning, and Rule 16 was amended in 1983 to provide for two types of pretrial conferences— 'scheduling and planning' and 'final.' * * * The rule states the purpose of the 'scheduling and planning' conference in clear case-management terms: expediting disposition, 'establishing early and continuing control so that the case will not be protracted because of lack of management,' 'discouraging wasteful pretrial activities,' 'improving the quality of the trial through more thorough preparation,' and facilitating settlement."[3]

1. See Marcus, Reining in the American Litigator: The New Role of American Judges, 27 Hast.Int'l & Compar.L.Rev. 3 (2003); Peckham, A Judicial Response to the Cost of Litigation: Case Management, Two–Stage Discovery Planning and Alternative Dispute Resolution, 37 Rutgers L. Rev. 253 (1985) (offering empirical evidence that managerial judging "substantially reduced" delay in federal district courts). This development has also been criticized. Resnik, Managerial Judges, 96 Harv.L.Rev. 374 (1983).

2. Solomon & Somerlot, American Bar Association, Caseflow Management in the Trial Court: Now and for the Future 1, 12–13, 24–28 (1987).

3. Sherman, A Process Model and Agenda for Civil Justice Reforms in the States, 46 Stan.L.Rev. 1553, 1564 (1994).

We will consider this expanded role of the pretrial conference in the first section of this chapter.

Promotion of settlement is also an increasingly significant aspect of judicial supervision of pretrial. At the end of Chapter II (supra p. 108), we briefly considered available alternatives to trial, including both processes that are outside the court system and those that have been made an integral part of pretrial procedures. As we observed there, settlement conferences with a judge have been a traditional vehicle for judicial promotion of settlement. However, the explosion of new settlement devices that has accompanied the ADR movement has led many courts to adopt other means of promoting settlement. In the second section of this chapter, we will consider some of the principal settlement devices that use intervention by third parties, and, in the third section, we will examine incentives to settle through shifting of attorney's fees and sanctions.

A. PRETRIAL CONFERENCE

Central to the relaxed standards of pleading adopted in the Federal Rules of Civil Procedure in 1938 was the premise that it is unreasonable to expect the parties to have full knowledge of all relevant facts at the pleading stage. Therefore it was understood that pleadings would be acceptable even if framed in general terms. It was during the discovery process, following the pleading stage, that the parties would be expected to obtain the bulk of the relevant factual information necessary for trial.

While the system adopted in the Federal Rules generally reduced the level of knowledge and information required at the pleading stage, it simultaneously attempted to increase dramatically the level of information possessed by the parties at trial. This seeming paradox was rationalized by a single overriding normative principle: The adjudicatory process should be viewed as a search for the truth, rather than purely as a game of competitive skill in mastering the technicalities of pleading or in orchestrating surprises at trial.

The one procedural device essential to achievement of these goals was the pretrial conference, provided for in Rule 16, a practice that found its origins in a procedure employed by the Circuit Court of Wayne County, Michigan in the 1930's.[4] At the pretrial conference, the parties were expected—*after* completion of discovery—to provide the type of factual detail no longer required in their pleadings. Also at the pretrial conference, the parties were to provide to the opposition information concerning how they intended to prove their cases at trial.

In its original form (changed in 1983 and further amended in 1993), the Rule provided that in any action, the Court, "in its discretion," may direct the attorneys for the parties to appear at a conference to consider:

(1) the simplification of the issues;

---

4. See Sunderland, The Theory and Practice of Pre–Trial Procedure, 36 Mich. L.Rev. 215 (1937).

(2) the necessity or desirability of amendments to the pleadings;

(3) the possibility of obtaining admissions of fact and of documents which will avoid unnecessary proof;

(4) the limitation of the number of expert witnesses;

(5) the advisability of a preliminary reference of issues to a master for findings to be used as evidence when the trial is to be by jury; and

(6) such other matters as may aid in the disposition of the action.

After the conference, the court was to issue "an order which recites the action taken at the conference, the amendments allowed to the pleadings, and the agreements made by the parties as to any of the matters considered, and which limits the issues for trial to those not disposed of by admissions or agreements of counsel." The pretrial order was intended to "control the subsequent course of the action, unless modified at the trial to prevent manifest injustice."

The pretrial conference authorized by Rule 16 was designed to familiarize the litigants and the court with issues actually involved in a lawsuit so that the parties could accurately appraise their cases and substantially reduce the danger of surprise at trial. See generally 6A C. Wright, A. Miller & M. Kane, Federal Practice and Procedure §§ 1522, 1522.1. According to Judge Charles Clark, Reporter for the original Advisory Committee that wrote the Federal Rules, "simplification of the issues" was "perhaps the over-all purpose of the entire rule. * * * The judge finds out what the case is all about, how much is admitted on each side, and how much not, and then he goes on to the question of manner of proof. This is pre-trial at its most effective level."[5]

A study conducted in the 1960's evaluated New Jersey's state pretrial conference device in the context of personal injury actions. The study concluded that the pretrial conference served a number of important and beneficial functions, including increasing the chance the case will be well presented, eliminating inefficiencies at trial, and improving the settlement process.[6]

In light of these beneficial functions, one might wonder why the original Rule 16 did not mandate the use of the pretrial conference in every case, rather than leaving the matter to the trial court's discretion. The answer is that "there always has been some question whether the time and effort consumed by the pretrial conference might not offset the benefits it supposedly yields and a concern that the time of judges and lawyers can be better spent in other pursuits."[7] In simple suits where trial would require a relatively brief period of time, a pretrial conference could consume more time than it saved. It was therefore thought wise to allow the judge to make the determination concerning the appropriate-

---

5. Clark, Objectives of Pre–Trial Procedure, 17 Ohio St.L.J. 163, 167 (1956).

6. M. Rosenberg, The Pretrial Conference and Effective Justice (1964).

7. 6A C. Wright, A. Miller & M. Kane, supra, § 1522.

ness of the conference on a case-by-case basis. However, certain of the busier districts, such as the District of Columbia and the Southern District of New York, adopted a local rule requiring a pretrial conference in all cases.

Rule 16 still provides that the holding of a pretrial conference lies in the court's discretion, but there are now mandatory aspects of the rule concerning scheduling. Rule 26(f) directs the parties to meet and confer regarding a number of topics "at least 21 days before a scheduling conference is held or a scheduling order is due under Rule 16(b)." This meeting is to yield a report to be submitted to the court within ten days of the meeting detailing a discovery plan for the case and possibly including other topics. See Official Form 35 for a blueprint of such a report. Rule 16(b) now provides that "[e]xcept in categories of actions exempted by district court rule as inappropriate, the district judge, or a magistrate judge when authorized by district court rule, shall, after receiving the report from the parties under Rule 26(f) * * * by a scheduling conference, telephone, mail, or other suitable means, enter a scheduling order" limiting the time for various procedural actions, including the filing of motions and the completion of discovery.

While the original Rule 16 contemplated the holding of only one conference, presumably at the close of discovery, in the more protracted and complex cases one conference proved to be inadequate to ensure efficient judicial management. Therefore Rule 16 now authorizes the holding of more than one conference, and provides for the holding of a "Final Pretrial Conference," to "be held as close to the time of trial as reasonable under the circumstances," for the purpose of "formulat[ing] a plan for trial, including a program for facilitating the admission of evidence."

The original Rule 16 made no express provision for sanctions for an attorney's failure to appear at or cooperate in a pretrial conference, but the Supreme Court recognized the trial judge's inherent authority to impose sanctions in such situations.[8] The rule now expressly provides for the imposition of sanctions in Rule 16(f).[9]

Notes and Questions

1. In Chapter I we noted the growing involvement of federal judges in controlling cases assigned to them and explored some aspects of judges' authority under Rule 16. Note the way in which the rule's requirement that the judge impose scheduling deadlines in every case tends to prompt judges to take control of cases from an early date. The managerial judging approach has attracted attention overseas; in the mid–1990s it was proposed as a new model for handling civil litigation in England. For discussion, see Marcus, "Deja Vu All Over Again?" An American Reaction to the Woolf Report, in Reform of Civil Procedure (A. Zuckerman & R. Cranston, eds., 1995) at 219.

---

8. See, e.g. Link v. Wabash R. Co., 370 U.S. 626, 82 S.Ct. 1386, 8 L.Ed.2d 734 (1962).

9. See Kothe v. Smith, supra p. 3.

2. As we saw in Band's Refuse Removal, Inc. v. Borough of Fair Lawn, supra p. 3, discovery may be used to probe an opponent's expected evidence for trial. Even if the parties don't focus their discovery on trial evidence, Rule 26(a)(3) requires disclosure at least 30 days before trial of the identities of likely witnesses and documents or other exhibits that the parties expect to offer at trial. It further provides that if the parties don't serve objections within 14 days after service of these disclosures most objections otherwise allowed by the Federal Rules of Evidence are waived.

As a part of case management under Rule 16, some courts require considerably more. Before the final pretrial conference, courts may require that the parties submit a statement that lists all undisputed facts and factual issues, identifies all disputed points of law and briefs them, lists all witnesses likely to be called together with a brief statement describing the substance of their testimony, lists all exhibits to be offered in evidence, and proposes voir dire questions, jury instructions and verdict forms. Some courts require that such specifics be provided in a joint pretrial statement. Preparing such statements call involve a great deal of effort for the lawyers. Is that effort wasted if the case settles on the courthouse steps? Would a lawyer be able to prepare properly for trial without making such an effort?

3. There have been cases where the appellate courts have found that district courts have gone too far in imposing pretrial requirements. For example, in McCargo v. Hedrick, 545 F.2d 393 (4th Cir.1976), the trial court's local rule on joint pretrial statements filled eleven single-spaced pages. After completing the 120–day discovery period allowed in this case, counsel for both sides began a 16–month effort to submit a pretrial statement that satisfied the rule, only to have each version rejected by the court. At the end of this time, the district court dismissed the case for failure to comply with the local rule. Noting that "[t]he facts of this case illustrate the burden put upon litigants and their counsel by a pretrial procedure that appears to have become an end in itself," id. at 396, the appellate court held that the local rule exceeded the district court's authority under Rule 16 as then written. It concluded (id. at 401):

> Ours is an adversary system of justice. Local Rule 2.08 is inquisitorial in tone and purpose. In our system lawyers worry about the whereabouts of witnesses. The court does not. Lawyers worry about proof. The court does not—except in the rare case of collusion. Lawyers get the case ready for trial. The court does not. Local Rule 2.08 subordinates the rule of the lawyer to that of the administering magistrate, reducing counsel to the role of clerical assistants who are to anticipate imaginatively what other matters ought to be embraced within an endless pretrial order.

4. If a final pretrial order is entered, it governs the action and may be changed only to prevent "manifest injustice." What does this mean? Should injustice that is not "manifest" be disregarded? One form of injustice can be surprise to the opponent, the matter that worried the appellate court in Band's Refuse Removal, Inc. v. Borough of Fair Lawn, supra p. 3. Recall the way in which Rule 15(b) treats that concern to allow amendment of the pleadings to conform to the evidence if the other party would not be prejudiced. See supra p. 217. Does Rule 16 impose on the party seeking to

change the final pretrial order a higher burden than one seeking to amend at trial under Rule 15(b)? See Wallin v. Fuller, 476 F.2d 1204, 1209 (5th Cir.1973) ("It is unlikely that the pretrial order under Rule 16 was intended to make the pleadings, and therefore Rule 15, obsolete").

But will a relaxed attitude undermine the purposes of the pretrial conference? "Unless pretrial orders are honored and enforced, the objectives of the pretrial conference to simplify issues and avoid unnecessary proof by obtaining admissions of fact will be jeopardized if not entirely nullified. * * * Disregard of these principles would bring back the days of trial by ambush and discourage timely preparation by the parties for trial." United States v. First National Bank of Circle, 652 F.2d 882, 886 (9th Cir.1981). Reacting to concerns about reliance and the importance that pretrial orders be enforced, courts have therefore forbidden the calling of witnesses not listed and excluded evidence not identified in the orders.

5. The use of sanctions under Rule 16 raises difficult issues concerning the court's power to require participation in a settlement conference, explored in the following case.

G. HEILEMAN BREWING CO.
v. JOSEPH OAT CORP.

United States Court of Appeal, Seventh Circuit, 1989.
871 F.2d 648.

Before BAUER, CHIEF JUDGE, CUMMINGS, WOOD, JR., CUDAHY, POSNER, COFFEY, FLAUM, EASTERBROOK, RIPPLE, MANION and KANNE, CIRCUIT JUDGES.

KANNE, CIRCUIT JUDGE.

May a federal district court order litigants—even those represented by counsel—to appear before it in person at a pretrial conference for the purpose of discussing the posture and settlement of the litigants' case? After reviewing the Federal Rules of Civil Procedure and federal district courts' inherent authority to manage and control the litigation before them, we answer this question in the affirmative and conclude that a district court may sanction a litigant for failing to comply with such an order.

I. BACKGROUND

A federal magistrate ordered Joseph Oat Corporation to send a "corporate representative with authority to settle" to a pretrial conference to discuss disputed factual and legal issues and the possibility of settlement. Although counsel for Oat Corporation appeared, accompanied by another attorney who was authorized to speak on behalf of the principals of the corporation, no principal or corporate representative personally attended the conference. The court determined that the failure of Oat Corporation to send a principal of the corporation to the pretrial conference violated its order. Consequently, the district court imposed a sanction of $5,860.01 upon Oat Corporation pursuant to Federal Rule of Civil Procedure 16(f). This amount represented the costs and attorneys' fees of the opposing parties attending the conference.

II. The Appeal

Oat Corporation appeals, claiming that the district court did not have the authority to order litigants represented by counsel to appear at the pretrial settlement conference. Specifically, Oat Corporation contends that, by negative implication, the language of Rule 16(a)(5) prohibits a district court from directing represented litigants to attend pretrial conferences. That is, because Rule 16 expressly refers to "attorneys for the parties and any unrepresented parties" in introductory paragraph (a), a district court may not go beyond that language to devise procedures which direct the pretrial appearance of parties represented by counsel. Consequently, Oat Corporation concludes that the court lacked the authority to order the pretrial attendance of its corporate representatives and, even if the court possessed such authority, the court abused its discretion to exercise that power in this case. Finally, Oat Corporation argues that the court abused its discretion to enter sanctions.

A. *Authority to Order Attendance*

First, we must address Oat Corporation's contention that a federal district court lacks the authority to order litigants who are represented by counsel to appear at a pretrial conference. Our analysis requires us to review the Federal Rules of Civil Procedure and district courts' inherent authority to manage the progress of litigation.

Rule 16 addresses the use of pretrial conferences to formulate and narrow issues for trial as well as to discuss means for dispensing with the need for costly and unnecessary litigation. As we stated in Link v. Wabash R.R., 291 F.2d 542, 547 (7th Cir.1961), aff'd, 370 U.S. 626, 82 S.Ct. 1386, 8 L.Ed.2d 734 (1962):

> Pre-trial procedure has become an integrated part of the judicial process on the trial level. Courts must be free to use it and to control and enforce its operation. Otherwise, the orderly administration of justice will be removed from control of the trial court and placed in the hands of counsel. We do not believe such a course is within the contemplation of the law.

The pretrial settlement of litigation has been advocated and used as a means to alleviate overcrowded dockets, and courts have practiced numerous and varied types of pretrial settlement techniques for many years. Since 1983, Rule 16 has expressly provided that settlement of a case is one of several subjects which should be pursued and discussed vigorously during pretrial conferences.

The language of Rule 16 does not give any direction to the district court upon the issue of a court's authority to order litigants who are represented by counsel to appear for pretrial proceedings. Instead, Rule 16 merely refers to the participation of trial advocates—attorneys of record and pro se litigants. However, the Federal Rules of Civil Procedure do not completely describe and limit the power of the federal courts. HMG Property Investors, Inc. v. Parque Indus. Rio Canas, Inc., 847 F.2d 908, 915 (1st Cir.1988).

The concept that district courts exercise procedural authority outside the explicit language of the rules of civil procedure is not frequently documented, but valid nevertheless. The Supreme Court has acknowledged that the provisions of the Federal Rules of Civil Procedure are not intended to be the exclusive authority for actions to be taken by district courts. Link v. Wabash R.R., 370 U.S. 626, 82 S.Ct. 1386, 8 L.Ed.2d 734 (1962).

* * *

In this case, we are required to determine whether a court's power to order the pretrial appearance of litigants who are represented by counsel is inconsistent with, or in derogation of, Rule 16. We must remember that Rule 1 states, with unmistakable clarity, that the Federal Rules of Civil Procedure "shall be construed to secure the just, speedy, and inexpensive determination of every action." This language explicitly indicates that the federal rules are to be liberally construed. There is no place in the federal civil procedural system for the proposition that rules having the force of statute, though in derogation of the common law, are to be strictly construed.

"[The] spirit, intent, and purpose [of Rule 16] is ... broadly remedial, allowing courts to actively manage the preparation of cases for trial." In re Baker, 744 F.2d 1438, 1440 (10th Cir.1984) (en banc), cert. denied, 471 U.S. 1014, 105 S.Ct. 2016, 85 L.Ed.2d 299 (1985). Rule 16 is not designed as a device to restrict or limit the authority of the district judge in the conduct of pretrial conferences. As the Tenth Circuit Court of Appeals sitting en banc stated in *Baker*, "the spirit and purpose of the amendments to Rule 16 always have been within the inherent power of the courts to manage their affairs as an independent constitutional branch of government." Id. at 1441.

We agree with this interpretation of Rule 16. The wording of the rule and the accompanying commentary make plain that the entire thrust of the amendment to Rule 16 was to urge judges to make wider use of their powers and to manage actively their dockets from an early stage. We therefore conclude that our interpretation of Rule 16 to allow district courts to order represented parties to appear at pretrial settlement conferences merely represents another application of a district judge's inherent authority to preserve the efficiency, and more importantly the integrity, of the judicial process.

* * *

B. Exercise of Authority to Order Attendance

Having determined that the district court possessed the power and authority to order the represented litigants to appear at the pretrial settlement conference, we now must examine whether the court abused its discretion to issue such an order.

At the outset, it is important to note that a district court cannot coerce settlement. Kothe v. Smith, 771 F.2d 667, 669 (2d Cir.1985).[8] In this case, considerable concern has been generated because the court ordered "corporate representatives with authority to settle" to attend the conference. In our view, "authority to settle," when used in the context of this case, means that the "corporate representative" attending the pretrial conference was required to hold a position within the corporate entity allowing him to speak definitively and to commit the corporation to a particular position in the litigation. We do not view "authority to settle" as a requirement that corporate representatives must come to court willing to settle on someone else's terms, but only that they come to court in order to consider the possibility of settlement.

As Chief Judge Crabb set forth in her decision which we now review:

> There is no indication ... that the magistrate's order contemplated requiring Joseph Oat ... to agree to any particular form of settlement or even to agree to settlement at all. The only requirement imposed by the magistrate was that the representative [of Oat Corporation] be present with full authority to settle, should terms for settlement be proposed that were acceptable to [Oat Corporation].

If this case represented a situation where Oat Corporation had sent a corporate representative and was sanctioned because that person refused to make an offer to pay money—that is, refused to submit to settlement coercion—we would be faced with a decidedly different issue—a situation we would not countenance.

The Advisory Committee Notes to Rule 16 state that "[a]lthough it is not the purpose of Rule 16(c)[9] to impose settlement negotiations on unwilling litigants, it is believed that providing a neutral forum for discussing [settlement] might foster it." These Notes clearly draw a distinction between being required to attend a settlement conference and being required to participate in settlement negotiations. Thus, under the scheme of pretrial settlement conferences, the corporate representative remains free, on behalf of the corporate entity, to propose terms of settlement independently—but he may be required to state those terms in a pretrial conference before a judge or magistrate.

As an alternative position, Oat Corporation argues that the court abused its discretion to order corporate representatives of the litigants to attend the pretrial settlement conference. Oat Corporation determined that because its business was a "going concern":

> It would be unreasonable for the magistrate to require the president of that corporation to leave his business [in Camden, New Jersey] to

---

8. Likewise, a court cannot compel parties to stipulate to facts. J.F. Edwards Constr. Co. v. Anderson Safeway Guard Rail Corp., 542 F.2d 1318 (7th Cir.1976) (per curiam). Nor can a court compel litigants to participate in a nonbinding summary jury trial. Strandell [v Jackson County], 838 F.2d [884] at 887 [(7th Cir.1987)]. In the same vein, a court cannot force a party to engage in discovery. Identiseal Corp. v. Positive Identification Sys., Inc., 560 F.2d 298 (7th Cir.1977).

travel to Madison, Wisconsin, to participate in a settlement conference. The expense and burden on the part of Joseph Oat to comply with this order was clearly unreasonable. Consequently, Oat Corporation believes that the district court abused its authority.

We recognize, as did the district court, that circumstances could arise in which requiring a corporate representative (or any litigant) to appear at a pretrial settlement conference would be so onerous, so clearly unproductive, or so expensive in relation to the size, value, and complexity of the case that it might be an abuse of discretion. Moreover, "[b]ecause inherent powers are shielded from direct democratic controls, they must be exercised with restraint and discretion." However, the facts and circumstances of this case clearly support the court's actions to require the corporate representatives of the litigants to attend the pretrial conference personally.

This litigation involved a claim for $4 million—a claim which turned upon the resolution of complex factual and legal issues. The litigants expected the trial to last from one to three months and all parties stood to incur substantial legal fees and trial expenses. This trial also would have preempted a large segment of judicial time—not an insignificant factor. Thus, because the stakes were high, we do not believe that the burden of requiring a corporate representative to attend a pretrial settlement conference was out of proportion to the benefits to be gained, not only by the litigants but also by the court.

Additionally, the corporation did send an attorney, Mr. Fitzpatrick, from Philadelphia, Pennsylvania to Madison, Wisconsin to "speak for" the principals of the corporation. It is difficult to see how the expenses involved in sending Mr. Fitzpatrick from Philadelphia to Madison would have greatly exceeded the expenses involved in sending a corporate representative from Camden to Madison. Consequently, we do not think the expenses and distance to be traveled are unreasonable in this case.

Furthermore, no objection to the magistrate's order was made prior to the date the pretrial conference resumed. Oat Corporation contacted the magistrate's office concerning the order's requirements and was advised of the requirements now at issue. However, Oat Corporation never objected to its terms, either when it was issued or when Oat Corporation sought clarification. Consequently, Oat Corporation was left with only one course of action: it had to comply fully with the letter and intent of the order and argue about its reasonableness later.

We thus conclude that the court did not abuse its authority and discretion to order a representative of the Oat Corporation to appear for the pretrial settlement conference on December 19.

C. Sanctions

Finally, we must determine whether the court abused its discretion by sanctioning Oat Corporation for failing to comply with the order to appear at the pretrial settlement conference. Oat Corporation argues that the instructions directing the appearance of corporate representatives were unclear and ambiguous. Consequently, it concludes that the sanctions were improper.

Absent an abuse of discretion, we may not disturb a district court's imposition of sanctions for failure of a party to comply with a pretrial order. The issue on review is not whether we would have imposed these costs upon Oat Corporation, but whether the district court abused its discretion in doing so.

Oat Corporation contends that the presence of Mr. Fitzpatrick, as an attorney authorized to speak on behalf of the principals of Oat Corporation, satisfied the requirement that its "corporate representative" attend the December 19 settlement conference. Oat Corporation argues that nothing in either the November 19, 1984 order or the December 14, 1984 order would lead a reasonable person to conclude that a representative or principal from the Joseph Oat Corporation was required to attend the conference personally—in effect arguing that sanctions cannot be imposed because the order failed to require a particular person to attend the conference.

We believe that Oat Corporation was well aware of what the court expected. While the November order may have been somewhat ambiguous, any ambiguity was eliminated by the magistrate's remarks from the bench on December 14, the written order of December 18, and the direction obtained by counsel from the magistrate's clerk.

* * *

III. Conclusion

We hold that Rule 16 does not limit, but rather is enhanced by, the inherent authority of federal courts to order litigants represented by counsel to attend pretrial conferences for the purpose of discussing settlement. Oat Corporation violated the district court's order requiring it to have a corporate representative attend the pretrial settlement conference on December 19, 1984. Under these circumstances, the district court did not abuse its discretion by imposing sanctions for Oat Corporation's failure to comply with the pretrial order.

Posner, Circuit Judge, dissenting.

Rule 16(a) of the Federal Rules of Civil Procedure authorizes a district court to "direct the attorneys for the parties and any *unrepresented* parties to appear before it for a [pretrial] conference." The word I have italicized could be thought to carry the negative implication that no represented party may be directed to appear—that was the panel's conclusion—but I hesitate to so conclude in a case that can be decided on a narrower ground.

The main purpose of the pretrial conference is to get ready for trial. For that purpose, only the attorneys need be present, unless a party is acting as his own attorney. The only possible reason for wanting a represented party to be present is to enable the judge or magistrate to explore settlement with the principals rather than with just their agents.

Some district judges and magistrates distrust the willingness or ability of attorneys to convey to their clients adequate information bearing on the desirability and terms of settling a case in lieu of pressing forward to trial. The distrust is warranted in some cases, I am sure; but warranted or not, it is what lies behind the concern that the panel opinion had stripped the district courts of a valuable settlement tool—and this at a time of heavy, and growing, federal judicial caseloads. The concern may well be exaggerated, however. The panel opinion may have had little practical significance; it is the rare attorney who will invite a district judge's displeasure by defying a request to produce the client for a pretrial conference.

The question of the district court's power to summon a represented party to a settlement conference is a difficult one. On the one hand, nothing in Rule 16 or in any other rule or statute confers such a power, and there are obvious dangers in too broad an interpretation of the federal courts' inherent power to regulate their procedure. One danger is that it encourages judicial high-handedness ("power corrupts"); several years ago one of the district judges in this circuit ordered Acting Secretary of Labor Brock to appear before him for settlement discussions on the very day Brock was scheduled to appear before the Senate for his confirmation hearing. The broader concern illustrated by the Brock episode is that in their zeal to settle cases judges may ignore the value of other people's time. One reason people hire lawyers is to economize on their own investment of time in resolving disputes. It is pertinent to note in this connection that Oat is a defendant in this case; it didn't want its executives' time occupied with this litigation.

On the other hand, die Not bricht Eisen ["necessity breaks iron"]. Attorneys often are imperfect agents of their clients, and the workload of our district courts is so heavy that we should hesitate to deprive them of a potentially useful tool for effecting settlement, even if there is some difficulty in finding a legal basis for the tool. Although few attorneys will defy a district court's request to produce the client, those few cases may be the very ones where the client's presence would be most conducive to settlement. If I am right that Rule 16(a) empowers a district court to summon unrepresented parties to a pretrial conference only because their presence may be necessary to get ready for trial, we need not infer that the draftsmen meant to forbid the summoning of represented parties for purposes of exploring settlement. The draftsmen may have been unaware that district courts were asserting a power to command the presence of a represented party to explore settlement. We should hesitate to infer inadvertent prohibitions.

The narrowly "legal" considerations bearing on the question whether district courts have the power asserted by the magistrate in this case are sufficiently equivocal to authorize—indeed compel—us to consider the practical consequences for settlement before deciding what the answer should be. Unfortunately we have insufficient information about those consequences to be able to give a confident answer, but fortunately we need not answer the question in this case—so clear is it that the magistrate abused his discretion, which is to say, acted unreasonably, in demanding that Oat Corporation send an executive having "full settlement authority" to the pretrial conference. This demand, which is different from a demand that a party who has not closed the door to settlement send an executive to discuss possible terms, would be defensible only if litigants had a duty to bargain in good faith over settlement before resorting to trial, and neither Rule 16 nor any other rule, statute, or doctrine imposes such a duty on federal litigants. There is no federal judicial power to coerce settlement. Oat had made clear that it was not prepared to settle the case on any terms that required it to pay money. That was its prerogative, which once exercised made the magistrate's continued insistence on Oat's sending an executive to Madison arbitrary, unreasonable, willful, and indeed petulant. This is apart from the fact that since no one officer of Oat may have had authority to settle the case, compliance with the demand might have required Oat to ship its entire board of directors to Madison. Ultimately Oat did make a money settlement, but there is no indication that it would have settled sooner if only it had complied with the magistrate's demand for the dispatch of an executive possessing "full settlement authority." * * *

COFFEY, CIRCUIT JUDGE, with whom EASTERBROOK, RIPPLE and MANION, CIRCUIT JUDGES, join, dissenting.

* * * Unlike the majority, I am convinced that Rule 16 does not authorize a trial judge to require a represented party litigant to attend a pretrial conference together with his or her attorney because the rule mandates in clear and unambiguous terms that only an unrepresented party litigant and attorneys may be ordered to appear.

[The opinion goes on to reject "inherent authority" to compel the presence of represented parties.]

EASTERBROOK, CIRCUIT JUDGE, with whom POSNER, COFFEY, and MANION, CIRCUIT JUDGES, join, dissenting.

Our case has three logically separate issues. First, whether a district court may demand the attendance of someone other than the party's counsel of record. Second, whether the court may insist that this additional person be an employee rather than an agent selected for the occasion. Third, whether the court may insist that the representative have "full settlement authority"—meaning the authority to agree to pay cash in settlement (maybe authority without cap, although that was not clear). Even if one resolves the first issue as the majority does, it does not follow that district courts have the second or third powers, or that their exercise here was prudent.

The proposition that a magistrate may require a firm to send an employee rather than a representative is puzzling. Corporate "employees" are simply agents of the firm. Corporations choose their agents and decide what powers to give them. Which agents have which powers is a matter of internal corporate affairs. Joseph Oat Corp. sent to the conference not only its counsel of record but also John Fitzpatrick, who had authority to speak for Oat. Now Mr. Fitzpatrick is an attorney, which raised the magistrate's hackles, but why should this count against him? Because Fitzpatrick is a part-time rather than a full-time agent of the corporation? Why can't the corporation make its own decision about how much of the agent's time to hire? Is Oat being held in contempt because it is too small to have a cadre of legal employees—because its general counsel practices with a law firm rather than being "in house"?

At all events, the use of outside attorneys as negotiators is common. * * *

As for the third subject, whether the representative must have "settlement authority": the magistrate's only reason for ordering a corporate representative to come was to facilitate settlement then and there. As I understand Magistrate Groh's opinion, and Judge Crabb's, the directive was to send a person with "full settlement authority". Fitzpatrick was deemed inadequate only because he was under instructions not to pay money. E.g.: "While Mr. Fitzpatrick claimed authority to speak for Oat, he stated that he had no authority to make a [monetary] offer. *Thus*, no representative of Oat or National having authority to settle the case was present at the conference as the order directed" (magistrate's opinion, emphasis added). On learning that Fitzpatrick did not command Oat's treasury, the magistrate ejected him from the conference and never listened to what he had to say on Oat's behalf, never learned whether Fitzpatrick might be receptive to others' proposals. (We know that Oat ultimately did settle the case for money, after it took part in and "prevailed" at a summary jury trial—participation and payment each demonstrating Oat's willingness to consider settlement.) The magistrate's approach implies that if the Chairman and CEO of Oat had arrived with instructions from the Board to settle the case without paying cash, and to negotiate and bring back for the Board's consideration any financial proposals, Oat still would have been in contempt.

Both magistrate and judge demanded the presence not of a "corporate representative" in the sense of a full-time employee but of a representative with "full authority to settle". Most corporations reserve power to agree (as opposed to power to discuss) to senior managers or to their boards of directors—the difference depending on the amounts involved. Heileman wanted $4 million, a sum within the province of the board rather than a single executive even for firms much larger than Oat. Fitzpatrick came with power to discuss and recommend; he could settle the case on terms other than cash; he lacked only power to sign a check. The magistrate's order therefore must have required either (a) changing the allocation of responsibility within the corporation, or (b) sending a quorum of Oat's Board.

Magistrate Groh exercised a power unknown even in labor law, where there is a duty to bargain in good faith. 29 U.S.C. § 158(d). Labor and management commonly negotiate through persons with the authority to discuss but not agree. The negotiators report back to management and the union, each of which reserves power to reject or approve the position of its agent. We know from Fed.R.Civ.P. 16—and especially from the Advisory Committee's comment to Rule 16(c) that the Rule's "reference to 'authority' is not intended to insist upon the ability to settle the litigation"—that the parties cannot be compelled to negotiate "in good faith". A defendant convinced it did no wrong may insist on total vindication. Rule 68, which requires a party who turns down a settlement proposal to bear costs only if that party does worse at trial, implies the same thing. Yet if parties are not obliged to negotiate in good faith, on what ground can they be obliged to come with authority to settle on the spot—an authority agents need not carry even when the law requires negotiation? The order we affirm today compels persons who have committed no wrong, who pass every requirement of Rules 11 and 68, who want only the opportunity to receive a decision on the merits, to come to court with open checkbooks on pain of being held in contempt.

Settling litigation is valuable, and courts should promote it. Is settlement of litigation more valuable than settlement of labor disputes, so that courts may do what the NLRB may not? The statutory framework—bona fide negotiations required in labor law but not in litigation—suggests the opposite. Does the desirability of settlement imply that rules of state law allocating authority within a corporation must yield? We have held in other cases that settlements must be negotiated within the framework of existing rules; the desire to get a case over and done with does not justify modifying generally applicable norms.

[Dissenting opinions of Judges Ripple and Manion omitted.]

Notes and Questions

1. The majority opinion in *Heileman* conceded that circumstances could arise in which requiring a corporate representative to appear "would be so onerous, so clearly unproductive, or so expensive in relation to the size, value, and complexity of the case that it might be an abuse of discretion." However, it found no such situation here, where the claim was sizable ($4 million) and turned on complex factual and legal issues, where the trial was expected to be lengthy (one to three months), and where the corporation had sent an attorney from Philadelphia to speak for the principals, whose expenses would not have exceeded sending a corporate representative from Camden. Would any of these facts, if changed, have made the attendance order impermissible?

2. Judge Posner, dissenting, expressed the concern "that in their zeal to settle cases judges may ignore the value of other people's time." Surely there are circumstances when an attorney can adequately represent a party and when requiring a nonattorney representative is unnecessarily wasteful. How does the majority opinion deal with this point? Do the efficiency and proportionality considerations identified by the majority provide appropriate guidance for case-by-case determinations?

3. Judge Easterbrook, also dissenting, argued that many firms send their lawyer to negotiate in collective bargaining or merger talks, and that a lawyer is no less suited to negotiating in a settlement conference. However, ADR places great importance on having in attendance the person who will make the ultimate decision to settle so that she can hear, see, and participate

in the proceedings, in short so that she can be affected by the discussion and interaction with the other side and the judge. Would an appropriate test be that if a lawyer is the sole representative she should be essentially the *alter ego* of the corporate decisionmaker, with the same knowledge, reactions, interests, and settlement authority?

4.   Professor Riskin has examined the advantages and disadvantages of client attendance at settlement conferences and ADR proceedings that offers useful guidance for courts. Riskin, The Represented Client in a Settlement Conference: The Lessons of *G. Heileman Brewing Co. v. Joseph Oat Corp.,* 69 Wash.U.L.Rev. 1059, 1099–1102 (1991). Advantages include giving the client a chance to tell his story in his own words, learning about the strengths and weaknesses of both sides, permitting him to act on new information, allowing cooperation and momentum to build in the offer process, clearing up miscommunications about facts and interests between lawyers and clients, and providing information to spot opportunities of problem-solving situations. Disadvantages include the risk that the client may give away valuable information that could leave him vulnerable to exploitation or weaken his case, that exposure to the other side's behavior will anger or harden some clients, or that direct communication will cause a flare-up and loss of objectivity. Riskin concludes that client attendance is likely to be useful in an ADR process that has such features as "participatory lawyer-client relationships, problem-solving negotiation, and judicial interventions emphasizing facilitation rather than pressure." Id. at 1106.

5.   Should there be an exception to the client attendance requirement when a named party has no real interest in the case? "Under standard insurance policy provisions, the insurance company has sole authority over the defense of cases, including whether to settle or go to trial. The insurance company representative, therefore, is the crucial person on the defense side for settlement negotiations. The insured defendant may have some interest in the case since its conduct is in question, but determination of that issue may have no monetary consequence to it." Sherman, Court–Mandated Alternative Dispute Resolution, 46 S.M.U.L.Rev. 2079, 2105 (1993) (arguing that settlement conference orders should not require an insured defendant to attend "when it has no realistic exposure over policy limits and when its consent to settle is not required"). Might not the parties still benefit from confronting the person on the other side of an accident, hopefully bringing some emotional closure that would make even the plaintiff more willing to settle?

In Kamaunu v. Kaaea, 57 P.3d 428, 430 n. 3 (Haw. 2002), the plaintiff sought and obtained sanctions against the defendant, alleging the failure of the insurer's representative to have adequate settlement authority and to make a genuine offer at a court-ordered settlement conference. The Hawaii Supreme Court noted that in cases of no-fault insurance, "the authority to settle a case generally lies with the defendant's insurer, especially where the settlement value does not exceed the insured's policy limits." It was thus unwilling to find that the defendant's presence at the settlement conference could make up for the insurer's representative not having adequate settlement authority "unless the defendant, in fact, had authority to settle the case." However, it found that the trial court's imposition of sanctions on defendant was actually not based on lack of a representative with settlement authority, but on "failure to make a monetary settlement offer and his firm intention to go to trial." It found that the fact that defendant made only a "walk-away" offer (a dismissal with each side bearing its own costs) was not grounds for sanctions. It quoted *Heileman* that sanctions would not be appropriate "[i]f this case represented a situation where [defendant] had sent a corporate representative and was sanctioned because that person refused to make an offer to pay money—that is, refused to submit to settlement coercion."

6.   Can a court require the insurer to attend a settlement conference? In *In re Novak*, 932 F.2d 1397 (11th Cir.1991), the district court in a medical malpractice action directed the defendant's lawyer to find out who at the defendant's insurer had "full settlement authority" after the lawyer stated in a pretrial conference that he would have to check with the insurer before increasing defendant's settlement offer. On being told that the person with such authority was Novak, the judge ordered him to appear for a settlement conference and fined him when he did not. The appellate court agreed with *Heileman* that there is inherent power to require a party to send a person with full settlement authority to a pretrial conference, but held that there is no similar authority to require a nonparty insurer to attend. It added, however, that the court could threaten sanctions against the insured party as a way to coerce cooperation from the party's insurer. See also *Universal Cooperatives, Inc. v. Tribal Co–Operative Marketing Devel. Fed. of India, Ltd.*, 45 F.3d 1194, 1196 (8th Cir.1995) (citing *Heileman*, upholding sanctions for failure to send an authorized corporate representative to settlement conference).

7.   Sending a person with settlement authority becomes more complicated when such authority resides in a body such as a city council or corporate board. See *Nueces County v. De Pena*, 953 S.W.2d 835 (Tex.App. 1997) (in suit against county, county judge could not be required to attend mediation although settlement authority lay in commissioners' court). Perhaps all that can be expected is that the representative be part of that body and that any settlement reached be subject to being confirmed by the body. Compare *In re United States*, 149 F.3d 332 (5th Cir.1998) (district court did not abuse its discretion in ordering the government to send a person with full settlement authority to mediation, at least where the government agreed to the mediation). The problems of requiring an insurer's representative or governmental official to attend a mediation with adequate settlement authority were arguably eased by 1993 amendments permitting availability by telephone.

8.   In 1993, Rule 16(c) was amended to provide that "[i]f appropriate, the court may require that a party or its representative be present or reasonably available by telephone in order to consider possible settlement of the dispute." The Advisory Committee Note also mentions that this might include "a representative from an insurance company." Citing *Heileman*, the Note states that the telephone provision "is not intended to limit the reasonable exercise of the court's inherent powers." Are the two really compatible? The Fifth Circuit, in *In re Stone*, 986 F.2d 898 (5th Cir.1993), recommended a "practical approach" to settlement authority requirements imposed on governmental bodies, such as allowing the official with ultimate authority to be fully prepared and available by telephone at the time of the

conference. But see Raad v. Wal–Mart Stores, Inc., 1998 WL 272879 (D.Neb. 1998) (upholding sanctions for nonattendance at mediation of corporate representative who only made himself available by telephone).

9. Rule 16(f) sanctions have been assessed for failure to comply with orders relating to the timing of settlement offers. The flood of asbestos cases lead federal district courts to adopt local rules requiring parties to settle by a certain date before the trial date. The purpose was to force parties to give earlier attention to settlement and to avoid last minute settlements just before or during the trial that are disruptive of a court's trial schedule and of the ability of parties in other cases to rely on trial dates. In Newton v. A.C. & S., 918 F.2d 1121 (3d Cir.1990), the district court set a deadline for settling asbestos cases of two weeks prior to the trial date, with sanctions to be imposed for later settlement. In these cases consolidated for appeal, the plaintiffs settled with some defendants before trial but after the settlement deadline, with others on the day trial was to begin, and with one defendant after several days of trial.

The appellate court approved the district court's use of deadlines as consistent with Rule 16 "to maximize the efficiency of the court system by insisting that attorneys and clients cooperate with the court and abandon practices which unreasonably interfere with the expeditious management of cases." It also approved the use of sanctions, but not as they were imposed in these cases. The district court levied fines only on the settling defendants. The appellate court said that, in the absence of a finding of fault, "disparate treatment of plaintiffs and defendants may not be countenanced." (Note the similarity to the one-sided imposition of sanctions for failing to settle in Kothe v. Smith, supra p. 3.) The court of appeals criticized the district judge's apparent belief that since the defendants "controlled the purse strings essential to a settlement," imposing fines against them alone "would be an effective measure to compel a relaxation of the purse strings and induce settlement." Can a court ever take into account the fact that defendant corporations or insurance companies are often repeat players and that fines could discourage them from delaying inevitable settlements?

In White v. Raymark Industries, Inc., 783 F.2d 1175 (4th Cir.1986), the district court assessed jurors' costs in the amount of $2,000 against a defendant pursuant to a local rule imposing costs on parties for settling cases without giving the clerk's office one day's notice. The Fourth Circuit upheld the assessment based on inherent judicial authority. It noted that "despite plaintiff's vigorous attempts to reach a settlement" in the week before the trial, the defendant's counsel was prohibited from agreeing on a settlement figure without permission of an official of the insurance carrier who could not be reached.

In State of Wisconsin v. American Family Mut. Ins. Co., 153 Wis.2d 477, 451 N.W.2d 429 (1990), the Wisconsin Supreme Court found no inherent authority for a trial court to impose a sanction on a party for disrupting its calendar by a last-minute settlement. Under the court's practice, in order to obtain a "stipulated" trial date, the parties had to agree that if the case were settled after a certain date, a penalty (in this case $20,000, the difference between the parties' offers) would be paid into the court's general fund. Had they chosen not to stipulate, the parties would have been given a "stacked" trial date which would normally involve having their case set with four other cases and running a risk of being unable to go to trial on that date. The Supreme Court found that the penalty was inconsistent with state statutes and precedents and actually restricted a party's ability to control prosecution of the case.

B. SETTLEMENT DEVICES USING INTERVENTION BY THIRD PARTIES

EDWARD F. SHERMAN, THE IMPACT ON LITIGATION STRATEGY OF INTEGRATING ALTERNATIVE DISPUTE RESOLUTION INTO THE PRETRIAL PROCESS, 168 F.R.D. 75, 75–77 (1996):

Alternative dispute resolution grew to prominence as an alternative to litigation. The principal form of nonbinding ADR—mediation—was first invoked in family law as a way to avoid the legal technicalities, expense, delay, and rigidity of remedies associated with litigation. The spread of the mediation movement to community disputes in the 1960s and 1970s was seen as a way to empower parties to resolve their own disputes without having to rely on the courts, police, or government agencies to frame the issues and devise solutions. Similarly, when the business community embraced "settlement promotion" through mediation and other ADR devices in the 1970s and 1980s, a prominent motivation was the desire to avoid the court system by making it possible for business persons to resolve their disagreements by less legalistic means.

Despite its antilitigation origins, ADR is rapidly becoming an integral part of the litigation process. Courts around the country are "annexing" a wide variety of ADR procedures that must be utilized before a lawsuit is allowed to proceed to trial. This institutionalization of ADR by the courts has raised a host of objections. ADR purists are concerned that it is contrary to the quality of voluntariness which many see as essential to the effectiveness of nonbinding ADR. There is also a concern that court-mandated ADR may coerce parties into settling without providing the safeguards that adjudication affords. Finally, there is a suspicion that the strengths of ADR in promoting problem solving and relationship building will be undermined by courts' emphasis on getting cases settled and clearing their dockets.

Reconciling the methodology, values, and objectives of ADR and trials within an integrated litigation process is no easy task. The procedural differences between a binding adjudicatory process (such as a trial) and a nonbinding facilitative process (like mediation) are considerable. These include such basic process features as the form of presentation, the kind of evidence and argumentation permitted, the role of the decisionmaker or audience, and the legal effect of the outcome. Of course, integrating ADR into the litigation process does not result in a single, amalgamated proceeding, and ADR processes do not mimic a trial. Attorneys must therefore anticipate having to participate in two very different procedures. It is difficult to engraft an ADR proceeding onto the usual pretrial process without affecting the way attorneys investigate and prepare their cases for both the ADR and the trial proceedings. Furthermore, the act of going through an ADR process, in which evidence and arguments are presented in a rather different manner than in a trial, can not help but affect the conduct of a subsequent trial.

A great deal of experimentation with different kinds of ADR processes has taken place in both federal and state courts over the past twenty-five years. These processes have in common the use of third-party neutrals to assist the parties in achieving settlement. The processes differ as to such features as the degree of procedural formality, the level of intrusiveness of the neutral, the time at which the process is invoked, and the manner of selecting the neutral. All of these processes are non-binding, and, unless the parties agree to a particular settlement, they will be entitled to go forward with a trial.

The principal ADR processes that have emerged can be roughly placed on a continuum from the least formal with the neutral playing primarily the role of facilitating discussion and consideration of settlement options (such as mediation) to the most formal with the neutral playing a "reality testing," "evaluative," or "fact-finding" role (such as court-annexed arbitration, mini-trial, and summary jury trial).[1] We will take them up in the order of least formal to most formal.

1. *Mediation*

Mediation (recall the discussion, supra p. 110) is a broad term used to describe the process by which a third party facilitates communication between parties to a dispute, and aids them in finding a solution. The "classical" format for mediation involves a mediator sitting at a table with the parties in an informal atmosphere. The mediator usually makes introductory remarks; then the parties or their counsel present their version of the dispute. This is followed by a dialogue guided by the mediator, which includes gathering information, identifying problems, generating options, and bargaining—the aim of which is to resolve the dispute and write a settlement agreement. At some stage, the mediator may also decide to move the parties into separate rooms with the mediator shuttling back and forth between them, conveying information, arguments and offers from the other side.

Participation in court-annexed mediation may not be voluntary. Statutes and court rules now often require parties to participate in mediation as part of the pre-trial process (see further discussion, infra p. 496). But although participation may be required, agreeing to settle is not, and settlement will only be achieved if the parties come to an

---

1. See further discussion in Rau, Sherman & Peppet, Processes of Dispute Resolution: The Role of Lawyers 545–78 (3d ed. 2002).

agreement as a result of the mediation.[2] "Mediation has emerged as the primary ADR process in the federal district courts," and over half of the 94 federal court districts offer or require mediation.[3]

Mediators may be selected in a variety of ways. Many court-annexed mediation programs allow the parties to select their own mediators, or, if they cannot agree, provide for selection by the court from a roster of qualified mediators. Some simply provide that the court will select the mediator. Because mediation has been an essentially private form of dispute resolution, governmental regulation is minimal. Unlike other professions—ranging from attorneys and psychologists to therapists and cosmetologists—mediators have not been subjected to governmental supervision over such matters as licensing, training, professional standards, and discipline. A number of professional mediation organizations certify mediators as having satisfied certain requirements as to training and experience, but there is no formal licensing of mediators. Court-annexed mediation programs typically require completion of a basic 40–hour training course in mediation, with advanced training required for certain kinds of cases like family law. A few state-court mediation programs have certification requirements for mediators, with their state Supreme Court or affiliate entities serving as the credentialing body (e.g., Florida, Virginia, Georgia, and Tennessee).

As courts began to annex mediation as an integral part of the trial process, lawyers have become the largest profession performing as mediators. Most are part-time, doing mediation as an adjunct to their law practice, although some confine their practice exclusively to mediation. In certain areas, non-lawyers also often serve as mediators (for example, psychologists in family disputes, social workers in juvenile or community matters, criminologists in victim-offender confrontations, engineers or architects in construction disputes, or labor specialists in labor/employment relations). Some courts have staff mediators to conduct mediations (for example, in California in family law cases). Prior experience in litigation is often desired in a mediator, particularly by parties' attorneys, and many full-time mediators are former litigators or judges. Typically mediators make known their fee schedules in advance, whether they are appointed by the court or selected by the parties. Mediator fees may be assessed by the court as costs, and are often split between the parties. See discussion in In re Atlantic Pipe Corporation, infra p. 496.

2. *Early Neutral Evaluation (ENE)*

The Early Neutral Evaluation (ENE) program, now used in a number of federal district courts, was first created by the U.S. District

2. There are, however, mediation-arbitration ("med-arb") hybrids that begin with mediation, but if the parties cannot reach a settlement, the mediator may decide the case as an arbitrator if agreed in advance by the parties. For a fuller discussion, see Rau, Sherman, & Peppet, *supra* note 1, at 545–78.

3. Plapinger & Stienstra, ADR and Settlement in the Federal District Courts: A Sourcebook for Judges and Lawyers, Alternative Dispute Resolution: The Litigator's Handbook, eds. Atlas, Huber & Trachte-Huber, 399 (ABA Section of Litigation 2000).

Court for the N.D. California.[4] Under it, a neutral—usually a respected lawyer with expertise in the subject matter of the case—meets with the parties and their lawyers for a couple of hours not long after the filing of the case and gives them a frank assessment of their cases. "Typically, one of the clients begins a narrative presentation of the case, without being led by the lawyer. After both sides have presented, the evaluator asks questions. The evaluator tries to help the parties to identify common ground, and to convert this to stipulations or informal agreements. The effort during the process is to isolate the areas of disagreement most central to the case."[5]

After the discussion, the evaluator leaves the room and writes her evaluation of the value of the case and two or three key analytical points. If the plaintiff wins, the evaluator ascribes a range of damages. Before giving the parties the evaluation, the evaluator asks if they wish to discuss settlement before they see it. Some 25% of cases have settled at this point. If they opt not to discuss settlement, the evaluator explains the evaluation. She then "outlines a case development plan, identifying key areas of disagreement and suggesting ways to posture the case and to conduct discovery as efficiently as possible. The evaluator is required to do case planning. The parties are required to listen, but not to agree. They may decide to come back for a follow-up settlement conference."[6]

3.   *Court–Annexed Arbitration*

In 1952, Pennsylvania adopted a court-supervised system of mandatory, non-binding arbitration for certain cases. The experiment was based on the premise that parties are more likely to settle if they are given an opportunity to present their cases in an abbreviated form to three neutral attorneys who would render a non-binding judgment. This would provide an opportunity to "reality test" by comparing the presentation of their case with that of their opponent and to see how neutrals who were familiar with the law would assess the cases.

A study of one of the programs in Pittsburgh found a high settlement rate and general satisfaction with the program by litigants and attorneys. "The private, informal arbitration procedure, conducted by three ordinary attorneys in business suits, sitting without a jury around a table in a small hearing room" clearly did not fit the trial paradigm of "a black-robed judge, conducting a public trial before a jury, in a formal courtroom environment."[7] Nevertheless, only a small percentage of litigants interviewed said they would have preferred to have a judge or

---

4. See Brazil, Kahn, Newman & Gold, Early Neutral Evaluation: An Experimental Effort to Expedite Dispute Resolution, 69 Judicature 279 (1986).

5. Lawyers Get Tips on Using Early Neutral Evaluation, 4 ADR Rep. 124, at 124–25 (April 12, 1990).

6. Id.

7. Adler, Hensler, & Nelson, Simple Justice: How Litigants Fare in the Pittsburgh Arbitration Program, 87–94 (1983).

jury hear their case.[8] The reason, the study concluded, was that the litigants were satisfied with a speedy, inexpensive procedure that provides a full hearing before an impartial third party:

> They wanted an opportunity to have their case heard and decided by an impartial third party. When this requirement was met, they reported that the arbitration process had been "fair." When asked why they had come to this conclusion, they were unlikely to offer elaborate rationales. "They heard us both out, listened the same to both sides," or "We got an equal chance to tell our stories," were typical responses.[9]

About half the states,[10] and a number of federal courts, now have court-annexed arbitration programs. Legislation in the 1980s authorized ten federal district courts to establish mandatory arbitration programs and another ten to implement voluntary programs.[11] The programs were generally well received, although doubts were expressed as to whether they were really cost-effective since a high percentage of cases will settle anyway.

The Civil Justice Reform Act of 1990[12] required each district court to study and develop a civil justice "expense and delay reduction" plan, including consideration of ADR programs. A number of the 94 federal district courts provided for court-annexed arbitration, either mandatory or voluntary. However, a Rand study of the effectiveness of the CJRA found no major effect of court-annexed arbitration on the time to disposition, lawyer work hours, or lawyer satisfaction.[13] In 1997, Congress permanently reauthorized the twenty district court arbitration programs.[14] Court-annexed arbitration continues to be one of several ADR alternatives in federal courts, but the Rand study noted "a marked shift in half of the pilot districts toward other structured and administratively supported ADR programs—especially mandatory or voluntary mediation and early neutral evaluation."[15]

In the typical federal court-annexed arbitration program, a roster of lawyers who are willing to serve as arbitrators is maintained by the court. A list of lawyers who have been randomly selected is submitted to counsel, who are instructed to strike one name and return the list to the

8. Id. at 9.

9. Id. at 9.

10. Melver & Keilitz, Court–Annexed Arbitration: An Introduction, 14 Just.Sys.J. 123 (1991).

11. See E. Plapinger & D. Stienstra, ADR and Settlement in the Federal District Courts 61–63 (Fed. Jud. Ctr. & CPR Inst. for Dispute Res. 1996)

12. 28 U.S.C.A. §§ 471–82.

13. See J. Kakalik, et al., Just, Speedy, and Inexpensive? An Evaluation of Judicial Case Management Under the Civil Justice Reform Act (Rand, Inst. of Civ. Just., 1996). However, there have been criticisms of the methodology and limited samples used in the Rand study. See Statement of Concerns Regarding the Rand ADR Study (CPR Inst. Of Disp. Res., March 14, 1997).

14. 111 Stat. 1173 (1997). However, the next year a bill requiring all federal district courts to use mandatory court-annexed arbitration in cases involving less than a certain dollar amount failed, and instead, the Alternative Dispute Resolution Act of 1998, 112 Stat. 2993 (1998), gave federal district courts power to refer cases to mediation and early neutral evaluation, but to court-annexed arbitration only if the parties consent.

15. Kakalik, supra note 13, at 17.

court. The three attorneys whose names remain are then asked to serve as the arbitration panel. At the hearing, counsel make a summarized presentation of their cases without live witnesses. The arbitrators confer and render a non-binding decision. The parties and their counsel may be given an opportunity to discuss the case informally with the arbitrators. Parties can demand a trial de novo within 30 days after entry of judgment if they post an amount equal to the arbitrators' fees (which was typically set at $75 per day of hearing for each arbitrator, a recognition that the lawyers were essentially serving pro bono). This amount is returned if the party obtains a judgment more favorable than the arbitration award; otherwise, it is forfeited to the government. Upon the filing of a de novo demand, the judgment entered on the arbitrators' award is vacated, and the award sealed pending the final outcome of the case.[16]

Notes and Questions

1. Court-annexed arbitration is generally expected to take place early in the litigation, without an opportunity for full discovery. It is viewed as a quick and inexpensive alternative to litigation: Judge Harry Edwards has referred to it as a "poor man's mini-trial." Edwards, Alternate Dispute Resolution: Panacea or Anathema?, 99 Harv.L.Rev. 668, 673 (1986). Can a case be properly arbitrated without full discovery? Parties are encouraged to "decide what discovery is crucial to the hearing and conduct that discovery in advance of arbitration." Handbook of Alternative Dispute Resolution 50 (State Bar of Texas 1987). One of the principal advantages of court-annexed arbitration as a settlement device is that it functions without a judge and thus frees up judicial time. It is also considerably less expensive than a trial. The form of presentation is through summarization of evidence in a relatively short proceeding, usually less than half a day. Under most federal court programs, the arbitrators are lawyers who serve with no, or little, compensation.

2. Should arbitrators have subpoena and other supervisory powers? In some state programs, they are selected immediately before the arbitration and thus have no opportunity to exercise such powers. In federal programs, they are usually assigned in advance and thus could enter orders governing such matters as a continuance and discovery. Under the Mandatory Arbitration Program of the D.C. Superior Court, arbitrators have the authority to issue subpoenas, rule on evidence, decide discovery disputes, compel the production of documents, enter judgment by default or consent, and stay execution of such judgments if the parties agree to schedule payments. Do you see any problem with these powers?

3. The rules of evidence in court-annexed arbitration have been relaxed. A local rule in the W.D. Tex. provides: "In receiving evidence, the arbitrators shall be guided by the Federal Rules of Evidence, but they shall not thereby be precluded from receiving evidence which they consider to be relevant and trustworthy and which is not privileged." Are there any

16. Meierhoefer & Seron, Court-Annexed Arbitration in the Western District of Texas 3 (1989).

constraints on what the arbitrators will hear under this rule? Can an arbitration provide a realistic trial run if lax rules of evidence permit material to be received that would not be admissible at trial?

4. Mandatory court-annexed arbitration has been challenged on various constitutional grounds, including the right to a jury trial, equal protection, and due process. None of these challenges has succeeded, primarily because there is a right to trial de novo, and courts have concluded that the benefits of settlement promotion outweigh the burden of participation. See Davis v. Gaona, 396 S.E.2d 218 (Ga.1990); Firelock, Inc. v. District Court of 20th Judicial Dist., 776 P.2d 1090 (Colo.1989); Kimbrough v. Holiday Inn, 478 F.Supp. 566 (E.D.Pa.1979).

5. What if a party refuses to come to court-annexed arbitration, or attends but refuses to participate? New England Merchants National Bank v. Hughes, 556 F.Supp. 712 (E.D.Pa.1983), denied a right to trial *de novo* to a defendant who offered no excuse for failing to appear, thus resulting in a final judgment for the plaintiff in the amount of $31,000 that the arbitrators had awarded. The court found no deprivation of the constitutional right to jury trial, observing that under those circumstances "the goals of the arbitration program and the authority of this Court would be seriously undermined" if the defendant were allowed to demand a trial. Compare Gilling v. Eastern Airlines, Inc., 680 F.Supp. 169 (D.N.J.1988) (modifying the sanction for nonparticipation from denial of a *de novo* trial to an order to reimburse the opposing party for all costs incurred in preparing for arbitration); Lyons v. Wickhorst, 727 P.2d 1019 (Cal.1986) (finding no power under state statutes to dismiss action with prejudice for not participating, but with disagreement among the justices as to whether such sanction might be constitutional).

6. Early studies indicated that the trial rate of cases diverted to court-annexed arbitration was substantially lower than the rate at which comparable cases would have gone to trial in the absence of the program. See Levine, Court–Annexed Arbitration, 16 J.Law Reform 537, 542–43 (1983). However, more recent studies have not demonstrated a statistically significant reduction in trial rates in most of the state programs. Keilitz, Court–Annexed Arbitration, in Nat'l Symposium on Court–Connected Dispute Resolution Research 43 (Nat'l Center for State Cts. and State Jus. Instit. 1994). Average appeal rates from arbitrators' judgments in state programs are 40 to 60%. Id. at 42–43. But the settlement rates of all cases are high, and it is difficult to determine to what degree the added effort involved in court-annexed arbitration results in more settlements. Court-annexed arbitration enjoys a high satisfaction rate among both litigants and attorneys. Not surprisingly, winners were more satisfied than losers; corporate litigants were also happier than individual litigants. Does the high satisfaction rate justify the process even if cost savings cannot be shown? Does it demonstrate that litigants can feel they have had their "day in court" without a full trial?

7. The Alternative Dispute Resolution Act of 1998, 28 U.S.C.A. §§ 654–58, directs every district to authorize at least one type of ADR by local rule, and provides specifics about how arbitration may be administered. The Act requires that litigant consent be obtained before referral to arbitration, and that there not be improper pressure to obtain consent. It also excludes

arbitration from use in actions alleging violation of a right secured by the Constitution, and limits it to cases in which the relief sought is less than $150,000 (although the court may presume damages are less than that amount unless counsel certifies that they exceed it). 28 U.S.C. §§ 654(b); 654(c). Fed. R. Civ. P. 45 can be used to subpoena witnesses to attend arbitration hearings, 28 U.S.C.A. § 656, and an arbitrator has the statutory power to conduct arbitration hearings and make awards. 28 U.S.C.A. § 655(a). Evidence about the arbitration or the award is generally inadmissible in the court proceeding. 28 U.S.C.A. § 657(c)(3).

4. *Summary Jury Trial*

A summary jury trial is a shortened trial, usually lasting less than a day, in which the lawyers summarize their cases before a jury empanelled under usual procedures. A judge or magistrate presides. Some brief testimony may be heard from key witnesses, such as the parties, but most of the testimony will be summarized by the attorneys based on depositions, other discovery, and affidavits. The jury verdict is only advisory and non-binding on the parties—although the jurors are not usually told this.

The summary jury trial was developed in 1980 by Judge Thomas Lambros, of the U.S. District Court for the Northern District of Ohio, for two personal injury suits that he believed should have settled: "The reason that they didn't was that counsel and their clients felt that they could obtain a better resolution from a jury than their pretrial settlement negotiations. It occurred to me that if only the parties could gaze into a crystal ball and be able to predict, with a reasonable amount of certainty, what a jury could do in their respective cases, the parties and counsel would be more willing to reach a settlement rather than going through the expense and aggravation of a full jury trial."[17]

Discovery should have been completed before a summary jury trial. The parties have to submit lists of the witnesses whose testimony will be summarized and must "present all procedural and evidentiary questions which foreseeably will arise during the course of the summary jury trial," on which the judge will rule, minimizing the need for objections.[18]

Judge Lambros described the hearing:[19]

The proceedings are not open to the public. Unless specifically ordered by the Court, the proceedings are not recorded. Counsel may, if so desired, arrange for a court reporter to be in attendance.

All evidence is presented through the attorneys, who may incorporate arguments on such evidence in their presentations. Opening and closing arguments are amalgamated with a narrative overview of the trial proofs. Generally, one hour of time is allotted to each side in the litigation, in which to present their case to the jury. This

---

17. Lambros, The Summary Jury Trial, 103 F.R.D. 461, 463 (1984).

18. Id. at 468.

19. Id. at 463; 468; 470–72.

time period may be broken up so that rebuttal time is available if desired.

No testimony is taken by sworn witnesses. Counsel simply summarize the anticipated testimony of trial witnesses and are free to present exhibits to the jury. While counsel may employ any effective and persuasive advocacy techniques, counsel are limited to presenting representations of evidence that would be admissible at trial. Representations of facts must be supportable by reference to discovery materials, including depositions, stipulations, documents, and formal admissions, or by a professional representation that counsel has spoken with the witness and is repeating that which the witness stated. Additionally, statements, reports, and depositions may be read from, but not at undue length.

* * *

Following counsels' presentation, the jury is given an abbreviated charge and then retires to deliberate. The jury may return a consensus verdict or separate, individual verdicts that list each juror's opinion of liability and damages. While consensus verdicts are encouraged, separate, individual verdicts do afford counsel substantial insight into the individual juror's perceptions and may suggest an equitable basis for settlement.

Notes and Questions

1. Summarization of evidence by lawyers, rather than live testimony, is central to the time-savings offered by the summary jury trial. This has been criticized in Brunet, Questioning the Quality of Alternative Dispute Resolution, 62 Tulane L.Rev. 1, 40 (1987), as an inferior form of presenting information:

> Most direct evidence presented to a judicial trial is one step removed from the actual event and can be only an imperfect perception. The attorney summations of evidence used in a summary jury trial add an additional layer of distance from the actual events that are the object of fact finding.
>
> Moreover, attorney witness summations cannot resolve factual questions of veracity and credibility. Any lawyer who has ever tried a case knows that the trier of fact has expertise in discerning witness credibility and veracity. A full trial achieves careful consideration of issues of witness believability. These advantages of trial are absent from summary jury trial. Attorney witness summaries simply are incomparable to actual consideration of witness demeanor. As Judge Posner has stated, "We do not need a jury of laymen to decide which of two lawyers is more credible." [Posner, The Summary Jury Trial and Other Methods of Alternative Dispute Resolution: Some Cautionary Observations, 53 U.Chi.L.Rev. 366, 374 (1986).]

On the other hand, it has to be remembered that a summary jury trial is not intended as a substitute for a trial, but as a device to provide "reality testing" conducive to a settlement short of trial. But see Marcus, Completing

Equity's Conquest? Reflections on the Future of Trial Under the Federal Rules of Civil Procedure, 50 U.Pitt.L.Rev. 725 (1988) (suggesting that, for some purposes, summary jury trial is analogous to trial). The issue is whether it can provide a sufficiently reliable overview to give some confidence that it will result in a fair settlement. Consider Sherman, Reshaping the Lawyer's Skills for Court–Supervised ADR, 51 Tex.Bar.J. 47, 47–49 (1988):

> The art of summarization is the centerpiece of court-supervised ADR proceedings. It is already familiar to attorneys who, in letters, memoranda, and briefs, are constantly called on to boil down information, synthesize it, and present it in a shortened form. Perhaps the closest analogues to this skill in litigation are found in closing argument to the jury, appellate argument, presentations to administrative agencies, and "written narrative statements."

> A genuine concern is that there is no opportunity for cross-examination which may be necessary to assess credibility when there is disputed testimony. Cross-examination, however, may take place on deposition. It is up to counsel to convey through his summarization the effect of the cross-examination and any discrepancies and flaws in the witness' total testimony. The ADR decision-maker, however, will not have the opportunity to observe the witness and assess his credibility, and, in certain cases, that can be a significant loss. For this reason, allowing brief appearances of witnesses or showing portions of a videotaped deposition seems desirable, and courts should be open to allowing such developments.

2. A check on counsels' inventiveness in a summary jury trial in describing the expected testimony is that they must have a basis for the assertions they make about the evidence. Lawyers often choose not to question their potential witness on deposition to bring out favorable details, preferring to wait until trial to have the witness tell the full story in its most favorable terms. Must attorneys now ensure that such details are covered in depositions so that they can be used in summary jury trials? Judge Lambros would allow summarized testimony not only of formal discovery like depositions, stipulations, documents, and admissions, but also "by a professional representation that counsel has spoken with the witnesses and is repeating that which the witness stated." Lambros, 103 F.R.D. at 471. Is there any check on a counsel's misstating what he has been told in private by a potential witness? Indeed, is there any check on a counsel's misstating or embellishing his summary of the deposition or other discovery? The primary check is the ability of the opposing counsel to set the record straight in her own presentation. Objections are possible, though not encouraged. Perhaps most importantly, it should be kept in mind that the summary jury verdict is advisory only, and a verdict that the other party will not accept because she feels she has been overreached in the summary jury trial is worth very little.

3. Although a summary jury trial provides perhaps the best estimate of how a jury would decide a case, questions have been raised as to whether it really results in a savings of effort. Most cases settle anyway. Moreover, using this method seems not to result in significant savings of attorney time (since full pretrial preparation is necessary) or judge time (since the judge

must rule on a variety of trial-related matters and must preside at the summary jury trial). For a skeptical examination of the claims of cost and time savings in a summary jury trial, see Posner, The Summary Jury Trial and Other Methods of Alternative Dispute Resolution: Some Cautionary Observations, 53 U.Chi.L.Rev. 366 (1986). Perhaps because so many resources go into a summary jury trial—which will be wasted if one of the parties will not accept the verdict—it has slipped behind mediation, ENE, and court-annexed arbitration as most-used ADR processes, with most federal courts that authorize it reporting only one or two a year. Plapinger & Stienstra, ADR and Settlement in the Federal District Courts: A Sourcebook for Judges and Lawyers, Alternative Dispute Resolution: The Litigators Handbook, eds. Atlas, Huber & Trachte–Huber, 399 (ABA Section of Litigation 2000).

4. If summary jury trials are non-binding, it is important that what is said in them and the jury's decision will be inadmissible in any later proceedings. As a form of compromise negotiations, the summary jury trial enjoys the protections of Fed.R.Evid. 408: "Evidence of (1) furnishing or offering or promising to furnish, or (2) accepting or offering or promising to accept, a valuable consideration in compromising or attempting to compromise a claim which was disputed as to either validity or amount, is not admissible to prove liability for or invalidity of the claim or its amount. Evidence of conduct or statements made in compromise negotiations is likewise not admissible." However, Rule 408 only goes to admissibility, and not discovery, and if the parties are to be assured that discovery may not be used in the future, by their opponent or third parties, as to what was said or decided in the summary jury trial, a privilege under common law or statute is necessary. For discussion of privilege issues in ADR, see A. Rau, E. Sherman, & S. Peppet, Processes of Dispute Resolution 279–96 461–514 (3d ed. 2002).

5. Note that the summary jury trial is closed to the public. Yet Judge Lambros says it is essential that the event take place in a courtroom, presided over by a judge or magistrate, using jurors summoned by public authorities. Should such events be closed to the public?

In Cincinnati Gas & Elec. Co. v. General Elec. Co., 117 F.R.D. 597 (S.D.Ohio 1987), affirmed, 854 F.2d 900 (6th Cir.1988), the court denied newspapers access to a summary jury trial. The newspapers argued that trials are public events, but the judge rejected the analogy (117 F.R.D. at 601):

> Because the purpose of the summary jury trial is settlement by means of giving the parties insights into the strengths and weaknesses of their case, the proceedings are markedly different. * * * As a matter of necessity, not all of the evidence that would be presented at trial will be covered by the summary proceeding. No live testimony and, thus, no testing of credibility or cross-examination of witnesses, is permitted. Moreover, given the flexibility of this procedure, the summary jury trial in the case deals with only selected issues; others, that will be tried on the merits, if this case goes to trial, are simply omitted from this procedure for the sake of simplicity and to focus on those issues that

appear to be central to any meaningful settlement discussions in this case.

* * * We readily agree that we attempt to have the proceeding mimic trial procedures to the degree possible, but this effort does not detract from the stated goal of settlement—to the contrary, the realism of the procedure is key to successful functioning.

Is it proper for a court to use its facilities for secret dispute resolution in this manner? Would it affect your answer to know that the underlying litigation in *Cincinnati Gas* concerned the safety of a nuclear reactor? Plaintiff alleged that due to poor design the reactor was unable to withstand the pressures generated by the nuclear steam supply system and therefore was unable to contain radioactive steam. After the secret summary jury trial, the case was settled for an amount reportedly exceeding $75 million. Should the press and residents of the area where the reactor is located have been given access to the evidence summarized during the summary jury trial? Federal Reserve Bank v. Carey–Canada, Inc., 123 F.R.D. 603, 607 (D.Minn. 1988), required the parties in an asbestos liability case to participate in a summary jury trial without their consent and followed *Cincinnati Gas* in closing it to the public.

6. If the summary jury trial is actually a private settlement device, does the court have authority to summon jurors to participate in it? In Hume v. M & C Management, 129 F.R.D. 506 (N.D.Ohio 1990), another judge in Judge Lambros' district, Judge Battisti, ruled that 28 U.S.C.A. § 1866(g), which empowers courts to summon jurors under threat of fine or imprisonment, does not authorize summoning them for summary jury trials. He further found that the basic jury statute, 28 U.S.C.A. § 1861, was not intended to apply to summary jury trials and expressed concern that summary jury trials could adversely affect the jury system by depleting the supply of jurors for real trials and demoralizing citizens assigned to participate in trials that are not real.

Following his order in *Hume*, Judge Battisti suspended all criminal and civil jury trials pending before him on the ground that the fact that some potential jurors might have served in summary jury trials "may impermissibly alter the jury selection process." United States v. Exum, 748 F.Supp. 512 (N.D.Ohio 1990). However, after the passage of the Civil Justice Reform Act of 1990, which provided that federal district courts should consider the use of ADR devices including the summary jury trial, see 28 U.S.C.A. § 473(a)(6), he vacated those orders. The CJRA is no longer in effect, but a number of federal district courts continue to have summary jury trial programs, relying on local court rules or court orders, FRCP 16 and 39(c), the inherent power of the court, and consent by the parties, as authority for conducting them.

5. *Mini–trial*

The term "mini-trial" was attached by a *New York Times* story to a formal settlement device created in 1977 in connection with a corporate dispute. It is not strictly speaking a trial at all, but a process that combines elements of adjudication with other processes such as negotiation and mediation. It refers to a proceeding, usually presided over by a neutral advisor, in which each side presents its case in shortened form to the persons who have ultimate settlement authority (often the Chief Executive Officers of corporate parties) as a prelude to settlement negotiations between them. The term is sometimes incorrectly used to refer to any form of shortened or summarized trial (rather than using the more specific titles, such as "summary jury trial" or "court-annexed arbitration").

The "mini-trial" was created for disputes involving corporate parties and has been primarily conducted by private organizations like the CPR Institute for Dispute Resolution, an association of corporations that promotes resolution of disputes without trials.[20] However, some courts have found it to be a useful settlement device, and it has been "court-annexed" in some cases by orders that the parties conduct a mini-trial.

A principal reason for creation of the mini-trial was to "return the dispute to the businessmen."[21] Often litigated matters result from business arrangements that have failed in some way, and the corporate managers shy away from them. Whether or not the corporate manager who oversees the litigation was personally responsible for the matter that is in litigation, he is unlikely to advance his career through association with that unhappy episode. Hence the tendency to leave the matter to the lawyers; if the case turns out unsuccessfully, the result can be blamed on them. Throughout the litigation the lawyers are likely to have to combat this tendency in order to prompt the client to take some responsibility for the conduct of the case. By shifting the responsibility for the outcome back to the client, advocates of the mini-trial argue, it can perform an important function. The process also directly involves the decision-makers who have settlement authority in the settlement process. The decision-makers may, for the first time, hear the weak points in their case when there is a summarized presentation of the evidence.

When mini-trial treatment is proposed, the parties may be expected to work out an agreement providing for specific procedures. For example, a Handbook prepared for the Center for Public Resources[22] lays out ground rules on presentations and includes a schedule calling for trial within six weeks, with only two weeks for discovery. The mini-trial itself is projected to last 2 ½ days: plaintiff's case-in-chief on the first afternoon, defendant's rebuttal and plaintiff's response on the following morning, defendant's case-in-chief on the second afternoon, and plaintiff's rebuttal and defendant's response on the second morning. Question and answer sessions for the neutral advisor are interspersed throughout,

20. See Fine, The CPR Legal Program Mini–Trial Workbook (Center for Public Resources, now CPR Institute for Dispute Resolution, 1985).

21. Olson, An Alternative for Large Case Dispute Resolution, 6 Litigation 22 (1980).

22. E. Green, The CPR Legal Program Mini–Trial Handbooks in Corporate Dispute Management 111–14 (1981).

and the third afternoon is reserved for negotiations without the advisor. If a settlement is not reached, the advisor may be summoned back to participate in negotiations.

Advantages of the mini-trial include the flexibility for parties to select their own timetable, location, rules and procedures, and neutral advisor; the benefit of directing presentations to the decision-making officials; and the salutary role of a respected neutral advisor in being able to go beyond the power of a judge to ask questions and provide reality-testing. Mini-trials still tend to be conducted by private organizations, like the CPR Institute for Dispute Resolution, and not pursuant to court order, although a number of local rules list the mini-trial among the authorized court-annexed ADR processes.

C. OBLIGATION TO PARTICIPATE IN SETTLEMENT PROCESSES

As ADR settlement procedures, particularly mediation, have increasingly provided an alternative to settlement conferences conducted by the judge, the question of mandatory participation and costs continues to arise. *Heileman*, supra p. 470, found that Rule 16 provided authority for federal judges to require parties to attend pretrial settlement conferences with settlement authority. But the ADR devices we have just discussed are a little different from a judicial settlement conference. They involve a third-party neutral and contemplate some form of presentation of arguments, and perhaps evidence, which might go beyond what is expected in just a pretrial conference with a judge. Rule 16 was amended in 1993 to include in the list of proper subjects for discussion at a pretrial conference "settlement and the use of special procedures to assist in revolving the dispute when authorized by statute or local rule." The limitation "when authorized by state or local rule" might be read as an indication that "special procedures" require more than just discussion in a settlement conference and therefore should be specifically authorized by statute or rule. Consider the following case:

IN RE ATLANTIC PIPE CORPORATION

United States Court of Appeals, First Circuit, 2002.
304 F.3d 135.

BOUDIN, CHIEF JUDGE, SELYA, CIRCUIT JUDGE, and GREENBERG, SENIOR CIRCUIT JUDGE, sitting by designation.

SELYA, CIRCUIT JUDGE.

[In a suit over a construction contract in the District of Puerto Rico, a third-party defendant (APC) sought mandamus to compel the judge to withdraw his order referring the case to mediation before Eric Green, a well-known law-professor mediator.]

There are four potential sources of judicial authority for ordering mandatory non-binding mediation of pending cases, namely, (a) the court's local rules, (b) an applicable statute, (c) the Federal Rules of Civil

Procedure, and (d) the court's inherent powers. Because the district court did not identify the basis of its assumed authority, we consider each of these sources.

A. THE LOCAL RULES

A district court's local rules may provide an appropriate source of authority for ordering parties to participate in mediation. See Rhea v. Massey–Ferguson, Inc., 767 F.2d 266, 268–69 (6th Cir.1985) (per curiam). In Puerto Rico, however, the local rules contain only a single reference to any form of alternative dispute resolution (ADR). That reference is embodied in the district court's Amended Civil Justice Expense and Delay Reduction Plan (CJR Plan). The district court adopted the CJR Plan on June 14, 1993, in response to the directive contained in the Civil Justice Reform Act of 1990 (CJRA), 28 U.S.C. 471–482. Rule V of the CJR Plan states: "Pursuant to 28 U.S.C. 473(b)(4), this Court shall adopt a method of Alternative Dispute Resolution ('ADR') through mediation by a judicial officer."

Such a program would allow litigants to obtain from an impartial third party—the judicial officer as mediator—a flexible non-binding, dispute resolution process to facilitate negotiations among the parties to help them reach settlement. In addition to specifying who may act as a mediator, Rule V also limits the proper procedure for mediation sessions and assures confidentiality.

The respondents concede that the mediation order in this case falls outside the boundaries of the mediation program envisioned by Rule V. It does so most noticeably because it involves mediation before a private mediator, not a judicial officer. Seizing upon this discrepancy, APC argues that the local rules limit the district court in this respect, and that the court exceeded its authority thereunder by issuing a non-conforming mediation order (i.e., one that contemplates the intervention of a private mediator). The respondents counter by arguing that the rule does not bind the district court because, notwithstanding the unambiguous promise of the CJR Plan (which declares that the district court "shall adopt a method of Alternative Dispute Resolution"), no such program has been adopted to date.

This is a powerful argument. APC does not contradict the respondents' assurance that the relevant portion of the CJR Plan has remained unimplemented, and we take judicial notice that there is no formal, ongoing ADR program in the Puerto Rico federal district court. Because that is so, we conclude that the District of Puerto Rico has no local rule in force that dictates the permissible characteristics of mediation orders. Consequently, APC's argument founders.

B. THE ADR ACT

There is only one potential source of statutory authority for ordering mandatory non-binding mediation here: the Alternative Dispute Resolution Act of 1998 (ADR Act), 28 U.S.C. 651–658. Congress passed the

ADR Act to promote the utilization of alternative dispute resolution methods in the federal courts and to set appropriate guidelines for their use. The Act lists mediation as an appropriate ADR process. Moreover, it sanctions the participation of "professional neutrals from the private sector" as mediators. Finally, the Act requires district courts to obtain litigants' consent only when they order arbitration, id. 652(a), not when they order the use of other ADR mechanisms (such as non-binding mediation).

Despite the broad sweep of these provisions, the Act is quite clear that some form of the ADR procedures it endorses must be adopted in each judicial district by local rule. In the absence of such local rules, the ADR Act itself does not authorize any specific court to use a particular ADR mechanism. Because the District of Puerto Rico has not yet complied with the Act's mandate, the mediation order here at issue cannot be justified under the ADR Act.

The respondents essay an end run around this lacuna: they contend (borrowing a phrase from the court below) that the "spirit" of the ADR Act authorizes the mediation order because the Act was intended to promote experimentation with ADR techniques. We reject this attempt to press the ADR Act into service by indirection.

Although the ADR Act was designed to promote the use of ADR techniques, Congress chose a very well-defined path: it granted each judicial district, rather than each individual judge, the authority to craft an appropriate ADR program. In other words, Congress permitted experimentation, but only within the disciplining format of district-wide local rules adopted with notice and a full opportunity for public comment. To say that the Act authorized each district judge to disregard a district-wide ADR plan (or the absence of one) and fashion innovative procedures for use in specific cases is simply too much of a stretch.

We add, however, that although the respondents cannot use the ADR Act as a justification, neither can APC use it as a nullification. Noting that the Act requires the adoption of local rules establishing a formal ADR program, APC equates the absence of such rules with the absence of power to employ an ADR procedure (say, mediation) in a specific case. But that is wishful thinking: if one assumes that district judges possessed the power to require mediation prior to the passage of the ADR Act, there is nothing in the Act that strips them of that power. After all, even the adoption of a federal procedural rule does not implicitly abrogate a district court's inherent power to act merely because the rule touches upon the same subject matter. See Chambers v. NASCO, Inc., 501 U.S. 32, 42–43, 111 S.Ct. 2123, 115 L.Ed.2d 27 (1991) (rejecting the argument that the adoption of various provisions of the Civil Rules eliminated the district court's inherent power to impose other sanctions); Link v. Wabash R.R., 370 U.S. 626, 630, 82 S.Ct. 1386, 8 L.Ed.2d 734 (1963) (explaining that neither the permissive language of Fed.R.Civ.P. 41(b) nor the policy behind it justified a conclusion that it was meant to limit the district courts' inherent power to dismiss a case for want of prosecution).

The case before us is analogous to *Chambers* and *Link*. Even though Congress may cabin the district courts' inherent powers, its intention to do so must be clear and unmistakable. Not so here: we know of nothing in either the ADR Act or the policies that undergird it that can be said to restrict the district courts' authority to engage in the case-by-case deployment of ADR procedures. Hence, we conclude that where, as here, there are no implementing local rules, the ADR Act neither authorizes nor prohibits the entry of a mandatory mediation order.

C. The Civil Rules

The respondents next argue that the district court possessed the authority to require mediation by virtue of the Federal Rules of Civil Procedure. They concentrate their attention on Fed.R.Civ.P. 16, which states in pertinent part that "the court may take appropriate action[ ] with respect to ... (9) settlement and the use of special procedures to assist in resolving the dispute when authorized by statute or local rule...." Fed.R.Civ.P. 16(c)(9). But the words "when authorized by statute or local rule" are a frank limitation on the district courts' authority to order mediation thereunder, and we must adhere to that circumscription. Because there is no statute or local rule authorizing mandatory private mediation in the District of Puerto Rico, Rule 16(c)(9) does not assist the respondents' cause.

D. Inherent Powers

Even apart from positive law, district courts have substantial inherent power to manage and control their calendars. This inherent power takes many forms. See Fed.R.Civ.P. 83(b) (providing that judges may regulate practice in any manner consistent with federal law and applicable rules). By way of illustration, a district court may use its inherent power to compel represented clients to attend pretrial settlement conferences, even though such a practice is not specifically authorized in the Civil Rules. See Heileman Brewing Co. v. Joseph Oat Corp., 871 F.2d 648, 650 (7th Cir.1989) (en banc).

Of course, a district court's inherent powers are not infinite. There are at least four limiting principles. First, inherent powers must be used in a way reasonably suited to the enhancement of the court's processes, including the orderly and expeditious disposition of pending cases. Second, inherent powers cannot be exercised in a manner that contradicts an applicable statute or rule. Third, the use of inherent powers must comport with procedural fairness. And, finally, inherent powers "must be exercised with restraint and discretion."

At one time, the inherent power of judges to compel unwilling parties to participate in ADR procedures was a hot-button issue for legal scholars. Although many federal district courts have forestalled further debate by adopting local rules that authorize specific ADR procedures and outlaw others, e.g., D.N.H. R. 53.1 (permitting mandatory mediation); D. Me. R. 83.11 (permitting only voluntary mediation); D. Mass. R. 16.4 (permitting mandatory summary jury trials but only voluntary mediation), the District of Puerto Rico is not among them. Thus, we have no choice but to address the question head-on.

We begin our inquiry by examining the case law. In Strandell v. Jackson County, 838 F.2d 884 (7th Cir.1987), the Seventh Circuit held that a district court does not possess inherent power to compel participation in a summary jury trial. In the court's view, Fed.R.Civ.P. 16 occupied the field and prevented a district court from forcing "an unwilling litigant [to] be sidetracked from the normal course of litigation." But the group that spearheaded the subsequent revision of Rule 16 explicitly rejected that interpretation. See Fed.R.Civ.P. 16, advisory committee's note (1993 Amendment) ("The [amended] rule does not attempt to resolve questions as to the extent a court would be authorized to require [ADR] proceedings as an exercise of its inherent powers."). Thus, we do not find *Strandell* persuasive on this point.

The *Strandell* court also expressed concern that summary jury trials would undermine traditional discovery and privilege rules by requiring certain disclosures prior to an actual trial. We find this concern unwarranted. Because a summary jury trial (like a non-binding mediation) does not require any disclosures beyond what would be required in the ordinary course of discovery, its principal disadvantage to the litigants is that it may prevent them from saving surprises for the time of trial. Since trial by ambush is no longer in vogue, that interest does not deserve protection.

Relying on policy arguments, the Sixth Circuit also has found that district courts do not possess inherent power to compel participation in summary jury trials. See In re NLO, Inc., 5 F.3d 154, 157–58 (6th Cir.1993). The court thought the value of a summary jury trial questionable when parties do not engage in the process voluntarily, and it worried that "too broad an interpretation of the federal courts' inherent power to regulate their procedure . . . encourages judicial high-handedness. . . . "

The concerns articulated by these two respected courts plainly apply to mandatory mediation orders. When mediation is forced upon unwilling litigants, it stands to reason that the likelihood of settlement is diminished. Requiring parties to invest substantial amounts of time and money in mediation under such circumstances may well be inefficient. Cf. Richard A. Posner, The Summary Jury Trial and Other Methods of Alternative Dispute Resolution: Some Cautionary Observations, 53 U. Chi. L.Rev. 366, 369–72 (1986) (offering a model to evaluate ADR techniques in terms of their capacity to encourage settlements).

The fact remains, however, that none of these considerations establishes that mandatory mediation is always inappropriate. There may well be specific cases in which such a protocol is likely to conserve judicial resources without significantly burdening the objectors' rights to a full, fair, and speedy trial. Much depends on the idiosyncracies of the particular case and the details of the mediation order.

In some cases, a court may be warranted in believing that compulsory mediation could yield significant benefits even if one or more parties object. After all, a party may resist mediation simply out of unfamiliarity with the process or out of fear that a willingness to submit would be perceived as a lack of confidence in her legal position. In such an instance, the party's initial reservations are likely to evaporate as the mediation progresses, and negotiations could well produce a beneficial outcome, at reduced cost and greater speed, than would a trial. While the possibility that parties will fail to reach agreement remains ever present, the boon of settlement can be worth the risk.

This is particularly true in complex cases involving multiple claims and parties. The fair and expeditious resolution of such cases often is helped along by creative solutions—solutions that simply are not available in the binary framework of traditional adversarial litigation. Mediation with the assistance of a skilled facilitator gives parties an opportunity to explore a much wider range of options, including those that go beyond conventional zero-sum resolutions. Mindful of these potential advantages, we hold that it is within a district court's inherent power to order non-consensual mediation in those cases in which that step seems reasonably likely to serve the interests of justice.

E. THE MEDIATION ORDER

Our determination that the district courts have inherent power to refer cases to non-binding mediation is made with a recognition that any such order must be crafted in a manner that preserves procedural fairness and shields objecting parties from undue burdens. We thus turn to the specifics of the mediation order entered in this case. As with any exercise of a district court's inherent powers, we review the entry of that order for abuse of discretion.

As an initial matter, we agree with the lower court that the complexity of this case militates in favor of ordering mediation. At last count, the suit involves twelve parties, asserting a welter of claims, counterclaims, cross-claims, and third-party claims predicated on a wide variety of theories. The pendency of nearly parallel litigation in the Puerto Rican courts, which features a slightly different cast of characters and claims that are related to but not completely congruent with those asserted here, further complicates the matter. Untangling the intricate web of relationships among the parties, along with the difficult and fact-intensive arguments made by each, will be time-consuming and will impose significant costs on the parties and the court. Against this backdrop, mediation holds out the dual prospect of advantaging the litigants and conserving scarce judicial resources.

* * *

APC posits that the appointment of a private mediator proposed by one of the parties is per se improper (and, thus, invalidates the order). We do not agree. The district court has inherent power to "appoint persons unconnected with the court to aid judges in the performance of specific judicial duties." In the context of non-binding mediation, the mediator does not decide the merits of the case and has no authority to coerce settlement. Thus, in the absence of a contrary statute or rule, it is perfectly acceptable for the district court to appoint a qualified and neutral private party as a mediator. The mere fact that the mediator was proposed by one of the parties is insufficient to establish bias in favor of that party.

We hasten to add that the litigants are free to challenge the qualifications or neutrality of any suggested mediator (whether or not nominated by a party to the case). APC, for example, had a full opportunity to present its views about the suggested mediator both in its opposition to the motion for mediation and in its motion for reconsideration of the mediation order. Despite these opportunities, APC offered no convincing reason to spark a belief that Professor Green, a nationally recognized mediator with significant experience in sprawling cases, is an unacceptable choice. When a court enters a mediation order, it necessarily makes an independent determination that the mediator it appoints is both qualified and neutral. Because the court made that implicit determination here in a manner that was procedurally fair (if not ideal), we find no abuse of discretion in its selection of Professor Green.[7]

APC also grouses that it should not be forced to share the costs of an unwanted mediation. We have held, however, that courts have the power under Fed.R.Civ.P. 26(f) to issue pretrial cost-sharing orders in complex litigation. See In re San Juan Dupont Plaza Hotel Fire Litig., 994 F.2d 956, 965 (1st Cir.1993). Given the difficulties facing trial courts in cases involving multiple parties and multiple claims, we are hesitant to limit that power to the traditional discovery context. This is especially true in complicated cases, where the potential value of mediation lies not only in promoting settlement but also in clarifying the issues remaining for trial.

The short of the matter is that, without default cost-sharing rules, the use of valuable ADR techniques (like mediation) becomes hostage to the parties' ability to agree on the concomitant financial arrangements. This means that the district court's inherent power to order private mediation in appropriate cases would be rendered nugatory absent the corollary power to order the sharing of reasonable mediation costs. To avoid this pitfall, we hold that the district court, in an appropriate case, is empowered to order the sharing of reasonable costs and expenses associated with mandatory non-binding mediation.

---

7. We say "not ideal" because, in an ideal world, it would be preferable for the district court, before naming a mediator, to solicit the names of potential nominees from all parties and to provide an opportunity for the parties to comment upon each others' proposed nominees.

The remainder of APC's arguments are not so easily dispatched. Even when generically appropriate, a mediation order must contain procedural and substantive safeguards to ensure fairness to all parties involved. The mediation order in this case does not quite meet that test. In particular, the order does not set limits on the duration of the mediation or the expense associated therewith.

We need not wax longiloquent. As entered, the order simply requires the parties to mediate; it does not set forth either a timetable for the mediation or a cap on the fees that the mediator may charge. The figures that have been bandied about in the briefs—$900 per hour or $9,000 per mediation day—are quite large and should not be left to the mediator's whim. Relatedly, because the mediator is to be paid an hourly rate, the court should have set an outside limit on the number of hours to be devoted to mediation. Equally as important, it is trite but often true that justice delayed is justice denied. An unsuccessful mediation will postpone the ultimate resolution of the case—indeed, the district court has stayed all discovery pending the completion of the mediation—and, thus, prolong the litigation. For these reasons, the district court should have set a definite time frame for the mediation.

The respondents suggest that the district court did not need to articulate any limitations in its mediation order because the mediation process will remain under the district court's ultimate supervision; the court retains the ability to curtail any excessive expenditures of time or money; and a dissatisfied party can easily return to the court at any time. While this might be enough of a safeguard in many instances, the instant litigation is sufficiently complicated and the mediation efforts are likely to be sufficiently expensive that, here, reasonable time limits and fee constraints, set in advance, are appropriate.

A court intent on ordering non-consensual mediation should take other precautions as well. For example, the court should make it clear (as did the able district court in this case) that participation in mediation will not be taken as a waiver of any litigation position. The important point is that the protections we have mentioned are not intended to comprise an exhaustive list, but, rather, to illustrate that when a district court orders a party to participate in mediation, it should take care to assuage legitimate concerns about the possible negative consequences of such an order.

To recapitulate, we rule that a mandatory mediation order issued under the district court's inherent power is valid in an appropriate case. We also rule that this is an appropriate case. We hold, however, that the district court's failure to set reasonable limits on the duration of the mediation and on the mediator's fees dooms the decree.

Notes and Questions

1.   The Seventh Circuit in Strandell v. Jackson County, 838 F.2d 884 (7th Cir. 1987), held that a district judge does not possess inherent power to compel participation in a summary jury trial. The plaintiff's attorney object-

ed that he would have to disclose work-product statements he had obtained from twenty-one witnesses which had been denied to defendants for failure to establish substantial need and undue hardship (see Rule 26(b)(3)). The court said mandatory participation in a summary jury trial would "affect seriously the well-established rules concerning discovery and work-product privilege." Is there a difference between being forced to participate in a mediation and a summary jury trial? Could the court in *Atlantic Pipe* have simply distinguished *Strandell* on the ground that a summary jury trial is a more formal proceeding than a mediation, requiring more formal presentation of evidence? *Atlantic Pipe* did not make this distinction, instead rejecting the *Strandell* rationale by saying that the only disadvantage of having to participate in an ADR proceeding is to be prevented "from saving surprises for the time of trial," which is not a legitimate interest.

Consider the following argument that plaintiff's being forced to reveal work product is not sufficiently prejudicial to warrant refusal to participate in a summary jury trial: "[In *Strandell*] the plaintiff's attorney was not required to put on any specific evidence in the summary jury trial. Given due regard for litigant autonomy, he would certainly have been entitled, for example, to hold back the work-product evidence for sole use at trial. Of course, that could mean that he would not do as well with the summary jury as he hoped he would do at trial. But that is a strategic choice he had to make—either hold back his work-product and possibly weaken his case in the summary jury trial, or risk all on the trial. Since the summary jury trial is nonbinding, all he risked was an adverse summary jury trial verdict that might conceivably weaken his bargaining position for settlement before trial." Sherman, Court–Mandated Alternative Dispute Resolution: What Form of Participation Should Be Required?, 46 S.M.U.L.Rev. 2079, 2101–02 (1993).

2.   The Sixth Circuit followed *Strandell* in In re NLO, Inc., 5 F.3d 154 (6th Cir.1993), holding that courts may not compel participation in a summary jury trial (id. at 158):

> Requiring participation in a pre-trial conference, even if settlement is explored, is permitted under Rule 16(a), and justifiably so, for it may facilitate settlement at very little expense to the parties and the court. A jury trial, even one of a summary nature, however, requires at minimum the time consuming process of assembling a panel and (one would hope) thorough preparation for argument by counsel, no matter how brief the actual proceeding. Compelling an unwilling litigant to undergo this process improperly interposes the tribunal into the normal adversarial course of litigation.

In Montgomery v. Louis Trauth Dairy, Inc., 164 F.R.D. 469 (S.D.Ohio 1996), the court held that the 1993 amendments to Rule 16 had effectively overruled In re NLO. Stressing that the district had a local rule authorizing mandatory summary jury trials, the judge refused the defendant's motion to be excused from participating in one. The court noted that Rule 16(c)(9) now says the court may "take appropriate action" with respect to "the use of special procedures to assist in resolving the dispute when authorized by statute or local rule." The Committee Note accompanying these changes referred to summary jury trials and also explained that the revisions would "clarify the court's power to enter appropriate orders at a conference notwithstanding the objection of a party."

3. *Atlantic Pipe* imposes due process restrictions on court-ordered mediation, and presumably other ADR procedures. Judges around the country have been routinely referring cases to mediation without concerning themselves with such matters as how long a mediation can last or how much the mediator's fee will be. Is a fee of $900 an hour or $9,000 per mediation day too high for due process? What other details of the mediation could offend due process?

4. In re African–American Slave Descendants' Litigation, 272 F.Supp.2d 755 (N.D. Ill. 2003), like *Atlantic Pipe*, involved a mediation order where there was no express local rule authorizing mandatory (as opposed to voluntary) mediation. The court found inherent powers lacking because, as set out in *Atlantic Pipe*, "the use of inherent powers must comport with procedural fairness," and mediation here would not "facilitate an expeditious end to the litigation" and mediation forced upon unwilling litigants diminishes the possibility of settlement and causes needless expense and time. Does this add additional fairness grounds to those set out in *Atlantic Pipe* for not permitting mandatory mediation?

5. Court orders often provide that the parties will attend the mediation and "participate in good faith." The vagueness of that standard, its possible intrusion on the right of parties not to settle, and difficulty in applying sanctions to enforce it have been considerably discussed. Compare Sherman, Court–Mandated Alternative Dispute Resolution: What Form of Participation Should be Required?, 46 SMU L. Rev. 2079, 2089–94 (1993) (proposing a "minimal meaningful participation" standard rather than "good faith") and Kovach, Lawyer Ethics in Mediation: Time for a Requirement of Good Faith, 4 Dispute Res. 9 (1997) (arguing that a good faith standard is necessary to accomplish the objectives of mediation). See also Lande, Using Dispute System Design Methods to Promote Good–Faith Participation in Court–Connected Mediation Programs, 50 UCLA L. Rev. 69 (2002).

D. INCENTIVES TO SETTLE THROUGH SHIFTING OF ATTORNEY'S FEES AND COSTS

MAREK v. CHESNY

Supreme Court of the United States, 1985.
473 U.S. 1, 105 S.Ct. 3012, 87 L.Ed.2d 1.

CHIEF JUSTICE BURGER delivered the opinion of the Court.

We granted certiorari to decide whether attorney's fees incurred by a plaintiff subsequent to an offer of settlement under Federal Rule of Civil Procedure 68 must be paid by the defendant under 42 U.S.C. § 1988, when the plaintiff recovers a judgment less than the offer.

I

Petitioners, three police officers, in answering a call on a domestic disturbance, shot and killed respondent's adult son. Respondent, in his own behalf and as administrator of his son's estate, filed suit against the officers in the United States District Court under 42 U.S.C. § 1983 and state tort law.

Prior to trial, petitioners made a timely offer of settlement "for a sum, including costs now accrued and attorney's fees, of ONE HUN-DRED THOUSAND ($100,000) DOLLARS." Respondent did not accept the offer. The case went to trial and respondent was awarded $5,000 on the state-law "wrongful death" claim, $52,000 for the § 1983 violation, and $3,000 in punitive damages.

Respondent filed a request for $171,692.47 in costs, including attorney's fees. This amount included costs incurred after the settlement offer. Petitioners opposed the claim for post-offer costs, relying on Federal Rule of Civil Procedure 68, which shifts to the plaintiff all "costs" incurred subsequent to an offer of judgment not exceeded by the ultimate recovery at trial. Petitioners argued that attorney's fees are part of the "costs" covered by Rule 68. The District Court agreed with petitioners and declined to award respondent "costs, including attorney's fees, incurred after the offer of judgment." The parties subsequently agreed that $32,000 fairly represented the allowable costs, including attorney's fees, accrued prior to petitioner's offer of settlement.[1] Respondent appealed the denial of post-offer costs.

The Court of Appeals reversed. The court rejected what it termed the "rather mechanical linking up of Rule 68 and section 1988." It stated that the District Court's reading of Rule 68 and § 1988, while "in a sense logical," would put civil rights plaintiffs and counsel in a "predicament" that "cuts against the grain of section 1988." Plaintiffs' attorneys, the court reasoned, would be forced to "think very hard" before rejecting even an inadequate offer, and would be deterred from bringing good faith actions because of the prospect of losing the right to attorney's fees if a settlement offer more favorable than the ultimate recovery were rejected. The court concluded that "[t]he legislators who enacted section 1988 would not have wanted its effectiveness blunted because of a little known rule of court."

We granted certiorari. We reverse.

II

Rule 68 provides that if a timely pretrial offer of settlement is not accepted and "the judgment finally obtained by the offeree is not more favorable than the offer, the offeree must pay *the costs incurred after the making of the offer*." Fed.Rule Civ.Proc. 68 (emphasis added). The plain purpose of Rule 68 is to encourage settlement and avoid litigation. Delta Air Lines, Inc. v. August, 450 U.S. 346, 352, 101 S.Ct. 1146, 1150, 67 L.Ed.2d 287 (1981). The Rule prompts both parties to a suit to evaluate the risks and costs of litigation, and to balance them against the

---

1. The District Court refused to shift to respondent any costs accrued by petitioners. Petitioners do not contest that ruling.

likelihood of success upon trial on the merits. This case requires us to decide whether the offer in this case was a proper one under Rule 68, and whether the term "costs" as used in Rule 68 includes attorney's fees awardable under 42 U.S.C. § 1988.

A

The first question we address is whether petitioners' offer was valid under Rule 68. Respondent contends that the offer was invalid because it lumped petitioners' proposal for damages with their proposal for costs. Respondent argues that Rule 68 requires that an offer must separately recite the amount that the defendant is offering in settlement of the substantive claim and the amount he is offering to cover accrued costs. Only if the offer is bifurcated, he contends, so that it is clear how much the defendant is offering for the substantive claim, can a plaintiff possibly assess whether it would be wise to accept the offer. * * *

If defendants are not allowed to make lump sum offers that would, if accepted, represent their total liability, they would understandably be reluctant to make settlement offers. As the Court of Appeals observed, "many a defendant would be unwilling to make a binding settlement offer on terms that left it exposed to liability for attorney's fees in whatever amount the court might fix on motion of the plaintiff."

Contrary to respondent's suggestion, reading the Rule in this way does not frustrate plaintiffs' efforts to determine whether defendants' offers are adequate. At the time an offer is made, the plaintiff knows the amount in damages caused by the challenged conduct. The plaintiff also knows, or can ascertain, the costs then accrued. A reasonable determination whether to accept the offer can be made by simply adding these two figures and comparing the sum to the amount offered. Respondent is troubled that a plaintiff will not know whether the offer on the substantive claim would be exceeded at trial, but this is so whenever an offer of settlement is made. In any event, requiring itemization of damages separate from costs would not in any way help plaintiffs know in advance whether the judgment at trial will exceed a defendant's offer.

* * *

B

The second question we address is whether the term "costs" in Rule 68 includes attorney's fees awardable under 42 U.S.C. § 1988. By the time the Federal Rules of Civil Procedure were adopted in 1938, federal statutes had authorized and defined awards of costs to prevailing parties for more than 85 years. See generally Alyeska Pipeline Service Co. v. Wilderness Society, 421 U.S. 240, 95 S.Ct. 1612, 44 L.Ed.2d 141 (1975). Unlike in England, such "costs" generally had not included attorney's fees; under the "American Rule," each party had been required to bear its own attorney's fees. The "American Rule" as applied in federal courts, however, had become subject to certain exceptions by the late 1930's. Some of these exceptions had evolved as a product of the "inherent power in the courts to allow attorney's fees in particular situations." But most of the exceptions were found in federal statutes that directed courts to award attorney's fees as part of costs in particular cases.

Section 407 of the Communications Act of 1934, for example, provided in relevant part that, "[i]f the petitioner shall finally prevail, he shall be allowed a reasonable attorney's fee, to be taxed and collected as a part of the costs of the suit." 47 U.S.C. § 407. There was identical language in Section 3(p) of the Railway Labor Act, 45 U.S.C. § 153(p) (1934 ed.). Section 40 of the Copyright Act of 1909, 17 U.S.C. § 40 (1934 ed.), allowed a court to "award to the prevailing party a reasonable attorney's fee as part of the costs." And other statutes contained similar provisions that included attorney's fees as part of awardable "costs." See, e.g., the Clayton Act, 15 U.S.C. § 15 (1934 ed.); the Securities Act of 1933, 15 U.S.C. § 77k(e) (1934 ed.); the Securities Exchange Act of 1934, 15 U.S.C. §§ 78i(e), 78r(a) (1934 ed.).

The authors of Federal Rule of Civil Procedure 68 were fully aware of these exceptions to the American Rule. The Advisory Committee's Note to Rule 54(d) contains an extensive list of the federal statutes which allowed for costs in particular cases; of the 25 "statutes as to costs" set forth in the final paragraph of the Note, no fewer than 11 allowed for attorney's fees as part of costs. Against this background of varying definitions of "costs," the drafters of Rule 68 did not define the term; nor is there any explanation whatever as to its intended meaning in the history of the Rule.

In this setting, given the importance of "costs" to the Rule, it is very unlikely that this omission was mere oversight; on the contrary, the most reasonable inference is that the term "costs" in Rule 68 was intended to refer to all costs properly awardable under the relevant substantive statute or other authority. In other words, all costs properly awardable in an action are to be considered within the scope of Rule 68 "costs." Thus, absent Congressional expressions to the contrary, where the underlying statute defines "costs" to include attorney's fees, we are satisfied such fees are to be included as costs for purposes of Rule 68.

Here, respondents sued under 42 U.S.C. § 1983. Pursuant to the Civil Rights Attorney's Fees Awards Act of 1976, 42 U.S.C. § 1988, a prevailing party in a § 1983 action may be awarded attorney's fees "as part of the costs." Since Congress expressly included attorney's fees as "costs" available to a plaintiff in a § 1983 suit, such fees are subject to the cost-shifting provision of Rule 68. This "plain meaning" interpretation of the interplay between Rule 68 and § 1988 is the only construction that gives meaning to each word in both Rule 68 and § 1988.[2]

---

2. Respondents suggest that *Roadway Express, Inc. v. Piper*, 447 U.S. 752, 100 S.Ct. 2455, 65 L.Ed.2d 488 (1980), requires a different result. *Roadway Express*, however, is not relevant to our decision today. In *Roadway*, attorney's fees were sought as part of costs under 28 U.S.C. § 1927, which allows the imposition of costs as a penalty on attorneys for vexatiously multiplying litigation. We held in *Roadway Express* that

Unlike the Court of Appeals, we do not believe that this "plain meaning" construction of the statute and the Rule will frustrate Congress' objective in § 1988 of ensuring that civil rights plaintiffs obtain "effective access to the judicial process." Merely subjecting civil rights plaintiffs to the settlement provision of Rule 68 does not curtail their access to the courts, or significantly deter them from bringing suit. Application of Rule 68 will serve as a disincentive for the plaintiff's attorney to continue litigation after the defendant makes a settlement offer. There is no evidence, however, that Congress, in considering § 1988, had any thought that civil rights claims were to be on any different footing from other civil claims insofar as settlement is concerned. Indeed, Congress made clear its concern that civil rights plaintiffs not be penalized for "helping to lessen docket congestion" by settling their cases out of court. See H.R.Rep.No. 94–1588, p. 7 (1976).

Moreover, Rule 68's policy of encouraging settlements is neutral, favoring neither plaintiffs nor defendants; it expresses a clear policy of favoring settlement of all lawsuits. Civil rights plaintiffs—along with other plaintiffs—who reject an offer more favorable than what is thereafter recovered at trial will not recover attorney's fees for services performed after the offer is rejected. But, since the Rule is neutral, many civil rights plaintiffs will benefit from the offers of settlement encouraged by Rule 68. Some plaintiffs will receive compensation in settlement where, on trial, they might not have recovered, or would have recovered less than what was offered. And, even for those who would prevail at trial, settlement will provide them with compensation at an earlier date without the burdens, stress, and time of litigation. In short, settlements rather than litigation will serve the interests of plaintiffs as well as defendants.

To be sure, application of Rule 68 will require plaintiffs to "think very hard" about whether continued litigation is worthwhile; that is precisely what Rule 68 contemplates. This effect of Rule 68, however, is in no sense inconsistent with the congressional policies underlying § 1983 and § 1988. Section 1988 authorizes courts to award only "reasonable" attorney's fees to prevailing parties. In Hensley v. Eckerhart, 461 U.S. 424, 103 S.Ct. 1933, 76 L.Ed.2d 40 (1983), we held that "the most critical factor" in determining a reasonable fee "is the degree of success obtained." We specifically noted that prevailing at trial "may say little about whether the expenditure of counsel's time was reasonable in relation to the success achieved." In a case where a rejected settlement offer exceeds the ultimate recovery, the plaintiff—although technically the prevailing party—has not received any monetary benefits from the post-offer services of his attorney. This case presents a good example: the $139,692 in post-offer legal services resulted in a recovery $8,000 less than petitioner's settlement offer. Given Congress' focus on the success

§ 1927 came with its own statutory definition of costs, and that this definition did not include attorney's fees. The critical distinction here is that Rule 68 does not come with a definition of costs; rather, it incorporates the definition of costs that otherwise applies to the case.

achieved, we are not persuaded that shifting the post-offer costs to respondent in these circumstances would in any sense thwart its intent under § 1988.

Rather than "cutting against the grain" of § 1988, as the Court of Appeals held, we are convinced that applying Rule 68 in the context of a § 1983 action is consistent with the policies and objectives of § 1988. Section 1988 encourages plaintiffs to bring meritorious civil rights suits; Rule 68 simply encourages settlements. There is nothing incompatible in these two objectives.

[Concurring opinions of JUSTICES POWELL and REHNQUIST omitted.]

JUSTICE BRENNAN, with whom JUSTICE MARSHALL and JUSTICE BLACKMUN join, dissenting.

The question presented by this case is whether the term "costs" as it is used in Rule 68 of the Federal Rules of Civil Procedure and elsewhere throughout the Rules refers simply to those taxable costs defined in 28 U.S.C. § 1920 and traditionally understood as "costs"— court's fees, printing expenses, and the like—or instead includes attorney's fees when an underlying fees-award statute happens to refer to fees "as part of" the awardable costs. Relying on what it recurrently emphasizes is the "plain language" of one such statute, 42 U.S.C. § 1988,[3] the Court today holds that a prevailing civil-rights litigant entitled to fees under that statute is per se barred by Rule 68 from recovering any fees for work performed after rejecting a settlement offer where he ultimately recovers less than the proffered amount in settlement.

I dissent. The Court's reasoning is wholly inconsistent with the history and structure of the Federal Rules, and its application to the over 100 attorney's fees statutes enacted by Congress will produce absurd variations in Rule 68's operation based on nothing more than picayune differences in statutory phraseology. Neither Congress nor the drafters of the Rules could possibly have intended such inexplicable variations in settlement incentives. Moreover, the Court's interpretation will "seriously undermine the purposes behind the attorney's fees provisions" of the civil-rights laws, Delta Air Lines, Inc. v. August, 450 U.S. 346, 378, 101 S.Ct. 1146, 1163, 67 L.Ed.2d 287 (1981) (REHNQUIST, J., dissenting)— provisions imposed by Congress pursuant to § 5 of the Fourteenth Amendment. * * *

I

The Court's "plain language" analysis goes as follows: Section 1988 provides that a "prevailing party" may recover "a reasonable attorney's

---

3. Civil Rights Attorney's Fees Awards Act of 1976, 42 U.S.C. § 1988. That section provides in relevant part that "[i]n any action or proceeding to enforce a provision of sections 1981, 1982, 1983, 1985, and 1986 of this title, title IX of Public Law 92– 318, or title VI of the Civil Rights Act of 1964, the court, in its discretion, may allow the prevailing party, other than the United States, a reasonable attorney's fee as part of the costs."

fee as part of the costs." Rule 68 in turn provides that, where an offeree obtains a judgment for less than the amount of a previous settlement offer, "the offeree must pay the costs incurred after the making of the offer." Because "attorney's fees" are "costs," the Court concludes, the "plain meaning" of Rule 68 per se prohibits a prevailing civil-rights plaintiff from recovering fees incurred after he rejected the proposed out-of-court settlement.

The Court's "plain language" approach is, as Judge Posner's opinion for the court below noted, "in a sense logical." However, while the starting point in interpreting statutes and rules is always the plain words themselves, "[t]he particular inquiry is not what is the abstract force of the words or what they may comprehend, but in what sense were they intended to be understood or what understanding they convey when used in the particular act." [2A C. Sands, Sutherland on Statutory Construction § 46.07, p. 110.] We previously have been confronted with "superficially appealing argument[s]" strikingly similar to those adopted by the Court today, and we have found that they "cannot survive careful consideration." Roadway Express, Inc. v. Piper, 447 U.S. 752, 758, 100 S.Ct. 2455, 2460, 65 L.Ed.2d 488 (1980). So here.

In *Roadway Express*, the petitioner argued that under 28 U.S.C. § 1927,[6] "costs" should be interpreted to include attorney's fees when the underlying fees-award statute provided for fees "as part of the costs." We rejected that argument, concluding that "costs" as it was used in § 1927 had a well-settled meaning limited to the traditional taxable items of costs set forth in 28 U.S.C. § 1920. * * *

The Court today restricts its discussion of *Roadway* to a single footnote, urging that that case "is not relevant to our decision" because "section 1927 came with its own statutory definition of costs" whereas "Rule 68 does not come with a definition of costs." But this purported "distinction" merely begs the question. As in *Roadway,* the question we face is whether a cost-shifting provision "come[s] with a definition of costs"—that set forth in § 1920 in an effort "to standardize the treatment of costs in federal courts"—or instead may vary wildly in meaning depending on the phraseology of the underlying fees-award statute. The parties' arguments in this case and in *Roadway* are virtually interchangeable, and our analysis is not much advanced simply by the conclusory statement that the cases are different.

For a number of reasons, "costs" as that term is used in the Federal Rules should be interpreted uniformly in accordance with the definition of costs set forth in § 1920:

First. The limited history of the costs provisions in the Federal Rules suggests that the drafters intended "costs" to mean only taxable

---

6. That section provided that any attorney "who so multiplies the proceedings in any case as to increase costs unreasonably and vexatiously may be required by the court to satisfy personally such excess costs." The section was amended after *Roadway Express* to require the payment of "excess costs, expenses, and attorneys' fees reasonably incurred because of such conduct."

costs traditionally allowed under the common law or pursuant to the statutory predecessor of § 1920. Nowhere was it suggested that the meaning of taxable "costs" might vary from case to case depending on the language of the substantive statute involved—a practice that would have cut against the drafters' intent to create uniform procedures applicable to "every action" in federal court. Fed.Rule Civ.Proc. 1.

Second. The Rules provide that "costs" may automatically be taxed by the clerk of the court on one day's notice, Fed.Rule Civ.Proc. 54(d)— strongly suggesting that "costs" were intended to refer only to those routine, readily determinable charges that could appropriately be left to a clerk, and as to which a single day's notice of settlement would be appropriate. Attorney's fees, which are awardable only by the court and which frequently entail lengthy disputes and hearings, obviously do not fall within that category.

Third. When particular provisions of the Federal Rules are intended to encompass attorney's fees, they do so explicitly. Eleven different provisions of the Rules authorize a court to award attorney's fees as "expenses" in particular circumstances, demonstrating that the drafters knew the difference, and intended a difference, between "costs," "expenses," and "attorney's fees."

Fourth. With the exception of one recent Court of Appeals opinion and two recent District Court opinions, the Court can point to no authority suggesting that courts or attorneys have ever viewed the cost-shifting provisions of Rule 68 as including attorney's fees. Yet Rule 68 has been in effect for 47 years, and potentially could have been applied to numerous fee statutes during this time. "The fact that the defense bar did not develop a practice of seeking" to shift or reduce fees under Rule 68 "is persuasive evidence that trial lawyers have interpreted the Rule in accordance with" the definition of costs in § 1920. Delta Air Lines, Inc. v. August, 450 U.S., at 360, 101 S.Ct., at 1154.

Fifth. We previously have held that words and phrases in the Federal Rules must be given a consistent usage and be read *in pari materia,* reasoning that to do otherwise would "attribute a schizophrenic intent to the drafters." Applying the Court's "plain language" approach consistently throughout the Rules, however, would produce absurd results that would turn statutes like § 1988 on their heads. * * * For example, Rule 54(d) provides that "costs shall be allowed as of course to the prevailing party unless the court otherwise directs." Similarly, the plain language of Rule 68 provides that a plaintiff covered by the Rule "must pay the costs incurred after the making of the offer"—language requiring the plaintiff to bear both his post-offer costs and the defendant's post-offer costs. If "costs" as used in these provisions were interpreted to include attorney's fees by virtue of the wording of § 1988, losing civil-rights plaintiffs would be required by the "plain language" of Rule 54(d) to pay the defendant's attorney's fees, and prevailing plaintiffs falling within Rule 68 would be required to bear the defendant's post-offer attorney's fees.

* * * If the word "costs" does subsume attorney's fees, this "would alter fundamentally the nature of" civil-rights attorney's fee legislation. Roadway Express, Inc. v. Piper, 447 U.S., at 762, 100 S.Ct., at 2462. To avoid this extreme result while still interpreting Rule 68 to include fees in some circumstances, however, the Court would have to "select on an ad hoc basis those features of § 1988 . . . that should be read into" Rule 68—a process of construction that would constitute nothing short of "standardless judicial lawmaking."[16]

Sixth. As with all of the Federal Rules, the drafters intended Rule 68 to have a uniform, consistent application in all proceedings in federal court. In accordance with this intent, Rule 68 should be interpreted to provide uniform, consistent incentives "to encourage the settlement of litigation." Delta Air Lines, Inc. v. August, supra, 450 U.S., at 352, 101 S.Ct., at 1150. Yet today's decision will lead to dramatically different settlement incentives depending on minor variations in the phraseology of the underlying fees-award statutes—distinctions that would appear to be nothing short of irrational and for which the Court has no plausible explanation.

Congress has enacted well over 100 attorney's fees statutes, many of which would appear to be affected by today's decision. As the Appendix to this dissent [listing these statutes] illustrates, Congress has employed a variety of slightly different wordings in these statutes. It sometimes has referred to the awarding of "attorney's fees as part of the costs," to "costs including attorney's fees," and to "attorney's fees and other litigation costs." Under the "plain language" approach of today's decision, Rule 68 will operate to include the potential loss of otherwise-recoverable attorney's fees as an incentive to settlement in litigation under these statutes. But Congress frequently has referred in other statutes to the awarding of "costs and a reasonable attorney's fee," of "costs together with a reasonable attorney's fee," or simply of "attorney's fees" without reference to costs. Under the Court's "plain language" analysis, Rule 68 obviously will not include the potential loss of otherwise-recoverable attorney's fees as a settlement incentive in litigation under these statutes because they do not refer to fees "as" costs.

The result is to sanction a senseless patchwork of fee-shifting that flies in the face of the fundamental purpose of the Federal Rules—the provision of uniform and consistent procedure in federal courts. Such a construction will "introduce into [Rule 68] distinctions unrelated to its goal . . . and [will] result in virtually random application of the Rule."

16. It also might be argued that a defendant may not recover post-offer attorney's fees under the "plain language" of Rule 68 because he is not the "prevailing party" within the meaning of § 1988. We have made clear, however, that a party may "prevail" under § 1988 on some elements of the litigation but not on others. Thus while the plaintiff would prevail for purposes of preoffer fees, the defendant could be viewed as the prevailing party for purposes of the postoffer fees. Shifting fees to the defendant in such circumstances would plainly violate § 1988 for the reasons set forth above in text, and the substantive standards of § 1988 must therefore override the otherwise "plain language" approach taken by the Court.

Roadway Express, Inc. v. Piper, supra, 447 U.S., at 761–762, 100 S.Ct., at 2461–2462. * * *

Although the Court's opinion fails to discuss any of the problems reviewed above, it does devote some space to arguing that its interpretation of Rule 68 "is in no sense inconsistent with the Congressional policies underlying § 1983 and § 1988." The Court goes so far as to assert that its interpretation fits in smoothly with § 1988 as interpreted by Hensley v. Eckerhart, 461 U.S. 424, 103 S.Ct. 1933, 76 L.Ed.2d 40 (1983).

The Court is wrong. Congress has instructed that attorney's fee entitlement under § 1988 be governed by a reasonableness standard. Until today the Court always has recognized that this standard precludes reliance on any mechanical "bright-line" rules automatically denying a portion of fees, acknowledging that such "mathematical approach[es]" provide "little aid in determining what is a reasonable fee in light of all the relevant factors." Although the starting point is always "the number of hours reasonably expended on the litigation," this "does not end the inquiry": a number of considerations set forth in the legislative history of § 1988 "may lead the district court to adjust the fee upward or downward." We also have emphasized that the district court "necessarily has discretion in making this equitable judgment" because of its "superior understanding of the litigation." Section 1988's reasonableness standard is, in sum, "acutely sensitive to the merits of an action and to antidiscrimination policy." Roadway Express, Inc. v. Piper, 447 U.S., at 762, 100 S.Ct., at 2462.

Rule 68, on the other hand, is not "sensitive" at all to the merits of an action and to antidiscrimination policy. It is a mechanical *per se* provision automatically shifting "costs" incurred after an offer is rejected, and it deprives a district court of all discretion with respect to the matter by using "the strongest verb of its type known to the English language—'must.'" Delta Air Lines, Inc. v. August, 450 U.S., at 369, 101 S.Ct., at 1158. The potential for conflict between § 1988 and Rule 68 could not be more apparent.[40]

Of course, a civil-rights plaintiff who unreasonably fails to accept a settlement offer, and who thereafter recovers less than the proffered amount in settlement, is barred under § 1988 itself from recovering fees for unproductive work performed in the wake of the rejection. This is because "the extent of a plaintiff's success is a crucial factor in determining the proper amount of an award of attorney's fees," hours that are "excessive, redundant, or otherwise unnecessary" must be excluded from that calculus. To this extent, the results might sometimes be the same under either § 1988's reasonableness inquiry or the Court's wooden application of Rule 68. Had the Court allowed the Seventh Circuit's

---

40. It might be argued that Rule 68's offer-of-judgment provisions merely serve to define one aspect of "reasonableness" within the meaning of Hensley v. Eckerhart, supra. This argument is foreclosed by Congress' rejection of *per se* "mathematical approach[es]" that would "end the inquiry" without allowing consideration of "all the relevant factors."

remand in the instant case to stand, for example, the District Court after conducting the appropriate inquiry might well have determined that much or even all of the respondent's post offer fees were not properly awardable.

But the results under § 1988 and Rule 68 will not always be congruent, because § 1988 mandates the careful consideration of a broad range of other factors and accords appropriate leeway to the district court's informed discretion. Contrary to the Court's protestations, it is not at all clear that "[t]his case presents a good example" of the smooth interplay of § 1988 and Rule 68, because there has never been an evidentiary consideration of the reasonableness or unreasonableness of the respondent's fee request. It is clear, however, that under the Court's interpretation of Rule 68 a plaintiff who ultimately recovers only slightly less than the proffered amount in settlement will *per se* be barred from recovering trial fees even if he otherwise "has obtained excellent results" in litigation that will have far-reaching benefit to the public interest. Today's decision necessarily will require the disallowance of some fees that otherwise would have passed muster under § 1988's reasonableness standard,[41] and there is nothing in § 1988's legislative history even vaguely suggesting that Congress intended such a result.

The Court argues, however, that its interpretation of Rule 68 "is neutral, favoring neither plaintiffs nor defendants." This contention is also plainly wrong. As the Judicial Conference Advisory Committee on the Federal Rules of Civil Procedure has noted twice in recent years, Rule 68 "is a 'one-way street,' available only to those defending against claims and not to claimants." Interpreting Rule 68 in its current version to include attorney's fees will lead to a number of skewed settlement incentives that squarely conflict with Congress' intent. To discuss but one example, Rule 68 allows an offer to be made any time after the complaint is filed and gives the plaintiff only 10 days to accept or reject. The Court's decision inevitably will encourage defendants who know they have violated the law to make "low-ball" offers immediately after suit is filed and before plaintiffs have been able to obtain the information they are entitled to by way of discovery to assess the strength of their claims and the reasonableness of the offers. The result will put severe pressure on plaintiffs to settle on the basis of inadequate information in order to avoid the risk of bearing all of their fees even if reasonable discovery might reveal that the defendants were subject to far greater liability. Indeed, because Rule 68 offers may be made recurrently without limitation, defendants will be well advised to make ever-slightly larger offers throughout the discovery process and before plaintiffs have conducted all reasonably necessary discovery.

* * *

---

41. Indeed, the "plain language" of § 1988 authorizes the inclusion as "costs" only of those attorney's fees that have been determined to be "reasonable," so the cost-shifting provisions of Rule 68 necessarily will come into play only with respect to reasonable attorney's fees.

Other difficulties will follow from the Court's decision. For example, if a plaintiff recovers less money than was offered before trial but obtains potentially far-reaching injunctive or declaratory relief, it is altogether unclear how the Court intends judges to go about quantifying the "value" of the plaintiff's success.[48] * * * These are difficult policy questions, and I do not mean to suggest that stronger settlement incentives would necessarily conflict with the effective enforcement of the civil-rights laws. But contrary to the Court's 4–paragraph discussion, the policy considerations do not all point in one direction, and the question of whether and to what extent attorney's fees should be included within Rule 68 has provoked sharp debate in Congress, on the Advisory Committee on the Federal Rules, and among commentators. The Court has offered up some interesting arguments based on an economic analysis of settlement incentives and aggregate results. But I believe Judge Posner had the better of this argument in concluding that the incentives created by interpreting Rule 68 in its current form to include attorney's fees would "cu[t] against the grain of section 1988," and that in any event a modification of Rule 68 to encompass fees is for Congress, not the courts.

Notes and Questions

1. *Marek* should be read against the backdrop of the American rule that the prevailing party is not entitled to recover attorneys' fees from the loser, as we have seen in Chapter II, supra p. 98. That rule is reflected in Rule 54(d), which provides that only costs as described in 28 U.S.C.A. § 1920 (which does not include attorneys' fees) are ordinarily recoverable by the prevailing party.

2. What is the effect of the American rule on settlement of cases? Does it cause parties who are confident of success nevertheless to settle for a reduced amount to avoid incurring further litigation costs? If so, is that a good thing? In England, where bilateral fee shifting is routine, it is not designed to offer full indemnity. Instead, "policymakers were concerned that giving full control over the accumulation of costs to the successful party would produce unfair and excessive fees. Requiring the loser to pay the full amount of fees might encourage the winner to prolong the litigation; on the other hand, requiring the winner to absorb a portion of the fees might encourage settlement or, at least, serve as a brake against dilatory tactics,

---

48. For example, a plaintiff who is unable to prove actual damages at trial and recovers only nominal damages of $1, but who nevertheless demonstrates the unconstitutionality of the challenged practice and obtains an injunction, is surely a "prevailing party" within the meaning of § 1988. If the plaintiff had earlier rejected an offer of $500 to "get rid" of the controversy, the damages portion of his suit will fall within Rule 68 as interpreted by today's decision. Yet we previously have emphasized that "a plaintiff who failed to recover damages but obtained injunctive relief, or vice versa, may recover a fee award based on all hours reasonably expended if the relief obtained justified that expenditure of attorney time." Hensley v. Eckerhart, supra, 461 U.S., at 435–436, n.11, 103 S.Ct., at 1940, n.11. Although courts must therefore evaluate the "value" of nonpecuniary relief before deciding whether the "judgment" was "more favorable than the offer" within the meaning of Rule 68, the uncertainty in making such assessments surely will add pressures on a plaintiff to settle his suit even if by doing so he abandons an opportunity to obtain potentially far-reaching nonmonetary relief—a discouraging incentive entirely at odds with Congress' intent.

harassment, or other abusive litigation practices." Tomkins & Willging, Taxation of Attorneys' Fees: Practices in English, Alaskan and Federal Courts 7–8 (1986).

3. Fee-shifting statutes like 42 U.S.C.A. § 1988 alter the American rule by providing that the prevailing party can recover attorneys' fees. Section 1988 has been interpreted to direct a pro-plaintiff attitude toward fee-shifting, making recovery of fees by plaintiffs routine, but allowing defendants to recover fees only if plaintiff sues without valid grounds or frivolously. See supra p. 103 n. 2. Other fee-shifting statutes have been read to be bilateral and permit winning plaintiffs and defendants equal opportunities to recover fees. See Fogerty v. Fantasy, Inc., 510 U.S. 517, 114 S.Ct. 1023, 127 L.Ed.2d 455 (1994) (refusing to find a pro-plaintiff bias in the fee-shifting provisions of the Copyright Act, 17 U.S.C.A. § 505).

4. In Alyeska Pipeline Serv. Co. v. Wilderness Society, 421 U.S. 240, 95 S.Ct. 1612, 44 L.Ed.2d 141 (1975), the Court held that Congress has not "extended any roving authority to the Judiciary to allow counsel fees as costs or otherwise whenever the courts might deem them warranted." The Court did acknowledge that there was authority to award fees to defendants where plaintiff has acted in bad faith in bringing the suit because that was a well established common law exception to the general rule against recovery of fees. Under *Alyeska,* implementing fee shifting by rule, which Marek v. Chesny seems to treat Rule 68 as doing, is arguably beyond the proper authority of the Judiciary. See Burbank, Proposals to Amend Rule 68—Time to Abandon Ship, 19 U. Mich. J.Law Ref. 425 (1986). We will address this issue again in connection with the problems of the scope of the federal rules considered in Chapter XI.

5. What happens when there is a verdict for the defendant? In Delta Air Lines, Inc. v. August, 450 U.S. 346, 351, 101 S.Ct. 1146, 67 L.Ed.2d 287 (1981), the Court held that "the plain language of Rule 68 confines its effects to * * * [cases] in which the plaintiff has obtained a judgment" which is not more favorable than the offer of judgment. Thus, Rule 68 is not applicable if the judgment is for the defendant. "There is irony in this interpretation of Rule 68: a plaintiff who suffers a defendant's judgment at trial might end up better off under the attorney's fee shifting provision than if there had been a plaintiff's verdict that was less favorable than the offer that the plaintiff turned down. The virtue of this literal interpretation of the rule, however, is to prevent defendants from making token, rather than serious, offers for small amounts (say $1) in order to invoke cost shifting in every case that results in a defendant's verdict. For this reason, proposals to change Rule 68 generally have chosen to leave the *Delta* interpretation intact." Sherman, From "Loser Pays" to Modified Offer of Judgment Rules, 76 Texas L. Rev. 1863, 1881 (1998). Note that a plaintiff who obtains a verdict on liability, but receives no damages, may still have to pay Rule 68 costs. See Tunison v. Continental Airlines Corp., 162 F.3d 1187 (D.C.Cir.1998) (although no damages were awarded, plaintiff was required to pay defendant's post-offer costs because plaintiff refused a Rule 68 offer and obtained a verdict).

6. In *Marek,* Justice Brennan relies heavily on Roadway Express, Inc. v. Piper, 447 U.S. 752, 100 S.Ct. 2455, 65 L.Ed.2d 488 (1980), which held that the word "costs" in 28 U.S.C.A. § 1927 (which authorized imposition of

"costs" on attorneys whose tactics unduly prolong or complicate litigation) did not include attorney's fees. The majority says that this case is distinguishable because § 1927 "came with its own statutory definition of costs." But in *Roadway Express,* Justice Powell, writing for the Court, said that "[s]ection 1927 * * * does not define the critical word. Only if 'costs' includes attorneys fees can § 1927 support the sanction in this case." Since costs were not understood to include fees in 1813, when the original version of § 1927 was enacted, the Court held that fees were not included in the term.

7. Should Rule 68 be interpreted to allow losing defendants in civil rights cases to recover their own attorney's fees if they made Rule 68 offers more favorable than the judgment won by the plaintiff? How would you argue against that result? See Crossman v. Marcoccio, 806 F.2d 329 (1st Cir.1986), cert. denied, 481 U.S. 1029, 107 S.Ct. 1955, 95 L.Ed.2d 527 (1987) (defendant's fees not shifted because they were not "properly awardable").

8. *Marek* was viewed by the plaintiff's bar, and particularly the pro bono and civil rights bar, as a backdoor way to deny prevailing plaintiffs their attorney's fees. Consider this strategic use of Rule 68 by defendants: "A defendant can put the plaintiff's recovery of his attorney's fees in jeopardy by making a lump sum offer and specifying that this sum is intended to include costs. The dilemma of a plaintiff's lawyer in such a situation can be intense: Any statutory attorney's fees the plaintiff might recover can be a negotiable item on the table, and his client, who has no liability for those statutory fee amounts if not awarded, has discretion to accept or reject the settlement offer." Sherman, supra note 5, 76 Texas L. Rev. at 1878–79. Evans v. Jeff D., 475 U.S. 717, 106 S.Ct. 1531, 89 L.Ed.2d 747 (1986), intensified this dilemma. There the defendant offered to settle only if the plaintiff's lawyer waived his statutory fees altogether, but offered terms very favorable to the client. The Supreme Court held that a settlement offer may link the relief on the merits to a waiver of statutory attorneys' fees, confirming "the possibility of a tradeoff between merits relief and attorney's fees." Id. at 733. Do these decisions improperly discourage access to the courts?

9. Rule 68 applies only if the judgment eventually obtained by plaintiff is "not more favorable" than the offer. If plaintiff seeks money, as in *Marek,* the comparison is relatively simple. But real difficulties can emerge in cases seeking equitable relief. Consider Spencer v. General Electric Company, 894 F.2d 651 (4th Cir.1990), an employment discrimination action in which plaintiff sued her employer after her supervisor harassed her at the workplace and pursued her outside the workplace, eventually raping her. Before trial, GE made a Rule 68 offer of $10,000 in damages, some job-related relief for plaintiff, and an injunction prohibiting GE from violating Title VII, but plaintiff rejected the offer. At trial, the court held that GE was not responsible for the actions of the supervisor off the premises, but found that it had violated Title VII by allowing a hostile environment in the workplace. Since plaintiff had not proven any losses resulting from that environment, however, the court awarded only one dollar in nominal damages. Moreover, because GE had voluntarily implemented an anti-harassment policy, the court denied injunctive relief.

Plaintiff sought $380,000 in attorneys' fees, but the district court allowed only $60,000 for pre-offer fees because the judgment that plaintiff obtained was less favorable than what GE had offered. On appeal, plaintiff argued that GE's adoption of the anti-harassment policy was prompted by her suit. Under established law, such actions in response to a suit may be considered in deciding whether a plaintiff is a "prevailing party" entitled to a fee award. Acknowledging this fact, the appellate court nevertheless held that Rule 68 precludes consideration of anything but the "judgment finally obtained." Accordingly, by adopting the anti-harassment program before judgment GE may have deprived plaintiff of the opportunity to recover post-offer attorneys' fees. If the district court had mandated the anti-harassment program by injunction, would plaintiff have been entitled to post-offer fees? Compare Leach v. Northern Telecom, Inc., 141 F.R.D. 420, 428 (E.D.N.C. 1991) ("If the monetary relief awarded falls short of that offered, but equitable relief is also awarded, the trial judge can then determine whether the relief awarded, as a package, is more or less favorable than that offered."). See also Note, Federal Rule 68 Offers of Judgment and Equitable Relief: Where Angels Fear To Tread, 70 Texas L.Rev. 465 (1991).

10.   The Civil Rights Act of 1991, Pub.L.No. 102–166, 105 Stat. 1071, "respond[ed] to a number of recent decisions of the United States Supreme Court that had sharply cut back on the scope and effectiveness of ... important [civil rights laws that ban discrimination in employment]." H.R.Rep.No. 102–40(II), at 2. *Marek* was one of those cases. Therefore, a Title VII employment discrimination case, Gudenkauf v. Stauffer Communications, Inc., 158 F.3d 1074 (10th Cir. 1998), held that the plaintiff's failure to do better than a Rule 68 offer of $7,500 would not prevent her from recovering her attorney's fees and costs as prevailing party. It noted that although 42 U.S.C. sec.2000e–2(k) of Title VII was not changed from stating that fees are to be awarded as part of the costs, the 1991 amendment to sec.(g)(2)(B), which provides that a court may award attorney's fees and costs, was intended to overrule *Marek*. "*Marek*," the House report said, "is particularly problematic in the context of Title VII, because it may impede private actions, which Congress has relied upon for enforcement of the statute's guarantees and advancement of the public's interest." Employment cases brought under the Fair Labor Standards Act (FLSA) and Age Discrimination in Employment Act (ADEA) have also been held not to be governed by *Marek* as to recovery of attorney's fees and costs despite a plaintiff's failure to do better than a Rule 68 offer. Dalal v. Alliant Techsystems, Inc., 182 F.3d 757 (10th Cir. 1999) (ADEA); Mogilevsky v. Bally Total Fitness Corp., 311 F.Supp.2d 212 (D. Mass. 2004) (FLSA).

11.   Courts have refused to extend *Marek* to settlement offers made outside of the context of Rule 68. Martino v. Massachusetts Bay Transportation Authority, 230 F.Supp.2d 195 (D.Mass. 2002) (failure of jury verdict of $50,000 to do better than $75,000 offer made orally in mediation would not prevent plaintiff from recovering attorney's fees and costs).

12.   Rule 68 only allows defendants to make offers to plaintiffs. Should plaintiffs get an equivalent opportunity to apply settlement pressure to defendants by making offers of judgment to them? Compare Cal.Code Civ.Proc. § 998 (allowing any party to make such an offer to any other party). Throughout the first half of the 1980s, there were proposals to

change Rule 68, generally designed to make it bilateral (i.e., to allow plaintiffs to make such offers as well), to provide explicitly for fee shifting in some situations, and to limit shifting to cases in which a party unreasonably rejected a Rule 68 offer. For an examination of the reform movement, see Simon, The Riddle of Rule 68, 54 Geo.Wash.L.Rev. 1 (1985). Further proposals for reform have been made. See Schwarzer, Fee–Shifting Offers of Judgment—An Approach to Reducing the Cost of Litigation, 76 Judicature 147 (1992); Rowe & Vidmar, Empirical Research on Offers of Settlement: A Preliminary Report, 51 Law & Contemp. Probs 13 (1988).

13. The House of Representatives passed a modified offer of judgment rule in 1995 that allowed either party to make an offer and, if refused and the ultimate judgment were not more favorable than the offer, the offeree would have to pay the offeror's costs, including attorney's fees. This led the American Bar Association to convene a task force to study the issue in light of expressed concerns that the bill would disproportionately impact plaintiffs who would be deterred from seeking access to the courts by the risk of having to pay the defendants' attorneys' fees. The task force concluded that allowing attorneys' fees to be shifted under an offer of judgment rule could promote settlement, but that safeguards were needed to mitigate the disproportionate adverse effect upon plaintiffs. It proposed a rule that included a fee shifting formula that gave an offeree a margin of error of 25% before cost shifting was triggered by not doing as well as the ultimate judgment obtained; limiting liability for the offeror's attorney's fees to an amount equal to the offeree's attorney's fees; and giving the court discretion to reduce or eliminate cost shifting to avoid undue hardship. Neither the House bill nor the ABA proposal became law. See Sherman, supra, 76 Tex.L.Rev. at 1185–1891.

14. An expanded "offer of judgment" rule has been part of the "tort reform" proposals urged by business interests in many states. The most sweeping was passed and signed into law in Texas, effective on January 1, 2004. It allows claimants or defendants to make offers and provides for the shifting of litigation expenses, including attorney's fees, fees of two testifying expert witnesses, and post-rejection litigation costs when the judgment is less favorable to the offeree by at least 20%. The Texas Supreme Court adopted rules implementing the procedure. 3 McDonald & Carlson, Texas Civil Practice, §§ 17.32–17.36 (2004). The approach in *Marek* is followed: "A party against whom litigation costs are awarded may not recover attorney fees and costs under another law incurred after the date the party rejected the settlement offer made the basis of the award." Tex.R.Civ.P. 167.4(f).

Chapter VIII

TRIAL

Cases that cannot be decided on the basis of pretrial submissions must go to trial unless settled. A thousand years ago, a trial had few of the aspects of modern trials. Indeed, the orientation of trial methods was anti-rational because people believed that they were not competent to decide questions of guilt or innocence. Thus, at least in criminal matters, trial might be by ordeal on the theory that the outcome would be determined by God. The Norman Conquest introduced trial by jury to England, but that also differed greatly from the current jury trial. The original version depended on a jury composed of people who already had information about the matter in dispute. Rather than receiving information about the dispute, the jurors were expected to investigate as necessary to acquire any further information they needed to resolve the controversy. See Marcus, The Tudor Treason Trials: Some Reflections on the Emergence of Forensic Themes, 1984 U.Ill.L.Rev. 675, 681–82. Gradually this model evolved into our current jury trial.

We have already discussed the pretrial conference, an event of increasing importance in organizing trials, in Chapter VII (supra pp. 466–70). In this chapter we examine the current handling of trials by first canvassing the phases of a jury trial. We then turn to the rules governing whether the right to jury trial exists under the Seventh Amendment, and the interaction of that right with the various devices by which the judge can control the jury's verdict.

A. THE PHASES OF A TRIAL

Modern jury trials are, in a sense, largely theatrical events. Mastering the techniques of this type of theater is the work of a lifetime. In law school, it is the work of courses on trial practice. Moreover, the legal rules that apply to in-court activities are assigned principally to the course on evidence, and beyond the scope of this book. This section briefly canvasses the phases of a trial to acquaint you with them in a general way. We will examine some of these topics more carefully later in the chapter.

1. Jury Selection

In jury trials, the first thing that must be done is to select a jury. This process involves questioning jurors about their possible biases or acquaintance with the parties or issues involved in the suit. Unlike the early English jury, the contemporary American jury should consist of persons entirely ignorant of the dispute. Juror selection can be extremely important, as the composition of the jury is thought by many to have a substantial effect on the outcome of the suit. For an examination of the process, see Jury Selection, infra p. 603.

2. Opening Statements

Because the jurors know nothing about the case, the lawyers get a chance to tell them something about it before the presentation of evidence begins. The presentation of the evidence is sometimes disjointed and difficult to follow because witnesses may be called in the order that is convenient for them, and they can only testify about events they know personally. Thus the jury might not appreciate the relation between a witness's story and the overall case unless it had been given some sort of roadmap to the whole case. The function of the opening statement is to provide that roadmap, but what the lawyers tell the jury is not itself evidence.

3. Presentation of Evidence

Needless to say, the presentation of evidence is the heart of a trial, and provides the focus of most of the forensic talents of the lawyers.

(a) *Sequence:* Because the jury is thought to be most attentive at the beginning of the trial, the question of sequence of presentation becomes important. The usual formulation is that the party with the burden of proof on an issue goes first (with the "case-in-chief"). When that is completed, the other side gets to present opposing evidence, to which the party with the burden of proof may respond with rebuttal evidence, which the other side may then rebut, until there is no further evidence to be presented. Customarily, this means that the plaintiff goes first with its case-in-chief on the claims against defendant. The defendant then responds with opposing evidence and, if there is a counterclaim, its case-in-chief on the counterclaim. Each successive round after that should be limited to material responsive to that presented by the opponent in its preceding opportunity to offer evidence.

(b) *Manner of presentation:* Our system relies on the witnesses—not the lawyers—to tell the jury what they know. Among other things, a "foundation" can be provided for documentary or other tangible evidence by testimony from a witness identifying an object. For an example, see Guenther v. Armstrong Rubber Co., infra p. 635, in which the dispute concerns testimony about whether a certain tire was the tire that exploded and injured the plaintiff.

There are several reasons for this method. For one thing, witnesses don't know what is relevant, and they need some direction from the lawyers. Moreover, some of the information that witnesses possess may be inadmissible. Using a question-and-answer format permits the opposing party to object to the question before the witness answers, thus keeping the information from the jury if the objection is sustained. Because the lawyer may exert too much influence over the witness, we generally insist that lawyers questioning witnesses who are not antagonistic to the lawyer's position use "non-leading" questions. See Fed. R.Evid. 611(c). A leading question is a question that suggests the answer the lawyer desires. Ordinarily these rules are relaxed to speed the testimony.

(c) *Exclusion of evidence:* The law of evidence allows litigants to prevent their opponents from presenting certain things to the jury. In general, the Federal Rules of Evidence incline toward allowing the jury to hear all relevant evidence unless its probative value is substantially outweighed by other factors. Detailed study of these rules must await a course on evidence, but general reference to some of them should be helpful by way of orientation.

Relevance and countervailing prejudice: We have already seen that Fed.R.Evid. 401 makes relevant any evidence that has *some* tendency to make a fact of consequence more or less likely. See supra p. 361 n.2. More refined analysis permits some evaluation of the probative value of relevant pieces of evidence. Under Fed.R.Evid. 403, relevant evidence may be excluded "if its probative value is substantially outweighed by the danger of unfair prejudice, confusion of the issues, or misleading the jury, or by considerations of undue delay, waste of time, or needless presentation of cumulative evidence." While courts are not quick to use this power, it permits particularized recalibration of the wide-open relevance standards of Rule 401. In some cases, it is used simply to speed up the trial by curtailing unnecessary proof.

More significantly, Rule 403 gives courts a tool to prevent the jury from learning about something that is relevant for one reason but which invites the jury to decide the case on a ground not authorized by law. The usual reason a party offers evidence is to prejudice the position of its opponent, so that is hardly a reason to exclude the evidence. When the main impact of the evidence is to invite a decision on a ground not authorized by law, however, the risk of distorting the outcome justifies exclusion of the evidence. For example, in a personal injury case a verdict for plaintiff was overturned. The appellate court noted that the case for liability was thin, but did not fault the trial court for allowing plaintiff to put on evidence regarding damages, including psychiatric testimony that persons with depression as severe as plaintiff's may commit suicide when confronted with other adversity. But the court found "much too inflammatory" plaintiff's further effort "to forge a direct link between a substantial award to him in this case and his continued life. The jury was clearly told that the plaintiff would commit suicide if their verdict was not a generous award to him." Gibson v.

Caterpillar Tractor Co., 20 Fed. R. Evid. Serv. 144 (4th Cir.1986). Was this relevant? Was the appellate court right in forbidding it?

More specifically, Rule 404 forbids "character" evidence offered to prove that on a certain occasion a person acted in conformity with his or her character. This provision emphasizes our belief that liability, civil or criminal, should depend on what a person did on a certain occasion, not an assessment of whether he is a "good" or "bad" person. This rule becomes particularly important in criminal cases, where the defendant's past convictions are usually excluded in order to avoid the risk that the jury would convict in order to get this "bad person" off the streets. But where a party testifies, evidence relevant to his character for truthfulness may be explored, and prior convictions (or other misconduct) are more readily admitted. See Fed.R.Evid. 608; 609.

Competence: Only persons who can perceive events and relate what they saw under oath are permitted to testify. Fed.R.Evid. 601; 603. Beyond that, Rule 602 permits a witness to testify only about matters within his personal knowledge.

Hearsay: Probably the best known evidence rule, the rule against hearsay is an important way of ensuring that the witness has personal knowledge, rather than simply repeating what somebody else said. It forbids a witness from proving something by means of an out-of-court assertion that it is true. See Fed.R.Evid. 801(c). In difficult cases, the application of this concept is extremely challenging. But even hearsay evidence is often admissible under one or more exceptions to the ban on hearsay. See Fed. R. Evid. 801(d); 803; 804.

Privileges: In Chapter V we examined some issues of privilege. In addition to the attorney-client privilege, the common law has recognized privileges for communications between a doctor and patient, priest and parishioner, husband and wife, and some others in confidential relationships. Unlike other rules of evidence, the ban on evidence of such communications is unrelated to its probative value. Instead, courts are forbidden to intrude into these relationships for policy reasons deemed to outweigh the value of such evidence to accurate decisions at trial.

Need to Object: The above rules are not self-executing, and a judge will rarely prevent a party from introducing improper evidence unless the other side objects. In the tumult of trial, lawyers often overlook grounds for objection, and even where they recognize that the evidence being offered is improper, lawyers may choose not to object for strategic reasons. As you should appreciate, effective use of the rules of evidence takes years to master.

When a party objects, the court must rule on the objection. If the objection is sustained, the witness is told not to answer the question. If the objection is overruled, the evidence is admitted. The objecting party may then argue on appeal or in support of a motion for a new trial that the objection should have been sustained. To succeed on that argument, however, the objecting party must be reasonably specific about the grounds for objection. For example, Perry Mason's perennial objection—

"irrelevant, incompetent and immaterial"—covers almost the entire gamut of evidence law and would likely be held to be too general to require a judge to survey all possible grounds for objection and determine whether any is applicable (a point seemingly always missed by Mason's perennial opponent, Hamilton Burger).

(d) *Motion for judgment as a matter of law:* At the close of the evidence, any party may move for judgment as a matter of law, formerly called a directed verdict. To prevail on such a motion, the party must show that the opposing party has failed to satisfy its burden of production, and that judgment should therefore be entered in the moving party's favor. The defendant may make this motion at the close of the plaintiff's case-in-chief without prejudice to the right to offer evidence if the motion is denied. If the motion is granted, the court need not submit the matter to the jury. See Fed.R.Civ.P. 50(a).

4. Argument

Once all the evidence is in and the parties have rested their cases, the lawyers are allowed to argue the case to the jury. Ordinarily the plaintiff gets to argue first, then the defendant responds, and the plaintiff gets the closing chance to address the jury.

The argument allows the lawyers to weave together all the evidence in the manner most favorable to their clients and to urge the jury to accept their view of the facts. They may also relate the evidence to the legal issues the judge will cover in the instructions. In doing so, they are accorded wide latitude in suggesting inferences that can be drawn from the evidence. There are, however, some limits beyond which they should not go. First, they are limited to "fair comment" on the evidence. Broad though this is, it excludes open invitations to decide the case on an improper ground. At some point, for instance, the lawyer for a local plaintiff will be reprimanded for suggesting to the jury that it decide for the plaintiff because the defendant is from another state. Second, the lawyer may not in argument try to offer new evidence to the jury; counsel must argue on the basis of the evidence actually received, rather than presenting additional information. Third, counsel are not to insinuate their personal beliefs into the case. Thus, defendant's lawyer may not assure the jury that "I wouldn't be here before you today if I didn't know in my heart that defendant has not wronged plaintiff."

5. Instructions

After the lawyers finish their closing arguments, the judge instructs the jury on the legal rules that govern the case. This activity gives the judge the "last word," and is the means by which the judge sets the scene for the jury to apply the law to the facts it finds. The respective roles of judge and jury are outlined in the following introductory instruction designed for the commencement of trial:

After the evidence has been heard and arguments and instructions are finished, you will meet to make your decision. You will determine the facts from all the testimony that you hear and the other evidence that is presented. You are the sole and exclusive judges of the facts. I must stress that you are required to accept the rules of law that I give you, whether you agree with them or not.

The law permits me to comment on the evidence in the case during the trial or while instructing the jury. Such comments are only expressions of my opinion as to the facts. You may disregard these comments entirely, because you are to determine for yourself the weight of the evidence and the credibility of each of the witnesses.

3 K. O'Malley, J. Grenig & W. Lee, Federal Jury Practice and Instructions § 101.10 (5th ed. 2000); see Thornburg, The Power and the Process: Instructions and the Civil Jury, 66 Fordham L. Rev. 1837 (1998).

Once the evidence is in, the judge is to be more specific about the way the jury should approach the evidence. As noted above, in federal court the judge may "comment" on the evidence by expressing an opinion about which party's evidence seemed forceful, truthful, etc. This practice rejects the view of some states that such comments invade the province of the jury. See Evans v. Wright, 505 F.2d 287, 289 (4th Cir.1974) ("a United States district judge is not a bump on a log"). But the jury remains the prime arbiter of factual issues, as revealed in the following instruction on the jury's role in evaluating the evidence. Keep these rules in mind as you examine the standards for taking the case from the jury:

As the sole judges of the facts, you must determine which of the witnesses you believe, what portion of their testimony you accept and what weight you attach to it. At times during the trial I sustained objections to questions asked without permitting the witness to answer or, where an answer has been made, instructed that it be stricken from the record and that you disregard it and dismiss it from your minds. You may not draw any inference from an unanswered question nor may you consider testimony which has been stricken in reaching your decision. The law requires that your decision be made solely upon the competent evidence before you. Such items as I exclude from your consideration were excluded because they are not legally admissible.

The law does not, however, require you to accept all of the evidence I admitted, even though it be competent. In determining what evidence you will accept you might make your own evaluation of the testimony given by each of the witnesses, and determine the degree of weight you choose to give to his testimony. The testimony of a witness may fail to conform to the facts as they occurred because he is intentionally telling a falsehood, because he did not accurately see or hear that about which he testifies, because his recollection of the event is faulty, or because he has not expressed himself clearly in giving his testimony. There is no magical formula by which one may evaluate testimony. You bring with you to this courtroom all of the experience and background of your lives. In your everyday affairs you determine for yourselves the reliability or unreliability of statements made to you by others. The same tests that you use in your everyday dealings are the tests which you apply in your deliberations. The interest or lack of interest of any witness in the outcome of this case, the bias or prejudice of a witness, if there be any, the age, the appearance, the manner in which the witness gives his testimony on the stand, the opportunity that the witness had to observe the facts concerning which he testifies, the probability or improbability of the witness' testimony when viewed in the light of all of the other evidence in the case, are all items to be taken into your consideration in determining the weight, if any, you will assign to that witness' testimony. If such considerations make it appear that there is a discrepancy in the evidence, you will have to consider whether the apparent discrepancy may not be reconciled by fitting the two stories together. If, however, that is not possible, you will then have to determine which of the conflicting versions you will accept.

2 E. Devitt & C. Blackmar, Federal Jury Practice and Instructions § 72.01 (3d ed. 1977).

In addition, the judge instructs the jury on the substantive rules that apply to the case. For example, the following is an instruction on the burden of persuasion. Recall the introduction to this subject in Chapter VI, supra p. 425:

Plaintiff _____ has the burden in a civil action, such as this, to prove every essential element of [plaintiff's] claim by a preponderance of the evidence. If plaintiff _____ should fail to establish any essential element of [plaintiff's] claim by a preponderance of the evidence, you should find for the defendant as to that claim.

"Establish by a preponderance of the evidence" means to prove that something is more likely so than not so. In other words, a preponderance of the evidence in the case means such evidence as, when considered and compared with the evidence opposed to it, has more convincing force, and produces in your minds belief that what is sought to be proved is more likely true than not true. This standard does not require proof to an absolute certainty, since proof to an absolute certainty is seldom possible in any case.

In determining whether any fact in issue has been proved by a preponderance of the evidence in the case, the jury may, unless otherwise instructed, consider the testimony of all witnesses, regardless of who may have called them, and all exhibits received in evidence, regardless of who may have produced them.

3 K.O'Malley, J. Grenig & W. Lee, supra, § 104.01. Further instructions would spell out the elements of plaintiff's case, and of any affirmative defenses, on which defendant would of course have the burden.

6. Jury Deliberation and Verdict

The judge's instructions will conclude with directions to the jury to retire to a jury room and deliberate. Ordinarily the first order of business for the jury is to select a foreperson who will chair the further deliberations. Then the jury is to deliberate. The following instruction summarizes the way in which the jurors are supposed to approach the deliberation process:

> It is your duty, as jurors, to consult with one another and to deliberate with a view to reaching an agreement, if you can do so without disregard of individual judgment. You must each decide the case for yourself, but only after an impartial consideration of the evidence in the case with your fellow jurors. In the course of your deliberations, do not hesitate to reexamine your own views, and change your opinion, if convinced it is erroneous. But do not surrender your honest conviction as to the weight or effect of evidence, solely because of the opinion of your fellow jurors, or for the mere purpose of returning a verdict.

> Remember at all times that you are not partisans. You are judges—judges of the facts. Your sole interest is to seek the truth from the evidence in the case.

3 K. O'Malley, J. Grenig & W. Lee, supra, § 106.01. Keep these guidelines in mind as you examine the materials on juror impeachment of the verdict, infra p. 681.

Once the jury reaches a verdict, it reports its decision on the verdict form it was given during the instructions. We will consider verdict forms in connection with Whitlock v. Jackson, infra p. 671. The judge then calls the parties into the courtroom, where the jury has reassembled, and asks the jurors if the verdict is their verdict. The loser may then have the jury "polled," which means that the judge will ask each juror individually if the verdict was his or her verdict. Unless there is dissent, the verdict will be accepted, and judgment entered thereon. When further consideration of the verdict may be necessary (as in a complicated plaintiff's verdict or where special verdicts are used), the judge may defer entering judgment until a later time.

7. Post–Trial Motions and Judgment

We will consider the standards governing post-trial motions in some detail. See infra pp. 606–71. There are two types of motions. First, there is the renewed motion for a judgment as a matter of law, formerly called judgment N.O.V. (notwithstanding the verdict), by which the dissatisfied litigant asks the court to enter judgment in its favor even though the jury decided the case the other way. As a prerequisite to such relief, in federal court the moving party must have made a motion for judgment as a matter of law at the close of "all the evidence." Fed. R. Civ. P. 50(b). Second, there is the motion for a new trial, in which the loser asks the court to set aside the verdict and order a retrial. See Fed.R.Civ.P. 59. The new trial motion may result in an order known as remittitur or additur, in which the judge orders that a new trial occur unless the other side agrees to a change in the amount of damages. If the verdict-winner accepts, judgment is entered in the amount selected by the judge.

B. SEVENTH AMENDMENT RIGHT TO JURY TRIAL

The Seventh Amendment to the United States Constitution provides:

> In suits at common law, where the value in controversy shall exceed twenty dollars, the right of trial by jury shall be preserved, and no fact tried by a jury, shall be otherwise re-examined in any Court of the United States, than according to the rules of the common law.

The Amendment contains two parts: one describing the circumstances under which a litigant has a right to a jury trial, and the other indicating what controls the court may impose upon a jury in a case in which the right is guaranteed. Thus, the second portion of the Amendment comes into play only after it has initially been determined that a right to a jury trial exists in the first place. Section C of this chapter, dealing with judicial control of the verdict, will examine the scope of the Amendment's second part. This section, on the other hand, focuses exclusively on the initial question of when a right to jury trial itself is guaranteed.

According to one commentator, the Seventh Amendment was added to the Bill of Rights in order to serve as a check on unrepresentative, unaccountable federal judges: "In 1789 there was a shared perception that guaranteeing the right to civil jury trials was important. Without an impartial jury, the individual citizen had no ability to check the power of the sovereign in a civil courtroom. Legislators and presidents are elected. Federal judges serve for life." Klein, The Myth of How to Interpret the Seventh Amendment Right to a Civil Jury Trial, 53 Ohio St. L.J. 1005, 1032 (1992). The same commentator asserts: "The Anti–Federalists distrusted the Federalists' assurance that civil juries were inviolate. The amendment the Anti–Federalists demanded reflected their belief that absent explicit language to the contrary, juries could slowly disappear from the civil courtroom, leaving judges as courtroom kings. The principle captured in the amendment is that this specter of unchecked authority was unacceptable." Id. at 1034. For analysis of the history of the Seventh Amendment's adoption, see Henderson, The Background of the Seventh Amendment, 80 Harv. L. Rev. 289 (1966); Wolfram, The Constitutional History of the Seventh Amendment, 57 Minn. L. Rev. 639 (1973).

By its terms, the Amendment appears to dictate a form of historical inquiry: Use of the word "preserved" has caused the Seventh Amendment to hold a unique position in the realm of constitutional interpretation. For many years following the Amendment's adoption, it was thought that its interpretation was to be governed by an exclusively historical test. See Dimick v. Schiedt, 293 U.S. 474, 476, 55 S.Ct. 296, 296, 79 L.Ed. 603 (1935), infra p. 658: "In order to ascertain the scope and meaning of the Seventh Amendment, resort must be had to the appropriate rules of the common law established at the time of the adoption of that constitutional provision in 1791." It is generally thought that the historical test was intended to look to the 1791 common law practice of England, rather than that of the states. See Wolfram, The Constitutional History of the Seventh Amendment, 57 Minn.L.Rev. 639, 640 (1973). Use of a strict historical test presents obvious problems. It is often difficult to determine what issues were, under the common law of England in 1791, "legal," for which a jury trial could be had, and which were "equitable," for which there was no right to jury trial.

Application of the historical test is further complicated by the merger of law and equity in the federal system. Attempting to determine what the English practice was in 1791 is sufficiently difficult without the additional burden of translating that practice into terms of merged procedures. See generally Redish, Seventh Amendment Right to Jury Trial: A Study in the Irrationality of Rational Decision Making, 70 Nw.U.L.Rev. 486 (1975). The cases in this section concern the Supreme Court's attempt to interpret the historically-oriented Seventh Amendment in light of modern procedural developments.

Before we turn to these problems, however, it is instructive, if only as background, to consider the question whether, wholly apart from its constitutional status, the continued widespread use of the civil jury makes practical sense. In this regard, it is interesting to note that England, the source of our concept of civil jury trial, has largely abandoned the concept.

The arguments against the civil jury can be grouped into three basic categories: delay caused by use of juries; juror incompetence; and juror prejudice. In the words of one commentator, "As a scientific method of settling disputes the general verdict rates a little higher than the ordeal, compurgation or trial by battle." L. Green, Judge and Jury 353 (1930). See also J. Frank, Courts on Trial 179 (1949).

In recent years, particular attention has been paid by both courts and commentators to problems that may arise from the use of juries in cases that are highly complex, either legally or factually. The issue is examined in detail infra at p. 597.

Not all commentators on the civil jury are critical, however. Professor Harry Kalven, for example, asserted that "there is much evidence that most people, once actually serving in a trial, become highly serious and responsible toward their task and toward the joint effort to deliberate through to a verdict." Kalven, The Dignity of the Civil Jury, 50 Va.L.Rev. 1055, 1062 (1964).

The English legal historian William Holdsworth listed what he saw as the basic advantages of the civil jury: (1) the jury can bring "average common sense" to bear upon the facts; (2) the findings of the jury do not result in the creation of binding precedent, thus permitting the jury to decide "hard cases" without making bad law; (3) a jury helps to preserve the dignity of the bench by relieving the judge of the responsibility of decision; (4) the jury members themselves are educated by their exposure to and participation in the administration of justice; and (5) the jury makes the law intelligible by constantly bringing the rules of the law to the touchstone of common sense. 1 W. Holdsworth, A History of English Law 348–50 (6th ed. 1938). According to a jury critic, "the argument for the jury system most frequently advanced * * * [is] that legal rules often work injustice, and that juries, through their general verdicts, wisely nullify those rules." J. Frank, supra at 127. Judge Frank rejected this defense, however, because "[i]t asserts that, desirably, each jury is a twelve-man ephemeral legislature, not elected by the voters, but empowered to destroy what the elected legislators have enacted or authorized." Id. at 129–30.

For additional defenses of the civil jury, see Note, Developments in the Law: The Civil Jury, 110 Harv. L. Rev. 1408 (1997). There it is argued that "the very fact that the civil jury is a democratic institution composed of laypersons fosters a sense of inclusion and participation that reflects and generates popular endorsement of the judicial system. The citizen jury confers legitimacy on judicial actions by identifying the actions of government with those of the people, both actually and vicariously." Id. at 1433. But see Lilly, The Decline of the American Jury, 72 U. Colo. L. Rev. 53 (2001): "[S]ubtle, long-term trends in the nature of litigation and the selection of juries pose serious questions about the potential of American juries to adequately perform their traditional roles."

BEACON THEATRES, INC. v. WESTOVER

Supreme Court of the United States, 1959.
359 U.S. 500, 79 S.Ct. 948, 3 L.Ed.2d 988.

JUSTICE BLACK delivered the opinion of the Court.

Petitioner, Beacon Theatres, Inc., sought by mandamus to require a district judge in the Southern District of California to vacate certain orders alleged to deprive it of a jury trial of issues arising in a suit brought against it by Fox West Coast Theatres, Inc. The Court of Appeals for the Ninth Circuit refused the writ, holding that the trial judge had acted within his proper discretion in denying petitioner's request for a jury. We granted certiorari, because "Maintenance of the jury as a fact-finding body is of such importance and occupies so firm a place in our history and jurisprudence that any seeming curtailment of the right to a jury trial should be scrutinized with the utmost care." Dimick v. Schiedt, 293 U.S. 474, 486, 55 S.Ct. 296, 301, 79 L.Ed. 603.

Fox had asked for declaratory relief against Beacon alleging a controversy arising under the Sherman Antitrust Act, 15 U.S.C. §§ 1, 2, and under the Clayton Act, 15 U.S.C. § 15, which authorizes suits for treble damages against Sherman Act violators. According to the complaint Fox operates a movie theatre in San Bernardino, California, and has long been exhibiting films under contracts with movie distributors. These contracts grant it the exclusive right to show "first run" pictures in the "San Bernardino competitive area" and provide for "clearance"— a period of time during which no other theatre can exhibit the same pictures. After building a drive-in theatre about 11 miles from San Bernardino, Beacon notified Fox that it considered contracts barring simultaneous exhibitions of first-run films in the two theatres to be overt acts in violation of the antitrust laws. Fox's complaint alleged that this notification, together with threats of treble damage suits against Fox and its distributors, gave rise to "duress and coercion" which deprived Fox of a valuable property right, the right to negotiate for exclusive first-run contracts. Unless Beacon was restrained, the complaint continued, irreparable harm would result. Accordingly, while its pleading was styled a "Complaint for Declaratory Relief," Fox prayed both for a declaration that a grant of clearance between the Fox and Beacon theatres is reasonable and not in violation of the antitrust laws, and for an injunction, pending final resolution of the litigation, to prevent Beacon from instituting any action under the antitrust laws against Fox and its distributors arising out of the controversy alleged in the complaint. Beacon filed an answer, a counterclaim against Fox, and a cross-claim against an exhibitor who had intervened. These denied the threats and asserted that there was no substantial competition between the two theatres, that the clearances granted were therefore unreasonable, and that a conspiracy existed between Fox and its distributors to manipulate contracts and clearances so as to restrain trade and monopolize first-run pictures in violation of the antitrust laws. Treble damages were asked.

Beacon demanded a jury trial of the factual issues in the case as provided by Federal Rule of Civil Procedure 38(b). The District Court, however, viewed the issues raised by the "Complaint for Declaratory Relief," including the question of competition between the two theatres, as essentially equitable. Acting under the purported authority of Rules 42(b) and 57, it directed that these issues be tried to the court before jury determination of the validity of the charges of antitrust violations made in the counterclaim and cross-claim. A common issue of the "Complaint for Declaratory Relief," the counterclaim, and the cross-claim was the reasonableness of the clearances granted to Fox, which depended, in part, on the existence of competition between the two theatres. Thus the effect of the action of the District Court could be, as the Court of Appeals believed, "to limit the petitioner's opportunity fully to try to a jury every issue which has a bearing upon its treble damage suit," for determination of the issue of clearances by the judge might "operate either by way of res judicata or collateral estoppel so as to conclude both parties with respect thereto at the subsequent trial of the treble damage claim."

* * *

[I]f Beacon would have been entitled to a jury trial in a treble damage suit against Fox it cannot be deprived of that right merely because Fox took advantage of the availability of declaratory relief to sue Beacon first. Since the right to trial by jury applies to treble damage suits under the antitrust laws, and is, in fact, an essential part of the congressional plan for making competition rather than monopoly the rule of trade, the Sherman and Clayton Act issues on which Fox sought a declaration were essentially jury questions.

Nevertheless the Court of Appeals refused to upset the order of the district judge. It held that the question of whether a right to jury trial existed was to be judged by Fox's complaint read as a whole. In addition to seeking a declaratory judgment, the court said, Fox's complaint can be read as making out a valid plea for injunctive relief, thus stating a claim traditionally cognizable in equity. A party who is entitled to maintain a suit in equity for an injunction, said the court, may have all the issues in his suit determined by the judge without a jury regardless of whether legal rights are involved. The court then rejected the argument that equitable relief, traditionally available only when legal remedies are inadequate, was rendered unnecessary in this case by the filing of the counterclaim and cross-claim which presented all the issues necessary to a determination of the right to injunctive relief. Relying on American Life Ins. Co. v. Stewart, 300 U.S. 203, 215, 57 S.Ct. 377, 380, 81 L.Ed. 605, decided before the enactment of the Federal Rules of Civil Procedure, it invoked the principle that a court sitting in equity could retain jurisdiction even though later a legal remedy became available. In such instances the equity court had discretion to enjoin the later lawsuit in order to allow the whole dispute to be determined in one case in one court. Reasoning by analogy, the Court of Appeals held it was not an abuse of discretion for the district judge, acting under Federal Rule of Civil Procedure 42(b), to try the equitable cause first even though this might, through collateral estoppel, prevent a full jury trial of the counterclaim and cross-claim which were as effectively stopped as by an equity injunction.

Beacon takes issue with the holding of the Court of Appeals that the complaint stated a claim upon which equitable relief could be granted. As initially filed the complaint alleged that threats of lawsuits by petitioner against Fox and its distributors were causing irreparable harm to Fox's business relationships. The prayer for relief, however, made no mention of the threats but asked only that pending litigation of the claim for declaratory judgment, Beacon be enjoined from beginning any lawsuits under the antitrust laws against Fox and its distributors arising out of the controversy alleged in the complaint. Evidently of the opinion that this prayer did not state a good claim for equitable relief, the Court of Appeals construed it to include a request for an injunction against threats of lawsuits. This liberal construction of a pleading is in line with Rule 8 of the Federal Rules of Civil Procedure. See Conley v. Gibson, 355 U.S. 41, 47–48. Assuming that the pleadings can be construed to support such a request and assuming additionally that the complaint can be read as alleging the kind of harassment by a multiplicity of lawsuits which would *traditionally* have justified equity to take jurisdiction and settle the case in one suit, we are nevertheless of the opinion that, under the Declaratory Judgment Act and the Federal Rules of Civil Procedure, neither claim can justify denying Beacon a trial by jury of all the issues in the antitrust controversy.

The basis of injunctive relief in the federal courts has always been irreparable harm and inadequacy of legal remedies. At least as much is required to justify a trial court in using its discretion under the Federal Rules to allow claims of equitable origins to be tried ahead of legal ones, since this has the same effect as an equitable injunction of the legal claims. And it is immaterial, in judging if that discretion is properly employed, that before the Federal Rules and the Declaratory Judgment Act were passed, courts of equity, exercising a jurisdiction separate from courts of law, were, in some cases, allowed to enjoin subsequent legal actions between the same parties involving the same controversy. This was because the subsequent legal action, though providing an opportunity to try the case to a jury, might not protect the right of the equity plaintiff to a fair and orderly adjudication of the controversy. Under such circumstances the legal remedy could quite naturally be deemed inadequate. Inadequacy of remedy and irreparable harm are practical terms, however. As such their existence today must be determined, not by precedents decided under discarded procedures, but in the light of the remedies now made available by the Declaratory Judgment Act and the Federal Rules.

Viewed in this manner, the use of discretion by the trial court under Rule 42(b) to deprive Beacon of a full jury trial on its counterclaim and cross-claim, as well as on Fox's plea for declaratory relief, cannot be justified. Under the Federal Rules the same court may try both legal and equitable causes in the same action. Thus any defenses, equitable or legal, Fox may have to charges of antitrust violations can be raised either in its suit for declaratory relief or in answer to Beacon's counterclaim. On proper showing, harassment by threats of other suits, or other suits actually brought, involving the issues being tried in this case, could be temporarily enjoined pending the outcome of this litigation. Whatever permanent injunctive relief Fox might be entitled to on the basis of the decision in this case could, of course, be given by the court after the jury renders its verdict. In this way the issues between these parties could be settled in one suit giving Beacon a full jury trial of every antitrust issue. By contrast, the holding of the court below while granting Fox no additional protection unless the avoidance of jury trial be considered as such, would compel Beacon to split his antitrust case, trying part to a judge and part to a jury. Such a result, which involves the postponement and subordination of Fox's own legal claim for declaratory relief as well as of the counterclaim which Beacon was compelled by the Federal Rules to bring, is not permissible.

* * * Since in the federal courts equity has always acted only when legal remedies were inadequate, the expansion of adequate legal remedies provided by the Declaratory Judgment Act and the Federal Rules necessarily affects the scope of equity. Thus, the justification for equity's deciding legal issues once it obtains jurisdiction, and refusing to dismiss a case, merely because subsequently a legal remedy becomes available, must be re-evaluated in the light of the liberal joinder provisions of the Federal Rules which allow legal and equitable causes to be brought and resolved in one civil action. Similarly the need for, and therefore, the availability of such equitable remedies as Bills of Peace, Quia Timet and Injunction must be reconsidered in view of the existence of the Declaratory Judgment Act as well as the liberal joinder provision of the Rules. This is not only in accord with the spirit of the Rules and the Act but is required by the provision in the Rules that "[t]he right of trial by jury as declared by the Seventh Amendment to the Constitution or as given by a statute of the United States shall be preserved . . . inviolate."

If there should be cases where the availability of declaratory judgment or joinder in one suit of legal and equitable causes would not in all respects protect the plaintiff seeking equitable relief from irreparable harm while affording a jury trial in the legal cause, the trial court will necessarily have to use its discretion in deciding whether the legal or equitable cause should be tried first. Since the right to jury trial is a constitutional one, however, while no similar requirement protects trials by the court, that discretion is very narrowly limited and must, wherever possible, be exercised to preserve jury trial. As this Court said in Scott v. Neely, 140 U.S. 106, 109–110, 11 S.Ct. 712, 714, 35 L.Ed. 358: "In the Federal courts this [jury] right cannot be dispensed with, except by the assent of the parties entitled to it; nor can it be impaired by any blending with a claim, properly cognizable at law, of a demand for equitable relief in aid of the legal action, or during its pendency." This long-standing principle of equity dictates that only under the most imperative circumstances, circumstances which in view of the flexible procedures of the Federal Rules we cannot now anticipate, can the right to a jury trial of legal issues be lost through prior determination of equitable claims. As we have shown, this is far from being such a case.

* * *

The judgment of the Court of Appeals is reversed.

Justice Frankfurter took no part in the consideration or decision of this case.

Justice Stewart, with whom Justice Harlan and Justice Whittaker concur, dissenting.

There can be no doubt that a litigant is entitled to a writ of mandamus to protect a clear constitutional or statutory right to a jury trial. But there was no denial of such a right here. The district judge simply exercised his inherent discretion, now explicitly confirmed by the Federal Rules of Civil Procedure, to schedule the trial of an equitable claim in advance of an action at law. Even an abuse of such discretion could not, I think, be attacked by the extraordinary writ of mandamus. In any event no abuse of discretion is apparent in this case.

The complaint filed by Fox stated a claim traditionally cognizable in equity. That claim, in brief, was that Beacon had wrongfully interfered with the right of Fox to compete freely with Beacon and other distributors for the licensing of films for first-run exhibition in the San Bernardino area. The complaint alleged that the plaintiff was without an adequate remedy at law and would be irreparably harmed unless the defendant were restrained from continuing to interfere—by coercion and threats of litigation—with the plaintiff's lawful business relationships.

The Court of Appeals found that the complaint, although inartistically drawn, contained allegations entitling the petitioner to equitable relief. That finding is accepted in the prevailing opinion today. If the complaint had been answered simply by a general denial, therefore, the issues would under traditional principles have been triable as a proceeding in equity. Instead of just putting in issue the allegations of the complaint, however, Beacon filed pleadings which affirmatively alleged the existence of a broad conspiracy among the plaintiff and other theatre owners to monopolize the first-run exhibition of films in the San Bernardino area, to refrain from competing among themselves, and to discriminate against Beacon in granting film licenses. Based upon these allegations, Beacon asked damages in the amount of $300,000. Clearly these conspiracy allegations stated a cause of action triable as of right by a jury. What was demanded by Beacon, however, was a jury trial not only of this cause of action, but also of the issues presented by the original complaint.

Upon motion of Fox the trial judge ordered the original action for declaratory and equitable relief to be tried separately to the court and in advance of the trial of the defendant's counterclaim and cross-claim for damages. The court's order, which carefully preserved the right to trial by jury upon the conspiracy and damage issues raised by the counterclaim and cross-claim, was in conformity with the specific provisions of the Federal Rules of Civil Procedure. Yet it is decided today that the Court of Appeals must compel the district judge to rescind it.

Assuming the existence of a factual issue common both to the plaintiff's original action and the defendant's counterclaim for damages, I cannot agree that the District Court must be compelled to try the counterclaim first. It is, of course, a matter of no great moment in what order the issues between the parties in the present litigation are tried. What is disturbing is the process by which the Court arrives at its decision—a process which appears to disregard the historic relationship between equity and law.

I

The Court suggests that "the expansion of adequate legal remedies provided by the Declaratory Judgment Act ... necessarily affects the scope of equity." Does the Court mean to say that the mere availability of an action for a declaratory judgment operates to furnish "an adequate remedy at law" so as to deprive a court of equity of the power to act? That novel line of reasoning is at least implied in the Court's opinion. But the Declaratory Judgment Act did not "expand" the substantive law. That Act merely provided a new statutory remedy, neither legal nor equitable, but available in the areas of both equity and law. When declaratory relief is sought, the right to trial by jury depends upon the basic context in which the issues are presented. If the basic issues in an action for declaratory relief are of a kind traditionally cognizable in equity, e.g., a suit for cancellation of a written instrument, the declaratory judgment is not a "remedy at law." If, on the other hand, the issues arise in a context traditionally cognizable at common law, the right to a jury trial of course remains unimpaired, even though the only relief demanded is a declaratory judgment.

Thus, if in this case the complaint had asked merely for a judgment declaring that the plaintiff's specified manner of business dealings with distributors and other exhibitors did not render it liable to Beacon under the antitrust laws, this would have been simply a "juxtaposition of parties" case in which Beacon could have demanded a jury trial. But the complaint in the present case, as the Court recognizes, presented issues of exclusively equitable cognizance, going well beyond a mere defense to any subsequent action at law. Fox sought from the court protection against Beacon's allegedly unlawful interference with its business relationships—protection which this Court seems to recognize might not have been afforded by a declaratory judgment, unsupplemented by equitable relief. The availability of a declaratory judgment did not, therefore, operate to confer upon Beacon the right to trial by jury with respect to the issues raised by the complaint.

II

The Court's opinion does not, of course, hold or even suggest that a court of equity may never determine "legal rights". For indeed it is precisely such rights which the Chancellor, when his jurisdiction has been properly invoked, has often been called upon to decide. Issues of fact are rarely either "legal" or "equitable." All depends upon the context in which they arise. * * *

Though apparently not disputing these principles, the Court holds, quite apart from its reliance upon the Declaratory Judgment Act, that Beacon by filing its counterclaim and cross-claim acquired a right to trial by jury of issues which otherwise would have been properly triable to the court. Support for this position is found in the principle that, "in the federal courts equity has always acted only when legal remedies were inadequate...." Yet that principle is not employed in its traditional sense as a limitation upon the exercise of power by a court of equity. This is apparent in the Court's recognition that the allegations of the complaint entitled Fox to equitable relief—relief to which Fox would not have been entitled if it had had an adequate remedy at law. Instead, the principle is employed today to mean that because it is possible under the counterclaim to have a jury trial of the factual issue of substantial competition, that issue must be tried by a jury, even though the issue was primarily presented in the original claim for equitable relief. This is a marked departure from long-settled principles.

It has been an established rule "that equitable jurisdiction existing at the filing of a bill is not destroyed because an adequate legal remedy may have become available thereafter." American Life Ins. Co. v. Stewart, 300 U.S. 203, 215, 57 S.Ct. 377, 380, 81 L.Ed. 605. It has also been long settled that the District Court in its discretion may order the trial of a suit in equity in advance of an action at law between the same parties, even if there is a factual issue common to both. In the words of Mr. Justice Cardozo, writing for a unanimous Court in American Life Ins. Co. v. Stewart, supra:

> "A court has control over its own docket.... In the exercise of a sound discretion it may hold one lawsuit in abeyance to abide the outcome of another, especially where the parties and the issues are the same.... If request had been made by the respondents to suspend the suits in equity till the other causes were disposed of, the District Court could have considered whether justice would not be done by pursuing such a course, the remedy in equity being exceptional and the outcome of necessity.... There would be many circumstances to be weighed, as, for instance, the condition of the court calendar, whether the insurer had been precipitate or its adversaries dilatory, as well as other factors. In the end, benefit and hardship would have to be set off, the one against the other, and a balance ascertained." 300 U.S. 203, 215–216, 57 S.Ct. 377, 380.[9]

III

The Court today sweeps away these basic principles as "precedents decided under discarded procedures." It suggests that the Federal Rules of Civil Procedure have somehow worked an "expansion of adequate legal remedies" so as to oust the District Courts of equitable jurisdiction, as well as to deprive them of their traditional power to control their own dockets. But obviously the Federal Rules could not and did not "expand" the substantive law one whit.

Like the Declaratory Judgment Act, the Federal Rules preserve inviolate the right to trial by jury in actions historically cognizable at common law, as under the Constitution they must. They do not create a right of trial by jury where that right "does not exist under the

---

9. It is arguable that if a case factually similar to American Life Ins. Co. v. Stewart were to arise under the Declaratory Judg- ment Act, the defendant would be entitled to a jury trial.

Constitution or statutes of the United States." Rule 39(a). Since Beacon's counterclaim was compulsory under the Rules, see Rule 13(a), it is apparent that by filing it Beacon could not be held to have waived its jury rights.[12] But neither can the counterclaim be held to have transformed Fox's original complaint into an action at law.

The Rules make possible the trial of legal and equitable claims in the same proceeding, but they expressly affirm the power of a trial judge to determine the order in which claims shall be heard. Rule 42(b). Certainly the Federal Rules were not intended to undermine the basic structure of equity jurisprudence, developed over the centuries and explicitly recognized in the United States Constitution.

———

DAIRY QUEEN, INC. v. WOOD, 369 U.S. 469, 82 S.Ct. 894, 8 L.Ed.2d 44 (1962):

JUSTICE BLACK delivered the opinion of the Court.

The United States District Court for the Eastern District of Pennsylvania granted a motion to strike petitioner's demand for a trial by jury in an action now pending before it on the alternative grounds that either the action was "purely equitable" or, if not purely equitable, whatever legal issues that were raised were "incidental" to equitable issues, and, in either case, no right to trial by jury existed.

* * *

At the outset, we may dispose of one of the grounds upon which the trial court acted * * *—that based upon the view that the right to trial by jury may be lost as to legal issues where those issues are characterized as "incidental" to equitable issues—for our previous decisions make it plain that no such rule may be applied in the federal courts. In Scott v. Neely, decided in 1891, this Court held that a court of equity could not even take jurisdiction of a suit "in which a claim properly cognizable only at law is united in the same pleadings with a claim for equitable relief." [140 U.S. 106, 117 (1891).] That holding, which was based upon both the historical separation between law and equity and the duty of the Court to insure "that the right to a trial by a jury in the legal action may be preserved intact," created considerable inconvenience in that it necessitated two separate trials in the same case whenever that case contained both legal and equitable claims. Consequently, when the procedure in the federal courts was modernized by the adoption of the Federal Rules of Civil Procedure in 1938, it was deemed advisable to abandon that part of the holding of Scott v. Neely which rested upon the separation of law and equity and to permit the joinder of legal and equitable claims in a single action. [The Court quoted Rule 18.]

---

12. This is not, of course, to suggest that the filing of a permissive "legal" counterclaim to an "equitable" complaint would amount to a waiver of jury rights on the issues raised by the counterclaim.

The Federal Rules did not, however, purport to change the basic holding of Scott v. Neely that the right to trial by jury of legal claims must be preserved. Quite the contrary, Rule 38(a) expressly reaffirms that constitutional principle. * * * Nonetheless, after the adoption of the Federal Rules, attempts were made indirectly to undercut that right by having federal courts in which cases involving both legal and equitable claims were filed decide the equitable claim first. The result of this procedure in those cases in which it was followed was that any issue common to both the legal and equitable claims was finally determined by the court and the party seeking trial by jury on the legal claim was deprived of that right as to these common issues. This procedure finally came before us in Beacon Theatres, Inc. v. Westover [359 U.S. 500, 79 S.Ct. 948, 3 L.Ed.2d 988 (1959)], a case which, like this one, arose from the denial of a petition for mandamus to compel a district judge to vacate his order striking a demand for trial by jury.

Our decision reversing that case not only emphasizes the responsibility of the Federal Courts of Appeals to grant mandamus where necessary to protect the constitutional right to trial by jury but also limits the issues open for determination here by defining the protection to which that right is entitled in cases involving both legal and equitable claims. The holding in *Beacon Theaters* was that where both legal and equitable issues are presented in a single case, "only under the most imperative circumstances, circumstances which in view of the flexible procedures of the Federal Rules we cannot now anticipate, can the right to a jury trial of legal issues be lost through prior determination of equitable claims." That holding, of course, applies whether the trial judge chooses to characterize the legal issues presented as "incidental" to the equitable issues or not. Consequently, in a case such as this where there cannot even be a contention of such "imperative circumstances," *Beacon Theaters* requires that any legal issues for which a trial by jury is timely and properly demanded be submitted to a jury. There being no question of the timeliness or correctness of the demand involved here, the sole question which we must decide is whether the action now pending before the District Court contains legal issues.

* * *

The District Court proceeding arises out of a controversy between petitioner and the respondent owners of the trademark "DAIRY QUEEN" with regard to a written licensing contract * * * under which petitioners agreed to pay some $150,000 for the exclusive right to use that trademark in certain portions of Pennsylvania. * * * In August 1960, the respondents wrote petitioner a letter in which they claimed that petitioner had committed "a material breach of that contract" by defaulting on the contract's payment provisions and notified petitioner of the termination of the contract and the cancellation of petitioner's right to use the trademark unless this claimed default was remedied immediately. When petitioner continued to deal with the trademark despite the notice of termination, the respondents brought an action based upon their view that a material breach of contract had occurred.

* * * [The complaint prayed for] (1) temporary and permanent injunctions to restrain petitioner from any future use of or dealing in the franchise and the trademark; (2) an accounting to determine the exact amount of money owing by petitioner and a judgment for that amount; and (3) an injunction pending accounting to prevent petitioner from collecting any money from "Dairy Queen" stores in the territory.

* * *

Petitioner's contention * * * is that insofar as the complaint requests a money judgment it presents a claim which is unquestionably legal. We agree with that contention. The most natural construction of the respondents' claim for a money judgment would seem to be that it is a claim that they are entitled to recover whatever was owed them under the contract as of the date of its purported termination plus damages for infringement of their trademark since that date. Alternatively, the complaint could be construed to set forth a full claim based upon both of these theories—that is, a claim that the respondents were entitled to recover both the debt due under the contract and damages for trademark infringement for the entire period of the alleged breach including that before the termination of the contract. Or it might possibly be construed to set forth a claim for recovery based completely on either one of these two theories—that is, a claim based solely upon the contract for the entire period both before and after the attempted termination on the theory that the termination, having been ignored, was of no consequence, or a claim based solely upon the charge of infringement on the theory that the contract, having been breached, could not be used as a defense to an infringement action even for the period prior to its termination. We find it unnecessary to resolve this ambiguity in the respondents' complaint because we think it plain that their claim for a money judgment is a claim wholly legal in its nature however the complaint is construed. As an action on a debt allegedly due under a contract, it would be difficult to conceive of an action of a more traditional legal character. And as an action for damages based upon a change of trademark infringement it would be no less subject to cognizance by a court of law.

The respondents' contention that this money claim is "purely equitable" is based primarily upon the fact that their complaint is cast in terms of an "accounting," rather than in terms of an action for "debt" or "damages." But the constitutional right to trial by jury cannot be made to depend upon the choice of words used in the pleadings. The necessary prerequisite to the right to maintain a suit for an equitable accounting, like all other equitable remedies, is, as we pointed out in *Beacon Theatres,* the absence of an adequate remedy at law. Consequently, in order to maintain such a suit on a cause of action cognizable at law, as this one is, the plaintiff must be able to show that "accounts between the parties" are of such a "complicated nature" that only a court of equity can satisfactorily unravel them. In view of the powers given to District Courts by Federal Rule of Civil Procedure 53(b) to appoint masters to assist the jury in those exceptional cases where the legal issues are too complicated for the jury adequately to handle alone, the burden of such a showing is considerably increased and it will indeed be a rare case in which it can be met. Be that as it may, this is certainly not such a case. A jury, under proper instructions from the court, could readily determine the recovery, if any, to be had here, whether the theory finally settled upon is that of breach of contract, that of trademark infringement, or any combination of the two. The legal remedy cannot be characterized as inadequate merely because the measure of damages may necessitate a look into petitioner's business records.

Nor is the legal claim here rendered "purely equitable" by the nature of the defenses interposed by petitioner. Petitioner's primary defense to the charge of breach of contract—that is, that the contract was modified by a subsequent oral agreement—presents a purely legal question having nothing whatever to do either with novation, as the district judge suggested, or reformation, as suggested by the respondents here. Such a defense goes to the question of just what, under the law, the contract between the respondents and petitioner is and, in an action to collect a debt for breach of a contract between these parties, petitioner has a right to have the jury determine not only whether the contract has been breached and the extent of the damages if any but also just what the contract is.

* * *

We conclude therefore that the district judge erred in refusing to grant petitioner's demand for a trial by jury on the factual issues related to the question of whether there has been a breach of contract. Since these issues are common with those upon which respondents' claim to equitable relief is based, the legal claims involved in the action must be determined prior to any final court determination of respondents' equitable claims. * * *

[Justice Stewart concurred in the result. Justices Frankfurter and White took no part in the consideration or decision of the case. Justice Harlan, joined by Justice Douglas, concurred separately: " * * * [W]hat is involved in this case is nothing more than a joinder in one complaint for prayers for both legal and equitable relief. In such circumstances, under principles long since established, the petitioner cannot be deprived of his constitutional right to a jury trial on the 'legal' claim contained in the complaint."]

Notes and Questions

1. Prior to *Beacon Theatres,* the Supreme Court had explicitly stated that the existence of the Seventh Amendment right to jury trial was to be determined by a historical analysis of common law practice prior to 1791, the year of the Amendment's adoption. See, e.g., Dimick v. Schiedt, 293 U.S. 474, 476, 55 S.Ct. 296, 296, 79 L.Ed. 603 (1935), infra p. 658. Since

historically there existed a right to jury trial in suits at law but not in equity, it was generally assumed that the Amendment's applicability was to be determined by an analysis of whether the case historically would have been deemed "legal" or "equitable". Do the decisions in *Beacon Theatres* and *Dairy Queen* reject this historical mode of inquiry? If not, do they modify it at all? See Redish, Seventh Amendment Right to Jury Trial: A Study in the Irrationality of Rational Decision Making, 70 Nw.U.L.Rev. 486, 496 (1975): "[T]he Court in *Beacon Theatres* appears to find that the Seventh Amendment's purpose was not to freeze the jury trial picture as it existed in 1791, but rather to dictate that in 'legal,' but not 'equitable,' cases there was to be a right to jury trial. Since equity acts only when the remedy at law is inadequate, the Court concluded that today the legal remedy in *Beacon Theatres* is not inadequate and, therefore, despite historical practice, the case is no longer equitable."

It should be noted that any attempt strictly to reproduce today the historical divisions between law and equity as of 1791 is no simple task, in part because "[b]efore the adoption of the [state and federal] constitutions the line between law and equity * * * was not a fixed and static one. There was a continual process of borrowing by one jurisdiction from the other; there were less frequent instances of a sloughing off of older functions * * *." F. James, Civil Procedure 340–41 (1965). See also Shapiro & Coquillette, The Fetish of Jury Trial in Civil Cases: A Comment on Rachal v. Hill, 85 Harv.L.Rev. 442, 449 (1971). On the pre-constitutional practice, see generally Wolfram, The Constitutional History of the Seventh Amendment, 57 Minn.L.Rev. 639 (1973). Recall Equitable Relief, supra p. 84.

2. One commentator has suggested that the decision in *Beacon Theatres* "fits well with the conception of the Constitution as a durable document providing continuingly useful standards for an evolving society." McCoid, Procedural Reform and the Right to Jury Trial: A Study of Beacon Theatres, Inc. v. Westover, 116 U.Pa.L.Rev. 1, 11 (1967). What point is he making?

3. Should either or both parties have a constitutional right to jury trial, where plaintiff sues for breach of contract and seeks both damages (legal relief) and specific performance (equitable relief)? How would a strict historical test (i.e. examination of the English practice in 1791, when law courts and equity courts were separate) apply? How would the approach taken in *Beacon Theatres* apply? Professors Wright and Kane contend that use of a purely historical test in such cases "must fail," because it attempts "to classify a hybrid form of lawsuit that could never have existed in ancient days." C. Wright & M. Kane Law of Federal Courts 660 (6th ed. 2002). Does this fact make it impossible to determine how the issue would have been resolved historically? They add that "[i]f the problem cannot be solved by history, resort must be had to policy, and the relevant policy, expressed in the Seventh Amendment, is favorable to jury trial." Id. Does the Seventh Amendment indicate a "policy" in favor of jury trial, even in a case where historically no such right existed?

4. Note that the suit in *Beacon Theatres* sought treble damages for violation of the federal antitrust laws. Obviously the federal antitrust statutes did not exist at common law prior to 1791. How, under a historical

test, can the Court assume that there exists a right to jury trial in a suit under these laws? We will consider this problem in Curtis v. Loether, infra p. 555.

5. Fox's original complaint in *Beacon Theatres* sought a declaratory judgment. Does the Court hold that declaratory judgment is a legal remedy? If so, why wasn't there a right to jury trial on Fox's suit, even absent the counterclaim? Note that if a declaratory judgment is not obeyed, the prevailing party can obtain an injunction. See 28 U.S.C.A. § 2201. Why wouldn't that remedy be adequate in any suit in which the plaintiff ultimately desired an injunction to compel compliance with the decision on the merits? See F. James, G. Hazard & J. Leubsdorf, Civil Procedure § 8.11 (5th ed. 2001) (reasoning that *Beacon* could support the conclusion that all claims are legal).

6. A considerably narrower interpretation of the Seventh Amendment than that adopted in *Beacon Theatres* and *Dairy Queen* is advocated in Schwartz, "Everything Depends on How You Draw the Lines": An Alternative Interpretation of the Seventh Amendment, 6 Seton Hall Const. L.J. 599 (1996). Schwartz argues that "the Seventh Amendment is not a guarantee of civil jury trial at all. Rather, it is an authorization to Congress to pass laws requiring jury trials in cases in which the legislature sees fit and an assurance that such laws will not violate the Constitution. When the Seventh Amendment dictated that the right to civil jury trial was preserved, it meant that it was not abolished." She relies on the fact that when the Constitution was going through the ratification process the Anti–Federalists argued that the document's silence as to the availability of civil jury rendered the use of juries impermissible. The amendment, she contends, was adopted in response to this concern. In support of this conclusion, Schwartz emphasizes Hamilton's response that the Constitution intended instead to leave the decision concerning the use of civil juries to Congress. Does this point support or undermine her position?

For the most part, the other of the first eight amendments included in the Bill of Rights were inserted not to emphasize congressional power to protect the rights in question but rather to insulate those rights from congressional interference. Should the Seventh Amendment, in contrast, be construed solely as the guarantee of congressional authority? Schwartz argues in support of such a distinction on the grounds that only the Seventh Amendment includes the word, "preserved." To what extent does use of this word support her position?

THE "CLEAN–UP" DOCTRINE

Note that the Court in *Dairy Queen,* in response to the argument "that the right to trial by jury may be lost as to legal issues where those issues are characterized as 'incidental' to equitable issues," stated that "our previous decisions make it plain that no such rule may be applied in the federal courts." This response has been criticized as historically inaccurate. F. James, Civil Procedure 374 n.14 (1965). In fact, the practice rejected by the Court, generally referred to as the "clean-up" doctrine, had a long history. See generally Levin, Equitable Clean–Up and the Jury: A Suggested Orientation, 100 U.Pa.Rev. 320 (1951). Why do you suppose equity courts had traditionally assumed authority to resolve "legal" matters that were deemed "incidental" to the primary equitable issues? See Levin, 100 U.Pa.L.Rev. at 320: "Sound considerations of policy lay behind * * * [the] 'clean-up rule,' considerations which loom large and real against the background of two entirely independent systems of trial courts." In light of this pragmatic rationale for the "clean-up" doctrine, might the Court in *Dairy Queen*, applying the approach taken in *Beacon Theatres*, have been able to reject its use in a system in which law and equity have been merged?

Four years after *Dairy Queen*, the Supreme Court itself relied on a form of the "clean-up" doctrine in Katchen v. Landy, 382 U.S. 323 (1966). A trustee in bankruptcy sought to recoup money which the bankrupt had paid to a claimant in the bankruptcy proceeding on the ground that it constituted a voidable preference. The claimant sought a jury trial, arguing that if he had chosen not to file a claim with the bankruptcy court, the trustee would have been forced to sue him, in which case petitioner could have obtained a jury trial.

Though the Court acknowledged that the claimant might be entitled to a jury trial in a plenary action on the preference, it rejected his claim to a right to a jury trial in the course of the bankruptcy proceeding. Acceptance of the jury trial argument, Justice White reasoned, would require that in every similar case "the proceedings on allowance of claims must be suspended and a plenary suit initiated, with all the delay and expense that course would entail." The Court rejected the jury trial right, because "incidental" legal questions could be handled by the bankruptcy court, acting as a court of equity. Is it possible to justify use of the "clean-up" rule in *Katchen* while rejecting its use in *Dairy Queen?*

The Court in *Katchen* distinguished *Beacon Theatres* and *Dairy Queen* on the ground that neither case had "involved a specific statutory scheme contemplating the prompt trial of a disputed claim without the intervention of a jury." Does this statement imply that the Court in *Katchen* was balancing the constitutional right to jury trial against the need for governmental convenience? See Comment, The Seventh Amendment and Civil Rights Statutes: History Adrift in a Maelstrom, 68 Nw.U.L.Rev. 503 (1973). If so, do you think this is a proper mode of constitutional analysis? Should a "statutory scheme" take precedence over a constitutional right? On the issue of the right to jury trial in bankruptcy cases, see infra pp. 581–97.

ROSS v. BERNHARD

Supreme Court of the United States, 1970.
396 U.S. 531, 90 S.Ct. 733, 24 L.Ed.2d 729.

JUSTICE WHITE delivered the opinion of the Court.

* * * Whether the [Seventh] Amendment guarantees the right to a jury trial in stockholders' derivative actions is the issue now before us.

Petitioners brought this derivative suit in federal court against the directors of their closed end investment company, the Lehman Corporation and the corporation's brokers, Lehman Brothers. They contended that Lehman Brothers controlled the corporation through an illegally large representation on the corporation's board of directors, in violation of the Investment Company Act of 1940, 15 U.S.C.A. §§ 80a–1 to 52, and used this control to extract excessive brokerage fees from the corporation. The directors of the corporation were accused of converting corporate assets and of "gross abuse of trust, gross misconduct, willful misfeasance, bad faith, [and] gross negligence." Both the individual defendants and Lehman Brothers were accused of breaches of fiduciary duty. * * * Petitioners requested that the defendants "account for and pay to the Corporation for their profits and gains and its losses." Petitioners also demanded a jury trial on the corporation's claims.

On motion to strike petitioners' jury trial demand, the District Court held that a shareholder's right to a jury on his corporation's cause of action was to be judged as if the corporation were itself the plaintiff. Only the shareholder's initial claim to speak for the corporation had to be tried to the judge. * * * The Court of Appeals reversed, holding that a derivative action was entirely equitable in nature, and no jury was available to try any part of it. * * *

We reverse the holding of the Court of Appeals that in no event does the right to a jury trial preserved by the Seventh Amendment extend to derivative actions brought by the stockholders of a corporation. We hold that the right to jury trial attaches to those issues in derivative actions as to which the corporation, if it had been suing in its own right, would have been entitled to a jury.

The Seventh Amendment preserves to litigants the right to jury trial in suits at common law—

"not merely suits, which the common law recognized among its old and settled proceedings, but suits in which legal rights were to be ascertained and determined, in contradistinction to those where equitable rights alone were recognized, and equitable remedies were administered.... In a just sense, the amendment then may well be construed to embrace all suits, which are not of equity and admiralty jurisdiction, whatever may be the peculiar form which they may assume to settle legal rights." Parsons v. Bedford, Breedlove & Robeson, 3 Pet. 433, 447, 7 L.Ed. 732 (1830).

However difficult it may have been to define with precision the line between actions at law dealing with legal rights and suits in equity dealing with equitable matters, some proceedings were unmistakably actions at law triable to a jury. The Seventh Amendment, for example, entitled the parties to a jury trial in actions for damages to a person or property, for libel and slander, for recovery of land, and for conversion of personal property. Just as clearly, a corporation, although an artificial being, was commonly entitled to sue and be sued in the usual forms of action, at least in its own State. Whether the corporation was viewed as an entity separate from its stockholders or as a device permitting its stockholders to carry on their business and to sue and be sued, a corporation's suit to enforce a legal right was an action at common law carrying the right to jury trial at the time the Seventh Amendment was adopted.

The common law refused, however, to permit stockholders to call corporate managers to account in actions at law. The possibilities for abuse, thus presented, were not ignored by corporate officers and directors. Early in the 19th century, equity provided relief both in this country and in England. Without detailing these developments, it suffices to say that the remedy in this country * * * provided redress not only against faithless officers and directors but also against third parties who had damaged or threatened the corporate properties and whom the corporation through its managers refused to pursue. The remedy made available in equity was the derivative suit, viewed in this country as a suit to enforce a corporate cause of action against officers, directors, and third parties. As elaborated in the cases, one precondition for the suit was a valid claim on which the corporation could have sued; another was that the corporation itself had refused to proceed after suitable demand, unless excused by extraordinary conditions. Thus the dual nature of the stockholder's action: first, the plaintiff's right to sue on behalf of the corporation and, second, the merits of the corporation's claim itself.

Derivative suits posed no Seventh Amendment problems where the action against the directors and third parties would have been by a bill in equity had the corporation brought the suit. Our concern is with cases based upon a legal claim of the corporation against directors or third parties. Does the trial of such claims at the suit of a stockholder and without a jury violate the Seventh Amendment?

* * *

What can be gleaned from this Court's opinions is not inconsistent with the general understanding, reflected by the state court decisions and secondary sources, that equity could properly resolve corporate claims of any kind without a jury when properly pleaded in derivative suits complying with the equity rules.

Such was the prevailing opinion when the Federal Rules of Civil Procedure were adopted in 1938. It continued until 1963 when the Court of Appeals for the Ninth Circuit, relying on the Federal Rules as construed and applied in Beacon Theatres, Inc. v. Westover, and Dairy Queen, Inc. v. Wood, required the legal issues in a derivative suit to be tried to a jury. * * *

Under [*Beacon Theatres* and *Dairy Queen*], where equitable and legal claims are joined in the same action, there is a right to jury trial on the legal claims which must not be infringed either by trying the legal issues as incidental to the equitable ones or by a court trial of a common issue existing between the claims. The Seventh Amendment question depends on the nature of the issue to be tried rather than the character of the overall action.[10] The principle of these cases bears heavily on derivative actions.

We have noted that the derivative suit has dual aspects: first, the stockholder's right to sue on behalf of the corporation, historically an equitable matter; second, the claim of the corporation against directors or third parties on which, if the corporation had sued and the claim presented legal issues, the company could demand a jury trial. * * * [L]egal claims are not magically converted into equitable issues by their presentation to a court of equity in a derivative suit. The claim pressed by the stockholder against directors or third parties "is not his own but the corporation's." Koster v. Lumbermens Mut. Cas. Co., 330 U.S. 518, 522, 67 S.Ct. 828, 831 (1947). The corporation is a necessary party to the action; without it the case cannot proceed. Although named a defendant, it is the real party in interest, the stockholder being at best the nominal plaintiff. The proceeds of the action belong to the corporation and it is bound by the result of the suit. The heart of the action is the corporate claim. If it presents a legal issue, one entitling the corporation to a jury trial under the Seventh Amendment, the right to a jury is not forfeited merely because the stockholder's right to sue must first be adjudicated as an equitable issue triable to the court. *Beacon* and *Dairy Queen* require no less.

If under older procedures, now discarded, a court of equity could properly try the legal claims of the corporation presented in a derivative suit, it was because irreparable injury was threatened and no remedy at law existed as long as the stockholder was without standing to sue and the corporation itself refused to pursue its own remedies. Indeed, from 1789 until 1938, the judicial code expressly forbade courts of equity from entertaining any suit for which there was an adequate remedy at law. * * * If, before 1938, the law had borrowed from equity, as it borrowed other things, the idea that stockholders could litigate for their recalcitrant corporation, the corporate claim, if legal, would undoubtedly have been tried to a jury.

Of course, this did not occur, but the Federal Rules had a similar impact. Actions are no longer brought as actions at law or suits in equity. Under the Rules there is only one action, a "civil action" in which all claims may be joined and all remedies are available. Purely procedural impediments to the presentation of any issue by any party, based on the difference between law and equity, were destroyed. In a civil action presenting a stockholder's derivative claim, the court after passing upon the plaintiff's right to sue on behalf of the corporation is now able to try the corporate claim for damages with the aid of a jury. Separable claims may be tried separately, Fed.Rule Civ.Proc. 42(b), or

10. As our cases indicate, the "legal" nature of an issue is determined by considering, first, the pre-merger custom with reference to such questions; second, the remedy sought; and, third, the practical abilities and limitations of juries. Of these factors, the first, requiring extensive and possibly abstruse historical inquiry, is obviously the most difficult to apply. See James, Right to a Jury Trial in Civil Actions, 72 Yale L.J. 655 (1963).

legal and equitable issues may be handled in the same trial. The historical rule preventing a court of law from entertaining a shareholder's suit on behalf of the corporation is obsolete; it is no longer tenable for a district court, administering both law and equity in the same action, to deny legal remedies to a corporation, merely because the corporation's spokesmen are its shareholders rather than its directors. Under the rules, law and equity are procedurally combined; nothing turns now upon the form of the action or the procedural devices by which the parties happen to come before the court. The "expansion of adequate legal remedies provided by ... the Federal Rules necessarily affects the scope of equity." Beacon Theatres, Inc. v. Westover.

Thus, for example, before-merger class actions were largely a device of equity, and there was no right to a jury even on issues that might, under other circumstances, have been tried to a jury. Although at least one post-merger court held that the device was not available to try legal issues, it now seems settled in the lower federal courts that class action plaintiffs may obtain a jury trial on any legal issues they present.

Derivative suits have been described as one kind of "true" class action. We are inclined to agree with the description, at least to the extent it recognizes that the derivative suit and the class action were both ways of allowing parties to be heard in equity who could not speak at law.[15] After adoption of the rules there is no longer any procedural obstacle to the assertion of legal rights before juries, however the party may have acquired standing to assert those rights. Given the availability in a derivative action of both legal and equitable remedies, we think the Seventh Amendment preserves to the parties in a stockholder's suit the same right to a jury trial that historically belonged to the corporation and to those against whom the corporation pressed its legal claims.

In the instant case we have no doubt that the corporation's claim is, at least in part, a legal one. The relief sought is money damages. There are allegations in the complaint of a breach of fiduciary duty, but there are also allegations of ordinary breach of contract and gross negligence. The corporation, had it sued on its own behalf, would have been entitled to a jury's determination, at a minimum, of its damages against its broker under the brokerage contract and of its rights against its own directors because of their negligence. Under these circumstances it is unnecessary to decide whether the corporation's other claims are also properly triable to a jury. Dairy Queen, Inc. v. Wood.

JUSTICE STEWART, with whom THE CHIEF JUSTICE and JUSTICE HARLAN join, dissenting.

15. Other equitable devices are used under the rules without depriving the parties employing them of the right to a jury trial on legal issues. For example, although the right to intervene may in some cases be limited, when intervention is permitted generally, the intervenor has a right to a jury trial on any legal issues he presents. A similar development seems to be taking place in the lower courts in interpleader actions. Before merger interpleader actions lay only in equity, and there was no right to a jury even on issues that might, under other circumstances, have been tried to a jury. This view continued for some time after merger.

In holding as it does that the plaintiff in a shareholder's derivative suit is constitutionally entitled to a jury trial, the Court today seems to rely upon some sort of ill-defined combination of the Seventh Amendment and the Federal Rules of Civil Procedure. Somehow the Amendment and the Rules magically interact to do what each separately was expressly intended not to do, namely, to enlarge the right to a jury trial in civil actions brought in the courts of the United States.

The Seventh Amendment, by its terms, does not extend, but merely preserves the right to a jury trial "[i]n Suits at common law." All agree that this means the reach of the Amendment is limited to those actions that were tried to the jury in 1791 when the Amendment was adopted.[1] Suits in equity, which were historically tried to the court, were therefore unaffected by it. Similarly, Rule 38 of the Federal Rules has no bearing on the right to a jury trial in suits in equity, for it simply preserves inviolate "[t]he right of trial by jury as declared by the Seventh Amendment." Thus this Rule, like the Amendment itself, neither restricts nor enlarges the right to jury trial. Indeed nothing in the Federal Rules can rightly be construed to enlarge the right of jury trial, for in the legislation authorizing the Rules, Congress expressly provided that they "shall neither abridge, enlarge, nor modify the substantive rights of any litigant." See 28 U.S.C. § 2072. I take this plain, simple, and straightforward language to mean that after the promulgation of the Federal Rules, as before, the constitutional right to a jury trial attaches only to suits at common law. So, apparently, has every federal court that has discussed the issue. Since, as the Court concedes, a shareholder's derivative suit could be brought only in equity, it would seem to me to follow by the most elementary logic that in such suits there is no constitutional right to a trial by jury. Today the Court tosses aside history, logic and over 100 years of firm precedent to hold that the plaintiff in a shareholder's derivative suit does indeed have a constitutional right to a trial by jury. This holding has a questionable basis in policy[5] and no basis whatever in the Constitution.

The Court begins by assuming the "dual nature" of the shareholder's action. While the plaintiff's right to get into court at all is conceded to be equitable, once he is there the Court says his claim is to be viewed as though it were the claim of the corporation itself. If the corporation would have been entitled to a jury trial on such a claim, then, it is said, so would the shareholder. This conceptualization is without any historical basis. For the fact is that a shareholder's suit was not originally viewed in this country, or in England, as a suit to enforce a corporate

---

1. Where a new cause of action is created by Congress, and nothing is said about how it is to be tried, the jury trial issue is determined by fitting the cause into its nearest historical analogy. See James, Right to a Jury Trial in Civil Actions, 72 Yale L.J. 655.

5. See, e.g., Frank, Courts on Trial 110 11 (1949). Certainly there is no consensus among commentators on the desirability of jury trials in civil actions generally. Particularly where the issues in the case are complex as they are likely to be in a derivative suit much can be said for allowing the court discretion to try the case itself. See discussion in 5 J. Moore, Federal Practice 38.02[1].

cause of action. Rather, the shareholder's suit was initially permitted only against the managers of the corporation—not third parties—and it was conceived of as an equitable action to enforce the right of a beneficiary against his trustee. The shareholder was not, therefore, in court to enforce indirectly the corporate right of action, but to enforce directly his own equitable right of action against an unfaithful fiduciary. Later the rights of the shareholder were enlarged to encompass suits against third parties harming the corporation, but "the postulated 'corporate cause of action' has never been thought to describe an actual historical class of suit which was recognized by courts of law." [Note, The Right to a Jury Trial in a Stockholder's Derivative Action, 74 Yale L.J. 725, 730 (1965)]. Indeed the commentators, including those cited by the Court as postulating the analytic duality of the shareholder's derivative suit, recognize that historically the suit has in practice always been treated as a single cause tried exclusively in equity. They agree that there is therefore no constitutional right to a jury trial even where there might have been one had the corporation itself brought the suit.

This has been not simply the "general" or "prevailing" view in the federal courts as the Court says, but the unanimous view with the single exception of the Ninth Circuit's 1963 decision in DePinto v. Provident Security Life Ins. Co., 323 F.2d 826, a decision that has since been followed by no court until the present case. The Court would have us discount all those decisions rendered before 1938, when the Federal Rules of Civil Procedure were adopted, because it says that before the promulgation of the Rules, "[p]urely procedural impediments" somehow blocked the exercise of a constitutional right. In itself this would seem a rather shaky premise upon which to build an argument. But the Court's position is still further weakened by the fact that any "[p]urely procedural impediments" to a jury trial in a derivative suit were eliminated, not in 1938, but at least as early as 1912. For Rule 23 of the Equity Rules of that year provided that if a "matter ordinarily determinable at law" arose in an equity suit it should "be determined in that suit according to the principles applicable, without sending the case or question to the law side of the court." These applicable principles included the right of jury trial. Consequently, when the Court said in United Copper Co. v. Amalgamated Copper Co., 244 U.S. 261, 264, 37 S.Ct. 509, 510, 61 L.Ed. 1119, that "it is clear" that the remedy of a stockholder seeking to enforce the rights of a corporation—whatever their nature—is not in law but in equity, it was not because there were "procedural impediments" to a jury trial on any "legal issues." Rather, it was because the suit itself was conceived of as a wholly equitable cause of action.

* * *

These pre–1938 cases, then, firmly establish the unitary, equitable basis of shareholders' derivative suits and in no way support the Court's holding here. But, the Court says, whatever the situation may have been before 1938, the Federal Rules of Civil Procedure of that year, at least as construed in our decisions more than 20 years later in Beacon Theatres, Inc. v. Westover, and Dairy Queen, Inc. v. Wood, in any event require the conclusion reached today. I can find nothing in either of these cases that leads to that conclusion.

* * *

It is true that in *Beacon Theatres* it was stated that the 1938 Rules did diminish the scope of federal equity jurisdiction in certain particulars. But the Court's effort to force the facts of this case into the mold of *Beacon Theatres* and *Dairy Queen* simply does not succeed. Those cases involved a combination of historically separable suits, one in law and one in equity. Their facts fit the pattern of cases where, before the Rules, the equity court would have disposed of the equitable claim and would then have either retained jurisdiction over the suit, despite the availability of adequate legal remedies, or enjoined a subsequent legal action between the same parties involving the same controversy.

But the present case is not one involving traditionally equitable claims by one party, and traditionally legal claims by the other. Nor is it a suit in which the plaintiff is asserting a combination of legal and equitable claims. For, as we have seen, a derivative suit has always been conceived of as a single, unitary, equitable cause of action. It is for this reason, and not because of "procedural impediments," that the courts of equity did not transfer derivative suits to the law side. In short, the cause of action is wholly a creature of equity. And whatever else can be said of *Beacon Theatres* and *Dairy Queen,* they did not cast aside altogether the historic division between equity and law.

If history is to be so cavalierly dismissed, the derivative suit can, of course, be artificially broken down into separable elements. But so then can any traditionally equitable cause of action, and the logic of the Court's position would lead to the virtual elimination of all equity jurisdiction. An equitable suit for an injunction, for instance, often involves issues of fact which, if damages had been sought, would have been triable to a jury. Does this mean that in a suit asking only for injunctive relief these factual issues must be tried to the jury, with the judge left to decide only whether, given the jury's findings, an injunction is the appropriate remedy? Certainly the Federal Rules make it possible to try a suit for an injunction in that way, but even more certainly they were not intended to have any such effect. Yet the Court's approach, it seems, would require that if any "legal issue" procedurally could be tried to a jury, it constitutionally must be tried to a jury.

The fact is, of course, that there are, for the most part, no such things as inherently "legal issues" or inherently "equitable issues." There are only factual issues, and, "like chameleons [they] take their color from surrounding circumstances."[12] Thus the Court's "nature of the issue" approach is hardly meaningful.

* * *

12.   James, supra n. 1, at 692. As Professor Moore has put it, "Whether issues are

The Court's decision today can perhaps be explained as a reflection of an unarticulated but apparently overpowering bias in favor of jury trials in civil actions. It certainly cannot be explained in terms of either the Federal Rules or the Constitution.

Notes and Questions

1. There is no doubt that historically, the *Ross* case would have been deemed purely equitable. Does the majority legitimately reach the conclusion that the right to jury trial applies? Does the approach to the law-equity distinction adopted in *Beacon Theatres* [supra p. 531] support the Court's conclusion?

2. One commentator has suggested that while in part *Ross* relied on historical analysis, "[a]t another point in its opinion * * * the Court gave reason to speculate that the historical test might be subject to substantial modification in future cases." Wolfram, The Constitutional History of the Seventh Amendment, 57 Minn.L.Rev. 639, 643 (1973). Professor Wolfram was referring to footnote 10 of the Court's opinion, where it noted that "the practical abilities and limitations of juries" was a factor relevant to the determination of the constitutional right to jury trial. With the exception of the case of an accounting, it had never been thought that the presence of the constitutional right was to be determined by an assessment of a jury's capabilities.

Professor Wolfram applauded this development: "If precedent is not an insurmountable obstacle, then one may hope that the time is near when the dead hand of the historical test will be lifted from the seventh amendment." 57 Minn.L.Rev. at 747. Do you agree with Professor Wolfram's sentiments? Does the language of the Seventh Amendment allow the court to ignore "the dead hand of the historical test"? Should that matter?

3. Professors Wright and Kane have commented that "[t]he lower courts have ignored the *Ross* footnote or cited it as a makeweight reference to support results that would have been reached had the footnote never been written." C. Wright & M. Kane, Law of Federal Courts 662 (6th ed. 2002). The one exception is the issue of the jury trial right in complex cases. This question is examined in detail infra at p. 597.

4. *Ross* shows that sometimes procedural innovation can give rise to a right to jury trial in a case where it would not have been available at common law. Procedural innovation can work the other way as well. Thus, in Parklane Hosiery Co. v. Shore, 439 U.S. 322, 99 S.Ct. 645, 58 L.Ed.2d 552 (1979), the Court abandoned the common law rule that collateral estoppel could only be asserted by one who was a party to the prior litigation whose results were urged as binding in the present suit. The Court therefore held that plaintiffs in a securities fraud action could rely on the findings of an earlier suit brought by the SEC against defendants. This issue is covered in Chapter XIII. See infra p. 1173.

legal or equitable may, of course, depend upon the manner in which they are presented...." 5 J. Moore, Federal Practice 38.04[1], n. 40. And he, along with virtually every other commentator, concludes that if the issues are presented in a shareholder's derivative suit they are equitable and the plaintiff has no constitutional right to have them tried by a jury. 5 J. Moore, Federal Practice 38.38[4].

Defendants in *Parklane* also argued that abandoning the requirement of mutuality for collateral estoppel deprived them of their right to a jury trial in the private securities fraud action since the earlier SEC suit had been tried to a judge. Pointing out that *Beacon Theatres* assumed that the judge's findings from a prior equitable action would bind the later litigation of the same issues between the same parties, the Court saw no reason for a different result where the party relying on estoppel had not been involved in the earlier proceeding:

> A litigant who has lost because of adverse factual findings in an equity action is equally deprived of a jury trial whether he is estopped from relitigating the factual issues against the same party or a new party. In either case, the party against whom estoppel is asserted has litigated questions of fact, and has had the facts determined against him in an earlier proceeding. In either case there is no further factfinding function for the jury to perform, since the common factual issues have been resolved in the previous action.

Only Justice Rehnquist dissented, reasoning that "the development of nonmutual estoppel is a substantial departure from the common law and its use in this case completely deprives petitioners of their right to have a jury determine contested issues of fact. I am simply unwilling to accept the Court's presumption that the complete extinguishment of petitioners' right to trial by jury can be justified as a mere change in 'procedural incident or detail.' " Justice Rehnquist based his conclusion on the great importance the framers of the Seventh Amendment placed on the jury trial.

Does *Parklane* signal a shift in attitude toward the right to jury trial? May other procedures be developed that deny a jury where it would have been available at common law?

5. In Lytle v. Household Manufacturing, Inc., 494 U.S. 545, 110 S.Ct. 1331, 108 L.Ed.2d 504 (1990), the Supreme Court refused to extend the reach of *Parklane*. The Court held that the Seventh Amendment precludes according collateral estoppel effect to a district court's determinations of issues that are common to both equitable and legal claims where the court resolved the equitable claims first solely because it had erroneously dismissed the legal claims. The plaintiff had sued under both Title VII of the Civil Rights Act of 1964 and 42 U.S.C.A. § 1981, alleging that the defendant had terminated his employment because of his race and had retaliated against him for filing a charge with the Equal Employment Opportunity Commission. The district court dismissed the § 1981 claim, to which the jury trial right applied, and conducted a bench trial on the Title VII claims, which it deemed equitable. While the court of appeals reversed the district court's dismissal of the § 1981 claim, it nevertheless held that that court's findings on the Title VII issue were collateral estoppel on the § 1981 claim.

In reversing, Justice Marshall, speaking for the Court, distinguished *Parklane* (494 U.S. at 550–52, 110 S.Ct. at 1336–37):

> Only the District Court's erroneous dismissal of the § 1981 claims enabled that court to resolve issues common to both claims, issues that otherwise would have been resolved by a jury. But for that erroneous ruling, this case would be indistinguishable from *Beacon Theatres* and *Dairy Queen*. It would be anomalous to hold that a district court may

not deprive a litigant of his right to a jury trial by resolving an equitable claim before a jury hears a legal claim raising common issues, but that a court may accomplish the same result by erroneously dismissing the legal claim. Such a holding would be particularly unfair here because [plaintiff] was required to join his legal and equitable claims to avoid the bar of res judicata.

CURTIS v. LOETHER

Supreme Court of the United States, 1974.
415 U.S. 189, 94 S.Ct. 1005, 39 L.Ed.2d 260.

JUSTICE MARSHALL delivered the opinion of the Court.

Section 812 of the Civil Rights Act of 1968 authorizes private plaintiffs to bring civil actions to redress violations of Title VIII, the fair housing provisions of the Act, and provides that "[t]he court may grant as relief, as it deems appropriate, any permanent or temporary injunction, temporary restraining order, or other order, and may award to the plaintiff actual damages and not more than $1,000 punitive damages...." The question presented in this case is whether the Civil Rights Act or the Seventh Amendment requires a jury trial upon demand by one of the parties in an action for damages and injunctive relief under this section.

Petitioner, a Negro woman, brought this action under § 812, claiming that respondents, who are white, had refused to rent an apartment to her because of her race, in violation of § 804(a) of the Act. In her complaint she sought only injunctive relief and punitive damages; a claim for compensatory damages was later added. * * * Respondents made a timely demand for jury trial in their answer. The District Court, however, held that jury trial was neither authorized by Title VIII nor required by the Seventh Amendment, and denied the jury request. * * *

The Court of Appeals reversed on the jury trial issue.

* * *

The legislative history on the jury trial question is sparse, and what little is available is ambiguous. There seems to be some indication that supporters of Title VIII were concerned that the possibility of racial prejudice on juries might reduce the effectiveness of civil rights damages actions. * * * We see no point to giving extended consideration to these arguments, however, for we think it is clear that the Seventh Amendment entitles either party to demand a jury trial in an action for damages in the federal courts under § 812.

* * * Although the thrust of the Amendment was to preserve right to jury trial as it existed in 1791, it has long been settled that the right extends beyond the common-law forms of action recognized at that time. Mr. Justice Story established the basic principle in 1830:

"The phrase 'common law,' found in this clause, is used in contradistinction to equity, and admiralty, and maritime jurisprudence...."

By *common law*, [the Framers of the Amendment] meant ... not merely suits, which the *common* law recognized among its old and settled proceedings, but suits in which *legal* rights were to be ascertained and determined, in contradistinction to those where equitable rights alone were recognized, and equitable remedies were administered.... In a just sense, the amendment then may well be construed to embrace all suits which are not of equity and admiralty jurisdiction, whatever might be the peculiar form which they may assume to settle legal rights." Parsons v. Bedford, 3 Pet. 433, 446–447 (1830) (emphasis in original).

Petitioner nevertheless argues that the Amendment is inapplicable to new causes of action created by congressional enactment. As the Court of Appeals observed, however, we have considered the applicability of the constitutional right to jury trial in actions enforcing statutory rights "as a matter too obvious to be doubted." * * * Whatever doubt may have existed should now be dispelled. The Seventh Amendment does apply to actions enforcing statutory rights, and requires a jury trial upon demand, if the statute creates legal rights and remedies, enforceable in an action for damages in the ordinary courts of law.

We think it is clear that a damages action under § 812 is an action to enforce "legal rights" within the meaning of our Seventh Amendment decisions. A damages action under the statute sounds basically in tort—the statute merely defines a new legal duty, and authorizes the courts to compensate a plaintiff for the injury caused by the defendant's wrongful breach. * * * [T]his cause of action is analogous to a number of tort actions recognized at common law. More important, the relief sought here—actual and punitive damages—is the traditional form of relief offered in the courts of law.

NLRB v. Jones & Laughlin Steel Corp., 301 U.S. 1, 57 S.Ct. 615, 81 L.Ed. 893 (1937), relied on by petitioner, lends no support to her statutory-rights argument. The Court there upheld the award of back pay without jury trial in an NLRB unfair labor practice proceeding, rejecting a Seventh Amendment claim on the ground that the case involved a "statutory proceeding" and "not a suit at common law or in the nature of such a suit." *Jones & Laughlin* merely stands for the proposition that the Seventh Amendment is generally inapplicable in administrative proceedings, where jury trials would be incompatible with the whole concept of administrative adjudication and would substantially interfere with the NLRB's role in the statutory scheme. Katchen v. Landy [supra pp. 544–45], also relied upon by petitioner, is to like effect. * * * These cases uphold congressional power to entrust enforcement of statutory rights to an administrative process or specialized court of equity free from the strictures of the Seventh Amendment. But when Congress provides for enforcement of statutory rights in an ordinary civil action in the district courts, where there is obviously no functional justification for denying the jury trial right, a jury trial must be available if the action involves rights and remedies of the sort typically enforced in an action at law.

* * *

We need not, and do not, go so far as to say that any award of monetary relief must necessarily be "legal" relief. A comparison of Title VIII with Title VII of the Civil Rights Act of 1964, where the courts of appeals have held that jury trial is not required in an action for reinstatement and back pay, is instructive, although we of course express no view on the jury trial issue in that context. In Title VII cases the courts of appeals have characterized back pay as an integral part of an equitable remedy, a form of restitution. But the statutory language on which this characterization is based—

> "[T]he court may enjoin the respondent from engaging in such unlawful employment practice, and order such affirmative action as may be appropriate, which may include, but is not limited to, reinstatement or hiring of employees, with or without back pay ... or any other equitable relief as the court deems appropriate," 42 U.S.C. § 2000e–5(g).

—contrasts sharply with § 812's simple authorization of an action for actual and punitive damages. In Title VII cases, also, the courts have relied on the fact that the decision whether to award back pay is committed to the discretion of the trial judge. There is no comparable discretion here: if a plaintiff proves unlawful discrimination and actual damages, he is entitled to judgment for that amount. Nor is there any sense in which the award here can be viewed as requiring the defendant to disgorge funds wrongfully withheld from the plaintiff. Whatever may be the merit of the "equitable" characterization in Title VII cases, there is surely no basis for characterizing the award of compensatory and punitive damages here as equitable relief.

We are not oblivious to the force of petitioner's policy arguments. Jury trials may delay to some extent the disposition of Title VIII damages actions. * * * We recognize, too, the possibility that jury prejudice may deprive a victim of discrimination of the verdict to which he or she is entitled. * * * More fundamentally, however, these considerations are insufficient to overcome the clear command of the Seventh Amendment.

Notes and Questions

1. After *Curtis,* what is left of the balancing approach to Seventh Amendment analysis arguably implied in footnote 10 of *Ross* and in Katchen v. Landy?

2. Does the Court in *Curtis* satisfactorily distinguish cases arising under Title VII of the 1964 Civil Rights Act from Title VIII cases? If a complaining party alleges that he was not hired because of his race, is it proper to characterize his damage claim as "backpay"? In section 102 of the Civil Rights Act of 1991, Pub. L. No. 102–166, 105 Stat. 1071 (1991),

Congress provided a statutory right to jury trial in Title VII actions when a complaining party seeks compensatory or punitive damages. However, Congress excluded backpay from the definition of "compensatory damages."

3. In Pernell v. Southall Realty, 416 U.S. 363, 94 S.Ct. 1723, 40 L.Ed.2d 198 (1974), the Supreme Court held that the Seventh Amendment guaranteed a right to jury trial in a landlord's suit to recover possession of real property from his tenant under § 16–1501 of the District of Columbia Code, stating:

> This Court has long assumed that actions to recover land, like actions for damages to a person or property, are actions at law triable to a jury. * * *

> Respondent suggests, however, that these precedents should be limited to actions to recover property where title is in issue and that actions brought under § 16–1501 should be distinguished * * *. The distinction between title to and possession of property, of course, was well recognized at common law. But however relevant it was for certain purposes, it had no bearing on the right to a jury trial.

> * * *

> In particular, ejectment became the principal means employed by landlords to evict tenants for overstaying the terms of their leases, nonpayment of rent, or other breach of lease covenants. * * *

> Notwithstanding this history, the Court of Appeals reasoned that an action under § 16–1501 was not the "equivalent" of an action of ejectment. * * * Since, in its opinion, neither § 16–1501 nor its equivalent existed at common law, the Court of Appeals held that the Seventh Amendment did not guarantee the right to jury trial.

> In our view, this analysis is fundamentally at odds with the test we have formulated for resolving Seventh Amendment questions.

The Court then quoted Parsons v. Bedford, which was relied on in *Curtis:* "whether or not a close equivalent to § 16–1501 existed in England in 1791 is irrelevant for Seventh Amendment purposes, for that Amendment requires trial by jury in actions unheard of at common law, provided that the action involves rights and remedies of the sort traditionally enforced in an action at law, rather than in an action in equity or admiralty."

4. According to one group of commentators:

> Read most broadly, *Curtis* and *Pernell* seem to indicate that a congressional indication that nonjury trial is preferable, unaccompanied by the creation of a specific statutory, nonjudicial proceeding, cannot insulate a particular action from the Seventh Amendment. However, that reading appears too broad. In both cases Congress was silent as to jury trial. Thus, the Supreme Court has not yet been faced with the situation in which Congress has expressed a strong preference for nonjury trial and has provided reasons supporting that preference. Read more narrowly, then, the cases do not foreclose the possibility that Congress can provide for a statutory cause of action that is not purely equitable to be enforced in the district courts without a jury trial.

J. Friedenthal, M. Kane & A. Miller, Civil Procedure 521 (3d ed. 1999). Do you agree with this analysis? If the cases were read as these commentators suggest, would that represent a principled construction of the Seventh Amendment?

5. Note that in Curtis v. Loether the proponents of jury trial are the defendants, while the party opposing it is the plaintiff. Consider how this alignment may reflect the arguments that might have moved Congress to desire that Title VIII claims not give rise to a jury trial. The actual outcome, however, may not have been as anticipated; one commentator reported that before Curtis v. Loether was decided, the usual plaintiff judgments ranged from $1,500 to $2,500, while after the decision they increased to a usual range on $10,000 to $50,000. See Susz, Federal Fair Housing, 89 Case & Comment 30, 30–31 (May–June 1984).

6. Note that Congress may choose to provide a *statutory* right to jury trial, when the Seventh Amendment does not itself dictate such a right. It is generally thought that there is no constitutional right to a non-jury trial. See 9 Wright & Miller, Federal Practice and Procedure § 2302.

————

TULL v. UNITED STATES, 481 U.S. 412, 107 S.Ct. 1831, 95 L.Ed.2d 365 (1987):

JUSTICE BRENNAN delivered the opinion of the Court.

[The government charged petitioner with dumping fill in wetlands in violation of the Clean Water Act, 33 U.S.C. §§ 1311; 1344; 1362. The Act authorizes both an injunction and a civil penalty of up to $10,000 per day during the period of the violation. The government sought both. Petitioner demanded a jury trial, but the trial court refused the demand. After a 15–day bench trial it found violations of the Act and fined petitioner $75,000, with further fines to follow unless petitioner undertook extremely expensive restoration efforts. The Supreme Court first held that petitioner had a right to jury trial on the question of violation of the Act.]

The petitioner analogizes this Government suit * * * to an action in debt within the jurisdiction of English courts of law. Prior to the enactment of the Seventh Amendment, English courts had held that a civil penalty suit was a particular species of an action in debt that was within the jurisdiction of the courts of law.

* * *

The Government argues, however, that—rather than an action in debt—the closer historical analogue is an action to abate a public nuisance.

* * *

Whether, as the Government argues, a public nuisance action is a better analogy than an action in debt is debatable. But we need not decide the question. As Pernell v. Southhall Realty [supra p. 558 n. 3] cautioned, the fact that the subject matter of a modern statutory action and an 18th-century English action are close equivalents "is irrelevant for Seventh Amendment purposes," because "that Amendment requires trial by jury in actions unheard of at common law." It suffices that we conclude that both the public nuisance action and the action in debt are appropriate analogies to the instant statutory action. * * *

We need not rest our conclusion on what has been called an "abstruse historical" search for the nearest 18th-century analogue. Ross v. Bernhard, [369 U.S. at 548] n.10. We reiterate our previously expressed view that characterizing the relief sought is "[m]ore important" than finding a precisely analogous common law cause of action in determining whether the Seventh Amendment guarantees a jury trial. Curtis v. Loether, supra p. 555.

A civil penalty was a type of remedy at common law that could only be enforced in courts of law. Remedies intended to punish culpable individuals, as opposed to those intended simply to extract compensation or restore the status quo, were issued by courts of law, not courts of equity. [This] action * * * is of this character. [The Act] does not direct that the "civil penalty" imposed be calculated solely on the basis of equitable determinations, such as the profits gained from violations of the statute, but simply imposes a maximum penalty of $10,000 per day of violation. * * * [The Act's] authorization of punishment to further retribution and deterrence clearly evidences that this subsection reflects more than a concern to provide equitable relief. * * * Because the nature of the relief authorized by [the Act] was traditionally available only in a court of law, the petitioner in this present action is entitled to a jury trial on demand.

The punitive nature of the relief sought in the present case is made apparent by a comparison with the relief sought in an action to abate a public nuisance. A public nuisance action was a classic example of the kind of suit that relied on the injunctive relief provided by courts of equity.

[The Court went on, however, to hold that there was no right to jury determination of the amount of civil penalties.]

The Seventh Amendment is silent on the question whether a jury must determine the remedy in a trial in which it must determine liability.[9] The answer must depend on whether the jury must shoulder this responsibility to preserve the "substance of the common-law right of trial by jury." Is a jury role necessary for that purpose? We do not think so. * * * The assessment of civil penalties * * * cannot be said to involve "the substance of a common-law right to a trial by jury," nor a "fundamental element of a jury trial."

9. Nothing in the Amendment's language suggests that the right to a jury trial extends to the remedy phase of a civil trial. * * * We have been presented with no evidence that the Framers meant to extend the right to a jury to the remedy phase of a civil trial.

Congress' assignment of the determination of the amount of civil penalties to trial judges therefore does not infringe on the constitutional right to a jury trial.

JUSTICE SCALIA, joined by JUSTICE STEVENS, concurring in part and dissenting in part.

[Justice Scalia agreed that petitioner was entitled to a jury trial on the question of violation, but disagreed with the majority about the assessment of the civil penalty.]

[I]n my view the right to trial by jury on whether a civil penalty of unspecified amount is assessable also involves a right to trial by jury on what the amount should be. * * *

While purporting to base its determination (quite correctly) upon historical practice, the Court creates a form of civil adjudication I have never encountered. I can recall no precedent for judgment of civil liability by jury but assessment of amount by the court. Even punitive damages are assessed by the jury when liability is determined in that fashion. * * * Since, as the Court correctly reasons, the proper analogue to a civil-fine action is the common-law action for debt, the government need only prove liability by a preponderance of the evidence; but must, as in any action for debt, accept the amount of award determined not by its own officials but by twelve private citizens. If that tends to discourage the government from proceeding in this fashion, I doubt that the Founding Fathers would be upset.

Notes and Questions

1. Does the Court in *Tull* abandon or rely on the historical test in reaching its decision? Does it purport to do both? *Can* it logically do both?

2. The Law–Fact Distinction: As *Tull* illustrates, even where the Seventh Amendment dictates a jury trial right, it does so only to issues of fact, not to issues of law. Distinguishing between the two has not always been an easy task. The Supreme Court devoted attention to this question in Markman v. Westview Instruments, Inc., 517 U.S. 370, 116 S.Ct. 1384, 134 L.Ed.2d 577 (1996), the Court held that construction of a patent, including terms of art, is exclusively within the province of the court, rather than the jury. In reaching this conclusion, the Court initially looked to historical practice. However, where such practice, either directly or by analogy, does not provide an answer, the Court will "consider both the relative interpretive skills of judges and juries and the statutory policies that ought to be furthered by the allocation." Such "functional considerations" may indicate that "as a matter of the sound administration of justice, one judicial actor is better positioned than another to decide the issue in question." Id. at 388, quoting Miller v. Fenton, 474 U.S. 104, 114, 106 S.Ct. 445, 451, 88 L.Ed.2d 405 (1985). *Markman* is defended in Kirgis, The Right to a Jury Decision On Questions of Fact Under the Seventh Amendment, 64 Ohio St. L. J. 1125 (2003). On the general issue of the law–fact distinction, see Sward, The Seventh Amendment and the Alchemy of Fact and Law, 33 Seton Hall L. Rev. 573 (2003).

3. In Feltner v. Columbia Pictures Television, Inc., 523 U.S. 340, 118 S.Ct. 1279, 140 L.Ed.2d 438 (1998), the Court held that the Seventh Amendment right to jury trial applied to the determination of the amount of damages in a suit under section 504(c) of the Copyright Act, 17 U.S.C. § 504(c). That provision permits a copyright owner "to recover, instead of actual damages and profits, an award of statutory damages ..., in a sum of not less than $500 or more than $20,000 as the court considers just." Although the Court held that Congress had not created a statutory right to jury trial in section 504(c), it nevertheless found that a jury trial right was provided by the Seventh Amendment.

The Court initially concluded that although the statutory right had not itself existed at common law, historical analogues did in fact exist, and those analogues demonstrated that historically such a right was one at law. The Court further pointed to the "general rule" that monetary relief is legal, and noted that "an award of statutory damages may serve purposes traditionally associated with legal relief, such as compensation and punishment." Because suits under the statute are suits at law, the Court held that the Seventh Amendment dictated a right to jury trial.

The Court further held that the jury trial right dictated that the jury find damages, as well as liability, because "there is overwhelming evidence that the consistent practice at common law was for juries to award damages." The fact that the damages were discretionary did not affect the constitutional requirement that the jury decide damages, because "there is historical evidence that cases involving discretionary monetary relief were tried before juries."

The Court rejected Columbia's reliance on *Tull*: "In *Tull* ... we were presented with no evidence that juries historically had determined the amount of civil penalties to be paid to the Government. Moreover, the awarding of civil penalties to the Government could be viewed as analogous to sentencing in a criminal proceeding.... Here, of course, there is no similar analogy, and there is clear and direct historical evidence that juries, both as a general matter and in copyright cases, set the amount of damages awarded to a successful plaintiff." How persuasive is the Court's asserted distinction of *Tull*? Might the Court's analogy of civil penalties to criminal sentencing prove too much? If a civil penalty is analogous to criminal sentencing, why do the traditional procedural protections of the criminal law (for example, requirement of proof beyond a reasonable doubt and the right to confront accusers) not also apply to civil penalty actions?

4. *Punitive Damages and the Law–Fact Distinction*: Should the question as to whether or not a punitive damage award should be deemed excessive be considered an issue of fact or of law? In BMW of North America, Inc. v. Gore, 517 U.S. 559, 116 S.Ct. 1589, 134 L.Ed.2d 809 (1996), the Supreme Court held that a punitive damage award may be unconstitutionally excessive. In Cooper Industries, Inc. v. Leatherman Tool Group, Inc., 532 U.S. 424, 1221 S.Ct. 1678, 149 L.Ed.2d 674 (2001), the Court held that "[b]ecause the jury's award of punitive damages does not constitute a finding of 'fact,' appellate review of the District Court's determination that an award is consistent with due process does not implicate the Seventh Amendment...." Id. at 437, 121 S. Ct. at 1686. Why should the award of

punitive damages be deemed a question of law? Is it that it is unlike the measure of actual damages, in that actual damage awards present a question of historical predictive fact, while punitive damages are comparable to civil fines? If, as the Court concludes, the award of punitive damages is not a finding of fact, why is it decided by the jury in the first place?

5. One method of tort reform attempted by numerous state legislatures in recent years has been the imposition of statutory caps on the amount of damages to be awarded in a variety of common law tort actions. Do such caps violate the Seventh Amendment in federal court diversity suits? One commentator believes that they do. See Murphy, Determining Compensation: The Tension Between Legislative Power and Jury Authority, 74 Tex. L. Rev. 345 (1995). Professor Murphy notes that "[b]efore adoption of the Seventh Amendment, English juries had long assessed compensatory damages because of their factfinding role." Should statutory caps be viewed as an invasion of the jury's traditional role? Consider the following response: Statutory caps on damages are properly viewed, not as a legislative interference with jury factfinding, but rather as a legislative alteration in the governing substantive law.

TEAMSTERS LOCAL NO. 391 v. TERRY

Supreme Court of the United States, 1990.
494 U.S. 558, 110 S.Ct. 1339, 108 L.Ed.2d 519.

JUSTICE MARSHALL delivered the opinion of the Court except as to Part III–A.

This case presents the question whether an employee who seeks relief in the form of backpay for a union's alleged breach of its duty of fair representation has a right to trial by jury. We hold that the Seventh Amendment entitles such a plaintiff to a jury trial.

I

McLean Trucking Company and the Chauffeurs, Teamsters, and Helpers Local Union No. 391 were parties to a collective-bargaining agreement that governed the terms and conditions of employment at McLean's terminals. The 27 respondents were employed by McLean as truckdrivers in bargaining units covered by the agreement, and all were members of the Union.

[Respondents objected to various employment practices used by McLean that impaired their seniority rights, alleging breaches of the collective bargaining agreement. They filed a grievance with the union, and the grievance committee ordered McLean to alter its practices. When their seniority rights were again impaired, respondents filed subsequent grievances. This time the union declined to refer them to the grievance committee on the ground that the relevant issues had been determined in the prior proceeding.]

In July 1983, respondents filed an action in District Court, alleging that McLean had breached the collective-bargaining agreement in violation of § 301 of the Labor Management Relations Act, 1947, and that the

Union had violated its duty of fair representation. Respondents requested a permanent injunction requiring the defendants to cease their illegal acts and to reinstate them to their proper seniority status; in addition, they sought, *inter alia,* compensatory damages for lost wages and health benefits. In 1986 McLean filed for bankruptcy; subsequently, the action against it was voluntarily dismissed, along with all claims for injunctive relief.

Respondents had requested a jury trial in their pleadings. The Union moved to strike the jury demand on the ground that no right to a jury trial exists in a duty of fair representation suit. The District Court denied the motion to strike. After an interlocutory appeal, the Fourth Circuit affirmed the trial court, holding that the Seventh Amendment entitled respondents to a jury trial of their claim for monetary relief. We granted the petition for certiorari to resolve a circuit conflict on this issue, and now affirm the judgment of the Fourth Circuit.

II

The duty of fair representation is inferred from unions' exclusive authority under the National Labor Relations Act, to represent all employees in a bargaining unit. The duty requires a union "to serve the interests of all members without hostility or discrimination toward any, to exercise its discretion with complete good faith and honesty, and to avoid arbitrary conduct." A union must discharge its duty both in bargaining with the employer and in its enforcement of the resulting collective bargaining agreement. Thus, the Union here was required to pursue respondents' grievances in a manner consistent with the principles of fair representation.

Because most collective-bargaining agreements accord finality to grievance or arbitration procedures established by the collective-bargaining agreement, an employee normally cannot bring a § 301 action against an employer unless he can show that the union breached its duty of fair representation in its handling of his grievance. Whether the employee sues both the labor union and the employer or only one of those entities, he must prove the same two facts to recover money damages: that the employer's action violated the terms of the collective-bargaining agreement and that the union breached its duty of fair representation.

III

We turn now to the constitutional issue presented in this case— whether respondents are entitled to a jury trial. * * *

To determine whether a particular action will resolve legal rights, we examine both the nature of the issues involved and the remedy sought. "First, we compare the statutory action to 18th-century actions brought in the courts of England prior to the merger of the courts of law and equity. Second, we examine the remedy sought and determine whether it is legal or equitable in nature." Tull [v. United States.] The second inquiry is the more important in our analysis.[4]

A

An action for breach of a union's duty of fair representation was unknown in 18th-century England; in fact, collective-bargaining was unlawful. We must therefore look for an analogous cause of action that existed in the 18th century to determine whether the nature of this duty of fair representation suit is legal or equitable.

The Union contends that this duty of fair representation action resembles a suit brought to vacate an arbitration award because respondents seek to set aside the result of the grievance process. In the 18th Century, an action to set aside an arbitration award was considered equitable. * * *

The arbitration analogy is inapposite, however, to the Seventh Amendment question posed in this case. No grievance committee has considered respondents' claim that the Union violated its duty of fair representation; the grievance process was concerned only with the employer's alleged breach of the collective-bargaining agreement. Thus, respondents' claim against the Union cannot be characterized as an action to vacate an arbitration award because " '[t]he arbitration proceeding did not, and indeed, could not, resolve the employee's claim against the union. . . . Because no arbitrator has decided the primary issue presented by this claim, no arbitration award need be undone, even if the employee ultimately prevails.' " DelCostello [v. Teamsters, 462 U.S. 151, 167 (1983)].

The Union next argues that respondents' duty of fair representation action is comparable to an action by a trust beneficiary against a trustee for breach of fiduciary duty. Such actions were within the exclusive jurisdiction of courts of equity. This analogy is far more persuasive than the arbitration analogy. Just as a trustee must act in the best interests of the beneficiaries, a union, as the exclusive representative of the workers, must exercise its power to act on behalf of the employees in good faith. Moreover, just as a beneficiary does not directly control the actions of a trustee, an individual employee lacks direct control over a union's actions taken on his behalf.

The trust analogy extends to a union's handling of grievances. In most cases, a trustee has the exclusive authority to sue third parties who

---

4. Justice Stevens' analysis emphasizes a third consideration, namely whether "the issues [presented by the claim] are typical grist for the jury's judgment." This Court, however, has never relied on this consideration "as an independent basis for extending the right to a jury trial under the Seventh Amendment." Tull v. United States [supra p. ___]. We recently noted that this consideration is relevant only to the determination "whether Congress has permissibly entrusted the resolution of certain disputes to an administrative agency or specialized court of equity, and whether jury trials would impair the functioning of the legislative scheme." Granfinanciera, S.A. v. Nordberg [infra p. 581]. No one disputes that an action for breach of the duty of fair representation may properly be brought in an Article III court; thus, the factor does not affect our analysis.

injure the beneficiaries' interest in the trust, including any legal claim the trustee holds in trust for the beneficiaries. The trustee then has the sole responsibility for determining whether to settle, arbitrate, or otherwise dispose of the claim. Similarly, the union typically has broad discretion in its decision whether and how to pursue an employee's grievance against an employer. Just as a trust beneficiary can sue to enforce a contract entered into on his behalf by the trustee only if the trustee "improperly refuses or neglects to bring an action against the third person," Restatement (Second) of Trusts, § 282(2), so an employee can sue his employer for a breach of the collective-bargaining agreement only if he shows that the union breached its duty of fair representation in its handling of the grievance.

Respondents contend that their duty of fair representation suit is less like a trust action than an attorney malpractice action which was historically an action at law. * * * We find that, in the context of the Seventh Amendment inquiry, the attorney malpractice analogy does not capture the relationship between the union and the represented employees as fully as the trust analogy does.

The attorney malpractice analogy is inadequate in several respects. Although an attorney malpractice suit is in some ways similar to a suit alleging a union's breach of its fiduciary duty, the two actions are fundamentally different. The nature of an action is in large part controlled by the nature of the underlying relationship between the parties. Unlike employees represented by a union, a client controls the significant decisions concerning his representation. Moreover, a client can fire his attorney if he is dissatisfied with his attorney's performance. This option is not available to an individual employee who is unhappy with a union's representation, unless a majority of the members of the bargaining unit share his dissatisfaction. Thus, we find the malpractice analogy less convincing than the trust analogy.

Nevertheless, the trust analogy does not persuade us to characterize respondents' claim as wholly equitable. The Union's argument mischaracterizes the nature of our comparison of the action before us to 18th-century forms of action. As we observed in Ross v. Bernhard, [supra p. 545], "The Seventh Amendment question depends on the nature of the *issue* to be tried rather than the character of the overall action." * * * [T]o recover from the Union here, respondents must prove both that McLean violated § 301 by breaching the collective-bargaining agreement and that the Union breached its duty of fair representation.[6] When

---

6. The dissent characterizes this opinion as "pars[ing] legal elements out of equitable claims". The question whether the Seventh Amendment analysis requires an examination of the nature of each element of a typical claim is not presented by this case. The claim we confront here is not typical; instead, it is a claim consisting of discrete issues that would normally be brought as two claims, one against the employer and one against the union. Had the employer remained a defendant in this action, the dissent would surely agree that the 301 claim against the employer was a separate claim. The Seventh Amendment analysis should not turn on the ability of the plaintiff to maintain his suit against both defendants, when the issues in the suit remain the same even when he can sue only the union. Consideration of the nature of

viewed in isolation, the duty of fair representation issue is analogous to a claim against a trustee for breach of fiduciary duty. The § 301 issue, however, is comparable to a breach of contract claim—a legal issue.

Respondents' action against the Union thus encompasses both equitable and legal issues. The first part of our Seventh Amendment inquiry, then, leaves us in equipoise as to whether respondents are entitled to a jury trial.

B

Our determination under the first part of the Seventh Amendment analysis is only preliminary. In this case, the only remedy sought is a request for compensatory damages representing backpay and benefits. Generally, an action for money damages was "the traditional form of relief offered in the courts of law." Curtis v. Loether, 415 U.S. 189, 196, 94 S.Ct. 1005, 1009, 39 L.Ed.2d 260 (1974). This Court has not, however, held that "any award of monetary relief must *necessarily* be 'legal' relief." *Ibid.* (emphasis added). Nonetheless, because we conclude that the remedy respondents seek has none of the attributes that must be present before we will find an exception to the general rule and characterize damages as equitable, we find that the remedy sought by respondents is legal.

First, we have characterized damages as equitable where they are restitutionary, such as in "action[s] for disgorgement of improper profits," *Tull,* 481 U.S., at 424, 107 S.Ct., at 1839. The backpay sought by respondents is not money wrongfully held by the Union, but wages and benefits they would have received from McLean had the Union processed the employees' grievances properly. Such relief is not restitutionary.

Second, a monetary award "incidental to or intertwined with injunctive relief" may be equitable. *Tull,* supra, 481 U.S., at 424, 107 S.Ct., at 1839. Because respondents seek only money damages, this characteristic is clearly absent from the case.[8]

The Union argues that the backpay relief sought here must nonetheless be considered equitable because this Court has labeled backpay awarded under Title VII, 42 U.S.C. § 2000e et seq. (1982 ed.), as

---

the two issues in this hybrid action is therefore warranted.

8. Both the Union and the dissent argue that the backpay award sought here is equitable because it is closely analogous to damages awarded to beneficiaries for a trustee's breach of trust. Such damages were available only in courts of equity because those courts had exclusive jurisdiction over actions involving a trustee's breach of his fiduciary duties.

The Union's argument, however, conflates the two parts of our Seventh Amendment inquiry. Under the dissent's approach, if the action at issue were analogous to an 18th-century action within the

exclusive jurisdiction of the courts of equity, we would necessarily conclude that the remedy sought was also equitable because it would have been unavailable in a court of law. This view would, in effect, make the first part of our inquiry dispositive. We have clearly held, however, that the second part of the inquiry he nature of the relief s more important to the Seventh Amendment determination. The second part of the analysis, therefore, should not replicate the "abstruse historical" inquiry of the first part, *Ross,* but requires consideration of the general types of relief provided by courts of law and equity.

equitable. It contends that the Title VII analogy is compelling in the context of the duty of fair representation because its backpay provision was based on the NLRA provision governing backpay awards for unfair labor practices. We are not convinced.

The Court has never held that a plaintiff seeking backpay under Title VII has a right to a jury trial. Assuming, without deciding, that such a Title VII plaintiff has no right to a jury trial, the Union's argument does not persuade us that respondents are not entitled to a jury trial here. Congress specifically characterized backpay under Title VII as a form of "equitable relief." 42 U.S.C. § 2000e–5(g) (1982 ed.) ("[T]he court may ... order such affirmative action as may be appropriate, which may include, but is not limited to, reinstatement or hiring of employees, with or without back pay ..., or any other equitable relief as the court deems appropriate"). See also Curtis v. Loether [supra p. 555] (distinguishing backpay under Title VII from damages under Title VIII, the fair housing provision of the Civil Rights Act, which the Court characterized as "legal" for Seventh Amendment purposes). Congress made no similar pronouncement regarding the duty of fair representation. Furthermore, the Court has noted that backpay sought from an employer under Title VII would generally be restitutionary in nature, in contrast to the damages sought here from the Union. Thus, the remedy sought in this duty of fair representation case is clearly different from backpay sought for violations of Title VII.

Moreover, the fact that Title VII's backpay provision may have been modeled on a provision in the NLRA concerning remedies for unfair labor practices does not require that the backpay remedy available here be considered equitable. The Union apparently reasons that if Title VII is comparable to one labor law remedy it is comparable to all remedies available in the NLRA context. Although both the duty of fair representation and the unfair labor practice provisions of the NLRA are components of national labor policy, their purposes are not identical. Unlike the unfair labor practice provisions of the NLRA, which are concerned primarily with the public interest in effecting federal labor policy, the duty of fair representation targets " 'the wrong done the individual employee.' " Electrical Workers v. Foust, 442 U.S. 42, 49, n. 12, 99 S.Ct. 2121, 2126, n. 12, 60 L.Ed.2d 698 (1979) (quoting Vaca v. Sipes, 386 U.S., at 182, n. 8, 87 S.Ct., at 912–913 n. 8) (emphasis deleted). Thus, the remedies appropriate for unfair labor practices may differ from the remedies for a breach of the duty of fair representation, given the need to vindicate different goals. Certainly, the connection between backpay under Title VII and damages under the unfair labor practice provision of the NLRA does not require us to find a parallel connection between Title VII backpay and money damages for breach of the duty of fair representation.

We hold, then, that the remedy of backpay sought in this duty of fair representation action is legal in nature. Considering both parts of the Seventh Amendment inquiry, we find that respondents are entitled to a jury trial on all issues presented in their suit.

IV

On balance, our analysis of the nature of respondents' duty of fair representation action and the remedy they seek convinces us that this action is a legal one. Although the search for an adequate 18th–century analog revealed that the claim includes both legal and equitable issues, the money damages respondents seek are the type of relief traditionally awarded by courts of law. Thus, the Seventh Amendment entitles respondents to a jury trial, and we therefore affirm the judgment of the Court of Appeals.

JUSTICE BRENNAN, concurring in part and concurring in the judgment.

I agree with the Court that respondents seek a remedy that is legal in nature and that the Seventh Amendment entitles respondents to a jury trial on their duty of fair representation claims. I therefore join Parts I, II, III–B, and IV of the Court's opinion. I do not join that part of the opinion which reprises the particular historical analysis this Court has employed to determine whether a claim is a "Suit at common law" under the Seventh Amendment, because I believe the historical test can and should be simplified.

The current test, first expounded in *Curtis v. Loether,* requires a court to compare the right at issue to 18th-century English forms of action to determine whether the historically analogous right was vindicated in an action at law or in equity, and to examine whether the remedy sought is legal or equitable in nature. However, this Court, in expounding the test, has repeatedly discounted the significance of the analogous form of action for deciding where the Seventh Amendment applies. I think it is time we dispense with it altogether.[1] I would decide Seventh Amendment questions on the basis of the relief sought. If the relief is legal in nature, i.e., if it is the kind of relief that historically was available from courts of law, I would hold that the parties have a constitutional right to a trial by jury—unless Congress has permissibly delegated the particular dispute to a non-Article III decisionmaker and jury trials would frustrate Congress' purposes in enacting a particular statutory scheme.[2]

I believe that our insistence that the jury trial right hinges in part on a comparison of the substantive right at issue to forms of action used in English courts 200 years ago needlessly convolutes our Seventh Amendment jurisprudence. For the past decade and a half, this Court has explained that the two parts of the historical test are not equal in

1. I therefore also do not join Part III of Justice Marshall opinion because it considers which 18th-century actions are comparable to the modern-day statutory claim brought here.

2. As the majority notes, ante at n. 4, where Congress has delegated a particular claim to an administrative agency or specialized court of equity, a court must consider whether the delegation is a permissi-

ble one and "whether jury trials would impair the functioning of the legislative scheme." Granfinanciera, S.A. v. Nordberg, 492 U.S. 33, 42, 109 S.Ct. 2782, 2790, 106 L.Ed.2d 26 (1989). These questions are not implicated in this case, as it is undisputed that an action for breach of the duty of fair representation may be brought in an Article III court.

weight, that the nature of the remedy is more important than the nature of the right. Since the existence of a right to jury trial therefore turns on the nature of the remedy, absent congressional delegation to a specialized decisionmaker,[3] there remains little purpose to our rattling through dusty attics of ancient writs. The time has come to borrow William of Occam's razor and sever this portion of our analysis.

We have long acknowledged that, of the factors relevant to the jury trial right, comparison of the claim to ancient forms of action, "requiring extensive and possibly abstruse historical inquiry, is obviously the most difficult to apply." Ross v. Bernhard, 396 U.S. 531, 538, n. 10, 90 S.Ct. 733, 738, n. 10, 24 L.Ed.2d 729 (1970). Requiring judges, with neither the training nor time necessary for reputable historical scholarship, to root through the tangle of primary and secondary sources to determine which of a hundred or so writs is analogous to the right at issue has embroiled courts in recondite controversies better left to legal historians. For example, in *Granfinanciera, S.A.,* [infra, p. 581], * * * both Justice White, in dissent, and I, writing for the Court, struggled with the question whether an equity court would have heard the suit that was comparable to the modern statutory action at issue. * * *

To be sure, it is neither unusual nor embarrassing for members of a court to disagree and disagree vehemently. But it better behooves judges to disagree within the province of judicial expertise. Furthermore, inquiries into the appropriate historical analogs for the rights at issue are not necessarily susceptible of sound resolution under the best of circumstances. * * *

In addition, modern statutory rights did not exist in the 18th-century and even the most exacting historical research may not elicit a clear historical analog. The right at issue here, for example, is a creature of modern labor law quite foreign to Georgian England. * * * I have grappled with this kind of inquiry for three decades on this Court and have come to the realization that engaging in such inquiries is impracticable and unilluminating.

To rest the historical test required by the Seventh Amendment solely on the nature of the relief sought would not, of course, offer the federal courts a rule that is in all cases self-executing. Courts will still be required to ask which remedies were traditionally available at law and which only in equity. But this inquiry involves fewer variables and simpler choices, on the whole, and is far more manageable than the

---

3. Even where Congress has assigned resolution of a dispute to a specialized forum, the right to a jury trial does not turn on whether the analogous 18th-century action was legal or equitable. As we explained in *Granfinanciera, S.A., supra,* at n. 4, a court first looks to the analogous historical form of action and the nature of the relief sought, allotting greater weight to the nature of the relief. If this inquiry leads the court to conclude that the party is entitled to a jury trial, the court must consider whether the party is asserting a public right or private right distinction contingent on the government's role in creating the right, and whether jury trials would impair the functioning of the legislative scheme. The result of the search for a historical analog is subordinate to the nature of the relief sought and irrelevant to the subsequent inquiry.

scholasticist debates in which we have been engaged. Moreover, the rule I propose would remain true to the Seventh Amendment, as it is undisputed that, historically, "[j]urisdictional lines [between law and equity] were primarily a matter of remedy." McCoid, Procedural Reform and the Right to Jury Trial: A Study of Beacon Theatres, Inc. v. Westover, 116 U.Pa.L.Rev. 1 (1967). See also Redish, Seventh Amendment Right to Jury Trial: A Study in the Irrationality of Rational Decision Making, 70 Nw.U.L.Rev. 486, 490 (1975) ("In the majority of cases at common law, the equitable or legal nature of a suit was determined not by the substantive nature of the cause of action but by the remedy sought").[7]

This is not to say that the resulting division between claims entitled to jury trials and claims not so entitled would exactly mirror the division between law and equity in England in 1791. But it is too late in the day for this Court to profess that the Seventh Amendment preserves the right to jury trial only in cases that would have been heard in the British law courts of the 18th century. * * *

Indeed, given this Court's repeated insistence that the nature of the remedy is always to be given more weight than the nature of the historically analogous right, it is unlikely that the simplified Seventh Amendment analysis I propose will result in different decisions than the analysis in current use. In the unusual circumstance that the nature of the remedy could be characterized equally as legal or equitable, I submit that the comparison of a contemporary statutory action unheard of in the 18th century to some ill-fitting ancient writ is too shaky a basis for the resolution of an issue as significant as the availability of a trial by jury. If, in the rare case, a tie-breaker is needed, let us break the tie in favor of jury trial.

7. There are, to be sure, some who advocate abolishing the historical test altogether. See, e.g., Wolfram, The Constitutional History of the Seventh Amendment, 57 Minn.L.Rev. 639, 742 47 (1973). Contrary to the intimations in Justice Kennedy's dissent, I am not among them. I believe that it is imperative to retain a historical test, for determining when parties have a right to jury trial, for precisely the same reasons Justice Kennedy, does. It is mandated by the language of the Seventh Amendment and it is a bulwark against those who would restrict a right our forefathers held indispensible. Like Justice Kennedy, I have no doubt that courts can and do look to legal history for the answers to constitutional questions, and therefore the Seventh Amendment test I propose today obligates courts to do exactly that.

Where Justice Kennedy and I differ is in our evaluations of which historical test provides the more reliable results. That three learned Justices of the Supreme Court can-not arrive at the same conclusion in this very case, on what is essentially a question of fact, does not speak well for the judicial solvency of the current test. My concern is not merely the competence of courts to delve into this peculiarly recalcitrant aspect of legal history and certainly not, as Justice Kennedy summarizes it, the "competence of the Court to understand legal history" in general. My concern is that all too often the first prong of the current test requires courts to measure modern statutory actions against 18th-century English actions so remote in form and concept that there is no firm basis for comparison. In such cases, the result is less the discovery of a historical analog than the manufacture of a historical fiction. By contrast, the nature of relief available today corresponds more directly to the nature of relief available in Georgian England. Thus the historical test I propose, focusing on the nature of the relief sought, is not only more manageable than the current test, it is more reliably grounded in history.

What Blackstone described as "the glory of the English law" and "the most transcendent privilege which any subject can enjoy," 3 W. Blackstone, Commentaries, was crucial in the eyes of those who founded this country. The encroachment on civil jury trial by colonial administrators was a "deeply divisive issue in the years just preceding the outbreak of hostilities between the colonies and England," and all thirteen States reinstituted the right after hostilities ensued. Wolfram, The Constitutional History of the Seventh Amendment, 57 Minn.L.Rev. 639, 654–655 (1973). "In fact, '[t]he right to trial by jury was probably the only one universally secured by the first American constitutions.'" Id., at 655 (quoting L. Levy, Freedom of Speech and Press in Early American History—Legacy of Suppression 281 (1963 reprint)). Fear of a federal government that had not guaranteed jury trial in civil cases, voiced first at the Philadelphia Convention in 1787 and regularly during the ratification debates, was the concern that precipitated the maelstrom over the need for a bill of rights in the United States Constitution.

* * *

We can guard this right and save our courts from needless and intractable excursions into increasingly unfamiliar territory simply by retiring that prong of our Seventh Amendment test which we have already cast into a certain doubt. If we are not prepared to accord the nature of the historical analog sufficient weight for this factor to affect the outcome of our inquiry, except in the rarest of hypothetical cases, what reason do we have for insisting that federal judges proceed with this arduous inquiry? It is time we read the writing on the wall, especially as we ourselves put it there.

JUSTICE STEVENS, concurring in part and concurring in the judgment.

Because I believe the Court has made this case unnecessarily difficult by exaggerating the importance of finding a precise common-law analogue to the duty of fair representation, I do not join Part III–A of its opinion. Ironically, by stressing the importance of identifying an exact analogue the Court has diminished the utility of looking for any analogue.

As I have suggested in the past, I believe the duty of fair representation action resembles a common law action against an attorney for malpractice more closely than it does any other form of action. Of course, this action is not an exact counterpart to a malpractice suit. Indeed, by definition, no recently recognized form of action—whether the product of express congressional enactment or of judicial interpretation—can have a precise analogue in 17th or 18th century English law. Were it otherwise the form of action would not in fact be "recently recognized."

But the Court surely overstates this action's similarity to an action against a trustee. Collective bargaining involves no settlor, no trust corpus, and no trust instrument executed to convey property to beneficiaries chosen at the settlor's pleasure. Nor are these distinctions reified matters of pure form. The law of trusts originated to expand the varieties of land ownership in feudal England, and evolved to protect the paternalistic beneficence of the wealthy, often between generations and always over time. Beneficiaries are protected from their own judgment. The attorney-client relationship, by contrast, advances the client's interests in dealings with adverse parties. Clients are saved from their lack of skill, but their judgment is honored. Union members, as a group, accordingly have the power to hire, fire, and direct the actions of their representatives—prerogatives anathema to the paternalistic forms of the equitable trust.[2]

Equitable reasoning calibrated by the sophisticated judgment of the jurist, the accountant, and the chancellor is thus appropriately invoked when the impact of a trustee's conduct on the future interests of contingent remaindermen must be reviewed. However, the common sense understanding of the jury, selected to represent the community, is appropriately invoked when disputes in the factory, the warehouse, and the garage must be resolved. In most duty of fair representation cases, the issues, which require an understanding of the realities of employment relationships, are typical grist for the jury's judgment. Indeed, the law defining the union's duty of fair representation has developed in cases tried to juries. * * *

As the Court correctly observed in Curtis v. Loether, "in an ordinary civil action in the district courts, where there is obviously no functional justification for denying the jury trial right, a jury trial must be available if the action involves rights and remedies of the sort typically enforced in an action at law." * * * Duty of fair representation suits are for the most part ordinary civil actions involving the stuff of contract and malpractice disputes. There is accordingly no ground for excluding these actions from the jury right.

In my view, the evolution of this doctrine through suits tried to juries, the useful analogy to common-law malpractice cases, and the well-recognized duty to scrutinize any proposed curtailment of the right to a jury trial "with the utmost care," provide a plainly sufficient basis for the Court's holding today. I therefore join its judgment and all of its opinion except for Part III–A.

JUSTICE KENNEDY, with whom JUSTICE O'CONNOR and JUSTICE SCALIA join, dissenting.

This case asks whether the Seventh Amendment guarantees the respondent union members a jury trial in a duty of fair representation action against their labor union. The Court is quite correct, in my view, in its formulation of the initial premises that must govern the case. Under Curtis v. Loether, the right to a jury trial in a statutory action depends on the presence of "legal rights and remedies." To determine whether rights and remedies in a duty of fair representation action are

---

2. Indeed, to make sense of the trust analogy, the majority must apparently be willing to assume that the union members, considered collectively, are both beneficiary and settlor, and that the settlor retains considerable power over the corpus, including the power to revoke the trust. That is an odd sort of trust.

legal in character, we must compare the action to the 18th-century cases permitted in the law courts of England, and we must examine the nature of the relief sought. I agree also with those Members of the Court who find that the duty of fair representation action resembles an equitable trust action more than a suit for malpractice.

I disagree with the analytic innovation of the Court that identification of the trust action as a model for modern duty of fair representation actions is insufficient to decide the case. The Seventh Amendment requires us to determine whether the duty of fair representation action "is more similar to cases that were tried in courts of law than to suits tried in courts of equity." Tull v. United States, 481 U.S. 412, 417, 107 S.Ct. 1831, 1835, 95 L.Ed.2d 365 (1987). Having made this decision in favor of an equitable action, our inquiry should end. Because the Court disagrees with this proposition, I dissent.

I

Both the union and the respondents identify historical actions to which they find the duty of fair representation action most analogous. * * *

Justice Marshall, speaking for four Members of the Court, states an important and correct reason for finding the trust model better than the malpractice analogy. He observes that the client of an attorney, unlike a union member or beneficiary, controls the significant decisions concerning his litigation and can fire the attorney if not satisfied. Put another way, although a lawyer acts as an agent of his client, unions and trustees do not serve as agents of their members and beneficiaries in the conventional sense of being subject to their direction and control in pursuing claims. An individual union member cannot require his union to pursue a claim and cannot choose a different representative. A trustee, likewise, may exercise proper discretion in deciding whether to press claims held in trust, and in general does not act as an agent of his beneficiaries. * * *

Further considerations fortify the conclusion that the trust analogy is the controlling one here. A union's duty of fair representation accords with a trustee's duty of impartiality. The duty of fair representation requires a union "to make an honest effort to serve the interests of all of [its] members, without hostility to any." Ford Motor Co. v. Huffman, 345 U.S. 330, 337, 73 S.Ct. 681, 686, 97 L.Ed. 1048 (1953). This standard may require a union to act for the benefit of employees who, as in this case, have antithetical interests. Trust law, in a similar manner, long has required trustees to serve the interests of all beneficiaries with impartiality.

A lawyer's duty of loyalty is cast in different terms. Although the union is charged with the responsibility of reconciling the positions of its members, the lawyer's duty of loyalty long has precluded the representation of conflicting interests. A lawyer, at least absent knowing waiver by the parties, could not represent both the respondents and the senior laid-off workers as the union has done in this case.

The relief available in a duty of fair representation action also makes the trust action the better model. To remedy a breach of the duty of fair representation, a court must issue an award "fashioned to make the injured employee whole." Electrical Workers v. Foust, 442 U.S. 42, 49, 99 S.Ct. 2121, 2126, 60 L.Ed.2d 698 (1979). The court may order an injunction compelling the union, if it is still able, to pursue the employee's claim, and may require monetary compensation, but it cannot award exemplary or punitive damages. This relief parallels the remedies prevailing in the courts of equity in actions against trustees for failing to pursue claims.

These remedies differ somewhat from those available in attorney malpractice actions. Because legal malpractice was a common law claim, clients sued their attorneys for breach of professional obligations in the law courts. No one maintains that clients could obtain from these courts the injunctive relief offered in duty of fair representation actions. The evidence suggests that compensatory damages in malpractice cases resembled the monetary relief now awarded in duty of fair representation actions. Yet, as a historical matter, juries did have the authority to award exemplary damages in at least some tort actions. * * *

For all these reasons, the suit here resembles a trust action, not a legal malpractice action. By this I do not imply that a union acts as a trustee in all instances or that trust law, as a general matter, should inform any particular aspects of federal labor law. Obvious differences between a union and a trustee will exist in other contexts. I would conclude only that, under the analysis directed by our precedents, the respondents may not insist on a jury trial. When all rights and remedies are considered, their action resembles a suit heard by the courts of equity more than a case heard by the courts of law. From this alone it follows that the respondents have no jury trial right on their duty of fair representation claims against the union.

II

The Court relies on two lines of precedents to overcome the conclusion that the trust action should serve as the controlling model. The first consists of cases in which the Court has considered simplifications in litigation resulting from modern procedural reforms in the federal courts. Justice Marshall asserts that these cases show that the Court must look at the character of individual issues rather than claims as a whole. The second line addresses the significance of the remedy in determining the equitable or legal nature of an action for the purpose of choosing the most appropriate analogy. Under these cases, the Court decides that the respondents have a right to a jury because they seek money damages. These authorities do not support the Court's holding.

A

In three cases we have found a right to trial by jury where there are legal claims that, for procedural reasons, a plaintiff could have or must have raised in the courts of equity before the systems merged. * * * [Justice Kennedy here discusses *Beacon Theatres, Dairy Queen,* and *Ross.*]

These three cases responded to the difficulties created by a merged court system. They stand for the proposition that, because distinct courts of equity no longer exist, the possibility or necessity of using former equitable procedures to press a legal claim no longer will determine the right to a jury. Justice Marshall reads these cases to require a jury trial whenever a cause of action contains legal issues and would require a jury trial in this case because the respondents must prove a breach of the collective-bargaining agreement as one element of their claim.

I disagree. The respondents, as shown above, are asserting an equitable claim. Having reached this conclusion, the *Beacon, Dairy Queen,* and *Ross* cases are inapplicable. Although we have divided self-standing legal claims from equitable declaratory, accounting, and derivative procedures, we have never parsed legal elements out of equitable claims absent specific procedural justifications. Actions which, beyond all question, are equitable in nature may involve some predicate inquiry that would be submitted to a jury in other contexts. For example, just as the plaintiff in a duty of fair representation action against his union must show breach of the collective-bargaining agreement as an initial matter, in an action against a trustee for failing to pursue a claim the beneficiary must show that the claim had some merit. But the question of the claim's validity, even if the claim raises contract issues, would not bring the jury right into play in a suit against a trustee.

Our own writing confirms the consistency of this view with respect to the action before us. We have not deemed the elements of a duty of fair representation action to be independent of each other. Proving breach of the collective-bargaining agreement is but a preliminary and indispensable step to obtaining relief in a duty of fair representation action. * * * The absence of distinct equitable courts provides no procedural reason for wresting one of these elements from the other.

B

The Court also rules that, despite the appropriateness of the trust analogy as a whole, the respondents have a right to a jury trial because they seek money damages. The nature of the remedy remains a factor of considerable importance in determining whether a statutory action had a legal or equitable analog in 1791, but we have not adopted a rule that a statutory action permitting damages is by definition more analogous to a legal action than to any equitable suit. In each case, we look to the remedy to determine whether, taken with other factors, it places an action within the definition of "suits at common law."

In *Curtis,* for example, we ruled that the availability of actual and punitive damages made a statutory anti-discrimination action resemble a legal tort action more than any equitable action. We made explicit that we did not "go so far as to say that any award of monetary relief must necessarily be 'legal' relief." Although monetary damages might cause some statutory actions to resemble tort suits, the presence of monetary damages in this duty of fair representation action does not make it more analogous to a legal action than to an equitable action. Indeed, as shown above, the injunctive and monetary remedies available make the duty of fair representation suit less analogous to a malpractice action than to a suit against a trustee.

* * *

* * * The courts of equity could and did award the kind of damages sought by the respondents here. The respondents' mere request for backpay in no way entitles them to a jury under the Seventh Amendment.

III

The Court must adhere to the historical test in determining the right to a jury because the language of the Constitution requires it. The Seventh Amendment "preserves" the right to jury trial in civil cases. We cannot preserve a right existing in 1791 unless we look to history to identify it. Our precedents are in full agreement with this reasoning and insist on adherence to the historical test. No alternatives short of rewriting the Constitution exist. * * * If we abandon the plain language of the Constitution to expand the jury right, we may expect Courts with opposing views to curtail it in the future.

It is true that a historical inquiry into the distinction between law and equity may require us to enter into a domain becoming less familiar with time. Two centuries have passed since the Seventh Amendment's ratification and the incompleteness of our historical records makes it difficult to know the nature of certain actions in 1791. The historical test, nonetheless, has received more criticism than it deserves. Although our application of the analysis in some cases may seem biased in favor of jury trials, the test has not become a nullity. We do not require juries in all statutory actions. * * *

I would hesitate to abandon or curtail the historical test out of concern for the competence of the Court to understand legal history. We do look to history for the answers to constitutional questions. Although opinions will differ on what this history shows, the approach has no less validity in the Seventh Amendment context than elsewhere.

If Congress has not provided for a jury trial, we are confined to the Seventh Amendment to determine whether one is required. Our own views respecting the wisdom of using a jury should be put aside. Like Justice Brennan, I admire the jury process. Other judges have taken the opposite view. See, e.g., J. Frank, Law and the Modern Mind 170–185

(1931). But the judgment of our own times is not always preferable to the lessons of history. Our whole constitutional experience teaches that history must inform the judicial inquiry. Our obligation to the Constitution and its Bill of Rights, no less than the compact we have with the generation that wrote them for us, do not permit us to disregard provisions that some may think to be mere matters of historical form.

* * *

Notes and Questions

1. Which historical analogy considered by the Court do you find to be closer to the cause of action provided in section 301? Should it matter, for purposes of determining the Seventh Amendment right?

2. Note that the Court in *Terry* indicates that in the two-part historical test outlined in *Tull*, "[t]he second inquiry is the more important in our analysis." Do you understand why? Under this weighted approach, what function does the first element of the test actually serve? Does it serve *any* real function?

3. In applying the second part of the *Tull* test, the Court distinguished the award of backpay under Title VII of the 1964 Civil Rights Act. How persuasive is the asserted basis of distinction?

4. *Terry* was deemed controlling in Wooddell v. International Brotherhood of Electrical Workers, Local 71, 502 U.S. 93, 112 S.Ct. 494, 116 L.Ed.2d 419 (1991). Plaintiff alleged that the Local had violated his rights under Title I of the Labor Management Reporting and Disclosure Act of 1959, by discriminating against him in job referrals in the operation of a hiring hall provided for in the Local's collective-bargaining contracts with electrical contractors. He sought injunctive relief, lost wages and benefits, additional compensatory damages, punitive damages, and attorney's fees. Plaintiff argued "that, although he seeks injunctive relief as well as damages, the injunctive relief is incidental to the damages, and not vice versa, and that his claim for lost wages cannot be treated as restitutionary incident to an order reinstating him to a job from which he has been terminated, as the damages sought are for pay for jobs to which the union failed to refer him." 502 U.S. at 97–98, 112 S.Ct. at 498. The Court agreed, holding that the jury trial right applied under *Terry*.

THE RIGHT TO JURY TRIAL IN STATUTORILY–CREATED ADMINISTRATIVE PROCEEDINGS

In NLRB v. Jones & Laughlin Steel Corp., 301 U.S. 1, 57 S.Ct. 615, 81 L.Ed. 893 (1937), discussed in Curtis v. Loether, supra p. 555, the Supreme Court denied a right to jury trial in an administrative proceeding for a back-pay order, despite the argument that an award of back pay was analogous to an award of damages at common law. The Court reasoned that the Seventh Amendment "has no application to cases where recovery of money damages is an incident to equitable relief even though damages might have been recovered in an action at law." The Court, in other words, relied on a form of the "clean-up" doctrine.

The Court also rejected the jury trial right because "[t]he instant case is not a suit at common law or in the nature of such a suit. The proceeding is one unknown at the common law. It is a statutory proceeding. Reinstatement of the employee and payment for time lost are requirements imposed for violation of the statute and are remedies appropriate to its enforcement."

In Atlas Roofing Co., Inc. v. Occupational Safety and Health Review Commission, 430 U.S. 442, 97 S.Ct. 1261, 51 L.Ed.2d 464 (1977), the Supreme Court held that the Seventh Amendment does not preclude Congress from assigning to an administrative agency the task of adjudicating violations of the Occupational Safety and Health Act of 1970. The Act "created a new statutory duty to avoid maintaining unsafe or unhealthy working conditions," and authorized the Commission to impose civil penalties on any employer maintaining any unsafe working condition. Recall Smith v. Western Electric Co., supra p. 86. Justice White, speaking for the Court, acknowledged the rule of Parsons v. Bedford, that the right to jury trial in a suit brought pursuant to a new statute is determined by analogy to common law practice. It had been argued "that a suit in federal court by the Government for civil penalties for violation of a statute is a suit for a money judgment which is classically a suit at common law, and that the defendant therefore has a Seventh Amendment right to a jury determination of all issues of fact in such a case." But the Court rejected this argument:

> At least in cases in which "public rights" are being litigated— e.g., cases in which the Government sues in its sovereign capacity to enforce public rights created by statutes within the power of Congress to enact—the Seventh Amendment does not prohibit Congress from assigning the factfinding function and initial adjudication to an administrative forum with which the jury would be incompatible.

> * * *

> Congress is not required by the Seventh Amendment to choke the already crowded federal courts with new types of litigation or prevented from committing some new types of litigation to administrative agencies with special competence in the relevant field. This is the case even if the Seventh Amendment would have required a jury where the adjudication of those rights is assigned to a federal court of law instead of an administrative agency.

In response to the argument "that the right to jury trial was never intended to depend on the identity of the forum to which Congress has chosen to submit a dispute; otherwise, * * * Congress could utterly destroy the right to a jury trial by always providing for administrative rather than judicial resolution of the vast range of cases that now arise in the courts," Justice White reasoned:

> Our prior cases support administrative factfinding in only those situations involving "public rights" * * *. Wholly private tort, con-

tract, and property cases as well as a vast range of other cases, are not at all implicated.

More to the point, it is apparent from the history of jury trial in civil matters that factfinding * * * was never the exclusive province of the jury under the English or American legal systems at the time of the adoption of the Seventh Amendment; and the question whether a fact would be found by a jury turned to a considerable degree on the nature of the forum in which a litigant found himself. Critical factfinding was performed without juries in suits in equity, and there were no juries in admiralty; nor were there juries in the military justice system.

* * *

The point is that the Seventh Amendment was never intended to establish the jury as the exclusive mechanism for factfinding in civil cases. It took the existing legal order as it found it * * *. We cannot conclude that the Amendment rendered Congress powerless—when it concluded that remedies available in courts of law were inadequate to cope with a problem within Congress' power to regulate—to create new public rights and remedies by statute and commit their enforcement, if it chose, to a tribunal other than a court of law—such as an administrative agency—in which facts are not found by juries.

Notes and Questions

1. Did the Court in *Curtis* adequately distinguish *Jones & Laughlin?*

2. Re-examine Justice Story's reasoning in Parsons v. Bedford, quoted in Ross v. Bernhard, supra p. 545, which the Court in Curtis v. Loether cites as establishing the "basic principle" that guides decisions in the area. Are NLRB v. Jones & Laughlin Steel Corp. or Atlas Roofing Co. v. OSHA consistent with *Parsons?* If not, is *Parsons'* continuing vitality undermined by these decisions?

3. Why is the fact that a so-called "public right", rather than a "private right", is involved so essential to the denial of the jury trial right in *Atlas Roofing?* Is there anything in the text of the Seventh Amendment to indicate the dichotomy's importance? Note that at common law, there is no evidence to indicate that the law-equity dichotomy, on which the jury trial right is largely determined, in any way turned on a distinction between "public" and "private" rights. Given the Court's emphasis on the "public"/"private" right distinction, is there any way logically to limit the distinction's effect to *administrative* proceedings? If a "public" right were adjudicated in a federal court, rather than before an administrative tribunal, should the Court's logic apply to deny a jury trial right? If not, should the distinction make any difference in an administrative proceeding, either?

4. Note that in *Atlas Roofing,* Justice White states that use of a jury would be "incompatible" with an administrative proceeding. Does this amount to a balancing of the Seventh Amendment right against competing

governmental interests? If so, is such a practice consistent with the Court's attitude towards balancing expressed in *Curtis?*

5. To support its conclusion concerning the absence of a right to jury trial, the Court in *Atlas Roofing* relied on Supreme Court precedents dating from the year 1856. According to one commentator, the fact that "[t]here is no attempt in *Atlas Roofing* to follow the classic doctrine that the scope of the seventh amendment is determined by reference to the common law of 1791" is "unusual". Kirst, Administrative Penalties and the Civil Jury: The Supreme Court's Assault on the Seventh Amendment, 126 U.Pa.L.Rev. 1281, 1282–83 (1978). Professor Kirst believes that *"Atlas* demonstrates how easily a modern court can misinterpret the seventh amendment if the analysis begins in the middle of the historical development." Id. at 1283.

GRANFINANCIERA, S.A. v. NORDBERG

Supreme Court of the United States, 1989.
492 U.S. 33, 109 S.Ct. 2782, 106 L.Ed.2d 26.

JUSTICE BRENNAN delivered the opinion of the Court.

The question presented is whether a person who has not submitted a claim against a bankruptcy estate has a right to a jury trial when sued by the trustee in bankruptcy to recover an allegedly fraudulent monetary transfer. We hold that the Seventh Amendment entitles such a person to a trial by jury, notwithstanding Congress' designation of fraudulent conveyance actions as "core proceedings" in 28 U.S.C. § 157(b)(2)(H) (1982 ed., Supp. IV).

I

The Chase & Sanborn Corporation filed a petition for reorganization under Chapter 11 in 1983. A Plan of Reorganization approved by the United States Bankruptcy Court for the Southern District of Florida vested in respondent Nordberg, the trustee in bankruptcy, causes of action for fraudulent conveyances. In 1985, respondent filed suit against petitioners Granfinanciera, S.A. and Medex, Ltda. in the United States District Court for the Southern District of Florida. The complaint alleged that petitioners had received $1.7 million from Chase & Sanborn's corporate predecessor within one year of the date its bankruptcy petition was filed, without receiving consideration or reasonably equivalent value in return. Respondent sought to avoid what it alleged were constructively and actually fraudulent transfers and to recover damages, costs, expenses, and interest under 11 U.S.C. §§ 548(a)(1) and (a)(2), 550(a)(1) (1982 ed. and Supp. V).

The District Court referred the proceedings to the Bankruptcy Court. Over five months later, and shortly before the Colombian Government nationalized Granfinanciera, respondent served a summons on petitioners in Bogota, Colombia. In their answer to the complaint following Granfinanciera's nationalization, both petitioners requested a "trial by jury on all issues so triable." The Bankruptcy Judge denied petitioners' request for a jury trial, deeming a suit to recover a fraudulent transfer "a core action that originally, under the English common law, as I understand it, was a non-jury issue." Following a bench trial, the court dismissed with prejudice respondent's actual fraud claim but entered judgment for respondent on the constructive fraud claim in the amount of $1,500,000 against Granfinanciera and $180,000 against Medex. The District Court affirmed, without discussing petitioners' claim that they were entitled to a jury trial.

The Court of Appeals for the Eleventh Circuit also affirmed. * * *

III

* * *

The form of our analysis is familiar. "First, we compare the statutory action to 18th-century actions brought in the courts of England prior to the merger of the courts of law and equity. Second, we examine the remedy sought and determine whether it is legal or equitable in nature." Tull v. United States. The second stage of this analysis is more important than the first. If, on balance, these two factors indicate that a party is entitled to a jury trial under the Seventh Amendment, we must decide whether Congress may assign and has assigned resolution of the relevant claim to a non-Article III adjudicative body that does not use a jury as factfinder.[4]

A

There is no dispute that actions to recover preferential or fraudulent transfers were often brought at law in late 18th-century England. * * * These actions, like all suits at law, were conducted before juries.

Respondent does not challenge this proposition or even contend that actions to recover fraudulent conveyances or preferential transfers were more than occasionally tried in courts of equity. He asserts only that courts of equity had concurrent jurisdiction with courts of law over fraudulent preference actions. While respondent's assertion that courts of equity sometimes provided relief in fraudulent preference actions is true, however, it hardly suffices to undermine petitioners' submission that the present action for *monetary* relief would not have sounded in equity two hundred years ago in England. * * *

4. This quite distinct inquiry into whether Congress has permissibly entrusted the resolution of certain disputes to an administrative agency or specialized court of equity, and whether jury trials would impair the functioning of the legislative scheme, appears to be what the Court contemplated when in Ross v. Bernhard it identified "the practical abilities and limitations of juries" as an additional factor to be consulted in determining whether the Seventh Amendment confers a jury trial right. * * * Contrary to Justice White's contention, we do not declare that the Seventh Amendment provides a right to a jury trial on all legal rather than equitable claims. If a claim that is legal in nature asserts a "public right," as we define that term in Part IV, then the Seventh Amendment does not entitle the parties to a jury trial if Congress assigns its adjudication to an administrative agency or specialized court of equity. The Seventh Amendment protects a litigant's right to a jury trial only if a cause of action is legal in nature and it involves a matter of "private right."

B

The nature of the relief respondent seeks strongly supports our preliminary finding that the right he invokes should be denominated legal rather than equitable. Our decisions establish beyond peradventure that "[i]n cases of fraud or mistake, as under any other head of chancery jurisdiction, a court of the United States will not sustain a bill in equity to obtain only a decree for the payment of money by way of damages, when the like amount can be recovered at law in an action sounding in tort or for money had and received." Buzard v. Houston, 119 U.S., at 352, 7 S.Ct., at 252, citing Parkersburg v. Brown, 106 U.S. 487, 500, 1 S.Ct. 442, 452, 27 L.Ed. 238 (1883). * * *

Respondent's fraudulent conveyance action plainly seeks relief traditionally provided by law courts or on the law side of courts having both legal and equitable dockets. Unless Congress may and has permissibly withdrawn jurisdiction over that action by courts of law and assigned it exclusively to non-Article III tribunals sitting without juries, the Seventh Amendment guarantees petitioners a jury trial upon request.

IV

Prior to passage of the Bankruptcy Reform Act of 1978, Pub.L. 95–598, 92 Stat. 2549 (1978 Act), "[s]uits to recover preferences constitute[d] no part of the proceedings in bankruptcy." Schoenthal v. Irving Trust Co. [287 U.S. 92, 94–95 (1932)]. Although related to bankruptcy proceedings, fraudulent conveyance and preference actions brought by a trustee in bankruptcy were deemed separate, plenary suits to which the Seventh Amendment applied. While the 1978 Act brought those actions within the jurisdiction of the bankruptcy courts, it preserved parties' rights to trial by jury as they existed prior to the effective date of the 1978 Act. 28 U.S.C. § 1480(a) (repealed). The 1984 Amendments, however, designated fraudulent conveyance actions "core proceedings," 28 U.S.C. § 157(b)(2)(H) (1982 ed., Supp. IV), which bankruptcy judges may adjudicate and in which they may issue final judgments, § 157(b)(1), if a district court has referred the matter to them. § 157(a). * * * The sole issue before us is whether the Seventh Amendment confers on petitioners a right to a jury trial in the face of Congress' decision to allow a non-Article III tribunal to adjudicate the claims against them.

A

In *Atlas Roofing*, we noted that "when Congress creates new statutory 'public rights,' it may assign their adjudication to an administrative agency with which a jury trial would be incompatible, without violating the Seventh Amendment's injunction that jury trial is to be 'preserved' in 'suits at common law.' " We emphasized, however, that Congress' power to block application of the Seventh Amendment to a cause of action has limits. Congress may only deny trials by jury in actions at law, we said, in cases where "public rights" are litigated: "Our prior cases support administrative factfinding in only those situations involving 'public rights,' e.g., where the Government is involved in its sovereign capacity under an otherwise valid statute creating enforceable public rights. Wholly private tort, contract, and property cases, as well as a vast range of other cases, are not at all implicated.''

We adhere to that general teaching. * * * Congress may devise novel causes of action involving public rights free from the strictures of the Seventh Amendment if it assigns their adjudication to tribunals without statutory authority to employ juries as factfinders. But it lacks the power to strip parties contesting matters of private right of their constitutional right to a trial by jury. As we recognized in *Atlas Roofing,* to hold otherwise would be to permit Congress to eviscerate the Seventh Amendment's guarantee by assigning to administrative agencies or courts of equity all causes of action not grounded in state law, whether they originate in a newly fashioned regulatory scheme or possess a long line of common-law forebears. The Constitution nowhere grants Congress such puissant authority. "[L]egal claims are not magically converted into equitable issues by their presentation to a court of equity," Ross v. Bernhard, nor can Congress conjure away the Seventh Amendment by mandating that traditional legal claims be brought there or taken to an administrative tribunal.

In certain situations, of course, Congress may fashion causes of action that are closely *analogous* to common-law claims and place them beyond the ambit of the Seventh Amendment by assigning their resolution to a forum in which jury trials are unavailable. * * * Unless a legal cause of action involves "public rights," Congress may not deprive parties litigating over that right of the Seventh Amendment's guarantee to a jury trial.

In *Atlas Roofing,* we noted that Congress may effectively supplant a common-law cause of action carrying with it a right to a jury trial with a statutory cause of action shorn of a jury trial right if that statutory cause of action inheres in or lies against the Federal Government in its sovereign capacity. Our case law makes plain, however, that the class of "public rights" whose adjudication Congress may assign to administrative agencies or courts of equity sitting without juries is more expansive than *Atlas Roofing*'s discussion suggests. Indeed, our decisions point to the conclusion that, if a statutory cause of action is legal in nature, the question whether the Seventh Amendment permits Congress to assign its adjudication to a tribunal that does not employ juries as factfinders requires the same answer as the question whether Article III allows Congress to assign adjudication of that cause of action to a non-Article III tribunal. For if a statutory cause of action, such as respondent's right to recover a fraudulent conveyance under 11 U.S.C. § 548(a)(2), is not a "public right" for Article III purposes, then Congress may not assign its adjudication to a specialized non-Article III court lacking "the essential attributes of the judicial power." Crowell v. Benson, 285 U.S., at 51, 52 S.Ct., at 292. And if the action must be tried under the auspices of an Article III court, then the Seventh Amendment affords the parties a right to a jury trial whenever the cause of action is legal in nature. Conversely, if Congress may assign the adjudication of a statutory cause of action to a non-Article III tribunal, then the Seventh Amendment poses no independent bar to the adjudication of that action by a nonjury factfinder. In addition to our Seventh Amendment precedents, we therefore rely as well on our decisions exploring the restrictions Article III places on Congress' choice of adjudicative bodies to resolve disputes over statutory rights to determine whether petitioners are entitled to a jury trial.

In our most recent discussion of the "public rights" doctrine as it bears on Congress' power to commit adjudication of a statutory cause of action to a non-Article III tribunal, we rejected the view that "a matter of public rights must at a minimum arise 'between the government and others.'" Northern Pipeline Construction Co. [v. Marathon Pipe Line Co., 458 U.S. 50 (1982)]. We held, instead, that the Federal Government need not be a party for a case to revolve around "public rights." Thomas v. Union Carbide Agricultural Products Co., 473 U.S., [568] at 586, (Brennan, J., concurring in judgment). The crucial question, in cases not involving the Federal Government, is whether "Congress, acting for a valid legislative purpose pursuant to its constitutional powers under Article I, [has] create[d] a seemingly 'private' right that is so closely integrated into a public regulatory scheme as to be a matter appropriate for agency resolution with limited involvement by the Article III judiciary." * * * If a statutory right is not closely intertwined with a federal regulatory program Congress has power to enact, and if that right neither belongs to nor exists against the Federal Government, then it must be adjudicated by an Article III court.[10] If the right is legal in nature, then it carries with it the Seventh Amendment's guarantee of a jury trial.

B

Although the issue admits of some debate, a bankruptcy trustee's right to recover a fraudulent conveyance under 11 U.S.C. § 548(a)(2)

---

10. In *Atlas Roofing,* we stated that "[i]n cases which do involve only 'private rights,' this Court has accepted factfinding by an administrative agency, without intervention by a jury, only as an adjunct to an Art. III court, analogizing the agency to a jury or a special master and permitting it in admiralty cases to perform the function of the special master." That statement, however, must be read in context. First, we referred explicitly only to Congress' power, where disputes concern private rights, to provide administrative factfinding instead of jury trials in *admiralty* cases. Civil causes of action in admiralty, however, are not suits at common law for Seventh Amendment purposes, and thus no constitutional right to a jury trial attaches. Second, our statement should not be taken to mean that Congress may assign at least the initial factfinding in all cases involving controversies entirely between private parties to administrative agencies or other tribu-

nals not involving juries, so long as they are established as adjuncts to Article III courts. If that were so, Congress could render the Seventh Amendment a nullity. Rather, that statement, citing Crowell v. Benson, means only that in *some* cases involving "private rights" *as that term was defined in* Crowell *and used in* Atlas Roofing amely, as encompassing all disputes to which the Federal Government is not a party in its sovereign capacity ay Congress dispense with juries as factfinders through its choice of adjudicative forum. Those cases in which Congress may decline to provide jury trials are ones involving statutory rights that are integral parts of a public regulatory scheme and whose adjudication Congress has assigned to an administrative agency or specialized court of equity. Whatever terminological distinctions *Atlas Roofing* may have suggested, we now refer to those rights as "public" rather than "private."

seems to us more accurately characterized as a private rather than a public right as we have used those terms in our Article III decisions. In *Northern Pipeline Construction Co.*, the plurality noted that the restructuring of debtor-creditor relations in bankruptcy "may well be a 'public right.' "[11] But the plurality also emphasized that state-law causes of action for breach of contract or warranty are paradigmatic private rights, even when asserted by an insolvent corporation in the midst of Chapter 11 reorganization proceedings. The plurality further said that "matters from their nature subject to 'a suit at common law or in equity or admiralty' " lie at the "protected core" of Article III judicial power (Rehnquist, J., concurring in judgment)—a point we reaffirmed in *Thomas*. There can be little doubt that fraudulent conveyance actions by bankruptcy trustees—suits which, we said in Schoenthal v. Irving Trust Co., "constitute no part of the proceedings in bankruptcy but concern controversies arising out of it"—are quintessentially suits at common law that more nearly resemble state-law contract claims brought by a bankrupt corporation to augment the bankruptcy estate than they do creditors' hierarchically ordered claims to a pro rata share of the bankruptcy *res*. They therefore appear matters of private rather than public right.

Our decision in Katchen v. Landy, under the Seventh Amendment rather than Article III, confirms this analysis. Petitioner, an officer of a bankrupt corporation, made payments from corporate funds within four months of bankruptcy on corporate notes on which he was an accommodation maker. When petitioner later filed claims against the bankruptcy estate, the trustee counterclaimed, arguing that the payments petitioner made constituted voidable preferences because they reduced his potential personal liability on the notes. We held that the bankruptcy court had jurisdiction to order petitioner to surrender the preferences and that it could rule on the trustee's claim without according petitioner a jury trial. Our holding did not depend, however, on the fact that "[bankruptcy] courts are essentially courts of equity" because "they characteristically proceed in summary fashion to deal with the assets of the bankrupt they are administering." Notwithstanding the fact that bankruptcy courts "characteristically" supervised summary proceedings, they were statutorily invested with jurisdiction at law as well, and could also oversee plenary proceedings. Our decision turned, rather, on the bankruptcy court's having "actual or constructive possession" of the bankruptcy estate, and its power and obligation to consider objections by the trustee in deciding whether to allow claims against the estate. * * *

Unlike Justice White, we do not view the Court's conclusion in *Katchen* as resting on an accident of statutory history. We read * * * *Katchen* as holding that, under the Seventh Amendment, a creditor's right to a jury trial on a bankruptcy trustee's preference claim depends

11. We do not suggest that the restructuring of debtor-creditor relations is in fact a public right. This thesis has met with substantial scholarly criticism, and we need not and do not seek to defend it here. Our point is that even if one accepts this thesis, the Seventh Amendment entitles petitioners to a jury trial.

upon whether the creditor has submitted a claim against the estate, not upon Congress' precise definition of the "bankruptcy estate" or upon whether Congress chanced to deny jury trials to creditors who have not filed claims and who are sued by a trustee to recover an alleged preference. Because petitioners here * * * have not filed claims against the estate, respondent's fraudulent conveyance action does not arise "as part of the process of allowance and disallowance of claims." Nor is that action integral to the restructuring of debtor-creditor relations. Congress therefore cannot divest petitioners of their Seventh Amendment right to a trial by jury. *Katchen* thus supports the result we reach today; it certainly does not compel its opposite.

The 1978 Act abolished the statutory distinction between plenary and summary bankruptcy proceedings, on which the Court relied in * * * *Katchen.* Although the 1978 Act preserved parties' rights to jury trials as they existed prior to the day it took effect, 28 U.S.C. § 1480(a) (repealed), in the 1984 Amendments Congress drew a new distinction between "core" and "non-core" proceedings and classified fraudulent conveyance actions as core proceedings triable by bankruptcy judges. 28 U.S.C. § 157(b)(2)(H) (1982 ed., Supp. IV). Whether 28 U.S.C. § 1411 (1982 ed., Supp. IV) purports to abolish jury trial rights in what were formerly plenary actions is unclear, and at any rate is not a question we need decide here. The decisive point is that in neither the 1978 Act nor the 1984 Amendments did Congress "creat[e] a new cause of action, and remedies therefor, unknown to the common law," because traditional rights and remedies were inadequate to cope with a manifest public problem. Rather, Congress simply reclassified a pre-existing common-law cause of action that was not integrally related to the reformation of debtor-creditor relations and that apparently did not suffer from any grave deficiencies. This purely taxonomic change cannot alter our Seventh Amendment analysis. Congress cannot eliminate a party's Seventh Amendment right to a jury trial merely by relabeling the cause of action to which it attaches and placing exclusive jurisdiction in an administrative agency or a specialized court of equity.

Nor can Congress' assignment be justified on the ground that jury trials of fraudulent conveyance actions would "go far to dismantle the statutory scheme," *Atlas Roofing,* n. 11, or that bankruptcy proceedings have been placed in "an administrative forum with which the jury would be incompatible." Id. To be sure, we owe some deference to Congress' judgment after it has given careful consideration to the constitutionality of a legislative provision. But respondent has adduced no evidence that Congress considered the constitutional implications of its designation of all fraudulent conveyance actions as core proceedings. Nor can it seriously be argued that permitting jury trials in fraudulent conveyance actions brought by a trustee against a person who has not entered a claim against the estate would "go far to dismantle the statutory scheme," as we used that phrase in *Atlas Roofing,* when our opinion in that case * * * plainly assumed that such claims carried with them a right to a jury trial. In addition, one cannot easily say that "the jury would be incompatible" with bankruptcy proceedings, in view of Congress' express provision for jury trials in certain actions arising out of bankruptcy litigation. And Justice White's claim that juries may serve usefully as checks only on the decisions of judges who enjoy life tenure, overlooks the extent to which judges who are appointed for fixed terms may be beholden to Congress or Executive officials, and thus ignores the potential for juries to exercise beneficial restraint on their decisions.

It may be that providing jury trials in some fraudulent conveyance actions—if not in this particular case, because respondent's suit was commenced after the Bankruptcy Court approved the debtor's plan of reorganization—would impede swift resolution of bankruptcy proceedings and increase the expense of Chapter 11 reorganizations.[17] But "these considerations are insufficient to overcome the clear command of the Seventh Amendment." Curtis v. Loether. * * *

V

We do not decide today whether the current jury trial provision permits bankruptcy courts to conduct jury trials in fraudulent conveyance actions like the one respondent initiated. Nor do we express any view as to whether the Seventh Amendment or Article III allows jury trials in such actions to be held before non-Article III bankruptcy judges subject to the oversight provided by the district courts pursuant to the 1984 Amendments. We leave those issues for future decisions. We do hold, however, that whatever the answers to these questions, the Seventh Amendment entitles petitioners to the jury trial they requested. Accordingly, the judgment of the Court of Appeals is reversed, and the case is remanded for further proceedings consistent with this opinion.

JUSTICE SCALIA, concurring in part and concurring in the judgment.

I join all but Part IV of the Court's opinion. I make that exception because I do not agree with the premise of its discussion: that "the Federal Government need not be a party for a case to revolve around 'public rights.'" In my view a matter of "public rights," whose adjudication Congress may assign to tribunals lacking the essential characteristics of Article III courts, "must at a minimum arise between the government and others." Northern Pipeline Construction Co. v. Mara-

---

17. Respondent argues, for example, that the prompt resolution of fraudulent transfer claims brought by bankruptcy trustees is often crucial to the reorganization process and that if, by demanding a jury trial, a party could delay those proceedings, it could alter the negotiating framework and unfairly extract more favorable terms for itself. It warrants notice, however, that the provision of jury trials in fraudulent conveyance actions has apparently not been attended by substantial difficulties under previous bankruptcy statutes; that respondent has not pointed to any discussion of this allegedly serious problem in the legislative history of the 1978 Act or the 1984 Amendments; that in many cases defendants would likely not request jury trials; that causes of action to recover preferences may be assigned pursuant to the plan of reorganization rather than pursued prior to the plan's approval, as was done in this very case; and that Congress itself, in enacting 28 U.S.C. 1411, explicitly provided for jury trials of personal injury and wrongful death claims, which would likely take much longer to try than most preference actions and which often involve large sums of money.

thon Pipe Line Co. * * * Until quite recently this has also been the consistent view of the Court. * * *

The notion that the power to adjudicate a legal controversy between two private parties may be assigned to a non-Article III, yet federal, tribunal is entirely inconsistent with the origins of the public rights doctrine. The language of Article III itself, of course, admits of no exceptions; it directs unambiguously that the "judicial Power of the United States, shall be vested in one supreme Court, and in such inferior Courts as the Congress may from time to time ordain and establish." In Murray's Lessee [v. Hoboken Land & Improvement Co., 18 How. 272 (1855)], however, we recognized a category of "public rights" whose adjudication, though a judicial act, Congress may assign to tribunals lacking the essential characteristics of Article III courts. * * *

I would return to the longstanding principle that the public rights doctrine requires, at a minimum, that the United States be a party to the adjudication. On that basis, I concur in the Court's conclusion in Part IV of its opinion that the Article III concomitant of a jury trial could not be eliminated here. Since I join the remainder of the Court's opinion, I concur in its judgment as well.

JUSTICE WHITE, dissenting.

The Court's decision today calls into question several of our previous decisions, strikes down at least one federal statute, and potentially concludes for the first time that the Seventh Amendment guarantees litigants in a specialized non-Article III forum the right to a jury trial. Because I cannot accept these departures from established law, I respectfully dissent.

I

Before I explore the Court's approach to analyzing the issues presented in this case, I first take up the question of the precedent that the Court most directly disregards today, Katchen v. Landy. Though the Court professes not to overrule this decision, and curiously, to be acting in reliance on it, there is simply no way to reconcile our decision in *Katchen* with what the Court holds today.

* * * This holding dispositively settles the question before us today: like the petitioner in *Katchen,* petitioners in this case have no Seventh Amendment right to a jury trial when respondent trustee seeks to avoid the fraudulent transfers they received.

In order to escape the force of *Katchen's* holding, the Court exploits the circumstances under which that decision was made. Most notably, at the time *Katchen* was decided, the Bankruptcy Act then in force (the 1898 Act) did not include actions to set aside voidable preferences among those proceedings covered by the Act. Thus, the clause of our opinion in *Katchen,* on which the Court today puts so much weight—"petitioner might be entitled to a jury trial on the issue of preference if he presented no claim in the bankruptcy proceeding and awaited a federal plenary action by the trustee,"—simply stated the truism that, under the 1898 Act in force at that time, if petitioner had not presented his claim to the bankruptcy court, that court would have had no jurisdiction to perform a summary adjudication of the preference.

That entitlement, however, on which the Court so heavily relies, was solely the product of the statutory scheme in existence at the time. If it were not, the next phrase appearing in the *Katchen* decision would make little sense: "[W]hen the same issue [i.e., validity of a preference] arises as part of the process of allowance and disallowance of claims, it is triable in equity." *Katchen* makes it clear that when Congress does commit the issue and recovery of a preference to adjudication in a bankruptcy proceeding, the Seventh Amendment is inapplicable. Only the limits of the 1898 Act prevented this from being the case in *all* instances, and thereby, left Katchen with the possibility of a jury trial right.

Today's Bankruptcy Code is markedly different. Specifically, under the 1984 Act, an action to recover fraudulently transferred property has been classified as a "core" bankruptcy proceeding. While in *Katchen*'s day, it was only in special circumstances that adjudicating a preference was committed to bankruptcy proceedings, today, Congress has expressly designated adjudication of a preference or a fraudulent transfer a "core" bankruptcy proceeding. The portion of *Katchen* on which the Court relies—"petitioner might be entitled to a jury trial on the issue of preference if he presented no claim in the bankruptcy proceeding and awaited a federal plenary action by the trustee," is therefore a relic of history.

* * *

The Court recognizes the distinction between the earlier law and the present Code, but calls the change a "purely taxonomic" one that "cannot alter our Seventh Amendment analysis." I disagree for two reasons. First, the change is significant because it illustrates the state of the law at the time of *Katchen,* and explains why that case came out as it did. It is hypocritical for the Court to rely on *Katchen*'s statement as to the existence of a jury trial entitlement for the petitioner's claim there, but then dismiss as "taxonomic" the change that wiped out that jury entitlement—or, at the very least, profoundly shifted the basis for it.

More fundamentally, the inclusion of actions to recover fraudulently conveyed property among core bankruptcy proceedings has meaning beyond the taxonomic. * * * [W]e have long recognized that the forum in which a claim is to be heard plays a substantial role in determining the extent to which a Seventh Amendment jury trial right exists. * * * The same is true here, and it counsels affirmance under our holding in *Katchen.*

In essence, the Court's rejection of *Katchen*—and its classification of the change effected by the 1984 Act as "taxonomic"—comes from its conclusion that the fraudulent conveyance action at issue here is not

" 'part of the process of allowance and disallowance of claims.' " The Court misses *Katchen*'s point, however: it was the fact that *Congress* had committed the determination and recovery of preferences to bankruptcy proceedings that was determinative in that case, not just the bare fact that the action "happened" to take place in the process of adjudicating claims. And the same determinative element is present here, for under the 1984 Act, Congress unmistakably intended to have fraudulent conveyances adjudicated and recovered in the Bankruptcy Court in accordance with that Court's usual procedures.

Perhaps in this respect the Court means something more akin to its later restatement of its position; namely, that the 1984 Act simply "reclassified a pre-existing common-law cause of action that was not integrally related to the reformation of debtor-creditor relations." The Court further indicates that it will pay little heed to the congressional inclusion of avoidance and recovery proceedings in core bankruptcy jurisdiction because that choice was not made "because [Congress found that] traditional rights and remedies were inadequate to cope with a manifest public problem." This misguided view of the congressional enactment is the crux of the problem with the Court's approach.

How does the Court determine that an action to recover fraudulently conveyed property is not "integrally related" to the essence of bankruptcy proceedings? Certainly not by reference to a current statutory definition of the core of bankruptcy proceedings—enacted by Congress under its plenary constitutional power, to establish bankruptcy laws. As discussed in the preceding paragraph, this vision of what is "integrally related" to the resolution of creditor-debtor conflicts includes the sort of action before us today.

* * *

One final observation with respect to *Katchen*. The Court attempts to distinguish *Katchen* by saying that a jury trial was not needed there because the funds in dispute were part of the "bankruptcy estate." "Our decision [in *Katchen*] turned ... on the bankruptcy court's having 'actual or constructive possession' of the bankruptcy estate," the Court writes. But obviously in this case, the Bankruptcy Court similarly had " 'actual or constructive possession' of the bankruptcy estate;" certainly it had as much constructive possession of the property sought as it had of the preference recovered in *Katchen*. Thus, it is as true here as it was in *Katchen* that the funds in dispute are part of the "bankruptcy estate." The Bankruptcy Code defines that estate to be comprised of "all the following property, wherever located and by whomever held," including "[a]ny interest in property that the trustee recovers under" the provision authorizing actions to recover fraudulently transferred property. 11 U.S.C. §§ 541(a)(3), 550 (1982 ed., Supp. V). Consequently, even if the Court is accurate in pinpointing the dispositive fact in the *Katchen* decision, that fact equally points towards a ruling for the trustee here.

In sum, I find that our holding in *Katchen,* and its underlying logic, dictate affirmance. The Court's decision today amounts to nothing less than a *sub silentio* overruling of that precedent.

II

Even if the question before us were one of first impression, however, and we did not have the decision in *Katchen* to guide us, I would dissent from the Court's decision. Under our cases, the determination of whether the Seventh Amendment guarantees a jury trial on petitioners' claims must turn on two questions: first, in what forum will those claims be heard; and second, what is the nature of those claims. A weighing of both of these factors must point towards application of the Seventh Amendment before that guarantee will attach.

Whatever the shortcomings of this opinion for failing to resolve the difficult balancing question, it remains superior to the Court's method of "balancing" these concerns, which amounts to no balancing at all—and instead focuses solely on the nature of [a] claim (*i.e.,* whether it is legal, and whether it concerns a public right) in determining if the Seventh Amendment applies.

A

To read the Court's opinion, one might think that the Seventh Amendment is concerned only with the nature of a claim. If a claim is legal, the Court announces, then the Seventh Amendment guarantees a jury trial on that claim. This is wrong. "[H]istory and our cases support the proposition that the right to a jury trial turns not solely on the nature of the issue to be resolved but also on the forum in which it is to be resolved," *Atlas Roofing Co.* Perhaps like *Katchen, Atlas Roofing* is no longer good law after today's decision. A further examination of the issue before us reveals, though, that it is the Court's decision today, and not our prior rulings, that is in error.

In the most obvious case, it has been held that the Seventh Amendment does not apply when a "suit at common law" is heard in a state court. Even with its exclusive focus on the claim at issue here, the Court does not purport to hold that a fraudulent conveyance action brought in state court would be covered by the Seventh Amendment, because that action was one at "common law" in the Court's view.

Nor does the Seventh Amendment apply in all federal forums. "[T]he Seventh Amendment is not applicable to administrative proceedings," for example. *Tull v. United States.* In these forums " 'where jury trials would be incompatible with the whole concept of administrative adjudication,' " the Seventh Amendment has no application. Thus, we have often looked at the character of the federal forum in which the claim will be heard, asking if a jury has a place in that forum, when determining if the Seventh Amendment's guarantee of a jury trial will apply there.

Most specifically relevant for this case, we have indicated on several previous occasions that bankruptcy courts—by their very nature, courts of equity—are forums in which a jury would be out of place. * * * "[T]he Court [has] recognized that a bankruptcy court has been traditionally viewed as a court of equity, and that jury trials would 'dismember' the statutory scheme of the Bankruptcy Act." Curtis v. Loether. *Atlas Roofing, Curtis,* and countless other cases have recognized that Congress has the power to "entrust enforcement of statutory rights to [a] ... specialized court of equity free from the strictures of the Seventh Amendment." *Curtis.* Prior cases emphatically hold that bankruptcy courts are such specialized courts of equity. Indeed, we have stated that "bankruptcy courts are inherently proceedings in equity." Katchen v. Landy.

* * * [I]n blithely ignoring the relevance of the forum Congress has designated to hear this action—focusing instead exclusively on the "legal" nature of petitioner's claim—the Court turns its back on a long line of cases that have rested, in varying degrees, on that point. The Court's decision today ignores our statement in *Atlas Roofing* that "even if the Seventh Amendment would have required a jury where the adjudication of [some types of] rights is assigned to a federal court of law instead of an administrative agency," this constitutional provision does not apply when Congress assigns the adjudication of these rights to specialized tribunals where juries have no place. Indeed, we observed in *Atlas Roofing* that it was even true in "English or American legal systems at the time of the adoption of the Seventh Amendment [that] the question whether a fact would be found by a jury turned to a considerable degree on the nature of the forum in which a litigant found himself."

The Court's decision also substantially cuts back on Congress' power to assign selected causes of action to specialized forums and tribunals (such as bankruptcy courts), by holding that these forums will have to employ juries when hearing claims like the one before us today—a requirement that subverts in large part Congress' decision to create such forums in the first place. Past decisions have accorded Congress far more discretion in making these assignments. * * * Yet to the extent that such disputes involve matters that are "legal" in nature—as they clearly do—the Court's decision today means that Congress cannot do what we said in * * * *Pernell* that it could.

Finally, the Court's ruling today ignores several additional reasons why juries have no place in bankruptcy courts and other "specialized courts of equity" like them. First, two of the principal rationales for the existence of the Seventh Amendment guarantee—the notions of "jury equity," and of juries serving as popular checks on life-tenured judges—are inapt in bankruptcy courts. * * *

Beyond its redundancy, a requirement that juries be used in bankruptcy courts would be disruptive, and would unravel the statutory scheme that Congress has created. The Court dismisses this prospect, and scoffs that it "can[not] seriously be argued that permitting jury trials" on this sort of claim would undermine the statutory bankruptcy scheme. Yet this argument has not only been "seriously" made, it was actually accepted by this Court in Curtis v. Loether. * * *

B

The above is not to say that Congress can vitiate the Seventh Amendment by assigning any claim that it wishes to a specialized tribunal in which juries are not employed. Our cases require a second inquiry—the one that the Court focuses exclusively upon—concerning the nature of the claim so assigned.

To resolve this query, the Court properly begins its analysis with a look at English practice of the 18th century. After conducting this review, the Court states with confidence that "in 18th-century England ... a court of equity would not have adjudicated" respondent's suit. While I agree that this action could have been brought at law—and perhaps even that it might have been so litigated in the most common case—my review of the English cases from the relevant period leaves me unconvinced that the chancery court would have *refused* to hear this action—the Court's conclusion today.

* * *

In sum, I do not think that a fair reading of the history—our understanding of which is inevitably obscured by the passage of time and the irretrievable loss of subtleties in interpretation—clearly proves or disproves that respondent's action would have sounded in equity in England in 1791.[9]

With the historical evidence thus in equipoise—and with the nature of the relief sought here not dispositive either—we should not hesitate to defer to Congress' exercise of its power under the express constitutional grant found in Art. I, § 8, cl. 4, authorizing Congress "[t]o establish ... uniform Laws on the subject of Bankruptcies." Congress has exercised that power, defining actions such as the one before us to be among the "core" of bankruptcy proceedings, triable in a bankruptcy court before a bankruptcy judge, and without a jury. I would defer to these decisions.

* * *

9. Nor do I think it clear, as the Court seems to, that simply because the remedy sought by respondent can be expressed in monetary terms, the relief he seeks is therefore "legal" in nature, and not equitable.

This Court has not accepted the view that "any award of monetary relief must necessarily be 'legal' relief." Curtis v. Loether. We have previously recognized that actions to disgorge improperly gained profits, Tull v. United States, to return funds rightfully belonging to another, *Curtis,* or to submit specific funds wrongfully withheld, Bowen v. Massachusetts, 487 U.S. 879, 893 6, 108 S.Ct. 2722, 2731 3, 101 L.Ed.2d 749 (1988), are all equitable actions even though the relief they seek is monetary because they are restitutionary in nature. Respondent's action against petitioners is of the same class, seeking a similar remedy.

Here the trustee is simply "ask[ing] the court to act in the public interest by restoring the status quo and ordering the return of that which rightfully belongs" to the estate; "[s]uch action is within the highest tradition of a court of equity." Porter v. Warner Co., 328 U.S. 395, 402, 66 S.Ct. 1086, 1091, 90 L.Ed. 1332 (1946). * * *

[T]he Court calls into question the long-standing assumption of our cases and the bankruptcy courts that the equitable proceedings of those courts, adjudicating creditor-debtor disputes, are adjudications concerning "public rights." * * * Yet today the Court calls all of this into doubt merely because these cases have been subjected to "substantial scholarly criticism." If no part of bankruptcy proceedings involve the adjudication of public rights, as the Court implies today, then *all* bankruptcy proceedings are saved from the strictures of the Seventh Amendment only to the extent that such proceedings are the decedents of earlier analogues heard in equity in 18th-century England. Because, as almost every historian has observed, this period was marked by a far more restrictive notion of equitable jurisdiction in bankruptcies, the Court's decision today may threaten the efficacy of bankruptcy courts as they are now constituted. I see no reason to use the Seventh Amendment as a tool to achieve this dubious result.

* * *

[The dissenting opinion of Justice Blackmun, joined by Justice O'Connor, is omitted.]

Notes and Questions

1. What is the rationale for application of the "public rights" doctrine to Seventh Amendment interpretation? Is it persuasive?

2. Does the majority successfully distinguish Katchen v. Landy? In Langenkamp v. Culp, 498 U.S. 42, 111 S.Ct. 330, 112 L.Ed.2d 343 (1990) (per curiam), the Supreme Court considered "the question whether creditors who submit a claim against a bankruptcy estate and are then sued by the trustee in bankruptcy to recover allegedly preferential monetary transfers are entitled to jury trial under the Seventh Amendment." Id. at 42–3, 111 S.Ct. at 330. The Court answered that question in the negative. In so doing, the Court distinguished *Granfinanciera* (498 U.S. at 4, 111 S.Ct. at 331):

> In *Granfinanciera* we recognized that by filing a claim against a bankruptcy estate the creditor triggers the process of "allowance and disallowance of claims," thereby subjecting himself to the bankruptcy court's equitable power. If the creditor is met, in turn, with a preference action from the trustee, that action becomes part of the claims-allowance process which is triable only in equity. In other words, the creditor's claim and the ensuing preference action by the trustee become integral to the restructuring of the debtor-creditor relationship through the bankruptcy court's *equity jurisdiction*. As such, there is no Seventh Amendment right to a jury trial. If a party does *not* submit a claim against the bankruptcy estate, however, the trustee can recover allegedly preferential transfers only by filing what amounts to a legal action to recover a monetary transfer. In those circumstances the preference defendant is entitled to a jury trial.

3. The majority in *Granfinanciera* concedes that it "owe[s] some deference to Congress' judgment" on constitutional issues, but denies the existence of evidence demonstrating that Congress had exercised any such judgment in the present case. It also denies that the provision of a jury trial

right would dismantle Congress's statutory scheme. Should the case have been decided differently if either or both of these questions had been resolved differently?

4. Note that the majority leaves unresolved "whether the Seventh Amendment or Article III allows jury trials * * * to be held before non-Article III bankruptcy judges * * *." In In re Ben Cooper, Inc., 896 F.2d 1394 (2d Cir.1990), vacated on other grounds, 498 U.S. 964, 111 S.Ct. 425, 112 L.Ed.2d 408 (1990), reinstated, 924 F.2d 36 (2d Cir.1991), the court held that the jury trial right applies in certain core proceedings, and that bankruptcy judges could properly conduct such proceedings. Though it conceded finding ambiguity in *Granfinanciera* on the issue, the court concluded "that *Granfinanciera* does not foreclose the possibility of jury trials in the bankruptcy court." The court initially found that "[d]espite the lack of a specific statutory provision, * * * the bankruptcy courts may conduct jury trials in core proceedings." 896 F.2d at 1402. The court held that "jury trials in core proceedings in the bankruptcy court do not violate Article III," 896 F.2d at 1403–04, reasoning: "The primary purpose of this Article is to ensure a federal judiciary free from pressure from the other branches of government. If anything, jurors are less likely to feel pressure from the executive and legislative branches than are bankruptcy judges, who depend on the other branches for reappointment to office." Id. at 1403.

Other federal courts, however, disagreed with these conclusions. For example, the court in In re United Missouri Bank of Kansas City, N.A., 901 F.2d 1449 (8th Cir.1990), held that Congress had neither expressly nor impliedly authorized bankruptcy courts to conduct jury trials. The court cited "the serious constitutional problems" to which the Second Circuit's interpretation, allowing an Article I court to conduct a jury trial, gives rise. Id. at 1457. To a similar effect, see Stansbury Poplar Place, Inc. v. Schwartzman, 13 F.3d 122 (4th Cir.1993).

In October, 1994, Congress enacted the Bankruptcy Reform Act of 1994, which included the following provision:

> If the right to a jury trial applies in a proceeding that may be heard under this section by a bankruptcy judge, the bankruptcy judge may conduct the jury trial if specially designated to exercise such jurisdiction by the district court and with the express consent of all the parties.

§ 112, Bankruptcy Reform Act of 1994, 103 P.L. 394; 108 Stat. 4106. On the issue of jury trials in bankruptcy proceedings, see generally Symposium, Jury Trials in Bankruptcy Courts, 65 Am. Bank. L.J. 1 (1991).

5. For a critical view of the Supreme Court's current doctrine concerning the role of the Seventh Amendment in administrative proceedings, see Redish & LaFave, Seventh Amendment Right to Jury Trial in Non–Article III Proceedings: A Study in Dysfunctional Constitutional Theory, 4 Wm. & Mary Bill of Rts. L.J. 407 (1995). There it is argued: "[T]he Court's exclusion of the jury trial right from most cases of congressional transfer of adjudication to a non-Article III forum can be rationalized only by means of a principle of functionalism. Under this principle, the Court allows the Congress to conclude that the needs of a particular legislative scheme require adjudication without jury trial. The Court does this, despite its assumption that absent such congressional action, the Seventh Amendment

would dictate existence of the jury trial right. Judicial revocation of an otherwise applicable constitutional right solely because of a congressional judgment of incompatibility of that right with a legislative scheme effectively inverts ... fundamental precepts of American constitutional theory."

See also Klein, The Validity of the Public Rights Doctrine in Light of the Historical Rationale of the Seventh Amendment, 21 Hastings Const. L.Q. 1013 (1994), where it is argued that the analysis dictating the absence of the Seventh Amendment right to non-Article III proceedings "rests on the faulty premise that the Seventh Amendment only applies to Article III courts." Professor Klein asserts that "the Seventh Amendment applies to the dispute resolution of all claims sounding in common law...."

COMPLEX CASES AND THE RIGHT TO JURY TRIAL

It has been argued that because jurors are generally incapable of comprehending all of the issues and evidence in so–called complex litigation, a "complexity" exception to the Seventh Amendment right to jury trial should be recognized in those cases. Is recognition of such an exception consistent with the Supreme Court's traditional approach to Seventh Amendment interpretation? Of what relevance is footnote 10 of *Ross* (supra p. 548)? Alternatively, it has been argued that use of a jury trial in complex cases violates the Fifth Amendment right to due process.

In In re Japanese Electronic Products Antitrust Litigation, 631 F.2d 1069 (3d Cir.1980), the Third Circuit rejected a generalized, historically-based exception to the jury trial right on the basis of complexity. However, the court found that "the principles that define the procedural requirement of due process would seem to impose some limitations on the range of cases that may be submitted to a jury." The court explained its reasoning in the following manner:

> The primary value promoted by due process in factfinding procedures is "to minimize the risk of erroneous decisions." A jury that cannot understand the evidence and the legal rules to be applied provides no reliable safeguard against erroneous decisions. Moreover, in the context of a completely adversary proceeding, like a civil trial, due process requires that "the decisionmaker's conclusion ... rest solely on the legal rules and evidence adduced at the hearing." Unless the jury can understand the legal rules and evidence, we cannot realistically expect that the jury will rest its decision on them.

* * *

> If a particular lawsuit is so complex that a jury cannot satisfy this requirement of due process but is nonetheless an action at law, we face a conflict between the requirements of the fifth and seventh amendments. In this situation, we must balance the constitutionally protected interests, as they are implicated in this particular context, and reach the most reasonable accommodation between the two constitutional provisions.

* * *

We believe that when a jury is unable to perform its decision-making task with a reasonable understanding of the evidence and legal rules, it undermines the ability of a district court to render basic justice.

The loss of the right to jury trial in a suit found too complex for a jury does not implicate the same fundamental concerns. The absence of a jury trial requirement in equitable and maritime actions indicates that federal courts can provide fair trials and can grant principles of basic justice without the aid of a jury.

* * *

We do not believe that a due process limitation allows the district courts a substantial amount of discretion to deny jury trials. Because preservation of the right to jury trial remains a constitutionally protected interest, denials of jury trial on grounds of complexity should be confined to suits in which due process clearly requires a nonjury trial. This implies a high standard. It is not enough that trial to the court would be preferable. The complexity of a suit must be so great that it renders the suit beyond the ability of a jury to decide by rational means with a reasonable understanding of the evidence and applicable legal rules.

Judge Gibbons dissented from this due process analysis:

[T]he majority has substituted for an express guarantee in the Bill of Rights a rule of district court discretion that in practice will be virtually unreviewable, and therefore largely unfettered.

* * *

The majority opinion attempts to objectify the factors that bear upon complexity, but in the end the factors which are identified will permit the exercise of trial court discretion. I fear that the exercise of that discretion will sometimes be influenced by unarticulated sympathies for or hostilities toward the underlying policies sought to be advanced in the lawsuit.

* * *

Part of my difficulty with the majority's position probably results from a perception of the nature of the judicial process and the role of juries in that process. It is often said that the judicial process involves the search for objective truth whether the trial is to the court or to a jury. * * * In the process of gaining public acceptance for the imposition of sanctions, the role of the jury is highly significant. * * * Any erosion of citizen participation in the sanctioning system is in the long run likely * * * to result in a reduction in the moral authority that supports the process.

In In re U.S. Financial Securities Litigation, 609 F.2d 411 (9th Cir.1979), cert. denied, 446 U.S. 929, 100 S.Ct. 1866, 64 L.Ed.2d 281 (1980), the court rejected any exception to the Seventh Amendment for complex cases. In so doing, it rejected reliance for such an exception on both footnote 10 of *Ross* and on the due process clause:

No Supreme Court decision prior to *Ross* even utilized a test even partially dependent upon an inquiry into the abilities of jurors.

* * *

While the Supreme Court has never specifically repudiated the third factor in the *Ross* footnote, it has never met with general acceptance by the courts. In the *Ross* decision itself, the Court did not consider the practical abilities and limitations of juries.

* * *

The appellees argued [in this case] that their rights to due process under the Fifth Amendment would be violated if this case was tried to a jury. * * *

We assume, without deciding, that there is such a right to a "competent" fact–finder. However, we do not agree with the two assumptions upon which the argument is based, that is, the complexity and the inability of a jury to serve as fact–finder.

* * *

Many cases appear overwhelmingly complicated in their early stages. Nevertheless, by the time such cases go to trial, what had initially appeared as an impossible array of facts and issues has been synthesized into a coherent theory by the efforts of counsel. * * *

Also, the trial judge has the power and the authority to control, manage and direct the course of complex cases. * * *

* * *

Not only do we refuse to read a complexity exception into the Seventh Amendment, but we also express grave reservations about whether a meaningful test could be developed were we to find such an exception.

Which position do you find more persuasive? See Lempert, Civil Juries and Complex Cases: Let's Not Rush to Judgment, 80 Mich.L.Rev. 68, 87–88 (1981): "[R]elying on the fifth amendment is discomfitting. Contrary to the usual canons of statutory construction, this approach prefers general language to specific language. * * * To rest the denial of the right to jury trial on due process grounds, one must see due process * * * as requiring the denial of one of the specific procedural guarantees of the Bill of Rights."

Certain scholars have argued in support of an historically-based exception to the jury trial right, even in cases seeking otherwise purely legal relief, on complexity grounds. For example, English legal scholar Lord Patrick Devlin, in an article derived from a study commissioned by a Washington, D.C. law firm that represented an amicus curiae opponent to jury trial in In re Japanese Antitrust Litigation, supra, expressed the view "that the practical abilities and limitations of juries would have been a factor very much in the mind of a Chancellor in 1791" in deciding whether to assert equitable jurisdiction, and that "if in any particular case he had thought the 'practical abilities' not up to the complexities of the case, he would have had the power to stop the suit at common law. And further, such a use of the power would not have been considered at all outrageous, but on the contrary as in tune with the accepted relationship between equity and the common law." Devlin, Jury Trial of Complex Cases: English Practices at the Time of the Seventh Amendment, 80 Colum.L.Rev. 43, 107 (1980).

Taking the opposite side of the historical debate, in an article commissioned by the lawyers for the plaintiffs in In re Japanese Antitrust Litigation, Professor (now Judge) Morris Arnold concluded:

> A diligent search of the available sources has not revealed any evidence of an eighteenth-century American or English belief that complexity was a ground for the exercise of equitable jurisdiction. In the nineteenth century, statements to that effect can be discovered but their lineage is in no sense ancient or otherwise distinguished. On the contrary, there is ample evidence that the jury was revered in most of the American colonies, so much so that jury trial found a regular place in Chancery, a practice that would have raised eyebrows in England. * * * There thus seems to be no good historical foundation for the argument that plaintiffs may be denied the right to a jury trial because their cases are complex.

Arnold, A Historical Inquiry Into the Right to Trial by Jury in Complex Civil Litigation, 128 U.Pa.L.Rev. 829, 848 (1980).

A response to Arnold's article argued "that Professor Arnold's conclusions rest upon an incomplete examination of the historical evidence." Campbell & Le Poidevin, Complex Cases and Jury Trials: A Reply to Professor Arnold, 128 U.Pa.L.Rev. 965 (1980). They criticized Arnold for focusing on the history of *American* "special affection" for the jury trial, when it is well established that it is *English* common law practice that determines the Seventh Amendment right. They agree with Lord Devlin's historical conclusions about the nature of English practice.

A number of years prior to this debate, Professor Fleming James stated what had been the generally accepted view of historical practice: "At no time in history was the line dividing equity from law altogether—or even largely—the product of a rational choice between issues which were better suited to court or to jury trial. * * * Rather, the choice between law and equity frequently was made upon consideration of other factors." F. James, Civil Procedure 344 (1965). Is this position reconcilable with that of Lord Devlin?

One non-historian legal scholar, commenting on this debate, concluded that "[a]s I read the evidence, it appears that the historical test gives little comfort to those who wish to read a complexity exception into the seventh amendment. There are a few early cases in which judges, choosing not to empanel juries, disparage the ability of jurors to deal with the litigation in question, but these cases appear to invoke disputes not remediable at law in the first instance. Even if one could discover a case where jury trial was denied although the action was unquestionably legal, it would not establish a *pattern* of denying jury trials in complex cases. The case would be more properly read as an aberrational decision that cannot be the measure of the right the framers of the seventh amendment intended to preserve." Lempert, Civil Juries and Complex Cases: Let's Not Rush to Judgment, 80 Mich.L.Rev. 68, 74 (1981). Professor Lempert further commented that "[w]hat is most notable about the attempts to find an eighteenth-century complexity exception to the right to jury trial is not the evidence presented, but that which is not given. * * * Had there been a complexity exception, we would expect to see a number of cases that make use of it, but we are not even presented with cases where counsel argued fruitlessly for one." Id. at 75.

One commentator has suggested that in most cases "[b]y implementing procedural devices already in place, courts can satisfy the requirements of both the Fifth Amendment and the Seventh Amendment, without unnecessarily balancing one against the other. Thus, jurors can decide complex cases without violating due process and retain their important role as a check on the government." Note, Taking the "Complexity" Out of Complex Litigation: Preserving the Constitutional Right to a Civil Jury Trial, 28 Val. U.L. Rev. 337, 359 (1993). The commentator places reliance on the use of masters, magistrates and court–appointed experts, as well as resort to special verdicts and the assumption by the trial judge of "an active role in determining how the trial will be structured." The same commentator suggests that "as a last resort, where a judge determines that a case is simply too complex for a traditional jury * * * a specially qualified jury must be implemented." Id. at 341. See also Lansing & Miley, The Right to a Jury Trial in Complex Commercial Litigation: A Comparative Law Perspective, 14 Loy. L.A. Int'l & Comp. L.J. 121 (1991); Bownes, Should Trial By Jury Be Eliminated in Complex Cases?, 1 Risk: Issues Health & Safety 75 (1990).

Another commentator has argued that "[s]pecial juries, chosen for their particular knowledge or experience, could help eliminate [the] current problems of jury confusion and lead to better decisions." Sutton, A More Rational Approach to Complex Civil Litigation in the Federal Courts: The Special Jury, 1990 U. Chi. Legal F. 575. See also Drazan, The Case for Special Juries in Toxic Tort Litigation, 72 Judicature 292 (1989). Should such a practice be found to violate the Seventh Amendment? Cf. Schwarzer, Reforming Jury Trials, 132 F.R.D. 575, 580 (1991):

> The process of calling prospective jurors is designed to produce a representative cross–section of the population for jury service. There is no right, however, to have a representative cross–section on any particular jury; indeed, there would be no way to achieve this result. Nor is there a right to a randomly selected jury. Thus, there is no reason why, from among a venire randomly called for service in

a case, one should not select those who by education and experience seem to be best qualified to decide the particular case.

Professor Steven Friedland has suggested that problems of juror competence may be reduced by encouraging a more active role for the jurors in the trial process. In performing such a role, jurors would "ask questions, take notes, or otherwise play a more active role in the system generally. . . . " Friedland, The Competency and Responsibility of Jurors in Deciding Cases, 85 Nw.U.L.Rev. 190, 218 (1990). See also Schwarzer, Reforming Jury Trials, 132 F.R.D. 575 (1991); Heuer & Penrod, Some Suggestions for the Critical Appraisal of a More–Active Jury, 85 Nw. U.L.Rev. 226 (1990).

For a more contemporary discussion of the question, see Lilly, The Decline of the American Jury, 72 U.Colo.L.Rev 53 (2001).

THE SEVENTH AMENDMENT AND JURY SIZE

To what extent does the constitutional right to jury trial guarantee a jury consisting of twelve members, as used at common law? In Williams v. Florida, 399 U.S. 78, 90 S.Ct. 1893, 26 L.Ed.2d 446 (1970), the Supreme Court held that a state could, consistently with the Sixth Amendment's right to jury trial in criminal cases as applied to the states through the Fourteenth Amendment's due process clause, employ a jury of six, or perhaps even fewer members.

In Colgrove v. Battin, 413 U.S. 149, 93 S.Ct. 2448, 37 L.Ed.2d 522 (1973), the Court upheld the constitutionality of a district court's local rule providing for a six-member jury in all civil cases:

> We can only conclude * * * that by referring to the "common law," the Framers of the Seventh Amendment were concerned with preserving the *right* of trial by jury in civil cases where it existed at common law, rather than the various incidents of trial by jury. In short, what was said in *Williams* with respect to the criminal jury is equally applicable here: constitutional history reveals no intention on the part of the Framers "to equate the constitutional and common-law characteristics of the jury."

> * * *

> In *Williams,* we rejected the notion that "the reliability of the jury as a factfinder . . . [is] a function of its size," * * * and nothing has been suggested to lead us to alter that conclusion.

> * * *

> Thus, while we express no view as to whether any number less than six would suffice, we conclude that a jury of six satisfies the Seventh Amendment's guarantee of trial by jury in civil cases.

A number of federal districts have provided by local rule for six-member juries. Cf. Rule 48. Acceptance of six-member juries has, however, been the subject of criticism:

If the jury size is reduced from twelve to six, [lawyers'] perception of the approximate balance between jury and bench trial will be disturbed. Henceforth, the "gamble" with a jury will be significantly greater than the "gamble" with a judge and, as a result, more lawyers might waive their right to a jury, perhaps a consequence not unexpected by those who initiated the reform.

In addition to the tendency to be less representative and to produce more varied damage verdicts, the six-member jury is likely to yield fewer examples of that treasured, paradoxical phenomenon—the hung jury. Hung juries almost always arise from situations in which there were originally several dissenters. Even if only one holds out, his having once been the member of a group is essential in sustaining him against the majority's efforts to make the verdict unanimous. Fewer hung juries can be expected in six-member juries for two reasons: first, * * * there will be fewer holders of minority positions on the jury; second, if a dissenter appears, he is more likely to be the only one on the jury. Lacking any associate to support his position, he is more likely to abandon it.

* * *

From the foregoing discussion, it would appear that the Court's holding in *Williams* rests on a poor foundation. In several important respects, the six-member jury performs differently than the twelve-member jury. The Court probably suspected that some differences in composition and performance would exist between the types of juries but thought them negligibly small. It would seem that the Court has underestimated their magnitude.

* * *

[T]he change in verdicts that might be expected from the deduction of the twelve-member jury to six members is by no means negligible.

Zeisel, . . . and Then There Were None: The Diminution of the Federal Jury, 38 U.Chi.L.Rev. 710 (1971); see also ABA Comm. On Federal Civil Procedure, The Importance of the Twelve–Member Jury in the Federal Courts, 205 F.R.D. 249 (2002) (arguing against shrinkage of the jury). Would the Court's logic in *Williams* and *Colgrove* also justify replacement of the traditional juror unanimity requirement with a majority-rule principle?

JURY SELECTION

Assuming there is a right to jury trial, one must select a jury. In general, litigants are entitled to fair and impartial jurors representing a cross-section of the community. Thiel v. Southern Pac. Co., 328 U.S. 217, 66 S.Ct. 984, 90 L.Ed. 1181 (1946). To implement this, the Juror Selection and Service Act of 1968, 28 U.S.C.A. §§ 1861 et seq., directs that the clerk of the court use a selection method that ensures that potential jurors are "selected at random from a fair cross section of the community." Ordinarily voter registration lists are employed for this purpose, although some have urged that they be supplemented because voter registration patterns vary significantly among different groups. See Kairys, Kadane & Lehockzy, Jury Representativeness: A Mandate for Multiple Source Lists, 65 Calif.L.Rev. 776 (1977).

The resulting group of potential jurors, often called the array, is summoned to the courthouse and directed to a jury assembly room, where the clerk determines whether the prospective jurors satisfy the statutory qualifications, such as the ability to understand the English language. See 28 U.S.C.A. § 1865(b). Qualifying persons are then given some instruction on the duties of jurors, assigned in groups of approximately fifty (called jury panels) and directed to report to specific courtrooms. Using a random process, the courtroom deputy clerk then selects enough prospective jurors from the panel to fill the seats in the jury box. Up to this point, except for challenges to the array on the ground that the selection method was not calculated to yield a fair cross section of the community, neither judges nor lawyers are involved in the jury selection process.

Once prospective jurors are seated in the jury box, the judge and lawyers address the question whether any of them should be excused "for cause." In general, the reasons for excusing jurors for cause relate to their ability to be fair and impartial. Thus, if a juror is acquainted with one of the parties or witnesses or lawyers that may be grounds for excusing the juror if it could affect his attitude toward the case. Similarly, a juror whose personal experiences might result in partiality may be excused. For example, a juror who has lost a limb in an accident may be inappropriate for a personal injury suit involving loss of a limb. Finally, some jurors may have such extensive personal commitments that these would distract them from jury service. For example, a juror who is raising three small children might on that ground be excused, but judges are increasingly strict in their willingness to allow such excuses. Lawyers, it should be noted, are not generally exempt from the civic duty to serve on juries. Any potential jurors who are excused are replaced with others from the panel selected at random by the courtroom deputy, and these are also screened to determine if they should be excused for cause.

Even if there is no ground for excusing jurors for cause, the jury selection process is not over because the parties retain what are called peremptory challenges. In federal court each side has three of these. See 28 U.S.C.A. § 1870. Traditionally it has been said that a party may excuse any juror using such a challenge for any reason whatsoever. Recent decisions severely limit the ability of parties to use peremptory challenges in a discriminatory manner. See Edmonson v. Leesville Concrete Co., 500 U.S. 614, 111 S.Ct. 2077, 114 L.Ed.2d 660 (1991) (race-based peremptory challenges in civil litigation between private parties violate the equal protection clause of the Constitution); J.E.B. v. Alabama *ex rel.* T.B., 511 U.S. 127, 114 S.Ct. 1419, 128 L.Ed.2d 89 (1994) (exclusion of all men from jury in paternity case unconstitutional because it discriminates on grounds of gender). Some suggest that untrammeled use of peremptory challenges is a thing of the past.

Decisions about excusing prospective jurors for cause or peremptorily should be based on information about them. To develop such information, jurors are questioned at the beginning of the trial in a process known as voir dire. Although voir dire is done by lawyers in many state courts, in federal court it is usually done by judges. See Fed.R.Civ.P. 47(a). Many lawyers feel that judicial control unduly limits their ability to get a "feel" for the jury, but judges justify the practice as a way to expedite voir dire and prevent lawyers from converting it into an indoctrination session. Judges will nevertheless entertain suggestions about areas for inquiry, and sometimes they are reversed for refusing such requests.

What happens if a juror fails to respond accurately in voir dire? In McDonough Power Equip., Inc. v. Greenwood, 464 U.S. 548, 104 S.Ct. 845, 78 L.Ed.2d 663 (1984), after the jury returned a verdict for plaintiff in a personal injury suit it was discovered that one juror had not revealed, during voir dire questioning about injuries to members of jurors' families, that his son had once been injured. The Supreme Court reversed a decision granting a new trial on this ground. It reasoned that the juror had acted in good faith, and that insisting on more than good faith asks for "something closer to perfection than our judicial system can be expected to give" because a litigant "is entitled to a fair trial, but not a perfect one."

The limitations on voir dire inquiry, and the possibility of inaccurate responses, have increasingly prompted lawyers to supplement voir dire with independent research. Indeed, judges may often refuse to allow inquiry into areas that might be pertinent to the decision whether to exercise a peremptory challenge because they have no bearing on whether a juror should be excused for cause. But the judge will usually inquire into background information about jurors such as their addresses, types of employment and educational backgrounds, and survey research can assist lawyers in using that information to make informed decisions about the exercise of peremptory challenges:

> One benefit of obtaining demographic correlates of trial-related attitudes is that during voir dire, jurors sometimes lie. * * * But background characteristics cannot be falsified. If the juror is a 54–year-old male registered Republican who is the proprietor of a sporting goods store, your printouts will tell you what he is likely to believe, even if he won't. On the other hand, your data will tell you only about the probabilities for this population, not how any particular 54–year-old male Republican entrepreneur will vote. Like a baseball manager deciding on which pinch hitter to use, you cannot know if on *this* occasion player A will outhit player B. But you can know that against this type of pitcher player A, on the average, does better than player B, and you play the percentages because in the long run you will come out ahead.

Saks, The Limits of Scientific Jury Selection: Ethical and Empirical, 17 Jurimetrics 3, 7–8 (1976).

Notes and Questions

1. As in so many other areas, the jury selection process relies in large part on the adversary initiative of the litigants rather than the court. Would complete control by the judge be more likely to assure impartial juries? Are the parties likely to try to get impartial jurors? Would plaintiff want to excuse a juror with a pro-plaintiff bias?

2. Assuming peremptory challenges may be used on any basis a party deems important, should voir dire be directed at the areas parties feel are significant to the exercise of the peremptory challenges? If judges imposed no limits on the subject matter of questions during voir dire, would there nevertheless be practical impediments to questioning about subjects jurors might be embarrassed to discuss?

3. Will judges' unwillingness to allow litigants a free hand in voir dire encourage them to rely more heavily on other juror investigation? Contacting prospective jurors outside of court may be unethical under rules against attempts to influence jurors improperly. Survey research avoids ethical problems. However, it is expensive because large numbers of people must be questioned about a variety of pertinent matters to determine the correlation between background characteristics and attitudes toward the issues involved in the case. Will limitations on voir dire magnify the advantages that wealthy litigants have over litigants who cannot afford such research? If so, what effect, if any, should that fact have?

C. JUDICIAL CONTROL OF THE VERDICT

1. Judgment as a Matter of Law (Formerly Directed Verdict and Judgment NOV)

Instructions to the jury are, of course, one form of judicial control, but judgment as a matter of law is a much more drastic form. Judgment as a matter of law is provided for in Rule 50(a) of the Federal Rules of Civil Procedure. The practice "enables the court to determine whether there is any question of fact to be submitted to the jury and whether any finding other than the one requested would be erroneous as a matter of law." 9A C. Wright & A. Miller, Federal Practice and Procedure § 2521 at 241. Motions for judgment as a matter of law may be made by either party at the close of her opponent's evidence. For the motion to be granted the court must find that there is insufficient evidence to go to the jury or that the evidence is so compelling that only one result could follow. In this way the motion for judgment as a matter of law acts effectively like a delayed summary judgment motion, in that it determines that there are no genuine issues of fact for the jury. Thus, while courts might be somewhat more hesitant to grant summary judgment than judgment as a matter of law because of the relative point in the litigation at which the two motions are made, essentially the same analysis concerning the meeting and shifting of the burden of production discussed in conjunction with summary judgment (see pp. 425–27, supra) applies to the motion for judgment as a matter of law. The party with the burden of production at trial must present enough evidence so that a reasonable jury could find for him. His opponent's motion for judgment as a matter of law asks the court to make this determination before sending the case to the jury. However, a party with the burden of production may present evidence so persuasive that a reasonable jury would have to find for him. In such an event, that party, too, can obtain a judgment as a matter of law.

Prior to its amendment in 1991, Rule 50 provided for two different motions to control the jury's verdict, directed verdict and judgment notwithstanding the verdict (generally described as "judgment n.o.v."). Under the prior Rule 50(a), a party could move for directed verdict before the case was submitted to the jury; under prior Rule 50(b), a party against whom a jury verdict was rendered could seek judgment n.o.v. Other than this difference in timing, the two motions were identical. In combining the two motions into a motion for judgment as a matter of law, the Advisory Committee expressed the view that the "directed verdict" terminology was both misleading and anachronistic. It believed that use of the phrase, "judgment as a matter of law", which also appears in Rule 56(e)'s description of the standard for awarding summary judgment, underscores the connection between the two rules and reveals the common identity of the motions for directed verdict and judgment n.o.v. The change, then, was, for all practical purposes, one in name only. In many state judicial systems, the traditional nomenclature is still used.

In analyzing the scope of the motion for judgment as a matter of law, two distinct issues must be considered: (1) whether the motion is consistent with constitutional dictates concerning the role of the jury, and (2) the method for determining whether there exists sufficient evidence for a "reasonable" jury to find for a particular party. The first case in this section, Galloway v. United States, presents both issues, while the final two cases raise different aspects of the second issue.

The courts have developed acronyms for the motion available under amended Rule 50. See, e.g., Weese v. Schukman, 98 F.3d 542, 545 (10th Cir.1996) (JML); McKeel v. City of Pine Bluff, 73 F.3d 207, 212 (8th Cir.1996) (JAML).

GALLOWAY v. UNITED STATES

Supreme Court of the United States, 1943.
319 U.S. 372, 63 S.Ct. 1077, 87 L.Ed. 1458.

JUSTICE RUTLEDGE delivered the opinion of the Court.

Petitioner seeks benefits for total and permanent disability by reason of insanity he claims existed May 31, 1919. On that day his policy of yearly renewable term insurance lapsed for nonpayment of premium.[1]

The suit was filed June 15, 1938. At the close of all the evidence the District Court granted the Government's motion for a directed verdict. Judgment was entered accordingly. The Circuit Court of Appeals affirmed. Both courts held the evidence legally insufficient to sustain a verdict for petitioner. He says this was erroneous and, in effect, deprived him of trial by jury, contrary to the Seventh Amendment.

The constitutional argument, as petitioner has made it, does not challenge generally the power of federal courts to withhold or withdraw from the jury cases in which the claimant puts forward insufficient evidence to support a verdict. The contention is merely that his case as made was substantial, the courts' decisions to the contrary were wrong, and therefore their effect has been to deprive him of a jury trial. * * * Upon the record and the issues as the parties have made them, the only question is whether the evidence was sufficient to sustain a verdict for petitioner. On that basis, we think the judgments must be affirmed.

I.

Certain facts are undisputed. Petitioner worked as a longshoreman in Philadelphia and elsewhere prior to enlistment in the Army November 1, 1917. He became a cook in a machine gun battalion. His unit arrived in France in April, 1918. He served actively until September 24. From then to the following January he was in a hospital with influenza. He then returned to active duty. He came back to the United States, and received honorable discharge April 29, 1919. He enlisted in the Navy January 15, 1920, and was discharged for bad conduct in July. The following December he again enlisted in the Army and served until May, 1922, when he deserted. Thereafter he was carried on the Army records as a deserter.

In 1930 began a series of medical examinations by Veterans' Bureau physicians. On May 19 that year his condition was diagnosed as "Moron, low grade; observation, dementia praecox, simple type." In November, 1931, further examination gave the diagnosis, "Psychosis with other diseases or conditions (organic disease of the central nervous system—type undetermined)." In July, 1934, still another examination was made, with diagnosis: "Psychosis manic and depressive insanity incompetent; hypertension, moderate; otitis media, chronic, left; varicose veins left, mild; abscessed teeth roots; myocarditis, mild."

Petitioner's wife, the nominal party in this suit, was appointed guardian of his person and estate in February, 1932. Claim for insurance

---

1. The contract was issued pursuant to the War Risk Insurance Act and insured against death or total permanent disability. Pursuant to statutory authority, T.D. 20 W.R., promulgated March 9, 1918, provided:

"Any impairment of mind or body which renders it impossible for the disabled person to follow continuously any substantially gainful occupation shall be deemed ... to be total disability.

"Total disability shall be deemed to be permanent whenever it is founded upon conditions which render it reasonably certain that it will continue throughout the life of the person suffering from it...."

benefits was made in June, 1934, and was finally denied by the Board of Veterans' Appeals in January, 1936. This suit followed two and a half years later.

Petitioner concededly is now totally and permanently disabled by reason of insanity and has been for some time prior to institution of this suit. It is conceded also that he was sound in mind and body until he arrived in France in April, 1918.

The theory of his case is that the strain of active service abroad brought on an immediate change, which was the beginning of a mental breakdown that has grown worse continuously through all the later years. Essential in this is the view it had become a total and permanent disability not later than May 31, 1919.

The evidence to support this theory falls naturally into three periods, namely, that prior to 1923; the interval from then to 1930; and that following 1930. It consists in proof of incidents occurring in France to show the beginnings of change; testimony of changed appearance and behavior in the years immediately following petitioner's return to the United States as compared with those prior to his departure; the medical evidence of insanity accumulated in the years following 1930; and finally the evidence of a physician, given largely as medical opinion, which seeks to tie all the other evidence together as foundation for the conclusion, expressed as of 1941, that petitioner's disability was total and permanent as of a time not later than May of 1919.

Documentary exhibits included military, naval and Veterans' Bureau records. Testimony was given by deposition or at the trial chiefly by five witnesses. One, O'Neill, was a fellow worker and friend from boyhood; two, Wells and Tanikawa, served with petitioner overseas; Lt. Col. Albert K. Mathews, who was an Army chaplain, observed him or another person of the same name at an Army hospital in California during early 1920; and Dr. Wilder, a physician, examined him shortly before the trial and supplied the only expert testimony in his behalf. The petitioner also put into evidence the depositions of Commander Platt and Lt. Col. James E. Matthews, his superior officers in the Navy and the Army, respectively, during 1920–22.

[Petitioner's fellow soldiers testified about various incidents in France demonstrating bizarre behavior on petitioner's part (including screaming a false alarm of a German attack while on guard duty on the Marne), and his friend testified about the dramatic change in petitioner's behavior after he returned from France.]

Lt. Col. (Chaplain) Mathews said he observed a Private Joseph Galloway, who was a prisoner for desertion and a patient in the mental ward at Fort MacArthur Station Hospital, California, during a six weeks period early in 1920. The chaplain's testimony gives strong evidence the man he observed was insane. However, there is a fatal weakness in this evidence. In his direct testimony, which was taken by deposition, the chaplain said he was certain that the soldier was petitioner. When confronted with the undisputed fact that petitioner was on active duty in the Navy during the first half of 1920, the witness at first stated that he might have been mistaken as to the time of his observation. Subsequently he reasserted the accuracy of his original statement as to the time of observation, but admitted that he might have been mistaken in believing that the patient-prisoner was petitioner. In this connection he volunteered the statement, "Might I add, sir, that I could not now identify that soldier if I were to meet him face to face, and that is because of the long lapse of time." The patient whom the witness saw was confined to his bed. The record is barren of other evidence, whether by the hospital's or the Army's records or otherwise, to show that petitioner was either patient or prisoner at Fort MacArthur in 1920 or at any other time.

Commander Platt testified that petitioner caused considerable trouble by disobedience and leaving ship without permission during his naval service in the first half of 1920. After "repeated warnings and punishments, leading to court martials," he was sentenced to a bad conduct discharge.

* * *

Dr. Wilder was the key witness. He disclaimed specializing in mental disease, but qualified as having given it "special attention." He first saw petitioner shortly before the trial, examined him "several times." He concluded petitioner's ailment "is a schizophrenic branch or form of praecox." Dr. Wilder heard the testimony and read the depositions of the other witnesses, and examined the documentary evidence. Basing his judgment upon this material, with inferences drawn from it, he concluded petitioner was born with "an inherent instability," though he remained normal until he went to France; began there "to be subjected to the strain of military life, then he began to go to pieces." In May, 1919, petitioner "was still suffering from the acuteness of the breakdown ... He is going down hill still, but the thing began with the breakdown ..." Petitioner was "definitely insane, yes, sir," in 1920 and "has been insane at all times, at least since July, 1918, the time of this episode on the Marne"; that is, "to the point that he was unable to adapt himself. I don't mean he has not had moments when he could not perform some routine tasks," but "from an occupational standpoint ... he has been insane." He could follow "a mere matter of routine," but would have no incentive, would not keep a steady job, come to work on time, or do anything he didn't want to do. * * *

However, the witness knew "nothing whatever except his getting married" about petitioner's activities between 1925 and 1930, and what he knew of them between 1922 and 1925 was based entirely on O'Neill's testimony and a paper not of record here. Dr. Wilder at first regarded knowledge concerning what petitioner was doing between 1925 and 1930 as not essential. "We have a continuing disease, quite obviously beginning during his military service, and quite obviously continuing in 1930, and the *minor incidents* don't seem to me—" (Emphasis added.) Counsel for the government interrupted to inquire, "Well, if he was continuously employed for eight hours a day from 1925 to 1930 would that have any bearing?" The witness replied, "It would have a great deal." Upon further questioning, however, he reverted to his first position, stating it would not be necessary or helpful for him to know what petitioner was doing from 1925 to 1930: "I testified from the information I had."

This, we think, is the crux of the case and distinguishes it from the cases on which petitioner has relied.[8] His burden was to prove total and permanent disability as of a date not later than May 31, 1919. He has undertaken to do this by showing incipience of mental disability shortly before that time and its continuance and progression throughout the succeeding years. He has clearly established incidence of total and permanent disability as of some period prior to 1938, when he began this suit.[9] For our purposes this may be taken as medically established by the Veterans' Bureau examination and diagnosis of July, 1934.

But if the record is taken to show that some form of mental disability existed in 1930, which later became total and permanent, petitioner's problem remains to demonstrate by more than speculative inference that this condition itself began on or before May 31, 1919 and continuously existed or progressed through the intervening years to 1930.

To show origin before the crucial date, he gives evidence of two abnormal incidents occurring while he was in France, one creating the disturbance before he came near the fighting front, the other yelling that the Germans were coming when he was on guard duty at the Marne. There is no other evidence of abnormal behavior during his entire service of more than a year abroad.

That he was court martialed for these sporadic acts and bound and gagged for one does not prove he was insane or had then a general breakdown in "an already fragile mental constitution," which the vicissitudes of a longshoreman's life had not been able to crack.

To these two incidents petitioner adds the testimony of O'Neill that he looked and acted like a wreck, compared with his former self, when he returned from France about a month before the crucial date, and O'Neill's vague recollections that this condition continued through the next two, three, four or five years.

O'Neill's testimony apparently takes no account of petitioner's having spent 101 days in a hospital in France with influenza just before he came home. But, given the utmost credence, as is required, it does no more than show that petitioner was subject to alternating periods of gaiety and depression for some indefinite period after his return, extend-

8. None of them exhibits a period of comparable length as to which evidence is wholly lacking and under circumstances which preclude inference the omission was unintentional.

9. He has not established a fixed date at which contemporaneous medical examination, both physical and mental, establishes totality and permanence prior to Dr. Wilder's examinations in 1941. Dr. Wilder testified that on the evidence concerning petitioner's behavior at the time of his discharge in 1919, and without reference to the testimony as to later conduct, including O'Neill's, he would reserve his opinion on whether petitioner was then "crazy"—"I wouldn't have enough—."

ing perhaps as late as 1922. But because of its vagueness as to time, dates, frequency of opportunity for observation, and specific incident, O'Neill's testimony concerning the period from 1922 to 1925 is hardly more than speculative.

We have then the two incidents in France followed by O'Neill's testimony of petitioner's changed condition in 1919 and its continuance to 1922.[11] * * * Then follows a chasm of eight years. The only evidence we have concerning this period is the fact that petitioner married his present guardian at some time within it, an act from which in the legal sense no inference of insanity can be drawn.

This period was eight years of continuous insanity, according to the inference petitioner would be allowed to have drawn. If so, he should have no need of inference. Insanity so long and continuously sustained does not hide itself from the eyes and ears of witnesses. The assiduity which produced the evidence of two "crazy" incidents during a year and a half in France should produce one during eight years or, for that matter, five years in the United States.

Inference is capable of bridging many gaps. But not, in these circumstances, one so wide and deep as this. Knowledge of petitioner's activities and behavior from 1922 or 1925 to 1930 was peculiarly within his ken and that of his wife, who has litigated this cause in his and presumably, though indirectly, in her own behalf. His was the burden to show continuous disability. What he did in this time, or did not do, was vital to his case. Apart from the mere fact of his marriage, the record is blank for five years and almost blank for eight. For all that appears, he may have worked full time and continuously for five and perhaps for eight, with only a possible single interruption.

No favorable inference can be drawn from the omission. It was not one of oversight or inability to secure proof. That is shown by the thoroughness with which the record was prepared for all other periods, before and after this one, and by the fact petitioner's wife, though she married him during the period and was available, did not testify. The only reasonable conclusion is that petitioner, or those who acted for him, deliberately chose, for reasons no doubt considered sufficient (and which we do not criticize, since such matters including tactical ones, are for the judgment of counsel) to present no evidence or perhaps to withhold evidence readily available concerning this long interval, and to trust to the genius of expert medical inference and judicial laxity to bridge this canyon.

11. Chaplain Mathews' testimony would be highly probative of insanity existing early in 1920, if petitioner were sufficiently identified as its subject. However, the bare inference of identity which might otherwise be drawn from the mere identity of names cannot be made reasonably in view of its overwhelming contradiction by other evidence presented by petitioner and the failure to produce records from Fort MacArthur Hospital or the Army or from persons who knew the fact that petitioner had been there at any time. The omission eloquently testifies in a manner which no inference could overcome that petitioner never was there. The chaplain's testimony therefore should have been stricken, had the case gone to the jury, and petitioner can derive no aid from it here.

In the circumstances exhibited, the former is not equal to the feat, and the latter will not permit it. No case has been cited and none has been found in which inference, however expert, has been permitted to make so broad a leap and take the place of evidence which, according to all reason, must have been at hand. To allow this would permit the substitution of inference, tenuous at best, not merely for evidence absent because impossible or difficult to secure, but for evidence disclosed to be available and not produced. This would substitute speculation for proof. Furthermore, the inference would be more plausible perhaps if the evidence of insanity as of May, 1919, were stronger than it is, such for instance as Chaplain Mathews' testimony would have furnished if it could be taken as applying to petitioner. But, on this record, the evidence of insanity as of that time is thin at best, if it can be regarded as at all more than speculative.

Beyond this, there is nothing to show totality or permanence. These come only by what the Circuit Court of Appeals rightly characterized as "long-range retroactive diagnosis." That might suffice, notwithstanding this crucial inference was a matter of opinion, if there were factual evidence over which the medical eye could travel and find continuity through the intervening years. But eight years are too many to permit it to skip, when the bridgeheads (if the figure may be changed) at each end are no stronger than they are here, and when the seer first denies, then admits, then denies again, that what took place in this time would make "a great deal" of difference in what he saw. Expert medical inference rightly can do much. But we think the feat attempted here too large for its accomplishment.

* * *

III.

What has been said disposes of the case as the parties have made it. For that reason perhaps nothing more need be said. But objection has been advanced that, in some manner not wholly clear, the directed verdict practice offends the Seventh Amendment.

It may be noted, first, that the Amendment has no application of its own force to this case. The suit is one to enforce a monetary claim against the United States. It hardly can be maintained that under the common law in 1791 jury trial was a matter of right for persons asserting claims against the sovereign.[17] Whatever force the Amendment has therefore is derived because Congress in the legislation cited has made it applicable. Even so, the objection made on the score of its requirements is untenable.

17. Neither the Amendment's terms nor its history suggest it was intended to extend to such claims. The Court of Claims has functioned for almost a century without affording jury trial in cases of this sort and without offending the requirements of the Amendment. McElrath v. United States, 102 U.S. 426, 26 L.Ed. 189; see Richardson, History, Jurisdiction and Practice of the Court of Claims (2d ed. 1885).

If the intention is to claim generally that the Amendment deprives the federal courts of power to direct a verdict for insufficiency of evidence, the short answer is the contention has been foreclosed by repeated decisions made here consistently for nearly a century. More recently the practice has been approved explicitly in the promulgation of the Federal Rules of Civil Procedure. Cf. Rule 50. The objection therefore comes too late.

Furthermore, the argument from history is not convincing. It is not that "the rules of the common law" in 1791 deprived trial courts of power to withdraw cases from the jury, because not made out, or appellate courts of power to review such determinations. The jury was not absolute master of fact in 1791. Then as now courts excluded evidence for irrelevancy and relevant proof for other reasons. The argument concedes they weighed the evidence, not only piecemeal but in toto for submission to the jury, by at least two procedures, the demurrer to the evidence and the motion for a new trial. The objection is not therefore to the basic thing, which is the power of the court to withhold cases from the jury or set aside the verdict for insufficiency of the evidence. It is rather to incidental or collateral effects, namely, that the directed verdict as now administered differs from both those procedures because, on the one hand, allegedly higher standards of proof are required and, on the other, different consequences follow as to further maintenance of the litigation. Apart from the standards of proof, the argument appears to urge that in 1791, a litigant could challenge his opponent's evidence, either by the demurrer, which when determined ended the litigation, or by motion for a new trial which if successful, gave the adversary another chance to prove his case; and therefore the Amendment excluded any challenge to which one or the other of these consequences does not attach.

The Amendment did not bind the federal courts to the exact procedural incidents or details of jury trial according to the common law in 1791, any more than it tied them to the common-law system of pleading or the specific rules of evidence then prevailing. Nor were "the rules of the common law" then prevalent, including those relating to the procedure by which the judge regulated the jury's role on questions of fact, crystalized in a fixed and immutable system. On the contrary, they were constantly changing and developing during the late eighteenth and early nineteenth centuries. In 1791 this process already had resulted in widely divergent common-law rules on procedural matters among the states, and between them and England. And none of the contemporaneous rules regarding judicial control of the evidence going to juries or its sufficiency to support a verdict had reached any precise, much less final, form. In addition, the passage of time has obscured much of the procedure which then may have had more or less definite form, even for historical purposes.

This difficulty, no doubt, accounts for the amorphous character of the objection now advanced, which insists, not that any single one of the features criticized, but that the cumulative total or the alternative effect of all, was embodied in the Amendment. The more logical conclusion, we think, and the one which both history and the previous decisions here support, is that the Amendment was designed to preserve the basic institution of jury trial in only its most fundamental elements, not the great mass of procedural forms and details, varying even then so widely among common-law jurisdictions.

Apart from the uncertainty and the variety of conclusion which follows from an effort at purely historical accuracy, the consequences flowing from the view asserted are sufficient to refute it. It may be doubted that the Amendment requires challenge to an opponent's case to be made without reference to the merits of one's own and at the price of all opportunity to have it considered. On the other hand, there is equal room for disbelieving it compels endless repetition of litigation and unlimited chance, by education gained at the opposing party's expense, for perfecting a case at other trials. The essential inconsistency of these alternatives would seem sufficient to refute that either or both, to the exclusion of all others, received constitutional sanctity by the Amendment's force. The first alternative, drawn from the demurrer to the evidence, attributes to the Amendment the effect of forcing one admission because another and an entirely different one is made,[28] and thereby compels conclusion of the litigation once and for all. The true effect of imposing such a risk would not be to guarantee the plaintiff a jury trial. It would be rather to deprive the defendant (or the plaintiff if he were the challenger) of that right; or, if not that, then of the right to challenge the legal sufficiency of the opposing case. The Amendment was not framed or adopted to deprive either party of either right. It is impartial in its guaranty of both. To posit assertion of one upon sacrifice of the other would dilute and distort the full protection intended. The admitted validity of the practice on the motion for a new trial goes far to demonstrate this.[29] It negatives any idea that the challenge must be made at such a risk as the demurrer imposed. As for the other alternative, it is not urged that the Amendment guarantees another trial whenever challenge to the sufficiency of evidence is sustained. That

28. By conceding the full scope of an opponent's evidence and asserting its insufficiency in law, which is one thing, the challenger must be taken, perforce the Amendment, also to admit he has no case, if the other's evidence is found legally sufficient, which is quite another thing. In effect, one must stake his case, not upon its own merit on the facts, but on the chance he may be right in regarding his opponent's as wanting in probative content. If he takes the gamble and loses, he pays with his own case, regardless of its merit and without opportunity for the jury to consider it. To force this choice and yet deny that afforded by the directed verdict would be to embed in the Constitution the hypertechnicality of common-law pleading and procedure in their heyday.

29. Under that practice the moving party receives the benefit of jury evaluation of his own case and of challenge to his opponent's for insufficiency. If he loses on the challenge, the litigation is ended. But this is not because, in making it, he is forced to admit his own is insufficient. It is rather for the reasons that the court finds the opposite party's evidence is legally sufficient and the jury has found it outweighs his own. There is thus no forced surrender of one right from assertion of another.

On the other hand, if the challenger wins, there is another trial. But this is because he has sought it, not because the Amendment guarantees it.

argument, in turn, is precluded by the practice on demurrer to the evidence.

Each of the classical modes of challenge, therefore, disproves the notion that the characteristic feature of the other, for effect upon continuing the litigation, became a part of the Seventh Amendment's guaranty to the exclusion of all others. That guaranty did not incorporate conflicting constitutional policies, that challenge to an opposing case must be made with the effect of terminating the litigation finally and, at the same time, with the opposite effect of requiring another trial. Alternatives so contradictory give room, not for the inference that one or the other is required, but rather for the view that neither is essential.

Finally, the objection appears to be directed generally at the standards of proof judges have required for submission of evidence to the jury. But standards, contrary to the objection's assumption, cannot be framed wholesale for the great variety of situations in respect to which the question arises. Nor is the matter greatly aided by substituting one general formula for another. It hardly affords help to insist upon "substantial evidence" rather than "some evidence" or "any evidence," or vice versa. The matter is essentially one to be worked out in particular situations and for particular types of cases. Whatever may be the general formulation, the essential requirement is that mere speculation be not allowed to do duty for probative facts, after making due allowance for all reasonably possible inferences favoring the party whose case is attacked. The mere difference in labels used to describe this standard, whether it is applied under the demurrer to the evidence or on motion for a directed verdict, cannot amount to a departure from "the rules of the common law" which the Amendment requires to be followed. If there is abuse in this respect, the obvious remedy is by correction on appellate review.

Judged by this requirement, or by any standard other than sheer speculation, we are unable to conclude that one whose burden, by the nature of his claim, is to show continuing and total disability for nearly twenty years supplies the essential proof of continuity when he wholly omits to show his whereabouts, activities or condition for five years, although the record discloses evidence must have been available, and, further, throws no light upon three additional years, except for one vaguely described and dated visit to his former home. Nothing in the Seventh Amendment requires it should be allowed to join forces with the jury system to bring about such a result. That guaranty requires that the jury be allowed to make reasonable inferences from facts proven in evidence having a reasonable tendency to sustain them. It permits expert opinion to have the force of fact when based on facts which sustain it. But it does not require that experts or the jury be permitted to make inferences from the withholding of crucial facts, favorable in their effects to the party who has the evidence of them in his peculiar knowledge and possession, but elects to keep it so. The words "total and permanent" are the statute's, not our own. They mean something more than incipient or occasional disability. We hardly need add that we give full credence to all of the testimony. But that cannot cure its inherent vagueness or supply essential elements omitted or withheld.

JUSTICE BLACK, with whom JUSTICE DOUGLAS and JUSTICE MURPHY concur, dissenting.

The Seventh Amendment to the Constitution provides:

> "In suits at common law, where the value in controversy shall exceed twenty dollars, the right of trial by jury shall be preserved, and no fact tried by a jury shall be otherwise re-examined in any Court of the United States, than according to the rules of the common law."

The Court here re-examines testimony offered in a common law suit, weighs conflicting evidence, and holds that the litigant may never take this case to a jury. The founders of our government thought that trial of fact by juries rather than by judges was an essential bulwark of civil liberty. For this reason, among others, they adopted Article III, § 2 of the Constitution, and the Sixth and Seventh Amendments. Today's decision marks a continuation of the gradual process of judicial erosion which in one hundred fifty years has slowly worn away a major portion of the essential guarantee of the Seventh Amendment.

The principal method by which judges prevented cases from going to the jury in the Seventeenth and Eighteenth Centuries was by the demurrer to the evidence, under which the defendant at the end of the trial admitted all facts shown by the plaintiff as well as all inferences which might be drawn from the facts, and asked for a ruling of the Court on the "law of the case." This practice fell into disuse in England in 1793, Gibson v. Hunter, 2 H.Bl. 187, and in the United States federal courts in 1826, Fowle v. Alexandria, 11 Wheat. 320, 6 L.Ed. 484. The power of federal judges to comment to the jury on the evidence gave them additional influence. The right of involuntary non-suit of a plaintiff, which might have been used to expand judicial power at jury expense was at first denied federal courts.

As Hamilton had declared in The Federalist, the basic judicial control of the jury function was in the court's power to order a new trial. In 1830, this Court said: "The only modes known to the common law to re-examine such facts, are the granting of a new trial by the court where the issue was tried, or to which the record was properly returnable; or the award of a venire facias de novo, by an appellate court, for some error of law which intervened in the proceedings." Parsons v. Bedford, supra, 3 Pet. at page 448, 7 L.Ed. 732. That retrial by a new jury rather than factual reevaluation by a court is a constitutional right of genuine value was restated as recently as Slocum v. New York Life Insurance Co., 228 U.S. 364, 33 S.Ct. 523, 57 L.Ed. 879.

A long step toward the determination of fact by judges instead of by juries was the invention of the directed verdict. In 1850, what seems to have been the first directed verdict case considered by this Court, Parks v. Ross, 11 How. 362, 374, 13 L.Ed. 730, was presented for decision. The

Court held that the directed verdict serves the same purpose as the demurrer to the evidence, and that since there was "no evidence whatever" on the critical issue in the case, the directed verdict was approved. The decision was an innovation, a departure from the traditional rule restated only fifteen years before in Greenleaf v. Birth, 1835, 9 Pet. 292, 299, 9 L.Ed. 132, in which this Court had said: "Where there is no evidence tending to prove a particular fact, the courts are bound so to instruct the jury, when requested; but they cannot legally give any instruction which shall take from the jury the right of weighing the evidence and determining what effect it shall have."

This new device contained potentialities for judicial control of the jury which had not existed in the demurrer to the evidence. In the first place, demurring to the evidence was risky business, for in so doing the party not only admitted the truth of all the testimony against him but also all reasonable inferences which might be drawn from it; and upon joinder in demurrer the case was withdrawn from the jury while the court proceeded to give final judgment either for or against the demurrant. Imposition of this risk was no mere technicality; for by making withdrawal of a case from the jury dangerous to the moving litigant's cause, the early law went far to assure that facts would never be examined except by a jury. Under the directed verdict practice the moving party takes no such chance, for if his motion is denied, instead of suffering a directed verdict against him, his case merely continues into the hands of the jury. The litigant not only takes no risk by a motion for a directed verdict, but in making such a motion gives himself two opportunities to avoid the jury's decision; for under the federal variant of judgment notwithstanding the verdict, the judge may reserve opinion on the motion for a directed verdict and then give judgment for the moving party after the jury was formally found against him. In the second place, under the directed verdict practice the courts soon abandoned the "admission of all facts and reasonable inferences" standard referred to, and created the so-called "substantial evidence" rule which permitted directed verdicts even though there was far more evidence in the case than a plaintiff would have needed to withstand a demurrer.

The substantial evidence rule did not spring into existence immediately upon the adoption of the directed verdict device. For a few more years federal judges held to the traditional rule that juries might pass finally on facts if there was "any evidence" to support a party's contention. The rule that a case must go to the jury unless there was "no evidence" was completely repudiated in Schuylkill and Dauphin Improvement Co. v. Munson, 1871, 14 Wall. 442, 447, 448, 20 L.Ed. 867, upon which the Court today relies in part. There the Court declared that "some" evidence was not enough—there must be evidence sufficiently persuasive to the judge so that he thinks "a jury can properly proceed." The traditional rule was given an ugly name, "the scintilla rule", to hasten its demise. For a time traces of the old formula remained, but the new spirit prevailed. The same transition from jury supremacy to jury subordination through judicial decisions took place in State courts.

* * *

Today the Court comes dangerously close to weighing the credibility of a witness and rejecting his testimony because the majority do not believe it.

The story thus briefly told depicts the constriction of a constitutional civil right and should not be continued.

* * *

The call for the true application of the Seventh Amendment is not to words, but to the spirit of honest desire to see that constitutional right preserved. Either the judge or the jury must decide facts and, to the extent that we take this responsibility, we lessen the jury function. Our duty to preserve this one of the Bill of Rights may be peculiarly difficult, for here it is our own power which we must restrain. * * * As for myself, I believe that a verdict should be directed, if at all, only when, without weighing the credibility of the witnesses, there is in the evidence no room whatever for honest difference of opinion over the factual issue in controversy. I shall continue to believe that in all other cases a judge should, in obedience to the command of the Seventh Amendment, not interfere with the jury's function. Since this is a matter of high constitutional importance, appellate courts should be alert to insure the preservation of this constitutional right even though each case necessarily turns on its peculiar circumstances.

* * *

This case graphically illustrates the injustice resulting from permitting judges to direct verdicts instead of requiring them to await a jury decision and then, if necessary, allow a new trial. The chief reason given for approving a directed verdict against this petitioner is that no evidence except expert medical testimony was offered for a five to eight year period. Perhaps, now that the petitioner knows he has insufficient evidence to satisfy a jury, he would be able to fill this time gap to meet any judge's demand. If a court would point out on a motion for new trial that the evidence as to this particular period was too weak, the petitioner would be given an opportunity to buttress the physician's evidence. If, as the Court believes, insufficient evidence has been offered to sustain a jury verdict for the petitioner, we should at least authorize a new trial.
* * *

I believe that there is a reasonable difference of opinion as to whether the petitioner was totally and permanently disabled by reason of insanity on May 31, 1919, and that his case therefore should have been allowed to go to the jury. The testimony of fellow soldiers, friends, supervisors, and of a medical expert whose integrity and ability is not challenged cannot be rejected by any process available to me as a judge.

Notes and Questions

1. Note that the Seventh Amendment contains two distinct clauses. The first concerns whether a constitutional right to jury trial exists at all. We have already considered the interpretation of that clause extensively in Section B of this chapter. The other clause, relevant only after one has initially concluded that the jury trial right applies, concerns the scope of the limitations that can be placed on performance of the jury's function. *Galloway*'s constitutional discussion primarily constitutes an interpretation of this latter clause to determine whether the directed verdict properly empowers the court to take the task of fact finding away from the jury in certain instances.

2. The Court's discussion of the constitutionality of the directed verdict is largely dicta, in light of its holding that the Seventh Amendment was inapplicable in *Galloway*. On what basis did the Court reach this conclusion? Is its reasoning persuasive? In answering, examine the language of the Seventh Amendment, and consider the approach to Seventh Amendment application adopted by Justice Story in Parsons v. Bedford, 28 U.S. (3 Pet.) 433, 447, 7 L.Ed. 732 (1830), used by the Court to the present day. See, e.g., Curtis v. Loether, supra pp. 555–56. If one were to assume that by its nature the right asserted in *Galloway* was "legal", should the Seventh Amendment apply, even though in 1791, at the time of the amendment's ratification, there were no suits against the sovereign? Consider the following argument: Because it is established that Congress need not allow private individuals to sue the government, it can take the lesser step of allowing such suits only on the condition that the individual waive his Seventh Amendment right to jury trial.

3. Justice Rutledge acknowledges that the directed verdict, at least in its modern form, did not exist at common law. Yet the second clause of the Seventh Amendment provides that jury fact finding may be reviewed only in accordance with procedures in existence at common law—i.e., at the time of the amendment's ratification in 1791. How, then, does Justice Rutledge reach the conclusion that the directed verdict is constitutional? What common law practices does he rely on to justify the directed verdict? In what ways did those practices differ from the modern directed verdict? Do you agree with Justice Rutledge that those differences are insufficient to distinguish those practices from the directed verdict?

4. What is the basis of Justice Black's dissent on the constitutional issue? Who do you think gets the better of the argument? Do you agree with Professor Cooper that the majority's response is "unduly facile"? Cooper, Directions for Directed Verdicts: A Compass for Federal Courts, 55 Minn. L.Rev. 903, 917 (1971). For a comprehensive examination of the history of the directed verdict and its predecessor, see id. at 909–27. See also Blume, Origin and Development of the Directed Verdict, 48 Mich.L.Rev. 555 (1950). For a critique of Justice Black's assumptions about early jury practices, see Woolhandler & Collins, The Article III Jury, 87 Va. L. Rev. 587 (2001) (arguing that Justice Black's view was incorrect that "pre-modern federal control of juries by the elaboration of law, the direction of verdicts, and the liberal use of commentary on the evidence along with new trials likely exceeded the overall level of modern judicial controls").

5. Assuming directed verdict is constitutional, was it properly invoked on the evidence presented in *Galloway?* To what extent is the decision to award directed verdict simply an illustration of the commonplace inference that when a party fails to produce evidence within its control the evidence would probably hurt the party's case (recall *Hammond Packing,* supra p. 420 n. 3). Even if this were true, would it justify a directed verdict, or simply influence the fact finder's decision? Would the jury have had to speculate in order to find for Galloway? If so, would that speculation have been anything more than the type of inferential process we normally expect juries to undertake? Is the majority or Justice Black more persuasive on this issue?

Justice Black argues that the majority improperly adopts a "substantial evidence" standard—unless the party with the burden of production produces "substantial evidence" to support its claim, directed verdict will be granted. Black says directed verdict should be granted only when the party opposing the motion has absolutely no supporting evidence—what he claims has been pejoratively labeled the "scintilla rule," since that was always the standard employed historically. How does Justice Rutledge respond to this contention? Consider how these differing standards may be applied in the next case.

6. Note that the attack on the directed verdict might also have been made against summary judgment. The English developed summary procedures in the 19th century in suits against debtors who failed to offer evidence to support their defenses. When the District of Columbia adopted a similar rule, the Supreme Court held that it did not violate the right of a debtor to trial by jury where the debtor failed to submit an affidavit showing that there was a real issue for trial:

> If it were true that the rule deprived the plaintiff in error of the right to trial by jury, we should pronounce it void without reference to cases. But it does not do so. It prescribes the means of making an issue. The purpose of the rule is to preserve the court from frivolous defenses and to defeat attempts to use formal pleading as means to delay the recovery of just demands.

Fidelity & Deposit Co. v. United States, 187 U.S. 315, 320, 23 S.Ct. 120, 122, 47 L.Ed. 194 (1902).

THE CONSTITUTIONALITY OF JUDGMENT AS A MATTER OF LAW AFTER VERDICT

Recall that prior to its amendment in 1991, Rule 50(a) provided for two distinct procedures, directed verdict (sought before the case is sent to the jury) and judgment n.o.v., or judgment notwithstanding the verdict (sought after the jury's verdict). Though the 1991 amendment replaced both procedures with the motion for judgment as a matter of law (see supra p. 607), the constitutional issues raised by the former judgment n.o.v. practice remain unchanged.

As was true of directed verdict, the motion for judgment n.o.v. faced a serious constitutional challenge under the Seventh Amendment. In fact, in Slocum v. New York Life Insurance Co., 228 U.S. 364, 33 S.Ct. 523, 57 L.Ed. 879 (1913), the Supreme Court, in an opinion by Justice

Van Devanter, held judgment n.o.v. to be unconstitutional, because it did not exist at common law. While at common law a court could order a new trial because of plaintiff's failure to present sufficient evidence, this was fundamentally different, the Supreme Court reasoned, from the court's entry of a judgment in defendant's favor. The Court also acknowledged the common law practice of demurrer to the evidence (discussed in *Galloway*), and, despite the controversy surrounding the issue in *Galloway* some thirty years later, assumed the validity of the directed verdict practice. However, the Court saw qualitative differences between these practices and the judgment n.o.v.:

> At the trial the defendant requested that a verdict in its favor be directed, and had the court indicated its purpose to do that, it would have been open to the plaintiff, under the then prevailing practice, to take a voluntary nonsuit, which would have enabled her to make a fuller and better presentation of her case, if the facts permitted, at another trial in a new suit.

If, on the other hand, the jury's verdict were rejected by the court and a verdict for the other party entered, the opportunity for a voluntary nonsuit would no longer be available. Today, a party could not take a voluntary nonsuit this late in the proceeding, without the court's permission. Fed.R.Civ.P. 41(a). In light of this fact, would the approach to Seventh Amendment interpretation adopted in *Galloway* lead to a finding that judgment n.o.v. is constitutional today?

Slocum has never been formally overruled. However, in Baltimore & Carolina Line, Inc. v. Redman, 295 U.S. 654, 55 S.Ct. 890, 79 L.Ed. 1636 (1935), the Court, once again in an opinion by Justice Van Devanter, effectively sapped the strength from *Slocum*. The Court found the case to present "[a] very different situation" from *Slocum,* because in *Redman* "[t]he trial court expressly reserved its ruling on the defendant's motions to dismiss and for a directed verdict * * *." This practice, the Court concluded, was valid at common law. Thus, when the trial judge invalidated the jury's verdict, he was not granting a motion for judgment n.o.v.; he was merely making a ruling on the directed verdict motion which he had reserved prior to trial.

In 2004, the Committee on Rules of Practice and Procedure published a proposal to amend Rule 50 to remove the requirement that the moving party must file the motion for judgment as a matter of law "at the close of all the evidence," in order to preserve the right to move again after verdict. Instead, the amendment would allow the motion to be made at any time before the case is submitted to the jury and after the opposing party has been fully heard on the issue. The accompanying Committee Note indicates that the continued requirement of a motion prior to submission to the jury satisfies the Seventh Amendment.

Notes and Questions

1. Why might a judge who has denied a motion for judgment as a matter of law under Rule 50(a) be willing to grant that motion when renewed by the moving party following the jury's verdict?

LAVENDER v. KURN

Supreme Court of the United States, 1946.
327 U.S. 645, 66 S.Ct. 740, 90 L.Ed. 916.

JUSTICE MURPHY delivered the opinion of the Court.

The Federal Employers' Liability Act permits recovery for personal injuries to an employee of a railroad engaged in interstate commerce if such injuries result "in whole or in part from the negligence of any of the officers, agents, or employees of such carrier, or by reason of any defect or insufficiency, due to its negligence, in its cars, engines, appliances, machinery, track, roadbed, works, boats, wharves, or other equipment." 45 U.S.C. § 51, 45 U.S.C.A. § 51.

Petitioner, the administrator of the estate of L. E. Haney, brought this suit under the Act against the respondent trustees of the St. Louis–San Francisco Railway Company (Frisco) and the respondent Illinois Central Railroad Company. It was charged that Haney, while employed as a switchtender by the respondents in the switchyard of the Grand Central Station in Memphis, Tennessee, was killed as a result of respondents' negligence. Following a trial in the Circuit Court of the City of St. Louis, Missouri, the jury returned a verdict in favor of petitioner and awarded damages in the amount of $30,000. Judgment was entered accordingly. On appeal, however, the Supreme Court of Missouri reversed the judgment, holding that there was no substantial evidence of negligence to support the submission of the case to the jury. We granted certiorari to review the propriety of the Supreme Court's action under the circumstances of this case.

It was admitted that Haney was employed by the Illinois Central, or a subsidiary corporation thereof, as a switchtender in the railroad yards near the Grand Central Station, which was owned by the Illinois Central. His duties included the throwing of switches for the Illinois Central as well as for the Frisco and other railroads using that station. * * *

The Illinois Central tracks run north and south directly past and into the Grand Central Station. About 2700 feet south of the station the Frisco tracks cross at right angles to the Illinois Central tracks. A westbound Frisco train wishing to use the station must stop some 250 feet or more west of this crossing and back into the station over a switch line curving east and north. The events in issue center about the switch several feet north of the main Frisco tracks at the point where the switch line branches off. This switch controls the tracks at this point.

It was very dark on the evening of December 21, 1939. At about 7:30 p.m. a westbound interstate Frisco passenger train stopped on the Frisco main line, its rear some 20 or 30 feet west of the switch. Haney, in the performance of his duties, threw or opened the switch to permit the train to back into the station. The respondents claimed that Haney was then required to cross to the south side of the track before the train passed the switch; and the conductor of the train testified that he saw Haney so cross. But there was also evidence that Haney's duties required him to wait at the switch north of the track until the train had cleared, close the switch, return to his shanty near the crossing and change the signals from red to green to permit trains on the Illinois Central tracks to use the crossing. The Frisco train cleared the switch, backing at the rate of 8 or 10 miles per hour. But the switch remained open and the signals still were red. Upon investigation Haney was found north of the track near the switch lying face down on the ground, unconscious. An ambulance was called, but he was dead upon arrival at the hospital.

Haney had been struck in the back of the head, causing a fractured skull from which he died. There were no known eye-witnesses to the fatal blow. Although it is not clear there is evidence that his body was extended north and south, the head to the south. Apparently he had fallen forward to the south; his face was bruised on the left side from hitting the ground and there were marks indicating that his toes had dragged a few inches southward as he fell. His head was about 5½ feet north of the Frisco tracks. Estimates ranged from 2 feet to 14 feet as to how far west of the switch he lay.

The injury to Haney's head was evidenced by a gash about two inches long from which blood flowed. The back of Haney's white cap had a corresponding black mark about an inch and a half long and an inch wide, running at an angle downward to the right of the center of the back of the head. A spot of blood was later found at a point 3 or 4 feet north of the tracks. The conclusion following an autopsy was that Haney's skull was fractured by "some fast moving small round object." One of the examining doctors testified that such an object might have been attached to a train backing at the rate of 8 or 10 miles per hour. But he also admitted that the fracture might have resulted from a blow from a pipe or club or some similar round object in the hands of an individual.

Petitioner's theory is that Haney was struck by the curled end or tip of a mail hook hanging down loosely on the outside of the mail car of the backing train. This curled end was 73 inches above the top of the rail, which was 7 inches high. The overhang of the mail car in relation to the rails was about 2 to 2½ feet. The evidence indicated that when the mail car swayed or moved around a curve the mail hook might pivot, its curled end swinging out as much as 12 to 14 inches. The curled end could thus be swung out to a point 3 to 3½ feet from the rail and about 73 inches above the top of the rail. Both east and west of the switch, however, was an uneven mound of cinders and dirt rising at its highest points 18 to 24 inches above the top of the rails. Witnesses differed as to how close the mound approached the rails, the estimates varying from 3 to 15 feet. But taking the figures most favorable to the petitioner, the mound extended to a point 6 to 12 inches north of the overhanging side of the mail car. If the mail hook end swung out 12 to 14 inches it would be 49 to 55 inches above the highest parts of the mound. Haney was 67½ inches tall. If he had been standing on the mound about a foot from the side of the mail car he could have been hit by the end of the mail hook, the exact point of contact depending upon the height of the mound at the particular point. His wound was about 4 inches below the top of his head, or 63½ inches above the point where he stood on the mound—well within the possible range of the mail hook end.

Respondents' theory is that Haney was murdered. They point to the estimates that the mound was 10 to 15 feet north of the rail, making it impossible for the mail hook end to reach a point of contact with Haney's head. Photographs were placed in the record to support the claim that the ground was level north of the rail for at least 10 feet. Moreover, it appears that the area immediately surrounding the switch was quite dark. Witnesses stated that it was so dark that it was impossible to see a 3–inch pipe 25 feet away. It also appears that many hoboes and tramps frequented the area at night in order to get rides on freight trains. Haney carried a pistol to protect himself. This pistol was found loose under his body by those who came to his rescue. It was testified, however, that the pistol had apparently slipped out of his pocket or scabbard as he fell. Haney's clothes were not disarranged and there was no evidence of a struggle or fight. No rods, pipes or weapons of any kind, except Haney's own pistol, were found near the scene. Moreover, his gold watch and diamond ring were still on him after he was struck. Six days later his unsoiled billfold was found on a high board fence about a block from the place where Haney was struck and near the point where he had been placed in an ambulance. It contained his social security card and other effects, but no money. His wife testified that he "never carried much money, not very much more than $10." Such were the facts in relation to respondents' theory of murder.

Finally, one of the Frisco foremen testified that he arrived at the scene shortly after Haney was found injured. He later examined the fireman's side of the train very carefully and found nothing sticking out or in disorder. In explaining why he examined this side of the train so carefully he stated that while he was at the scene of the accident "someone said they thought that train No. 106 backing in to Grand Central Station is what struck this man" and that Haney "was supposed to have been struck by something protruding on the side of the train." The foreman testified that these statements were made by an unknown Illinois Central switchman standing near the fallen body of Haney. The foreman admitted that the switchman "didn't see the accident." This testimony was admitted by the trial court over the strenuous objections of respondents' counsel that it was mere hearsay falling outside the res gestae rule.

The jury was instructed that Frisco's trustees were liable if it was found that they negligently permitted a rod or other object to extend out from the side of the train as it backed past Haney and that Haney was killed as the direct result of such negligence, if any. The jury was further told that Illinois Central was liable if it was found that the company negligently maintained an unsafe and dangerous place for Haney to work, in that the ground was high and uneven and the light insufficient and inadequate, and that Haney was injured and killed as a direct result of the said place being unsafe and dangerous. This latter instruction as to Illinois Central did not require the jury to find that Haney was killed by something protruding from the train.

The [Missouri] Supreme Court, in upsetting the jury's verdict against both the Frisco trustees and the Illinois Central, admitted that "It could be inferred from the facts that Haney could have been struck by the mail hook knob *if* he were standing on the south side of the mound and the mail hook extended out as far as 12 or 14 inches." But it held that "all reasonable minds would agree that it would be mere speculation and conjecture to say that Haney was struck by the mail hook" and that "plaintiff failed to make a submissible case on that question." It also ruled that there "was no substantial evidence that the uneven ground and insufficient light were cause or contributing causes of the death of Haney." Finally, the Supreme Court held that the testimony of the foreman as to the statement made to him by the unknown switchman was inadmissible under the *res gestae* rule since the switchman spoke from what he had heard rather than from his own knowledge.

We hold, however, that there was sufficient evidence of negligence on the part of both the Frisco trustee and the Illinois Central to justify the submission of the case to the jury and to require appellate courts to abide by the verdict rendered by the jury.

The evidence we have already detailed demonstrates that there was evidence from which it might be inferred that the end of the mail hook struck Haney in the back of the head, an inference that the [State] Supreme Court admitted could be drawn. That inference is not rendered unreasonable by the fact that Haney apparently fell forward toward the main Frisco track so that his head was 5½ feet north of the rail. He may well have been struck and then wandered in a daze to the point where he fell forward. The testimony as to blood marks some distance away from his head lends credence to that possibility, indicating that he did not fall immediately upon being hit. When that is added to the evidence most favorable to the petitioner as to the height and swing-out of the hook, the height and location of the mound and the nature of Haney's duties, the inference that Haney was killed by the hook cannot be said to be unsupported by probative facts or to be so unreasonable as to warrant taking the case from the jury.

It is true that there is evidence tending to show that it was physically and mathematically impossible for the hook to strike Haney. And there are facts from which it might reasonably be inferred that Haney was murdered. But such evidence has become irrelevant upon appeal, there being a reasonable basis in the record for inferring that the hook struck Haney. The jury having made that inference, the respondents were not free to relitigate the factual dispute in a reviewing court. Under these circumstances it would be an undue invasion of the jury's historic function for an appellate court to weigh the conflicting evidence, judge the credibility of witnesses and arrive at a conclusion opposite from the one reached by the jury.

It is no answer to say that the jury's verdict involved speculation and conjecture. Whenever facts are in dispute or the evidence is such that fair-minded men may draw different inferences, a measure of speculation and conjecture is required on the part of those whose duty it is to settle the dispute by choosing what seems to them to be the most reasonable inference. Only when there is a complete absence of probative facts to support the conclusion reached does a reversible error appear. But where, as here, there is an evidentiary basis for the jury's verdict, the jury is free to discard or disbelieve whatever facts are inconsistent with its conclusion. And the appellate court's function is exhausted when that evidentiary basis becomes apparent, it being immaterial that the court might draw a contrary inference or feel that another conclusion is more reasonable.

We are unable, therefore, to sanction a reversal of the jury's verdict against Frisco's trustees. Nor can we approve any disturbance in the verdict as to Illinois Central. The evidence was uncontradicted that it was very dark at the place where Haney was working and the surrounding ground was high and uneven. The evidence also showed that this area was entirely within the domination and control of Illinois Central despite the fact that the area was technically located in a public street of the City of Memphis. It was not unreasonable to conclude that these conditions constituted an unsafe and dangerous working place and that such conditions contributed in part to Haney's death, assuming that it resulted primarily from the mail hook striking his head.

* * *

The judgment of the Supreme Court of Missouri is reversed and the case is remanded for whatever further proceedings may be necessary not inconsistent with this opinion.

The Chief Justice and Justice Frankfurter concur in the result.

Justice Reed dissents.

Justice Jackson took no part in the consideration or decision of this case.

Notes and Questions

1. If you were a member of the jury in *Lavender,* how would you have decided how the decedent had been killed? Could your decision be anything more than speculation? Do you agree with the comment that "a study of the evidence in [*Lavender*] would lead me at least to the conclusion that there was no more reason for attributing the accident to the railroad's negligence, than to the deceased man's negligence, or the vicious act of a third person, or a combination of circumstances involving no fault on anyone's part"? Jaffe, Res Ipsa Loquitur Vindicated, 1 Buffalo L.Rev. 1, 14 (1951). If so, does it follow that the Court's decision to allow the case to go to the jury was wrong?

Consider the argument in James, Sufficiency of the Evidence and Jury–Control Devices Available Before Verdict, 47 Va.L.Rev. 218, 221–22 (1961):

> Where from the proven facts the nonexistence of the fact to be inferred appears to be just as probable as its existence (or more probable than its existence), then the conclusion that it exists is a matter of speculation, surmise, and conjecture, and a jury will not be allowed to draw it. This test suggests mathematical precision, but the suggestion is spurious. For one thing, we lack the quantitative data about most matters which would be needed to make meaningful statements in terms of probabilities. * * *

> Another flaw in the test as usually formulated lies in the possibility that courts may not mean it to be taken literally anyhow. * * *

> It appears then that the test, formulated in terms which suggest objective, scientific precision, is in fact one which gives the courts little guidance and great latitude. * * * Instead, courts are constantly asserting or assuming broad generalizations about human behavior and all sorts of other matters which either rest on their own very fallible notions about such things * * * or spring from considerations of policy and expediency.

How does the decision in *Lavender* respond to this kind of argument? Could the Court's opinion fairly be characterized as saying that it is incorrect to take cases away from the jury when the jury's conclusion would be no more than speculation, because the *only* occasions when a court *should* send a case to a jury are those in which an element of speculation is required? Does the fact the jury has such difficulty choosing between plaintiff's version and defendant's version mean that plaintiff has offered substantial evidence?

2. *Lavender* was a suit under the Federal Employers' Liability Act, a law enacted by Congress to provide special protection to railroad workers against railroad negligence. As Professor Cooper states, "it is no secret that FELA cases involve special reasons for allowing juries a wide discretion in fact inference and in law application * * *. The consequence of a mistaken denial of recovery for the injured plaintiff is disaster; the consequence of a verdict imposing liability after dispensing with any real requirement of negligence is that one more easily anticipated cost is added to the many costs of railroading. Although it may sometimes seem that railroads are less than ideally situated for absorbing or redistributing extra costs, there can be no question that they are far better situated than their injured workmen. That the seventh amendment is appropriately applied to preserve this area for jury justice does not mean that it is appropriately applied to require allowing an equivalent scope of jury freedom in areas where it may be more capricious or arbitrary." 55 Minn.L.Rev. at 926–27. See also Jaffe, supra, 1 Buffalo L.Rev. at 14–15: "We must not go too fast in drawing conclusions from Lavender v. Kurn. The FELA serves as a glorified workmen's compensation, and the Supreme Court has gone very far in dispensing with meaningful notions of both negligence and actual causation." Jaffe adds, however, "that there are similar trends in the automobile and railroad crossing cases." Id. at 15. Is there anything in the *Lavender* opinion to indicate that it was intended to be limited to FELA cases? For a discussion of the reasons for *not*

limiting *Lavender* to FELA cases, see C. Wright & M. Kane, Law of Federal Courts 689–90 (6th ed. 2002).

A number of courts to have specifically considered the question have confined *Lavender* to cases arising under pro-plaintiff congressional statutes, such as the FELA and the Jones Act (authorizing negligence suits by seamen). See, e.g., Boeing Co. v. Shipman, 411 F.2d 365, 370–73 (5th Cir.1969):

> FELA cases * * * are statutory negligence actions. * * * [I]t is clear that the congressional intent in enacting the FELA was to secure jury determinations in a larger proportion of cases than would be true of ordinary common law actions.
>
> * * *
>
> As a corollary to the unique statutory context of FELA actions, it is apparent that in the general run of cases federal courts have rejected the legendary "scintilla" test. * * * [T]he FELA test should not be employed as a vehicle to re-establish the "scintilla" rule which has been so firmly rejected by the federal judiciary.
>
> Although the Supreme Court has not answered the question of law, no Circuit Court of the United States * * * has held that the FELA test of sufficiency of evidence is applicable in non-FELA cases. * * *

The court then articulated what it considered the applicable standard in non-FELA cases (id. at 374–75):

> On motions for directed verdict and for judgment notwithstanding the verdict the Court should consider all of the evidence—not just that evidence which supports the non-mover's case—but in the light and with all reasonable inferences most favorable to the party opposed to the motion. If the facts and inferences point so strongly and overwhelmingly in favor of one party that the Court believes that reasonable men could not arrive at a contrary verdict, granting of the motions is proper. * * * A mere scintilla of evidence is insufficient to present a question for the jury. The motions for directed verdict and judgment n.o.v. should not be decided by which side has the better of the case, nor should they be granted only when there is a complete absence of probative facts to support a jury verdict. There must be a conflict in substantial evidence to create a jury question. However, it is the function of the jury as the traditional finder of the facts, and not the Court, to weigh conflicting evidence and inferences, and determine the credibility of witnesses.

See also Farpella–Crosby v. Horizon Health Care, 97 F.3d 803, 805 (5th Cir. 1996) (applying *Boeing* standard). Does it make sense to decide a directed verdict motion without looking at the evidence presented by the movant, as well as by the nonmovant?

In Boeing Co. v. Shipman, supra, Judge Rives dissented on the rejection of *Lavender*. Though he expressed no doubt "that the so-called 'scintilla' test has been firmly rejected by the Supreme Court and other federal courts in all jury cases including FELA cases," he also noted that the use of the term "substantial evidence" is "misleading," if not "erroneous," because "[t]he word 'substantial,' used in its legal sense, can equally well connote either a *qualitative* or a *quantitative* meaning." He further noted "that, notwithstanding all the variations which the Supreme Court has played on its sufficiency theme, I have been unable to find a single instance in which the Supreme Court has used 'substantial' in any of its articulations of the constitutional standard." 411 F.2d at 393–94. Certain courts have applied the *Lavender* standard to non-FELA cases as well. See, e.g., Howard v. McCrory Corp., 601 F.2d 133 (4th Cir.1979); Wratchford v. S. J. Groves & Sons Co., 405 F.2d 1061 (4th Cir.1969); Lones v. Detroit, Toledo and Ironton R. Co., 398 F.2d 914 (6th Cir.1968), cert. denied, 393 U.S. 1063, 89 S.Ct. 714, 21 L.Ed.2d 705 (1969).

3.   Compare *Lavender* to the Supreme Court's decision in an earlier FELA case, Pennsylvania R. Co. v. Chamberlain, 288 U.S. 333, 53 S.Ct. 391, 77 L.Ed. 819 (1933). This was an action to recover for the death of a brakeman, alleged to have been caused by the railroad's negligence. The brakeman was riding on a string of two cars while assisting in the breaking and making up of trains in the yard. Immediately behind him was a string of nine cars. Both strings were descending from a hump in the track through the force of gravity. His body was found next to the track some distance past the hump, and plaintiff's theory was that the railroad employees piloting the nine-car string allowed it to hit his string, causing him to be thrown off the cars and killed. However, the three employees riding the nine-car string testified that their string never collided with his string, and their testimony was corroborated by other employees in a position to see.

The only witness to testify for plaintiff was one Bainbridge, who said he was standing close to the hump. He saw the deceased riding at the rear of his string as it went by him and then saw the nine-car string pass by at a somewhat greater speed. Bainbridge looked away, heard a "loud crash" (which he said was not an unusual event in the yard and did not cause him to turn around at once), and when he turned around again, saw the two strings together, still moving, and the deceased no longer in sight. Later he heard shouts and went to the spot where the deceased's body was found.

The Supreme Court affirmed a directed verdict in favor of the defendant. It conceded that "where there is a direct conflict of testimony upon a matter of fact, the question must be left to the jury to determine, without regard to the number of witnesses upon either side." However, it found that "here there really is no conflict in the testimony as to the facts" because the defendant's witnesses all flatly testified that there was no collision between the two strings and "Bainbridge did not say there was such a collision." It concluded that the case "belong[s] to that class of cases where proven facts give equal support to each of two inconsistent inferences; in which event, neither of them being established, judgment, as a matter of law, must go against the party upon whom rests the necessity of sustaining one of those inferences as against the other, before he is entitled to recover." A verdict in plaintiff's favor, said the Court, "would have rested upon mere speculation and conjecture." Is it possible to reconcile this holding with that of *Lavender*? If not, which of the two makes more sense as a measure of the sufficiency of the evidence?

The *Chamberlain* decision also went on to characterize Bainbridge's testimony:

Not only is Bainbridge's testimony considered as a whole suspicious, insubstantial and insufficient, but his statement that when he turned shortly after hearing the crash the two strings were moving together is simply incredible, if he meant thereby to be understood as saying that he saw the two in contact. * * * [H]e was paying slight and only occasional attention to what was going on. The cars were eight or nine hundred feet from where he stood and moving almost directly away from him, his angle of vision being only 3° 33″ from a straight line. At that sharp angle and from that distance, near dusk of a misty evening (as the proof shows), the practical impossibility of the witness being able to see whether the front of the nine-car string was in contact with the back of the two-car string is apparent. And, certainly, in the light of these conditions, no verdict based upon a statement so unbelievable reasonably could be sustained as against the positive testimony to the contrary of unimpeached witnesses, all in a position to see, as this witness was not, the precise relations of the cars to one another. The fact that these witnesses were employees of the petitioner, under the circumstances here disclosed, does not impair this conclusion.

What contrary arguments could be made on plaintiff's behalf concerning the nature and strength of Bainbridge's testimony? Is this argument by the Court concerning the incredibility of Bainbridge's testimony and his inability to have had sense perception a different rationale from its earlier argument that the evidence was insufficient because it gave equal support to two inconsistent inferences?

4. Also compare to *Lavender* another FELA case, Brady v. Southern Ry. Co., 320 U.S. 476, 64 S.Ct. 232, 88 L.Ed. 239 (1943), where the Court, in affirming a state court holding that the plaintiff's case should not have been submitted to a jury, stated: "The weight of the evidence under the Employers' Liability Act must be more than a scintilla before the case may be properly left to the discretion of the trier of fact * * *. When the evidence is such that without weighing the credibility of the witnesses there can be but one reasonable conclusion as to the verdict, the court should determine the proceedings by non-suit, directed verdict or otherwise in accordance with the applicable practice without submission to the jury * * *." *Lavender* was decided three years later. Are the two decisions inconsistent? Some decisions have read *Brady* to overrule *Lavender*'s invocation of the scintilla rule, even in FELA cases. See, e.g., Aparicio v. Norfolk & Western Railway Co., 84 F.3d 803, 810 (6th Cir. 1996). However, while the standard under the FELA now appears to demand more than a scintilla, it nevertheless continues to be less demanding than the traditional burden. Mullahon v. Union Pacific R.R., 64 F.3d 1358, 1363 (9th Cir. 1995) (referring to standard in FELA cases as "less stringent.").

5. *The "Substantial Evidence" and "Scintilla" Rules:* Recall the discussion in Justice Black's dissent in *Galloway* concerning these alternative approaches to the measure of the sufficiency of the evidence. Would it be accurate to characterize *Lavender* as an illustration of the "scintilla" rule and *Chamberlain* as an illustration of the "substantial evidence" rule? According to Professor James, "[i]t is a judicial legend that there once was a 'scintilla rule' under which a verdict could be directed only where there was literally no evidence for proponent, but if there ever was such a notion all

that remains of it today is its universal repudiation." 47 Va.L.Rev. at 218–19. Today, it seems reasonably clear that the general trend in the courts has been toward the use of the substantial evidence test and increased court control. As one modern court of appeals has phrased the standard, "[j]udgment as a matter of law is proper when the record contains no proof beyond speculation to support the verdict." Larson v. Miller, 76 F.3d 1446, 1452 (8th Cir. 1996) (en banc). See also Sassaman v. Heart City Toyota, 879 F.Supp. 901, 907 (N.D.Ind.1994) ("a mere scintilla of evidence is not sufficient to support the jury's verdict."). Thus, to the extent *Lavender* does represent adoption of the "scintilla" rule, it appears to have been limited to its specific context.

6. *Judgment as a matter of law in employment discrimination suits:* In addition to FELA suits, courts have developed judgment as a matter of law standards that are specific to a number of federal statutes creating substantive causes of action for discrimination in employment. Included are suits under the Age Discrimination in Employment Act (ADEA), 29 U.S.C.§§ 621–634, which prohibits age discrimination against workers, and suits for racial or gender-based discrimination pursuant to Title VII of the Civil Rights Act of 1964, 42 U.S.C. § 2000e et seq.

One who sues for violation of these statutory protections bears an initial burden to establish a prima facie case of discrimination. Meeting this burden is "not onerous." Sanchez v. Puerto Rico Oil Co., 37 F.3d 712, 719 (1st Cir. 1994). "All that is needed is the production of admissible evidence which, if uncontradicted, would justify a legal conclusion of discrimination." Id. "Once the plaintiff establishes the prima facie requirements, a rebuttable presumption that the employer engaged in intentional age based discrimination attaches. * * * The burden then shifts to the employer to articulate a legitimate, nondiscriminatory reason for the decision. If the employer meets its burden, the presumption of discrimination vanishes." Brennan v. GTE Government Systems Corp., 150 F.3d 21, 25 (1st Cir. 1998). At that point, the court, in ruling on a motion for judgment as a matter of law, asks "whether the evidence as a whole would permit a reasonable factfinder to conclude that the proffered reason was pretextual and the true reason was an age-based animus." Id. This "three-step" burden-shifting framework was originally set out by the Supreme Court in McDonnell Douglas Corp. v. Green, 411 U.S. 792, 93 S.Ct. 1817, 36 L.Ed.2d 668 (1973), and Texas Department of Community Affairs v. Burdine, 450 U.S. 248, 101 S.Ct. 1089, 67 L.Ed.2d 207 (1981).

In St. Mary's Honor Center v. Hicks, 509 U.S. 502, 113 S.Ct. 2742, 125 L.Ed.2d 407 (1993), the Supreme Court discussed how to assess a motion for judgment as a matter of law in light of this burden-shifting framework. The Court stated: "The fact finder's disbelief of the reasons put forward by the defendant (particularly if disbelief is accompanied by a suspicion of mendacity) may, together with the elements of the prima facie case, suffice to show intentional discrimination. Thus, rejection of the defendant's proffered reasons will permit the trier of fact to infer the ultimate fact of intentional discrimination." 509 U.S. at 511.

In Reeves v. Sanderson Plumbing Products, Inc., 530 U.S. 133, 120 S.Ct. 2097, 147 L.Ed.2d 105 (2000), the Supreme Court reaffirmed *Hicks*, holding that "a plaintiff's prima facie case, combined with sufficient evidence to find that the employer's asserted justification is false, may permit the trier of fact to conclude that the employer unlawfully discriminated." Id. at 148. The Court added, however, that "[t]his is not to say that such a showing by the plaintiff will *always* be adequate to sustain a jury's finding of liability. Certainly there will be instances where, although the plaintiff has established a prima facie case and set forth sufficient evidence to reject the defendant's explanation, no rational factfinder could conclude that the action was discriminatory. For instance, an employer would be entitled to judgment as a matter of law if the record conclusively revealed some other, nondiscriminatory reason for the employer's decision, or if the plaintiff created only a weak issue of fact as to whether the employer's reason was untrue and there was abundant and uncontroverted independent evidence that no discrimination had occurred." Id. Contrast the standards for judgment as a matter of law in Title VII cases with the pleading requirements imposed in suits brought pursuant to the same statute, discussed in Swierkiewicz v. Sorema N.A., 534 U.S. 506, 122 S.Ct. 992, 152 L.Ed.2d 1 (2002), supra p. 177.

JUDGMENT AS A MATTER OF LAW AND LAW APPLICATION

Note that in *Lavender* plaintiff also sought to recover on the theory that the Illinois Central Railroad negligently maintained an unsafe place for Haney to work. Besides raising questions of historical fact, this claim called for the application of a reasonableness standard to the historical facts as found. Particularly in negligence actions, the jury has an important function to play in this law application process even where there is no dispute as to the historical facts. See generally Weiner, The Civil Jury and the Law–Fact Distinction, 54 Calif.L.Rev. 1867 (1966).

For example, in Sioux City & P. Railroad Co. v. Stout, 84 U.S. (17 Wall.) 657, 21 L.Ed. 745 (1873), plaintiff, a small child, was injured by an unlocked railroad turntable on which he was playing. Because there was no dispute about the location of the turntable, the absence of a lock, and other circumstances, the railroad contended that the question whether it had been guilty of negligence was a question of law for the judge. The Supreme Court disagreed:

> It is true, in many cases, that where the facts are undisputed the effect of them is for the judgment of the court, and not for the decision of the jury. This is true in that class of cases where the existence of such facts comes in question rather than where deductions or inferences are to be made from the facts. If a deed be given in evidence, a contract proven, or its breach testified to, the existence of such deed, contract, or breach, there being nothing in derogation of the evidence, is no doubt to be ruled as a question of law. In some cases, too, the necessary inference from the proof is so certain that it may be ruled as a question of law. If a sane man voluntarily throws himself in contact with a passing engine, there being nothing to counteract the effect of this action, it may be ruled as a matter of law that the injury to him resulted from his own fault, and that no action can be sustained by him or his representatives. * * * But these are extreme cases. The range between them is

almost infinite in variety and extent. It is in relation to these
intermediate cases that the opposite rule prevails. Upon the facts
proven in such cases, it is a matter of judgment and discretion, of
sound inference, what is the deduction to be drawn from the
undisputed facts. Certain facts we may suppose to be clearly established from which one sensible, impartial man would infer that
proper care had not been used, and that negligence existed; another
man equally sensible and equally impartial would infer that proper
care had been used, and that there was no negligence. It is this class
of cases and those akin to it that the law commits to the decisions of
a jury. * * * It is assumed that twelve men know more of the
common affairs of life than does one man, that they can draw wiser
and safer conclusions from admitted facts thus occurring than can a
single judge.

BURDEN SHIFTING AND SUBSTANTIVE POLICY

While the issues of directed verdict standards and burden shifting
are essentially procedural issues, as the discussion of FELA cases (supra
p. 628 n. 2) demonstrates, substantive policy considerations have influenced these issues. The classic illustration is Summers v. Tice, 199 P.2d
1 (Cal.1948). Plaintiff was injured when two hunters negligently shot in
his direction. It was impossible to determine which of the two shots
caused the injury. The defendants nevertheless were held liable as joint
tortfeasors. In order to avoid liability, then, one of the defendants would
have to demonstrate that his shot did not cause plaintiff's injury,
thereby imposing full damages on the other defendant. What are the
likely reasons for such a rule? To what dangers, if any, might it give
rise?

Summers, in modified form, was relied on by the California Supreme
Court in Sindell v. Abbott Laboratories, 607 P.2d 924 (Cal.1980), cert.
denied sub nom. Upjohn Co. v. Sindell, 449 U.S. 912, 101 S.Ct. 285, 66
L.Ed.2d 140 (1980). The plaintiff, the daughter of a woman who had
taken the drug DES as a miscarriage preventative during pregnancy,
sued many years later claiming she developed cancer as a result of her
mother's ingestion of the drug. She sued eleven named drug companies,
as well as other unnamed manufacturers of DES, claiming all had acted
negligently in the sale and handling of the drug. However, she was
unable to establish which of the companies—named or unnamed—
manufactured the specific drug ingested by her mother. The state
supreme court refused to dismiss the complaint:

> The most persuasive reason for finding plaintiff states a cause
> of action is that advanced in Summers: as between an innocent
> plaintiff and negligent defendants, the latter should bear the cost of
> the injury. Here, as in Summers, plaintiff is not at fault in failing to
> provide evidence of causation, and although the absence of such
> evidence is not attributable to the defendants either, their conduct
> in marketing a drug the effects of which are delayed for many years
> played a significant role in creating the unavailability of proof.

From a broader policy standpoint, defendants are better able to bear the cost of injury resulting from the manufacture of a defective product. * * *

Where, as here, all defendants produced a drug from an identical formula and the manufacturer of the DES which caused plaintiff's injuries cannot be identified through no fault of plaintiff, a modification of the rule of *Summers* is warranted. * * *

[W]e hold it to be reasonable in the present context to measure the likelihood that any of the defendants supplied the product which allegedly injured plaintiff by the percentage which the DES sold by each of them for the purpose of preventing miscarriage bears to the entire production of the drug sold by all for that purpose. * * *

Each defendant will be held liable for the proportion of the judgment represented by its share of the market unless it demonstrates that it could not have made the product which caused plaintiff's injuries. * * *

Under this approach, each manufacturer's liability would approximate its responsibility for the injuries caused by its own products.

Is this a perversion of purely procedural factfinding devices in individual cases, or does it represent a legitimate blending of substantive social policy with a procedural mechanism? Cf. Goldman v. Johns–Manville Sales Corp., 514 N.E.2d 691 (Ohio 1987) (market share liability theory rejected where it could not be shown that all products to which injured party was exposed were completely fungible). For a thorough, more recent discussion of the market share theory, see Kurczi v. Eli Lilly and Co., 113 F.3d 1426 (6th Cir. 1997).

GUENTHER v. ARMSTRONG RUBBER CO.

United States Court of Appeals, Third Circuit, 1969.
406 F.2d 1315.

Before McLAUGHLIN, STALEY and VAN DUSEN, CIRCUIT JUDGES.

GERALD McLAUGHLIN, CIRCUIT JUDGE.

This is an ordinary products liability negligence claim. It is in the Federal courts solely by reason of diversity of citizenship between the parties. It has one rather unusual situation which was the sole reason for the direction of verdict below in favor of the defendant and is the only question on appeal.

The facts are simple. Plaintiff-appellant is a mechanic who on May 21, 1965 was employed by Sears Roebuck & Company at its place of business in the Pittsburgh, Pennsylvania area. His main work was installing automobile tires and batteries. On the particular day he was in the process of putting four summer tires on an automobile. He first removed the four tires which were on the car. Without any complications he then put on three of the new ones. As he was adjusting the fourth tire, it exploded and threw him about six feet away. He was unconscious for a few seconds. He was later taken to the Pittsburgh Hospital where he was given emergency treatment. Robert W. Small, the Sears Service Center Manager at the time, was a witness on behalf of the plaintiff. He said he was in the Service building when the explosion occurred and that he rushed from his office to the tire center. Mr. Guenther was on the floor about four feet from the tire machine. There was a tire on the machine. After Mr. Guenther was removed to the ambulance, Mr. Small had the tire taken to his office where he checked out its serial numbers.

In November 1966, Messrs. Drozness, plaintiff's expert, and Dunlop, the defense expert, examined the tire in Mr. Small's office. That tire was in the court at the trial. It was admitted on behalf of the defendant regarding that tire "This is our tire, our experts have told you that." Mr. Drozness was called as an expert on behalf of the plaintiff. The defense asked for an offer of proof. Plaintiff's attorney stated that Mr. Drozness "has already been identified by Mr. Small as having examined the tire involved in the accident. I am going to put him on to testify that it had a broken bead, that he went over the history of the mounting procedure used by Mr. Guenther and as a basis of that, he concludes that this is a manufacturer's defect." In response to the court's query, plaintiff's attorney continued to outline his theory of the defendant's liability, stating as to the jury, "If they accept Small's testimony and they accept the tire as given by Mr. Drozness which has a broken bead in it and if they are on the basis of a hypothetical inquiry wherein I intend to tell him, repeat how the Plaintiff put it on the machine and everything and that it had no apparent defects." The attorney went on to say he expected to develop that in the expert's opinion the tire had not been damaged by handling and that the broken bead was a manufacturer's defect. The defense attorney objected to the testimonial offer and was sustained by the judge.

Plaintiff, as a witness, carefully outlined the steps he had taken in mounting the fourth tire. He said that after he had the tire in position and he started to put air into it "Well, it started to come up, the bead, and when it hit the rim it just let loose and exploded." The tire which Mr. Small had testified was on the machine and which he had brought to his office was a "white wall". Mr. Guenther testified that the tire he was mounting and which exploded was a "black wall". He said it was a fifteen inch and that the white wall in court was a thirteen inch. He was asked "How do you remember that the one you were mounting was black?" He answered "I just remember it was." He said he remembered it was fifteen inch because the automobile was a Chrysler "55 or 56" which takes "15 inch".

With respect to the identification of the white wall tire in court, the defense attorney, addressing the court with reference to the proposed evidence of Mr. Drozness, said "He is going to say he examined a tire, how is he going to identify it?" Plaintiff's counsel answered, "Small has already said the tire Drozness examined is the tire in Court." The judge commented "That may be sufficient identity if Drozness examined the tire Small produced." Defense counsel said, "Judge, it seems to me that they are going to rely on Small to establish the identity." The judge asked "Well, with that offer, do you object to his testimony?" Counsel replied "I certainly do your Honor." The judge sustained the motion for a directed verdict in favor of the defendant.

Later, in denying the motion for a new trial, the judge specifically found as to the tire produced by Sears Roebuck manager Small which was marked as a trial exhibit, that, "This tire was admittedly manufactured by Defendant. It is this tire which Plaintiff's expert examined and would testify was defective." The court concluded that "To allow this is to fly directly in the face of Plaintiff's clear and unequivocal denial that this was the tire that injured him. We believe that Plaintiff is bound by this testimony." The judge therefore upheld his trial conclusion of a directed verdict in favor of the defendant. The lower court decision centered entirely upon the testimony of the plaintiff that it was a "black wall" tire which exploded, threw him six feet and rendered him unconscious.

* * *

The foundation of plaintiff's cause is that he was injured by a bursting tire which he had been adjusting on the tire machine in front of him and which was still on the machine after it had exploded. There is a disagreement between plaintiff and his witness Small as to whether that particular tire was a "black wall" or a "white wall". On such detail we do not think it is the function of the court to conclude plaintiff's cause of action by directing a verdict against him. In this instance no reason appears why a jury should not be able to readily resolve the problem in dispute at this time in this appeal.

It is also urged for appellant that his claim should have been allowed to go to the jury * * * founded on evidence that the defendant made from 75 to 80 per cent of the tires the particular Sears Roebuck store had for sale. It is true that the trial court in holding that plaintiff's evidence of identification failed, relied on Kamosky v. Owens–Illinois Glass Co., 89 F.Supp. 561 (M.D.Pa.1950), affd. p.c. 185 F.2d 674 (3 Cir.1950). It is also true that in *Kamosky* there was only a 10 to 15 per cent likelihood of liability of the alleged offending article. Even so as we see it there was no justification for allowing plaintiff's case on that so-called probability hypothesis to go to the jury. The latter's verdict would at best be a guess. It could not be reasonably supported.

The judgment of the District Court will be reversed and the case remanded for a new trial on the merits.

Notes and Questions

1. The facts of *Guenther* present a problem of proof similar to that found in what has been referred to by academics as the "blue bus" hypothetical:

While driving late at night on a dark, two-laned road, a person confronts an oncoming bus speeding down the centerline of the road in the opposite direction. In the glare of the headlights, the person sees that the vehicle is a bus, but cannot otherwise identify it. He swerves to avoid a collision, and his car hits a tree. The bus speeds past without stopping. The injured person later sues the Blue Bus Company. He proves, in addition to the facts stated above, that the Blue Bus Company owns and operates 80% of the buses that run on the road where the accident occurred. Can he win?

Nesson, The Evidence or the Event? On Judicial Proof and the Acceptability of Verdicts, 98 Harv.L.Rev. 1357, 1378 (1985). For a case strikingly similar to this example, see Smith v. Rapid Transit, Inc., 58 N.E.2d 754 (Mass.1945).

In commenting on this hypothetical, Professor Nesson writes: "one can conclude from the evidence that the plaintiff was probably injured by a blue bus, and yet not be entirely satisfied with the conclusion that a blue bus injured the plaintiff. The evidence seems not to be about the specific event in question, but rather about a class of events (all cases involving unidentified busses). It suggests only that the defendant causes a majority but not all of a class of events. It offers no basis for a leap to a conclusion about any specific event. Although the information about the class suggests it is more probable than not that the defendant caused any given accident, a finding for any one plaintiff would logically extend to every plaintiff in the class." Nesson, Agent Orange Meets the Blue Bus, 66 B.U.L.Rev. 521, 522 (1986).

2. In the *Kamosky* case, mentioned in the *Guenther* opinion, the plaintiff attempted to establish that a bottle involved in an accident was one of defendant's by producing evidence that (1) defendant had manufactured the overwhelming portion of the new bottles used by the bottler from whom ultimately the bottle in question had been obtained, and (2) between 10% and 15% of the bottles used by the bottler during the relevant time period were in fact new bottles. On this evidence, the court directed a verdict for the defendant, and a motion to set aside the directed verdict was denied: "Such was clearly not substantial evidence from which the jury, without guessing, might find that Owens did manufacture, produce, handle, or process the bottle which exploded." Do you agree with the trial court in *Guenther* that the two cases are indistinguishable?

3. Would the *Guenther* court have reached the same conclusion on plaintiff's "probability" argument had 99.9% of the tires in the store in question been manufactured by the defendant? *Should* it reach the same conclusion in such a case? Cf. Nesson, 66 B.U.L.Rev. at 522, n.3: "At some point, high probability alone is sufficient to produce an acceptable verdict. In the blue bus hypothetical * * * evidence indicating a 55% likelihood that the plaintiff should recover presents a problem, whereas evidence indicating a 95% likelihood might not. Reaching a conclusion involves putting doubt aside. The difficulty of doing so will vary with the intensity of the doubt, the degree to which we are concerned about making a mistake, and the rationalizations we have to help us conclude."

For a comparison with *Guenther*, consider Kramer v. Weedhopper of Utah, Inc., 490 N.E.2d 104 (Ill.App.1986). The case was a products liability suit, turning largely on the question of who had distributed an allegedly defective bolt used on an airplane that had crashed. Defendant Lawrence had distributed 90% of the bolts used by the airplane manufacturer, while Hughes Aviation supplied the remainder. No other evidence existed to demonstrate who had distributed the bolt. Lawrence was granted summary judgment, but the appellate court reversed:

> The parties here do not seriously dispute that the elements of a product liability action may be proved inferentially or by direct or circumstantial evidence. The dispute centers, instead, on whether the fact that Lawrence supplied 90% of the bolts * * * is sufficient circumstantial evidence to avoid entry of summary judgment. Circumstantial evidence consists of facts or circumstances which give rise to a reasonable inference of the truth of an underlying fact. * * * Such evidence must have reasonable probative force; the jury will not be allowed to engage in conjecture, surmise or speculation. * * *

> The focus must then be on what quantum of evidence is sufficient for an inference to be reasonable. This measure has eluded specific standardization and enumeration. * * * Generally, the test of reasonableness resolves into a question of probability: is the inferred occurrence more probable than not, or is it merely possible.

> * * * Evidence showing that defendant was the exclusive distributor of a product would strongly support plaintiff's case when defendant's identification can be proved only circumstantially; but when two suppliers of an allegedly dangerous product exist, under circumstances which show that a defendant supplied 90% of the parts used, this evidence is sufficient to withstand a motion for summary judgment.

> * * * Defendant was allegedly the most probable cause of plaintiff's injury. The defects in plaintiff's proof are such that affect the weight which should be accorded the evidence, not whether the evidence initially poses a genuine material triable question of fact.

One judge dissented, arguing: "Liability is not based on a balancing of probabilities, but on a finding of fact." He relied in part on *Guenther* for his decision that plaintiff's evidence was insufficient to go to the jury.

4. Should probability evidence be limited to issues of identification? Plaintiff is cut on his arm by flying glass, caused by defendant's negligence. A scar forms at the location of the injury, and, a number of years later, a skin cancer develops on the exact location of the scar. Expert witnesses testify that there is no medical basis on which to believe that such an injury is likely to give rise to skin cancer. Should the court grant a directed verdict on the causation issue? Cf. Kramer Service, Inc. v. Wilkins, 186 So. 625 (Miss.1939), in which the court precluded recovery for such a cancer by a plaintiff whose expert witness testified the trauma could cause skin cancer, but only in one of a hundred cases. The court reasoned that "[p]ossibilities will not sustain a verdict."

5. To what extent does the question of whether there exists sufficient evidence for a case to go to the jury lend itself to the application of mathematical-statistical probability theory? See generally Cullison, Probability Analysis of Judicial Fact–Finding: A Preliminary Outline of The Subjective Approach, 1 Tol.L.Rev. 538 (1969).

Professor Nesson has argued: " '[P]robability' as we use the term in law, particularly in the civil standard of proof, is not a hard-edged mathematical concept. It is, rather, a concept that incorporates less rigid ideas of justice and reflects the judicial function of resolving disputes in the real world, where values shift and knowledge is uncertain. An outcome is 'probable' if it best accomplishes a just and acceptable resolution of the dispute. Probability, as a legal concept in the law of proof, suggests wisdom, probity, and approbation—not favorable betting odds." Nesson, Agent Orange Meets the Blue Bus: Factfinding at the Frontier of Knowledge, 66 B.U.L.Rev. 521 (1986). See also Tribe, Trial by Mathematics: Precision and Ritual in the Legal Process, 84 Harv.L.Rev. 1329 (1971).

To illustrate his point, Nesson cites a portion of the "Agent Orange" litigation, in which former servicemen sued the government for damages they claimed to have incurred as a result of their use of the defoliant, Agent Orange, in Vietnam. In re "Agent Orange" Prod. Liab. Litig., 611 F.Supp. 1223 (E.D.N.Y.1985), affirmed on other grounds, 818 F.2d 187 (2d Cir.1987), cert. denied, 487 U.S. 1234, 108 S.Ct. 2898, 101 L.Ed.2d 931 (1988). Though the plaintiffs involved in the class action recovered a large amount as part of a settlement, the court granted summary judgment against those plaintiffs who had opted out of the class, because "[i]n Judge Weinstein's view, the epidemiological studies on Agent Orange so clearly failed to prove any causative link between exposure to Agent Orange and cancers, birth defects, and other illnesses, that * * * [none] of the * * * opt-out plaintiffs presented a factual dispute." 66 B.U.L.Rev. at 525. Nesson is critical of the court's approach:

> [Judge Weinstein's] view reflects an erroneous and hard-edged statistical concept of probability, which obscures the differences between law and science. Although he has settled the Agent Orange cases, his approach, if it becomes dogma, will gravely incapacitate the dispute-resolving powers of courts in toxic tort cases. It leaves entirely to defendants the range between what jurors and members of the public can rationally believe, and what statisticians can prove.

While there were no studies linking the chemical in Agent Orange to cancer in humans (though there were such studies as to animals), Nesson notes that "[t]he etiology of cancer is not yet known; scientists cannot explain at a cellular level the mechanism of causation." 66 B.U.L.Rev. at 526. He draws a distinction between "scientific proof" and "legal proof" (66 B.U.L.Rev. at 529–30):

> An imaginative scientist exploring the hypothesis that a given toxic agent causes cancer is very likely to suspend scientific judgment on the ultimate question of causation until more testing or study can be done to eliminate alternative hypotheses. A doctor or lawyer or judge, on the other hand, often does not have the luxury of postponing a decision. Often he makes a judgment once he reaches a reasonable working conclusion. Likewise, we ask juries to come to conclusions without insisting on waiting for scientific demonstration. The legal standard of proof would seem to require only a rational basis for the expert's opinion—a standard far short of scientific demonstration.

In response, Professor Ronald Allen writes:

If the issue was whether any rational jury could find for the plaintiff, then Weinstein did his job—no rational jury could so find based upon the evidence before the court. If, by contrast, the issue was whether *any* jury could find for the plaintiff, then obviously Weinstein did not do his job. The only way to find out if a jury would return a plaintiff's verdict is to let it hear the case. * * *

Now [under Nesson's view] we see that "what actually happened" does not matter. Rather, whatever a jury decided will be promulgated as "what actually happened" no matter how irrational or lawless it might be. I do not believe the rest of us are that gullible. We know that there is the risk that any small group of people making a decision might act in an irrational fashion. There is also a risk that such a group might reach a result for the wrong reason. In either case, such decisions should not be allowed precisely because they diverge from reality as we are able to reconstruct it. It is a tenet of our civilization that legal rights and obligations should, in general, rest on as accurate a reconstruction of reality as is feasible in the context of any particular dispute.

Allen, Rationality, Mythology, and the "Acceptability of Verdicts" Thesis, 66 B.U.L.Rev. 541, 561–62 (1986).

Might the court in the *Agent Orange* case have appropriately utilized the burden-shifting approach employed by the California Supreme Court in Summers v. Tice and the DES litigation [supra p. 634]? Were the causation problems in *Summers* comparable to those in *Agent Orange*?

6.   In cases like *Agent Orange,* could the causation problem be solved by using a different procedural device? Professor David Rosenberg has argued that the class action offers a solution because it permits the judicial system to aggregate exposed individuals into a group and impose on the defendant who is responsible for their exposure liability equal to the population-wide increase in the incidence of disease due to the exposure. This money could then create a fund that could be used to compensate those suffering from the disease even though there is no way to be certain which of them would not have gotten the disease in the absence of exposure. See Rosenberg, The Causal Connection in Mass Exposure Cases: A "Public Law" Vision of the Tort System, 97 Harv.L.Rev. 851 (1984). Would this be fair to defendants? Should courts countenance a device that transfers money from defendants to people they have not injured?

7.   *Proving damages by means of statistical sampling*: Certain courts adjudicating class actions (see chapter IV, supra) have utilized statistical sampling methods as a means of determining damages of individual class members after deciding liability issues collectively. For example, in Hilao v. Estate of Marcos, 103 F.3d 767 (9th Cir. 1996), the court upheld the use of such a method to determine damages of individual class members in a class suit against the estate of the former dictator of the Philippines. The district court adjudicated, in front of a jury, 137 damage claims selected randomly by computer from a list of 9,541 claims by class members. The number of randomly selected cases was chosen on the basis of the testimony of a statistical expert. The district court then extrapolated those awards across the sub-classes that had been established prior to the adjudication of damages. The majority on the appellate court, in rejecting a due process

challenge to this methodology, noted that while the district court's methodology was unorthodox, "it can be justified by the extraordinarily unusual nature of this case." Id. at 786. Judge Rymer, in dissent, argued: "Even in the context of a class action, individual causation and individual damages must still be proved individually * * *. There is little question that Marcos caused tremendous harm to many people, but the question is which people, and how much. That, I think, is a question on which the defendant has a right to due process." Id. at 788.

Other federal courts have been far less accepting of class damage proof by means of statistical sampling. See In re Fibreboard Corp., 893 F.2d 706 (5th Cir. 1990) (noting that "there will inevitably be individual class members whose recovery will be greater or lesser than it would have been if tried alone" and that "persons who would have had their claims rejected may recover," and therefore expressing "profound disquiet" over the constitutionality of the practice); Cimino v. Raymark Industries, Inc., 151 F.3d 297 (5th Cir. 1998) (finding the practice to violate Seventh Amendment right to jury trial). Compare Blue Cross and Blue Shield of New Jersey, Inc. v. Philip Morris USA Inc., 344 F.3d 211 (2d Cir. 2003) (accepting the practice).

In what ways, if any, does the use of statistical sampling to prove classwide damages differ from the use of naked statistics to prove liability in an individual case?

8. While the court in *Guenther* rejected plaintiff's "probability" argument as a basis for denying a directed verdict motion, it ultimately reversed the granting of the directed verdict, because a jury could reasonably believe plaintiff's witness, rather than plaintiff's own recollection, on the nature of the exploding tire. Would the jury have been "guessing" any less in making this judgment than in deciding, on the basis of the applicable statistics, whether the tire had actually been manufactured by the defendant? Is the jury "guessing" any less when it decides the cause of the switchman's death in *Lavender*? Do you think the Supreme Court that decided *Lavender* would have affirmed a grant of directed verdict in *Guenther*?

It is often said that issues of credibility are to be decided by the jury, rather than on a motion for directed verdict. While this is generally accurate, the situation is somewhat more complicated. In the words of one group of commentators:

[A]n assertion that credibility is at issue, resting alone, will not suffice to prevent the court from directing a verdict if all of the objective or indisputable evidence indicates that a particular piece of testimony is incredible. Conversely, uncontradicted, disinterested testimony may support the entry of a directed verdict, since the jury should not be allowed to disbelieve that testimony. The court is not weighing the evidence under these circumstances, rather it is determining that there is not sufficient evidence to create an issue of credibility. * * *

Less clear, however, is the question whether a directed verdict may be entered because the evidence presented is inherently incredible or because some of the evidence of physical facts suggests that other testimony is incredible and should be ignored. Some courts seem to be willing to make this assessment; others refuse to do so.

J. Friedenthal, M. Kane & A. Miller, Civil Procedure 568–69 (3d ed. 1999). The issue of the jury's proper role in assessing credibility is also examined in connection with the discussion of summary judgment. See pp. 455–56 supra.

2. Motion for New Trial

AHERN v. SCHOLZ

United States Court of Appeals First Circuit, 1996.
85 F.3d 774.

Before TORRUELLA, CHIEF JUDGE, BOWNES, SENIOR CIRCUIT JUDGE, and STAHL, CIRCUIT JUDGE.

TORRUELLA, CHIEF JUDGE.

The parties in this breach of contract case, a successful musician and his former manager, dispute whether royalties from record albums have been accounted for and paid to each other. The appeal is from a final judgment by the district court after a jury trial, disposing of all claims in respect to all parties.

In this case, the parties dispute many of the facts and the inferences to be drawn from them. Thus we start with a sketch of the basic facts, and address the individual issues in more detail below. Appellant and cross-appellee Donald Thomas Scholz ("Scholz") is a musician, composer, and record producer who was, and is, a member of the musical group BOSTON ("BOSTON"). In late 1975, Scholz entered into three agreements with appellee and cross-appellant Paul F. Ahern ("Ahern"), who was engaged in the business of promoting and managing music groups, and his then partner, Charles McKenzie ("McKenzie") (collectively, the "1975 Agreements"). First, Scholz made a recording agreement (the "Recording Agreement") with Ahern and McKenzie d/b/a P.C. Productions, to which Bradley Delp, the lead singer of BOSTON, was also a party. Second was a management agreement (the "Management Agreement"), also between Scholz and P.C. Productions, under which Ahern and McKenzie were appointed Scholz' exclusive personal managers worldwide. The third agreement was a songwriter agreement made between Scholz and Ahern, under which Scholz was obligated to furnish Ahern his exclusive songwriting services for a period of five years.

In early 1976, CBS Records ("CBS") and Ahern Associates, a business name of Ahern and McKenzie, entered into a recording agreement for the exclusive recording services of BOSTON. The group's first album (the "first album") was released in 1976, and sold approximately 11 million copies—one of the highest-selling debut albums ever. Its second album (the "second album") was released in August 1978, and sold approximately 6 million copies.

In 1978, Scholz and the other members of BOSTON entered into a modification agreement with Ahern and P.C. Productions, dated April 24, 1978. Among other things, the First Modification Agreement modified the 1975 Agreements and changed the financial relationship between Scholz and his managers. Ahern and McKenzie dissolved their partnership. A few years later, in May of 1981, Ahern and Scholz, individually and under various business names, entered into a further modification agreement (the "Further Modification Agreement" or "FMA"), which is at the heart of this dispute. Ahern ceased to be Scholz' manager.

In 1982, with the third album not yet released, CBS cut off the payment of royalties generated from the first and second albums. In 1983, CBS brought suit against Scholz, Ahern, and the members of BOSTON for failure to timely deliver record albums. Scholz' counsel in that action was Donald S. Engel ("Engel"); Ahern had his own counsel. While that litigation was pending, the third album was released by MCA Records ("MCA") in 1986 and sold well over 4 million copies. At the close of trial—seven years after the CBS litigation began—the jury found that Scholz was not in breach of contract. Scholz incurred legal fees of about $3.4 million dollars.

In February 1991, Ahern commenced this action against Scholz for breach of the FMA claiming a failure to pay royalties due under the third album. Scholz asserted various affirmative defenses and counterclaims against Ahern, including breach of the FMA. During trial, Engel, Scholz' lead trial counsel, was twice called as a witness. At the close of the evidence, the court granted Scholz' directed verdict dismissing Ahern's Count III for fraud and IV for breach of implied covenant of good faith and fair dealing. The court also granted Ahern's motion for directed verdict dismissing Scholz' First, Second, and Third Counterclaims and his Third, Fourth, and Fifth affirmative defenses. Only the parties' respective breach of contract claims went to the jury. The jury found that Scholz breached section 5.2.1 of the FMA to pay Ahern royalties from the third album, and found that Ahern had not breached the FMA to account for and pay Scholz royalties due from the first and second albums. It awarded Ahern $547,007 in damages.

The trial court sitting without a jury also found Scholz had breached the FMA, and heard Ahern's Count II for declaratory relief and Count V for violation of Mass. Gen. L. ch. 93A and Scholz' Fifth Counterclaim for recision of contract for failure to obtain a license. The court denied the declaratory relief Ahern sought in Count I, and awarded him costs, interest and attorney's fees pursuant to Count V for violation of Mass. Gen. L. ch. 93A §§ 2 & 11. The court denied the relief sought by Scholz in his Fifth Counterclaim and held that he waived his Counts VI and VII at oral argument. After a hearing on Ahern's bill of costs and application for reasonable attorney's fees and interest, the court awarded Ahern $265,000 in attorney's fees and $135,000 in costs.

The district court denied, without a hearing, Scholz' motion for a new trial, motion to amend the court's memorandum and order and judgment entered thereon, motion to admit new evidence, and motion to amend the court's memorandum and order and the judgment entered thereon regarding Scholz' Sixth Counterclaim. This appeal followed.

Appellant first argues that the district court erred in denying his motion for a new trial, made pursuant to Fed.R.Civ.P. 59(a). We therefore review the record below to determine whether the evidence required that the district court grant the motion for a new trial. In reviewing the record of the 16–day trial, we note that both parties presented extensive evidence. The jury heard testimony regarding a history that spans two decades, involves at least seven contracts, includes detailed numerical accounting, and references more than half a dozen other legal battles. The parties called a total of fifteen witnesses, seven of whom, including Ahern, Scholz, and Engel, Scholz' counsel, testified twice. In short, the jury faced a complex and sometimes conflicting set of facts in making its decision as to whether either, neither, or both parties breached the 1981 Further Modification Agreement. Ultimately, we find that the jury's verdict was not against the clear weight of the evidence, and the district court did not abuse its discretion in so finding.

A. STANDARD OF REVIEW

"A verdict may be set aside and new trial ordered 'when the verdict is against the clear weight of the evidence, or is based upon evidence which is false, or will result in a clear miscarriage of justice.' " Phav v. Trueblood, Inc., 915 F.2d 764, 766 (1st Cir.1990) (quoting Torres–Troche v. Municipality of Yauco, 873 F.2d 499 (1st Cir.1989)); see Fed.R.Civ.P. 59(a) * * *. In reaching its decision, "the district court has broad legal authority to determine whether or not a jury's verdict is against the 'clear weight of the evidence.' " de Perez [v. Hospital del Maestro], 910 F.2d at 1006. Nonetheless, "the trial judge's discretion, although great, must be exercised with due regard to the rights of both parties to have questions which are fairly open resolved finally by the jury at a single trial." Coffran v. Hitchcock Clinic, Inc., 683 F.2d 5, 6 (1st Cir.), cert. denied, 459 U.S. 1087, 103 S.Ct. 571, 74 L.Ed.2d 933 (1982); Thus, the district court judge "cannot displace a jury's verdict merely because he disagrees with it or would have found otherwise in a bench trial." "The mere fact that a contrary verdict may have been equally—or even more easily—supportable furnishes no cognizable ground for granting a new trial." Freeman v. Package Mach. Co., 865 F.2d 1331, 1333–34 (1st Cir.1988).

Our review is circumscribed: we will disturb the district court's ruling on appellant's motion for a new trial only where there has been a clear abuse of discretion. In order to determine whether such an abuse occurred here, we must review the record below. We do this not in the role of "a thirteenth juror," assessing the credibility of witnesses and weighing testimony, but rather to isolate the factual basis for the trial court's ruling and provide the foundation for our action today. "So long as a reasonable basis exists for the jury's verdict, we will not disturb the district court's ruling on appeal."

With our standard of review established, we turn to Scholz' argument and the record below. We address each of the two breach of contract claims the jury decided in turn.

B. Did Ahern Breach the FMA?

Scholz argues that Ahern breached his obligations under the 1981 FMA to both account for and pay to Scholz, every six months, his share of the royalties from the compositions on the first and second albums: indeed, Ahern admitted at trial that he had failed to make some payments he owed Scholz under the FMA. The jury and the trial court disagreed with Scholz, however, and found that Ahern's breach of the FMA was not material. The question facing us, then, is whether the district court abused its discretion in finding that the jury's decision was not against the weight of the evidence. After careful review of the record, we find no abuse of discretion in the lower court's decision not to disturb the jury's finding.

Scholz argues at some length on appeal that Ahern's breach was by definition material, both for his failure to account and his failure to pay. As for the first contention, we note that while Scholz' reading of the FMA as requiring that Ahern render Scholz direct accountings every six months is a convincing one, it is not the only plausible one. Indeed, Ahern contends that the FMA only required him to send irrevocable letters of direction to various entities involved directing them to send Scholz his share of the royalties when collected. In the end, it would not be against the clear weight of the evidence to find that letters of directions would satisfy Ahern's accounting obligations under the FMA, and that such letters were sent. Therefore, Ahern's failure to account every six months was not a material breach.

As for the second contention, Scholz supports his position that Ahern's failure to pay constitutes a separate, material breach by drawing on both New York and Massachusetts case law. He points to the Second Circuit's refusal to overturn summary judgment in ARP Films, Inc. v. Marvel Entertainment Group, Inc., 952 F.2d 643, 649 (2d Cir.1991). In that case, where plaintiffs failed to account and pay royalties in excess of $400,000, the court stated that the district court correctly concluded that the breach by plaintiffs in failing to make the payments and provide the reports required * * * was material as a matter of law, thus authorizing Marvel to terminate the contract. [The parties' agreement] explicitly singled out plaintiffs' obligation to provide "prompt accounting" for distributions as a term and condition of the agreement, the substantial breach of which authorized Marvel to terminate the license provided by the agreement. In addition, failure to tender payment is generally deemed a material breach of contract. Finally, as the district court found, and the subsequent accounting confirmed, the amounts withheld from Marvel by plaintiffs were very substantial. * * * Scholz argues that Ahern's breach, spanning thirteen years, is more egregious than these cases of a six-month failure to pay concession and rental fees, four-month failure to pay license and lease fees, and seven-month failure to pay (and five-month failure to account). Therefore, Scholz concludes, Ahern's failure to pay Scholz at least $459,000 is clearly a substantial breach.

We are not convinced. We remind appellant that under our standard of review, we do not sit as a juror, evaluating credibility and weighing evidence, as he seems to ask us to do. Rather, we simply weigh whether the district court committed a clear abuse of its discretion in determining that the jury verdict was not against the clear weight of the evidence. Our review of the record reveals that Ahern's counsel presented testimony questioning, to varying degrees, nine of the thirteen items of the estimate Scholz' accounting expert made of how much Ahern owed Scholz. Phillip Ames ("Ames"), a certified public accountant who served as business manager for both Ahern and BOSTON from 1976 through sometime in 1981 or 1982, made several estimates of how much Ahern owed Scholz, which he labeled "ball park figures." While we note that Ames' final estimate was $277,000, for a total of $459,000 with interest, we cannot assume that the jury accepted this figure as gospel. Given that Ahern sought over a million dollars in principal and interest from Scholz, the jury may reasonably have found that the Ames figure was not a substantial breach in the particular context of this case. It may have determined that the amount of money Ahern owed, taken in the perspective of the contract, Ahern's obligations, and the total amounts of money concerned, was not so significant a breach as to violate "an essential and inducing feature of the contract." Finally, addressing the case law Scholz relies on for support, we note that here, unlike in those cases, the amount of money owed was in question.

Ultimately, examining the record in full, the evidence clearly provides the jury and trial court with a basis for finding that Ahern did not substantially breach the FMA. As this Circuit stated on another occasion,

> We can understand how a jury might have decided for [defendant] on the basis of this evidence. But the jury did not do this; it decided for [plaintiff]. We do not see how one could say that the jury clearly made a mistake. We do not see how one could say that the evidence overwhelmingly favored the [defendant]. Rather, the evidence simply was mixed and contradictory. de Perez, 910 F.2d at 1008.

Therefore we cannot say that the district court committed a clear breach of its discretion on this point.

* * *

[The court ultimately reversed on other grounds and remanded for retrial].

Notes and Questions

1. How does the standard for granting the motion for new trial differ from that employed when judgment as a matter of law is sought after a verdict has been returned? See Rule 59(a)(1). At a minimum, it is said that the court may weigh the evidence in ruling on a motion for new trial. But how can this be consistent with the right to jury trial? Keep in mind the historical directive embodied in the Seventh Amendment's second clause. See *Galloway*, supra p. 607.

The famous English judge, Lord Mansfield, said that "[t]rials by jury, in civil causes, could not subsist now without a power, *somewhere*, to grant new trials. * * * It is an absolute necessity to justice, that there should, upon many occasions, be opportunities of reconsidering the cause by a new trial." Bright v. Eynon, 97 Eng.Rep. 365 (K.B. 1757). As an American judge put it, "the exercise of this power is not in derogation of the right of trial by jury but is one of the historic safeguards of that right." Aetna Casualty & Surety Co. v. Yeatts, 122 F.2d 350, 353 (4th Cir.1941).

2. It is often said that there is effectively no appellate review of a trial judge's *grant* of a motion for a new trial. Why? Keep in mind that as a general rule, appeal may be taken only from final judgments. On the other hand, it has been suggested that, at least as a theoretical matter, appellate review of a *grant* of a new trial is more appropriate than review of a *denial*, because "[i]f a new trial is denied, the trial judge has accepted the verdict of the jury and these are the most compelling reasons for an appellate court not to interfere. But if a new trial is granted, the verdict of the jury has gone for naught and the appellate court can interfere more freely to resolve the difference between the judge and the jury." C. Wright & M. Kane, The Law of Federal Courts 684 (6th ed. 2002). Does this argument make sense in light of the fact that by the time the appellate court gets the case, there will be a *second* jury decision?

The court in *Ahern* states that an appellate court will reverse a denial of a new trial motion because the verdict was against the weight of the evidence only if the district judge committed abuse of discretion. But consider the approach of the court in Lind v. Schenley Industries, Inc., 278 F.2d 79, 88 (3d Cir.), cert. denied, 364 U.S. 835, 81 S.Ct. 58, 5 L.Ed.2d 60 (1960):

> It is frequently stated that a motion for a new trial [on the ground that the verdict is against the weight of the evidence] ordinarily is non-reviewable because within the discretion of the trial court. * * * But this discretion must still be exercised in accordance with ascertainable legal standards and if an appellate court is shown special or unusual circumstances which clearly indicate an abuse of discretion in that the trial court failed to apply correctly the proper standards, reversal is possible. * * * Concededly appellate courts rarely find that the trial court abused its discretion.

Plaintiff in *Lind* was a former employee of defendant who claimed that his superior, Kaufman, had orally promised him a special commission that would have been more than five times his salary and would have made him the highest paid employee in the company. He sued for the commission. Defendant denied that the promise had been made, but the jury found in plaintiff's favor. The trial judge granted defendant a judgment n.o.v. and, in the alternative, a new trial should the judgment n.o.v. be overturned. The appellate court reversed the judgment n.o.v. and held that the new trial was improper:

> Where a trial is long and complicated and deals with a subject matter not lying within the ordinary knowledge of jurors a verdict should be scrutinized more closely by the trial judge than is necessary where the litigation deals with material which is familiar and simple,

the evidence relating to ordinary commercial practices. An example of subject matter unfamiliar to a layman would be a case requiring a jury to pass upon the nature of an alleged newly discovered organic compound in an infringement action. A prime example of subject matter lying well within the comprehension of jurors is presented by the circumstances at bar.

The subject matter of the litigation before us is simple and easily comprehended by an intelligent layman. The jury's main function was to determine the veracity of the witnesses: i.e., what testimony should be believed. If Lind's testimony and that of Mrs. Kennan, Kaufman's secretary [who claimed she witnessed the promise], was deemed credible, Lind presented a convincing, indeed an overwhelming case. We must conclude that the jury did believe this testimony and that the court below substituted its judgment for that of the jury on this issue and thereby abused legal discretion.

Is this approach sensible?

3. Should the court, ruling on a motion for new trial, concern itself with distortion in the outcome due to poor lawyering? Consider Vance v. Texas A & M University System, 117 F.R.D. 93 (S.D.Tex.1987), in which the judge granted a mistrial on the ground plaintiff's lawyer was "completely unorganized and ineffective." The judge reasoned that "[a] trial judge is not a mere observer of the proceedings, nor an umpire. He or she has the affirmative duty to ensure that litigants have a full and complete opportunity to present their case to the trier of fact for determination." Recall Band's Refuse Removal, Inc. v. Borough of Fair Lawn, supra p. 3. Is this attitude consistent with the proper role of the judge outlined there?

4. The above discussion relates to new trials granted because the judge concludes that the verdict is against the clear weight of the evidence. Verdict losers may also argue that they deserve a new trial because of errors in the handling of the trial. See, e.g., People v. Hutchinson, infra p. 682. How should the court address such arguments? See Rule 61. Should the judge's uneasiness with the result bear on his assessment of the importance of the errors?

THE INTERSECTION BETWEEN JUDGMENT AS A MATTER OF LAW AND MOTION FOR NEW TRIAL

Rules 50(b), (c) and (d) establish a framework for the intersection between the motions for judgment as a matter of law and new trial. Rule 50(b) provides that in renewing a motion for a judgment as a matter of law after verdict, the movant "may alternatively request a new trial or join a motion for new trial under Rule 59." Rule 50(c)(1) provides that if the court grants the renewed motion for judgment as a matter of law, it "shall also rule on the motion for a new trial, if any, by determining whether it should be granted if the judgment is thereafter vacated or reversed, and shall specify the grounds for granting or denying the motion for new trial." Rule 50(c)(2), on the other hand, provides an opportunity for the party who won at trial but lost on the motion for judgment as a matter of law against it to move for a new trial.

Rule 50(d) provides that "[i]f the motion for judgment as a matter of law is denied, the party who prevailed on that motion may, as appellee, assert grounds entitling the party to a new trial in the event the appellate court concludes that the trial court erred in denying the motion for judgment." The Rule further provides that "[i]f the appellate court reverses the judgment, nothing in this rule precludes it from determining that the appellee is entitled to a new trial, or from directing the trial court to determine whether a new trial shall be granted."

Consider initially the alternative new trial motion procedure provided for in Rule 50(b). Can you imagine circumstances under which the trial court would deny the motion for judgment as a matter of law, but nevertheless grant the alternative motion for new trial? The most obvious possibility is that while the court does not believe that the non-movant's evidence is so deficient that it would be unreasonable for the jury to find for that party, the court is nevertheless firmly convinced that a verdict on behalf of the non-movant is against the clear weight of the evidence. In other words, because the standard for granting a new trial on the grounds that the verdict is against the clear weight of the evidence is less deferential to the jury than is the standard employed on a motion for judgment as a matter of law, it is conceivable that the court would believe that the non-movant's evidence failed to satisfy the former standard, even though it satisfied the latter standard. Also, a trial court may choose to grant the alternative motion for new trial under Rule 50(b), despite denying the motion for judgment as a matter of law, because it believes that it committed an error at trial—for example, in improperly refusing to admit some of the non-movant's evidence.

Rule 50(c)(1) concerns the situation in which the trial court has granted the renewed motion for judgment as a matter of law under Rule 50(b). The provision requires the trial court also to rule, hypothetically, on the motion for new trial. At the trial level, the ruling on the alternative new trial motion is hypothetical, because the court's granting of the motion for judgment as a matter of law has the effect of mooting the merits of the new trial motion: Having had judgment entered in his favor as a matter of law, the movant of course no longer is interested in having its new trial motion granted. The rule requires the hypothetical ruling, however, to take account of the possibility that the trial court's grant of the motion for judgment as a matter of law will ultimately be reversed on appeal. Rule 50(c)(1) provides that in such an event, if the trial court has conditionally granted the new trial motion, "the new trial shall proceed unless the appellate court has otherwise ordered." If, on the other hand, the trial court denied the alternative new trial motion, "the appellee on appeal may assert error in that denial."

Consider also the role played by Rule 50(c)(2). Note that while Rule 50(c)(1) concerns post-trial motions by the party who *lost* at trial, Rule 50(c)(2) relates to the party who *won* at trial but then *lost* on the motion for judgment as a matter of law that has been made against it. The provision allows that party, who now stands to be the loser, to seek a new trial. Why might a court that has just granted a motion for judgment as a matter of law against that party nevertheless grant the party's motion for new trial? Presumably, it would not be because the trial court thought that the verdict was against the clear weight of the evidence; to the contrary, the verdict at trial was actually *in favor* of the party now moving for a new trial, so this ground for new trial would be completely irrelevant. The court, however, may nevertheless believe that a new trial is warranted, because of legal errors that it committed at trial that may have caused the party who had judgment as a matter of law granted against it to present an inadequate case—for example, due to the improper exclusion of valuable evidence.

Rule 50(d) concerns the situation in which the trial court has denied the motion for judgment as a matter of law. The provision allows the appellee—i.e., the party who both won at trial and defeated the motion for judgment as a matter of law in the trial court—to argue that in the event the trial court's denial of judgment as a matter of law is reversed he should nevertheless be granted a new trial. Can you understand why, purely as a strategic matter, appellees might be reluctant to make such an argument to the appellate court?

One issue that has arisen concerns the ability of the appellate court to enter judgment on behalf of the party who made a motion for judgment as a matter of law when the appellate court has reversed the trial court's denial of that motion. If the appellee has argued that it should be granted a new trial in the event that the appellate court reverses the denial of the judgment as a matter of law, and the appellate court nevertheless enters judgment for the appellant, it would necessarily mean that the appellate court had rejected the appellee's request for a new trial. The question is whether Rule 50(d) authorizes the appellate court to reject the request for a new trial itself, or instead requires it to remand to the trial court to rule on such a request.

In Neely v. Martin K. Eby Construction Co., Inc., 386 U.S. 317, 87 S.Ct. 1072, 18 L.Ed.2d 75 (1967), the Supreme Court held that the appellate court, where it reverses a denial of a motion for judgment as a matter of law, may simply direct entry of judgment for the appellant, even when the appellee has asked for a new trial in the event the denial of judgment as a matter of law is reversed.

Justice White, writing for the majority, conceded that often the request for a new trial should be ruled upon by the trial court, rather than by the appellate court, "because of the trial judge's firsthand knowledge of witnesses, testimony, and issues—because of his 'feel' for the overall case." He added that "obviously judgment for defendant-appellant should not be ordered where the plaintiff-appellee urges grounds for a nonsuit or new trial which should more appropriately be addressed to the trial court." However, he further noted that "these considerations do not justify an ironclad rule that the court of appeals should never order dismissal or judgment for defendant where plaintiff's verdict has been set aside on appeal. Such a rule would not serve the purpose of Rule 50 to speed litigation and to avoid unnecessary retrials."

Justice White noted one example where entry of judgment for the appellant would be appropriate: "situations where the defendant's grounds for setting aside the jury's verdict raise questions of subject matter jurisdiction or dispositive issues of law which, if resolved in defendant's favor, must necessarily terminate the litigation." Further, he pointed to situations in which the asserted basis for new trial by appellee would concern pure issues of law, for which no deference to the trial court would be required.

Justice Black dissented. He did so in part on the grounds that in such a situation the appellate court "is entirely powerless to order the trial court to dismiss the case, thus depriving the verdict winner of any opportunity to present a motion for new trial to the trial judge who is thoroughly familiar with the case."

Consider the language of Rule 50(d). Does it authorize the appellate court to enter judgment on behalf of appellant where the appellee has argued that it should be granted a new trial in the event that the trial court's denial of judgment as a matter of law is reversed?

Less than a year after deciding *Neely,* the Supreme Court emphasized the need to remand to the trial court where it has greater expertise in Iacurci v. Lummus Co., 387 U.S. 86, 87 S.Ct. 1423, 18 L.Ed.2d 581 (1967). The jury there returned a verdict for plaintiff and answered yes to one of five parts of an interrogatory to the jury about ways in which defendant might have been negligent, failing to answer the other four parts. The appellate court, inferring from the jury's silence on the other four parts of the interrogatory to the jury that it found no negligence as to those matters, directed entry of judgment for defendant upon finding that the evidence was insufficient to justify a verdict for plaintiff on the ground selected by the jury. The Supreme Court vacated and remanded with directions that the new trial issue be sent back to the district judge: "Under these circumstances, we think the Court of Appeals erred in directing entry of judgment for respondent; the case should have been remanded to the Trial Judge, who was in the best position to pass upon the question of a new trial in light of the evidence, his charge to the jury, and the jury's verdict and interrogatory answers." How often will that not be true?

Professor Louis has concluded that "[a]fter *Iacurci,* the courts of appeals should ordinarily reject only those requests for a new trial, the grant of which by the trial court would constitute an abuse of discretion." Louis, Post–Verdict Rulings on the Sufficiency of the Evidence: Neely v. Martin K. Eby Construction Co. Revisited, 1975 Wisc.L.Rev. 503, 516. Would that approach have justified the action by the court of appeals in *Neely*? Should it be an abuse of discretion to grant plaintiff a new trial where plaintiff has failed to satisfy the burden of production in the first trial?

In Weisgram v. Marley Co., 528 U.S. 440, 120 S.Ct. 1011, 145 L.Ed.2d 958 (2000), the Supreme Court held that Rule 50(d) authorizes an appellate court to direct the entry of judgment as a matter of law when it determines that evidence was erroneously admitted at trial and that the remaining, properly admitted evidence is insufficient to constitute a submissible case. The Court rejected plaintiff's argument that under such circumstances the appellate court may not order entry of judgment for the verdict loser, instead having to remand the case to the case to the trial court for a new trial determination. It found unpersuasive plaintiff's argument "that allowing courts of appeals to direct the entry of judgment for defendants will punish plaintiffs who could have shored up their cases by other means had they known their expert testimony would be found inadmissable," because it viewed both parties on notice as to the possibility that judgment would be entered contrary to the jury verdict due to exclusion of evidence. The Court found *Neely*'s reasoning applicable to the situation in *Weisgram*.

A number of commentators have criticized the decision in *Neely*. See, e.g., Note, Post–Verdict Motions Under Rule 50: Protecting the Verdict Winner, 53 Minn.L.Rev. 358 (1968); Note, Civil Procedure— Federal Rule 50(d)—Disposition of Cases by the Court of Appeals After Granting Judgment Notwithstanding the Verdict, 47 N.C.L.Rev. 162 (1968). Professor Louis, however, has defended it. Though he asserts that "courts of appeals should ordinarily not make such discretionary determinations," he finds that this does not "establish or even suggest that they cannot screen out cases beyond the scope of legitimate discretion. Admittedly the courts have sometimes attempted to overreach this function, and may seek to do so in the future. But the Supreme Court has thwarted such efforts in the past and presumably would continue to do so." Louis, supra, 1975 Wisc.L.Rev. at 520.

RELIEF FROM JUDGMENT UNDER RULE 60(b)

A motion for new trial under Rule 59 must be made "not later than 10 days after the entry of the judgment." Rule 59(b). However, Rule 60(b) provides a mechanism by which a party may obtain relief from a judgment at a later time. Note that it only applies to *final* judgment; the court usually may reconsider any earlier decision before final judgment.

What are the competing policy considerations that might influence a court's predisposition towards motions under Rule 60(b)? See Comment, Rule 60(b): Survey and Proposal for General Reform, 60 Calif.L.Rev. 531, 533 (1972): "Rule 60(b) is an attempt to reconcile the values of finality and doing individual justice. * * * Besides helping to keep societal peace and protecting an individual litigant from harassment, finality lends stability and predictability to judicial activity—qualities essential to any institution charged with settling disputes authoritatively. On the other hand, the rigidity of absolute finality could be intolerable."

While Rule 60(b) provides that motions must be made "within a reasonable time" and for mistake, excusable neglect, newly discovered evidence, and fraud "not more than one year after the judgment," it also provides that the Rule does not limit a court's power "to entertain an independent action." Generally an independent action is allowed where a party has been denied an opportunity to present his claims fairly. But this second action is limited by the doctrine of res judicata, which is said to preclude relitigation in an independent action not only of issues actually litigated but also of issues open to litigation in the prior action. See Comment, supra, 60 Calif.L.Rev. at 542–43. How often will this option be available?

Because finality furthers highly important values, relief under Rule 60(b) is extremely difficult to obtain. Nevertheless, it is useful to consider some of the rule's provisions:

Mistake: Rule 60(b)(1) allows a party to ask that judgment be set aside on grounds of "mistake, inadvertence, surprise, or excusable neglect." Except for default cases, where such relief may often be obtained on the ground that defendant failed through mistake to file an answer (recall Shepard Claims Serv. v. William Darrah & Assoc., supra p. 191), it is difficult to justify such relief on the ground that a party simply made a mistake, and bad lawyering ordinarily will not provide a basis for granting relief on this ground.

Newly discovered evidence: Rule 60(b)(2) authorizes setting aside a judgment where the loser presents newly discovered evidence. The standard for allowing relief under this provision is the same as the approach under Rule 59 to a motion for a new trial on grounds of newly discovered evidence. See 11 C. Wright & A. Miller, Federal Practice & Procedure § 2859. What factors should the court consider in evaluating such a motion? Consider that the rule indicates that the proffered material be evidence, be newly discovered, and not have been discoverable in time with due diligence.

Fraud: Rule 60(b)(3) provides that fraud or other misconduct of a party is a ground for setting aside a final judgment or order. The rule abandons the former idea that relief should only be accorded for "extrinsic" fraud, but concern about making relief readily available persists. Consider how often the loser may claim that the winner's witnesses lied during the trial. Should this be a ground for a second trial? If so, what is the purpose of a trial in which the jury is supposed to determine the truth?

The Supreme Court early announced that "the mischief of retrying every case in which the judgment or decree [was] rendered on false testimony * * * would be greater, by reason of the endless nature of the strife, than any compensation arising from doing justice in individual cases." United States v. Throckmorton, 98 U.S. (8 Otto) 61, 68–69, 25 L.Ed. 93 (1878). Since then, courts have relaxed their attitude, but the difficulties confronting the moving party are reflected in the following observations by Justice Brennan, at the time a member of the New Jersey Supreme Court:

> Perjured testimony that warrants disturbance of a final judgment must be shown by clear, convincing and satisfactory evidence to have been, not false merely, but to have been willfully and purposely falsely given, and to have been material to the issue tried and not

merely cumulative but probably to have controlled the result. Further, a party seeking to be relieved from the judgment must show that the fact of the falsity of the testimony could not have been discovered by reasonable diligence in time to offset it at the trial * * *.

Shammas v. Shammas, 88 A.2d 204, 209 (N.J.1952).

Particular difficulty arises if the alleged perjury came not from a party but from some other witness. In Harre v. A.H. Robins Co., 750 F.2d 1501 (11th Cir.1985), one of defendant's experts claimed that he had performed tests on the Dalkon Shield contraceptive device, which was produced by defendant, and determined that it did not cause infections in women, but later testimony by the same witness in another case showed that he had not done any such experiments. Stressing the fact that the same lawyer represented defendant in both cases, the appellate court directed a new trial. It reasoned that the issue on which the witness testified—defect of the product—was the "ultimate issue in the case" and that the lawyers knew or should have known of the falsity of the testimony. The witness himself was later indicted for obstructing justice but was acquitted. See Harre v. A.H. Robins Co., 866 F.2d 1303 (11th Cir.1989). On the other hand, in Metlyn Realty Corp. v. Esmark, Inc., 763 F.2d 826 (7th Cir.1985), the trial court approved the settlement of a class action after a hearing in which an expert gave his opinion on the value of corporate shares in issue. After the court approved the settlement, objectors moved to set aside the resulting judgment on the ground that the witness had lied about his experience. The appellate court upheld denial of the Rule 60 motion, noting that "[e]xpert witnesses such as Levy are free agents. Parties and counsel have an obligation not to deceive the court about the witness and to correct statements they know to be false, but they are not responsible for the details of the witness's testimony."

In Pumphrey v. K.W. Thompson Tool Co., 62 F.3d 1128 (9th Cir. 1995), the court upheld relief under Rule 60(b) to set aside a judgment for fraud on the court. Defendant in that product liability action had not revealed that, in addition to the test film it showed at trial in which the product did not malfunction, there was another test film showing the very malfunction in question. Indeed, "[t]he trial video was made because the test shown on the original video did not turn out as planned." Id. at 1131. Because defendant's general counsel was involved in this chicanery, and defendant also answered interrogatories falsely, there was fraud on the court. See also Lonsdorf v. Seefeldt, 47 F.3d 893 (7th Cir.1995) (relief justified because document used at trial had been altered).

Other Reasons: Rule 60(b)(6) provides that a party may be relieved from a final judgment for "any other reason justifying relief from the operation of the judgment." Do you think it is wise to include such an open-ended authorization? See United States v. Buck, 281 F.3d 1336, 1340 (10th Cir. 2002) ("If there is ever to be closure to litigation, such motions should be granted only for compelling reasons.'') The provision was added as part of the 1946 amendment, in part in response to an article, Moore & Rogers, Federal Relief From Civil Judgments, 55 Yale L.J. 623, 688 (1946), which argued:

> [I]t is productive of harsh and inequitable results to enumerate exclusive situations when relief can be afforded by motion; and when this is done, courts will invent some means of escape as by the doctrine of inherent power, or the doctrine that the term of the court gives power.

Note that the one-year time limit in Rule 60(b) applies only to reasons (1), (2), and (3), i.e., mistake, etc., newly discovered evidence, and fraud, etc. Can it be avoided by simply filing under reason (6)? The answer is, not if the real reason is one of the other specified reasons, which is likely in most cases. As stated in Stradley v. Cortez, 518 F.2d 488, 493–94 (3d Cir.1975): "[P]laintiff can use Rule 60(b)(6) as a means of avoiding the time bars * * * only upon a showing that (1) the reason for the relief sought under 60(b)(6) is not embraced within the various provisions of 60(b)(1–5) and (2) exceptional circumstances exist which warrant the granting of relief." See also United States v. Buck, 281 F.3d 1336 (10th Cir. 2002).

Courts have emphasized that "a motion under Rule 60(b) is not a second opportunity for the losing party to make its strongest case, to rehash arguments or to dress up arguments that previously failed." Kustom Signals, Inc. v. Applied Concepts, Inc., 247 F.Supp.2d 1233, 1235 (D. Kan. 2003). For a hard-nosed application of the requirements of Rule 60(b), consider Brandon v. Chicago Board of Education, 143 F.3d 293 (7th Cir.1998). Plaintiff filed an ADA action in August, 1995, and the clerk's office somehow entered the wrong name and address for his lawyer while docketing the case. Accordingly, from that point forward all communications from the court were sent to a lawyer with a name similar to plaintiff's lawyer and an office near the office of plaintiff's lawyer. This lawyer sent the notices back to the clerk, explaining that this was not his case, but the clerk's office still did not catch the error. As a result, plaintiff's actual lawyer never received two status hearing notices and the court dismissed for nonprosecution when counsel did not appear. The dismissal was also misdirected by the clerk's office.

In late 1996, counsel for plaintiff visited the clerk's office and discovered that "his case had been quite active without him." He promptly filed a Rule 60(b) motion, but it was by then one year and three days after the date the case had been dismissed. Plaintiff argued that this should not matter because he could rely on the fallback provisions of Rule 60(b)(6), but the court of appeals ruled that Rule 60(b)(1) was the pertinent provision because it applies to errors by the court as well as those of the parties. Accordingly, Rule 60(b)(6) could not apply. Probably the lawyer should have wondered about the case much sooner, but this case nevertheless emphasizes the limitations on relief under Rule 60(b).

On the general issue, see Kane, Relief From Federal Judgments: A Morass Unrelieved by a Rule, 30 Hastings L.J. 41 (1978); Wham, Federal District Court Rule 60(b): A Humane Rule Gone Wrong, 49 A.B.A.J. 566 (1963).

The Supreme Court has recognized that Rule 60(b) may play an important role in allowing modifications of decrees in institutional reform litigation. See Rufo v. Inmates of Suffolk County Jail, 502 U.S. 367, 380, 112 S.Ct. 748, 758, 116 L.Ed.2d 867 (1992): "The upsurge in institutional reform litigation since Brown v. Board of Education * * * has made the ability of a district court to modify a decree in response to changed circumstances all the more important. Because such decrees often remain in place for extended periods of time, the likelihood of significant changes occurring during the life of the decree is increased." The Court noted that "[t]he experience of the district and circuit courts in implementing and modifying such decrees has demonstrated that a flexible approach is often essential to achieving the goals of reform litigation." Id. The Court therefore held that modification, under Rule 60(b)(5), of consent decrees in institutional reform litigation is not to be measured by the "grievous wrong" standard that had previously been employed in other contexts.

In United States v. Beggerly, 524 U.S. 38, 118 S.Ct. 1862, 141 L.Ed.2d 32 (1998), the Court addressed the requirements for an independent action to set aside a judgment. In 1979, the government had sought to quiet its title to an island in the Gulf of Mexico from some 200 people who claimed ownership interests in the island. The government's position was that no such interests could exist because the United States never patented the property. During discovery, defendants sought proof of their title, but the government reported that a search of official records included nothing showing that the island had ever been granted to private landowners. The claimants settled with the government, and judgment was entered in accordance with the settlement.

Some years later, a specialist hired by claimants found materials in the National Archives that they argued showed that the island was granted to a private party before it became part of the United States. That would mean that the title did not pass to the United States in the Louisiana Purchase, and might mean that claimants' title to the land was superior to the government's. They filed a suit asking the court to set aside the earlier judgment and award much more than the settlement amount. Although the district court dismissed for lack of jurisdiction, the Court of Appeals reversed on the ground that the suit satisfied the requirements for an "independent action" identified in Rule 60(b).

The Supreme Court reversed. The Court agreed that the district court could entertain the suit without an independent basis for jurisdiction, for ancillary jurisdiction would justify entertaining the suit to set aside the judgment entered by the federal court. But this suit did not satisfy the requirements for a meritorious independent action. All claimants alleged was that the government had failed to provide relevant information in the earlier case, and that would at best come under Rule 60(b)(3), which is subject to a one-year limitation. Independent actions should be reserved for those cases of "injustices which * * * are deemed sufficiently gross to demand a departure" from res judicata. Although fraud would suffice, the Court held that claimants' allegations in this case "do not approach this demanding standard."

3. *Remittitur and Additur*

DIMICK v. SCHIEDT

Supreme Court of the United States, 1935.
293 U.S. 474, 55 S.Ct. 296, 79 L.Ed. 603.

JUSTICE SUTHERLAND delivered the opinion of the Court.

This is an action brought by respondent (plaintiff) against petitioner (defendant) in the federal District Court for the District of Massachusetts to recover damages for a personal injury resulting from the alleged negligent operation of an automobile on a public highway in Massachusetts. The jury returned a verdict in favor of respondent for the sum of $500. Respondent moved for a new trial on the grounds that the verdict was contrary to the weight of the evidence, that it was a compromise verdict, and that the damages allowed were inadequate. The trial court ordered a new trial upon the last-named ground, unless petitioner would consent to an increase of the damages to the sum of $1,500. Respondent's consent was neither required nor given. Petitioner, however, consented to the increase, and, in accordance with the order of the court, a denial of the motion for new trial automatically followed. Respondent appealed to the Circuit Court of Appeals, where the judgment was reversed; the court holding that the conditional order violated the Seventh Amendment of the Federal Constitution in respect of the right of trial by jury. That court recognized the doctrine, frequently stated by this court, that in the case of an excessive verdict it is within the power of the trial court to grant defendant's motion for a new trial unless plaintiff remit the amount deemed to be excessive, but held that the trial court was without power to condition the allowance of plaintiff's motion for a new trial upon the refusal of defendant to consent to an increase in the amount of damages.

* * *

Section 269 of the Judicial Code, as amended, U.S.C. title 28, § 391 (28 U.S.C.A. § 391), confers upon all federal courts power to grant new trials "in cases where there has been a trial by jury, for reasons for which new trials have usually been granted in the courts of law ..."

In order to ascertain the scope and meaning of the Seventh Amendment, resort must be had to the appropriate rules of the common law established at the time of the adoption of that constitutional provision in 1791. A careful examination of the English reports prior to that time fails to disclose any authoritative decision sustaining the power of an

English court to increase, either absolutely or conditionally, the amount fixed by the verdict of a jury in an action at law, with certain exceptions.

* * *

From the foregoing, and from many other English authorities which we have examined but deem it unnecessary to cite, we conclude that, while there was some practice to the contrary in respect of *decreasing* damages, the established practice and the rule of the common law, as it existed in England at the time of the adoption of the Constitution, forbade the court to *increase* the amount of damages awarded by a jury in actions such as that here under consideration.

We could well rest this opinion upon that conclusion, were it not for the contention that our federal courts from a very early day have upheld the authority of a trial court to deny a motion for new trial because damages were found to be excessive, if plaintiff would consent to remit the excessive amount, and that this holding requires us to recognize a similar rule in respect of increasing damages found to be grossly inadequate. There is a decision by Mr. Justice Story, sitting on circuit, authorizing such a remittitur, as early as 1822. Blunt v. Little, Fed.Cas. No. 1,578, 3 Mason, 102. There, the jury returned a verdict for $2,000 damages, suffered as a result of a malicious arrest. Defendant moved for a new trial on the ground that the damages were excessive. The court asserted its power to grant a new trial upon that ground, but directed that the cause should be submitted to another jury unless plaintiff was willing to remit $500 of the damages. This view of the matter was accepted by this court in Northern Pacific R. Co. v. Herbert, 116 U.S. 642, 646, 647, 6 S.Ct. 590, 29 L.Ed. 755, and has been many times reiterated.

Since the decision of Mr. Justice Story in 1822, this court has never expressed doubt in respect of the rule, and it has been uniformly applied by the lower federal courts. It is, however, remarkable that in none of these cases was there any real attempt to ascertain the common-law rule on the subject. Mr. Justice Story, in the *Blunt* Case, cited two English cases antedating the Constitution in support simply of his conclusion that the court had power to grant a new trial for excessive damages, and thereupon announced without more that, unless the plaintiff should be willing to remit $500 of his damages, the cause would be submitted to another jury. For the latter conclusion, no authority whatever was cited. The plaintiff remitted the amount, and the motion was overruled.

* * *

In the last analysis, the sole support for the decisions of this court and that of Mr. Justice Story, so far as they are pertinent to cases like that now in hand, must rest upon the practice of some of the English judges—a practice which has been condemned as opposed to the principles of the common law by every *reasoned* English decision, both before and after the adoption of the Federal Constitution, which we have been able to find.

In the light reflected by the foregoing review of the English decisions and commentators, it therefore may be that, if the question of remittitur were now before us for the first time, it would be decided otherwise. But, first announced by Mr. Justice Story in 1822, the doctrine has been accepted as the law for more than a hundred years and uniformly applied in the federal courts during that time. And, as it finds some support in the practice of the English courts prior to the adoption of the Constitution, we may assume that in a case involving a remittitur, which this case does not, the doctrine would not be reconsidered or disturbed at this late day.

Nevertheless, this court in a very special sense is charged with the duty of construing and upholding the Constitution; and, in the discharge of that important duty, it ever must be alert to see that a doubtful precedent be not extended by mere analogy to a different case if the result will be to weaken or subvert what it conceives to be a principle of the fundamental law of the land.

That rule applies with peculiar force to the present case * * *. That is to say, the power to conditionally increase the verdict of a jury does not follow as a necessary corollary from the power to conditionally decrease it. As the court below correctly pointed out, in the case of a conditional remittitur, "a jury has already awarded a sum in excess of that fixed by the court as a basis for a remittitur, which, at least, finds some support in the early English practice; while in the second case no jury has ever passed on the increased amount, and the practice has no precedent according to the rules of the common law."

* * *

The controlling distinction between the power of the court and that of the jury is that the former has the power to determine the law and the latter to determine the facts. In dealing with questions like the one now under consideration, that distinction must be borne steadily in mind. Where the verdict returned by a jury is palpably and grossly inadequate or excessive, it should not be permitted to stand; but, in that event, both parties remain entitled, as they were entitled in the first instance, to have a jury properly determine the question of liability and the extent of the injury by an assessment of damages. Both are questions of fact. Where the verdict is excessive, the practice of substituting a remission of the excess for a new trial is not without plausible support in the view that what remains is included in the verdict along with the unlawful excess—in the sense that it has been found by the jury—and that the remittitur has the effect of merely lopping off an excrescence. But, where the verdict is too small, an increase by the court is a bald addition of something which in no sense can be said to be included in the verdict. When, therefore, the trial court here found that the damages awarded by the jury were so inadequate as to entitle plaintiff to a new trial, how can it be held, with any semblance of reason, that that court, with the consent of the defendant only, may, by assessing an additional amount of damages, bring the constitutional right of the plaintiff to a jury trial to an end in respect of a matter of fact which no jury has ever passed upon either explicitly or by implication? To so hold is obviously to compel the plaintiff to forego his constitutional right to the verdict of a jury and accept "an assessment partly made by a jury which has acted improperly, and partly by a tribunal which has no power to assess." [Lionel Barber & Co. v. Deutsche Bank, [1919] A.C. 304, 335.]

It is said that the common law is susceptible of growth and adaptation to new circumstances and situations, and that the courts have power to declare and effectuate what is the present rule in respect of a given subject without regard to the old rule; and some attempt is made to apply that principle here. The common law is not immutable, but flexible, and upon its own principles adapts itself to varying conditions. But here we are dealing with a constitutional provision which has in effect adopted the rules of the common law in respect of trial by jury as these rules existed in 1791. To effectuate any change in these rules is not to deal with the common law, *qua* common law, but to alter the Constitution. * * *

It is worthy of note that, while for more than a century the federal courts have followed the approved practice of conditioning the allowance of a new trial on the consent of plaintiff to remit excessive damages, no federal court, so far as we can discover, has ever undertaken similarly to increase the damages, although there are numerous cases where motions for new trial have been made and granted on the ground that the verdict was inadequate. This, it is true, is but negative evidence; but it is negative evidence of more than ordinary value. For, when we consider that during the great length of time mentioned the federal courts were constantly applying the rule in respect of the remission of excessive damages, the circumstance that the practice here in question in respect of inadequate damages was never followed or, apparently, its approval even suggested, seems highly significant as indicating a lack of judicial belief in the existence of the power.

JUSTICE STONE [joined by CHIEF JUSTICE HUGHES and JUSTICES BRANDEIS and CARDOZO], dissenting:

I think the judgment should be reversed.

What the trial court has done is to deny a motion for a new trial, for what seemed to it a good reason: That the defendant had given his binding consent to an increased recovery, which the court thought to be adequate, and thus to remove any substantial ground for awarding a new trial. In denying the motion, the trial judge relied on two rules of the common law which have received complete acceptance for centuries. One is that the court has power to act upon a motion to set aside the verdict of a jury because inadequate or excessive, and in its discretion to grant or deny a new trial. The other, which is implicit in the first, is that it has power to determine, as a matter of law, the upper and lower limits within which recovery by a plaintiff will be permitted and the authority to set aside a verdict which is not within those limits.

As a corollary to these rules is the further one of the common law, long accepted in the federal courts, that the exercise of judicial discretion in denying a motion for a new trial, on the ground that the verdict is too small or too large, is not subject to review on writ of error or appeal. This is but a special application of the more general rule that an appellate court will not re-examine the facts which induced the trial court to grant or deny a new trial.

If the effect of what is now decided is to liberalize the traditional common-law practice so that the denial of a motion for a new trial, made on the ground that the verdict is excessive or inadequate, is subject to some sort of appellate review, the change need not be regarded as unwelcome, even though no statute has authorized it. But the question remains whether, in exercising this power of review, the trial judge should be reversed.

The decision of the Court is rested on the ground that the Constitution prohibits the trial judge from adopting the practice. Accordingly, I address myself to the question of power without stopping to comment on the generally recognized advantages of the practice as a means of securing substantial justice and bringing the litigation to a more speedy and economical conclusion than would be possible by a new trial to a jury, or the extent to which that or analogous practice has been adopted and found useful in the courts of the several states. The question is a narrow one: Whether there is anything in the Seventh Amendment or in the rules of the common law, as it had developed before the adoption of the amendment, which would require a federal appellate court to set aside the denial of the motion merely because the particular reasons which moved the trial judge to deny it are not shown to have similarly moved any English judge before 1791.

There is nothing in its history or language to suggest that the amendment had any purpose but to preserve the essentials of the jury trial as it was known to the common law before the adoption of the Constitution. For that reason this Court has often refused to construe it as intended to perpetuate in changeless form the *minutiae* of trial practice as it existed in the English courts in 1791. From the beginning, its language has been regarded as but subservient to the single purpose of the amendment, to preserve the essentials of the jury trial in actions at law, serving to distinguish them from suits in equity and admiralty, and to safeguard the jury's function from any encroachment which the common law did not permit.

Thus interpreted, the Seventh Amendment guarantees that suitors in actions at law shall have the benefits of trial of issues of fact by a jury, but it does not prescribe any particular procedure by which these benefits shall be obtained, or forbid any which does not curtail the function of the jury to decide questions of fact as it did before the adoption of the amendment. It does not restrict the court's control of the jury's verdict, as it had previously been exercised, and it does not confine the trial judge, in determining what issues are for the jury and what for the court, to the particular forms of trial practice in vogue in 1791.

Thus this Court has held that a federal court, without the consent of the parties, may constitutionally appoint auditors to hear testimony, examine books and accounts, and frame and report upon issues of fact, as an aid to the jury in arriving at its verdict, Ex parte Peterson, 253 U.S. 300, 40 S.Ct. 543, 64 L.Ed. 919; it may require both a general and a special verdict and set aside the general verdict for the plaintiff and direct a verdict for the defendant on the basis of the facts specially found, Walker v. New Mexico & Southern Pacific R. Co., 165 U.S. 593, 17 S.Ct. 421, 41 L.Ed. 837; and it may accept so much of the verdict as declares that the plaintiff is entitled to recover, and set aside so much of it as fixes the amount of the damages, and order a new trial of that issue alone, Gasoline Products Co., Inc. v. Champlin Refining Co., 283 U.S. 494, 51 S.Ct. 513, 75 L.Ed. 1188. Yet none of these procedures was known to the common law. In fact, the very practice, so firmly imbedded in federal procedure, of making a motion for a new trial directly to the trial judge, instead of to the court *en banc,* was never adopted by the common law. But this Court has found in the Seventh Amendment no bar to the adoption by the federal courts of these novel methods of dealing with the verdict of a jury, for they left unimpaired the function of the jury to decide issues of fact, which it had exercised before the adoption of the amendment.

If we apply that test to the present case, it is evident that the jury's function has not been curtailed. After the issues of fact had been submitted to the jury and its verdict taken, the trial judge was authorized to entertain a motion to set aside the verdict and, as an incident, to determine the legal limits of a proper verdict. A denial of the motion out of hand, however inadequate the verdict, was not an encroachment upon the province of the jury as the common law defined it. It would seem not to be any the more so here because the exercise of the judge's discretion was affected by his knowledge of the fact that a proper recovery had been assured to the plaintiff by the consent of the defendant. Thus the plaintiff has suffered no infringement of a right by the denial of his motion. The defendant has suffered none because he has consented to the increased recovery, of which he does not complain.

It is upon these grounds, as well as the further one that the denial of a new trial may not be reviewed upon appeal, that this Court has upheld the practice of the remittitur.

The defendant, who has formally consented to pay the increased amount, cannot complain. The plaintiff has suffered no denial of a right because the court, staying its hand, has left the verdict undisturbed, as it lawfully might have done if the defendant had refused to pay more than the verdict. The fact that in one case the recovery is less than the amount of the verdict, and that in the other it is greater, would seem to be without significance. For in neither does the jury return a verdict for the amount actually recovered, and in both the amount of recovery was fixed, not by the verdict, but by the consent of the party resisting the motion for a new trial.

The question with which we are now concerned—what considerations shall govern an appellate review of this discretionary action of the trial court—is one unknown to the common law, which provided for no such review. We are afforded but a meager and fragmentary guide if our review is to be controlled by the Seventh Amendment, read as though it had incorporated by reference the particular details of English trial practice exhibited by the law books in 1791. * * *

If our only guide is to be this scant record of the practice of controlling the jury's verdict, however fragmentary the state of its development at this period, and if we must deny any possibility of change, development, or improvement, then it must be admitted that search of the legal scrap heap of a century and a half ago may commit us to the incongruous position in which we are left by the present decision: A federal trial court may deny a motion for a new trial where the plaintiff consents to decrease the judgment to a proper amount, but it is powerless to deny the motion if its judgment is influenced by the defendant's consent to a comparable increase in the recovery.

But I cannot agree that we are circumscribed by so narrow and rigid a conception of the common law. * * * When the Constitution was adopted, the common law was something more than a miscellaneous collection of precedents. It was a system, then a growth of some five centuries, to guide judicial decision. One of its principles, certainly as important as any other, and that which assured the possibility of the continuing vitality and usefulness of the system, was its capacity for growth and development, and its adaptability to every new situation to which it might be needful to apply it. "This flexibility and capacity for growth and adaptation is," as the Court declared in Hurtado v. California, 110 U.S. 516, 530, 4 S.Ct. 111, 118, 28 L.Ed. 232, "the peculiar boast and excellence of the common law."

* * * If this Court could thus, in conformity to common law, substitute a new rule for an old one because it was more consonant with modern conditions, it would seem that no violence would be done to the common law by extending the principle of the remittitur to the case where the verdict is inadequate, although the common law had made no rule on the subject in 1791; and that we could not rightly refuse to apply to either the principle of general application, that it is competent to exercise a discretionary power to grant or withhold relief in any way which is not unjust.

* * *

To me it seems an indefensible anachronism for the law to reject the like principle of decision, in reviewing on appeal denials of motions for new trials, where the plaintiff has consented to decrease the judgment or the defendant has consented to increase it by the proper amount, or to apply it in the one case and reject it in the other. It is difficult to see upon what principle the denial of a motion for a new trial, which for centuries has been regarded as so much a matter of discretion that it is not disturbed when its only support may be a bad or inadequate reason, may nevertheless be set aside on appeal when it is supported by a good one: That the defendant has bound himself to pay an increased amount of damages which the court judicially knows is within the limits of a proper verdict.

Notes and Questions

1. "Remittitur is the procedure by which a trial judge gives a plaintiff who has received an excessively favorable jury verdict the option of accepting a specified reduction in the jury verdict or submitting to a new trial. Since its approval by a federal court in 1822, remittitur has been accepted and employed by the courts of the United States. Despite this century and a half of use, the procedures and standards utilized by the federal courts have been, and still are, far from uniform." Note, Remittitur Practice in the Federal Courts, 76 Colum.L.Rev. 299 (1976). Note, however, the possible limits of the remittitur concept. For example, in Tronzo v. Biomet, Inc., 236 F.3d 1342 (Fed Cir. 2001), the court rejected plaintiff's argument that it was unconstitutional legal error for the district court to fail to award him a new trial after he had rejected a reduction in his award and instead directly implement the reduction. The Federal Circuit held that the judicially imposed reduction in damages did not constitute a remittitur: "[I]n the present case, the district court did not reweigh any evidence, nor did it exercise its discretion in computing the damages award. Instead, the court awarded the maximum damages possible given the lack of competent evidence in the record. * * * Thus, representing this issue to the jury would have been pointless because, as a matter of law, the compensatory damages award could not exceed [the amount] already awarded." How persuasive is the court's distinction between cases in which the district court reduces damages as excessive (remittitur) and those in which the district court reduces damages due to "the lack of competent evidence in the record" supporting the award? If there exists competent evidence supporting the jury's award, should the court be granting remittitur in the first place?

Contrast the situation in *Tronzo* with that in Ross v. Kansas City Power & Light Co., 293 F.3d 1041 (8th Cir. 2002), where the court held a plaintiff was not entitled to remittitur's option of a new trial when the district court reduced the award of punitive damages because it was deemed to be unconstitutionally excessive. "[T]he court's mandatory [and constitutionally dictated] review of a punitive damages award," the court concluded, "does not implicate the Seventh Amendment. The plaintiff's consent to a constitutional reduction of a punitive damages award is 'irrelevant' because the court must decide the issue as a matter of law." See also Cooper Industries, Inc. v. Leatherman Tool Group, Inc., 532 U.S. 424, 437, 121 S.Ct. 167, 149 L.Ed.2d 674 (2001) ("Because the jury's award of punitive damages does not constitute a finding of 'fact,' appellate review of the district court's determination that an award is consistent with due process does not implicate.... Seventh Amendment concerns....") What, according to the Court in Dimick, are the bases for distinguishing between additur and remittitur for purposes of the Seventh Amendment? Are they persuasive?

2. On what grounds does Justice Stone dissent? Compare his analysis to that of Justice Rutledge, speaking for the Court, in *Galloway,* supra p. 607. Note that *Galloway* was decided a number of years after *Dimick.* Though *Galloway* itself concerned the constitutionality of only the directed verdict, might the opinion's reasoning be relied upon to uphold the modern use of additur? It should be noted, however, that the Supreme Court has never taken this step. Thus, *Dimick* remains controlling in the federal courts. However, many state courts, not bound by the Seventh Amendment, have upheld the constitutionality of additur under state constitutional jury trial provisions. See, e.g., Fisch v. Manger, 130 A.2d 815 (N.J.1957). Sometimes they use it aggressively. See Cunningham, Judge Tacks $5.3 Million Onto Jury's Award, S.F. Recorder, July 18, 2002 at 1 (judge increased $713,000 for pain and suffering by $5.5 million).

3. One scholar has argued that, despite the reasoning in *Dimick*, remittitur is unconstitutional. Thomas, Re–Examining the Constitutionality of Remittitur Under the Seventh Amendment, 64 Ohio St. L. J. 731 (2003). According to Professor Thomas, "[t]he study of the English cases at the time of the Seventh Amendment's adoption shows that remittitur as presently practiced by the federal courts did not exist at common law in 1791." Id. at 793. Even if one were to accept an "evolving" view of the Seventh Amendment right, she argues, remittitur should be deemed unconstitutional because "[w]hen faced with the possibility of a new trial or alternatively, a remittitur, the plaintiff has no real choice to take a new trial ... because even if the second trial results in a verdict that is greater or the same as the previous jury's verdict, the same judge will oversee the case, and that judge has already determined the maximum amount that a reasonable jury could award under the facts." Id. at 734.

4. Although *Dimick* remains good law, the additur practice has nevertheless been utilized sporadically in the federal courts. See Liriano v. Hobart Corp., 170 F.3d 264 (2d Cir.1999) (upholding district court's "adjustment" of a jury verdict to include a hospital bill); E.E.O.C. v. Massey Yardley Chrysler Plymouth, Inc., 117 F.3d 1244 (11th Cir. 1997). In Hattaway v. McMillian, 903 F.2d 1440 (11th Cir.1990), the federal trial court had ordered an additur pursuant to a Florida statute. While the appellate court expressly acknowledged "that the order of an additur by a federal court violates the seventh amendment right to a jury trial in civil cases," citing *Dimick*, it found the additur order to be non–appealable. In so holding it relied, by analogy, on a long line of decisions, reaffirmed in Donovan v. Penn Shipping Co., 429 U.S. 648, 97 S.Ct. 835, 51 L.Ed.2d 112 (1977) (per curiam), which "forbid the plaintiff from accepting a remittitur—even under protest—and then appealing the order granting the remittitur." 903 F.2d at 1451. Though the court acknowledged "that there are no federal cases applying these principles [of non–appealability] to an additur order," and that on the merits "the district court erred in ordering the defendant to choose between accepting either the additur or a new trial," it nevertheless left "untouched the district court's judgment on this issue." Id. See also Sulzer Carbomedics, Inc. v. Oregon Cardio–Devices, Inc., 257 F.3d 449 (5th Cir. 2001).

Does the *Donovan* rule make any sense in its original context of remittitur? If a party agrees to a remittitur only under protest, can that party rationally be deemed to have voluntarily waived any objection? What alternative does a plaintiff who finds a remittitur unacceptable have? If the plaintiff refuses to agree to the remittitur, the trial judge will order a new trial—a non–appealable interlocutory order. As a practical matter, then, under the *Donovan* rule, how often is a plaintiff likely to be able to obtain appellate review of a trial court's conditional order of remittitur? If the answer is almost never, is that necessarily a bad result? (It should be noted, however, that when the trial court *denies* a defendant's motion for new trial, that decision will be subject to appellate review as part of the normal process of appeal from the final judgment in favor of the plaintiff). See also Anderson v. Roberson, 249 F.3d 539, 542 (6th Cir. 2001) ("a district court order giving the plaintiff a choice between remittitur or a new trial is not a final, appealable order.")

Does any basis exist on which to distinguish the appealability of an additur order from a remittitur order? Note that in the case of a remittitur, the party seeking appellate review—the plaintiff—was victorious at trial and continues to retain an award of damages while in the case of additur the party seeking appellate review is the defendant, who lost at trial as well as on the additur motion. Is that a proper basis of distinction, for purposes of appealability? How relevant is the fact that any appeal from a remittitur can challenge only the propriety of remittitur in that particular case, while an appeal from an additur challenges what is unambiguously an unconstitutional order by the trial court?

Note that where a trial court has, purportedly through the use of remittitur, denied an entire award of punitive damages, an appeals court may view the trial court's decision as a judgment as a matter of law, and therefore appealable. See Hill v. Marshall, 962 F.2d 1209 (6th Cir.1992).

5.   On occasion state courts, who are not bound by the Seventh Amendment but nevertheless generally employ a historically-based standard pursuant to applicable state constitutional provisions, have upheld additur. For example, in Jehl v. Southern Pacific Co., 427 P.2d 988 (Cal.1967), the California Supreme Court upheld the use of additur, describing the practice as "the fraternal twin [of] remittitur" and as "a logical step in the growth of the law relating to unliquidated damages as remittitur was at an earlier date." Id. at 995; 994.

6.   In Gibeau v. Nellis, 18 F.3d 107 (2d Cir.1994), the court held that nominal damages had to be awarded in a civil rights case pursuant to § 1983 where liability had been found by the jury, even though the jury awarded no damages. The court reached this conclusion, despite its recognition that, under *Dimick*, "a federal court's increase of a jury award would constitute impermissible additur where it would violate the Seventh Amendment right to a jury trial." Id. at 110. The court found *Dimick* inapplicable, because its decision that nominal damages had to be awarded was compelled by substantive law. For a contrary decision, holding that *Dimick* precludes reversal of a jury's failure to award nominal damages in a civil rights case, see Walker v. Anderson Electrical Connectors, 944 F.2d 841 (11th Cir.1991).

7.   In his dissent in *Dimick*, Justice Stone argues that the power to determine the upper and lower limits of acceptable verdicts is implicit in the power to set aside the verdict of a jury and grant a retrial. Is this "greater includes the lesser" argument persuasive? Would it justify a judge's decision

to instruct the jury on the upper and lower limits of acceptable recoveries during a second trial? If so, should the judge so instruct the jury in the first trial?

8. Is there some reason why the jury's mistake about the amount of damages should be peculiarly vulnerable to meddling after-the-fact by the judge? Should judges be allowed to change verdicts to reflect other disagreements with the jury's decision? Consider Akermanis v. Sea–Land Serv., Inc., 688 F.2d 898 (2d Cir.1982), where the jury determined that plaintiff's contributory negligence was a four percent cause of the accident for which it found plaintiff had suffered damages totalling $528,000. On defendant's motion for a new trial, the judge found no fault with the jury's measurement of damages, but concluded that the four percent figure for plaintiff's responsibility was "clear and serious error." Finding that 25 percent would be more appropriate, the trial judge granted defendant's motion conditioned on reduction in the verdict to reflect the increase of plaintiff's responsibility to 25 percent. Plaintiff accepted.

The court of appeals held that this procedure was invalid under Dimick v. Schiedt:

> [W]e note a fundamental difference between the use of remittitur to decrease a determination of damages and its use here to increase a contributory negligence percentage. Though both have the same ultimate consequence of reducing the amount of the judgment that the plaintiff is invited to accept as the price of avoiding a new trial, the means by which the reduction is accomplished differ in a way that is critical to determining the lawfulness of the technique. A conditional reduction of a damage calculation leaves in the judgment a portion of what the jury awarded, a circumstance that the Supreme Court considered crucial to its willingness to permit remittitur while rejecting additur in *Dimick*. In this case, however, the conditional adjustment of the contributory negligence percentage inserts into the judgment something beyond what the jury found: a conclusion that the plaintiff's negligence was responsible for a greater share of the accident than the jury had thought. In *Dimick*, the four dissenters thought it was needlessly artificial to deny a trial judge the authority to condition a new trial order on payment of an additur while permitting him to use the device of remittitur. In either circumstance, they argued, the judge is simply conditioning the new trial order on the minimum adjustment necessary to render the verdict within the bounds of reasonableness. But their view did not prevail. We are therefore bound to apply the rationale of the *Dimick* majority, which, as we understand it, precludes any adjustment that extends a jury's finding, even if that extension results in a reduced monetary judgment.

Does this case correctly read *Dimick?* Would the *Dimick* dissenters have approved what the judge did in this case?

9. *Determining when remittitur is appropriate*: As is the case in ruling on a motion for a judgment as a matter of law, a trial court is not permitted to usurp the jury's factfinding function merely because the court would have awarded less had it been the factfinder. Rather, according to one court, "[r]emittitur is appropriate only when the error in the verdict results from a

specific misconception on the part of the jury and can be mechanically corrected without resolving a disputed issue of fact." Control Terminals, Inc. v. Airline Management Group, Inc., 931 F.2d 62 (10th Cir.1991). Another phrasing of the test is whether the amount of damages found by the jury is so excessive and exorbitant as to show passion and prejudice on the part of the jury. See, e.g., Gorsalitz v. Olin Mathieson Chemical Corp., 429 F.2d 1033 (5th Cir.1970). It has been suggested that the use of remittitur has increased in recent years. See Comment, Appellate Control of Excessive Jury Verdicts Since Gasperini v. Center for Humanities: From Nisi Prius Courts to "Gasperini Hearings," 66 U.Cin. L. Rev. 1323 (1998) (referring to "[t]he current unbridled use of remittitur by federal trial and appellate courts)." For a critical view of this development, see Dooley, Our Jury, Our Selves: The Power, Perception and Politics of the Civil Jury, 80 Cornell L. Rev. 321 (1995); Comment, Gasperini v. Center for Humanities: Clarifying Federal Appellate Review or Judicial License in Tort Reform?, 32 New England L. Rev. 853 (1998).

A number of federal courts have sought to determine whether a jury award is excessive through resort to so-called "comparability" analysis, i.e., reviewing damage awards by comparison to amounts awarded in other similar cases. See, e.g., Mathie v. Fries, 121 F.3d 808, 813–14 (2d Cir.1997) ("the determination of whether a damage award exceeds a reasonable range 'should not be made in a vacuum,' but should include consideration of the amounts awarded in other, comparable cases."); Hetzel v. County of Prince William, 89 F.3d 169, 173 (4th Cir. 1996) (instructing district court, upon remand, to examine awards in cases "which are comparable to what would be an appropriate award"). Cf. Gasperini v. Center for Humanities, Inc., 518 U.S. 415, 116 S.Ct. 2211, 135 L.Ed.2d 659 (1996), infra p. 975. According to one commentator, use of comparability analysis "has become a widespread practice among federal courts." Elsevier, Out-of-Line: Federal Courts Using Comparability to Review Damage Awards, 33 Georgia L. Rev. 243 (1997).

The same commentator refers to the use of comparability analysis as "a highly suspect, if not unconstitutional, practice." Id. at 244. He suggests that "in practice a comparability analysis can be easily manipulated, thereby allowing a court to justify its assertion that a damage award is excessive." Id. at 257. Pursuant to the analysis used by the Court in Dimick v. Schiedt, how would a court properly go about deciding whether a particular version of remittitur practice violated the Seventh Amendment?

10. *Deciding the size of the remittitur.* Once a court decides that a remittitur is appropriate because the jury's award of damages is excessive, it must decide the amount of damages to be reduced. There are three basic methods for determining this amount: by reducing the award to (1) the minimum amount the jury might have awarded, (2) the amount the court itself believes should have been awarded, and (3) the maximum amount that a reasonable jury could have awarded. It has been argued that "[i]t is questionable whether an actual measuring rod can be constructed" and that "it may be that judicial corrections of jury awards in this area can only reflect the personal predictions of particular judges or groups of judges." Comment, Remittitur Review: Constitutionality and Efficiency in Liquidated and Unliquidated Damage Cases, 43 U.Chi.L.Rev. 376, 394 (1976). See also Carlin, Remittiturs and Additurs, 49 W.Va.L.Q. 1 (1942).

A leading treatise asserts that the "maximum recovery" rule is the only standard that "has any reasonable claim of being consistent with the Seventh Amendment." 11 C. Wright, A. Miller & M. Kane, Federal Practice & Procedure § 2815. Do you agree? It has been argued that "[t]he maximum recovery rule would * * * be the most effective [standard] in reducing caseloads." Note, Remittitur Practice in the Federal Courts, 76 Colum.L.Rev. 299, 309 (1976). Why? See id. The same commentator contends, however, that the "maximum recovery" rule is "the most inequitable in terms of fairness to the defendant." Id. Why? See Note, Constitutional Law—Right to Jury Trial—Judicial Use of Additurs in Correcting Insufficient Damage Verdicts, 21 Va.L.Rev. 666, 672 (1935). In defense of the "maximum recovery" rule, the court in Earl v. Bouchard Transportation Co., Inc., 917 F.2d 1320 (2d Cir.1990), argued that "[t]o obtain a 'fair' judgment on damages in a case such as this, the law has traditionally deferred to the decision of a jury of laymen drawn from the community at large, and not to the 'seasoned judgment' of the trial judge." Id. at 1329.

The intermediate standard was forcefully advocated by Professor J.W. Moore, who reasoned that the standard "gives the defendant the benefit of the full supervisory power of the trial court, and yet the plaintiff still has his option to refuse to remit. And it moderately serves the function of remittitur aimed at avoiding the judicial waste of a new trial, for the plaintiff still has a strong incentive to remit." 6A Moore's Federal Practice ¶ 59.08[7] (2d ed. 1989). Professor Moore attacked the maximum recovery standard, because if "the trial court fixes the residue at the lowest amount that it would permit a verdict to stand, this constitutes a considerable intrusion upon the jury's function and the plaintiff's incentive in remitting is reduced to a minimum." Id.

Why might a court employ the "minimum recovery" standard? See Meissner v. Papas, 35 F.Supp. 676, 677 (E.D.Wis.1940) ("in order to protect the party obliged to pay against a judge's assessment of damages, the court determines from the evidence the lowest amount that an impartial jury properly instructed would reasonably award"). Might a defendant properly support use of such a rule by arguing "that but for the procedure of remittitur he would be entitled to a new trial"? Note, Remittitur Practice in the Federal Courts, 76 Colum.L.Rev. 299, 309 (1976).

11. Recall the discussion of pain and suffering awards in note 5 after Carey v. Piphus, supra p. 68. Is this sort of compensation inherently resistant to judicial scrutiny because it depends so largely on the jury's determination of a proper amount of compensation? Does the prospect of judicial revision of pain and suffering awards remove some concerns about the untrammeled nature of jury discretion in the area?

Empirical research indicates that post-trial revisions of the amount awarded significantly reduce the amount collected in cases where plaintiffs win verdicts. See generally M. Shanley & M. Peterson, Post–Trial Adjustments to Jury Awards (1987). Examining all plaintiff verdicts, this study of state courts in California and Illinois found that the amount actually paid plaintiff was lower than the amount awarded plaintiff in 25% of cases involving plaintiff verdicts. Most such reductions were the result of settlements, but nearly a quarter were by court action, which tended to occur more often in cases with high verdicts. As to those, the authors report that "[v]erdicts reduced by the courts involved the largest verdicts and quite substantial reductions in jury awards. The average verdict in such trials is nearly $780,000, but the average payment by defendants is less than half that amount." Id. at 45. Does this evidence on judges' actual reductions indicate that efforts to devise caps for such awards are unnecessary?

12. *Partial new trial*: Another new trial possibility is that the trial court may conclude that a new trial is appropriate only as to certain issues, such as the amount of damages. In Gasoline Products Co. v. Champlin Refining Co., 283 U.S. 494, 51 S.Ct. 513, 75 L.Ed. 1188 (1931), the Court stated that a partial new trial "may not properly be resorted to unless it clearly appears that the issue to be retried is so distinct and separable from the others that a trial of it alone may be had without injustice." What sort of injustice might be relevant? In *Dimick*, would a retrial limited to the amount of damages be proper? Recall that the Court labeled the jury decision there a "compromise verdict." What was the nature of the compromise?

4. The Nature of the Verdict

WHITLOCK v. JACKSON

United States District Court, Southern District of Indiana, 1991.
754 F.Supp. 1394.

McKINNEY, DISTRICT JUDGE.

This action was brought by Eileen Whitlock, as administratrix of the estate of her brother, Richard Gaisor. The suit alleged that on August 20, 1986, the defendants arrested Gaisor and inflicted serious injuries that caused his death. The suit alleged numerous violations of both state and federal laws, and sought compensatory and punitive damages. Following a trial, the jury returned a verdict in favor of the plaintiff and against the defendants for the sum of $29,700.

The plaintiff now argues that inconsistencies in the jury's answers to special interrogatories require an additur or, in the alternative, a new trial. The plaintiff's motion raises two broad issues. First, did the plaintiff's failure to object to the alleged inconsistencies constitute a waiver, thus preventing review? Second, if no waiver occurred, are there in fact inconsistencies in the interrogatories that require a new trial?

A. WAIVER

The defendants assert that the plaintiff's failure to object to the allegedly inconsistent answers to interrogatories prior to the jury's discharge constitutes waiver of the issue. In support of this argument, the defendants cite Strauss v. Stratojac Corp., 810 F.2d 679 (7th Cir. 1987), wherein the Seventh Circuit held that the failure to raise a timely objection did indeed constitute a waiver pursuant to Rule 49(b).[2] Citation

2. In addition, the court in *Strauss* qualified its holding somewhat, stating, "We realize that, at some future date, we might encounter a case where the inconsis- tency in the special interrogatories is so obvious that it would be proper to hold that the trial judge had an independent respon-

to *Strauss*, however, presupposes either that the special interrogatories in the case at bar were submitted under Rule 49(b), or that the waiver doctrine is equally applicable under both Rule 49(a) and (b).

Rule 49(a) governs "special verdicts," and states in relevant part that district courts may require a jury to return "a special written finding upon each issue of fact ... or it may use such other method of submitting the issues and requiring the written findings thereon as it deems most appropriate." Rule 49(b) governs "general verdicts accompanied by answers to interrogatories," and provides in part that a district court "may submit to the jury, together with the appropriate forms for a general verdict, written interrogatories upon one or more issues of fact...."

In the case at bar the Court did not clearly indicate whether it was proceeding under Rule 49(a) or (b). The "verdict form" submitted to the jury in this cause contained numerous specialized questions, requiring either a "yes" or "no" answer or an amount of damages. However, no actual verdict was given to the jury, and the "final verdict" in this case was completed by the Court.

In Bonin v. Tour West, Inc., 896 F.2d 1260, 1262 (10th Cir.1990), the district court used a verdict form that mirrors the form used in the case at bar. The verdict form in *Bonin* required the jury to answer "yes" or "no" to questions regarding negligence, proportion fault among the parties, and then assess damages. The defendant in *Bonin* argued that the plaintiffs waived their right to contest any inconsistencies in the jury's answers because no objection was made prior to the discharge of the jury. In reviewing the verdict form, the court of appeals stated, "The court, here, did not submit a general verdict coupled with written interrogatories under Rule 49(b) to the jury. Rather, the court gave the jury a special verdict in the form described in Rule 49(a)."

Similarly, the procedure employed by this Court closely parallels the procedure employed under Rule 49(a). This is especially true in that no "general verdict" was given to the jury, and that Rule 49(a) provides the more flexible approach whereby a district court may require "special written finding(s) upon each issue of fact" or it may use "such other method ... as it deems most appropriate."

While the need to distinguish between Rule 49(a) and (b) may appear inconsequential, it is in fact critical. As the court went on to say in *Bonin*: Unlike Rule 49(b), Rule 49(a) does not contain a specific direction to send the jury back for further deliberations in the event of an inconsistency in the jury's answers. Therefore, Rule 49(a) does not require a party to object to the inconsistencies in order to preserve his right to challenge the inconsistencies in a subsequent motion or on appeal. Id. (citation omitted).

Thus, the defendants' reflexive citation to *Strauss* and the Rule 49(b) standard is incorrect if the *Bonin* analysis is applied in the Seventh

sibility to act despite trial counsel's silence."

Circuit. Unfortunately, this issue has not been clearly resolved. In Bates v. Jean, 745 F.2d 1146, 1150 (7th Cir.1984), the Seventh Circuit ruled that a pro se plaintiff who failed to object to inconsistent verdicts under Rule 49(a) was not precluded from arguing inconsistency on appeal. However, the plaintiff's pro se status was the motivation for the appellate court's ruling, not the application of Rule 49(a).

In fact, the *Bates* court noted that the circuit courts of appeal are split on their interpretation of the waiver doctrine under Rule 49(a), and expressly refused to decide the issue. * * *

The split among the circuits is apparent. * * *

Absent a clear directive on the waiver issue from the Seventh Circuit, this Court is instructed to give "respectful consideration" to the decisions of other circuits. Given the split in the circuits, this consideration requires choosing one alternative over another. For several reasons, this Court is compelled to reject waiver under Rule 49(a).

First, the greater weight of authority supports rejecting the waiver approach. The majority of the circuits so hold, and it is respectfully submitted that those circuits holding otherwise have done so on insufficient authority. * * * The second reason compelling this Court to reject waiver as a bar involves the Seventh Amendment. It has been said that the Seventh Amendment creates a "delicate balance" between judge and jury which must be maintained, as explained in Mercer v. Long Mfg. N.C., Inc., 671 F.2d 946, 948 n. 1 (5th Cir.1982). The *Mercer* court stated:

> The legal error resulting from the entry of a judgment based on inconsistent special interrogatories is one which undermines the validity and integrity of the judgment and may, in fact, run afoul of the Seventh Amendment by allowing the District Court to usurp the jury's function. The Seventh Amendment creates a delicate balance.

Finally, the language of Rule 49(a) and (b) differs in a pivotal way, thus supporting waiver only under Rule 49(b) practice. Rule 49(b) states in relevant part, "When the answers are inconsistent with each other and one or more is likewise inconsistent with the general verdict, judgment shall not be entered, but the court shall return the jury for further consideration of its answers and verdict or shall order a new trial." Rule 49(a) is devoid of any direction that the jury shall be returned "for further consideration." Given that Rule 49(a) does not provide for this procedure, it is difficult to understand how the failure to object waives any rights under the Rule.

In commenting on practice under Rule 49(a), one scholar has flatly stated, "It would appear that a party does not waive his right to object to inconsistencies in the special interrogatories on appeal if he does not object at trial." 5A J. Moore & J. Lucas, Moore's Federal Practice § 49.03[4] (2d ed. 1990). For all the foregoing reasons, this Court agrees. Accordingly, the plaintiff has not waived the right to challenge alleged inconsistencies in the special interrogatories.

B. ALLEGED INCONSISTENCIES

Having found no waiver occurred, the Court must address the plaintiff's claim of inconsistencies in the special interrogatories.

This cause was put to the jury against three defendants: Indiana State Police Sgt. Donald Jackson, and Marion County Sheriff Deputies Glenn Thompson and Terrence Cress. Recovery was sought against defendant Jackson on the basis of the Fourth Amendment (unreasonable excessive force in a seizure), the Fifth and Fourteenth Amendments (denial of medical treatment in violation of due process), wrongful death, and assault and battery. Recovery was sought against defendants Cress and Thompson under the Fifth and Fourteenth Amendments (excessive force in violation of due process), wrongful death, and assault and battery.

The jury declined to hold the defendants liable for any constitutional violations, nor did the jury find the defendants' acts to have proximately caused the death of Gaisor, who died from a ruptured aneurism. Instead, the jury found the defendants liable for battery only, and awarded compensatory damages of $3,700 against Jackson, $1,500 against Cress, and $2,000 against Thompson. Additionally, the jury awarded punitive damages of $10,000 against Jackson, $4,000 against Cress, and $8,500 against Thompson. Judgment was entered accordingly.

The plaintiff's motion argues an inconsistency exists in that the jury awarded punitive damages, but failed to find a violation of constitutional proportions. The plaintiff argues that the "verdict form is inconsistent in that it must have simultaneously found that the actions of the defendants violated the constitutional rights of the plaintiff."

The starting point for resolving this issue is that in considering a motion for a new trial the Court is required to harmonize the answers on a special verdict if possible under a fair reading of them. In addition, the Court must search for a reasonable way to read the verdicts as expressing a coherent view of the case, and if there is any way to view a case that makes the jury's answers to the special interrogatories consistent, they must be resolved that way even if strained.

In the case at bar, the plaintiff essentially argues that it was inconsistent for the jury to have found that the defendants battered the plaintiff, and that the defendants should be liable for punitive damages, but not find the defendants liable for torts of a constitutional magnitude. The Court disagrees, as demonstrated by reviewing the jury's findings as to each defendant.

As for defendant Jackson, the jury found his conduct constituted battery, but declined to find unreasonable excessive force in a seizure (Fourth Amendment), or a denial of medical treatment violative of due process (Fifth and Fourteenth Amendments). The defendant correctly points out that the evidence supports a finding that Jackson struck Gaisor after Gaisor was handcuffed and in police custody. Thus, it was not inconsistent for the jury to find that the seizure was lawfully conducted, but that thereafter Jackson battered Gaisor.

This analysis relies on the premise that the Fourth Amendment protects against unreasonable force during an arrest, but that after the arrest has been effected the Fourth Amendment drops out and Fifth Amendment substantive due process protections are triggered. * * *

Thus, no legal reason prevented the jury from denying relief on Fourth Amendment grounds if it found that Gaisor was battered after his seizure was effected. Given that the jury's conclusions can be so reconciled, the Court will not inquire further. If the plaintiff had sought recovery from Jackson on the basis of Fifth Amendment substantive due process for use of unreasonably excessive force, an instruction reflecting this fact should have been submitted, and an objection should have been made if the Court failed to offer the tendered instruction.

It was not inconsistent for the jury to find a state law battery violation, and to additionally find that the defendants did not violate the Constitution by using unreasonably excessive force. A plaintiff's constitutional protection "is not co-extensive with that afforded the common law tort action for battery." Santiago v. Yarde, 487 F.Supp. 52, 54 (S.D.N.Y.1980). The often-stated rule applicable here is that not every wrong rises to the level of a constitutional violation for the purposes of 42 U.S.C. § 1983.

The imposition of punitive damages in this case presents a much closer question, but does not alter the result. The punitive damages instruction given to the jury allowed for the imposition of punitive damages for various alternative reasons, including "malice." The instructions and special interrogatories allowed the jury to find the defendants intentionally touched Gaisor in a rude manner, and that this was done with malice, yet determine that this touching did not involve unreasonably reckless and excessive force. Such a determination is not necessarily inconsistent given the conflicting nature of the testimony. The number of times the defendants struck Gaisor was in dispute, as was the amount of force used. Given that this Court must make every effort to view the jury's answers to the special interrogatories as consistent, the jury could properly have believed the defendants' version that only minimal force was used, and that reckless and excessive force was not involved.

The answers to interrogatories imply that the jury found the force used on Gaisor constituted battery and involved malice. This is not the same as finding the force was constitutionally excessive. The fact that the jury found the defendants' acts were not the proximate cause of Gaisor's death speaks loudly on this point. Accordingly, the jury could have found that Thompson and Cress each struck a blow to Gaisor, and did so maliciously, yet concluded that such conduct did not involve reckless and excessive force. In other words, evidence of a single blow of modest force delivered with malicious intent might not carry the day on a claim that the defendants' conduct on the whole involved reckless and excessive force.

Furthermore, the jury was instructed that it could award punitive damages "to deter others from like offenses." Therefore, the award of punitive damages in this case could have been rooted in a desire to deter other police officers from engaging in similar batteries. Arguably this "deterrent" aspect of punitive damages involves a reason for awarding punitive damages, which comes into play only after the jury has found malice or the like. Nevertheless, the jury was entitled to award punitive damages as a deterrent to others without finding the defendants' conduct constitutionally prohibited.

Thus, it is speculation to graft upon the jury's imposition of punitive damages the additional conclusion that Gaisor's constitutional rights were violated. To so hold, in view of the plaintiff's argument, would have required instructing the jury that if it found that Gaisor was battered, and if it found that punitive damages were appropriate, it also must find Fifth and Fourteenth Amendment violations. The plaintiff has not presented this Court with any supporting authority for such an instruction.

Lost in the plaintiff's argument for a new trial is an understanding of the message contained in the jury's verdict. The plaintiff's complaint sought recovery on the basis of alleged constitutional violations, wrongful death, and state tort claims. The jury returned a verdict in the plaintiff's favor on the battery claim only, plus a modest award of punitive damages. The evidence showed that on the night of Gaisor's arrest, he had been drinking, he disobeyed a police directive to discard a whiskey bottle, and was combative with police, both at the time of his arrest and later at the hospital.

Accordingly, in awarding approximately $30,000 in damages, including an award of punitive damages, the jury stated that Gaisor had been wronged, and that the defendants acted improperly. However, the jury verdict is just as significant for what it did not say. It did not say that Gaisor's constitutional rights were violated, or that the defendants were responsible for Gaisor's death. The answers to interrogatories reflect this fact and are not inconsistent.

C. CONCLUSION

In conclusion, the Court finds that the plaintiff did not waive the right to object to any alleged inconsistencies in the special interrogatories. However, the Court has reviewed the jury's responses to these interrogatories and for the reasons discussed herein finds that they may be viewed as consistent. Accordingly, the plaintiff's motion for additur or for a new trial is DENIED.

Notes and Questions

1. The practice set out in Rule 49(a) is known as the "special verdict." It was developed as an alternative to the general verdict, under which the

jury provides nothing more than its ultimate verdict. In contrast, under the procedure set out in Rule 49(a), the judge propounds a series of written questions to the jury about the facts of the case and enters a verdict based on her assessment of those answers. What is the rationale for Rule 49(a)? Is it a good idea? See Brodin, Accuracy, Efficiency, and Accountability in the Litigation Process—The Case for the Fact Verdict, 59 U. Cin. L. Rev. 15, 22 (1990), suggesting that routine use of the special verdict "has the significant potential for enhancing the reliability and efficiency of our judicial dispute resolution process." See also Sutton, A More Rational Approach to Complex Civil Litigation in the Federal Courts: The Special Jury, 1990 U. Chi. Legal F. 575; Faulkner, Using the Special Verdict to Manage Complex Cases and Avoid Compromise Verdicts, 21 Ariz. St.L.J. 297 (1989).

2.   Does Rule 49(a) reflect a fundamental mistrust of the jury system? If so, in what way does it control the jury more than the general verdict procedure does? Justices Black and Douglas, strong supporters of the civil jury, characterized the special verdict as "but another means utilized by courts to weaken the constitutional power of juries and to vest judges with more power to decide cases according to their own judgments." Minority Statement of Justices Black and Douglas, Opposing the 1963 Amendments to the Federal Rules of Civil Procedure, 374 U.S. 861, 865 (1963). The jurist traditionally associated with support of the special verdict procedure is Judge Jerome Frank, long a critic of the jury system. Consider his views in Courts on Trial: Myth and Reality in American Justice 141 (1949):

> A special verdict would seem to do away with some of the most objectionable features of trial by jury. The division of functions between jury and judge is apparently assured, the one attending to the facts alone, the other to the legal rules alone. The jury seems, by this device, to be shorn of its power to ignore the rules or to make rules to suit itself. * * * The finding of facts, says Sunderland, "is much better done by means of the special verdict. Every advantage which the jury is popularly supposed to have over the [judge] as a trier of facts is retained, with the very great additional advantage that the analysis and separation of the facts in the case which the court and the attorney must necessarily effect in employing the special verdict, materially reduce the chance of error. It is easy to make mistakes in dealing at large with aggregates of facts. The special verdict compels detailed consideration. But above all it enables the public, the parties and the court to see what the jury has really done. * * * The morale of the jury also is aided by throwing off the cloak of secrecy, for only through publicity is there developed the proper feeling of responsibility in public servants. So far, then, as the facts go, they can be much more effectively, conveniently, and usefully tried by abandoning the general verdict. * * * The special verdict is devised for the express purpose of escaping the sham of false appearances."

3.   Do you see any disadvantages of the special verdict? Consider the argument in C. Wright & M. Kane, Law of Federal Courts 678 (6th ed. 2002):

> The use of special verdicts is intended to emphasize the facts, prevent the jury from acting on bias, and make the law more scientific.

Little is gained, however, by making the law more scientific if, in the process, it becomes harder to achieve substantial justice. Some of the most famous students of the judicial process have argued that one of the purposes of the jury system is to permit the jury to temper strict rules of law by the demands and necessities of substantial justice, thereby adding a much needed element of flexibility. Those who share this conception of the role of the jury rightly fear that it will be limited or defeated by the special verdict practice * * *.

Consider also the response to this type of argument by Judge Frank:

The general-verdict jury trial, in practice, negates that which the dogma of precise legal predictability maintains to be the nature of law. A better instrument could scarcely be imagined for achieving uncertainty, capriciousness, lack of uniformity, disregard of former decisions—utter unpredictability.

* * *

[T]o preserve the self-delusion of legal fixity, certainty and impartiality, in many cases we hand over the determination of legal rights and liabilities to the whims of twelve men casually gathered together.

The demand for an impossible legal stability, resulting from an infantile longing to find a father-substitute in the law, thus actually leads, in the use of the jury, to a capriciousness that is unnecessary and socially harmful.

J. Frank, Law and the Modern Mind 186–92 (1930).

Should the jury be thought to possess authority to "nullify" unjust legal rules by means of the general verdict? Consider the following argument: "Many may applaud when a jury, under the protection and guise of its general verdict, effectively repeals the law of contributory negligence and replaces it with a crude form of case-by-case, comparative negligence. Perhaps many of those same individuals, however, would be outraged by a jury's blatant disregard of a judge's instructions in a civil rights action because the jurors do not agree with the application of section 1983 to a suit by a black against a local police officer. Yet if we accept the jury's power to disregard the law and do what it deems to be 'justice' in the former, does it not become intellectually awkward to deny it in the latter? Even if the answer is no, it must be realized that if we are to allow the former it is, as a practical matter, virtually impossible to prevent the latter." Redish, Seventh Amendment Right to Jury Trial: A Study in the Irrationality of Rational Decision Making, 70 Nw.U.L.Rev. 486, 508 (1975).

4. Whatever their impact on jury nullification, special verdicts may be especially appropriate in complex cases: "Special verdicts reduce jury confusion in factually and legally complex cases by identifying and organizing the issues in the case and by simplifying the instructions given to the jury." Note, Resolving Inconsistencies in Federal Special Verdicts, 53 Ford.L.Rev. 1089, 1090–91 (1985). Several federal courts have agreed. In SCM Corp. v. Xerox Corp., 463 F.Supp. 983 (D.Conn.1978), affirmed and remanded, 645 F.2d 1195 (2d Cir.1981), cert. denied, 455 U.S. 1016, 102 S.Ct. 1708, 72 L.Ed.2d 132 (1982), an antitrust suit involving 215 days of evidence presentation, the trial judge stated that "the sheer volume and complexity of the

evidence necessitated focusing the jury's attention on specific issues to be sure that orderly decision-making occurred." Id. at 988.

5. Other than possible interferences with the jury's "law-making" function, does the special verdict have any disadvantages? Is there any value to cloaking jury decision-making in secrecy? Are there any risks to finding out more about the jury's reasoning process? Consider Sunderland, Verdicts, General and Special, 29 Yale L.J. 253, 262 (1920):

> The real objection to the special verdict is that it is an honest portrayal of the truth, and the truth is too awkward a thing to fit the technical demands of the record. The record must be absolutely flawless, but such a result is possible only by concealing, not by excluding mistakes. This is the great technical merit of the general verdict. It covers up all the shortcomings which frail human nature is unable to eliminate from the trial of a case. In the abysmal abstraction of the general verdict concrete details are swallowed up, and the eye of the law, searching anxiously for the realization of logical perfection, is satisfied. In short, the general verdict is valued for what it does, not for what it is. It serves as the great procedural opiate, which draws the curtain upon human errors and soothes us with the assurance that we have attained the unattainable.

6. What is the difference between Rules 49(a) and 49(b)? See Lavoie v. Pacific Press & Shear Co., 975 F.2d 48, 53 (2d Cir.1992): "The distinction between the two provisions is that under Rule 49(a) the jury answers primarily factual questions for the benefit of the trial court which then applies the law to those answers. Under Rule 49(b), the jury after being fully instructed answers the interrogatories, renders a general verdict and the trial court enters judgment on the jury's verdict." Why might a judge prefer to use Rule 49(b), instead of Rule 49(a)?

Rule 49(b) has been the subject of heavy criticism. Judge John R. Brown has argued that "Rule 49(b) offers, so far as I can see, nothing but trouble because it seeks to mold a general verdict and special answers with the high likelihood of conflict which extinguishes both. Rule 49(a), on the other hand, if used with skill and resourcefulness, melds the general *charge* (not verdict) with the special answers to specific controlling issues of fact or legal fact." Brown, Federal Special Verdicts: The Doubt Eliminator, 44 F.R.D. 338, 339–40 (1967).

7. *Whitlock* deals with the issue of whether a plaintiff's failure to object to allegedly inconsistent jury answers to interrogatories constitutes waiver of that objection. The court in *Whitlock* sides with those courts that have found the waiver principle, which is expressly incorporated into Rule 49(b), inapplicable to cases employing Rule 49(a). As to the role of waiver under Rule 49(b), see, e.g., Diamond Shamrock Corp. v. Zinke & Trumbo, Ltd., 791 F.2d 1416 (10th Cir.1986). What are the competing considerations? Is there some basis for finding waiver under Rule 49(b) when the party fails to object to the inconsistencies prior to dismissal of the jury that is inapplicable to the situation under Rule 49(a)? Does the text of the rule resolve the waiver issue under Rule 49(a)?

8. A different waiver issue may also arise concerning the relationship between Rules 49(a) and 49(b). Note that Rule 49(a) explicitly provides that

if, in giving the verdict form to the jury "the court omits any issue of fact raised by the pleadings or by the evidence, each party waives the right to a trial by jury of the issue so omitted unless before the jury retires the party demands its submission to the jury." Rule 49(b) does not contain a similar waiver provision. See Bradway v. Gonzales, 26 F.3d 313 (2d Cir.1994).

9. When, as in *Whitlock*, the answers are alleged to be inconsistent, "jury verdicts must be interpreted so as to avoid inconsistency wherever possible * * *." Freeman v. Chicago Park District, 189 F.3d 613, 615 (7th Cir. 1999). Courts believe that they "should do what we can to save the verdict against the spectre of inconsistency." American Casualty Co. v. B. Cianciolo, Inc., 987 F.2d 1302 (7th Cir. 1993).

10. The use of special verdicts or interrogatories poses problems as to how narrow or broad the questions should be. In Texas, where the jury is not allowed to render a general verdict but must answer questions that the judge will then convert into a verdict, an ordinary case once generated dozens of issues, with a separate question as to each claim or defense. In negligence cases, for example, the jury was required to answer as to each act of negligence alleged (e.g., speeding, failure to apply brakes, failure to keep a proper lookout, etc.), forcing them to agree on the specific act of negligence. All answers had to be consistent, and it is not surprising that the practice was favored by the defense bar. For an argument against requiring unanimity on such specifics by a present Supreme Court Justice, see Ginsburg, Special Findings and Jury Unanimity in Federal Courts, 65 Colum. L. Rev.256 (1965). However, "broad-form" submission of questions is now required in Texas (which is consistent with the usual practice in federal courts under Rule 49). See Lemos v. Montez, 680 S.W.2d 798, 801 (Tex. 1984); Tex.R.Civ.P. 277. Use of questions has the advantage over a general verdict of guiding the jury's deliberations and obtaining precise answers that may be necessary pursuant to the substantive law, as in the case of comparative negligence or responsibility. Thus, the Texas Pattern Jury Charge book suggests the following questions for a basic automobile negligence case [1 Tex. Pattern Jury Charges §§ 4.1; 4.3; 8.2 (2003)]:

> Did the negligence, if any, of those named below proximately cause the [occurrence] [injury] [occurrence or injury] in question?

> a. Don Davis [defendant] _____
> b. Paul Payne [plaintiff] _____
> c. Sam Settlor [if plaintiff has previously settled with another person claimed to be responsible] _____
> d. Responsible Ray [a responsible third party] _____
> e. Connie Contributor [a contribution defendant] _____

> What percent of the negligence that caused the [occurrence] [injury] [occurrence or injury] do you find to be attributable to each of those listed below and found by you, in your answer to Question _____ [4.1 or other applicable liability question], to have been negligent?

a.	Don Davis	_____	%
b.	Paul Payne	_____	%
c.	Sam Settlor	_____	%
d.	Responsible Ray	_____	%
	Total	100	%

What sum of money, if paid now in cash, would fairly and reasonably compensate Paul Payne for his injuries, if any, that resulted from the occurrence in question?

Consider the elements of damages listed below and none other. Consider each element separately. Do not award any sum of money on any element if you have otherwise, under some other element, awarded a sum of money for the same loss. That is, do not compensate twice for the same loss, if any. Do not include interest or any amount of damages you find.

a. Physical pain and mental anguish.

b. Loss of earning capacity.

c. Disfigurement.

d. Physical impairment.

e. Medical care expenses.

Do not reduce the amounts, if any, in your answers because of the negligence, if any, of *Paul Payne.*

Answer in dollars and cents for damagnes, if any, that—
were sustained in the past;   Answer: _____
in reasonable probability will
be sustained in the future.   Answer: _____

5. *Juror Impeachment of the Verdict*

SOPP v. SMITH, 377 P.2d 649 (Cal.1963):

Schauer, J.

[Plaintiff in a negligence action arising out of an automobile accident sought a new trial on the basis of a juror's affidavit that after all the evidence had been presented, he took a drive to the scene of the accident and tested the claims of some of the witnesses. The trial court denied the motion on the grounds that the affidavit was inadmissible. The California Supreme Court affirmed on the basis of the rule in Kollert v. Cundiff, 50 Cal.2d 768, 329 P.2d 897 (1958): "It is the general rule in California that affidavits of jurors may not be used to impeach a verdict."]

The *Kollert* case also points out that California recognizes two exceptions to the rule, one created by statute (resort to chance, Code Civ.Proc. § 657, subd. 2), and the other by judicial decision (bias or disqualification of a juror concealed by false answers on *voir dire*), * * * and further emphasizes that "The problem involves the balancing of two conflicting policies. It is, of course, necessary to prevent instability of verdicts, fraud, and harassment of jurors, and, on the other hand, it is desirable to give the losing party relief from wrongful conduct by the jury. * * * "Having thus expressly recognized and considered the conflicting policies, we rejected plaintiffs' plea to create a further exception.

PETERS, J.

I dissent.

The majority, following the rule of stare decisis, adhere to a court created doctrine first announced by Judge Mansfield in Vaise v. Delaval, 1 Term R. 11, 99 Eng.Rep. 944 (K.B.1785). That rule is that affidavits of jurors may not be used to impeach their verdict. The only reason given by the majority, other than stare decisis, is public policy, at best a vague and uncertain guide * * *.

Dean Wigmore has demonstrated to a certainty that before 1785 the rule was well settled that jurors could, as to overt acts showing misconduct, impeach their own verdict. The Dean has also pointed out that the only reason given by Judge Mansfield for adopting the new rule was his belief that under no circumstances should a witness be heard to allege his own turpitude. That doctrine, involving the admissibility of voluntary confessions, has long been overruled in practically all American jurisdictions, including California.

* * *

Wigmore demonstrates to a certainty that there is no reason in law or logic for continuing the rule * * *.

Iowa has taken the lead in liberalizing the Mansfield rule. At least 12 jurisdictions, by judicial decision, have modified the strict Mansfield rule. * * *

The Iowa rule is based upon the distinction between extrinsic or overt acts which may be corroborated or disproved, such as access to improper matter or an illegal method of reaching a verdict, and intrinsic matters which "inhere in the verdict itself" and hence are known only to the individual juror, such as misunderstanding or prejudice. Because matters which "inhere" in the verdict, including the thought processes and motives of the juror in reaching his decision, are not readily capable of being either corroborated or disproved they should be excluded.

* * *

I would hold that as to overt acts of misconduct a juror, on motion for a new trial, may testify to such misconduct, and that the trial court erred in excluding such testimony from its consideration.

PEOPLE v. HUTCHINSON

Supreme Court of California, 1969.
455 P.2d 132.

TRAYNOR, CHIEF JUSTICE.

[Convicted of possession of marijuana for sale, defendant argued on appeal that there was insufficient evidence to support his conviction and that the trial court committed prejudicial error in refusing to consider a juror's affidavit he offered in support of his motion for a new trial.]

* * *

In support of his motion for a new trial defendant submitted an affidavit of a juror alleging misconduct on the part of the bailiff.[1] The trial court refused to consider the affidavit on the ground that: "They [the jury] can't impeach their own verdict."

The rule that jurors cannot impeach their verdicts, although almost universally assailed by the commentators as without foundation in logic or policy, has been a common law rule in this state since our first volume of reports. The rule first sprang full blown and unprecedented from the opinion of Lord Mansfield in Vaise v. Delaval (1785) 1 T.R. 11, 99 Eng.Rep. 944, and was based on an extension of the principle *nemo turpitudinem suam allegans audietur*—no man shall be heard to allege his own turpitude.[2] With several exceptions, the rule was adopted by the courts in American jurisdictions, including California, even though the principle on which it was originally based was largely repudiated as applied to other areas of the law of evidence. (See 8 Wigmore, Evidence (McNaughton rev. 1961) § 2352, p. 696.)

* * * The rule owes its continuing vitality, not to statute, but to the force of stare decisis (see Sopp v. Smith (1963) 59 Cal.2d 12, 15–16, 27 Cal.Rptr. 593, 377 P.2d 649 (dissenting opinion, Peters, J.)); and to a variety of legal arguments and public policies that, like the discredited

---

1. "I hereby certify and declare that I was a juror on the above-entitled case and that the following is my recollection of the activities of the bailiff in regard to this case. The Judge stated from the Bench that we would go to dinner at 6:00 p.m., if we had not reached a verdict. At 6:00 p.m. we were not taken to dinner.

"It was not until about 6:30 when the bailiff came in, and at our request. At this time inquiry of him was made as to when we would get to dinner. At this point he replied words to the effect: 'If you go out to eat, you will be locked up overnight.' At some time during the deliberations in the late afternoon, after 6:30, the bailiff came in and said words to this effect: 'If you knew what was going on out there, you would be shivering in your boots.' At one time when he entered, around 7:00, he seemed quite angry and put out. He said words, 'This is it.' We replied, 'Give us a few more minutes and we can come to a verdict.' He gave us about five or ten minutes and said if we had not reached a verdict that was it. I feel that we were definitely rushed by the bailiff. When the bailiff came in the last time, I felt we just had to make up our minds and that was it when he came in. He had come in three times and each time he seemed and spoke in a more angry manner. It was my opinion that the entire jury was uncertain as to how to proceed. As a result of his actions, everyone said, 'Hurry up.' It is my opinion that I hurried my verdict and agreed to the compromise verdict in order to prevent the jury from being locked up overnight.

"There were about four of us who felt from the beginning of deliberations that he was not guilty. I was the last holdout on the jury. The verdict for the lesser included was my verdict and was the verdict of the entire jury. I heard no vulgarity. I would not desire to sit on another jury if it was handled in the same way that this jury was handled by the bailiff."

2. 12 The jurors in Vaise v. Delaval had reached their verdict by lot, conduct that Lord Mansfield classed as a very high misdemeanor.

policy against self-stultifying testimony, cannot withstand careful analysis.

In Kollert v. Cundiff, 50 Cal.2d 768, 773–774, 329 P.2d 897, 900, we stated the rationale presently underlying the rule: "The problem involves the balancing of two conflicting policies. It is, of course, necessary to prevent instability of verdicts, fraud, and harassment of jurors, and, on the other hand, it is desirable to give the losing party relief from wrongful conduct by the jury. The court in McDonald v. Pless, 238 U.S. 264, 267–269, 35 S.Ct. 783, 785, 59 L.Ed. 1300, after discussing these policies and stating that the wrong to the individual was the lesser of two evils, concluded that as a general rule the affidavits [of jurors] should be excluded but that there might be instances where the rule could not be applied without 'violating the plainest principles of justice.' " Upon further deliberation we have concluded that there is no substantial conflict of policies and that the wrong to the individual cannot be considered the lesser of two evils.

In the Evidence Code the Legislature has determined that certain facts may be proved to impeach a verdict. "Upon an inquiry as to the validity of a verdict, any otherwise admissible evidence may be received as to statements made, or conduct, conditions, or events occurring, either within or without the jury room, of such a character as is likely to have influenced the verdict improperly. No evidence is admissible to show the effect of such statement, conduct, condition, or event upon a juror either in influencing him to assent to or dissent from the verdict or concerning the mental processes by which it was determined." (Evid. Code, § 1150, subd. (a).) This distinction between proof of overt acts, objectively ascertainable, and proof of the subjective reasoning processes of the individual juror, which can be neither corroborated nor disproved, has been advocated by commentators, adopted by the Uniform Rules of Evidence (rules 41 and 44) and the Model Code of Evidence (rule 301), and has been the basic limitation on proof set by the leading decisions allowing jurors to impeach their verdicts.

Although section 1150 does not alter the rule against impeachment of a verdict by the jurors, its limitation of impeachment evidence to proof of overt conduct, conditions, events, and statements, as suggested by the commentators, vitiates the major policy arguments supporting the common law rule. (See Sopp v. Smith, supra, 59 Cal.2d 12, 15–20, 27 Cal.Rptr. 593, 377 P.2d 649 (dissenting opinion, Peters, J.).) This limitation prevents one juror from upsetting a verdict of the whole jury by impugning his own or his fellow jurors' mental processes or reasons for assent or dissent. The only improper influences that may be proved under section 1150 to impeach a verdict, therefore, are those open to sight, hearing, and the other senses and thus subject to corroboration. "[T]hese facts can be easily proved or disproved. There is invariably little disagreement as to their occurrence." (Report of the New Jersey Supreme Court Committee on Evidence (1963) 80.) Experience in other jurisdictions that recognize the competency of a juror to impeach his verdict indicates that the admission of jurors' affidavits within the limits set by section 1150 will not result in the widespread upsetting of verdicts. Experience in this state with the present exceptions "indicates that the fears of jury tampering are unrealistic" (6 Cal.Law Revision Com. Reports (1964) 611), and there is no reason to believe that permitting proof of other overt misconduct is more likely to encourage post verdict tampering with the jury than do the present exceptions.

Admission of jurors' affidavits within the limits set by section 1150 protects the stability of verdicts, and allows proof by the best evidence of misconduct on the part of either jurors or third parties that should be exposed, misconduct upon which no verdict should be based. The content and conduct of deliberations may already be exposed by jurors at the trial of one who attempted corruptly to influence the verdict, or, in the case of the present two exceptions to the rule, at motion for new trial. Admission of this best evidence of misconduct or improper influence at a motion for new trial, therefore, would not present a breach in the post verdict privacy of jury deliberations. It would merely insure that evidence of misconduct will be available to the courts, freeing them to determine the substantive questions of whether the particular misconduct is a recognized ground for new trial and whether it has prejudiced the losing party. Admission of jurors' affidavits should also have a further prophylactic effect of stripping from all prejudicial misconduct whatever veil of post verdict secrecy is now reserved for the proper deliberations of the jury. "[T]o hear such proof would have a tendency to diminish such practices and to purify the jury room, by rendering such improprieties capable and probable of exposure, and consequently deterring jurors from resorting to them." (Wright v. Illinois, etc., Tel. Co., 20 Iowa 195, 211.)

We therefore hold that jurors are competent witnesses to prove objective facts to impeach a verdict under section 1150 of the Evidence Code. To the extent that Sopp v. Smith; Kollert v. Cundiff and similar cases are contrary to our conclusion herein, they are overruled.

The bailiff's remarks and the tone of their delivery constitute statements and conduct that are "likely to have influenced the verdict improperly." The affidavit of the juror is therefore admissible to prove the statements and conduct of the bailiff. Since the trial court refused to consider this competent evidence, defendant is entitled to a redetermination of his motion for new trial.

The order granting probation and the order denying the motion for new trial are vacated with directions to the trial court to hear and determine the motion for new trial in accordance with this opinion and to take such further proceedings as are appropriate.

McComb, Peters, Tobriner, Mosk, Burke and Sullivan, JJ., concur.

Notes and Questions

1. The rationale for the traditional rule established by Lord Mansfield in Vaise v. Delaval was described by the Supreme Court in McDonald v. Pless, 238 U.S. 264, 267–68, 35 S.Ct. 783, 784, 59 L.Ed. 1300 (1915):

[L]et it once be established that verdicts solemnly made and publicly returned into court can be attacked and set aside on the testimony of those who took part in their publication and all verdicts could be, and many would be, followed by an inquiry in the hope of discovering something which might invalidate the finding. Jurors would be harassed and beset by the defeated party in an effort to secure from them evidence of facts which might establish misconduct sufficient to set aside a verdict. If evidence thus secured could be thus used, the result would be to make what was intended to be a private deliberation, the constant subject of public investigation—to the destruction of all frankness and freedom of discussion and conference.

Do these arguments justify the *total* ban of juror impeachment established by the *Delaval* rule? What if, during the course of deliberations, one juror pulls out a gun and orders every other juror to vote for the plaintiff? Could one of the jurors impeach the verdict on the basis of this evidence under the *Delaval* rule? Note that the *Delaval* rule "addresses itself to the question of whether a juror shall be allowed to testify to misconduct committed by his own jury panel. The * * * rule distinguishes sharply between the testimony of a juror and that of an outsider. Although a juror would be forbidden to file an affidavit or testify about an irregularity in the jury room, 'some person having seen the transaction through a window, or by some such other means' would be allowed to testify in court or file an affidavit concerning it." Carlson & Sumberg, Attacking Jury Verdicts: Paradigms for Rule Revision, 1977 Ariz.St.L.J. 247, 249 [quoting *Delaval*]. Does this distinction make sense?

2. Should the judge feel some responsibility to ensure that the jury has not misbehaved in reaching its verdict? Consider Peterson v. Wilson, 141 F.3d 573 (5th Cir.1998), in which the trial judge met with the jurors without notice to counsel after the jury returned a plaintiff's verdict, and discussed the verdict with the jurors. Later, she sua sponte granted a motion for a new trial, explaining that "comments the jurors made to the court after returning the verdict [demonstrated] that the jury completely disregarded the Court's instructions." The court of appeals held that this violated Federal Rule of Evidence 606(b) (note 5 infra), for "—with the possible exception of an instance in which the court's professional curiosity has been piqued but on which no subsequent action is taken by the court—such a meeting is highly irregular if not absolutely impermissible, and, more importantly, that impeachment of the jury verdict on the basis of information obtained in such a discussion constitutes abuse of discretion per se."

3. In Ballard v. Uribe, 715 P.2d 624 (Cal.1986), Justice Mosk (who had concurred in Justice Traynor's opinion in *Hutchinson*) wrote in a separate concurring opinion:

I must express my apprehension at an incipient trend, that of losing parties attempting to impeach jury verdicts. * * * Giving such appeals and petitions any credence prevents the finality of judgments, places additional burdens on the judicial process, and contributes to disenchantment with the tort system.

Most juror affidavits * * * delve into the subjective concerns of the jurors during their deliberations. When deference is given to such affidavits, encouragement is given to opposing counsel in future cases to engage in postverdict competition to obtain juror affidavits revealing discussions that took place behind the closed doors of the deliberation room. Generally the party with the most resources will win that contest. If affidavits purportedly relating jury discussions are permissible, in the interest of accuracy we may as well install recording devices in jury rooms.

See also In re Hamilton, 84 Cal.Rptr.2d 403 (Cal.1999) (Chin, J., concurring) ("fishing expeditions by litigants who lost at trial must not transform the quest for misconduct claims into the witch hunts of the next millennium.").

4. The so-called "Iowa rule", discussed in Justice Peters' dissent in *Sopp*, was developed as an attempt to bridge the interests served by the *Delaval* rule on the one hand and the competing interest in a fair and accurate verdict, on the other. Does it successfully achieve this goal? Could a juror impeach his verdict in the circumstances described in note 1 under the Iowa rule? See Carlson & Sumberg, supra, 1977 Ariz.St.L.J. at 257:

A key to understanding the Iowa rule lies in appreciating which matters do, and which matters do not, "inhere in the verdict." Although there is some disagreement over the precise meaning of the phrase, matters that inhere in the verdict usually are deemed to be those which are personal to the juror, such as his mental operations, emotions, and personal reactions to the arguments of counsel.

5. Federal Rule of Evidence 606(b) provides:

Inquiry into validity of verdict or indictment. Upon an inquiry into the validity of a verdict or indictment, a juror may not testify as to any matter or statement occurring during the course of the jury's deliberations or to the effect of anything upon that or any other juror's mind or emotions as influencing the juror to assent to or dissent from the verdict or indictment or concerning the juror's mental processes in connection therewith, except that a juror may testify on the question whether extraneous prejudicial information was improperly brought to the jury's attention or whether any outside influence was improperly brought to bear upon any juror. Nor may a juror's affidavit or evidence of any statement by him concerning a matter about which the juror would be precluded from testifying be received for these purposes.

To what extent is this Rule similar to either the *Delaval* or Iowa rules? To what extent does it differ? For a discussion of the history and policy of Rule 606(b), see Mueller, Jurors' Impeachment of Verdicts and Indictments in Federal Court Under Rule 606(b), 57 Neb.L.Rev. 920 (1978).

6. Consider how the three rules would apply to the following hypotheticals:

(a) The quotient verdict: The jurors reached a verdict by writing down the amount each thought plaintiff should recover (even if zero) and dividing the total amount by the number of jurors. Cf. Scogin v. Century Fitness, Inc., 780 F.2d 1316 (8th Cir.1985) (evidence of quotient verdict "does not concern extraneous prejudicial information or outside influence being brought to bear upon any juror").

(b) The notes the jury made while calculating damages indicate that it was confused and as a result awarded the wrong amount. See Ohanian v. Avis Rent A Car System, Inc., 779 F.2d 101 (2d Cir.1985) ("To use jurors' notes to impeach a verdict would, as the Supreme Court in McDonald v. Pless feared, 'make what was intended to be a private deliberation, the constant subject of public investigation—to the destruction of all frankness and freedom of discussion and conference.' ").

(c) After the verdict is returned and the jury excused, a juror reports that the jury actually intended to award plaintiff a much higher amount. See Attridge v. Cencorp Div. of Dover Technologies Intern., Inc., 836 F.2d 113 (2d Cir.1987), in which the verdict said that plaintiff should recover $100,000 and his wife $50,000 but that plaintiff was 80% responsible for his injury so that the net amounts would be $20,000 and $10,000. Two jurors then reported that the jury intended that plaintiff and his wife receive $100,000 and $50,000 net. After determining from juror interviews that all jurors concurred in these reports, the trial court entered judgment for the larger amounts. The appellate court affirmed, reasoning that "[R]ule 606(b), by its own terms, does not extend to juror testimony on the veracity of the verdict. Rather, juror testimony is admissible to show that the verdict delivered was not that actually agreed upon." The court distinguished Continental Cas. Co. v. Howard, 775 F.2d 876 (7th Cir.1985), in which the foreman of the jury submitted an affidavit stating that the jury intended to award plaintiff $369,500 rather than $9,500, which is what the verdict had said. The appellate court there upheld refusal to consider this affidavit on the ground that there was no assertion the jury had reached a different verdict, but only that it intended plaintiff recover more, and as such that it was an attempt to testify about the jury's thought processes. In 2004, a proposed amendment to Rule 606(b) was published; if adopted, it would allow juror affidavits on whether the verdict "is the result of a clerical mistake."

(d) A juror attempts to impeach his verdict by stating that for many hours he had been the last holdout in favor of the ultimate losing party, when his boss, who was also a member of the jury, said to him: "Remember, you have a job, Sam." At that point he switched his vote.

(e) A juror testifies that during a break in deliberation, the bailiff called him aside and, in discussing an especially recalcitrant juror, pulled his gun out, took out a bullet, and said he could "put her out of her misery." The juror did not tell the recalcitrant juror, but testifies that "it really shook me up." See Sea Hawk Seafoods, Inc. v. Alyeska Pipeline Service Co., 206 F.3d 900 (9th Cir. 2000).

7. A number of years ago, commentators noted that "[s]ome courts are developing new exceptions to the no-impeachment rule for civil cases, and recently enacted codes of evidence are broadly replacing the rule in both civil and criminal litigation in other jurisdictions. However, the most dramatic developments have been in the constitutional area. They point to the probable demise of the [Delaval] rule, at least where activities in the jury room deprive an accused of his constitutional rights in a criminal prosecution." Carlson & Sumberg, supra, 1977 Ariz.St.L.J. at 267.

In Tanner v. United States, 483 U.S. 107, 107 S.Ct. 2739, 97 L.Ed.2d 90 (1987), the Court rejected such arguments by a convicted criminal defendant who relied on a juror affidavit that several jurors were drunk or stoned or both. The juror asserted that he "felt like * * * the jury was one big party." He detailed a rather troubling picture: Four of the jurors customarily drank one to three pitchers of beer at lunch, the foreperson, an alcoholic, usually had a carafe of wine at lunch, four jurors regularly smoked marijuana during the trial, one juror sold a quarter pound of marijuana to another juror in the courthouse during the trial, and one juror took cocaine five times during the trial while another used that drug two or three times. Despite arguments by the dissent that this evidence indicated a violation of due process, the majority held that, like matters of alleged mental or physical incompetence, the evidence related to something "internal" to the verdict and that it was therefore inadmissible.

In Robles v. Exxon Corp., 862 F.2d 1201 (5th Cir.), cert. denied, 490 U.S. 1051, 109 S.Ct. 1967, 104 L.Ed.2d 434 (1989), the court held that a judge's receiving testimony from the jurors after they have returned their verdict, for the purposes of ascertaining that the jury misunderstood its instructions, is absolutely prohibited by Rule 606(b).

Chapter IX

CHOOSING THE FORUM— GEOGRAPHICAL LOCATION

Until this point, we have given little attention to the location of the court in which the case is to proceed. In a country the size of the United States, that factor can of course be quite important, as can the question whether the case is in federal or state court. The plaintiff's preferences with regard to location and court system may result from a variety of strategic factors, but they are subject to a number of legal limitations. We turn to those limitations now. In this chapter we consider the geographical location of the court. In the next chapter we address the choice between state and federal court.

In early English procedure, the method for obtaining jurisdiction was often rather primitive, if direct—under the writ of *capias ad respondendum,* the sheriff simply arrested the defendant and put him in jail, there to await trial. Gradually that method was abandoned and, "in the case of a suit against a man, jurisdiction is regarded as established by service [of process], without the need of keeping him in prison to await judgment. It is enough that the personal service shows that he could have been seized and imprisoned." Tyler v. Judges of the Court of Registration, 175 Mass. 71, 55 N.E. 812, 814 (1900) (Holmes, C.J.). Nevertheless, jurisdiction has continued to plague lawyers, judges and law students. Many, no doubt, would agree with the judge who observed that "the legal issues raised in these cases are rather dull. If Judge Wapner had to worry about personal jurisdiction, 'The People's Court' would not be on television." Hall's Specialties, Inc. v. Schupbach, 758 F.2d 214, 215 (7th Cir.1985). On the other hand, another court has referred to "the heart of a federal court's ability to practice its trade, namely personal jurisdiction." Hugel v. McNell, 886 F.2d 1, 2 (1st Cir.1989).

A. THE TRADITIONAL FORMULATION: THE "POWER" THEORY OF JURISDICTION

PENNOYER v. NEFF

Supreme Court of the United States, 1877.
95 U.S. (5 OTTO) 714, 24 L.Ed. 565.

JUSTICE FIELD delivered the opinion of the Court.

[In November, 1865, J.H. Mitchell sued Neff in the Circuit Court of Multnomah County, Oregon, claiming that Neff owed him $253.14 for legal work performed in 1862 and 1863. Shortly after filing the suit, Mitchell submitted his affidavit asserting that Neff was a California resident, but that Mitchell did not know his address. Mitchell also averred that Neff owned property in Oregon, although the record does not reveal what that property was. On the basis of the affidavit, the Oregon court directed that Neff be served by publication. Where the defendant's place of residence was known, the Code of Oregon provided that he either be personally served outside the state or that the summons and complaint be mailed to him. But since Neff's address was unknown, the only notice of the suit required was publication once a week for six weeks in the Pacific Christian Advocate, a paper of general circulation in Multnomah County. When Neff failed to answer, Mitchell obtained a default judgment in early 1866. A month later, Neff acquired title to a tract of land in Oregon. Mitchell then executed against this land and bought it at the sheriff's sale for $341.60, presumably the amount of the judgment plus interest and costs. Three days later, on August 10, 1866, he transferred title to Pennoyer.

In September, 1874, Neff sued Pennoyer in federal court in Oregon to recover title to the land, which he alleged was worth $15,000. He contended that the judgment in Mitchell's suit was invalid because the Oregon court had not, despite substituted service under the Oregon procedure, had jurisdiction.]

The Code of Oregon provides for such service [by publication] when an action is brought against a non-resident and absent defendant, who has property within the state. It also provides, where the action is for the recovery of money or damages, for the attachment of the property of the non-resident. And it also declares that no natural person is subject to the jurisdiction of a court of the State, "unless he appear in the court, or be found within the State, or be a resident thereof, or have property therein; and, in the last case, only to the extent of such property at the time the jurisdiction attached." Construing this latter provision to mean, that, in an action for money or damages where a defendant does not appear in the court, and is not found within the State, and is not a resident thereof, but has property therein, the jurisdiction of the court extends only over such property, the declaration expresses a principle of general, if not universal, law. The authority of every tribunal is necessarily restricted by the territorial limits of the State in which it is established. Any attempt to exercise authority beyond those limits would be deemed in every other forum, as has been said by this Court, an illegitimate assumption of power, and be resisted as mere abuse. In this case against the plaintiff, the property here in controversy sold under the judgment rendered was not attached, nor in any way brought under the jurisdiction of the court. Its first connection with the case was caused by a levy of the execution. It was not, therefore, disposed of pursuant to any adjudication, but only in enforcement of a personal judgment, having no relation to the property, rendered against a non-resident without service of process upon him in the action, or his appearance therein.

[The lower court had ruled for Neff on the ground that the affidavit used to prove service by publication was defective because it came from the editor, and the statute called for the affidavit of "the printer, or his foreman, or his principal clerk." The Supreme Court found the affidavit of the editor sufficient.]

* * *

If, therefore, we were confined to the rulings of the court below upon the defects in the affidavits mentioned, we should be unable to uphold its decision. But it was also contended in that court, and is insisted upon here, that the judgment in the State court against the plaintiff was void for want of personal service of process on him, or of his appearance in the action in which it was rendered, and that the premises in controversy could not be subjected to the payment of the demand of a resident creditor except by a proceeding *in rem;* that is, by a direct proceeding against the property for that purpose. If these positions are sound, the ruling of the Circuit Court as to the invalidity of that judgment must be sustained, notwithstanding our dissent from the reasons upon which it was made. And that they are sound would seem to follow from two well-established principles of public law respecting the jurisdiction of an independent State over persons and property. The several States of the Union are not, it is true, in every respect independent, many of the rights and powers which originally belonged to them being now vested in the government created by the Constitution. But, except as restrained and limited by that instrument, they possess and exercise the authority of independent States, and the principles of public law to which we have referred are applicable to them. One of these principles is, that every State possesses exclusive jurisdiction and sovereignty over persons and property within its territory. As a consequence, every State has the power to determine for itself the civil *status* and capacities of its inhabitants; to prescribe the subjects upon which they may contract, the forms and solemnities with which their contracts shall be executed, the rights and obligations arising from them, and the mode in which their validity shall be determined and their obligations enforced; and also to regulate the manner and conditions upon which property situated within such territory, both personal and real, may be acquired, enjoyed, and transferred. The other principle of public law referred to follows from the one mentioned; that is, that no State can exercise direct jurisdiction and authority over persons or property without its territory. Story, Confl. Laws, c. 2; Wheat. Int. Law, pt. 2, c. 2. The several States are of equal dignity and authority, and the independence of one implies the exclusion of power from all others. And so it is laid down by jurists, as an elementary principle, that the laws of one State have no operation outside of its territory, except so far as is allowed by comity; and that no tribunal established by it can extend its process beyond that territory so as to subject either persons or property to its decisions. "Any exertion of authority of this sort beyond this limit," says Story, "is a mere nullity, and incapable of binding such persons or property in any other tribunals." Story, Confl. Laws, sect. 539.

But as contracts made in one State may be enforceable only in another State, and property may be held by non-residents, the exercise of the jurisdiction which every State is admitted to possess over persons and property within its own territory will often affect persons and property without it. To any influence exerted in this way by a State affecting persons resident or property situated elsewhere, no objection can be justly taken; whilst any direct exertion of authority upon them, in an attempt to give ex-territorial operation to its laws, or to enforce an exterritorial jurisdiction by its tribunals, would be deemed an encroachment upon the independence of the State in which the persons are domiciled or the property is situated, and be resisted as usurpation.

Thus the State, through its tribunals, may compel persons domiciled within its limits to execute, in pursuance of their contracts respecting property elsewhere situated, instruments in such form and with such solemnities as to transfer the title, so far as such formalities can be complied with; and the exercise of this jurisdiction in no manner interferes with the supreme control over the property by the State within which it is situated.

So the State, through its tribunals, may subject property situated within its limits owned by non-residents to the payment of the demand of its own citizens against them; and the exercise of this jurisdiction in no respect infringes upon the sovereignty of the State where the owners are domiciled. Every State owes protection to its own citizens; and, when non-residents deal with them, it is a legitimate and just exercise of authority to hold and appropriate any property owned by such non-residents to satisfy the claims of its citizens. It is in virtue of the State's jurisdiction over the property of the non-resident situated within its limits that its tribunals can inquire into that non-resident's obligations to its own citizens, and the inquiry can then be carried only to the extent necessary to control the disposition of the property. If the non-resident have no property in the State, there is nothing upon which the tribunals can adjudicate.

* * *

If, without personal service, judgments *in personam*, obtained *ex parte* against non-residents and absent parties, upon mere publication of process, which, in the great majority of cases, would never be seen by the parties interested, could be upheld and enforced, they would be the constant instruments of fraud and oppression. Judgments for all sorts of claims upon contracts and for torts, real or pretended, would be thus obtained, under which property would be seized, when the evidence of the transactions upon which they were founded, if they ever had any existence, had perished.

Substituted service by publication, or in any other authorized form, may be sufficient to inform parties of the object of proceedings taken where property is once brought under the control of the court by seizure or some equivalent act. The law assumes that property is always in the possession of its owner, in person or by agent; and it proceeds upon the theory that its seizure will inform him, not only that it is taken into the custody of the court, but that he must look to any proceedings authorized by law upon such seizure for its condemnation and sale. Such service may also be sufficient in cases where the object of the action is to reach and dispose of property in the State, or of some interest therein, by enforcing a contract or a lien respecting the same, or to partition it among different owners, or, when the public is a party, to condemn and appropriate it for a public purpose. In other words, such service may answer in all actions which are substantially proceedings *in rem*. But where the entire object of the action is to determine the personal rights and obligations of the defendants, that is, where the suit is merely *in personam*, constructive service in this form upon a non-resident is ineffectual for any purpose. Process from the tribunals of one State cannot run into another State, and summon parties there domiciled to leave its territory and respond to proceedings against them. Publication of process or notice within the State where the tribunal sits cannot create any greater obligation upon the non-resident to appear. Process sent to him out of the State, and process published within it, are equally unavailing in proceedings to establish his personal liability.

The want of authority of the tribunals of a State to adjudicate upon the obligations of non-residents, where they have no property within its limits, is not denied by the court below; but the position is assumed, that, where they have property within the State, it is immaterial whether the property is in the first instance brought under the control of the court by attachment or some other equivalent act, and afterwards applied by its judgment to the satisfaction of demands against its owner; or such demands be first established in a personal action, and the property of the non-resident be afterwards seized and sold on execution. But the answer to this position has already been given in the statement, that the jurisdiction of the court to inquire into and determine his obligations at all is only incidental to its jurisdiction over the property. Its jurisdiction in that respect cannot be made to depend upon facts to be ascertained after it has tried the cause and rendered the judgment. If the judgment be previously void, it will not become valid by the subsequent discovery of property of the defendant, or by his subsequent acquisition of it. The judgment, if void when rendered, will always remain void: it cannot occupy the doubtful position of being valid if property be found, and void if there be none. Even if the position assumed were confined to cases where the non-resident defendant possessed property in the State at the commencement of the action, it would still make the validity of the proceedings and judgment depend upon the question whether, before the levy of the execution, the defendant had or had not disposed of the property. If before the levy the property should be sold, then, according to this position, the judgment would not be binding. This doctrine would introduce a new element of uncertainty in judicial proceedings. The contrary is the law: the validity of every judgment depends upon the jurisdiction of the court before it is rendered, not upon what may occur subsequently. * * *

The force and effect of judgments rendered against non-residents without personal service of process upon them, or their voluntary appearance, have been the subject of frequent consideration in the courts of the United States and of the several States, as attempts have been made to enforce such judgments in States other than those in which they were rendered, under the provision of the Constitution requiring that "full faith and credit shall be given in each State to the public acts, records, and judicial proceedings of every other State;" and the act of Congress providing for the mode of authenticating such acts, records, and proceedings, and declaring that, when thus authenticated, "they shall have such faith and credit given to them in every court within the United States as they have by law or usage in the courts of the State from which they are or shall be taken." In the earlier cases, it was supposed that the act gave to all judgments the same effect in other States which they had by law in the State where rendered. But this view was afterwards qualified so as to make the act applicable only when the court rendering the judgment had jurisdiction of the parties and of the subject matter, and not to preclude an inquiry into the jurisdiction of the court in which the judgment was rendered, or the right of the State itself to exercise authority over the person or the subject-matter.

* * *

Since the adoption of the Fourteenth Amendment to the Federal Constitution, the validity of such judgments may be directly questioned, and their enforcement in the State resisted on the ground that proceedings in a court of justice to determine the personal rights and obligations of parties over whom that court has no jurisdiction do not constitute due process of law. Whatever difficulty may be experienced in giving to those terms a definition which will embrace every permissible exertion of power affecting private rights, and exclude such as is forbidden, there can be no doubt of their meaning when applied to judicial proceedings. They then mean a course of legal proceedings according to those rules and principles which have been established in our systems of jurisprudence for the protection and enforcement of private rights. To give such proceedings any validity, there must be a tribunal competent by its constitution—that is, by the law of its creation—to pass upon the subject-matter of the suit; and, if that involves merely a determination of the personal liability of the defendant, he must be brought within its jurisdiction by service of process within the State, or his voluntary appearance.

Except in cases affecting the personal status of the plaintiff, and cases in which that mode of service may be considered to have been assented to in advance, as hereinafter mentioned, the substituted service of process by publication, allowed by the law of Oregon and by similar laws in other States, where actions are brought against non-residents, is effectual only where, in connection with process against the person for commencing the action, property in the State is brought under the control of the court, and subjected to its disposition by process adapted to that purpose, or where the judgment is sought as a means of reaching such property or affecting some interest therein; in other words, where the action is in the nature of a proceeding *in rem.* * * *

It is true that, in a strict sense, a proceeding *in rem* is one taken directly against property, and has for its object the disposition of the property, without reference to the title of individual claimants; but, in a larger and more general sense, the terms are applied to actions between parties, where the direct object is to reach and dispose of property owned by them, or of some interest therein. Such are cases commenced by attachment against the property of debtors, or instituted to partition real estate, foreclose a mortgage, or enforce a lien. So far as they affect property in the State, they are substantially proceedings *in rem* in the broader sense which we have mentioned.

* * *

To prevent any misapplication of the views expressed in this opinion, it is proper to observe that we do not mean to assert, by anything we have said, that a State may not authorize proceedings to determine the *status* of one of its citizens towards a non-resident, which would be binding within the State, though made without service of process or personal notice to the non-resident. The jurisdiction which every State possesses to determine the civil *status* and capacities of all its inhabitants involves authority to prescribe the conditions on which proceedings affecting them may be commenced and carried on within its territory. The State, for example, has absolute right to prescribe the conditions upon which the marriage relation between its own citizens shall be created, and the causes for which it may be dissolved. One of the parties guilty of acts for which, by the law of the State, a dissolution may be granted, may have removed to a State where no dissolution is permitted. The complaining party would, therefore, fail if a divorce were sought in the State of the defendant; and if application could not be made to the tribunals of the complainant's domicile in such case, and proceedings be there instituted without personal service of process or personal notice to the offending party, the injured citizen would be without redress.

Neither do we mean to assert that a State may not require a non-resident entering into a partnership or association within its limits, or making contracts enforceable there, to appoint an agent or representative in the State to receive service of process and notice in legal proceedings instituted with respect to such partnership, association, or contracts, or to designate a place where such service may be made and notice given, and provide, upon their failure, to make such appointment or to designate such place that service may be made upon a public officer designated for that purpose, or in some other prescribed way, and that judgments rendered upon such service may not be binding upon the non-residents both within and without the state. * * * Nor do we doubt that a State, on creating corporations or other institutions for pecuniary or charitable purposes, may provide a mode in which their conduct may be investigated, their obligations enforced, or their charters revoked, which shall require other than personal service upon their officers or members. Parties becoming members of such corporations or institutions would hold their interest subject to the conditions prescribed by law.

In the present case, there is no feature of this kind, and, consequently, no consideration of what would be the effect of such legislation in enforcing the contract of a non-resident can arise. The question here respects only the validity of a money judgment rendered in one State, in an action upon a simple contract against the resident of another, without service of process upon him, or his appearance therein.

[Dissenting opinion of Justice Hunt omitted.]

Notes and Questions

1. As befits an epic case, Pennoyer v. Neff involves some interesting characters, as Professor Perdue has chronicled. See Perdue, Sin, Scandal, and Substantive Due Process: Personal Jurisdiction and *Pennoyer* Reconsidered, 62 Wash.L.Rev. 479 (1987). Marcus Neff was an illiterate settler who came to Oregon from Iowa by wagon train in 1848 and experienced difficulties qualifying for land for settlers under the Oregon Donation Act. In 1862 he consulted Mitchell for legal services, the nature of which is not clear. Mitchell did not sue for payment until three years later, by which time Neff had moved to California. Mitchell himself was born John Hipple and, while a teacher in Pennsylvania, had been forced to marry a 15 year old student he had seduced. In 1860 he changed his name and headed west, leaving his wife behind but taking along $4,000 of client money from his legal practice and his current paramour. He abandoned the paramour in California and moved to Oregon, where he established a successful law practice and married again without divorcing his first wife. In 1872 Mitchell was elected to the U.S. Senate, and after losing his seat in 1879 he was elected again in 1885 despite scandal due to the publication of love letters from a recent adulterous relationship. Sylvester Pennoyer was also a successful politician. Elected Governor of Oregon in 1887, and still smarting from his loss to Neff, he used his inaugural address to decry the Supreme Court's decision against him as an example of federal judicial usurpation of state power.

2. *Terminology:* Justice Field distinguishes *in personam* and *in rem* jurisdiction. In theory, a judgment is *in personam* when it makes the defendant personally liable. As we have seen in Chapter II, such a judgment might declare that the defendant is liable to pay money to the plaintiff (damages), or it might order defendant to begin or cease certain activity (injunction). In either instance, the judgment is "personal" to the defendant.

Jurisdiction *in rem,* in contrast, focuses on property (the *res*) and permits the court to dispose of the property in accordance with the outcome of the litigation. In practice, this distinction often blurs. The most common form of *in personam* judgment, for money damages, may ordinarily be enforced (as was done in this case) against property of the defendant, so that *in personam* judgments often have an impact on property. A judgment *in rem,* meanwhile, is effective only to the extent that it extinguishes the claimed rights of persons in the property involved, so that it has a personal impact on them despite the description. Whatever the shortcomings of the dichotomy, it is central to the jurisdictional approach of *Pennoyer:*

(a) Jurisdiction *in personam:* A court can enter a valid judgment *in personam* only, the Court held, when jurisdiction has been obtained by personal service of process in the state, although it does not matter that the defendant was present in the state only briefly. The *reductio ad absurdum* on this score to date is Grace v. MacArthur, 170 F.Supp. 442 (E.D.Ark.1959), in which defendant, a passenger on a nonstop Braniff Airlines flight from Memphis, Tennessee, to Dallas, Texas, was served while the plane was over Pine Bluff, Arkansas. The court held that this service was sufficient to subject him to Arkansas jurisdiction, although it recognized "that a time may come, and may not be far distant, when commercial aircraft will fly at altitudes so high that it would be unrealistic to consider them as being within the territorial limits of the United States or of any particular State while flying at such altitudes."

This sort of jurisdiction is popularly known as "transient" jurisdiction, because it permits a state to exercise jurisdiction over a defendant even if he was only present in the state for a short period if he was served there. Against the background of *capias ad respondendum,* it may seem eminently reasonable to conclude that service alone is sufficient to support jurisdiction. Nevertheless, most other countries do not authorize transient jurisdiction. *Pennoyer*'s casual acceptance of the sufficiency of transient jurisdiction was forcefully challenged in Ehrenzweig, The Transient Rule of Personal Jurisdiction: The "Power" Myth and Forum Conveniens, 65 Yale L.J. 289 (1956). Professor Ehrenzweig showed that, before *Pennoyer,* personal service had been neither essential nor sufficient to support jurisdiction, which he contended depended on issues of convenience and submission by defendant to the power of the court. *Pennoyer*'s prohibition on process beyond the state, however, undermined this flexible structure and paved the way for cases like Grace v. MacArthur, which involved no elements of either convenience or submission by the defendant to jurisdiction of the court. Is there any persuasive justification for treating personal service, without more, as sufficient for jurisdiction? We return to the current validity of transient jurisdiction in Burnham v. Superior Court, infra p. 809.

(b) Jurisdiction *in rem:* Personal service in the jurisdiction is not necessary, however, for the state to exercise its power over property in the state. The presence of property in a state under traditional practice could conceivably give rise to two distinct forms of jurisdiction: *in rem* and *quasi in rem.* In the case of *in rem* jurisdiction, the physical presence of the property within the state vests the state with jurisdiction to adjudicate the rights of any individual—whether in the state or not—in that property. Though this form of jurisdiction conceivably allows the state to adjudicate the rights of individuals located anywhere in the world, it does so only for rights in that particular property.

In rem jurisdiction, standing alone, conferred no authority to assess damages against an individual or in any way control the individual's personal rights apart from his interest in the property. *In rem* jurisdiction appeared in two forms: "pure" *in rem* and actions "in the nature of rem" (sometimes also inexactly referred to as *quasi in rem*). In "pure" *in rem* actions, the state sought to bind the rights of the entire world in a piece of property within the state's borders. For example, consider an action to quiet title; unless the action could bind the entire world, its goal of preserving the uninhibited alienability of property would be undermined. In an action in the nature of rem, while the state sought to bind merely rights in a particular piece of property, it did so only as to specifically named individuals. Thus, a suit to specifically enforce a contract for the sale of land could be viewed either as an *in personam* action (i.e., to determine and control the defendant's personal rights in the property), or as an action in the nature of rem (i.e., to adjudicate rights in property located within the state). Usually, the plaintiff would characterize the action in one form or the other, depending upon which form of jurisdiction provided the state with authority to adjudicate: If the property was located in the state but the defendant was not subject to service, the state could properly characterize the case as in the nature of rem; if, on the other hand, the property was beyond the state's borders but the defendant was subject to service of process, the state would likely deem the case to be *in personam*.

Although as already noted actions in the nature of rem were also sometimes referred to as *quasi in rem,* it is important not to confuse that form of jurisdiction with the more common category of cases described as *quasi in rem*. In these cases, the action is purely *in personam*; the substance of the case has nothing to do with defendant's property. However, for whatever reason, the state lacks authority to assert *in personam* jurisdiction over the defendant. In such a case, the plaintiff was allowed to assert jurisdiction over the defendant's property within the state by attachment, garnishment, or other process available at the beginning of a suit to allow seizure of property to secure any judgment plaintiff ultimately obtains on the *in personam* claim. For example, *A* from Illinois sues *B* from New York in Illinois state court for damages of $50,000 for breach of a personal services contract. *B* is not subject to *in personam* jurisdiction in Illinois, but does own a piece of property in that state worth $25,000. Though the property is irrelevant to the substance of the case, *A* is able to sue *B* in Illinois for $25,000—the value of the property—by attaching it at the time suit was filed. If successful, *A* is still able to sue *B* in some other jurisdiction for the remaining amount. *B*, in turn, is traditionally allowed to make a "limited appearance" in Illinois: i.e., to appear to defend the suit up to the value of the property, without implicitly consenting to full *in personam* jurisdiction. On the scope of *in rem* and *quasi in rem* jurisdiction, see generally Developments in the Law: State–Court Jurisdiction, 73 Harv. L.Rev. 909, 948–66 (1960). Which of these forms of jurisdiction was employed in *Pennoyer?*

As we shall see, *quasi in rem* jurisdiction generated its own *reductio ad absurdum:* In Seider v. Roth, 17 N.Y.2d 111, 269 N.Y.S.2d 99, 216 N.E.2d

312 (1966), the court held that the obligation of an insurer to defend and indemnify the nonresident defendant in an auto accident case is property of the insured that is present in New York if the insurance company does business there, and that the presence of such "property" justifies the exercise of jurisdiction in a suit against the defendant no matter where the accident occurred or where the defendant lives. We shall return to this problem in Rush v. Savchuk, infra p. 803 n. 1.

3. What is the source of the rules on which the Court relies in *Pennoyer?* As Justice Field foresees, the Due Process Clause of the 14th Amendment would thereafter permit attacks on jurisdiction as a violation of due process, and in fact due process is the rubric under which the Court has since handled jurisdiction issues. But that amendment did not become effective until 1868, after Mitchell's judgment was entered. Instead, the Court in *Pennoyer* relied on principles of "public law" derived from the international sphere. How relevant are these concepts about the relations of independent nations to the relations of the states of the United States? To the degree they are relevant, what do they have to do with due process, which normally protects the individual against overreaching by the government? For an argument that the due process inquiry should be limited to unfair inconvenience to defendant, see Redish, Due Process, Federalism, and Personal Jurisdiction: A Theoretical Evaluation, 75 Nw.U.L.Rev. 1112 (1981); see also Conison, What Does Due Process Have to Do With Jurisdiction?, 46 Rutgers L. Rev. 1071 (1994) (surveying gradual constitutionalization of jurisdictional limitations).

4. If the proper focus is on the relative rights of states as sovereigns, are limitations on jurisdiction designed to protect defendants or states? If it is the latter, why should these limitations evaporate once the defendant appears in the lawsuit (or flies over the state in an airplane)?

5. Whatever their source, how well do the postulates upon which the *Pennoyer* Court relies work as a description of the American judicial system? Justice Field asserts confidently that every state has "exclusive jurisdiction" of persons and property within it and, as a corollary, that no state may exercise "direct" jurisdiction over persons or property outside it. But consider:

(a) If Mitchell had managed to serve Neff in Oregon, couldn't he insist that California give the resulting judgment full faith and credit? If so, he could enforce it against Neff's property in California. Could California, by asserting its "exclusive" jurisdiction over property in California, refuse to enforce the judgment? See U.S. Const., Art. IV § 1.

(b) If Neff were served with process while temporarily in Oregon, would he be subject to Oregon's "exclusive" jurisdiction? In Milliken v. Meyer, 311 U.S. 457, 61 S.Ct. 339, 85 L.Ed. 278 (1940), the Court held that a state may exercise jurisdiction over one of its citizens even while the citizen is out of the state.

(c) If Mitchell had attached Neff's Oregon property before judgment was entered by the Oregon court, it appears that Justice Field would have been satisfied. But a piece of property worth $15,000 was a very significant interest in 1866. How realistic is it to say that Oregon is only exercising "indirect" jurisdiction over Neff when it takes that property away from him?

For a careful dissection of *Pennoyer*'s premises, see Hazard, A General Theory of State–Court Jurisdiction, 1965 S.Ct.Rev. 241, 265–68.

6.   Justice Field himself carefully carves out two exceptions. First, he emphasizes that a state retains the right to determine the status of its citizens, a doctrine that normally is important in family law litigation. One theoretical explanation for this exception is that marital status is somehow a res, so that the jurisdiction is *in rem*. True, a divorce decree is not *in personam* in that it neither orders the defendant to pay money nor directs him to do or cease doing anything. But it is hard to imagine a judicial action that has a more personal effect on the defendant. Nevertheless, the courts have pursued the *in rem* reasoning to create the "divisible divorce"—the divorce plaintiff's state has jurisdiction to decree the divorce (*in rem*) but not to decide questions of alimony or child support obligations involving an absent defendant (*in personam*). See, e.g., Estin v. Estin, 334 U.S. 541, 68 S.Ct. 1213, 92 L.Ed. 1561 (1948); Wasserman, Divorce and Domicile: Time to Sever the Knot, 39 Will. & Mary L. Rev. 1 (1997) (tracing the difficulties caused by tying jurisdiction to domicile and proposing solving these problems by statutory action).

The other exception is consent. We treat issues raised by private consent to jurisdiction infra at p. 833. The consent envisioned by the *Pennoyer* Court turned on a state's right to refuse outsiders access to the state, a refusal it could withdraw in return for their submission to its jurisdiction. Because this idea illustrates the way the Court and the states tried to cope with the difficulties caused by the *Pennoyer* construct, we treat it in some detail.

FRAUDULENT INDUCEMENT INTO THE FORUM

It should be apparent that *Pennoyer*'s general requirement of service within the forum was often an obstacle to the exercise of jurisdiction. But the parallel idea that service within the forum was always sufficient for jurisdiction led to troubling results when plaintiff enticed defendant into the state to effect service. In reaction, the courts developed the doctrine of fraudulent inducement, which would invalidate service where plaintiff has lured defendant into the jurisdiction with falsehoods. See, e.g., Wyman v. Newhouse, 93 F.2d 313 (2d Cir.1937) (in suit growing out of adulterous affair between plaintiff and defendant, plaintiff's repeated pleas that defendant come to visit her one last time invalidated service on defendant as he alighted from airplane). This doctrine limits the ability of a plaintiff to invoke the power of a distant state through subterfuge.

The fraudulent inducement doctrine is most difficult to apply to situations where defendant has come into the jurisdiction to negotiate a resolution of an admitted dispute, for in such cases there is no doubt that a dispute exists between the parties and that it may result in litigation. Courts nevertheless have applied the doctrine. For example, in E/M Lubricants, Inc. v. Microfral, S.A.R.L., 91 F.R.D. 235 (N.D.Ill.1981), plaintiff licensed defendant, a French corporation, to use and market plaintiff's patented processes for the treatment of metals. When a dispute arose about defendant's obligation to make certain minimum royalty payments, there was much correspondence attempting to resolve the dispute. Eventually defendant's president suggested that since he was planning a visit to the United States on other business he could meet with plaintiff's president to discuss the dispute, and plaintiff's president agreed to meet in Chicago. On the night before the scheduled meeting, however, defendant's president was served with summons and complaint at his hotel. Defendant moved to dismiss, to which plaintiff responded that the meeting had been defendant's idea and that, in any event, it had not decided to sue until after the meeting was arranged, so there had been no fraud.

The court granted the motion to dismiss. It held the fact that defendant had proposed the meeting irrelevant because its president came to Illinois only to discuss settlement. Compare Schwarz v. Artcraft Silk Hosiery Mills, 110 F.2d 465 (2d Cir.1940) (service in New York at outset of negotiations valid because defendant had come to New York to visit his summer home on Long Island). Accepting plaintiff's claim that it had not decided to sue until the meeting was arranged, the court decided that plaintiff's failure to advise defendant of its change of heart then was deceitful because the earlier discussions gave rise to a duty to speak. The court in *Microfral* found this result compelled by policy as well:

> First and most significantly, it is in the interest of justice to promote the speedy and amicable resolution of disputes as an alternative to legal battle. Conduct such as that engaged in by plaintiff in this case does not further that interest. Out-of-state persons in the shoes of [defendant] will simply forgo the opportunity to negotiate a settlement rather than risk subjecting themselves to service in an unfavorable jurisdiction. It is significant that the interest in informal dispute resolution is compromised whether the plaintiff induces reliance through misrepresentation of his intention from the outset or, as in the instant case, through failure to disclose a subsequent change of heart.

> Second, there are enforcement problems if plaintiffs are permitted to escape the reach of the fraudulent enticement doctrine merely by asserting that they did not form the intent to sue until after they had agreed to negotiate. It is extremely easy for a plaintiff to make such an assertion and extremely difficult to disprove it.

But see Sawyer v. LaFlamme, 185 A.2d 466 (Vt.1962), where the court upheld service in the office of plaintiff's lawyer after negotiations had broken down, reasoning that the negotiations were in good faith and there had accordingly been no fraud. If plaintiff in *Microfral* had waited until after negotiations were completed (unsuccessfully) would that have made a difference?

———

HARRIS v. BALK, 198 U.S. 215, 25 S.Ct. 625, 49 L.Ed. 1023 (1905):

JUSTICE PECKHAM delivered the opinion of the Court:

[While Harris, a resident of North Carolina, was in Maryland on a business trip in 1896, he was served with a writ of garnishment issued by a Maryland court at the request of one Epstein, a Maryland resident. Epstein had a claim for over $300 against another North Carolinian named Balk, and the writ garnished a $180 debt that Harris owed Balk. Harris did not contest the Maryland proceedings and paid the $180 to an attorney for Epstein. Upon his return to North Carolina, barely a week after being garnished in Maryland, Harris was sued by Balk in North Carolina on the $180 debt. Harris defended on the ground that his obligation was extinguished by payment to Epstein. Balk argued, however, that Maryland never obtained jurisdiction because Harris was not a resident of Maryland and Balk had no property there, the situs of the debt being North Carolina, where the loan was made. The North Carolina courts refused to accord the Maryland judgment full faith and credit and ordered Harris to pay $180 to Balk. The Supreme Court held that North Carolina had to enforce the Maryland judgment.]

Attachment is the creature of the local law; that is, unless there is a law of the state providing for and permitting the attachment, it cannot be levied there. If there be a law of the state providing for the attachment of the debt, then, if the garnishee be found in that state, and process be personally served upon him therein, we think the court thereby acquires jurisdiction over him, and can garnish the debt due from him to the debtor of the plaintiff, and condemn it, provided the garnishee could himself be sued by his creditor in that state. We do not see how the question of jurisdiction vel non can properly be made to depend upon the so-called original situs of the debt, or upon the character of the stay of the garnishee, whether temporary or permanent, in the state where the attachment is issued. Power over the person of the garnishee confers jurisdiction on the courts of the state where the writ issues. If, while temporarily there, his creditor might sue him there and recover the debt, then he is liable to process of garnishment, no matter where the situs of the debt was originally. We do not see the materiality of the expression "situs of the debt," when used in connection with attachment proceedings. If by situs is meant the place of the creation of the debt, that fact is immaterial. If it be meant that the obligation to pay the debt can only be enforced at the situs thus fixed, we think it plainly untrue. The obligation of the debtor to pay his debt clings to and accompanies him wherever he goes. He is as much bound to pay his debt in a foreign state when therein sued upon his obligation by his creditor, as he was in the state where the debt was contracted. We speak of ordinary debts, such as the one in this case. It would be no defense to such suit for the debtor to plead that he was only in the foreign state casually or temporarily. His obligation to pay would be the same whether he was there in that way or with an intention to remain. It is nothing but the obligation to pay which is garnished or attached.

This obligation can be enforced by the courts of the foreign state after personal service of process therein, just as well as by the courts of the domicil of the debtor. If the debtor leaves the foreign state without appearing, a judgment by default may be entered, upon which execution may issue, or the judgment may be sued upon in any other state where the debtor might be found. In such a case the situs is unimportant. It is not a question of possession in the foreign state, for possession cannot be taken of a debt or of the obligation to pay it, as tangible property might be taken possession of. Notice to the debtor (garnishee) and the commencement of the suit, and notice not to pay to his creditor, is all that can be given, whether the garnishee be a mere casual and temporary comer, or a resident of the state where the attachment is laid. His obligation to pay his creditor is thereby arrested, and a lien created upon the debt itself. We can see no reason why the attachment could not be thus laid, provided the creditor of the garnishee could himself sue in that state, and its laws permitted the attachment.

There can be no doubt that Balk, as a citizen of the state of North Carolina, had the right to sue Harris in Maryland to recover the debt which Harris owed him. Being a citizen of North Carolina, he was entitled to all the privileges and immunities of citizens of the several states, one of which is the right to institute actions in the courts of another state.

* * *

It seems to us, therefore, that the judgment against Harris in Maryland, condemning the $180 which he owed to Balk, was a valid judgment, because the court had jurisdiction over the garnishee by personal service of process within the state of Maryland.

It ought to be and it is the object of courts to prevent the payment of any debt twice over. Thus, if Harris, owing a debt to Balk, paid it under a valid judgment against him, to Epstein, he certainly ought not to be compelled to pay it a second time, but should have the right to plead his payment under the Maryland judgment. It is objected, however, that the payment by Harris to Epstein was not under legal compulsion. Harris in truth owed the debt to Balk, which was attached by Epstein. He had, therefore, as we have seen, no defense to set up against the attachment of the debt. Jurisdiction over him personally had been obtained by the Maryland court. As he was absolutely without defense, there was no reason why he should not consent to a judgment impounding the debt, which judgment the plaintiff was legally entitled to, and which he could not prevent. There was no merely voluntary payment within the meaning of that phrase as applicable here.

But most rights may be lost by negligence, and if the garnishee were guilty of negligence in the attachment proceeding, to the damage of Balk, he ought not to be permitted to set up the judgment as a defense. Thus it is recognized as the duty of the garnishee to give notice to his own creditor, if he would protect himself, so that the creditor may have the opportunity to defend himself against the claim of the person suing out the attachment. * * * While the want of notification by the garnishee to his own creditor may have no effect upon the validity of the judgment against the garnishee (the proper publication being made by the plaintiff), we think it has and ought to have an effect upon the right of the garnishee to avail himself of the prior judgment and his payment thereunder. This notification by the garnishee is for the purpose of making sure that his creditor shall have an opportunity to defend the claim made against him in the attachment suit. Fair dealing requires this at the hands of the garnishee. In this case, while neither the defendant nor the garnishee appeared, the court, while condemning the credits attached, could not, by the terms of the Maryland statute, issue the writ of execution unless the plaintiff gave bond or sufficient security before the court awarding the execution, to make restitution of the money paid if the defendant should, at any time within a year and a day, appear in the action and show that the plaintiff's claim, or some part thereof, was not due to the plaintiff. The defendant in error, Balk, had notice of this attachment, certainly within a few days after the issuing thereof and the entry of judgment thereon, because he sued the plaintiff in error to recover his debt within a few days after his [Harris'] return to North Carolina, in which suit the judgment in Maryland was set up by Harris as a plea in bar to Balk's claim. Balk, therefore, had an opportunity for a year and a day after the entry of the judgment to litigate the question of his liability in the Maryland court, and to show that he did not owe the debt, or some part of it, as was claimed by Epstein. He, however, took no proceedings to that end, so far as the record shows, and the reason may be supposed to be that he could not successfully defend the claim, because he admitted in this case that he did, at the time of the attachment proceeding, owe Epstein some $344.

Notes and Questions

1. If the reasoning of this case seems convoluted, keep in mind that when Epstein filed his suit such stratagems were necessary to solve the jurisdictional problems caused by *Pennoyer*. Would the *Pennoyer* Court have looked favorably on this exercise of jurisdiction?

2. From the perspective of Balk, and consistent with *Pennoyer*'s outlook, Maryland's jurisdiction is *quasi-in-rem*. What is it from the perspective of Harris? Suppose that Maryland garnishment procedures resembled *capias ad respondendum* (supra p. 690) and required the sheriff to imprison the garnishee until he paid the money into court. If Maryland lacks jurisdiction, what does Harris do to extricate himself and avoid double liability?

3. Aside from providing a pretext to get around *Pennoyer, in rem* jurisdiction serves other functions. As we have seen in Chapter II, pre-judgment attachment can secure the plaintiff's right ultimately to recover and post-judgment garnishment can provide a means for enforcing judgments once entered. Beyond that, jurisdiction in rem can often serve very important interests of the state. The Court recognized these interests in Arndt v. Griggs, 134 U.S. 316, 10 S.Ct. 557, 33 L.Ed. 918 (1890):

If a state has no power to bring a non-resident into its courts for any purposes by publication, it is impotent to perfect the titles of real estate within its limits held by its own citizens; and a cloud cast upon such title by a claim by a non-resident will remain for all time a cloud, unless such non-resident shall voluntarily come into its courts for the purpose of having it adjudicated. But no such imperfections attend the sovereignty of the state. * * * The well-being of every community requires that the title to real estate therein shall be secure, and that there be convenient and certain methods of determining any unsettled questions respecting it. The duty of accomplishing this is local in its nature.

Do any of these justifications for exercise of *in rem* jurisdiction apply in Harris v. Balk?

4. The Court reasons that the debt can be attached in Maryland while Harris is there because Balk could then sue him there to collect on the debt. Does Balk's ability to sue Harris in Maryland if he serves him there have anything to do with the situs of the debt? Is there any reason to say that intangible property has a situs for purposes of exercise of *quasi-in-rem* jurisdiction?

5. Was notice to Balk critical to the Maryland court's jurisdiction? If so, shouldn't it be Epstein's responsibility to provide notice?

6. What if Balk denies that he owes money to Epstein? Can he contest the Maryland proceedings without consenting to jurisdiction there over Epstein's entire claim? See supra p. 699 for a discussion of limited appearances.

7. Note that the Court cautions that "[w]e speak of ordinary debts, such as the one in this case." Under substantive law, such as that relating to negotiable instruments, enforcement of an obligation often entails possession of a document evidencing the obligation. Where that is true, the debt would not follow the debtor, and possession of the document would be a prerequisite to exercise of jurisdiction over the obligation.

———

HESS v. PAWLOSKI, 274 U.S. 352, 47 S.Ct. 632, 71 L.Ed. 1091 (1927):

JUSTICE BUTLER delivered the Opinion of the Court.

[Plaintiff sued defendant, a Pennsylvania resident, in Massachusetts for personal injuries sustained in an auto accident in Massachusetts. Defendant objected to jurisdiction, but his objection was rejected and judgment was entered against him. Jurisdiction was based on a Massachusetts statute providing that the acceptance by a nonresident of the "privilege" of operating a motor vehicle in that state "shall be deemed equivalent to an appointment by such nonresident of the registrar or his successor in office, to be his true and lawful attorney upon whom may be served all lawful processes in any action or proceeding against him, growing out of any accident or collision in which said nonresident may be involved while operating a motor vehicle [in Massachusetts]." Service on the registrar would then be effective to subject defendant to Massachusetts jurisdiction provided plaintiff also "forthwith" sent notice of the service and a copy of the process to defendant by registered mail and obtained a signed return receipt. After plaintiff obtained jurisdiction in this manner, defendant sought Supreme Court review on the ground that he was not subject to Massachusetts jurisdiction. The Supreme Court upheld jurisdiction.]

The process of a court of one State cannot run into another and summon a party there domiciled to respond to proceedings against him. Notice sent outside the state to a nonresident is unavailing to give jurisdiction in an action against him personally for money recovery. Pennoyer v. Neff, 95 U.S. 714, 24 L.Ed. 565. There must be actual service within the State of notice upon him or upon some one authorized to accept service for him. A personal judgment rendered against a nonresident, who has neither been served with process nor appeared in the suit, is without validity. The mere transaction of business in a State by nonresident natural persons does not imply consent to be bound by the process of its courts. Flexner v. Farson, 248 U.S. 289, 39 S.Ct. 97, 63 L.Ed. 250. The power of a State to exclude foreign corporations, although not absolute, but qualified, is the ground on which such an implication is supported as to them. Pennsylvania Fire Insurance Co. v. Gold Issue Mining Co., 243 U.S. 93, 96, 37 S.Ct. 344, 61 L.Ed. 610. But a State may not withhold from nonresident individuals the right of doing business therein. The privileges and immunities clause of the Constitution, § 2, Art. IV, safeguards to the citizens of one State the right "to pass through, or to reside in any other state for purposes of trade, agriculture, professional pursuits, or otherwise." And it prohibits state legislation discriminating against citizens of other states.

Motor vehicles are dangerous machines; and, even when skillfully and carefully operated, their use is attended by serious dangers to persons and property. In the public interest the State may make and enforce regulations reasonably calculated to promote care on the part of all, residents and nonresidents alike, who use its highways. The measure in question operates to require a nonresident to answer for his conduct in the State where arise causes of action alleged against him, as well as to provide for a claimant a convenient method by which he may sue to enforce his rights. Under the statute the implied consent is limited to proceedings growing out of accidents or collisions on a highway in which the nonresident may be involved. It is required that he shall actually receive and receipt for notice of the service and a copy of the process. And it contemplates such continuances as may be found necessary to give reasonable time and opportunity for defense. It makes no hostile discrimination against nonresidents, but tends to put them on the same footing as residents. Literal and precise equality in respect of this matter is not attainable; it is not required. The State's power to regulate the use of its highways extends to their use by nonresidents as well as by residents. And, in advance of the operation of a motor vehicle on its highway by a nonresident, the State may require him to appoint one of its officials as his agent on whom process may be served in proceedings growing out of such use. Kane v. New Jersey, 242 U.S. 160, 167, 37 S.Ct. 30, 61 L.Ed. 222. That case recognized power of the State to exclude a nonresident until the formal appointment is made. And, having the power so to exclude, the State may declare that the use of the highway by the nonresident is the equivalent of the appointment of the registrar as agent on whom process may be served. The difference between the formal and implied appointment is not substantial, so far as concerns the application of the due process clause of the Fourteenth Amendment.

Notes and Questions

1. Is the Court's emphasis on the automobile's dangerousness a non-sequitur in light of its emphasis on defendant's implied consent as the basis for finding jurisdiction? Cf. Henry L. Doherty & Co. v. Goodman, 294 U.S. 623, 55 S.Ct. 553, 79 L.Ed. 1097 (1935), where the Supreme Court, relying in part on *Hess*, upheld Iowa's authority to assert jurisdiction over a nonresident individual by means of service of process on the individual's agent within the state. Defendant, though never personally within the state, had established an office in the state for dealing in securities. The Court noted that "Iowa treats the business of dealing in corporate securities as exceptional and subjects it to special regulation." Should that factor be relevant in determining the applicability of *Hess*'s implied consent analysis?

2. Kane v. New Jersey, 242 U.S. 160, 37 S.Ct. 30, 61 L.Ed. 222 (1916), upheld a state requirement that nonresidents who used its highways register, pay a fee, and appoint an agent for service of process. As in *Hess*, the Court emphasized the dangerousness of the car in concluding that the requirement was a reasonable regulation of the use of the highways. To what extent is that sort of state interest in regulating the activity involved essential to its right to condition permission to engage in the activity on consent to jurisdiction? Could Massachusetts exclude people on bicycles or on foot? Cf. Edwards v. California, 314 U.S. 160, 62 S.Ct. 164, 86 L.Ed. 119 (1941) (state statute excluding indigents violates commerce clause).

3. Did Justice Field have implied consent in mind in *Pennoyer?* Consider the analysis of Justice Frankfurter in Olberding v. Illinois Central Ry. Co., 346 U.S. 338, 74 S.Ct. 83, 98 L.Ed. 39 (1953), rejecting a similar argument that defendant had waived his right to object on venue grounds (statutory limitations on the location of suit, see infra p. 840) by driving his truck in the state:

> The defendant may protest to high heaven his unwillingness to be sued and it avails him not. The liability rests on the inroad which the automobile has made on the decision of Pennoyer v. Neff, 95 U.S. 714, as it has on so many aspects of our social scene. The potentialities of damage by a motorist, in a population as mobile as ours, are such that those whom he injures must have opportunities of redress against him provided only that he is afforded an opportunity to defend himself. We have held that this is a fair rule of law as between a resident injured party (for whose protection these statutes are primarily intended) and a non-resident motorist, and that the requirements of due process are therefore met. Hess v. Pawloski, 274 U.S. 352. But to conclude from this holding that the motorist, who never consented to anything and whose

consent is altogether immaterial, has actually agreed to be sued and has thus waived his federal venue rights is surely to move in the world of Alice in Wonderland.

4.   The Massachusetts statute limited the implied consent to claims arising out of driving in the state. Was that limitation constitutionally required? In Pennsylvania Fire Ins. Co. v. Gold Issue Mining & Milling Co., 243 U.S. 93, 37 S.Ct. 344, 61 L.Ed. 610 (1917), the Court held that a state could constitutionally require that foreign corporations wishing to be authorized to do business consent to suit in all actions, of whatever nature, not just those arising out of the business done in the state. Compare Bendix Autolite Corp. v. Midwesco Enterprises, Inc., 486 U.S. 888, 108 S.Ct. 2218, 100 L.Ed.2d 896 (1988) (state may not deny protection of statute of limitations to foreign corporation that refuses to consent to jurisdiction over unrelated suits); Note, Registration Statutes, Personal Jurisdiction, and the Problem of Predictability, 103 Colum.L.Rev. 1163 (2003) (arguing that due process precludes general jurisdiction based on corporate registration statutes). Could the state infer such a consent from corporations that did not register but did engage in business? In *Gold Issue,* the Court distinguished cases in which consent was implied, not actual. If the state could not infer such consent, would that not reward those corporations who evaded their obligation to register?

5.   The consent theory can founder where the state does not have the power to exclude the defendant. Why? In Flexner v. Farson, 248 U.S. 289, 39 S.Ct. 97, 63 L.Ed. 250 (1919), the court refused to allow the consent theory to be applied to a partnership because, under the privileges and immunities clause of the Constitution, the individual partners had the right (not shared by corporations) to engage in business in the state. The Court watered down this holding in Henry L. Doherty & Co. v. Goodman, 294 U.S. 623, 55 S.Ct. 553, 79 L.Ed. 1097 (1935), described in note 1 above.

JURISDICTION OVER CORPORATE DEFENDANTS

Corporations presented special difficulties for the *Pennoyer* analysis. Like the automobile, they came to have greater and greater importance in society in the decades after *Pennoyer* was decided. Because they were fictional entities, however, it was difficult to say that they could be found in any particular place for purposes of service. Initially, it was assumed that a corporation could be sued in the state in which it was incorporated, but as corporations began to grow and engage in interstate activities that hardly seemed sufficient. Two types of solutions were found. First, states enacted comprehensive requirements that all corporations engaging in business within their borders register and appoint agents for service of process. Failing that, many of these statutes provided that corporations which engaged in business but did not register would be deemed impliedly to have consented to service on a state official. This was permissible because corporations, unlike individuals, have been held to have no rights under the privileges and immunities clause.

Second, there developed a doctrine of corporate "presence"—a corporation was present wherever it engaged in a sufficient amount of activities, and it could therefore be served like a natural person who was present. Unhappily, this approach used the same label and looked to the same facts as the implied consent theory—"doing business." It is important to note that under the "presence" analysis, whether plaintiff's claim was related to defendant's activities within the state was logically irrelevant. This fact derived from the analogy of the corporate "presence" doctrine to an individual's physical presence within a state as a basis for *in personam* jurisdiction: Under the "transient" principle, an individual physically present within a state could be subjected to jurisdiction for any suit; similarly, if a corporation were deemed "present," no relationship between the suit and the corporation's in-state activity need be established. Thus, the analysis of "doing business" turned exclusively on an examination of purely quantitative factors, primarily the total amount and continuity of the corporation's business activities in the state. "Continuous and substantial" commercial activity was necessary to constitute presence. See, e.g., the opinion of Judge Cardozo in Tauza v. Susquehanna Coal Company, 115 N.E. 915 (N.Y.1917).

Given these difficulties in adapting *Pennoyer* to suits against corporations, it is not surprising that the Court broke away from *Pennoyer* in a suit against a corporation.

B. THE SHIFT TO MINIMUM CONTACTS

INTERNATIONAL SHOE CO. v. WASHINGTON

Supreme Court of the United States, 1945.
326 U.S. 310, 66 S.Ct. 154, 90 L.Ed. 95.

CHIEF JUSTICE STONE delivered the opinion of the Court.

The questions for decision are (1) whether, within the limitations of the due process clause of the Fourteenth Amendment, appellant, a Delaware corporation, has by its activities in the State of Washington rendered itself amenable to proceedings in the courts of that state to recover unpaid contributions to the state unemployment compensation fund exacted by state statutes, Washington Unemployment Compensation Act, Washington Revised Statutes, § 9998—103a through § 9998—123a, 1941 Supp., and (2) whether the state can exact those contributions consistently with the due process clause of the Fourteenth Amendment.

The statutes in question set up a comprehensive scheme of unemployment compensation, the costs of which are defrayed by contributions required to be made by employers to a state unemployment compensation fund. The contributions are a specified percentage of the wages payable annually by each employer for his employees' services in the state. The assessment and collection of the contributions and the fund are administered by respondents. Section 14(c) of the Act (Wash.Rev. Stat. 1941 Supp., § 9998—114c) authorizes respondent Commissioner to issue an order and notice of assessment of delinquent contributions upon prescribed personal service of the notice upon the employer if found within the state, or, if not so found, by mailing the notice to the employer by registered mail at his last known address. That section also authorizes the Commissioner to collect the assessment by distraint if it is not paid within ten days after service of the notice. By §§ 14e and 6b the order of assessment may be administratively reviewed by an appeal tribunal within the office of unemployment upon petition of the employer, and this determination is by § 6(i) made subject to judicial review on questions of law by the state Superior Court, with further right of appeal in the state Supreme Court as in other civil cases.

appeal

In this case notice of assessment for the years in question was personally served upon a sales solicitor employed by appellant in the State of Washington, and a copy of the notice was mailed by registered mail to appellant at its address in St. Louis, Missouri. Appellant appeared specially before the office of unemployment and moved to set aside the order and notice of assessment on the ground that the service upon appellant's salesman was not proper service upon appellant; that appellant was not a corporation of the State of Washington and was not doing business within the state; that it had no agent within the state upon whom service could be made; and that appellant is not an employer and does not furnish employment within the meaning of the statute.

service in Wash personall

St. Louis registered

why appeal

The motion was heard on evidence and a stipulation of facts by the appeal tribunal which denied the motion and ruled that respondent Commissioner was entitled to recover the unpaid contributions. That action was affirmed by the Commissioner; both the Superior Court and the Supreme Court affirmed. Appellant in each of these courts assailed the statute as applied, as a violation of the due process clause of the Fourteenth Amendment, and as imposing a constitutionally prohibited burden on interstate commerce. The cause comes here on appeal, appellant assigning as error that the challenged statutes as applied infringe the due process clause of the Fourteenth Amendment and the commerce clause.

Statute violate due process : Commerce claus

The facts as found by the appeal tribunal and accepted by the state Superior Court and Supreme Court, are not in dispute. Appellant is a Delaware corporation, having its principal place of business in St. Louis, Missouri, and is engaged in the manufacture and sale of shoes and other footwear. It maintains places of business in several states, other than Washington, at which its manufacturing is carried on and from which its merchandise is distributed interstate through several sales units or branches located outside the State of Washington.

Appellant has no office in Washington and makes no contracts either for sale or purchase of merchandise there. It maintains no stock of merchandise in that state and makes there no deliveries of goods in intrastate commerce. During the years from 1937 to 1940, now in question, appellant employed eleven to thirteen salesmen under direct supervision and control of sales managers located in St. Louis. These salesmen resided in Washington; their principal activities were confined to that state; and they were compensated by commissions based upon the amount of their sales. The commissions for each year totaled more than $31,000. Appellant supplies its salesmen with a line of samples, each consisting of one shoe of a pair, which they display to prospective purchasers. On occasion they rent permanent sample rooms, for exhibiting samples, in business buildings, or rent rooms in hotels or business buildings temporarily for that purpose. The cost of such rentals is reimbursed by appellant.

The authority of the salesmen is limited to exhibiting their samples and soliciting orders from prospective buyers, at prices and on terms fixed by appellant. The salesmen transmit the orders to appellant's office in St. Louis for acceptance or rejection, and when accepted the merchandise for filling the orders is shipped f.o.b. from points outside Washington to the purchasers within the state. All the merchandise shipped into Washington is invoiced at the place of shipment from which collections are made. No salesman has authority to enter into contracts or to make collections.

The Supreme Court of Washington was of opinion that the regular and systematic solicitation of orders in the state by appellant's salesmen, resulting in a continuous flow of appellant's product into the state, was sufficient to constitute doing business in the state so as to make appellant amenable to suit in its courts. But it was also of opinion that there were sufficient additional activities shown to bring the case within the rule frequently stated, that solicitation within a state by the agents of a foreign corporation plus some additional activities there are sufficient to render the corporation amenable to suit brought in the courts of the state to enforce an obligation arising out of its activities there. The court found such additional activities in the salesmen's display of samples sometimes in permanent display rooms, and the salesmen's residence within the state, continued over a period of years, all resulting in a substantial volume of merchandise regularly shipped by appellant to purchasers within the state. The court also held that the statute as applied did not invade the constitutional power of Congress to regulate interstate commerce and did not impose a prohibited burden on such commerce. Appellant's argument, renewed here, that the statute imposes an unconstitutional burden on interstate commerce need not detain us.

* * *

Appellant also insists that its activities within the state were not sufficient to manifest its "presence" there and that in its absence the state courts were without jurisdiction, that consequently it was a denial of due process for the state to subject appellant to suit. It refers to those cases in which it was said that the mere solicitation of orders for the purchase of goods within a state, to be accepted without the state and filled by shipment of the purchased goods interstate, does not render the corporation seller amenable to suit within the state. And appellant further argues that since it was not present within the state, it is a denial of due process to subject it to taxation or other money exaction. It thus denies the power of the state to lay the tax or to subject appellant to a suit for its collection.

Pennoyer v. Neff

Historically the jurisdiction of courts to render judgment in personam is grounded on their de facto power over the defendant's person. Hence his presence within the territorial jurisdiction of court was prerequisite to its rendition of a judgment personally binding him. Pennoyer v. Neff, 95 U.S. 714, 733, 24 L.Ed. 565. But now that the capias ad respondendum has given way to personal service of summons or other form of notice, due process requires only that in order to subject a defendant to a judgment in personam, if he be not present within the territory of the forum, he have certain minimum contacts with it such that the maintenance of the suit does not offend "traditional notions of fair play and substantial justice." Milliken v. Meyer, 311 U.S. 457, 463, 61 S.Ct. 339, 343, 85 L.Ed. 278.

Since the corporate personality is a fiction, although a fiction intended to be acted upon as though it were a fact, it is clear that unlike an individual its "presence" without, as well as within, the state of its origin can be manifested only by activities carried on in its behalf by those who are authorized to act for it. To say that the corporation is so far "present" there as to satisfy due process requirements, for purposes of taxation or the maintenance of suits against it in the courts of the state, is to beg the question to be decided. For the terms "present" or "presence" are used merely to symbolize those activities of the corporation's agent within the state which courts will deem to be sufficient to satisfy the demands of due process. Those demands may be met by such contacts of the corporation with the state of the forum as make it reasonable, in the context of our federal system of government, to require the corporation to defend the particular suit which is brought there. An "estimate of the inconveniences" which would result to the corporation from a trial away from its "home" or principal place of business is relevant in this connection.

"Presence" in the state in this sense has never been doubted when the activities of the corporation there have not only been continuous and systematic, but also give rise to the liabilities sued on, even though no consent to be sued or authorization to an agent to accept service of process has been given. Conversely it has been generally recognized that the casual presence of the corporate agent or even his conduct of single or isolated items of activities in a state in the corporation's behalf are not enough to subject it to suit on causes of action unconnected with the activities there. To require the corporation in such circumstances to defend the suit away from its home or other jurisdiction where it carries on more substantial activities has been thought to lay too great and unreasonable a burden on the corporation to comport with due process.

While it has been held in cases on which appellant relies that continuous activity of some sort within a state is not enough to support the demand that the corporation be amenable to suits unrelated to that activity, there have been instances in which the continuous corporate operations within a state were thought so substantial and of such a nature as to justify suit against it on causes of action arising from dealings entirely distinct from those activities.

Finally, although the commission of some single or occasional acts of the corporate agent in a state sufficient to impose an obligation or liability on the corporation has not been thought to confer upon the state authority to enforce it, Rosenberg Bros. & Co. v. Curtis Brown Co., 260 U.S. 516, 43 S.Ct. 170, 67 L.Ed. 372, other such acts, because of their nature and quality and the circumstances of their commission, may be deemed sufficient to render the corporation liable to suit. Cf. Kane v. New Jersey, 242 U.S. 160, 37 S.Ct. 30, 61 L.Ed. 222; Hess v. Pawloski, [274 U.S. 352]. True, some of the decisions holding the corporation amenable to suit have been supported by resort to the legal fiction that it has given its consent to service and suit, consent being implied from its presence in the state through the acts of its authorized agents. But more realistically it may be said that those authorized acts were of such a nature as to justify the fiction.

It is evident that the criteria by which we mark the boundary line between those activities which justify the subjection of a corporation to suit, and those which do not, cannot be simply mechanical or quantitative. The test is not merely, as has sometimes been suggested, whether the activity, which the corporation has seen fit to procure through its agents in another state, is a little more or a little less. Whether due process is satisfied must depend rather upon the quality and nature of the activity in relation to the fair and orderly administration of the laws which it was the purpose of the due process clause to insure. That clause does not contemplate that a state may make binding a judgment in personam against an individual or corporate defendant with which the state has no contacts, ties, or relations. Cf. Pennoyer v. Neff, supra.

But to the extent that a corporation exercises the privilege of conducting activities within a state, it enjoys the benefits and protection of the laws of that state. The exercise of that privilege may give rise to obligations; and, so far as those obligations arise out of or are connected with the activities within the state, a procedure which requires the corporation to respond to a suit brought to enforce them can, in most instances, hardly be said to be undue.

Applying these standards, the activities carried on in behalf of appellant in the State of Washington were neither irregular nor casual. They were systematic and continuous throughout the years in question. They resulted in a large volume of interstate business, in the course of which appellant received the benefits and protection of the laws of the state, including the right to resort to the courts for the enforcement of its rights. The obligation which is here sued upon arose out of those very activities. It is evident that these operations establish sufficient contacts or ties with the state of the forum to make it reasonable and just according to our traditional conception of fair play and substantial justice to permit the state to enforce the obligations which appellant has incurred there. Hence we cannot say that the maintenance of the present suit in the State of Washington involves an unreasonable or undue procedure.

JUSTICE BLACK delivered the following opinion.

* * *

[I]t is unthinkable that the vague due process clause was ever intended to prohibit a State from regulating or taxing a business carried on within its boundaries simply because this is done by agents of a corporation organized and having its headquarters elsewhere. To read this into the due process clause would in fact result in depriving a State's citizens of due process by taking from the State the power to protect them in their business dealings within its boundaries with representatives of a foreign corporation. Nothing could be more irrational or more designed to defeat the function of our federative system of government. Certainly a State, at the very least, has power to tax and sue those dealing with its citizens within its boundaries, as we have held before. Were the Court to follow this principle, it would provide a workable standard for cases where, as here, no other questions are involved. The Court has not chosen to do so, but instead has engaged in an unnecessary discussion in the course of which it has announced vague Constitutional criteria applied for the first time to the issue before us. It has thus introduced uncertain elements confusing the simple pattern and tending to curtail the exercise of State powers to an extent not justified by the Constitution.

* * *

I believe that the Federal Constitution leaves to each State, without any "ifs" or "buts", a power to tax and to open the doors of its courts for its citizens to sue corporations whose agents do business in those States. Believing that the Constitution gave the States that power, I think it a judicial deprivation to condition its exercise upon this Court's notion of "fair play," however appealing that term may be. Nor can I stretch the meaning of due process so far as to authorize this Court to deprive a State of the right to afford judicial protection to its citizens on the ground that it would be more "convenient" for the corporation to be sued somewhere else.

There is a strong emotional appeal in the words "fair play", "justice", and "reasonableness." But they were not chosen by those who wrote the original Constitution or the Fourteenth Amendment as a measuring rod for this Court to use in invalidating State or Federal laws passed by elected legislative representatives. * * * For application of this natural law concept, whether under the terms "reasonableness", "justice", or "fair play", makes judges the supreme arbiters of the country's laws and practices.

Notes and Questions

1. Chief Justice Stone goes to some lengths to expose the difficulties created by previous theories for jurisdiction over foreign corporations. While one could argue that the new minimum contacts formulation announced in

International Shoe applies only to corporate defendants, in fact it was held to apply generally to all defendants.

2. What factors are relevant to a minimum contacts determination whether to exercise jurisdiction over defendant? Obviously plaintiff will have information bearing on some of those factors when the lawsuit is filed, but on others plaintiff will need to do discovery. In Insurance Corp. of Ireland, Ltd. v. Compagnie des Bauxites de Guinee, 456 U.S. 694, 102 S.Ct. 2099, 72 L.Ed.2d 492 (1982), infra p. 829, the Court upheld the power of a court to compel defendant to respond to discovery regarding its contacts with the forum.

3. The Court's decision does not seem keyed to the precise facts of the case before it, and it provides little insight into proper disposition of jurisdictional challenges in other types of cases. Consider the following alternative scenarios:

(a) A Washington resident buys a pair of International Shoe shoes at a shoe store in Seattle and is injured in Seattle due to an alleged defect in the shoes. Can he sue International Shoe in Washington to recover for his injuries?

(b) An Oregon resident visiting in Washington buys a pair of International Shoe shoes at a shoe store in Seattle, takes them home to Oregon, and is injured there due to an alleged defect in the shoes. Can she sue International Shoe in Oregon to recover for her injuries? Can she sue in Washington?

(c) A Washington resident visiting in St. Louis buys a pair of International Shoe shoes there, takes them home to Washington and is injured there due to an alleged defect in the shoes. Can he sue International Shoe in Washington to recover for his injuries?

(d) An Oregon shoe retailer meets with International Shoe sales representatives in Seattle and places an order for 100 pairs of International Shoe shoes. International Shoe accepts the order and ships the shoes to Oregon. The retailer sells some, and customers who discover defects in the shoes return them. Can the Oregon retailer sue International Shoe in Oregon to get back the money she paid for the shoes and to recover damages for injury to her business reputation?

(e) Assume the Oregon retailer in the previous example had not paid for the shoes when she received the complaints and that she then refused to pay. Can International Shoe sue her in St. Louis for payment? In Rosenberg Bros. & Co. v. Curtis Brown Co., 260 U.S. 516, 43 S.Ct. 170, 67 L.Ed. 372 (1923), cited in *International Shoe,* an Oklahoma retailer of clothing which regularly purchased a large part of its merchandise from New York, was sued in New York when it failed to pay for some of the merchandise. The Court held that New York could not exercise jurisdiction. It reasoned that "[t]he only business alleged to have been transacted by the company in New York, either then or theretofore, related to such purchases of goods by officers of a foreign corporation. Visits on such business, even if occurring at regular intervals, would not warrant the inference that the corporation was present within the jurisdiction of the State."

(f) If one of the customers of the Oregon retailer in (d) above was injured in Oregon due to the alleged defects in the shoes, could he sue in Oregon to recover for his injuries? If so, would that affect the right of the Oregon resident in (b) above, who bought her shoes in Seattle, to sue in Oregon for injuries received there due to alleged defects in International Shoe shoes?

4. As should be apparent, much development of the minimum contacts standard would be necessary to make it workable. Justice Black castigated the majority for creating a "natural law" standard infinitely manipulable by judges. His concern, obviously, was that judges would invalidate exercises of state power, as had occurred during the 1920's and 1930's with regard to a great deal of New Deal and similar regulatory legislation. Was his concern realistic? Consider that the jurisdiction decision is usually made by an elected state court judge confronted with a local plaintiff (and constituent), often injured, suing a distant defendant, often a large corporation. In what direction is judicial power likely to be abused?

––––––––

McGEE v. INTERNATIONAL LIFE INS. CO., 355 U.S. 220, 78 S.Ct. 199, 2 L.Ed.2d 223 (1957):

Opinion of the Court by JUSTICE BLACK, announced by JUSTICE DOUGLAS.

Petitioner, Lulu B. McGee, recovered a judgment in a California state court against respondent, International Life Insurance Company, on a contract of insurance. Respondent was not served with process in California but by registered mail at its principal place of business in Texas. The California court based its jurisdiction on a state statute which subjects foreign corporations to suit in California on insurance contracts with residents of that State even though such corporations cannot be served with process within its borders. [Cal. Ins. Code, §§ 1610–1620.]

Unable to collect the judgment in California petitioner went to Texas where she filed suit on the judgment in a Texas court. But the Texas courts refused to enforce her judgment holding it was void under the Fourteenth Amendment because service of process outside California could not give the courts of that State jurisdiction over respondent. Since the case raised important questions, not only to California but to other States which have similar laws, we granted certiorari. It is not controverted that if the California court properly exercised jurisdiction over respondent the Texas courts erred in refusing to give its judgment full faith and credit.

The material facts are relatively simple. In 1944, Lowell Franklin, a resident of California, purchased a life insurance policy from the Empire Mutual Insurance Company, an Arizona corporation. In 1948 the respondent agreed with Empire Mutual to assume its insurance obligations. Respondent then mailed a reinsurance certificate to Franklin in California offering to insure him in accordance with the terms of the policy he

Suicide refused to pay (margin annotation)

held with Empire Mutual. He accepted this offer and from that time until his death in 1950 paid premiums by mail from his California home to respondent's Texas office. Petitioner, Franklin's mother, was the beneficiary under the policy. She sent proofs of his death to the respondent but it refused to pay claiming that he had committed suicide. It appears that neither Empire Mutual nor respondent has ever had any office or agent in California. And so far as the record before us shows, respondent has never solicited or done any insurance business in California apart from the policy involved here.

Since Pennoyer v. Neff, 95 U.S. 714, 24 L.Ed. 565, this Court has held that the Due Process Clause of the Fourteenth Amendment places some limit on the power of state courts to enter binding judgments against persons not served with process within their boundaries. But just where this line of limitation falls has been the subject of prolific controversy, particularly with respect to foreign corporations. In a continuing process of evolution this Court accepted and then abandoned "consent," "doing business," and "presence" as the standard for measuring the extent of state judicial power over such corporations. More recently in International Shoe Co. v. State of Washington, 326 U.S. 310, 66 S.Ct. 154, 90 L.Ed. 95, the Court decided that "due process requires only that in order to subject a defendant to a judgment in personam, if he be not present within the territory of the forum, he have certain minimum contacts with it such that the maintenance of the suit does not offend 'traditional notions of fair play and substantial justice.' "

Looking back over this long history of litigation a trend is clearly discernible toward expanding the permissible scope of state jurisdiction over foreign corporations and other nonresidents. In part this is attributable to the fundamental transformation of our national economy over the years. Today many commercial transactions touch two or more States and may involve parties separated by the full continent. With this increasing nationalization of commerce has come a great increase in the amount of business conducted by mail across state lines. At the same time modern transportation and communication have made it much less burdensome for a party sued to defend himself in a State where he engages in economic activity.

holding (margin annotation)

Turning to this case we think it apparent that the Due Process Clause did not preclude the California court from entering a judgment binding on respondent. It is sufficient for purposes of due process that the suit was based on a contract which had substantial connection with that State. The contract was delivered in California, the premiums were mailed from there and the insured was a resident of that State when he died. It cannot be denied that California has a manifest interest in providing effective means of redress for its residents when their insurers refuse to pay claims. These residents would be at a severe disadvantage if they were forced to follow the insurance company to a distant State in order to hold it legally accountable. When claims were small or moderate individual claimants frequently could not afford the cost of bringing an action in a foreign forum—thus in effect making the company judgment proof. Often the crucial witnesses—as here on the company's defense of suicide—will be found in the insured's locality. Of course there may be inconvenience to the insurer if it is held amenable to suit in California where it had this contract but certainly nothing which amounts to a denial of due process. There is no contention that respondent did not have adequate notice of the suit or sufficient time to prepare its defenses and appear.

Notes and Questions

1.   In terms of general attitude toward the extent of jurisdiction, *McGee* represented the apogee of liberality by the Supreme Court. In support of this expansive view, Justice Black cites the "fundamental transformation of our national economy" that has occurred since *Pennoyer*. Certainly state lines seem insignificant in terms of the geographic organization of significant parts of our country. One need only consider metropolitan areas that include parts of several states, such as New York and Philadelphia, to recognize that for many purposes our society is not organized along state lines. Should state lines simply be irrelevant, with the burden on the defendant the only significant factor? Would that place due process limitations on the power of a large state to require its own citizens to defend in a distant court of that state?

2.   The Court's opinion suggests that the focus should be on balancing the inconvenience to the plaintiff of suing elsewhere and the inconvenience to the defendant of defending in the forum. How often will such a balance turn out to favor dismissal where the plaintiff is local?

3.   The Court also appears, in keeping with the regulatory tradition of *International Shoe*, to place weight on the state's interest in affording redress against foreign insurance companies. Is this analogous to the emphasis in Hess v. Pawloski (supra p. 706) on the dangerousness of automobiles and the state's consequent interest in regulation? Why should that have a bearing on the defendant's due process rights? How does the Court determine whether the state has such an interest? In *McGee* the state had recently passed a statute regarding suits against insurers, suggesting such an interest. If there had only been a general provision for suits against nonresident corporations, would the same state interest argument have applied? Do insurers have less due process rights than other businesses?

4.   Several years before *McGee*, the Court was presented with a jurisdictional challenge in Mullane v. Central Hanover Bank & Trust Co., 339 U.S. 306, 70 S.Ct. 652, 94 L.Ed. 865 (1950). That case arose in a New York state court when a bank that acted as trustee for trust funds under testamentary trusts (i.e., created pursuant to a will) with a large number of beneficiaries sought an "accounting," a judicial determination that its handling of the trusts complied with its obligations to the beneficiaries. Success on the petition for an accounting would extinguish any claims the beneficiaries might have against the bank for mishandling the trusts. The Court rejected a jurisdictional challenge:

> We are met at the outset with a challenge to the power of the State—the right of its courts to adjudicate at all as against those beneficiaries who reside without the State of New York. It is contended

that the proceeding is one *in personam* in that the decree affects neither title to nor possession of any *res*, but adjudges only personal rights of the beneficiaries to surcharge their trustee for negligence or breach of trust. Accordingly, it is said, under the strict doctrine of Pennoyer v. Neff, 95 U.S. 714, 24 L.Ed. 565, the Surrogate [the New York state-court judge] is without jurisdiction as to nonresidents upon whom personal service of process was not made.

Distinctions between actions *in rem* and those *in personam* are ancient and originally expressed in procedural terms what seems really to have been a distinction in the substantive law of property under a system quite unlike our own. The legal recognition and rise in economic importance of incorporeal or intangible forms of property have upset the ancient simplicity of property law and the clarity of its distinctions, while new forms of proceedings have confused the old procedural classification. American courts have sometimes classed certain actions as *in rem* because personal service of process was not required, and at other times have held personal service of process not required because the action was *in rem*.

Judicial proceedings to settle fiduciary accounts have been sometimes termed *in rem,* or more indefinitely *quasi in rem,* or more vaguely still, "in the nature of a proceeding *in rem.*" It is not readily apparent how the courts of New York did or would classify the present proceeding, which has some characteristics and is wanting in some features of proceedings both *in rem* and *in personam.* But in any event we think that the requirements of the Fourteenth Amendment to the Federal Constitution do not depend upon a classification for which the standards are so elusive and confused generally and which, being primarily for state courts to define, may and do vary from state to state. Without disparaging the usefulness of distinctions between actions *in rem* and those *in personam* in many branches of law, or on other issues, or the reasoning which underlies them, we do not rest the power of the State to resort to constructive service in this proceeding upon how its courts or this Court may regard this historic antithesis. It is sufficient to observe that, whatever the technical definition of its chosen procedure, the interest of each state in providing means to close trusts that exist by the grace of its laws and are administered under the supervision of its courts is so insistent and rooted in custom as to establish beyond doubt the right of its courts to determine the interests of all claimants, resident or nonresident, provided its procedure accords full opportunity to appear and be heard.

Does this decision presage *McGee*'s expansive view of jurisdiction? Does it show that the former distinction between in rem and in personam jurisdiction should no longer matter? Keep that point in mind for Shaffer v. Heitner, infra p. 791.

5. Later in the same term in which it decided *McGee,* the Court sounded a note of caution on overbroad extensions of state court jurisdiction in Hanson v. Denckla, 357 U.S. 235, 78 S.Ct. 1228, 2 L.Ed.2d 1283 (1958). This extraordinarily complicated case revolved around the validity of a trust set up in Delaware by Dora Donner, a woman from Pennsylvania who later

moved to Florida and died there. The corpus of the trust consisted of securities, and Donner reserved the income from the securities for life. She also retained a good deal of control over the handling of the trust, and provided that she could, by exercising a "power of appointment," designate the person who would receive the corpus upon her death. After she moved to Florida, Donner exercised the power of appointment to designate the children of one of her three daughters to receive the corpus. After she died, the other two daughters challenged that disposition in the Florida courts, which held that the trust was invalid because Donner retained too much control over it. To reach that result, it had to find jurisdiction over the Delaware trustee, the Wilmington Trust Co., which was an indispensable party under Florida law.

The Supreme Court reversed on the ground that Florida's exercise of jurisdiction over the trustee was unconstitutional. Chief Justice Warren, writing for the Court, recognized the progressive relaxation of limitations on jurisdiction, but cautioned that "it is a mistake to assume that this trend heralds the eventual demise of all restrictions on the personal jurisdiction of state courts. Those restrictions are more than a guarantee of immunity from inconvenient or distant litigation. They are a consequence of territorial limitations on the power of the respective States. However minimal the burden of defending in a foreign tribunal, a defendant may not be called upon to do so unless he has the 'minimal contacts' with that state that are a prerequisite to its exercise of power over him."

Even though the trustee continued to follow Donner's directions after she moved to Florida (the reason Florida held the trust invalid), and presumably to remit the income from the trust to her on a regular basis, the Court found minimum contacts absent: "The unilateral activity of those who claim some relationship with a nonresident defendant cannot satisfy the requirement of contact with the forum State. The application of that rule will vary with the quality and nature of the defendant's activity, but it is essential in each case that there be some act by which the defendant purposefully avails itself of the privilege of conducting activities within the forum State, thus invoking the benefits and protections of its laws."

This *purposeful availment* requirement seems to be derived from some of the reasoning in *International Shoe:* "[T]o the extent that a corporation exercises the privilege of conducting activities within a state, it enjoys the benefits and protection of the laws of that state. The exercise of that privilege may give rise to obligations, and, so far as those obligations arise out of or are connected with the activities within the state, a procedure which requires the corporation to respond to a suit brought to enforce them can, in most instances, hardly be said to be undue." See supra p. 714.

Nevertheless, the facts in *Hanson* seemed a great deal like *McGee,* and the trustee's long-term business relationship with Donner no more tenuous a thread than the sending of a single insurance policy to Mr. Franklin in California. In *Hanson,* the Court saw distinctions. It noted the special interest California had in providing effective redress for its residents against insurers and the fact the insurance contract had "substantial connection" with California. Chief Justice Warren acknowledged that "[f]rom Florida Mrs. Donner carried on several bits of trust administration that may be compared to the mailing of premiums in *McGee*. But the record discloses no instance in which the *trustee* performed any acts in Florida that bear the same relationship to the agreement as the solicitation in *McGee*." How persuasive are these distinctions? For nearly 20 years many believed that *Hanson* was an aberration, designed to accomplish with jurisdictional rhetoric Donner's desire that her grandchildren receive the corpus. Indeed, had the trustee failed to remit moneys due Donner, it seems likely that the Court would have upheld Florida jurisdiction in her suit to collect the sums. But when the Court again addressed the subject, it showed that it was serious about the analytical framework of *Hanson*. Before we examine those developments, however, we shall turn to the states' response to the relaxation of the due process formula.

6. How should *McGee*'s approach be applied in Gray v. American Radiator & Standard Sanitary Corp., 176 N.E.2d 761 (Ill.1961)? Plaintiff in that case was injured in Illinois due to the explosion of a water heater manufactured by defendant American Radiator at its plant in Pennsylvania. She also sued Titan Valve Manufacturing Co., an Ohio company that manufactured safety valves and supplied them to American Radiator, claiming that the valve in the water heater that exploded was manufactured by Titan. Titan objected to jurisdiction on the ground that it did no business in Illinois and had no agent in the state. It argued that its sales of valves to American Radiator outside Illinois was not a proper basis for jurisdiction. The court disagreed:

> In the case at bar defendant does not claim that the present use of its product in Illinois is an isolated instance. While the record does not disclose the volume of Titan's business or the territory in which appliances incorporating its valves are marketed, it is a reasonable inference that its commercial transactions, like those of other manufacturers, result in substantial use and consumption in this State. To the extent that its business may be directly affected by transactions occurring here it enjoys benefits from the laws of this State, and it has undoubtedly benefited, to a degree, from the protection which our law has given to the marketing of hot water heaters containing its valves. Where the alleged liability arises, as in this case, from the manufacture of products presumably sold in contemplation of use here, it should not matter that the purchase was made from an independent middleman or that someone other than the defendant shipped the product into this State.

> With the increasing specialization of commercial activity and the growing interdependence of business enterprises it is seldom that a manufacturer deals directly with consumers in other States. The fact that the benefit he derives from its laws is an indirect one, however, does not make it any the less essential to the conduct of his business; and it is not unreasonable, where a cause of action arises from alleged defects in his product, to say that the use of such products in the ordinary course of commerce is sufficient contact with this State to justify a requirement that he defend here.

> As a general proposition, if a corporation elects to sell its products for ultimate use in another State, it is not unjust to hold it answerable there for any damage caused by defects in those products. Advanced

means of distribution and other commercial activity have made possible these modern methods of doing business, and have largely effaced the economic significance of State lines. By the same token, today's facilities for transportation and communication have removed much of the difficulty and inconvenience formerly encountered in defending lawsuits brought in other States.

This justification for exercising jurisdiction has come to be known as the *stream of commerce* theory, positing that if a commercial actor puts its products into the stream of commerce with the expectation that they will be marketed in the forum it may be sued in the forum for injuries allegedly resulting there. Is this analysis consistent with *McGee*? Does it comport with the "purposeful availment" analysis of Hanson v. Denckla, supra note 5? We will return to these questions in connection with World–Wide Volkswagen Corp. v. Woodson, infra p. 730, and Asahi Metal Industry Co. v. Superior Court, infra p. 765.

C. THE STATES' RESPONSE—LONG–ARM STATUTES

As we have seen, the states responded to *Pennoyer* by creatively fitting their jurisdictional statutes within its framework, particularly by expanding the concept of consent. The relaxation of *Pennoyer* that culminated in *International Shoe* similarly had an effect on state law regarding exercise of jurisdiction. There is no constitutional requirement that a state actually exercise its jurisdiction to the maximum extent permitted by due process, although some legislatures decided to do so. Consider California's straightforward approach: "A court of this state may exercise jurisdiction on any basis not inconsistent with the Constitution of this state or of the United States." Cal.Code Civ.Proc. § 410.10.

Most states, however, were more circumspect, enacting statutes that described with some particularity the kinds of cases in which their courts were to exercise jurisdiction. The first comprehensive effort in this regard was the Illinois long-arm statute of 1955 (originally codified as Ill.Rev.Stats. ch. 110, § 17), which provided as follows:

> (1) Any person, whether or not a citizen or resident of this State, who in person or through an agent does any of the acts hereinafter enumerated, thereby submits said person, and, if an individual, his personal representative, to the jurisdiction of the courts of this State as to any cause of action arising from the doing of any of said acts:
>
>> (a) The transaction of any business within this State;
>>
>> (b) The commission of a tortious act within this State;
>>
>> (c) The ownership, use, or possession of any real estate in this State;
>>
>> (d) Contracting to insure any person, property or risk located within this State at the time of contracting.

The Illinois statute served as a model for the statutes in other states. In Gray v. American Radiator & Standard Sanitary Corp., 176 N.E.2d 761

(Ill.1961) (also discussed supra p. 722 n.6), the Illinois Supreme Court adopted an expansive interpretation of the provision for jurisdiction on claims arising out of "[t]he commission of a tortious act within this State." Plaintiff there had been injured in Illinois when a water heater exploded. Plaintiff sued not only American Radiator, a Pennsylvania company that manufactured the water heater, but also Titan Valve Manufacturing Co., an Ohio company that supplied American Radiator with valves, including the one in the water heater that exploded. Titan argued that if it had committed a "tortious act," it must have done so in Ohio. Since it had never done any business in Illinois, and sent the valves it sold to American Radiator, it contended that it could not be sued in Illinois.

The court rejected Titan's argument:

> The wrong in the case at bar did not originate in the conduct of a servant physically present here, but arose instead from acts performed at the place of manufacture. Only the consequences occurred in Illinois. It is well established, however, that in law the place of a wrong is where the last event takes place which is necessary to render the actor liable. Restatement, Conflict of Laws, sec. 377. A second indication that the place of injury is the determining factor is found in rules governing the time within which an action must be brought. In applying statutes of limitation our court has computed the period from the time when the injury is done. We think it is clear that the alleged negligence in manufacturing the valve cannot be separated from the resulting injury; and that for present purposes, like those of liability and limitations, the tort was committed in Illinois.
>
> Titan seeks to avoid this result by arguing that instead of using the word "tort," the legislature employed the term "tortious act"; and that the latter refers only to the act or conduct, separate and apart from any consequences thereof. We cannot accept the argument. To be tortious an act must cause injury. The concept of injury is an inseparable part of the phrase. In determining legislative intention courts will read words in their ordinary and popularly understood sense. We think the intent should be determined less from technicalities of definition than from considerations of general purpose and effect. To adopt the criteria urged by defendant would tend to promote litigation over extraneous issues concerning the elements of a tort and the territorial incidence of each, whereas the test should be concerned more with those substantial elements of convenience and justice presumably contemplated by the legislature. As we observed in Nelson v. Miller, 11 Ill.2d 378, 143 N.E.2d 673, the statute contemplates the exertion of jurisdiction over nonresident defendants to the extent permitted by the due-process clause.

Titan's argument seemed to have some force; the New York statute modeled on the Illinois provision was interpreted as Titan had argued. In

Feathers v. McLucas, 209 N.E.2d 68 (N.Y.1965), the New York court explicitly disagreed with the Illinois court's approach in *Gray*:

> The language of paragraph 2 [of the New York long-arm statute]—conferring personal jurisdiction over a nondomiciliary "if, in person or through an agent, he … commits a tortious act *within the state*"—is too plain and precise to permit it to be read * * * as if it were synonymous with "commits a tortious act *without* the state which causes injury within the state." The mere occurrence of the injury in this State certainly cannot serve to transmute an out-of-state tortious act into one committed here within the sense of the statutory wording.

But it may often be difficult to discern why the legislature would want to close the courthouse door on local plaintiffs seeking compensation from distant defendants. In New York, the New York Legislature responded to the more restrictive interpretation of the New York court by amending its statute to cover tortious acts outside New York causing injury within, so long as defendant "expects or should reasonably expect the act to have consequences in the state and derives substantial revenue from interstate or international commerce."

Notes and Questions

1. The Illinois court said that it was interpreting the term "tortious act" in its "ordinary and popularly understood sense." Is this persuasive? It also invoked "considerations of general purpose and effect." Would it be reasonable to expect that the Illinois legislature would endorse the interpretation given the statute by the court?

Ultimately the Illinois legislature amended its long-arm statute, and it now appears as § 2–209 of the Illinois Code of Civil Procedure. Subsection (a) repeats the original provisions (quoted supra p. 723) and adds the following additional acts, where the cause of action arises from them (the original (a) through (d) having been renumbered (1) through (4)), among others:

> (7) The making or performance of any contract or promise substantially connected with this State;

> (10) The acquisition or ownership, possession or control of any asset or thing of value present within this State when ownership, possession or control was acquired;

> (11) The breach of any fiduciary duty within this State;

> (12) The performance of duties as a director or officer of a corporation organized under the laws of this State or having its principal place of business within this State.

Subsection (b) authorizes jurisdiction "in any action arising within or without this State against any person who:

> (1) Is a natural person present within this State when served;

(2) Is a natural person domiciled or resident within this State when the cause of action arose, the action was commenced, or process was served;

(3) Is a corporation organized under the laws of this State; or

(4) Is a natural person or corporation doing business within this State."

Finally, subsection (c) states that "[a] court may also exercise jurisdiction on any other basis now or hereafter permitted by the Illinois Constitution and the Constitution of the United States."

Do these amendments indicate that the court in *Gray* was correct in its interpretation of the original Act? Should the original provisions of the Act continue to be interpreted the same way given the passage of these amendments?

2.   The *Gray* analysis seemed to permit suit in Illinois on any tort that allegedly had an injurious effect there. But in Green v. Advance Ross Elec. Corp., 427 N.E.2d 1203 (Ill.1981), the court retreated some from that view. Plaintiff there was a Delaware corporation headquartered in Illinois claimed jurisdiction there over a former employee for alleged breaches of fiduciary duty that occurred outside Illinois, arguing that the tort had an impact inside Illinois because it harmed the company's financial condition. The Illinois Supreme Court found this effect "too remote," reasoning that plaintiff's interpretation "would be tantamount to permitting a corporation operating nationwide to sue employees, suppliers, customers and perhaps others, at the company's State of incorporation or at its headquarters no matter how far away they lived and worked or their contact with the corporation was."

3.   Other problems can arise from the use of the phrase "tortious act." Until the trial is completed, how can the court know whether defendant has committed a tort? Whatever Titan did in Ohio or Illinois has not been proved to be a tort. Must there be two trials? The problem was early disposed of in Illinois when the statute was interpreted to apply whenever the act as alleged would be tortious. Nelson v. Miller, 143 N.E.2d 673 (Ill.1957); see Currie, The Growth of the Long Arm: Eight Years of Extended Jurisdiction in Illinois, 1963 U.Ill.L.F. 533, 539. Still, the use of substantive law terms in a long-arm statute invites further difficulties.

4.   As a fallback for its statutory interpretation, the court in *Gray* asserts that it has already, in Nelson v. Miller, interpreted its long-arm statute to go to the maximum extent permitted by due process. Many state courts have thus interpreted their statutes (see World–Wide Volkswagen v. Woodson, infra p. 731 n. 7), and this alternative route should be kept in mind. But if the legislature wanted to take the California route it could have done so explicitly; shouldn't the courts exercise some caution? Consider the Illinois Supreme Court's later views on the subject before the legislature adopted the changes described in note 1: "We do not, however, regard this observation as the equivalent of declaring that the construction and application of section 17(1)(b) depend entirely on decisions determining in what circumstances due process requirements would permit long-arm jurisdiction. * * * A statute worded in the way ours is should have a fixed meaning

without regard to changing concepts of due process." Green v. Advance Ross Elec. Corp., 427 N.E.2d 1203 (Ill.1981).

5.   Notwithstanding expansive interpretations of long-arm statutes, it is important to keep in mind that they must be satisfied in order for a court to exercise jurisdiction, whether or not the exercise of jurisdiction would be constitutional. As with the due process analysis of prejudgment seizure (see supra pp. 27–66), the starting point for issues of personal jurisdiction is statutory authorization for the assertion of jurisdiction; only when that is satisfied does the question of due process limitations arise.

PERSONAL JURISDICTION IN FEDERAL COURT

At this point, students often suggest that the easy solution to these jurisdictional problems is to sue in federal court. We will deal in the next chapter with subject matter jurisdiction, which governs access to federal court. The personal jurisdiction issue bears separate treatment here, however, because in most cases those jurisdictional problems are identical in state and federal court.

The congruence of personal jurisdiction issues between state and federal courts is hardly obvious, however, and those who assume that there simply is no personal jurisdiction problem in federal court have sensible grounds for their reaction. *Pennoyer,* after all, emphasized the sovereign power of any state over all found within it, so it would seem that the United States could, without encountering any problems of personal jurisdiction, exercise jurisdiction through its courts over anyone served in the country, just as Oregon could have properly exercised jurisdiction over anyone served in that state. Indeed, less than a year after the decision in *Pennoyer,* the Supreme Court suggested that Congress could have created a single federal trial court with nationwide personal jurisdiction. United States v. Union Pacific R. Co., 98 U.S. (8 Otto) 569, 25 L.Ed. 143 (1878). Although Congress did not do so, there is certainly room to debate the need for the state-by-state organization that Congress did adopt for the U.S. district courts. Moreover, it has broken almost half the states into more than one district, with California, New York and Texas divided into four districts each. Certainly one could reasonably surmise that these federal courts would not be subject to the same personal jurisdiction limitations as the courts of the states in which they sit, particularly since the 14th Amendment, with its due process clause, applies only to the states and not to the federal government (although the 5th Amendment due process clause does apply to the federal government).

But the reality is different, and raises some extremely slippery issues. Rule 4(k)(1)(A) authorizes exercise of personal jurisdiction by a federal court only to the extent a state court of the state in which it sits, under the state's long-arm statute, could exercise jurisdiction. This normally will invoke an *International Shoe* analysis of minimum contacts with the state even when the plaintiff asserts a federal claim in federal court. Accordingly, with some exceptions noted below, the problems of statutory interpretation and due process are the same whether the case is in federal or state court. Some cavil about this situation, see Berger, Acquiring In Personam Jurisdiction in Federal Question Cases: Procedural Frustration Under Federal Rule of Civil Procedure 4, 1982 Utah L.Rev. 285, but for our purposes it is a working assumption.

One important exception is that Congress has, in some instances, authorized nationwide service of process in specific statutes. See Rule 4(k)(1)(D). Many of these provisions are designed to facilitate the assertion of the claims created by the statutory scheme. See, e.g., 15 U.S.C.A. § 25 (antitrust claims); 15 U.S.C.A. §§ 77v(a); 78aa (securities claims). In other situations, nationwide service is designed to provide a forum in federal court that can bind all interested parties where jurisdictional problems might make that impossible in state court. See, e.g., 28 U.S.C.A. §§ 1335 (interpleader); 28 U.S.C.A. §§ 1695 (derivative actions); 1697 (multiparty, multiforum litigation); cf. Bankruptcy Rule 7004(d) (authorizing nationwide service in connection with bankruptcy proceedings).

Are there no constitutional protections against unfair inconvenience where nationwide service is permitted? Some have argued that the due process clause of the 5th Amendment, which does bind the United States, should be read to impose similar limitations on nationwide service. Compare Republic of Panama v. BCCI Holdings, 119 F.3d 935 (11th Cir.1997) (5th amendment does limit federal court assertion of jurisdiction in extraordinarily inconvenient district) with F.T.C. v. Jim Walter Corp., 651 F.2d 251 (5th Cir.1981) (rejecting 5th Amendment limitation on federal court jurisdiction). See generally Fullerton, Constitutional Limits on Nationwide Personal Jurisdiction in the Federal Courts, 79 Nw.U.L.Rev. 1 (1984).

Another exception is Rule 4(k)(1)(B), which authorizes service within 100 miles of the federal courthouse, even though outside the state, where a third party complaint is asserted under Rule 14, or where additional parties are necessary for full adjudication under Rule 19. This is known as "bulge jurisdiction." In Coleman v. American Export Isbrandtsen Lines, Inc., 405 F.2d 250 (2d Cir.1968), the court explained that the provision of bulge jurisdiction was designed "to allow complicated controversies to be ended by a single lawsuit if all the necessary third parties could be found within 100 miles of the courthouse."

The special jurisdictional features of a federal court are also invoked by Rule 4(k)(2), with respect to claims based on federal law against any defendant "who is not subject to the jurisdiction of the courts of general jurisdiction of any state." One situation in which this provision would apply is where the forum state's long-arm statute does not authorize exercise of jurisdiction although that would be constitutional, and there are not sufficient contacts with any other state to permit it to exercise jurisdiction. Another is where the defendant's contacts with any particular state are insufficient to support jurisdiction, but its contacts with the country as a whole are sufficient. But how does a plaintiff show that jurisdiction is not possible in any other state? In ISI International, Inc.

v. Borden Ladner Gervais LLP, 256 F.3d 548 (7th Cir.2001), the court decided that "[a] defendant who wants to preclude use of Rule 4(k)(2) has only to name some other state in which the suit could proceed. Naming a more appropriate state would amount to a consent to personal jurisdiction there. * * * If, however, the defendant contends that he cannot be sued in the forum state and refuses to identify any other where suit is possible, then the federal court is entitled to use Rule 4(k)(2)" Id. at 552; see also United States v. Swiss American Bank, 191 F.3d 30 (1st Cir.1999) (requiring the plaintiff invoking Rule 4(k)(2) jurisdiction to certify that, based on available information, defendant is not subject to jurisdiction in any state, and then placing the burden on defendant to show that it does have sufficient contacts with some specific state).

Pendent personal jurisdiction: The existence of some federal authorizations for nationwide personal jurisdiction explains the emergence of the doctrine of "pendent personal jurisdiction." "Pendent personal jurisdiction is typically found where one or more federal claims for which there is nationwide personal jurisdiction are combined in the same suit with one or more state or federal claims for which there is not nationwide personal jurisdiction." Action Embroidery Corp. v. Atlantic Embroidery, Inc., 368 F.3d 1174, 1180–81 (9th Cir.2004). "Pendent personal jurisdiction * * * exists when a court possesses personal jurisdiction over a defendant for one claim, lacks an independent basis for personal jurisdiction over the defendant for another claim that arises out of the same nucleus of operative fact, and then, because it possesses personal jurisdiction over the first claim, asserts personal jurisdiction over the second claim." United States v. Botefuhr, 309 F.3d 1263, 1272 (10th Cir.2002).

D. REFINING THE MINIMUM CONTACTS ANALYSIS

Since *International Shoe*, courts have sometimes said that issues of personal jurisdiction depended on "gestalt factors," Ticketmaster–New York, Inc. v. Alioto, 26 F.3d 201, 209 (1st Cir.1994), and that resolving these questions was "more an art than a science." Donatelli v. National Hockey League, 893 F.2d 459, 468 n. 7 (1st Cir.1990). After nearly twenty years of silence, the Supreme Court began deciding personal jurisdiction cases again in 1977. As it decided more cases, it refined the minimum contacts standard, although in some ways these refinements resembled what Professor Hazard called "arbitrary particularization." Hazard, A General Theory of State–Court Jurisdiction, 1965 Sup.Ct.Rev. 241, 283. As you examine these cases, you will note a seeming evolution of the Supreme Court's thinking since its attitude toward personal jurisdiction reached its seeming high-water mark in McGee v. International Life Ins. Co. (supra p. 717). It is not so clear that the shifts in the Court's decisions have been reflected in lower court decisions. Thus, Professor Solimine reviewed nearly 1,000 published personal jurisdiction decisions in the lower courts during the period 1970 to 1994 and found that the changes were actually modest. See Solimine, The Quiet Revolution in Personal Jurisdiction, 73 Tulane L. Rev. 1 (1998).

WORLD–WIDE VOLKSWAGEN CORP. v. WOODSON

Supreme Court of the United States, 1980.
444 U.S. 286, 100 S.Ct. 559, 62 L.Ed.2d 490.

JUSTICE WHITE delivered the opinion of the Court.

The issue before us is whether, consistently with the Due Process Clause of the Fourteenth Amendment, an Oklahoma court may exercise in personam jurisdiction over a nonresident automobile retailer and its wholesale distributor in a products-liability action, when the defendants' only connection with Oklahoma is the fact that an automobile sold in New York to New York residents became involved in an accident in Oklahoma.

I

Respondents Harry and Kay Robinson purchased a new Audi automobile from petitioner Seaway Volkswagen, Inc. (Seaway), in Massena, N.Y., in 1976. The following year the Robinson family, who resided in New York, left that State for a new home in Arizona. As they passed through the State of Oklahoma, another car struck their Audi in the rear, causing a fire which severely burned Kay Robinson and her two children.[1]

The Robinsons subsequently brought a products-liability action in the District Court for Creek County, Okla., claiming that their injuries resulted from defective design and placement of the Audi's gas tank and fuel system. They joined as defendants the automobile's manufacturer, Audi NSU Auto Union Aktiengesellschaft (Audi); its importer, Volkswagen of America, Inc. (Volkswagen); its regional distributor, petitioner World–Wide Volkswagen Corp. (World–Wide); and its retail dealer, petitioner Seaway. Seaway and World–Wide entered special appearances,[3] claiming that Oklahoma's exercise of jurisdiction over them would offend the limitations on the State's jurisdiction imposed by the Due Process Clause of the Fourteenth Amendment.

The facts presented to the District Court showed that World–Wide is incorporated and has its business office in New York. It distributes vehicles, parts, and accessories, under contract with Volkswagen, to retail dealers in New York, New Jersey, and Connecticut. Seaway, one of these retail dealers, is incorporated and has its place of business in New York. Insofar as the record reveals, Seaway and World–Wide are fully independent corporations whose relations with each other and with Volkswagen and Audi are contractual only. Respondents adduced no

---

1. The driver of the other automobile does not figure in the present litigation.

3. Volkswagen also entered a special appearance in the District Court, but unlike World–Wide and Seaway did not seek re-

view in the Supreme Court of Oklahoma and is not a petitioner here. Both Volkswagen and Audi remain as defendants in the litigation pending before the District Court in Oklahoma.

evidence that either World–Wide or Seaway does any business in Oklahoma, ships or sells any products to or in that State, has an agent to receive process there, or purchases advertisements in any media calculated to reach Oklahoma. In fact, as respondents' counsel conceded at oral argument, there was no showing that any automobile sold by World–Wide or Seaway has ever entered Oklahoma with the single exception of the vehicle involved in the present case. Despite the apparent paucity of contacts between petitioners and Oklahoma, the District Court rejected their constitutional claim and reaffirmed that ruling in denying petitioners' motion for reconsideration. Petitioners then sought a writ of prohibition in the Supreme Court of Oklahoma to restrain the District Judge, respondent Charles S. Woodson, from exercising in personam jurisdiction over them. They renewed their contention that, because they had no "minimal contacts" with the State of Oklahoma, the actions of the District Judge were in violation of their rights under the Due Process Clause.

The Supreme Court of Oklahoma denied the writ, holding that personal jurisdiction over petitioners was authorized by Oklahoma's "long-arm" statute, Okla.Stat., Tit. 12, § 1701.03(a)(4) (1971).[7] Although the court noted that the proper approach was to test jurisdiction against both statutory and constitutional standards, its analysis did not distinguish these questions, probably because § 1701.03(a)(4) has been interpreted as conferring jurisdiction to the limits permitted by the United States Constitution. The court's rationale was contained in the following paragraph:

> "In the case before us, the product being sold and distributed by the petitioners is by its very design and purpose so mobile that petitioners can foresee its possible use in Oklahoma. This is especially true of the distributor, who has the exclusive right to distribute such automobile in New York, New Jersey and Connecticut. The evidence presented below demonstrated that goods sold and distributed by the petitioners were used in the State of Oklahoma, and under the facts we believe it reasonable to infer, given the retail value of the automobile, that the petitioners derive substantial income from automobiles which from time to time are used in the State of Oklahoma. This being the case, we hold that under the facts presented, the trial court was justified in concluding that the petitioners derive substantial revenue from goods used or consumed in this State."

7. This subsection provides:

"A court may exercise personal jurisdiction over a person, who acts directly or by an agent, as to a cause of action or claim for relief arising from the person's ... causing tortious injury in this state by an act or omission outside this state if he regularly does or solicits business or engages in any other persistent course of conduct, or derives substantial revenue from goods used or consumed or services rendered, in this state...."

The State Supreme Court rejected jurisdiction based on § 1701.03(a)(3), which authorizes jurisdiction over any person "causing tortious injury in this state by an act or omission in this state." Something in addition to the infliction of tortious injury was required.

We granted certiorari to consider an important constitutional question with respect to state-court jurisdiction and to resolve a conflict between the Supreme Court of Oklahoma and the highest courts of at least four other States. We reverse.

II

The Due Process Clause of the Fourteenth Amendment limits the power of a state court to render a valid personal judgment against a nonresident defendant. Kulko v. California Superior Court, 436 U.S. 84, 91, 98 S.Ct. 1690, 1696, 56 L.Ed.2d 132 (1978). A judgment rendered in violation of due process is void in the rendering State and is not entitled to full faith and credit elsewhere. Pennoyer v. Neff, 95 U.S. 714, 732–733, 24 L.Ed. 565 (1877). Due process requires that the defendant be given adequate notice of the suit, Mullane v. Central Hanover Trust Co., 339 U.S. 306, 313–314, 70 S.Ct. 652, 657, 94 L.Ed. 865 (1950), and be subject to the personal jurisdiction of the court, International Shoe Co. v. Washington, 326 U.S. 310, 66 S.Ct. 154, 90 L.Ed. 95 (1945). In the present case, it is not contended that notice was inadequate; the only question is whether these particular petitioners were subject to the jurisdiction of the Oklahoma courts.

As has long been settled, and as we reaffirm today, a state court may exercise personal jurisdiction over a nonresident defendant only so long as there exist "minimum contacts" between the defendant and the forum State. International Shoe Co. v. Washington, supra, at 316, 66 S.Ct., at 158. The concept of minimum contacts, in turn, can be seen to perform two related, but distinguishable, functions. It protects the defendant against the burdens of litigating in a distant or inconvenient forum. And it acts to ensure that the States, through their courts, do not reach out beyond the limits imposed on them by their status as coequal sovereigns in a federal system.

The protection against inconvenient litigation is typically described in terms of "reasonableness" or "fairness." We have said that the defendant's contacts with the forum State must be such that maintenance of the suit "does not offend 'traditional notions of fair play and substantial justice.' " International Shoe Co. v. Washington, at 316, 66 S.Ct., at 158, quoting Milliken v. Meyer, 311 U.S. 457, 463, 61 S.Ct. 339, 342, 85 L.Ed. 278 (1940). The relationship between the defendant and the forum must be such that it is "reasonable ... to require the corporation to defend the particular suit which is brought there." 326 U.S., at 317, 66 S.Ct., at 158. Implicit in this emphasis on reasonableness is the understanding that the burden on the defendant, while always a primary concern, will in an appropriate case be considered in light of other relevant factors, including the forum State's interest in adjudicating the dispute, see McGee v. International Life Ins. Co., 355 U.S. 220, 223, 78 S.Ct. 199, 201, 2 L.Ed.2d 223 (1957); the plaintiff's interest in obtaining convenient and effective relief, see Kulko v. California Superior Court, 436 U.S., at 92, 98 S.Ct., at 1697, at least when that interest is not adequately protected by the plaintiff's power to choose the forum, cf.

Shaffer v. Heitner, 433 U.S. 186, 211, n. 37, 97 S.Ct. 2569, 2583, n. 37, 53 L.Ed.2d 683 (1977); the interstate judicial system's interest in obtaining the most efficient resolution of controversies; and the shared interest of the several States in furthering fundamental substantive social policies, see Kulko v. California Superior Court, supra, 436 U.S., at 93, 98, 98 S.Ct., at 1697, 1700.

The limits imposed on state jurisdiction by the Due Process Clause, in its role as a guarantor against inconvenient litigation, have been substantially relaxed over the years. As we noted in McGee v. International Life Ins. Co., 355 U.S., at 222–223, 78 S.Ct., at 201, this trend is largely attributable to a fundamental transformation in the American economy: "Today many commercial transactions touch two or more States and may involve parties separated by the full continent. With this increasing nationalization of commerce has come a great increase in the amount of business conducted by mail across state lines. At the same time modern transportation and communication have made it much less burdensome for a party sued to defend himself in a State where he engages in economic activity."

The historical developments noted in *McGee*, of course, have only accelerated in the generation since that case was decided.

Nevertheless, we have never accepted the proposition that state lines are irrelevant for jurisdictional purposes, nor could we, and remain faithful to the principles of interstate federalism embodied in the Constitution. The economic interdependence of the States was foreseen and desired by the Framers. In the Commerce Clause, they provided that the Nation was to be a common market, a "free trade unit" in which the States are debarred from acting as separable economic entities. But the Framers also intended that the States retain many essential attributes of sovereignty, including, in particular, the sovereign power to try causes in their courts. The sovereignty of each State, in turn, implied a limitation on the sovereignty of all of its sister States—a limitation express or implicit in both the original scheme of the Constitution and the Fourteenth Amendment.

Hence, even while abandoning the shibboleth that "[t]he authority of every tribunal is necessarily restricted by the territorial limits of the State in which it is established," Pennoyer v. Neff, 95 U.S., at 720, we emphasized that the reasonableness of asserting jurisdiction over the defendant must be assessed "in the context of our federal system of government," International Shoe Co. v. Washington, 326 U.S., at 317, 66 S.Ct., at 158, and stressed that the Due Process Clause ensures not only fairness, but also the "orderly administration of the laws," id., at 319, 66 S.Ct., at 159. As we noted in Hanson v. Denckla, 357 U.S. 235, 250–251, 78 S.Ct. 1228, 2 L.Ed.2d 1283 (1958):

> "As technological progress has increased the flow of commerce between the States, the need for jurisdiction over nonresidents has undergone a similar increase. At the same time, progress in communications and transportation has made the defense of a suit in a

foreign tribunal less burdensome. In response to these changes, the requirements for personal jurisdiction over nonresidents have evolved from the rigid rule of Pennoyer v. Neff, 95 U.S. 714, 24 L.Ed. 565, to the flexible standard of International Shoe Co. v. Washington, 326 U.S. 310, 66 S.Ct. 154, 90 L.Ed. 95. But it is a mistake to assume that this trend heralds the eventual demise of all restrictions on the personal jurisdiction of state courts. Those restrictions are more than a guarantee of immunity from inconvenient or distant litigation. They are a consequence of territorial limitations on the power of the respective States."

Thus, the Due Process Clause "does not contemplate that a state may make binding a judgment in personam against an individual or corporate defendant with which the state has no contacts, ties, or relations." International Shoe Co. v. Washington, 326 U.S., at 319, 66 S.Ct., at 159. Even if the defendant would suffer minimal or no inconvenience from being forced to litigate before the tribunals of another State; even if the forum State has a strong interest in applying its law to the controversy; even if the forum State is the most convenient location for litigation, the Due Process Clause, acting as an instrument of interstate federalism, may sometimes act to divest the State of its power to render a valid judgment. Hanson v. Denckla, 357 U.S., at 251, 254, 78 S.Ct., at 1238, 1240.

III

Applying these principles to the case at hand, we find in the record before us a total absence of those affiliating circumstances that are a necessary predicate to any exercise of state-court jurisdiction. Petitioners carry on no activity whatsoever in Oklahoma. They close no sales and perform no services there. They avail themselves of none of the privileges and benefits of Oklahoma law. They solicit no business there either through salespersons or through advertising reasonably calculated to reach the State. Nor does the record show that they regularly sell cars at wholesale or retail to Oklahoma customers or residents or that they indirectly, through others, serve or seek to serve the Oklahoma market. In short, respondents seek to base jurisdiction on one, isolated occurrence and whatever inferences can be drawn therefrom: the fortuitous circumstance that a single Audi automobile, sold in New York to New York residents, happened to suffer an accident while passing through Oklahoma.

It is argued, however, that because an automobile is mobile by its very design and purpose it was "foreseeable" that the Robinsons' Audi would cause injury in Oklahoma. Yet "foreseeability" alone has never been a sufficient benchmark for personal jurisdiction under the Due Process Clause. In Hanson v. Denckla [supra p. 720 n. 5], it was no doubt foreseeable that the settlor of a Delaware trust would subsequently move to Florida and seek to exercise a power of appointment there; yet we held that Florida courts could not constitutionally exercise jurisdiction over a Delaware trustee that had no other contacts with the forum State. In Kulko v. California Superior Court, 436 U.S. 84, 98 S.Ct. 1690, 56 L.Ed.2d 132 (1978), it was surely "foreseeable" that a divorced wife would move to California from New York, the domicile of the marriage, and that a minor daughter would live with the mother. Yet we held that California could not exercise jurisdiction in a child-support action over the former husband who had remained in New York.

If foreseeability were the criterion, a local California tire retailer could be forced to defend in Pennsylvania when a blowout occurs there, see Erlanger Mills, Inc. v. Cohoes Fibre Mills, Inc., 239 F.2d 502, 507 (C.A.4 1956); a Wisconsin seller of a defective automobile jack could be haled before a distant court for damage caused in New Jersey, Reilly v. Phil Tolkan Pontiac, Inc., 372 F.Supp. 1205 (N.J.1974); or a Florida soft-drink concessionaire could be summoned to Alaska to account for injuries happening there, see Uppgren v. Executive Aviation Services, Inc., 304 F.Supp. 165, 170–171 (Minn.1969). Every seller of chattels would in effect appoint the chattel his agent for service of process. His amenability to suit would travel with the chattel.[11] * * *

This is not to say, of course, that foreseeability is wholly irrelevant. But the foreseeability that is critical to due process analysis is not the mere likelihood that a product will find its way into the forum State. Rather, it is that the defendant's conduct and connection with the forum State are such that he should reasonably anticipate being haled into court there. The Due Process Clause, by ensuring the "orderly administration of the laws," International Shoe Co. v. Washington, 326 U.S., at 319, 66 S.Ct., at 159, gives a degree of predictability to the legal system that allows potential defendants to structure their primary conduct with some minimum assurance as to where that conduct will and will not render them liable to suit. When a corporation "purposefully avails itself of the privilege of conducting activities within the forum State," Hanson v. Denckla, 357 U.S., at 253, 78 S.Ct., at 1240, it has clear notice that it is subject to suit there, and can act to alleviate the risk of burdensome litigation by procuring insurance, passing the expected costs on to customers, or, if the risks are too great, severing its connection with the State. Hence if the sale of a product of a manufacturer or distributor such as Audi or Volkswagen is not simply an isolated occurrence, but arises from the efforts of the manufacturer or distributor to serve directly or indirectly, the market for its product in other States, it is not unreasonable to subject it to suit in one of those States if its allegedly defective merchandise has there been the source of injury to its owner or

---

11. Respondents' counsel, at oral argument, sought to limit the reach of the foreseeability standard by suggesting that there is something unique about automobiles. It is true that automobiles are uniquely mobile, that they did play a crucial role in the expansion of personal jurisdiction through the fiction of implied consent, e.g., Hess v. Pawloski, 274 U.S. 352, 47 S.Ct. 632, 71 L.Ed. 1091 (1927), and that some of the cases have treated the automobile as a "dangerous instrumentality." But today, under the regime of *International Shoe,* we see no difference for jurisdictional purposes between an automobile and any other chattel. The "dangerous instrumentality" concept apparently was never used to support personal jurisdiction; and to the extent it has relevance today it bears not on jurisdiction but on the possible desirability of imposing substantive principles of tort law such as strict liability.

to others. The forum State does not exceed its powers under the Due Process Clause if it asserts personal jurisdiction over a corporation that delivers its products into the stream of commerce with the expectation that they will be purchased by consumers in the forum State. Cf. Gray v. American Radiator & Standard Sanitary Corp., 22 Ill.2d 432, 176 N.E.2d 761 (1961).

But there is no such or similar basis for Oklahoma jurisdiction over World–Wide or Seaway in this case. Seaway's sales are made in Massena, N.Y. World–Wide's market, although substantially larger, is limited to dealers in New York, New Jersey, and Connecticut. There is no evidence of record that any automobiles distributed by World–Wide are sold to retail customers outside this tri-state area. It is foreseeable that the purchasers of automobiles sold by World–Wide and Seaway may take them to Oklahoma. But the mere "unilateral activity of those who claim some relationship with a nonresident defendant cannot satisfy the requirement of contact with the forum State." Hanson v. Denckla, at 253, 78 S.Ct., at 1239–1240.

In a variant on the previous argument, it is contended that jurisdiction can be supported by the fact that petitioners earn substantial revenue from goods used in Oklahoma. The Oklahoma Supreme Court so found, drawing the inference that because one automobile sold by petitioners had been used in Oklahoma, others might have been used there also. While this inference seems less than compelling on the facts of the instant case, we need not question the court's factual findings in order to reject its reasoning.

This argument seems to make the point that the purchase of automobiles in New York, from which the petitioners earn substantial revenue, would not occur but for the fact that the automobiles are capable of use in distant States like Oklahoma. Respondents observe that the very purpose of an automobile is to travel, and that travel of automobiles sold by petitioners is facilitated by an extensive chain of Volkswagen service centers throughout the country, including some in Oklahoma. However, financial benefits accruing to the defendant from a collateral relation to the forum State will not support jurisdiction if they do not stem from a constitutionally cognizable contact with that State. In our view, whatever marginal revenues petitioners may receive by virtue of the fact that their products are capable of use in Oklahoma is far too attenuated a contact to justify that State's exercise of in personam jurisdiction over them.

Because we find that petitioners have no "contacts, ties, or relations" with the State of Oklahoma, International Shoe Co. v. Washington, supra, 326 U.S., at 319, 66 S.Ct., at 159, the judgment of the Supreme Court of Oklahoma is reversed.

JUSTICE MARSHALL, with whom JUSTICE BLACKMUN joins, dissenting.

* * *

The majority apparently acknowledges that if a product is purchased in the forum State by a consumer, that State may assert jurisdiction over everyone in the chain of distribution. With this I agree. But I cannot agree that jurisdiction is necessarily lacking if the product enters the State not through the channels of distribution but in the course of its intended use by the consumer. We have recognized the role played by the automobile in the expansion of our notions of personal jurisdiction. Unlike most other chattels, which may find their way into States far from where they were purchased because their owner takes them there, the intended use of the automobile is precisely as a means of traveling from one place to another. In such a case, it is highly artificial to restrict the concept of the "stream of commerce" to the chain of distribution from the manufacturer to the ultimate consumer.

I sympathize with the majority's concern that the persons ought to be able to structure their conduct so as not to be subject to suit in distant forums. But that may not always be possible. Some activities by their very nature may foreclose the option of conducting them in such a way as to avoid subjecting oneself to jurisdiction in multiple forums. This is by no means to say that all sellers of automobiles should be subject to suit everywhere; but a distributor of automobiles to a multi-state market and a local automobile dealer who makes himself part of a nationwide network of dealerships can fairly expect that the cars they sell may cause injury in distant States and that they may be called on to defend a resulting lawsuit there.

In light of the quality and nature of petitioners' activity, the majority's reliance on Kulko v. California Superior Court, supra, is misplaced. Kulko involved the assertion of state-court jurisdiction over a nonresident individual in connection with an action to modify his child custody rights and support obligations. His only contact with the forum State was that he gave his minor child permission to live there with her mother. In holding that exercise of jurisdiction violated the Due Process Clause, we emphasized that the cause of action as well as the defendant's actions in relation to the forum State arose *"not from the defendant's commercial transactions in interstate commerce,* but rather from his personal, domestic relations," 436 U.S., at 97, 98 S.Ct., at 1699 (emphasis supplied), contrasting Kulko's actions with those of the insurance company in McGee v. International Life Ins. Co., 355 U.S. 220, 78 S.Ct. 199, 2 L.Ed.2d 223 (1957), which were undertaken for commercial benefit.

Manifestly, the "quality and nature" of commercial activity is different, for purposes of the *International Shoe* test, from actions from which a defendant obtains no economic advantage. Commercial activity is more likely to cause effects in a larger sphere, and the actor derives an economic benefit from the activity that makes it fair to require him to answer for his conduct where its effects are felt. The profits may be used to pay the costs of suit, and knowing that the activity is likely to have effects in other States the defendant can readily insure against the costs of those effects, thereby sparing himself much of the inconvenience of defending in a distant forum. Of course, the Constitution forbids the exercise of jurisdiction if the defendant had no judicially cognizable contacts with the forum. But as the majority acknowledges, if such contacts are present the jurisdictional inquiry requires a balancing of various interests and policies. I believe such contacts are to be found here and that, considering all of the interests and policies at stake, requiring petitioners to defend this action in Oklahoma is not beyond the bounds of the Constitution. Accordingly, I dissent.

[Dissenting opinion of Justice Blackmun omitted.]

Justice Brennan, dissenting.

* * *

[T]he interest of the forum State and its connection to the litigation is strong. The automobile accident underlying the litigation occurred in Oklahoma. The plaintiffs were hospitalized in Oklahoma when they brought suit. Essential witnesses and evidence were in Oklahoma. The State has a legitimate interest in enforcing its laws designed to keep its highway system safe, and the trial can proceed at least as efficiently in Oklahoma as anywhere else.

The petitioners are not unconnected with the forum. Although both sell automobiles within limited sales territories, each sold the automobile which in fact was driven to Oklahoma where it was involved in an accident.[8] It may be true, as the Court suggests, that each sincerely intended to limit its commercial impact to the limited territory, and that each intended to accept the benefits and protection of the laws only of those States within the territory. But obviously these were unrealistic hopes that cannot be treated as an automatic constitutional shield.

An automobile simply is not a stationary item or one designed to be used in one place. An automobile is *intended* to be moved around. Someone in the business of selling large numbers of automobiles can hardly plead ignorance of their mobility or pretend that the automobiles stay put after they are sold. It is not merely that a dealer in automobiles foresees that they will move. The dealer actually intends that the purchasers will use the automobiles to travel to distant States where the dealer does not directly "do business." The sale of an automobile does *purposefully* inject the vehicle into the stream of interstate commerce so that it can travel to distant States.

* * *

The Court accepts that a State may exercise jurisdiction over a distributor which "serves" that State "indirectly" by "deliver[ing] its products into the stream of commerce with the expectation that they will be purchased by consumers in the forum State." It is difficult to see why

---

8. On the basis of this fact the state court inferred that the petitioners derived substantial revenue from goods used in Oklahoma. The inference is not without support. Certainly, were use of goods ac- cepted as a relevant contact, a plaintiff would not need to have an exact count of the number of petitioners' cars that are used in Oklahoma.

the Constitution should distinguish between a case involving goods which reach a distant State through a chain of distribution and a case involving goods which reach the same State because a consumer, using them as the dealer knew the customer would, took them there. In each case the seller purposefully injects the goods into the stream of commerce and those goods predictably are used in the forum State.[12]

Furthermore, an automobile seller derives substantial benefits from States other than its own. A large part of the value of automobiles is the extensive, nationwide network of highways. Significant portions of that network have been constructed by and are maintained by the individual States, including Oklahoma. The States, through their highway programs, contribute in a very direct and important way to the value of petitioners' businesses. Additionally, a network of other related dealerships with their service departments operates throughout the country under the protection of the laws of the various States, including Oklahoma, and enhances the value of petitioners' businesses by facilitating their customers' traveling.

Thus, the Court errs in its conclusion, that "petitioners have *no* 'contacts, ties, or relations' " with Oklahoma. There obviously are contacts, and, given Oklahoma's connection to the litigation, the contacts are sufficiently significant to make it fair and reasonable for the petitioners to submit to Oklahoma's jurisdiction.

It may be that affirmance of the judgment * * * would approach the outer limits of *International Shoe*'s jurisdictional principle. But that principle, with its almost exclusive focus on the rights of defendants, may be outdated. * * *

The model of society on which the *International Shoe* Court based its opinion is no longer accurate. Business people, no matter how local their businesses, cannot assume that goods remain in the business' locality. Customers and goods can be anywhere else in the country usually in a matter of hours and always in a matter of a very few days.

In answering the question whether or not it is fair and reasonable to allow a particular forum to hold a trial binding on a particular defendant, the interests of the forum State and other parties loom large in today's world and surely are entitled to as much weight as are the interests of the defendant. The "orderly administration of the laws" provides a firm basis for according some protection to the interests of plaintiffs and States as well as of defendants. Certainly, I cannot see how a defendant's right to due process is violated if the defendant suffers no inconvenience.

* * *

Given the tremendous mobility of goods and people, and the inability of businessmen to control where goods are taken by customers (or

---

12. The manufacturer in the case cited by the Court, Gray v. American Radiator & Standard Sanitary Corp., 22 Ill. 2d 432, 176 N.E.2d 761 (1961), had no more control over which States its goods would reach than did the petitioners in this case.

retailers), I do not think that the defendant should be in complete control of the geographical stretch of his amenability to suit. Jurisdiction is no longer premised on the notion that non-resident defendants have somehow impliedly consented to suit. People should understand that they are held responsible for the consequences of their actions and that in our society most actions have consequences affecting many States. When an action in fact causes injury in another State, the actor should be prepared to answer for it there unless defending in that State would be unfair for some reason other than that a state boundary must be crossed.[19]

In effect the Court is allowing defendants to assert the sovereign rights of their home States. The expressed fear is that otherwise all limits on personal jurisdiction would disappear. But the argument's premise is wrong. I would not abolish limits on jurisdiction or strip state boundaries of all significance; I would still require the plaintiff to demonstrate sufficient contacts among the parties, the forum, and the litigation to make the forum a reasonable State in which to hold the trial.

I would also, however, strip the defendant of an unjustified veto power over certain very appropriate fora—a power the defendant justifiably enjoyed long ago when communication and travel over long distances were slow and unpredictable and when notions of state sovereignty were impractical and exaggerated. But I repeat that is not today's world. If a plaintiff can show that his chosen forum State has a sufficient interest in the litigation (or sufficient contacts with the defendant), then the defendant who cannot show some real injury to a constitutionally protected interest should have no constitutional excuse not to appear.[21]

Notes and Questions

1. You may have wondered why plaintiffs would sue the objecting defendants as well as Audi and Volkswagen of America, and why these defendants would pursue the jurisdiction question to the Supreme Court. The curious explanation is that the Robinsons' lawyer wanted to keep the case in state court because juries in the county where the accident happened were known to be friendly to plaintiffs. Because the Robinsons were still technically New Yorkers for purposes of diversity of citizenship (see infra pp. 860–68), it was necessary to sue a New York defendant such as Seaway or World–Wide Volkswagen to prevent removal on grounds of diversity. Audi and Volkswagen of America underwrote the cost of appealing to the Supreme Court so that they could get the case removed to federal court. After removal, the federal jury returned a defense verdict. For a history of the case, see Adams, *World–Wide Volkswagen v. Woodson*—The Rest of the Story, 72 Neb.L.Rev. 1122 (1993).

19. One consideration that might create some unfairness would be if the choice of forum also imposed on the defendant an unfavorable substantive law which the defendant could justly have assumed would not apply.

21. Frequently, of course, the defendant will be able to influence the choice of forum through traditional doctrines, such as venue or *forum non conveniens*, permitting the transfer of litigation.

2. In Kulko v. Superior Court, 436 U.S. 84, 98 S.Ct. 1690, 56 L.Ed.2d 132 (1978), discussed in Justice Marshall's dissent, plaintiff and defendant were married in 1959 in California while defendant was there on a three-day stopover on his way to Korea for a tour of military duty. Both were New Yorkers, and plaintiff wife returned to New York right after the marriage. As soon as he was done with his military service in Korea, defendant husband returned to New York to live with plaintiff, who soon gave birth to a son and a daughter. In 1972 they separated and plaintiff moved to San Francisco. Under a written settlement agreement (executed in New York), the children were to remain in New York with their father, except for vacations which they would spend with their mother in California, defendant would pay plaintiff $3,000 per year in child support for those periods, and plaintiff waived alimony. Plaintiff then went to Haiti and obtained a divorce there that incorporated the agreement. She then returned to California and remarried.

As the 1973 Christmas vacation visit approached, the daughter told defendant that she wanted to stay with her mother in California, so he bought her a one-way airplane ticket to California, and she remained there. In 1976, the son called plaintiff and said he wanted to stay with her also, so she sent him a ticket. As soon as the son arrived in California, plaintiff filed suit there to establish the Haitian divorce as a California judgment and increase defendant's support obligations. Under the "divisible divorce" idea (see supra p. 701 n. 6), California could only increase those obligations if it had jurisdiction over defendant. The California courts upheld jurisdiction.

The Supreme Court reversed. Anxious not to "discourage parents from entering into reasonable visitation agreements," the Court held that defendant's purchase of a ticket for his daughter was insufficient to support jurisdiction: "A father who agrees, in the interests of family harmony and his children's preferences, to allow them to spend more time in California than was required under a separation agreement can hardly be said to have 'purposefully availed himself' of the 'benefits and protections' of California's laws." The Court also held that defendant was not subject to California jurisdiction on the theory that he had, by sending his daughter there, caused an effect in that state. Without rejecting the idea that an effect in the state is often sufficient, the Court reasoned that this "effects" theory "was intended to reach wrongful activity outside of the State causing injury within the State or commercial activity affecting state residents." Finally, the Court rejected the idea that California's interest in the case supported jurisdiction: "[W]hile the presence of the children and one parent in California arguably might favor application of California law in a lawsuit in New York, the fact that California is the 'center of gravity' for choice of law purposes does not mean that California has personal jurisdiction over the defendant." Should this case have any effect outside the family law area? Does it stand for the proposition that non-commercial activities are subject to narrower jurisdictional rules?

3. In *World–Wide Volkswagen*, the Court places great stress on the sovereignty issue in personal jurisdiction. Two years later, however, it watered down this idea in Insurance Corp. of Ireland, Ltd. v. Compagnie des Bauxites de Guinee, 456 U.S. 694, 102 S.Ct. 2099, 72 L.Ed.2d 492 (1982), in upholding a finding of jurisdiction entered as a discovery sanction because

defendant had consented to disposition of the jurisdictional issue by the American court (see infra p. 829 for discussion of this aspect of the case):

> It is true that we have stated that the requirement of personal jurisdiction, as applied to state courts, reflects an element of federalism and the character of state sovereignty vis-a-vis other States. * * * The restriction on state sovereign power described in *World–Wide Volkswagen Corp.,* however, must be seen as ultimately a function of the individual liberty interest preserved by the Due Process Clause. That Clause is the only source of the personal jurisdiction requirement and the Clause itself makes no mention of federalism concerns. Furthermore, if the federalism concept operated as an independent restriction on the sovereign power of the court, it would not be possible to waive the personal jurisdiction requirement.

Does this signal the demise of the sovereignty concern in jurisdiction analysis? If so, does that mean that the decision in *World–Wide Volkswagen* was wrong? In the above passage, the Court says that the only source of the sovereignty principle is due process. Is the full faith and credit clause an alternative source? For an argument that this constitutional provision should be considered, see Abrams & Dimond, Toward a Constitutional Framework for the Control of State Court Jurisdiction, 69 Minn.L.Rev. 75 (1984).

4. Although the sovereignty concept does not easily fit within the traditional confines of a due process analysis, does it serve a useful purpose as a rigid limitation on a state's ability to manipulate concepts of "fairness," due to the concerns voiced by Justice Black in *International Shoe?* Professor Louis, for example, praised *World–Wide Volkswagen* and other recent restrictive decisions as a way to counterbalance "the relentless prod of local interest, [which ensures that] the state's long arm will inevitably reach farther and farther":

> In effect, what the Court has done in these cases is to turn the clock back to an earlier time when jurisdiction, like substantive tort law, was concerned more with the defendant's conduct and less with notions of social welfare and convenient risk allocation. A defendant must now act with respect to the forum state or have some control over and derive some benefit from the acts of those for which he is to be jurisdictionally charged. If the affiliating acts are limited in scope or territory, the jurisdictional risk will be correspondingly limited to claims arising specifically from them and to forums directly involved or affected.

> * * *

> The Court must set the limits of due process somewhere and no doubt believes that its mechanical approach will usually produce the right result, or at least will produce few very wrong and unfair ones. Thus, justice would only rarely be served if the state courts were permitted to search under a balancing approach for the random exception, which they, in their obvious self-interest, would perhaps too often erroneously purport to find. The potential sources of that self-interest are certainly numerous. For example, an affirmative jurisdictional finding may (1) allow the creation or augmentation of an estate or fund for

tax or local creditor purposes, (2) allow the assertion of state regulatory or taxing authority, (3) provide a local forum for state residents, (4) allow more sympathetic, and possibly more liberal, local juries and judges to decide issues and assess damages, (5) allow the choice of local substantive law, and (6) obviate the need for local attorneys to seek out, rely upon and divide their fees with out-of-state counsel.

Louis, The Grasp of Long Arm Jurisdiction Finally Exceeds Its Reach: A Comment on World–Wide Volkswagen Corp. v. Woodson and Rush v. Savchuk, 58 N.C.L.Rev. 407, 431 (1980).

5. The Court couches its general approach in terms of foreseeability. Is this analysis circular? Consider Redish, Due Process, Federalism, and Personal Jurisdiction: A Theoretical Evaluation, 75 Nw.U.L.Rev. 1112 (1981): "If the law were to tell potential litigants that they may be sued in any convenient forum, regardless of their previous contact with the forum, the litigants' reasonable expectations would have to change." Or is circularity in the eyes of the beholder? Consider West American Insurance Company v. Westin, Inc., 337 N.W.2d 676 (Minn.1983), in which the court held that *World–Wide Volkswagen* required reconsideration of two of its earlier decisions upholding jurisdiction over Wisconsin drinking establishments that served Minnesota 18–year-olds in suits by persons injured by those patrons after they returned to Minnesota: "It might be argued that [the earlier decisions] provided this foreseeability. This line of reasoning fails because it is essentially circular. The ultimate question in this case is whether [the earlier decisions] are still good law. To answer this query by arguing that after *World–Wide,* these cases make jurisdiction by Minnesota courts 'reasonably foreseeable' is to say that [the earlier decisions] are valid because [they] are valid." But if all the Wisconsin tavern owners were in fact aware of the earlier decisions, why wouldn't that fact satisfy *World–Wide?*

6. *World–Wide* was the first products liability personal jurisdiction decision by the Supreme Court. In that setting, the Court tells us that a manufacturer or distributor should foresee being sued in areas it "seeks to serve." How broad are such areas? World–Wide was the distributor for the states of New York, New Jersey and Connecticut. If it supplied a retailer in Camden, New Jersey, just across the Delaware River from Philadelphia, Pa., and the retailer advertised in the Philadelphia media, would it be found to have sought to serve Pennsylvania? Would that extend also to Delaware if the Philadelphia media reached there?

7. In *World–Wide Volkswagen*, the Court says that due process permits jurisdiction over "a corporation that delivers its products into the stream of commerce with the expectation that they will be purchased by consumers in the forum State. Cf. Gray v. American Radiator & Standard Sanitary Corp." Recall that in Gray v. American Radiator (supra p. 722 n. 6), the Illinois court upheld jurisdiction in Illinois over an Ohio company that supplied valves to a Pennsylvania company that manufactured water heaters using those valves when one of the water heaters exploded in Illinois, causing the plaintiff's injuries. The reasoning that jurisdiction is proper in such situations is often called the *stream of commerce* theory. Does the Court endorse that theory in *World–Wide Volkswagen?* We will return to this issue in Asahi Metal Industry Co. v. Superior Court, infra p. 765.

GENERAL AND SPECIFIC JURISDICTION

It does seem that the Court expects in *World–Wide Volkswagen* that Audi and World–Wide should be subject to Oklahoma jurisdiction in the Robinsons' case. Indeed, that seems to follow from the Court's implicit conclusion that they do "seek to serve" Oklahoma. Yet the Robinsons' purchase of a car in New York appears unrelated to their seeking to serve Oklahoma. If these defendants are subject to suit in Oklahoma on this claim that did not result from their contacts with Oklahoma, does this mean that Audi and Volkswagen of America are subject to suit by anyone on any claim in Oklahoma?

That would entail a finding that they are subject to *general jurisdiction*, a subject we will examine below, see infra p. 821, but it is worthwhile to introduce the concept now. In their article Jurisdiction to Adjudicate: A Suggested Analysis, 79 Harv.L.Rev. 1121 (1966), Professors von Mehren and Trautman introduced the idea that jurisdiction cases should be classified as involving either general or specific jurisdiction, and the Supreme Court has sometimes adhered to this dichotomy. The concept is that specific jurisdiction exists where the claim arises out of or is related to the defendant's contacts with the forum, while general jurisdiction permits all claims, of whatever origin, to be asserted against the defendant.

The problem is to apply the dichotomy to defendants in the position of Audi and Volkswagen of America. It seems unlikely that the Court intended that a manufacturer be subject to general jurisdiction in every state it seeks to serve. But how does the Robinsons' claim arise out of these defendants' contacts with Oklahoma? For another example of this problem, consider Buckeye Boiler Co. v. Superior Court, 71 Cal.2d 893, 80 Cal.Rptr. 113, 458 P.2d 57 (1969). Plaintiff was injured by the explosion in California of a boiler manufactured by defendant. Defendant regularly supplied boilers to one purchaser in California, generating gross sales of $25,000 to $35,000 per year. The problem was that the boiler that injured the plaintiff was of a different type from those sold to the California purchaser. Moreover, there was no indication that defendant had ever sold any of this type of boiler in California, and there was no explanation how the boiler that injured the plaintiff came to be in California.

The court nevertheless held that jurisdiction was proper, emphasizing the uncertainty about how the boiler reached California and the fact that defendant marketed boilers throughout the nation, so that it could have expected one of them to reach California: "But whether the pressure tank that injured plaintiff is one of a number of tanks sent into California by Buckeye through a 'chain of sales' or is the subject of an isolated California transaction apart from Buckeye's sales to [the known buyer in California], plaintiff's cause of action appears to arise from Buckeye's economic activity in California, the totality of its sales of pressure tanks to California customers or to other customers for foreseeable resale or use in California." Since the burden is ordinarily on the plaintiff to establish jurisdiction, however, shouldn't the uncertainty about how this boiler got to California cut against exercise of jurisdiction? Would the same reasoning have applied if the product that exploded had been a toaster that defendant also manufactured and distributed only in the Northeast?

It may be that foreseeability provides a solution to this problem. The Court says that the foreseeability that matters is the ability to foresee being haled into court in the forum. Does that foresight relate to the kind of claim being made? In terms of fundamental fairness, are Audi and Volkswagen of America worse off because the product liability suit against them in Oklahoma happens to have been filed by the Robinsons instead of some Oklahoman who bought his car there? The burden of defense on them, and the legal and factual issues that are to be resolved, are essentially the same. Thus, it might be said that specific jurisdiction includes types of claims rather than requiring that this precise claim results from the defendant's contacts with the forum. But that resolution, if it works, still leaves problems with *Buckeye Boiler* because defendant there did not distribute the offending product in the forum at all. To justify the same result there, one must conclude that the substantial similarity between different makes of boilers (as opposed to toasters) justifies jurisdiction. For further discussion, see infra p. 825 n. 1.

CALDER v. JONES, 465 U.S. 783, 104 S.Ct. 1482, 79 L.Ed.2d 804 (1984):

JUSTICE REHNQUIST delivered the opinion of the Court.

[In its October 9, 1979, issue, the National Enquirer (published by a Florida corporation that had its principal place of business in that state) printed a story about Shirley Jones, an entertainer who lives and works in California. The story made a number of uncomplimentary assertions about Jones, including a report that she drank so heavily as to prevent her from fulfilling her professional obligations. Jones sued the Enquirer for libel in California state court. Perhaps because some 12% of its nationwide circulation of 5 million is sold in California, nearly twice the distribution of any other state, the paper answered without raising any objection to jurisdiction.

Jones also sued Calder, the paper's editor, and South, the reporter whose byline appeared on the story. Both were Florida residents, and they objected to California jurisdiction. South frequently travels to California on business but claimed he did his research on this story by telephone from Florida to California, although the trial court found that he made one visit to the state in connection with the story. Calder, who "oversees just about every function of the Enquirer," reviewed and approved the subject for the story and edited the article in final form. He also refused Jones' demand for a retraction. But he had visited California only twice—once on pleasure and once to testify at the trial of the unrelated libel suit against the Enquirer brought by entertainer Carol Burnett.]

The Supreme Court unanimously upheld jurisdiction, but declined to premise it on South's numerous telephone calls to California and visit to that state.]

The Due Process Clause of the Fourteenth Amendment to the United States Constitution permits personal jurisdiction over a defendant in any State with which the defendant has "certain minimum contacts ... such that the maintenance of the suit does not offend 'traditional notions of fair play and substantial justice.' " International Shoe Co. v. Washington, 326 U.S. 310, 316, 66 S.Ct. 154, 158, 90 L.Ed. 95 (1945). In judging minimum contacts, a court properly focuses on "the relationship among the defendant, the forum, and the litigation." Shaffer v. Heitner, 433 U.S. 186, 204, 97 S.Ct. 2569, 2579, 53 L.Ed.2d 683 (1977). The plaintiff's lack of "contacts" will not defeat otherwise proper jurisdiction, see Keeton v. Hustler Magazine, Inc., 465 U.S. 770, 779–81, 104 S.Ct. 1473, 1480–1482, 79 L.Ed.2d 790 (1984), but they may be so manifold as to permit jurisdiction when it would not exist in their absence. Here, the plaintiff is the focus of the activities of the defendants out of which the suit arises. See McGee v. International Life Ins. Co., 355 U.S. 220, 78 S.Ct. 199, 2 L.Ed.2d 223 (1957).

The allegedly libelous story concerned the California activities of a California resident. It impugned the professionalism of an entertainer whose television career was centered in California. The article was drawn from California sources, and the brunt of the harm, in terms both of respondent's emotional distress and the injury to her professional reputation, was suffered in California. In sum, California is the focal point both of the story and of the harm suffered. Jurisdiction over petitioners is therefore proper in California based on the "effects" of their Florida conduct in California. World–Wide Volkswagen Corp. v. Woodson, 444 U.S. 286, 297–298, 100 S.Ct. 559, 567–568, 62 L.Ed.2d 490 (1980).

Petitioners argue that they are not responsible for the circulation of the article in California. A reporter and an editor, they claim, have no direct economic stake in their employer's sales in a distant State. Nor are ordinary employees able to control their employer's marketing activity. The mere fact that they can "foresee" that the article will be circulated and have an effect in California is not sufficient for an assertion of jurisdiction. World–Wide Volkswagen Corp. v. Woodson, 444 U.S., at 295, 100 S.Ct., at 566. They do not "in effect appoint the [article their] agent for service of process." World–Wide Volkswagen Corp. v. Woodson, 444 U.S., at 296, 100 S.Ct., at 566. Petitioners liken themselves to a welder employed in Florida who works on a boiler which subsequently explodes in California. Cases which hold that jurisdiction will be proper over the manufacturer, Buckeye Boiler Co. v. Superior Court, 71 Cal.2d 893, 80 Cal.Rptr. 113, 458 P.2d 57 (1969); Gray v.

American Radiator & Standard Sanitary Corp., 22 Ill.2d 432, 176 N.E.2d 761 (1961), should not be applied to the welder who has no control over and derives no direct benefit from his employer's sales in that distant State.

Petitioners' analogy does not wash. Whatever the status of their hypothetical welder, petitioners are not charged with mere untargeted negligence. Rather, their intentional, and allegedly tortious, actions were expressly aimed at California. Petitioner South wrote and petitioner Calder edited an article that they knew would have a potentially devastating impact upon respondent. And they knew that the brunt of that injury would be felt by respondent in the State in which she lives and works and in which the National Enquirer has its largest circulation. Under the circumstances, petitioners must "reasonably anticipate being haled into court there" to answer for the truth of the statements made in their article. World–Wide Volkswagen Corp. v. Woodson, 444 U.S., at 297, 100 S.Ct., at 567; Kulko v. Superior Court, 436 U.S. 84, 97–98, 98 S.Ct. 1690, 1699–1700, 56 L.Ed.2d 132 (1978); Shaffer v. Heitner, 433 U.S. 186, 216, 97 S.Ct. 2569, 2586, 53 L.Ed.2d 683 (1977). An individual injured in California need not go to Florida to seek redress from persons who, though remaining in Florida, knowingly cause the injury in California. Petitioners are correct that their contacts with California are not to be judged according to their employer's activities there. On the other hand, their status as employees does not somehow insulate them from jurisdiction. Each defendant's contacts with the forum State must be assessed individually. In this case, petitioners are primary participants in an alleged wrongdoing intentionally directed at a California resident, and jurisdiction over them is proper on that basis.

Notes and Questions

1. Keeton v. Hustler Magazine, Inc., 465 U.S. 770, 104 S.Ct. 1473, 79 L.Ed.2d 790 (1984), a companion case to *Calder,* was also a libel suit against a nationally distributed publication. Plaintiff, a New York resident, had first sued defendant, an Ohio corporation, in Ohio. When this suit was dismissed on statute of limitations grounds (considered "procedural" and therefore not on the merits for res judicata purposes), the only state in which the limitations period had not yet run was New Hampshire. Even though she had no prior contacts with New Hampshire, plaintiff filed a second libel suit there. Defendant regularly sold 10,000 to 15,000 copies of its magazine, a very small proportion of the total distribution, in New Hampshire. Under the "single publication rule" (that all damages sustained in all jurisdictions are recoverable in one action), plaintiff sought in the second suit to recover for injuries suffered from the nationwide circulation of the defamation. Reasoning that "the New Hampshire tail is too small to wag so large an out-of-state dog," the lower courts dismissed the case for lack of personal jurisdiction.

The Supreme Court reversed. It found that "regular monthly sales of thousands of magazines cannot by any stretch of the imagination be characterized as random, isolated or fortuitous." Despite the single publication rule, New Hampshire's unusually long statute of limitations, and plaintiff's lack of contacts with the forum, jurisdiction was therefore proper in New Hampshire. The Court reasoned that New Hampshire had a sufficient interest in redressing injuries that occurred within the state because its residents were allegedly misled about plaintiff, and that her reputation was harmed by these misrepresentations even though she was otherwise unknown in New Hampshire. Plaintiff's lack of contacts, although not irrelevant to the issue of state interest, did not foreclose jurisdiction. The Court refused to consider choice of law issues because "any potential unfairness of applying New Hampshire's statute of limitations to all aspects of this nationwide suit has nothing to do with jurisdiction of the Court to adjudicate the claims," and choice of law concerns "should not distort the jurisdictional inquiry."

In Gordy v. Daily News, L.P., 95 F.3d 829 (9th Cir.1996), Berry Gordy, former president of Motown Records, filed suit in California claiming a story in the New York Daily News defamed him. The story was not about California activities of Gordy and did not mention California. More than 99% of the circulation of the paper was distributed within 300 miles of New York City. But the News did deliver 13 copies of its daily edition and 18 copies of its Sunday edition to California recipients. The court upheld jurisdiction:

> The prime targeting arises, of course, from the fact that Gordy is an individual who lives in California * * *. We have no desire to republish the alleged libel, but it was of a nature that clearly would have a severe impact on Gordy as an individual. It is reasonable to expect the bulk of the harm from defamation of an individual to be felt at his domicile. Targeting also occurs because the Daily News regularly distributes from 13 to 18 copies of its publication in California, and the defamatory column contained in those copies causes harm in California.

Contrast Schwarzenegger v. Fred Martin Motor Co., 374 F.3d 797 (9th Cir.2004) (Ohio car dealership did not target California when it used a picture of California Governor Arnold Schwarzenegger as the "Terminator" in an advertisement run in a local newspaper in Ohio that was not distributed in California).

2. In both *Calder* and *Keeton,* the media defendants argued that personal jurisdiction should be more circumscribed in defamation cases against the media to avoid chilling First Amendment interests. Lower courts had in the past shown some sympathy to this argument, but the Supreme Court rejected it unequivocally in *Calder:* "The infusion of such considerations would needlessly complicate an already imprecise inquiry. Moreover, the potential chill on protected First Amendment activity stemming from libel and defamation actions is already taken into account in the constitutional limitations on the substantive law governing such suits. To reintroduce those concerns at the jurisdictional stage would be a form of double counting."

3. In *Calder,* the Court uses a number of phrases to explain why jurisdiction over Calder and South is different from jurisdiction over the welder who negligently produces a boiler. It says, for example, that they were "primary participants" who are "not charged with mere untargeted negligence." How many other employees of a defendant charged with an intentional tort would be similarly covered by the Court's reasoning? Does it

cover non-employees? Suppose that South gathered information for his story from other Floridians who knew Jones. Could they be sued in California when their stories were printed in the Enquirer? Is there something unfair about subjecting someone to jurisdiction in places where material is circulated if he has no control over that circulation? Consider the case of Harry Reems, a star of X-rated movies, who was prosecuted for obscenity in Tennessee when Deep Throat, a movie in which he appeared as an actor, was distributed widely by the makers of the movie. Was it fair to subject him to prosecution in Tennessee for activities before a camera in Florida (where the movie was made) when he had no role in the distribution of the film? See A. Dershowitz, The Best Defense 155–74 (1982).

In Madara v. Hall, 916 F.2d 1510 (11th Cir.1990), a rock star gave a telephonic interview from New York, his home, to a magazine published in California that was distributed nationwide. When he was sued in Florida for comments made in the interview about a Florida resident, the court held that jurisdiction was not proper: "Simply giving an interview to a reporter is not enough to cause Hall to anticipate being haled into court in Florida. Hall was not the magazine's publisher and did not control its circulation and distribution. * * * Hall's mere awareness, if he indeed was aware, that a small number of copies of the magazine might find their way to Florida is not enough to justify the exercise of personal jurisdiction." Compare Sinatra v. National Enquirer, Inc., 854 F.2d 1191 (9th Cir.1988), in which the court upheld suit in California against a Swiss clinic for statements in an article concerning plaintiff's alleged treatment at the clinic. The clinic pursued California clients through advertising and intended to receive further advertising benefit in California via publication of its name in the National Enquirer article.

4. In Kulko v. Superior Court (supra p. 741 n. 2), the Court refused to permit California jurisdiction on an effects test, but *Calder* adopts one. In *Calder*, all the indicators mentioned by the Court point toward jurisdiction in California. Thus, we are told that the article "concerned the California activities of a California resident," and that "the brunt of the harm" was California. How many of these factors need to coalesce to justify jurisdiction on the Court's effects test? Consider:

(a) Suppose Jones lived in Arizona when she was not making TV programs. Would jurisdiction then be permissible in both Arizona and California? Would it be permissible in either?

(b) Suppose Jones sometimes acted in plays in New York. New York has the second largest circulation of the National Enquirer. Would jurisdiction be permissible there?

5. Does the effects analysis give plaintiff too much control over jurisdiction? Consider Burt v. Board of Regents, 757 F.2d 242 (10th Cir.1985). Plaintiff doctor had done his medical residency at the University of Nebraska and then moved to Colorado. He asked Dr. Connolly, the head of the University's Department of Orthopedic Surgery, to provide a reference, and Dr. Connolly said uncomplimentary things about plaintiff. Plaintiff sued Connolly in Colorado, and a divided court of appeals upheld jurisdiction:

Nor are we persuaded by Dr. Connolly's claim that it violates due process to hale him into court in Colorado because the letter was, in effect, solicited by Dr. Burt, who gave Dr. Connolly's name to the hospitals. Dr. Burt solicited a letter of reference; he did not solicit a malicious falsehood. Taking Dr. Burt's allegations as true, as we must on a motion to dismiss, we hold that no due process notions of fairness are violated by requiring one who intentionally libels another to answer for the truth of his statements in any state where the libel causes harm to the victim. To the extent that Dr. Connolly's statements damage Dr. Burt's reputation and his ability to practice his profession, the damage occurred in Colorado.

Judge Seth dissented:

> In the case before us, the letter was, of course, sent to Colorado but the "focal" point of the story was Nebraska. The letter was about what had taken place in Nebraska, not Colorado. The story was certainly not drawn from Colorado sources. The action was initiated by plaintiff. We thus have but half a *Calder*.

The Supreme Court granted certiorari in *Burt*, but later dismissed the case as moot. See also Brainerd v. Governors of the University of Alberta, 873 F.2d 1257 (9th Cir.1989) (suit allowed in Arizona for allegedly defamatory statement by vice president of Canadian university about a former faculty member in response to inquiry by the faculty member's present employer, the University of Arizona).

Contrast Reynolds v. International Amateur Athletic Federation, 23 F.3d 1110 (6th Cir.1994), in which a world champion sprinter sued the IAAF for suspending him when a drug test after a track meet in Monaco proved positive. Reynolds sued in Ohio, alleging that, as a result of the IAAF press release announcing the suspension, he had lost some $4 million in endorsement and appearance fees in Ohio. The court held that jurisdiction was not proper under *Calder* because: the press release concerned Reynolds' activities in Monaco, not Ohio, Reynolds' reputation was international rather than centered in Ohio, the IAAF itself did not publish the report in Ohio, Ohio was not the "focal point" of the press release, and there was no evidence that the IAAF knew of the contracts or of their Ohio origin.

6. It might be suggested that *Calder* only applies to defamation cases, but this limitation has not been adopted:

> The Supreme Court did not intend the *Calder* "effects" test to apply only to libel cases. However, the "effects" of the intentional tort of libel in the forum state (i.e., the plaintiff's residence) are perhaps more pronounced than the "effects" of most other intentional torts. Nevertheless, the key to *Calder* is that the effects of an alleged intentional tort are to be assessed as part of the analysis of the defendant's relevant contacts with the forum. Whether these effects, either alone or in combination with other contacts, are sufficient to support in personam jurisdiction will turn upon the particular facts of each case.

Wallace v. Herron, 778 F.2d 391 (7th Cir.1985).

With business torts, one could argue that the necessary impact occurs at the headquarters of a business no matter where the wrongdoing actually occurs. Recall Green v. Advance Ross, Inc., supra p. 726 n.2. The courts have generally not adopted this approach:

We believe that for *Calder* to apply, the plaintiff must allege facts sufficient to meet a three-prong test. First, the defendant must have committed an intentional tort. Second, the plaintiff must have felt the brunt of the harm caused by that tort in the forum, such that the forum can be said to be the focal point of the harm suffered by the plaintiff as a result of the tort. Third, the defendant must have expressly aimed his tortious conduct at the forum, such that the forum can be said to be the focal point of the tortious activity.

IMO Industries, Inc. v. Kiekert AG, 155 F.3d 254, 256 (3d Cir.1998). Plaintiff there, a multinational corporation with headquarters in New Jersey, sued defendant, a German company, in New Jersey. Plaintiff alleged that defendant had tortiously interfered with its attempt to sell its wholly-owned Italian subsidiary to one of defendant's competitors by sending letters to a New York investment firm threatening to revoke a licensing agreement it had with plaintiff's subsidiary. The court concluded that plaintiff had not pointed to sufficient facts indicating that defendant "expressly aimed" its tortious conduct at New Jersey. "To the contrary, the focus of the dispute— i.e., the proposed sale of an Italian company to a French company and a claim of rights by a German company pursuant to a license agreement apparently governed by German law—and the alleged contacts by [defendant] (i.e., its correspondence) all appeared to be focused outside the forum."

Compare Indianapolis Colts v. Metropolitan Baltimore Football Club Limited Partnership, 34 F.3d 410 (7th Cir.1994). After the owner of the Baltimore Colts National Football League moved the team to Indianapolis, fans in Baltimore obtained a franchise in the Canadian Football League and prepared to launch a new football team to be called the "Baltimore CFL Colts." The Indianapolis Colts sued in Indiana, claiming trademark infringement, and the court upheld jurisdiction:

> The Indiana Colts use the trademarks they seek to defend in this suit mainly in Indiana. If the trademarks are impaired, as the suit alleges, the injury will be felt mainly in Indiana. By choosing a name that might be found to be confusingly similar to that of the Indianapolis Colts, the defendants assumed the risk of injuring valuable property located in Indiana. Since there can be no tort without an injury, the state in which the injury occurs is the state in which the tort occurs, and someone who commits a tort in Indiana should, one might suppose, be amenable to suit there. This conclusion is supported by the Supreme Court's decision in Calder v. Jones.

The court noted as well that defendants intended to broadcast games involving the new Baltimore team nationwide via cable TV.

7. In Yahoo! Inc. v. La Ligue Contre Le Racisme Et L'Antisemitisme, 379 F.3d 1120 (9th Cir.2004), defendants had sued Yahoo in a French court and obtained an order from that court directing plaintiff to remove—on pain of a fine of 100,000 French Francs per day—certain anti-semitic and Nazi items from the server it maintained in California. Defendants' French suit was based on French laws prohibiting access to Nazi items, which postings on Yahoo made possible from France. Defendants had the French complaint and order served in California by the U.S. Marshals Service. Plaintiff then sued the parties who filed the French suit in an American court, seeking a

declaratory judgment that the French order was not enforceable in the United States because it violated the free-speech guarantees of the First Amendment. The court held there was no jurisdiction because *Calder* requires "something more" than a foreign act with forseeable effects in the forum. To rely on "express aiming" under *Calder*, it concluded, plaintiff must allege that the conduct was wrongful. But the French court had upheld defendants' position under French law and, as a result, a "we cannot say here that the parties did anything wrongful, sufficient for a finding of 'express aiming,' in bringing this suit against Yahoo!." Id. at 1126. A dissenting judge argued that "though wrongful conduct will satisfy [*Calder*], it is not necessarily required." Id. at 1127. The court later granted rehearing en banc. See 399 F.3d 1010.

BURGER KING CORP. v. RUDZEWICZ

Supreme Court of the United States, 1985.
471 U.S. 462, 105 S.Ct. 2174, 85 L.Ed.2d 528.

JUSTICE BRENNAN delivered the opinion of the Court.

The State of Florida's long-arm statute extends jurisdiction to "[a]ny person, whether or not a citizen or resident of this state," who, inter alia, "[b]reach[es] a contract in this state by failing to perform acts required by the contract to be performed in this state," so long as the cause of action arises from the alleged contractual breach. Fla.Stat. § 48.193(1)(g) (Supp.1984). The United States District Court for the Southern District of Florida, sitting in diversity, relied on this provision in exercising personal jurisdiction over a Michigan resident who allegedly had breached a franchise agreement with a Florida corporation by failing to make required payments in Florida. The question presented is whether this exercise of long-arm jurisdiction offended "traditional conception[s] of fair play and substantial justice" embodied in the Due Process Clause of the Fourteenth Amendment.

I

[Burger King, a Florida corporation headquartered in Florida, operates 3,000 restaurants, 80% through a franchise operation called the "Burger King System" that prescribes uniform standards for format and building design as well as food preparation. Franchisees are therefore required to attend training seminars at Burger King University in Miami and at Whopper College Regional Training Centers around the country. They are subject to "exacting regulation of virtually every conceivable aspect of their operations by Burger King." Ultimate authority rests with Burger King headquarters in Miami, but day-to-day monitoring is conducted through a network of district offices.]

The instant litigation grows out of Burger King's termination of one of its franchisees, and is aptly described by the franchisee as "a divorce proceeding among commercial partners." The appellee John Rudzewicz, a Michigan citizen and resident, is the senior partner in a Detroit accounting firm. In 1978, he was approached by Brian MacShara, the son of a business acquaintance, who suggested that they jointly apply to

Burger King for a franchise in the Detroit area. MacShara proposed to serve as the manager of the restaurant if Rudzewicz would put up the investment capital; in exchange, the two would evenly share the profits. Believing that MacShara's idea offered attractive investment and tax-deferral opportunities, Rudzewicz agreed to the venture.

Rudzewicz and MacShara jointly applied for a franchise to Burger King's Birmingham, Michigan district office in the autumn of 1978. Their application was forwarded to Burger King's Miami headquarters, which entered into a preliminary agreement with them in February 1979. During the ensuing four months it was agreed that Rudzewicz and MacShara would assume operation of an existing facility in Drayton Plains, Michigan. MacShara attended the prescribed management courses in Miami during this period, and the franchisees purchased $165,000 worth of restaurant equipment from Burger King's Davmor Industries division in Miami. Even before the final agreements were signed, however, the parties began to disagree over site-development fees, building design, computation of monthly rent, and whether the franchisees would be able to assign their liabilities to a corporation they had formed. During these disputes Rudzewicz and MacShara negotiated both with the Birmingham district office and with the Miami headquarters.[7] With some misgivings, Rudzewicz and MacShara finally obtained limited concessions from the Miami headquarters, signed the final agreements, and commenced operations in June 1979. By signing the final agreements, Rudzewicz obligated himself personally to payments exceeding $1 million over the 20–year franchise relationship.

The Drayton Plains facility apparently enjoyed steady business during the summer of 1979, but patronage declined after a recession began later that year. Rudzewicz and MacShara soon fell far behind in their monthly payments to Miami. Headquarters sent notices of default, and an extended period of negotiations began among the franchisees, the Birmingham district office, and the Miami headquarters. After several Burger King officials in Miami had engaged in prolonged but ultimately unsuccessful negotiations with the franchisees by mail and by telephone, headquarters terminated the franchise and ordered Rudzewicz and MacShara to vacate the premises. They refused and continued to occupy and operate the facility as a Burger King restaurant.

[Burger King sued Rudzewicz and McShara for breach of contract, and for tortiously infringing its trademarks and service marks by continuing to operate the Drayton Plains facility. Defendants filed a counterclaim accusing Burger King of violation of Michigan's Franchise Investment Law. After a 3–day bench trial, the district court entered judgement in Burger King's favor for $228,875 in contract damages and ordered defendants to cease operating the restaurant and turn the keys

---

7. Although Rudzewicz and MacShara dealt with the Birmingham district office on a regular basis, they communicated directly with the Miami headquarters in forming the contracts; moreover, they learned that the district office had "very little" decision-making authority and accordingly turned directly to headquarters in seeking to resolve their disputes.

over to Burger King, meanwhile rejecting their counterclaim. McShara did not appeal, and Rudzewicz settled the trademark infringement aspects of the judgment. Accordingly, the Court noted that it did not need to address the extent to which the tortious act provisions of Florida's long-arm statute could apply to out-of-state trademark infringement under Calder v. Jones, supra p. 745.]

II

A

The Due Process Clause protects an individual's liberty interest in not being subject to the binding judgments of a forum with which he has established no meaningful "contacts, ties, or relations." International Shoe Co. v. Washington, 326 U.S., at 319, 66 S.Ct., at 160.[13] By requiring that individuals have "fair warning that a particular activity may subject [them] to the jurisdiction of a foreign sovereign," Shaffer v. Heitner, 433 U.S. 186, 218, 97 S.Ct. 2569, 2587, 53 L.Ed.2d 683 (1977) (Stevens, J., concurring in judgment), the Due Process Clause "gives a degree of predictability to the legal system that allows potential defendants to structure their primary conduct with some minimum assurance as to where that conduct will and will not render them liable to suit," World–Wide Volkswagen Corp. v. Woodson, 444 U.S. 286, 297, 100 S.Ct. 559, 567, 62 L.Ed.2d 490 (1980).

Where a forum seeks to assert specific jurisdiction over an out-of-state defendant who has not consented to suit there, this "fair warning" requirement is satisfied if the defendant has "purposefully directed" his activities at residents of the forum, Keeton v. Hustler Magazine, Inc., 465 U.S. 770, 774, 104 S.Ct. 1473, 1478, 79 L.Ed.2d 790 (1984), and the litigation results from alleged injuries that "arise out of or relate to" those activities, Helicopteros Nacionales de Colombia, S.A. v. Hall, 466 U.S. 408, 414, 104 S.Ct. 1868, 1872, 80 L.Ed.2d 404 (1984).[15] Thus "[t]he forum State does not exceed its powers under the Due Process Clause if it asserts personal jurisdiction over a corporation that delivers its products into the stream of commerce with the expectation that they will be purchased by consumers in the forum State" and those products subsequently injure forum consumers. World–Wide Volkswagen Corp. v. Woodson, supra, 444 U.S., at 297–298, 100 S.Ct., at 567–568. Similarly, a publisher who distributes magazines in a distant State may fairly be held accountable in that forum for damages resulting there from an allegedly

---

13. Although this protection operates to restrict state power, it "must be seen as ultimately a function of the individual liberty interest preserved by the Due Process Clause" rather than as a function "of federalism concerns." Insurance Corp. of Ireland, Ltd. v. Compagnie des Bauxites de Guinee, 456 U.S. 694, 702–703, n. 10, 102 S.Ct. 2099, 2104–2105, n. 10, 72 L.Ed.2d 492 (1982).

15. "Specific" jurisdiction contrasts with "general" jurisdiction, pursuant to which "a State exercises personal jurisdiction over a defendant in a suit not arising out of or related to the defendant's contacts with the forum." Helicopteros Nacionales de Colombia, S.A. v. Hall, 466 U.S. 408, 414, n. 9, 104 S.Ct. 1868, 1872, n. 9, 80 L.Ed.2d 404 (1984); see also Perkins v. Benguet Consolidated Mining Co., 342 U.S. 437, 72 S.Ct. 413, 96 L.Ed. 485 (1952).

defamatory story. Keeton v. Hustler Magazine, Inc., supra; see also Calder v. Jones, 465 U.S. 783, 104 S.Ct. 1482, 79 L.Ed.2d 804 (1984) (suit against author and editor). And with respect to interstate contractual obligations, we have emphasized that parties who "reach out beyond one state and create continuing relationships and obligations with citizens of another state" are subject to regulation and sanctions in the other State for the consequences of their activities. Travelers Health Assn. v. Virginia, 339 U.S. 643, 647, 70 S.Ct. 927, 929, 94 L.Ed. 1154 (1950). See also McGee v. International Life Insurance Co., 355 U.S. 220, 222–223, 78 S.Ct. 199, 200–201, 2 L.Ed.2d 223 (1957).

We have noted several reasons why a forum legitimately may exercise personal jurisdiction over a nonresident who "purposefully directs" his activities toward forum residents. A State generally has a "manifest interest" in providing its residents with a convenient forum for redressing injuries inflicted by out-of-state actors. Id., at 223, 78 S.Ct., at 201; see also Calder v. Jones, 465 U.S., at 776, 104 S.Ct., at 1479. Moreover, where individuals "purposefully derive benefit" from their interstate activities, Kulko v. California Superior Court, 436 U.S. 84, 96, 98 S.Ct. 1690, 1699, 56 L.Ed.2d 132 (1978), it may well be unfair to allow them to escape having to account in other States for consequences that arise proximately from such activities; the Due Process Clause may not readily be wielded as a territorial shield to avoid interstate obligations that have been voluntarily assumed. And because "modern transportation and communications have made it much less burdensome for a party sued to defend himself in a State where he engages in economic activity," it usually will not be unfair to subject him to the burdens of litigating in another forum for disputes relating to such activity. McGee v. International Life Insurance Co., 355 U.S., at 223, 78 S.Ct., at 201.

Notwithstanding these considerations, the constitutional touchstone remains whether the defendant purposefully established "minimum contacts" in the forum State. Although it has been argued that foreseeability of causing injury in another State should be sufficient to establish such contacts there when policy considerations so require, the Court has consistently held that this kind of foreseeability is not a "sufficient benchmark" for exercising personal jurisdiction. World–Wide Volkswagen Corp. v. Woodson, 444 U.S., at 295, 100 S.Ct., at 566. Instead, "the foreseeability that is critical to due process analysis . . . is that the defendant's conduct and connection with the forum State are such that he should reasonably anticipate being haled into court there." Id., at 297, 100 S.Ct., at 567. * * *

This "purposeful availment" requirement ensures that a defendant will not be haled into a jurisdiction solely as a result of "random," "fortuitous," or "attenuated" contacts, Keeton v. Hustler Magazine, Inc., supra, 465 U.S., at 774, 104 S.Ct., at 1478; World–Wide Volkswagen Corp. v. Woodson, 444 U.S., at 299, 100 S.Ct., at 568, or of the "unilateral activity of another party or a third person," Helicopteros Nacionales de Colombia, S.A. v. Hall, supra, 466 U.S., at 417, 104 S.Ct.,

at 1873. Jurisdiction is proper, however, where the contacts proximately
result from actions by the defendant himself that create a "substantial
connection" with the forum State. McGee v. International Life Insurance
Co., supra, 355 U.S., at 223, 78 S.Ct., at 201. Thus where the defendant
"deliberately" has engaged in significant activities within a State, Keeton v. Hustler Magazine, Inc., 465 U.S., at 781, 104 S.Ct., at 1481, or has
created "continuing obligations" between himself and residents of the
forum, Travelers Health Assn. v. Virginia, 339 U.S., at 648, 70 S.Ct., at
929, he manifestly has availed himself of the privilege of conducting
business there, and because his activities are shielded by "the benefits
and protections" of the forum's laws it is presumptively not unreasonable to require him to submit to the burdens of litigation in that forum
as well.

Jurisdiction in these circumstances may not be avoided merely
because the defendant did not physically enter the forum State. Although territorial presence frequently will enhance a potential defendant's affiliation with a State and reinforce the reasonable foreseeability
of suit there, it is an inescapable fact of modern commercial life that a
substantial amount of business is transacted solely by mail and wire
communications across state lines, thus obviating the need for physical
presence within a State in which business is conducted. So long as a
commercial actor's efforts are "purposefully directed" toward residents
of another State, we have consistently rejected the notion that an
absence of physical contacts can defeat personal jurisdiction there.

Once it has been decided that a defendant purposefully established
minimum contacts within the forum State, these contacts may be considered in light of other factors to determine whether the assertion of
personal jurisdiction would comport with "fair play and substantial
justice." International Shoe Co. v. Washington, 326 U.S., at 320, 66
S.Ct., at 160. Thus courts in "appropriate case[s]" may evaluate "the
burden on the defendant," "the forum State's interest in adjudicating
the dispute," "the plaintiff's interest in obtaining convenient and effective relief," "the interstate judicial system's interest in obtaining the
most efficient resolution of controversies," and the "shared interest of
the several States in furthering fundamental substantive social policies."
World–Wide Volkswagen Corp. v. Woodson, supra, 444 U.S., at 292, 100
S.Ct., at 564. These considerations sometimes serve to establish the
reasonableness of jurisdiction upon a lesser showing of minimum contacts than would otherwise be required. On the other hand, where a
defendant who purposefully has directed his activities at forum residents
seeks to defeat jurisdiction, he must present a compelling case that the
presence of some other considerations would render jurisdiction unreasonable. Most such considerations usually may be accommodated
through means short of finding jurisdiction unconstitutional. For example, the potential clash of the forum's law with the "fundamental
substantive social policies" of another State may be accommodated
through application of the forum's choice-of-law rules. Similarly, a
defendant claiming substantial inconvenience may seek a change of

venue. Nevertheless, minimum requirements inherent in the concept of "fair play and substantial justice" may defeat the reasonableness of jurisdiction even if the defendant has purposefully engaged in forum activities. World–Wide Volkswagen Corp. v. Woodson, 444 U.S., at 292, 100 S.Ct., at 564. As we previously have noted, jurisdictional rules may not be employed in such a way as to make litigation "so gravely difficult and inconvenient" that a party unfairly is at a "severe disadvantage" in comparison to his opponent.

B

(1)

Applying these principles to the case at hand, we believe there is substantial record evidence supporting the District Court's conclusion that the assertion of personal jurisdiction over Rudzewicz in Florida for the alleged breach of his franchise agreement did not offend due process. At the outset, we note a continued division among lower courts respecting whether and to what extent a contract can constitute a "contact" for purposes of due process analysis. If the question is whether an individual's contract with an out-of-state party alone can automatically establish sufficient minimum contacts in the other party's home forum, we believe the answer clearly is that it cannot. The Court long ago rejected the notion that personal jurisdiction might turn on "mechanical" tests, or on "conceptualistic ... theories of the place of contracting or of performance." Instead, we have emphasized the need for a "highly realistic" approach that recognizes that a "contract" is "ordinarily but an intermediate step serving to tie up prior business negotiations with future consequences which themselves are the real object of the business transaction." It is these factors—prior negotiations and contemplated future consequences, along with the terms of the contract and the parties' actual course of dealing—that must be evaluated in determining whether the defendant purposefully established minimum contacts within the forum.

In this case, no physical ties to Florida can be attributed to Rudzewicz other than MacShara's brief training course in Miami.[22] Rudzewicz did not maintain offices in Florida and, for all that appears from the record, has never even visited there. Yet this franchise dispute grew

---

22. The Eleventh Circuit held that MacShara's presence in Florida was irrelevant to the question of Rudzewicz's minimum contacts with that forum, reasoning that "Rudzewicz and MacShara never formed a partnership" and "signed the agreements in their individual capacities." The two did jointly form a corporation through which they were seeking to conduct the franchise, however. They were required to decide which one of them would travel to Florida to satisfy the training requirements so that they could commence business, and Rudzewicz participated in the decision that MacShara would go there. We have previously noted that when commercial activities are "carried on in behalf of" an out-of-state party those activities may sometimes be ascribed to the party, International Shoe Co. v. Washington, 326 U.S. 310, 320, 66 S.Ct. 154, 160, 90 L.Ed. 95 (1945), at least where he is a "primary participan[t]" in the enterprise and has acted purposefully in directing those activities, Calder v. Jones, 465 U.S., at 790, 104 S.Ct., at 1487. Because MacShara's matriculation at Burger King University is not pivotal to the disposition of this case, we need not resolve the permissible bounds of such attribution.

directly out of "a contract which had a *substantial* connection with that State." McGee v. International Life Insurance Co., 355 U.S., at 223, 78 S.Ct., at 201 (emphasis added). Eschewing the option of operating an independent local enterprise, Rudzewicz deliberately "reach[ed] out beyond" Michigan and negotiated with a Florida corporation for the purchase of a long-term franchise and the manifold benefits that would derive from affiliation with a nationwide organization. Travelers Health Assn. v. Virginia, 339 U.S., at 647, 70 S.Ct., at 929. Upon approval, he entered into a carefully structured 20–year relationship that envisioned continuing and wide-reaching contacts with Burger King in Florida. In light of Rudzewicz's voluntary acceptance of the long-term and exacting regulation of his business from Burger King's Miami headquarters, the "quality and nature" of his relationship to the company in Florida can in no sense be viewed as "random," "fortuitous," or "attenuated." Rudzewicz's refusal to make the contractually required payments in Miami, and his continued use of Burger King's trademarks and confidential business information after his termination, caused foreseeable injuries to the corporation in Florida. For these reasons it was, at the very least, presumptively reasonable for Rudzewicz to be called to account there for such injuries.

The Court of Appeals concluded, however, that in light of the supervision emanating from Burger King's district office in Birmingham, Rudzewicz reasonably believed that "the Michigan office was for all intents and purposes the embodiment of Burger King" and that he therefore had no "reason to anticipate a Burger King suit outside of Michigan." This reasoning overlooks substantial record evidence indicating that Rudzewicz most certainly knew that he was affiliating himself with an enterprise based primarily in Florida. The contract documents themselves emphasize that Burger King's operations are conducted and supervised from the Miami headquarters, that all relevant notices and payments must be sent there, and that the agreements were made in and enforced from Miami. Moreover, the parties' actual course of dealing repeatedly confirmed that decisionmaking authority was vested in the Miami headquarters and that the district office served largely as an intermediate link between the headquarters and the franchisees. When problems arose over building design, site-development fees, rent computation, and the defaulted payments, Rudzewicz and MacShara learned that the Michigan office was powerless to resolve their disputes and could only channel their communications to Miami. Throughout these disputes, the Miami headquarters and the Michigan franchisees carried on a continuous course of direct communications by mail and by telephone, and it was the Miami headquarters that made the key negotiating decisions out of which the instant litigation arose. See n.7, supra.

Moreover, we believe the Court of Appeals gave insufficient weight to provisions in the various franchise documents providing that all disputes would be governed by Florida law. The franchise agreement, for example, stated:

"This Agreement shall become valid when executed and accepted by BKC at Miami, Florida; it shall be deemed made and entered into in the State of Florida and shall be governed and construed under and in accordance with the laws of the State of Florida. The choice of law designation does not require that all suits concerning this Agreement be filed in Florida."

The Court of Appeals reasoned that choice-of-law provisions are irrelevant to the question of personal jurisdiction, relying on Hanson v. Denckla for the proposition that "the center of gravity for choice-of-law purposes does not necessarily confer the sovereign prerogative to assert jurisdiction." This reasoning misperceives the import of the quoted proposition. The Court in *Hanson* and subsequent cases has emphasized that choice-of-law analysis—which focuses on all elements of a transaction, and not simply on the defendant's conduct—is distinct from minimum-contacts jurisdictional analysis—which focuses at the threshold solely on the defendant's purposeful connection to the forum. Nothing in our cases, however, suggests that a choice-of-law provision should be ignored in considering whether a defendant has "purposefully invoked the benefits and protections of a State's laws" for jurisdictional purposes. Although such a provision standing alone would be insufficient to confer jurisdiction, we believe that, when combined with the 20–year interdependent relationship Rudzewicz established with Burger King's Miami headquarters, it reinforced his deliberate affiliation with the forum State and the reasonable foreseeability of possible litigation there. As Judge Johnson argued in his dissent below, Rudzewicz "purposefully availed himself of the benefits and protections of Florida's laws" by entering into contracts expressly providing that those laws would govern franchise disputes.

(2)

Nor has Rudzewicz pointed to other factors that can be said persuasively to outweigh the considerations discussed above and to establish the unconstitutionality of Florida's assertion of jurisdiction. We cannot conclude that Florida had no "legitimate interest in holding [Rudzewicz] answerable on a claim related to" the contacts he had established in that State. Keeton v. Hustler Magazine, Inc., 465 U.S., at 776, 104 S.Ct., at 1479; see also McGee v. International Life Insurance Co., 355 U.S., at 223, 78 S.Ct., at 201 (noting that State frequently will have a "manifest interest in providing effective means of redress for its residents").[25] Moreover, although Rudzewicz has argued at some length that Michigan's Franchise Investment Law, Mich.Comp.Laws § 445.1501 et seq. (1979), governs many aspects of this franchise relationship, he has not

---

25. Complaining that "when Burger King is the plaintiff, you won't 'have it your way' because it sues all franchisees in Miami," Rudzewicz contends that Florida's interest in providing a convenient forum is negligible given the company's size and ability to conduct litigation anywhere in the country. We disagree. Absent compelling considerations, a defendant who has purposefully derived commercial benefit from his affiliations in a forum may not defeat jurisdiction there simply because of his adversary's greater net wealth.

demonstrated how Michigan's acknowledged interest might possibly render jurisdiction in Florida unconstitutional.[26] Finally, the Court of Appeals' assertion that the Florida litigation "severely impaired [Rudzewicz's] ability to call Michigan witnesses who might be essential to his defense and counterclaim" is wholly without support in the record. And even to the extent that it is inconvenient for a party who has minimum contacts with a forum to litigate there, such considerations most frequently can be accommodated through a change of venue. Although the Court has suggested that inconvenience may at some point become so substantial as to achieve constitutional magnitude, this is not such a case.

The Court of Appeals also concluded, however, that the parties' dealings involved "a characteristic disparity of bargaining power" and "elements of surprise," and that Rudzewicz "lacked fair notice" of the potential for litigation in Florida because the contractual provisions suggesting to the contrary were merely "boilerplate declarations in a lengthy printed contract." Rudzewicz presented many of these arguments to the District Court, contending that Burger King was guilty of misrepresentation, fraud, and duress; that it gave insufficient notice in its dealings with him; and that the contract was one of adhesion. After a 3–day bench trial, the District Court found that Burger King had made no misrepresentations, that Rudzewicz and MacShara "were and are experienced and sophisticated businessmen," and that "at no time" did they "ac[t] under economic duress or disadvantage imposed by" Burger King. Federal Rule of Civil Procedure 52(a) requires that "[f]indings of fact shall not be set aside unless clearly erroneous," and neither Rudzewicz nor the Court of Appeals have pointed to record evidence that would support a "definite and firm conviction" that the District Court's findings are mistaken. To the contrary, Rudzewicz was represented by counsel throughout these complex transactions and, as Judge Johnson observed in dissent below, was himself an experienced accountant "who for five months conducted negotiations with Burger King over the terms of the franchise and lease agreements, and who obligated himself personally to contracts requiring over time payments that exceeded $1 million." Rudzewicz was able to secure a modest reduction in rent and other concessions from Miami headquarters; moreover, to the extent that Burger King's terms were inflexible, Rudzewicz presumably decided that the advantages of affiliating with a national organization provided sufficient commercial benefits as to offset the detriments.[28]

---

26. Rudzewicz has failed to show how the District Court's exercise of jurisdiction in this case might have been at all inconsistent with Michigan's interests. To the contrary, the court found that Burger King had fully complied with Michigan law, and there is nothing in Michigan's franchise act suggesting that Michigan would attempt to assert exclusive jurisdiction to resolve franchise disputes affecting its residents. In any event, minimum-contacts analysis presup-poses that two or more States may be interested in the outcome of a dispute, and the process of resolving potentially conflicting "fundamental substantive social policies," World–Wide Volkswagen Corp. v. Woodson, 444 U.S., at 292, 100 S.Ct., at 564, can usually be accommodated through choice-of-law rules rather than through outright preclusion of jurisdiction in one forum.

28. We do not mean to suggest that the jurisdictional outcome will always be the

III

Notwithstanding these considerations, the Court of Appeals apparently believed that it was necessary to reject jurisdiction in this case as a prophylactic measure, reasoning that an affirmance of the District Court's judgment would result in the exercise of jurisdiction over "out-of-state consumers to collect payments due on modest personal purchases" and would "sow the seeds of default judgments against franchisees owing smaller debts." We share the Court of Appeals' broader concerns and therefore reject any talismanic jurisdictional formulas; "the facts of each case must [always] be weighed" in determining whether personal jurisdiction would comport with "fair play and substantial justice." Kulko v. California Superior Court, 436 U.S., at 92, 98 S.Ct., at 1696–1697. The "quality and nature" of an interstate transaction may sometimes be so "random," "fortuitous," or "attenuated" that it cannot fairly be said that the potential defendant "should reasonably anticipate being haled into court" in another jurisdiction. We also have emphasized that jurisdiction may not be grounded on a contract whose terms have been obtained through "fraud, undue influence, or overweening bargaining power" and whose application would render litigation "so gravely difficult and inconvenient that [a party] will for all practical purposes be deprived of his day in court." The Bremen v. Zapata Off–Shore Co., 407 U.S., at 12, 18, 92 S.Ct., at 1914, 1917. Cf. Fuentes v. Shevin, 407 U.S. 67, 94–96, 92 S.Ct. 1983, 2001–2002, 32 L.Ed.2d 556 (1972); National Equipment Rental, Ltd. v. Szukhent, 375 U.S. 311, 329, 84 S.Ct. 411, 421, 11 L.Ed.2d 354 (1964) (Black, J., dissenting) (jurisdictional rules may not be employed against small consumers so as to "crippl[e] their defense"). Just as the Due Process Clause allows flexibility in ensuring that commercial actors are not effectively "judgment proof" for the consequences of obligations they voluntarily assume in other States, so too does it prevent rules that would unfairly enable them to obtain default judgments against unwitting customers.

For the reasons set forth above, however, these dangers are not present in the instant case. Because Rudzewicz established a substantial and continuing relationship with Burger King's Miami headquarters, received fair notice from the contract documents and the course of dealing that he might be subject to suit in Florida, and has failed to demonstrate how jurisdiction in that forum would otherwise be fundamentally unfair, we conclude that the District Court's exercise of jurisdiction pursuant to Florida Stat. § 48.193(1)(g) (Supp.1984) did not offend due process. The judgment of the Court of Appeals is accordingly

same in franchise cases. Some franchises may be primarily intrastate in character or involve different decisionmaking structures, such that a franchisee should not reasonably anticipate out-of-state litigation. Moreover, commentators have argued that franchise relationships may sometimes involve unfair business practices in their inception and operation. For these reasons, we reject Burger King's suggestion for "a general rule, or at least a presumption, that participation in an interstate franchise relationship" represents consent to the jurisdiction of the franchisor's principal place of business.

reversed, and the case is remanded for further proceedings consistent with this opinion.

It is so ordered.

JUSTICE POWELL took no part in the consideration or decision of this case.

JUSTICE STEVENS, with whom JUSTICE WHITE, joins, dissenting.

In my opinion there is a significant element of unfairness in requiring a franchisee to defend a case of this kind in the forum chosen by the franchisor. It is undisputed that respondent maintained no place of business in Florida, that he had no employees in that State, and that he was not licensed to do business there. Respondent did not prepare his french fries, shakes, and hamburgers in Michigan, and then deliver them into the stream of commerce "with the expectation that they [would] be purchased by consumers in" Florida. To the contrary, respondent did business only in Michigan, his business, property, and payroll taxes were payable in that state, and he sold all of his products there.

Throughout the business relationship, respondent's principal contacts with petitioner were with its Michigan office. Notwithstanding its disclaimer, the Court seems ultimately to rely on nothing more than standard boilerplate language contained in various documents to establish that respondent " 'purposefully availed himself of the benefits and protections of Florida's laws.' " Such superficial analysis creates a potential for unfairness not only in negotiations between franchisors and their franchisees but, more significantly, in the resolution of the disputes that inevitably arise from time to time in such relationships. Judge Vance's opinion for the Court of Appeals for the Eleventh Circuit adequately explains why I would affirm the judgment of that court. I particularly find the following more persuasive than what this Court has written today:

> "Nothing in the course of negotiations gave Rudzewicz reason to anticipate a Burger King suit outside of Michigan. The only face-to-face or even oral contact Rudzewicz had with Burger King throughout months of protracted negotiations was with representatives of the Michigan office. Burger King had the Michigan office interview Rudzewicz and MacShara, appraise their application, discuss price terms, recommend the site which the defendants finally agreed to, and attend the final closing ceremony. There is no evidence that Rudzewicz ever negotiated with anyone in Miami or even sent mail there during negotiations. He maintained no staff in the state of Florida, and as far as the record reveals, he has never even visited the state.

> "The contracts contemplated the startup of a local Michigan restaurant whose profits would derive solely from food sales made to customers in Drayton Plains. The sale, which involved the use of an intangible trademark in Michigan and occupancy of a Burger King facility there, required no performance in the state of Florida. Under

the contract, the local Michigan district office was responsible for providing all of the services due Rudzewicz, including advertising and management consultation. Supervision, moreover, emanated from that office alone. To Rudzewicz, the Michigan office was for all intents and purposes the embodiment of Burger King. He had reason to believe that his working relationship with Burger King began and ended in Michigan, not at the distant and anonymous Florida headquarters. . . .

"Given that the office in Rudzewicz' home state conducted all of the negotiations and wholly supervised the contract, we believe that he had reason to assume that the state of the supervisory office would be the same state in which Burger King would file suit. Rudzewicz lacked fair notice that the distant corporate headquarters which insulated itself from direct dealings with him would later seek to assert jurisdiction over him in the courts of its own home state. . . .

"Just as Rudzewicz lacked notice of the possibility of suit in Florida, he was financially unprepared to meet its added costs. The franchise relationship in particular is fraught with potential for financial surprise. The device of the franchise gives local retailers the access to national trademark recognition which enable them to compete with better-financed, more efficient chain stores. This national affiliation, however, does not alter the fact that the typical franchise store is a local concern serving at best a neighborhood or community. Neither the revenues of a local business nor the geographical range of its market prepares the average franchise owner for the cost of distant litigation. . . ."

Notes and Questions

1. Isn't a fast food outlet much more local than a three-state distributor of cars like World–Wide Volkswagen? Indeed, isn't it more local than an auto retailer like Seaway? Yet the Court here upholds jurisdiction in part because defendants "reached out" beyond Michigan for "the manifold benefits that would derive from affiliation with a nationwide organization." But in *World–Wide Volkswagen* the Court had rejected the argument that a local retailer relied upon the existence of a nationwide net of service facilities as justifying jurisdiction in Oklahoma. Are the two cases consistent? Is it significant that Justice Brennan dissented in *World–Wide Volkswagen?*

In *Burger King* the Court cites Travelers Health Ass'n v. Virginia, 339 U.S. 643, 70 S.Ct. 927, 94 L.Ed. 1154 (1950), on the nationwide organization point. The defendant there was a mail-order health insurance business that solicited numerous residents of Virginia who joined the association. Pursuant to its "Blue Sky" law regarding securities, Virginia ordered the Association to cease soliciting Virginians. On appeal, the Supreme Court upheld Virginia's jurisdiction to do so, noting that "[t]he Association did not engage in mere isolated or short-lived transactions. Its insurance certificates, systematically and widely delivered in Virginia following solicitation based on recommendations of Virginians, create continuing obligations between the

Association and each of the many certificate holders in the state." Is this case really support for the outcome in *Burger King?* Compare McGee v. International Life Ins. Co., supra p. 717.

2. When did Rudzewicz "reach out" to Florida? When he filed the initial application at the Birmingham, Michigan, district office of Burger King? When he negotiated by letter with headquarters in Florida? When he signed the franchise agreement? When he and MacShara began operating the outlet?

3. Justice Brennan proceeds essentially by a two-step analysis, looking first to purposeful availment and, if that is satisfied, determining whether the exercise of jurisdiction would be reasonable. After enumerating several factors that bear on reasonableness, he says that "[t]hese considerations sometimes serve to establish the reasonableness of jurisdiction upon a lesser showing of minimum contacts than would otherwise be required." Does this comment mean that state interest and absence of burden on defendant lower the threshold of purposeful availment? Is that consistent with *World–Wide Volkswagen?*

4. With respect to reasonableness, the Court says that if defendant "purposefully has directed his activities at forum residents" jurisdiction is appropriate unless it presents "a compelling case that some other considerations would render jurisdiction unreasonable." Although purposeful availment is obviously the more significant hurdle in most cases, courts do sometimes dismiss on reasonableness grounds. For example, in Benton v. Cameco Corp., 375 F.3d 1070 (10th Cir.2004), a Colorado resident sued a Canadian corporation in Colorado after the defendant declined to go forward with a tentative agreement to sell plaintiff uranium. The parties had negotiated a memorandum of understanding that conditioned defendant's obligation to proceed on its review of some 18 contracts plaintiff claimed to have to sell uranium to utilities. Members of defendant's staff therefore spent two days in Colorado reviewing these contracts, after which defendant's board of directors declined to go forward with the deal, prompting plaintiff to sue for breach of contract. The court held that purposeful availment had been satisfied, but that jurisdiction was improper under the reasonableness standard. The court stressed that defendant was from another country, that Canadian law would govern the controversy, and that many of the witnesses would be Canadian. Colorado's interest in affording relief to its resident did not suffice under these circumstances, particularly given the weakness of the showing of purposeful availment: "We have already concluded that Cameco's contacts with Colorado were quite limited, barely satisfying the minimum contacts standard. As a result, Cameco need not make a particularly strong showing in order to defeat jurisdiction." Id. at 1080. Is this what Justice Brennan was getting at when he spoke of the relationship between the strength of the showings on the purposeful availment and reasonableness prongs (supra note 3)? Keep this case in mind in relation to Asahi Metal Industry Co. v. Superior Court, infra p. 765.

5. In *Burger King,* the Court finds that the choice-of-law provision in the franchise agreement constituted some purposeful availment by defendants of Florida law. How realistic is that analysis? The franchise agreement could have provided for appointment of a Florida agent for service of process,

National Equipment Rental, Inc. v. Szukhent, infra p. 833, and might validly have required that disputes be adjudicated in a certain jurisdiction to the exclusion of all others. See Carnival Cruise Lines, Inc. v. Shute, infra p. 835. Since the agreement in this case did not include any such provisions, does the provision regarding choice of law really notify defendant that he may be sued in Florida?

6.   The Court also treats as significant the fact that defendant entered into "a carefully structured 20–year relationship that envisioned continuing and wide-reaching contacts with Burger King." To get an idea how pervasive that influence might be, consider the following description of the level of control McDonalds exerts over its franchisees:

> In 1958 [McDonalds] put together an operations and training manual for the company that was seventy-five pages long, specifying how almost everything should be done. Hamburgers were always to be placed on the grill in six neat rows; french fries had to be exactly 0.28 inches thick. The McDonalds operations manual today has ten times the number of pages and weighs about four pounds. Known within the company as "the Bible," it contains precise instructions on how various appliances should be used, how each item on the menu should look, and how employees should greet customers. Operators who disobey these rules can lose their franchises. Cooking instructions are not only printed in the manual, they are often designed into the machines. A McDonalds kitchen is full of buzzers and flashing lights that tell employees what to do.

Schlosser, Fast Food Nation 69 (2002). How often will a contractual relationship be so intimate?

7.   For some time before *Burger King* was decided, commentators hoped for clear rules for the handling of jurisdictional issues in breach of contract cases. In Professor Louis' view, *"Burger King* is not the definitive contract case we had hoped for, and it sheds only a little more light on the basic problem than its predecessors." Louis, Jurisdiction Over Those Who Breach Their Contracts: The Lessons of *Burger King*, 72 N.C.L.Rev. 55 (1993). He found that tort and contract cases are actually not approached differently; "jurisdiction over the person in both tort and contract cases is readily established when the claim arises out of the personal activities of the defendant within the forum state or out of the regular shipment of defendant's goods into, or the plaintiff's goods out of, the forum state. Jurisdiction is much more difficult to establish if the defendant has not personally entered the state, the defendant's contacts with the state are few or irregular, and the defendant is a purchaser, particularly a consumer-purchaser." Id. at 63.

ASAHI METAL INDUSTRY CO.
v. SUPERIOR COURT

Supreme Court of the United States, 1987.
480 U.S. 102, 107 S.Ct. 1026, 94 L.Ed.2d 92.

JUSTICE O'CONNOR announced the judgment of the Court and delivered the unanimous opinion of the Court with respect to Part I, the opinion of the Court with respect to Part II–B, in which the CHIEF JUSTICE, JUSTICE BRENNAN, JUSTICE WHITE, JUSTICE MARSHALL, JUSTICE BLACKMUN, JUSTICE POWELL and JUSTICE STEVENS join, and an opinion with respect to Parts II–A and III, in which the CHIEF JUSTICE, JUSTICE POWELL, and JUSTICE SCALIA join.

[In 1978 Gary Zurcher, a Californian, was injured when the rear tire of his Honda motorcycle burst while he was riding it on a freeway in California. He sued to recover for his injuries in a state court in California. One of the defendants was Cheng Shin Rubber Industry Co., a Taiwanese company that manufactured the tube used in the tire that burst. Cheng Shin in turn filed a cross-complaint (like a Rule 14 third party complaint) against Asahi Metal Indus. Co., a Japanese company that supplied tube valve assemblies to Cheng Shin. Asahi challenged jurisdiction. Meanwhile, Zurcher settled his claims.

In connection with the jurisdictional issue, it appeared that Asahi shipped valves from Japan to Cheng Shin in Taiwan, where they were incorporated into tire tubes. Between 1978 and 1982, Asahi's sales to Cheng Shin ranged between 100,000 and 500,000 units per year and accounted for approximately 1% of Asahi's income. Cheng Shin used valves from other suppliers as well, and marketed its tire tubes throughout the world. There was no indication how many Asahi valves reached California, and Asahi denied that the valve on Zurcher's motorcycle was one of its products. Cheng Shin submitted the affidavit of its purchasing manager, who asserted that Asahi was aware its valve assemblies would be used in products sold in California. The affidavit of the president of Asahi, on the other hand, averred that it "never contemplated that its limited sales of tire valves to Cheng Shin in Taiwan would subject it to lawsuits in California."

The California Supreme Court held jurisdiction proper in California. 39 Cal.3d 35, 216 Cal.Rptr. 385, 702 P.2d 543 (1985). The Supreme Court reversed.]

II

A

The Due Process Clause of the Fourteenth Amendment limits the power of a state court to exert personal jurisdiction over a nonresident defendant. "[T]he constitutional touchstone" of the determination whether an exercise of personal jurisdiction comports with due process "remains whether the defendant purposefully established 'minimum contacts' in the forum State." Burger King Corp. v. Rudzewicz, 471 U.S. 462, 474, 105 S.Ct. 2174, 2183, 85 L.Ed.2d 528 (1985). Most recently we have reaffirmed the oft-quoted reasoning of Hanson v. Denckla, 357 U.S. 235, 253, 78 S.Ct. 1228, 1239, 2 L.Ed.2d 1283 (1958), that minimum contacts must have a basis in "some act by which the defendant purposefully avails itself of the privilege of conducting activities within the forum State, thus invoking the benefits and protections of its laws." Burger King, 471 U.S., at 475, 105 S.Ct., at 2183. "Jurisdiction is proper

... where the contacts proximately result from actions by the defendant *himself* that create a 'substantial connection' with the forum State." Ibid., quoting McGee v. International Life Insurance Co., 355 U.S. 220, 223, 78 S.Ct. 199, 201, 2 L.Ed.2d 223 (1957) (emphasis in original).

Applying the principle that minimum contacts must be based on an act of the defendant, the Court in World–Wide Volkswagen Corp. v. Woodson, 444 U.S. 286, 100 S.Ct. 559, 62 L.Ed.2d 490 (1980), rejected the assertion that a *consumer's* unilateral act of bringing the defendant's product into the forum State was a sufficient constitutional basis for personal jurisdiction over the defendant. * * *

Since *World–Wide Volkswagen,* lower courts have been confronted with cases in which the defendant acted by placing a product in the stream of commerce, and the stream eventually swept defendant's product into the forum State, but the defendant did nothing else to purposefully avail itself of the market in the forum State. Some courts have understood the Due Process Clause, as interpreted in *World–Wide Volkswagen,* to allow an exercise of personal jurisdiction to be based on no more than the defendant's act of placing the product in the stream of commerce. Other courts have understood the Due Process Clause and the above-quoted language in *World–Wide Volkswagen* to require the action of the defendant to be more purposefully directed at the forum State than the mere act of placing a product in the stream of commerce.

The reasoning of the Supreme Court of California in the present case illustrates the former interpretation of *World–Wide Volkswagen.* The Supreme Court of California held that, because the stream of commerce eventually brought some valves Asahi sold Cheng Shin into California, Asahi's awareness that its valves would be sold in California was sufficient to permit California to exercise jurisdiction over Asahi consistent with the requirements of the Due Process Clause. The Supreme Court of California's position was consistent with those courts that have held that mere foreseeability or awareness was a constitutionally sufficient basis for personal jurisdiction if the defendant's product made its way into the forum State while still in the stream of commerce.

Other courts, however, have understood the Due Process Clause to require something more than that the defendant was aware of its product's entry into the forum State through the stream of commerce in order for the State to exert jurisdiction over the defendant. * * * In Humble v. Toyota Motor Co., 727 F.2d 709 (C.A.8 1984), an injured car passenger brought suit against Arakawa Auto Body Company, a Japanese corporation that manufactured car seats for Toyota. Arakawa did no business in the United States, it had no office, affiliate, subsidiary, or agent in the United States; it manufactured its component parts outside the United States and delivered them to Toyota Motor Company in Japan. The Court of Appeals, adopting the reasoning of the District Court in that case, noted that although it "does not doubt that Arakawa could have foreseen that its product would find its way into the United

States," it would be "manifestly unjust" to require Arakawa to defend itself in the United States.

We now find this latter position to be consonant with the requirements of due process. The "substantial connection" between the defendant and the forum State necessary for a finding of minimum contacts must come about by *an action of the defendant purposefully directed toward the forum State.* The placement of a product into the stream of commerce, without more, is not an act of the defendant purposefully directed toward the forum State. Additional conduct of the defendant may indicate an intent or purpose to serve the market in the forum State, for example, designing the product for the market in the forum State, advertising in the forum State, establishing channels for providing regular advice to customers in the forum State, or marketing the product through a distributor who has agreed to serve as the sales agent in the forum State. But a defendant's awareness that the stream of commerce may or will sweep the product into the forum State does not convert the mere act of placing the product into the stream into an act purposefully directed toward the forum State.

Assuming, *arguendo,* that respondents have established Asahi's awareness that some of the valves sold to Cheng Shin would be incorporated into tire tubes sold in California, respondents have not demonstrated any action by Asahi to purposefully avail itself of the California market. Asahi does not do business in California. It has no office, agents, employees, or property in California. It does not advertise or otherwise solicit business in California. It did not create, control, or employ the distribution system that brought its valves to California. Cf. Hicks v. Kawasaki Heavy Industries, 452 F.Supp. 130 (M.D.Pa.1978). There is no evidence that Asahi designed its product in anticipation of sales in California. Cf. Rockwell International Corp. v. Costruzioni Aeronautiche Giovanni Agusta, 553 F.Supp. 328 (E.D.Pa.1982). On the basis of these facts, the exertion of personal jurisdiction over Asahi by the Superior Court of California exceeds the limits of Due Process.

B

The strictures of the Due Process Clause forbid a state court from exercising personal jurisdiction over Asahi under circumstances that would offend "traditional notions of fair play and substantial justice." International Shoe Co. v. Washington, 326 U.S., at 316, 66 S.Ct., at 158.

We have previously explained that the determination of the reasonableness of the exercise of jurisdiction in each case will depend on an evaluation of several factors. A court must consider the burden on the defendant, the interests of the forum state, and the plaintiff's interest in obtaining relief. It must also weigh in its determination "the interstate judicial system's interest in obtaining the most efficient resolution of controversies; and the shared interest of the several States in furthering fundamental substantive social policies." World–Wide Volkswagen, 444 U.S., at 292, 100 S.Ct., at 564.

A consideration of these factors in the present case clearly reveals the unreasonableness of the assertion of jurisdiction over Asahi, even apart from the question of the placement of goods in the stream of commerce.

Certainly the burden on the defendant in this case is severe. Asahi has been commanded by the Supreme Court of California not only to traverse the distance between Asahi's headquarters in Japan and the Superior Court of California in and for the County of Solano, but also to submit its dispute with Cheng Shin to a foreign nation's judicial system. The unique burdens placed upon one who must defend oneself in a foreign legal system should have significant weight in assessing the reasonableness of stretching the long arm of personal jurisdiction over national borders.

When minimum contacts have been established, often the interests of the plaintiff and the forum in the exercise of jurisdiction will justify even the serious burdens placed on the alien defendant. In the present case, however, the interests of the plaintiff and the forum in California's assertion of jurisdiction over Asahi are slight. All that remains is a claim for indemnification asserted by Cheng Shin, a Taiwanese corporation, against Asahi. The transaction on which the indemnification claim is based took place in Taiwan; Asahi's components were shipped from Japan to Taiwan. Cheng Shin has not demonstrated that it is more convenient for it to litigate its indemnification claim against Asahi in California rather than in Taiwan or Japan.

Because the plaintiff is not a California resident, California's legitimate interests in the dispute have considerably diminished. The Supreme Court of California argued that the State had an interest in "protecting its consumers by ensuring that foreign manufacturers comply with the state's safety standards." 39 Cal.3d, at 49, 216 Cal.Rptr., at 392, 702 P.2d, at 550. The State Supreme Court's definition of California's interest, however, was overly broad. The dispute between Cheng Shin and Asahi is primarily about indemnification rather than safety standards. Moreover, it is not at all clear at this point that California law should govern the question whether a Japanese corporation should indemnify a Taiwanese corporation on the basis of a sale made in Taiwan and a shipment of goods from Japan to Taiwan. The possibility of being haled into a California court as a result of an accident involving Asahi's components undoubtedly creates an additional deterrent to the manufacture of unsafe components; however, similar pressures will be placed on Asahi by the purchasers of its components as long as those who use Asahi components in their final products, and sell those products in California, are subject to the application of California tort law.

World–Wide Volkswagen also admonished courts to take into consideration the interests of the "several States," in addition to the forum state, in the efficient judicial resolution of the dispute and the advancement of substantive policies. In the present case, this advice calls for a court to consider the procedural and substantive policies of other nations whose interests are affected by the assertion of jurisdiction by the California court. The procedural and substantive interests of other nations in a state court's assertion of jurisdiction over an alien defendant will differ from case to case. In every case, however, those interests, as well as the Federal interest in its foreign relations policies, will be best served by a careful inquiry into the reasonableness of the assertion of jurisdiction in the particular case, and an unwillingness to find the serious burdens on an alien defendant outweighed by minimal interests on the part of the plaintiff or the forum State. "Great care and reserve should be exercised when extending our notions of personal jurisdiction into the international field." United States v. First National City Bank, 379 U.S. 378, 404, 85 S.Ct. 528, 542, 13 L.Ed.2d 365 (1965) (Harlan, J., dissenting).

Considering the international context, the heavy burden on the alien defendant, and the slight interests of the plaintiff and the forum State, the exercise of personal jurisdiction by a California court over Asahi in this instance would be unreasonable and unfair.

JUSTICE BRENNAN, with whom JUSTICE WHITE, JUSTICE MARSHALL, and JUSTICE BLACKMUN join, concurring in part and in the judgment.

I do not agree with the plurality's interpretation of the stream-of-commerce theory, nor with its conclusion that Asahi did not "purposely avail itself of the California market." I do agree, however, with the Court's conclusion in Part II–B that the exercise of personal jurisdiction over Asahi in this case would not comport with "fair play and substantial justice," International Shoe Co. v. Washington, 326 U.S. 310, 320, 66 S.Ct. 154, 160, 90 L.Ed. 95 (1945). This is one of those rare cases in which "minimum requirements inherent in the concept of 'fair play and substantial justice' ... defeat the reasonableness of jurisdiction even [though] the defendant has purposefully engaged in forum activities." Burger King Corp. v. Rudzewicz, 471 U.S. 462, 477–478, 105 S.Ct. 2174, 2184–2185, 85 L.Ed.2d 528 (1985). I therefore join Parts I and II–B of the Court's opinion, and write separately to explain my disagreement with Part II–A.

* * * The stream of commerce refers not to unpredictable currents or eddies, but to the regular and anticipated flow of products from manufacture to distribution to retail sale. As long as a participant in this process is aware that the final product is being marketed in the forum State, the possibility of a lawsuit there cannot come as a surprise. Nor will the litigation present a burden for which there is no corresponding benefit. A defendant who has placed goods in the stream of commerce benefits economically from the retail sale of the final product in the forum State, and indirectly benefits from the State's laws that regulate and facilitate commercial activity. These benefits accrue regardless of whether that participant directly conducts business in the forum State, or engages in additional conduct directed toward that State. Accordingly, most courts and commentators have found that jurisdiction premised on the placement of a product into the stream of commerce is consistent

with the Due Process Clause, and have not required a showing of additional conduct.

The plurality's endorsement of what appears to be the minority view among Federal Courts of Appeals represents a marked retreat from its analysis in World–Wide Volkswagen v. Woodson, 444 U.S. 286, 100 S.Ct. 559, 62 L.Ed.2d 490 (1980). * * *

[In *World–Wide Volkswagen,* the Court referred as an example] to Gray v. American Radiator & Standard Sanitary Corp., 22 Ill.2d 432, 176 N.E.2d 761 (1961) [supra p. 722, n. 6], a well-known stream-of-commerce case in which the Illinois Supreme Court applied the theory to assert jurisdiction over a component-parts manufacturer that sold no components directly in Illinois, but did sell them to a manufacturer who incorporated them into a final product that was sold in Illinois.

The Court in *World–Wide Volkswagen* thus took great care to distinguish "between a case involving goods which reach a distant State through a chain of distribution and a case involving goods which reach the same State because a consumer ... took them there." 444 U.S., at 306–307, 100 S.Ct., at 584 (Brennan, J., dissenting). The California Supreme Court took note of this distinction, and correctly concluded that our holding in *World–Wide Volkswagen* preserved the stream-of-commerce theory.

In this case, the facts found by the California Supreme Court support its finding of minimum contacts. The Court found that "[al]though Asahi did not design or control the system of distribution that carried its valve assemblies into California, Asahi was aware of the distribution system's operation, and it knew that it would benefit economically from the sale in California of products incorporating its components." Accordingly, I cannot join the plurality's determination that Asahi's regular and extensive sales of component parts to a manufacturer it knew was making regular sales of the final product in California is insufficient to establish minimum contacts with California.

JUSTICE STEVENS, with whom JUSTICE WHITE and JUSTICE BLACKMUN join, concurring in part and concurring in the judgment.

The judgment of the Supreme Court of California should be reversed for the reasons stated in Part II–B of the Court's opinion. While I join Parts I and II–B, I do not join Part II–A for two reasons. First, it is not necessary to the Court's decision. * * * [T]his case fits within the rule that "minimum requirements inherent in the concept of 'fair play and substantial justice' may defeat the reasonableness of jurisdiction even if the defendant has purposefully engaged in forum activities." Burger King, 471 U.S., at 477–478, 105 S.Ct., at 2184–2185 (quoting International Shoe Co. v. Washington, 326 U.S. 310, 320, 66 S.Ct. 154, 160, 90 L.Ed. 95 (1945)). Accordingly, I see no reason in this case for the Court to articulate "purposeful direction" or any other test as the nexus between an act of a defendant and the forum State that is necessary to establish minimum contacts.

Second, even assuming that the test ought to be formulated here, Part II–A misapplies it to the facts of this case. The Court seems to assume that an unwavering line can be drawn between "mere awareness" that a component will find its way into the forum State and "purposeful availment" of the forum's market. Over the course of its dealings with Cheng Shin, Asahi has arguably engaged in a higher quantum of conduct than "[t]he placement of a product into the stream of commerce, without more...." Whether or not this conduct rises to the level of purposeful availment requires a constitutional determination that is affected by the volume, the value, and the hazardous character of the components. In most circumstances I would be inclined to conclude that a regular course of dealing that results in deliveries of over 100,000 units annually over a period of several years would constitute "purposeful availment" even though the item delivered to the forum State was a standard product marketed throughout the world.

Notes and Questions

1. Focus carefully on the Justices' voting patterns, particularly with regard to Part II A of Justice O'Connor's opinion. The Court unanimously concluded that jurisdiction over the claim asserted against Asahi was unconstitutional. Is it clear what the basis for that conclusion was?

2. Recall that in *World–Wide Volkswagen*, the Court appeared to speak favorably of the stream of commerce theory for jurisdiction. See supra p. 743 n.7. Does *Asahi* change that? Some lower courts have said it does not. See Dehmlow v. Austin Fireworks, 963 F.2d 941, 947 (7th Cir.1992) ("Because the Supreme Court established the stream of commerce theory, and a majority of the Court has not yet rejected it, we consider that theory to be determinative."); Nuovo Pignone v. Storman Asia M/V, 310 F.3d 374 (5th Cir.2002) (defendant's act in putting a product into the stream of commerce suffices for jurisdiction when the product allegedly causes an injury in the forum). Others have adopted Justice O'Connor's analysis requiring something more than foreseeability. See ALS Scan, Inc. v. Digital Serv. Consultants, Inc., 293 F.3d 707 (4th Cir.2002); Boit v. Gar–Tec Products, Inc., 967 F.2d 671, 683 (1st Cir.1992). See also Pennzoil Prod. Co. v. Colelli & Assoc., Inc., 149 F.3d 197 (3d Cir.1998) (court finds that "the clear satisfaction of both the O'Connor and Brennan standards obviates any need to adopt one over the other"); Bridgeport Music, Inc. v. Still N the Water Pub., 327 F.3d 472, 479 (6th Cir.2003) (most lower courts have avoided choosing, but this court now expresses a preference for the O'Connor view).

3. Which approach to purposeful availment *should* the Court adopt? Consider:

(a) Justice O'Connor says that "additional conduct" is necessary beyond placing a product in the stream of commerce. This idea seems to correspond to the notion that a purchaser's unilateral action in bringing a product to the forum State does not constitute a relevant contact. Is this a fair analogy? What would be necessary to justify jurisdiction for Zurcher's claim against Cheng Shin?

Consider Lesnick v. Hollingsworth & Vose Co., 35 F.3d 939 (4th Cir. 1994), in which the court held jurisdiction improper under *Asahi*. Plaintiff's late husband had smoked cigarettes manufactured by Lorillard, Inc. He died of mesothelioma, a form of cancer caused by exposure to asbestos fibers. In the 1950's Lorillard, a New York company with plants in New Jersey and Kentucky, entered into an arrangement with defendant, a Massachusetts company, to develop a "Micronite Filter" for cigarettes using asbestos fibers. They jointly owned the resulting patent, and defendant sold some 10 billion asbestos-containing filters to Lorillard during the 1950's knowing that they would be incorporated into cigarettes and sold throughout the country. The court concluded that this collaborative arrangement between defendant and Lorillard was not in any way directed toward Maryland, where plaintiff's husband lived and bought the cigarettes that plaintiff claimed caused his mesothelioma. Accordingly, jurisdiction was improper (id. at 945):

> To permit a state to assert jurisdiction over any person in the country whose product is sold in the state simply because a person must expect that to happen destroys the notion of individual sovereignties inherent in our system of federalism. Such a rule would subject defendants to judgment in locations based on the activity of third persons and not the deliberate conduct of the defendant, making it impossible for defendants to plan and structure their business contacts and risks.

(b) Justice Brennan urges that any foreseeable delivery of a product into the forum State before ultimate sale should be sufficient to establish purposeful availment with respect to the forum. Consider Humble v. Toyota Motor Co., a case discussed by Justice O'Connor. Would it be legitimate to require the component supplier in that case to defend in this country? Suppose that a small Japanese steel producer filled a small spot order of steel from Toyota. Should it be subject to suit anywhere Toyota distributes cars on a claim that its steel was incorporated into a car sold in the forum, and that its steel was defective? Note, in connection with this issue, that Asahi denied manufacturing the valve on the tire that exploded and caused Zurcher's injuries. Assuming that plaintiff may assert a claim against Toyota for a defect in the car, why should jurisdiction be distended to permit plaintiff to sue the component manufacturer also?

4. The above discussion focuses on producers of components that are incorporated into products distributed by the end producer, as in *Asahi*. The *Asahi* "stream of commerce plus" reasoning has also been applied to manufacturers of finished products. In Parry v. Ernst Home Center Corp., 779 P.2d 659 (Utah 1989), plaintiff was injured in Utah using a tool manufactured in Japan by Hirota, a Japanese company. Hirota had sold the tool to an exporter for sale in the United States, and it had been sold to plaintiff's daughter in Idaho. The court found that jurisdiction over Hirota was improper because it had not undertaken any of the "additional conduct" Justice O'Connor identified as necessary to justify liability. See also Boit v. Gar–Tec Products, Inc., 967 F.2d 671 (1st Cir.1992) (plaintiffs could not sue Indiana manufacturer of tool in Maine for damages sustained there due to alleged defect in tool, which plaintiffs bought through a specialty tool catalogue).

5.   Under Justice O'Connor's view, how would jurisdiction over defendant have been justified in Gray v. American Radiator, supra p. 722 n.6? Could jurisdiction in Oklahoma have been justified over Audi of Germany in World–Wide Volkswagen v. Woodson, supra p. 730? Ever since MacPherson v. Buick Motor Co., 217 N.Y. 382, 111 N.E. 1050 (1916) and Henningsen v. Bloomfield Motors, Inc., 32 N.J. 358, 161 A.2d 69 (1960) abandoned the privity requirement for negligence and products liability suits, consumers have had a substantive method for seeking recovery from manufacturers of defective products. Does *Asahi* impose an inappropriate jurisdictional hurdle in their way? See Wiseman, Reconstructing the Citadel: The Advent of Jurisdictional Privity, 54 Ohio St. L. Rev. 403, 443 (1993) ("The synergy developed between the law of products liability, as codified in the Restatement [of Torts], and personal jurisdiction * * * has now been not so neatly undone by a plurality of the Supreme Court in *Asahi*.").

6.   It appears that the entire Court agreed that allowing the case to proceed against Asahi would have violated the reasonableness prong of the jurisdictional inquiry. Is jurisdiction over Asahi in California more unreasonable than jurisdiction over Hustler in New Hampshire in Keeton v. Hustler Co. (supra p. 747 n. 1)? Is the fact that Asahi is a foreign corporation a decisive matter? Would the reasonableness prong have been satisfied for Cheng Shin's indemnity claim against Asahi if Zurcher had not settled? Wouldn't California jurisdiction have been reasonable for a claim by Zurcher against Asahi?

7.   How should *Asahi* be applied in cases where the out-of-state defendant advertises in the state inviting residents to sample its wares elsewhere? Usually such cases involve a plaintiff injured at defendant's distant establishment. In Shute v. Carnival Cruise Lines, 897 F.2d 377, 380–87 (9th Cir.1990), rev'd on other grounds, 499 U.S. 585, 111 S.Ct. 1522, 113 L.Ed.2d 622 (1991), plaintiffs from the state of Washington booked a Carnival cruise that began in Los Angeles through a travel agent near their home. (The Supreme Court's approach to this case is considered below. See Forum Selection Clauses, infra p. 834) After being injured during the cruise, plaintiffs sued in their home state. Carnival Lines was not registered to do business in Washington, and owned no property and maintained no office there. Its ships had never called at Washington ports. It did, however, advertise its cruises in local Washington newspapers and provide brochures to local travel agents for distribution to potential customers. It also periodically held seminars for travel agents in the state to inform them about its cruises and encourage them to sell tickets. It paid travel agents a 10% commission for selling tickets. Slightly over 1% of its cruise business was derived from residents of Washington.

The Ninth Circuit upheld jurisdiction, using a three-part analysis. First, it concluded that defendant's act of soliciting business in Washington should be considered purposeful availment to the extent it resulted in transaction of business with residents. Second, the court held that the claim arose out of the defendant's solicitation of business in Washington even though the claim was for negligence on the ship in international waters off Mexico. The court used a "but for" analysis, concluding that the plaintiffs would not have bought a ticket on defendant's cruise but for its solicitation activities directed at Washington travel agents. Finally, drawing on the "presumption of reasonableness" it found in Burger King Corp. v. Rudzewicz, supra p. 752, the court held that defendant had not presented a compelling case that the exercise of jurisdiction would be unreasonable.

Contrast Nowak v. Tak How Investments, Ltd., 94 F.3d 708 (1st Cir.1996), a suit filed in Massachusetts to recover for the drowning of a Massachusetts resident at the Hong Kong Holiday Inn, which was operated by defendant. Defendant had no other business activities besides operation of that hotel, but it had advertised the hotel in some publications that circulated in Massachusetts. The court did not treat this advertising activity as sufficient, and rejected the Ninth Circuit's "but for" causation standard, favoring a proximate causation standard:

> First, proximate or legal cause clearly distinguishes between foreseeable and unforeseeable risks of harm. Foreseeability is a critical component of the due process inquiry, particularly in evaluating purposeful availment, and we think it also informs the relatedness prong. * * * Adherence to a proximate cause standard is likely to enable defendants better to anticipate which conduct might subject them to a state's jurisdiction than a more tenuous link in the chain of causation. * * *
>
> A "but for" requirement, on the other hand, has in itself no limiting principle; it literally embraces every event that hindsight can logically identify in the causative chain. True, as the Ninth Circuit has noted, courts can use the reasonableness prong to keep Pandora's jar from opening too wide. But to say that the harm that might be done by one factor can be prevented by another is not, after all, an affirmative justification for the former.

Under this standard, the court concluded that jurisdiction was proper because this guest was in Hong Kong due to special rates that were offered to her husband's employer to persuade the employer to have employees stay at this hotel. The court added that "we intend to emphasize the importance of proximate causation, but to allow a slight loosening of that standard when circumstances dictate." It also noted that "it will not always be easy to apply this flexible approach to the particular circumstances, but that is a function of the complexity of this area of the law." Which approach is most in keeping with *Asahi*?

8.   One consideration stressed in the Court's reasonableness analysis is the fact that Asahi is a foreign company. Is the Court's application of the reasonableness prong peculiarly applicable to defendants from other countries? Are all other countries the same for this purpose? In Aristech Chem. Intern. Ltd. v. Acrylic Fabricators Ltd., 138 F.3d 624 (6th Cir.1998), a suit against a Canadian company, the district court in Kentucky found that purposeful availment was satisfied and that the claim arose out of the contacts, but that the exercise of jurisdiction would be unreasonable. The court of appeals disagreed and reversed (id. at 628):

> The Supreme Court has warned that the burden of mounting a defense in a foreign legal system is "unique" and should be afforded "significant weight in assessing the reasonableness of stretching the long arm of personal jurisdiction over national borders." But we think a Canadian defendant such as AFL bears a substantially lighter burden than does a Japanese defendant—or, for that matter, most other foreign

defendants. First, only a short plane flight separates Ontario from Kentucky. * * * Moreover, a Canadian defendant litigating in the United States finds a judicial system "rooted in the same common law traditions as that of Canada."

PAVLOVICH v. SUPERIOR COURT

Supreme Court of California, 2002.
58 P.3d 2.

Brown, J.

"The Internet is an international network of interconnected computers" which "enable[s] tens of millions of people to communicate with one another and to access vast amounts of information from around the world." (*Reno v. American Civil Liberties Union* (1997) 521 U.S. 844, 849–850 [117 S.Ct. 2329, 2334, 138 L.Ed.2d 874].) "The best known category of communication over the Internet is the World Wide Web, which allows users to search for and retrieve information stored in remote computers, as well as, in some cases, to communicate back to designated sites. In concrete terms, the Web consists of a vast number of documents stored in different computers all over the world." (*Id.* at p. 852 [117 S.Ct. at p. 2335].) On the Web, "documents, commonly known as Web 'pages,' are ... prevalent." (*Ibid.*) These pages are located at Web sites and have addresses marking their location on the Web. (See *ibid.*) If a Web page is freely accessible, then anyone with access to a computer connected to the Internet may view that page. With its explosive growth over the past two decades, the Internet has become " 'a unique and wholly new medium of worldwide human communication.' " (*Id.* at p. 850 [117 S.Ct. at p. 2334].)

Not surprisingly, the so-called Internet revolution has spawned a host of new legal issues as courts have struggled to apply traditional legal frameworks to this new communication medium. Today, we join this struggle and consider the impact of the Internet on the determination of personal jurisdiction. In this case, a California court exercised personal jurisdiction over a defendant based on a posting on an Internet Web site. Under the particular facts of this case, we conclude the court's exercise of jurisdiction was improper.

I

Digital versatile discs (DVD's) "provide high quality images, such as motion pictures, digitally formatted on a convenient 5–inch disc...." Before the commercial release of DVD's containing motion pictures, the Content Scrambling System (CSS), a system used to encrypt and protect copyrighted motion pictures on DVD's, was developed. The CSS technology prevents the playing or copying of copyrighted motion pictures on DVD's without the algorithms and keys necessary to decrypt the data stored on the disc.

Real party in interest DVD Copy Control Association, Inc. (DVD CCA) is a nonprofit trade association organized under the laws of the

State of Delaware with its principal place of business in California. The DVD industry created DVD CCA in December 1998 to control and administer licensing of the CSS technology. In September 1999, DVD CCA hired its staff, and, in December 1999, it began administering the licenses. Soon thereafter, DVD CCA acquired the licensing rights to the CSS technology and became the sole licensing entity for this technology in the DVD video format.

Petitioner Matthew Pavlovich is currently a resident of Texas and the president of Media Driver, LLC, a technology consulting company in Texas. During the four years before he moved to Texas, he studied computer engineering at Purdue University in Indiana, where he worked as a systems and network administrator. Pavlovich does not reside or work in California. He has never had a place of business, telephone listing, or bank account in California and has never owned property in California. Neither Pavlovich nor his company has solicited any business in California or has any business contacts in California.

At Purdue, Pavlovich was the founder and project leader of the LiVid video project (LiVid), which operated a Web site located at "livid.on.openprojects.net." The site consisted of a single page with text and links to other Web sites. The site only provided information; it did not solicit or transact any business and permitted no interactive exchange of information between its operators and visitors.

According to Pavlovich, the goal of LiVid was "to improve video and DVD support for Linux and to . . . combine the resources and the efforts of the various individuals that were working on related things. . . ." To reach this goal, the project sought to defeat the CSS technology and enable the decryption and copying of DVD's containing motion pictures. Consistent with these efforts, LiVid posted the source code of a program named DeCSS on its Web site as early as October 1999. DeCSS allows users to circumvent the CSS technology by decrypting data contained on DVD's and enabling the placement of this decrypted data onto computer hard drives or other storage media.

At the time LiVid posted DeCSS, Pavlovich knew that DeCSS "was derived from CSS algorithms" and that reverse engineering these algorithms was probably illegal. He had also "heard" that "there was an organization which you had to file for or apply for a license" to the CSS technology. He did not, however, learn that the organization was DVD CCA or that DVD CCA had its principal place of business in California until after DVD CCA filed this action.

In its complaint, DVD CCA alleged that Pavlovich misappropriated its trade secrets by posting the DeCSS program on the LiVid Web site because the "DeCSS program . . . embodies, uses, and/or is a substantial derivation of confidential proprietary information which DVD CCA licenses. . . ." The complaint sought injunctive relief but did not seek monetary damages. In response, Pavlovich filed a motion to quash service of process, contending that California lacked jurisdiction over his person. DVD CCA opposed, contending that jurisdiction was proper because Pavlovich "misappropriated DVD CCA's trade secrets knowing that such actions would adversely impact an array of substantial California business enterprises-including the motion picture industry, the consumer electronics industry, and the computer industry." In a brief order, the trial court denied Pavlovich's motion, citing *Calder v. Jones* (1984) 465 U.S. 783 [104 S.Ct. 1482, 79 L.Ed.2d 804] (*Calder*), and *Panavision Intern., L.P. v. Toeppen* (9th Cir. 1998) 141 F.3d 1316 (*Panavision*).

* * *

We granted review to determine whether the trial court properly exercised jurisdiction over Pavlovich's person based solely on the posting of the DeCSS source code on the LiVid Web site. We conclude it did not.

[The court summarized due process limitations on personal jurisdiction.]

"The purposeful availment inquiry ... focuses on the defendant's intentionality. This prong is only satisfied when the defendant purposefully and voluntarily directs his activities toward the forum so that he should expect, by virtue of the benefit he receives, to be subject to the court's jurisdiction based on" his contacts with the forum. Thus, the " 'purposeful availment' requirement ensures that a defendant will not be haled into a jurisdiction solely as a result of 'random,' 'fortuitous,' or 'attenuated' contacts, or of the 'unilateral activity of another party or a third person.'.]" (*Burger King [v. Rudzewicz]*, 471 U.S. at p. 475 [105 S.Ct. at p. 2183].) "When a [defendant] 'purposefully avails itself of the privilege of conducting activities within the forum State,' it has clear notice that it is subject to suit there, and can act to alleviate the risk of burdensome litigation by procuring insurance, passing the expected costs on to customers, or, if the risks are too great, severing its connection with the State." (*World–Wide Volkswagen Corp. v. Woodson* (1980) 444 U.S. 286, 297 [100 S.Ct. 559, 567, 62 L.Ed.2d 490] (*World–Wide Volkswagen*).)

* * *

Although *Calder* involved a libel claim, courts have applied the effects test to other intentional torts, including business torts. (See *IMO Industries, Inc. v. Kiekert AG* (3d Cir. 1998) 155 F.3d 254, 259–260, 261 (*IMO*) [supra pp. 750–51 n.6] [courts must consider *Calder* in intentional tort cases].) Indeed, courts have "struggled somewhat with *Calder*'s import, recognizing that the case cannot stand for the broad proposition that a foreign act with foreseeable effects in the forum state always gives rise to specific jurisdiction."

Despite this struggle, most courts agree that merely asserting that a defendant knew or should have known that his intentional acts would cause harm in the forum state is not enough to establish jurisdiction under the effects test. Instead, the plaintiff must also "point to contacts which demonstrate that the defendant *expressly aimed* its tortious conduct at the forum...." (*IMO*, *supra*, 155 F.3d at p. 265.)

* * *

In this case, Pavlovich's sole contact with California is LiVid's posting of the DeCSS source code containing DVD CCA's proprietary information on an Internet Web site accessible to any person with Internet access. Pavlovich never worked in California. He owned no property in California, maintained no bank accounts in California, and had no telephone listings in California. Neither Pavlovich nor his company solicited or transacted any business in California. The record also contains no evidence of any LiVid contacts with California.

Although we have never considered the scope of personal jurisdiction based solely on Internet use, other courts have considered this issue, and most have adopted a sliding scale analysis. "At one end of the spectrum are situations where a defendant clearly does business over the Internet. If the defendant enters into contracts with residents of a foreign jurisdiction that involve the knowing and repeated transmission of computer files over the Internet, personal jurisdiction is proper. At the opposite end are situations where a defendant has simply posted information on an Internet Web site which is accessible to users in foreign jurisdictions. A passive Web site that does little more than make information available to those who are interested in it is not grounds for the exercise [of] personal jurisdiction. The middle ground is occupied by interactive Web sites where a user can exchange information with the host computer. In these cases, the exercise of jurisdiction is determined by examining the level of interactivity and commercial nature of the exchange of information that occurs on the Web site." (*Zippo Mfg. Co. v. Zippo Dot Com, Inc.* (W.D.Pa. 1997) 952 F.Supp. 1119, 1124.)

Here, LiVid's Web site merely posts information and has no interactive features. There is no evidence in the record suggesting that the site targeted California. Indeed, there is no evidence that any California resident ever visited, much less downloaded the DeCSS source code from, the LiVid Web site. Thus, Pavlovich's alleged "conduct in ... posting [a] passive Web site[] on the Internet is not," by itself, "sufficient to subject" him "to jurisdiction in California." " 'Creating a site, like placing a product into the stream of commerce, may be felt nationwide-or even worldwide-but, without more, it is not an act purposefully directed toward the forum state.' " (*Cybersell [v. Cybersell, Inc.* (9th Cir.) 130 F.3d 414,] 418.) Otherwise, "personal jurisdiction in Internet-related cases would almost always be found in any forum in the country."

Nonetheless, DVD CCA contends posting the misappropriated source code on an Internet Web site is sufficient to establish purposeful availment in this case because Pavlovich knew the posting would harm not only a licensing entity but also the motion picture, computer and consumer electronics industries centered in California. According to DVD CCA, this knowledge establishes that Pavlovich intentionally targeted California and is sufficient to confer jurisdiction under the *Calder* effects test. Although the question is close, we disagree.

[The court concluded that Pavlovich's knowledge that some entity owned the licensing rights to CSS technology did not support jurisdiction because DVD CCA only began administering licenses two months after Pavlovich posted the misappropriated code.]

Thus, the only question in this case is whether Pavlovich's knowledge that his tortious conduct may harm certain industries centered in California-i.e., the motion picture, computer, and consumer electronics industries-is sufficient to establish express aiming at California. As explained below, we conclude that this knowledge, by itself, cannot establish purposeful availment under the effects test.

First, Pavlovich's knowledge that DeCSS could be used to illegally pirate copyrighted motion pictures on DVD's and that such pirating would harm the motion picture industry in California does not satisfy the express aiming requirement. As an initial matter, we question whether these effects are even relevant to our analysis, because DVD CCA does not assert a cause of action premised on the illegal pirating of copyrighted motion pictures. In any event, "the mere 'unilateral activity of those who claim some relationship with a nonresident defendant cannot satisfy the requirement of contact with the forum State.'" (*World–Wide Volkswagen, supra*, 444 U.S. at p. 298 [100 S.Ct. at p. 567].) Thus, the foreseeability that third parties may use DeCSS to harm the motion picture industry cannot, by itself, satisfy the express aiming requirement. Because nothing in the record suggests that Pavlovich encouraged Web site visitors to use DeCSS to illegally pirate copyrighted motion pictures, his mere "awareness" they might do so does not show purposeful availment. (See *Asahi Metal Industry Co. v. Superior Court* (1987) 480 U.S. 102, 112 [107 S.Ct. 1026, 1032, 94 L.Ed.2d 92] (plur. opn. of O'Connor, J.) [the mere awareness that third parties will sweep the defendant's product into the forum state does not convert its act of selling the product to third parties "into an act purposefully directed toward the forum State"].)

Second, Pavlovich's knowledge of the effects of his tortious conduct on the consumer electronics and computer industries centered in California is an even more attenuated basis for jurisdiction. According to DVD CCA, Pavlovich knew that posting DeCSS would harm the consumer electronics and computer industries in California, because many licensees of the CSS technology resided in California. The record, however, indicates that Pavlovich did not know that any of DVD CCA's licensees resided in California. At most, the record establishes that Pavlovich should have guessed that these licensees resided in California because there are many consumer electronic and computer companies in California. DVD CCA's argument therefore boils down to the following syllogism: jurisdiction exists solely because Pavlovich's tortious conduct had a foreseeable effect in California. But mere foreseeability is not enough for jurisdiction. Otherwise, the commission of any intentional tort affecting industries in California would subject a defendant to jurisdiction in California. We decline to adopt such an expansive interpretation of the effects test.

Cases citing a defendant's knowledge of the effects of its tortious conduct on an industry centered in the forum state to support a finding of jurisdiction under the effects test are inapposite. In exercising jurisdiction, those courts concluded that the defendant's knowledge of industry-wide effects in the forum state *in conjunction with other* evidence of express aiming at the forum state established purposeful availment under the effects test.[6] Thus, those cases merely hold that such knowledge is relevant to any determination of personal jurisdiction. They do not establish that such knowledge, by itself, establishes express aiming. Indeed, DVD CCA does not cite, and we have not found, any case where a court exercised jurisdiction under the effects test based solely on the defendant's knowledge of industry-wide effects in the forum state.

This dearth of supporting case law is understandable when we consider the ramifications of a contrary holding. According to DVD CCA, California should exercise jurisdiction over Pavlovich because he *should have known* that third parties *may* use the misappropriated code to illegally copy movies on DVD's and that licensees of the misappropriated technology resided in California. In other words, DVD CCA is asking this court to exercise jurisdiction over a defendant because he *should have known* that his conduct *may* harm—not a California plaintiff—but industries associated with that plaintiff. As a practical matter, such a ruling makes foreseeability of harm the sole basis for jurisdiction in contravention of controlling United States Supreme Court precedent. (See *Burger King [v. Rudzewicz], supra*, 471 U.S. at p. 474 [105 S.Ct. at p. 2183].)

Indeed, such a broad interpretation of the effects test would effectively eliminate the purposeful availment requirement in the intentional tort context for select plaintiffs. In most, if not all, intentional tort cases, the defendant is or should be aware of the industries that may be affected by his tortious conduct. Consequently, any plaintiff connected to industries centered in California—i.e., the motion picture, computer, and consumer electronics industries-could sue an out-of-state defendant in California for intentional torts that *may* harm those industries. For example, any creator or purveyor of technology that enables copying of movies or computer software—including a student in Australia who develops a program for creating backup copies of software and distributes it to some of his classmates or a store owner in Africa who sells a device that makes digital copies of movies on videotape—would be

6. (See *Panavision, supra*, 141 F.3d at p. 1322 [the defendant "engaged in a scheme to register [a forum resident's] trademarks as his domain names for the purpose of extorting money from" that resident]; *Cable News Network v. GoSMS.com, Inc.* (S.D.N.Y. 2000) 56 U.S.P.Q.2d 1959, 1963 [2000 WL 1678039, *4] [the defendant "transmitted infringing content to" forum residents]; *3DO Co. v. Poptop Software Inc.* (N.D.Cal. 1998) 49 U.S.P.Q.2d 1469, 1472, 1998 WL 962202 [the defendants "encourage[d] and facilitate[d] users" in the forum state "to *download* allegedly infringing copies" from its Web site and used a server in the forum state to operate the site].)

subject to suit in California because they should have known their conduct may harm the motion picture or computer industries in California.[7] Indeed, DVD CCA's interpretation would subject any defendant who commits an intentional tort affecting the motion picture, computer, or consumer electronics industries to jurisdiction in California even if the plaintiff was not a California resident. Under this logic, plaintiffs connected to the auto industry could sue any defendant in Michigan, plaintiffs connected to the financial industry could sue any defendant in New York, and plaintiffs connected to the potato industry could sue any defendant in Idaho. Because finding jurisdiction under the facts in this case would effectively subject all intentional tortfeasors whose conduct may harm industries in California to jurisdiction in California, we decline to do so.

We, however, emphasize the narrowness of our decision. A defendant's knowledge that his tortious conduct may harm industries centered in California is undoubtedly relevant to any determination of personal jurisdiction and may support a finding of jurisdiction. We merely hold that this knowledge *alone* is insufficient to establish express aiming at the forum state as required by the effects test. Because the only evidence in the record even suggesting express aiming is Pavlovich's knowledge that his conduct may harm industries centered in California, due process requires us to decline jurisdiction over his person.

In addition, we are not confronted with a situation where the plaintiff has no other forum to pursue its claims and therefore do not address that situation. DVD CCA has the ability and resources to pursue Pavlovich in another forum such as Indiana or Texas. Our decision today does not foreclose it from doing so. Pavlovich may still face the music—just not in California.

WE CONCUR: KENNARD, WERDEGAR, MORENO, J.J.

BAXTER, J.

I respectfully dissent. That this case involves a powerful new medium of electronic communication, usable for good or ill, should not blind us to the essential facts and principles. The record indicates that, by intentionally posting an unlicensed decryption code for the Content Scrambling System (CSS) on their Internet Web sites, defendant and his network of "open source" associates sought to undermine and defeat the very purposes of the licensed CSS encryption technology, i.e., *copyright protection* for movies recorded on digital versatile discs (DVD's) and *limitation of playback* to operating systems licensed to unscramble the encryption code. The intended targets of this effort were not individual persons or businesses, but entire industries. Defendant knew at least two of the intended targets—the movie industry and the computer industry involved in producing the licensed playback systems-either were centered in California or maintained a particularly substantial presence here.

---

7. Pavlovich claims-and DVD CCA does not dispute-that DeCSS may be used for legitimate, and not just illegal, purposes.

Thus, Pavlovich is no different from the student or store owner in the hypothetical.

Thus, the record amply supports the trial court's conclusion, for purposes of specific personal jurisdiction, that defendant's intentional act, even if committed outside California, was "expressly aimed" at California.

[Justice Baxter supplemented the majority's description of the allegations of the complaint: As early as October, 1999, a resident of Norway had posted DeCSS on the Web. The same program appeared on the Web site operated by Pavlovich shortly thereafter, and Web sites in at least 11 states and 11 countries either directly posted the code or provided links to sites where it was posted. Wholesale copying of DVD's using DeCSS would destroy the movies' copyrights and the market for DVD-based products. Plaintiff therefore sued Pavlovich and 20 other named individuals, as well as 500 Doe defendants, for misappropriation of trade secrets. The complaint sought a declaratory judgment that defendants had misappropriated trade secrets and an injunction against distribution of plaintiff's proprietary information about CSS technology.

The dissent also detailed information from Pavlovich's deposition. He said that LiVid was seeking "to develop an open source DVD player for Liunx" so "we could play ... DVDs on the systems that we had bought that had DVD drives." He insisted that anyone who buys a DVD should have the freedom to duplicate it. He admitted having heard that one needed a license to use the DeCSS code, but did not seek one because "more than likely a license would not allow us to release the source code and things like that that didn't follow the same development path as open source followed." He also understood that DeCSS had been obtained by reverse engineering, and wrote in an e-mail dated Oct. 1, 1999, that "[r]everse engineering is illegal in most (if not all) of the countries that developers of this project live in." He also testified that he knew that Hollywood was where the movie industry is centered and that Silicon Valley is a top technology hot spot.]

For purposes of minimum contacts analysis, the following facts are either undisputed or fairly inferable from the record: The DeCSS source code was posted on defendant Pavlovich's LiVid Web site as part of a widespread effort to defeat the CSS encryption system jointly developed by the movie and DVD industries for their mutual protection and benefit. DeCSS was posted on the LiVid Web site despite Pavlovich's assumption that DeCSS illegally infringed the licensed trade secret represented by CSS. Pavlovich, a technical expert in this area, knew CSS was intended to protect copyrighted materials on DVD's from unauthorized duplication, and also to limit DVD playback to systems with CSS technology. Indeed LiVid's goal in defeating CSS was to develop an alternative, and presumably competitive, "open source" DVD playback system. Thus, the intended injurious effects of posting DeCSS were aimed directly at the computer hardware industry involved in producing CSS-encrypted DVD players-an industry Pavlovich knew was heavily concentrated in California.

Moreover, Pavlovich knew the purpose of CSS was to protect copyrighted movies from pirating, and that the widespread availability of DeCSS undermined that interest. Thus, even if he did not personally pirate copyrighted material for commercial gain, Pavlovich, by publishing material he understood as an infringement of the CSS trade secret, took an action calculated to harm the movie industry, which Pavlovich knew was centered in California.

Accordingly, the necessary minimum contacts required by *Calder*, *supra*, 465 U.S. 783, are present. Pavlovich engaged in " '(1) intentional actions (2) expressly aimed at the forum state (3) causing harm, the brunt of which is suffered-and which the defendant knows is likely to be suffered-in the forum state.' " (*Panavision*, *supra*, 141 F.3d 1316, 1321.) Accordingly, he should reasonably anticipate he would be haled into *California's* courts to account for his conduct.

The majority ascribe undue significance to the fact that Pavlovich acted through a new and rapidly burgeoning medium of interstate and international communication-the Internet. They assert that the mere posting of information on a passive Internet Web site, which is accessible from anywhere but is directed at no particular audience, cannot be an action targeted at a particular forum. Otherwise, they worry, mere use of the Internet would subject the user to personal jurisdiction in any forum where the site was accessible.

I agree that *mere* operation of an Internet Web site cannot expose the operator to suit in any jurisdiction where the site's contents might be read, or where resulting injury might occur. Communication by a universally accessible Internet Web site cannot be equated with "express aiming" at the entire world.

However, defendants who aim conduct at particular jurisdictions, expecting and intending that injurious effects will be felt in those specific places, cannot shield themselves from suit there simply by using the Internet, or some other generalized medium of communication, as the means of inflicting the harm.[4]

In such circumstances, the defendant is not exposed to universal and unpredictable jurisdiction. He faces suit only in a particular forum where he directed his injurious conduct, and where he must reasonably anticipate being called to account.

The cases cited by the majority for the proposition that operation or use of a passive Internet Web site cannot create personal jurisdiction in a

---

4. The majority imply that the maintenance of a passive Internet Web site cannot be considered "express aiming" at any jurisdiction because such a site is just a way of allowing interested persons to search for and retrieve information stored in remote computers. But the maintenance of a Web site that includes content intended and expected to harm particular individuals, entities, or interests in specific places is no more "passive" in this regard than television broadcasts which all or none may watch as they choose (see *Indianapolis Colts, Inc. v. Baltimore Football Club Limited Partnership* [supra p. 751 n.6]) or a recorded toll-free telephone message which all or none may hear as they choose (cf. *Inset Systems, Inc.*, *supra*, 937 F.Supp. 161, 165).

state foreign to the operator's location are inapposite. Those decisions hold that personal jurisdiction cannot be based on *mere accessibility* to a Web site by residents of the forum state or otherwise conclude, on their individual facts, that particular *uses* of the Internet did not establish the geographic specificity, knowledge, and intent necessary for "express aiming."[5]

Next, the majority accept Pavlovich's argument that he cannot have expressly aimed his conduct at California because he knew neither the specific identity nor the location of the CSS *licensing agency* (now California-based plaintiff DVD CCA) at the time DeCSS was posted on the LiViD Web site. But knowledge of this exact kind is unnecessary to establish personal jurisdiction. When a foreign defendant, by intentional conduct directed toward the forum, establishes the necessary minimum contacts with that jurisdiction, he or she may be exposed to litigation there for any " 'controversy [that] is *related to* or *"arises out of"* [those] contacts....' " The *plaintiff* need not be the exact person or entity toward whom the defendant's conduct was directed.

* * *

I believe that the unusual and unprecedented facts of this case demonstrate *purposeful activity* directed toward this forum sufficient to establish minimum contacts under the *Calder* test. As a result of his actions, defendant Pavlovich should reasonably have anticipated being haled into court in this state, and recognition of California's jurisdiction thus meets constitutional standards of fairness.

5. (E.g., *Jewish Defense Organization, Inc. v. Superior Court* (1999) 72 Cal.App.4th 1045, 1059 [85 Cal.Rptr.2d 611, 620] [assertion by plaintiff, who lives in New York and travels frequently, that he "spends 'considerable professional time' in California" is insufficient to show California was targeted when plaintiff was allegedly defamed by an individual and organization, both located in New York, using Internet services provided by companies with offices in California]; *Cybersell, Inc. v. Cybersell, Inc.* (9th Cir. 1997) 130 F.3d 414 (*Cybersell*) [Floridians' mere use of an allegedly infringing mark on a passive Web site home page promoting their business did not subject users to personal jurisdiction in Arizona, where mark's owners were located; there was no evidence defendants sought Arizona business or otherwise targeted Arizona with knowledge that harm would be suffered there]; *GTE New Media Service Inc. v. BellSouth Corp.* (D.C. Cir. 2000) 199 F.3d 1343 [mere evidence that foreign defendants sought to maximize use, within District of Columbia as elsewhere, of their Internet "yellow pages" service did not create District of Columbia jurisdiction for suit by competing Internet "yellow pages" service provider]; *Bensusan Restaurant Corp. v. King* (S.D.N.Y. 1996) 937 F.Supp. 295, affd. (2d Cir. 1997) 126 F.3d 25 [use of allegedly infringing logotype on Web site promoting independent Blue Note jazz club, which was located in Missouri, did not create New York personal jurisdiction in trademark infringement suit by owner-operator of Blue Note jazz clubs in New York and elsewhere]; see also, e.g., *Nam Tai Electronics, Inc. v. Titzer* (2001) 93 Cal.App.4th 1301 [113 Cal.Rptr.2d 769] [defendant Colorado resident, who posted alleged commercial libels against plaintiff Hong Kong company on an Internet bulletin board provided by Yahoo!, a California corporation, was not subject to California jurisdiction at plaintiff's behest simply because Yahoo!'s Web site was "maintained" in California and defendant's service agreement with Yahoo! stated that California jurisdiction would apply to disputes between Yahoo! and defendant].)

For purposes of this case, which does not involve direct *commercial* use of the Internet, I find little utility in those federal decisions that look to " 'the nature and quality of commercial activity that an entity conducts over the Internet' " to determine personal jurisdiction.

The posting of the DeCSS source code on Pavlovich's LiVid Web site was done with the *specific goal* of negating, by illegal means, the licensed CSS technology Pavlovich knew had been jointly developed by the movie and DVD industries for their mutual protection. Pavlovich's immediate aim, he acknowledged, was to promote development of alternative DVD playback systems not dependent on CSS licensure. However, he also knew CSS was intended to afford crucial copyright protection to DVD movies. He has denied any personal desire to pirate movies, or to encourage others to do so. But by deciding to display the DeCSS source code without restriction on the universally accessible Web site, Pavlovich offered visitors to the site the patent opportunity to exploit this information as they chose.

By taking this calculated action, Pavlovich thus not only foresaw, but must have *intended*, the natural and probable consequences he knew would befall the affected industries. These consequences included *both* the competitive injury Pavlovich admitted he intended to inflict upon the DVD industry, which is substantially present in California, *and* the loss of copyright protection to the movie industry he knew is primarily associated with this state.

We Concur: George, C.J., and Chin, J.

Notes and Questions

1. As this case demonstrates, courts have struggled with the jurisdictional issues that can result from activities on the Internet. Should Internet cases be considered different from other cases? Recall the emphasis on improved methods of travel and communication in McGee v. International Life Ins. Co., supra p. 717. Should the flexibility of electronic communications lead to further relaxation of the limitations on territorial jurisdiction because it will be easier for defendants to respond to suits in distant places? It might become possible to use electronic means to relieve parties of the need to attend trials in person. See Carrington, Virtual Civil Litigation: A Visit to John Bunyan's Celestial City, 98 Colum. L. Rev. 1516, 1524–29 (1998) (discussing "virtual trials"). In Edwards v. Logan, 38 F.Supp.2d 463 (W.D.Va.1999), a prisoner confined in New Mexico sued officials at a Virginia prison where he was formerly confined. The court ordered that his jury trial occur by video conferencing, noting that "courts are beginning to use video conferencing to conduct judicial business." It did, however, recognize that there is still a preference for actual presence at trial. See also F.T.C. v. Swedish Match North America, Inc., 197 F.R.D. 1 (D.C.D.C.2000) (permitting plaintiff to present a distant witness by live video feed).

Ordinarily the stress in Internet jurisdiction cases is on the greater ability it provides for affecting parties in distant places. Some see the existing doctrinal framework as well suited to the new problems: "[T]he Internet is no different from the myriad of ways that people from one place injure people in other places. * * * Since the replacement of strict territorialism [in the wake of *International Shoe*, supra p. 710], such interstate activity no longer confounds the courts. There is a rich and complex body of law to test the legitimacy of sovereign claims to regulate and redress interstate claims." Stein, The Unexceptional Problem of Jurisdiction in Cyberspace, 32 Int'l Lawyer 1167, 1180 (1998).

Others are less sanguine about adapting current principles to Internet situations. Consider that "the ease and relative inexpensiveness involved in placing a Web page on the Internet mean that such activity cannot legitimately be viewed as true purposeful availment of those forums [the Internet reaches]. The defendant has not made the type of temporal or financial commitment required in the use of a preexisting communications technology." Redish, Of New Wine in Old Bottles: Personal Jurisdiction, the Internet, and the Nature of Constitutional Evolution, 38 Jurimetrics 575, 590 (1998). As a consequence, the purposeful availment standard may be unsuited to determining jurisdictional issues related to Internet activities (id. at 580):

> [B]ecause of the dramatic and unique ease with which those out-of-staters may make use of the Internet to inflict such harm, it will often be impossible realistically to characterize their activities as the purposeful availment of the jurisdiction's benefits and privileges, i.e, the conscious decision affirmatively to connect oneself with the forum state for the purpose of acquiring benefits and privileges from that state. Use of this standard will therefore effectively prevent individual states from protecting their citizens against Internet harm. At least in the context of the Internet, then, the purposeful availment test fails the traditional utilitarian calculus of procedural due process, which seeks to draw an appropriate balance between the competing interests of state and litigant.

For further discussion of these issues, see Symposium, Personal Jurisdiction in the Internet Age, 98 Nw.U.L.Rev. 409 (2004).

2. The majority and dissent in *Pavlovich* do not seem divided on the legal principles to use, but only on the way to apply them. The majority sees the question as "close," but concludes that the purposeful availment test has not been satisfied. It stresses defendant's ignorance of the location of plaintiff's principal place of business and the absence of any evidence that he encouraged illegal pirating of DVDs. Is this reasoning persuasive? What was defendant's purpose in posting the source code if not to facilitate circumvention of DVD encription? How likely is it that defendant—a computer expert and enthusiast for open access—did not either know where plaintiff was located or support misuse of the misappropriated code? The majority also points out that there was no evidence that anyone from California had actually downloaded the code from defendant's site. How likely is it that there had been no such downloads? Defendants sometimes resist jurisdiction by showing that there have been no hits from the forum state on their websites. See, e.g., Cybersell v. Cybersell, 130 F.3d 414 (9th Cir.1997) (defendant only had one hit from forum state, and that was from plaintiff). Probably defendants can get this information from their webmaster or network administrator. How easily can plaintiffs get this information?

On the other hand, is there a limiting principle to the dissent's analysis? The dissent agrees that "mere operation of an Internet Web site cannot expose the operator to suit in any jurisdiction where the site's contents might be read, or where resulting injury might occur." Is the dissent's analysis sufficient to distinguish the Australian student and the African store owner suggested by the majority? How about Jon Johansen, the Norweigen who first posted DeCss? Compare Core–Vent Corp. v. Nobel Industries AB, 11 F.3d 1482 (9th Cir.1993) ("publication of a commercial libel in a worldwide medical journal did not permit suit against Swedish writers in California."). Is California the only state in which Pavlovich could be sued under the dissent's effects analysis? Would the dissent's analysis, as the majority argues, "effectively eliminate the purposeful availment requirement in the intentional tort context" for Internet activities? How would it apply to a person who releases a virus on the Internet that causes millions of dollars in damage in the forum? In Inset Systems, Inc. v. Instruction Set, Inc., 937 F.Supp. 161 (D.Conn.1996), the court upheld jurisdiction on the ground that defendant's otherwise passive website contained a toll-free telephone number, and that numerous forum residents could access it because "[o]nce posted on the Internet, unlike radio and television advertising, the advertisement is available continuously to any Internet user."

Contrast Panavision International, L.P. v. Toeppen, 141 F.3d 1316 (9th Cir.1998). Plaintiff Panavision was a California company in the motion picture and television camera and photographic equipment business. Defendant was a "cyber pirate" who had registered the Web domain name Panavision.com and then offered to "settle" his "dispute" with Panavision for $13,000 in return for transferring the domain name to plaintiff. Plaintiff sued in Los Angeles instead, claiming dilution of its trademark. The court held that jurisdiction was established (id. at 1322):

> Toeppen engaged in a scheme to register Panavision's trademarks as his domain names for the purpose of extorting money from Panavision. His conduct, as he knew it likely would, had the effect of injuring Panavision in California where Panavision has its principal place of business and where the movie and television industry is centered.

Is *Pavlovich* distinguishable?

3. In *Pavlovich*, both the majority and the dissent seem to agree that the circumstances giving rise to the suit were extraordinary. Most of the cases that have come up have fallen into more predictable categories:

Defamation: In Blumenthal v. Drudge, 992 F.Supp. 44 (D.D.C.1998), the court held that a White House staffer could sue Matt Drudge, the Internet columnist, in D.C. Drudge solicited contributions of information from people in D.C., focused much of his column on activities in the capitol, and visited the District to promote his column. Contrast Young v. New Haven Advocate, 315 F.3d 256 (4th Cir.2002), in which a Connecticut newspaper published an article about the transfer of inmates to a prison in Virginia that was posted in its Web site and could be read there. Plaintiff, the warden of the Virginia prison, claimed that the article was libelous, but except for Internet access no copies of the newspaper were distributed in Virginia. The court held there was no jurisdiction. Compare Gordy v. Daily News, supra p. 748 n. 1. In Griffis v. Luban, 646 N.W.2d 527 (Minn.2002), cert. denied, 538 U.S. 906, 123 S.Ct. 1483, 155 L.Ed.2d 225 (2003), plaintiff sued defendant in Alabama for posting uncomplimentary assertions about plaintiff on an Internet newsgroup site for those interested in archeology. The Minnesota court held that plaintiff's Alabama default judgment was not entitled to full faith and credit because jurisdiction was not warranted under *Calder*. The postings were about archaeology and directed, not to Alabama, but to an Internet community likely spread across the country and the world.

Trademark infringement: In Zippo Manuf. Co. v. Zippo Dot Com, Inc., 952 F.Supp. 1119 (W.D.Pa.1997), plaintiff manufactured tobacco lighters in Pennsylvania. Defendant operated an Internet news service in California to which customers could subscribe and, for a fee, view and/or download Internet newsgroup messages stored on defendant's server in California. Plaintiff objected to defendant's use of the word "Zippo" in its domain name. The court found jurisdiction warranted because defendant had contracted with approximately 3,000 individuals and seven Internet access providers in Pennsylvania, and these interactions formed one basis for plaintiff's claims of infringement. Would there be any way that defendant could operate without thus being subject to jurisdiction in Pennsylvania? Contrast Carefirst of Maryland v. Carefirst Pregnancy Centers, Inc., 334 F.3d 390 (4th Cir.2003), in which a Maryland plaintiff sued a defendant that used the same name in Illinois. Defendant's website sought donations for its Chicago-area activities, but it had only received $1,500 (0.0174%) of its contributions from Maryland residents. The court used the *Zippo* analysis, but held that jurisdiction was improper. Even though defendant's site was "semi-interactive," it did not satisfy this test. In reaching this conclusion, the court recognized that Maryland was the focal point of plaintiff's injuries. But the overall content of defendant's site was "strongly local" in character, directed to the Chicago area. Accordingly, "when [defendant] set up its generally accessible, semi-interactive Internet website, it did not thereby direct electronic activity into Maryland with the manifest intent of engaging in business or other interactions within that state in particular." Id. at 401. The fact that defendant relied on a Maryland company as a web server and to facilitate its acquisition of domain names was de minimis, particularly since the servers themselves were actually located in Massachusetts.

4. In GTE New Media Serv., Inc. v. BellSouth Corp., 199 F.3d 1343 (D.C.Cir.2000), plaintiff claimed that defendant regional phone companies had entered into a conspiracy to persuade Netscape and Yahoo to link exclusively to defendants' Internet Yellow Pages service. Plaintiff provided similar services, but Netscape and Yahoo ceased referring Internet users to plaintiff's service pursuant to this arrangement. Plaintiff claimed that this alleged antitrust violation legitimated jurisdiction in the District of Columbia, although it identified no physical contacts between defendants and the district. The court disagreed:

> [P]ersonal jurisdiction surely cannot be based solely on the ability of District residents to access the defendants' websites, for this does not by itself show any persistent course of conduct by the defendants in the District. Access to a website reflects nothing more than a telephone call by a District resident to the defendants' computer servers, all of which apparently are operated outside of the District. And, as this court has held, mere receipt of telephone calls outside the District does not constitute persistent conduct "in the district" within the meaning of the [District's] long-arm statute.

Finally, GTE appears to suggest that, when a District resident accesses the defendant's Yellow Pages websites, the defendants are somehow "transacting business" within the District. This is a far-fetched claim on this record. Access to an Internet Yellow Page site is akin to searching a telephone book—the consumer pays nothing to use the search tool, and any resulting business is between the consumer and a business found in the Yellow Pages, not between the consumer and the provider of the Yellow Pages. In short, there is nothing here to indicate that District residents actually engage in any business transactions with the defendants.

5. What should be the scope of jurisdiction if defendant does transact business over the Web? In CompuServe, Inc. v. Patterson, 89 F.3d 1257 (6th Cir.1996), defendant entered into an online agreement with plaintiff to market various programs he had developed. The contract said it was governed by the law of Ohio, where plaintiff's headquarters were located. When defendant sent e-mail messages to plaintiff accusing it of infringing his common law trademarks and stealing his programs, it sued in Ohio seeking a declaration it had not violated his rights. The court upheld jurisdiction, emphasizing that defendant was "far more than a purchaser of services." The court was circumspect about possible implications of its holding, however (id. at 1268):

> We need not and do not hold that Patterson would be subject to suit in any state where his software was purchased or used; that is not the case before us. We also do not have before us an attempt by another party from a third state to sue Patterson in Ohio for, say, a "computer virus" caused by his software, and thus we need not address whether personal jurisdiction could be found on those facts. Finally, we need not and do not hold that Compuserve may * * * sue any regular subscriber to its service for nonpayment in Ohio, even if the subscriber is a native Alaskan who has never left home.

6. The dissent says (see ftn. 5) that Pavlovich's use of the Internet was noncommercial. Should noncommercial uses of the Internet be treated differently? In Barrett v. The Catacombs Press, 44 F.Supp.2d 717 (E.D.Pa. 1999), plaintiff sued defendant for defamation in Pennsylvania, where he resided, because defendant posted messages about plaintiff on various Web sites. The underlying dispute between plaintiff and defendant had to do with fluoridation; plaintiff favored it and defendant was opposed. Defendant resided in Oregon and had accessed the Web from there, and the court refused to find that her postings concerning plaintiff's own Internet activities established a connection with Pennsylvania. Although defendant's postings were different from maintaining a passive Web page, the court found them akin to a passive Web site.

7. Courts frequently distinguish between "active" and "passive" web sites when assessing jurisdictional issues. See, e.g., Mink v. AAAA Development LLC, 190 F.3d 333 (5th Cir.1999). Is this distinction really meaningful? "From a purely conceptual perspective, it is difficult to understand how the affirmative act of opening a Web page can accurately be described as a 'passive' act." Redish, supra note 1, at 591.

E.   PRESENCE OF DEFENDANT'S PROPERTY

SHAFFER v. HEITNER

Supreme Court of the United States, 1977.
433 U.S. 186, 97 S.Ct. 2569, 53 L.Ed.2d 683.

JUSTICE MARSHALL delivered the opinion of the Court.

The controversy in this case concerns the constitutionality of a Delaware statute that allows a court of that State to take jurisdiction of a lawsuit by sequestering any property of the defendant that happens to be located in Delaware. Appellants contend that the sequestration statute as applied in this case violates the Due Process Clause of the Fourteenth Amendment both because it permits the state courts to exercise jurisdiction despite the absence of sufficient contacts among the defendants, the litigation, and the State of Delaware and because it authorizes the deprivation of defendants' property without providing adequate procedural safeguards. We find it necessary to consider only the first of these contentions.

I

Appellee Heitner, a nonresident of Delaware, is the owner of one share of stock in the Greyhound Corp., a business incorporated under the laws of Delaware with its principal place of business in Phoenix, Ariz. On May 22, 1974, he filed a shareholder's derivative suit in the Court of Chancery for New Castle County, Del., in which he named as defendants Greyhound, its wholly owned subsidiary Greyhound Lines, Inc., and 28 present or former officers or directors of one or both of the corporations. In essence, Heitner alleged that the individual defendants had violated their duties to Greyhound by causing it and its subsidiary to engage in actions that resulted in the corporations being held liable for substantial damages in a private antitrust suit and a large fine in a criminal contempt action. The activities which led to these penalties took place in Oregon.

Simultaneously with his complaint, Heitner filed a motion for an order of sequestration of the Delaware property of the individual defendants pursuant to Del.Code Ann., Tit. 10, § 366 (1975). This motion was accompanied by a supporting affidavit of counsel which stated that the individual defendants were nonresidents of Delaware. The affidavit identified the property to be sequestered as

> "common stock, 3% Second Cumulative Preferred Stock and stock unit credits of the Defendant Greyhound Corporation, a Delaware corporation, as well as all options and all warrants to purchase said stock issued to said individual Defendants and all contractual (sic) obligations, all rights, debts or credits due or accrued to or for the benefit of any of the said Defendants under any type of written agreement, contract or other legal instrument of any kind whatever between any of the individual Defendants and said corporation."

The requested sequestration order was signed the day the motion was filed. Pursuant to that order, the sequestrator "seized" approximately 82,000 shares of Greyhound common stock belonging to 19 of the defendants, and options belonging to another 2 defendants. These seizures were accomplished by placing "stop transfer" orders or their equivalents on the books of the Greyhound Corp. So far as the record shows, none of the certificates representing the seized property was physically present in Delaware. The stock was considered to be in Delaware, and so subject to seizure, by virtue of Del.Code Ann., Tit. 8, § 169 (1975), which makes Delaware the situs of ownership of all stock in Delaware corporations.

All 28 defendants were notified of the initiation of the suit by certified mail directed to their last known addresses and by publication in a New Castle County newspaper. The 21 defendants whose property was seized (hereafter referred to as appellants) responded by entering a special appearance for the purpose of moving to quash service of process and to vacate the sequestration order. They contended that the ex parte sequestration procedure did not accord them due process of law and that the property seized was not capable of attachment in Delaware. In addition, appellants asserted that under the rule of International Shoe Co. v. Washington, 326 U.S. 310, 66 S.Ct. 154, 90 L.Ed. 95 (1945), they did not have sufficient contacts with Delaware to sustain the jurisdiction of that State's courts.

The Court of Chancery rejected these arguments in a letter opinion which emphasized the purpose of the Delaware sequestration procedure:

> "The primary purpose of 'sequestration' as authorized by 10 Del.C. § 366 is not to secure possession of property pending a trial between resident debtors and creditors on the issue of who has the right to retain it. On the contrary, as here employed, 'sequestration' is a process used to compel the personal appearance of a nonresident defendant to answer and defend a suit brought against him in a court of equity. It is accomplished by the appointment of a sequestrator by this Court to seize and hold property of the nonresident located in this State subject to further Court order. If the defendant enters a general appearance, the sequestered property is routinely released, unless the plaintiff makes special application to continue its seizure, in which event the plaintiff has the burden of proof and persuasion."

This limitation on the purpose and length of time for which sequestered property is held, the court concluded, rendered inapplicable the due process requirements enunciated in Sniadach v. Family Finance Corp., 395 U.S. 337, 89 S.Ct. 1820, 23 L.Ed.2d 349 (1969); Fuentes v. Shevin, 407 U.S. 67, 92 S.Ct. 1983, 32 L.Ed.2d 556 (1972) [supra p. 29]:; and Mitchell v. W. T. Grant Co., 416 U.S. 600, 94 S.Ct. 1895, 40 L.Ed.2d 406 (1974) [supra p. 42]. The court also found no state-law or federal constitutional barrier to the sequestrator's reliance on Del.Code Ann., Tit. 8, § 169 (1975). Finally, the court held that the statutory Delaware situs of the stock provided a sufficient basis for the exercise of quasi in rem jurisdiction by a Delaware court.

On appeal, the Delaware Supreme Court affirmed the judgment of the Court of Chancery.

II

The Delaware courts rejected appellants' jurisdictional challenge by noting that this suit was brought as a *quasi in rem* proceeding. Since *quasi in rem* jurisdiction is traditionally based on attachment or seizure of property present in the jurisdiction, not on contacts between the defendant and the State, the courts considered appellants' claimed lack of contacts with Delaware to be unimportant. This categorical analysis assumes the continued soundness of the conceptual structure founded on the century-old case of Pennoyer v. Neff, 95 U.S. 714, 24 L.Ed. 565 (1877).

[The Court reviewed *Pennoyer* and the jurisdictional developments since 1878, finding that "the relationship among the defendant, the forum, and the litigation, rather than the mutually exclusive sovereignty of the States on which the rules of *Pennoyer* rest, became the central concern of the inquiry into personal jurisdiction."]

No equally dramatic change has occurred in the law governing jurisdiction *in rem*. There have, however, been intimations that the collapse of the *in personam* wing of *Pennoyer* has not left that decision unweakened as a foundation for *in rem* jurisdiction. Well-reasoned lower court opinions have questioned the proposition that the presence of property in a State gives that State jurisdiction to adjudicate rights to the property regardless of the relationship of the underlying dispute and the property owner to the forum. The overwhelming majority of commentators have also rejected *Pennoyer*'s premise that a proceeding "against" property is not a proceeding against the owners of that property. Accordingly, they urge that the "traditional notions of fair play and substantial justice" that govern a State's power to adjudicate in personam should also govern its power to adjudicate personal rights to property located in the State. See, e.g., von Mehren & Trautman, Jurisdiction to Adjudicate: A Suggested Analysis, 79 Harv.L.Rev. 1121 (1966); Traynor, Is This Conflict Really Necessary?, 37 Texas L.Rev. 657 (1959); Ehrenzweig, The Transient Rule of Personal Jurisdiction: The "Power" Myth and Forum Conveniens, 65 Yale L.J. 289 (1956).

Although this Court has not addressed this argument directly, we have held that property cannot be subjected to a court's judgment unless reasonable and appropriate efforts have been made to give the property owners actual notice of the action. Walker v. City of Hutchinson, 352 U.S. 112, 77 S.Ct. 200, 1 L.Ed.2d 178 (1956); Mullane v. Central Hanover Bank & Trust Co., 339 U.S. 306, 70 S.Ct. 652, 94 L.Ed. 865 (1950). This conclusion recognizes, contrary to *Pennoyer,* that an adverse judgment *in rem* directly affects the property owner by divesting him of his rights in the property before the court. Moreover, in *Mullane* we held that Fourteenth Amendment rights cannot depend on the classification of an action as *in rem* or *in personam,* since that is

> "a classification for which the standards are so elusive and confused generally and which, being primarily for state courts to define, may and do vary from state to state."

It is clear, therefore, that the law of state-court jurisdiction no longer stands securely on the foundation established in *Pennoyer.* We think that the time is ripe to consider whether the standard of fairness and substantial justice set forth in *International Shoe* should be held to govern actions *in rem* as well as *in personam.*

III

The case for applying to jurisdiction *in rem* the same test of "fair play and substantial justice" as governs assertions of jurisdiction in personam is simple and straightforward. It is premised on recognition that "[t]he phrase, 'judicial jurisdiction over a thing', is a customary elliptical way of referring to jurisdiction over the interests of persons in a thing." Restatement (Second) of Conflict of Laws § 56, Introductory Note (1971) (hereafter Restatement). This recognition leads to the conclusion that in order to justify an exercise of jurisdiction *in rem,* the basis for jurisdiction must be sufficient to justify exercising "jurisdiction over the interests of persons in a thing."[23] The standard for determining whether an exercise of jurisdiction over the interests of persons is consistent with the Due Process Clause is the minimum-contacts standard elucidated in *International Shoe.*

This argument, of course, does not ignore the fact that the presence of property in a State may bear on the existence of jurisdiction by providing contacts among the forum State, the defendant, and the litigation. For example, when claims to the property itself are the source of the underlying controversy between the plaintiff and the defendant,[24] it would be unusual for the State where the property is located not to have jurisdiction. In such cases, the defendant's claim to property located in the State would normally indicate that he expected to benefit from the State's protection of his interest. The State's strong interests in assuring the marketability of property within its borders and in provid-

---

23. It is true that the potential liability of a defendant in an *in rem* action is limited by the value of the property, but that limitation does not affect the argument. The fairness of subjecting a defendant to state-court jurisdiction does not depend on the size of the claim being litigated.

24. This category includes true *in rem* actions and the first type of *quasi in rem* proceedings. See n. 17, supra. [Footnote 17 provides as follows: "A judgment *in rem* affects the interests of all persons in designated property. A judgment *quasi in rem*

affects the interests of particular persons in designated property. The latter is of two types. In one the plaintiff is seeking to secure a pre-existing claim in the subject property and to extinguish or establish the nonexistence of similar interests of particular persons. In the other the plaintiff seeks to apply what he concedes to be the property of the defendant to the satisfaction of a claim against him. Restatement, Judgments, 5–9." Hanson v. Denckla, 357 U.S. 235, 246 n. 12, 78 S.Ct. 1228, 1235, 2 L.Ed.2d 1283 (1958).]

ing a procedure for peaceful resolution of disputes about the possession of that property would also support jurisdiction, as would the likelihood that important records and witnesses will be found in the State.[28] The presence of property may also favor jurisdiction in cases such as suits for injury suffered on the land of an absentee owner, where the defendant's ownership of the property is conceded but the cause of action is otherwise related to rights and duties growing out of that ownership.[29]

It appears, therefore, that jurisdiction over many types of actions which now are or might be brought *in rem* would not be affected by a holding that any assertion of state-court jurisdiction must satisfy the *International Shoe* standard.[30] For the type of *quasi in rem* action typified by Harris v. Balk [supra p. 703] and the present case, however, accepting the proposed analysis would result in significant change. These are cases where the property which now serves as the basis for state-court jurisdiction is completely unrelated to the plaintiff's cause of action. Thus, although the presence of the defendant's property in a State might suggest the existence of other ties among the defendant, the State, and the litigation, the presence of the property alone would not support the State's jurisdiction. If those other ties did not exist, cases over which the State is now thought to have jurisdiction could not be brought in that forum.

Since acceptance of the *International Shoe* test would most affect this class of cases, we examine the arguments against adopting that standard as they relate to this category of litigation. Before doing so, however, we note that this type of case also presents the clearest illustration of the argument in favor of assessing assertions of jurisdiction by a single standard. For in cases such as *Harris* and this one, the only role played by the property is to provide the basis for bringing the defendant into court. Indeed, the express purpose of the Delaware sequestration procedure is to compel the defendant to enter a personal appearance.[33] In such cases, if a direct assertion of personal jurisdiction over the defendant would violate the Constitution, it would seem that an indirect assertion of that jurisdiction should be equally impermissible.

The primary rationale for treating the presence of property as a sufficient basis for jurisdiction to adjudicate claims over which the State would not have jurisdiction if *International Shoe* applied is that a wrongdoer "should not be able to avoid payment of his obligations by the expedient of removing his assets to a place where he is not subject to an

---

28. We do not suggest that these illustrations include all the factors that may affect the decision, nor that the factors we have mentioned are necessarily decisive.

29. Cf. Dubin v. Philadelphia, 34 Pa.D. & C. 61 (1939). If such an action were brought under the *in rem* jurisdiction rather than under a long-arm statute, it would be a *quasi in rem* action of the second type. See n. [24], supra.

30. We do not suggest that jurisdictional doctrines other than those discussed in text, such as the particularized rules governing adjudications of status, are inconsistent with the standard of fairness.

33. This purpose is emphasized by Delaware's refusal to allow any defense on the merits unless the defendant enters a general appearance, thus submitting to full *in personam* liability.

in personam suit." Restatement § 66, Comment a. This justification, however, does not explain why jurisdiction should be recognized without regard to whether the property is present in the State because of an effort to avoid the owner's obligations. Nor does it support jurisdiction to adjudicate the underlying claim. At most, it suggests that a State in which property is located should have jurisdiction to attach that property, by use of proper procedures, as security for a judgment being sought in a forum where the litigation can be maintained consistently with *International Shoe.* Moreover, we know of nothing to justify the assumption that a debtor can avoid paying his obligations by removing his property to a State in which his creditor cannot obtain personal jurisdiction over him. The Full Faith and Credit Clause, after all, makes the valid *in personam* judgment of one State enforceable in all other States.[36]

It might also be suggested that allowing *in rem* jurisdiction avoids the uncertainty inherent in the *International Shoe* standard and assures a plaintiff of a forum.[37] We believe, however, that the fairness standard of *International Shoe* can be easily applied in the vast majority of cases. Moreover, when the existence of jurisdiction in a particular forum under *International Shoe* is unclear, the cost of simplifying the litigation by avoiding the jurisdictional question may be the sacrifice of "fair play and substantial justice." That cost is too high.

We are left, then, to consider the significance of the long history of jurisdiction based solely on the presence of property in a State. Although the theory that territorial power is both essential to and sufficient for jurisdiction has been undermined, we have never held that the presence of property in a State does not automatically confer jurisdiction over the owner's interest in that property. This history must be considered as supporting the proposition that jurisdiction based solely on the presence of property satisfies the demands of due process, cf. Ownbey v. Morgan, 256 U.S. 94, 111, 41 S.Ct. 433, 438, 65 L.Ed. 837 (1921), but it is not decisive. "[T]raditional notions of fair play and substantial justice" can be as readily offended by the perpetuation of ancient forms that are no longer justified as by the adoption of new procedures that are inconsistent with the basic values of our constitutional heritage. Cf. Sniadach v. Family Finance Corp., 395 U.S., at 340, 89 S.Ct., at 1822. The fiction that an assertion of jurisdiction over property is anything but an assertion of jurisdiction over the owner of the property supports an ancient form without substantial modern justification. Its continued acceptance would serve only to allow state-court jurisdiction that is fundamentally unfair to the defendant.

36. Once it has been determined by a court of competent jurisdiction that the defendant is a debtor of the plaintiff, there would seem to be no unfairness in allowing an action to realize on that debt in a State where the defendant has property, whether or not that State would have jurisdiction to determine the existence of the debt as an original matter.

37. This case does not raise, and we therefore do not consider, the question whether the presence of a defendant's property in a State is a sufficient basis for jurisdiction when no other forum is available to the plaintiff.

We therefore conclude that all assertions of state-court jurisdiction must be evaluated according to the standards set forth in *International Shoe* and its progeny.

IV

The Delaware courts based their assertion of jurisdiction in this case solely on the statutory presence of appellants' property in Delaware. Yet that property is not the subject matter of this litigation, nor is the underlying cause of action related to the property. Appellants' holdings in Greyhound do not, therefore, provide contacts with Delaware sufficient to support the jurisdiction of that State's courts over appellants. If it exists, that jurisdiction must have some other foundation.

Appellee Heitner did not allege and does not now claim that appellants have ever set foot in Delaware. Nor does he identify any act related to his cause of action as having taken place in Delaware. Nevertheless, he contends that appellants' positions as directors and officers of a corporation chartered in Delaware provide sufficient "contacts, ties, or relations", International Shoe Co. v. Washington, 326 U.S., at 319, 66 S.Ct., at 160, with that State to give its courts jurisdiction over appellants in this stockholder's derivative action. This argument is based primarily on what Heitner asserts to be the strong interest of Delaware in supervising the management of a Delaware corporation. That interest is said to derive from the role of Delaware law in establishing the corporation and defining the obligations owed to it by its officers and directors. In order to protect this interest, appellee concludes, Delaware's courts must have jurisdiction over corporate fiduciaries such as appellants.

This argument is undercut by the failure of the Delaware Legislature to assert the state interest appellee finds so compelling. Delaware law bases jurisdiction, not on appellants' status as corporate fiduciaries, but rather on the presence of their property in the State. Although the sequestration procedure used here may be most frequently used in derivative suits against officers and directors, the authorizing statute evinces no specific concern with such actions. Sequestration can be used in any suit against a nonresident and reaches corporate fiduciaries only if they happen to own interests in a Delaware corporation, or other property in the State. But as Heitner's failure to secure jurisdiction over seven of the defendants named in his complaint demonstrates, there is no necessary relationship between holding a position as a corporate fiduciary and owning stock or other interests in the corporation. If Delaware perceived its interest in securing jurisdiction over corporate fiduciaries to be as great as Heitner suggests, we would expect it to have enacted a statute more clearly designed to protect that interest.

Moreover, even if Heitner's assessment of the importance of Delaware's interest is accepted, his argument fails to demonstrate that Delaware is a fair forum for this litigation. The interest appellee has identified may support the application of Delaware law to resolve any controversy over appellants' actions in their capacities as officers and directors.[44] But we have rejected the argument that if a State's law can properly be applied to a dispute, its courts necessarily have jurisdiction over the parties to that dispute.

> "[The State] does not acquire . . . jurisdiction by being the 'center of gravity' of the controversy, or the most convenient location for litigation. The issue is personal jurisdiction, not choice of law. It is resolved in this case by considering the acts of the [appellants]." Hanson v. Denckla, 357 U.S. 235, 254, 78 S.Ct. 1228, 1240, 2 L.Ed.2d 1283 (1958).

Appellee suggests that by accepting positions as officers or directors of a Delaware corporation, appellants performed the acts required by Hanson v. Denckla. He notes that Delaware law provides substantial benefits to corporate officers and directors, and that these benefits were at least in part the incentive for appellants to assume their positions. It is, he says, "only fair and just" to require appellants, in return for these benefits, to respond in the State of Delaware when they are accused of misusing their power.

But like Heitner's first argument, this line of reasoning establishes only that it is appropriate for Delaware law to govern the obligations of appellants to Greyhound and its stockholders. It does not demonstrate that appellants have "purposefully avail[ed themselves] of the privilege of conducting activities within the forum State," Hanson v. Denckla, at 253, 78 S.Ct., at 1240, in a way that would justify bringing them before a Delaware tribunal. Appellants have simply had nothing to do with the State of Delaware. Moreover, appellants had no reason to expect to be haled before a Delaware court. Delaware, unlike some States, has not enacted a statute that treats acceptance of a directorship as consent to jurisdiction in the State.

* * *

Delaware's assertion of jurisdiction over appellants in this case is inconsistent with that constitutional limitation on state power. The judgment of the Delaware Supreme Court must, therefore, be reversed.

JUSTICE REHNQUIST took no part in the consideration or decision of this case.

JUSTICE POWELL, concurring.

I agree that the principles of International Shoe Co. v. Washington, 326 U.S. 310, 66 S.Ct. 154, 90 L.Ed. 95 (1945), should be extended to govern assertions of *in rem* as well as *in personam* jurisdiction in a state court. I also agree that neither the statutory presence of appellants' stock in Delaware nor their positions as directors and officers of a

---

44. In general, the law of the State of incorporation is held to govern the liabilities of officers or directors to the corporation and its stockholders. See Restatement [Second, Conflict of Laws] § 309. The ratio- nale for the general rule appears to be based more on the need for a uniform and certain standard to govern the internal affairs of a corporation than on the perceived interest of the State of incorporation.

Delaware corporation can provide sufficient contacts to support the Delaware courts' assertion of jurisdiction in this case.

I would explicitly reserve judgment, however, on whether the ownership of some forms of property whose situs is indisputably and permanently located within a State may, without more, provide the contacts necessary to subject a defendant to jurisdiction within the State to the extent of the value of the property. In the case of real property, in particular, preservation of the common-law concept of *quasi in rem* jurisdiction arguably would avoid the uncertainty of the general *International Shoe* standard without significant cost to " 'traditional notions of fair play and substantial justice.' "

Subject to the foregoing reservation, I join the opinion of the Court.

JUSTICE STEVENS, concurring in the judgment.

The Due Process Clause affords protection against "judgments without notice." International Shoe Co. v. Washington, 326 U.S. 310, 324, 66 S.Ct. 154, 162, 90 L.Ed. 95 (opinion of Black, J.). Throughout our history the acceptable exercise of *in rem* and *quasi in rem* jurisdiction has included a procedure giving reasonable assurance that actual notice of the particular claim will be conveyed to the defendant. Thus, publication, notice by registered mail, or extraterritorial personal service has been an essential ingredient of any procedure that serves as a substitute for personal service within the jurisdiction.

The requirement of fair notice also, I believe, includes fair warning that a particular activity may subject a person to the jurisdiction of a foreign sovereign. If I visit another State, or acquire real estate or open a bank account in it, I knowingly assume some risk that the State will exercise its power over my property or my person while there. My contact with the State, though minimal, gives rise to predictable risks.

Perhaps the same consequences should flow from the purchase of stock of a corporation organized under the laws of a foreign nation, because to some limited extent one's property and affairs then become subject to the laws of the nation of domicile of the corporation.

* * *

How the Court's opinion may be applied in other contexts is not entirely clear to me. I agree with Justice Powell that it should not be read to invalidate *quasi in rem* jurisdiction where real estate is involved. I would also not read it as invalidating other long-accepted methods of acquiring jurisdiction over persons with adequate notice of both the particular controversy and the fact that their local activities might subject them to suit. My uncertainty as to the reach of the opinion, and my fear that it purports to decide a great deal more than is necessary to dispose of this case, persuade me merely to concur in the judgment.

JUSTICE BRENNAN, concurring in part and dissenting in part.

I join Parts I–III of the Court's opinion. I fully agree that the minimum-contacts analysis developed in International Shoe Co. v. Washington, 326 U.S. 310, 66 S.Ct. 154, 90 L.Ed. 95 (1945), represents a far more sensible construct for the exercise of state-court jurisdiction than the patchwork of legal and factual fictions that has been generated from the decision in Pennoyer v. Neff, 95 U.S. 714, 24 L.Ed. 565 (1877). It is precisely because the inquiry into minimum contacts is now of such overriding importance, however, that I must respectfully dissent from Part IV of the Court's opinion.

[Justice Brennan argued that the Court's resolution of the propriety of Delaware's assertion of jurisdiction on a minimum contacts basis was an advisory opinion because no effort had been made below to assert jurisdiction on this basis.]

* * *

Nonetheless, because the Court rules on the minimum-contacts question, I feel impelled to express my view. While evidence derived through discovery might satisfy me that minimum contacts are lacking in a given case, I am convinced that as a general rule a state forum has jurisdiction to adjudicate a shareholder derivative action centering on the conduct and policies of the directors and officers of a corporation chartered by that State. Unlike the Court, I therefore would not foreclose Delaware from asserting jurisdiction over appellants were it persuaded to do so on the basis of minimum contacts.

It is well settled that a derivative lawsuit as presented here does not inure primarily to the benefit of the named plaintiff. Rather, the primary beneficiaries are the corporation and its owners, the shareholders. "The cause of action which such a plaintiff brings before the court is not his own but the corporation's. . . . Such a plaintiff often may represent an important public and stockholder interest in bringing faithless managers to book." Koster v. Lumbermens Mutual Cas. Co., 330 U.S. 518, 67 S.Ct. 828, 91 L.Ed. 1067 (1947).

Viewed in this light, the chartering State has an unusually powerful interest in insuring the availability of a convenient forum for litigating claims involving a possible multiplicity of defendant fiduciaries and for vindicating the State's substantive policies regarding the management of its domestic corporations. I believe that our cases fairly establish that the State's valid substantive interests are important considerations in assessing whether it constitutionally may claim jurisdiction over a given cause of action.

In this instance, Delaware can point to at least three interrelated public policies that are furthered by its assertion of jurisdiction. First, the State has a substantial interest in providing restitution for its local corporations that allegedly have been victimized by fiduciary misconduct, even if the managerial decisions occurred outside the State. The importance of this general state interest in assuring restitution for its own residents previously found expression in cases that went outside the then-prevailing due process framework to authorize state-court jurisdiction over nonresident motorists who injure others within the State. Hess

v. Pawloski, 274 U.S. 352, 47 S.Ct. 632, 71 L.Ed. 1091 (1927). More recently, it has led States to seek and to acquire jurisdiction over nonresident tortfeasors whose purely out-of-state activities produce domestic consequences. E.g., Gray v. American Radiator & Standard Sanitary Corp., 22 Ill.2d 432, 176 N.E.2d 761 (1961). Second, state courts have legitimately read their jurisdiction expansively when a cause of action centers in an area in which the forum State possesses a manifest regulatory interest. E.g., McGee v. International Life Ins. Co., 355 U.S. 220, 78 S.Ct. 199, 2 L.Ed.2d 223 (1957) (insurance regulation); Travelers Health Ass'n v. Virginia, 339 U.S. 643, 70 S.Ct. 927, 94 L.Ed. 1154 (1950) (blue sky laws). * * * Finally, a State like Delaware has a recognized interest in affording a convenient forum for supervising and overseeing the affairs of an entity that is purely the creation of that State's law. For example, even following our decision in *International Shoe*, New York courts were permitted to exercise complete judicial authority over nonresident beneficiaries of a trust created under state law, even though, unlike appellants here, the beneficiaries personally entered into no association whatsoever with New York. Mullane v. Central Hanover Bank & Trust Co., 339 U.S. 306, 313, 70 S.Ct. 652, 656, 94 L.Ed. 865 (1950). I, of course, am not suggesting that Delaware's varied interests would justify its acceptance of jurisdiction over any transaction touching upon the affairs of its domestic corporations. But a derivative action which raises allegations of abuses of the basic management of an institution whose existence is created by the State and whose powers and duties are defined by state law fundamentally implicates the public policies of that forum.

To be sure, the Court is not blind to these considerations. It notes that the State's interests "may support the application of Delaware law to resolve any controversy over appellants' actions in their capacities as officers and directors." But this, the Court argues, pertains to choice of law, not jurisdiction. I recognize that the jurisdictional and choice-of-law inquiries are not identical. Hanson v. Denckla, 357 U.S. 235, 254, 78 S.Ct. 1228, 1240, 2 L.Ed.2d 1283 (1958). But I would not compartmentalize thinking in this area quite so rigidly as it seems to me the Court does today, for both inquiries "are often closely related and to a substantial degree depend upon similar considerations." Id., at 258, 78 S.Ct., at 1242 (Black, J., dissenting). In either case an important linchpin is the extent of contacts between the controversy, the parties, and the forum State. While constitutional limitations on the choice of law are by no means settled, important considerations certainly include the expectancies of the parties and the fairness of governing the defendants' acts and behavior by rules of conduct created by a given jurisdiction. See, e.g., Restatement (Second) of Conflict of Laws § 6 (1971) (hereafter Restatement). These same factors bear upon the propriety of a State's exercising jurisdiction over a legal dispute. At the minimum, the decision that it is fair to bind a defendant by a State's laws and rules should prove to be highly relevant to the fairness of permitting that same State to accept jurisdiction for adjudicating the controversy.

Furthermore, I believe that practical considerations argue in favor of seeking to bridge the distance between the choice-of-law and jurisdictional inquiries. Even when a court would apply the law of a different forum, as a general rule it will feel less knowledgeable and comfortable in interpretation, and less interested in fostering the policies of that foreign jurisdiction, than would the courts established by the State that provides the applicable law. Obviously, such choice-of-law problems cannot entirely be avoided in a diverse legal system such as our own. Nonetheless, when a suitor seeks to lodge a suit in a State with a substantial interest in seeing its own law applied to the transaction in question, we could wisely act to minimize conflicts, confusion, and uncertainty by adopting a liberal view of jurisdiction, unless considerations of fairness or efficiency strongly point in the opposite direction.

This case is not one where, in my judgment, this preference for jurisdiction is adequately answered. Certainly nothing said by the Court persuades me that it would be unfair to subject appellants to suit in Delaware. The fact that the record does not reveal whether they "set foot" or committed "act[s] related to [the] cause of action" in Delaware, is not decisive, for jurisdiction can be based strictly on out-of-state acts having foreseeable effects in the forum State. E.g., McGee v. International Life Ins. Co., supra. I have little difficulty in applying this principle to nonresident fiduciaries whose alleged breaches of trust are said to have substantial damaging effect on the financial posture of a resident corporation. Further, I cannot understand how the existence of minimum contacts in a constitutional sense is at all affected by Delaware's failure statutorily to express an interest in controlling corporate fiduciaries. To me this simply demonstrates that Delaware did not elect to assert jurisdiction to the extent the Constitution would allow. Nor would I view as controlling or even especially meaningful Delaware's failure to exact from appellants their consent to be sued. Once we have rejected the jurisdictional framework created in Pennoyer v. Neff, I see no reason to rest jurisdiction on a fictional outgrowth of that system such as the existence of a consent statute, expressed or implied.

I, therefore, would approach the minimum-contacts analysis differently than does the Court. Crucial to me is the fact that appellants voluntarily associated themselves with the State of Delaware, "invoking the benefits and protections of its laws", Hanson v. Denckla, 357 U.S., at 253, 78 S.Ct., at 1240; International Shoe Co. v. Washington, 326 U.S., at 319, 66 S.Ct., at 159, by entering into a long-term and fragile relationship with one of its domestic corporations. They thereby elected to assume powers and to undertake responsibilities wholly derived from that State's rules and regulations, and to become eligible for those benefits that Delaware law makes available to its corporations' officials. E.g., Del.Code Ann., Tit. 8, § 143 (1975) (interest-free loans); § 145 (1975 ed. and Supp.1976) (indemnification). While it is possible that countervailing issues of judicial efficiency and the like might clearly favor a different forum, they do not appear on the meager record before us; and, of course, we are concerned solely with "minimum" contacts, not the "best" contacts. I thus do not believe that it is unfair to insist that appellants make themselves available to suit in a competent forum that Delaware might create for vindication of its important public policies directly pertaining to appellants' fiduciary associations with the State.

Notes and Questions

1. The Court elaborated on *Shaffer* three years later in Rush v. Savchuk, 444 U.S. 320, 100 S.Ct. 571, 62 L.Ed.2d 516 (1980). Plaintiff there had been a passenger in a single-car accident in Indiana, where he then lived, and sued the driver, who was also from Indiana. By the time suit was filed, plaintiff had moved to Minnesota, and plaintiff sued there. One reason why plaintiff sued in Minnesota was that under Indiana law plaintiff's claim was barred by the guest statute and the statute of limitations. It appeared, however, that Minnesota might apply its own law, which had a longer limitations period and no guest statute.

Plaintiff did not serve defendant in Minnesota. Instead, he used a Minnesota procedure that permitted him to garnish State Farm Insurance Co., which had issued defendant a liability policy, because Minnesota law treated that obligation of the insurer as property of the defendant that was present in the state and subject to garnishment. Without questioning Minnesota's assertion that there was property present, the Court held the exercise of jurisdiction invalid:

> The Minnesota Supreme Court was of the view that the insurance policy was so important to the litigation that it provided contacts sufficient to satisfy due process. The insurance policy is not the subject matter of the case, however, nor is it related to the operative facts of the negligence action. The contractual arrangements between the defendant and the insurer pertain only to the conduct, not the substance of the litigation, and accordingly do not affect the court's jurisdiction unless they demonstrate ties between the defendant and the forum.

> In fact, the fictitious presence of the insurer's obligation in Minnesota does not, without more, provide a basis for concluding that there is any contact in the *International Shoe* sense between Minnesota and the insured. To say that "a debt follows the debtor" is simply to say that intangible property has no actual situs, and a debt may be sued on wherever there is jurisdiction over the debtor. State Farm is "found," in the sense of doing business, in all 50 States and the District of Columbia. Under appellee's theory, the "debt" owed to Rush would be "present" in each of those jurisdictions simultaneously. It is apparent that such a "contact" can have no jurisdictional significance.

2. In the first sentence of its opinion in *Shaffer*, the Court announces that the case is about "the constitutionality of a Delaware statute." Does the Court hold the statute itself unconstitutional? There is some precedent for such treatment. Thus, in Wuchter v. Pizzutti, 276 U.S. 13, 48 S.Ct. 259, 72 L.Ed. 446 (1928), the Court invalidated jurisdiction over a nonresident motorist under a statute similar to the one involved in Hess v. Pawloski (supra p. 706), because this statute did not require actual mailed notice to the defendant, even though the defendant in the case before the Court had

in fact been given notice by mail. Is the Court in *Shaffer* similarly holding the statute unconstitutional and invalidating jurisdiction even though (as Justice Brennan points out) there may be a constitutionally sufficient basis for jurisdiction over at least some of these defendants? Does the fact that a long-arm statute would authorize jurisdiction in some cases beyond the state's constitutional power invalidate all exercises of jurisdiction under the statute?

A possible explanation is that the Delaware sequestration statute is held invalid because it infringes the meaningful opportunity to be heard by holding shares in Delaware corporations hostage to coerce a general appearance. Note that, in the Delaware courts, defendants stressed procedural due process attacks on pre-seizure notice and hearing. Although parties with no contacts with Delaware could, like defendants here, appear specially and contest the procedure, the real impact on many shareholders in Delaware corporations (a group including a large segment of American society) would be in effect to deny them any real opportunity to protect their rights to that property. In this sense, holding the statute unconstitutional serves to guard the interests protected by the procedural due process arguments. Are there risks to holding long-arm statutes unconstitutional because in some cases they might overreach due process? Should the Court hold that jurisdiction over these defendants is improper without examination of their actual contacts with Delaware?

3. Do these defendants actually have property in Delaware? Obviously Delaware says they do, but all the other 49 states say that a share of corporate stock is physically embodied in the share certificate and therefore not in Delaware unless the certificate is present there. Given this disparity in determination of location of property, does the Court have to treat Delaware's deviant rule as significant for jurisdictional purposes?

The Court has never addressed constitutional limitations on a state's right to claim that there is property within its limits in a case involving personal jurisdiction issues, but it confronted similar issues in Western Union Tel. Co. v. Pennsylvania, 368 U.S. 71, 82 S.Ct. 199, 7 L.Ed.2d 139 (1961), when Pennsylvania claimed that all undelivered wire orders to send money that originated in Pennsylvania should escheat to the state. While disavowing any claim to the money, Western Union challenged Pennsylvania's right to claim the funds on the ground that other states (such as the state to which the money was to be sent) could claim that the money was located there and make similar escheat claims. The Supreme Court did not dispute the power of a state to claim abandoned property, but held that Pennsylvania had denied Western Union due process because it could not guarantee that no other state would make a conflicting and duplicative claim. Is the Constitution a basis for challenging a state's claim that property is present only when there is a similar risk of double exposure? Couldn't the dual location of stock lead to similar duplicative liability? Compare Blackstone v. Miller, 188 U.S. 189, 23 S.Ct. 277, 47 L.Ed. 439 (1903), upholding multiple death taxation of intangible personal property. On multiple taxation of such property, see generally R. Rotunda & J. Nowak, Constitutional Law: Substance and Procedure §§ 13.2; 13.3 (2d ed. 1992).

4. The Court refers to the tripartite division of the Restatement of Judgments among true *in rem, quasi in rem* type I and *quasi in rem* type II. Does this division really have a bearing on the jurisdictional determination?

(a) How many actions are genuine *in rem* actions? The Restatement Second of Judgments, § 6, Comment b, identifies four: admiralty libels in rem, proceedings leading to the forfeiture of a thing to the government, title clearance or registration proceedings, and proceedings to settle an estate. Is jurisdiction of the state where the property is located guaranteed in these cases?

(b) *Quasi in rem* type I: Is jurisdiction always permissible in cases falling into this category? If so, would it be permissible in a specific performance action against a nonresident purchaser? Does it matter what type of property is involved? What if plaintiff claims that defendant fraudulently obtained $100,000 of plaintiff's money in State A and deposited it in an account in State B? Can plaintiff support jurisdiction in State B on the basis of presence of the bank account? Would that depend on whether plaintiff could establish a right to *that* $100,000, as opposed to an award of that amount in damages?

(c) *Quasi in rem* type II: At first blush it would seem that in these cases the presence of property is irrelevant to the jurisdictional determination. But the Court tells us in footnote 29 that some cases that would be denominated type II still involve a pertinent connection between the property and the claim that might make the presence of the property relevant. Thus, it cites Dubin v. Philadelphia, a case in which the court held a nonresident owner of property subject to jurisdiction in a suit by a person injured on the property, relying on an analogy to Hess v. Pawloski (supra p. 706): "It is just as important that nonresident owners of Philadelphia real estate should keep their property in such shape as not to injure our citizens as it is that nonresident owners of cars should drive about our streets with equal care. It is only a short step beyond this to assert that defendants in both classes of cases should be answerable in this forum." Does this mean that the presence of property is relevant for jurisdictional purposes where, on analogy to *Hess*, it would justify an inference of consent to jurisdiction?

5. The Court also says that there is no due process problem with allowing local enforcement of a foreign judgment without making a minimum contacts analysis. Why?

6. Taking its cue from the Court, the Delaware legislature quickly passed a statute making acceptance of the position as director of a Delaware corporation consent to suit there on claims of malfeasance in that position. In Armstrong v. Pomerance, 423 A.2d 174 (Del.1980), the court rejected a challenge to this statute by directors of a corporation who had never conducted any business in Delaware because defendants were on notice of their exposure to suit. In terms of Justice Stevens' concern that defendant have "fair notice" about susceptibility to suit (adopted by the Court in *Burger King*, supra p. 752), why does that matter? Isn't that the same kind of circularity that plagues the foreseeability analysis of *World–Wide Volkswagen?* See p. 743 n. 5. Greyhound responded to this statute by switching its state of incorporation to Arizona. Perdue, The Story of *Shaffer v. Heither*: Allocating Jurisdictional Authority Among the States, in Civil Procedure

Stories (2004), at 129, 147. Beginning in 2004, an amendment to the statute broadened the implied consent to officers of the corporation. See Tit. 10, Del. Code § 3114.

7. After *Shaffer*, one might have expected quasi-in-rem jurisdiction to disappear, but it did not. A survey published in 1990 showed that New York and some other states have continued to use the doctrine where due process would allow assertion of jurisdiction, but "gaps" in their long-arm statutes precluded that. Mushlin, The New Quasi-in-rem Jurisdiction: New York's Revival of a Doctrine Whose Time Has Passed, 55 Brooklyn L. Rev. 1059 (1990). Professor Mushlin argues that this is undesirable because it deprives defendants of the use of their property pending resolution of the litigation, and because it improperly overrides the choice of the legislature in adopting a narrow long-arm statute. See also Note, Shaffer, Burnham, and New York's Continuing Use of QIR–2 Jurisdiction: A Resurrection of the Power Theory, 45 Emory L.J. 239 (1996).

8. The Anticybersquatting Consumer Protection Act, enacted in 1999, provides remedies against those who improperly obtain rights to Internet domain names based on other parties' trademarks. In cases in which personal jurisdiction over the registrant of the domain name is not possible, the Act permits "an in rem civil action against a domain name in the judicial district in which the domain name registrar, domain name registry, or other domain name authority that registered or assigned the domain name is location." 15 U.S.C.A. § 1125(d)(2)(A). In Porsche Cars North America, Inc. v. Porsche.Net, 302 F.3d 248 (4th Cir.2002), the court held that domain names are property subject to seizure under the Act, and that this seizure would be permissible whether or not the purported owner of the domain name was subject to personal jurisdiction. In another domain name case, it held that *Shaffer* was satisfied because claims to the property are the source of the underlying controversy. Harrods Ltd. v. Sixty Internet Domain Names, 302 F.3d 214, 224–25 (4th Cir.2002). For discussion, see Allen, In Rem Jurisdiction from *Pennoyer* to *Shaffer* to the Anticybersquatting Consumer Protection Act, 11 Geo. Mason L. Rev. 243 (2002).

9. Should *Shaffer* have overturned such a time-honored procedure as attachment jurisdiction on due process grounds? Keep in mind Justice Marshall's treatment of the evolving nature of "traditional notions of fair play and substantial justice" as you read Burnham v. Superior Court, infra p. 809.

CHOICE OF LAW

Law school courses in Conflicts of Law examine in detail the many doctrines that bear on selection of the law to decide cases. With 50 separate jurisdictions, the United States presents a fertile field for conflicts of law. Except for limitations imposed by jurisdiction and venue, a plaintiff can forum shop for favorable law. Thus, efforts to defeat personal jurisdiction may, as in Rush v. Savchuk (supra p. 803 n. 1), seem to be animated by concerns about choice of law. But the Supreme Court has repeatedly separated issues of choice of law from those of personal jurisdiction. This Note provides only an overview of the choice of law problem.

Choice of Law Principles: Because the handling of choice of law problems has evolved to different points in different states, it is necessary to canvass the history of these different approaches. Early in the 20th century, under the influence of Professor Beale of Harvard, the prevailing choice of law analysis relied on vested rights concepts resulting in fairly rigid rules that determined which law should be applied to decide a case. Thus, in a suit growing out of an accident, the rules called for application of the law of the place of the accident. Similar rules governed selection of the law in actions for breach of contract (e.g. law of the state where the contract was executed or breached).

These rigid rules had the advantage of ease of application, but they also had serious disadvantages when they led to results that seemed to make no sense. Taking Rush v. Savchuk (supra p. 803 n.1) as an example, it seems difficult to justify the availability of the guest statute defense as depending on whether the accident (involving two Indianans) happened in Indiana or just across the state line in Illinois, assuming Illinois had abandoned the guest statute. Similarly, it would seem odd to apply the guest statute to an accident just inside Indiana involving two Illinois residents. Some refinement of the analysis looking to a determination whether Indiana had an interest in application of its guest statute seemed in order.

One of the leading proponents of change was Professor Brainerd Currie of the University of Chicago. He developed an elaborate method of determining governmental interests designed, at a minimum, to identify cases in which only one state had a real interest in applying its law. To take the Rush v. Savchuk example, so long as both parties involved in the accident are Indianans, it may well be that Illinois has no interest in applying its more liberal rule to permit the passenger to recover from his host even though the accident occurred in Illinois. Similarly, were the accident in Indiana, involving two Illinoisians, it would seem that Indiana has no interest in applying its guest statute to deny the Illinois passenger recovery, while Illinois' abandonment of the guest statute seems to show that it desires to allow recovery.

Currie's methods were often not easy to apply, but they furthered a revolution in conflicts jurisprudence that at least one commentator has described as "without parallel in the history of the common law." Hill, The Judicial Function in Choice of Law, 85 Colum. L. Rev. 1585, 1588 (1985). The dust has yet to settle, however, and the question whether "interest analysis" is a legitimate choice of law tool remains highly controversial. Obviously this book cannot resolve these ongoing disputes. Instead, it can give some of the flavor of the policy-oriented approach that is evolving around the Restatement (Second) of Conflict of Laws (1971). This Restatement, adopted after 17 years of drafting, calls for application of the law of the state that, with respect to a given issue, is most significantly related to the occurrence and the parties. In section 6 it enumerates a list of factors that should be considered in identifying the state that is most significantly related:

(a) the needs of the interstate and international systems,

(b) the relevant policies of the forum,

(c) the relevant policies of other interested states and the relative interests of those states in the determination of the particular issue,

(d) the protection of justified expectations,

(e) the basic policies underlying the particular field of law,

(f) certainty, predictability and uniformity of result, and

(g) ease in the determination and application of the law to be applied.

Later sections prescribe specific factors to consider in certain types of cases. See, e.g., §§ 145 (torts); 188 (contracts). Suffice it to say that these principles afford state courts substantial latitude in selecting the law to be applied.

Two further points should be made. First, after all the analysis is done, the reality is that courts have a strong tendency to apply their own law, and usually do so. Second, these rules are said to apply only to matters of "substance," leaving matters of "procedure" to local law in the court in which the case is pending. We shall attempt to distinguish between these two concepts in detail in Chapter XI, dealing with the *Erie* problem, and note here that similar issues can arise in connection with selection of the law of different states. Thus, in Keeton v. Hustler Magazine, Inc. (supra p. 747 n. 1), the dismissal of the first suit brought by plaintiff in Ohio on statute of limitations grounds was not considered res judicata because it was made on a "procedural" ground.

Constitutional Limitations: States are not totally free to apply their own law, however. Instead, due process requires that "for a State's substantive law to be selected in a constitutionally permissible manner, that State must have a significant contact or significant aggregation of contacts, creating state interests, such that choice of its law is neither arbitrary nor fundamentally unfair." Allstate Ins. Co. v. Hague, 449 U.S. 302, 101 S.Ct. 633, 66 L.Ed.2d 521 (1981).

As applied by the courts, this standard is less demanding than the normal minimum contacts standard for personal jurisdiction. In *Allstate,* for instance, plaintiff's husband, a Wisconsin resident, had been killed in a collision in Wisconsin involving two other Wisconsin residents, neither of whom had insurance. But decedent had policies of insurance, issued in Wisconsin on each of the family's three cars (registered in Wisconsin), and each policy had $15,000 coverage for injuries caused by an uninsured motorist. The issue was whether plaintiff should be permitted to "stack" those three policies, thereby obtaining a total recovery of $45,000. Under the law of Wisconsin, stacking was not allowed. Plaintiff had, however, moved to Minnesota after her husband died, and she sued the insurance company there. The Minnesota Supreme Court, concluding that allowing stacking is the "better rule," permitted the higher recovery, and the

Supreme Court rejected the insurance company's due process arguments. In an opinion joined by three other justices, Justice Brennan identified three connections between Minnesota and the claim that together permitted application of Minnesota law: (1) The husband worked in Minnesota, commuting there every work day (although he was not on his way to work when he was killed), (2) Allstate was doing business at all times in Minnesota, so that it was familiar with Minnesota's laws (although this fact hardly put it on notice that Minnesota law would be applied to *this* case), and (3) Plaintiff became a Minnesota resident before the suit was filed (although this was clearly her unilateral activity).

It is unlikely that these factors would have provided a basis for jurisdiction over either of the Wisconsin drivers involved in the accident, so that State courts appear to have more freedom in choice of law than in extensions of personal jurisdiction. For a criticism of *Hague,* see Brilmayer, Legitimate Interests in Multistate Problems: As Between State and Federal Law, 79 Mich.L.Rev. 1315 (1981). For our purposes, it seems likely that a state which has a constitutional basis for exercising jurisdiction would generally be able constitutionally to apply its own law as well if its choice of law analysis points in that direction (as it usually does). In Phillips Petroleum Co. v. Shutts, 472 U.S. 797, 105 S.Ct. 2965, 86 L.Ed.2d 628 (1985), however, the court held that although a state could entertain personal jurisdiction over a nationwide class action on grounds of consent, it could not constitutionally apply its law over defendant's objections to decide the rights of class members who had no contact with the forum.

F. PERSONAL SERVICE WITHIN THE JURISDICTION

BURNHAM v. SUPERIOR COURT

Supreme Court of the United States, 1990.
495 U.S. 604, 110 S.Ct. 2105, 109 L.Ed.2d 631.

JUSTICE SCALIA announced the judgment of the Court and delivered an opinion in which THE CHIEF JUSTICE and JUSTICE KENNEDY join, and in which JUSTICE WHITE joins with respect to Parts I, II–A, II–B, and II–C.

The question presented is whether the Due Process Clause of the Fourteenth Amendment denies California courts jurisdiction over a nonresident, who was personally served with process while temporarily in that State, in a suit unrelated to his activities in the State.

I

Petitioner Dennis Burnham married Francie Burnham in 1976, in West Virginia. In 1977 the couple moved to New Jersey, where their two children were born. In July 1987 the Burnhams decided to separate. They agreed that Mrs. Burnham, who intended to move to California, would take custody of the children. Shortly before Mrs. Burnham departed for California that same month, she and petitioner agreed that she would file for divorce on grounds of "irreconcilable differences."

In October 1987, petitioner filed for divorce in New Jersey state court on grounds of "desertion." Petitioner did not, however, obtain an issuance of summons against his wife, and did not attempt to serve her with process. Mrs. Burnham, after unsuccessfully demanding that petitioner adhere to their prior agreement to submit to an "irreconcilable differences" divorce, brought suit for divorce in California state court in early January 1988.

In late January, petitioner visited southern California on business, after which he went north to visit his children in the San Francisco Bay area, where his wife resided. He took the older child to San Francisco for the weekend. Upon returning the child to Mrs. Burnham's home on January 24, 1988, petitioner was served with a California court summons and a copy of Mrs. Burnham's divorce petition. He then returned to New Jersey.

Later that year, petitioner made a special appearance in the California Superior Court, moving to quash the service of process on the ground that the court lacked personal jurisdiction over him because his only contacts with California were a few short visits to the State for the purposes of conducting business and visiting his children. The Superior Court denied the motion, and the California Court of Appeal denied mandamus relief, rejecting petitioner's contention that the Due Process Clause prohibited California courts from asserting jurisdiction over him because he lacked "minimum contacts" with the State. The court held it to be "a valid jurisdictional predicate for *in personam* jurisdiction" that the "defendant [was] present in the forum state and personally served with process." We granted certiorari.

II

A

* * *

To determine whether the assertion of personal jurisdiction is consistent with due process, we have long relied on the principles traditionally followed by American courts in marking out the territorial limits of each State's authority. That criterion was first announced in Pennoyer v. Neff, in which we stated that due process "mean[s] a course of legal proceedings according to those rules and principles which have been established in our systems of jurisprudence for the protection and enforcement of private rights," including the "well-established principles of public law respecting the jurisdiction of an independent State over persons and property." In what has become the classic expression of the criterion, we said in International Shoe Co. v. Washington, 326 U.S. 310, 66 S.Ct. 154, 90 L.Ed. 95 (1945), that a State court's assertion of personal jurisdiction satisfies the Due Process Clause if it does not violate " 'traditional notions of fair play and substantial justice.' " Since *International Shoe,* we have only been called upon to decide whether these "traditional notions" permit States to exercise jurisdiction over absent defendants in a manner that deviates from the rules of jurisdiction applied in the 19th century. We have held such deviations permissible, but only with respect to suits arising out of the absent defendant's contacts with the State.[1] The question we must decide today is whether due process requires a similar connection between the litigation and the defendant's contacts with the State in cases where the defendant is physically present in the State at the time process is served upon him.

B

Among the most firmly established principles of personal jurisdiction in American tradition is that the courts of a State have jurisdiction over nonresidents who are physically present in the State. The view developed early that each State had the power to hale before its courts any individual who could be found within its borders, and that once having acquired jurisdiction over such a person by properly serving him with process, the State could retain jurisdiction to enter judgment against him, no matter how fleeting his visit. That view had antecedents in English common-law practice, which sometimes allowed "transitory" actions, arising out of events outside the country, to be maintained against seemingly nonresident defendants who were present in England. Justice Story believed the principle, which he traced to Roman origins, to be firmly grounded in English tradition: "[B]y the common law[,] personal actions, being transitory, may be brought in any place, where the party defendant may be found," for "every nation may . . . rightfully exercise jurisdiction over all persons within its domains." J. Story, Commentaries on the Conflict of Laws §§ 554, 543 (1846). See also §§ 530–538; Picquet v. Swan, supra, at 611–612 (Story, J.) ("Where a party is within a territory, he may justly be subjected to its process, and bound personally by the judgment pronounced, on such process, against him").

Recent scholarship has suggested that English tradition was not as clear as Story thought. Accurate or not, however, judging by the evidence of contemporaneous or near-contemporaneous decisions one must conclude that Story's understanding was shared by American courts at the crucial time for present purposes: 1868, when the Fourteenth Amendment was adopted. * * *

1. We have said that "[e]ven when the cause of action does not arise out of or relate to the foreign corporation's activities in the forum State, due process is not offended by a State's subjecting the corporation to its *in personam* jurisdiction when there are sufficient contacts between the State and the foreign corporation." Helicopteros Nacionales de Colombia v. Hall, 466 U.S., at 414, 104 S.Ct., at 1872. Our only holding supporting that statement, however, involved "regular service of summons upon [the corporation's] president while he was in [the forum State] acting in that capacity." See Perkins v. Benguet Consolidated Mining Co., 342 U.S. 437, 440, 72 S.Ct. 413, 415, 96 L.Ed. 485 (1952). It may be that whatever special rule exists permitting "continuous and systematic" contacts, id., at 438, 72 S.Ct., at 414, to support jurisdiction with respect to matters unrelated to activity in the forum, applies *only* to corporations, which have never fitted comfortably in a jurisdictional regime based primarily upon "de facto power over the defendant's person." International Shoe Co. v. Washington, 326 U.S. 310, 316, 66 S.Ct. 154, 158, 90 L.Ed. 95 (1945). We express no views on these matters—and, for simplicity's sake, omit reference to this aspect of "contacts"-based jurisdiction in our discussion.

Decisions in the courts of many States in the 19th and early 20th centuries held that personal service upon a physically present defendant sufficed to confer jurisdiction, without regard to whether the defendant was only briefly in the State or whether the cause of action was related to his activities there. [Justice Scalia cited more than ten state court decisions between 1881 and 1904.] Although research has not revealed a case deciding the issue in every State's courts, that appears to be because the issue was so well settled that it went unlitigated. Opinions from the courts of other States announced the rule in dictum. Most States, moreover, had statutes or common-law rules that exempted from service of process individuals who were brought into the forum by force or fraud, or who were there as a party or witness in unrelated judicial proceedings. These exceptions obviously rested upon the premise that service of process conferred jurisdiction. Particularly striking is the fact that, as far as we have been able to determine, *not one* American case from the period (or, for that matter, not one American case until 1978) held, or even suggested, that in-state personal service on an individual was insufficient to confer personal jurisdiction. Commentators were also seemingly unanimous on the rule.

This American jurisdictional practice is, moreover, not merely old; it is continuing. It remains the practice of, not only a substantial number of the States, but as far as we are aware *all* the States and the federal government—if one disregards (as one must for this purpose) the few opinions since 1978 that have erroneously said, on grounds similar to those that petitioner presses here, that this Court's due-process decisions render the practice unconstitutional. We do not know of a single State or federal statute, or a single judicial decision resting upon State law, that has abandoned in-State service as a basis of jurisdiction. Many recent cases reaffirm it. [Justice Scalia cited 14 state court decisions between 1979 and 1989.]

C

Despite this formidable body of precedent, petitioner contends, in reliance on our decisions applying the *International Shoe* standard, that in the absence of "continuous and systematic" contacts with the forum, see note 1, supra, a nonresident defendant can be subjected to judgment only as to matters that arise out of or relate to his contacts with the forum. This argument rests on a thorough misunderstanding of our cases.

[Justice Scalia recounted the evolution from the 19th century view that a state could not exercise in personam jurisdiction unless the defendant were personally served within the state to the *International Shoe* rule that jurisdiction was proper even though personal service was not accomplished. "As *International Shoe* suggests, the defendant's litigation-related 'minimum contacts' may take the place of physical presence as the basis for jurisdiction."]

Nothing in *International Shoe* or the cases that have followed it, however, offers support for the very different proposition petitioner seeks to establish today: that a defendant's presence in the forum is not only unnecessary to validate novel, non-traditional assertions of jurisdiction, but is itself no longer sufficient to establish jurisdiction. That proposition is unfaithful to both elementary logic and the foundations of our due process jurisprudence. The distinction between what is needed to support novel procedures and what is needed to sustain traditional ones is fundamental, as we observed over a century ago:

> "[A] process of law, which is not otherwise forbidden, must be taken to be due process of law, if it can show the sanction of settled usage both in England and in this country; but it by no means follows that nothing else can be due process of law.... [That which], in substance, has been immemorially the actual law of the land ... therefor[e] is due process of law. But to hold that such a characteristic is essential to due process of law, would be to deny every quality of the law but its age, and to render it incapable of progress or improvement. It would be to stamp upon our jurisprudence the unchangeableness attributed to the laws of the Medes and Persians." Hurtado v. California, 110 U.S. 516, 528–529, 4 S.Ct. 111, 117–118, 28 L.Ed. 232 (1884).

The short of the matter is that jurisdiction based on physical presence alone constitutes due process because it is one of the continuing traditions of our legal system that define the due process standard of "traditional notions of fair play and substantial justice." That standard was developed by *analogy* to "physical presence," and it would be perverse to say it could now be turned against that touchstone of jurisdiction.

D

Petitioner's strongest argument, though we ultimately reject it, relies upon our decision in Shaffer v. Heitner, 433 U.S. 186, 97 S.Ct. 2569, 53 L.Ed.2d 683 (1977). * * *

It goes too far to say, as petitioner contends, that *Shaffer* compels the conclusion that a State lacks jurisdiction over an individual unless the litigation arises out of his activities in the State. *Shaffer,* like *International Shoe,* involved jurisdiction over an *absent defendant,* and it stands for nothing more than the proposition that when the "minimum contact" that is a substitute for physical presence consists of property ownership it must, like other minimum contacts, be related to the litigation. Petitioner wrenches out of its context our statement in *Shaffer* that "all assertions of state-court jurisdiction must be evaluated according to the standards set forth in *International Shoe* and its progeny." When read together with the two sentences that preceded it, the meaning of this statement becomes clear:

> "The fiction that an assertion of jurisdiction over property is anything but an assertion of jurisdiction over the owner of the

property supports an ancient form without substantial modern justification. Its continued acceptance would serve only to allow state-court jurisdiction that is fundamentally unfair to the defendant.

"We *therefore conclude* that all assertions of state-court jurisdiction must be evaluated according to the standards set forth in *International Shoe* and its progeny." Ibid. (emphasis added).

Shaffer was saying, in other words, not that all bases for the assertion of *in personam* jurisdiction (including, presumably, in-state service) must be treated alike and subjected to the "minimum contacts" analysis of *International Shoe;* but rather that *quasi in rem* jurisdiction, that fictional "ancient form," and *in personam* jurisdiction, are really one and the same and must be treated alike—leading to the conclusion that *quasi in rem* jurisdiction, i.e., that form of *in personam* jurisdiction based upon a "property ownership" contact and by definition unaccompanied by personal, in-state service, must satisfy the litigation-relatedness requirement of *International Shoe.* The logic of *Shaffer*'s holding—which places all suits against absent nonresidents on the same constitutional footing, regardless of whether a separate Latin label is attached to one particular basis of contact—does not compel the conclusion that physically present defendants must be treated identically to absent ones. As we have demonstrated at length, our tradition has treated the two classes of defendants quite differently, and it is unreasonable to read *Shaffer* as casually obliterating that distinction. *International Shoe* confined its "minimum contacts" requirement to situations in which the defendant "be not present within the territory of the forum," and nothing in *Shaffer* expands that requirement beyond that.

It is fair to say, however, that while our holding today does not contradict *Shaffer,* our basic approach to the due process question is different. We have conducted no independent inquiry into the desirability or fairness of the prevailing in-state service rule, leaving that judgment to the legislatures that are free to amend it; for our purposes, its validation is its pedigree, as the phrase "*traditional notions* of fair play and substantial justice" makes clear. *Shaffer* did conduct such an independent inquiry, asserting that " 'traditional notions of fair play and substantial justice' can be as readily offended by the perpetuation of ancient forms that are no longer justified as by the adoption of new procedures that are inconsistent with the basic values of our constitutional heritage." Perhaps that assertion can be sustained when the "perpetuation of ancient forms" is engaged in by only a very small minority of the States. Where, however, as in the present case, a jurisdictional principle is both firmly approved by tradition and still favored, it is impossible to imagine what standard we could appeal to for the judgment that it is "no longer justified." While in no way receding from or casting doubt upon the holding of *Shaffer* or any other case, we reaffirm today our time-honored approach. For new procedures, hitherto unknown, the Due Process Clause requires analysis to determine whether "traditional notions of fair play and substantial justice" have been offended. *International Shoe,* 326 U.S., at 316, 66 S.Ct., at 158. But a doctrine of personal jurisdiction that dates back to the adoption of the Fourteenth Amendment and is still generally observed unquestionably meets that standard.

III

A few words in response to Justice Brennan's concurrence: It insists that we apply "contemporary notions of due process" to determine the constitutionality of California's assertion of jurisdiction. But our analysis today comports with that prescription, at least if we give it the only sense allowed by our precedents. The "contemporary notions of due process" applicable to personal jurisdiction are the enduring *"traditional notions of fair play and substantial justice"* established as the test by *International Shoe.* By its very language, that test is satisfied if a state court adheres to jurisdictional rules that are generally applied and have always been applied in the United States.

But the concurrence's proposed standard of "contemporary notions of due process" requires more: it measures state-court jurisdiction not only against traditional doctrines in this country, including current state-court practice, but against each Justice's subjective assessment of what is fair and just. Authority for that seductive standard is not to be found in any of our personal jurisdiction cases. It is, indeed, an outright break with the test of "traditional notions of fair play and substantial justice," which would have to be reformulated *"our* notions of fair play and substantial justice."

The subjectivity, and hence inadequacy, of this approach becomes apparent when the concurrence tries to explain *why* the assertion of jurisdiction in the present case meets its standard of continuing-American-tradition-*plus*-innate-fairness. [Although Justice Brennan points up the benefits Mr. Burnham derived from the State of California during his visit there, "[t]hree days' worth of these benefits strike us as powerfully inadequate to establish, as an abstract matter, that it is 'fair' for California to decree the ownership of all Mr. Burhham's worldly goods acquired during the ten years of his marriage, and the custody over his children." Justice Brennan's argument that the fact Mr. Burnham can appear in California courts creates an "asymmetry" repaired by upholding jurisdiction, moreover, would "justify the exercise of jurisdiction over *everyone, whether or not* he ever comes to California." Although Justice Brennan's argument that fairness is satisfied because those who visit a state have a "reasonable expectation" of being sued there is persuasive, that is true only because "it is just tradition masquerading as 'fairness.' " The continuing tradition is what makes the exercise of jurisdiction fair.]

The difference between us and Justice Brennan has nothing to do with whether "further progress [is] to be made" in the "evolution of our legal system." It has to do with whether changes are to be adopted as progressive by the American people or decreed as progressive by the

Justices of this Court. Nothing we say today prevents individual States
from limiting or entirely abandoning the in-state-service basis of jurisdiction. And nothing prevents an overwhelming majority of them from
doing so, with the consequence that the "traditional notions of fairness"
that this Court applies may change. But the states have overwhelmingly
declined to adopt such limitation or abandonment, evidently not considering it to be progress. The question is whether, armed with no authority
other than individual Justices' perceptions of fairness that conflict with
both past and current practice, this Court can compel the states to make
such a change on the ground that "due process" requires it. We hold
that it cannot.

* * *

Because the Due Process Clause does not prohibit the California
courts from exercising jurisdiction over petitioner based on the fact of in-
state service of process, the judgment is

Affirmed.

JUSTICE WHITE, concurring in part and concurring in the judgment.

I join Part I and Parts II–A, II–B, and II–C of Justice Scalia's
opinion and concur in the judgment of affirmance. The rule allowing
jurisdiction to be obtained over a non-resident by personal service in the
forum state, without more, has been and is so widely accepted throughout this country that I could not possibly strike it down, either on its
face or as applied in this case, on the ground that it denies due process of
law guaranteed by the Fourteenth Amendment. Although the Court has
the authority under the Amendment to examine even traditionally
accepted procedures and declare them invalid, e.g., Shaffer v. Heitner,
433 U.S. 186, 97 S.Ct. 2569, 53 L.Ed.2d 683 (1977), there has been no
showing here or elsewhere that as a general proposition the rule is so
arbitrary and lacking in common sense in so many instances that it
should be held violative of due process in every case. Furthermore, until
such a showing is made, which would be difficult indeed, claims in
individual cases that the rule would operate unfairly as applied to the
particular non-resident involved need not be entertained. At least this
would be the case where presence in the forum state is intentional,
which would almost always be the fact. Otherwise, there would be
endless, fact-specific litigation in the trial and appellate courts, including
this one. Here, personal service in California, without more, is enough,
and I agree that the judgment should be affirmed.

JUSTICE BRENNAN, with whom JUSTICE MARSHALL, JUSTICE BLACKMUN,
and JUSTICE O'CONNOR join, concurring in the judgment.

* * *

I

I believe that the approach adopted by Justice Scalia's opinion
today—reliance solely on historical pedigree—is foreclosed by our deci-

sions in *International Shoe Co. v. Washington,* 326 U.S. 310, 66 S.Ct. 154, 90 L.Ed. 95 (1945), and *Shaffer v. Heitner,* 433 U.S. 186, 97 S.Ct. 2569, 53 L.Ed.2d 683 (1977). In *International Shoe,* we held that a state court's assertion of personal jurisdiction does not violate the Due Process Clause if it is consistent with " 'traditional notions of fair play and substantial justice.' "[2] In *Shaffer,* we stated that "*all* assertions of state-court jurisdiction must be evaluated according to the standards set forth in *International Shoe* and its progeny." The critical insight of *Shaffer* is that all rules of jurisdiction, even ancient ones, must satisfy contemporary notions of due process. * * * We recognized [in *Shaffer*] that " '[t]raditional notions of fair play and substantial justice' can be as readily offended by the perpetuation of ancient forms that are no longer justified as by the adoption of new procedures that are inconsistent with the basic values of our constitutional heritage."

* * *

II

Tradition, though alone not dispositive, is of course *relevant* to the question whether the rule of transient jurisdiction is consistent with due process. Tradition is salient not in the sense that practices of the past are automatically reasonable today; indeed, under such a standard, the legitimacy of transient jurisdiction would be called into question because the rule's historical "pedigree" is a matter of intense debate. [Justice Brennan's footnotes challenged Justice Scalia's version of the pre-*Pennoyer* acceptance of transient jurisdiction.] * * *

Rather, I find the historical background relevant because, however murky the jurisprudential origins of transient jurisdiction, the fact that American courts have announced the rule for perhaps a century (first in dicta, more recently in holdings) provides a defendant voluntarily present in a particular State *today* "clear notice that [he] is subject to suit" in the forum. *World–Wide Volkswagen Corp. v. Woodson,* 444 U.S. 286, 297, 100 S.Ct. 559, 567, 62 L.Ed.2d 490 (1980). Regardless of whether Justice Story's account of the rule's genesis is mythical, our common understanding *now,* fortified by a century of judicial practice, is that jurisdiction is often a function of geography. The transient rule is consistent with reasonable expectations and is entitled to a strong presumption that it comports with due process. * * *[11]

2. Our reference in *International Shoe* to " 'traditional notions of fair play and substantial justice,' " 326 U.S., at 316, 66 S.Ct., at 158, meant simply that those concepts are indeed traditional ones, not that, as Justice Scalia's opinion suggests, their specific *content* was to be determined by tradition alone. We recognized that contemporary societal norms must play a role in our analysis. See, e.g., 326 U.S., at 317, 66 S.Ct., at 158–159 (considerations of "rea-sonable[ness], in the context of our federal system of government").

11. As the Restatement suggests, there may be cases in which a defendant's involuntary or unknowing presence in a State does not support the exercise of personal jurisdiction over him. The facts of the instant case do not require us to determine the outer limits of the transient jurisdiction rule.

By visiting the forum State, a transient defendant actually "avail[s]" himself of significant benefits provided by the State. His health and safety are guaranteed by the State's police, fire, and emergency medical services; he is free to travel on the State's roads and waterways; he likely enjoys the fruits of the State's economy as well. * * * Subject only to the doctrine of *forum non conveniens,* an out-of-state plaintiff may use state courts in all circumstances in which those courts would be available to state citizens. Without transient jurisdiction, an asymmetry would arise: a transient would have the full benefit of the power of the forum State's courts as a plaintiff while retaining immunity from their authority as a defendant.

The potential burdens on a transient defendant are slight. " '[M]odern transportation and communications have made it much less burdensome for a party sued to defend himself' " in a State outside his place of residence. That the defendant has already journeyed at least once before to the forum—as evidenced by the fact that he was served with process there—is an indication that suit in the forum likely would not be prohibitively inconvenient. Finally, any burdens that do arise can be ameliorated by a variety of procedural devices.[13] For these reasons, as a rule the exercise of personal jurisdiction over a defendant based on his voluntary presence in the forum will satisfy the requirements of due process. See n. 11, supra.

In this case, it is undisputed that petitioner was served with process while voluntarily and knowingly in the State of California. I therefore concur in the judgment.

JUSTICE STEVENS, concurring in the judgment.

As I explained in my separate writing, I did not join the Court's opinion in Shaffer v. Heitner, 433 U.S. 186, 97 S.Ct. 2569, 53 L.Ed.2d 683 (1977), because I was concerned by its unnecessarily broad reach. Id., at 217–219, 97 S.Ct., at 2586–2588 (opinion concurring in judgment). The same concern prevents me from joining either Justice Scalia's or Justice Brennan's opinion in this case. For me, it is sufficient to note that the historical evidence and consensus identified by Justice Scalia, the considerations of fairness identified by Justice Brennan, and the common sense displayed by Justice White, all combine to demonstrate that this is, indeed, a very easy case.* Accordingly, I agree that the judgment should be affirmed.

---

13. For example, in the federal system, a transient defendant can avoid protracted litigation of a spurious suit through a motion to dismiss for failure to state a claim or through a motion for summary judgment. Fed.Rules Civ.Proc. 12(b)(6) and 56. He can use relatively inexpensive methods of discovery, such as oral deposition by telephone (Rule 30(b)(7)), deposition upon written questions (Rule 31), interrogatories (Rule 33), and requests for admission (Rule 36), while enjoying protection from harassment (Rule 26(c)), and possibly obtaining costs and attorney's fees for some of the work involved (Rule 37(a)(4), (b)–(d)). Moreover, a change of venue may be possible. 28 U.S.C. § 1404. In state court, many of the same procedural protections are available, as is the doctrine of *forum non conveniens,* under which the suit may be dismissed. See generally Abrams, Power, Convenience, and the Elimination of Personal Jurisdiction in the Federal Courts, 58 Ind.L.J. 1, 23–25 (1982).

* Perhaps the adage about hard cases making bad law should be revised to cover easy cases.

Notes and Questions

1. Would jurisdiction have been proper in this case if defendant had not been personally served in California? California would have a significant interest in adjudicating this claim by one of its residents. Moreover, defendant did have contacts with California including at least one visit to his estranged family there. At the time of this visit he was aware of the prospect of litigation concerning the divorce. Should these factors have sufficed to justify assertion of California jurisdiction without reference to personal service in California? Compare Kulko v. Superior Court, supra p. 744 n. 2.

2. Note the disagreement between Justices Scalia and Brennan concerning the proper due process test. Is Justice Scalia's emphasis on the "pedigree" of transient jurisdiction the proper test? A similar showing could be made concerning the pedigree of quasi-in-rem jurisdiction. Consider Pyrolusite Manganese Co. v. Ward, 73 Ga. 491, 492 (1884): "No one ever dreamed that the attachment laws of the several States authorizing attachments against non-resident defendants, were violative of the Constitution of the United States. Argument is unnecessary." Contrast the approach to pedigree in Shaffer v. Heitner (supra p. 791) and recall Fuentes v. Shevin (supra p. 29), which invalidated attachment statutes on procedural due process grounds.

Justice Scalia justifies the "pedigree" approach by focusing on the word "traditional" in the *International Shoe* formula. Is this justified? Consider the following criticism:

> By focusing solely on the word, "traditional," Justice Scalia has ignored the words that follow. The Court did not say that due process dictates merely adherence to traditional judicial *practices of asserting jurisdiction*. Rather, it expressly referred to "traditional *notions of fair play and substantial justice*." Far from locking in a mindless equation of traditional jurisdictional practice with due process, then, the *International Shoe* Court was attempting to introduce into jurisdictional analysis the traditional due process concern with fundamental procedural fairness. Justice Scalia's construction is therefore one hundred eighty degrees away from an accurate perception of the *International Shoe* Court's intent.

Redish, Tradition, Fairness, and Personal Jurisdiction: Due Process and Constitutional Theory After Burnham v. Superior Court, 22 Rutgers L.J. 675, 682 (1991).

3. If one evaluates transient jurisdiction under contemporary standards of fairness, should it be upheld? Are Justice Brennan's reasons for sustaining jurisdiction based on personal service sufficient to uphold it where jurisdiction could not be upheld without such service?

(a) Justice Brennan concludes that by visiting California defendant availed himself of the protections of California law. Unless that has some bearing on the claims asserted in the case, should this contact matter? If this contact does suffice, why does personal service in the state matter?

(b) Justice Brennan argues that a century of judicial practice upholding jurisdiction based on personal service should create reasonable expectations supporting jurisdiction on these grounds. Is this really, as Justice Scalia says, "tradition masquerading as 'fairness.' ' "? Should the same arguments be available to uphold attachment jurisdiction?

(c) Justice Brennan says that transient jurisdiction overcomes an asymmetry that would otherwise exist since the transient could sue the forum resident in its courts while the resident could not sue the transient. But isn't that asymmetry a consequence of limitations on state court jurisdiction? Since the transient need not personally enter the state to sue the resident there, how does the transient jurisdiction doctrine solve the asymmetry? Cf. Adam v. Saenger (infra p. 834) (by filing suit in California plaintiff consented to jurisdiction on defendant's cross-complaint against him).

4. As you reflect on contemporary reactions to transient jurisdiction, consider also the following observations:

> If the rule becomes a recognized part of domestic relations law, will it deter a parent from visiting children, particularly in a case like *Burnham* in which a parent's trip to California was primarily for business purposes? Will parents seek to avoid *Burnham* by flying children to visit them rather than travelling to the state of residence of the former spouse? Will this added cost decrease the frequency of visits or adversely affect the children? Will a parent enter into a previsit contract with the other parent agreeing not to serve process during the visit? Will such terms be included as a matter of course in initial divorce-custody decrees?

Zeppos, People's Court, 44 Vand.L.Rev. 847, 856–57 (1991). Should these issues bear on the constitutional question presented in *Burnham?*

5. Does *Burnham* hold that service within the jurisdiction always suffices to uphold jurisdiction? Would jurisdiction on this basis have been constitutionally sufficient in Grace v. MacArthur (supra p. 698 n. 2(a))? Note carefully Justice White's concurrence and Justice Brennan's footnote 11. Would jurisdiction depend upon the manner in which a transient traversed the state? Consider the Robinsons in World–Wide Volkswagen Corp. v. Woodson (supra p. 730): Would there be any limitation on Oklahoma jurisdiction in suits against them if they were served while passing through Oklahoma on their way to Arizona from New York?

6. Justice Scalia mentions immunity from service. Rather outdated procedures accorded immunity from service to persons who were in the jurisdiction only to participate in a trial. When *capias ad respondendum* was used, the desire for such immunity was understandable in that the witness might be seized by the sheriff before testifying. More recently, immunity has been justified on the ground that witnesses would otherwise be deterred from coming into the jurisdiction to testify. But how often will the possibility of service actually deter them? Consider Mr. Calder, of Calder v. Jones, supra p. 745. Would he have refused to come to California to testify in Carol Burnett's suit against the National Enquirer for fear that Shirley Jones would serve him with the summons and complaint in her suit? In Kadic v. Karadzic, 70 F.3d 232 (2d Cir.1995), cert. denied, 518 U.S. 1005, 116 S.Ct. 2524, 135 L.Ed.2d 1048 (1996), plaintiffs suing Rodovan Karadzic for violations of international law in Bosnia served process on him at the U.N. in New York. The Second Circuit rejected Karadzic's argument that the U.N. headquarters agreement exempted him from service: "Fed.R.Civ.P. 4(e)(2)

specifically authorizes personal service of a summons and complaint upon an individual physically present within a judicial district of the United States, and such personal service comports with the requirements of due process for the assertion of personal jurisdiction. See Burnham v. Superior Court.''

7. How should *Burnham* be applied if defendant is a corporation or other similar entity? Recall that serving corporate defendants presented difficult problems under the *Pennoyer* regime. See Jurisdiction Over Corporate Defendants, supra p. 709. What constitutional limitations exist now over jurisdiction based on service in the forum on a corporate officer or employee? Compare First American Corp. v. Price Waterhouse LLP, 154 F.3d 16 (2d Cir.1998), in which a British accounting partnership assigned one of its partners to work on an extended basis in New York, where he was served with a subpoena by litigants anxious to obtain documents from the partnership. Service on a partner sufficed under New York law as service on the partnership. Citing *Burnham*, the court concluded that the assertion of personal jurisdiction over the British partnership satisfied due process. It noted that the rule authorizing service on a partnership by serving a partner was "a venerable one," and that the partnership should have known it was risking exposure to New York jurisdiction by sending its partner to work in New York.

G. THE GENERAL JURISDICTION ALTERNATIVE

HELICOPTEROS NACIONALES de COLOMBIA, S.A. v. HALL, 466 U.S. 408, 104 S.Ct. 1868, 80 L.Ed.2d 404 (1984):

JUSTICE BLACKMUN delivered the opinion of the Court.

[Four Americans working on a pipeline in Peru were killed in a helicopter crash. The pipeline was being constructed by their employer, a Texas-based joint venture called Consorcio/WSH, and they had been hired in Texas. The helicopter that crashed was owned and operated by Helicopteros Nacionales de Colombia, S.A. (Helicol), a Colombian corporation that had contracted with Consorcio/WSH to move personnel, materials and equipment to the job site. In negotiating the contract, Helicol's president met with representatives of Consorcio/WSH in Houston, Texas, and Helicol had been paid over $5 million for its services under the contract. Beyond that, Helicol's only contact with Texas had been its purchase of helicopters (80% of its fleet) from Bell Helicopter Co. of Ft. Worth, Tex., for more than $4 million. In connection with that, Helicol had sent prospective pilots to Ft. Worth for training by Bell and to ferry helicopters to South America.

Plaintiffs, relatives of the four Americans, filed a wrongful death action in Texas against Consorcio/WSH, Bell and Helicol, and the jury returned a verdict against Helicol for over $1 million. The Supreme Court reversed on the ground that Helicol was not subject to jurisdiction in Texas.]

Even when the cause of action does not arise out of or relate to the foreign corporation's activities in the forum State,[9] due process is not offended by a State's subjecting the corporation to its *in personam* jurisdiction when there are sufficient contacts between the State and the foreign corporation. Perkins v. Benguet Consolidated Mining Co., 342 U.S. 437, 72 S.Ct. 413, 96 L.Ed. 485 (1952); see Keeton v. Hustler Magazine, Inc., 465 U.S., at 778–780, 104 S.Ct., at 1480–1481. In *Perkins,* the Court addressed a situation in which state courts had asserted general jurisdiction over a defendant foreign corporation. During the Japanese occupation of the Philippine Islands, the president and general manager of a Philippine mining corporation maintained an office in Ohio from which he conducted activities on behalf of the company. He kept company files and held directors' meetings in the office, carried on correspondence relating to the business, distributed salary checks drawn on two active Ohio bank accounts, engaged an Ohio bank to act as transfer agent, and supervised policies dealing with the rehabilitation of the corporation's properties in the Philippines. In short, the foreign corporation, through its president, "ha[d] been carrying on in Ohio a continuous and systematic, but limited, part of its general business," and the exercise of general jurisdiction over the Philippine corporation by an Ohio court was "reasonable and just."

All parties to the present case concede that respondents' claims against Helicol did not "arise out of," and are not related to, Helicol's activities within Texas. We thus must explore the nature of Helicol's contacts with the State of Texas to determine whether they constitute the kind of continuous and systematic general business contacts the Court found to exist in *Perkins.* We hold that they do not.

It is undisputed that Helicol does not have a place of business in Texas and never has been licensed to do business in the State. Basically, Helicol's contacts with Texas consisted of sending its chief executive officer to Houston for a contract-negotiation session; accepting into its New York bank account checks drawn on a Houston bank; purchasing helicopters, equipment, and training services from Bell Helicopter for substantial sums; and sending personnel to Bell's facilities in Fort Worth for training.

The one trip to Houston by Helicol's chief executive officer for the purpose of negotiating the transportation-services contract with Consorcio/WSH cannot be described or regarded as a contact of a "continuous and systematic" nature, as *Perkins* described it, and thus cannot support an assertion of in personam jurisdiction over Helicol by a Texas court. Similarly, Helicol's acceptance from Consorcio/WSH of checks drawn on a Texas bank is of negligible significance for purposes of determining whether Helicol had sufficient contacts in Texas. There is no indication that Helicol ever requested that the checks be drawn on a Texas bank or

---

9. When a State exercises personal jurisdiction over a defendant in a suit not arising out of or related to the defendant's contacts with the forum, the State has been said to be exercising "general jurisdiction" over the defendant. See von Mehren & Trautman, [Jurisdiction to Adjudicate: A Suggested Analysis], 79 Harv.L.Rev., at 1136–1144.

that there was any negotiation between Helicol and Consorcio/WSH with respect to the location or identity of the bank on which checks would be drawn. Common sense and everyday experience suggest that, absent unusual circumstances, the bank on which a check is drawn is generally of little consequence to the payee and is a matter left to the discretion of the drawer. Such unilateral activity of another party or a third person is not an appropriate consideration when determining whether a defendant has sufficient contacts with a forum State to justify an assertion of jurisdiction.

banking

The Texas Supreme Court focused on the purchases and the related training trips in finding contacts sufficient to support an assertion of jurisdiction. We do not agree with that assessment, for the Court's opinion in Rosenberg Bros. & Co. v. Curtis Brown Co., 260 U.S. 516, 43 S.Ct. 170, 67 L.Ed. 372 (1923) (Brandeis, J., for a unanimous tribunal), makes clear that purchases and related trips, standing alone, are not a sufficient basis for a State's assertion of jurisdiction.

Texas Supreme Court focused on purchase + training trips

The defendant in *Rosenberg* was a small retailer in Tulsa, Okla., who dealt in men's clothing and furnishings. It never had applied for a license to do business in New York, nor had it at any time authorized suit to be brought against it there. It never had an established place of business in New York and never regularly carried on business in that State. Its only connection with New York was that it purchased from New York wholesalers a large portion of the merchandise sold in its Tulsa store. The purchases sometimes were made by correspondence and sometimes through visits to New York by an officer of the defendant. The Court concluded: "Visits on such business, even if occurring at regular intervals, would not warrant the inference that the corporation was present within the jurisdiction of [New York]."

Business trips not jurisdiction

This Court in *International Shoe* acknowledged and did not repudiate its holding in *Rosenberg*. See 326 U.S., at 318, 66 S.Ct., at 159. In accordance with *Rosenberg*, we hold that mere purchases, even if occurring at regular intervals, are not enough to warrant a State's assertion of in personam jurisdiction over a nonresident corporation in a cause of action not related to those purchase transactions.[12] Nor can we conclude that the fact that Helicol sent personnel into Texas for training in connection with the purchase of helicopters and equipment in that State in any way enhanced the nature of Helicol's contacts with Texas. The training was a part of the package of goods and services purchased by Helicol from Bell Helicopter. The brief presence of Helicol employees in

mere purchases not enough

training part of purchase

12. This Court in *International Shoe* cited *Rosenberg* for the proposition that "the commission of some single or occasional acts of the corporate agent in a state sufficient to impose an obligation or liability on the corporation has not been thought to confer upon the state authority to enforce it." Arguably, therefore, *Rosenberg* also stands for the proposition that mere purchases are not a sufficient basis for ei- ther general or specific jurisdiction. Because the case before us is one in which there has been an assertion of general jurisdiction over a foreign defendant, we need not decide the continuing validity of *Rosenberg* with respect to an assertion of specific jurisdiction, i.e., where the cause of action arises out of or relates to the purchases by the defendant in the forum State.

Texas for the purpose of attending the training sessions is no more a significant contact than were the trips to New York made by the buyer for the retail store in *Rosenberg.*

BRENNAN, J. dissenting.

[Justice Brennan chastised the majority for limiting its consideration to general jurisdiction.]

* * *

[T]he Court refuses to consider any distinction between contacts that are "related to" the underlying cause of action and contacts that "give rise" to the underlying cause of action. In my view, however, there is a substantial difference between these two standards for asserting specific jurisdiction. Thus, although I agree that the respondents' cause of action did not formally "arise out of" specific activities initiated by Helicol in the State of Texas, I believe that the wrongful death claim filed by the respondents is significantly related to the undisputed contacts between Helicol and the forum. On that basis, I would conclude that the Due Process Clause allows the Texas courts to assert specific jurisdiction over this particular action.

The wrongful death action filed by the respondents was premised on a fatal helicopter crash that occurred in Peru. Helicol was joined as a defendant in the lawsuit because it provided transportation services, including the particular helicopter and pilot involved in the crash, to the joint venture that employed the decedents. Specifically, the respondents claimed in their original complaint that "Helicol is . . . legally responsible for its own negligence through its pilot employee." Viewed in light of these allegations, the contacts between Helicol and the State of Texas are directly and significantly related to the underlying claim filed by the respondents. The negotiations that took place in Texas led to the contract in which Helicol agreed to provide the precise transportation services that were being used at the time of the crash. Moreover, the helicopter involved in the crash was purchased by Helicol in Texas, and the pilot whose negligence was alleged to have caused the crash was actually trained in Texas. This is simply not a case, therefore, in which a state court has asserted jurisdiction over a nonresident defendant on the basis of wholly unrelated contacts with the forum. Rather, the contacts between Helicol and the forum are directly related to the negligence that was alleged in the respondents' original complaint.[4] Because Helicol should have expected to be amenable to suit in the Texas courts for claims directly related to these contacts, it is fair and reasonable to allow the assertion of jurisdiction in this case.

* * *

4. The jury specifically found that "the pilot failed to keep the helicopter under proper control," that "the helicopter was flown into a treetop fog condition, whereby the vision of the pilot was impaired," that "such flying was negligence," and that "such negligence . . . was a proximate cause of the crash." On the basis of these findings, Helicol was ordered to pay over $1 million in damages to the respondents.

Limiting the specific jurisdiction of a forum to cases in which the cause of action formally arose out of the defendant's contacts with the State would subject constitutional standards under the Due Process Clause to the vagaries of the substantive law or pleading requirements of each State. For example, the complaint filed against Helicol in this case alleged negligence based on pilot error. Even though the pilot was trained in Texas, the Court assumes that the Texas courts may not assert jurisdiction over the suit because the cause of action "did not 'arise out of,' and [is] not related to," that training. If, however, the applicable substantive law required that negligent training of the pilot was a necessary element of a cause of action for pilot error, or if the respondents had simply added an allegation of negligence in the training provided for the Helicol pilot, then presumably the Court would concede that the specific jurisdiction of the Texas courts was applicable.

Our interpretation of the Due Process Clause has never been so dependent upon the applicable substantive law or the State's formal pleading requirements. At least since *International Shoe*, supra, the principal focus when determining whether a forum may constitutionally assert jurisdiction over a nonresident defendant has been on fairness and reasonableness to the defendant. To this extent, a court's specific jurisdiction should be applicable whenever the cause of action arises out of or relates to the contacts between the defendant and the forum. It is eminently fair and reasonable, in my view, to subject a defendant to suit in a forum with which it has significant contacts directly related to the underlying cause of action.

Notes and Questions

1. Note that the Court adopts the dichotomy between specific jurisdiction and general jurisdiction. Recall General and Specific Jurisdiction, supra p. 744. Before turning to general jurisdiction, reflect on the ways in which concepts of specific jurisdiction should be applied. Justice Brennan accuses the Court of limiting specific jurisdiction to cases in which the plaintiff's claim "arises out of" the defendant's forum contacts. Since the parties did not try to approach the case on a specific jurisdiction theory, it is difficult to know whether Justice Brennan is right. Professor Brilmayer, however, has argued that the critical question for specific jurisdiction problems is whether the contacts have substantive relevance to plaintiff's claim whether or not there is a jurisdictional problem in the case:

> A contact is related to the controversy if it is the geographical qualification of a fact relevant to the merits. A forum occurrence which would ordinarily be alleged as part of a comparable domestic complaint is a related contact. In contrast, an occurrence in the forum State of no relevance to a totally domestic cause of action is an unrelated contact, a purely jurisdictional allegation with no substantive purpose. If a fact is irrelevant in a purely domestic dispute, it does not suddenly become related to the controversy simply because there are multistate elements.

Brilmayer, How Contacts Count: Due Process Limitations on State Court Jurisdiction, 1980 Sup.Ct.Rev. 77, 82. It this a desirable standard?

Professor Twitchell criticized this approach as underinclusive. In World–Wide Volkswagen v. Woodson (supra p. 730), for example, it would seem that Audi's sales of cars in Oklahoma lacked that sort of relationship to the claim by the Robinsons, who bought their car in New York. She feels that specific jurisdiction should reach such a case:

> [T]he fact that this accident occurred within the forum, coupled with similarity between the manufacturer's conduct in the forum and the conduct underlying the plaintiff's cause of action, * * * makes exercising jurisdiction over this claim particularly reasonable. Having sold and serviced identical cars in the state, the manufacturer will have foreseen such suits and insured against them. Furthermore, the forum has a very strong interest in regulating the manufacturer's conduct in this suit, not just because this particular automobile malfunctioned there, but because state residents are buying many similar cars and operating them on the forum's highways. The fact that the car was not actually sold within the state is, in this context, fortuitous. A court need not decide whether it is fair to hold the manufacturer subject to jurisdiction on all causes of action in the forum in order to decide that it is fair in this particular case. Specific jurisdiction, in which the nature of the cause of action is taken into account when considering fairness, not general jurisdiction, is the key to proper jurisdictional analysis under these circumstances.

Twitchell, The Myth of General Jurisdiction, 101 Harv.L.Rev. 610, 661–62 (1988). Did the Court implicitly endorse this analysis in *World–Wide Volkswagen?*

In response, Professor Brilmayer argued that substantive relevance is a critical element of a sensible test. See Brilmayer, Related Contacts and Personal Jurisdiction, 101 Harv.L.Rev. 1444 (1988). With regard to defective products cases, she raises the "tricky problem of what constitutes adequate similarity. Must it be the identical product that is distributed? A similar make or model? * * * Would assertion of specific jurisdiction require that a similar product sent into the forum state have an identical defect?" With regard to defendant's ability to foresee suit of the character of the suit brought, she adds that "[i]f one assumes that awareness of potential liability to suit on *some* cause of action in the forum entails awareness of potential liability on *other* causes of action that did not arise in the forum, then one risks turning specific jurisdiction into general jurisdiction. Under this view, the defendant should be equally unsurprised by any cause of action brought against him or her in the forum: the very definition of general jurisdiction." Id. at 1460–61.

2. Could plaintiffs in *Helicopteros* have made a specific jurisdiction argument? Would it matter if they claimed the accident in Peru resulted from deficient training in Texas? If decedents' employer, Consorcio/WSH, had filed a third party indemnity complaint against Helicopteros, would that have been within specific jurisdiction because of its relation to the contract negotiated in Texas? Compare Asahi Metal Indus. Co. v. Superior Court (supra p. 765).

3. Specific jurisdiction analysis looks to purposeful availment and reasonableness. How should those subjects be addressed when plaintiff relies on

general jurisdiction? In Metropolitan Life Ins. Co. v. Robertson–Ceco Corp., 84 F.3d 560 (2d Cir.), cert. denied, 519 U.S. 1006, 117 S.Ct. 508, 136 L.Ed.2d 398 (1996), the majority upheld dismissal on the ground that the exercise of jurisdiction would be unreasonable even though jurisdiction was premised on general jurisdiction. Met Life sued in Vermont, claiming that defendant had negligently constructed a building it owned in Miami, Fla. All agreed that no activities on which Met Life sued occurred in Vermont, but Met Life asserted that defendant's unrelated activities in Vermont sufficed for general jurisdiction. Those activities included sales of nearly $4 million over a four-year period, an ongoing relationship with independent dealers for its products, and advertising and product support activities in the state. Although recognizing that "this is a close case," the court held that in the aggregate these activities justified a finding that general jurisdiction could apply. It nevertheless upheld dismissal on reasonableness grounds, finding that exceptional circumstances justified rejection of jurisdiction. Judge Walker dissented, arguing that the reasonableness factors should be limited to application of forum non conveniens and not applied to general jurisdiction. Under the majority's reasoning, is general jurisdiction really a separate category of personal jurisdiction? Would the majority hold that one can't always sue International Shoe Co. in St. Louis, where it is headquartered? Keep these questions in mind when you reach the materials on transfer and discretionary decline of jurisdiction on grounds of convenience, infra p. 847.

4. General jurisdiction is necessary only when specific jurisdiction cannot be justified. In Nichols v. G.D. Searle & Co., 991 F.2d 1195, 1200 (4th Cir.1993), the court observed that "because specific jurisdiction has expanded tremendously, plaintiffs may now generally bring their claims in the forum where they arose. As a result, 'obsolescing notions of general jurisdiction,' which functioned primarily to ensure that a forum was available for plaintiffs to bring their claims, have been rendered largely unnecessary. Thus, broad constructions of general jurisdiction should generally be disfavored." Is there any continuing theoretical justification for allowing general jurisdiction in a state that has no significant relation to the dispute? Some would suggest that it offers a safe harbor; one can always sue International Shoe Co. at its headquarters in St. Louis rather than risk successful jurisdictional objections elsewhere. Is this concern satisfied by the ability to sue a corporation in its state of incorporation and to sue an individual in his or her state of domicile? In any event, does this argument justify allowing more than one place to have general jurisdiction over a defendant?

5. In *Helicopteros*, the level of defendant's activity in the forum is fairly minimal; the case gives little insight about the level of activity necessary to support general jurisdiction. Beyond saying that "substantial activity" is necessary, the cases do not afford a very precise test, and in some cases the level of activity found sufficient has been quite low. For example, in Bryant v. Finnish National Airline, 15 N.Y.2d 426, 260 N.Y.S.2d 625, 208 N.E.2d 439 (1965), plaintiff was a New Yorker who was injured at Orly airport in Paris due to defendant's alleged negligence. Defendant flew no planes to or from the United States, and none of its officers, directors or shareholders was American. It did, however, have a one-and-a-half room New York office staffed by three full-time and four part-time employees to receive and process reservations for travel on Finnair inside Europe. This

office had no authority to sell tickets or receive payment for travel in Europe on defendant's planes, but it did do some publicity for defendant in New York. Using the doing business rubric, the court applied a "pragmatic test" to justify jurisdiction over this unrelated claim: "The New York office is one of many maintained by defendant in various parts of the world, it has a lease on a New York office, it employs several people and it has a bank account here, it does public relations and publicity work for defendant including maintaining contacts with other airlines and travel agencies and, while it does not make reservations or sell tickets, it transmits requests for space to defendant in Europe and helps to generate business. These things should be enough."

Contrast Nichols v. G.D. Searle & Co., 991 F.2d 1195 (4th Cir.1993), in which 116 plaintiffs from other states sued Searle in Maryland for injuries allegedly caused by one of its products. Although Searle was headquartered in Illinois, it did have 17 to 21 employees regularly working in Maryland to market its products there, and it had annual sales in that state ranging from $9 million to $13 million. Noting that none of the plaintiffs' claims arose in Maryland, the court upheld dismissal for lack of jurisdiction because Searle's activities were insufficient to support general jurisdiction. It reasoned that advertising and soliciting activities alone should not suffice to support general jurisdiction.

The Supreme Court has provided little guidance on the level of activity that is sufficient to support general jurisdiction. Presumably it must be as much as would be required to support specific jurisdiction over a claim arising out of the contacts involved. Beyond that, the line is hard to draw. Perkins v. Benguet Consol. Min. Co., discussed by the Court in *Helicopteros*, is obviously an unusual case in that the company's headquarters were in effect in Ohio for the duration of World War II. In Rush v. Savchuk, supra p. 803 n. 1, the Court asserted that "State Farm is 'found,' in the sense of doing business, in all 50 states," citing the Insurance Almanac as support. In Keeton v. Hustler Magazine, Inc., supra p. 747 n. 1, the Court upheld jurisdiction in New Hampshire over a defendant that distributed 10,000 to 15,000 magazines monthly in New Hampshire, but noted that "respondent's activities in the forum may not be so substantial as to support jurisdiction over a cause of action unrelated to those activities." Would California have general jurisdiction over the National Enquirer? See Calder v. Jones, supra p. 745. Would Burger King Corporation (see Burger King Corp. v. Rudzewicz, supra p. 752) be subject to general jurisdiction, like State Farm, throughout the country?

Professor Twitchell argued that the courts should adopt a "home base" solution, ordinarily at corporate headquarters. See Twitchell, supra, 101 Harv.L.Rev. at 667–70. Thereafter, however, she became uneasy about her proposal: "Doing business jurisdiction plays a vital role in resolving multi-party disputes, and situates some cases in fora that might well be reasonable although the jurisdictional exercise would not pass constitutional muster under current specific-jurisdiction case law. Doing-business jurisdiction thus provides a practical solution to thorny constitutional debates." Twitchell, Why We Keep Doing Business With Doing–Business Jurisdiction, 2001 U. Chi. L.F. 171, 203. Nonetheless, the doctrine has produced serious problems of predictability. See id. at 203–13; Rhodes, Clarifying General Jurisdiction,

34 Seton Hall L.Rev. 807 (2004) (survey of general jurisdiction holdings based on a review of approximately 3,000 cases).

6. With natural persons, the state of defendant's domicile may exercise jurisdiction that is analogous to general jurisdiction. To some extent this idea is inherent in *Pennoyer*'s affirmation that a state has jurisdiction over its citizens. It was partly confirmed in Blackmer v. United States, 284 U.S. 421, 52 S.Ct. 252, 76 L.Ed. 375 (1932), which upheld the power of the United States to subpoena an American in France. In Milliken v. Meyer, 311 U.S. 457, 61 S.Ct. 339, 85 L.Ed. 278 (1940), the Court applied the same idea to state court jurisdiction over an absent citizen: "Domicile in the state is alone sufficient to bring an absent defendant within the reach of the state's jurisdiction for purposes of a personal judgment by means of appropriate substituted service. * * * As in the case of the authority of the United States over its absent citizens, the authority of a state over one of its citizens is not terminated by the mere fact of his absence from the state." Is state "citizenship" really analogous to national citizenship? In general, one is said to be a citizen of a state until he establishes domicile elsewhere, but all that requires is that he establish residence in that state and intend to remain there indefinitely. Doesn't this make it too easy for a defendant to defeat jurisdiction? On the other hand, a person retains his childhood citizenship until establishing an adult domicile (see Mas v. Perry, infra p. 861), so that he may remain subject to general jurisdiction at his parents' domicile long after he has severed any contact with it. Would a general jurisdiction standard for natural persons looking to substantial contacts be preferable?

7. The term "general jurisdiction" is used to describe a very different concept in connection with subject matter jurisdiction, where we will find that some courts (like the federal courts) are allowed only to hear claims of certain types or involving certain minimum or maximum amounts, while others are courts of "general jurisdiction" and may hear claims of all types. Be careful not to confuse the two ideas.

H. LITIGATING JURISDICTION

INSURANCE CORPORATION OF IRELAND, LTD. v. COMPAGNIE DES BAUXITES DE GUINEE, 456 U.S. 694, 102 S.Ct. 2099, 72 L.Ed.2d 492 (1982):

JUSTICE WHITE delivered the opinion of the Court.

[Compagnie des Bauxites de Guinee, a Delaware corporation owned jointly by a Pennsylvania company and the Republic of Guinee, operated bauxite mines in that country. In connection with those operations, it obtained $20 million worth of business interruption insurance, $10 million from an American insurance company and the additional $10 million ("excess" coverage) from 21 foreign insurers on the London insurance market. As a result of mechanical problems at the mine, it lost over $10 million due to a stoppage of work. When the insurers denied that this loss was covered, Compagnie des Bauxites sued in U.S. District Court in Pennsylvania. The American insurer did not challenge jurisdiction, but the foreign insurers raised lack of jurisdiction as a defense in their answers and moved for summary judgment on that ground. Plaintiffs served discovery asking for copies of all business interruption insurance policies that the foreign insurers had issued covering risks in Pennsylvania or delivered in Pennsylvania. After protracted discovery wrangles, including defendants' offer to make 4 million files available in London, the district court ordered them to produce the requested information in Pennsylvania. When they refused, the district court found it had jurisdiction as a sanction under Rule 37(b)(2)(A). On appeal, defendants argued that the trial court could not bootstrap itself into jurisdiction through use of sanctions if it had no jurisdiction. The Supreme Court affirmed.]

The personal jurisdiction requirement recognizes and protects an individual liberty interest. It represents a restriction on judicial power not as a matter of sovereignty, but as a matter of individual liberty. Thus, the test for personal jurisdiction requires that "the maintenance of the suit ... not offend 'traditional notions of fair play and substantial justice.'" International Shoe Co. v. Washington, 326 U.S. 310, 316, 66 S.Ct. 154, 158, 90 L.Ed. 95 (1945), quoting Milliken v. Meyer, 311 U.S. 457, 463, 61 S.Ct. 339, 342, 85 L.Ed. 278 (1940).

Because the requirement of personal jurisdiction represents first of all an individual right, it can, like other such rights, be waived. In McDonald v. Mabee, [243 U.S. 90, 37 S.Ct. 343, 61 L.Ed. 608 (1917)], the Court indicated that regardless of the power of the State to serve process, an individual may submit to the jurisdiction of the court by appearance. A variety of legal arrangements [has] been taken to represent express or implied consent to the personal jurisdiction of the court. In National Equipment Rental, Ltd. v. Szukhent, 375 U.S. 311, 316, 84 S.Ct. 411, 414, 11 L.Ed.2d 354 (1964), we stated that "parties to a contract may agree in advance to submit to the jurisdiction of a given court," and in Petrowski v. Hawkeye–Security Insurance Co., 350 U.S. 495, 76 S.Ct. 490, 100 L.Ed. 639 (1956), the Court upheld the personal jurisdiction of a District Court on the basis of a stipulation entered into by the defendant. In addition, lower federal courts have found such consent implicit in agreements to arbitrate. Furthermore, the Court has upheld state procedures which find constructive consent to the personal jurisdiction of the state court in the voluntary use of certain state procedures. See Adam v. Saenger, 303 U.S. 59, 67–68, 58 S.Ct. 454, 458, 82 L.Ed. 649 (1938). Finally, unlike subject-matter jurisdiction, which even an appellate court may review sua sponte, under Rule 12(h), Federal Rules of Civil Procedure, "[a] defense of lack of jurisdiction over the person ... is waived" if not timely raised in the answer or a responsive pleading.

In sum, the requirement of personal jurisdiction may be intentionally waived, or for various reasons a defendant may be estopped from raising the issue. These characteristics portray it for what it is—a legal right protecting the individual. The plaintiff's demonstration of certain historical facts may make clear to the court that it has personal jurisdiction over the defendant as a matter of law—i.e., certain factual showings will have legal consequences—but this is not the only way in which the personal jurisdiction of the court may arise. The actions of the defendant may amount to a legal submission to the jurisdiction of the court, whether voluntary or not.

The expression of legal rights is often subject to certain procedural rules: The failure to follow those rules may well result in a curtailment of the rights. Thus, the failure to enter a timely objection to personal jurisdiction constitutes, under Rule 12(h)(1), a waiver of the objection. A sanction under Rule 37(b)(2)(A) consisting of a finding of personal jurisdiction has precisely the same effect. As a general proposition, the Rule 37 sanction applied to a finding of personal jurisdiction creates no more of a due process problem than the Rule 12 waiver.

[The Court noted that discovery sanctions do not violate due process where they are based upon a presumption of fact that the evidence not produced would support the adversary's position. Instead, due process would be offended only if the sanction were imposed solely to punish a party for disobeying the court's order. See supra p. 420 n. 3.]

Petitioners argue that a sanction consisting of a finding of personal jurisdiction differs from all other instances in which a sanction is imposed * * * because a party need not obey the orders of a court until it is established that the court has personal jurisdiction over that party. If there is no obligation to obey a judicial order, a sanction cannot be applied for the failure to comply. Until the court has established personal jurisdiction, moreover, any assertion of judicial power over the party violates due process.

This argument again assumes that there is something unique about the requirement of personal jurisdiction, which prevents it from being established or waived like other rights. A defendant is always free to ignore the judicial proceedings, risk a default judgment, and then challenge that judgment on jurisdictional grounds in a collateral proceeding. By submitting to the jurisdiction of the court for the limited purpose of challenging jurisdiction, the defendant agrees to abide by that court's determination on the issue of jurisdiction: That decision will be res judicata on that issue in any further proceedings.

Notes and Questions

1. When did the foreign insurers submit to the court's jurisdiction to decide the personal jurisdiction issue? Cf. Fed.R.Civ.P. 12(h). From that moment on, could they ever have withdrawn that consent? As *Bauxites* suggests, defendants who wish to challenge personal jurisdiction may have to make some hard choices about how best to protect their rights. Since a judgment entered by a court without jurisdiction is not entitled to full faith and credit, defendant may chose to disregard the litigation, permit its default to be entered, and defend against enforcement of the judgment on the ground it is invalid for lack of jurisdiction. *Pennoyer* shows that the validity of the judgment can be litigated later even in the state that entered the judgment. The problem with this approach is that the defendant may be uncertain about how the jurisdictional question will be resolved, given the elasticity of the minimum contacts calculus. If defendant defaults but is

wrong about the first court's jurisdiction, it is too late to defend on the merits when that court's default judgment is enforced elsewhere. Thus, a defendant with a valid defense on the merits takes a risk in permitting its default to be entered.

2. The alternative, obviously, is to litigate jurisdiction as a defense in the distant court where the first action is filed. Should that obviously be the first choice of most defendants, as it was the choice made by defendants in *Bauxites*? If the distant court rejects the jurisdiction argument, defendant has no remedy except appeal. Baldwin v. Iowa State Traveling Men's Ass'n, 283 U.S. 522, 51 S.Ct. 517, 75 L.Ed. 1244 (1931), held that a defendant who has litigated jurisdiction and lost is estopped later to claim that the judgment is not entitled to full faith and credit due to lack of jurisdiction. Cf. Durfee v. Duke, 375 U.S. 106, 84 S.Ct. 242, 11 L.Ed.2d 186 (1963) (estoppel to relitigate subject matter jurisdiction). But it may not be possible to appeal until after trial. As explained in Chapter XII, in many court systems (including the federal courts) there is no right to appeal pretrial rulings like denial of a motion to dismiss for lack of personal jurisdiction until final judgment is entered. Compare Cal.Code Civ.Proc. § 418.10(c) (requiring that defendant seek immediate review by petitioning an appellate court for a writ of mandate or waive objections to jurisdiction).

Accordingly, the defendant usually will have to put on a defense at trial before getting a chance to persuade an appellate court that defending in this jurisdiction is unfairly burdensome. Of course, defendant can take some solace in the hope that the defense will be successful, thereby ending its worries about the case, while the opportunity to overturn an unsuccessful result on the merits with the jurisdictional argument still exists if the trial turns out unfavorably. It may be, however, that the defendant has no right to such an option. In Western Life Indem. Co. v. Rupp, 235 U.S. 261, 35 S.Ct. 37, 59 L.Ed. 220 (1914), the Court upheld the constitutionality of a state court rule requiring defendant whose objection to jurisdiction was rejected to waive the jurisdiction objection as a precondition to the right to defend on the merits.

3. As *Bauxites* also makes clear, a defendant must take care to avoid losing its objections to jurisdiction unintentionally. Fed.R.Civ.P. 12(h) requires only that the jurisdiction issue be raised at the first opportunity, whether that be a Rule 12 motion or the answer. State court rules may require a *special appearance* to avoid submitting to the jurisdiction of the court by entering a general appearance. See Tex. R. Civ. P. 120a (special appearance required to object to jurisdiction; any other appearance results in consent to jurisdiction).

Even the right to make a special appearance may be a matter of legislative grace, not constitutional right. In York v. Texas, 137 U.S. 15, 11 S.Ct. 9, 34 L.Ed. 604 (1890), the Court upheld a Texas rule (abandoned in 1962) that even an objection to jurisdiction was a general appearance. Reasoning that the entry of a judgment which is void for lack of jurisdiction deprives defendant of nothing, the Court found no violation of due process in denying defendant the opportunity to contest jurisdiction: "It certainly is more convenient that a defendant be permitted to object to the service, and raise the question of jurisdiction, in the first instance, in the court in which the suit is pending. But mere convenience is not substance of right." This attitude reflects an age in which questions of jurisdiction were thought, under the influence of *Pennoyer,* to be clear cut. How realistic is it today to say that a defendant who loses the right to defend on the merits by guessing wrong about jurisdiction loses nothing? Isn't the right to defend on the merits entitled to some recognition?

4. Once a proper objection to jurisdiction has been made, there may be factual matters that are uncertain, and discovery in aid of jurisdiction may be available to develop information for use on the jurisdictional challenge, as in *Bauxites.* Frequently that discovery has nothing to do with the substantive merits of the plaintiff's claim. Should courts routinely grant such discovery? See Carefirst of Maryland v. Carefirst Pregnancy Centers, 334 F.3d 390 (4th Cir.2003) (if the plaintiff offers only speculative or conclusory assertions about contacts with the forum, the district court may deny jurisdictional discovery). In *Bauxites*, was plaintiff's discovery proper? Was plaintiff relying on general or specific jurisdiction? Was it a mistake for defendants to move to dismiss in *Bauxites*? Should their lawyer have alerted them to the possibility of discovery before they filed their motion?

5. Finally, a very practical note: It should be clear that jurisdictional issues may often turn on factual material; very often that information is supplied by affidavits prepared by the lawyer for the defendant or its employees to sign. Lawyers should be extremely careful in the preparation of these affidavits. Often they will necessarily describe events that lie at the heart of the substantive dispute between the parties. Whatever the disposition of the jurisdiction issue, the affidavits remain. They are signed under oath by persons who may be critical witnesses at trial. Because they are prepared early in the litigation, at a time when attention is centered on the jurisdictional problem, they may be inexact or incomplete about matters that later prove to be critical to the merits. Accordingly, mark well the adage that early affidavits usually come back to haunt a litigant. Where possible, obtain affidavits from persons who won't be witnesses on the merits. Always draft the affidavits with extreme care.

CONSENT TO SUIT IN FORUM

Entering a general appearance constitutes consent to proceeding in the jurisdiction selected by plaintiff. Defendant may consent to jurisdiction in advance of suit. For example, in National Equipment Rental, Ltd. v. Szukhent, 375 U.S. 311, 84 S.Ct. 411, 11 L.Ed.2d 354 (1964), two Michigan farmers signed National Equipment's form lease for farm equipment. The form provided that they appointed one Florence Weinberg of Long Island City, New York, their agent "for the purpose of accepting service of any process within the State of New York." They were not acquainted with Weinberg, who was the wife of an officer of National Equipment. When problems developed with the equipment, National Equipment sued the farmers in New York, serving Ms. Weinberg. The farmers claimed that the agency was not valid, particularly in light of Ms. Weinberg's conflict of interest. In a 5–4 decision, the Court disagreed: "Under well-settled general principles of the law of agency Florence Weinberg's prompt acceptance and transmittal to the respondents of the summons and complaint was itself sufficient to validate the agency, even though there was no explicit previous promise on her part to do so." In dissent, Justice Black decried the invitation to insert such a clause in all form contracts. Should the Court have looked to equality of bargaining power between the parties? Cf. D.H. Overmyer Co. v. Frick Co., 405 U.S. 174, 92 S.Ct. 775, 31 L.Ed.2d 124 (1972) (consent to entry of judgment without prior notice and hearing valid only if bargained for among parties of equal bargaining power). Should the Court have treated the absence of such a provision in the form franchise agreement as significant in its treatment of the choice of law clause in Burger King Corp. v. Rudzewicz, supra p. 752?

By filing a lawsuit, a plaintiff is deemed to have consented to jurisdiction of the court he has selected with respect to defendant's claims against him. Thus, in Adam v. Saenger, 303 U.S. 59, 58 S.Ct. 454, 82 L.Ed. 649 (1938), the Court held that California's provision that the plaintiff's attorney is his agent for service of process on a cross-complaint sufficed to establish California jurisdiction entitling a default judgment entered on the cross-complaint to full faith and credit in plaintiff's home state of Texas. How broad is this consent? Cf. Fed. R.Civ.P. 13(b). Should it apply to claims asserted against the plaintiff by additional parties brought into the action by the defendant? See Nobel Floral, Inc. v. Pasero, 130 Cal.Rptr.2d 881 (Cal.Ct.App.2003) (nonresident who filed suit in California thereby consented to jurisdiction in a later separate suit in California arising from the same transaction).

In Phillips Petroleum Co. v. Shutts, 472 U.S. 797, 105 S.Ct. 2965, 86 L.Ed.2d 628 (1985), the Court held that a similar consent principle permits nationwide class actions, even though the individual class members do not take action to participate in the suit. It stressed that "States place fewer burdens upon absent class plaintiffs than they do upon absent defendants in nonclass suits" because class members "may sit back and allow the litigation to run its course, content in knowing that there are safeguards provided for his protection." It also noted that counterclaims against unnamed class members are extremely rare.

FORUM SELECTION CLAUSES

Another aspect of consent involves the advance choice of the forum for any possible disputes, commonly called a forum selection clause. In The M/S Bremen v. Zapata Off–Shore Co., 407 U.S. 1, 92 S.Ct. 1907, 32 L.Ed.2d 513 (1972), an American company had entered into such a contract with a German company in a contract to tow an oil drilling rig from Louisiana to Italy, designating London as the chosen forum. Notwithstanding, the American company filed an action in a U.S. District Court. Recognizing "present-day commercial realities and expanding international trade," the Supreme Court held that the clause should be enforced and the American suit should be dismissed. So a forum selection clause can trump otherwise valid jurisdiction.

In Carnival Cruise Lines, Inc. v. Shute, 499 U.S. 585, 111 S.Ct. 1522, 113 L.Ed.2d 622 (1991), the Court applied the same reasoning to a forum selection clause that was on the back of a cruise line passenger ticket. Although the passengers came from the state of Washington and the cruise in question originated in Los Angeles, the clause said that any suit had to be filed in Florida. The Court found the clause reasonable because Carnival Cruise Lines had its headquarters in Florida and many of its cruises originated there, and because a cruise line would have a "special interest in limiting the fora in which it could potentially be liable to suit." It also observed that "it stands to reason that passengers who purchase tickets containing a forum clause like that at issue in this case benefit in the form of reduced fares reflecting the savings that the cruise line enjoys." Because the clause was not fundamentally unfair, the Court held that the plaintiffs' suit in Washington had to be dismissed. For an example outside the admiralty area, see Caspi v. The Microsoft Network, 732 A.2d 528 (N.J. Super. Ct.1999) (holding that a forum selection clause in the on-line subscription contract for the Microsoft Network is binding).

Is use of forum selection clauses in consumer contracts fair? For criticism, see Purcell, Geography as a Litigation Weapon: Consumers, Forum–Selection Clauses, and the Rehnquist Court, 40 U.C.L.A.L. Rev. 423 (1992).

I. THE REQUIREMENT OF NOTICE

Recall that in *Pennoyer* it was unclear whether the Due Process clause (which had not even gone into effect at the pertinent time) would require notice to the defendant, and that in *Harris v. Balk*, supra p. 703, the Court seemed to say that the garnishee, not the plaintiff, had the obligation to give notice to be protected by the binding effect of the judgment.

In Mullane v. Central Hanover Bank & Trust Co., 339 U.S. 306, 70 S.Ct. 652, 94 L.Ed. 865 (1950), the Court directly addressed due process notice requirements. In that case, a bank sought an "accounting," a decision that its handling as trustee of combined trust funds containing bequests being administered for a large number of beneficiaries was proper. The effect of the decree would be to extinguish any right of any beneficiary to sue the bank for mishandling the accounts. The only notice given of the proceeding was publication in a newspaper four times of a brief and cryptic advertisement that did not even identify the beneficiaries. This notice effort could be contrasted with the bank's regular correspondence with many of the beneficiaries to remit income and conduct like business. The Court held that this published notice did not satisfy due process.

The Court began by recognizing that "[p]ersonal service of written notice within the jurisdiction is the classic form of notice always adequate in any type of proceeding," but also that alternative means could be used in situations in which that form is impracticable. The fundamental rule is a realistic one that takes account of the demands of the given situation:

> An elementary and fundamental requirement of due process in any proceeding which is to be accorded finality is notice reasonably calculated, under all the circumstances, to apprise interested parties of the pendency of the action and afford them an opportunity to present their objections. The notice must be of such nature as reasonably to convey the required information, and it must afford a reasonable time for those interested to make their appearance. But if with due regard for the practicalities and peculiarities of the case these conditions are reasonably met the constitutional requirements are satisfied. "The criterion is not the possibility of conceivable injury, but the just and reasonable character of the requirements, having reference to the subject with which the statute deals."

The Court added that "[t]he means employed must be such as one desirous of actually informing the absentee might reasonably adopt to accomplish it." Measured by these standards, the newspaper publication by the bank was inadequate. "Chance alone brings to the attention of even a local resident an advertisement in small type inserted in the back pages of a newspaper, and if he makes his home outside the area of the newspaper's normal circulation the odds that the information will never reach him are large indeed."

The Court recognized that notice in some instances might be "reinforced by steps likely to attract the parties attention to the proceeding." For example, seizure of tangible property would be likely to come to the owner's attention. Cf. Fuentes v. Shevin, supra p. 29. And it may often be permissible to use constructive means of notice with regard to persons missing or unknown. But the bank had names and addresses for many of the beneficiaries, and as to them "we find no tenable ground for dispensing with a serious effort to inform them personally of the accounting, at least by ordinary mail to the record addresses." Notice to some might often be a reasonable substitute for notice to all:

> The individual interest does not stand alone but is identical with that of a class. The rights of each in the integrity of the fund and the fidelity of the trustee are shared by many other beneficiaries. Therefore notice reasonably certain to reach most of those interested in objecting is likely to safeguard the interests of all, since any objections sustained would inure to the benefit of all. We think that under such circumstances reasonable risks that notice might not actually reach every beneficiary are justifiable.

Notes and Questions

1. Although *Mullane* suggested that seizure of property might be sufficient to give notice in *in rem* proceedings, in Walker v. City of Hutchinson, 352 U.S. 112, 77 S.Ct. 200, 1 L.Ed.2d 178 (1956) the Court held that mailed notice to the owner is required in state condemnation proceedings.

2. If the defendant's name and address are known, what means of notice are sufficient? The Court in *Mullane* notes that personal service is the "classic form" of notice, and that first class mail is usually sufficient, but it also acknowledges that posting on property may be sufficient. In Greene v. Lindsey, 456 U.S. 444, 102 S.Ct. 1874, 72 L.Ed.2d 249 (1982), tenants at a public housing project challenged the state processes for serving notice of eviction proceedings. The procedure authorized posting on the door of the apartment, but plaintiffs offered testimony that notices were often torn off doors, and the trial court so found. On this basis the Court, while recognizing that posting may often be sufficient, found the procedure a denial of due process in plaintiffs' case, and that only mailed notice would suffice. Justice O'Connor retorted in dissent:

> The Court * * * holds that notice via the mails is so far superior to posted notice that the difference is of constitutional dimension. How the Court reaches this judgment remains a mystery, especially since the Court is unable, on the present record, to evaluate the risks that notice mailed to public housing projects might fail due to loss, misdelivery, lengthy delay, or theft. Furthermore, the advantages of the mails over posting, if any, are far from obvious. It is no secret, after all, that unattended mailboxes are subject to plundering by thieves. Moreover, unlike the use of the mails, posting notice at least gives assurance that the notice has gotten as far as the tenant's door.

Should there be a constitutional difference between posting and mailing?

3. In Dusenbery v. United States, 534 U.S. 161, 122 S.Ct. 694, 151 L.Ed.2d 587 (2002), plaintiff, who was in a federal prison on drug charges, claimed that he had been denied due process due to inadequate notice of the government's administrative forfeiture of his automobile and nearly $22,000 in cash, which were seized when he was arrested. The government had sent notice by certified mail to the prison, where it was signed for by prison mailroom staff. But plaintiff said he never got the notice, and that he was accordingly denied due process. The Court, reasoning that *"Mullane* supplies the appropriate analytical framework," held that the procedure used to distribute mail was sufficient even though there was no record that plaintiff had actually received the notice. Plaintiff said the government should have made a "special effort" to make certain that he got the notice, but the majority reasoned that "the Due Process Clause does not require such heroic efforts * * *; it requires only that the Government's effort be 'reasonably calculated' to apprise a party of the pendency of the action." Although the prison's method of distributing mail had been upgraded to minimize the risk of the sort of error plaintiff contended had occurred in his case, the majority said that "the Government ought not be penalized and told to 'try harder' simply because the [Bureau of Prisons] has since upgraded its policies." Four justices dissented.

4. The Court acknowledges in *Mullane* that notice is not required for those who are too difficult to identify or locate. How much effort is required to identify such persons? In Mennonite Board of Missions v. Adams, 462 U.S. 791, 103 S.Ct. 2706, 77 L.Ed.2d 180 (1983), the Court held that a mortgagee is entitled to notice of proceedings to sell the mortgaged property for

nonpayment of taxes. It had no difficulty deciding that the mortgagee was reasonably identifiable:

> In this case, the mortgage on file with the county recorder identified the mortgagee only as "MENNONITE BOARD OF MISSIONS a corporation, of Wayne County, in the State of Ohio." We assume that the mortgagee's address could have been ascertained by reasonably diligent efforts. Simply mailing a letter to "Mennonite Board of Missions, Wayne County, Ohio," quite likely would have provided actual notice, given "the well-known skill of postal officials and employees in making proper delivery of letters defectively addressed." We do not suggest, however, that a government body is required to undertake extraordinary efforts to discover the identity and whereabouts of a mortgagee whose identity is not in the public record.

How much guidance does this give others trying to decide whether they have made sufficient efforts to locate parties with an interest? Should they ask the court to approve their efforts? In certain kinds of proceedings, such as actions to quiet title and to close an estate, judicial approval is sometimes necessary to establish that sufficient efforts have been made to identify and notify those who are interested.

5. The *Mullane* Court's recognition that, because the beneficiaries constituted "a class," notice was only required to those who could be identified provided a foundation for Rule 23's notice provisions regarding class actions. See Rule 23(c)(2). In Eisen v. Carlisle & Jacquelin, 417 U.S. 156, 94 S.Ct. 2140, 40 L.Ed.2d 732 (1974), the trial judge certified a class action on behalf of six million persons who traded in odd lots of shares on the New York Stock Exchange (blocks of less than 100 or not in multiples of 100 shares). It directed notice of the action (including the right to opt out) be sent to all individuals who had ten or more such trades during the four years in question and to 5,000 others, selected at random, as well as requiring advertisements in a number of papers. Citing *Mullane,* the Supreme Court held that this did not comply with Fed.R.Civ.P. 23(c)(2), which requires "individual notice to all members who can be identified through reasonable effort." About 2.25 million class members could be identified. Was this notice constitutionally required? Would it be necessary if there were no right to opt out?

6. If a person entitled to receive notice does not, is he bound by the judgment?

MANNER OF SERVING PROCESS

The ordinary way to give the defendant notice of the action is through service of the summons and complaint. On one level, of course, that represents the exercise of the court's power over the individual. When *capias ad respondendum* was the method for exercise of that power, service had to be by the sheriff, in person, and notice was not a problem. Given *Pennoyer*'s emphasis on power, notice remained a secondary consideration. Service of process today is still an exercise of the court's power through the summons, which directs the defendant to file an answer. The primary purpose of service provisions, however, is to guarantee that the defendant gets notice of the suit.

As *Mullane* suggests, the variety of methods available for service of process has increased since the day when only the sheriff could do so. Although state procedures may differ, see Hanna v. Plumer, infra p. 949, Fed.R.Civ.P. 4 touches on most of the likely methods. It allows service to be made in most civil cases by any person not a party who is over the age of 18. Rule 4(c)(2). If the defendant is an individual located in a federal judicial district, Rule 4(e) states that service may be accomplished by any means authorized by the law of the state in which the court in which the suit is pending sits, or by the law of the state in which the person is served. It also authorizes service by personal delivery, or by leaving the summons and complaint at the defendant's "usual place of abode" with a person of "suitable age and discretion then residing therein." Rule 4(f) provides directions for service of individuals in foreign countries, and there are further specifics regarding service on corporations (Rule 4(h)), the United States (Rule 4(i)), foreign governments (Rule 4(j)), and infants and incompetent persons (Rule 4(g)).

As amended in 1993, Rule 4(d) offers an alternative route: the plaintiff may ask the defendant to waive formal service. Rule 4(d)(2) imposes a "duty to avoid unnecessary costs of serving the summons" on a party who receives notice and a request to waive service in the prescribed way by first class mail. It also rewards the defendant who waives service by according a longer time to answer than defendant would have if formally served. Some states go even further. See, e.g., Cal.Code Civ.Proc. § 415.40 (summons may be served on person outside state by first-class mail, and service is effective without action of defendant on tenth day after mailing). Compare Brockmeyer v. May, 383 F.3d 798 (9th Cir.2004) (service by regular mail in England is permitted by the Hague Convention on the Service Abroad of Judicial and Extrajudicial Documents but valid in federal court only if affirmatively authorized by some provision of federal law). A defendant in this country who fails to waive service in response to a request made pursuant to Rule 4(d) shall be assessed costs, which Rule 4(a)(5) says include the costs subsequently incurred in effecting service in a more traditional way along with a reasonable attorneys' fee incurred for the motion to recover the costs.

Should service by e-mail suffice? The easy answer is that Rule 4 does not presently authorize service of process by e-mail. (Rule 5(b)(2)(D) authorizes use of e-mail to serve later filings in some circumstances.) In Rio Properties, Inc. v. Rio International Interlink, Inc., 284 F.3d 1007 (9th Cir.2002), the court upheld a court order authorizing service of process by e-mail under 4(f)(3) on a company with offices in Costa Rica, but the circumstances were quite unusual. Plaintiff asserted a claim that defendant's gambling Web site infringed the trademark of plaintiff's Las Vegas casino. Plaintiff made a variety of efforts to serve defendant by more conventional means but failed. Indeed, defendant had publicly indicated that it generally preferred communication through its e-mail address to any other means. Under these circumstances, the appellate court ruled, the district judge acted properly in authorizing service by e-mail. See also Popular Ent., LLC v. Webcom Media Group, Inc., 225 F.R.D. 560 (E.D.Tenn.2004) (services by e-mail warranted).

The person who serves the summons and complaint then makes out a proof of service (Rule 4(*l*)) attesting that service has been accomplished and how it was done. This document is filed, which may be important because Rule 4(m) provides that the action is subject to dismissal unless service is accomplished within 120 days of filing of the action.

As Rule 12(b)(5) indicates, a defendant who does not waive service can contest the sufficiency of service, and such a contest can raise a variety of factual issues. Where, for example, is defendant's "usual place of abode"? Was it sufficient to leave the summons and complaint with the secretary of the president of the defendant corporation? The variety of factual disputes that can arise is beyond the scope of this book, but it is worth noting that courts in general are not receptive to arguments about the manner of service made by defendants who clearly have received notice of the action (although they may be receptive to defendant's objections to the jurisdiction of the court). Where default is involved, however, they are more likely to entertain arguments about whether the manner of service actually gave defendant notice of the suit.

J. VENUE

Venue, meaning place of trial, places a further geographical limitation on plaintiff's options in selecting a forum. Although "[t]erritorial jurisdiction and venue were largely indistinguishable concepts for more than the first half of the existence of the federal courts," Clermont, Restating Territorial Jurisdiction and Venue for State and Federal Courts, 66 Cornell L.Rev. 411, 430 (1981), due to relaxation of restrictions on jurisdiction federal venue requirements now place an additional hurdle in the plaintiff's way. Indeed, some have gone so far as to suggest that "[j]urisdiction must become venue." Ehrenzweig, From State Jurisdiction to Interstate Venue, 50 Ore.L.Rev. 103, 113 (1971).

Before federal venue requirements were adopted, all states had venue limitations of their own, usually limiting the counties in which suit could be brought. Although there are some variations, these statutes tend to look to one or more of the following factors: (1) the location of property involved in the action, (2) the place where the cause of action arose, (3) the location of some particular event or fact, (4) defendant's residence, (5) plaintiff's residence, (6) defendant's place of business, and (7) plaintiff's place of business. See generally Stevens, Venue Statutes: Diagnosis and Proposed Cure, 49 Mich.L.Rev. 307 (1951).

Read 28 U.S.C.A. §§ 1391; 1392 and consider the factors employed there. The Supreme Court has explained that "[i]n most instances, the purpose of statutorily specified venue is to protect the defendant against the risk that a plaintiff will select an unfair or inconvenient place of trial." Leroy v. Great Western United Corp., 443 U.S. 173, 183–84, 99 S.Ct. 2710, 2716, 61 L.Ed.2d 464 (1979). Before 1966, venue in federal court generally turned on residence of defendants, but this produced "venue gaps" when there was no state in which all defendants resided.

In 1966 Congress sought to solve this problem by authorizing venue in the district "where the claim arose." This provision was changed, in turn, in 1990.

BATES v. C & S ADJUSTERS, INC.

United States Court of Appeals, Second Circuit, 1992.
980 F.2d 865.

Before: OAKES, NEWMAN, and PIERCE, CIRCUIT JUDGES.

JON O. NEWMAN, CIRCUIT JUDGE:

This appeal concerns venue in an action brought under the Fair Debt Collection Practices Act, 15 U.S.C. §§ 1692–1692o (1988). Specifically, the issue is whether venue exists in a district in which the debtor resides and to which a bill collector's demand for payment was forwarded. The issue arises on an appeal by Phillip E. Bates from the May 21, 1992, judgment of the District Court for the Western District of New York, dismissing his complaint because of improper venue. We conclude that venue was proper under 28 U.S.C.A. § 1391(b)(2) and therefore reverse and remand.

Bates commenced this action in the Western District of New York upon receipt of a collection notice from C & S Adjusters, Inc. ("C & S"). Bates alleged violations of the Fair Debt Collection Practices Act, and demanded statutory damages, costs, and attorney's fees. The facts relevant to venue are not in dispute. Bates incurred the debt in question while he was a resident of the Western District of Pennsylvania. The creditor, a corporation with its principal place of business in that District, referred the account to C & S, a local collection agency which transacts no regular business in New York. Bates had meanwhile moved to the Western District of New York. When C & S mailed a collection notice to Bates at his Pennsylvania address, the Postal Service forwarded the notice to Bates' new address in New York.

In its answer, C & S asserted two affirmative defenses and also counterclaimed for costs, alleging that the action was instituted in bad faith and for purposes of harassment. C & S subsequently filed a motion to dismiss for improper venue, which the District Court granted.

1. VENUE AND THE 1990 AMENDMENTS TO 28 U.S.C. § 1391(b)

Bates concedes that the only plausible venue provision for this action is 28 U.S.C.A. § 1391(b)(2), which allows an action to be brought in "a judicial district in which a substantial part of the events or omissions giving rise to the claim occurred." Prior to 1990, section 1391 allowed for venue in "the judicial district . . . in which the claim arose." 28 U.S.C. § 1391(b) (1988). This case represents our first opportunity to consider the significance of the 1990 amendments.

Prior to 1966, venue was proper in federal question cases, absent a special venue statute, only in the defendant's state of citizenship. If a plaintiff sought to sue multiple defendants who were citizens of different states, there might be no district where the entire action could be brought. Congress closed this "venue gap" by adding a provision allowing suit in the district "in which the claim arose." This phrase gave rise to a variety of conflicting interpretations. Some courts thought it meant that there could be only one such district; others believed there could be several. Different tests developed, with courts looking for "substantial contacts," the "weight of contacts," the place of injury or performance, or even to the boundaries of personal jurisdiction under state law.

The Supreme Court gave detailed attention to section 1391(b) in *Leroy v. Great Western United Corp.*, 443 U.S. 173, 99 S.Ct. 2710, 61 L.Ed.2d 464 (1979). The specific holding of *Leroy* was that Great Western, a Texas corporation, which had attempted to take over an Idaho corporation, could not bring suit in Texas against Idaho officials who sought to enforce a state anti-takeover law. Although the effect of the Idaho officials' action might be felt in Texas, the Court rejected this factor as a basis for venue, since it would allow the Idaho officials to be sued anywhere a shareholder of the target corporation could allege that he wanted to accept Great Western's tender offer. The Court made several further observations: (1) the purpose of the 1966 statute was to close venue gaps and should not be read more broadly than necessary to close those gaps; (2) the general purpose of the venue statute was to protect defendants against an unfair or inconvenient trial location; (3) location of evidence and witnesses was a relevant factor; (4) familiarity of the Idaho federal judges with the Idaho anti-takeover statute was a relevant factor; (5) plaintiff's convenience was not a relevant factor; and (6) in only rare cases should there be more than one district in which a claim can be said to arise.

Subsequent to *Leroy* and prior to the 1990 amendment to section 1391(b), most courts have applied at least a form of the "weight of contacts" test. Courts continued to have difficulty in determining whether more than one district could be proper.

Against this background, we understand Congress' 1990 amendment to be at most a marginal expansion of the venue provision. The House Report indicates that the new language was first proposed by the American Law Institute in a 1969 Study, and observes:

> The great advantage of referring to the place where things happened ... is that it avoids the litigation breeding phrase "in which the claim arose." It also avoids the problem created by the frequent cases in which substantial parts of the underlying events have occurred in several districts.

H.R.Rep. No. 734, 101st Cong., 2d Sess. 23, reprinted in 1990 U.S.C.C.A.N. 6860, 6869. Thus it seems clear that *Leroy*'s strong admonition against recognizing multiple venues has been disapproved. Many of the factors in *Leroy*—for instance, the convenience of defendants and the location of evidence and witnesses—are most useful in distinguishing between two or more plausible venues. Since the new statute does not, as a general matter, require the District Court to determine the best venue, these factors will be of less significance. Apart from this point, however, *Leroy* and other precedents remain important sources of guidance.

2. FAIR DEBT COLLECTION PRACTICES ACT

Under the version of the venue statute in force from 1966 to 1990, at least three District Courts held that venue was proper under the Fair Debt Collection Practices Act in the plaintiff's home district if a collection agency had mailed a collection notice to an address in that district or placed a phone call to a number in that district. None of these cases involved the unusual fact, present in this case, that the defendant did not deliberately direct a communication to the plaintiff's district.

We conclude, however, that this difference is inconsequential, at least under the current venue statute. The statutory standard for venue focuses not on whether a defendant has made a deliberate contact—a factor relevant in the analysis of personal jurisdiction[1]—but on the location where events occurred. Under the new version of section 1391(b)(2), we must determine only whether a "substantial part of the events ... giving rise to the claim" occurred in the Western District of New York.

In adopting this statute, Congress was concerned about the harmful effect of abusive debt practices on consumers. See 15 U.S.C. § 1692(a) ("Abusive debt collection practices contribute to the number of personal bankruptcies, to marital instability, to the loss of jobs, and to invasions of individual privacy."). This harm does not occur until receipt of the collection notice. Indeed, if the notice were lost in the mail, it is unlikely that a violation of the Act would have occurred.[2] Moreover, a debt collection agency sends its dunning letters so that they will be received. Forwarding such letters to the district to which a debtor has moved is an important step in the collection process. If the bill collector prefers not to be challenged for its collection practices outside the district of a debtor's original residence, the envelope can be marked "do not forward." We conclude that receipt of a collection notice is a substantial part of the events giving rise to a claim under the Fair Debt Collection Practices Act.

The relevant factors identified in *Leroy* add support to our conclusion. Although "bona fide error" can be a defense to liability under the

---

1. C & S has waived whatever claim it might have had that the District Court lacked personal jurisdiction over it. Waiver resulted from C & S's failure to allege lack of personal jurisdiction in its answer or motion to dismiss. See Fed.R.Civ.P. 12(b)(2), (h).

2. Although we need not decide the issue today, we note that at least one court has indicated that a plaintiff's cause of action might not accrue until receipt of the collection notice for purposes of the Act's one-year statute of limitations, 15 U.S.C.

§ 1692k(d) (1988). See Seabrook v. Onondaga Bureau of Medical Economics, Inc., 705 F.Supp. 81, 83 (N.D.N.Y.1989) ("more likely" that statute would start to run only "on the date the debtor received the communication"). But see Mattson v. U.S. West Communications, Inc., 967 F.2d 259, 261 (8th Cir.1992) (statute starts to run on date of mailing); Drumright v. Collection Recovery, Inc., 500 F.Supp. 1 (M.D.Tenn.1980) (statute starts to run on date of mailing for some violations).

Act, 15 U.S.C. § 1692k(c), the alleged violations of the Act turn largely not on the collection agency's intent, but on the content of the collection notice. The most relevant evidence—the collection notice—is located in the Western District of New York. Because the collection agency appears not to have marked the notice with instructions not to forward, and has not objected to the assertion of personal jurisdiction, trial in the Western District of New York would not be unfair.

Notes and Questions

1. Defendant C & S is a corporation. Why isn't its venue objection overcome by 28 U.S.C.A. § 1391(c)? Note that under this provision venue has become jurisdiction rather than the other way around, as Professor Ehrenzweig urged (see supra p. 840). Should venue provide greater limits on suits against non-corporate defendants than personal jurisdiction requirements?

As interpreted by the Second Circuit, how does the venue requirement of § 1391(b)(2) compare to personal jurisdiction analysis? Could it be said that defendant C & S purposefully availed with respect to New York in a way that would support jurisdiction in New York? Would it be important that under some views (see the court's footnote 2) the claim was not actionable until receipt of the letter?

2. How should venue be handled when the defendant is an organizational entity but not a corporation? For purposes of diversity of citizenship federal court subject matter jurisdiction, voluntary associations like labor unions are not considered separate legal entities and therefore are generally considered citizens of the state in which any member resides. See infra p. 867 n. 10. In Denver and Rio Grande Western R.R. Co. v. Brotherhood of Railroad Trainmen, 387 U.S. 556, 87 S.Ct. 1746, 18 L.Ed.2d 954 (1967), the Court held that Congress left it to the courts to determine the residence of such an entity for purposes of venue, and that it should be viewed as having a separate existence for that purpose. Accordingly, it should be held to reside in any district where it is doing business, which the Court took to mean "any district in which its duly authorized officers or agents are engaged in representing or acting for employee members." See also Penrod Drilling Co. v. Johnson, 414 F.2d 1217 (5th Cir.1969) (doing business approach used to determine residence for venue purposes of partnership).

3. Is the court's application of § 1391(b)(2) in *Bates* persuasive? Consider the explanation of this provision offered by another court: "[T]he current statutory language still favors the defendant in a venue dispute by requiring that the events or omissions supporting a claim be 'substantial.' Events or omissions that might only have some tangential connection with the dispute in litigation are not enough. * * * The test for determining venue is not the defendant's 'contacts' with a particular district, but rather the location of those 'events or omissions giving rise to the claim,' theoretically a more easily demonstrable circumstance than where a 'claim arose.'" Cottman Transmission Systems, Inc. v. Martino, 36 F.3d 291 (3d Cir.1994). Compare the Supreme Court's decision in *Leroy,* discussed in the court's opinion. In that case, Idaho officials acting pursuant to an Idaho anti-takeover law directed a cease and desist order to a company headquartered

in Texas to prevent it from undertaking an impending tender offer for shares of a company with substantial Idaho operations. The company sued in Texas, asserting that the Idaho officials lacked authority to prevent the tender offer. Would the result be the same under the new statute?

4. For a contrast to *Bates*, consider Database America, Inc. v. Bellsouth Advertising & Publishing Corp., 825 F.Supp. 1216 (D.N.J.1993). Plaintiff, a New Jersey company, was in the business of marketing information drawn from a number of sources including the telephone yellow pages. Defendant, which compiles and publishes yellow pages for nine southeastern states, sent a letter to plaintiff asserting that plaintiff was violating defendant's copyright and instructing plaintiff to stop doing so. Plaintiff responded with a suit in New Jersey seeking a declaratory judgment that it had not infringed or that the copyright was not valid. The court concluded that venue was not proper under § 1392(b)(2):

> [I]t is difficult to accept the assertion that merely sending a cease and desist letter into a forum, in a declaratory judgment action for non-infringement and/or copyright invalidity, constitutes "substantial" activity as the term is used in Section 1391(b)(2). While such a letter may provoke an alleged infringer to file such a lawsuit, the letter itself has nothing to do with whether the copyright is valid or whether infringement has occurred. In other words, * * * the cease and desist letter does not constitute a "substantial" activity "giving rise to the claim[s]."

Id. at 1225. The court emphasized that the only elements of copyright infringement are ownership of a valid copyright and copying of parts of an original copyrighted work, and concluded that all such activities by defendant had occurred in Georgia, where it was headquartered. But usually in an action for declaratory relief the plaintiff must demonstrate that there is a genuine controversy between the parties; wouldn't the cease and desist letter matter for that? Does the nature of the claim asserted in *Bates* lead to a different result?

5. In other instances, the new statute may create difficulties similar to those we have already encountered in jurisdiction cases. "The ALI's test for transactional venue is more liberal than the 'in which the claim arose' test, but hardly comes warranted as less likely to be 'litigation breeding.'" Oakley, Recent Statutory Changes in the Law of Federal Jurisdiction and Venue: The Judicial Improvements Acts of 1988 and 1990, 24 U.C.Davis L.Rev. 735, 775 (1991). Consider:

Where does an omission occur? In Burger King Corp. v. Rudzewicz (supra p. 752), would it be fair to say that defendant's failure to make payments that the contract said should be made in Florida was an omission in Florida? Compare Cottman Transmission Systems, Inc. v. Martino, 36 F.3d 291 (3d Cir.1994), in which plaintiff franchisor claimed that defendant franchisee had violated his contract by continuing to operate transmission repair facilities in Michigan, thereby violating plaintiff's trademark rights. The court held that defendant's alleged failure to pay license fees in Pennsylvania, where plaintiff was headquartered, and his failure to return advertising items to Pennsylvania, did not support venue in Pennsylvania. "The omissions that Cottman cites—Martino's failure to return various materials and failure to remit payments—actually occurred in Michigan, not in Pennsylvania. Even though the result was Cottman's non-receipt of those items in Pennsylvania, the omissions bringing about this result actually occurred in Michigan." Id. at 295.

Where does an "event" occur? In Calder v. Jones (supra p. 745), did the events occur in Florida, where the allegedly defamatory story was written and published, or in California, where the defamation was circulated? When the action upon which the claim is based has been done on the Internet, where should venue treat it as having occurred? For example, how would venue have been handled in Pavlovich v. Superior Court, supra p. 776, if the suit had been filed in federal court?

What events or omissions "give rise to" a claim so as to matter for venue purposes? Should inquiry be limited to those that form a basis for liability under the applicable substantive law? Recall Justice Brennan's resistance to that standard for relatedness in the personal jurisdiction context in Helicopteros Nacionales de Colombia v. Hall (supra p. 821). Should events not essential to liability be disregarded? Should only matters that are properly included in the complaint be considered?

What is a "substantial part" of these events or omissions? In proposing this standard, the American Law Institute admitted that "[i]t is true that there may be controversy over what constitutes 'a substantial part,'" but concluded that this prospect did not matter because "this is most likely to occur when a plaintiff is taking a deliberate chance in an effort to gain a desired forum." In Keeton v. Hustler Magazine (supra p. 747 n. 1), plaintiff sued in New Hampshire although only a small portion of defendant's sales containing the allegedly defamatory article occurred there. Was that a substantial part? If not, were the sales of National Enquirers in California a substantial part in Calder v. Jones (supra p. 745)?

6. What is the focus of the third venue option, sometimes called the fallback option? "Subsection 3 is meant to cover the cases in which no substantial part of the events happened in the United States and in which all the defendants do not reside in the same state." H.R.Rep. No. 734, 101st Cong., 2d Sess.

7. Besides the general venue statute, Congress has provided special venue provisions in a number of areas. See generally 15 C. Wright, A. Miller & E. Cooper, Federal Practice & Procedure §§ 3816–25.

8. Note that if personal jurisdiction can be obtained but the federal venue limitations preclude suit in a forum, it may still be possible to sue in state court if the venue rules are different there.

9. *Local actions*: As 28 U.S.C.A. § 1392 suggests, there is a distinction for venue purposes between actions that are "local" and other actions, which are known as "transitory." The idea is that if the action relates to specific property, it should proceed only in the place where the property is located. This objective can cause substantial problems for plaintiffs. For example, in Livingston v. Jefferson, 15 F.Cas. 660, 1 Brock 203 (C.C.D.Va. 1811), plaintiff sued former president Thomas Jefferson in Virginia, Jefferson's residence, charging him with trespass to lands in Louisiana, and Jefferson objected that such a local action could only be brought in Louisiana. Chief Justice Marshall, sitting on circuit, found the difference to be that "actions

are deemed transitory, where transactions on which they are founded, might have taken place anywhere, but are local where their cause is in its nature necessarily local." While recognizing that application of the rule might mean that "the injured party may have a clear right without a remedy in a case where the person who has done the wrong, and who ought to make the compensation, is within the power of the court," but the property is located in a jurisdiction where jurisdiction is not available, Marshall sustained the objection to jurisdiction. The only justification he cited besides history was the possibility that a survey might be essential to resolution of the claim.

The importance of the distinction between local and transitory actions has abated in recent years. For example, in Raphael J. Musicus, Inc. v. Safeway Stores, Inc., 743 F.2d 503 (7th Cir.1984), the court rejected a venue objection to a suit in Illinois to void subleases Safeway had entered into for commercial property in Montana and Nebraska and to void Safeway's option to renew its leases to the land. The court said the distinction between local and transitory actions "is the same as that between *in personam* and *in rem* jurisdiction," and that so long as a personal judgment against the defendant would suffice a transitory action could be brought. Since plaintiff did not seek to recover possession by order of the Illinois court (although it could later seek to do so in a separate proceeding based on the relief obtained from the Illinois court), the venue objection was unjustified.

K.   DISCRETIONARY DECLINE OF JURISDICTION

PIPER AIRCRAFT CO. v. REYNO

Supreme Court of the United States, 1981.
454 U.S. 235, 102 S.Ct. 252, 70 L.Ed.2d 419.

JUSTICE MARSHALL delivered the opinion of the Court.

These cases arise out of an air crash that took place in Scotland. Respondent, acting as representative of the estates of several Scottish citizens killed in the accident, brought wrongful-death actions against petitioners that were ultimately transferred to the United States District Court for the Middle District of Pennsylvania. Petitioners moved to dismiss on the ground of forum non conveniens. After noting that an alternative forum existed in Scotland, the District Court granted their motions. The United States Court of Appeals for the Third Circuit reversed. The Court of Appeals based its decision, at least in part, on the ground that dismissal is automatically barred where the law of the alternative forum is less favorable to the plaintiff than the law of the forum chosen by the plaintiff. Because we conclude that the possibility of an unfavorable change in law should not, by itself, bar dismissal, and because we conclude that the District Court did not otherwise abuse its discretion, we reverse.

I

A

In July 1976, a small commercial aircraft crashed in the Scottish highlands during the course of a charter flight from Blackpool to Perth.

The pilot and five passengers were killed instantly. The decedents were all Scottish subjects and residents, as are their heirs and next of kin. There were no eyewitnesses to the accident. At the time of the crash the plane was subject to Scottish air traffic control.

The aircraft, a twin-engine Piper Aztec, was manufactured in Pennsylvania by petitioner Piper Aircraft Co. (Piper). The propellers were manufactured in Ohio by petitioner Hartzell Propeller, Inc. (Hartzell). At the time of the crash the aircraft was registered in Great Britain and was owned and maintained by Air Navigation and Trading Co., Ltd. (Air Navigation). It was operated by McDonald Aviation, Ltd. (McDonald), a Scottish air taxi service. Both Air Navigation and McDonald were organized in the United Kingdom. The wreckage of the plane is now in a hangar in Farnsborough, England.

The British Department of Trade investigated the accident shortly after it occurred. A preliminary report found that the plane crashed after developing a spin, and suggested that mechanical failure in the plane or the propeller was responsible. At Hartzell's request, this report was reviewed by a three-member Review Board, which held a 9–day adversary hearing attended by all interested parties. The Review Board found no evidence of defective equipment and indicated that pilot error may have contributed to the accident. The pilot, who had obtained his commercial pilot's license only three months earlier, was flying over high ground at an altitude considerably lower than the minimum height required by his company's operations manual.

In July 1977, a California probate court appointed respondent Gaynell Reyno administratrix of the estates of the five passengers. Reyno is not related to and does not know any of the decedents or their survivors; she was a legal secretary to the attorney who filed this lawsuit. Several days after her appointment, Reyno commenced separate wrongful-death actions against Piper and Hartzell in the Superior Court of California, claiming negligence and strict liability. Air Navigation, McDonald, and the estate of the pilot are not parties to this litigation. The survivors of the five passengers whose estates are represented by Reyno filed a separate action in the United Kingdom against Air Navigation, McDonald, and the pilot's estate. Reyno candidly admits that the action against Piper and Hartzell was filed in the United States because its laws regarding liability, capacity to sue, and damages are more favorable to her position than are those of Scotland. Scottish law does not recognize strict liability in tort. Moreover, it permits wrongful-death actions only when brought by a decedent's relatives. The relatives may sue only for "loss of support and society."

On petitioners' motion, the suit was removed to the United States District Court for the Central District of California. Piper then moved for transfer to the United States District Court for the Middle District of Pennsylvania, pursuant to 28 U.S.C. § 1404(a). Hartzell moved to dismiss for lack of personal jurisdiction, or in the alternative, to transfer.[5]

---

5. The District Court concluded that it could not assert personal jurisdiction over Hartzell consistent with due process. However, it decided not to dismiss Hartzell be-

In December 1977, the District Court quashed service on Hartzell and transferred the case to the Middle District of Pennsylvania. Respondent then properly served process on Hartzell.

B

In May 1978, after the suit had been transferred, both Hartzell and Piper moved to dismiss the action on the ground of forum non conveniens. The District Court granted these motions in October 1979. It relied on the balancing test set forth by this Court in Gulf Oil Corp. v. Gilbert, 330 U.S. 501, 67 S.Ct. 839, 91 L.Ed. 1055 (1947), and its companion case, Koster v. Lumbermens Mut. Cas. Co., 330 U.S. 518, 67 S.Ct. 828, 91 L.Ed. 1067 (1947). In those decisions, the Court stated that a plaintiff's choice of forum should rarely be disturbed. However, when an alternative forum has jurisdiction to hear the case, and when trial in the chosen forum would "establish ... oppressiveness and vexation to a defendant ... out of all proportion to plaintiff's convenience," or when the "chosen forum [is] inappropriate because of considerations affecting the court's own administrative and legal problems," the court may, in the exercise of its sound discretion, dismiss the case. *Koster,* supra, at 524, 67 S.Ct., at 831–832. To guide trial court discretion, the Court provided a list of "private interest factors" affecting the convenience of the litigants, and a list of "public interest factors" affecting the convenience of the forum. *Gilbert,* supra, 330 U.S. at 508–509, 67 S.Ct., at 843.[6]

[The district court granted the motion. With regard to private interests, it acknowledged that evidence about the design and manufacture of the plane was in the United States, but otherwise found the connections with Scotland "compelling." Moreover, it found plaintiff's choice of forum unimportant since all the real parties in interest were foreign. Concerning public interests, it determined that Pennsylvania law would apply to the claim against Piper and Scottish law to the claim against Hartzell.[8] This disparity, it concluded, would confuse the jury and, to the extent Scottish law had to be applied, the court as well.]

cause the corporation would be amenable to process in Pennsylvania.

6. The factors pertaining to the private interests of the litigants included the "relative ease of access to sources of proof; availability of compulsory process for attendance of unwilling, and the cost of obtaining attendance of willing, witnesses; possibility of view of premises, if view would be appropriate to the action; and all other practical problems that make trial of a case easy, expeditious and inexpensive." *Gilbert,* 330 U.S., at 508, 67 S.Ct., at 843. The public factors bearing on the question included the administrative difficulties flowing from court congestion; the "local interest in having localized controversies decided at home"; the interest in having the trial of a

diversity case in a forum that is at home with the law that must govern the action; the avoidance of unnecessary problems in conflict of laws, or in the application of foreign law; and the unfairness of burdening citizens in an unrelated forum with jury duty.

8. Under Klaxon v. Stentor Electric Mfg. Co., 313 U.S. 487, 61 S.Ct. 1020, 85 L.Ed. 1477 (1941), a court ordinarily must apply the choice-of-law rules of the State in which it sits. However, where a case is transferred pursuant to 28 U.S.C. § 1404(a), it must apply the choice-of-law rules of the State from which the case was transferred. Van Dusen v. Barrack, 376 U.S. 612, 84 S.Ct. 805, 11 L.Ed.2d 945 (1964). Relying on these two cases, the District Court concluded that California choice-

C

On appeal, the United States Court of Appeals for the Third Circuit reversed and remanded for trial. The decision to reverse appears to be based on two alternative grounds. First, the Court held that the District Court abused its discretion in conducting the *Gilbert* analysis. Second, the Court held that dismissal is never appropriate where the law of the alternative forum is less favorable to the plaintiff. [The appellate court bolstered this point by deciding that American law would apply to the claims against both defendants.[10]]

II

The Court of Appeals erred in holding that plaintiffs may defeat a motion to dismiss on the ground of forum non conveniens merely by showing that the substantive law that would be applied in the alternative forum is less favorable to the plaintiffs than that of the present forum. The possibility of a change in substantive law should ordinarily not be given conclusive or even substantial weight in the forum non conveniens inquiry.

We expressly rejected the position adopted by the Court of Appeals in our decision in Canada Malting Co. v. Paterson Steamships, 285 U.S. 413, 52 S.Ct. 413, 76 L.Ed. 837 (1932). That case arose out of a collision between two vessels in American waters. The Canadian owners of cargo lost in the accident sued the Canadian owners of one of the vessels in Federal District Court. The cargo owners chose an American court in large part because the relevant American liability rules were more favorable than the Canadian rules. The District Court dismissed on grounds of forum non conveniens. The plaintiffs argued that dismissal was inappropriate because Canadian laws were less favorable to them. This Court nonetheless affirmed:

> "We have no occasion to enquire by what law the rights of the parties are governed, as we are of the opinion that, under any view of that question, it lay within the discretion of the District Court to decline to assume jurisdiction over the controversy.... '[T]he court

of-law rules would apply to Piper, and Pennsylvania choice-of-law rules would apply to Hartzell. It further concluded that California applied a "governmental interests" analysis in resolving choice-of-law problems, and that Pennsylvania employed a "significant contacts" analysis. The court used the "governmental interests" analysis to determine that Pennsylvania liability rules would apply to Piper, and the "significant contacts" analysis to determine that Scottish liability rules would apply to Hartzell. [This is the Court's footnote.—Eds.]

10. The Court of Appeals agreed with the District Court that California choice-of-

law rules applied to Piper, and that Pennsylvania choice-of-law rules applied to Hartzell, see n. 8, supra. It did not agree, however, that California used a "governmental interests" analysis and that Pennsylvania used a "significant contacts" analysis. Rather, it believed that both jurisdictions employed the "false conflicts" test. Applying this test, it concluded that Ohio and Pennsylvania had a greater policy interest in the dispute than Scotland, and that American law would apply to both Piper and Hartzell. [This is the Court's footnote.—Eds.]

will not take cognizance of the case if justice would be as well done by remitting the parties to their home forum.' "

The Court further stated that "[t]here was no basis for the contention that the District Court abused its discretion."

It is true that *Canada Malting* was decided before *Gilbert,* and that the doctrine of forum non conveniens was not fully crystallized until our decision in that case. However, *Gilbert* in no way affects the validity of *Canada Malting.* Indeed, by holding that the central focus of the forum non conveniens inquiry is convenience, *Gilbert* implicitly recognized that dismissal may not be barred solely because of the possibility of an unfavorable change in law. Under *Gilbert,* dismissal will ordinarily be appropriate where trial in the plaintiff's chosen forum imposes a heavy burden on the defendant or the court, and where the plaintiff is unable to offer any specific reasons of convenience supporting his choice. If substantial weight were given to the possibility of an unfavorable change in law, however, dismissal might be barred even where trial in the chosen forum was plainly inconvenient.

The Court of Appeals' decision is inconsistent with this Court's earlier forum non conveniens decisions in another respect. Those decisions have repeatedly emphasized the need to retain flexibility. In *Gilbert,* the Court refused to identify specific circumstances "which will justify or require either grant or denial of remedy." Similarly, in *Koster,* the Court rejected the contention that where a trial would involve inquiry into the internal affairs of a foreign corporation, dismissal was always appropriate. "That is one, but only one, factor which may show convenience." And in Williams v. Green Bay & Western R. Co., 326 U.S. 549, 557, 66 S.Ct. 284, 288, 90 L.Ed. 311 (1946), we stated that we would not lay down a rigid rule to govern discretion, and that "[e]ach case turns on its facts." If central emphasis were placed on any one factor, the forum non conveniens doctrine would lose much of the very flexibility that makes it so valuable.

In fact, if conclusive or substantial weight were given to the possibility of a change in law, the forum non conveniens doctrine would become virtually useless. Jurisdiction and venue requirements are often easily satisfied. As a result, many plaintiffs are able to choose from among several forums. Ordinarily, these plaintiffs will select that forum whose choice-of-law rules are most advantageous. Thus, if the possibility of an unfavorable change in substantive law is given substantial weight in the forum non conveniens inquiry, dismissal would rarely be proper.

* * *

At least where the foreign plaintiff named an American manufacturer as defendant,[17] a court could not dismiss the case on grounds of forum

---

17. In fact, the defendant might not even have to be American. A foreign plaintiff seeking damages for an accident that occurred abroad might be able to obtain service of process on a foreign defendant who does business in the United States. Under the Court of Appeals' holding, dismissal would be barred if the law in the

non conveniens where dismissal might lead to an unfavorable change in law. The American courts, which are already extremely attractive to foreign plaintiffs, would become even more attractive. The flow of litigation into the United States would increase and further congest already crowded courts.

The Court of Appeals based its decision, at least in part, on an analogy between dismissals on grounds of forum non conveniens and transfers between federal courts pursuant to § 1404(a). In Van Dusen v. Barrack, 376 U.S. 612, 84 S.Ct. 805, 11 L.Ed.2d 945 (1964), this Court ruled that a § 1404(a) transfer should not result in a change in the applicable law. Relying on dictum in an earlier Third Circuit opinion interpreting *Van Dusen,* the court below held that principle is also applicable to a dismissal on forum non conveniens grounds. However, § 1404(a) transfers are different than dismissals on the ground of forum non conveniens.

Congress enacted § 1404(a) to permit change of venue between federal courts. Although the statute was drafted in accordance with the doctrine of forum non conveniens, it was intended to be a revision rather than a codification of the common law. Norwood v. Kirkpatrick, 349 U.S. 29, 75 S.Ct. 544, 99 L.Ed. 789 (1955). District courts were given more discretion to transfer under § 1404(a) than they had to dismiss on grounds of forum non conveniens. The reasoning employed in Van Dusen v. Barrack is simply inapplicable to dismissals on grounds of forum non conveniens. That case did not discuss the common-law doctrine. Rather, it focused on "the construction and application" of § 1404(a). Emphasizing the remedial purpose of the statute, *Barrack* concluded that Congress could not have intended a transfer to be accompanied by a change in law. The statute was designed as a "federal housekeeping measure," allowing easy change of venue within a unified federal system. The Court feared that if a change in venue were accompanied by a change in law, forum-shopping parties would take unfair advantage of the relaxed standards for transfer. The rule was necessary to ensure the just and efficient operation of the statute.

We do not hold that the possibility of an unfavorable change in law should never be a relevant consideration in a forum non conveniens inquiry. Of course, if the remedy provided by the alternative forum is so clearly inadequate or unsatisfactory that it is no remedy at all, the unfavorable change in law may be given substantial weight; the district court may conclude that dismissal would not be in the interests of justice.[22] In these cases, however, the remedies that would be provided by

alternative forum were less favorable to the plaintiff—even though none of the parties are American, and even though there is absolutely no nexus between the subject matter of the litigation and the United States.

22. At the outset of any forum non conveniens inquiry, the court must determine whether there exists an alternative forum. Ordinarily, this requirement will be satisfied when the defendant is "amenable to process" in the other jurisdiction. *Gilbert,* 330 U.S., at 506–507, 67 S.Ct., at 842. In rare circumstances, however, where the remedy offered by the other forum is clearly unsatisfactory, the other forum may not be

the Scottish courts do not fall within this category. Although the relatives of the decedents may not be able to rely on a strict liability theory, and although their potential damages award may be smaller, there is no danger that they will be deprived of any remedy or treated unfairly.

III

The Court of Appeals also erred in rejecting the District Court's *Gilbert* analysis. The Court of Appeals stated that more weight should have been given to the plaintiff's choice of forum, and criticized the District Court's analysis of the private and public interests. However, the District Court's decision regarding the deference due plaintiff's choice of forum was appropriate. Furthermore, we do not believe that the District Court abused its discretion in weighing the private and public interests.

A

The District Court acknowledged that there is ordinarily a strong presumption in favor of the plaintiff's choice of forum, which may be overcome only when the private and public interest factors clearly point towards trial in the alternative forum. It held, however, that the presumption applies with less force when the plaintiff or real parties in interest are foreign.

The District Court's distinction between resident or citizen plaintiffs and foreign plaintiffs is fully justified. In *Koster,* the Court indicated that a plaintiff's choice of forum is entitled to greater deference when the plaintiff has chosen the home forum. 330 U.S., at 524, 67 S.Ct., at 831–832.[23] When the home forum has been chosen, it is reasonable to assume that this choice is convenient. When the plaintiff is foreign, however, this assumption is much less reasonable. Because the central purpose of any forum non conveniens inquiry is to ensure that the trial is convenient, a foreign plaintiff's choice deserves less deference.[24]

an adequate alternative, and the initial requirement may not be satisfied. Thus, for example, dismissal would not be appropriate where the alternative forum does not permit litigation of the subject matter of the dispute. Cf. Phoenix Canada Oil Co. Ltd. v. Texaco, Inc., 78 F.R.D. 445 (Del. 1978) (court refuses to dismiss, where alternative forum is Ecuador, it is unclear whether Ecuadorean tribunal will hear the case, and there is no generally codified Ecuadorean legal remedy for the unjust enrichment and tort claims asserted).

23. Citizens or residents deserve somewhat more deference than foreign plaintiffs, but dismissal should not be automatically barred when a plaintiff has filed suit in his home forum. As always, if the balance of conveniences suggests that trial in the chosen forum would be unnecessarily burdensome for the defendant or the court, dismissal is proper.

24. Respondent argues that since plaintiffs will ordinarily file suit in the jurisdiction that offers the most favorable law, establishing a strong presumption in favor of both home and foreign plaintiffs will ensure that defendants will always be held to the highest possible standard of accountability for their purported wrongdoing. However, the deference accorded a plaintiff's choice of forum has never been intended to guarantee that the plaintiff will be able to select the law that will govern the case.

B

The forum non conveniens determination is committed to the sound discretion of the trial court. It may be reversed only when there has been a clear abuse of discretion; where the court has considered all relevant public and private interest factors, and where its balancing of these factors is reasonable, its decision deserves substantial deference.

(1)

In analyzing the private interest factors, the District Court stated that the connections with Scotland are "overwhelming." This characterization may be somewhat exaggerated. Particularly with respect to the question of relative ease of access to sources of proof, the private interests point in both directions. As respondent emphasizes, records concerning the design, manufacture, and testing of the propeller and plane are located in the United States. She would have greater access to sources of proof relevant to her strict liability and negligence theories if trial were held here.[25] However, the District Court did not act unreasonably in concluding that fewer evidentiary problems would be posed if the trial were held in Scotland. A large proportion of the relevant evidence is located in Great Britain.

The Court of Appeals found that the problems of proof could not be given any weight because Piper and Hartzell failed to describe with specificity the evidence they would not be able to obtain if trial were held in the United States. It suggested that defendants seeking forum non conveniens dismissal must submit affidavits identifying the witnesses they would call and the testimony these witnesses would provide if the trial were held in the alternative forum. Such detail is not necessary. Piper and Hartzell have moved for dismissal precisely because many crucial witnesses are located beyond the reach of compulsory process, and thus are difficult to identify or interview. Requiring extensive investigation would defeat the purpose of their motion. Of course, defendants must provide enough information to enable the District Court to balance the parties' interests. Our examination of the record convinces us that sufficient information was provided here. Both Piper and Hartzell submitted affidavits describing the evidentiary problems they would face if the trial were held in the United States.[27]

The District Court correctly concluded that the problems posed by the inability to implead potential third-party defendants clearly supported holding the trial in Scotland. Joinder of the pilot's estate, Air

25. In the future, where similar problems are presented, district courts might dismiss subject to the condition that defendant corporations agree to provide the records relevant to the plaintiff's claims.

27. The affidavit provided to the District Court by Piper states that it would call the following witnesses: the relatives of the decedents; the owners and employees of McDonald; the persons responsible for the training and licensing of the pilot; the persons responsible for servicing and maintaining the aircraft; and two or three of its own employees involved in the design and manufacture of the aircraft.

Navigation, and McDonald is crucial to the presentation of petitioners' defense. If Piper and Hartzell can show that the accident was caused not by a design defect, but rather by the negligence of the pilot, the plane's owners, or the charter company, they will be relieved of all liability. It is true, of course, that if Hartzell and Piper were found liable after a trial in the United States, they could institute an action for indemnity or contribution against these parties in Scotland. It would be far more convenient, however, to resolve all claims in one trial. The Court of Appeals rejected this argument. Forcing petitioners to rely on actions for indemnity or contributions would be "burdensome" but not "unfair." Finding that trial in the plaintiff's chosen forum would be burdensome, however, is sufficient to support dismissal on grounds of forum non conveniens.

(2)

The District Court's review of the factors relating to the public interest was also reasonable. On the basis of its choice-of-law analysis, it concluded that if the case were tried in the Middle District of Pennsylvania, Pennsylvania law would apply to Piper and Scottish law to Hartzell. It stated that a trial involving two sets of laws would be confusing to the jury. It also noted its own lack of familiarity with Scottish law. Consideration of these problems was clearly appropriate under *Gilbert;* in that case we explicitly held that the need to apply foreign law pointed towards dismissal. The Court of Appeals found that the District Court's choice-of-law analysis was incorrect, and that American law would apply to both Hartzell and Piper. Thus, lack of familiarity with foreign law would not be a problem. Even if the Court of Appeals' conclusion is correct, however, all other public interest factors favored trial in Scotland.

Scotland has a very strong interest in this litigation. The accident occurred in its airspace. All of the decedents were Scottish. Apart from Piper and Hartzell, all potential plaintiffs and defendants are either Scottish or English. As we stated in *Gilbert,* there is "a local interest in having localized controversies decided at home." Respondent argues that American citizens have an interest in ensuring that American manufacturers are deterred from producing defective products, and that additional deterrence might be obtained if Piper and Hartzell were tried in the United States, where they could be sued on the basis of both negligence and strict liability. However, the incremental deterrence that would be gained if this trial were held in an American court is likely to be insignificant. The American interest in this accident is simply not sufficient to justify the enormous commitment of judicial time and resources that would inevitably be required if the case were to be tried here.

[Opinions of Justice Stevens, dissenting (joined by Justice Brennan), and Justice White, concurring in part and dissenting in part, omitted. Neither Justice Powell nor Justice O'Connor took part in the decision.]

Notes and Questions

1. *Transfer:* Plaintiff originally sued in state court in California, but since defendants removed to federal court it was possible to transfer to Pennsylvania, where Piper's plant is located. Under 28 U.S.C.A. § 1404(a), transfer is permitted only to a district where the action might have been brought, which has been interpreted to mean a district in which plaintiff could satisfy both personal jurisdiction and venue requirements as to all defendants. Hoffman v. Blaski, 363 U.S. 335, 80 S.Ct. 1084, 4 L.Ed.2d 1254 (1960). Why was Pennsylvania such a jurisdiction?

§ 1404(a) directs the court to transfer "[f]or the convenience of parties and witnesses, in the interest of justice." In general, it is said that the showing for a transfer need not be so compelling as that required for a forum non conveniens dismissal. How should the California court have evaluated these factors in connection with Piper's transfer motion? What information would it need to make its decision?

Hartzell moved to dismiss in the California federal court on the ground that it was not subject to personal jurisdiction there. Recall Asahi Metal Industry Co. v. Superior Court, supra p. 765. Assuming that there was no valid basis for jurisdiction over Hartzell in California, the California federal court nevertheless could transfer because 28 U.S.C.A. § 1406(a) permits transfer where suit is filed in a district that is not a proper venue. In Goldlawr, Inc. v. Heiman, 369 U.S. 463, 82 S.Ct. 913, 8 L.Ed.2d 39 (1962), the Court held that this allowed transfer even if jurisdiction were improper in the original district because that would "remov[e] whatever obstacles may impede an expeditious and orderly adjudication of cases and controversies on their merits." *Should* a court without jurisdiction do so? In Nichols v. G.D. Searle & Co., 991 F.2d 1195 (4th Cir.1993), the court upheld the district court's refusal to transfer, reasoning that "a district court acts within its discretion when it finds that the interest of justice is not served by allowing a plaintiff whose attorney committed an obvious error in filing the plaintiff's action in the wrong court, and thereby imposed substantial unnecessary costs on both the defendant and the legal system, simply to transfer his/her action to the proper court, with no cost to him/herself or his/her attorney." Id. at 1201. Compare Cottman Transmission Systems, Inc. v. Martino, 36 F.3d 291 (3d Cir.1994) (it was an abuse of discretion to transfer as to one defendant because venue was improper with respect to it while retaining claim against another defendant where the two claims were directly connected; claims against both should have been transferred).

Given the ultimate disposition of the case, it would seem that the California federal court might better have dismissed the entire action on forum non conveniens grounds. Where the showing of inconvenience is sufficient to justify dismissal, is transfer nevertheless preferable? The consensus has been that, in federal court, the court should transfer rather than dismiss no matter how forceful the showing, an attitude that compounds choice of law problems (see note 2 below).

Yet another transfer provision is 28 U.S.C.A. § 1407, which authorizes the Judicial Panel on Multidistrict Litigation to transfer all cases raising common questions of fact or law to a single district for all pretrial purposes. This provision has been used in connection with several suits resulting from crashes of large airplanes, where hundreds of people have been injured or killed. In Lexecon v. Milberg Weiss Bershad Hynes & Lerach, 523 U.S. 26, 118 S.Ct. 956, 140 L.Ed.2d 62 (1998), the Court disallowed a practice that had been used frequently by the lower courts, which allowed the judge who received a transfer under § 1407 to use § 1404(a) to keep the cases so transferred for pretrial purposes for all purposes, including trial.

2. *Choice of law:* Choice of law complications arise after transfer. The problem is whether the defendant should get "a change of law as a bonus for a change of venue" if transfer is granted. See Wells v. Simonds Abrasive Co., 345 U.S. 514, 522, 73 S.Ct. 856, 860, 97 L.Ed. 1211 (1953) (Jackson, J., dissenting). In Van Dusen v. Barrack, 376 U.S. 612, 84 S.Ct. 805, 11 L.Ed.2d 945 (1964), the Court interpreted the statute as preserving the plaintiff's choice of law resulting from the freedom to select the initial forum under broad venue provisions, so that the transferee court applies the law that would have been applied in the transferor court. In some ways this seems illogical. Consider Marcus, Conflicts Among Circuits and Transfer Within the Federal Judicial System, 93 Yale L.J. 677, 698 (1984):

> The transfer section is intended, on a case-by-case basis, to accomplish the original objective of venue provisions and limit a plaintiff's ability to impose undue geographical burdens on a defendant. Once plaintiff's original choice of forum has been overridden by a transfer, the reason for giving plaintiff a broad choice of venues in the first place ceases to apply. Indeed, any connection between the convenience of the forum and the choice of law would point to preferring the law of the transferee. Ironically, however, even though his choice of location has been taken away from him, plaintiff's incidental choice of law is still protected under a theory of acquired rights.

This outcome, however, merely recognizes that, within constitutional limits on choice of law, states may select the law to apply. There is no federal principle that overrides that choice, and § 1404(a) was not intended to be one. Indeed, in Ferens v. John Deere Co., 494 U.S. 516, 110 S.Ct. 1274, 108 L.Ed.2d 443 (1990), the Court held that transferor law applies even if the *plaintiff* makes the § 1404(a) motion. The Court reasoned that otherwise plaintiffs would not make such motions, and that defendants who chose not to make them would thereby inflict on plaintiffs (and the court) the inconvenience of trial in a distant forum. Justice Scalia dissented, arguing that it was "unlikely that Congress meant to provide the plaintiff with a vehicle by which to appropriate the law of a distant and inconvenient forum in which he does not intend to litigate, and to carry that prize back to the State in which he wishes to try the case." But where, as with Hartzell, the original forum lacked jurisdiction or venue, the law of the transferee will apply after the transfer. Ellis v. Great Southwestern Corp., 646 F.2d 1099 (5th Cir. 1981).

3. The district court in Pennsylvania concluded that Pennsylvania law would apply to the claim against Piper, and the Court of Appeals concluded that Ohio law would apply to the claim against Hartzell. The Supreme Court does not reject these conclusions. Does the fact that American law would be applied indicate that there is an American interest in having this case decided under American law? Under Klaxon Co. v. Stentor Electric Mfg. Co.,

313 U.S. 487, 61 S.Ct. 1020, 85 L.Ed. 1477 (1941), a district court sitting in a diversity case must apply the choice of law rules of the state in which it sits. Does forum non conveniens threaten to undermine this system? Consider Stein, Forum Non Conveniens and the Redundancy of Court–Access Doctrine, 133 U.Pa.L.Rev. 781, 827–28 (1985): "[T]he district court in *Reyno* would not have been permitted to disregard Pennsylvania's interest analysis for choice-of-law purposes simply because it believed that Scottish interests in the controversy were paramount. Nonetheless, the very same result— application of Scottish law in a Scottish court—was achieved for the very same reason—paramount Scottish interests."

Balanced against an American interest in applying American law is the spectre of a flood of essentially foreign cases clogging American courts. How realistic is this concern? Consider the views of an English judge in Smith Kline & French Laboratories Ltd. v. Bloch, [1983] 1 W.L.R. 730 (C.A. 1982):

> As a moth is drawn to the light, so is a litigant drawn to the United States. If he can only get his case into their courts, he stands to win a fortune. At no cost to himself, and at no risk of having to pay anything to the other side. The lawyers there will conduct the case "on spec" as we say, or on a "contingency fee" as they say. * * * There is also in the United States a right to trial by jury. These are prone to award fabulous damages. They are notoriously sympathetic and know that the lawyers will take their 40 per cent. All this means that the defendant can be readily forced into a settlement. The plaintiff holds all the cards.

4. While upholding dismissal, the Court reiterates the ordinary refrain that the plaintiff's choice of forum is not to be disturbed except upon a compelling showing. Similar language can be found in transfer cases under § 1404(a). Why should plaintiff be accorded this solicitude in close cases (i.e., where the choice of forum seems highly questionable)?

In *Reyno,* the Court avoids this roadblock by saying that the plaintiff's choice is not important when she is foreign. Does this mean a non-American, or a person not suing in her home state? In any event, why should it matter? Had one of the victims of the crash had a daughter living in Los Angeles who filed a wrongful death action there, would the fact that she had sued at home invoke the presumption in her favor? If the presumption depends on the presence of witnesses and evidence in the forum, then what does the fact that it is plaintiff's home add to the weight of those factors?

In Iragorri v. United Technologies Corp., 274 F.3d 65 (2d Cir.2001), the court explored the weight the court should give to plaintiff's interest in suing in the forum. Plaintiffs were U.S. domiciliaries but nationals of Colombia suing for an injury that was inflicted in Colombia. They sued in Connecticut, although they lived in Florida, because two of the defendants had headquarters there. The district court dismissed on forum non conveniens grounds, but the appellate court vacated for further consideration. It found the Supreme Court's observations about suit in this country by foreigners to be "part of a broader principle under which the degree of deference to be given to a plaintiff's choice of forum moves on a sliding scale. * * * The more it appears that a domestic or foreign plaintiff's choice of form has been dictated by reasons that the law recognizes as valid, the greater the deference that will be given to the plaintiff's forum choice." This, in turn, should look to whether there is a "bona fide connection" between the suit and the U.S. The fact that plaintiffs here were not living in Connecticut should not be controlling since they had to sue where they could get personal jurisdiction. Compare Iragorri v. International Elevator, Inc., 203 F.3d 8 (1st Cir.2000) (upholding dismissal of the same plaintiffs' claim against a different defendant arising out of the same incident in Colombia).

5. Note that the court may, while dismissing, require defendant to make certain concessions to plaintiff in connection with litigation elsewhere. Courts often require stipulations waiving statutes of limitation or consenting to jurisdiction before agreeing to dismiss on forum non conveniens grounds. There are limits on the power to insist on such conditions. In In re Union Carbide Corp. Gas Plant Disaster at Bhopal, India, 809 F.2d 195 (2d Cir.), cert. denied, 484 U.S. 871, 108 S.Ct. 199, 98 L.Ed.2d 150 (1987), the district judge required Union Carbide to agree to discovery in India according to the Federal Rules of Civil Procedure, which are much broader than Indian practice, as a condition for dismissing. Is it appropriate for an American court thus to supplant Indian procedure? The appellate court revoked the condition because "[b]asic justice requires that both sides be treated equally."

6. The Court says that, even where dismissal otherwise is appropriate, it may be denied if the foreign remedy is "no remedy at all." What does this mean? In footnote 22, it favorably cites a case that refused to dismiss unjust enrichment tort claims because the law of Ecuador, the alternative forum, did not recognize such claims. But why isn't Scotland's decision not to allow strict liability claims similarly a bar to dismissal? See Aquinda v. Texaco, Inc., 303 F.3d 470 (9th Cir.2002) (upholding dismissal of suit for environmental harm by citizens of Ecuador despite plaintiffs' contentions that there were no parallel claims under local law and that the courts in Ecuador were not independent).

7. It should be obvious that the forum non conveniens decision and the transfer decision require consideration of a great variety of factors that must be evaluated with reference to a very general standard. Yet the Court emphasizes that the trial court's decision should not be disturbed unless it is an abuse of discretion. Given all the effort put into policing jurisdictional and venue decisions, is it appropriate for the appellate courts to abdicate responsibility in this manner? Would a district court decision *not* to dismiss in *Reyno* have been an abuse of discretion?

8. Would the outcome have been different had the case not been removed to federal court? Although there is a uniform act that would permit conditional dismissals to effect something like a § 1404(a) transfer, the act has not been widely adopted by states and, even if it were, the act would not permit state courts to transfer to other state courts. At the time this suit was filed, California law precluded forum non conveniens dismissals of suits by California residents. Had a California state court dismissed on forum non conveniens grounds, plaintiff would have had to file a new suit in Pennsylvania and there would have been no question that California choice of law rules would not apply with respect to Piper. Should *Van Dusen* (supra note 2) be interpreted to have the same result where the case is removed? See Caribbean Wholesales & Serv. Corp. v. US JVC Corp., 855 F.Supp. 627 (S.D.N.Y.1994) (*Van Dusen* inapplicable if action would have been dismissed on forum non conveniens grounds in state court).

Chapter X

CHOOSING THE FORUM—STATE v. FEDERAL COURT

Putting aside questions of geographical location, plaintiff must also select a court with authority to decide the case. Court systems may assign different authority to different courts. Thus, many states have simplified small claims courts with jurisdiction over claims up to a certain dollar limit, and some direct that certain types of claims (such as divorce or probate matters) be handled by specialized courts. Most states have one court of "general" jurisdiction as well.

Problems of selecting the proper court raise issues entirely separate from the problems of personal jurisdiction we considered in the previous chapter. Hence, one may say generally that plaintiff must select a court that has personal jurisdiction over the defendant and subject matter jurisdiction over the claim. Do not confuse the two concepts.

The various allocations of jurisdiction in state court systems are beyond the scope of this book. Instead, we will focus on the limited subject matter jurisdiction of the federal courts. For most purposes, the existence of federal jurisdiction is the same whether the plaintiff has initially sued in federal court, or the defendant has "removed" the case to federal court from state court.

A. DIVERSITY OF CITIZENSHIP

In the Judiciary Act of 1789 Congress vested federal courts with jurisdiction of cases in which there was diversity of citizenship in the predecessor to 28 U.S.C.A. § 1332. In Strawbridge v. Curtiss, 7 U.S. (3 Cranch) 267, 2 L.Ed. 435 (1806), the Court held that the statute required "complete diversity," that no defendant come from the same state as any plaintiff. Read Article III §§ 1 and 2 of the Constitution, section 1332 and Rule 8(a)(1).

MAS v. PERRY

United States Court of Appeals, Fifth Circuit, 1974.
489 F.2d 1396.

Before WISDOM, AINSWORTH and CLARK, CIRCUIT JUDGES.

AINSWORTH, CIRCUIT JUDGE.

This case presents questions pertaining to federal diversity jurisdiction under 28 U.S.C.A. § 1332, which, pursuant to article III, section 2 of the Constitution, provides for original jurisdiction in federal district courts of all civil actions that are between, inter alia, citizens of different States or citizens of a State and citizens of foreign states and in which the amount in controversy is more than $10,000.

Appellees Jean Paul Mas, a citizen of France, and Judy Mas were married at her home in Jackson, Mississippi. Prior to their marriage, Mr. and Mrs. Mas were graduate assistants, pursuing coursework as well as performing teaching duties, for approximately nine months and one year, respectively, at Louisiana State University in Baton Rouge, Louisiana. Shortly after their marriage, they returned to Baton Rouge to resume their duties as graduate assistants at LSU. They remained in Baton Rouge for approximately two more years, after which they moved to Park Ridge, Illinois. At the time of the trial in this case, it was their intention to return to Baton Rouge while Mr. Mas finished his studies for the degree of Doctor of Philosophy. Mr. and Mrs. Mas were undecided as to where they would reside after that.

Upon their return to Baton Rouge after their marriage, appellees rented an apartment from appellant Oliver H. Perry, a citizen of Louisiana. This appeal arises from a final judgment entered on a jury verdict awarding $5,000 to Mr. Mas and $15,000 to Mrs. Mas for damages incurred by them as a result of the discovery that their bedroom and bathroom contained "two-way" mirrors and that they had been watched through them by the appellant during three of the first four months of their marriage.

At the close of the appellees' case at trial, appellant made an oral motion to dismiss for lack of jurisdiction. The motion was denied by the district court. Before this Court, appellant challenges the final judgment below solely on jurisdictional grounds, contending that appellees failed to prove diversity of citizenship among the parties and that the requisite jurisdictional amount is lacking with respect to Mr. Mas. Finding no merit to these contentions, we affirm. Under section 1332(a)(2), the federal judicial power extends to the claim of Mr. Mas, a citizen of France, against the appellant, a citizen of Louisiana. Since we conclude that Mrs. Mas is a citizen of Mississippi for diversity purposes, the district court also properly had jurisdiction under section 1332(a)(1) of her claim.

It has long been the general rule that complete diversity of parties is required in order that diversity jurisdiction obtain; that is, no party on one side may be a citizen of the same State as any party on the other side. Strawbridge v. Curtiss, 7 U.S. (3 Cranch) 267, 2 L.Ed. 435 (1806). This determination of one's State citizenship for diversity purposes is controlled by federal law, not by the law of any State. As is the case in other areas of federal jurisdiction, the diverse citizenship among adverse parties must be present at the time the complaint is filed. Jurisdiction is unaffected by subsequent changes in the citizenship of the parties. The burden of pleading the diverse citizenship is upon the party invoking federal jurisdiction, and if the diversity jurisdiction is properly challenged, that party also bears the burden of proof.

To be a citizen of a State within the meaning of section 1332, a natural person must be both a citizen of the United States, and a domiciliary of that State. For diversity purposes, citizenship means domicile; mere residence in the State is not sufficient.

A person's domicile is the place of "his true, fixed, and permanent home and principal establishment, and to which he has the intention of returning whenever he is absent therefrom...." A change of domicile may be effected only by a combination of two elements: (a) taking up residence in a different domicile with (b) the intention to remain there.

It is clear that at the time of her marriage, Mrs. Mas was a domiciliary of the State of Mississippi. While it is generally the case that the domicile of the wife—and, consequently, her State citizenship for purposes of diversity jurisdiction—is deemed to be that of her husband, we find no precedent for extending this concept to the situation here, in which the husband is a citizen of a foreign state but resides in the United States. Indeed, such a fiction would work absurd results on the facts before us. If Mr. Mas were considered a domiciliary of France—as he would be since he had lived in Louisiana as a student-teaching assistant prior to filing this suit—then Mrs. Mas would also be deemed a domiciliary, and thus, fictionally at least, a citizen of France. She would not be a citizen of any State and could not sue in a federal court on that basis; nor could she invoke the alienage jurisdiction to bring her claim in federal court, since she is not an alien. On the other hand, if Mrs. Mas's domicile were Louisiana, she would become a Louisiana citizen for diversity purposes and could not bring suit with her husband against appellant, also a Louisiana citizen, on the basis of diversity jurisdiction. These are curious results under a rule arising from the theoretical identity of person and interest of the married couple.

An American woman is not deemed to have lost her United States citizenship solely by reason of her marriage to an alien. 8 U.S.C. § 1489. Similarly, we conclude that for diversity purposes a woman does not have her domicile or State citizenship changed solely by reason of her marriage to an alien.

Mrs. Mas's Mississippi domicile was disturbed neither by her year in Louisiana prior to her marriage nor as a result of the time she and her husband spent at LSU. Though she testified that after her marriage she had no intention of returning to her parents' home in Mississippi, Mrs.

Mas did not effect a change of domicile since she and Mr. Mas were in Louisiana only as students and lacked the requisite intention to remain there. Until she acquires a new domicile, she remains a domiciliary, and thus a citizen, of Mississippi.[2]

Appellant also contends that Mr. Mas's claim should have been dismissed for failure to establish the requisite jurisdictional amount for diversity cases of more than $10,000. In their complaint Mr. and Mrs. Mas alleged that they had each been damaged in the amount of $100,000. As we have noted, Mr. Mas ultimately recovered $5,000.

It is well settled that the amount in controversy is determined by the amount claimed by the plaintiff in good faith. Federal jurisdiction is not lost because a judgment of less than the jurisdictional amount is awarded. That Mr. Mas recovered only $5,000 is, therefore, not compelling. As the Supreme Court stated in St. Paul Mercury Indemnity Co. v. Red Cab Co., 303 U.S. 283, 288–290, 58 S.Ct. 586, 590–591, 82 L.Ed. 845:

> The sum claimed by the plaintiff controls if the claim is apparently made in good faith.

> It must appear to a legal certainty that the claim is really for less than the jurisdictional amount to justify dismissal. The inability of the plaintiff to recover an amount adequate to give the court jurisdiction does not show his bad faith or oust the jurisdiction. . . .

> . . . His good faith in choosing the federal forum is open to challenge not only by resort to the face of his complaint, but by the facts disclosed at trial, and if from either source it is clear that his claim never could have amounted to the sum necessary to give jurisdiction there is no injustice in dismissing the suit.

Having heard the evidence presented at the trial, the district court concluded that the appellees properly met the requirements of section 1332 with respect to jurisdictional amount. Upon examination of the record in this case, we are also satisfied that the requisite amount was in controversy.

Thus the power of the federal district court to entertain the claims of appellees in this case stands on two separate legs of diversity jurisdiction: a claim by an alien against a State citizen; and an action between citizens of different States. We also note, however, the propriety of having the federal district court entertain a spouse's action against a defendant, where the district court already has jurisdiction over a claim, arising from the same transaction, by the other spouse against the same defendant. In the case before us, such a result is particularly desirable. The claims of Mr. and Mrs. Mas arise from the same operative facts, and

---

2. The original complaint in this case was filed within several days of Mr. and Mrs. Mas's realization that they had been watched through the mirrors, quite some time before they moved to Park Ridge, Illinois. Because the district court's jurisdiction is not affected by actions of the parties subsequent to the commencement of the suit, the testimony concerning Mr. and Mrs. Mas's moves after that time is not determinative of the issue of diverse citizenship, though it is of interest insofar as it supports their lack of intent to remain permanently in Louisiana.

there was almost complete interdependence between their claims with respect to the proof required and the issues raised at trial. Thus, since the district court had jurisdiction of Mr. Mas's action, sound judicial administration militates strongly in favor of federal jurisdiction of Mrs. Mas's claim.

Notes and Questions

1. Since the above decision, 28 U.S.C.A. § 1332(a) has been amended to provide that "an alien admitted to the United States for permanent residence shall be deemed the citizen of the state in which such alien is domiciled." Had this provision been in effect when Mas v. Perry was filed, would the result have been different? See Singh v. Daimler–Benz, AG, 800 F.Supp. 260, 262 (E.D.Pa.1992), affirmed, 9 F.3d 303 (3d Cir.1993) ("The clear language of § 1332 establishes that when an alien receives permanent resident status the alien is no longer an alien for diversity purposes, but is instead a citizen of the state in which he or she resides"); Miller v. Thermarite Pty. Ltd., 793 F.Supp. 306, 307 (S.D.Ala.1992) ("it is clear that the statute affects only the status of those aliens with 'green cards' ").

The goal of the statutory change was to prevent suits in federal court based on diversity of citizenship when the parties were both permanent residents of the same state. Read literally, however, the statute expanded federal subject matter jurisdiction by creating the possibility there might be diversity in an action between a resident alien and an alien domiciled in a different state or a nonresident alien. That, however, would raise constitutional problems. See C. Wright & M. Kane, Law of Federal Courts 156 (6th ed. 2002) (concluding that the power of Congress to open courts to suit between resident aliens domiciled in different states is "extremely doubtful"). In Saadeh v. Farouki, 107 F.3d 52 (D.C.Cir.1997), the court held that the statute did not authorize this expansion of federal jurisdiction, partly to avoid constitutional difficulties. Compare Singh v. Daimler–Benz AG, 9 F.3d 303 (3d Cir.1993) (finding that statute allows suit in federal court between aliens because one was domiciled in American state).

2. Why is there federal jurisdiction for cases involving citizens of different states? The historical record is rather thin on the question, but the usual reason offered is that diversity jurisdiction was intended to afford a safety valve against local prejudice against outsiders. If that is true, why should it not be sufficient to justify federal jurisdiction that there is a risk of local prejudice against husband Mas? In terms of this purpose, the complete diversity requirement is hard to justify: "[W]ho can say whether a Vermont jury, concentrating attention on the one Vermont defendant, would shut its eyes to the merits of the complainants' case, or, realizing that its fellow citizen was only one of a crowd, would deal fairly and squarely with all? A theory so little founded on realities could hardly be expected to furnish a satisfactory answer to a new and difficult question." Friendly, The Historic Basis of Diversity Jurisdiction, 41 Harv.L.Rev. 483, 509 (1928). A similar rule is generally said to apply with regard to suits involving aliens; diversity does not exist if there are aliens on both sides of the case. Ruhrgas AG v. Marathon Oil Co., 526 U.S. 574, 119 S.Ct. 1563, 143 L.Ed.2d 760 (1999) (joinder of alien plaintiff and alien defendant defeats complete diversity).

3. Whatever the wisdom of the complete diversity rule, the Court made clear in State Farm Fire & Cas. Co. v. Tashire, supra p. 268, that it is not constitutionally required. It upheld the requirement of "minimal diversity" in the federal interpleader statute: "Article III poses no obstacle to the legislative extension of federal jurisdiction, founded on diversity, so long as any two adverse parties are not co-citizens."

4. As Mas v. Perry demonstrates, the trigger for diversity jurisdiction is the concept of domicile, which is slightly different from residence. In a highly mobile society like ours, does this difference matter? The idea, as indicated in Mas v. Perry, is that a person must be present in a new state with the intention to remain before domicile changes. In Poucher v. Intercounty Appliance Corp., 336 F.Supp.2d 251 (E.D.N.Y.2004), the court therefore held that there was no diversity between a prisoner incarcerated in California and a New York corporation because plaintiff had been a New Yorker before beginning his involuntary stay in California. Compare Rishell v. Jane Phillips Episcopal Memorial Medical Center, 12 F.3d 171 (10th Cir.1993) (finding an exception to the normal rule requiring conscious intention to change domicile in case of a move involving an incompetent person is incapable of forming the necessary intent to change domicile).

How should this test apply to the wife in Mas v. Perry? One possibility would be to consider her to share the domicile of her husband, France. If so, she would fall into what might be called the "expatriate exception" to diversity jurisdiction. See Newman–Green, Inc. v. Alfonzo–Larrain, 490 U.S. 826, 828, 109 S.Ct. 2218, 104 L.Ed.2d 893 (1989) ("The problem in this case is that Bettison, although a United States citizen, has no domicile in any State. He is therefore 'stateless' for purposes of § 1332(a)(2)."). But in an era of bicoastal marriages, the notion that wives always share their husbands' domicile seems outdated. Alternatively, should she still be considered a Mississippi citizen even though she has no intention to return? She says she has not decided where to live for the long term; could she be regarded as "stateless" even though she remains in the U.S.?

5. It should be apparent that diversity jurisdiction is often manipulable. 28 U.S.C.A. § 1359 seeks to control such manipulation: "A district court shall not have jurisdiction of a civil action in which any party, by assignment or otherwise, has been improperly or collusively made or joined to invoke the jurisdiction of such court." In Kramer v. Caribbean Mills, Inc., 394 U.S. 823, 89 S.Ct. 1487, 23 L.Ed.2d 9 (1969), a Panamanian corporation assigned its claim against a Haitian corporation to a Texas lawyer in return for one dollar and a promise that the Texan would remit 95% of any amounts he recovered. The assignment was admittedly intended to create diversity, but it was evidently valid as a matter of Texas law. The Court nevertheless held that this strategy would not create diversity for jurisdictional purposes: "If federal jurisdiction could be created by assignments of this kind, which are easy to arrange and involve few disadvantages for the assignor, then a vast quantity of ordinary contract and tort litigation could be channelled into the federal courts at the will of one of the parties." At the same time, the Court was careful to note that "where the transfer of a claim is absolute, with the transferor retaining no interest in the subject matter, then the transfer is not 'improperly or collusively made,' regardless of the transferor's motive."

6. Before 1988, there was much opportunity to create or defeat diversity when a claim was made on behalf of an estate by selecting an executor or administrator of the desired citizenship. Cf. Piper Aircraft Co. v. Reyno, supra p. 847. In 1988, Congress amended 28 U.S.C.A. § 1332(c) to provide that for purposes of diversity the representative of an estate would be deemed a citizen of the same state as the decedent. For discussion, see Nicolas, Fighting the Probate Mafia: A Dissection of the Probate Exception to Federal Court Jurisdiction, 74 S.Cal.L.Rev. 1479 (2001).

7. Problems have also arisen in determining whether there is diversity when plaintiff names fictitious "John Doe" defendants. Recall Swartz v. Gold Dust Casinos, supra p. 218. In general, it is said that for a plaintiff to sue Doe defendants in federal court on grounds of diversity she must plead that they are of diverse citizenship. See C. Wright & M. Kane, Law of Federal Courts 190 (6th ed. 2002). For purposes of removal on grounds of diversity of a case originally filed in state court, 28 U.S.C.A. § 1441(a) provides that defendants sued under fictitious names shall be disregarded.

8. Given the fatal consequences of lack of subject matter jurisdiction, defendants may be tempted to lull plaintiffs into thinking that jurisdiction is proper until it is too late to file suit in state court. For example, in Itel Containers Intern. Corp. v. Puerto Rico Marine Mgmt., Inc., 108 F.R.D. 96 (D.N.J.1985), the court found that defense counsel had knowingly concealed the absence of diversity from plaintiff and the court in hopes that the statute of limitations would run before the truth was discovered. This effort involved filing inadequate responses to plaintiff's complaint, providing misleading answers to interrogatories and even filing a counterclaim over which defendant knew the court had no jurisdiction. When the truth was discovered on the eve of trial, the court held that defendant's attorneys should be sanctioned for violating Rules 7, 11 and 26(g) and imposed a sanction of over $40,000 on them personally. See also Wojan v. General Motors Corp., 851 F.2d 969 (7th Cir.1988) (after dismissing for lack of diversity, court retains jurisdiction to punish defendant for falsely admitting existence of diversity); Note, Second Bites at the Jurisdictional Apple: A Proposal for Preventing False Assertions of Diversity of Citizenship, 41 Hast.L.J. 1417 (1990) (urging estoppel against belated challenges to existence of diversity). Is it wise to have rules of subject matter jurisdiction that invite such chicanery?

9. Regarding corporate parties, section 1332(c) provides that a corporation is a citizen of any state in which it is incorporated and "the state where it has its principal place of business." Determining where a corporation's principal place of business is located is sometimes challenging. Courts usually use a "total activity" test, looking to where the bulk of corporate activity takes place. C. Wright & M. Kane, Law of Federal Courts 169–70 (6th ed. 2002). This analysis can sometimes lead to surprising results. In Teal Energy USA, Inc. v. GT, Inc., 369 F.3d 873 (5th Cir.2004), the court held there was no jurisdiction over a suit between a corporation with its headquarters in Canada and another that was incorporated in Nevada and held no certificate to transact business in Texas because they should both be considered Texas citizens for diversity purposes. The Canadian company was the subsidiary of another Canadian company created to do business in the U.S. and doing most of that business in Texas. Even though all decisions about its activities were made at headquarters in Calgary, Canada, the "total

activity" test indicated that its main activities were in Texas. The Nevada corporation had all its assets and officers in Texas, and the absence of authority to do business in that state did not prevent it from being a Texas citizen. See also Ghaderi v. United Airlines, Inc., 136 F.Supp.2d 1041 (N.D.Cal.2001) (United Airlines, though headquartered in Chicago, Ill., should be considered a California citizen because California is home to the largest proportion of United employees and the company derives more income from California than from any other state). As the size and economic power of California grow, will corporations that do substantial business there all be considered California citizens? Would that result conflict with the purposes of diversity jurisdiction?

10. Other groupings of people may cause more difficulty. Unlike corporations, unincorporated associations are not treated as separate entities for diversity purposes, and in determining diversity one must consider the citizenship of all members of the association. See United Steelworkers of America v. R.H. Bouligny, Inc., 382 U.S. 145, 86 S.Ct. 272, 15 L.Ed.2d 217 (1965). In Carden v. Arkoma Associates, 494 U.S. 185, 110 S.Ct. 1015, 108 L.Ed.2d 157 (1990), the Court refused to liken a limited partnership to a corporation and therefore to consider only the citizenship of the full partners. Even though the limited partners had little or no right to influence the operation of the enterprise, and were therefore in a position similar to the shareholders of a corporation, the Court held that their citizenship should be counted for purposes of determining the existence of diversity. In Cresswell v. Sullivan & Cromwell, 922 F.2d 60 (2d Cir.1990), the court decided that defendant law firm could not be sued in federal court on diversity grounds because it was a partnership including U.S. nationals who are domiciled abroad. See also Indiana Gas Co. v. Home Ins. Co., 141 F.3d 314 (7th Cir.), cert. denied, 525 U.S. 931, 119 S.Ct. 339, 142 L.Ed.2d 280 (1998) (holding that the underwriting syndicate known as Lloyd's of London has the citizenship, for diversity purposes, of every "name," or investor, and that presence of one from Indiana would defeat diversity in suit brought by Indiana plaintiff); compare Certain Interested Underwriters at Lloyd's of London v. Layne, 26 F.3d 39 (6th Cir.1994) (as real party in interest, only Lloyd's need be considered in determining diversity).

In Navarro Savings Ass'n v. Lee, 446 U.S. 458, 100 S.Ct. 1779, 64 L.Ed.2d 425 (1980), the Court held that for a Massachusetts business trust only the citizenship of the trustees need be considered in determining diversity because they possess "certain customary powers to hold, manage, and dispose of assets for the benefit of others." See also Supreme Tribe of Ben–Hur v. Cauble, 255 U.S. 356, 41 S.Ct. 338, 65 L.Ed. 673 (1921) (in class action only the citizenship of the class representatives need be considered in determining diversity). Compare Cote v. Wadel, 796 F.2d 981 (7th Cir.1986), in which the court held that a law firm organized as a professional corporation should be treated as such: "To paraphrase Gertrude Stein, for purposes of diversity jurisdiction a corporation is a corporation is a corporation."

11. Even where diversity is present, federal courts have traditionally refused to entertain certain kinds of cases. One category is cases involving domestic relations issues. In Ankenbrandt v. Richards, 504 U.S. 689, 112 S.Ct. 2206, 119 L.Ed.2d 468 (1992), plaintiff sued her former husband on behalf of their children, for damages for abuse of the children while they

were visiting their father. The district court dismissed, but the Supreme Court reversed. While concluding that "[t]he domestic relations exception * * * divests the federal courts of power to issue divorce, alimony, and child custody decrees," the Court found this exception inapplicable to plaintiffs' suit for money. Compare Congleton v. Holy Cross Child Placement Agency, Inc., 919 F.2d 1077 (5th Cir.1990) (challenge by birth mother to contract under which she gave up child for adoption was really not just a breach of contract action but an effort to obtain custody of child and therefore beyond federal jurisdiction). Another category in which federal courts refuse jurisdiction despite diversity involves cases regarding probating of an estate. See In re Marshall, 392 F.3d 1118 (9th Cir.2004) (despite diversity, federal court lacked jurisdiction over claim by widow Anna Nichole Smith for tortious interference with her receipt of a gift from her aged husband because the claim had to be asserted in a Texas probate court).

12. Plaintiffs can cure jurisdictional problems created by the lack of complete diversity by dismissing as to the nondiverse defendant unless that defendant is indispensable under Rule 19(b). In Newman–Green, Inc. v. Alfonzo–Larrain, 490 U.S. 826, 109 S.Ct. 2218, 104 L.Ed.2d 893 (1989), the Court held that Rule 21 permits this solution even if the case is on appeal when the lack-of-diversity problem appears. Compare Grupo Dataflux v. Atlas Global Group, L.P., 541 U.S. 567, 124 S.Ct. 1920, 158 L.Ed.2d 866 (2004), holding that the departure of two non-diverse partners from plaintiff partnership due to commercial developments before trial could not cure the lack of diversity at the beginning of the lawsuit. Four justices dissented, arguing that jurisdiction should be found because there had been minimal diversity throughout, and complete diversity by the time of trial.

AMOUNT IN CONTROVERSY

To qualify for federal jurisdiction on grounds of diversity, plaintiff must establish not only complete diversity but also that more than $75,000 is in controversy. From the outset, there has been such a monetary minimum for federal jurisdiction. In 1789, it was set at $500. It was increased to $2,000 in 1887, $3,000 in 1911, to $10,000 in 1958, to $50,000 in 1988, and to $75,000 in 1996. There have been suggestions to "index" the figure so it could fluctuate in accordance with the Consumer Price Index or some similar measure of inflation. The idea behind this minimum is to exclude inconsequential cases from the federal courts while keeping the federal court doors open to all and not just the well-to-do.

In Mas v. Perry, defendant argued that plaintiff husband, who had recovered only $5,000, had not satisfied the jurisdictional minimum requirement. Rejecting this argument, the court quoted the governing standard from St. Paul Mercury Indem. Co. v. Red Cab Co., 303 U.S. 283, 58 S.Ct. 586, 82 L.Ed. 845 (1938). See p. 863 supra. Reread that standard and consider the difficulties that arise in applying it, discussed below.

Notes and Questions

1. In Mas v. Perry, both husband and wife claimed $100,000 in damages and yet the jury awarded them only $5,000 and $15,000 respective-

ly. Is reference to the amount they ultimately recovered a sensible way of determining good faith? Would the suit have satisfied the jurisdictional minimum requirements if defendant had spied on them only once? If so, would jurisdiction be proper if they had merely been brushing their teeth on that occasion?

2. Suppose defendant in Mas v. Perry had failed to return plaintiffs' security deposit of $150. Could they have satisfied the jurisdictional minimum requirements in a suit for the return of their security deposit by adding a claim for punitive damages of $100,000, or alleging that they suffered severe mental distress as a result and seeking $100,000 compensation for that? In such a situation the court would be faced with two somewhat separate questions. First, as a matter of applicable substantive law, is this sort of recovery permitted? Second, if so, is this claim made in good faith? The questions tend to blend in practice. For example, in Kahal v. J.W. Wilson & Assoc., Inc., 673 F.2d 547 (D.C.Cir.1982), plaintiff alleged that his former employer owed him some $4,000 for overtime wages and liquidated damages. Alleging that defendant had engaged in "a pattern of past practice of willful and wanton aggravated oppression, malice and wicked conduct," plaintiff also prayed for $25,000 in punitive damages. Under the applicable law, however, punitive damages were only available in "rare" cases aggravated by particularly egregious conduct. Because plaintiff's interrogatory answers only impugned defendant's motives and provided no specifics showing such egregious conduct, the court upheld dismissal of the claim for lack of jurisdiction. Compare Cabral v. Willard, 333 F.Supp.2d 1108 (D.Kan.2004) (it was not clear to a legal certainty that plaintiff could not recover more than $75,000 even though her total medical expenses were less than $4,000 and she had not sought medical treatment for pain in the seven months since the last visit to her chiropractor).

3. How carefully should the court scrutinize the claim? Consider Scherer v. Equitable Life Assur. Society, 347 F.3d 394 (2d Cir.2003), in which defendant argued that the amount in controversy requirement was not satisfied because almost all of plaintiff's claims were barred by res judicata, leaving claims insufficient to uphold jurisdiction. The court stressed that jurisdiction had to be determined based on the allegations of the complaint, and rejected defendant's arguments (id. at 397–98):

> [A]ffirmative "defenses asserted on the merits" may not be used to whittle down the amount in controversy. Were such defenses to affect the jurisdictional amount, we have said, "doubt and uncertainty would surround the jurisdictional base of most diversity litigation from complaint to final judgment[, and i]ssues going to a federal court's power to decide would be hopelessly confused with the merits themselves." Even where the complaint itself "discloses the existence of a valid defense," we have declined to consider it in determining whether the jurisdictional test is met.

> The rule that affirmative defenses may not be used in determining the jurisdictional amount does not appear to depend on whether a colorable argument against the defense has been advanced. * * *

> This may seem paradoxical: if it can be said "to a legal certainty" that the defense in question is a winning defense, ought it not be

considered for amount-in-controversy purposes? One plausible answer is that because affirmative defenses can be waived the court cannot *at the time of filing* be certain that any given affirmative defense will be applied to the case.

4. Actions for nonmonetary relief pose great problems. In general, the amount in controversy is to be determined by reference to the value of the relief sought. But courts are split on whether the relief should be valued from the plaintiff's perspective (value to plaintiff) or the defendant's (cost to defendant). For example, in Glenwood Light & Water Co. v. Mutual Light, Heat & Power Co., 239 U.S. 121, 36 S.Ct. 30, 60 L.Ed. 174 (1915), plaintiff sued to restrain defendant from erecting poles and wires in a way that would injure plaintiff's poles and wires. The trial court dismissed because the cost to defendant of changing its method would be less than the jurisdictional amount, but the Supreme Court reversed, holding that plaintiff's right to conduct its business free of wrongful interference had a value far in excess of the jurisdictional amount. Contrast Ronzio v. Denver & Rio Grande R.R., 116 F.2d 604, 606 (10th Cir.1940). There plaintiffs sued the railroad to quiet title to water rights that were worth far less than the jurisdictional amount to plaintiffs but a good deal more to defendant, and the court upheld jurisdiction. See C. Wright & M. Kane, Law of Federal Courts § 34 (6th ed. 2002) (supporting jurisdiction if amount exceeds jurisdictional minimum from either plaintiff's viewpoint or defendant's viewpoint).

5. The joinder rules lead to ironic results regarding aggregation of claims to satisfy the jurisdictional minimum. Thus, not only does Rule 18 allow plaintiff to combine all the claims it has against defendant, no matter how unrelated, into one suit, but the jurisdictional amount issue is resolved with reference to the aggregate total of all the claims. Where several plaintiffs can join under Rule 20 because their claims all derive from the same transaction or occurrence, however, they cannot aggregate these related claims to satisfy the jurisdictional minimum. Similarly, in class actions the Supreme Court held that the claims of class members may not be aggregated to meet the jurisdictional minimum. Snyder v. Harris, 394 U.S. 332, 89 S.Ct. 1053, 22 L.Ed.2d 319 (1969). The Class Action Fairness Act of 2005, however, added § 1332(d), which authorizes jurisdiction over certain class actions in which an aggregate of at least $5 million is sought by the class.

6. Related problems arise with respect to a counterclaim by defendant. If it is permissive, it cannot be added to the amount of the claim to satisfy the amount in controversy requirement where the plaintiff's claim is less than the jurisdictional amount. Even if it is compulsory, considering the counterclaim would run afoul of the notion that jurisdiction must be determined from the face of the plaintiff's complaint. Cf. Louisville & Nashville R.R. v. Mottley, infra p. 871, but see Spectacor Management Group v. Brown, 131 F.3d 120 (3d Cir.1997), cert. denied, 523 U.S. 1120, 118 S.Ct. 1799, 140 L.Ed.2d 939 (1998) (holding that compulsory counterclaim is included in "the substance of the controversy"). In removal situations, a stronger argument can be made for considering the counterclaim if it is compulsory under state law and the defendant would, in effect, be marooned in state court because plaintiff sued there first and has a claim insufficient to satisfy the jurisdictional minimum. Nevertheless, it is difficult to generalize

confidently about the treatment of counterclaims. See generally 14B C. Wright, A. Miller & E. Cooper, Federal Practice & Procedure § 3706.

7. Under *St. Paul Mercury*, the court is not to dismiss unless it concludes that plaintiff's damage claim is not asserted in good faith. Should it impose sanctions under Rule 11 in every instance in which dismissal is appropriate?

8. Until 1980, 28 U.S.C.A. § 1331 also included a requirement that the jurisdictional amount be in controversy for federal question cases, but the requirement was deleted in that year. Why should Congress have removed the limitation for these cases, but left it in place for diversity cases?

B. FEDERAL QUESTION

Article III, § 2 of the Constitution vested the Supreme Court with judicial power extending to "all Cases, in Law and Equity, arising under this Constitution, the Laws of the United States, and Treaties made, or which shall be made, under their Authority." But Congress did not vest the lower federal courts with general jurisdiction over cases raising federal questions until 1875, when it passed the predecessor to 28 U.S.C.A. § 1331: "The district courts shall have original jurisdiction of all civil actions arising under the Constitution, laws, or treaties of the United States."

LOUISVILLE & NASHVILLE R.R. v. MOTTLEY

Supreme Court of the United States, 1908.
211 U.S. 149, 29 S.Ct. 42, 53 L.Ed. 126.

JUSTICE MOODY delivered the opinion of the Court.

The appellees (husband and wife), being residents and citizens of Kentucky, brought this suit in equity in the circuit court of the United States for the western district of Kentucky against the appellant, a railroad company and a citizen of the same state. The object of the suit was to compel the specific performance of the following contract:

Louisville, Ky., Oct. 2d, 1871.

The Louisville & Nashville Railroad Company, in consideration that E. L. Mottley and wife, Annie E. Mottley, have this day released company from all damages or claims for damages for injuries received by them on the 7th of September, 1871, in consequence of a collision of trains on the railroad of said company at Randolph's Station, Jefferson County, Kentucky, hereby agrees to issue free passes on said railroad and branches now existing or to exist, to said E. L. & Annie E. Mottley for the remainder of the present year, and thereafter to renew said passes annually during the lives of said Mottley and wife or either of them.

The bill alleged that in September, 1871, plaintiffs, while passengers upon the defendant railroad, were injured by the defendant's negligence, and released their respective claims for damages in consideration of the agreement for transportation during their lives, expressed in the contract. It is alleged that the contract was performed by the defendant up to January 1, 1907, when the defendant declined to renew the passes. The bill then alleges that the refusal to comply with the contract was based solely upon that part of the act of Congress of June 29, 1906, which forbids the giving of free passes or free transportation. The bill further alleges: First, that the act of Congress referred to does not prohibit the giving of passes under the circumstances of this case; and, second, that, if the law is to be construed as prohibiting such passes, it is in conflict with the 5th Amendment of the Constitution, because it deprives the plaintiffs of their property without due process of law. The defendant demurred to the bill. The judge of the circuit court overruled the demurrer, entered a decree for the relief prayed for, and the defendant appealed directly to this court.

Two questions of law were raised by the demurrer to the bill, were brought here by appeal, and have been argued before us. They are, first, whether that part of the act of Congress of June 29, 1906, which forbids the giving of free passes or the collection of any different compensation for transportation of passengers than that specified in the tariff filed, makes it unlawful to perform a contract for transportation of persons who, in good faith, before the passage of the act, had accepted such contract in satisfaction of a valid cause of action against the railroad; and, second, whether the statute, if it should be construed to render such a contract unlawful, is in violation of the 5th Amendment of the Constitution of the United States. We do not deem it necessary, however, to consider either of these questions, because, in our opinion, the court below was without jurisdiction of the cause. Neither party has questioned that jurisdiction, but it is the duty of this court to see to it that the jurisdiction of the circuit court, which is defined and limited by statute, is not exceeded. This duty we have frequently performed of our own motion.

There was no diversity of citizenship, and it is not and cannot be suggested that there was any ground of jurisdiction, except that the case was a "suit ... arising under the Constitution or laws of the United States." [The Court here cited the predecessor to 28 U.S.C.A. § 1331.] It is the settled interpretation of these words, as used in this statute, conferring jurisdiction, that a suit arises under the Constitution and laws of the United States only when the plaintiff's statement of his own cause of action shows that it is based upon those laws or that Constitution. It is not enough that the plaintiff alleges some anticipated defense to his cause of action, and asserts that the defense is invalidated by some provision of the Constitution of the United States. Although such allegations show that very likely, in the course of the litigation, a question under the Constitution would arise, they do not show that the suit, that is, the plaintiff's original cause of action, arises under the Constitution. * * * [I]n Boston & M. Consol. Copper & S. Min. Co. v. Montana Ore Purchasing Co. 188 U.S. 632, 47 L.Ed. 626, 23 Sup.Ct. 434, the plaintiff brought suit in the circuit court of the United States for the conversion of copper ore and for an injunction against its continuance. The plaintiff then alleged, for the purpose of showing jurisdiction, in substance, that the defendant would set up in defense certain laws of the United States. The cause was held to be beyond the jurisdiction of the circuit court, the court saying, by Mr. Justice Peckham:

> "It would be wholly unnecessary and improper, in order to prove complainant's cause of action, to go into any matters of defense which the defendants might possibly set up, and then attempt to reply to such defense, and thus, if possible, to show that a Federal question might or probably would arise in the course of the trial of the case. To allege such defense and then make an answer to it before the defendant has the opportunity to itself plead or prove its own defense is inconsistent with any known rule of pleading, so far as we are aware, and is improper.

> "The rule is a reasonable and just one that the complainant in the first instance shall be confined to a statement of its cause of action, leaving to the defendant to set up in his answer what his defense is, and, if anything more than a denial of complainant's cause of action, imposing upon the defendant the burden of proving such defense."

* * *

The application of this rule to the case at bar is decisive against the jurisdiction of the circuit court.

Notes and Questions

1. Note that the Court raised subject matter jurisdiction on its own motion. Unlike personal jurisdiction, subject matter jurisdiction is never waived during the course of the case; the parties cannot by agreement confer this type of jurisdiction on a court that does not have it. See Fed.R.Civ.P. 12(h)(3). Is there a reason why the two types of jurisdiction should be treated so differently?

The difference is not so striking in all cases, however. In Ruhrgas AG v. Marathon Oil Co., 526 U.S. 574, 119 S.Ct. 1563, 143 L.Ed.2d 760 (1999), the district court dismissed a removed action for lack of personal jurisdiction even though there were objections to the court's subject-matter jurisdiction. Citing an earlier Supreme Court decision that said subject-matter jurisdiction must be established before a decision on the merits, the court of appeals reversed on the ground that personal jurisdiction may never be resolved before subject-matter jurisdiction. Holding that "there is no unyielding jurisdictional hierarchy," the Supreme Court reversed unanimously. Although subject-matter jurisdictional limitations are not waivable and personal jurisdiction limitations may easily be waived, "[t]hese distinctions do not mean that subject-matter jurisdiction is ever and always the more 'fundamental.'" Accordingly, although usually subject-matter jurisdiction question would come first, a district court has discretion to turn to personal jurisdiction if the subject-matter jurisdiction question presents particularly thorny problems. See Idleman, The Emergence of Jurisdictional Resequencing in the Federal Courts, 87 Cornell L.Rev. 1 (2001) (criticizing this approach).

2. It is generally said that the court's jurisdiction must be determined from the plaintiff's complaint, so the Court's adoption of the *well-pleaded complaint rule* to determine whether there is federal question jurisdiction seems natural. Yet even the Supreme Court has seemed ambivalent about the rule:

> It is possible to conceive of a rational jurisdictional system in which the answer as well as the complaint would be consulted before a determination was made whether the case "arose under" federal law, or in which original and removal jurisdiction were not co-extensive. Indeed, until the 1887 amendments to the 1875 Act [granting federal question jurisdiction to the federal courts], the well-pleaded complaint rule was not applied in full force to cases removed from state court; the defendant's petition for removal could furnish the necessary guarantee that the case necessarily presented a substantial question of federal law. Commentators have repeatedly proposed that some mechanism be established to permit removal of cases in which a federal defense may be dispositive. But those proposals have not been adopted.

Franchise Tax Board v. Construction Laborers Vacation Trust, 463 U.S. 1, 10 n. 9, 103 S.Ct. 2841, 2847 n. 9, 77 L.Ed.2d 420, 431 n. 9 (1983). For an attack on the rule, see Doernberg, There's No Reason For It: It's Just Our Policy: Why the Well–Pleaded Complaint Rule Sabotages the Purpose of Federal Question Jurisdiction, 38 Hast.L.J. 597 (1987). Nonetheless, the Court adheres to the view that "Congress has not authorized removal based on a defense, or anticipated defense federal in character." Rivet v. Regions Bank, 522 U.S. 470, 118 S.Ct. 921, 923 (1998).

Are there justifications for the rule that outweigh its drawbacks? Consider:

(a) The rule requires that the court determine whether the complaint is "well pleaded," so it should disregard superfluous references to federal law that the plaintiff has inserted in an effort to obtain federal jurisdiction. In 1908, it was still thought that distinctions between "ultimate facts" and "mere evidence" could be drawn in a meaningful way, but the adoption of Rule 8(a)(2) shows that the federal system has moved away from that idea. Moreover, as we have seen in Chapter III, distinguishing between matters that are part of plaintiff's pleading burden and those which are affirmative defenses is often difficult. Putting aside these difficulties of application, the rule invites circumvention by the adept; "[i]t is too late in the day to deny that inventive pleading plays some part in conferring jurisdiction upon the federal courts." American Invs–Co Countryside, Inc. v. Riverdale Bank, 596 F.2d 211, 216 (7th Cir.1979).

(b) Assuming that distinctions between proper and improper pleading, and between defenses and claims, can be made, do those distinctions provide a sensible guiding line for federal jurisdiction? Is there less federal interest in a federal defense than a federal issue properly included in plaintiff's complaint? Consider a libel action against a newspaper which claims that the First Amendment protects its right to publish. Although the freedom of speech issue is a defense, it is surely one in which there is a great federal interest. Indeed, the Supremacy Clause, U.S. Const. art. VI, commands state judges to hear the First Amendment defense. Was Congress anxious to assure access to a federal judge for litigants raising such issues when it created federal question jurisdiction?

3. Could a federal-law counterclaim be a basis for federal-question jurisdiction? Consider the Supreme Court's analysis of a slightly different question in The Holmes Group, Inc. v. Vornado Air Circulation Systems, Inc., 535 U.S. 826, 122 S.Ct. 1889, 153 L.Ed.2d 13 (2002):

> Allowing a counterclaim to establish "arising under" jurisdiction would also contravene the longstanding policies underlying our precedents. First, since the plaintiff is "the master of the complaint," the well-pleaded-complaint rule enables him, "by eschewing claims based on federal law, ... to have the cause heard in state court." The rule proposed by respondent, in contrast, would leave acceptance or rejection of a state forum to the master of the counterclaim. It would allow a defendant to remove a case brought in state court under state law, thereby defeating a plaintiff's choice of forum, simply by raising a federal counterclaim. Second, conferring this power upon the defendant would radically expand the class of removable cases, contrary to the "[d]ue regard for the rightful independence of state governments" that our cases addressing removal require. And finally, allowing responsive pleadings by the defendant to establish "arising under" jurisdiction would undermine the clarity and ease of administration of the well-pleaded-complaint doctrine, which serves as a "quick rule of thumb" for resolving jurisdictional conflicts.

4. Having lost their federal court judgment on jurisdictional grounds in 1908, the Mottleys promptly sued in a Kentucky state court, raising the same arguments. The state court held for them and ordered the railroad to resume issuing free passes to them. The railroad appealed and the Supreme Court again took away the Mottleys' victory, reaching the merits and rejecting both their statutory construction and constitutional arguments. Louisville & Nashville N.R. v. Mottley, 219 U.S. 467, 31 S.Ct. 265, 55 L.Ed. 297 (1911). How could the Court have had authority under Article III to hear the appeal in light of its decision in 1908 that the case did not arise under federal law?

The answer is that the constitutional provision is interpreted to be broader than § 1331, even though it is worded in a very similar fashion, and Congress has granted the Court broader appellate jurisdiction. See 28 U.S.C.A. § 1257. The broad interpretation of Article III is grounded on Osborn v. Bank of the United States, 22 U.S. (9 Wheat.) 738, 6 L.Ed. 204 (1824). The issue there was the validity of a statute by which Congress had, as the Court read it, granted federal courts jurisdiction over any action to which the Bank of the United States was a party. Chief Justice Marshall, writing for the Court, found this acceptable because the bank was a federal creation, so that in any case there would be a question whether it could sue—a federal issue. But once that question was resolved, it would not likely arise again. This fact did not trouble Marshall: "The question forms an original ingredient in every cause. Whether it be in fact relied on or not, in the defense, it is still a part of the cause, and may be relied upon." Far from rejecting federal jurisdiction based on an affirmative defense, then, Marshall's view would uphold federal jurisdiction as to possible defenses that were in fact never raised.

In American National Red Cross v. S.G., 505 U.S. 247, 112 S.Ct. 2465, 120 L.Ed.2d 201 (1992), the Court held that the federal statute chartering the Red Cross conferred original federal court jurisdiction because it authorized the organization "to sue or be sued in courts of law and equity, State or Federal, within the jurisdiction of the United States." Regarding the constitutionality of this interpretation, the Court said: "As long ago as *Osborn,* the Court held that Article III's 'arising under' jurisdiction is broad enough to authorize Congress to confer federal court jurisdiction over actions involving federally chartered corporations."

Does the *Osborn* view overextend federal judicial power? For example, it would seemingly permit all land disputes in western states to gain admission to the federal courts, even though their outcome would be controlled by state law, because they depend ultimately upon federal land grants, surely a curious result. Whether or not this breadth is proper, it is obviously much greater than § 1331. Thus, there is no question that a newspaper with the First Amendment defense in a libel suit may seek Supreme Court review if that defense is rejected. See, e.g., New York Times Co. v. Sullivan, 376 U.S. 254, 84 S.Ct. 710, 11 L.Ed.2d 686 (1964).

5. The application of the well-pleaded complaint rule was blurred further by the adoption of the Declaratory Judgment Act, since that would allow a party in the position of the Mottleys properly to include reference to the federal defense in a declaratory judgment action seeking a determination that the defense is not valid. In other words, in a real sense their mention of the federal issue would be "well pleaded." However, in Skelly Oil Co. v. Phillips Petroleum Co., 339 U.S. 667, 70 S.Ct. 876, 94 L.Ed. 1194 (1950), the Court ruled that the Declaratory Judgment Act did not permit circumvention of the rule in such circumstances. Noting that to rule otherwise would "turn into the federal courts a vast current of litigation indubitably arising under State law," the Court emphasized that the Act did not broaden federal jurisdiction: "To sanction suits for declaratory relief as within the jurisdiction of the District Courts merely because, as in this case, artful pleading anticipates a defense based on federal law would contravene the whole trend of jurisdictional legislation by Congress, disregard the effective functioning of the federal judicial system and distort the limited procedural purpose of the Declaratory Judgment Act." Accordingly, there is federal question jurisdiction only when the declaratory judgment defendant's coercive action would itself be within federal jurisdiction. For a criticism of this decision, see M. Redish, Federal Jurisdiction: Tensions in the Allocation of Judicial Power 108–10 (2d ed.1990).

Is the result in *Skelly Oil* compelled by *Mottley?* Whatever the risk that the plaintiff's forecast about which issues will be raised might prove wrong in the *Mottley* situation, isn't the requirement that the declaratory judgment plaintiff show an actual dispute between the parties about federal law sufficient? In Franchise Tax Board v. Construction Laborers Vacation Trust, 463 U.S. 1, 103 S.Ct. 2841, 77 L.Ed.2d 420 (1983), the state taxing authority sought a declaratory judgment in state court that, despite the federal Employment Retirement Income Security Act (ERISA), it could collect unpaid state income taxes by levying on taxpayers' funds held in trust pursuant to ERISA by defendants. As the board alleged in its complaint, defendants took the position that ERISA precluded such action, and it seemed clear that this was the only disputed legal issue in the case. But when defendants removed the case to federal court, the Supreme Court somewhat reluctantly held that *Skelly Oil* should be extended to apply to actions brought under state declaratory judgment acts as well: "The issue is an important one, which affects thousands of federally regulated trusts and all non-federal tax collection systems, and it must eventually receive a definitive, uniform resolution. Nevertheless, for reasons involving perhaps more history than logic, we hold that the lower federal courts had no jurisdiction to decide the question in the case before us." Should proper declaratory judgment actions be treated differently?

MERRELL DOW PHARMACEUTICALS, INC. v. THOMPSON

Supreme Court of the United States, 1986.
478 U.S. 804, 106 S.Ct. 3229, 92 L.Ed.2d 650.

JUSTICE STEVENS delivered the opinion of the Court.

The question presented is whether the incorporation of a federal standard in a state-law private action, when Congress has intended that there not be a federal private action for violations of that federal standard, makes the action one "arising under the Constitution, laws, or treaties of the United States," 28 U.S.C. § 1331.

I

The Thompson respondents are residents of Canada and the Mac-Tavishes reside in Scotland. They filed virtually identical complaints against petitioner, a corporation, that manufactures and distributes the drug Bendectin. The complaints were filed in the Court of Common Pleas in Hamilton County, Ohio. Each complaint alleged that a child was born with multiple deformities as a result of the mother's ingestion of Bendectin during pregnancy. In five of the six counts, the recovery of substantial damages was requested on common-law theories of negligence, breach of warranty, strict liability, fraud, and gross negligence. In Count IV, respondents alleged that the drug Bendectin was "misbranded" in violation of the Federal Food, Drug, and Cosmetic Act (FDCA), 52 Stat. 1040, as amended, 21 U.S.C. § 301 et seq. (1982 ed., Supp.II), because its labeling did not provide adequate warning that its use was potentially dangerous. Paragraph 26 alleged that the violation of the FDCA "in the promotion" of Bendectin "constitutes a rebuttable presumption of negligence." Paragraph 27 alleged that the "violation of said federal statutes directly and proximately caused the injuries suffered" by the two infants.

Petitioner filed a timely petition for removal from the state court to the Federal District Court alleging that the action was "founded, in part, on an alleged claim arising under the laws of the United States." After removal, the two cases were consolidated. Respondents filed a motion to remand to the state forum on the ground that the federal court lacked subject-matter jurisdiction. Relying on our decision in Smith v. Kansas City Title & Trust Co., 255 U.S. 180 (1921), the District Court held that Count IV of the complaint alleged a cause of action arising under federal law and denied the motion to remand. It then granted petitioner's motion to dismiss on forum non conveniens grounds.

The Court of Appeals for the Sixth Circuit reversed. * * * [N]oting "that the FDCA does not create or imply a private right of action for individuals injured as a result of violations of the Act," it explained:

> "Federal question jurisdiction would, thus, exist only if plaintiffs' right to relief depended necessarily on a substantial question of federal law. Plaintiffs' causes of action referred to the FDCA merely as one available criterion for determining whether Merrell Dow was negligent. Because the jury could find negligence on the part of Merrell Dow without finding a violation of the FDCA, the plaintiffs' causes of action did not depend necessarily upon a question of federal law. Consequently, the causes of action did not arise under federal law and, therefore, were improperly removed to federal court."

We granted certiorari, and we now affirm.

II

Article III of the Constitution gives the federal courts power to hear cases "arising under" federal statutes. That grant of power, however, is not self-executing, and it was not until the Judiciary Act of 1875 that Congress gave the federal courts general federal-question jurisdiction. Although the constitutional meaning of "arising under" may extend to all cases in which a federal question is "an ingredient" of the action, Osborn v. Bank of the United States, 9 Wheat. 738, 823, 6 L.Ed. 204 (1824), we have long construed the statutory grant of federal-question jurisdiction as conferring a more limited power.

Under our longstanding interpretation of the current statutory scheme, the question whether a claim "arises under" federal law must be determined by reference to the "well-pleaded complaint." A defense that raises a federal question is inadequate to confer federal jurisdiction. Louisville & Nashville N.R. Co. v. Mottley, 211 U.S. 149, 29 S.Ct. 42, 53 L.Ed. 126 (1908). Since a defendant may remove a case only if the claim could have been brought in federal court, 28 U.S.C. § 1441(b), moreover, the question for removal jurisdiction must also be determined by reference to the "well-pleaded complaint."

As was true in Franchise Tax Board [v. Construction Laborers Vacation Trust, 463 U.S. 1 (1983)], the propriety of the removal in this case thus turns on whether the case falls within the original "federal question" jurisdiction of the federal courts. There is no "single, precise definition" of that concept; rather, "the phrase 'arising under' masks a welter of issues regarding the interrelation of federal and state authority and the proper management of the federal judicial system."

This much, however, is clear. The "vast majority" of cases that come within this grant of jurisdiction are covered by Justice Holmes' statement that a " 'suit arises under the law that creates the cause of action.' " Id., at 8–9, quoting American Well Works Co. v. Layne & Bowler Co., 241 U.S. 257, 260 [Holmes, J.]. Thus, the vast majority of cases brought under the general federal-question jurisdiction of the federal courts are those in which federal law creates the cause of action.

We have, however, also noted that a case may arise under federal law "where the vindication of a right under state law necessarily turned on some construction of federal law."[5] * * *

This case does not pose a federal question of the first kind; respondents do not allege that federal law creates any of the causes of action that they have asserted. This case thus poses what Justice Frankfurter called the "litigation-provoking problem," Textile Workers v. Lincoln Mills, 353 U.S. 448, 470 (1957) (dissenting opinion)—the presence of a federal issue in a state-created cause of action.

In undertaking this inquiry into whether jurisdiction may lie for the presence of a federal issue in a nonfederal cause of action, it is, of course, appropriate to begin by referring to our understanding of the statute conferring federal-question jurisdiction. We have consistently emphasized that, in exploring the outer reaches of § 1331, determinations about federal jurisdiction require sensitive judgments about congressional intent, judicial power, and the federal system. * * *

In this case, both parties agree with the Court of Appeals' conclusion that there is no federal cause of action for FDCA violations. For purposes of our decision, we assume that this is a correct interpretation of the FDCA. Thus, as the case comes to us, it is appropriate to assume that, under the settled framework for evaluating whether a federal cause of action lies, some combination of the following factors is present: (1) the plaintiffs are not part of the class for whose special benefit the statute was passed; (2) the indicia of legislative intent reveal no congressional purpose to provide a private cause of action; (3) a federal cause of action would not further the underlying purposes of the legislative scheme; and (4) the respondents' cause of action is a subject traditionally relegated to

5. The case most frequently cited for that proposition is Smith v. Kansas City Title & Trust Co., 255 U.S. 180 (1921). In that case the Court upheld federal jurisdiction of a shareholder's bill to enjoin the corporation from purchasing bonds issued by the federal land banks under the authority of the Federal Farm Loan Act on the ground that the federal statute that authorized the issuance of the bonds was unconstitutional. The Court stated:

"The general rule is that where it appears from the bill or statement of the plaintiff that the right to relief depends upon the construction or application of the Constitution or laws of the United States, and that such federal claim is not merely colorable, and rests upon a reasonable foundation, the District Court has jurisdiction under this provision."

The effect of this view, expressed over Justice Holmes' vigorous dissent, on his *American Well Works* formulation has been often noted.

state law. In short, Congress did not intend a private federal remedy for violations of the statute that it enacted.

[The Court pointed out that it had concluded in prior cases that implying a private federal remedy would "flout congressional intent" in situations that did not satisfy its four-part test. To permit a federal court to entertain a state-law claim based on a federal statute that would not support a direct federal claim, it concluded, would similarly "flout" congressional intent.]

III

Petitioner advances three arguments to support its position that, even in the face of this congressional preclusion of a federal cause of action for a violation of the federal statute, federal-question jurisdiction may lie for the violation of the federal statute as an element of a state cause of action.

First, petitioner contends that the case represents a straightforward application of the statement in *Franchise Tax Board* that federal-question jurisdiction is appropriate when "it appears that some substantial, disputed question of federal law is a necessary element of one of the well-pleaded state claims." *Franchise Tax Board*, however, did not purport to disturb the long-settled understanding that the mere presence of a federal issue in a state cause of action does not automatically confer federal-question jurisdiction.[11] Indeed, in determining that federal-question jurisdiction was not appropriate in the case before us, we stressed Justice Cardozo's emphasis on principled, pragmatic distinctions: " 'What is needed is something of that common-sense accommodation of judgment to kaleidoscopic situations which characterizes the law in its treatment of causation ... a selective process which picks the substantial causes out of the web and lays the other ones aside.' " Id., at 20–21 (quoting Gully v. First National Bank, 299 U.S. 109, 117–118 (1936)).

Far from creating some kind of automatic test, *Franchise Tax Board* thus candidly recognized the need for careful judgments about the exercise of federal judicial power in an area of uncertain jurisdiction. Given the significance of the assumed congressional determination to preclude federal private remedies, the presence of the federal issue as an element of the state tort is not the kind of adjudication for which jurisdiction would serve congressional purposes and the federal system. This conclusion is fully consistent with the very sentence relied on so heavily by petitioner. We simply conclude that the congressional determination that there should be no federal remedy for the violation of this

---

11. See, e.g., Gully v. First National Bank, 299 U.S. 109, 115 (1936) ("Not every question of federal law emerging in a suit is proof that a federal law is the basis of the suit"); id., at 118 ("If we follow the ascent far enough, countless claims of right can be discovered to have their source or their operative limits in the provisions of a federal statute or in the Constitution itself with its circumambient restrictions upon legislative power. To set bounds to the pursuit, the courts have formulated the distinction between controversies that are basic and those that are collateral, between disputes that are necessary and those that are merely possible. We shall be lost in a maze if we put that compass by").

federal statute is tantamount to a congressional conclusion that the presence of a claimed violation of the statute as an element of a state cause of action is insufficiently "substantial" to confer federal-question jurisdiction.[12]

Second, petitioner contends that there is a powerful federal interest in seeing that the federal statute is given uniform interpretations, and that federal review is the best way of insuring such uniformity. In addition to the significance of the congressional decision to preclude a federal remedy, we do not agree with petitioner's characterization of the federal interest and its implications for federal-question jurisdiction. To the extent that petitioner is arguing that state use and interpretation of the FDCA pose a threat to the order and stability of the FDCA regime, petitioner should be arguing, not that federal courts should be able to review and enforce state FDCA-based causes of action as an aspect of federal-question jurisdiction, but that the FDCA preempts state-court jurisdiction over the issue in dispute. Petitioner's concern about the uniformity of interpretation, moreover, is considerably mitigated by the fact that, even if there is no original district court jurisdiction for these kinds of action, this Court retains power to review the decision of a federal issue in a state cause of action.

Finally, petitioner argues that, whatever the general rule, there are special circumstances that justify federal-question jurisdiction in this case. Petitioner emphasizes that it is unclear whether the FDCA applies to sales in Canada and Scotland; there is, therefore, a special reason for having a federal court answer the novel federal question relating to the extraterritorial meaning of the Act.

We reject this argument. * * * The novelty of an FDCA issue is not sufficient to give it status as a federal cause of action; nor should it be sufficient to give a state-based FDCA claim status as a jurisdiction-triggering federal question.[15]

---

12. Several commentators have suggested that our § 1331 decisions can best be understood as an evaluation of the nature of the federal interest at stake. See, e.g., Shapiro, Jurisdiction and Discretion, 60 N.Y.U.L.Rev. 543, 568 (1985); C. Wright, Federal Courts 96 (4th ed. 1983), Cohen, The Broken Compass: The Requirement That a Case Arise "Directly" Under Federal Law, 115 U.Pa.L.Rev. 890, 916 (1967).

Focusing on the nature of the federal interest, moreover, suggests that the widely perceived "irreconcilable" conflict between the finding of federal jurisdiction in Smith v. Kansas City Title & Trust Co., 255 U.S. 180 (1921), and the finding of no jurisdiction in Moore v. Chesapeake & Ohio R. Co., 291 U.S. 205 (1934), see, e.g., M. Redish, Federal Jurisdiction: Tensions in the Allocation of Judicial Power 67 (1980), is far from clear. For the difference in results can be seen as manifestations of the differences in the nature of the federal issues at stake. In *Smith,* as the Court emphasized, the issue was the constitutionality of an important federal statute. In *Moore,* in contrast, the Court emphasized that the violation of the federal standard as an element of state tort recovery did not fundamentally change the state tort nature of the action. * * *

15. Petitioner also contends that the Court of Appeals opinion rests on the view that federal-question jurisdiction was inappropriate because, whatever the role of the federal issue in the FDCA-related count, the plaintiff could recover on other, strictly state-law claims. See 766 F.2d at 1006 (noting that "the jury could find negligence on the part of Merrell Dow without finding a violation of the FDCA"). To the extent that the opinion can be read to express such a view, we agree that it was erroneous. * * *

IV

We conclude that a complaint alleging a violation of a federal statute as an element of a state cause of action, when Congress has determined that there should be no private, federal cause of action for the violation, does not state a claim "arising under the Constitution, laws, or treaties of the United States." 28 U.S.C. § 1331.

JUSTICE BRENNAN, with whom JUSTICE WHITE, JUSTICE MARSHALL, and JUSTICE BLACKMUN join, dissenting.

* * *

I

While the majority of cases covered by § 1331 may well be described by Justice Holmes' adage that "a suit arises under the law that creates the cause of action," American Well Works Co. v. Layne & Bowler Co., 241 U.S. 257, 260, 36 S.Ct. 585, 586, 60 L.Ed. 987 (1916), it is firmly settled that there may be federal question jurisdiction even though both the right asserted and the remedy sought by the plaintiff are state created. The rule as to such cases was stated in what Judge Friendly described as "[t]he path-breaking opinion" in Smith v. Kansas City Title & Trust Co., 255 U.S. 180 (1921). In *Smith,* a shareholder of the defendant corporation brought suit in the federal court to enjoin the defendant from investing corporate funds in bonds issued under the authority of the Federal Farm Loan Act. The plaintiff alleged that Missouri law imposed a fiduciary duty on the corporation to invest only in bonds that were authorized by a valid law and argued that, because the Farm Loan Act was unconstitutional, the defendant could not purchase bonds issued under its authority. Although the cause of action was wholly state created, the Court held that there was original federal jurisdiction over the case:

> "The general rule is that where it appears from the bill or statement of the plaintiff that the right to relief depends upon the construction or application of the Constitution or laws of the United States, and that such federal claim is not merely colorable, and rests upon a reasonable foundation, the District Court has jurisdiction under [the statute granting federal question jurisdiction]."

The continuing vitality of *Smith* is beyond challenge.[1] * * *

For the reasons we have stated, however, there is no federal-question jurisdiction even with that possible error corrected.

1. Some commentators have argued that the result in *Smith* conflicts with our decision in Moore v. Chesapeake & Ohio Ry., 291 U.S. 205 (1934).

[Justice Brennan described *Moore*, in which an injured railroad worker claimed that his injury was caused by the railroad's failure to comply with the Federal Safety Appliance Act.]

In one sense, the Court is correct [in its ftn. 12] in asserting that we can reconcile *Smith* and *Moore* on the ground that the "nature" of the federal interest was more significant in *Smith* than in *Moore*. Indeed, as the Court appears to believe, we could reconcile many of the seemingly inconsistent results that have been reached under § 1331 with such a test. But this is so only because a test based upon an ad hoc evaluation of the importance of the federal issue is infinitely malleable: at what point does a

There is, to my mind, no question that there is federal jurisdiction over the respondents' fourth cause of action under the rule set forth in *Smith* and reaffirmed in *Franchise Tax Board*. Respondents pleaded that petitioner's labeling of the drug Bendectin constituted "misbranding" in violation of §§ 201 and 502(f)(2), and (j) of the Federal Food, Drug, and Cosmetics Act (FDCA), and that this violation "directly and proximately caused" their injuries. Respondents asserted in the complaint that this violation established petitioner's negligence per se and entitled them to recover damages without more. No other basis for finding petitioner negligent was asserted in connection with this claim. As pleaded, then, respondents' "right to relief depend[ed] upon the construction or application of the Constitution or laws of the United States." *Smith*, 255 U.S., at 199. * * * Petitioner's principal defense is that the Act does not govern the branding of drugs that are sold in foreign countries. It is certainly not immediately obvious whether this argument is correct. Thus, the statutory question is one which "discloses a need for determining the meaning or application of [the FDCA]," and the claim raised by the fourth cause of action is one "arising under" federal law within the meaning of § 1331.

II

The Court apparently does not disagree with any of this—except, of course, for the conclusion. According to the Court, if we assume that Congress did not intend for there to be a private federal cause of action under a particular federal law (and, presumably, a fortiori if Congress' decision not to create a private remedy is express), we must also assume that Congress did not intend for there to be federal jurisdiction over a state cause of action that is determined by that federal law. Therefore, assuming—only because the parties have made a similar assumption— that there is no private cause of action under the FDCA,[4] the Court holds that there is no federal jurisdiction over the plaintiff's claim. * * *

federal interest become strong enough to create jurisdiction? * * * However, the inevitable—and undesirable—result of a test such as that suggested in the Court's footnote 12 is that federal jurisdiction turns in every case on an appraisal of the federal issue, its importance and its relation to state law issues. Yet it is precisely because the Court believes that federal jurisdiction would be "ill-served" by such a case-by-case appraisal that it rejects petitioners' claim that the difficulty and importance of the statutory issue presented by their claim suffices to confer jurisdiction under § 1331. The Court cannot have it both ways.

My own view is in accord with those commentators who view the results in *Smith* and *Moore* as irreconcilable. * * * Professor Redish [concluded] after comparing the vitality of *Smith* and *Moore* that "the principle enunciated in *Smith* is the one widely followed by modern lower feder-

al courts." Redish [Federal Jurisdiction: Tensions in the Allocation of Judicial Power] 67. Finally, as noted in text, the commentators have also preferred *Smith*. *Moore* simply has not survived the test of time; it is presently moribund, and, to the extent that it is inconsistent with the well-established rule of the *Smith* case, it ought to be overruled.

4. It bears emphasizing that the Court does not hold that there is no private cause of action under the FDCA. * * * Under the Court's analysis, however, if a party persuaded a court that there is a private cause of action under the FDCA, there would be federal jurisdiction under *Smith* and *Franchise Tax Board* over a state cause of action making violations of the FDCA actionable. Such jurisdiction would apparently exist even if the plaintiff did not seek the federal remedy.

The Court nowhere explains the basis for this conclusion. Yet it is hardly self-evident. Why should the fact that Congress chose not to create a private federal remedy mean that Congress would not want there to be federal jurisdiction to adjudicate a state claim that imposes liability for violating the federal law? Clearly, the decision not to provide a private federal remedy should not affect federal jurisdiction unless the reasons Congress withholds a federal remedy are also reasons for withholding federal jurisdiction. Thus, it is necessary to examine the reasons for Congress' decisions to grant or withhold both federal jurisdiction and private remedies, something the Court has not done.

A

In the early days of our Republic, Congress was content to leave the task of interpreting and applying federal laws in the first instance to the state courts; with one shortlived exception, Congress did not grant the inferior federal courts original jurisdiction over cases arising under federal law until 1875. The reasons Congress found it necessary to add this jurisdiction to the district courts are well known. First, Congress recognized "the importance, and even necessity of uniformity of decisions throughout the whole United States, upon all subjects within the purview of the constitution." Concededly, because federal jurisdiction is not always exclusive and because federal courts may disagree with one another, absolute uniformity has not been obtained even under § 1331. However, while perfect uniformity may not have been achieved, experience indicates that the availability of a federal forum in federal question cases has done much to advance that goal.

In addition, § 1331 has provided for adjudication in a forum that specializes in federal law and that is therefore more likely to apply that law correctly. Because federal question cases constitute the basic grist for federal tribunals, "the federal courts have acquired a considerable expertise in the interpretation and application of federal law." By contrast, "it is apparent that federal question cases must form a very small part of the business of [state] courts." As a result, the federal courts are comparatively more skilled at interpreting and applying federal law, and are much more likely correctly to divine Congress' intent in enacting legislation.[6]

These reasons for having original federal question jurisdiction explain why cases like this one and *Smith*—i.e., cases where the cause of

---

6. Another reason Congress conferred original federal question jurisdiction on the district courts was its belief that state courts are hostile to assertions of federal rights. Although this concern may be less compelling today than it once was, the American Law Institute reported as recently as 1969 that "it is difficult to avoid concluding that federal courts are more likely to apply federal law sympathetically and understandingly than are state courts." * * *

One might argue that this Court's appellate jurisdiction over state court judgments in cases arising under federal law can be depended upon to correct erroneous state court decisions and to insure that federal law is interpreted and applied uniformly. However, * * * having served on this Court for 30 years, it is clear to me that, realistically, it cannot even come close to "doing the whole job" and that § 1331 is essential if federal rights are to be adequately protected.

action is a creature of state law, but an essential element of the claim is federal—"arise under" federal law within the meaning of § 1331. * * * [T]he possibility that the federal law will be incorrectly interpreted in the context of adjudicating the state law claim implicates the concerns that led Congress to grant the district courts power to adjudicate cases involving federal questions in precisely the same way as if it was federal law that "created" the cause of action. It therefore follows that there is federal jurisdiction under § 1331.

B

The only remaining question is whether the assumption that Congress decided not to create a private cause of action alters this analysis in a way that makes it inappropriate to exercise original federal jurisdiction.

[Justice Brennan rejected the majority's reasoning. The increased complexity of federal legislation, he concluded, indicated that the expertise of federal courts would be desirable. The increased volume of federal litigation might be a motive for narrowing § 1331, but it was not a good reason. Finally, more careful scrutiny of legislative intent did not cut against federal jurisdiction because the statute explicitly authorizes a variety of enforcement actions by the Food and Drug Administration in federal court, suggesting that Congress favored adjudication in federal court.]

It may be that a decision by Congress not to create a private remedy is intended to preclude all private enforcement. If that is so, then a state cause of action that makes relief available to private individuals for violations of the FDCA is pre-empted. But if Congress' decision not to provide a private federal remedy does not pre-empt such a state remedy, then, in light of the FDCA's clear policy of relying on the federal courts for enforcement, it also should not foreclose federal jurisdiction over that state remedy. Both § 1331 and the enforcement provisions of the FDCA reflect Congress' strong desire to utilize the federal courts to interpret and enforce the FDCA, and it is therefore at odds with both these statutes to recognize a private state law remedy for violating the FDCA but to hold that this remedy cannot be adjudicated in the federal courts.

The Court's contrary conclusion requires inferring from Congress' decision not to create a private federal remedy that, while some private enforcement is permissible in state courts, it is "bad" if that enforcement comes from the federal courts. But that is simply illogical. Congress' decision to withhold a private right of action and to rely instead on public enforcement reflects congressional concern with obtaining more accurate implementation and more coordinated enforcement of a regulatory scheme. These reasons are closely related to the Congress' reasons for giving federal courts original federal question jurisdiction. Thus, if anything, Congress' decision not to create a private remedy strengthens the argument in favor of finding federal jurisdiction over a state remedy that is not preempted.

Notes and Questions

1. The reasonably easy starting point in identifying federal question cases is Justice Holmes' observation that where federal law creates a claim, it arises under federal law. Thus, had the Court concluded that the FDCA gave rise to an implied private cause of action (a matter of federal common law, which is covered in Chapter XI), there would be no question that § 1331 would provide federal jurisdiction over that claim. Moreover, under the Supremacy Clause, state courts would have concurrent jurisdiction to entertain such federal claims as well. See Redish & Muench, Adjudication of Federal Causes of Action in State Court, 75 Mich.L.Rev. 311 (1976). Congress can, however, specify that there is exclusive federal jurisdiction over federal claims, thereby ousting state courts of jurisdiction.

The fact that Congress has authorized a suit does not mean, however, that the resulting claim necessarily falls within § 1331. In Shoshone Mining Co. v. Rutter, 177 U.S. 505, 20 S.Ct. 726, 44 L.Ed. 864 (1900), Congress had created a mechanism for resolving disputes about mining claims and provided that adverse claimants could bring suit in a "court of competent jurisdiction." The legislation specified, however, that such suits should be determined by "local customs or rules of miners in the several mining districts, so far as the same are applicable and not inconsistent with the laws of the United States." Focusing on this provision, the Court held that such claims do not arise under federal law.

Given trends in federal regulation since 1900, however, it is not likely that there will be many instances in which Congress authorizes a suit without providing some rules for decision of the case. Where it does, however, that does not mean that federal jurisdiction is always absent. In Textile Workers Union v. Lincoln Mills, 353 U.S. 448, 77 S.Ct. 912, 1 L.Ed.2d 972 (1957), for example, the Court confronted § 301 of the Labor Management Relations Act, 29 U.S.C.A. § 185, which explicitly grants federal courts jurisdiction over suits to enforce collective bargaining agreements between employers and unions. Stressing the need for national uniformity in enforcement of such agreements, the Court found that "the legislation does more than confer jurisdiction in the federal courts": "The question then is, what is the substantive law to be applied in suits under § 301(a)? We conclude that the substantive law to apply in suits under § 301(a) is federal law, which the courts must fashion from the policy of our national labor laws."

2. If the plaintiffs in *Merrell Dow* had initially sued in federal court, claiming that the FDCA provided a private cause of action, would the court have had jurisdiction? The fact that the purported federal claim may prove meritless does not preclude subject matter jurisdiction from attaching. In Bell v. Hood, 327 U.S. 678, 66 S.Ct. 773, 90 L.Ed. 939 (1946), the Court rejected an attempt to link the jurisdictional inquiry to a determination whether the complaint states a claim for relief. To decide if there is federal question jurisdiction, the court "must look to the way the complaint is drawn to see if it is drawn so as to claim a right to recover under the Constitution and laws of the United States. * * * [I]t is well settled that the failure to state a proper cause of action calls for a judgment on the merits and not a dismissal for want of jurisdiction." The Court went on, however, to

distinguish cases "where the alleged claim under the Constitution or federal statutes clearly appears to be immaterial and made solely for the purpose of obtaining jurisdiction, or where the claim is wholly insubstantial and frivolous." In such cases, dismissal for lack of jurisdiction is proper. How easily can this distinction be drawn? Why does it matter?

In In re Bendectin Litigation, 857 F.2d 290 (6th Cir.1988), the court held that there was federal question jurisdiction over claims made by nondiverse plaintiffs who sued Merrell Dow in federal court claiming injuries caused by Bendectin. The court reasoned that "[a] straightforward reading of plaintiffs' complaints gives the undeniable impression that plaintiffs intended to allege an implied cause of action under the FDCA." Id. at 300. Noting that, unlike the plaintiffs in Merrell Dow v. Thompson, these plaintiffs "never conceded that there was no implied cause of action under the FDCA," it concluded that these seemingly federal claims were not "wholly insubstantial": "Until this court or the Supreme Court holds that there is no implied private right of action under the FDCA, the opposite position cannot be deemed either frivolous or unsubstantial." Id.

3. The problem area involves claims that are created by state law which turn to some extent on interpretation of federal law. Professor Mishkin has suggested that jurisdiction depends upon "a substantial claim founded 'directly' upon federal law." Mishkin, The Federal "Question" in the District Court, 53 Colum. L. Rev. 157, 165 (1953). In Gully v. First National Bank, 299 U.S. 109, 57 S.Ct. 96, 81 L.Ed. 70 (1936), the Court, in an opinion by Justice Cardozo, explained its approach as follows:

> To bring a case within the statute, a right or immunity created by the Constitution or laws of the United States must be an element, and an essential one, of the plaintiff's cause of action. * * * The right or immunity must be such that it will be supported if the Constitution or laws of the United States are given one construction or effect, and defeated if they receive another.

Putting aside the majority's emphasis in *Merrell Dow* on the assumed congressional purpose not to create a private cause of action, what test is the Court applying there?

4. Is *Merrell Dow* distinguishable from Moore v. Chesapeake & Ohio Ry. (described in footnote 1 of Justice Brennan's opinion)? It should be noted that in *Moore* the ultimate effect of the Court's holding that plaintiff's claim did not arise under federal law was that jurisdiction was proper for his suit in Indiana, where he lived, because finding a federal claim would have required plaintiff to sue defendant at its home in Virginia under then-existing venue rules. Is it distinguishable from Smith v. Kansas City Title & Trust Co., upon which Justice Brennan relies? Regarding *Smith*, consider the following analysis: "In Smith v. Kansas City Title & Trust Co., the stakes were high, the issue urgent, and the case of national importance: the marketability of a bond program for the relief of farmers was impaired until the Supreme Court resolved the constitutionality of enabling legislation." Oakley, Federal Jurisdiction and the Problem of the Litigative Unit: When Does What "Arise Under" Federal Law?, 76 Texas L. Rev. 1829, 1838 (1998).

In City of Chicago v. International College of Surgeons, 522 U.S. 156, 118 S.Ct. 523, 139 L.Ed.2d 525 (1997), the Court held that a federal law element of a state law claim sufficed to create jurisdiction under § 1331. Curiously, the case involved an effort by the City to get the state law claim into federal court. The International College of Surgeons (ICS) sought review in state court of the decision of the Chicago Landmarks Commission to designate two buildings the College owned as landmarks (which meant that it could not develop the property in the way it wanted). Among the grounds for overturning the Commission's decision were federal constitutional contentions based on the takings clause, due process clause and equal protection clause of the Fifth and Fourteenth amendments. The City removed and the district court eventually granted it summary judgment. But the Seventh Circuit reversed on the ground there was no federal question jurisdiction.

The Supreme Court held that jurisdiction was proper:

> In this case, there can be no question that ICS's state court complaint raised a number of issues of federal law in the form of various federal constitutional challenges to the Landmarks and Designation Ordinances and to the manner in which the Commission conducted the administrative proceedings. It is true, as ICS asserts, that the federal constitutional claims were raised by way of a cause of action created by state law, namely, the Illinois Administrative Review Law. As we have explained, however, "[e]ven though state law creates [a party's] causes of action, its case might still 'arise under' the laws of the United States if a well-pleaded complaint established that its right to relief under state law requires resolution of a substantial question of federal law."

Justice Ginsburg dissented, emphasizing her view that the proceeding authorized under the Illinois law as appellate in nature, and that federal courts should not entertain "cross-system appeals."

5. How should the well-pleaded complaint rule be applied in *Merrell Dow?* Would it matter whether Ohio law requires explicit reference to the FDCA to state a claim for misbranding? Compare Smith v. Industrial Valley Title Ins. Co., 957 F.2d 90 (3d Cir.1992), in which plaintiffs sued title insurance companies for conversion and unfair trade practices under state law on the ground that the companies had charged an IRS "reporting fee" in violation of an Internal Revenue Code prohibition on charging a customer for complying with the Code's reporting requirement. After defendants tried to remove to federal court, a majority of the appellate court held that there was no federal jurisdiction even though a violation of the federal Internal Revenue Code was an "essential element of each state cause of action." The majority said that *Merrell Dow* held that "a private federal remedy * * * is a prerequisite for finding federal jurisdiction in this circumstance." A dissenting judge urged that this case was different because the Code violation was "more than just an 'element' of the state law claims. The federal statute forms the fundamental foundation of the state law claims." See Note, Mr. *Smith* Goes to Federal Court: Federal Question Jurisdiction Post *Merrell Dow*, 115 Harv.L.Rev. 2272 (2002) (reporting that the lower courts have "split nearly evenly" on whether *Smith* jurisdiction is allowed only in situations in which there is an implied private federal cause of action).

6. Justice Brennan articulates a number of purposes for federal question jurisdiction. Are they persuasive? Do they apply less forcefully to federal defenses?

7. The majority concludes that allowing federal jurisdiction would "flout" congressional intent and make it "meaningless." Why does allowing federal jurisdiction over this state law claim have that effect? Why wouldn't state court jurisdiction have the same effect? See M. Redish, Federal Jurisdiction: Tensions in the Allocation of Judicial Power 104 (2d ed. 1990) ("a congressional decision not to provide a federal remedy does not necessarily imply congressional disapproval of the provision of a federal forum for adjudication of a state cause of action turning on the interpretation of that federal statute").

8. Justice Brennan suggests that the pervasive regulation of the FDCA may preempt state law remedies in the area. Preemption occurs when state law is inconsistent with federal law (and therefore invalid under the Supremacy Clause), or when federal law so pervasively regulates a subject that it is said to "occupy" the whole area, leaving no room for state law to operate.

Should preemption be a ground for exercising federal jurisdiction? Ordinarily preemption is said to be a defense and therefore, under *Mottley,* it provides no basis for federal jurisdiction under § 1331, even where the preemption issue is raised in a declaratory judgment action, as the Court held in *Franchise Tax Board.* But there are limits:

> One corollary of the well-pleaded complaint rule developed in the case law, however, is that Congress may so completely pre-empt a particular area, that any civil complaint raising this select group of claims is necessarily federal in character. For 20 years, this Court has singled out claims pre-empted by § 301 of the Labor Management Relations Act (LMRA), 29 U.S.C.A. § 185, for such special treatment. Avco Corp. v. Machinists, 390 U.S. 557, 88 S.Ct. 1235, 20 L.Ed.2d 126 (1968).

> "The necessary ground of decision [in *Avco*] was that the preemptive force of § 301 is so powerful as to displace entirely any state cause of action 'for violation of contracts between an employer and a labor organization.' Any such suit is purely a creature of federal law, notwithstanding the fact that state law would provide a cause of action in the absence of § 301."

Metropolitan Life Ins. Co. v. Taylor, 481 U.S. 58, 64, 107 S.Ct. 1542, 1546–47, 95 L.Ed.2d 55 (1987) (quoting *Franchise Tax Board*); see Butero v. Royal Maccabees Life Ins. Co., 174 F.3d 1207, 1211 (11th Cir.1999) (referring to "super preemption"). Thus, in *Taylor* the Court held that plaintiff's state law claim regarding benefits under employee benefit plan had been "displaced" by the Employee Retirement Security Act (ERISA), 29 U.S.C.A. §§ 1001 et seq., because the legislative history said that they should be handled "in similar fashion to those brought under section 301 of the Labor–Management Relations Act," which the Court took to be a "specific reference to the *Avco* rule." See also Beneficial Nat. Bank v. Anderson, 539 U.S. 1, 123 S.Ct. 2058, 156 L.Ed.2d 1 (2003) (National Bank Act completely preempts state-law usury claim against a bank). Compare Caterpillar Inc. v. Williams, 482 U.S. 386, 107 S.Ct. 2425, 96 L.Ed.2d 318 (1987), in which the

Court found that LMRA § 301 did not displace claims by employees for violation of independent contractual undertakings. See also Willy v. Coastal Corp., 855 F.2d 1160 (5th Cir.1988) (federal environmental laws do not displace state-law claims).

9.   Except in cases where federal law displaces state claims, plaintiff is ordinarily free to rely solely on state law grounds and thereby defeat federal jurisdiction. But in a footnote in Federated Department Stores, Inc. v. Moitie, 452 U.S. 394, 101 S.Ct. 2424, 69 L.Ed.2d 103 (1981), the Court suggested that "artful pleading" could not be used to avoid federal jurisdiction. In Rivet v. Regions Bank, 522 U.S. 470, 118 S.Ct. 921, 139 L.Ed.2d 912 (1998), however, the Court ruled that unless there is a completely preemptive federal statute (see note 8 above) the well-pleaded complaint rule precludes consideration of claims not raised. For discussion, see Miller, Artful Pleading: A Doctrine in Search of Definition, 76 Texas L. Rev. 1781 (1998); Rogazzo, Reconsidering the Artful Pleading Doctrine, 44 Hast.L.J. 273, 303–16 (1993). *Moitie* is reproduced in connection with a different issue infra p. 1111.

10.   *Postscript on Merrell Dow*: The stimulus for the fight about federal-court jurisdiction was the federal court's application of forum non conveniens; Ohio state courts had not accepted the view that prevailed in the federal courts. Recall Piper Aircraft Co. v. Reyno, supra p. 847. But in Chambers v. Merrell-Dow Pharmaceuticals, 519 N.E.2d 370 (Ohio 1988)— also raising Bendectin claims by British plaintiffs—the Ohio Supreme Court adopted a view like the federal rule, and the cases were dismissed.

C.   THE PENUMBRA OF FEDERAL JUDICIAL POWER—SUPPLEMENTAL JURISDICTION

Having found a ground for exercise of federal jurisdiction, one is left with the question of the extent of that jurisdiction. Regarding the constitutional scope of federal-question jurisdiction, the Supreme Court early took a broad view. In Osborn v. Bank of the United States, 22 U.S. 738, 6 L.Ed. 204 (1824), the Court held that Congress could grant the federal courts jurisdiction over "a whole case," so long as a federal issue was an "ingredient in the original cause" asserted. Even though it early interpreted the diversity-jurisdiction statute to require complete diversity (Strawbridge v. Curtiss, supra p. 860), the Court held that the Constitution required only minimal diversity. See Tashire v. State Farm Fire & Cas. Co., supra p. 865 n.3.

Over time, broadened concepts of joinder of claims built on *Osborn* in federal-question cases to produce *pendent claim jurisdiction*, which included not only a claim arising under federal law but also other claims based entirely on state law arising from the same set of circumstances. In United Mine Workers of America v. Gibbs, 383 U.S. 715, 86 S.Ct. 1130, 16 L.Ed.2d 218 (1966), the Court endorsed the use of that jurisdiction because, "[u]nder the Rules, the impulse is toward entertaining the broadest possible scope of action consistent with fairness to the parties; joinder of claims, parties, and remedies is strongly encouraged."

Against that background, it announced the following test for the scope of a "case" under Article III:

> Pendent jurisdiction, in the sense of judicial power, exists whenever there is a claim "arising under [the] Constitution, the Laws of the United States, and Treaties made, or which shall be made, under their Authority ...," U.S. Const., Art III. § 2, and the relationship between that claim and the state claim permits the conclusion that the entire action before the court comprises but *one constitutional "case."* The federal claim must have substance sufficient to confer subject matter jurisdiction on the court. The state and federal claims must derive from a common nucleus of operative fact. (emphasis added)

As we shall see, this concept is central to supplemental jurisdiction. Consider the way in which the substantive law makes various facts "operative" for purposes of this analysis. How often will joinder be permissible under the rules but go beyond the limits of the "constitutional case"? Compare Rules 18 and 20.

In diversity cases, federal-court jurisdiction depends on the characteristics of the parties rather than the nature of the claims asserted, so the pendent claim problem ordinarily would not arise. But within a single "constitutional case" there might be claims against diverse and nondiverse parties. A plaintiff who wanted to sue in federal court might choose to sue only the diverse defendants. In such circumstances, the doctrine of *ancillary jurisdiction* developed to permit parties other than the original plaintiff to assert related state-law claims against nondiverse opponents, including counterclaims against the plaintiff. Recall Wigglesworth v. Teamsters Local No. 592, supra p. 207. In Owen Equipment & Erection Co. v. Kroger, 437 U.S. 365, 98 S.Ct. 2396, 57 L.Ed.2d 274 (1978), the Supreme Court indicated that the constitutional scope of this jurisdiction also turned on the *Gibbs* "common nucleus of operative fact" analysis, but held on statutory grounds that ancillary jurisdiction should not permit the plaintiff to circumvent the complete diversity limitations on federal-court jurisdiction even though it enabled other parties to add nondiverse parties to the litigation. *Kroger* therefore affirmed the right of a defendant to assert a Rule 14 third-party claim against a nondiverse opponent because it arose out of the same accident that was the basis for the plaintiff's suit. But it also held that the plaintiff could not assert a claim against the impleaded third party—even though such a claim was authorized by Rule 14—because there was no diversity between the plaintiff and the third party. Otherwise, the Court observed, "the plaintiff could defeat the statutory requirement of complete diversity by the simple expedient of suing only those defendants who were of diverse citizenship and waiting for them to implead nondiverse defendants."

Similar issues arose in connection with the amount-in-controversy requirement for diversity jurisdiction, and the Court refused to permit joinder of multiple plaintiffs to satisfy that requirement. To the contrary, it held that each plaintiff must individually satisfy that requirement.

Clark v. Paul Gray, Inc., 306 U.S. 583, 59 S.Ct. 744, 83 L.Ed. 1001 (1939). In a state-law class action, the requirement could not be satisfied by combining the claims of all the class members. Snyder v. Harris, 394 U.S. 332, 89 S.Ct. 1053, 22 L.Ed.2d 319 (1969). Zahn v. International Paper Co., 414 U.S. 291, 94 S.Ct. 505, 38 L.Ed.2d 511 (1973), held further that even if the named class representative in a state-law class action had a sufficient claim, that circumstance did not provide jurisdiction for the claims of the other class members, each of whom also had to satisfy the requirement.

The interaction of pendent and ancillary jurisdiction with broadened joinder produced the *pendent party* problem. Adding nondiverse litigants to the case could further the sort of efficiencies that United Mine Workers v. Gibbs, supra, extolled. Nonetheless, in Aldinger v. Howard, 427 U.S. 1, 96 S.Ct. 2413, 49 L.Ed.2d 276 (1976), the Court held that a plaintiff with a federal claim against one defendant could not add a nondiverse defendant sued only on a related state-law claim because that was different from adding a nonfederal claim against a defendant who was already facing a federal claim: "The addition of a completely new party would run counter to the well-established principle that federal courts, as opposed to state trial courts of general jurisdiction, are courts of limited jurisdiction marked out by Congress."

At least in a case like *Aldinger* the party who wanted to sue all the defendants in one action could sue in state court, for there was concurrent jurisdiction over the federal claim asserted in that case. But in Finley v. United States, 490 U.S. 545, 109 S.Ct. 2003, 104 L.Ed.2d 593 (1989), the Court held that there could be no federal-court jurisdiction over claims against nondiverse defendants arising out of the incident even though plaintiff's Federal Torts Claims Act claim against the United States could not be asserted in state court. In *Finley* the Court announced that it would interpret most grants of federal-court jurisdiction as forbidding exercise of jurisdiction over pendent parties, but observed that Congress could change this result by statute. In 1990 Congress adopted the Supplemental Jurisdiction Act, largely in reaction to *Finley*.

ROSARIO ORTEGA v. STAR–KIST FOODS, INC.

United States Court of Appeals, First Circuit, 2004.
370 F.3d 124, cert. granted, ___ U.S. ___, 125 S.Ct. 314.

Before BOUDIN, Chief Judge, TORRUELLA and LYNCH, Circuit Judges.

LYNCH, Circuit Judge.

In April 1999, Beatriz Blanco–Ortega, then nine years old, cut her right pinky finger on a can of Star–Kist tuna. That is not normally the stuff of lawsuits in federal court, but her injuries were more than trivial and led to surgery, the prospect of future surgery, and minor permanent disability and scarring. Beatriz, along with her parents and sister, sued in federal court, asserting diversity jurisdiction. 28 U.S.C. § 1332. The claims of Beatriz's family members were composed of emotional distress damages, with the mother asserting medical expenses as well. Plaintiffs' choice of federal court was no doubt influenced by the fact that civil jury trials are unavailable in the local courts of Puerto Rico.

The case raises two issues. First is the classic question whether each of the plaintiffs meets the amount-in-controversy requirement for diversity jurisdiction. * * * As to the injured child, Beatriz, we reverse and hold that it is not a legal certainty that she could not recover an award over $75,000. But we uphold the district court's conclusion that none of Beatriz's family members satisfies the amount-in-controversy requirement.

The second question is whether Beatriz's family members may nonetheless remain as plaintiffs under the supplemental jurisdiction statute, 28 U.S.C. § 1367. This is a very difficult question, new to this court, on which the circuits have split. We hold that by limiting supplemental jurisdiction to "civil action[s] of which the district courts have original jurisdiction," § 1367(a), Congress preserved the traditional rule that each plaintiff in a diversity action must separately satisfy the amount-in-controversy requirement. Accordingly, we affirm the dismissal of Beatriz's family members' claims for lack of subject-matter jurisdiction.

* * *

II

A.   AMOUNT-IN-CONTROVERSY REQUIREMENT

[Because Beatriz had to undergo general-anesthetic surgery and eight weeks of painful physical therapy, as well as suffering a lifelong partial disability and the possibility of further problems later in life, her claim satisfied the amount-in-controversy requirement. But her family members relied on emotional distress claims that could not.]

B.   SUPPLEMENTAL JURISDICTION UNDER § 1367

This leaves the issue of supplemental jurisdiction. Beatriz's family members cannot file their own suits against Star–Kist in federal court. The question is whether the supplemental jurisdiction statute, 28 U.S.C. § 1367, allows them to proceed in federal court nonetheless on the basis of Beatriz's jurisdictionally sufficient claim.

Though simple to state, the question has not been answered in this circuit, and its proper resolution is far from clear. The courts of appeals are sharply divided over whether § 1367 allows parties who cannot themselves satisfy § 1332's amount-in-controversy requirement to sue in federal court by joining forces with a plaintiff who can. The Supreme Court once granted certiorari to resolve the matter, but it ultimately split 4–4 and affirmed without opinion. See *Free v. Abbott Labs., Inc.*, 529 U.S. 333, 120 S.Ct. 1578, 146 L.Ed.2d 306 (2000).

The problem has actually arisen in two contexts, each of which is the subject of a circuit split. First, there are cases—like Beatriz's—

involving the ordinary joinder of additional plaintiffs under Fed.R.Civ.P. 20. *Compare Stromberg Metal Works, Inc. v. Press Mech., Inc.,* 77 F.3d 928, 932 (7th Cir.1996) (where one plaintiff satisfies the amount-in-controversy requirement, § 1367 permits jurisdiction over transactionally related claims by co-plaintiffs who do not), *with Meritcare, Inc. v. St. Paul Mercury Ins. Co.,* 166 F.3d 214, 216 (3d Cir.1999) (each co-plaintiff must independently satisfy the amount-in-controversy requirement). Second, there are cases involving the claims of absent class members in diversity-only class actions. *Compare Allapattah Serv., Inc. v. Exxon Corp.,* 333 F.3d 1248, 1254 (11th Cir.2003) (section 1367 authorizes jurisdiction over all class members' claims if the named plaintiffs satisfy the amount-in-controversy requirement) *with Trimble v. Asarco, Inc.,* 232 F.3d 946, 962 (8th Cir.2000) (section 1367 does not extend jurisdiction over class members who do not independently meet the amount-in-controversy requirement). Because the same statutory language applies in both contexts, some courts have lumped the two together for purposes of § 1367. Our case involves only Rule 20 joinder, however, and we express no view regarding the application of § 1367 in class actions.

Even aside from the circuit split, this is an area where courts are wise to tread carefully. The problem of pendent-party jurisdiction implicates some of the most sensitive and enduring issues in the law of federal jurisdiction, and it directly affects the allocation of judicial business among the state and federal courts. In the end, certainty can come only from Congress or the Supreme Court. * * *

1. Background

Before 1990, it is clear, Beatriz's family members could not have joined in Beatriz's diversity suit unless they each stood to recover more than the minimum amount required for jurisdiction. * * * That rule is now commonly associated with *Clark v. Paul Gray, Inc.,* 306 U.S. 583, 59 S.Ct. 744, 83 L.Ed. 1001 (1939). Even after *United Mine Workers v. Gibbs,* 383 U.S. 715, 86 S.Ct. 1130, 16 L.Ed.2d 218 (1966), in which the Supreme Court approved pendent-claim jurisdiction in federal-question cases, *Clark* remained good law: "[M]ultiple plaintiffs with separate and distinct claims must each satisfy the jurisdictional-amount requirement for suit in the federal courts." *Zahn v. Int'l Paper Co.,* 414 U.S. 291, 294, 94 S.Ct. 505, 38 L.Ed.2d 511 (1973); *see also Aldinger v. Howard,* 427 U.S. 1, 15–16, 96 S.Ct. 2413, 49 L.Ed.2d 276 (1976) (distinguishing pendent-party jurisdiction from the type of pendent-claim jurisdiction permitted in *Gibbs*). If the *Clark* rule applies in this case, we should affirm the dismissal as to Beatriz's family members but vacate as to Beatriz, thereby leaving Beatriz free to choose between proceeding alone in federal court or voluntarily dismissing her complaint and re-filing together with her family in the Puerto Rico courts.

Whether *Clark* continues to apply today depends on how one reads 28 U.S.C. § 1367, the supplemental jurisdiction statute, which was enacted by Congress in 1990. In relevant part, § 1367 provides:

(a) Except as provided in subsections (b) and (c) or as expressly provided otherwise by Federal statute, in any civil action of which the district courts have original jurisdiction, the district courts shall have supplemental jurisdiction over all other claims that are so related to claims in the action within such original jurisdiction that they form part of the same case or controversy under Article III of the United States Constitution. Such supplemental jurisdiction shall include claims that involve the joinder or intervention of additional parties.

(b) In any civil action of which the district courts have original jurisdiction founded solely on section 1332 of this title, the district courts shall not have supplemental jurisdiction under subsection (a) over claims by plaintiffs against persons made parties under Rule 14, 19, 20, or 24 of the Federal Rules of Civil Procedure, or over claims by persons proposed to be joined as plaintiffs under Rule 19 of such rules, or seeking to intervene as plaintiffs under Rule 24 of such rules, when exercising supplemental jurisdiction over such claims would be inconsistent with the jurisdictional requirements of section 1332.

The impetus for Congress's adoption of § 1367 was the Supreme Court's 5–4 decision in *Finley v. United States,* 490 U.S. 545, 109 S.Ct. 2003, 104 L.Ed.2d 593 (1989). *Finley* did not deal with the amount-in-controversy requirement. Rather, the plaintiff in *Finley* had filed suit against the United States under the Federal Tort Claims Act (FTCA), 28 U.S.C. § 1346(b), alleging that the government's failure to maintain certain airport runway lights had contributed to the death of her husband and children in an airplane accident. Later, she amended her complaint to add state-law tort claims against two new defendants, a municipality and a utility company. No independent basis for federal subject-matter jurisdiction existed over those claims. The Supreme Court acknowledged that the plaintiff could not have brought her entire action in state court because federal jurisdiction in FTCA cases is exclusive, but it held nevertheless that the district court lacked jurisdiction over the "pendent-party" state-law claims. The Court concluded by noting that Congress was free to reverse that result if it wished.

Congress did so in § 1367. The text of the statute, however, can be read to do more than overturn *Finley.* The jurisdictional grant, which appears in section (a), is not limited to cases like *Finley* involving exclusive federal jurisdiction, or even to federal-question cases generally. Instead, subsection (a) permits the district courts to hear any claim arising from the same constitutional case or controversy "in any civil action of which the district courts have original jurisdiction." Subsection (b) then creates an exception to that grant for certain claims in diversity cases. The result is a jurisdictional grant of such apparent breadth that, as one commentator succinctly put it, "the statute has created confusion in a number of areas in which principles were thought to be well established."

2. Section 1367 and the Clark Rule

One such area of confusion involves the continued validity of *Clark* in the wake of § 1367. The case law on this issue is split between two competing interpretations of § 1367.

The first, adopted by the Seventh Circuit in *Stromberg,* turns on Congress's failure to include Rule 20 plaintiffs among those parties who cannot rely on supplemental jurisdiction where doing so would be inconsistent with § 1332. *See* § 1367(b) (restricting supplemental jurisdiction over parties joined as plaintiffs under Rules 19 or 24, but omitting Rule 20 plaintiffs). On this reading, § 1367 overturns *Clark* and extends supplemental jurisdiction over claims asserted by diversity plaintiffs who cannot meet the amount-in-controversy requirement, provided that at least one plaintiff in the action has a jurisdictionally sufficient claim. *See Stromberg,* 77 F.3d at 930–32.

The second interpretation, originally suggested in an article by Professor Pfander[9] and later adopted by the Tenth Circuit in *Leonhardt* [*v. W. Sugar Co.,* 160 F.3d 631 (10th Cir. 1998),] emphasizes the requirement in § 1367(a) that the district court must first have "original jurisdiction" over an action before supplemental jurisdiction can apply. On this reading, § 1367 *preserves* the rule in *Clark* and thus does not supply supplemental jurisdiction where, as in this case, only one of the named plaintiffs meets the amount in controversy. Although *Leonhardt* was a class action case, the Third Circuit subsequently endorsed its reasoning in *Meritcare* [*v. St. Paul Mercury Ins.Co.,* 160 F.3d 214 (3d Cir.1999)], a Rule 20 joinder case with facts analogous to the case at bar.

We recognize that plausible textual arguments can be made in favor of either of these readings. For the reasons that follow, however, we conclude that *Leonhardt* and *Meritcare* embody the better reading of § 1367.

a. Text of § 1367

* * *

The first sentence of § 1367 specifies that supplemental jurisdiction can only apply in a "civil action of which the district courts have original jurisdiction." § 1367(a). That phrase unambiguously invokes the language that Congress has used for more than two hundred years to confer jurisdiction on the federal district courts in civil cases. Nearly every jurisdictional grant in Title 28 provides that "the district courts shall have original jurisdiction" of "civil action[s]" within the scope of the grant. *See, e.g.,* 28 U.S.C. §§ 1331 (federal questions), 1332 (diversity), 1335 (interpleader), 1337 (antitrust), 1338 (intellectual property), 1339 (postal matters), 1340 (internal revenue). Such grants, in turn, have been the subject of judicial interpretation for centuries. *E.g., Strawbridge v. Curtiss,* 7 U.S. (3 Cranch) 267, 2 L.Ed. 435 (1806). By invoking the concept of a district court's "original jurisdiction" over a "civil

---

9. Pfander, Supplemental Jurisdiction and Section 1367: The Case for a Sympa-   thetic Textualism, 148 U.Pa.L.Rev. 109 (1999).

action," Congress presumptively incorporated into § 1367 the longstanding, judicially developed doctrines that determine whether those statutes confer "original jurisdiction" over a particular civil action.

That is important because, under well-settled law, joinder and aggregation have different implications for the existence of "original jurisdiction" in federal-question and diversity cases. Under the federal-question statute, 28 U.S.C. § 1331, the original jurisdiction of the district courts is triggered if the action "aris[es] under the Constitution, laws, or treaties of the United States." All that is required is the federal question. Joinder questions arise only after "original jurisdiction" is established, and only to the extent that the court seeks to decide non-federal questions incident to disposition of the federal question.

Under § 1332, by contrast, joinder and aggregation questions can actually *determine* whether the district court has "original jurisdiction" over the action. Joinder affects original jurisdiction through the complete diversity rule of *Strawbridge v. Curtiss, supra.* Aggregation issues affect original jurisdiction because *Clark* prohibits multiple plaintiffs from combining their claims to clear the amount-in-controversy bar. *Strawbridge* and *Clark,* in turn, are binding interpretations of the diversity statute.

Thus, Congress preserved both *Clark* and *Strawbridge* by providing that, before supplemental jurisdiction can attach, the district court must first have "original jurisdiction" over the action. In a diversity case, if the *Clark* rule is not met, or if the parties are not completely diverse, then the "original jurisdiction" requirement in § 1367(a) is not satisfied and supplemental jurisdiction will not attach. On the other hand, if the parties are completely diverse and each plaintiff separately meets the amount-in-controversy requirement, then § 1332 is satisfied and the "original jurisdiction" requirement is met. If so, § 1367 will support any transactionally related claims that the plaintiffs may wish to bring—but only so long as § 1367(b) is satisfied, and only as long as original jurisdiction is not destroyed. This last qualification is important because it precludes a plaintiff from, for example, using § 1367 to circumvent *Strawbridge* by amending her complaint to add a nondiverse party after "original jurisdiction" is initially established.

* * *

We are persuaded to adopt this reading of the statutory text for several reasons. First, it gives effect to Congress's requirement that the district court must have "original jurisdiction" over the "civil action" before supplemental jurisdiction can apply. Congress could have applied a different test in § 1367(a)—for example, it could have permitted supplemental jurisdiction whenever any single *claim* in the action would have supported original jurisdiction if it had been brought by itself.[11] But

---

11. The dissent would apply such a test in this case. According to the dissent, § 1367 authorizes supplemental jurisdiction whenever the district court has "original jurisdiction over a *claim.*" (emphasis added). The problem with the dissent's theory

that is not what the statute says.[12]

* * *

Given this background, it is significant that Congress included the same "original jurisdiction" requirement in § 1367. Congress purposefully employed language in § 1367(a) that had already been interpreted in § 1441 to incorporate the traditional doctrines of federal jurisdiction—including *Strawbridge* and *Clark.*

Another advantage of our interpretation of § 1367 is that it aligns statutory supplemental jurisdiction with the judicially developed doctrines of pendent and ancillary jurisdiction as they existed prior to *Finley.* Congress took the opportunity in § 1367 to codify the doctrines of pendent and ancillary jurisdiction under a single heading. Neither of those doctrines permitted a diversity plaintiff to circumvent the requirements of § 1332 simply by joining her claim in an action brought by another, jurisdictionally competent diversity plaintiff.[13] We see no indication in § 1367 that Congress wanted to alter that rule. Notably, where Congress *did* intend to alter existing law in § 1367, it took pains to do so directly and unequivocally. *See* § 1367(a) (repudiating *Finley* in a separate sentence: "Such supplemental jurisdiction shall include claims that involve the joinder or intervention of additional parties.").

Finally, our interpretation explains the omission of Rule 20 plaintiffs from § 1367(b). This was the "apparent incongruity" on which the

is that § 1367(a) does not refer to original jurisdiction over "claims." Rather, the statute requires a *"civil action* of which the district courts have original jurisdiction." § 1367(a) (emphasis added).

That distinction is critical. The Supreme Court has never held that original jurisdiction exists over a "civil action" under § 1332 simply because *one claim* in the action is between diverse parties and exceeds the jurisdictional minimum. On the contrary, original jurisdiction does not lie unless *all* of the parties in the case are diverse. Similarly, § 1332 is not satisfied, and original jurisdiction over the "civil action" does not exist, unless *each* plaintiff independently satisfies the amount-in-controversy requirement. Because the complaint in this case fails this requirement, original jurisdiction over the "civil action" is absent and § 1367 is inapplicable.

12. The dissent argues that a single claim is sufficient to create original jurisdiction over a "civil action" under § 1332 because courts are not normally required to dismiss the entire action when a jurisdictional flaw is discovered. Rather, a court may simply dismiss the offending parties. *See, e.g., Newman–Green, Inc. v. Alfonzo–Larrain,* 490 U.S. 826, 836, 109 S.Ct. 2218,

104 L.Ed.2d 893 (1989) (courts of appeals may cure jurisdictional defects by dismissing dispensable nondiverse parties); *Clark,* 306 U.S. at 590, 59 S.Ct. 744 (dismissing parties who failed to meet the amount-in-controversy requirement but retaining jurisdiction over the party that satisfied it). This argument confuses the *existence* of original jurisdiction with remedies for its absence. Original jurisdiction over the "civil action" may be *achieved* by dismissing certain dispensable parties. But as long as the offending parties are present, original jurisdiction over the "civil action" cannot exist, regardless of whether any single claim in the action would satisfy § 1332 by itself.

13. The doctrine of pendent jurisdiction, which allowed plaintiffs to assert non-federal claims in federal court, was applicable only in federal-question cases. Ancillary jurisdiction, by contrast, applied in both federal-question and diversity cases, but that doctrine "typically involve[d] claims *by a defending party* haled into court against his will." [*Owen Equip., & Erection Co v.*] *Kroger,* 437 U.S. at 376, 98 S.Ct. 2396 (emphasis added). Moreover, the Court in *Kroger* made clear that a party could not resort to ancillary jurisdiction where doing so would effectively circumvent the complete diversity rule.

Seventh Circuit relied in *Stromberg*. *Stromberg* reasoned that because Congress omitted claims by Rule 20 plaintiffs from § 1367(b), it must have intended to allow permissively joined plaintiffs to bring claims that § 1332 would not otherwise support. In our view, there is a better explanation. The permissive joinder of a nondiverse party, whether in the original complaint or afterwards, destroys complete diversity and thus deprives the court of "original jurisdiction." Likewise, "original jurisdiction" is destroyed by the joinder of a Rule 20 plaintiff who, like Beatriz's family members, cannot satisfy the amount-in-controversy requirement. Supplemental jurisdiction in such a case fails at the threshold of § 1367(a), so there was simply no need for Congress to include Rule 20 plaintiffs in subsection (b) in order to preserve *Clark* or *Strawbridge*.

A few courts have rejected this reading of § 1367 on the ground that nothing in the statute suggests the phrase "original jurisdiction" has a different meaning in diversity cases than in federal-question cases. That argument is misplaced. The requirement of "original jurisdiction" in § 1367(a) has the same meaning in every case: that some underlying statutory grant of original jurisdiction must be satisfied. What differs between federal question and diversity cases is not the meaning of "original jurisdiction" but rather the requirements of sections 1331 and 1332. Under § 1331, the sole issue is whether a federal question appears on the face of the plaintiff's well-pleaded complaint; the identity of the parties and the amounts they stand to recover are largely irrelevant. Section 1332, by contrast, predicates original jurisdiction on the identity of the parties (*i.e.,* complete diversity) and their ability to meet the amount-in-controversy requirement. So the "original jurisdiction" language in § 1367 operates differently in federal-question and diversity cases not because the meaning of that term varies, but because the requirements of the underlying statutes are different.

Nor does this reading of the statute make § 1367(b) superfluous. By itself, § 1367(a) would authorize a wide variety of supplemental claims in diversity cases—counterclaims by defendants, cross-claims among plaintiffs, claims by and against intervenors, and so on. Section § 1367(b) is important because it ensures that this authorization does not functionally undermine the requirements of § 1332. Suppose, for example, that the defendant in a diversity case impleads a nondiverse party under Fed.R.Civ.P. 14. Section 1367(b) would prevent the plaintiff from asserting a non-federal claim against the impleaded party. This example, of course, is *Owen Equip. & Erection Co. v. Kroger,* 437 U.S. 365, 98 S.Ct. 2396, 57 L.Ed.2d 274 (1978), in which the Supreme Court held that permitting ancillary (now supplemental) jurisdiction over such a claim would allow diversity plaintiffs to "defeat the statutory requirement of complete diversity by the simple expedient of suing only those defendants who were of diverse citizenship and waiting for them to implead nondiverse defendants." Section 1367(b) codifies *Kroger's* anticircumvention rationale, not merely as against parties impleaded under Rule 14, but in a variety of situations in which "original jurisdiction" may technically exist but the exercise of supplemental jurisdiction "would be inconsistent with the jurisdictional requirements of section 1332." Nothing about our interpretation of § 1367(a) obviates this provision.

Admittedly, our reading of § 1367 is not perfect. One difficulty is that while § 1367(b) does not mention Rule 20 plaintiffs, it does refer to "claims by persons proposed to be joined as plaintiffs under Rule 19"—a reference that is technically unnecessary under our reading of the statute, since the joinder of a nondiverse party as an indispensable plaintiff would likewise destroy original jurisdiction under § 1332. And, on policy grounds, there are certainly litigation efficiencies to be gained by an interpretation of § 1367 that would permit Beatriz's family members' claims to proceed in federal court alongside her own.

But no reading of § 1367 is perfect—the alternative approach embodied in *Stromberg,* for example, accords no significance to Congress's use of the term "original jurisdiction." In light of the historical and legal context to Congress's enactment of § 1367, including the settled interpretation of § 1441 and the established limits on pendent and ancillary jurisdiction, we conclude that Congress intended to preserve the *Clark* anti-aggregation rule by requiring that the district courts must have "original jurisdiction" over the "civil action" before supplemental jurisdiction will lie.

b.   Section 1367 and the Complete Diversity Rule

There is a further reason why we reject the alternative reading of § 1367 set out in the Seventh Circuit's opinion in *Stromberg.* As we have said, *Stromberg's* reading of the statutory text is, while imperfect, at least plausible. Yet it also has surprising and far-reaching consequences: if § 1367 permits the permissive joinder of plaintiffs who cannot meet the amount-in-controversy requirement, then it also permits the joinder of non-diverse plaintiffs. Nothing in the statute distinguishes between the *Clark* amount-in-controversy requirement and the complete diversity rule in *Strawbridge.* So if *Stromberg's* interpretation of § 1367 is correct, Congress overturned nearly 200 years of case law interpreting § 1332 and authorized a potentially huge expansion of the federal docket. Moreover, it did so not by amending the diversity statute itself, but instead by failing to mention Rule 20 plaintiffs in § 1367(b).[16]

We do not think Congress intended § 1367 to work such a revolution in the law of diversity jurisdiction. Congress has long maintained a policy of *restricting* diversity jurisdiction, not expanding it, chiefly by raising the amount-in-controversy bar. Indeed, the same congressional Federal Courts Study Committee that proposed overturning *Finley* and codifying supplemental jurisdiction also proposed *eliminating* most forms of diversity jurisdiction. Congress did not accept that proposal, to be

16. *Stromberg* itself recognized that "[s]upplemental jurisdiction has the potential to move from complete to minimal diversity." Nevertheless, the court concluded that § 1367(b) is adequate to protect the interests served by the *Strawbridge* complete diversity rule. Like many commentators, we disagree.

sure, but that hardly suggests it wanted to *expand* diversity jurisdiction. On the contrary, only a few years after enacting § 1367, Congress again raised the amount-in-controversy bar in an effort to reduce the diversity caseload in the federal courts. The Supreme Court, too, has repeatedly admonished that in light of the burgeoning federal caseload, diversity jurisdiction must be narrowly construed.

Against this background, it is implausible to us that Congress undermined *Strawbridge* and overturned *Clark* by such an unlikely and obscure device as the omission of Rule 20 plaintiffs from § 1367(b).

Moreover, Congress has continued to regard *Strawbridge* as good law even after § 1367. Since 1990, Congress has enacted at least two statutes limiting the rule of complete diversity. Each time, Congress has done so clearly and conspicuously, carefully circumscribing the situations in which *Strawbridge* will not apply. *See* Multiparty, Multiforum Trial Jurisdiction Act of 2002, Pub.L. No. 107–273, § 11020(b)(1)(A), 116 Stat. 1758 (codified at 28 U.S.C. § 1369) (granting the district courts original jurisdiction over "any civil action involving minimal diversity" between adverse parties arising from any single accident in which 75 natural persons died, and further defining "minimal diversity" in the case of both natural and corporate parties).[18] * * *

Congress thus knows how to limit *Strawbridge* clearly when it wishes, and it would have had little reason to enact these statutes if it believed that it had already undermined the complete diversity rule in the supplemental jurisdiction statute. Plainly it did not so believe, and that understanding informs our choice among plausible interpretations of § 1367.

c. Legislative History of § 1367

Finally, the legislative history of § 1367 strongly corroborates the conclusion that Congress did not intend to repudiate *Clark* or *Strawbridge*. Resort to legislative history is appropriate where, as here, the text of a statute is susceptible to two textually plausible interpretations. That is particularly true in this case, given that our sister circuits have reached conflicting answers to the same question based on the same statutory text.

The legislative history of § 1367 is somewhat muddled in its details, but one fact is certain: Congress did not believe that § 1367 would make significant changes to the law of diversity jurisdiction. The House Judiciary Committee report—the only congressional report concerning the provision that became § 1367—stated that the bill was intended to "essentially restore the pre-*Finley* understandings of the authorization for and limits on ... supplemental jurisdiction." H. Rep. No. 101–734, at 28 (Sept. 10, 1990). * * *

---

18. The dissent points to the Multiparty, Multiforum Trial Jurisdiction Act (MMTJA) as evidence that Congress is backing away from its long history of restricting diversity jurisdiction. We disagree. Our conclusion is that Congress is keenly aware of the limits on diversity jurisdiction and expects those limits to apply except where, as in the MMTJA, it specifically and unambiguously alters them.

At no point in the legislative process did any member of Congress suggest that § 1367 would overturn *Clark,* undercut the complete diversity rule, or otherwise dramatically expand federal diversity jurisdiction.[19]

III.

We hold that § 1367 does not authorize jurisdiction over Beatriz's family members' claims. Those claims would have been barred under *Clark* before 1990, and we conclude that Congress did not upset that rule when it overturned *Finley* and codified the prior law of pendent and ancillary jurisdiction in § 1367.[20]

TORRUELLA, Circuit Judge.

* * *

It is because I believe that a court's role is limited to applying the statute, not changing the statute, that I respectfully dissent. In doing so, I join the majority of our sister circuits that have interpreted 28 U.S.C. § 1367 to grant a district court jurisdiction to hear a plaintiff's claim that does not meet the amount-in-controversy, if a co-plaintiff's claim satisfies the amount-in-controversy requirement.

I.   *Joinder and class actions*

Before analyzing § 1367 and its meaning, one observation must be made. The majority [argues] that the class action context differs from the Rule 20 joinder context. Such a characterization is misguided for several reasons.

---

19. We express no view on the related but distinct issue of whether § 1367 overturns the Supreme Court's holding in *Zahn v. International Paper Co.,* 414 U.S. 291, 94 S.Ct. 505, 38 L.Ed.2d 511 (1973), that each class member in a diversity-only class action must meet the jurisdictional amount in controversy. The application of § 1367 to diversity-only class actions is a different problem for several reasons, including because (1) the complete diversity rule applies with diminished force in the class-action context, *see Supreme Tribe of Ben–Hur v. Cauble,* 255 U.S. 356, 366, 41 S.Ct. 338, 65 L.Ed. 673 (1921); (2) section 1367(b) does not mention Rule 23 at all, while it mentions Rule 20 at least as to defending parties; and (3) there are conflicting signals in the legislative history as to whether Congress intended to overrule *Zahn.*

20. The dissent argues that Congress could not have intended this result because it is too similar to the outcome in *Finley,* which Congress meant to overturn. The analogy to *Finley,* however, is both inaccurate and unpersuasive. *Finley* involved an exclusively federal claim under the FTCA; this case is predicated only on diversity. That is a critical difference: the rules of pendent jurisdiction have always been more flexible in federal-question cases than in diversity cases, *see supra* note 13, no doubt to facilitate a federal forum for claims arising under federal law. The federal interest in Beatriz's family members' ability to assert their state-law claims in federal court is much more attenuated.

In *Finley,* moreover, there was no forum available in which the federal plaintiff could assert all of her claims. In this case, by contrast, such a forum is readily available: the courts of Puerto Rico. It was the plaintiffs who chose to sue in federal court. Against that background, the dissent's judicial efficiency arguments ring hollow. *Cf. Kroger,* 437 U.S. at 376, 98 S.Ct. 2396 ("A plaintiff cannot complain if ancillary jurisdiction does not encompass all of his possible claims in a case such as this one, since it is he who has chosen the federal rather than the state forum. . . .").

First, the majority opinion fails to acknowledge that for § 1367 purposes, *Clark* and *Zahn* stand for the same principle. In *Clark v. Paul Gray, Inc.,* the Supreme Court held that each plaintiff's claim must meet the amount-in-controversy requirement. In *Zahn v. Int'l Paper Co.,* the Supreme Court held that each class member's claim must meet the amount-in-controversy requirement. Thus, *Clark* "is the nonclass analog to *Zahn.* Section 1367, on its face, overrules *Clark,* just as it overrules *Zahn.*"

This position has been adopted by every circuit court to consider the issue. As the Seventh Circuit noted, "§ 1367 does not distinguish class actions from other cases . . . [and section 1367] affects *Clark* and *Zahn* equally." *Stromberg Metal Works,* 77 F.3d at 931. * * *

Second, if a distinction were to be made between class actions and joinder, the distinction would favor allowing supplemental jurisdiction in joinder situations, and not in class action situations, as "it is hard to avoid remarking that allowing thousands of small claims into federal court via the class device is a substantially greater expansion of jurisdiction than is allowing a single pendent party." *Stromberg Metal Works,* 77 F.3d at 931. Thus, it is "easy to imagine wanting to overturn *Clark* but not *Zahn;* it is much harder to imagine wanting to overturn *Zahn* but not *Clark,* and we have no reason to believe that Congress harbored such a secret desire."

II.   The plain meaning of § 1367

When interpreting a statute, the starting point is the statute's text. Section 1367(a) provides that district courts shall have supplemental jurisdiction over claims that form part of the same case or controversy as any civil action of which the court has original jurisdiction. For diversity purposes, a district court has original jurisdiction if the plaintiff's citizenship differs from the defendant's and the claim exceeds $75,000.

Section 1367(b) creates exceptions to § 1367(a) if (1) jurisdiction is based on diversity (§ 1332), (2) the plaintiff is the party seeking to assert supplemental jurisdiction against persons made parties under Rule 14 (third-party practice), 19 (mandatory joinder), 20 (permissive joinder), or 24 (intervention) of the Federal Rules of Civil Procedure or persons proposed to be joined as plaintiffs or intervene as plaintiffs under Rules 19 and 24 respectively, and exercising jurisdiction over the supplemental claims would be inconsistent with the statutory requirements of diversity jurisdiction under § 1332.

Section 1367(c) creates further exceptions, notably awarding a district court discretion to decline supplemental jurisdiction if the supplemental jurisdiction claim predominates over the claim that has original jurisdiction.[26]

26. Section 1367(c) states: "(c) The district courts may decline to exercise supplemental jurisdiction over a claim . . . if—(1) the claim raises a novel or complex issue of State law, (2) the claim substantially predominates over the claim or claims over which the district court has original jurisdiction, (3) the district court has dismissed

Applying § 1367(a) to the present case is straightforward. Before supplemental jurisdiction can apply, a district court must have original jurisdiction over a claim. In this case, the district court has jurisdiction over Beatriz's claims because Beatriz is a citizen of a different state than Star–Kist and has alleged claims for which it is not a legal certainty that the damages are less than $75,000. *See* 28 U.S.C. § 1332. Since the district court has jurisdiction over Beatriz's claims, it may assert supplemental jurisdiction over Beatriz's family members' claims if they arise out of the same case or controversy. *See* 28 U.S.C. § 1367(a). There is no dispute that all of the claims in this case arise out of the same case or controversy.

Supplemental jurisdiction may attach unless one of the exceptions applies. *See* 28 U.S.C. § 1367(b) & (c). The exceptions pertaining to Federal Rule of Civil Procedure 14 (third-party practice), Rule 19 (mandatory joinder), Rule 20 (permissive joinder), or Rule 24 (intervention) are inapplicable to this case as there are no claims by plaintiffs *against* persons made parties under those rules. The further exception pertaining to Federal Rule of Civil Procedure 19 does not apply as Beatriz's family members are not indispensable parties. The last exception pertaining to Federal Rule of Civil Procedure Rule 24 does not apply as the family members are not seeking to intervene. Thus, none of the exceptions in § 1367(b) apply.

The exceptions in § 1367(c) also do not apply. The claims of Beatriz's family members do not raise novel or complex issues of Commonwealth law, their claims do not substantially predominate Beatriz's claims, and there do not tend to be any compelling reasons for declining jurisdiction. Thus, a plain, straightforward reading of § 1367 results in the district court having jurisdiction over Beatriz's family members' claims.

III.   The majority opinion's alternative approach

The majority opinion disagrees with this conclusion, however, by arguing that the term "original jurisdiction" in § 1367(a) has two distinct meanings. In federal-question cases, § 1367 applies if *at least one* claim qualifies for "original jurisdiction." But, in diversity cases, the majority argues, § 1367 applies only if *all* claims qualify for original jurisdiction. This contrived reading of § 1367 is wrong for several reasons.

First, the majority's interpretation of § 1367(a) violates "the basic canon of statutory construction that identical terms within an Act bear the same meaning." In this case, not only does the majority opinion define identical terms differently, it defines the same term differently. There is "nothing in the text of subsection (a) to suggest, even remotely, that there is such a difference in meaning."

all claims over which it has original juris-   there are other compelling reasons for de-
diction, or (4) in exceptional circumstances,   clining jurisdiction."

[The majority also overlooks the doctrine that "original jurisdiction" may exist even if some of the claims asserted do not fall within it; the jurisdictionally insufficient claims may be dismissed while jurisdiction is retained over the others.] Thus, the fact that a case contains claims that destroy diversity does not prevent the court from maintaining jurisdiction over the claims that qualify for "original jurisdiction."

The very language of § 1367 incorporates this concept. Section 1367(a) states that a court shall have supplemental jurisdiction over all other claims that are "so related to claims in the action." The "other claims" join the related claims (those qualifying for original jurisdiction) as part of the civil action.

In this case, Beatriz's claims qualified for "original jurisdiction." On remand, it will be undisputed that Beatriz's claims constitute "a civil action of which the district courts have original jurisdiction." Once the majority opinion concluded that the district court had "original jurisdiction" over the "civil action" consisting of Beatriz's claims, it should have turned to § 1367's statement that "in any civil action of which the district courts have original jurisdiction [(Beatriz's claims)], the district courts shall have supplemental jurisdiction over all other [related] claims [(Beatriz's family's claims)]." Instead of taking this step, the majority opinion attempts to redefine the practice of interpreting § 1332 claims to achieve a result contrary to that dictated by § 1367.

Further, the majority's interpretation of § 1367(a) violates "[t]he cardinal principle of statutory construction . . . to give effect, if possible, to every clause and word of a statute, . . . rather than to emasculate an entire section." The majority's interpretation of § 1367(a) eviscerates portions of § 1367(b). As the majority is forced to admit, its interpretation of § 1367 makes the Rule 19 exception in § 1367(b) "unnecessary." What the majority does not admit is that its interpretation makes other provisions of § 1367 superfluous. For example, according to the majority's interpretation of § 1367, "original jurisdiction" would not exist over a claim made by a plaintiff against a non-diverse defendant joined under Rule 20 of the Federal Rules of Civil Procedure. The majority's interpretation cannot be correct, however, because section 1367(b) specifically excepts supplemental jurisdiction over a claim made by a plaintiff against a non-diverse defendant joined under Rule 20. The only reason § 1367(b) would contain such an exception is if § 1367(a) provides jurisdiction for joined claims against non-diverse defendants. If, as the majority contends, " 'original jurisdiction' under subsection (a) were determined by looking at all the claims in the complaint, there would have been no jurisdiction under § 1332 (and hence no 'original jurisdiction') in the first place." Thus, the exclusion of supplemental jurisdiction of claims by non-diverse parties joined under Rule 20 would be surplusage.

IV. Congressional intent & legislative history

Recognizing that its interpretation of § 1367 results in an "imperfect" reading based on "presumptions," the majority opinion attempts to buttress its position by referring to Congressional intent and legislative history. The majority opinion begins by noting that "Congress has long maintained a policy of restricting diversity jurisdiction." Relying on "long maintained" policy is problematic for several reasons. First, Congressional action in the past sheds little light on what the 101st Congress believed when it passed § 1367. Rather than speculate on what was done in the past, it is more fruitful to look at the actions of the Congress that adopted § 1367. In 1990, the same Congress that passed § 1367 was given the *Report of the Federal Courts Study Committee* which recommended "diversity jurisdiction should be virtually eliminated." This recommendation was *rejected* by Congress. We should not achieve through judicial action what the Federal Courts Study Committee could not convince Congress to achieve. Ultimately, it is not unreasonable to believe that Congress read the plain language of § 1367, recognized that it allowed diversity jurisdiction for supplemental plaintiffs, and voted for it.

Second, the continued validity of Congress's "long maintained policy" of restricting diversity jurisdiction is called into question by Congress's expansion of federal jurisdiction based upon minimal diversity in the Multiparty Multi–Forum Trial Jurisdiction Act in 2002. *See* 28 U.S.C. § 1369.

Third, and perhaps most convincing is the fact that a proposed amendment achieving the majority's result in this case, that would limit supplemental jurisdiction in Rule 20 & 23 cases has been circulating in Congress since 1998. This amendment has done nothing more than circulate for six years. Congress has reasonably rejected that view.

* * *

Perhaps the most relevant piece of legislative history is the fact that Congress passed § 1367 in reaction to the Supreme Court's holding in *Finley,* which held that a plaintiff suing the United States in a Federal Tort Claims Act case could not join a defendant, against whom there were only state law claims, without an independent basis for federal jurisdiction. Had *Finley* not been overturned by § 1367, a plaintiff, such as the one in *Finley,* would have been required to either (1) split the case in two and bring the federal claim in federal court and the state claims in state court, or (2) forsake one of the two claims. To prevent such a result, Congress enacted § 1367.

The majority opinion in this case achieves a result similar to that Congress was trying to avoid by overruling *Finley.* As in *Finley,* the plaintiffs in this case must either (1) pursue Beatriz's claims in federal court and her family's claims in state court, (2) dispose of her family's claims altogether, or (3) pursue all of the claims in state court. The first option leads to a waste of judicial resources and a potential for inconsistent verdicts. The second option deprives Beatriz's family of their day in court. The third option, not present in *Finley,* deprives Beatriz of a federal forum and of her right to a trial by jury, as her case would not receive a jury trial in the Commonwealth courts. As Congress showed by overturning *Finley,* being faced with these options should be avoided.

Ultimately, as the majority concedes, the legislative history is muddled and can be used to support or to contradict either position. In the end, the unclear legislative history leaves us where we started: with the text of the statute.

V.   Conclusion

* * *

I am comforted by and conclude with a statement by the Supreme Court in *Finley:* "Whatever we say regarding the scope of jurisdiction conferred by a particular statute can of course be changed by Congress" or, in this case, by the Supreme Court.

Notes and Questions

1. As both the majority and Judge Torruella point out, the Supreme Court could clear up the interpretation of § 1367, and by granting certiorari in this case it indicated an intention to do so. On the same day it granted certiorari in this case, it also granted certiorari in Allapattah Services, Inc. v. Exxon Corp., 333 F.3d 1248 (11th Cir.2003), which directly presented the question whether supplemental jurisdiction could be used in class actions for the claims of class members that could not satisfy the amount-in-controversy requirement. As of the time this book went to press, the Court had not decided these cases. As noted in *Rosario,* the Court had earlier heard but failed to decide a case raising the class-action question.

2. The majority reserves judgment on whether § 1367 should be held to permit supplemental jurisdiction over claims of unnamed class members that don't satisfy the amount in controversy requirement, while holding that the statute does not affect plaintiffs joined under Rule 20. Is there really a difference between the two situations? If so, would it make sense for the statute to forbid joinder under Rule 20, even for the members of the same family, but to permit state-law class actions into federal court? The Class Action Fairness Act of 2005 added 28 U.S.C.A. § 1332(d), which gives the federal courts jurisdiction over certain state-law class actions in which over $5 million is sought in the aggregate on behalf of the class, without regard to the size of individual claims. The Act explicitly invokes minimal diversity jurisdiction, providing that such a case may be in federal court so long as any member of the plaintiff class is a citizen of a state different from any defendant. The House Report accompanying § 1367, in contrast, said that it "is not intended to affect the jurisdictional requirements of 28 U.S.C. § 1332 in diversity-only class actions, as those requirements were interpreted prior to *Finley [v. United States,* supra p. 892]," and cited Zahn v. International Paper Co., supra p. 892, which held that each class member must satisfy the amount-in-controversy requirement.

3. The dissent in *Rosario* points to the Multiparty, Multiforum Trial Jurisdiction Act, 28 U.S.C. § 1369, as showing that Congress has been tending toward undercutting the complete-diversity rule. Like the Class Action Fairness Act, this provision relies on minimal diversity to permit

federal-court jurisdiction in litigation arising from accidents in which at least 75 people are killed. Examine § 1369. Does it support the dissent's arguments? If § 1367 is interpreted as the dissent argues, would § 1369 be necessary?

4. The majority says that "[t]he problem of pendent-party jurisdiction implicates some of the most sensitive and enduring issues in the law of federal jurisdiction." The Supreme Court similarly said that adding parties is more problematical than adding claims in Aldinger v. Howard, supra p. 892. But hasn't Congress rejected that argument by adopting the last sentence of § 1367(a)? Why should the courts' reluctance to add parties be pertinent to interpretation of the statute?

5. The majority argues that the dissent's view would undercut the complete-diversity requirement and produce a "revolution in the law of diversity jurisdiction." Is there any indication in the language of the statute that Congress wanted to preserve the complete-diversity requirement? What is the purpose of § 1367(b)? According to the House Report that accompanied the legislation, "[t]he net effect of subsection (b) is to implement the principal rationale of Owen Equipment Co. v. Kroger, 437 U.S. 365 (1978)." H.R.Rep. No. 734, 101st Cong, 2d Sess., at 29 n.16. As explained supra p. 891, *Kroger* forbade use of ancillary jurisdiction in ways that would defeat the complete-diversity requirement. Does Judge Torruella deny that the complete diversity rule could be undermined by his approach to the statute?

§ 1367(b) clearly does forbid claims against additional defendants joined under Rule 20 unless there is an independent basis for federal-court jurisdiction. So even Beatriz could not sue a nondiverse defendant in federal court as a co-defendant in her suit against Star–Kist. Indeed, her original suit included a claim against Star–Kist Caribe, Inc., the branch of Star–Kist that does business in Puerto Rico, but because that defendant was a Puerto Rico citizen for diversity purposes all claims against it had to be dismissed. Is there a reason why Congress would have wanted to prevent Beatriz from using supplemental jurisdiction to sue Star–Kist Caribe in federal court, but have wanted to allow her parents and sister to join in her suit against Star–Kist Foods?

Could it be that Congress made a mistake in omitting plaintiffs joined under Rule 20 from § 1367(b)? Law professors involved in drafting the statute observed that "[w]e can only hope that the federal courts will plug that potentially gaping hold in the complete diversity requirement." Rowe, Burbank & Mengler, Compounding or Creating Confusion about Supplemental Jurisdiction, 40 Emory L.J. 943, 961 n.1 (1991). Early on, some courts did. See Ware v. Jolly Roger Rides, Inc., 857 F.Supp. 462, 464 (D.Md.1994) ("§ 1367 does not change the complete diversity requirement.").

6. How should courts approach interpretation of a statute that appears to include a "mistake" by Congress? Judge Torruella argues that the fact bills to "correct" § 1367 have been proposed in Congress but not adopted shows that it does not agree that it made a mistake in the first place. Should the failure of a recent Congress to amend legislation adopted by an earlier Congress affect the interpretation of that legislation?

One view is that if Congress has made a mistake it is up to Congress to correct the mistake. Certainly that should be true if the "mistake" was one of policy; courts ought not give effect in their interpretation of statutes to their view that Congress made a policy mistake in adopting certain legislation. Whether courts always heed that limit can be debated. Some say that courts invoke congressional intent as a method of altering statutory language to give effect to their policy views. Might that be a problem in *Rosario*?

Professor Pfander's article offered a way out of the difficulty, by focusing on the term "original jurisdiction" in § 1367(a), and the majority adopts this view in *Rosario*. Ordinarily one looks into the murky area of congressional intent only after finding that the statute itself is ambiguous. Does the majority's view in *Rosario* provide a satisfactory ground for looking beyond the words of the statute? Consider the views of the court in Olden v. LaFarge Corp., 383 F.3d 495, 504 (6th Cir.2004):

> It is the structure of this statute which makes its meaning unambiguous. The first part of the statute (§ 1367(a)) contains a sweeping grant of supplemental jurisdiction giving the courts supplemental jurisdiction over all claims not excluded by the second part (S 1367(b)). The second part of the statute contains all of the exclusions. Given this structure, it defies logic to suggest that the inclusive section of the statute, containing the sweeping grant of supplemental jurisdiction, also contains a completely unspoken, yet critically important exclusion. This is particularly true where there is no doubt that the unspoken exclusion would fit naturally into the express list of exclusions in the second part. Congress was not using 28 U.S.C. § 1367 as an opportunity to play "Hide the Ball," "Where's Waldo?" or "Find the Hidden Exclusion." To argue that the alternative interpretation is viable enough to make this statute ambiguous only begs the question of the meaning of the word "ambiguity."

7. It is clear that Congress intended § 1367(a) to extend supplemental jurisdiction to the limits of the "constitutional case" under Article III. This feature contrasts with §§ 1331 and 1332, which have both been construed not to go to the constitutional limit in their grants of jurisdiction. If the dissent in *Rosario* is right, could a vacationer from Star–Kist's home state who was similarly injured by a can of Star–Kist tuna in Puerto Rico join in Beatriz's suit despite the absence of diversity? The "common nucleus of operative fact" test does not offer much guidance. Consider the following argument that there has been "a good deal of circularity and question-begging":

> Cases delineating the scope of a constitutional "case" for purposes of ancillary jurisdiction offer little help. Here courts speak of the "same transaction or occurrence." This phrase, too, is ambiguous. For example, assume a traffic accident, followed by a fist fight between the drivers. Driver A sues driver B for negligence in causing the accident; driver B counterclaims for battery arising out of the postaccident fight. On a purely linguistic or conceptual level, these two incidents could be characterized as either being part of the same occurrence or not. Courts that define the phrase in terms of evidentiary overlap would probably decline to find these incidents to be part of the same occurrence, because there likely will be little, if any, evidentiary overlap. Yet courts that define the

phrase in terms of the broader concept of "logical relationship" would quite probably find that the incidents are, in fact, part of the same occurrence.

Redish, Reassessing the Allocation of Judicial Business Between State and Federal Courts: Federal Jurisdiction and the "Martian Chronicles," 78 Va.L.Rev. 1769, 1822–23 (1992).

8. A court that may exercise supplemental jurisdiction may also decline to do so pursuant to § 1367(c). Judge Torruella argues that this provision would provide no ground for declining to exercise jurisdiction over the claims of the other family members in *Rosario*. Is this correct? In United Mine Workers v. Gibbs, supra pp. 890–91, the Court emphasized that the district courts had broad discretion to decline to exercise pendent jurisdiction. In Executive Software North America, Inc. v. United States District Court, 24 F.3d 1545 (9th Cir.1994), the court took a narrower view of the statute: "once it is determined that the assertion of supplemental jurisdiction is permissible under section 1367(a) and (b), section 1367(c) provides the only valid basis upon which the district court may decline jurisdiction." Thus, a court may only decline jurisdiction if it identifies a factual predicate in the case that corresponds to one of those enumerated in the statute. Other courts have recognized limits to authority under § 1367(c) to dismiss. See Montano v. City of Chicago, 375 F.3d 593 (7th Cir.2004) (holding that failure to exercise supplemental jurisdiction over state-law claims was an abuse of discretion). But the fact that § 1367(c) might apply in a case does not require dismissal. See Motorola Credit Corp. v. Uzan, 388 F.3d 39 (2d Cir.2004) (district court was not required to decline to exercise supplemental jurisdiction over state-law claims after dismissing all federal claims because the court was fully conversant with the facts and had conducted a trial on the merits).

9. § 1367(d) tolls the running of the limitations period for a party that has invoked supplemental jurisdiction during the time the federal case is pending and for 30 days thereafter, permitting the party to file all the claims in state court if proceeding in federal court becomes impossible. As the Supreme Court explained in Jinks v. Richland County, 538 U.S. 456, 123 S.Ct. 1667, 155 L.Ed.2d 631 (2003):

> Prior to the enactment of § 1367(d), [prospective plaintiffs] had the following unattractive options: (1) They could file a single federal-court action, which would run the risk that the federal court would dismiss the state-law claims after the limitations period had expired; (2) they could file a single state-law action, which would abandon their right to a federal forum; (3) they could file separate, timely actions in federal and state court and ask that the state-court litigation be stayed pending resolution of the federal case, which would increase litigation costs with no guarantee that the state court would oblige. Section 1367(d) replaces this selection of inadequate choices with the assurance that state-law claims asserted under § 1367(a) will not become time barred while pending in federal court.

10. The Supplemental Jurisdiction Act has gotten a lot of scholarly attention; "it is difficult to think of another topic in civil procedure that has commanded more scholarly attention in the past thirteen years." Freer, The Cauldron Boils: Supplemental Jurisdiction, Amount in Controversy, and

Diversity of Citizenship Class Actions, 53 Emory L.J. 55, 57–58 (2004). For further reading on § 1367, see Symposium, A Reappraisal of the Supplemental Jurisdiction Statute, 74 Ind.L.J. 1–250 (1998); and exchange of articles between law professors critical of the statute and others involved in drafting it, 40 Emory L.J. 943–1014 (1991), and a colloquy among five other law professors on the same topic, 41 Emory L.J. 1–113 (1992).

D. REMOVAL

Plaintiffs who could sue in federal court sometimes choose to sue in state court instead. Sometimes they do so because federal court does not offer jurisdiction for all the claims or parties they wish to include in the suit. For example, in Rosario Ortega v. Star–Kist Foods, supra p. 892, if Beatriz wants to proceed in the same suit as her parents and sister, under the First Circuit's interpretation she will have to do so in a Puerto Rico court in the absence of subject matter jurisdiction in federal court over the claims for the other family members.

But often the suit filed in state court could as easily have been filed in federal court. Should defendants then be permitted to overrule plaintiff's choice to litigate in state court and take the case to federal court? That is what removal allows. Removal jurisdiction is "quite an anomalous jurisdiction, giving a defendant sued in a court of competent jurisdiction, the right to elect a forum of its own choosing. The procedure was unknown to the common law, nor is removal mentioned in the Constitution. Nevertheless there has been provision for removal of cases from state courts to federal courts from the First Judiciary Act, in 1789, to the present day, and the constitutionality of removal is entirely settled." C. Wright & M. Kane, Law of Federal Courts 225 (6th ed. 2002). In a sense, the addition of removal jurisdiction to the original jurisdiction provided by 28 U.S.C. §§ 1331 and 1332 means that there is a de facto preference for litigation in federal court in cases where federal jurisdictional requirements are satisfied. Plaintiff may initially file there without consulting defendant, and defendant may remove to federal court without the assent of plaintiff. So if either plaintiff or defendant wants the case in federal court, it will be.

In *Rosario Ortega*, plaintiffs wanted to be in federal court because they would not have a jury trial in the Puerto Rico courts. Even though federal court offers many advantages, plaintiffs often strongly prefer to avoid it. Walker, Keep Your Case in State Court, Trial, Sept., 2004, at 22 explains why:

> Plaintiff attorneys' preference for state courts is undisputed and understandable. Reasons for avoiding federal court range from the mundane (greater familiarity with state procedure) to the strategic (greater likelihood of securing justice for clients).

> In most cases, local judges are elected by the very people whose disputes they will hear, motivating speedy and fair adjudication. Federal judges are appointed for life, and their courts are clogged with criminal cases. The so-called war on drugs has so overburdened

the federal judiciary that getting a civil case tried at all in many federal courts is nearly impossible.

To reduce their burgeoning dockets, federal courts have increasingly engaged in stringent control of discovery, aggressive encouragement of settlement, and more frequent granting of summary judgment. As a result, litigation in federal court is more expensive and time-consuming. Moreover, plaintiffs whose cases are removed to federal court are substantially less successful than those who originally filed there. Finally, but significantly, lawsuits in federal court are increasingly being consolidated into multidistrict, pretrial litigation proceedings, where they often languish for years.

Defense attorneys are not oblivious to these facts; upon receiving a state court complaint, they frequently search for any conceivable basis to remove the lawsuit to federal court.

The bottom line is that removal is a subject that a defendant is likely to examine with care upon being sued in state court. A plaintiff lawyer who wishes to remain in state court may therefore give serious thought to configuring her suit in a way that will make it nonremovable, and also to look carefully to whether defendant has used the proper procedure in removing if it attempts to do so.

Read 28 U.S.C. §§ 1441, 1446, and 1447, and consider the following questions.

Notes and Questions

1. Suppose your client, a Californian, is injured in a single-car crash in California while driving a new car manufactured by Ford Motor Co., a citizen of Delaware and Michigan. There is good reason to believe that the crash was caused by a defect in the car's steering.

(a) If it were urgently important that your client's case remain in state court, but not necessary that it be a California state court, how would you assure that Ford could not remove? See 28 U.S.C. § 1441(b) and recall Merrell Dow Pharmaceuticals v. Thompson, supra p. 877; compare Spencer v. U.S. District Court, 393 F.3d 867 (9th Cir.2004) (amendment to add local, diverse, defendant after removal does not mandate remand even though case would not have been removable if the local defendant had originally been sued). Why should in-state defendants be forbidden to remove on grounds of diversity? Recall that diversity jurisdiction is said to exist to protect against local prejudice. If it should not be available to in-state defendants, should local plaintiffs similarly be forbidden to file in federal courts on grounds of diversity? What if they simply go to another state and sue there in federal court?

(b) If it were important to bring the case in a California state court, would there be any way to prevent Ford from removing? How about initially requesting less than $75,000 in damages? Should this suffice to defeat removal if California state-court procedure permits a plaintiff to increase the amount sought later in the suit? In Hollenbeck v. Outboard Marine Corp., 201 F.Supp.2d 990 (E.D. Mo. 2001), the complaint attempted to limit the damages claim to less than $75,000 for "as long as removal potential exists." State law allowed plaintiff to amend to increase the damage claim later, and the body of the complaint alleged present damages of at least $160,000. Removal was allowed.

(c) If plaintiff had purchased the car from a local car dealer two weeks before the accident, there might be a claim against the dealer in connection with the failure of the car's steering. If plaintiff sues the local dealer as well, should that affect removability? See Poulos v. Naas Foods, Inc., 959 F.2d 69, 72–73 (7th Cir.1992) (if a nondiverse defendant was fraudulently joined, and there is no possibility of success against it, then the case is removable despite the presence of the nondiverse defendant); Smallwood v. Illinois Central R.R. Co., 385 F.3d 568 (5th Cir.2004) (renaming fraudulent joinder doctrine "improper joinder"). How can the federal court determine whether a defendant has been fraudulently joined without passing on the merits of the claim against that defendant? Would passing on the merits involve the exercise of subject matter jurisdiction? Given the absence of diversity, where would that jurisdiction come from? Cf. Rule 11.

Could the same fraudulent or improper joinder reasoning be applied if plaintiff joined another plaintiff in a state-court suit with the result that the case could not be removed? Suppose, in Rosario Ortega v. Star–Kist Foods, Inc., supra p. 892, that plaintiffs had wanted to ensure that the case would not be removable. Should joining the claims of all four family members accomplish that objective? Would there be a ground for concluding that this joinder was not proper? Should it matter whether Puerto Rico law recognizes a claim by family members under such circumstances?

(d) Assume that plaintiff does sue the dealer and thus defeats removal. Six months later the dealer files a motion for summary judgment on the ground that there is no evidence that it was responsible for any fault in the car's steering. After this motion is filed plaintiff and the dealer reach a settlement under which plaintiff will consent to dismissal of her claim against the dealer in return for payment of a sum of money. Would dismissal of the dealer affect removability? See 28 U.S.C.A. § 1446(b). Would it matter if the dealer agreed to defer the dismissal until a year and a day after plaintiff filed the suit?

In Tedford v. Warner–Lambert Co., 327 F.3d 423 (5th Cir. 2003), plaintiff orchestrated the addition of a non-diverse defendant but executed a post-dated notice of nonsuit as to that defendant that became effective one day after the time to remove had expired. Reasoning that "[s]trict application of the one-year limit would encourage plaintiffs to join nondiverse defendants for 366 days simply to avoid federal court," the court concluded that "Tedford's forum manipulation justifies application of an equitable exception" to the one-year limitation on removal.

(e) Assume that plaintiff does not sue the dealer, and Ford removes the case. A week later, plaintiff amends the complaint to reduce the prayer for damages below the jurisdictional minimum. May plaintiff then obtain a remand to state court? See St. Paul Mercury Indem. Co. v. Red Cab Co., 303 U.S. 283, 58 S.Ct. 586, 82 L.Ed. 845 (1938) (plaintiff's reduction of the amount sought below the jurisdictional minimum did not deprive the court of removal jurisdiction, for that is determined by the circumstances in the case at the time of removal and not by later events).

(f) Assume that plaintiff does not sue the dealer, and Ford removes the case. Six months later, plaintiff learns through discovery that the steering was significantly damaged in dealer preparation. Can plaintiff add a claim against the dealer at that point? See 28 U.S.C. § 1447(e). How should the court decide whether to permit addition of the dealer? Should it matter that, due to the statute of limitations, it is too late to file a separate suit against the dealer in state court?

2. Congress has decreed that certain types of cases are not removable even though plaintiff could file initially in federal court. See, e.g., 28 U.S.C.A. § 1445(a) (Federal Employers' Liability Act and Jones Act cases); 1445(c) (worker's compensation proceedings); compare Breuer v. Jim's Concrete of Brevard, Inc., 538 U.S. 691, 123 S.Ct. 1882, 155 L.Ed.2d 923 (2003) (action under the Fair Labor Standards Act may be removed; nothing in that statute forbids removal). Why would Congress want to guarantee plaintiffs in some cases a choice of forum that defendant could not veto?

3. The Supreme Court has emphasized that removal is limited to the grounds authorized in § 1441. Owing to concerns about mass torts, federal courts began in the 1990s to permit removal of state-court cases that overlapped with federal-court proceedings under the All Writs Act, 28 U.S.C. § 1651, which authorizes federal courts to issue "all writs necessary or appropriate in aid of their respective jurisdictions." In Syngenta Crop Protection, Inc. v. Henson, 537 U.S. 28, 123 S.Ct. 366, 154 L.Ed.2d 368 (2002), the Supreme Court rejected this practice. In that case, the state-court plaintiff had intervened in the federal-court case, participated in settlement negotiations, and stipulated to dismissal with prejudice in federal court. Then, evidently at a hearing defendant was not notified would occur, plaintiff's lawyer told the state-court judge that only certain claims were included in the settlement of the federal action, and the state-court judge said that the state-court case could proceed. On learning of this development, defendant removed to the federal court, which had retained jurisdiction over its case, on the ground that plaintiff's actions threatened to disrupt the proceedings in federal court. The Supreme Court ruled that this was improper because "[t]he right to removal is entirely a creature of statute," and "the All Writs Act does not confer jurisdiction on the federal courts."

This sort of tension between cases in state and federal court has grown in importance. Thus, 28 U.S.C.A. § 1369, adopted in 2002, creates a new form of original federal-court jurisdiction for multiparty, multiforum situations in which the minimal diversity requirement is satisfied and there is litigation resulting from an accident that led to the death of 75 people. 28 U.S.C.A. § 1441(e) contains removal provisions to handle that situation. In early 2005, Congress passed the Class Action Fairness Act of 2005, which responded to perceived improprieties in the handling of some state-court class action. The Act added 28 U.S.C.A. § 1453, which authorizes removal of state-law class actions in which more than $5 million is sought on behalf of the class as a whole unless more than two-thirds of the class members and all the "primary defendants" are citizens of the state in which the action was filed.

4. To remove, a defendant must file a notice of removal in the federal court, signed pursuant to Rule 11, containing a statement of the grounds for removal. How does defendant do that? Does the complaint provide enough information? See Ardison v. Villa, 248 F.2d 226, 227 (10th Cir.1957) ("The manifest purpose of starting the period for removal from the date of service of the 'initial pleading' is to enable the defendant to intelligently ascertain removability from the face of such initial pleading.").

(a) What if defendant can't tell whether there is diversity of citizenship from the complaint? In Lovern v. General Motors Corp., 121 F.3d 160 (4th Cir.1997), plaintiff sued in a Virginia state court claiming that his injuries in an auto accident were magnified by defects in the seatbelt, and the complaint did not state plaintiff's citizenship. Thereafter G.M. obtained the police report about the accident, which stated that plaintiff was a resident of Virginia, and later it received his interrogatory answers, which said the same thing. 28 days after it got the police report, and 8 days after receipt of the interrogatory answers, G.M. removed. By then, 88 days had passed since it was served.

The appellate court held that the removal was timely under the portion of 28 U.S.C.A. § 1446(b) that permits removal in cases not originally removable on later receipt of a paper by defendant from which "it may first be ascertained that the case is one which is removable." Although it would seem that the case was originally removable, whether or not G.M. realized it, the court said the clock starts running only "where an initial pleading reveals a ground for removal," or at least that it does not start running if "such details are obscured or omitted." The court also said that it would not "require courts to inquire into the subjective knowledge of the defendant, an inquiry that could degenerate into a mini-trial regarding who knew what and when," and added that the court could instead "rely on the face of the initial pleading" and that the time to remove would start running only when the right to remove was "apparent within the four corners of the initial pleading." Does this make sense? Would it mean that plaintiffs who want protection against belated removal must include in their pleadings material not required by state-court pleading rules? Must the complaint say "This case is removable"?

(b) What if defendant can't be certain that the amount-in-controversy requirement is satisfied? In Singer v. State Farm Mut. Auto. Ins. Co., 116 F.3d 373 (9th Cir.1997), defendant removed even though the complaint did not state the amount of damages sought. California law forbids personal injury plaintiffs from including such a prayer in the complaint, and an earlier Ninth Circuit case had held that in the absence of such a prayer defendant's assertion that the amount in controversy requirement is satisfied does not suffice to invoke removal jurisdiction. In *Singer*, the court held that defendant's demonstration from material beyond the complaint that the claim exceeded the jurisdictional minimum (a point that plaintiff did not dispute) sufficed. Compare Williams v. Best Buy Co., 269 F.3d 1316 (11th Cir.2001), in which the complaint did not specify the amount of damages sought. Defendant removed after plaintiff refused to stipulate that she did not seek in excess of $75,000. On appeal from the district court's later grant of summary judgment in favor of defendant, the appellate court vacated the judgment and remanded for a determination whether the jurisdictional minimum was really satisfied.

5. *Timing for removal*: As note 4 above suggests, the defendant is under tight time pressures in deciding whether to remove. 28 U.S.C. § 1446(b) permits a defendant 30 days to file a petition to remove.

(a) Suppose plaintiff faxes a copy of the complaint to defendant but takes no further action for 30 days. Has defendant's 30 days to remove expired? The statute says the time to remove starts running from the date of "receipt by the defendant, through service or otherwise, of a copy of the initial pleading." In Murphy Brothers, Inc. v. Michetti Pipe Stringing, Inc., 526 U.S. 344, 119 S.Ct. 1322, 143 L.Ed.2d 448 (1999), the plaintiff faxed a file-stamped copy of the complaint to defendant but did not serve defendant for some time thereafter. When defendant removed within 30 days of formal service, plaintiff contended it was too late because more than 30 days had passed since it faxed the complaint to defendant. The Supreme Court held that the time for removal cannot start running until the defendant is formally served with summons, relying on "a bedrock principle: An individual or entity named as a defendant is not obliged to engage in litigation unless notified of the action, and brought under a court's authority, by formal process."

(b) Should uncertainty about whether the case is removable affect the running of the time to remove? In Krentz v. Robertson, 228 F.3d 897 (8th Cir. 2000), the court held that "the thirty-day time limit of section 1446(b) begins running upon receipt of the initial complaint only when the complaint explicitly discloses the plaintiff is seeking damages in excess of the federal judicial amount." The court thought that this rule would promote certainty and also said that it "prevents a plaintiff from disguising the amount of damages until after the thirty-day time limit has run to avoid removal to federal court." A later district court decision noted the practical implications for plaintiffs who sue in jurisdictions that forbid stating in the complaint how much the plaintiff wants in damages. There, plaintiffs may have to serve a separate notice setting out the amount sought as well as serving the complaint in order to start the 30–day period. Nguyen v. Kautz, 125 F. Supp. 2d 364 (S.D. Iowa 2000).

(c) Suppose defendant does not remove within 30 days. Ordinarily that would prevent any later removal. However, 28 U.S.C. § 1446(b) permits removal after the 30–day period has elapsed based on later developments in the state-court case that make it removable "[i]f the case stated by the initial pleading is not removable." But what if it was not clear initially whether the case was removable, and defendant was wrong to conclude that it was not? If that mistake precludes later removal based on developments in the state-court case, should the risk of losing that opportunity prompt defendants to file removal notices whenever they can consistent with Rule 11?

(d) If the case was removable as originally filed, should any later development in the state-court case revive the right to remove after the 30 days has elapsed? Suppose plaintiff amends the prayer to seek 100 times as much in damages. Suppose plaintiff amends the complaint to add several federal-law claims. If there was diversity and the amount-in-controversy requirement was satisfied in the original complaint is defendant forever barred from removing? A leading treatise reports that courts usually do revive the right to remove where the development "changes the character of the litigation so as to make it substantially a new suit" and concludes that this result is fair because "a willingness on the part of the defendant to remain in a state court to litigate a particular claim should not be interpreted as a willingness on his part to remain in a state court to adjudicate a completely different claim." 14C Fed. Prac. & Pro. § 3732 at 321 (3d ed. 1998).

(e) Why impose such time pressures on defendants? What is the effect on the state-court case of the filing of a notice of removal? See 28 U.S.C. § 1446(d).

6. Courts often say that removal jurisdiction should be strictly construed. E.g., Takeda v. Northwestern Nat'l Life Ins. Co., 765 F.2d 815, 818 (9th Cir.1985) ("We strictly construe the removal statute against removal jurisdiction."). Does that make sense? Congress has made certain claims nonremovable in order to assure plaintiffs an absolute choice between state and federal court. See note 2 above. If Congress has not done so more generally, should the courts nevertheless incline against exercising removal jurisdiction? Would it be proper to construe §§ 1331 and 1332 narrowly to limit exercise of jurisdiction when the plaintiff wants to be in federal court?

7. What should be the scope of supplemental jurisdiction in removed actions? Professor Steinman concludes that supplemental jurisdiction should be available even though 28 U.S.C.A. § 1367(a) speaks only of actions commenced in federal court. She sees § 1367(b), which curtails supplemental jurisdiction in diversity cases, as having a more limited application in removed cases, however, because it speaks only of claims by or against parties added pursuant to the Federal Rules of Civil Procedure, not state analogues. "Consequently, § 1367(b)'s limitations can apply only to claims asserted or proposed to be asserted post-removal; it does not govern claims (such as counterclaims, cross-claims or third-party claims) asserted in a state court action prior to removal." Steinman, Supplemental Jurisdiction in § 1441 Removed Cases: An Unsurveyed Frontier of Congress' Handiwork, 35 Ariz.L.Rev. 305, 330 (1993). If this is correct, would a case be removable on the basis of minimum diversity where the nondiverse parties are joined pursuant to state joinder rules? Professor Steinman concludes that would not satisfy the requirement of §§ 1441(a) and (b) that removal will be allowed only in a "civil action" of which the district courts have original jurisdiction. Id. at 332.

8. If plaintiff knows the case will be removable, should that sometimes incline plaintiff toward filing in federal court? Consider the following advice for lawyers seeking a temporary restraining order or preliminary injunction: "A removal petition by the defendant will take the case to federal court and will eat up irreplaceable time doing so. The safest course is to file in federal court if there is a reasonable basis to be there." Gohn & Oliver, In Pursuit of the Elusive TRO, 19 Litigation 25, 25–26 (Summer 1993)

9. *"Separate and independent" federal claim*: 28 U.S.C. § 1441(c) permits defendant to remove the "entire case" if it includes a "separate and independent claim or cause of action within the jurisdiction conferred by

section 1331." The notion is that state joinder rules (if they resemble, for example, Rule 18) may permit joinder of completely unrelated state and federal claims in instances in which the state-law claims could not be included in a federal-court suit because they are beyond the scope of supplemental jurisdiction under 28 U.S.C. § 1367(c), which is limited to additional claims within the same "case or controversy." But if supplemental jurisdiction would allow removal whenever the state-law claims are within the same case or controversy (see supra note 7), what constitutional ground is there for § 1441(c) to permit removal of additional claims? For discussion, see C. Wright & M. Kane, Law of Federal Courts § 39 (6th ed. 2002); Porter v. Roosa, 259 F.Supp.2d 638, 653–54 (S.D. Ohio 2003) (declaring that there is "no constitutional use for § 1441(c)").

10. *Remand*: 28 U.S.C. § 1447(c) permits plaintiff to move to remand a case that was not properly removed. Ordinarily the federal court may not remand unless the removal itself was improper. Thermtron Products, Inc. v. Hermansdorfer, 423 U.S. 336, 96 S.Ct. 584, 46 L.Ed.2d 542 (1976) (remand due to docket congestion in federal court not authorized); compare Carnegie–Mellon University v. Cohill, 484 U.S. 343, 108 S.Ct. 614, 98 L.Ed.2d 720 (1988) (federal court that has dismissed federal claim in removed case and determined not to exercise supplemental jurisdiction over state-law claims under 28 U.S.C. § 1367(c)(3) could remand those claims rather than dismiss them). The new multiparty, multiforum jurisdiction provided by 28 U.S.C.A. § 1369, however, permits a federal court to remand the damages part of a case after it has determined liability. See 28 U.S.C.A. § 1441(e)(2).

But appellate review of a decision to remand is difficult to obtain. 28 U.S.C. § 1447(d) provides that an order remanding a case "is not reviewable on appeal or otherwise." In *Thermtron,* supra, the Supreme Court justified overlooking the immunity to review on the ground that the district court there did not invoke the grounds for remand listed in the statute. In Things Remembered, Inc. v. Petrarca, 516 U.S. 124, 116 S.Ct. 494, 133 L.Ed.2d 461 (1995), the Court explained that "[a]s long as a district court's remand is based on a timely raised defect in removal procedure or on lack of subject-matter jurisdiction—the grounds for removal recognized in § 1447(c)—a court of appeals lacks jurisdiction to entertain an appeal of the remand order under § 1447(d)." Id. at 497.

If remand is denied, review is not immediately available under 28 U.S.C. § 1291, limiting appeals to "final decisions." See Chp. XII. Sometimes later developments in the federal-court case may preclude review even then. In Caterpillar Inc. v. Lewis, 519 U.S. 61, 117 S.Ct. 467, 136 L.Ed.2d 437 (1996), the Court held that an erroneous denial of a motion to remand is not ground for reversal after trial if the defect in federal jurisdiction is cured before trial. When the case was initially removed there was incomplete diversity, but the district court denied a motion to remand. Thereafter, all claims involving the nondiverse defendant were settled and dismissed. At trial, defendant prevailed. Seeing the problem as a "statutory flaw" that was cured by the time trial began, the Court concluded that it was insufficient to invalidate the result at trial when balanced against an "overriding consideration" that "[o]nce a diversity case has been tried in federal court, * * * considerations of finality, efficiency, and economy become overwhelming." To wipe out a verdict where there is no objection to the conduct of the trial "would impose an exorbitant cost on our dual court system."

Chapter XI

CHOOSING THE LAW TO BE APPLIED IN FEDERAL COURT

A. CHOOSING BETWEEN STATE AND FEDERAL LAW

SWIFT v. TYSON

Supreme Court of the United States, 1842.
41 U.S. (16 Pet.) 1, 10 L.Ed. 865.

JUSTICE STORY delivered the opinion of the Court.

[Plaintiff sued in federal court in New York, jurisdiction premised on diversity of citizenship, to enforce a bill of exchange. The issue in the case was whether a pre-existing debt constituted consideration for an endorsement of the bill, making the endorsee a "holder in due course." This issue, in turn, depended largely on whether the applicable substantive common law applied was based on general principles derived by the federal court (in which event valid consideration would be found) or was to be determined on the basis of New York decisions (in which event it was assumed that consideration would be rejected).

Defendant argued that the federal court had to apply the New York decisions because of the Rules of Decision Act, originally section 34 of the Judiciary Act of 1789, 1 Stat. 92 (now codified, in slightly modified form, in 28 U.S.C.A. § 1652), which provided that "the laws of the several states, except where the constitution, treaties, or statutes of the United States shall otherwise require or provide, shall be regarded as rules of decision in trials at common law in the courts of the United States in cases where they apply." There was no doubt that the Act required federal courts to apply state statutes. The question for the Court to decide in this case was whether state common law also constituted "laws" for purposes of the Rules of Decision Act.

Justice Story concluded that, with certain exceptions, state judge-made common law did not fall within the concept of "laws" in the Rules of Decision Act.]

* * *

[T]he courts of New York do not found their decisions upon this point upon any local statute, or positive, fixed, or ancient local usage: but they deduced the doctrine from the general principles of commercial law. * * * In the ordinary use of language it will hardly be contended that the decisions of Courts constitute laws. They are, at most, only evidence of what the laws are, and are not themselves laws. They are often reexamined, reversed, and qualified by the Courts themselves, wherever they are found to be either defective, or ill-founded, or otherwise incorrect. The laws of a state are more usually understood to mean the rules and enactments promulgated by the legislative authority thereof, or long established local customs having the force of laws. In all the various cases, which have hitherto come before us for decision, this Court have uniformly supposed, that the true interpretation of the thirty-fourth section limited its application to state laws strictly local, that is to say, to the positive statutes of the state, and the construction thereof adopted by the local tribunals, and to rights and titles to things having a permanent locality, such as the rights and titles to real estate, and other matters immovable and intraterritorial in their nature and character. It never has been supposed by us, that the section did apply, or was designed to apply, to questions of a more general nature, not at all dependent upon local statutes or local usages of a fixed and permanent operation, as for example, to the construction of ordinary contracts or other written instruments and especially to questions of general commercial law, where the state tribunals are called upon to perform the like functions as ourselves, that is, to ascertain upon general reasoning and legal analogies, what is the true exposition of the contract or instruments, or what is the just rule furnished by the principles of commercial law to govern the case. And we have not now the slightest difficulty in holding, that this section, upon its true intendment and construction, is strictly limited to local statutes and local usages of the character before stated, and does not extend to contracts and other instruments of a commercial nature, the true interpretation and effect whereof are to be sought, not in the decisions of local tribunals, but in the general principles and doctrines of commercial jurisprudence.

ERIE RAILROAD CO. v. TOMPKINS

Supreme Court of the United States, 1938.
304 U.S. 64, 58 S.Ct. 817, 82 L.Ed. 1188.

JUSTICE BRANDEIS delivered the opinion of the Court.

The question for decision is whether the oft-challenged doctrine of Swift v. Tyson shall now be disapproved.

Tompkins, a citizen of Pennsylvania, was injured on a dark night by a passing freight train of the Erie Railroad Company while walking along its right of way at Hughestown in that state. He claimed that the accident occurred through negligence in the operation, or maintenance, of the train; that he was rightfully on the premises as licensee because on a commonly used beaten footpath which ran for a short distance alongside the tracks; and that he was struck by something which looked like a door projecting from one of the moving cars. To enforce that claim he brought an action in the federal court for Southern New York, which had jurisdiction because the company is a corporation of that state. It denied liability; and the case was tried by a jury.

The Erie insisted that its duty to Tompkins was no greater than that owed to a trespasser. It contended, among other things, that its duty to Tompkins, and hence its liability, should be determined in accordance with the Pennsylvania law; that under the law of Pennsylvania, as declared by its highest court, persons who use pathways along the railroad right of way—that is, a longitudinal pathway as distinguished from a crossing—are to be deemed trespassers; and that the railroad is not liable for injuries to undiscovered trespassers resulting from its negligence, unless it be wanton or willful. Tompkins denied that any such rule had been established by the decisions of the Pennsylvania courts; and contended that, since there was no statute of the state on the subject, the railroad's duty and liability is to be determined in federal courts as a matter of general law.

The trial judge refused to rule that the applicable law precluded recovery. The jury brought in a verdict of $30,000; and the judgment entered thereon was affirmed by the Circuit Court of Appeals, which held that it was unnecessary to consider whether the law of Pennsylvania was as contended, because the question was one not of local, but of general, law, and that "upon questions of general law the federal courts are free, in absence of a local statute, to exercise their independent judgment as to what the law is; and it is well settled that the question of the responsibility of a railroad for injuries caused by its servants is one of general law.... Where the public has made open and notorious use of a railroad right of way for a long period of time and without objection, the company owes to persons on such permissive pathway a duty of care in the operation of its trains.... It is likewise generally recognized law that a jury may find that negligence exists toward a pedestrian using a permissive path on the railroad right of way if he is hit by some object projecting from the side of the train."

The Erie had contended that application of the Pennsylvania rule was required, among other things, by section 34 of the Federal Judiciary Act of September 24, 1789, c. 20, 28 U.S.C. § 725, 28 U.S.C.A. § 725, which provides:

> "The laws of the several States, except where the Constitution, treaties, or statutes of the United States otherwise require or provide, shall be regarded as rules of decision in trials at common law, in the courts of the United States, in cases where they apply."

Because of the importance of the question whether the federal court was free to disregard the alleged rule of the Pennsylvania common law, we granted certiorari.

First. Swift v. Tyson, 16 Pet. 1, 18, 10 L.Ed. 865, held that federal courts exercising jurisdiction on the ground of diversity of citizenship need not, in matters of general jurisprudence, apply the unwritten law of the state as declared by its highest court; that they are free to exercise an independent judgment as to what the common law of the state is—or should be * * *.

The federal courts assumed, in the broad field of "general law," the power to declare rules of decision which Congress was confessedly without power to enact as statutes. Doubt was repeatedly expressed as to the correctness of the construction given section 34, and as to the soundness of the rule which it introduced. But it was the more recent research of a competent scholar, who examined the original document, which established that the construction given to it by the Court was erroneous; and that the purpose of the section was merely to make certain that, in all matters except those in which some federal law is controlling, the federal courts exercising jurisdiction in diversity of citizenship cases would apply as their rules of decision the law of the state, unwritten as well as written.[5]

Criticism of the doctrine became widespread after the decision of Black & White Taxicab & Transfer Co. v. Brown & Yellow Taxicab & Transfer Co., 276 U.S. 518, 48 S.Ct. 404, 72 L.Ed. 681, 57 A.L.R. 426. There, Brown & Yellow, a Kentucky corporation owned by Kentuckians, and the Louisville & Nashville Railroad, also a Kentucky corporation, wished that the former should have the exclusive privilege of soliciting passenger and baggage transportation at the Bowling Green, Kentucky, railroad station; and that the Black & White, a competing Kentucky corporation, should be prevented from interfering with that privilege. Knowing that such a contract would be void under the common law of Kentucky, it was arranged that the Brown & Yellow reincorporate under the law of Tennessee, and that the contract with the railroad should be executed there. The suit was then brought by the Tennessee corporation in the federal court for Western Kentucky to enjoin competition by the Black & White; an injunction issued by the District Court was sustained by the Court of Appeals; and this Court, citing many decisions in which the doctrine of Swift & Tyson had been applied, affirmed the decree.

Second. Experience in applying the doctrine of Swift v. Tyson, had revealed its defects, political and social; and the benefits expected to flow from the rule did not accrue. Persistence of state courts in their own opinions on questions of common law prevented uniformity; and the impossibility of discovering a satisfactory line of demarcation between the province of general law and that of local law developed a new well of uncertainties.

On the other hand, the mischievous results of the doctrine had become apparent. Diversity of citizenship jurisdiction was conferred in order to prevent apprehended discrimination in state courts against those not citizens of the state. Swift v. Tyson introduced grave discrimination by noncitizens against citizens. It made rights enjoyed under the

---

5. Charles Warren, New Light on the History of the Federal Judiciary Act of 1789   (1923) 37 Harv. L. Rev. 49, 51–52, 81–88, 108.

unwritten "general law" vary according to whether enforcement was sought in the state or in the federal court; and the privilege of selecting the court in which the right should be determined was conferred upon the noncitizen.[9] Thus, the doctrine rendered impossible equal protection of the law. In attempting to promote uniformity of law throughout the United States, the doctrine had prevented uniformity in the administration of the law of the state.

The discrimination resulting became in practice far-reaching. This resulted in part from the broad province accorded to the so-called "general law" as to which federal courts exercised an independent judgment. In addition to questions of purely commercial law, "general law" was held to include the obligations under contracts entered into and to be performed within the state, the extent to which a carrier operating within a state may stipulate for exemption from liability for his own negligence or that of his employee; the liability for torts committed within the state upon persons resident or property located there, even where the question of liability depended upon the scope of a property right conferred by the state; and the right to exemplary or punitive damages. * * *

In part the discrimination resulted from the wide range of persons held entitled to avail themselves of the federal rule by resort to the diversity of citizenship jurisdiction. Through this jurisdiction individual citizens willing to remove from their own state and become citizens of another might avail themselves of the federal rule. And, without even change of residence, a corporate citizen of the state could avail itself of the federal rule by reincorporating under the laws of another state, as was done in the *Taxicab* Case.

The injustice and confusion incident to the doctrine of Swift v. Tyson have been repeatedly urged as reasons for abolishing or limiting diversity of citizenship jurisdiction. Other legislative relief has been proposed. If only a question of statutory construction were involved, we should not be prepared to abandon a doctrine so widely applied throughout nearly a century. But the unconstitutionality of the course pursued has now been made clear, and compels us to do so.

Third. Except in matters governed by the Federal Constitution or by acts of Congress, the law to be applied in any case is the law of the state. And whether the law of the state shall be declared by its Legislature in a statute or by its highest court in a decision is not a matter of federal concern. There is no federal general common law. Congress has no power to declare substantive rules of common law applicable in a state whether they be local in their nature or "general," be they commercial law or a part of the law of torts. And no clause in the Constitution purports to confer such a power upon the federal courts. * * *

___

9. It was even possible for a nonresident plaintiff defeated on a point of law in the highest court of a State nevertheless to win out by taking a nonsuit and renewing the controversy in the federal court.

The fallacy underlying the rule declared in Swift v. Tyson is made clear by Mr. Justice Holmes.[23] The doctrine rests upon the assumption that there is "a transcendental body of law outside of any particular State but obligatory within it unless and until changed by statute," that federal courts have the power to use their judgment as to what the rules of common law are; and that in the federal courts "the parties are entitled to an independent judgment on matters of general law":

"but law in the sense in which courts speak of it today does not exist without some definite authority behind it. The common law so far as it is enforced in a State, whether called common law or not, is not the common law generally but the law of that State existing by the authority of that State without regard to what it may have been in England or anywhere else . . . . .

"the authority and only authority is the State, and if that be so, the voice adopted by the State as its own [whether it be of its Legislature or of its Supreme Court] should utter the last word."

Thus the doctrine of Swift v. Tyson is, as Mr. Justice Holmes said, "an unconstitutional assumption of powers by the Courts of the United States which no lapse of time or respectable array of opinion should make us hesitate to correct." In disapproving that doctrine we do not hold unconstitutional section 34 of the Federal Judiciary Act of 1789 or any other act of Congress. We merely declare that in applying the doctrine this Court and the lower courts have invaded rights which in our opinion are reserved by the Constitution to the several States.

Fourth. The defendant contended that by the common law of Pennsylvania as declared by its highest court in Falchetti v. Pennsylvania R. Co., 307 Pa. 203, 160 A. 859, the only duty owed to the plaintiff was to refrain from willful or wanton injury. The plaintiff denied that such is the Pennsylvania law. In support of their respective contentions the parties discussed and cited many decisions of the Supreme Court of the state. The Circuit Court of Appeals ruled that the question of liability is one of general law; and on that ground declined to decide the issue of state law. As we hold this was error, the judgment is reversed and the case remanded to it for further proceedings in conformity with our opinion.

Reversed.

Justice Cardozo took no part in the consideration or decision of this case.

Justice Butler (dissenting).

* * *

No constitutional question was suggested or argued below or here. And as a general rule, this Court will not consider any question not

---

23. Kuhn v. Fairmont Coal Co., 215 U.S. 349, 370–372, 30 S. Ct. 140, 54 L.Ed. 228; Black & White Taxicab, etc., Co. v. Brown & Yellow Taxicab, etc., Co., 276 U.S. 518, 532–536, 48 S. Ct. 404, 408, 409, 72 L.Ed. 681, 57 A.L.R. 426.

raised below and presented by the petition. Here it does not decide either of the questions presented, but, changing the rule of decision in force since the foundation of the government, remands the case to be adjudged according to a standard never before deemed permissible.

* * *

This Court has often emphasized its reluctance to consider constitutional questions and that legislation will not be held invalid as repugnant to the fundamental law if the case may be decided upon any other ground. In view of grave consequences liable to result from erroneous exertion of its power to set aside legislation, the Court should move cautiously, seek assistance of counsel, act only after ample deliberation, show that the question is before the Court, that its decision cannot be avoided by construction of the statute assailed or otherwise, indicate precisely the principle or provision of the Constitution held to have been transgressed, and fully disclose the reasons and authorities found to warrant the conclusion of invalidity. * * *

So far as appears, no litigant has ever challenged the power of Congress to establish the rule as construed. It has so long endured that its destruction now without appropriate deliberation cannot be justified. There is nothing in the opinion to suggest that consideration of any constitutional question is necessary to a decision of the case. By way of reasoning, it contains nothing that requires the conclusion reached. Admittedly, there is no authority to support that conclusion. Against the protest of those joining in this opinion, the Court declines to assign the case for reargument. It may not justly be assumed that the labor and argument of counsel for the parties would not disclose the right conclusion and aid the Court in the statement of reasons to support it. Indeed, it would have been appropriate to give Congress opportunity to be heard before divesting it of power to prescribe rules of decision to be followed in the courts of the United States.

The course pursued by the Court in this case is repugnant to the Act of Congress of August 24, 1937, 50 Stat. 751, 28 U.S.C.A. §§ 17 and note, 349a, 380a and note, 401. It declares: "That whenever the constitutionality of any Act of Congress affecting the public interest is drawn in question in any court of the United States in any suit or proceeding to which the United States, or any agency thereof, or any officer or employee thereof, as such officer or employee, is not a party, the court having jurisdiction of the suit or proceeding shall certify such fact to the Attorney General. In any such case the court shall permit the United States to intervene and become a party for presentation of evidence (if evidence is otherwise receivable in such suit or proceeding) and argument upon the question of the constitutionality of such Act. In any such suit or proceeding the United States shall, subject to the applicable provisions of law, have all the rights of a party and the liabilities of a party as to court costs to the extent necessary for a proper presentation of the facts and law relating to the constitutionality of such Act." Section 1, 28 U.S.C.A. § 401. That provision extends to this Court. If defendant had applied for and obtained the writ of certiorari upon the claim that, as now held, Congress has no power to prescribe the rule of decision, section 34 as construed, it would have been the duty of this Court to issue the prescribed certificate to the Attorney General in order that the United States might intervene and be heard on the constitutional question. Within the purpose of the statute and its true intent and meaning, the constitutionality of that measure has been "drawn in question." Congress intended to give the United States the right to be heard in every case involving constitutionality of an act affecting the public interest. In view of the rule that, in the absence of challenge of constitutionality, statutes will not here be invalidated on that ground, the Act of August 24, 1937 extends to cases where constitutionality is first "drawn in question" by the Court. No extraordinary or unusual action by the Court after submission of the cause should be permitted to frustrate the wholesome purpose of that Act. * * *

I am of opinion that the constitutional validity of the rule need not be considered, because under the law, as found by the courts of Pennsylvania and generally throughout the country, it is plain that the evidence required a finding that plaintiff was guilty of negligence that contributed to cause his injuries, and that the judgment below should be reversed upon that ground.

JUSTICE McREYNOLDS, concurs in this opinion.

JUSTICE REED (concurring in part).

I concur in the conclusion reached in this case, in the disapproval of the doctrine of Swift v. Tyson, and in the reasoning of the majority opinion, except in so far as it relies upon the unconstitutionality of the "course pursued" by the federal courts.

* * *

To decide the case now before us and to "disapprove" the doctrine of Swift v. Tyson requires only that we say that the words "the laws" include in their meaning the decisions of the local tribunals. As the majority opinion shows, by its reference to Mr. Warren's researches and the first quotation from Mr. Justice Holmes, that this Court is now of the view that "laws" includes "decisions," it is unnecessary to go further and declare that the "course pursued" was "unconstitutional," instead of merely erroneous.

The "unconstitutional" course referred to in the majority opinion is apparently the ruling in Swift v. Tyson that the supposed omission of Congress to legislate as to the effect of decisions leaves federal courts free to interpret general law for themselves. (I am not at all sure whether, in the absence of federal statutory direction, federal courts would be compelled to follow state decisions. There was sufficient doubt about the matter in 1789 to induce the first Congress to legislate.) No former opinions of this Court have passed upon it. * * * If the opinion commits this Court to the position that the Congress is without power to declare what rules of substantive law shall govern the federal courts, that conclusion also seems questionable. The line between procedural and substantive law is hazy but no one doubts federal power over procedure. The Judiciary Article and the "necessary and proper" clause of Article One may fully authorize legislation, such as this section of the Judiciary Act.

In this Court, stare decisis, in statutory construction, is a useful rule, not an inexorable command. It seems preferable to overturn an established construction of an Act of Congress, rather than, in the circumstances of this case, to interpret the Constitution.

Notes and Questions

1. One of the interesting aspects of the *Erie* decision is that neither party had at any point argued that the doctrine of Swift v. Tyson should be overruled. Is it appropriate for the Court to resolve a case on the basis of a ground not raised by either party? See Friendly, In Praise of *Erie*—and of the New Federal Common Law, 39 N.Y.U.L. Rev. 383, 399 n. 71 (1964) (arguing that both sides were sufficiently aware of the possibility the Court would abandon *Swift*). Is it appropriate for the Court to reach an issue of this import when a narrower basis of decision was available? As a practical matter, *was* a narrower basis of decision available? Why do you suppose the Court chose to resolve the broad question of the *Swift* doctrine's validity?

2. According to one scholar, corporations were significantly benefited by the general federal common law recognized in *Swift*. E. Purcell, Brandeis and the Progressive Constitution 66 (2000). "In two common types of cases—for example, tort suits brought by injured employees and insurance actions brought by individual claimants—the federal common law grew distinctly more favorable toward business in the late nineteenth century and was far more favorable then the common law of many states." Id.

3. According to Professor Purcell, "[t]he federal general common law resonated broadly as a political issue because it implicated one of the fundamental divisions that separated Populists and Progressives from their conservative opponents." This was because the former "saw Swift as a license for judicial subjectivism and biased decision making," while the latter "saw it as a guarantor of security and the reign of common law principles." Hostility towards *Swift* also "grew from the states' rights tradition that rejected both diversity jurisdiction and the federal common law as intrusions on state sovereignty." E. Purcell, Brandeis and the Progressive Constitution 67 (2000).

4. Justice Brandeis asserts that if it were not for the constitutional difficulties caused by *Swift,* he would have been reluctant to overturn that decision. What, according to Brandeis, were the constitutional problems with the *Swift* doctrine? Are these concerns legitimate? See Keefe, Gilhooley, Bailey & Day, Weary *Erie*, 34 Cornell L.Q. 494, 497 (1949): "It is difficult to determine exactly what was unconstitutional about the *Tyson* doctrine. Unquestionably Article III of the Constitution designates the federal courts as proper forums to litigate suits between 'Citizens of different States.' Given jurisdiction, it would logically follow that a federal court would have the constitutional power to determine the controversy by any reasonable

method. The choice of 'federal common law' rather than the law of a particular state is clearly not so unreasonable as to be unconstitutional.''

According to Professor Borchers, "the drafting and ratification history [of the Constitution] supports the conclusion that diversity was intended at least in part as a protection against aberrational state laws, particularly those regarding commercial transactions." Borchers, The Origins of Diversity Jurisdiction, the Rise of Legal Positivism, and a Brave New World for *Erie* and *Klaxon*, 72 Tex. L. Rev. 79, 81 (1993). For a defense of *Swift* against *Erie*'s attack, see Corr, Thoughts on the Vitality of *Erie*, 41 Am. U. L. Rev. 1087 (1992). Professor Corr describes what he refers to as "the fragility of the *Erie* majority's position." Id. at 1091.

5. Has *Erie*'s constitutional predicate been eroded by subsequent developments? Consider the comments of Professor Thomas Merrill:

> Although the framers may have intended that the federal government would be a government of limited powers, in the years since *Erie* the Supreme Court has permitted those powers to expand so much that the federal government has authority to regulate in virtually any area it chooses. * * * The Court's acquiescence in the transformation of the federal government from one of limited powers to one of plenary authority might be illustrated with the facts of *Erie* itself. The issue there—the standard of care that a railroad owes to a pedestrian walking on a railroad right of way—is one that Congress today could clearly resolve by legislation enacted pursuant to its power to regulate interstate commerce. Since the issue therefore falls within the enumerated powers of the federal government (now viewed as plenary rather than limited), there would seem to be no reason for objecting *on the grounds of federalism* if a federal court decided to formulate a rule of decision governing the issue.
>
> The answer to this objection is that the federalism principle identified by *Erie* still exists but has been silently transformed from a general constraint on the powers of the federal government into an attenuated constraint that applies principally to one branch of that government— the federal judiciary. * * * With respect to judicial power, however, the federalism principle still has force.

Merrill, The Common Law Powers of Federal Courts, 52 U.Chi.L.Rev. 1, 14– 15 (1985); see also Mishkin, Some Further Last Words on *Erie*—The Thread, 87 Harv.L.Rev. 1682 (1974).

Is there any textual or theoretical basis for drawing the constitutional distinction suggested by Professor Merrill? Is there any policy argument to support the distinction?

6. If one were to reject the constitutional basis of *Erie,* might one nevertheless support the doctrine, purely as a matter of political philosophy or social policy?

7. What weight should have been given to the newly discovered historical evidence cited by Brandeis concerning the intent of the drafters of the Rules of Decision Act? Historian Charles Warren had discovered an earlier draft of the Rules of Decision Act, never adopted, which provided that "the statute law of the several states in force for the time being and their

unwritten or common law now in use, whether by adoption from the common law of England, the ancient statutes of the same or otherwise" would serve as rules of decision in federal court. On the basis of this draft (and solely on that basis), Warren concluded that the change in the final version of the statute to "laws of the several states" was intended as merely a shorthand for what had been contained in the earlier draft. Warren, New Light on the History of the Federal Judiciary Act of 1789, 37 Harv.L.Rev. 49, 84–88 (1923). Is this the only conceivable explanation for the change in statutory wording?

For an argument that the drafters of section 34 of the Judiciary Act of 1789 did not intend to require use of state law in diversity cases, see W. Ritz, Rewriting the History of the Judiciary Act of 1789, 134 (1990). See also Holt, To Establish Justice: Politics, the Judiciary Act of 1789, and the Invention of the Federal Courts, 1989 Duke L.J. 1421, 1506–07.

One modern commentator has asserted the "bias" that Professor Warren "brought to the issue of the proper authority of federal courts hearing diversity cases to deviate from state common law." Corr, Thoughts on the Vitality of *Erie*, 41 Am. U. L. Rev. 1087, 1093 (1992). According to Professor Corr, "[i]t is an understatement to say that Warren's general view of federalism was that federal courts, below the level of the Supreme Court, should have almost no role to play." Id.

8. What were Justice Brandeis' concerns about the unfairness of the *Swift* doctrine? Note that he states that the *Swift* doctrine "rendered impossible equal protection of the law." It is clear, however, that by this reference he did not intend to invoke the constitutional requirement of equal protection, for at that time no one had seriously suggested that a guarantee of equal protection was included within the Fifth Amendment. Bolling v. Sharpe, 347 U.S. 497, 74 S.Ct. 693, 98 L.Ed. 884 (1954), reaching this conclusion, was not decided until 16 years later. What Brandeis was undoubtedly referring to was the unfairness inherent in the unequal treatment that is said to result from the evil of forum shopping. What is so bad about forum shopping? For example, what was so terrible about the *Black & White Taxicab* case? Might the injustice caused by that decision have been avoided by means short of the abolition of the *Swift* doctrine?

9. Examine Justice Brandeis' attack on what he considered to be Story's legal philosophy underlying the *Swift* doctrine. In what way is it thought that Story's philosophy manifests itself in the *Swift* doctrine? Is it accurate to infer this legal philosophy from *Swift*? Recall that in *Swift* Story recognized certain exceptions, where state common law *would* be followed. Does the existence of these exceptions cast doubt on the inference of a particular philosophy of law from Story's adoption of the *Swift* doctrine? For a discussion of the *Erie* Court's attack on the legal philosophy underlying *Swift*, see Rutherglen, Reconstructing *Erie*: A Comment on the Perils of Legal Positivism, 10 Const. Comm. 285 (1993).

10. Whatever philosophical assumptions underlay Justice Story's reasoning, was *Swift* an unreasonable interpretation of the Rules of Decision Act? As of 1789, when the statute was originally adopted, where would judges look to find authority to decide questions not governed by statute or "local" law? Judge Fletcher argues that "[i]n such cases, depending on the

nature of the dispute, a number of different kinds of law could provide the relevant rules for decision. The general common law was by far the most important of these nonlocal and nonfederal laws. That it was not explicitly referred to in section 34 does not prove that it was not expected to be applied. Rather, the fact that it was not mentioned probably suggests quite the opposite—that its applicability was so obvious as to go without saying." Fletcher, The General Common Law and Section 34 of the Judiciary Act of 1789: The Example of Marine Insurance, 97 Harv.L.Rev. 1513, 1517 (1984). But the hegemony of the general common law was fragmented during the 19th century, and the concept of law changed to one in which legal rules had force only by virtue of the governmental authority behind them, a view now known as "positivism." Was this development inevitable? Was it undesirable? Should this 19th century development have an impact on the interpretation of a statute enacted in 1789?

11. After *Erie,* are federal courts required to adhere to state law on every issue that may arise in a case? Does the decision attempt to draw any distinctions among different types of issues? Does Justice Reed suggest a possible solution? On these questions, consider the relevance of the *York* case, below.

There is one piece of background that should be added, however. Before 1938, the federal courts were generally directed to follow state procedure under a series of statutes called the Process Acts and the Conformity Act. See generally Burbank, The Rules Enabling Act of 1934, 130 U.Pa.L.Rev. 1015, 1036–42 (1982). The objective was to make sure that the procedure employed in a state was the same, whether the case was in state or federal court. In 1934 Congress passed the Rules Enabling Act, which authorized the Supreme Court to promulgate rules of practice and procedure for use in all federal courts to supplant the former requirement that federal courts use state procedure. Thus Justice Reed could observe that "no one doubts federal power over procedure." These rules were drafted by a committee headed by Dean Charles Clark of Yale Law School and became effective in 1938. After 1938, many states chose to model their procedural rules after the Federal Rules. See Oakley & Coon, The Federal Rules in State Courts: A Survey of State Court Systems of Civil Procedure, 61 Wash.L.Rev. 1367 (1986).

GUARANTY TRUST CO. v. YORK

Supreme Court of the United States, 1945.
326 U.S. 99, 65 S.Ct. 1464, 89 L.Ed. 2079.

JUSTICE FRANKFURTER delivered the opinion of the Court.

* * *

In May, 1930, Van Sweringen Corporation issued notes to the amount of $30,000,000. Under an indenture of the same date, petitioner, Guaranty Trust Co., was named trustee with power and obligations to enforce the rights of the noteholders in the assets of the Corporation and of the Van Sweringen brothers. In October, 1930, petitioner, with other banks, made large advances to companies affiliated with the Corporation and wholly controlled by the Van Sweringens. In October, 1931, when it was apparent that the Corporation could not meet its obligations, Guaranty co-operated in a plan for the purchase of the outstanding notes on the basis of cash for 50% of the face value of the notes and twenty shares of Van Sweringen Corporation's stock for each $1,000 note. This exchange offer remained open until December 15, 1931.

Respondent York received $6,000 of the notes as a gift in 1934, her donor not having accepted the offer of exchange. In April, 1940, three accepting noteholders began suit against petitioner, charging fraud and misrepresentation. Respondent's application to intervene in that suit was denied, and summary judgment in favor of Guaranty was affirmed. Hackner v. Morgan, 130 F.2d 300. After her dismissal from the *Hackner* litigation, respondent, on January 22, 1942, began the present proceedings.

The suit, instituted as a class action on behalf of non-accepting noteholders and brought in a federal court solely because of diversity of citizenship, is based on an alleged breach of trust by Guaranty in that it failed to protect the interests of the noteholders in assenting to the exchange offer and failed to disclose its self-interest when sponsoring the offer. Petitioner moved for summary judgment, which was granted, upon the authority of the *Hackner* case. On appeal, the Circuit Court of Appeals, one Judge dissenting, found that the *Hackner* decision did not foreclose this suit, and held that in a suit brought on the equity side of a federal district court that court is not required to apply the State statute of limitations that would govern like suits in the courts of a State where the federal court is sitting even though the exclusive basis of federal jurisdiction is diversity of citizenship. * * *

In view of the basis of the decision below, it is not for us to consider whether the New York statute would actually bar this suit were it brought in a State court. Our only concern is with the holding that the federal courts in a suit like this are not bound by local law.

We put to one side the considerations relevant in disposing of questions that arise when a federal court is adjudicating a claim based on a federal law. Our problem only touches transactions for which rights and obligations are created by one of the States, and for the assertion of which, in case of diversity of the citizenship of the parties, Congress has made a federal court another available forum.

Our starting point must be the policy of federal jurisdiction which Erie R. Co. v. Tompkins embodies. In overruling Swift v. Tyson, 16 Pet. 1, 10 L.Ed. 865, Erie R. Co. v. Tompkins did not merely overrule a venerable case. It overruled a particular way of looking at law which dominated the judicial process long after its inadequacies had been laid bare. Law was conceived as a "brooding omnipresence" of Reason, of which decisions were merely evidence and not themselves the controlling formulations. Accordingly, federal courts deemed themselves free to ascertain what Reason, and therefore Law, required wholly independent of authoritatively declared State law, even in cases where a legal right as the basis for relief was created by State authority and could not be created by federal authority and the case got into a federal court merely because it was "between Citizens of different States" under Art. III, § 2 of the Constitution of the United States.

* * *

In exercising their jurisdiction on the ground of diversity of citizenship, the federal courts, in the long course of their history, have not differentiated in their regard for State law between actions at law and suits in equity. Although § 34 of the Judiciary Act of 1789 directed that the "laws of the several States ... shall be regarded as rules of decision in trials of common law ...", this was deemed, consistently for over a hundred years, to be merely declaratory of what would in any event have governed the federal courts and therefore was equally applicable to equity suits. Indeed, it may fairly be said that the federal courts gave greater respect to State-created "substantive rights" in equity than they gave them on the law side, because rights at law were usually declared by State courts and as such increasingly flouted by extension of the doctrine of Swift v. Tyson, while rights in equity were frequently defined by legislative enactment and as such known and respected by the federal courts.

Partly because the States in the early days varied greatly in the manner in which equitable relief was afforded and in the extent to which it was available, Congress provided that "the forms and modes of proceeding in suits ... of equity" would conform to the settled uses of courts of equity. But this enactment gave the federal courts no power that they would not have had in any event when courts were given "cognizance," by the first Judiciary Act, of suits in "equity". From the beginning there has been a good deal of talk in the cases that federal equity is a separate legal system. And so it is, properly understood. The suits in equity of which the federal courts have had "cognizance" ever since 1789 constituted the body of law which had been transplanted to this country from the English Court of Chancery. But this system of equity "derived its doctrines, as well as its powers, from its mode of giving relief." Langdell, Summary of Equity Pleading (1877) xxvii. In giving federal courts "cognizance" of equity suits in cases of diversity jurisdiction, Congress never gave, nor did the federal courts ever claim, the power to deny substantive rights created by State law or to create substantive rights denied by State law.

This does not mean that whatever equitable remedy is available in a State court must be available in a diversity suit in a federal court, or conversely, that a federal court may not afford an equitable remedy not available in a State court. Equitable relief in a federal court is of course subject to restrictions: the suit must be within the traditional scope of equity as historically evolved in the English Court of Chancery, a plain, adequate and complete remedy at law must be wanting, explicit Congressional curtailment of equity powers must be respected, see, e.g., Norris–LaGuardia Act, 47 Stat. 70, 29 U.S.C. § 101 et seq., 29 U.S.C.A. § 101 et seq.; the constitutional right to trial by jury cannot be evaded. That a State may authorize its courts to give equitable relief unhampered by any or all such restrictions cannot remove these fetters from the federal courts. State law cannot define the remedies which a federal court must give simply because a federal court in diversity jurisdiction is available as an alternative tribunal to the State's courts. Contrariwise, a federal court may afford an equitable remedy for a substantive right recognized by a State even though a State court cannot give it. Whatever contradiction or confusion may be produced by a medley of judicial phrases severed from their environment, the body of adjudications concerning equitable relief in diversity cases leaves no doubt that the federal courts enforced State-created substantive rights if the mode of proceeding and remedy were consonant with the traditional body of equitable remedies, practice and procedure, and in so doing they were enforcing rights created by the States and not arising under any inherent or statutory federal law.

And so this case reduces itself to the narrow question whether, when no recovery could be had in a State court because the action is barred by the statute of limitations, a federal court in equity can take cognizance of the suit because there is diversity of citizenship between the parties. Is the outlawry, according to State law, of a claim created by the States a matter of "substantive rights" to be respected by a federal court of equity when that court's jurisdiction is dependent on the fact that there is a State-created right, or is such statute of "a mere remedial character," which a federal court may disregard?

Matters of "substance" and matters of "procedure" are much talked about in the books as though they defined a great divide cutting across the whole domain of law. But, of course, "substance" and "procedure" are the same key-words to very different problems. Neither "substance" nor "procedure" represents the same invariants. Each implies different variables depending upon the particular problem for which it is used. And the different problems are only distantly related at best, for the terms are in common use in connection with situations turning on such different considerations as those that are relevant to questions pertaining to ex post facto legislation, the impairment of the obligations of contract, the enforcement of federal rights in the State courts and the multitudinous phases of the conflict of laws.

Here we are dealing with a right to recover derived not from the United States but from one of the States. When, because the plaintiff happens to be a nonresident, such a right is enforceable in a federal as well as in a State court, the forms and mode of enforcing the right may at times, naturally enough, vary because the two judicial systems are not identical. But since a federal court adjudicating a state-created right solely because of the diversity of citizenship of the parties is for that purpose, in effect, only another court of the State, it cannot afford recovery if the right to recover is made unavailable by the State nor can it substantially affect the enforcement of the right as given by the State.

And so the question is not whether a statute of limitations is deemed a matter of "procedure" in some sense. The question is whether such a statute concerns merely the manner and the means by which a right to recover, as recognized by the State, is enforced, or whether such statutory limitation is a matter of substance in the aspect that alone is relevant to our problem, namely, does it significantly affect the result of a litigation for a federal court to disregard a law of a State that would be controlling in an action upon the same claim by the same parties in a State court?

It is therefore immaterial whether statutes of limitation are characterized either as "substantive" or "procedural" in State court opinions in any use of those terms unrelated to the specific issue before us. Erie R. Co. v. Tompkins was not an endeavor to formulate scientific legal terminology. It expressed a policy that touches vitally the proper distribution of judicial power between State and federal courts. In essence, the intent of that decision was to insure that, in all cases where a federal court is exercising jurisdiction solely because of the diversity of citizenship of the parties, the outcome of the litigation in the federal court should be substantially the same, so far as legal rules determine the outcome of a litigation, as it would be if tried in a State court. The nub of the policy that underlies Erie R. Co. v. Tompkins is that for the same transaction the accident of a suit by a non-resident litigant in a federal court instead of in a State court a block away, should not lead to a substantially different result. And so, putting to one side abstractions regarding "substance" and "procedure", we have held that in diversity cases the federal courts must follow the law of the State as to burden of proof, Cities Service Oil Co. v. Dunlap, 308 U.S. 208, 60 S.Ct. 201, 84 L.Ed. 196, as to conflict of laws, Klaxon Co. v. Stentor Co., 313 U.S. 487, 61 S.Ct. 1020, 85 L.Ed. 1477, as to contributory negligence, Palmer v. Hoffman, 318 U.S. 109, 117, 63 S.Ct. 477, 482, 87 L.Ed. 645, 144 A.L.R. 719. And see Sampson v. Channell, 1 Cir., 110 F.2d 754, 128 A.L.R. 394. Erie R. Co. v. Tompkins has been applied with an eye alert to essentials in avoiding disregard of State law in diversity cases in the federal courts. A policy so important to our federalism must be kept free from entanglements with analytical or terminological niceties.

Plainly enough, a statute that would completely bar recovery in a suit if brought in a State court bears on a State created right vitally and not merely formally or negligibly. As to consequences that so intimately affect recovery or non-recovery a federal court in a diversity case should follow State law. The fact that under New York law a statute of limitations might be lengthened or shortened, that a security may be foreclosed though the debt be barred, that a barred debt may be used as a set-off, are all matters of local law properly to be respected by federal courts sitting in New York when their incidence comes into play there. Such particular rules of local law, however, do not in the slightest change the crucial consideration that if a plea of the statute of limitations would bar recovery in a State court, a federal court ought not to afford recovery.

* * *

To make an exception to Erie R. Co. v. Tompkins on the equity side of a federal court is to reject the considerations of policy which, after long travail, led to that decision. * * *

Diversity jurisdiction is founded on assurance to non-resident litigants of courts free from susceptibility to potential local bias. The Framers of the Constitution, according to Marshall, entertained "apprehensions" lest distant suitors be subjected to local bias in State courts, or, at least, viewed with "indulgence the possible fears and apprehensions" of such suitors. Bank of the United States v. Deveaux, 5 Cranch 61, 87, 3 L.Ed. 38. And so Congress afforded out-of-State litigants another tribunal, not another body of law. The operation of a double system of conflicting laws in the same State is plainly hostile to the reign of law. Certainly, the fortuitous circumstance of residence out of a State of one of the parties to a litigation ought not to give rise to a discrimination against others equally concerned but locally resident. The source of substantive rights enforced by a federal court under diversity jurisdiction, it cannot be said too often, is the law of the States. Whenever that law is authoritatively declared by a State, whether its voice be the legislature or its highest court, such law ought to govern in litigation founded on that law, whether the forum of application is a State or a federal court and whether the remedies be sought at law or may be had in equity.

* * *

The judgment is reversed and the case is remanded for proceedings not inconsistent with this opinion.

JUSTICE ROBERTS and JUSTICE DOUGLAS took no part in the consideration or decision of this case.

[Dissenting opinion of JUSTICE RUTLEDGE, joined by JUSTICE MURPHY, omitted.]

Notes and Questions

1. Note that in deciding whether federal or state law is to be applied, Justice Frankfurter draws a distinction between matters of "substance" and matters of "procedure." Why is this distinction important for purposes of the choice between state and federal law? To what extent was the distinction a part of the *Erie* decision itself?

2. What standard does Justice Frankfurter adopt in order to determine whether a legal rule is substantive or procedural for purposes of the *Erie* doctrine? What policy or policies mentioned in *Erie* is he attempting to foster? How does he apply this standard to the facts of *York?* Professor Henry Hart noted what he considered "the triviality of the [*Erie*] principle" emphasized in *York,* and argued that "[t]he more faithfully it is carried out the more completely the constitutional and statutory grants of diversity

jurisdiction are emptied of intelligible meaning." Hart, the Relations Between State and Federal Law, 54 Colum.L.Rev. 489, 512 (1954). What do you think this means? He also contended that "[t]he principle passes over the essential rationale of the *Erie* opinion—the need of recognizing the state courts as organs of coordinate authority with other branches of the state government in the discharge of the constitutional functions of the states * * *." Do you agree that this concern, rather than the policy emphasized in *York*, constituted "the essential rationale of the *Erie* opinion"?

3. Note that Justice Frankfurter indicates that adoption of the *Erie* test he employs "does not mean that whatever equitable remedy is available in a State court must be available in a diversity suit in a federal court, or conversely, that a federal court may not afford an equitable remedy not available in a State court." Is this conclusion consistent with the case's test?

More generally, what significance should be attributed to Justice Frankfurter's recognition that federal equity is a separate system? Consider the views of Professors Wright and Kane [C. Wright & M. Kane, The Law of Federal Courts 401–02 (6th ed. 2002)]:

> [T]here is language in the opinion that seems to suggest that the doctrine of "equitable remedial rights" persists, and that a federal court sitting in equity is free to grant or withhold remedies without regard to what a state court would do in a similar case. Probably this is true where an Act of Congress has taken away jurisdiction to grant an injunction in particular cases [as with the Norris–La Guardia Act] or where the constitutional right to trial by jury might be abridged. It seems equally true that federal courts are free to use procedural devices made available by statutes or the Federal Rules despite the absence of similar procedures in the states. Beyond those situations it is difficult to believe that the federal court is free to fashion an independent law of remedies in equitable actions.

For a discussion of the application of the *Erie* doctrine to the availability of equitable remedies in diversity cases, see Crump, The Twilight Zone of the *Erie* Doctrine: Is There Really a Different Choice of Equitable Remedies in the "Court a Block Away"?, 1991 Wis. L. Rev. 1233.

4. Is the *York* test a wise one? Professors Wright and Kane have suggested that the *York* test was plagued with "inevitable difficulties," because "[a]pplied literally, very little would remain of the Federal Rules of Civil Procedure in diversity cases, for almost every procedural rule may have a substantial effect on the outcome of a case. If the test was not to be carried to its literal limits, however, there was confusion as to how far it was to go." C. Wright & M. Kane, The Law of Federal Courts 380 (6th ed. 2002). Cf. Fed.R.Civ.P. 61. Is Professor Wright correct in his assertion that application of *York* to the Federal Rules of Civil Procedure would leave very little of the Federal Rules in diversity cases? Examine, for example, Rules 15(c) and 35(a). Under the *York* test, could a federal court in a diversity case apply these rules when the state in which it sits does not do so?

Note that *York* itself did not involve a Federal Rule of Civil Procedure. Does the opinion provide some basis on which to determine whether the test of that case was intended to be applied to Federal Rules? If it were, what harm would result? Is there a logical basis on which not to extend the case's test to the Federal Rules of Civil Procedure?

5.   How would the *York* test apply to the following hypothetical case: The federal court requires that all movants' briefs be filed with a red brief cover; no brief with a cover any color other than red will be accepted. The state court, on the other hand, has a similar rule, but the required color is blue. A defendant, moving for summary judgment in federal court, employs a blue brief cover, and argues that, on the basis of *York,* the federal court sitting in diversity is required to follow the state practice of employing blue covers. Cf. Loya v. Desert Sands Unified School Dist., 721 F.2d 279 (9th Cir.1983) (for purposes of statute of limitations, complaint on long paper should be considered filed on date received though district court rejected it because of local rule requiring use of short paper); Cintron v. Union Pacific R.R., 813 F.2d 917 (9th Cir.1987) (complaint timely filed even though rejected by clerk because it lacked two holes in the top as required by local rules).

EFFORTS TO APPLY *YORK*

In three post-*York* decisions decided on the same day in 1949, the Court applied that case's principle to three very different situations:

(1) Cohen v. Beneficial Industrial Loan Corp., 337 U.S. 541, 69 S.Ct. 1221, 93 L.Ed. 1528 (1949): In a stockholders' derivative action, defendants contended that a state statute, which required that plaintiffs in stockholder derivative actions owning less than a specified percentage of the corporation's stock were required to post a bond, should be applied to the plaintiffs. The district court held the New Jersey statute inapplicable, and the court of appeals reversed. The Supreme Court, relying on *York,* found the New Jersey statute applicable. Was this a proper application of *York?* The plaintiffs had argued that Rule 23 of the Federal Rules of Civil Procedure, which imposed no bond requirement, "deals with plaintiff's right to maintain such an action in federal court and that therefore the subject is recognized as procedural and the federal rule alone prevails." (Stockholder derivative actions are today more specifically regulated by Rule 23.1.) The Supreme Court, however, held that none of the provisions of Rule 23 conflicted with the state statute.

(2) Ragan v. Merchants Transfer & Warehouse Co., Inc., 337 U.S. 530, 69 S.Ct. 1233, 93 L.Ed. 1520 (1949): In a personal injury action in federal district court in Kansas, the complaint was filed in federal court within Kansas' two-year statute of limitations, but service was not made on the defendant until after the statutory period had run. Rule 3 of the Federal Rules of Civil Procedure provides that "[a] civil action is commenced by filing a complaint with the court." Kansas law, however, stated that the statute of limitations was not tolled until actual service of the summons on the defendant, rather than when the complaint was filed. Defendant argued, on the basis of Kansas law, that the statute of limitations had run. The Supreme Court, relying on both *Erie* and *York,* held state law applicable:

Erie R. Co. v. Tompkins was premised on the theory that in diversity cases the rights enjoyed under local law should not vary because enforcement of those rights was sought in the federal court rather than in the state court. If recovery could not be had in the state court, it should be denied in the federal court. Otherwise, those authorized to invoke the diversity jurisdiction would gain advantages over those confined to state court. Guaranty Trust Co. v. York applied that principle to statutes of limitations on the theory that, where one is barred from recovery in the state court, he should likewise be barred in the federal court.

It is conceded that if the present case were in a Kansas court it would be barred. The theory of Guaranty Trust Co. v. York would therefore seem to bar it in the federal court * * *. The force of that argument is sought to be avoided by the argument that the Federal Rules of Civil Procedure determine the manner in which an action is commenced in the federal courts—a matter of procedure which the principle of Erie R. Co. v. Tompkins does not control. It is accordingly argued that since the suit was properly commenced in the federal court before the Kansas statute of limitations ran, it tolled the statute.

* * * [Here] there can be no doubt that the suit was properly commenced in the federal court. But in the present case we look to local law to find the cause of action on which suit is brought. Since that cause of action is created by local law, the measure of it is to be found only in local law. It carries the same burden and is subject to the same defenses in the federal court as in the state court. * * * Otherwise there is a different measure of the cause of action in one court than in the other, and the principle of Erie R. Co. v. Tompkins is transgressed.

Is this decision a correct application of *York*?

For many years, it was widely thought that *Ragan* stood for the proposition that the Federal Rules of Civil Procedure were just as subject to the *Erie* doctrine as were purely judge-made rules. On the basis of the quoted excerpt, do you agree? In Walker v. Armco Steel Corp., 446 U.S. 740, 100 S.Ct. 1978, 64 L.Ed.2d 659 (1980), the Court held that *Ragan* had done no such thing. *Walker* is examined in detail, infra at p. ___.

(3) Woods v. Interstate Realty Co., 337 U.S. 535, 69 S.Ct. 1235, 93 L.Ed. 1524 (1949): The issue in the case was whether a federal court, sitting in diversity, was bound to apply a Mississippi "door closing" statute—a law prohibiting out-of-state corporations doing business in the state from suing in state court unless they had first qualified by consenting to service within the state. The statute provided that a foreign corporation failing to designate an agent for service within the state "shall not be permitted to bring or maintain any action or suit in any of the courts of this state." Relying on its earlier post-*York* decision in Angel v. Bullington, 330 U.S. 183, 67 S.Ct. 657, 91 L.Ed. 832 (1947), the Supreme Court held that the state statute had to be followed. It

relied on *York* for the proposition "that for purposes of diversity jurisdiction a federal court is 'in effect only another court of the State. * * *.'"

The Court reasoned:

The *York* case was premised on the theory that a right which local law creates but which it does not supply with a remedy is no right at all for purposes of enforcement in a federal court in a diversity case; that where in such cases one is barred from recovery in the state court, he should likewise be barred in the federal court. The contrary result would create discriminations against citizens of the State in favor of those authorized to invoke the diversity jurisdiction of the federal courts. It was that element of discrimination that Erie R. Co. v. Tompkins was designed to eliminate.

Justice Rutledge dissented in all three cases:

I think the three decisions taken together demonstrate the extreme extent to which the Court is going in submitting the control of diversity litigation in the federal courts to the states rather than to Congress, where it properly belongs. This is done in the guise of applying the rule of Erie R. Co. v. Tompkins * * *. But in my opinion it was never the purpose of that decision to put such matters as those involved here outside the power of Congress to regulate and to confer that authority exclusively upon the states.

Is Justice Rutledge correct in suggesting that the three decisions put such matters "outside the power of Congress to regulate"? What if Congress amended the Rules of Decision Act to exempt these areas from state control, or simply passed new statutes dealing with these areas? Recall that the Rules of Decision Act requires the application of state law, except where an Act of Congress, among other things, otherwise provides. To answer these questions we must first determine exactly what it was that the Court in *York* was interpreting and applying when it established its rule. Reexamine Justice Frankfurter's opinion in *York.* Was he interpreting the Rules of Decision Act? The Constitution? What difference, if any, would it make if he had been interpreting the latter, rather than the former? Could a persuasive argument be fashioned that Justice Frankfurter appears to be interpreting neither? If so, from where does he derive the legal principle he ultimately establishes?

How, under the test of *York,* should one determine whether use of a different rule in federal court would "significantly affect the result of a litigation"? Must it be clear, *a priori,* that the plaintiff will win if one standard is employed and lose if the other standard is used? How would *York* itself have been decided under that approach? Should we say instead that the test is that state law must be employed if under one standard a party will definitely lose while the other standard would at least give that party a chance to win? How would *York* be decided under this approach?

On this issue, consider Bernhardt v. Polygraphic Co. of America, Inc., 350 U.S. 198, 76 S.Ct. 273, 100 L.Ed. 199 (1956), in which the question was whether a federal court could enforce an arbitration provision in a contract even though under Vermont law the arbitration clause could be revoked at any time before an award was made. The Supreme Court initially held that the United States Arbitration Act did not control the case. The court of appeals had held that federal common law, rather than Vermont law, controlled the issue of whether the case would go to arbitration, because "[a]rbitration is merely a form of trial * * *." The Supreme Court disagreed, holding that Vermont law had to be used:*

> If the federal court allows arbitration where the state court would disallow it, the outcome of litigation might depend on the courthouse where suit is brought. For the remedy by arbitration, whatever its merits or shortcomings, substantially affects the cause of action created by the State. The nature of the tribunal where suits are tried is an important part of the parcel of rights behind a cause of action. The change from a court of law to an arbitration panel may make a radical difference in ultimate result. Arbitration carries no right to trial by jury that is guaranteed both by the Seventh Amendment and by * * * the Vermont Constitution. Arbitrators do not have the benefit of judicial instruction on the law; they need not give their reasons for their results; the record of their proceedings is not as complete as it is in a court trial; and judicial review of an award is more limited than judicial review of a trial * * *. We said in the *York* case that "The nub of the policy that underlies Erie R. Co. v. Tompkins is that for the same transaction the accident of a suit by a non-resident litigant in a federal court instead of in a State court a block away should not lead to a substantially different result." There would in our judgment be a resultant discrimination if the parties suing on a Vermont cause of action in the federal court were remitted to arbitration, while those suing in the Vermont court could not be.

Is *Bernhardt* a proper application of the *York* test? Is it clear, *a priori*, whether plaintiff or defendant would be helped by resort to arbitration, rather than to judicial procedure? Should that matter, in light of the *Erie* policies *York* was designed to foster? Was it clear in *York* itself whether plaintiff or defendant would be helped by use of a different standard in federal court? How about in *Cohen, Ragan* or *Woods?* Should those cases be distinguished from *Bernhardt* on this basis?

ERIE AND CONFLICT OF LAWS

As we saw in the discussion of choice of law in Chapter IX (supra p. 806), state courts do not always apply the law of their own state. Under

---

* Note that *Bernhardt* is no longer good law on this point because the Federal Arbitration Act, 9 U.S.C.A. §§ 1 et seq., has been held to preempt state-law limitations on the enforcement of agreements to arbitrate if they are included in agreements affecting commerce. See Southland Corp. v. Keating, 465 U.S. 1, 104 S.Ct. 852, 79 L.Ed.2d 1 (1984).

certain circumstances, a court may decide that the law of another state is to be applied. States have employed a variety of criteria to determine which state's law is to be invoked.

A federal court, sitting in diversity, knows, after *Erie,* that in most cases it must apply substantive state law, rather than "general" common law. However, because a diversity case always involves citizens of at least two states, the federal court will be required to determine *which* state's law to apply. May a federal court, as a matter of federal common law, choose its own conflict of laws rule to decide which state's law to apply, or, under *Erie,* must it employ the conflict of laws rule of the state in which it sits?

The Supreme Court decided this question in the post-*Erie,* pre-*York* decision of Klaxon Co. v. Stentor Electric Manufacturing Co., 313 U.S. 487, 61 S.Ct. 1020, 85 L.Ed. 1477 (1941):

> We are of opinion that the prohibition declared in Erie R. Co. v. Tompkins, against * * * independent determinations by the federal courts, extends to the field of conflict of laws. The conflict of laws rule to be applied by the federal court in [a particular state] must conform to those prevailing in [that state's] courts. Otherwise, the accident of diversity of citizenship would constantly disturb equal administration of justice in coordinate state and federal courts sitting side by side. * * * Any other ruling would do violence to the principle of uniformity within a state, upon which the *Tompkins* decision is based.

Is *Klaxon* a proper application of *Erie?* Would it have been decided the same way following *York?*

Consider the following criticism of *Klaxon* by Professor Hart: "In [its holding in *Klaxon*] the Court has paralyzed the capacities of the federal courts to further one of the central desiderata of a federal system. Uniformity throughout the * * * states is occasionally desirable, and where that is so a uniform federal substantive law provides the best means of securing it. But uniformity of obligation as between particular individuals, regardless of the laws of litigation, is almost invariably desirable; and the essence of this can be achieved without enacting uniform substantive laws. The promotion of this kind of uniformity, so far as this can be done without sacrifice of greater values, is one of the functions of the principles of the conflict of laws." Hart, The Relations Between State and Federal Law, 54 Colum.L.Rev. 489, 513–14 (1954).

Is Professor Hart's criticism persuasive? Consider the following language from the *Klaxon* opinion: "Whatever lack of uniformity this [decision] may produce between federal courts in different states is attributable to our federal system, which leaves to a state, within the limits permitted by the Constitution, the right to pursue local policies diverging from those of its neighbors. It is not for the federal courts to thwart such local policies by enforcing an independent 'general law' of conflict of laws." Is this statement, though written thirteen years prior to Professor Hart's article, nevertheless responsive to his criticism? Does it suggest other forum-shopping concerns by enabling plaintiffs to seek a state with favorable law?

The Court continues to adhere to the *Klaxon* holding. See, e.g., Keeton v. Hustler Magazine, Inc., 465 U.S. 770, 104 S.Ct. 1473, 79 L.Ed.2d 790 (1984) (supra p. 747 n.1); Day & Zimmermann, Inc. v. Challoner, 423 U.S. 3, 96 S.Ct. 167, 46 L.Ed.2d 3 (1975). On the validity of *Klaxon,* see generally Horowitz, Toward a Federal Common Law of Choice of Law, 14 U.C.L.A.L.Rev. 1191 (1967); Weintraub, The Erie Doctrine and State Conflict of Laws Rules, 39 Ind.L.J. 228 (1964); Baxter, Choice of Law and the Federal System, 16 Stan.L.Rev. 1 (1963). For an argument that *Klaxon* "should be replaced with an approach that calls on diversity courts to apply an independent choice–of–law approach focusing on substantive values," see Borchers, The Origins of Diversity Jurisdiction, the Rise of Legal Positivism, and a Brave New World for *Erie* and *Klaxon,* 72 Tex. L. Rev. 79, 132 (1993).

The American Law Institute has recommended adoption of a "coherent and uniform federal choice of law code" for complex federal court litigation, in contravention of *Klaxon.* American Law Institute, Complex Litigation Project, ch. 6 Introductory Note (1994). The ALI argued that "[t]he rationale for developing federal choice of law standards for complex litigation is to decrease forum shopping and to reduce the extremely complicated inquiry now needed to ascertain and apply the numerous state choice of law rules that may be relevant in a consolidated action." Id. See also Lowenfeld, Mass Torts and the Conflict of Laws: The Airline Disaster, 1989 U. Ill. L. Rev. 157; Mullenix, Federalizing Choice of Law for Mass–Tort Litigation, 70 Tex. L. Rev. 1623 (1992); Mullenix, Class Resolution of the Mass–Tort Case: A Proposed Federal Procedure Act, 64 Tex. L. Rev. 1039 (1986); Vairo, Multi–Tort Cases: Cause for More Darkness on the Subject, Or a New Role for Federal Common Law?, 54 Ford. L. Rev. 167 (1985); Weintraub, Methods for Resolving Conflict-of-Laws Problems in Mass Tort Litigation, 1989 U. Ill. L. Rev. 129. Can complex cases, which often involve numerous parties from a number of states, properly be distinguished from more traditional litigation for purposes of choice of law? Is the rationale of *Klaxon* any less relevant in this context?

Arguably more controversial than *Klaxon* was the Court's decision the same day in Griffin v. McCoach, 313 U.S. 498, 61 S.Ct. 1023, 85 L.Ed. 1481 (1941). An interpleader action was filed in federal court in Texas, pursuant to the federal interpleader statute. Though subject matter jurisdiction in the case was based on diversity of citizenship, with the substantive claim deriving from state law, the action could not have been brought in state court in Texas, because the suit required use of the nationwide service of process provided for by the federal interpleader statute, not available to any state court because of due process limitations. Nevertheless, the Supreme Court, relying on *Klaxon,* held that the federal court must apply the Texas conflict of laws rules. Professor Wright suggests that "[e]ven if the *Klaxon* doctrine is accepted, there is ground to argue that Griffin v. McCoach goes too far * * *." C. Wright & M. Kane, The Law of Federal Courts 392 (6th ed. 2002). Do you agree?

BYRD v. BLUE RIDGE RURAL ELECTRIC COOPERATIVE, INC.

Supreme Court of the United States, 1958.
356 U.S. 525, 78 S.Ct. 893, 2 L.Ed.2d 953.

JUSTICE BRENNAN delivered the opinion of the Court.

[Plaintiff filed a diversity suit in federal district court in South Carolina for injuries allegedly caused by defendant's negligence. Plaintiff was a lineman in a construction crew of a contractor who had contracted to build power lines for the defendant, an electric company. Plaintiff was injured while connecting power lines on the job. The trial court denied defendant's motion to dismiss, and plaintiff won a jury verdict.]

One of respondent's affirmative defenses was that under the South Carolina Workmen's Compensation Act [§ 72–111], the petitioner—because the work contracted to be done by his employer was work of the kind also done by the respondent's own construction and maintenance crews—had the status of a statutory employee of the respondent and was therefore barred from suing the respondent at law because obliged to accept statutory compensation benefits as the exclusive remedy for his injuries. Two questions concerning this defense are before us: (1) whether the Court of Appeals erred in directing judgment for respondent without a remand to give petitioner an opportunity to introduce further evidence; and (2) whether petitioner, state practice notwithstanding, is entitled to a jury determination of the factual issues raised by this defense.

I.

* * *

Relying on the decisions of the Supreme Court of South Carolina, * * * the Court of Appeals held that the statute granted respondent immunity from the action if the proofs established that the respondent's own crews had constructed lines and substations which, like the work contracted to the petitioner's employer, were necessary for the distribution of the electric power which the respondent was in the business of selling. * * *

However, instead of ordering a new trial at which the petitioner might offer his own proof pertinent to a determination according to the correct interpretation, the Court of Appeals made its own determination on the record and directed a judgment for the respondent.

* * *

We believe that the Court of Appeals erred. We do not agree with the petitioner's argument in this Court that the respondent's evidence was insufficient to withstand the motion to strike the defense and that he is entitled to our judgment reinstating the judgment of the District Court. But the petitioner is entitled to have the question determined in the trial court. This would be necessary even if petitioner offered no proof of his own. Although the respondent's evidence was sufficient to withstand the motion under the meaning given the statute by the Court of Appeals, it presented a fact question, which, in the circumstances of this case to be discussed infra, is properly to be decided by a jury. This is clear not only because of the issue of the credibility of the [respondent's] manager's vital testimony [concerning use of respondent's employees on construction projects], but also because, even should the jury resolve that issue as did the Court of Appeals, the jury on the entire record—consistent with the view of the South Carolina cases that this question is in each case largely one of degree and of fact—might reasonably reach an opposite conclusion from the Court of Appeals as to the ultimate fact whether the respondent was a statutory employer.

At all events, the petitioner is plainly entitled to have an opportunity to try the issue under the Court of Appeals' interpretation. * * *

II.

A question is also presented as to whether on remand the factual issue is to be decided by the judge or by the jury. The respondent argues on the basis of the decision of the Supreme Court of South Carolina in Adams v. Davison–Paxon Co., 230 S.C. 532, 96 S.E.2d 566, that the issue of immunity should be decided by the judge and not by the jury. That was a negligence action brought in the state trial court against a store owner by an employee of an independent contractor who operated the store's millinery department. The trial judge denied the store owner's motion for a directed verdict made upon the ground that § 72–111 barred the plaintiff's action. The jury returned a verdict for the plaintiff. The South Carolina Supreme Court reversed, holding that it was for the judge and not the jury to decide on the evidence whether the owner was a statutory employer, and that the store owner had sustained his defense. * * *

The respondent argues that this state-court decision governs the present diversity case and "divests the jury of its normal function" to decide the disputed fact question of the respondent's immunity under § 72–111. This is to contend that the federal court is bound under Erie R. Co. v. Tompkins, 304 U.S. 64, 58 S.Ct. 817, 82 L.Ed. 1188, to follow the state court's holding to secure uniform enforcement of the immunity created by the State.

First. It was decided in Erie R. Co. v. Tompkins that the federal courts in diversity cases must respect the definition of state-created rights and obligations by the state courts. We must, therefore, first examine the rule in Adams v. Davison–Paxon Co. to determine whether it is bound up with these rights and obligations in such a way that its application in the federal court is required.

The Workmen's Compensation Act is administered in South Carolina by its Industrial Commission. The South Carolina courts hold that, on judicial review of actions of the Commission under § 72–111, the question whether the claim of an injured workman is within the Commission's jurisdiction is a matter of law for decision by the court, which makes its own findings of fact relating to that jurisdiction. The South Carolina Supreme Court states no reasons in Adams v. Davison–Paxon Co. why, although the jury decides all other factual issues raised by the cause of action and defenses, the jury is displaced as to the factual issue raised by the affirmative defense under § 72–111. A State may, of course, distribute the functions of its judicial machinery as it sees fit. The decisions relied upon, however, furnish no reason for selecting the judge rather than the jury to decide this single affirmative defense in the negligence action. They simply reflect a policy that administrative determination of "jurisdictional facts" should not be final but subject to judicial review. The conclusion is inescapable that the *Adams* holding is grounded in the practical consideration that the question had theretofore come before the South Carolina courts from the Industrial Commission and the courts had become accustomed to deciding the factual issue of immunity without the aid of juries. We find nothing to suggest that this rule was announced as an integral part of the special relationship created by the statute. Thus the requirement appears to be merely a form and mode of enforcing the immunity, Guaranty Trust Co. of New York v. York, and not a rule intended to be bound up with the definition of the rights and obligations of the parties. * * *

Second. But cases following *Erie* have evinced a broader policy to the effect that the federal courts should conform as near as may be—in the absence of other considerations—to state rules even of form and mode where the state rules may bear substantially on the question whether the litigation would come out one way in the federal court and another way in the state court if the federal court failed to apply a particular local rule. E.g., Guaranty Trust Co. of New York v. York, supra; Bernhardt v. Polygraphic Co., 350 U.S. 198, 76 S.Ct. 273, 100 L.Ed. 199. Concededly the nature of the tribunal which tries issues may be important in the enforcement of the parcel of rights making up a cause of action or defense, and bear significantly upon achievement of uniform enforcement of the right. It may well be that in the instant personal-injury case the outcome would be substantially affected by whether the issue of immunity is decided by a judge or a jury. Therefore, were "outcome" the only consideration, a strong case might appear for saying that the federal court should follow the state practice.

But there are affirmative countervailing considerations at work here. The federal system is an independent system for administering justice to litigants who properly invoke its jurisdiction. An essential characteristic of that system is the manner in which, in civil common-law actions, it distributes trial functions between judge and jury and, under the influence—if not the command[10]—of the Seventh Amendment, assigns the decisions of disputed questions of fact to the jury. The policy of uniform enforcement of state-created rights and obligations, see, e.g., Guaranty Trust Co. of New York v. York, supra, cannot in every case exact compliance with a state rule—not bound up with rights and obligations—which disrupts the federal system of allocating functions between judge and jury. Herron v. Southern Pacific Co., 283 U.S. 91, 51 S.Ct. 383, 75 L.Ed. 857. Thus the inquiry here is whether the federal policy favoring jury decisions of disputed fact questions should yield to the state rule in the interest of furthering the objective that the litigation should not come out one way in the federal court and another way in the state court.

We think that in the circumstances of this case the federal court should not follow the state rule. It cannot be gainsaid that there is a strong federal policy against allowing state rules to disrupt the judge-jury relationship in the federal courts. In Herron v. Southern Pacific Co., supra, the trial judge in a personal-injury negligence action brought in the District Court for Arizona on diversity grounds directed a verdict for the defendant when it appeared as a matter of law that the plaintiff was guilty of contributory negligence. The federal judge refused to be bound by a provision of the Arizona Constitution which made the jury the sole arbiter of the question of contributory negligence. This Court sustained the action of the trial judge, holding that "state laws cannot alter the essential character or function of a federal court" because that function "is not in any sense a local matter, and state statutes which would interfere with the appropriate performance of that function are not binding upon the federal court under either the Conformity Act or the 'Rules of Decision' Act." Perhaps even more clearly in light of the influence of the Seventh Amendment, the function assigned to the jury "is an essential factor in the process for which the Federal Constitution provides." Concededly the *Herron* case was decided before Erie R. Co. v. Tompkins, but even when Swift v. Tyson was governing law and allowed federal courts sitting in diversity cases to disregard state decisional law, it was never thought that state statutes or constitutions were similarly to be disregarded. Yet *Herron* held that state statutes and constitutional provisions could not disrupt or alter the essential character or function of a federal court.

Third. We have discussed the problem upon the assumption that the outcome of the litigation may be substantially affected by whether the issue of immunity is decided by a judge or a jury. But clearly there is not present here the certainty that a different result would follow, cf. Guaranty Trust Co. of New York v. York, supra, or even the strong possibility that this would be the case, cf. Bernhardt v. Polygraphic Co.,

---

10. Our conclusion makes unnecessary the consideration of—and we intimate no view upon—the constitutional question whether the right of jury trial protected in federal courts by the Seventh Amendment embraces the factual issue of statutory immunity when asserted, as here, as an affirmative defense in a common-law negligence action.

supra. There are factors present here which might reduce that possibility. The trial judge in the federal system has powers denied the judges of many States to comment on the weight of evidence and credibility of witnesses, and discretion to grant a new trial if the verdict appears to him to be against the weight of the evidence. We do not think the likelihood of a different result is so strong as to require the federal practice of jury determination of disputed factual issues to yield to the state rule in the interest of uniformity of outcome.

The Court of Appeals did not consider other grounds of appeal raised by the respondent because the ground taken disposed of the case. We accordingly remand the case to the Court of Appeals for the decision of the other questions, with instructions that, if not made unnecessary by the decision of such questions, the Court of Appeals shall remand the case to the District Court for a new trial of such issues as the Court of Appeals may direct.

Reversed and remanded.

[The opinions of Justice Whitaker, concurring in part and dissenting in part, and of Justices Frankfurter and Harlan, dissenting, are omitted.]

Notes and Questions

1.   In what way does the test of *Byrd* differ from that of *York?* To what extent does the alteration in the test to be applied reflect a change in the particular underlying policies intended to be fostered? See Redish & Phillips, *Erie* and the Rules of Decision Act: In Search of the Appropriate Dilemma, 91 Harv.L.Rev. 356, 365 (1977): "The most striking departure from [*York*] was the *Byrd* Court's significant emphasis on the relationship between the federal and state system, coupled with a relative disregard of more litigant-oriented concerns." Does the *Byrd* test reflect such a change?

2.   It has been suggested that "[t]he Court's approach [in *Byrd*] recognized the relevance of three distinct interests in applying *Erie:* The state's interest in not having its substantive policies undermined in diversity cases, the federal courts' interest in administering justice in accord with the dictates of significant federal principles, and the litigants' interest in not having the outcome of the case turn exclusively on the forum in which the case was brought." Redish & Phillips, supra, 91 Harv.L.Rev. at 364. Examine the Court's opinion in *Byrd* closely. Exactly how are these three factors to be weighed? Is there some degree of ambiguity on the point in the opinion? See id.

Some lower courts after *Byrd* all but excluded consideration of the potential effect on outcome, instead focusing exclusively on a weighing of competing state and federal interests. See, for example, the decision in Allstate Insurance Co. v. Charneski, 286 F.2d 238 (7th Cir.1960). The diversity case was brought by Allstate in federal court in Wisconsin. Allstate sought a declaratory judgment that there was no insurance coverage for the car operated by one defendant at the time of collision with another defendant. The court noted that "the Supreme Court of Wisconsin has declared it to be the public policy of that state that an insurance company may not bring a separate declaratory judgment action under the Wisconsin Uniform

Declaratory Judgment Act as being in contravention of the legislative policy declared in its direct action statute. Such state policy commands that all issues arising in a negligence action, including insurance policy coverage, be determined in a single action." The court was therefore "required to determine whether in a diversity action under the Federal Declaratory Judgments Act * * * a federal district court can assume jurisdiction in contravention of the declared state policy of Wisconsin." It noted that "[t]he different outcome of this case in a state and federal court would result in forum shopping, for no such case can be brought in Wisconsin. However, under the *Byrd* standards, outcome determination is not a mechanical solution. A proper line of inquiry must assess the competing policy goals of the two sovereigns." The court concluded that the state had a strong policy that "would be seriously weakened if we allow in federal courts that which the state courts disallow." The federal interest, on the other hand, was found to be "slight". The court therefore held that state law must be applied.

3.   What potential problems do you see with application of the *Byrd* balancing test? Professors Wright and Kane have noted that "there was considerable difficulty in applying the *Byrd* test. Able courts—and judges within a single court—were divided in situations that were distinguishable but perhaps not really different. * * * The difficulty in applying the *Byrd* test probably stemmed from the fact that there is no scale to say with assurance in a particular case that the federal interest asserted is more or less important than the interest in preserving uniformity of result with the state court. Even if there were such a scale, the weights to be put in it must be whatever the judges say they are." C. Wright & M. Kane, The Law of Federal Courts 404–05 (6th ed. 2002). According to Professor John Ely, "[t]he [*Byrd*] opinion exhibits a confusion that exceeds even that normally surrounding a balancing test, and lower courts understandably experienced considerable difficulty in applying it." Ely, The Irrepressible Myth of Erie, 87 Harv.L.Rev. 693, 709 (1974). For an attempt to develop a more "refined," structured and predictable balancing test, see Redish & Phillips, supra, 91 Harv.L.Rev. at 384–400.

4.   What are the competing federal and state interests in *Byrd* itself? Note that the Court cites the federal interest in "distribut[ing] trial functions between judge and jury and, under the influence—if not the command—of the Seventh Amendment, assign[ing] the decisions of disputed questions of fact to the jury." The Seventh Amendment provides in relevant part that "[i]n suits at common law, where the value in controversy shall exceed twenty dollars, the right of trial by jury shall be preserved * * *." See discussion in Chapter VIII, supra pp. 529–606. Thus, while apparently federal practice in this case would have assigned the disputed issue to the jury, rather than the judge, the Court at no point decides that this allocation is in fact dictated by the Seventh Amendment. If the Court had resolved that question in the affirmative, what role, if any, would have remained for the Court's balancing test? The Court apparently believed that it need not resolve the constitutional question, because even if the Seventh Amendment did not "command" the result, its "influence" was sufficiently great to weigh heavily on the federal side of the balance. How can a constitutional provision that does not dictate a particular result nevertheless "influence"

the outcome? The Seventh Amendment, for example, requires that certain matters be resolved by a jury, and says absolutely nothing about the method of resolving other issues. If the Court in *Byrd* had held that the Seventh Amendment did not require use of a jury on the disputed issue, how could it have had any residual "influence" toward that end?

If one were to exclude the Seventh Amendment's "influence," what remains on the federal side of the balance? The Court notes that "[t]he federal system is an independent system for administering justice to litigants who properly invoke its jurisdiction." Is this a distinct federal interest for purposes of balancing? At various times, lower federal courts relied on this statement to reject use of state law in favor of a distinct federal standard in diversity cases. For example, in Monarch Insurance Co. v. Spach, 281 F.2d 401 (5th Cir.1960), the court refused to follow a Florida rule regarding admissibility of evidence for impeachment purposes where the party seeking to impeach failed to present the impeaching materials to the opposing litigant. Applying *Byrd,* the court identified the federal interest as "the indispensable necessity that a tribunal, if it is to be an independent federal court administering law, must have the capacity to regulate the manner by which cases are to be presented in the search for the truth of the cause." It has been suggested that this interest "might be thought to prove too much; its logic would authorize federal court rejection of purely substantive state standards where, in the federal court's opinion, to apply them would cause an injustice." Redish & Phillips, supra, 91 Harv.L.Rev. at 390. The same authors also articulated the counter-argument: "A court's integrity is to a degree dependent upon its authority to control matters that are intimately bound up with its daily internal operations. In this sense, a court's power to determine the fairest procedures is qualitatively different from its authority to develop principles of substantive law." Id. at 391. Which of these two positions do you accept? In employing the interest as part of a balancing test, must one accept one view or the other? See id. at 391–92.

5. In developing the balancing test, what was the Court in *Byrd* interpreting? The Rules of Decision Act? The Constitution? Something else?

HANNA v. PLUMER

Supreme Court of the United States, 1965.
380 U.S. 460, 85 S.Ct. 1136, 14 L.Ed.2d 8.

CHIEF JUSTICE WARREN delivered the opinion of the Court.

The question to be decided is whether, in a civil action where the jurisdiction of the United States district court is based upon diversity of citizenship between the parties, service of process shall be made in the manner prescribed by state law or that set forth in Rule 4(d)(1) of the Federal Rules of Civil Procedure.

On February 6, 1963, petitioner, a citizen of Ohio, filed her complaint in the District Court for the District of Massachusetts, claiming damages in excess of $10,000 for personal injuries resulting from an automobile accident in South Carolina, allegedly caused by the negligence of one Louise Plumer Osgood, a Massachusetts citizen deceased at the time of the filing of the complaint. Respondent, Mrs. Osgood's executor and also a Massachusetts citizen, was named as defendant. On February 8, service was made by leaving copies of the summons and the complaint with respondent's wife at his residence, concededly in compliance with Rule 4(d)(1),* which provides:

> "The summons and complaint shall be served together. The plaintiff shall furnish the person making service with such copies as are necessary. Service shall be made as follows:

> "(1) Upon an individual other than an infant or an incompetent person, by delivering a copy of the summons and of the complaint to him personally or by leaving copies thereof at his dwelling house or usual place of abode with some person of suitable age and discretion then residing therein...."

Respondent filed his answer on February 26, alleging, inter alia, that the action could not be maintained because it had been brought "contrary to and in violation of the provisions of Massachusetts General Laws (Ter. Ed.) Chapter 197, Section 9." That section provides:

> "Except as provided in this chapter, an executor or administrator shall not be held to answer to an action by a creditor of the deceased which is not commenced within one year from the time of his giving bond for the performance of his trust, or to such an action which is commenced within said year unless before the expiration thereof the writ in such action has been served by delivery in hand upon such executor or administrator or service thereof accepted by him or a notice stating the name of the estate, the name and address of the creditor, the amount of the claim and the court in which the action has been brought has been filed in the proper registry of probate...." Mass.Gen.Laws Ann., c. 197, § 9 (1958).

On October 17, 1963, the District Court granted respondent's motion for summary judgment, citing Ragan v. Merchants Transfer & Warehouse Co., 337 U.S. 530, 69 S.Ct. 1233, 93 L.Ed. 1520 [supra p. 937], and Guaranty Trust Co. of New York v. York, 326 U.S. 99, 65 S.Ct. 1464, 89 L.Ed. 2079 [supra p. 930], in support of its conclusion that the adequacy of the service was to be measured by § 9, with which, the court held, petitioner had not complied. On appeal, petitioner admitted noncompliance with § 9, but argued that Rule 4(d)(1) defines the method by which service of process is to be effected in diversity actions. The Court of Appeals for the First Circuit, finding that "[r]elatively recent amendments [to § 9] evince a clear legislative purpose to require personal notification within the year,"[1] concluded that the conflict of state and federal rules was over "substantive rather than a procedural matter,"

---

* The parallel provisions now appear in Rule 4(e)(2).—Eds.

1. Section 9 is in part a statute of limitations, providing that an executor need not "answer to an action...which is not commenced within one year from the time of his giving bond..." This part of the statute, the purpose of which is to speed the settlement of estates, is not involved in this case, since the action clearly was timely commenced. Cf. Guaranty Trust Co. v. York, supra; Ragan v. Merchants Transfer Co., supra.

Section 9 also provides for the manner of service. Generally, service of process must

and unanimously affirmed. * * *"substantive rather than a procedural matter," and unanimously affirmed. * * *

We conclude that the adoption of Rule 4(d)(1), designed to control service of process in diversity actions, neither exceeded the congressional mandate embodied in the Rules Enabling Act nor transgressed constitutional bounds, and that the Rule is therefore the standard against which the District Court should have measured the adequacy of the service. Accordingly, we reverse the decision of the Court of Appeals.

The Rules Enabling Act, 28 U.S.C. § 2072 provides, in pertinent part:

> "The Supreme Court shall have the power to prescribe, by general rules, the forms of process, writs, pleadings, and motions, and the practice and procedure of the district courts of the United States in civil actions.

> "Such rules shall not abridge, enlarge or modify any substantive right and shall preserve the right of trial by jury...."

Under the cases construing the scope of the Enabling Act, Rule 4(d)(1) clearly passes muster. Prescribing the manner in which a defendant is to be notified that a suit has been instituted against him, it relates to the "practice and procedure of the district courts."

> "The test must be whether a rule really regulates procedure,—the judicial process for enforcing rights and duties recognized by substantive law and for justly administering remedy and redress for disregard or infraction of them." Sibbach v. Wilson & Co., 312 U.S. 1, 14, 61 S.Ct. 422, 426, 85 L.Ed. 479....

* * *

Thus were there no conflicting state procedure, Rule 4(d)(1) would clearly control. However, respondent, focusing on the contrary Massachusetts rule, calls to the Court's attention another line of cases, a line which—like the Federal Rules—had its birth in 1938. Erie R. Co. v. Tompkins, overruling Swift v. Tyson, held that federal courts sitting in diversity cases, when deciding questions of "substantive" law, are bound by state court decisions as well as state statutes. The broad command of *Erie* was therefore identical to that of the Enabling Act: federal courts are to apply state substantive law and federal procedural law. However, as subsequent cases sharpened the distinction between substance and procedure, the line of cases following *Erie* diverged markedly from the

be made by "delivery in hand," although there are two alternatives: acceptance of service by the executor, or filing of a notice of claim the components of which are set out in the statute, in the appropriate probate court. The purpose of this part of the statute, which is involved here, is, as the court below noted, to insure that executors will receive actual notice of claims. Actual notice is or course also the goal of Rule 4(d)(1); however, the Federal Rule reflects a determination that this goal can be achieved by a method less cumbersome than that prescribed in § 9. In this case the goal seems to have been achieved; although the affidavit filed by respondent in the District Court asserts that he had not been serviced in hand nor had he accepted service, it does not allege lack of actual notice.

line construing the Enabling Act. Guaranty Trust Co. of New York v. York made it clear that *Erie*-type problems were not to be solved by reference to any traditional or common-sense substance-procedure distinction:

> "And so the question is not whether a statute of limitations is deemed a matter of 'procedure' in some sense. The question is ... does it significantly affect the result of a litigation for a federal court to disregard a law of a State that would be controlling in an action upon the same claim by the same parties in a State court?"

Respondent, by placing primary reliance on *York* and *Ragan*, suggests that the *Erie* doctrine acts as a check on the Federal Rules of Civil Procedure, that despite the clear command of Rule 4(d)(1), *Erie* and its progeny demand the application of the Massachusetts rule. Reduced to essentials, the argument is: (1) *Erie*, as refined in *York*, demands that federal courts apply state law whenever application of federal law in its stead will alter the outcome of the case. (2) In this case, a determination that the Massachusetts service requirements obtain will result in immediate victory for respondent. If, on the other hand, it should be held that Rule 4(d)(1) is applicable, the litigation will continue, with possible victory for petitioner. (3) Therefore, *Erie* demands application of the Massachusetts rule. The syllogism possesses an appealing simplicity, but is for several reasons invalid.

In the first place, it is doubtful that, even if there were no Federal Rule making it clear that in-hand service is not required in diversity actions, the *Erie* rule would have obligated the District Court to follow the Massachusetts procedure. "Outcome-determination" analysis was never intended to serve as a talisman. Byrd v. Blue Ridge Rural Elec. Cooperative. Indeed, the message of *York* itself is that choices between state and federal law are to be made not by application of any automatic, "litmus paper" criterion, but rather by reference to the policies underlying the *Erie* rule.

The *Erie* rule is rooted in part in a realization that it would be unfair for the character or result of a litigation materially to differ because the suit had been brought in a federal court. * * * The decision was also in part a reaction to the practice of "forum-shopping" which had grown up in response to the rule of Swift v. Tyson. That the *York* test was an attempt to effectuate these policies is demonstrated by the fact that the opinion framed the inquiry in terms of "substantial" variations between state and federal litigation. Not only are nonsubstantial, or trivial, variations not likely to raise the sort of equal protection problems which troubled the Court in *Erie*: they are also unlikely to influence the choice of a forum. The "outcome-determination" test therefore cannot be read without reference to the twin aims of the *Erie* rule: discouragement of forum-shopping and avoidance of inequitable administration of the laws.[9]

9. The Court of Appeals seemed to frame the inquiry in terms of how "important" § 9 is to the State. In support of its suggestion that § 9 serves some interest the

The difference between the conclusion that the Massachusetts rule is applicable, and the conclusion that it is not, is of course at this point "outcome-determinative" in the sense that if we hold the state rule to apply, respondent prevails, whereas if we hold that Rule 4(d)(1) governs, the litigation will continue. But in this sense every procedural variation is "outcome-determinative." For example, having brought suit in a federal court, a plaintiff cannot then insist on the right to file subsequent pleadings in accord with the time limits applicable in state courts, even though enforcement of the federal timetable will, if he continues to insist that he must meet only the state time limit, result in determination of the controversy against him. So it is here. Though choice of the federal or state rule will at this point have a marked effect upon the outcome of the litigation, the difference between the two rules would be of scant, if any, relevance to the choice of a forum. Petitioner, in choosing her forum, was not presented with a situation where application of the state rule would wholly bar recovery;[10] rather, adherence to the state rule would have resulted only in altering the way in which process was served.[11] Moreover, it is difficult to argue that permitting service of defendant's wife to take the place of in hand service of defendant himself alters the mode of enforcement of state-created rights in a fashion sufficiently "substantial" to raise the sort of equal protection problems to which the *Erie* opinion alluded.

There is, however, a more fundamental flaw in respondent's syllogism: the incorrect assumption that the rule of Erie R. Co. v. Tompkins constitutes the appropriate test of the validity and therefore the applicability of a Federal Rule of Civil Procedure. The *Erie* rule has never been

State regards as vital to its citizens, the court noted that something like § 9 has been on the books in Massachusetts a long time, that § 9 has been amended a number of times and that § 9 is designed to make sure that executors receive actual notice. See note 1, supra. The apparent lack of relation among these three observations is not surprising, because it is not clear to what sort of question the Court of Appeals was addressing itself. One cannot meaningfully ask how important something is without first asking important for what purpose? *Erie* and its progeny make clear that when a federal court sitting in a diversity case is faced with a question of whether or not to apply state law, the importance of a state rule is indeed relevant, but only in the context of asking whether application of the rule would make so important a difference to the character or result of the litigation that failure to enforce it would unfairly discriminate against citizens of the forum State, or whether application of the rule would have so important an effect upon the fortunes of one or both of the litigants that failure to enforce it would be likely to cause a plaintiff to choose the federal court.

10. See Guaranty Trust Co. of New York v. York, supra, 326 U.S. at 108–109, 65 S.Ct. at 1469; Ragan v. Merchants Transfer & Warehouse Co., supra, 337 U.S. at 532, 69 S.Ct. at 1234; Woods v. Interstate Realty Co., 337 U.S. at 538, 69 S.Ct. at 1237. Similarly, a federal court's refusal to enforce the New Jersey rule involved in Cohen v. Beneficial Indus. Loan Corp., 337 U.S. 541, 69 S.Ct. 1221, 93 L.Ed. 1528, requiring the posting of security by plaintiffs in stockholders' derivative actions, might well impel a stockholder to choose to bring suit in the federal, rather than the state, court.

11. Cf. Monarch Insurance Co. of Ohio v. Spach, 281 F.2d 401, 412 (C.A.5th Cir. 1960). We cannot seriously entertain the thought that one suing an estate would be led to choose the federal court because of a belief that adherence to Rule 4(d)(1) is less likely to give the executor actual notice than § 9, and therefore more likely to produce a default judgment. Rule 4(d)(1) is well designed to give actual notice, as it did in this case.

invoked to void a Federal Rule. It is true that there have been cases where this Court has held applicable a state rule in the face of an argument that the situation was governed by one of the Federal Rules. But the holding of each such case was not that *Erie* commanded displacement of a Federal Rule by an inconsistent state rule, but rather that the scope of the Federal Rule was not as broad as the losing party urged, and therefore, there being no Federal Rule which covered the point in dispute, *Erie* commanded the enforcement of state law. * * * Here, of course, the clash is unavoidable; Rule 4(d)(1) says—implicitly, but with unmistakable clarity—that in-hand service is not required in federal courts. At the same time, in cases adjudicating the validity of Federal Rules, we have not applied the *York* rule or other refinements of *Erie,* but have to this day continued to decide questions concerning the scope of the Enabling Act and the constitutionality of specific Federal Rules in light of the distinction set forth in *Sibbach.*

Nor has the development of two separate lines of cases been inadvertent. The line between "substance" and "procedure" shifts as the legal context changes. "Each implies different variables depending upon the particular problem for which it is used." Guaranty Trust Co. of New York v. York. It is true that both the Enabling Act and the *Erie* rule say, roughly, that federal courts are to apply state "substantive" law and federal "procedural" law, but from that it need not follow that the tests are identical. For they were designed to control very different sorts of decisions. When a situation is covered by one of the Federal Rules, the question facing the court is a far cry from the typical, relatively unguided *Erie* choice: the court has been instructed to apply the Federal Rule, and can refuse to do so only if the Advisory Committee, this Court, and Congress erred in their prima facie judgment that the Rule in question transgresses neither the terms of the Enabling Act nor constitutional restrictions.[13]

We are reminded by the *Erie* opinion that neither Congress nor the federal courts can, under the guise of formulating rules of decision for federal courts, fashion rules which are not supported by a grant of federal authority contained in Article I or some other section of the Constitution; in such areas state law must govern because there can be no other law. But the opinion in *Erie,* which involved no Federal Rule and dealt with a question which was "substantive" in every traditional sense (whether the railroad owed a duty of care to Tompkins as a trespasser or a licensee), surely neither said nor implied that measures like Rule 4(d)(1) are unconstitutional. For the constitutional provision for a federal court system (augmented by the Necessary and Proper Clause) carries with it congressional power to make rules governing the practice and pleading in those courts, which in turn includes a power to regulate matters which, though falling within the uncertain area between substance and procedure, are rationally capable of classification as either. Neither *York* nor the cases following it ever suggested that the

---

13. Sibbach v. Wilson & Co., supra, 312 U.S. at 13–15, 61 S.Ct. at 426–427.

rule there laid down for coping with situations where no Federal Rule applies is coextensive with the limitation on Congress to which *Erie* had adverted. Although this Court has never before been confronted with a case where the applicable Federal Rule is in direct collision with the law of the relevant State, courts of appeals faced with such clashes have rightly discerned the implications of our decisions.

"One of the shaping purposes of the Federal Rules is to bring about uniformity in the federal courts by getting away from local rules. This is especially true of matters which relate to the administration of legal proceedings, an area in which federal courts have traditionally exerted strong inherent power, completely aside from the powers Congress expressly conferred in the Rules. The purpose of the *Erie* doctrine, even as extended in *York* and *Ragan,* was never to bottle up federal courts with 'outcome-determinative' and 'integral-relations' stoppers—when there are 'affirmative countervailing [federal] considerations' and when there is a Congressional mandate (the Rules) supported by constitutional authority." Lumbermen's Mutual Casualty Co. v. Wright, 322 F.2d 759, 764 (C.A.5th Cir. 1963).

Erie and its offspring cast no doubt on the long-recognized power of Congress to prescribe housekeeping rules for federal courts even though some of those rules will inevitably differ from comparable state rules. * * * Thus, though a court, in measuring a Federal Rule against the standards contained in the Enabling Act and the Constitution, need not wholly blind itself to the degree to which the Rule makes the character and result of the federal litigation stray from the course it would follow in state courts, Sibbach v. Wilson & Co., it cannot be forgotten that the *Erie* rule, and the guidelines suggested in *York,* were created to serve another purpose altogether. To hold that a Federal Rule of Civil Procedure must cease to function whenever it alters the mode of enforcing state-created rights would be to disembowel either the Constitution's grant of power over federal procedure or Congress' attempt to exercise that power in the Enabling Act. Rule 4(d)(1) is valid and controls the instant case.

Reversed.

Justice Black concurs in the result.

Justice Harlan, concurring.

It is unquestionably true that up to now *Erie* and the cases following it have not succeeded in articulating a workable doctrine governing choice of law in diversity actions. I respect the Court's effort to clarify the situation in today's opinion. However, in doing so I think it has misconceived the constitutional premises of *Erie* and has failed to deal adequately with those past decisions upon which the courts below relied.

Erie was something more than an opinion which worried about "forum-shopping and avoidance of inequitable administration of the laws," although to be sure these were important elements of the decision. I have always regarded that decision as one of the modern corner-stones of our federalism, expressing policies that profoundly touch the allocation of judicial power between the state and federal systems. *Erie* recognized that there should not be two conflicting systems of law controlling the primary activity of citizens, for such alternative governing authority must necessarily give rise to a debilitating uncertainty in the planning of everyday affairs. And it recognized that the scheme of our Constitution envisions an allocation of law-making functions between state and federal legislative processes which is undercut if the federal judiciary can make substantive law affecting state affairs beyond the bounds of congressional legislative powers in this regard. Thus, in diversity cases *Erie* commands that it be the state law governing primary private activity which prevails.

The shorthand formulations which have appeared in some past decisions are prone to carry untoward results that frequently arise from oversimplification. The Court is quite right in stating that the "outcome-determinative" test of Guaranty Trust Co. of New York v. York, if taken literally, proves too much, for any rule, no matter how clearly "procedural," can affect the outcome of litigation if it is not obeyed. In turning from the "outcome" test of *York* back to the unadorned forum-shopping rationale of *Erie*, however, the Court falls prey to like oversimplification, for a simple forum-shopping rule also proves too much; litigants often choose a federal forum merely to obtain what they consider the advantages of the Federal Rules of Civil Procedure or to try their cases before a supposedly more favorable judge. To my mind the proper line of approach in determining whether to apply a state or a federal rule, whether "substantive" or "procedural," is to stay close to basic principles by inquiring if the choice of rule would substantially affect those primary decisions respecting human conduct which our constitutional system leaves to state regulation. If so, *Erie* and the Constitution require that the state rule prevail, even in the face of a conflicting federal rule.

The Court weakens, if indeed it does not submerge, this basic principle by finding, in effect, a grant of substantive legislative power in the constitutional provision for a federal court system (compare Swift v. Tyson), and through it, setting up the Federal Rules as a body of law inviolate. * * * So long as a reasonable man could characterize any duly adopted federal rule as "procedural," the Court, unless I misapprehend what is said, would have it apply no matter how seriously it frustrated a State's substantive regulation of the primary conduct and affairs of its citizens. Since the members of the Advisory Committee, the Judicial Conference, and this Court who formulated the Federal Rules are presumably reasonable men, it follows that the integrity of the Federal Rules is absolute. Whereas the unadulterated outcome and forum-shopping tests may err too far toward honoring state rules, I submit that the Court's "arguably procedural, ergo constitutional" test moves too fast and far in the other direction.

The courts below relied upon this Court's decisions in Ragan v. Merchants Transfer & Warehouse Co., and Cohen v. Beneficial Indus.

Loan Corp. Those cases deserve more attention than this Court has given them, particularly *Ragan* which, if still good law, would in my opinion call for affirmance of the result reached by the Court of Appeals. Further, a discussion of these two cases will serve to illuminate the "diversity" thesis I am advocating.

In *Ragan* a Kansas statute of limitations provided that an action was deemed commenced when service was made on the defendant. Despite Federal Rule 3 which provides that an action commences with the filing of the complaint, the Court held that for purposes of the Kansas statute of limitations a diversity tort action commenced only when service was made upon the defendant. The effect of this holding was that although the plaintiff had filed his federal complaint within the state period of limitations, his action was barred because the federal marshal did not serve a summons on the defendant until after the limitations period had run. I think that the decision was wrong. At most, application of the Federal Rule would have meant that potential Kansas tort defendants would have to defer for a few days the satisfaction of knowing that they had not been sued within the limitations period. The choice of the Federal Rule would have had no effect on the primary stages of private activity from which torts arise, and only the most minimal effect on behavior following the commission of the tort. In such circumstances the interest of the federal system in proceeding under its own rules should have prevailed.

Cohen v. Beneficial Indus. Loan Corp. held that a federal diversity court must apply a state statute requiring a small stockholder in a stockholder derivative suit to post a bond securing payment of defense costs as a condition to prosecuting an action. Such a statute is not "outcome determinative"; the plaintiff can win with or without it. The Court now rationalizes the case on the ground that the statute might affect the plaintiff's choice of forum but as has been pointed out, a simple forum-shopping test proves too much. The proper view of *Cohen* is in my opinion, that the statute was meant to inhibit small stockholders from instituting "strike suits," and thus it was designed and could be expected to have a substantial impact on private primary activity. Anyone who was at the trial bar during the period when *Cohen* arose can appreciate the strong state policy reflected in the statute.* I think it wholly legitimate to view Federal Rule 23 as not purporting to deal with the problem. But even had the Federal Rules purported to do so, and in so doing provided a substantially less effective deterrent to strike suits, I think the state rule should still have prevailed. That is where I believe the Court's view differs from mine; for the Court attributes such overriding force to the Federal Rules that it is hard to think of a case where a conflicting state rule would be allowed to operate, even though the state rule reflected policy considerations which, under *Erie*, would lie within the realm of state legislative authority.

---

* Justice Harlan, as a practicing lawyer, argued *Cohen* for defendants.—Eds.

It remains to apply what has been said to the present case. The Massachusetts rule provides that an executor need not answer suits unless in-hand service was made upon him or notice of the action was filed in the proper registry of probate within one year of his giving bond. The evident intent of this statute is to permit an executor to distribute the estate which he is administering without fear that further liabilities may be outstanding for which he could be held personally liable. If the Federal District Court in Massachusetts applies Rule 4(d)(1) of the Federal Rules of Civil Procedure instead of the Massachusetts service rule, what effect would that have on the speed and assurance with which estates are distributed? As I see it, the effect would not be substantial. It would mean simply that an executor would have to check at his own house or the federal courthouse as well as the registry of probate before he could distribute the estate with impunity. As this does not seem enough to give rise to any real impingement on the vitality of the state policy which the Massachusetts rule is intended to serve, I concur in the judgment of the Court.

JOHN H. ELY, THE IRREPRESSIBLE MYTH OF *ERIE*

87 Harvard Law Review 693, 697–98; 699; 710; 712–14; 717–18 (1974).

My suggestion in this Article will be that the indiscriminate admixture of all questions respecting choices between federal and state law in diversity cases, under the single rubric of "the *Erie* doctrine" or "the *Erie* problem," has served to make a major mystery out of what are really three distinct and rather ordinary problems of statutory and constitutional interpretation. Of course there will be occasions with respect to all three on which reasonable persons will differ, but that does not make the problems mysterious or even very unusual. The United States Constitution, I shall argue, constitutes the relevant text only where Congress has passed a statute creating law for diversity actions, and it is in this situation alone that *Hanna*'s "arguably procedural" test controls. Where a nonstatutory rule is involved, the Constitution necessarily remains in the background, but is functionally irrelevant because the applicable statutes are significantly more protective of the prerogatives of state law. Thus, where there is no relevant Federal Rule of Civil Procedure or other Rule promulgated pursuant to the Enabling Act and the federal rule in issue is therefore wholly judge-made, whether state or federal law should be applied is controlled by the Rules of Decision Act, the statute construed in *Erie* and *York*. Where the matter in issue is covered by a Federal Rule, however, the Enabling Act—and not the Rules of Decision Act itself or the line of cases construing it—constitutes the relevant standard. To say that, however, and that is one of the things *Hanna* said, is by no means to concede the validity of all Federal Rules, for the Enabling Act contains significant limiting language of its own. The Court has correctly sensed that language cannot be construed to protect state prerogatives as strenuously as the Rules of Decision Act protects them in the absence of a Federal Rule. However, the Court's recent appreciation that the Enabling Act constitutes the only check on the Rules—that "Erie" does not stand there as a backstop—should lead it in an appropriate case to take the Act's limiting language more seriously than it has in the past.

* * *

[W]hatever *Hanna*'s other merits or demerits, the major point of the Court's opinion was its separation for purposes of analysis of the Rules of Decision Act, the Enabling Act, and the constitutional demands to which the *Erie* opinion had alluded.

* * *

The majority's main point, that the Rules Enabling Act alone was the appropriate measure of a Federal Rule of Civil Procedure, was sufficient to decide the case. It saw fit, however, to add a considered dictum on the question of what law would have been applicable had there been no such Rule and thus had a genuine *Erie* problem been presented.

Since "rules of decision" is hardly self-defining and the legislative history is sparse, the Court approached this issue by seeking "the policies underlying the *Erie* rule." It noted that the *Erie* opinion had evidenced concern with federal-state forum shopping, and went on to lay considerable stress on that concern in construing the Rules of Decision Act. But while the likelihood of forum shopping may turn out to be a handy touchstone for identifying those situations exhibiting the evils against which the Act was directed, forum shopping is not an evil per se. It is evil only if something evil flows from it; indeed, the very idea of the diversity jurisdiction was to provide an alternative to state court. Thus, unless the Rules of Decision Act was a pointless exercise, the First Congress must have seen something else wrong with allowing federal courts to formulate their own rules of decision and thereby to create a separate regime for those nonresident plaintiffs who wish to avail themselves of it.

* * *

What *Erie* mentioned, and *Hanna* picked up, was simple unfairness. The Court was referring to the unfairness of affording a nonresident plaintiff suing a resident defendant a unilateral choice of the rules by which the lawsuit was to be determined. But there is another unfairness, one not tied to the vicissitudes of the removal provisions—the unfairness of subjecting a person involved in litigation with a citizen of a different state of a body of law different from that which applies when his next door neighbor is involved in similar litigation with a citizen. The *Erie* opinion suggested a denial of equal protection was involved, but surely that was a metaphor. It would not be irrational to fight bias against out-of-staters by giving them access to a body of law, developed by persons beholden to no particular state, unavailable in suits between cocitizens. Not irrational, but the founders of our Republic—by not including any such power in the Constitution, and even more clearly by enacting the

Rules of Decision Act—refused to do it. Bias against out-of-staters was to be resisted, but only by providing an unbiased tribunal. To provide more, or at least so it was felt, would create an unfairness in the other direction.

The point of the *Hanna* dictum is that it is difficult to find unfairness of a sort that would have troubled the framers of the Rules of Decision Act, or of a sort whose elimination would justify disrupting a federal court's routine, when the difference between the federal and state rules is trivial, when their requirements are essentially fungible. The problem with the previously prevailing rhetoric was that it is possible to speak of enforcing a rule in either of two senses—exacting compliance on the one hand, or sanctioning a noncomplying party on the other. Thus, whenever the sanction for noncompliance is dismissal, there is a sense in which "enforcement" of the rule can be outcome determinative. But it is a backhanded sense, and one that implicates the concerns that gave rise to the Rules of Decision Act only when the underlying mandate thus enforced is sufficiently more or less burdensome than its state counterpart to support a plausible claim of unfairness. The Court therefore suggested by its examples that a federal court may adhere to its own rules in diversity cases insofar, but only insofar, as they are neither materially more or less difficult for the burdened party to comply with than their state counterparts, nor likely to generate an outcome different from that which would result were the case litigated in the state court system and the state rules followed.

* * *

[I]n the context of the Rules of Decision Act, a rejuvenated outcome determination test—augmented a little and clipped a little, so as to intercept the more preposterous implications of its earlier formulations—was just what was called for. And that is what *Hanna* provided.

Hanna's main point, however, was that when the application of a Federal Rule is at issue, the Rules Enabling Act—and not the Rules of Decision Act as construed by Erie R.R. v. Tompkins and other cases— should determine whether federal or state law is to be applied. Although it is a different question how closely the two statutes should be read to track each other, this point seems plainly correct. The Enabling Act provides that "[a]ll laws in conflict with" Rules promulgated under its authority "shall be of no further force or effect," and the Rules of Decision Act is a law. But even if that language were not there, the Enabling Act is much more recent; it is specifically designed to control the validity of the Rules; and it contains language directed to the same general concern—protection of the prerogatives of state law—as the Rules of Decision Act. It indicates it is the only statutory test of a Federal Rule, and there is every reason to believe it means it.

Notes and Questions

1. Consider Professor Ely's explication of *Hanna*. Is his interpretation of the decision accurate? What is the Court's test for determining the constitutional scope of *Erie?* What is the rationale for this approach?

2. When will the Court's constitutional test be relevant? Under what circumstances, according to the Court, is the test of the Rules of Decision Act to be used?

3. What is the actual holding in *Hanna?* Need the Court have examined the proper standard under the Rules of Decision Act in order to decide the case?

4. The Court in *Hanna* does not expressly overrule *Byrd.* What, if anything, is left of *Byrd* after *Hanna?* In answering, consider specifically footnote 9 in the Court's opinion. Does this reveal anything about the continued vitality of the *Byrd* test? Consider the following argument: *Byrd* and *Hanna* are incompatible in their perspectives on the interpretation of the Rules of Decision Act, because they focus on fundamentally different interests and concerns.

5. In the years after *Hanna,* lower federal courts often continued to employ the *Byrd* balancing tests, particularly on issues concerning the relationship between judge and jury. See, e.g., Mayer v. Gary Partners and Co., Ltd., 29 F.3d 330 (7th Cir.1994). Other federal courts attempted to combine *Byrd* and *Hanna.* For example, in Szantay v. Beech Aircraft Corp., 349 F.2d 60 (4th Cir.1965), the court, in holding that a South Carolina door-closing statute did not deprive the federal court of diversity jurisdiction, inquired "whether the [state] rule embodies important policies that would be frustrated by the application of a different federal jurisdictional rule and, if so, is this policy to be overridden because of a stronger federal policy?" The Court, however, also made mention of *Hanna*'s redefinition of outcome determination.

Another example is Yarber v. Allstate Insurance Co., 674 F.2d 232 (4th Cir.1982). A Virginia statute permits a plaintiff to take one voluntary nonsuit without prejudice to recommencement of the same action and, in a saving provision, provides a six-month grace period following the nonsuit, during which time the action may be restarted free of the bar of any statute of limitations that would otherwise have run, but only if suit is filed in the same state court in which the nonsuit was taken. The issue for *Erie* doctrine purposes was "whether a federal court sitting in diversity must honor Virginia's restriction of the court within which a nonsuited plaintiff may recommence in order to invoke the saving provision." Though the case was decided many years after *Hanna,* the court nevertheless relied partially on *Byrd* in holding that "[b]ecause we construe the restriction to be an integral part of the several policies served by Virginia's statute of limitations, we hold that it must be applied."

The Third Circuit, attempting to blend *Hanna* and *Byrd,* developed the following test in Jarvis v. Johnson, 668 F.2d 740, 743–44 (3d Cir.1982):

> [W]e must approach a problem such as is presented by the instant case by considering how the constitutional and policy concerns that motivated the Court in *Erie* and its progeny are implicated by the application or nonapplication of the particular state rule at issue. * * * [T]hese concerns include (1) the effect of application of the state or federal rule on the outcome of the litigation; (2) the likelihood that divergent state and federal rules will result in forum shopping; and (3) the existence of an overriding federal interest in the application of the federal rule.

Is this an accurate characterization of the state of the law under the Supreme Court precedents?

6. In what way does *Hanna*'s approach to the Rules of Decision Act differ from *York?* How would the *York* test have resolved the *Hanna* case? Does your answer reveal how the two differ? Is *Hanna* closer to *York* than it is to *Byrd?*

7. Note that in its explication of the Rules of Decision Act test, the Court in *Hanna* referred to "discouragement of forum-shopping and the avoidance of inequitable administration of the laws." Are these distinct concerns, or do they simply represent different means of characterizing the same interest? See McCoid, Hanna v. Plumer: The Erie Doctrine Takes Shape, 51 Va.L.Rev. 884, 889 (1965): "Opposition to forum shopping was based solely on the unfairness which resulted from the opportunity of some litigants to choose advantageously between two court systems applying different law. * * * The real aim of the uniformity policy, then, is what the Chief Justice describes as 'evidence of inequitable administration of the laws' and lack of 'equal protection.' " In this regard, consider also the *Walker* decision, infra p. 972.

8. The *Hanna* Court's approach to the Rules of Decision Act focuses on the dangers of forum-shopping. Exactly what are those dangers? How significant are they? Consider Redish & Phillips, *Erie* and the Rules of Decision Act: In Search of the Appropriate Dilemma, 91 Harv.L.Rev. 356, 375 (1977):

> [T]here is serious doubt about the severity of the discrimination the test is attempting to avoid, since similar disparities between litigants go unquestioned in other contexts. * * * The existence of an option afforded plaintiff and denied defendant * * * is a commonly accepted litigation phenomenon. For example, a plaintiff invariably has the choice of timing in bringing a suit (within the confines established by the applicable statute of limitations), and often, in light of relaxed due process limits on personal jurisdiction, a wide choice of locale. It can generally be expected that a plaintiff will choose the timing and locale simultaneously most convenient to him and most inconvenient to the defendant.

In his separate opinion, Justice Harlan argues that the forum-shopping approach proves too much, since it logically would lead to the end of the Federal Rules of Civil Procedure in situations when the state did not provide the same rule. Is his point valid?

9. Can the motivation behind a Federal Rule affect its validity in diversity cases? Consider Fed.R.Evid. 407. As originally adopted, it forbade evidence of subsequent remedial measures to prove negligence. The goal was to promote such corrective measures. Many states which have comparable rules, however, had held them inapplicable to products liability cases, so that federal courts entertaining suits under the law of those states must decide whether to apply the rule. In Moe v. Avions Marcel Dassault–Breguet Aviation, 727 F.2d 917 (10th Cir.1984), the court found that state law should control because "[t]he purpose of Rule 407 is not to seek the truth or to expedite trial proceedings; rather, in our view, it is one designed to promote state policy in a substantive law area." In Flaminio v. Honda Motor Co.,

Ltd., 733 F.2d 463 (7th Cir.1984), the court admitted that the rule is based primarily on social policy but held it valid: "[T]he substantive judgment that underlies Rule 407 is entwined with procedural considerations. It is only because juries are believed to overreact to evidence of subsequent remedial measures that the admissibility of such evidence could deter defendants from taking such measures. * * * Congress' judgment that juries are apt to give too much weight to such evidence is a procedural judgment, that is, a judgment concerning procedures designed to enhance accuracy or reduce expense in the adjudicative process." In 1997, Rule 407 was amended to apply explicitly to proof of product defects.

How significant is it that the Federal Rules of Evidence were themselves originally adopted by Congress as a statute, so that they are not subject to the limitations of the Rules Enabling Act? See Hottle v. Beech Aircraft Corp., 47 F.3d 106 (4th Cir.1995), a product liability action, in which the court held that defendants' internal manuals were properly excluded from evidence pursuant to Virginia law even though they would be admissible under the Federal Rules of Evidence. The court reasoned, citing *Byrd*, that "where a state's procedural rule is bound up with substantive policy, a federal court is to apply the state rule." Id. at 109. Because Virginia persisted in its rule as an expression of its substantive policy concerning what is the standard of care, state law should be applied. This was necessary because "application of the federal rule of evidence, although beyond argument procedural, may encroach upon a State's substantive law." Id. at 110. After *Hanna*, is this the proper approach to take to the question of whether a Federal Rule, promulgated pursuant to the Rules Enabling Act, supersedes conflicting state law in a diversity case? See infra at pp. 967–68.

10. How would Justice Harlan resolve *Erie* issues? Is he interpreting the Constitution, the Rules of Decision Act, the Rules Enabling Act, or something else? Why does he concur, rather than dissent, in *Hanna*?

11. How should the following case be resolved after *Hanna*: State law requires that prior to actual litigation of medical malpractice claims, the plaintiff's claim be presented to a malpractice screening panel, consisting of selected attorneys and judges. The panel presents a recommendation, admissible at trial, concerning the merits of the claim. The rule reflects a state policy interest in providing a measure of protection for physicians and in encouraging reduction in malpractice insurance rates and health care costs, thought to be increased by unduly large jury verdicts in malpractice suits. Federal practice makes no provision for the use of such a screening panel procedure. In a diversity malpractice suit in federal court, defendant seeks dismissal because plaintiff failed to follow the screening panel procedure as prescribed by state law. See, e.g., Edelson v. Soricelli, 610 F.2d 131 (3d Cir.1979) (divided court holds that state requirement of arbitration should be applied in medical malpractice case).

FEDERAL PROCEDURAL STATUTES AND HANNA–ERIE

Under the logic of *Hanna*, how should the Court resolve a difference between federal and state procedural standards when the federal standard is neither embodied in a Federal Rule of Civil Procedure nor merely a judge-made product, but rather is embodied in a distinct federal statute? Should the standard of the Rules of Decision Act control? How would Professor Ely suggest such cases should be decided?

On this question, consider the Supreme Court's decision in Stewart Organization, Inc. v. Ricoh Corp., 487 U.S. 22, 108 S.Ct. 2239, 101 L.Ed.2d 22 (1988). This diversity suit involved a contract that contained a forum-selection clause, providing that any dispute arising out of the contract could be brought only in a court located in Manhattan. The suit, however, was filed in the Northern District of Alabama. Relying on the contractual forum-selection clause, defendant moved, pursuant to the venue transfer statute, 28 U.S.C. § 1404(a) [see supra p. 856 n. 1], to transfer the case to the Southern District of New York, or to dismiss for improper venue under 28 U.S.C.A. § 1406. The district court denied the motion, reasoning that the motion was controlled by Alabama law and that Alabama looks unfavorably upon contractual forum-selection clauses. The court of appeals reversed.

The Supreme Court, in an opinion by Justice Marshall, held that federal, not state, law controlled:

> A District Court's decision whether to apply a federal statute such as § 1404(a) in a diversity action * * * involves a considerably less intricate analysis than that which governs the "relatively unguided *Erie* choice." Hanna v. Plumer. Our cases indicate that when the federal law sought to be applied is a congressional statute, the first and chief question for the District Court's determination is whether the statute is "sufficiently broad to control the issue before the Court." This question involves a straightforward exercise in statutory interpretation to determine if the statute covers the point in dispute.

> If the District Court determines that a federal statute covers the point in dispute, it proceeds to inquire whether the statute represents a valid exercise of Congress' authority under the Constitution. If Congress intended to reach the issue before the Court, and if it enacted its intention into law in a manner that abides with the Constitution, that is the end of the matter * * *. Thus, a District Court sitting in diversity must apply a federal statute that controls the issue before the court and that represents a valid exercise of Congress' constitutional power.

On the basis of this analysis, the Court held that § 1404(a) controlled.

Would Professor Ely agree with the Court's analysis? For an examination of the problems raised by Stewart Organization, Inc. v. Ricoh Corp., see Freer, Erie's Mid–Life Crisis, 63 Tulane L.Rev. 1087 (1989). Professor Freer argues that in *Stewart*, the Court was "interpreting federal legislation too broadly, employing it in [a] situation[ ] in which Congress did not clearly intend it to apply." Id. at 1090. Such an overextension, he asserts, "raises obvious separation of powers concerns," and illustrates how the federal courts are "stacking the deck against the application of state law." Id. On the general subject, see also Heiser, Forum Selection Clauses in State Courts: Limitations on Enforcement After *Stewart* and *Carnival Cruise*, 45 Fla. L. Rev. 361 (1993); Maltz, Choice of Forum and Choice of Law in the Federal Courts: A Reconsideration of *Erie* Principles, 79 Ky. L.J. 231, 245–52 (1991).

In Jinks v. Richland County, 538 U.S. 456, 123 S.Ct. 1667 (2003), the Court addressed a challenge to 28 U.S.C. § 1367(d)'s tolling provision for cases in which the federal court declines to exercise supplemental jurisdiction. Defendant argued that Congress had no constitutional power to toll limitations for state-law claims asserted in state court. The Court disagreed, holding that this legislation could be viewed as "necessary" within the Necessary and Proper Clause:

> As to the "necessity": The federal Courts can assuredly exist and function in the absence of § 1367(d), but we long ago rejected the view that the Necessary a Proper Clause demands that an Act of Congress be "absolutely necessary" to the exercise of an enumerated power. Rather, it suffices that § 1367(d) is "conducive to the due administration of justice" in federal court, and is "plainly adapted" to that end. Section 1367(d) is conducive to the administration of justice because it provides an alternative to the unsatisfactory options that federal judges faced when they decided whether to retain jurisdiction over supplemental state-law claims that might be time barred in state court. [The court summarized the alternatives that existed before adoption of the statute.] By providing a straightforward tolling rule in place of this regime, § 1367(d) unquestionably promotes fair and efficient operation of the federal courts and is therefore conducive the administration of justice.

> And it is conducive to the administration of justice for another reason: It eliminates a serious impediment to access to the federal courts on the part of plaintiffs pursuing federal and state-law claims that "derive from a common nucleus of operative fact." * * *

> "We are also persuaded * * * that § 1367(d) is plainly adapted" to the power of Congress to establish the lower federal courts and provide for the fair and efficient exercise of their Article III powers. There is no suggestion by either of the parties that Congress enacted § 1367(d) as a "pretext" for "the accomplishment of objects not entrusted to the [federal] government," nor is the connection between § 1367(d) and Congress's authority over the federal courts so attenuated as to undermine the enumeration of powers set forth in Article I § 8.

BURLINGTON NORTHERN RAILROAD CO. v. WOODS, 480 U.S. 1, 107 S.Ct. 967, 94 L.Ed.2d 1 (1987):

JUSTICE MARSHALL delivered the opinion of the Court.

[A tort action for personal injuries was removed to federal district court in Alabama on the basis of diversity of citizenship. Based on a jury verdict, the court entered judgment of over $300,000 in favor of plaintiffs, and defendant posted bond to stay the judgment pending appeal. The Court of Appeals for the Eleventh Circuit affirmed and granted plaintiff's request to impose, under Alabama's mandatory affirmance penalty statute, a penalty of 10% of the amount of the judgment. The purpose of the Alabama rule was to penalize frivolous appeals and appeals interposed for delay. The Supreme Court held the Alabama statute to be inapplicable because it was in conflict with Rule 38 of the Federal Rules of Appellate Procedure, which provided: "If the court of appeals shall determine that an appeal is frivolous, it may award just damages and single or double costs to the appellee."]

The Rule must * * * be applied if it represents a valid exercise of Congress' rule-making authority, which originates in the Constitution and has been bestowed on this Court by the Rules Enabling Act, 28 U.S.C.A. § 2072.

The constitutional constraints on the exercise of this rulemaking authority define a test of reasonableness. Rules regulating matters indisputably procedural are *a priori* constitutional. Rules regulating matters "which, though falling within the uncertain area between substance and procedure, are rationally capable of classification as either," also satisfy this constitutional standard [citing *Hanna*]. The Rules Enabling Act, however, contains an additional requirement. The Federal Rule must not "abridge, enlarge or modify any substantive right. . . ." The cardinal purpose of Congress in authorizing the development of a uniform and consistent system of rules governing federal practice and procedure suggests that Rules which incidentally affect litigants' substantive rights do not violate this provision if reasonably necessary to maintain the integrity of that system of rules. Moreover, the study and approval given each proposed Rule by the Advisory Committee, the Judicial Conference, and this Court, and the statutory requirement that the Rule be reported to Congress for a period of review before taking effect give the Rules presumptive validity under both the constitutional and statutory constraints.

* * *

[Rule 38's] discretionary mode of operation unmistakably conflicts with the mandatory provision of Alabama's affirmance penalty statute. Moreover, the purposes underlying the Rule are sufficiently co-extensive with the asserted purposes of the Alabama statute to indicate that the Rule occupies the statute's field of operation so as to preclude its application in federal diversity actions.

Petitioner nevertheless argues that, because Alabama has a similar Appellate Rule which may be applied in state court alongside the affirmance penalty statute, see Ala.Rule App.Pro. 38, a federal court sitting in diversity could impose the mandatory penalty and likewise remain free to exercise its discretionary authority under Federal Rule 38. This argument, however, ignores the significant possibility that a Court of Appeals may, in any given case, find a limited justification for imposing penalties in an amount *less than* 10% of the lower court's judgment. Federal Rule 38 adopts a case-by-case approach to identifying and deterring frivolous appeals; the Alabama statute precludes any exercise of discretion within its scope of operation. * * *

Federal Rule 38 regulates matters which can reasonably be classified as procedural, thereby satisfying the constitutional standard for validity. Its displacement of the Alabama statute also satisfies the statutory constraints of the Rules Enabling Act. The choice made by the drafters of the Federal Rules in favor of a discretionary procedure affects only the process of enforcing litigants' rights and not the rights themselves.

Notes and Questions

1. In 1988, Congress amended the Rules Enabling Act. As amended, 28 U.S.C.A. § 2072 provides as follows:

> (a) The Supreme Court shall have the power to prescribe general rules of practice and procedure and rules of evidence for cases in the United States district courts (including proceedings before magistrates thereof) and courts of appeals.

> (b) Such rules shall not abridge, enlarge or modify any substantive right. All laws in conflict with such rules shall be of no further force or effect after such rules have taken effect.

In other new provisions, Congress spelled out procedures for the amendment of the rules and their submission to Congress before they become effective. See 28 U.S.C.A. §§ 2073; 2074. It is unlikely that these changes will have a significant effect on the issues decided in *Hanna* and *Burlington Northern*. But see note 3 infra.

Note that § 2072(b) contains what is known as the Supersession Clause, which nullifies laws in conflict with rules adopted pursuant to the Rules Enabling Act. In Henderson v. United States, 517 U.S. 654, 116 S.Ct. 1638, 134 L.Ed.2d 880 (1996), the Court applied the Supersession Clause to override the requirement of the Suits in Admiralty Act, 46 U.S.C.A. § 742, that suits be served on the United States "forthwith." The Court's reasoning was that Fed. R. Civ. P. 4(m) guarantees plaintiffs 120 days to serve the complaint, while the "forthwith" requirement of the statute, although not precise in number of days, calls for service good deal sooner. Accordingly, the rule and the statute conflict irreconcilably. The government took the position that the service requirement of the statute was jurisdictional because it dealt with waiver of sovereign immunity, but the Court did not accept this argument, viewing service as separate from the court's jurisdiction. Justice Thomas, joined by Chief Justice Rehnquist and Justice O'Connor, dissented on the ground that prompt service is a condition for waiver of sovereign immunity.

2. Contrast the approach of both *Hanna* and *Burlington Northern* to the Rules Enabling Act with the interpretation adopted by the Supreme Court in Sibbach v. Wilson & Co., 312 U.S. 1, 61 S.Ct. 422, 85 L.Ed. 479 (1941). In a personal injury suit in federal court defendant moved, pursuant to Rule 35(a) of the Federal Rules of Civil Procedure, for an order requiring plaintiff to submit to a physical examination by court-appointed physicians.

Plaintiff refused, and was judged to be in contempt pursuant to Rule 37. The issue was whether, in a diversity case, Rule 35 or possibly contrary state law controlled on the availability of a physical examination.

Plaintiff argued that the applicable Rules violated the limits imposed by the Rules Enabling Act, since they violated a state substantive right not to be forced to submit to a physical examination. The Supreme Court rejected the argument. The Court noted that the plaintiff "admits, and, we think, correctly, that Rules 35 and 37 are rules of procedure." This admission proved fatal to plaintiff's argument, for according to the Court "[t]he test [of the Enabling Act] must be whether a rule really regulates procedure,—the judicial process for enforcing rights and duties recognized by substantive law and for justly administering remedy and redress for disregard or infraction of them." This much, the Court said, plaintiff had admitted.

3. Professor Ely has suggested the following construction of the Enabling Act (Ely, supra, 87 Harv.L.Rev. at 718–19; 724–27):

> In thus delegating authority to the Court, the Act begins with a checklist approach—anything that relates to process, writs, pleadings, motions, or to practice and procedure generally, is authorized; anything else is not. Thus far, no limitation is imposed that was not imposed by the Constitution. The second sentence, however, provides that "Such rules shall not abridge, enlarge or modify any substantive right...." The Act therefore contains, as the Court used to say the Constitution contained, limitations of both the checklist and enclave variety. Not only must a Rule be procedural; it must in addition abridge, enlarge or modify no substantive right.

* * *

> We were all brought up on sophisticated talk about the fluidity of the line between substance and procedure. But the realization that the terms carry no monolithic meaning at once appropriate to all the contexts in which courts have seen fit to employ them need not imply that they can have no meaning at all. And they are the terms the Enabling Act uses. We have, I think, some moderately clear notion of what a procedural rule is—one designed to make the process of litigation a fair and efficient mechanism for the resolution of disputes. Thus, one way of doing things may be chosen over another because it is thought to be more likely to get at the truth, or better calculated to give the parties a fair opportunity to present their sides of the story, or because, and this may point quite the other way, it is a means of promoting the efficiency of the process. Or the protection of the process may proceed at wholesale, as by keeping the size of the docket at a level consistent with giving those cases that are heard the attention they deserve. The most helpful way, it seems to me, of defining a substantive rule—or more particularly a substantive right, which is what the Act refers to—is as a right granted for one or more nonprocedural reasons, for some purpose or purposes not having to do with the fairness or efficiency of the litigation process.

* * *

Of course it is not at all unlikely that with respect to a given rule the legislature or other rulemaker will have had two (or more) goals in mind—one relating to the management of litigation and one relating to some other concern. Under the definitions suggested above, such a rule would be both procedural and substantive. This conclusion strikes me as not at all troublesome, however, and indeed fits precisely what I am suggesting is the proper interpretation of the Enabling Act. Thus, statutes of limitations are passed not simply for the substantive purpose of relieving people's minds after the passage of the designated period, but also for procedural purposes to keep down the size of the docket and to ensure that cases will not be tried on evidence so stale as to cast doubt on its trustworthiness. They are therefore procedural, which means * * * that a Federal Rule prescribing such a limitation would satisfy the Enabling Act's first sentence. It should not get by the second sentence, however, for the substantive rights established by state statutes of limitations would be abridged by applying such a Federal Rule.

How does Professor Ely's suggested interpretation of the Rules Enabling Act compare to the interpretation employed in *Hanna?* In *Sibbach?* How persuasive is Ely's suggested interpretation? Does it make sense to assume that, by insertion of the second sentence precluding a Federal Rule from abridging a "substantive" right, Congress intended to protect *state-created* substantive rights, in light of the fact that the Enabling Act was adopted in 1934, four years prior to *Erie?* See generally Burbank, The Rules Enabling Act of 1934, 130 U.Pa.L.Rev. 1015 (1982). If Professor Ely's reading of "substantive right" is anachronistic, does the recent re-enactment of the Enabling Act (see note 1 supra) have a bearing on its current force?

Assuming that Congress sought to insulate substantive interests it had created against dilution through procedural rules, could the scope of rulemaking authority shift as Congress becomes more active in adopting legislation dealing with procedural issues? Recent legislation such as the Private Securities Litigation Reform Act of 1995 includes provisions regulating matters previously covered by the Federal Rules of Civil Procedure. See Requirements of the Private Securities Litigation Reform Act, supra p. 170. For an argument that "the increasing reach of Congress' procedural legislation * * * expand[s] the scope of matters to be considered 'substantive' within the meaning of the REA," see Kelleher, Taking "Substantive Rights" (In the Rules Enabling Act) More Seriously, 74 Notre Dame L. Rev. 47 (1998).

4. Professor Perdue has suggested that "[t]he Rules Enabling Act may constrain courts, even where they are not directly interpreting a Federal Rule of Civil Procedure but are instead creating a federal common law rule of 'practice and procedure.'" Thus, she concludes, "[t]he constraints of the Rules Enabling Act should apply regardless of whether courts are interpreting a promulgated Federal Rule of Civil Procedure or creating a common law rule of procedure." Perdue, The Sources and Scope of Federal Procedural Common Law: Some Reflections on Erie and Gasperini, 46 U. Kan. L. Rev. 751, 760 (1998). She acknowledges that "[s]ome might recoil at this argument that jumbles Rules Enabling Act cases with Rules of Decision Act cases," but argues that if the source of authority to create a common law procedural rule "is the general power to create rules for the court's opera-

tion, then such a common law rule should be constrained by the Rules Enabling Act." How persuasive is this analysis?

5. After *Burlington Northern*, to what extent are the Federal Rules of Civil Procedure likely to be superseded in diversity cases by contrary state law? Consider Douglas v. NCNB Texas National Bank, 979 F.2d 1128 (5th Cir.1992). A state court suit, brought by a borrower to recover for prime rate fraud, was removed to federal court by the defendant lender. The lender filed an answer but no counterclaims. The action was later dismissed. The lender's assignee subsequently sued in federal court to collect on the notes, and the borrower defended on the grounds that these claims had been compulsory counterclaims under Rule 13(a) in the borrower's prior suit. The court rejected the borrower's argument, finding Rule 13(a) inapplicable because it conflicted with a lender's "substantive right" under Texas law "to elect judicial or nonjudicial foreclosure in the event of a default." The court noted that "the state's compulsory counterclaim rule * * * does not require the secured party to counterclaim to collect on the debt if the creditor has a contractual right to pursue a nonjudicial foreclosure." 979 F.2d at 1129. Was the court correct in characterizing the state right as "substantive"? If so, should it have concluded that, under *Burlington Northern*, the Federal Rule's impact on the state right was merely "incidental"?

In Carota v. Johns Manville Corp., 893 F.2d 448 (1st Cir.1990), the court held that a Massachusetts law authorizing admission into evidence of out-of-court settlements is substantive. Pursuant to the limits imposed in the Enabling Act, the First Circuit held that the Massachusetts law supersedes the contrary directive in Federal Rule of Evidence 408, which provides in relevant part:

> Evidence of (1) furnishing or offering or promising to furnish or (2) accepting or offering or promising to accept, a valuable consideration in compromising or attempting to compromise a claim which was disputed as to either validity or amount, is not admissible to prove liability for or invalidity of the claim or its amount.

In holding that it was not error for the district court in this diversity case to have admitted the evidence of third party out-of-court settlements, the court reasoned:

> Generally, rules of evidence are procedural, since they describe the admissibility, relevancy, weight and sufficiency of information utilized at trial to define substantive rights. The law of damages, however, is substantive since it prescribes what, if any, money a plaintiff will receive as compensation for injury. * * *
>
> Certain matters do not fall neatly into the substantive/procedural dichotomy, but rather fall within a twilight zone between both classifications. The present case presents such a matter. Out of court settlement evidence is "rationally capable of classification as either" substantive or procedural. *Hanna*. * * *
>
> But when a state permits the admission of out of court settlement evidence with the intent that such admission affect the damage award, then we must deem the issue substantive. If a state has a substantive policy to have a jury hear out of court settlement evidence when

determining damage awards, we will not contravene that state law in a diversity action.

893 F.2d at 450–51. Compare the treatment of Fed.R.Evid. 407, supra p. 962 n. 9. The court made no mention of *Burlington Northern*. Are the two decisions consistent?

6. Was the Court in *Burlington Northern* correct in finding a conflict between the Alabama statute and Rule 38? See generally, Whitten, *Erie* and the Federal Rules: A Review and Reappraisal After *Burlington Northern Railroad v. Woods,* 21 Creighton L.Rev. 1 (1987). Professor Whitten suggests that "the one constant in the Court's decisions dealing with Federal Rules-state law conflicts from *Sibbach* through *Burlington Northern* has been its refusal to provide significant content to the Act's substantive rights restriction." Id. Is *Burlington Northern* an appropriate case for application of the Enabling Act's "substantive rights" restriction?

7. In Business Guides, Inc. v. Chromatic Communications Enterprises, Inc., 498 U.S. 533, 111 S.Ct. 922, 112 L.Ed.2d 1140 (1991), the Supreme Court, in an opinion by Justice O'Connor, upheld imposition of sanctions against a party under Rule 11 of the Federal Rules of Civil Procedure. Rule 11 then provided that signature on a paper filed in court is a certification, made after reasonable inquiry, that the paper is well grounded in fact and warranted by existing law or a good faith argument for its extension or modification. See the discussion of Rule 11 in Chapter III, supra pp. 143–56. In *Business Guides,* the Court held that Rule 11 applies to represented parties who themselves sign the certification, and that as so construed the Rule does not violate the Rules Enabling Act. The Court first noted "that any Rules Enabling Act challenge to Rule 11 has a large hurdle to get over," because "the Rules do not go into effect until Congress has had at least seven months to look them over." 498 U.S. at 550, 111 S.Ct. at 933. Moreover, the Court held that the Enabling Act challenge to Rule 11 failed under the *Burlington Northern* standard: "There is little doubt that Rule 11 is reasonably necessary to maintain the integrity of the system of federal practice and procedure, and that any effect on substantive rights is incidental." Id. at 552, 111 S.Ct. at 934. In rejecting the argument that Rule 11 represents "impermissible fee-shifting" and as a result affects substantive rights, the Court reasoned that "Rule 11 sanctions are not tied to the outcome of litigation; the relevant inquiry is whether a specific filing was, if not successful, at least well founded. Nor do sanctions shift the entire cost of litigation; they shift only the cost of a discrete event." Id. The Court ultimately concluded that "[i]mposing monetary sanctions on parties that violate the Rule may confer a benefit on other litigants, but the Rules Enabling Act is not violated by such incidental effects on substantive rights."

In dissent, Justice Kennedy argued that, as construed by the majority, Rule 11 constitutes a "potential incursion into matters reserved to the States * * *." The majority's application of Rule 11 to a represented party, as opposed to its attorney, he argued, "creates a new tort of 'negligent prosecution' or 'accidental abuse of process,' applicable to any represented party ignorant enough to sign a pleading or other Rule 11 paper." He concluded that "[w]hether or not Rule 11 as construed by the majority exceeds our rulemaking authority, these concerns weigh in favor of a reasonable, alternative interpretation * * *."

In Willy v. Coastal Corp., 503 U.S. 131, 112 S.Ct. 1076, 117 L.Ed.2d 280 (1992), the Court held that Rule 11 sanctions may be imposed on a plaintiff for behavior while his case is pending in federal court even though it is later determined that the case was never properly removed because there was no federal subject matter jurisdiction. Although plaintiff argued that federal courts could not sanction litigants in cases over which they lacked subject matter jurisdiction, the Court held that Rule 11 was intended to apply in such situations and could be constitutionally applied: "The interest in having rules of procedure obeyed * * * does not disappear upon a subsequent determination that the court was without subject-matter jurisdiction. Courts do make mistakes. * * * [W]here * * * an immediate appeal is not authorized, there is no constitutional infirmity under Article III in requiring those practicing before the courts to conduct themselves in compliance with the applicable procedural rules in the interim * * *."

8. One commentator has argued that "the Federal Rules of Civil Procedure do not, by and large, contain preclusion law and * * * they cannot validly prescribe such law." Burbank, *Semtek*, Forum Shopping, and Federal Common Law, 77 Notre Dame L. Rev. 1027 (2002). Is this accurate? Consider Rule 13(a), concerning compulsory counterclaims. Does that rule have a preclusive effect beyond the court in which the rule has been invoked? Does Rule 13(a) violate the Rules Enabling Act's directive that the Rules not abridge, enlarge or modify a substantive right? What would the test adopted in *Burlington Northern* say about Rule 13(a)? Reconsider this question in connection with Semtek, Inc. v. Lockheed Martin Corp., infra p. 1133.

WALKER v. ARMCO STEEL CORP., 446 U.S. 740, 100 S.Ct. 1978, 64 L.Ed.2d 659 (1980):

JUSTICE MARSHALL delivered the opinion of the Court.

[Plaintiff, a carpenter, was injured on August 22, 1975, when an allegedly defective nail manufactured by defendant shattered. The complaint in this diversity case was filed in federal district court in Oklahoma on August 19, 1977, but service of process was not made on respondent's authorized service agent until December 1, 1977. Defendant moved to dismiss on the ground that the action was barred by the applicable Oklahoma statute of limitations. Although the complaint had been filed within the 2-year Oklahoma statute of limitations, state law did not deem the action "commenced" for purposes of the statute of limitations until service of the summons on the defendant. In response to defendant's motion to dismiss, plaintiff admitted that his case would be foreclosed in state court, but argued that Rule 3 of the Federal Rules of Civil Procedure governs the manner in which an action is commenced for all purposes, including the tolling of the state statute of limitations. The Supreme Court unanimously held that state law controlled, finding the case indistinguishable from *Ragan,* supra p. 937, and therefore upheld dismissal of plaintiff's case.]

There is no indication that [Rule 3] was intended to toll a state statute of limitations, much less that it purported to displace state tolling rules for purposes of state statutes of limitations. In our view, in diversity actions Rule 3 governs the date from which various timing requirements of the Federal Rules begin to run, but does not affect state statutes of limitations.

In contrast to Rule 3, the Oklahoma statute is a statement of a substantive decision by that State that actual service on, and accordingly actual notice by, the defendant is an integral part of the several policies served by the statute of limitations. * * * The statute of limitations establishes a deadline after which the defendant may legitimately have peace of mind; it also recognizes that after a certain period of time it is unfair to require the defendant to attempt to piece together his defense to an old claim. A requirement of actual service promotes both of those functions of the statute. * * * It is these policy aspects which make the service requirement an "integral" part of the statute of limitations both in this case and in *Ragan.* * * * Rule 3 does not replace such policy determinations found in state law. Rule 3 and [state law] can exist side by side, therefore, each controlling its own intended sphere of coverage without conflict.

Since there is no direct conflict between the Federal Rule and the state law, the *Hanna* analysis does not apply. Instead, the policies behind *Erie* and *Ragan* control the issue whether, in the absence of a federal rule directly on point, state service requirements which are an integral part of the statute of limitations should control in an action based on state law which is filed in federal court under diversity jurisdiction. * * * It is sufficient to note that although in this case failure to apply the state service law might not create any problem of forum shopping, the result would be an "inequitable administration of the law." Hanna v. Plumer. There is simply no reason why, in the absence of a controlling federal rule, an action based on state law which concededly would be barred in the state courts by the state statute of limitations should proceed through litigation to judgment in federal court solely because of the fortuity that there is diversity of citizenship between the litigants.

Notes and Questions

1. The Court in *Walker* rejected the argument that *Hanna* had over-ruled *Ragan.* Do you agree?

2. Note the Court's emphasis on how "integral" the state's commencement rule is to the statute of limitations. Does the Court in *Walker* return to *Byrd,* in lieu of *Hanna?* Reconsider the effect on *Byrd* of footnote 9 in *Hanna.* Would the *Hanna* Court have given any weight to the importance of the state policy in the manner that the *Walker* Court did?

3. How different is the Court's analysis from that in *York?* Note that the Court in *Walker* found no likelihood of forum shopping as the result of

the use of a separate federal standard, yet nevertheless held that state law must be applied. How do you think the *Hanna* Court would have decided *Walker* under the Rules of Decision Act?

4. The Court in *Walker* found Rule 3 inapplicable to the statute of limitations issue. If the Rule were amended to provide explicitly that an action commenced for purposes of the tolling of the statute of limitations when it was filed, rather than when service was made, how do you think the Court would have held? How would the test of *Sibbach* apply?

5. In Chambers v. NASCO, Inc., 501 U.S. 32, 111 S.Ct. 2123, 115 L.Ed.2d 27 (1991), the Court held that a district judge in a diversity case possessed "inherent power" to impose sanctions—unauthorized by rule or statute—on a party for acting in bad faith, despite a contrary rule in state court in which the district court sat. Plaintiff in that case sued for specific performance of a contract to buy defendant's television station. Defendant responded with a variety of dishonest devices to defeat the suit, including lying to the judge. After entering judgment for plaintiff, the district court imposed plaintiff's entire attorney's fees and litigation expenses—nearly $1 million—on defendant as a sanction even though there was no statute or federal rule to support such action.

The Supreme Court affirmed. Justice White, speaking for the majority, reasoned:

> Only when there is a conflict between state and federal substantive law are the concerns of Erie R. Co. v. Tompkins at issue. As we explained in Hanna v. Plumer, the "outcome determinative" test of *Erie* and Guaranty Trust Co. v. York "cannot be read without reference to the twin aims of the *Erie* rule: discouragement of forum-shopping and avoidance of inequitable administration of the laws." * * * [N]either of these twin aims is implicated by the assessment of attorney's fees as a sanction for bad-faith conduct before the court which involved disobedience of the court's orders and the attempt to defraud the court itself. * * * [T]he imposition of sanctions under the bad-faith exception depends not on which party wins the lawsuit, but on how the parties conduct themselves during the litigation. Consequently, there is no risk that the exception will lead to forum-shopping. Nor is it inequitable to apply the exception to citizens and noncitizens alike, when the party, by controlling his or her conduct in litigation, has the power to determine whether sanctions will be assessed.

Justice Kennedy, joined by the Chief Justice and Justice Souter, dissented. He argued that "the Court upholds the wholesale shift of respondent's attorney's fees to petitioner, even though the District Court opinion reveals that petitioner was sanctioned at least in part for his so-called breach of contract. The extension of inherent authority to sanction a party's prelitigation conduct * * * turns the *Erie* doctrine upside down by punishing petitioner's primary conduct contrary to [state] law." Justice Kennedy viewed the district court's opinion as penalizing pre-litigation conduct, even though the majority rejected such an interpretation. "The inherent power exercised here," Justice Kennedy concluded, "violates the fundamental tenet of federalism announced in *Erie* by regulating primary behavior that the

Constitution leaves to the exclusive province of States." Justice Scalia dissented on an unrelated issue.

Is *Chambers* consistent with the approach to the Rules of Decision Act employed in *Walker*? Is Justice White correct in asserting that *Erie* concerns are implicated "[o]nly when there is a conflict between state and federal substantive law"? Do you agree with him that when the outcome of a case is not likely to be affected by the use of different rules in state and federal court, forum-shopping is not likely to be encouraged? For example, would plaintiff's choice of forum likely be influenced by different sanction rules for bad faith conduct in a case such as *Chambers,* where the defendant was ultimately found to have acted in blatantly bad faith? Should it matter?

What approach to *Erie* is Justice Kennedy advocating?

GASPERINI v. CENTER FOR HUMANITIES, INC.

Supreme Court of the United States, 1996.
518 U.S. 415, 116 S.Ct. 2211, 135 L.Ed.2d 659.

JUSTICE GINSBURG delivered the opinion of the Court.

Under the law of New York, appellate courts are empowered to review the size of jury verdicts and to order new trials when the jury's award "deviates materially from what would be reasonable compensation." N.Y. Civ. Prac. Law and Rules (CPLR) § 5501(c) (McKinney 1995). Under the Seventh Amendment, which governs proceedings in federal court, but not in state court, "the right of trial by jury shall be preserved, and no fact tried by a jury, shall be otherwise re-examined in any Court of the United States, than according to the rules of the common law." U.S. Const., Amdt. 7. The compatibility of these provisions, in an action based on New York law but tried in federal court by reason of the parties' diverse citizenship, is the issue we confront in this case. We hold that New York's law controlling compensation awards for excessiveness or inadequacy can be given effect, without detriment to the Seventh Amendment, if the review standard set out in CPLR § 5501(c) is applied by the federal trial court judge, with appellate control of the trial court's ruling limited to review for "abuse of discretion."

I

Petitioner William Gasperini, a journalist for CBS News and the Christian Science Monitor, began reporting on events in Central America in 1984. He earned his living primarily in radio and print media and only occasionally sold his photographic work. During the course of his seven-year stint in Central America, Gasperini took over 5,000 slide transparencies, depicting active war zones, political leaders, and scenes from daily life. In 1990, Gasperini agreed to supply his original color transparencies to The Center for Humanities, Inc. (Center) for use in an educational videotape, *Conflict in Central America.* Gasperini selected 300 of his slides for the Center; its videotape included 110 of them. The Center agreed to return the original transparencies, but upon the completion of the project, it could not find them.

Gasperini commenced suit in the United States District Court for the Southern District of New York, invoking the court's diversity jurisdiction pursuant to 28 U.S.C. § 1332. He alleged several state-law claims for relief, including breach of contract, conversion, and negligence. The Center conceded liability for the lost transparencies and the issue of damages was tried before a jury.

At trial, Gasperini's expert witness testified that the "industry standard" within the photographic publishing community valued a lost transparency at $1,500. This industry standard, the expert explained, represented the average license fee a commercial photograph could earn over the full course of the photographer's copyright, i.e., in Gasperini's case, his lifetime plus 50 years. Gasperini estimated that his earnings from photography totaled just over $10,000 for the period from 1984 through 1993. He also testified that he intended to produce a book containing his best photographs from Central America.

After a three-day trial, the jury awarded Gasperini $450,000 in compensatory damages. This sum, the jury foreperson announced, "is [$]1500 each, for 300 slides." Moving for a new trial under Federal Rule of Civil Procedure 59, the Center attacked the verdict on various grounds, including excessiveness. Without comment, the District Court denied the motion.

The Court of Appeals for the Second Circuit vacated the judgment entered on the jury's verdict. 66 F.3d 427 (1995). Mindful that New York law governed the controversy, the Court of Appeals endeavored to apply CPLR § 5501(c), which instructs that, when a jury returns an itemized verdict, as the jury did in this case, the New York Appellate Division "shall determine that an award is excessive or inadequate if it deviates materially from what would be reasonable compensation." * * * Surveying Appellate Division decisions that reviewed damage awards for lost transparencies, the Second Circuit concluded that testimony on industry standard alone was insufficient to justify a verdict; prime among other factors warranting consideration were the uniqueness of the slides' subject matter and the photographer's earning level.

Guided by Appellate Division rulings, the Second Circuit held that the $450,000 verdict "materially deviates from what is reasonable compensation." Some of Gasperini's transparencies, the Second Circuit recognized, were unique, notably those capturing combat situations in which Gasperini was the only photographer present. But others "depicted either generic scenes or events at which other professional photojournalists were present." No more than 50 slides merited a $1,500 award, the court concluded, after "[g]iving Gasperini every benefit of the doubt." Absent evidence showing significant earnings from photographic endeavors or concrete plans to publish a book, the court further determined, any damage award above $100 each for the remaining slides would be excessive. Remittiturs "presen[t] difficult problems for appellate courts," the Second Circuit acknowledged, for court of appeals judges review the evidence from "a cold paper record." Nevertheless, the

Second Circuit set aside the $450,000 verdict and ordered a new trial, unless Gasperini agreed to an award of $100,000.

This case presents an important question regarding the standard a federal court uses to measure the alleged excessiveness of a jury's verdict in an action for damages based on state law. We therefore granted certiorari.

II

Before 1986, state and federal courts in New York generally invoked the same judge-made formulation in responding to excessiveness attacks on jury verdicts: courts would not disturb an award unless the amount was so exorbitant that it "shocked the conscience of the court." As described by the Second Circuit: "The standard for determining excessiveness and the appropriateness of remittitur in New York is somewhat ambiguous. Prior to 1986, New York law employed the same standard as the federal courts, which authorized remittitur only if the jury's verdict was so excessive that it 'shocked the conscience of the court.'"

In both state and federal courts, trial judges made the excessiveness assessment in the first instance, and appellate judges ordinarily deferred to the trial court's judgment.

In 1986, as part of a series of tort reform measures, New York codified a standard for judicial review of the size of jury awards. Placed in CPLR § 5501(c), the prescription reads:

> "In reviewing a money judgment ... in which it is contended that the award is excessive or inadequate and that a new trial should have been granted unless a stipulation is entered to a different award, the appellate division shall determine that an award is excessive or inadequate if it deviates materially from what would be reasonable compensation."

As stated in Legislative Findings and Declarations accompanying New York's adoption of the "deviates materially" formulation, the lawmakers found the "shock the conscience" test an insufficient check on damage awards; the legislature therefore installed a standard "invit[ing] more careful appellate scrutiny." At the same time, the legislature instructed the Appellate Division, in amended § 5522, to state the reasons for the court's rulings on the size of verdicts, and the factors the court considered in complying with § 5501(c). In his signing statement, then-Governor Mario Cuomo emphasized that the CPLR amendments were meant to ratchet up the review standard: "This will assure greater scrutiny of the amount of verdicts and promote greater stability in the tort system and greater fairness for similarly situated defendants throughout the State."

New York state-court opinions confirm that § 5501(c)'s "deviates materially" standard calls for closer surveillance than "shock the conscience" oversight.

Although phrased as a direction to New York's intermediate appellate courts, § 5501(c)'s "deviates materially" standard, as construed by New York's courts, instructs state trial judges as well. Application of § 5501(c) at the trial level is key to this case.

To determine whether an award "deviates materially from what would be reasonable compensation," New York state courts look to awards approved in similar cases. * * * The "deviates materially" standard, however, in design and operation, influences outcomes by tightening the range of tolerable awards.

III

In cases like Gasperini's, in which New York law governs the claims for relief, does New York law also supply the test for federal court review of the size of the verdict? The Center answers yes. The "deviates materially" standard, it argues, is a substantive standard that must be applied by federal appellate courts in diversity cases. The Second Circuit agreed. Gasperini, emphasizing that § 5501(c) trains on the New York Appellate Division, characterizes the provision as procedural, an allocation of decisionmaking authority regarding damages, not a hard cap on the amount recoverable. Correctly comprehended, Gasperini urges, § 5501(c)'s direction to the Appellate Division cannot be given effect by federal appellate courts without violating the Seventh Amendment's reexamination clause.

As the parties' arguments suggest, CPLR § 5501(c), appraised under Erie R. Co. v. Tompkins, 304 U.S. 64, 58 S.Ct. 817, 82 L.Ed. 1188 (1938), and decisions in *Erie*'s path, is both "substantive" and "procedural": "substantive" in that § 5501(c)'s "deviates materially" standard controls how much a plaintiff can be awarded; "procedural" in that § 5501(c) assigns decisionmaking authority to New York's Appellate Division. Parallel application of § 5501(c) at the federal appellate level would be out of sync with the federal system's division of trial and appellate court functions, an allocation weighted by the Seventh Amendment. The dispositive question, therefore, is whether federal courts can give effect to the substantive thrust of § 5501(c) without untoward alteration of the federal scheme for the trial and decision of civil cases.

A

Federal diversity jurisdiction provides an alternative forum for the adjudication of state-created rights, but it does not carry with it generation of rules of substantive law. As *Erie* read the Rules of Decision Act: "Except in matters governed by the Federal Constitution or by Acts of Congress, the law to be applied in any case is the law of the State." 304 U.S., at 78, 58 S.Ct., at 822. Under the *Erie* doctrine, federal courts sitting in diversity apply state substantive law and federal procedural law.

Classification of a law as "substantive" or "procedural" for Erie purposes is sometimes a challenging endeavor.[7] Guaranty Trust Co. v. York, 326 U.S. 99, 65 S.Ct. 1464, 89 L.Ed. 2079 (1945), an early interpretation of *Erie*, propounded an "outcome-determination" test. * * * A later pathmarking case, qualifying *Guaranty Trust*, explained that the "outcome-determination" test must not be applied mechanically to sweep in all manner of variations; instead, its application must be guided by "the twin aims of the *Erie* rule: discouragement of forum-shopping and avoidance of inequitable administration of the laws." Hanna v. Plumer, 380 U.S. 460, 468, 85 S.Ct. 1136, 1142, 14 L.Ed.2d 8 (1965).

Informed by these decisions, we address the question whether New York's "deviates materially" standard, codified in CPLR § 5501(c), is outcome-affective in this sense: Would "application of the [standard] ... have so important an effect upon the fortunes of one or both of the litigants that failure to [apply] it would [unfairly discriminate against citizens of the forum state, or] be likely to cause a plaintiff to choose the federal court"? Id., at 468, n. 9, 85 S.Ct., at 1142, n. 9.

We start from a point the parties do not debate. Gasperini acknowledges that a statutory cap on damages would supply substantive law for *Erie* purposes. Although CPLR § 5501(c) is less readily classified, it was designed to provide an analogous control.

New York's Legislature codified in § 5501(c) a new standard, one that requires closer court review than the common law "shock the conscience" test. More rigorous comparative evaluations attend application of § 5501(c)'s "deviates materially" standard. To foster predictability, the legislature required the reviewing court, when overturning a verdict under § 5501(c), to state its reasons, including the factors it considered relevant. see CPLR § 5522(b). We think it a fair conclusion that CPLR § 5501(c) differs from a statutory cap principally "in that the maximum amount recoverable is not set by statute, but rather is determined by case law." In sum, § 5501(c) contains a procedural instruction, but the State's objective is manifestly substantive. Cf. S.A. Healy Co. v. Milwaukee Metropolitan Sewerage Dist., 60 F.3d 305, 310 (C.A.7 1995).

---

7. Concerning matters covered by the Federal Rules of Civil Procedure, the characterization question is usually unproblematic: It is settled that if the Rule in point is consonant with the Rules Enabling Act, 28 U.S.C. § 2072, and the Constitution, the Federal Rule applies regardless of contrary state law. Federal courts have interpreted the Federal Rules, however, with sensitivity to important state interests and regulatory policies. See, e.g., Walker v. Armco Steel Corp., 446 U.S. 740, 750–752, 100 S.Ct. 1978, 1985–1986, 64 L.Ed.2d 659 (1980) (reaffirming decision in Ragan v. Merchants Transfer & Warehouse Co., 337 U.S. 530, 69 S.Ct. 1233, 93 L.Ed. 1520 (1949), that state law rather than Rule 3 determines when a diversity action commences for the purposes of tolling the state statute of limitations; Rule 3 makes no reference to the tolling of state limitations, the Court observed, and accordingly found no direct conflict ; S.A. Healy Co. v. Milwaukee Metropolitan Sewerage Dist., 60 F.3d 305, 310–312 (C.A.7 1995) (state provision for offers of settlement by plaintiffs is compatible with Federal Rule 68, which is limited to offers by defendants).

It thus appears that if federal courts ignore the change in the New York standard and persist in applying the "shock the conscience" test to damage awards on claims governed by New York law, " 'substantial' variations between state and federal [money judgments]" may be expected. See *Hanna*, 380 U.S., at 467–468, 85 S.Ct., at 1142. We therefore agree with the Second Circuit that New York's check on excessive damages implicates what we have called *Erie*'s "twin aims."[12] Just as the *Erie* principle precludes a federal court from giving a state-created claim "longer life ... than [the claim] would have had in the state court," *Ragan*, 337 U.S., at 533–534, 69 S.Ct., at 1235, so *Erie* precludes a recovery in federal court significantly larger than the recovery that would have been tolerated in state court.

B

CPLR § 5501(c), as earlier noted, is phrased as a direction to the New York Appellate Division. Acting essentially as a surrogate for a New York appellate forum, the Court of Appeals reviewed Gasperini's award to determine if it "deviate[d] materially" from damage awards the Appellate Division permitted in similar circumstances. The Court of Appeals performed this task without benefit of an opinion from the District Court, which had denied "without comment" the Center's Rule 59 motion. Concentrating on the authority § 5501(c) gives to the Appellate Division, Gasperini urges that the provision shifts fact-finding responsibility from the jury and the trial judge to the appellate court. Assigning such responsibility to an appellate court, he maintains, is incompatible with the Seventh Amendment's re-examination clause, and therefore, Gasperini concludes, § 5501(c) cannot be given effect in federal court. Although we reach a different conclusion than Gasperini, we agree that the Second Circuit did not attend to "[a]n essential characteristic of [the federal-court] system," *Byrd v. Blue Ridge Rural Elec. Cooperative, Inc.*, 356 U.S. 525, 537, 78 S.Ct. 893, 901, 2 L.Ed.2d 953 (1958), when it used § 5501(c) as "the standard for [federal] appellate review."

That "essential characteristic" was described in *Byrd*, a diversity suit for negligence in which a pivotal issue of fact would have been tried by a judge were the case in state court. The *Byrd* Court held that, despite the state practice, the plaintiff was entitled to a jury trial in federal court. In so ruling, the Court said that the *Guaranty Trust* "outcome-determination" test was an insufficient guide in cases presenting countervailing federal interests [such as what *Byrd* described as "the manner in which, in civil common-law actions, [the federal system] distributes trial functions between judge and jury and, under the influence—if not the command—of the Seventh Amendment, assigns the decisions of disputed questions of fact to the jury."]

---

12. For rights that are state-created, state law governs the amount properly awarded as punitive damages, subject to an ultimate federal constitutional check for ex- orbitancy. An evenhanded approach would require federal court deference to endeavors like New York to control compensatory damages for excessiveness.

The Seventh Amendment, which governs proceedings in federal court, but not in state court, bears not only on the allocation of trial functions between judge and jury, the issue in *Byrd*; it also controls the allocation of authority to review verdicts, the issue of concern here. The Amendment reads:

"In suits at common law, where the value in controversy shall exceed twenty dollars, the right of trial by jury shall be preserved, and no fact tried by a jury, shall be otherwise re-examined in any Court of the United States, than according to the rules of the common law."

Byrd involved the first clause of the Amendment, the "trial by jury" clause. This case involves the second, the "re-examination" clause. In keeping with the historic understanding, the re-examination clause does not inhibit the authority of trial judges to grant new trials "for any of the reasons for which new trials have heretofore been granted in actions at law in the courts of the United States." Fed. Rule Civ. Proc. 59(a). That authority is large. "The trial judge in the federal system," we have reaffirmed, "has . . . discretion to grant a new trial if the verdict appears to [the judge] to be against the weight of the evidence." *Byrd*, 356 U.S., at 540, 78 S.Ct., at 902. This discretion includes overturning verdicts for excessiveness and ordering a new trial without qualification, or conditioned on the verdict winner's refusal to agree to a reduction (remittitur). See Dimick v. Schiedt, 293 U.S. 474, 486–487, 55 S.Ct. 296, 301, 79 L.Ed. 603 (1935) [supra p. 658] (recognizing that remittitur withstands Seventh Amendment attack, but rejecting additur as unconstitutional).

In contrast, appellate review of a federal trial court's denial of a motion to set aside a jury's verdict as excessive is a relatively late, and less secure, development. Such review was once deemed inconsonant with the Seventh Amendment's re-examination clause. * * *

Before today, we have not "expressly [held] that the Seventh Amendment allows appellate review of a district court's denial of a motion to set aside an award as excessive." Browning–Ferris Industries of Vt., Inc. v. Kelco Disposal, Inc., 492 U.S. 257, 279, n. 25, 109 S.Ct. 2909, 2922, n. 25, 106 L.Ed.2d 219 (1989). [The Court held that the Seventh Amendment does not preclude such appellate review.]

* * *

C

In *Byrd*, the Court faced a one-or-the-other choice: trial by judge as in state court, or trial by jury according to the federal practice.[21] In the case before us, a choice of that order is not required, for the principal state and federal interests can be accommodated. The Second Circuit correctly recognized that when New York substantive law governs a

---

21. The two-trial rule posited by Justice Scalia surely would be incompatible with the existence of the federal system [as] an independent system for administering jus-tice, Byrd v. Blue Ridge Rural Elec. Coop., Incorporated, 356 U.S. 525, 537, 78 S.Ct. 893, 901, 2 L.Ed.2d 953 (1958).

claim for relief, New York law and decisions guide the allowable damages. But that court did not take into account the characteristic of the federal-court system that caused us to reaffirm: "The proper role of the trial and appellate courts in the federal system in reviewing the size of jury verdicts is ... a matter of federal law." Donovan v. Penn Shipping Co., 429 U.S. 648, 649, 97 S.Ct. 835, 837, 51 L.Ed.2d 112 (1977).

New York's dominant interest can be respected, without disrupting the federal system, once it is recognized that the federal district court is capable of performing the checking function, i.e., that court can apply the State's "deviates materially" standard in line with New York case law evolving under CPLR § 5501(c).[22] We recall, in this regard, that the "deviates materially" standard serves as the guide to be applied in trial as well as appellate courts in New York.

Within the federal system, practical reasons combine with Seventh Amendment constraints to lodge in the district court, not the court of appeals, primary responsibility for application of § 5501(c)'s "deviates materially" check. Trial judges have the "unique opportunity to consider the evidence in the living courtroom context," while appellate judges see only "the cold paper record."

District court applications of the "deviates materially" standard would be subject to appellate review under the standard the Circuits now employ when inadequacy or excessiveness is asserted on appeal: abuse of discretion. In light of *Erie*'s doctrine, the federal appeals court must be guided by the damage-control standard state law supplies, but as the Second Circuit itself has said: "If we reverse, it must be because of an abuse of discretion.... The very nature of the problem counsels restraint.... We must give the benefit of every doubt to the judgment of the trial judge."

IV

It does not appear that the District Court checked the jury's verdict against the relevant New York decisions demanding more than "industry standard" testimony to support an award of the size the jury returned in this case. * * * Accordingly, we vacate the judgment of the Court of Appeals and instruct that court to remand the case to the District Court so that the trial judge, revisiting his ruling on the new trial motion, may test the jury's verdict against CPLR § 5501(c)'s "deviates materially" standard.

---

22. Justice Scalia finds in Federal Rule of Civil Procedure 59 a federal standard for new trial motions in direct collision with, and leaving no room for the operation of, a state law like CPLR § 5501(c). The relevant prescription, Rule 59(a), has remained unchanged since the adoption of the Federal Rules by this Court in 1937. Rule 59(a) is as encompassing as it is uncontroversial. It is indeed hornbook law that a most usual ground for a Rule 59 motion is that he damages are excessive. See C. Wright, Law of Federal Courts 676–677 (5th ed. 1994). Whether damages are excessive for the claim-in-suit must be governed by some law. And there is no candidate for that governance other than the law that gives rise to the claim for relief there, the law of New York. See 28 U.S.C. § 2072(a) and (b) Supreme Court shall have the power to prescribe general rules of procedure such rules shall not abridge, enlarge or modify any substantive right.

JUSTICE STEVENS, dissenting.

[Justice Stevens explained that he essentially agreed with the Court's *Erie* analysis. Thus, he felt that "[a] state-law ceiling on allowable damages, whether fixed by dollar limit or by a standard that forbids any award that 'deviates materially from what would be reasonable compensation,' is a substantive rule of decision that federal courts must apply in diversity cases governed by New York law." He also concluded that "there is no conceivable conflict between Federal Rule of Civil Procedure 59 and the application of the New York damages limit [since Rule 59's directive] that new trials could be granted 'for any of the reasons for which trials have heretofore been granted in actions at law in courts of the United States' * * *] hardly constitutes a command that federal courts must always substitute federal limits on the size of judgments for those set by the several States." Justice Stevens disagreed, however, on the need to vacate the Second Circuit's decision and remand to the district court for it to apply the New York standard. He felt that the appellate court could do so without violating the Seventh Amendment, and that "there is no reason to suppose that the Court of Appeals has reached a conclusion with which the District Court could permissibly disagree on remand." Accordingly, he would affirm the decision of the Second Circuit.]

JUSTICE SCALIA, with whom the CHIEF JUSTICE and JUSTICE THOMAS join, dissenting.

Today the Court overrules a longstanding and well-reasoned line of precedent that has for years prohibited federal appellate courts from reviewing refusals by district courts to set aside civil jury awards as contrary to the weight of the evidence. [Justice Scalia concludes that such review is not permitted.]

* * *

II

The Court's holding that federal courts of appeals may review district court denials of motions for new trials for error of fact is not the only novel aspect of today's decision. The Court also directs that the case be remanded to the District Court, so that it may "test the jury's verdict against CPLR § 5501(c)'s 'deviates materially' standard." This disposition contradicts the principle that "[t]he proper role of the trial and appellate courts in the federal system in reviewing the size of jury verdicts is . . . a matter of federal law." Donovan v. Penn Shipping Co., 429 U.S. 648, 649, 97 S.Ct. 835, 837, 51 L.Ed.2d 112 (1977) (per curiam).

The Court acknowledges that state procedural rules cannot, as a general matter, be permitted to interfere with the allocation of functions in the federal court system. Indeed, it is at least partly for this reason that the Court rejects direct application of § 5501(c) at the appellate level as inconsistent with an " 'essential characteristic' " of the federal court system—by which the Court presumably means abuse-of-discretion review of denials of motions for new trials. But the scope of the Court's concern is oddly circumscribed. The "essential characteristic" of the federal jury, and, more specifically, the role of the federal trial court in reviewing jury judgments, apparently counts for little. The Court approves the "accommodat[ion]" achieved by having district courts review jury verdicts under the "deviates materially" standard, because it regards that as a means of giving effect to the state's purposes "without disrupting the federal system." But changing the standard by which trial judges review jury verdicts does disrupt the federal system, and is plainly inconsistent with "the strong federal policy against allowing state rules to disrupt the judge-jury relationship in federal court." Byrd v. Blue Ridge Rural Elec. Co-op., Incorporated, 356 U.S. 525, 538, 78 S.Ct. 893, 901, 2 L.Ed.2d 953 (1958). The Court's opinion does not even acknowledge, let alone address, this dislocation.

We discussed precisely the point at issue here in Browning–Ferris Industries of Vt., Inc. v. Kelco Disposal, Inc., 492 U.S. 257, 109 S.Ct. 2909, 106 L.Ed.2d 219 (1989), and gave an answer altogether contrary to the one provided today. *Browning-Ferris* rejected a request to fashion a federal common-law rule limiting the size of punitive-damages awards in federal courts, reaffirming the principle of Erie R. Co. v. Tompkins, 304 U.S. 64, 58 S.Ct. 817, 82 L.Ed. 1188 (1938), that "[i]n a diversity action, or in any other lawsuit where state law provides the basis of decision, the propriety of an award of punitive damages ... and the factors the jury may consider in determining their amount, are questions of state law." But the opinion expressly stated that "[f]ederal law ... will control on those issues involving the proper review of the jury award by a federal district court and court of appeals." "In reviewing an award of punitive damages," it said, "the role of the district court is to determine whether the jury's verdict is within the confines of state law, and to determine, by reference to federal standards developed under Rule 59, whether a new trial or remittitur should be ordered." The same distinction necessarily applies where the judgment under review is for compensatory damages: State substantive law controls what injuries are compensable and in what amount; but federal standards determine whether the award exceeds what is lawful to such degree that it may be set aside by order for new trial or remittitur.

The Court does not disavow those statements in *Browning-Ferris* (indeed, it does not even discuss them), but it presumably overrules them, at least where the state rule that governs "whether a new trial or remittitur should be ordered" is characterized as "substantive" in nature. That, at any rate, is the reason the Court asserts for giving § 5501(c) dispositive effect. The objective of that provision, the Court states, "is manifestly substantive" since it operates to "contro[l] how much a plaintiff can be awarded" by "tightening the range of tolerable awards." Although "less readily classified" as substantive than "a statutory cap on damages," it nonetheless "was designed to provide an analogous control," by making a new trial mandatory when the award "deviat[es] materially" from what is reasonable.

I do not see how this can be so. It seems to me quite wrong to regard this provision as a "substantive" rule for *Erie* purposes. The "analog[y]" to "a statutory cap on damages" fails utterly. There is an absolutely fundamental distinction between a *rule of law* such as that, which would ordinarily be imposed upon the jury in the trial court's instructions, and a *rule of review*, which simply determines how closely the jury verdict will be scrutinized for compliance with the instructions. A tighter standard for reviewing jury determinations can no more plausibly be called a "substantive" disposition than can a tighter appellate standard for reviewing trial-court determinations. The one, like the other, provides additional assurance *that the law has been complied with*; but the other, like the one, *leaves the law unchanged*.

The Court commits the classic *Erie* mistake of regarding whatever changes the outcome as substantive. That is not the only factor to be considered. Outcome-determination "was never intended to serve as a talisman," Hanna v. Plumer, 380 U.S. 460, 466–467, 85 S.Ct. 1136, 1141, 14 L.Ed.2d 8 (1965), and does not have the power to convert the most classic elements of the *process* of assuring that the law is observed into the substantive law itself. The right to have a jury make the findings of fact, for example, is generally thought to favor plaintiffs, and that advantage is often thought significant enough to be the basis for forum selection. But no one would argue that *Erie* confers a right to a jury in federal court wherever state courts would provide it; or that, were it not for the Seventh Amendment, *Erie* would require federal courts to dispense with the jury whenever state courts do so.

In any event, the Court exaggerates the difference that the state standard will make. It concludes that different outcomes are likely to ensue depending on whether the law being applied is the state "deviates materially" standard of § 5501(c) or the "shocks the conscience" standard. Of course it is not the federal *appellate* standard but the federal *district-court* standard for granting new trials that must be compared with the New York standard to determine whether substantially different results will obtain—and it is far from clear that the district-court standard *ought* to be "shocks the conscience." Indeed, it is not even clear (as the Court asserts) that "shocks the conscience" is the standard (erroneous or not) actually applied by the district courts of the Second Circuit. The Second Circuit's test for reversing a grant of a new trial for an excessive verdict is whether the award was "clearly within the maximum limit of a reasonable range." [Justice Scalia cited a variety of district court articulations of the standard for review of a verdict for excessiveness.] In sum, it is at least highly questionable whether the consistent outcome differential claimed by the Court even exists. What seems to me far more likely to produce forum-shopping is the consistent difference between the state and federal *appellate* standards, which the Court leaves untouched. Under the Court's disposition, the Second Circuit reviews only for abuse of discretion, whereas New York's appellate courts engage in a *de novo* review for material deviation, giving the defendant a double shot at getting the damages award set aside. The only result that would produce the conformity the Court erroneously believes *Erie* requires is the one adopted by the Second Circuit and rejected by the Court: *de novo* federal appellate review under the § 5501(c) standard.

To say that application of § 5501(c) in place of the federal standard will not consistently produce disparate results is not to suggest that the decision the Court has made today is not a momentous one. The principle that the state standard governs is of great importance, since it bears the potential to destroy the uniformity of federal practice and the integrity of the federal court system. Under the Court's view, a state rule that directed courts "to determine that an award is excessive or inadequate if it deviates *in any degree* from *the proper measure of compensation*" would have to be applied in federal courts, effectively requiring federal judges to determine the amount of damages *de novo*, and effectively taking the matter away from the jury entirely. Or consider a state rule that allowed the defendant a second trial on damages, with judgment ultimately in the amount of the lesser of two jury awards. Under the reasoning of the Court's opinion, even such a rule as that would have to be applied in the federal courts.

The foregoing describes why I think the Court's *Erie* analysis is flawed. But in my view, one does not even reach the *Erie* question in this case. The standard to be applied by a district court in ruling on a motion for a new trial is set forth in Rule 59 of the Federal Rules of Civil Procedure, which provides that "[a] new trial may be granted ... for any of the reasons for which new trials have heretofore been granted in actions at law *in the courts of the United States*" (emphasis added). That is undeniably a federal standard.[12] Federal district courts in the Second Circuit have interpreted that standard to permit the granting of new trials where "it is quite clear that the jury has reached a seriously erroneous result" and letting the verdict stand would result in a "miscarriage of justice." Assuming (as we have no reason to question) that this is a correct interpretation of what Rule 59 requires, it is undeniable that the federal rule is " 'sufficiently broad' to cause a 'direct collision' with the state law or, implicitly, to 'control the issue' before the court, thereby leaving no room for the operation of that law." Burlington Northern R. Co. v. Woods, 480 U.S. 1, 4–5, 107 S.Ct. 967, 969, 94 L.Ed.2d 1 (1987). It is simply not possible to give controlling effect both to the federal standard and the state standard in reviewing the jury's award. That being so, the court has no choice but to apply the Federal Rule, which is an exercise of what we have called Congress's "power to regulate matters which, though falling within the uncertain area be-

---

12. I agree with the Court's entire progression of reasoning in the footnote 22, leading up to the conclusion that *state* law must determine "[w]hether damages are excessive." But the question of whether damages are excessive is quite separate from the question of when a jury award may be set aside for excessiveness. It is the latter that is governed by Rule 59; as *Browning-Ferris* said, district courts are "to determine, by reference to *federal standards developed under Rule 59*, whether a new trial or remittance should be ordered," 492 U.S. at 279, 109 S.Ct., at 2922 (emphasis added).

tween substance and procedure, are rationally capable of classification as either," *Hanna*, 380 U.S., at 472, 85 S.Ct., at 1144.

Notes and Questions

1. *Postscript*: On remand, the district judge employed the New York standard and granted a much more modest remittitur than the reduction to $100,000 the Second Circuit had endorsed. Gasperini v. Center for Humanities, Inc., 972 F.Supp. 765 (S.D.N.Y.1997). The judge explained his new figure by pointing out that the lost slides were selected from over 5,000 for their relationship with the topics covered in the video. Accordingly, he reasoned that he "should consider what our trial jury considered, namely the actual facts of this case, rather than prior lost photograph cases essentially involving professional libraries which make photographs available without any editorial commitment on the part of the photographer, or any pre-selection except by topic." Notwithstanding the miscellaneous nature of their selection process, he noted, these libraries have pegged the liquidated sum for lost photographs at $1,500 per slide on their printed forms or receipts, which seemed to him some evidence of the value of these items. Against this background, the district judge found strong reasons to set a high value for many of Gasperini's slides:

> Included in the loss are photographs taken by Mr. Gasperini while he was held a hostage of the Contras in the Nicaraguan jungle, and while he was under fire from helicopter gun ships in El Salvador. They include major historical figures at scenes of historical interest and portray the vivid aftermath of war. Most of the photographs represent scenes and images which are impossible to recreate. The jury has a right to consider the superior quality of Mr. Gasperini's work, and the uniqueness of the lost slides as well as the fact that most of them were irreplaceable.

Accordingly, the judge found that all but 70 of the slides could reasonably be valued at $1,500, and that the remaining slides could be valued at $200 per slide, justifying a remittitur of $375,000.

That left the fact that the Court of Appeals had already set the remittitur at $100,000. The judge reasoned that "[w]hile that conclusion must be considered, it is entitled to little weight because the attorneys did not argue the issue of amount, and the exhibits in evidence, which are most critical in evaluating damages, were not even sent to the Court of Appeals, nor were they requested by that Court." When defendant appealed, the Court of Appeals essentially agreed, noting that "[t]he district court was better positioned to review the reasonableness of the jury verdict, and we owe deference to its decision," noting that its earlier decision was based on a "cold paper record," and that the Supreme Court's intervening decision had emphasized that appellate review was limited to determining whether the district judge had committed an abuse of discretion. Gasperini v. Center for Humanities, Inc., 149 F.3d 137, 142 (2d Cir.1998). It did vacate the district judge's decision for "one relatively minor error," including ten slides Gasperini claimed his mother had delivered to defendant but that the jury evidently concluded defendant had not received, and remanded for a recalculation with that mistake removed.

2. Does *Gasperini* represent a significant shift in analysis of *Erie* problems? Consider the following thoughts:

> *Gasperini* does suggest some changes in what the Supreme Court is saying about approaches to *Erie-Hanna* issues, but the basic framework for analysis that has prevailed since *Hanna* appears very much intact. The two differences of particular note seem to be a degree of emphasis on construing possibly applicable Federal Rules with sensitivity to important state interests to avoid "direct conflicts" with state law when possible, and more centrally the clear preservation of *Byrd* interest analysis in a subset of cases involving judge-made federal procedural rules. As best we may be able to tell on the basis of *Gasperini* itself and subsequent lower-court decisions, the *Hanna* "twin aims" approach remains applicable to such decisional-rule cases—*unless* an "essential characteristic" of the federal judicial system presenting a "countervailing federal interest" is involved.

Rowe, Not Bad for Government Work: Does Anyone Else Think the Supreme Court is Doing a Halfway Decent Job in Its *Erie-Hanna* Jurisprudence?, 73 Notre Dame L. Rev. 963, 1014 (1998).

Do you agree that the Court, in interpreting the Rules of Decision Act, continues to employ *Hanna*, "unless an 'essential characteristic' of the federal judicial system presenting a 'countervailing federal interest' is involved"? If so, is such an approach consistent with the analysis contained in either *Hanna* or *Byrd*? Can the two approaches be reconciled into a single test? See footnote 9 in *Hanna;* cf. McClain v. Owens–Corning Fiberglas Corp., 139 F.3d 1124, 1125 (7th Cir. 1998) (expressing view that *Hanna* overruled *Byrd*). Under the Court's approach, why did it apply *Byrd* to the issue of the scope of appellate review, but not to the issue of the remittitur standard? In applying *Hanna's* forum-shopping analysis to the remittitur standard, did the Court reach the correct conclusion?

For other discussions, see Floyd, *Erie* Awry: A Comment on Gasperini v. Center for Humanities, Inc., 1997 B.Y.U.L. Rev. 267; Freer, Some Thoughts on the State of Erie After *Gasperini*, 76 Texas L. Rev. 1637 (1998); Perdue, The Sources and Scope of Federal Procedural Common Law: Some Reflections on Erie and Gasperini, 46 U. Kan. L. Rev. 751 (1998).

3. Was the Seventh Amendment the source of the standard for new trial used in federal court? The Court concludes that applying the revised standard adopted by the New York Legislature does not violate the Seventh Amendment. At some point, however, the second clause of that constitutional provision must limit the power of the judge to alter or reject the verdict. Yet the Seventh Amendment would not apply in state court. Thus, although it might prevent a federal judge from applying a state standard that intruded too deeply into the jury's function, it would not explain the use by federal and state judges of the same standard. Did the Court in *Gasperini* deal adequately with the issue of the Seventh Amendment's relevance? Note that where the Constitution controls, conflicting state law is necessarily preempted. See Continent Trend Resources, Inc. v. OXY USA, Inc., 101 F.3d 634 (10th Cir. 1996); Hayes v. Cha, 338 F. Supp.2d 470 (D.N.J. 2004).

4. Was the Court correct in concluding that Rule 59 did not prescribe the standard to be used by the federal courts? The rule does say that the

federal court should use the rules that "heretofore" were established in the federal courts, which does not seem to include a new one adopted by New York State in 1986. Here is the explanation offered by Dean Charles Clark, who acted as Reporter of the committee that drafted the Federal Rules of Civil Procedure, at a program designed to introduce the new rules to lawyers:

> We first thought we might try to state in detail, categorically, all the reasons for new trials, but if you are familiar with the subject you know that the annotations to the federal statutes dealing with those subjects cover pages and pages. It therefore did not seem practical to attempt to state the grounds, so we listed them generally.

Proceedings of the Institute on Federal Rules 324 (1938).

Some lower courts have suggested that a distinct federal standard does exist. Thus, in Atlas Food Systems and Services, Inc. v. Crane National Vendors, 99 F.3d 587, 595 (4th Cir.1996), the court concluded that "while a jury is authorized to award punitive damages on a framework of liability and the factors supplied by state law, the judgment a jury makes as to the *amount* is reviewable by federal trial courts under Federal Rule of Civil Procedure 59 less deferentially than are factual findings which may be measured against the factual record." (emphasis in original) The court did not cite *Gasperini*, and it certainly did not seem to believe that its starting point in making this determination to be state law. See also Tormenia v. First Investors Realty Co., Inc., 251 F.3d 128, 138 (3d.Cir.2000) (employing federal "shock the conscience" standard in diversity case); Miksis v. Howard, 106 F.3d 754, 764 (7th Cir.1997) ("We use federal standards to determine excessiveness of verdicts in diversity cases").

Does Rule 59 provide sufficient detail to displace pertinent state law? Compare the Court's conclusion in Stewart Organizations, Inc. v. Ricoh Corp., supra p. 964, that 28 U.S.C.A. § 1404(a) displaced a state-law rule denying effect to a forum selection clause in a contract because Congress intended a "flexible and multifaceted analysis" to govern transfer that would be upset were state law to apply.

5. Does the Court hold that the standard for ruling on a new trial motion is generally derived from the law of the state that provides the substantive law used to decide the case? How should a federal court in New York handle a motion for a new trial in a case governed by Connecticut law? This could easily happen under *Klaxon*, supra p. 941, if New York choice of law rules would direct the application of Connecticut law. But a New York court might well treat the standard for granting a new trial as "procedural" within the meaning of its choice of law rules, and therefore subject to New York law, since procedural matters are usually governed by the forum's law. Should a federal court therefore apply the New York standard because a New York court would?

6. If Rule 59 generally does prescribe some federally-controlled standard for granting new trials, is there a reason why it should not apply in *Gasperini*? Perhaps Rule 59 should be interpreted narrowly to avoid a conflict with the substantive impulse of the New York Legislature. In footnote 7, the Court points out that the Federal Rules have been "interpreted with sensitivity to important state interests and regulatory policies,"

citing Walker v. Armco Steel Corp., supra p. 972. But note what it had said in a footnote in *Walker*:

> This is not to suggest that the Federal Rules of Civil Procedure are to be narrowly construed in order to avoid a "direct collision" with state law. The Federal Rules should be given their plain meaning. If a direct collision with state law arises from that plain meaning, then the analysis developed in Hanna v. Plumer applies.

446 U.S. at 750 n.9; 100 S.Ct. at 1985 n.9. Did the Court really employ this caution in *Gasperini*?

The Court also cites S.A. Healy Co. v. Milwaukee Metropolitan Sewerage Dist., 60 F.3d 305 (7th Cir.1995), cert. denied, 516 U.S. 1010, 116 S.Ct. 566, 133 L.Ed.2d 491 (1995), as exemplifying the correct "sensitivity." Plaintiff there sought to recover double its taxable costs plus prejudgment interest on them because it had made an offer of judgment to defendant but defendant had not accepted it, and plaintiff had then obtained a judgment superior to the offer. A Wisconsin statute authorized such consequences for offers by plaintiffs, but Rule 68 does not. The court found "no direct conflict" between the state statute and Rule 68 because the federal rule is limited to offers by defendants. Could the decision by the federal rulemakers *not* to give the same consequences to offers by plaintiffs come into play here? (In this connection, is it worth noting that there were formal proposals in the mid–1980s to amend Rule 68 to make it applicable to offers by plaintiffs, but that these were not adopted?) Judge Posner concluded that "there is no inconsistency when a plaintiff's demand rather than a defendant's offer is in issue."

Finding no direct conflict, the court in *Healy* returned to "first principles," and asked whether the state-law rule is "so likely to dictate outcomes that it will cause a lot of forum shopping" and whether it is "so entwined with procedures prescribed by the federal rules that it is likely to impair the integrity of federal procedure if it is applied in diversity cases?" Finding that defendants would have an added incentive to remove were a rule so favorable to plaintiffs not applicable in federal court, and that the application of the Wisconsin statute would not "tread on the toes of Rule 68" (as it would had defendant made an offer of judgment and invoked the state provision), the court applied the state statute.

Since *Gasperini*, lower courts have on occasion struggled with the task of determining whether a Federal Rule of Civil Procedure actually controls a particular issue. See Cohen v. Office Depot, Inc., 184 F.3d 1292 (11th Cir. 1999) (Rule 8(a) (3), concerning the pleading of remedies, precludes use of state statute requiring leave of court to include prayer for punitive damages); Vaught v. Showa Denko K.K., 107 F.3d 1137 (5th Cir. 1997) (Rule 23 does not concern tolling of statute of limitations); Senger Brothers Nursery, Inc. v. E.I. Dupont De Nemours & Co., 184 F.R.D. 674 (M.D.Fla.1999) (Rule 23, concerning class actions, does not conflict with state statute of limitations).

7. If Rule 59 does prescribe a standard for granting new trials, is there any justification under Burlington Northern Railroad Co. v. Woods, supra, p. 965 for refusing to apply it in *Gasperini*? Does § 5501(c) create a "substan-

tive right" which the federal rule may not alter pursuant to 28 U.S.C.A. § 2072(b)?

8. C.P.L.R. § 5501(c) governs determinations whether the verdict is inadequate as well as whether the verdict is excessive. If the New York Legislature directs that judges should use additur if the jury returns an inadequate verdict, should federal courts do the same? Recall Dimick v. Schiedt, supra p. 658.

B. DETERMINING STATE LAW

MASON v. AMERICAN EMERY WHEEL WORKS

United States Court of Appeals, First Circuit, 1957.
241 F.2d 906.

Before MAGRUDER, CHIEF JUDGE, and WOODBURY and HARTIGAN, CIRCUIT JUDGES.

MAGRUDER, CHIEF JUDGE.

[While at work in Mississippi, plaintiff was injured by an emery wheel manufactured by defendant, a Rhode Island corporation. Plaintiff sued in federal court in Rhode Island, alleging that the emery wheel was unreasonably dangerous. In its answer, defendant raised lack of privity. When evidence at trial showed that the emery wheel had passed through several owners before it was sold to plaintiff's employer, the trial court granted defendant's motion to dismiss on the ground that Mississippi still required privity to sue a manufacturer for such injuries.]

Since the injury was inflicted in Mississippi, the district court, no doubt correctly under now familiar authorities, deemed itself to be obliged to apply the Mississippi local law to determine the tort liability, if any, of a manufacturer to one not in privity of contract with him. The district court came to the conclusion "reluctantly" that it was bound by the Mississippi law as declared in Ford Motor Co. v. Myers, 1928, 151 Miss. 73, 117 So. 362; that the "harsh rule" of Mississippi as so declared, "contrary to the great weight of authority" elsewhere, was that a manufacturer was not liable for negligence in the manufacture of appliances which could and would become highly dangerous when put to the uses for which they are intended, where there is no privity of contract between the user and the manufacturer.

Ford Motor Co. v. Myers was the only Mississippi case relied upon, or even referred to, by the district court. In that case the Supreme Court of Mississippi, in a half-page opinion, did in fact apply what was at one time the prevailing rule, in holding that Ford Motor Company as the manufacturer of a truck owed no duty of care to a remote subvendee of the truck who was injured when the truck collapsed and plunged into a ditch because of a defect which could have been detected by reasonable inspection by the manufacturer before the vehicle left the factory.

At a time when the federal courts were applying their own notions of the federal common law of torts, under Swift v. Tyson, the court in

Huset v. J.I. Case Threshing Machine Co., 8 Cir., 1903, 120 F. 865, 868, 61 L.R.A. 303, declared as a general rule that "a contractor, manufacturer, or vendor is not liable to third parties who have no contractual relations with him for negligence in the construction, manufacture, or sale of the articles he handles." At this late date it is hardly necessary to spend much time on the merit or justification for that supposed general rule. * * *

MacPherson v. Buick Motor Co., [217 N.Y. 382, 111 N.E. 1050 (1916)] started a new trend in this particular field of the law, and its substantive result has found favor in § 395 of the American Law Institute Restatement of Torts. If the Supreme Court of Mississippi had recently reconsidered the rule it applied in Ford Motor Co. v. Myers, and had decided to adhere to it on the ground of stare decisis, no doubt the federal courts would have had to accept the local law as so declared. But it would be gratuitous and unwarranted to assume that the Supreme Court of Mississippi would now so hold, when we bear in mind the readiness of other courts, in conservative jurisdictions at that, to overrule their earlier holdings and to bring their jurisprudence into accord with what is now the overwhelming weight of authority. * * *

Of course it is not necessary that a case be explicitly overruled in order to lose its persuasive force as an indication of what the law is. A decision may become so overloaded with illogical exceptions that by erosion of time it may lose its persuasive or binding force even in the inferior courts of the same jurisdiction. And where, as in Ford Motor Co. v. Myers, the Supreme Court of Mississippi, twenty or thirty years ago, applied an old rule which has since been generally discredited elsewhere, it is relevant to consider what the Supreme Court of Mississippi has subsequently said on the point. We think that appellant herein rightly stresses the importance of E.I. Du Pont De Nemours & Co. v. Ladner, 1954, 221 Miss. 378, 73 So.2d 249. In that very recent case, the Supreme Court of Mississippi was able to dispose of the particular issue on another ground without the necessity of expressly overruling its earlier decision in Ford Motor Co. v. Myers. But the court did take occasion, in a long and careful opinion, to indicate its awareness of the modern trend in the area * * *; it stated that, whatever may have been the rule originally, "the principle seems now to be well established by the decisions of many courts that a person who has had no direct contractual relations with a manufacturer may nevertheless recover from such manufacturer for damages to property caused by the negligence of the manufacturer in the same manner that such a remote vendee or other third person can recover for personal injuries." And it quoted, with apparent approval, many more recent authorities in support of the "modern doctrine". We think it is fair to infer from this latest expression by the Supreme Court of Mississippi that it is prepared to reconsider and revise the rule it applied in Ford Motor Co. v. Myers whenever it may have before it a case that squarely presents the issue. We have no doubt that when this occasion does come to pass, the Supreme Court of

Mississippi will declare itself in agreement with the more enlightened and generally accepted modern doctrine.

A judgment will be entered vacating the order of the District Court, dismissing the complaint and remanding the case to the District Court for further proceedings not inconsistent with this opinion.

HARTIGAN, CIRCUIT JUDGE (concurring).

I concur in the opinion of the court but I am constrained to comment briefly. We were informed in oral argument by counsel for the appellee that the district court in deciding this case had before it both the *Ford* and the *Du Pont* decisions. Moreover, the district court knew from the official Mississippi report that the *MacPherson* case, then approximately twelve years old, had been considered and rejected by the Mississippi Supreme Court sitting in the *Ford* case. Therefore, "reluctantly" Judge Day adopted the *Ford* holding since it, as the only binding and conclusive statement of Mississippi law on the issue, had not been expressly modified or overruled. * * *

We, however, have inferred from pure dicta in the *Du Pont* case and from the status of the law elsewhere on this issue that Mississippi is prepared to discard the *Ford* rule and adopt the modern rule. I believe this is a sound inference since the dicta in the *Du Pont* case, though not expressly mentioning *Ford,* is sufficiently clear and the *Ford* rule is sufficiently outdated. Yet, in doing so I realize that we present a difficult problem for district judges when they must apply the *Erie* doctrine to situations wherein the considerations as between conflicting holdings and dicta are not as clearly defined as they are here. The question of how clear dicta must be to prevail over a prior controlling decision does not lend itself to easy solution.

Notes and Questions

1. Why was a federal court in Rhode Island applying the law of Mississippi in this case?

2. If you were a practicing attorney in Mississippi in 1954 (when the accident in *Mason* occurred), and a client asked you to describe the state's law on the requirement of privity in tort cases, what would you have said?

3. In deciding what the state law is, should a federal court, in a diversity case, deem itself bound by state lower-court decisions where there is no applicable state supreme court decision? Might such a practice lead to a type of reverse forum-shopping? Could the same be said of reliance on antiquated state supreme court decisions? In Commissioner v. Estate of Bosch, 387 U.S. 456, 465, 87 S.Ct. 1776, 1782, 18 L.Ed.2d 886 (1967), in a context not directly involving *Erie,* the Court stated that "the State's highest court is the best authority on its own law. If there be no decision by that court then federal authorities must apply what they find to be the state law after giving 'proper regard' to relevant rulings of other courts of the State. In this respect, it may be said to be, in effect, sitting as a state court." According to Judge Jerome Frank, the test should be: "What would be the decision of reasonably intelligent lawyers, sitting as judges of the highest

[state] court, and fully conversant with state 'jurisprudence?' '' Cooper v. American Airlines, Inc., 149 F.2d 355, 359 (2d Cir.1945). See also Valley Forge Insurance Co. v. Jefferson, 628 F.Supp. 502, 510 (D.Del.1986): "Where a state's highest court has not spoken, a federal court sitting in diversity has a duty to decide a case as it believes the state's highest court would have done." One court of appeals concluded that the proper approach to determine state common law in the absence of an applicable decision of the state supreme court was to look "to other sources: (1) lower state court decisions and Supreme Court dicta, (2) the lower court ruling in this case, (3) the general rule on the issue, (4) the rule in other states looked to by [the state's] courts, and (5) other available legal sources, such as treatises and law review commentaries." Nicolson v. Life Insurance Co. of the Southwest, 783 F.2d 1316, 1319 (5th Cir.1986). Federal courts have often emphasized, however, that in making this determination their function is not to adopt the rule that it would choose for itself, but rather to adopt the rule that the federal court believes the state court itself would adopt. See, e.g., Nichols v. Anderson, 837 F.2d 1372, 1375 (5th Cir.1988). See generally C. Wright & M. Kane, Law of Federal Courts § 58 (6th ed. 2002).

Note that one source considered by the court in *Mason* is the Restatement of Torts. Does the pertinence of that source depend on a decision by Mississippi to be bound by decisions of the American Law Institute, which promulgates Restatements? Consider Title I, § 4 of the Virgin Islands Code:

> The rules of the common law, as expressed in the restatements of the law approved by the American Law Institute, and to the extent not so expressed, as generally understood and applied in the United States, shall be the rules of decision of the courts of the Virgin Islands in cases to which they apply, in the absence of local laws to the contrary.

4. After *Mason,* the Fifth Circuit held that privity was not a bar under Mississippi law. Grey v. Hayes–Sammons Chemical Co., 310 F.2d 291 (5th Cir.1962). Ultimately, the Mississippi Supreme Court overruled *Ford Motor Co.* and rejected the privity requirement. State Stove Mfg. Co. v. Hodges, 189 So.2d 113 (Miss.1966), cert. denied sub nom. Yates v. Hodges, 386 U.S. 912, 87 S.Ct. 860, 17 L.Ed.2d 784 (1967). Does this mean the *Mason* court was right?

In Clark, Ascertaining the Laws of the Several States: Positivism and Judicial Federalism After *Erie,* 145 U.Pa.L.Rev. 1459 (1997), the author reasons that "a federal court's 'prediction' of state law frequently devolves into little more than a choice among competing policy considerations. No matter how pure a federal court's intentions may be, legal indeterminacy necessarily requires courts to exercise some degree of policymaking discretion." Id. at 1499. As an example of particularly problematical activity by federal judges, he cites *Mason,* noting that "for nine years (from 1957 to 1966), federal courts recognized and applied 'substantive rules of common law' that Mississippi had yet to adopt (and might have never adopted)." Id. at 1515.

5. In Salve Regina College v. Russell, 499 U.S. 225, 111 S.Ct. 1217, 1219, 113 L.Ed.2d 190 (1991), the Supreme Court considered the question "whether a federal court of appeals may review a district court's determination of state law under a standard less probing than that applied to a

determination of federal law." Most courts of appeals had adopted a policy of deferring to district court interpretations of state law if the district judge was interpreting the law of the state in which he sat. See, e.g., Norton v. St. Paul Fire & Marine Ins. Co., 902 F.2d 1355, 1357 (8th Cir.1990). In an opinion by Justice Blackmun, the Supreme Court decided that this rule of deference was improper:

> Independent appellate review of legal issues best serves the dual goals of doctrinal coherence and economy of judicial administration. District judges preside alone over fast-paced trials: of necessity they devote much of their energy and resources to hearing witnesses and reviewing evidence. Similarly, the logistical burdens of trial advocacy limit the extent to which trial counsel is able to supplement the district judge's legal research with memoranda and briefs. Thus, trial judges often must resolve complicated legal questions without benefit of "extended reflection [or] extensive information."

> Courts of appeals, on the other hand, are structurally suited to the collaborative judicial process that promotes decisional accuracy. With the record having been constructed below and settled for purposes of the appeal, appellate judges are able to devote their primary attention to legal issues.

* * *

> Independent appellate review necessarily entails a careful consideration of the district court's legal analysis, and an efficient and sensitive appellate court at least will naturally consider this analysis in undertaking its review. * * * Any expertise possessed by the district court will inform the structure and content of its conclusions of law and thereby become evident to the reviewing court. * * * Independent review, however, does not admit of unreflective reliance on a lower court's inarticulable intuitions.

The Court also concluded that "appellate deference to the district court's determination of state law is inconsistent with the principles underlying this Court's decision in *Erie*," 499 U.S. at 233, because "deferential appellate review invites divergent development of state law among the federal trial courts even within a single state. Moreover, by denying a litigant access to meaningful review of state-law claims, appellate courts that defer to the district courts' state-law determinations create a dual system of enforcement of state-created rights, in which the substantive rule applied to a dispute may depend on the choice of forum." Id. at 234

Chief Justice Rehnquist, joined by Justices White and Stevens, dissented: "A district court's insights are particularly valuable to an appellate court in a case such as this where the state law is unsettled." Id. at 241. Consider the strength of this argument if the district judge had served on the state supreme court before appointment to the federal bench.

6. In Yohannon v. Keene Corp., 924 F.2d 1255 (3d Cir.1991), the Third Circuit expressed the exasperation probably often felt by federal courts in attempting to discern unclear state law:

Since [state supreme] courts often do not speak clearly or precisely to the issue in question, a federal court sitting in diversity must often take on the mantle of the soothsayers of old and predict what the supreme court of a particular state would do if it were presented with the issue that controls the case before the federal court. Such contemporary predictions are just as chancy a business as the divination of dreams that heathen kings of ancient biblical lands so often called upon their counselors to interpret in the stories of the Old Testament. Like them, in taking on the task, we hope that our prophecy will find favor in the eyes of the authority that may one day brand it true or false.

The growing popularity of unpublished opinions can make the task of determining state law even more difficult. For example, in Exxon Co. v. Banque De Paris Et Des Pays–Bas, 889 F.2d 674 (5th Cir.1989), an action on a letter of credit, the Fifth Circuit initially decided that the obligation to pay had been terminated even though the expiration date had not been reached. Five weeks after this decision, a state intermediate appellate court rendered an unreported opinion, adopting a different view of state law. On petition for rehearing, the Fifth Circuit refused to consider this decision because under Texas law an unreported opinion may not be cited as precedent. Meanwhile, the Texas Supreme Court denied a motion to publish the appellate court decision, but the state appellate court that had rendered the decision granted a similar motion and published the decision.

The Supreme Court then vacated the Fifth Circuit's judgment and remanded for reconsideration in light of the now-published state court decision. Uncertain about what the Texas Supreme Court's refusal to order the lower court opinion published meant about its attitude toward the decision itself, the Fifth Circuit certified the question to the Texas Supreme Court, which declined to answer the certified question on the ground that the answer depended on unresolved issues of fact. Thus rebuffed, the Fifth Circuit concluded that the state appellate court opinion should be followed and that it dictated a different result.

7. *Certification*: When a state so authorizes by statute, court rule, or constitution, a federal court may refer uncertain or unsettled questions of state law to the state's highest court for decision. Under this procedure, the case itself remains in federal court. The procedure is discretionary with the federal court. "Most state high courts now offer federal courts faced with questions of state law * * * the opportunity to 'certify' those questions of state law to the state high court." Nash, Evaluating the Power of Federal Courts to Certify Questions of State Law, 88 Cornell L. Rev. 1682, 1674 (2003). Some federal courts are enthusiastic about using this opportunity : "Where there is any doubt as to the application of state law, a federal court should certify the question to the state supreme court to avoid making unnecessary Erie 'guesses' and to offer the state court the opportunity interpret or change existing law." Mosher v. Speedstar Div. of AMCA Int'l, Inc., 52 F.3d 913, 916–17 (11th Cir. 1995). The use of certification in diversity cases is somewhat controversial. See, e.g., Mattis, Certification of Questions of State Law: An Impractical Tool in the Hands of the Federal Courts, 23 U.Miami L.Rev. 717 (1969). Why might this be so?

C. THE "CONVERSE-*ERIE*" PROBLEM

DICE v. AKRON, CANTON & YOUNGSTOWN R.R.

Supreme Court of the United States, 1952.
342 U.S. 359, 72 S.Ct. 312, 96 L.Ed. 398.

Opinion of the Court by JUSTICE BLACK, announced by JUSTICE DOUG-LAS.

Petitioner, a railroad fireman, was seriously injured when an engine in which he was riding jumped the track. Alleging that his injuries were due to respondent's negligence, he brought this action for damages under the Federal Employers' Liability Act, 35 Stat. 65, 45 U.S.C. § 51 et seq., in an Ohio court of common pleas. Respondent's defenses were (1) a denial of negligence and (2) a written document signed by petitioner purporting to release respondent in full for $924.63. Petitioner admitted that he had signed several receipts for payments made him in connection with his injuries but denied that he had made a full and complete settlement of all his claims. He alleged that the purported release was void because he had signed it relying on respondent's deliberately false statement that the document was nothing more than a mere receipt for back wages.

After both parties had introduced considerable evidence the jury found in favor of petitioner and awarded him a $25,000 verdict. The trial judge later entered judgment notwithstanding the verdict. In doing so he reappraised the evidence as to fraud, found that petitioner had been "guilty of supine negligence" in failing to read the release, and accordingly held that the facts did not "sustain either in law or equity the allegations of fraud by clear, unequivocal and convincing evidence." This judgment notwithstanding the verdict was reversed by the Court of Appeals of Summit County, Ohio, on the ground that under federal law, which controlled, the jury's verdict must stand because there was ample evidence to support its finding of fraud. The Ohio Supreme Court, one judge dissenting, reversed the Court of Appeals' judgment and sustained the trial court's action, holding that: (1) Ohio, not federal, law governed; (2) under that law petitioner, a man of ordinary intelligence who could read, was bound by the release even though he had been induced to sign it by the deliberately false statement that it was only a receipt for back wages; and (3) under controlling Ohio law factual issues as to fraud in the execution of this release were properly decided by the judge rather than by the jury. We granted certiorari because the decision of the Supreme Court of Ohio appeared to deviate from previous decisions of this Court that federal law governs cases arising under the Federal Employers' Liability Act.

First. We agree with the Court of Appeals of Summit County, Ohio, and the dissenting judge in the Ohio Supreme Court and hold that validity of releases under the Federal Employers' Liability Act raises a federal question to be determined by federal rather than state law. Congress in § 1 of the Act granted petitioner a right to recover against his employer for damages negligently inflicted. State laws are not controlling in determining what the incidents of this federal right shall be. Manifestly the federal rights affording relief to injured railroad employees under a federally declared standard could be defeated if states were permitted to have the final say as to what defenses could and could not be properly interposed to suits under the Act. Moreover, only if federal law controls can the federal Act be given that uniform application throughout the country essential to effectuate its purposes. Releases and other devices designed to liquidate or defeat injured employees' claims play an important part in the federal Act's administration. Their validity is but one of the many interrelated questions that must constantly be determined in these cases according to a uniform federal law.

Second. In effect the Supreme Court of Ohio held that an employee trusts his employer at his peril, and that the negligence of an innocent worker is sufficient to enable his employer to benefit by its deliberate fraud. Application of so harsh a rule to defeat a railroad employee's claim is wholly incongruous with the general policy of the Act to give railroad employees a right to recover just compensation for injuries negligently inflicted by their employers. And this Ohio rule is out of harmony with modern judicial and legislative practice to relieve injured persons from the effect of releases fraudulently obtained. We hold that the correct federal rule is that announced by the Court of Appeals of Summit County, Ohio, and the dissenting judge in the Ohio Supreme Court—a release of rights under the Act is void when the employee is induced to sign it by the deliberately false and material statements of the railroad's authorized representatives made to deceive the employee as to the contents of the release. The trial court's charge to the jury correctly stated this rule of law.

Third. Ohio provides and has here accorded petitioner the usual jury trial of factual issues relating to negligence. But Ohio treats factual questions of fraudulent releases differently. It permits the judge trying a negligence case to resolve all factual questions of fraud "other than fraud in the factum." The factual issue of fraud is thus split into fragments, some to be determined by the judge, others by the jury.

It is contended that since a state may consistently with the Federal Constitution provide for trial of cases under the Act by a nonunanimous verdict, Minneapolis & St. Louis R. Co. v. Bombolis, 241 U.S. 211, 36 S.Ct. 595, 60 L.Ed. 961, Ohio may lawfully eliminate trial by jury as to one phase of fraud while allowing jury trial as to all other issues raised. The *Bombolis* case might be more in point had Ohio abolished trial by jury in all negligence cases including those arising under the federal Act. But Ohio has not done this. It has provided jury trials for cases arising under the federal Act but seeks to single out one phase of the question of fraudulent releases for determination by a judge rather than by a jury.

We have previously held that "The right to trial by jury is 'a basic and fundamental feature of our system of federal jurisprudence'" and that it is "part and parcel of the remedy afforded railroad workers under the Employers' Liability Act." Bailey v. Central Vermont R. Co., 319 U.S. 350, 354, 63 S.Ct. 1062, 1064, 87 L.Ed. 1444. We also recognized in that case that to deprive railroad workers of the benefit of a jury trial where there is evidence to support negligence "is to take away a goodly portion of the relief which Congress has afforded them." It follows that the right to trial by jury is too substantial a part of the rights accorded by the Act to permit it to be classified as a mere "local rule of procedure" for denial in the manner that Ohio has here used. Brown v. Western R. Co., 338 U.S. 294, 70 S.Ct. 105, 94 L.Ed. 100.

The trial judge and the Ohio Supreme Court erred in holding that petitioner's rights were to be determined by Ohio law and in taking away petitioner's verdict when the issues of fraud had been submitted to the jury on conflicting evidence and determined in petitioner's favor. The judgment of the Court of Appeals of Summit County, Ohio, was correct and should not have been reversed by the Supreme Court of Ohio. The cause is reversed and remanded to the Supreme Court of Ohio for further action not inconsistent with this opinion.

JUSTICE FRANKFURTER, whom JUSTICE REED, JUSTICE JACKSON and JUSTICE BURTON join, concurring for reversal but dissenting from the Court's opinion.

Ohio, as do many other States, maintains the old division between law and equity as to the mode of trying issues, even though the same judge administers both. The Ohio Supreme Court has told us what, on one issue, is the division of functions in all negligence actions brought in the Ohio courts: "Where it is claimed that a release was induced by fraud (other than fraud in the factum) or by mistake, it is ... necessary, before seeking to enforce a cause of action which such release purports to bar, that equitable relief from the release be secured." Thus, in all cases in Ohio, the judge is the trier of fact on this issue of fraud, rather than the jury. It is contended that the Federal Employers' Liability Act requires that Ohio courts send the fraud issue to a jury in the cases founded on that Act. To require Ohio to try a particular issue before a different fact-finder in negligence actions brought under the Employers' Liability Act from the fact-finder on the identical issue in every other negligence case disregards the settled distribution of judicial power between Federal and State courts where Congress authorizes concurrent enforcement of federally-created rights.

It has been settled ever since the Second Employers' Liability Cases (Mondou v. New York, N.H. & H.R. Co., 223 U.S. 1, 32 S.Ct. 169, 56 L.Ed. 327), that no State which gives its courts jurisdiction over common law actions for negligence may deny access to its courts for a negligence action founded on the Federal Employers' Liability Act. Nor may a State discriminate disadvantageously against actions for negligence under the Federal Act as compared with local causes of action in negligence. Conversely, however, simply because there is concurrent jurisdiction in Federal and State courts over actions under the Employers' Liability Act, a State is under no duty to treat actions arising under that Act differently from the way it adjudicates local actions for negligence, so far as the mechanics of litigation, the forms in which law is administered, are concerned. This surely covers the distribution of functions as between judge and jury in the determination of the issues in a negligence case.

In 1916 the Court decided without dissent that States in entertaining actions under the Federal Employers' Liability Act need not provide a jury system other than that established for local negligence actions. States are not compelled to provide the jury required of Federal courts by the Seventh Amendment. Minneapolis & St. L.R. Co. v. Bombolis, 241 U.S. 211, 36 S.Ct. 595, 60 L.Ed. 961. In the thirty-six years since this early decision after the enactment of the Federal Employers' Liability Act, 35 Stat. 65 (1908), the *Bombolis* case has often been cited by this Court but never questioned. Until today its significance has been to leave to States the choice of the fact-finding tribunal in all negligence actions, including those arising under the Federal Act. * * *

Although a State must entertain negligence suits brought under the Federal Employers' Liability Act if it entertains ordinary actions for negligence, it need conduct them only in the way in which it conducts the run of negligence litigation. The *Bombolis* case directly establishes that the Employers' Liability Act does not impose the jury requirements of the Seventh Amendment on the States pro tanto for Employers' Liability litigation. If its reasoning means anything, the *Bombolis* decision means that, if a State chooses not to have a jury at all, but to leave questions of fact in all negligence actions to a court, certainly the Employers' Liability Act does not require a State to have juries for negligence actions brought under the Federal Act in its courts. Or, if a State chooses to retain the old double system of courts, common law and equity—as did a good many States until the other day, and as four States still do—surely there is nothing in the Employers' Liability Act that requires traditional distribution of authority for disposing of legal issues as between common law and chancery courts to go by the board. And, if States are free to make a distribution of functions between equity and common law courts, it surely makes no rational difference whether a State chooses to provide that the same judge preside on both the common law and the chancery sides in a single litigation, instead of in separate rooms in the same building. So long as all negligence suits in a State are treated in the same way, by the same mode of disposing equitable, non-jury, and common law, jury issues, the State does not discriminate against Employers' Liability suits nor does it make any inroad upon substance.

Ohio and her sister States with a similar division of functions between law and equity are not trying to evade their duty under the Federal Employers' Liability Act; nor are they trying to make it more difficult for railroad workers to recover, than for those suing under local law. The States merely exercise a preference in adhering to historic ways of dealing with a claim of fraud; they prefer the traditional way of making unavailable through equity an otherwise valid defense. The State judges and local lawyers who must administer the Federal Employers' Liability Act in State courts are trained in the ways of local practice; it multiplies the difficulties and confuses the administration of justice to require, on purely theoretical grounds, a hybrid of State and Federal practice in the State courts as to a single class of cases. Nothing in the Employers' Liability Act or in the judicial enforcement of the Act for over forty years forces such judicial hybridization upon the States. The fact that Congress authorized actions under the Federal Employers' Liability Act to be brought in State as well as in Federal courts seems a strange basis for the inference that Congress overrode State procedural arrangements controlling all other negligence suits in a State, by imposing upon State courts to which plaintiffs choose to go the rules prevailing in the Federal courts regarding juries. Such an inference is admissible, so it seems to me, only on the theory that Congress included as part of the right created by the Employers' Liability Act an assumed likelihood that trying all issues to juries is more favorable to plaintiffs. At least, if a plaintiff's right to have all issues decided by a jury rather than the court is "part and parcel of the remedy afforded railroad workers under the Employers Liability Act," the *Bombolis* case should be overruled explicitly instead of left as a derelict bound to occasion collisions on the waters of the law. We have put the questions squarely because they seem to be precisely what will be roused in the minds of lawyers properly pressing their clients' interests and in the minds of trial and appellate judges called upon to apply this Court's opinion.

Even though the method of trying the equitable issue of fraud which the State applies in all other negligence cases governs Employers' Liability cases, two questions remain for decision: Should the validity of the release be tested by a Federal or a State standard? And if by a Federal one, did the Ohio courts in the present case correctly administer the standard? If the States afford courts for enforcing the Federal Act, they must enforce the substance of the right given by Congress. They cannot depreciate the legislative currency issued by Congress—either expressly or by local methods of enforcement that accomplish the same result. In order to prevent diminution of railroad workers' nationally-uniform right to recover, the standard for the validity of a release of contested liability must be Federal. * * * The admitted fact that the injured worker signed the release is material in tending to show the release to be valid, but presumptions must not be drawn from that fact so as to hobble the plaintiff's showing that it would be unjust to allow a formally good defense to prevail.

The judgment of the Ohio Supreme Court must be reversed for it applied the State rule as to validity of releases, and it is not for us to interpret Ohio decisions in order to be assured that on a matter of substance the State and Federal criteria coincide. Moreover, we cannot say with confidence that the Ohio trial judge applied the Federal standard correctly. * * *

Notes and Questions

1. In what sense is *Dice* a "converse-*Erie*" case?

2. What did the *Dice* Court mean when it stated: "The *Bombolis* case might be more in point had Ohio abolished trial by jury in all negligence cases including those arising under the federal Act"?

3. Is there any constitutional limitation on what procedures Congress may require state courts to follow in adjudicating federal suits? Could Congress constitutionally require state judges to stand on one leg while adjudicating federal cases? If not, could it require state judges to follow the Federal Rules of Evidence in such cases?

4. What is Justice Frankfurter's reasoning to support his conclusion that the state court need not employ federal procedures? Is his reasoning persuasive?

5. Under Georgia state practice, great factual detail was required in a complaint. This was in contrast to federal procedure where, under Rule 8(a) of the Federal Rules of Civil Procedure, a considerably more liberal pleading system is applied. Georgia state courts dismissed a complaint brought under the Federal Employers' Liability Act because it failed to meet the requirements of Georgia pleading practice. Plaintiff, in the United States Supreme Court, argued that in adjudicating this federal cause of action, the Georgia courts should be required to follow federal pleading practice. What result? See Brown v. Western Railway of Alabama, 338 U.S. 294, 70 S.Ct. 105, 94 L.Ed. 100 (1949). Noting that "[t]o what extent rules of practice and procedure may themselves dig into 'substantive rights' is a troublesome question at best," the Court held: "Strict local rules of pleading cannot be used to impose unnecessary burdens upon rights of recovery authorized by federal laws. 'Whatever springes the State may set for those who are endeavoring to assert rights that the State confers, the assertion of federal rights, when plainly and reasonably made, is not to be defeated under the name of local practice.'" What other local practices must give way in cases asserting federal rights? Must state courts permit discovery using all the devices available in federal court? Cf. Sibbach v. Wilson & Co., supra p. 967 n. 2.

Consider Johnson v. Fankell, 520 U.S. 911, 117 S.Ct. 1800, 138 L.Ed.2d 108 (1997), in which the Court distinguished Dice v. Akron R.R. and held that a state court did not have to follow federal law regarding the timing of an appeal. In a § 1983 civil rights suit in state court, defendants tried to appeal after the trial court denied their motion to dismiss on qualified immunity grounds. When the state supreme court dismissed their appeal, they obtained certiorari arguing that state courts should have to handle this question in the same way the federal courts would, and allow immediate review. Although there is no doubt that under Mitchell v. Forsyth, 472 U.S. 511, 105 S.Ct. 2806, 86 L.Ed.2d 411 (1985), an immediate appeal would be allowed in federal court to protect officials against groundless suits, the Court unanimously affirmed, saying that the immediate appealability in federal court "is a federal procedural right that simply does not apply in a nonfederal forum." In *Dice*, the Court held that the F.E.L.A. implicitly required a jury trial. The federal appealability doctrine, by way of contrast, "is found in [28 U.S.C.] § 1291, which obviously has no application to state courts." The Court also noted that immediate appealability was designed in part to protect state officials in such cases, and that the state's decision to provide less protection implicated no federal interest.

6. Is *Dice* arguably inconsistent with *Byrd*, supra, p. 943? If so, can the two be reconciled?

7. Limitations issues can raise particularly difficult problems. These problems have surfaced in connection with federal claims for which Congress has not specified a limitations period. For civil rights and securities fraud suits, which fall in this category, the federal courts "borrowed" limitations periods from state law. This practice of borrowing from state law raised difficulties because the limitations period could vary from state to state and because related provisions of state law (such as a requirement that service be effected within the limitations period) were sometimes different from normal federal practice. See generally Marcus, Fraudulent Concealment in Federal Court: Toward a More Disparate Standard?, 71 Geo.L.J. 829, 836–55 (1983) (discussing the difficulties in such cases where state and federal law differ regarding the events that suspend the running of limitations).

In DelCostello v. Teamsters, 462 U.S. 151, 103 S.Ct. 2281, 76 L.Ed.2d 476 (1983), a labor case, the Supreme Court broke away from borrowing from state law in order to provide nationwide uniformity of limitations periods. Plaintiff in that case was an employee asserting a "hybrid" claim under federal labor statutes against both his employer and union. Congress had not specified a limitations period for the claim. Rather than borrow from state law for "hybrid" claims, the Court borrowed the six month limitations period from another federal labor statute. But that statute also required service within six months. In West v. Conrail, 481 U.S. 35, 107 S.Ct. 1538, 95 L.Ed.2d 32 (1987), the Court held that this service requirement did not apply to "hybrid" suits by employees: "when the underlying cause of action is based on federal law and the absence of an express federal statute of limitations makes it necessary to borrow a limitations period from another statute, the action is not barred if it has been 'commenced' in compliance with Rule 3 within the borrowed period."

"Hybrid" labor suits can also be filed in state court, however; does this mean that Rule 3 applies to suits filed in state court as well? In Cannon v. Kroger Co., 832 F.2d 303 (4th Cir.1987), plaintiff filed such a "hybrid" claim in state court, using a state court procedure that permits a plaintiff to file an application for an extension of time to file the complaint, which is not due for another 20 days. After she filed and served her complaint, defendants removed to federal court and moved to dismiss on the ground that the action was not commenced in time. The appellate court upheld dismissal of the suit:

> After *West*, there can be no question that commencement of a "hybrid" claim brought in district court is to be assessed in accordance with the Federal Rules of Civil Procedure. Unlike appellant, we can perceive no justification for allowing a different result simply because the underlying action is initiated in a state court. The substantive rights involved remain purely federal in nature. Moreover, the choice of a forum in no way diminishes the subtle balance of interests [that prompted the Supreme Court to borrow a uniform limitations period]. The application of alternative state law procedures must inevitably intrude

into the balance and threaten the goal of uniform adjudication. We conclude, therefore, that the statute of limitations applicable to "hybrid" actions runs until the action is properly commenced under the dictates of the Federal Rules of Civil Procedure.

Is this reasoning persuasive? Why wouldn't it apply equally well to federal claims with uniform congressionally set limitations periods? In this connection, it should be noted that some lower courts have read the Supreme Court's decision in DelCostello v. Teamsters, supra, as an invitation to re-examine decisions borrowing from state law for other federal claims. See In re Data Access Sys. Securities Litig., 843 F.2d 1537 (3d Cir.1988) (adopting analogous federal limitations period for federal securities fraud action). Should Rule 3 apply to all federal claims filed in state court? Recall Walker v. Armco Steel Corp., supra p. 972 (stating that Rule 3 was not intended to toll statutes of limitations). Can *Walker* be reconciled with these decisions involving federal claims? For a criticism of this approach, see Burbank, Of Rules and Discretion: The Supreme Court, Federal Rules and Procedural Common Law, 63 Notre Dame L.Rev. 693 (1988).

8. In Felder v. Casey, 487 U.S. 131, 108 S.Ct. 2302, 101 L.Ed.2d 123 (1988), the Supreme Court held invalid the Wisconsin Supreme Court's reliance on the state's notice-of-claim statute to bar a suit brought under the federal civil rights laws, 42 U.S.C.A. § 1983. The state statute provided that before suit may be brought in state court against a state or local governmental entity or officer, the plaintiff must notify the defendant of the circumstances and amount of the claim within 120 days of the injury. Justice Brennan, writing for the Court, reasoned:

> The decision to subject state subdivisions to liability for violations of federal rights * * * was a choice that Congress, not the Wisconsin legislature, made, and it is a decision that the State has no authority to override. Thus, however understandable or laudable the State's interest in controlling liability expenses might otherwise be, it is patently incompatible with the compensatory goals of the federal legislation, as are the means the State has chosen to effectuate it.

* * *

> This burdening of a federal right, moreover, is not the natural or permissible consequence of an otherwise neutral, uniformly applicable state rule. Although it is true that the notice-of-claim statute does not discriminate between state and federal causes of action against local governments, the fact remains that the law's protection extends only to governmental defendants and thus conditions the right to bring suit against the very persons and entities Congress intended to subject to liability. We therefore cannot accept the suggestion that this requirement is simply part of "the vast body of procedural rules, rooted in policies unrelated to the definition of any particular substantive cause of action, that forms no essential part of 'the cause of action' as applied to any given plaintiff." * * * [The] defendant-specific focus of the notice requirement serves to distinguish it, rather starkly, from rules uniformly applicable to all suits, such as rules governing service of process or substitution of parties * * *. That state courts will hear the entire § 1983 cause of action once a plaintiff complies with the notice-of-claim

statute, therefore, in no way alters the fact that the statute discriminates against the precise type of claim Congress has created.

Justice O'Connor, joined by the Chief Justice, dissented.

How do you think the Court would have held had the state's notice-of-claim statute applied to every suit brought in state court? How *should* the Court have held? Assume a state judicial system provides for little or no discovery. Should the Supreme Court hold that in a § 1983 suit the state court must make available all of the discovery devices provided for in the Federal Rules of Civil Procedure?

9. In American Dredging Co. v. Miller, 510 U.S. 443, 114 S.Ct. 981, 127 L.Ed.2d 285 (1994), the Court held that a Louisiana statute that precluded application of forum non conveniens only in claims for injury brought pursuant to the Jones Act, 46 U.S.C.A. § 688, was applicable despite the existence of federal forum non conveniens doctrine and an interest in uniform application of maritime law. Plaintiff, a seaman injured on the Delaware River, sued defendant, which was headquartered in New Jersey, in a Louisiana state court, for injuries under the Jones Act and general maritime law. Although the state trial court dismissed pursuant to federal forum non conveniens law, the Louisiana Supreme Court held that forum non conveniens was not available due to a Louisiana statute that requires the doctrine's application in every other type of case but forbids it in maritime injury cases.

The Supreme Court affirmed, holding that forum non conveniens is not a "characteristic feature" of admiralty or a doctrine whose application is necessary to maintain the "proper harmony" of maritime law. It concluded that the doctrine had not been unique to admiralty, although early cases invoking it were most frequently admiralty cases, and that any disuniformity would not be a matter of importance since the doctrine was basically a question of venue and therefore "a matter that goes to process rather than substantive rights." Justice Kennedy dissented, emphasizing the "undue risk" that ship owners and operators run of being sued in inconvenient venues and concluding that disuniformity on such a question could not be justified by any interest of Louisiana in view of its willingness to apply the doctrine in all other cases. He reasoned that "[t]he reverse-*Erie* metaphor, while perhaps of use in other contexts, is not a sure guide for determining when a specific state law has displaced an essential feature of the general maritime law. Procedural or substantive, the forum non conveniens defense promotes comity and trade. The States are not free to undermine those goals."

D. FEDERAL COMMON LAW

1. The Source and Legitimacy of Federal Common Law

In *Erie*, Justice Brandeis wrote that "[t]here is no federal general common law." However, the very same day, the Supreme Court held that federal common law controlled the issue of the apportionment of an interstate stream. Hinderlider v. La Plata River & Cherry Creek Ditch Co., 304 U.S. 92, 58 S.Ct. 803, 82 L.Ed. 1202 (1938).

Justice Jackson later attempted to explain the distinction between the form of federal common law rejected in *Erie* and that which continues to exist:

> The federal Courts have no *general* common law, as in a sense they have no general or comprehensive jurisprudence of any kind, because many subjects of private law are ordinarily within the province of the states and not of the federal government. But this is not to say that whenever we have occasion to decide a federal question which cannot be answered from federal statutes alone we may not resort to all of the source materials of the common law, or that when we have fashioned an answer it does not become a part of the federal non-statutory or common law.

D'Oench, Duhme & Co. v. FDIC, 315 U.S. 447, 469, 62 S.Ct. 676, 687, 86 L.Ed. 956 (1942) (Jackson, J., concurring). Is the distinction Justice Jackson draws persuasive?

Recall that the Rules of Decision Act, 28 U.S.C.A. § 1652, provides: "The laws of the several states, except where the Constitution or treaties of the United States or Acts of Congress otherwise require or provide, shall be regarded as rules of decision in civil actions in the courts of the United States, in cases where they apply." By its terms, does this Act authorize the creation of *any* federal common law, "general" or otherwise? See M. Redish, Federal Jurisdiction: Tensions in the Allocation of Judicial Power 121–25 (2d ed. 1990). Can you fashion any arguments which allow you to construe the Rules of Decision Act to authorize the creation of federal common law? Consider this view: "Far from being a limitation on the authority of the federal courts, the Rules of Decision Act is an explicit grant of authority: It directs the federal courts to apply state law with regard to any issue that is not governed by a pertinent and valid federal rule. It reminds the federal courts that if a valid federal rule exists—whether constitutional, statutory, or judge-made—the federal rule shall govern." Westen & Lehman, Is There Life for *Erie* After the Death of Diversity?, 78 Mich.L.Rev. 311, 314 (1980). Westen and Lehman find the statute's failure to mention federal common law unimportant because "the distinction between federal common law and federal statutory law is merely a difference in emphasis." Id. at 369. Compare Redish, Continuing the *Erie* Debate: A Response to Westen and Lehman, 78 Mich.L.Rev. 959, 963–64 (1980): "[W]hat possible difference does it make that the distinction between common and statutory law is one 'in emphasis' (if indeed that is an accurate characterization)? A congressional statute is *still* an 'Act of Congress,' and federal common law is still *not* an 'Act of Congress.' "

The validity of substantive federal common law is challenged in M. Redish, The Federal Courts in the Political Order: Judicial Jurisdiction and American Political Theory 30 (1991): "[J]udicial recognition of the power to create substantive federal common law * * * violates the inescapable textual command of the [Rules of Decision] Act, and effectively renders the Act a nullity, results that are wholly unacceptable under [a] separation-of-powers analysis * * *." Federal common law, in its post-*Erie* form, is defended in Rutherglen, Reconstructing *Erie:* A Comment on the Perils of Legal Positivism, 10 Const.Comm. 285 (1993). See also Weinberg, Federal Common Law, 83 Nw.U.L.Rev. 805 (1989); Brown, Federal Common Law and the Role of the Federal Courts in Private Law Adjudication—A (New) *Erie* Problem?, 12 Pace L. Rev. 229 (1992), and Merrill, The Judicial Prerogative, 12 Pace L. Rev. 327 (1992).

On this issue, consider the relevance of one of the Supreme Court's classic "federal common law" decisions, Clearfield Trust Co. v. United States, 318 U.S. 363, 63 S.Ct. 573, 87 L.Ed. 838 (1943). The case involved a stolen check that had been mailed, but was not received by its intended recipient. An unknown person presented the check to a J.C. Penney store for cashing, and endorsed it with the name of the intended recipient. J.C. Penney endorsed the check over to Clearfield Trust, which accepted it for purposes of collection. Clearfield endorsed the check with a guaranty of all prior endorsements, collected the amount of the check from the Federal Reserve and paid it to J.C. Penney. Neither Penney nor Clearfield had suspected forgery. Federal officials did not inform any of the interested parties of the forgery until eight months after they had learned that the intended recipient had not received the check.

The United States sued Clearfield on Clearfield's express guaranty of prior endorsements. The district court held that the rights of the parties were to be determined by the law of Pennsylvania. Since the United States had unreasonably delayed giving notice of the forgery, it was barred from recovery under Pennsylvania law and the district court dismissed the complaint. The Court of Appeals for the Third Circuit reversed, and the Supreme Court affirmed the reversal, rejecting the district court's conclusion that Pennsylvania law controlled:

> The rights and duties of the United States on commercial paper which it issues are governed by federal rather than local law. When the United States disburses its funds or pays its debts, it is exercising a constitutional function or power * * *. The authority to issue the check had its origin in the Constitution and the statutes of the United States and was in no way dependent on the laws of Pennsylvania or of any other state.

Having decided that federal law applied, the Court held that "[i]f it is shown that the drawee on learning of the forgery did not give prompt notice of it and that damage resulted, recovery of the drawee is barred." By contrast, under Pennsylvania law damage arising from the delay need not have been shown before recovery could be had. Since neither Clearfield nor Penney had shown any damage caused directly by the government's delay, the Court found for the government.

Does this decision provide an arguable basis for avoiding the bar of the Rules of Decision Act? Is it persuasive? Cf. Mishkin, the Variousness of "Federal Law": Competence and Discretion in the Choice of National and State Rules for Decision, 105 U.Pa.L.Rev. 797, 800 (1957): "At the very least, effective Constitutionalism requires recognition of power in the federal courts to declare, as a matter of common law or 'judicial legislation,' rules which may be necessary to fill interstitially or otherwise effectuate the statutory patterns enacted in the large by Congress." Is this persuasive? Does it successfully circumvent the problem of the Rules of Decision Act?

Contrast with *Clearfield Trust* cases in which some congressional delegation of power can be found. For example, in Textile Workers Union v. Lincoln Mills, 353 U.S. 448, 77 S.Ct. 912, 1 L.Ed.2d 972 (1957), the Supreme Court found that in suits under the Labor Management Relations Act, Congress not only created federal jurisdiction for actions to enforce collective bargaining agreements but also intended that federal courts develop rules of substantive law to decide such cases in order to achieve national uniformity:

> The Labor Management Relations Act expressly furnishes some substantive law. It points out what parties may or may not do in certain situations. Other problems will lie in the penumbra of express statutory mandates. Some will lack express statutory sanction but will be solved by looking at the policy of the legislation and fashioning a remedy that will effectuate that policy. The range of judicial inventiveness will be determined by the nature of the problem. Federal interpretation of the federal law will govern, not state law. But state law, if compatible with the purpose of [the federal act], may be resorted to in order to find the rule that will best effectuate the federal policy. Any state law applied, however, will be absorbed as federal law and will not be an independent source of private rights.

> It is not uncommon for federal courts to fashion federal law where federal rights are concerned. See Clearfield Trust Co. v. United States, 318 U.S. 363, 366–67. Congress has indicated by [the federal act] the purpose to follow that course here. There is no constitutional difficulty. Article III, § 2, extends that judicial power to cases "arising under ... the Laws of the United States...." The power of Congress to regulate these labor-management controversies under the Commerce Clause is plain.

2.   *The Common Law of Federal "Proprietary" Interests*

UNITED STATES v. KIMBELL FOODS, INC.

Supreme Court of the United States, 1979.
440 U.S. 715, 99 S.Ct. 1448, 59 L.Ed.2d 711.

JUSTICE MARSHALL delivered the opinion of the Court.

We granted certiorari in these cases to determine whether contractual liens arising from certain federal loan programs take precedence over private liens, in the absence of a federal statute setting priorities. To resolve this question, we must decide first whether federal or state law governs the controversies; and second, if federal law applies, whether this Court should fashion a uniform priority rule or incorporate state commercial law. We conclude that the source of law is federal, but that a national rule is unnecessary to protect the federal interests underlying the loan programs. Accordingly, we adopt state law as the appropriate federal rule for establishing the relative priority of these competing federal and private liens.

I

A

No. 77–1359 involves two contractual security interests in the personal property of O. K. Super Markets, Inc. Both interests were perfected pursuant to Texas' Uniform Commercial Code (UCC). The United States' lien secures a loan guaranteed by the Small Business Administration (SBA). The private lien, which arises from security agreements that preceded the federal guarantee, secures advances respondent made after the federal guarantee.

In 1968, O.K. Super Markets borrowed $27,000 from Kimbell Foods, Inc., a grocery wholesaler. Two security agreements identified the supermarket's equipment and merchandise as collateral. The agreements also contained a standard "dragnet" clause providing that this collateral would secure future advances from Kimbell to O. K. Super Markets. Kimbell properly perfected its security interests by filing financing statements with the Texas Secretary of State according to Texas law.

In February 1969, O.K. Super Markets obtained a $300,000 loan from Republic National Bank of Dallas (Republic). The bank accepted as security the same property specified in Kimbell's 1968 agreements, and filed a financing statement with the Texas Secretary of State to perfect its security interest. The SBA guaranteed 90% of this loan under the Small Business Act, which authorizes such assistance but, with one exception, does not specify priority rules to govern the SBA's security interests.

O.K. Super Markets used the Republic loan proceeds to satisfy the remainder of the 1968 obligation and to discharge an indebtedness for inventory purchased from Kimbell on open account. Kimbell continued credit sales to O.K. Super Markets until the balance due reached $18,258.57 on January 15, 1971. Thereupon, Kimbell initiated state proceedings against O.K. Super Markets to recover this inventory debt.

Shortly before Kimbell filed suit, O.K. Super Markets had defaulted on the SBA-guaranteed loan. Republic assigned its security interest to the SBA in late December 1970, and recorded the assignment with Texas authorities on January 21, 1971. The United States then honored its guarantee and paid Republic $252,331.93 (90% of the outstanding indebtedness) on February 3, 1971. That same day, O.K. Super Markets, with the approval of its creditors, sold its equipment and inventory and placed the proceeds in escrow pending resolution of the competing claims to the funds. Approximately one year later, the state court entered judgment against O.K. Super Markets, and awarded Kimbell $24,445.37, representing the inventory debt, plus interest and attorney's fees.

Kimbell thereafter brought the instant action to foreclose on its lien, claiming that its security interest in the escrow fund was superior to the SBA's. The District Court held for the Government. On determining that federal law controlled the controversy, the court applied principles developed by this Court to afford federal statutory tax liens special priority over state and private liens where the governing statute does not specify priorities. Under these rules, the lien "first in time" is "first in right." However, to be considered first in time, the nonfederal lien must be "choate," that is, sufficiently specific, when the federal lien arises. A state-created lien is not choate until the "identity of the lien or, the property subject to the lien, and the amount of the lien are established." United States v. New Britain, 347 U.S. 81, 84, 74 S.Ct. 367, 369, 98 L.Ed. 520 (1954). Failure to meet any one of these conditions forecloses priority over the federal lien, even if under state law the nonfederal lien was enforceable for all purposes when the federal lien arose.

Because Kimbell did not reduce its lien to judgment until February 1972, and the federal lien had been created either in 1969, when Republic filed its financing statement, or in 1971, when Republic recorded its assignment, the District Court concluded that respondent's lien was inchoate when the federal lien arose. Alternatively, the court held that even under state law, the SBA lien was superior to Kimbell's claim because the future advance clauses in the 1968 agreements were not intended to secure the debts arising from O.K. Super Market's subsequent inventory purchases.

The Court of Appeals reversed. It agreed that federal law governs the rights of the United States under its SBA loan program, and that the "first in time, first in right" priority principle should control the competing claims. However, the court refused to extend the choateness rule to situations in which the Federal Government was not an involuntary creditor of tax delinquents, but rather a voluntary commercial lender. Instead, it fashioned a new federal rule for determining which lien was first in time, and concluded that "in the context of competing state security interests arising under the U.C.C.," the first to meet UCC perfection requirements achieved priority.

The Court of Appeals then considered which lien qualified as first perfected. Disagreeing with the District Court, the court determined that, under Texas law, the 1968 security agreements covered Kimbell's future advances, and that the liens securing those advances dated from the filing of the security agreements before the federal lien arose. But the Court of Appeals did not adopt Texas law. Rather, it proceeded to decide whether the future advances should receive the same treatment under federal common law. After surveying three possible approaches, the court held that Kimbell's future advances dated back to the 1968 agreements, and therefore took precedence over Republic's 1969 loan.

B

At issue in No. 77–1644 is whether a federal contractual security interest in a tractor is superior to a subsequent repairman's lien in the same property.

* * *

The Court of Appeals * * * first ruled that "the rights and liabilities of the parties to a suit arising from FHA loan transactions must, under the rationale of the *Clearfield Trust* doctrine, be determined with reference to federal law." See Clearfield Trust Co. v. United States, 318 U.S. 363, 63 S.Ct. 573, 87 L.Ed. 838 (1943). In fashioning a federal rule for assessing the sufficiency of the FHA's financing statement, the court elected to follow the Model UCC rather than to incorporate Georgia law. And, it determined that the description of the collateral was adequate under the Model UCC to perfect the FHA's security interest.

The Court of Appeals then addressed the priority question and concluded that neither state law nor the first-in-time, first-in-right and choateness doctrines were appropriate to resolve the conflicting claims. In their place, the court devised a special "federal commercial law rule," using the Model UCC and the Tax Lien Act of 1966 as guides. This rule would give priority to repairman's liens over the Government's previously perfected consensual security interests when the repairman continuously possesses the property from the time his lien arises. Applying its rule, the Court of Appeals concluded that Crittenden's lien for only the final $543.81 repair bill took precedence over the FHA's security interest.

II

This Court has consistently held that federal law governs questions involving the rights of the United States arising under nationwide federal programs. * * *

Guided by these principles, we think it clear that the priority of liens stemming from federal lending programs must be determined with reference to federal law. The SBA and FHA unquestionably perform federal functions within the meaning of *Clearfield*. Since the agencies derive their authority to effectuate loan transactions from specific Acts of Congress passed in the exercise of a "constitutional function or power," Clearfield Trust Co. v. United States, supra, their rights, as well, should derive from a federal source. When Government activities "aris[e] from and bea[r] heavily upon a federal ... program," the Constitution and Acts of Congress " 'require' otherwise than that state law govern of its own force." United States v. Little Lake Misere Land Co., 412 U.S. 580, 592, 593, 93 S.Ct. 2389, 2397, 37 L.Ed.2d 187 (1973). In such contexts, federal interests are sufficiently implicated to warrant the protection of federal law.

That the statutes authorizing these federal lending programs do not specify the appropriate rule of decision in no way limits the reach of federal law. It is precisely when Congress has not spoken " 'in an area comprising issues substantially related to an established program of government operation,' " id., at 593, 93 S.Ct., at 2397, that *Clearfield* directs federal courts to fill the interstices of federal legislation "according to their own standards."

Federal law therefore controls the Government's priority rights. The more difficult task, to which we turn, is giving content to this federal rule.

III

Controversies directly affecting the operations of federal programs, although governed by federal law, do not inevitably require resort to uniform federal rules. Whether to adopt state law or to fashion a nationwide federal rule is a matter of judicial policy "dependent upon a variety of considerations always relevant to the nature of the specific governmental interests and to the effects upon them of applying state law." United States v. Standard Oil Co., 332 U.S. 301, 310, 67 S.Ct. 1604, 1609, 91 L.Ed. 2067 (1947).

Undoubtedly, federal programs that "by their nature are and must be uniform in character throughout the Nation" necessitate formulation of controlling federal rules. United States v. Yazell, 382 U.S. 341, 354, 86 S.Ct. 500, 507, 15 L.Ed.2d 404 (1966). Conversely, when there is little need for a nationally uniform body of law, state law may be incorporated as the federal rule of decision. Apart from considerations of uniformity, we must also determine whether application of state law would frustrate specific objectives of the federal programs. If so, we must fashion special rules solicitous of those federal interests. Finally, our choice-of-law inquiry must consider the extent to which application of a federal rule would disrupt commercial relationships predicated on state law.

The Government argues that effective administration of its lending programs requires uniform federal rules of priority. It contends further that resort to any rules other than first in time, first in right and choateness would conflict with protectionist fiscal policies underlying the programs. We are unpersuaded that, in the circumstances presented here, nationwide standards favoring claims of the United States are necessary to ease program administration or to safeguard the Federal Treasury from defaulting debtors. Because the state commercial codes "furnish convenient solutions in no way inconsistent with adequate protection of the federal interest[s]," United States v. Standard Oil Co., we decline to override intricate state laws of general applicability on which private creditors base their daily commercial transactions.

Incorporating state law to determine the rights of the United States as against private creditors would in no way hinder administration of the SBA and FHA loan programs. In United States v. Yazell, supra, this Court rejected the argument, similar to the Government's here, that a need for uniformity precluded application of state coverture rules to an SBA loan contract. Because SBA operations were "specifically and in great detail adapted to state law," the federal interest in supplanting "important and carefully evolved state arrangements designed to serve multiple purposes" was minimal. Our conclusion that compliance with state law would produce no hardship on the agency was also based on the SBA's practice of "individually negotiat[ing] in painfully particularized detail" each loan transaction. These observations apply with equal force here and compel us again to reject generalized pleas for uniformity as substitutes for concrete evidence that adopting state law would adversely affect administration of the federal programs.

Although the SBA Financial Assistance Manual on which this Court relied in *Yazell* is no longer "replete with admonitions to follow state law carefully," SBA employees are still instructed to, and indeed do, follow state law. * * *

Thus, the agencies' own operating practices belie their assertion that a federal rule of priority is needed to avoid the administrative burdens created by disparate state commercial rules. The programs already conform to each State's commercial standards. By using local lending offices and employees who are familiar with the law of their respective localities, the agencies function effectively without uniform procedures and legal rules.

Nevertheless, the Government maintains that requiring the agencies to assess security arrangements under local law would dictate close scrutiny of each transaction and thereby impede expeditious processing of loans. We disagree. Choosing responsible debtors necessarily requires individualized selection procedures, which the agencies have already implemented in considerable detail. Each applicant's financial condition is evaluated under rigorous standards in a lengthy process. Agency employees negotiate personally with borrowers, investigate property offered as collateral for encumbrances, and obtain local legal advice on the adequacy of proposed security arrangements. In addition, they adapt the terms of every loan to the parties' needs and capabilities. Because each application currently receives individual scrutiny, the agencies can readily adjust loan transactions to reflect state priority rules, just as they consider other factual and legal matters before disbursing Government funds. As we noted in United States v. Yazell, these lending programs are distinguishable from "nationwide act[s] of the Federal Government, emanating in a single form from a single source." Since there is no indication that variant state priority schemes would burden current methods of loan processing, we conclude that considerations of administrative convenience do not warrant adoption of a uniform federal law.

* * *

IV

Accordingly, we hold that, absent a congressional directive, the relative priority of private liens and consensual liens arising from these Government lending programs is to be determined under nondiscriminatory state laws. In No. 77–1359, the Court of Appeals found that Texas law gave preference to respondent Kimbell's lien. We therefore affirm the judgment in that case. Although the issue was contested, the Court of Appeals in No. 77–1644 did not decide whether and to what extent Georgia treats repairman's liens as superior to previously perfected consensual liens. Nor did the court assess the sufficiency of the FHA's financing statement under Georgia law. Because "[t]he federal judges who deal regularly with questions of state law in their respective districts and circuits are in a better position than we to determine how local courts would dispose of [such] issues," Butner v. United States, 440 U.S. 48, 58, 99 S.Ct. 914, 919, 59 L.Ed.2d 136, we vacate the judgment in No. 77–1644 and remand for resolution of these issues.

Notes and Questions

1. In O'Melveny & Myers v. FDIC, 512 U.S. 79, 114 S.Ct. 2048, 129 L.Ed.2d 67 (1994), the Court held that state law, rather than federal law, governs the issue of the imputation of corporate officers' knowledge of fraud to a corporation asserting a federal cause of action. "The remote possibility that corporations may go into federal receivership," the court stated, "is no conceivable basis for adopting a special federal common-law rule divesting States of authority over the entire law of imputation." Judicial lawmaking is inappropriate, the Court held, absent a "significant conflict between some federal policy or interest and the use of state law." According to one commentator, *"O'Melveny & Myers* represents a strong statement by the Supreme Court substantially restricting courts' ability to fashion federal common law." Rosenberg, The Ultimate Independence of the Federal Courts: Defying the Supreme Court in the Exercise of Federal Common Law Powers, 36 Conn. L. Rev. 425, 451 (2004). According to Professor Rosenberg, *O'Melveny & Myers'* "significant conflict" prerequisite "strengthens the Court's prior holding in *Kimbell Foods*, and reiterates the Court's preference for legislatively-created law at either the federal or the state level." Id. See also Atherton v. FDIC, 519 U.S. 213, 117 S.Ct. 666, 136 L.Ed.2d 656 (1997), holding that federal common law did not control the issue of the standard of care and directors of federally issued savings institutions, because application of state law standard of care to such institutions would not conflict with or threaten federal policies of interests.

Do *Kimbell Foods* and *O'Melveny* overrule the *Clearfield Trust* principle (described supra, p. 1007? If not, what modification, if any, do they impose?

2. In addition to what has been labeled the area of "proprietary" federal interests, involved in both *Clearfield* and *Kimbell Foods,* federal common law has been developed in the following types of cases: those in which the state is a party, those involving maritime law, and those having an impact on international relations. See Hill, The Law–Making Power of the Federal Courts: Constitutional Preemption, 67 Colum.L.Rev. 1024 (1967). For a discussion of these applications of federal common law, see M. Redish, Federal Jurisdiction: Tensions in the Allocation of Judicial Power 125–48 (2d ed. 1990); C. Wright & M. Kane, The Law of Federal Courts § 60 (6th ed. 2002). In addition, on occasion the Supreme Court has inferred private remedies from statutes or constitutional provisions which do not on their

face provide for such remedies. These exercises could be deemed a form of federal common law, and are discussed in the subsection that follows.

3. In Boyle v. United Technologies Corp., 487 U.S. 500, 108 S.Ct. 2510, 101 L.Ed.2d 442 (1988), the Court considered whether the "military contractor" defense, recognized under federal common law, applied in a diversity tort action, brought by the father of a military pilot killed in a crash, against the private company that had constructed his helicopter. In holding that such a defense could be utilized, Justice Scalia, writing for the Court, stated:

> In most fields of activity, to be sure, this Court has refused to find federal pre-emption of state law in the absence of either a clear statutory prescription, or a direct conflict between federal and state law. But we have held that a few areas, involving "uniquely federal interests," are so committed by the Constitution and laws of the United States to federal control that state law is preempted and replaced, where necessary, by federal law of a content prescribed (absent explicit statutory directive) by the courts—so-called "federal common law."

> The dispute in the present case borders upon two areas that we have found to involve such "uniquely federal interests." We have held that obligations to and rights of the United States under its contracts are governed exclusively by federal law. * * *

> Another area that we have found to be of peculiarly federal concern, warranting the displacement of state law, is the civil liability of federal officials for actions taken in the course of their duty. * * *

> We think the reasons for considering these closely related areas to be of "uniquely federal" interest apply as well to the civil liabilities arising out of the performance of federal procurement contracts. * * *

> Moreover, it is plain that the Federal Government's interest in the procurement of equipment is implicated by suits such as the present one—even though the dispute is one between private parties.

In dissent, Justice Brennan, joined by Justices Marshall and Blackmun, argued: "In my view, this Court lacks both authority and expertise to fashion [a government contractor defense]. * * * I would leave that exercise of legislative power to Congress, where our Constitution places it * * *."

In its subsequent decision in Kamen v. Kemper Financial Services, Inc., 500 U.S. 90, 111 S.Ct. 1711, 114 L.Ed.2d 152 (1991), however, the Supreme Court declined to fashion a distinct federal common law rule obliging the representative shareholder in a derivative action founded on the Investment Company Act of 1940 (ICA), 15 U.S.C.A. §§ 80a–1(a) et seq., to make a demand on the board of directors even when such a demand would be excused as futile under state law. Justice Marshall, speaking for the Court, concluded that "[b]ecause the scope of the demand requirement embodies the incorporating State's allocation of governing powers within the corporation, and because a futility exception to demand does not impede the purposes of the Investment Company Act, we decline to displace state law with a uniform rule abolishing the futility exception in federal derivative actions." He explained further:

> It is clear that the contours of the demand requirement in a derivative action founded on the ICA are governed by *federal* law.

Because the ICA is a federal statute, any common law rule necessary to effectuate a private cause of action under that statute is necessarily federal in character.

It does not follow, however, that the content of such a rule must be wholly the product of a federal court's own devising. Our cases indicate that a court should endeavor to fill the interstices of federal remedial schemes with uniform federal rules only when the scheme in question evidences a distinct need for nationwide legal standards, or when express provisions in analogous statutory schemes embody congressional policy choices readily applicable to the matter at hand, see, e.g., Boyle v. United Technologies Corp. Otherwise, we have indicated that federal courts should "incorporat[e] [state law] as the federal rule of decision," unless "application of [the particular] state law [in question] would frustrate specific objectives of the federal programs." United States v. Kimbell Foods, Inc. The presumption that state law should be incorporated into federal common law is particularly strong in areas in which private parties have entered legal relationships with the expectation that their rights and obligations would be governed by state-law standards.

Corporation law is one such area.

* * *

Because a futility exception to demand does not impede the regulatory objectives of the ICA, a court that is entertaining a derivative action under that statute must apply the demand futility exception as it is defined by the law of the State of incorporation.

Chapter XII

APPEALS

A. THE VALUE OF APPELLATE REVIEW

Before considering the avenues available to obtain appellate review, it is appropriate to examine the general values and costs involved in invoking the appellate process. Such an inquiry is necessary because the answer to this threshold question influences the way we will construe the various methods of obtaining appellate review.

The starting point is: why provide any appeal at all? Why not simply rely on the judgment and discretion of the trial judge to resolve the case? Consider the following defense of the value of appeal, made by Professor Paul Carrington:

> The judge responsible for making primary decisions must necessarily make a heavy investment of time and interest in particular disputes and individuals that come before him; his limited perspective and his limited opportunity for reflection makes it impossible for him to coordinate successfully with his colleagues. Vanity and pride of opinion are additional obstacles; even very sensitive, intelligent, and self-disciplined judges must be troubled at times by their own involvement of ego.

Carrington, Crowded Dockets and the Courts of Appeals: The Threat to the Function of Review and the National Law, 82 Harv.L.Rev. 542, 551 (1969). Because "[t]he trial judge is in a unique position of authority over the day-to-day actions of individuals," Carrington contends, "[m]egalomania is an occupational hazard of the judicial office." Review by a court remote "from the firing line of a trial" provides the objective supervision "essential to the goal of law." Id. at 550–51.

It has also been argued that "even if trial judges are capable of maintaining necessary objectivity, and their decisions are usually correct * * * preserving the appearance of justice in the eyes of the litigants who would otherwise view themselves as victims of arbitrary individuals is an equally important goal. A viable appellate process legitimizes the decisions of the lower courts, and thereby preserves faith in the functioning of the legal system." Redish, The Pragmatic Approach to Appealability in the Federal Courts, 75 Colum.L.Rev. 89, 97 (1975). See also R. Leflar, Internal Operating Procedures of Appellate Courts 9–10 (1976).

Even if one is persuaded that an appeal to an independent court serves the interests of justice and promotes confidence in the judicial system, should that right be extended to all cases? It might be argued that some cases are not serious enough to warrant the expenditure of further judicial effort and the delay in finality that is incident to an appeal. But what criteria should be used for allowing an appeal—the amount in controversy, the issues at stake, the nature of the cause of action, the kind of trial court in which the case arose? The answer varies from jurisdiction to jurisdiction, depending on standards set by the legislative body, court rule, or the applicable constitution.

In many jurisdictions, "appeal as of right" is granted only to an intermediate appellate court, with a further appeal to the highest court discretionary with that court. The United States Supreme Court has declined to find that a right to appeal is an element of due process guaranteed under the Fifth and Fourteenth Amendments. See, e.g., Griffin v. Illinois, 351 U.S. 12, 18, 76 S.Ct. 585, 590, 100 L.Ed. 891 (1956). Cf. Bankers Life and Casualty Co. v. Crenshaw, 486 U.S. 71, 108 S.Ct. 1645, 100 L.Ed.2d 62 (1988) (state statute requiring unsuccessful appellants in certain cases to pay an additional 15% of the judgment does not violate equal protection); Burlington Northern Railroad Co. v. Woods, supra p. 965. Compare Fuentes v. Shevin, supra p. 29 (regarding due process right to pre-seizure hearing in trial court). Thus in federal courts the right to appeal derives from statute or court rule. Some state constitutions, however, assure a constitutional right to appeal from state court judgments.

One commentator, who has urged a significant cutback in the scope of appeal as of right in the federal courts, questions many of the assumptions underlying the arguments in support of appellate review. Professor Dalton argues that "on several counts there is reason to question the intuitively appealing notion that the threat of reversal induces trial judges to self-correct. Some judges just don't take the threat seriously, because the ratio of reversal to total cases is so small, because they regard reversals as inevitable or arbitrary, or because they think it inappropriate to concern themselves with what might happen on appeal. For others, appellate review is a pressing concern, but their response to it may have little to do with improving case outcomes. Where the name of the game is to avoid reversal by toeing the appellate court line, victory will bring juster justice only if the appellate court has drawn the line in the right place * * *." Dalton, Taking the Right to Appeal (More or Less) Seriously, 95 Yale L.J. 62, 92 (1985). He argues further that "even if appeal of right does promote self-correction by trial judges, any consequent gain in accuracy may be more than offset by harm done to the trial court as an institution. The more we underscore the fact that trial courts are hierarchically inferior to appellate courts, the more we feed the notion that they are inferior in other ways as well." Id. at 92–93. For an argument from a "liberal" judge (presently sitting on the court of appeals) that the time has come to ration appeals, see Parker & Chapman, Accepting Reality: The Time for Adopting Discretionary Review in the Courts of Appeals Has Arrived, 50 S.M.U. L. Rev. 573 (1997).

Are these arguments persuasive? Consider the response of Professor Carrington in The Function of the Civil Appeal: A Late–Century View, 38 So.Car.L.Rev. 411, 431 (1987):

> Professor Harlan Dalton contends that the appeal of right is a disparagement of the trial judge and unlikely to make that judge more attentive to direction from higher courts. His argument rests in part on intuition and in part on the self-analysis of trial judges. My intuitions are contrary to his. * * * More important in my view, however, is the signal sent to the litigants by the recognition of the right of appeal, which does shape their perception of the fairness of the proceeding and the power or prerogative of the trial judge. We send the wrong message to a litigant when we tell him that he is dependent on the reactions of a single judge whose decisions will be reviewed by higher authority only as an act of grace. The idea of law is that the individual judge is accountable for the principled exercise of power. Discretionary accountability may look to the skeptic very much like no accountability at all.

One federal judge, expressing the belief "that federal courts of appeals are so inundated by the volume of appeals that appeals of right can no longer be given the full deliberative process to which they are entitled," has suggested "guidelines that allow a court of appeals to deny review of only those cases that are patently frivolous or those in which the district court opinion appears on its face to be correct as a matter of law or fact." Lay, A Proposal for Discretionary Review in Federal Courts of Appeals, 34 Sw. L.J. 1151, 1155 (1981). How persuasive is the caseload argument? Is it a satisfactory response to suggest that we should simply appoint more appellate judges? Should we consider abolishing the civil rights jurisdiction of the federal courts because of the resultant caseload burdens? If we accept the abstract value of the right to appeal, can the two situations be distinguished?

Judge Lay noted that "[t]he tremendous increase of federal appeals has prompted various responses. * * * The latest experiment has been the Second Circuit's Civil Appeals Mediation Plan, which fosters attempts to settle cases before the appeal process takes place." He also notes that "[t]he most universally adopted innovation has been the screening of cases either for limitation of the time for oral argument or for complete elimination of argument. Various summary techniques have been developed for deciding cases screened for no argument. Central court staffs have been enlarged to work principally on these cases. In many courts of appeals, staff memoranda, written by first-year law clerks, are utilized as the court opinion in no-argument and even some argument cases." Id. at 1153. Do these developments amount, as a practical matter, to the replacement of the statutory right of appeal with a discretionary system of review? Are summary appellate procedures more reliable than summary trial procedures?

Similar concerns about growing caseloads have prompted most federal courts of appeals to adopt the practice of deciding some cases by unpublished opinions and orders. This practice is intended for cases raising issues that are extremely fact-specific or of insufficient general interest to warrant publication. These decisions tend to be much briefer than published opinions, and some have criticized this trend as inconsistent with the responsibility of appellate courts to make reasoned decisions. One empirical study reported that such decisions were generally of lower quality than published opinions. See Reynolds & Richman, An Evaluation of Limited Publication in the United States Courts of Appeals: The Price of Reform, 48 U.Chi.L.Rev. 573, 598–604 (1981). Moreover, there is at least a risk that an informal market in such opinions may develop, enabling some litigants to acquire insight into the attitudes of the appellate court that is denied those who have access only to reported opinions. But the local rules of the courts of appeals usually provide that these decisions may not be cited as precedent, so there is no problem with access to legal authority. Nevertheless, one court held that such a nonpublication rule was unconstitutional. See Anastasoff v. United States, 223 F.3d 898 (8th Cir. 2000) (later vacated as moot). In 2003, a proposed Fed. App. R. 32.1 that would limit nonpublication rules was published for comment. See Preliminary Draft of Proposed Amendments to Federal Rules of Appellate Proedure, 217 F.R.D. 1, 31–32 (2003). This proposal sparked strong opposition among many judges, and no rule had been adopted at the time of publication of this book.

In light of all of these issues, we might ask whether the statutory right of appeal in the federal system should be formally transformed into a discretionary practice, at least in certain classes of cases. What types of cases might best lend themselves to such treatment?

At the present time, the right of appeal in the federal courts is governed primarily by 28 U.S.C.A. § 1291, which provides that "[t]he courts of appeals * * * shall have jurisdiction of all final decisions of the district courts * * *." As a textual matter, does this statute actually guarantee a right of appeal? In the federal system it is generally assumed that § 1291 does guarantee such a right. Therefore most of the doctrinal developments on the question of appellate review in the federal courts concern *when* an appeal is to be allowed, rather than *whether* it is to be allowed. As the quoted portion of § 1291 indicates, appellate federal courts generally have jurisdiction only over *final* judgments. The next section concerns the concept of finality, as well as the judge-made and statutory exceptions to it. As you address these issues, consider the extent to which delaying appeals may have the same effect as denying the right to appeal altogether.

B. THE PROBLEM OF APPEALABILITY

1. *The "Final Judgment" Rule: Judicial Expansion and Contraction*

Under section 1291 of the Judicial Code (28 U.S.C.A. § 1291), the federal courts of appeals have jurisdiction over "appeals from all final decisions" of the district courts. This limitation of appeals to final decisions reflects a long-held policy of requiring that the appeal of any issues in a case be reserved until there is a final decision in the lower court. Justice Frankfurter commented on the policy underlying the final decision rule in Cobbledick v. United States, 309 U.S. 323, 324–25, 60 S.Ct. 540, 541, 84 L.Ed. 783 (1940):

> Finality as a condition of review is an historical characteristic of federal appellate procedure. It was written into the first Judiciary Act and has been departed from only when observance of it would practically defeat the right to any review at all. Since the right to a judgment from more than one court is a matter of grace and not a necessary ingredient of justice, Congress from the very beginning has, by forbidding piecemeal disposition on appeal of what for practical purposes is a single controversy, set itself against enfeebling judicial administration.

In addition, the final judgment rule is said to "preserve[ ] the primacy of the district court as the arbiter of the proceedings before it." MDK, Inc. v. Mike's Train House, Inc., 27 F.3d 116, 119 (4th Cir.1994).

What is meant by a "final decision"? The Supreme Court has defined it as a judgment that "ends the litigation on the merits and leaves nothing for the court to do but execute the judgment." Catlin v. United States, 324 U.S. 229, 233, 65 S.Ct. 631, 633, 89 L.Ed. 911 (1945). Two such examples are the granting of a Rule 12(b)(6) motion to dismiss and the granting of a Rule 12(c) motion for judgment on the pleadings where the answer admitted all the essential allegations of the claim made in the complaint. In these situations there would be nothing further for the court to do but to execute the judgment (unless, of course, it also granted the party losing the motion the right to replead).

Some orders clearly do not satisfy the test—for example, denial of a motion for summary judgment, Forsyth v. Kleindienst, 599 F.2d 1203 (3d Cir.1979), cert. denied, 453 U.S. 913, 101 S.Ct. 3147, 69 L.Ed.2d 997 (1981); grant of a request that a party be ordered to produce materials through discovery, Alexander v. United States, 201 U.S. 117, 26 S.Ct. 356, 50 L.Ed. 686 (1906); an order disqualifying counsel, Firestone Tire & Rubber Co. v. Risjord, 449 U.S. 368, 101 S.Ct. 669, 66 L.Ed.2d 571 (1981); and an order consolidating or severing claims, Garber v. Randell, 477 F.2d 711 (2d Cir.1973).

On the other hand, in certain situations the test of finality is not so easily applied, as the following decision illustrates.

QUACKENBUSH v. ALLSTATE INSURANCE COMPANY

Supreme Court of the United States, 1996.
517 U.S. 706, 116 S.Ct. 1712, 135 L.Ed.2d 1.

JUSTICE O'CONNOR delivered the opinion of the Court.

In this case, we consider whether an abstention-based remand order is appealable as a final order under 28 U.S.C. § 1291. * * *

I

Petitioner, the Insurance Commissioner for the State of California, was appointed trustee over the assets of the Mission Insurance Company and its affiliates (Mission companies) in 1987, after those companies were ordered into liquidation by a California court. In an effort to gather the assets of the defunct Mission companies, the Commissioner filed the instant action against respondent Allstate Insurance Company in state court, seeking contract and tort damages for Allstate's alleged breach of certain reinsurance agreements, as well as a general declaration of Allstate's obligations under those agreements.

Allstate removed the action to federal court on diversity grounds and filed a motion to compel arbitration under the Federal Arbitration Act, 9 U.S.C. § 1 et seq. (1988 ed. and Supp. V). The Commissioner sought remand to state court, arguing that the District Court should abstain from hearing the case under Burford [v. Sun Oil Co., 319 U.S. 315, 63 S. Ct. 1098, 87 L.Ed. 1424 (1943)], because its resolution might interfere with California's regulation of the Mission insolvency. Specifically, the Commissioner indicated that Allstate would be asserting its right to set off its own contract claims against the Commissioner's recovery under the contract, that the viability of these setoff claims was a hotly disputed question of state law, and that this question was currently pending before the state courts in another case arising out of the Mission insolvency.

The District Court observed that "California has an overriding interest in regulating insurance insolvencies and liquidations in a uniform and orderly manner," and that in this case "this important state interest could be undermined by inconsistent rulings from the federal and state courts." Based on these observations, and its determination that the setoff question should be resolved in state court, the District Court concluded this case was an appropriate one for the exercise of Burford abstention. The District Court did not stay its hand pending the California courts' resolution of the setoff issue, but instead remanded the entire case to state court. * * *

After determining that appellate review of the District Court's remand order was not barred by 28 U.S.C. § 1447(d) and that the remand order was appealable under 28 U.S.C. § 1291 as a final collateral order, see 47 F.3d, at 353–354 (citing Moses H. Cone Memorial Hospital

v. Mercury Constr. Corp., 460 U.S. 1, 103 S.Ct. 927, 74 L.Ed.2d 765 (1983)), the Court of Appeals for the Ninth Circuit vacated the District Court's decision and ordered the case sent to arbitration. The Ninth Circuit concluded that federal courts can abstain from hearing a case under *Burford* only when the relief being sought is equitable in nature, and therefore held that abstention was inappropriate in this case because the Commissioner purported to be seeking only legal relief.

* * *

II

We first consider whether the Court of Appeals had jurisdiction to hear Allstate's appeal under 28 U.S.C. § 1291, which confers jurisdiction over appeals from "final decisions" of the district courts, and 28 U.S.C. § 1447(d), which provides that "[a]n order remanding a case to the State court from which it was removed is not reviewable on appeal or otherwise."

We agree with the Ninth Circuit and the parties that § 1447(d) interposes no bar to appellate review of the remand order at issue in this case. * * *

Finding no affirmative bar to appellate review of the District Court's remand order, we must determine whether that review may be obtained by appeal under § 1291. The general rule is that "a party is entitled to a single appeal, to be deferred until final judgment has been entered, in which claims of district court error at any stage of the litigation may be ventilated." Digital Equipment Corp. v. Desktop Direct, Inc., 511 U.S. 863, 868, 114 S.Ct. 1992, 1996, 128 L.Ed.2d 842 (1994). Accordingly, we have held that a decision is ordinarily considered final and appealable under § 1291 only if it "ends the litigation on the merits and leaves nothing for the court to do but execute the judgment." Catlin v. United States, 324 U.S. 229, 233, 65 S.Ct. 631, 633, 89 L.Ed. 911 (1945).

* * *

The application of these principles to the appealability of the remand order before us is controlled by our decision in Moses H. Cone Memorial Hospital v. Mercury Constr. Corp., supra. The District Court in that case entered an order under Colorado River Water Conservation Dist. v. United States, 424 U.S. 800, 96 S.Ct. 1236, 47 L.Ed.2d 483 (1976), staying a federal diversity suit pending the completion of a declaratory judgment action that had been filed in state court. The Court of Appeals held that this stay order was appealable under § 1291, and we affirmed that determination on two independent grounds.

We first concluded that the abstention-based stay order was appealable as a "final decision" under § 1291 because it put the litigants " 'effectively out of court.' " 460 U.S., at 11, n. 11, 103 S.Ct., at 934, n. 11 (quoting Idlewild Bon Voyage Liquor Corp. v. Epstein, 370 U.S. 713, 715, n. 2, 82 S.Ct. 1294, 1296, n. 2, 8 L.Ed.2d 794 (1962) (per curiam)), and because its effect was "precisely to surrender jurisdiction of a federal suit to a state court." These standards do not reflect our oft-repeated definition of finality, but in *Moses H. Cone* we found their application to be compelled by precedent.

* * *

The District Court's order remanding on grounds of *Burford* abstention is in all relevant respects indistinguishable from the stay order we found to be appealable in *Moses H. Cone*. No less than an order staying a federal court action pending adjudication of the dispute in state court, it puts the litigants in this case " 'effectively out of court,' " *Moses H. Cone* supra, and its effect is "precisely to surrender jurisdiction of a federal suit to a state court." Indeed, the remand order is clearly more "final" than a stay order in this sense. When a district court remands a case to a state court, the district court disassociates itself from the case entirely, retaining nothing of the matter on the federal court's docket.

* * *

[The Court alternatively relied on the "collateral order" doctrine, discussed infra pp. 1029–50]

We have previously stated that "an order remanding a removed action does not represent a final judgment reviewable by appeal." Thermtron Products, Inc. v. Hermansdorfer, 423 U.S., at 352–353, 96 S.Ct., at 594. Petitioner asks that we adhere to that statement and hold that appellate review of the District Court's remand order can only be obtained through a petition for writ of mandamus. To the extent *Thermtron* would require us to ignore the implications of our later holding in *Moses H. Cone*, however, we disavow it.

* * *

Admittedly, remand orders like the one entered in this case do not meet the traditional definition of finality—they do not "en[d] the litigation on the merits and leav[e] nothing for the court to do but execute the judgment," *Catlin*, 324 U.S., at 233, 65 S.Ct., at 633. But because the District Court's remand order is functionally indistinguishable from the stay order we found appealable in *Moses H. Cone*, we conclude that it is appealable. * * *

[The Court held that abstention was appropriate. The concurring opinions of Justices Scalia and Kennedy are omitted.]

Notes and Questions

1. Though the order in *Quackenbush* was not a technically final order, the Supreme Court authorized appeal from the district court to the court of appeals under § 1291, in part because pursuant to that order the litigants are "effectively out of court." For a discussion of the concept of practical, as opposed to technical, finality, see Redish, The Pragmatic Approach to Appealability in the Federal Courts, 75 Colum. L. Rev. 89 (1975).

2. In *Quackenbush*, the Court relies on Moses H. Cone Memorial Hospital v. Mercury Construction Corporation, 460 U.S. 1, 103 S.Ct. 927, 74

L.Ed.2d 765 (1983). There a hospital and a contractor had entered into a contract for the construction of additions to the hospital. The contract included provisions for binding arbitration of certain claims. After a dispute arose, the hospital filed an action in state court, seeking declarations that the contractor had lost the right to arbitration and that the hospital was not liable to the contractor. It also sought a stay of arbitration. The contractor filed suit in federal court, seeking an order compelling arbitration under § 4 of the Federal Arbitration Act. On the hospital's motion, the federal court stayed the contractor's suit, pending resolution of the hospital's state court suit, under the doctrine of Colorado River Water Conservation Dist. v. United States, 424 U.S. 800, 96 S.Ct. 1236, 47 L.Ed.2d 483 (1976) (stay of federal suit in deference to parallel litigation pending in state court is appropriate under exceptional circumstances in the interests of "wise judicial administration"). The Court of Appeals, after finding that it had jurisdiction under § 1291 to review the stay, reversed the stay and remanded the case.

A majority of the Supreme Court, in an opinion by Justice Brennan, found the stay order appealable under § 1291:

> [T]he District Court predicated its stay order on its conclusion that the federal and state actions involved "the identical issue of arbitrability of the claims * * *." That issue of arbitrability was the only substantive issue present in the federal suit. Hence, stay of the federal suit pending resolution of the state suit meant that there would be no further litigation in the federal forum; the state court's judgment on the issue would be res judicata. Thus, * * * Mercury [Construction Corp.] was "effectively out of court." Hence, as the Court of Appeals held, this stay order amounts to a dismissal of the suit.

Obviously, a stay is in no sense a technically final order, a fact acknowledged by the Court. But this fact alone did not prevent the stay order from being deemed "final" for purposes of § 1291; the test was whether the losing party was *effectively* out of court" (emphasis added).

Compare United States v. Jose, 519 U.S. 54, 117 S.Ct. 463, 136 L.Ed.2d 364 (1996), in which the Court held that a district court order enforcing an IRS summons but requiring the IRS to provide five days' notice before transferring information thus obtained to any IRS office other than the one that seized the material was immediately appealable. The IRS had appealed, claiming that the notice proviso was beyond the district court's authority, but the court of appeals dismissed the appeal on the ground that there was nothing in the record indicating that the IRS actually intended any such revelation. Without addressing the underlying arguments made by the IRS, the Court rejected the appealability conclusion per curiam:

> We think it clear, however, that the District Court's final order is indeed final. It is a decision dispositively granting in part and denying in part the remedy requested. The IRS prevailed to the extent that the District Court enforced the summonses. The Service did not prevail to the extent that the District Court imposed a condition—an unqualified requirement that the IRS provide five days' notice to the trustee before transferring summoned information from its Examination Division to

any other IRS office. With that disposition, the District Court completed its adjudication.

3. One area in which some believed that the concept of practical finality authorized appeal under § 1291 was the so-called "death knell" cases, in which a district court had denied certification of a class action brought by an individual plaintiff possessing a relatively minimal personal claim. The order denying certification in no way ended the plaintiff's individual personal suit. However, it was argued that when the individual claim was so small that, as a practical matter, the suit would not proceed, the denial of certification should be deemed the "death knell" of the action and therefore appealable under the practical finality doctrine.

The "death knell" doctrine was first employed in Eisen v. Carlisle & Jacquelin, 370 F.2d 119 (2d Cir.1966), cert. denied, 386 U.S. 1035, 87 S.Ct. 1487, 18 L.Ed.2d 598 (1967) (*"Eisen* I"), which allowed an appeal from an order of the district court dismissing a class action, but permitting plaintiff to litigate his individual claims. Because plaintiff's individual claims amounted to $70, the court reasoned that "[t]he alternatives are to appeal now or to end the lawsuit for all practical purposes * * * [for] [w]e can safely assume that no lawyer of competence is going to undertake this complex and costly case to recover $70 for Mr. Eisen." The court therefore concluded that "[i]f the appeal is dismissed, not only will Eisen's claim never be adjudicated, but no appellate court will be given the chance to decide if this class action was proper * * *." The court stated the governing rule: "Where the effect of a district court's order, if not reviewed, is the death knell of the action, review should be allowed."

In Coopers & Lybrand v. Livesay, 437 U.S. 463, 98 S.Ct. 2454, 57 L.Ed.2d 351 (1978), the Supreme Court rejected the death knell doctrine: "A threshold inquiry of this kind may, it is true, identify some orders that would truly end the litigation prior to final judgment; allowing an immediate appeal from those orders may enhance the quality of justice afforded a few litigants. But this incremental benefit is outweighed by the impact of such an individualized jurisdictional inquiry on the judicial system's overall capacity to administer justice."

In 1998 the Supreme Court amended Rule 23 by adding subdivision (f), which authorizes immediate appeal of the district court's ruling on class certification, at the discretion of the court of appeals. For a discussion of the case law applying Rule 23(f), see Waters, Common Law Courts In an Age of Equity Procedure: Redefining Appellate Review for the Mass Tort Era, 80 N.C.L. Rev. 527 (2002); Solimine & Hines, Deciding to Decide: Class Action Certification and Interlocutory Review by the United States Court of Appeals Under Rule 23(f), 41 Will. & Mary L. Rev. 1531 (2000).

4. Consider the relevance to the pragmatic finality inquiry of the Supreme Court's decision in Gillespie v. United States Steel Corp., 379 U.S. 148, 85 S.Ct. 308, 13 L.Ed.2d 199 (1964). There the plaintiff, mother of a seaman who drowned while working on defendant's ship, sued in federal court pursuant to the Jones Act, 46 U.S.C.A. § 688 (a federal statute authorizing negligence actions by seamen) and the Ohio Wrongful Death Statute, the latter on behalf of the decedent's brother and sisters, as well as herself. The district court held the Jones Act to be plaintiff's exclusive

remedy, and struck all references to Ohio law. On appeal, the Sixth Circuit conceded that the order appeared not to be final, but nevertheless reasoned that "[t]he unnecessary expense in time and money, the duplication of effort, the frustration of being required to award the verdict * * * and the piecemeal litigation compelled in the trial court, all as a result of appellate inaction now, are self-evident * * *." The court therefore proceeded to decide the merits of the appeal.

The Supreme Court, in an opinion by Justice Black, affirmed:

> [O]ur cases long have recognized that whether a ruling is "final" within the meaning of § 1291 is frequently so close a question that decision of that issue either way can be supported with equally forceful arguments and that it is impossible to devise a formula to resolve all marginal cases coming within what might be called the "twilight zone" of finality. Because of this difficulty this Court has held that the requirement of finality is to be given a "practical rather than a technical construction." Cohen v. Beneficial Industrial Loan Corp., 337 U.S., at 546. Dickinson v. Petroleum Conversion Corp., 338 U.S. 507, 511, pointed out that in deciding the question of finality the most important competing considerations are "the inconvenience and costs of piecemeal review on the one hand and the danger of denying justice by delay on the other." Such competing considerations are shown by the record in the case before us. * * * [I]t seems clear now that the case is before us that the eventual costs * * * will certainly be less if we now pass on the questions presented here rather than send the case back with those issues undecided. Moreover, delay of perhaps a number of years in hearing the brother's and sisters' rights determined might work a great injustice on them, since the claims for recovery for their benefit have been effectively cut off so long as the District Judge's ruling stands.

Justice Harlan, dissenting, argued that "the decision of the District Court * * * lacked the essential quality of finality; it involved but interstitial rulings in an action not yet tried."

Is Justice Black's decision an *interpretation* of the finality requirement of 28 U.S.C.A. § 1291, or is it an *exception* to it? If the latter, is it appropriate, as an institutional matter, for the Court to establish such an exception to a congressional directive? Cf. Swint v. Chambers County Comm'n, 514 U.S. 35, 115 S.Ct. 1203, 131 L.Ed.2d 60 (1995) (pendent appellate jurisdiction not permitted, despite economies it would produce, because such a practice "drift[s] away from the statutory instructions Congress has given to control the timing of appellate proceedings"). The broad language in *Gillespie,* suggesting an *ad hoc* cost-benefit approach to finality, has been criticized. See C. Wright & M. Kane, Law of Federal Courts 752 (6th ed. 2002). Couldn't the Court's argument that "the eventual costs * * * will certainly be less if we now pass on the questions presented here" be made in every case in which the intermediate appellate court allowed an interlocutory appeal? Wholly apart from institutional considerations, how advisable is the use of a pragmatic balancing approach to determine appealability?

Despite *Coopers & Lybrand,* the standard employed in *Gillespie* is still occasionally employed to authorize an appeal. See, e.g., American Export

Lines, Inc. v. Alvez, 446 U.S. 274, 279 & n. 7, 100 S.Ct. 1673, 1675–76 & n. 7, 64 L.Ed.2d 284 (1980); Boughton v. Cotter Corp., 10 F.3d 746, 751–52 (10th Cir.1993); Bender v. Clark, 744 F.2d 1424 (10th Cir.1984). But see Stubblefield v. Windsor Capital Group, 74 F.3d 990, 996 (10th Cir. 1996) ("It is unclear whether the *Gillepsie* doctrine is still viable.") The courts using it have stressed that the doctrine is a limited one, to be invoked only in truly "unique instances" in order to preserve the vitality of § 1291. Boughton v. Cotter Corp., 10 F.3d at 752. See also Utah v. Kennecott Corp., 14 F.3d 1489, 1496 (10th Cir.1994) (appeal from denial of approval of proposed settlement consent decree does not fall within "practical finality" doctrine, because "[t]he case at hand is neither unique nor exceptional"); Quinn v. CGR, 828 F.2d 1463, 1467 (10th Cir.1987) ("practical finality" doctrine to be applied only in the "most exceptional circumstances").

5.   The Third Circuit has held that "considerations unique to bankruptcy appeals have led us consistently in those cases to construe finality in a more pragmatic, functional sense than with the typical appeal." In re Professional Insurance Management, 285 F.3d 268, 279 (3d Cir. 2002). This is "because these proceedings often are protracted and involve numerous parties with different claims. To delay resolution of discrete claims until after final approval of a reorganization plan, for example, would waste time and resources, particularly if the appeal resulted in reversal of a bankruptcy court order necessitating re-appraisal of the entire plan." In re White Beauty View, Inc., 841 F.2d 524, 526 (3d Cir. 1988). Does this analysis represent proper application of the pragmatic finality concept?

6.   When an order contemplates some further action, as in determining the nature of injunctive relief, finality is more difficult to determine. In Brown Shoe Co. v. United States, 370 U.S. 294, 82 S.Ct. 1502, 8 L.Ed.2d 510 (1962), the district court ordered the parties to submit a detailed plan for divestiture in a suit challenging a merger under the antitrust laws. The Court found the order final because the divestiture disposed of all issues in the complaint, and the fact that the detailed plan involved further negotiation in light of market conditions did not prevent its appealability. Similarly, in Budinich v. Becton Dickinson & Co., 486 U.S. 196, 108 S.Ct. 1717, 100 L.Ed.2d 178 (1988), the Court held that a district court order was final for purposes of § 1291, even though the recoverability or amount of attorney's fees for the litigation remained to be determined. See also Forgay v. Conrad, 47 U.S. (6 How.) 201, 12 L.Ed. 404 (1848), where Chief Justice Taney held that a judgment directing immediate delivery of physical property to the opposing party is appealable, even though the lower court had also ordered an accounting that had not yet taken place. Key to the decision in *Forgay* and cases that have followed it was "the fact that there had been a conclusive adjudication of the rights and liabilities of the parties with immediate delivery of possession of the subject matter of the suit." Radio Station WOW, Inc. v. Johnson, 326 U.S. 120, 125 n. 2, 65 S.Ct. 1475, 1478 n. 2, 89 L.Ed. 569 (1945).

Where damages are sought, a similar situation can arise. Thus an order, such as a summary judgment or a default judgment, may be entered in plaintiff's favor on liability, but the issue of damages will still have to be determined by trial. Such an order is not final until an order as to damages has been entered. Guarantee Co. of North America v. Mechanics' Sav. Bank & Trust Co., 173 U.S. 582, 19 S.Ct. 551, 43 L.Ed. 818 (1899).

2. Exceptions to the Final Judgment Rule

It is important to note that the final judgment rule of § 1291 by no means exhausts the conceivable sources of appellate review. There exist several statutory and judge-made exceptions to the final judgment rule, and those will be examined in the following sections.

In 1990, Congress amended the Rules Enabling Act to provide that the rules "shall define when a ruling of a district court is final for the purposes of appeal under section 1291 of this title." 28 U.S.C. § 2072(c). In 1992, Congress enacted a statute giving the Supreme Court power to prescribe rules to provide for an appeal for an interlocutory decision not already provided for in existing provisions. 28 U.S.C. § 1292(e). Exercising this power, the Supreme Court in 1998 adopted Rule 23(f) authorizing discretionary appeal of class certification decisions.   23(F)

a. The "Collateral Order" Doctrine

COHEN v. BENEFICIAL INDUSTRIAL LOAN CORPORATION, 337 U.S. 541, 69 S.Ct. 1221, 93 L.Ed. 1528 (1949):

JUSTICE JACKSON delivered the opinion of the Court.

[Petitioner's decedent was one of Beneficial's 16,000 shareholders, owning 100 shares which were worth less than $9,000. In 1943 he filed a derivative action in U.S. District Court in New Jersey against the corporation and certain of its managers and directors, claiming that they had violated their duties to the corporation by enriching themselves at the corporation's expense. In 1945 New Jersey enacted a statute that made derivative-action plaintiffs owning less than a specified percentage of the corporation's stock liable for defendants' costs, including attorneys' fees, if defendants won the suit. The new statute also required such plaintiffs to post a bond to cover these costs as a condition for proceeding with a derivative action, and was explicitly made applicable to pending actions. Beneficial moved to require petitioner to post a $125,000 bond, but the district court held that the state law did not apply to suits in federal court. Eventually the Supreme Court held that the security-for-expenses requirement did apply in federal court, see supra p. 937, but first it had to deal with objections to appealability.]

At the threshold we are met with the question whether the District Court's order refusing to apply the statute was an appealable one. Title 28 U.S.C. § 1291, provides, as did its predecessors, for appeal only "from all final decisions of the district courts," except when direct appeal to this Court is provided. Section 1292 allows appeals also from certain interlocutory orders, decrees and judgments, not material to this case except as they indicate the purpose to allow appeals from orders other than final judgments when they have a final and irreparable effect on the rights of the parties. It is obvious that, if Congress had allowed

If owns 100 shares sue Δ breached fiduciary duty

Statute

π - $125 bond

Fed District

state law does not apply to suits in federal court

Δ Issue

1291 final

Issue

appeals only from those final judgments which terminate an action, this order would not be appealable.

The effect of the statute is to disallow appeal from any decision which is tentative, informal or incomplete. Appeal gives the upper court a power of review, not one of intervention. So long as the matter remains open, unfinished or inconclusive, there may be no intrusion by appeal. But the District Court's action upon this application was concluded and closed and its decision final in that sense before the appeal was taken.

Nor does the statute permit appeals, even from fully consummated decisions, where they are but steps towards final judgment in which they will merge. The purpose is to combine in one review all stages of the proceeding that effectively may be reviewed and corrected if and when final judgment results. But this order of the District Court did not make any step toward final disposition of the merits of the case and will not be merged in final judgment. When that time comes, it will be too late effectively to review the present order and the rights conferred by the statute, if it is applicable, will have been lost, probably irreparably. We conclude that the matters embraced in the decision appealed from are not of such an interlocutory nature as to affect, or to be affected by, decision of the merits of this case.

This decision appears to fall in that small class which finally determine claims of right separable from, and collateral to, rights asserted in the action, too important to be denied review and too independent of the cause itself to require that appellate consideration be deferred until the whole case is adjudicated. The Court has long given this provision of the statute this practical rather than a technical construction.

We hold this order appealable because it is a final disposition of a claimed right which is not an ingredient of the cause of action and does not require consideration with it. But we do not mean that every order fixing security is subject to appeal. Here it is the right to security that presents a serious and unsettled question. If the right were admitted or clear and the order involved only an exercise of discretion as to the amount of security, a matter the statute makes subject to reconsideration from time to time, appealability would present a different question.

DIGITAL EQUIPMENT CORPORATION
v. DESKTOP DIRECT, INC.

Supreme Court of the United States, 1994.
511 U.S. 863, 114 S.Ct. 1992, 128 L.Ed.2d 842.

JUSTICE SOUTER delivered the opinion of the Court.

Section 1291 of the Judicial Code confines appeals as of right to those from "final decisions of the district courts." 28 U.S.C. § 1291. This case raises the question whether an order vacating a dismissal predicated on the parties' settlement agreement is final as a collateral order even without a district court's resolution of the underlying cause of action.

See Cohen v. Beneficial Loan Corp., 337 U.S. 541, 546, 69 S.Ct. 1221, 1225–1226, 93 L.Ed. 1528 (1949). We hold that an order denying effect to a settlement agreement does not come within the narrow ambit of collateral orders.

I

Respondent, Desktop Direct, Inc. (Desktop) sells computers and like equipment under the trade name "Desktop Direct." Petitioner, Digital Equipment Corporation is engaged in a similar business and in late 1991 began using that trade name to market a new service it called "Desktop Direct from Digital." In response, Desktop filed this action in the United States District Court for the District of Utah, charging Digital with unlawful use of the Desktop Direct name. Desktop sent Digital a copy of the complaint, and negotiations between officers of the two corporations ensued. Under a confidential settlement reached on March 25, 1992, Digital agreed to pay Desktop a sum of money for the right to use the "Desktop Direct" trade name and corresponding trademark, and for waiver of all damages and dismissal of the suit. That same day, Desktop filed a notice of dismissal in the District Court.

Several months later, Desktop moved to vacate the dismissal and rescind the settlement agreement, alleging misrepresentation of material facts during settlement negotiations. The District Court granted the motion, concluding "that a fact finder could determine that [Digital] failed to disclose material facts to [Desktop] during settlement negotiations which would have resulted in rejection of the settlement offer." After the District Court declined to reconsider that ruling or stay its order vacating dismissal, Digital appealed. The Court of Appeals for the Tenth Circuit dismissed the appeal for lack of jurisdiction, holding that the District Court order was not appealable under § 1291, because it neither "end[ed] the litigation on the merits" nor "[fell] within the long-recognized 'collateral order' exception to the final judgment requirement." Applying the three-pronged test for determining when "collateral order" appeal is allowed, see *Cohen*, supra; Coopers & Lybrand v. Livesay, 437 U.S. 463, 98 S.Ct. 2454, 57 L.Ed.2d 351 (1978), the Court of Appeals concluded that any benefits claimed under the settlement agreement were insufficiently "important" to warrant the immediate appeal as of right. Although Digital claimed what it styled a "right not to go to trial," the court reasoned that any such privately negotiated right as Digital sought to vindicate was different in kind from an immunity rooted in an explicit constitutional or statutory provision or "compelling public policy rationale," the denial of which has been held to be immediately appealable. 993 F.2d at 758–760.

The Tenth Circuit recognized that it was thus deviating from the rule followed in some other Courts of Appeals * * *. We granted certiorari, to resolve this conflict and now affirm.

II

A

The collateral order doctrine is best understood not as an exception to the "final decision" rule laid down by Congress in § 1291, but as a "practical construction" of it, *Cohen*, supra, 337 U.S., at 546, 69 S.Ct., at 1225–1226; see, e.g., *Coopers & Lybrand*, supra, 437 U.S., at 468, 98 S.Ct., at 2457–2458. We have repeatedly held that the statute entitles a party to appeal not only from a district court decision that "ends the litigation on the merits and leaves nothing more for the court to do but execute the judgment," Catlin v. United States, 324 U.S. 229, 233, 65 S.Ct. 631, 633, 89 L.Ed. 911 (1945), but also from a narrow class of decisions that do not terminate the litigation, but must, in the interest of "achieving a healthy legal system," cf. Cobbledick v. United States, 309 U.S. 323, 326, 60 S.Ct. 540, 541, 84 L.Ed. 783 (1940), nonetheless be treated as "final." The latter category comprises only those district court decisions that are conclusive, that resolve important questions completely separate from the merits, and that would render such important questions effectively unreviewable on appeal from final judgment in the underlying action. See generally *Coopers & Lybrand*, supra. Immediate appeals from such orders, we have explained, do not go against the grain of § 1291, with its object of efficient administration of justice in the federal courts, see generally Richardson–Merrell, Inc. v. Koller, 472 U.S. 424, 105 S.Ct. 2757, 86 L.Ed.2d 340 (1985).

But we have also repeatedly stressed that the "narrow" exception should stay that way and never be allowed to swallow the general rule, that a party is entitled to a single appeal, to be deferred until final judgment has been entered, in which claims of district court error at any stage of the litigation may be ventilated, see United States v. Hollywood Motor Car Co., 458 U.S. 263, 270, 102 S.Ct. 3081, 3085, 73 L.Ed.2d 754 (1982). We have accordingly described the conditions for collateral order appeal as stringent, see, e.g., Midland Asphalt Corp. v. United States, 489 U.S. 794, 799, 109 S.Ct. 1494, 1498, 103 L.Ed.2d 879 (1989), and have warned that the issue of appealability under § 1291 is to be determined for the entire category to which a claim belongs, without regard to the chance that the litigation at hand might be speeded, or a "particular injustic[e]" averted, Van Cauwenberghe v. Biard, 486 U.S. 517, 529, 108 S.Ct. 1945, 1953, 100 L.Ed.2d 517 (1988), by a prompt appellate court decision. See also *Richardson-Merrell*, supra, 472 U.S., at 439, 105 S.Ct., at 2764 (this Court "has expressly rejected efforts to reduce the finality requirement of § 1291 to a case-by-case [appealability] determination"); Carroll v. United States, 354 U.S. 394, 405, 77 S.Ct. 1332, 1339, 1 L.Ed.2d 1442 (1957).

B

Here, the Court of Appeals accepted Digital's claim that the order vacating dismissal (and so rescinding the settlement agreement) was the "final word on the subject addressed," and held the second *Cohen* condition, separability, to be satisfied, as well. Neither conclusion is beyond question, but each is best left untouched here, both because Desktop has made no serious effort to defend the Court of Appeals judgment on those points and because the failure to meet the third condition of the *Cohen* test, that the decision on an "important" question be "effectively unreviewable" upon final judgment, would in itself suffice to foreclose immediate appeal under § 1291. Turning to these dispositive factors, we conclude, despite Digital's position that it holds a "right not to stand trial" requiring protection by way of immediate appeal, that rights under private settlement agreements can be adequately vindicated on appeal from final judgement.

C

The roots of Digital's argument that the settlement with Desktop gave it a "right not to stand trial altogether" (and that such a right per se satisfies the third *Cohen* requirement) are readily traced to Abney v. United States, 431 U.S. 651, 97 S.Ct. 2034, 52 L.Ed.2d 651 (1977), where we held that § 1291 entitles a criminal defendant to appeal an adverse ruling on a double jeopardy claim, without waiting for the conclusion of his trial. After holding the second *Cohen* requirement satisfied by the distinction between the former jeopardy claim and the question of guilt to be resolved at trial, we emphasized that the Fifth Amendment not only secures the right to be free from multiple punishments, but by its very terms embodies the broader principle, " 'deeply ingrained . . . in the Anglo–American system of jurisprudence,' " that it is intolerable for " 'the State, with all its resources . . . [to] make repeated attempts to convict an individual [defendant], thereby subjecting him to embarrassment, expense and ordeal and compelling him to live in a continuing state of anxiety and insecurity.' " 431 U.S., at 661–662, 97 S.Ct., at 2041. We found that immediate appeal was the only way to give "full protection" to this constitutional right "not to face trial at all."

Abney's rationale was applied in Nixon v. Fitzgerald, 457 U.S. 731, 742, 102 S.Ct. 2690, 2697, 73 L.Ed.2d 349 (1982), where we held to be similarly appealable an order denying the petitioner absolute immunity from suit for civil damages arising from actions taken while petitioner was President of the United States. Seeing this immunity as a "functionally mandated incident of the President's unique office, rooted in the . . . separation of powers and supported by our history," we stressed that it served "compelling public ends," and would be irretrievably lost if the former President were not allowed an immediate appeal to vindicate this right to be free from the rigors of trial. Next, in Mitchell v. Forsyth, 472 U.S. 511, 105 S.Ct. 2806, 86 L.Ed.2d 411 (1985), we held that similar considerations supported appeal under § 1291 from decisions denying government officials qualified immunity from damages suits. An "essential attribute," of this freedom from suit for past conduct not violative of clearly established law, we explained, is the "entitlement not to stand trial or face the other burdens of litigation," one which would be "effectively lost if a case [were] erroneously permitted to go to trial."

Echoing the reasoning of Nixon v. Fitzgerald, supra (and Harlow v. Fitzgerald, 457 U.S. 800, 102 S.Ct. 2727, 73 L.Ed.2d 396 (1982)), we explained that requiring an official with a colorable immunity claim to defend a suit for damages would be "peculiarly disruptive of effective government," and would work the very "distraction ... from ... dut[y], inhibition of discretionary action, and deterrence of able people from public service" that qualified immunity was meant to avoid. See also Puerto Rico Aqueduct & Sewer Authority v. Metcalf & Eddy, Inc., 506 U.S. 139, 113 S.Ct. 684, 121 L.Ed.2d 605 (1993) (State's Eleventh Amendment immunity from suit in federal court may be vindicated by immediate appeal under § 1291).

D

Digital puts this case on all fours with *Mitchell*. It maintains that it obtained dual rights under the settlement agreement with Desktop, not only a broad defense to liability but the "right not to stand trial," the latter being just like the qualified immunity held immediately appealable in *Mitchell*. As in *Mitchell*, that right must be enforceable on collateral order appeal, Digital asserts, or an adverse trial ruling will destroy it forever.

While Digital's argument may exert some pull on a narrow analysis, it does not hold up under the broad scrutiny to which all claims of immediate appealability under § 1291 must be subjected. To be sure, *Abney* and *Mitchell* are fairly cited for the proposition that orders denying certain immunities are strong candidates for prompt appeal under § 1291. But Digital's larger contention, that a party's ability to characterize a district court's decision as denying an irreparable "right not to stand trial" altogether is sufficient as well as necessary for a collateral order appeal, is neither an accurate distillation of our case law nor an appealing prospect for adding to it. Even as they have recognized the need for immediate appeals under § 1291 to vindicate rights that would be "irretrievably lost," *Richardson–Merrell*, if review were confined to final judgments only, our cases have been at least as emphatic in recognizing that the jurisdiction of the courts of appeals should not, and cannot, depend on a party's agility in so characterizing the right asserted. This must be so because the strong bias of § 1291 against piecemeal appeals almost never operates without some cost. A fully litigated case can no more be untried than the law's proverbial bell can be unrung, and almost every pretrial or trial order might be called "effectively unreviewable" in the sense that relief from error can never extend to rewriting history. Thus, erroneous evidentiary rulings, grants or denials of attorney disqualification, see, e.g., *Richardson–Merrell*, supra, and restrictions on the rights of intervening parties, see Stringfellow v. Concerned Neighbors in Action, 480 U.S. 370, 107 S.Ct. 1177, 94 L.Ed.2d 389 (1987), may burden litigants in ways that are only imperfectly reparable by appellate reversal of a final district court judgment, cf. Carroll, 354 U.S., at 406, 77 S.Ct., at 1339–1340; Parr v. United States, 351 U.S. 513, 519–520, 76 S.Ct. 912, 916–917, 100 L.Ed. 1377 (1956);

and other errors, real enough, will not seem serious enough to warrant reversal at all, when reviewed after a long trial on the merits, see *Stringfellow*, supra. In still other cases, see Coopers & Lybrand v. Livesay, 437 U.S. 463, 98 S.Ct. 2454, 57 L.Ed.2d 351 (1978), an erroneous district court decision will, as a practical matter, sound the "death knell" for many plaintiffs' claims that might have gone forward if prompt error correction had been an option. But if immediate appellate review were available every such time, Congress's final decision rule would end up a pretty puny one, and so the mere identification of some interest that would be "irretrievably lost" has never sufficed to meet the third *Cohen* requirement. See generally Lauro Lines, s.r.l. v. Chasser, 490 U.S. 495, 499, 109 S.Ct. 1976, 1978, 104 L.Ed.2d 548 (1989) ("It is always true, however, that 'there is value ... in triumphing before trial, rather than after it'") (quoting United States v. MacDonald, 435 U.S. 850, 860, n. 7, 98 S.Ct. 1547, 1553, n. 7, 56 L.Ed.2d 18 (1978)).

Nor does limiting the focus to whether the interest asserted may be called a "right not to stand trial" offer much protection against the urge to push the § 1291 limits. We have, after all, acknowledged that virtually every right that could be enforced appropriately by pretrial dismissal might loosely be described as conferring a "right not to stand trial," see, e.g., Midland Asphalt, 489 U.S., at 501, 109 S.Ct., at 1269; Van Cauwenberghe v. Biard, 486 U.S. 517, 524, 108 S.Ct. 1945, 1950–1951, 100 L.Ed.2d 517 (1988). Allowing immediate appeals to vindicate every such right would move § 1291 aside for claims that the district court lacks personal jurisdiction, see *Van Cauwenberghe*, that the statute of limitations has run, that the movant has been denied his Sixth Amendment right to speedy trial, see *MacDonald*, supra, that an action is barred on claim preclusion principles, that no material fact is in dispute and the moving party is entitled to judgment as a matter of law, or merely that the complaint fails to state a claim. Such motions can be made in virtually every case, see generally *MacDonald*, supra, 435 U.S., at 862, 98 S.Ct., at 1553–1554; United States v. Hollywood Motor Car Co., 458 U.S., at 270, 102 S.Ct. at 3085 and it would be no consolation that a party's meritless summary judgment motion or res judicata claim was rejected on immediate appeal; the damage to the efficient and congressionally mandated allocation of judicial responsibility would be done, and any improper purpose the appellant might have had in saddling its opponent with cost and delay would be accomplished. Cf. *Richardson–Merrell*, 472 U.S., at 434, 105 S.Ct., at 2762–2763 (appeals from "entirely proper" decisions impose the same costs as do appeals from "injudicious" ones). Thus, precisely because candor forces us to acknowledge that there is no single, "obviously correct way to characterize" an asserted right, *Lauro Lines*, 490 U.S., at 500, 109 S.Ct., at 1979, we have held that § 1291 requires courts of appeals to view claims of a "right not to be tried" with skepticism, if not a jaundiced eye.

In *Midland Asphalt*, for example, we had no trouble in dispatching a defendant's claim of entitlement to an immediate appeal from an order denying dismissal for alleged violation of Federal Rule of Criminal

Procedure 6(e), forbidding disclosure of secret grand jury information. Noting " 'a crucial distinction between a right not to be tried and a right whose remedy requires the dismissal of charges,' " we observed that Rule 6(e) "contains no hint," of an immunity from trial, and we contrasted that Rule with the Fifth Amendment's express provision that "[n]o person shall to held to answer" for a serious crime absent grand jury indictment. Only such an "explicit statutory or constitutional guarantee that trial will not occur," we suggested, could be grounds for an immediate appeal of right under § 1291.

The characterization issue surfaced again (and more ominously for Digital, see infra) in Lauro Lines s.r.l. v. Chasser, supra, where a defendant sought to appeal under § 1291 from an order denying effect to a contractual provision that a Neapolitan court would be the forum for trying all disputes arising from the parties' cruise-ship agreement. While we realized of course that the value of the forum-selection clause would be diminished if the defendant could be tried before appealing, we saw the contractual right to limit trial to an Italian forum as "different in kind" from the entitlement to "avoid suit altogether" that Abney, and Mitchell held could be "adequately vindica[ted]" only on immediate appeal.

E

As Digital reads the cases, the only things standing in the way of an appeal to perfect its claimed rights under the settlement agreement are the lone statement in Midland Asphalt, to the effect that only explicit statutory and constitutional immunities may be appealed immediately under § 1291, and language (said to be stray) repeated in many of our collateral order decisions, suggesting that the "importance" of the right asserted is an independent condition of appealability. The first, Digital explains, cannot be reconciled with Mitchell's holding, that denial of qualified immunity (which we would be hard-pressed to call "explicitly ... guarantee[d]" by a particular constitutional or statutory provision) is a collateral order under § 1291; as between Mitchell and the Midland Asphalt dictum, Digital says, the dictum must give way. As for the second obstacle, Digital adamantly maintains that "importance" has no place in a doctrine justified as supplying a gloss on Congress's "final decision" language.

1

These arguments miss the mark. First, even if Mitchell could not be squared fully with the literal words of the Midland Asphalt sentence (but cf. Lauro Lines, 490 U.S., at 499, 109 S.Ct., at 1978–1979, noting that Midland Asphalt was a criminal case and Mitchell was not), that would be only because the qualified immunity right is inexplicit, not because it lacks a good pedigree in public law. Indeed, the insight that explicitness may not be needed for jurisdiction consistent with § 1291 only leaves Digital with the unenviable task of explaining why other rights that might fairly be said to include an (implicit) "right to avoid trial" aspect are less in need of protection by immediate review, or more readily vindicated on appeal from final judgment, than the (claimed) privately negotiated right to be free from suit. It is far from clear, for example, why § 1291 should bless a party who bargained for the right to avoid trial, but not a party who "purchased" the right by having once prevailed at trial and now pleads res judicata, or a party who seeks shelter under the statute of limitations, which is usually understood to secure the same sort of "repose" that Digital seeks to vindicate here, or a party not even subject to a claim on which relief could be granted.

Digital answers that the status under § 1291 of these other (seemingly analogous) rights should not give us pause, because the text and structure of this particular settlement with Desktop confer what no res judicata claimant could ever have, an express right not to stand trial. But we cannot attach much significance one way or another to the supposed clarity of the agreement's terms in this case. To ground a ruling here on whether this settlement agreement in terms confers the prized "right not to stand trial" (a point Desktop by no means concedes) would flout our own frequent admonitions, that availability of collateral order appeal must be determined at a higher level of generality. Indeed, just because it would be the rare settlement agreement that could not be construed to include (at least an implicit) freedom-from-trial "aspect," we decide this case on the assumption that if Digital prevailed here, any district court order denying effect to a settlement agreement could be appealed immediately. * * *

2

The more fundamental response, however, to the claim that an agreement's provision for immunity from trial can distinguish it from other arguable rights to be trial-free is simply that such a right by agreement does not rise to the level of importance needed for recognition under § 1291. This, indeed, is the bone of the fiercest contention in the case. In disparaging any distinction between an order denying a claim grounded on an explicit constitutional guarantee of immunity from trial and an order at odds with an equally explicit right by private agreement of the parties, Digital stresses that the relative "importance" of these rights, heavily relied upon by the Court of Appeals, is a rogue factor. No decision of this Court, Digital maintains, has held an order unappealable as "unimportant" when it has otherwise met the three *Cohen* requirements, and whether a decided issue is thought "important," it says, should have no bearing on whether it is "final" under § 1291.

If "finality" were as narrow a concept as Digital maintains, however, the Court would have had little reason to go beyond the first factor in *Cohen*. And if "importance" were truly aberrational, we would not find it featured so prominently in the *Cohen* opinion itself, which describes the "small class" of immediately appealable prejudgment decisions in terms of rights that are "too important to be denied review" right away. To be sure, Digital may validly question whether "importance" is a factor "beyond" the three *Cohen* conditions or whether it is best considered, as we have sometimes suggested it should be, in connection with the second, "separability," requirement, but neither enquiry could lead to the conclusion that "importance" is itself unimportant. To the contrary, the third *Cohen* question, whether a right is "adequately vindicable" or "effectively reviewable," simply cannot be answered without a judgment about the value of the interests that would be lost through rigorous application of a final judgment requirement.

While there is no need to decide here that a privately conferred right could never supply the basis of a collateral order appeal, * * * there are surely sound reasons for treating such rights differently from those originating in the Constitution or statutes. When a policy is embodied in a constitutional or statutory provision entitling a party to immunity from suit (a rare form of protection), there is little room for the judiciary to gainsay its "importance." Including a provision in a private contract, by contrast, is barely a prima facie indication that the right secured is "important" to the benefitted party (contracts being replete with boilerplate), let alone that its value exceeds that of other rights not embodied in agreements (e.g., the right to be free from a second suit based on a claim that has already been litigated), or that it qualifies as "important" in *Cohen*'s sense, as being weightier than the societal interests advanced by the ordinary operation of final judgment principles. Where statutory and constitutional rights are concerned, "irretrievabl[e] los[s]" can hardly be trivial, and the collateral order doctrine might therefore be understood as reflecting the familiar principle of statutory construction that, when possible, courts should construe statutes (here § 1291) to foster harmony with other statutory and constitutional law. But it is one thing to say that the policy of § 1291 to avoid piecemeal litigation should be reconciled with policies embodied in other statutes or the Constitution, and quite another to suggest that this public policy may be trumped routinely by the expectations or clever drafting of private parties.

* * *

Nor are we swayed by Digital's last-ditch effort to come within *Cohen*'s sense of "importance" by trying to show that settlement-agreement "immunities" merit first-class treatment for purposes of collateral order appeal, because they advance the public policy favoring voluntary resolution of disputes. It defies common sense to maintain that parties' readiness to settle will be significantly dampened (or the corresponding public interest impaired) by a rule that a district court's decision to let allegedly barred litigation go forward may be challenged as a matter of right only on appeal from a judgment for the plaintiff's favor.

III

A

Even, finally, if the term "importance" were to be exorcized from the *Cohen* analysis altogether, Digital's rights would remain "adequately vindicable" or "effectively reviewable" on final judgment to an extent that other immunities, like the right to be free from a second trial on a criminal charge, are not. As noted already, experience suggests that freedom from trial is rarely the sine qua non * * * of a negotiated settlement agreement. Avoiding the burden of a trial is no doubt a welcome incident of out-of-court dispute resolution (just as it is for parties who prevail on pretrial motions), but in the run of the mill cases this boon will rarely compare with the " 'embarrassment' " and " 'anxiety' " averted by a successful double jeopardy claimant, see *Abney*, or the " 'distraction from . . . dut[y],' " *Mitchell*, avoided by qualified immunity. Judged within the four corners of the settlement agreement, avoiding trial probably pales in comparison with the benefit of limiting exposure to liability (an interest that is fully vindicable on appeal from final judgment). In the rare case where a party had a special reason, apart from the generic desire to triumph early, for having bargained for an immunity from trial, e.g., an unusual interest in preventing disclosure of particular information, it may seek protection from the district court.

The case for adequate vindication without immediate appeal is strengthened, moreover, by recognizing that a settling party has a source of recompense unknown to trial immunity claimants dependent on public law alone. The essence of Digital's claim here is that Desktop, for valuable consideration, promised not to sue, and we have been given no reason to doubt that Utah law provides for the enforcement of that promise in the same way that other rights arising from private agreements are enforced, through an action for breach of contract. And as for Digital's suggestion, that Desktop is using this proceeding not to remedy a fraud but merely to renege on a promise because it now thinks it should have negotiated a better deal, when a party claims fraud or otherwise seeks recision of a settlement for such improper purposes, its opponent need not rely on a court of appeals for protection. See Fed.Rule Civ.Proc. 11 (opponent may move for sanction when litigation is motivated by an "improper purpose, such as . . . unnecessary delay or needless increase in the cost of litigation").

B

In preserving the strict limitations on review as of right under § 1291, our holding should cause no dismay, for the law is not without its safety valve to deal with cases where the contest over a settlement's enforceability raises serious legal questions taking the case out of the ordinary run. While Digital's insistence that the District Court applied a fundamentally wrong legal standard in vacating the dismissal order here may not be considered in deciding appealability under § 1291, it plainly is relevant to the availability of the discretionary interlocutory appeal from particular district court orders "involv[ing] a controlling question of law as to which there is substantial ground for difference of opinion," provided for in § 1292(b) of Title 28. Indeed, because we suppose that a defendant's claimed entitlement to a privately negotiated "immunity from suit" could in some instances raise "a controlling question of law . . . [which] . . . may materially advance the ultimate termination of the litigation," the discretionary appeal provision (allowing courts to consider the merits of individual claims) would seem a better vehicle for vindicating serious contractual interpretation claims than the blunt, categorical instrument of § 1291 collateral order appeal.

IV

The words of § 1291 have long been construed to recognize that certain categories of pre-judgment decisions exist for which it is both justifiable and necessary to depart from the general rule, that "the whole case and every matter in controversy in it [must be] decided in a single appeal." McLish v. Roff, 141 U.S. 661, 665–666, 12 S.Ct. 118, 119–120, 35 L.Ed. 893 (1891). But denying effect to the sort of (asserted) contractual right at issue here is far removed from those immediately appealable decisions involving rights more deeply rooted in public policy, and the rights Digital asserts may, in the main, be vindicated through means less disruptive to the orderly administration of justice than immediate, mandatory appeal. We accordingly hold that a refusal to enforce a settlement agreement claimed to shelter a party from suit altogether does not supply the basis for immediate appeal under § 1291.

Notes and Questions

1. The collateral order doctrine of Cohen v. Beneficial Industrial Loan Corp., 337 U.S. 541, 69 S.Ct. 1221, 93 L.Ed. 1528 (1949), applied in *Digital*, was restated in Coopers & Lybrand v. Livesay, 437 U.S. 463, 98 S.Ct. 2454, 57 L.Ed.2d 351 (1978), in the following manner: "[T]he order must conclusively determine the disputed question, resolve an important issue completely separate from the merits of the action, and be effectively unreviewable on appeal from a final judgment."

2. Is the collateral order doctrine an *interpretation* of the finality requirement of § 1291, or an *exception* to it? Are there elements of *both* present? To the extent the rule constitutes an exception to § 1291, does its creation represent a proper performance of the judicial function?

3. Does it make sense for the Court to require that the order be "completely separate from the merits" for it to be appealable? See Comment, Collateral Orders and Extraordinary Writs as Exceptions to the Finality Rule, 51 Nw.U.L.Rev. 746, 757 (1957):

> It would seem that the only real function of this requirement is to limit the number of interlocutory appeals, since the question of whether an order is collateral is capable of fairly accurate determination and but few orders fall within the definition. However, from the standpoint of the litigant this is hardly a justification for the requirement. Whether or not an order is collateral has no relation to the potential injury he may be forced to suffer.

See also Note, Appealability in the Federal Courts, 75 Harv.L.Rev. 351, 365 (1961).

4. The Supreme Court applied the collateral order doctrine to allow appeal in Sell v. United States, 539 U.S. 166, 123 S.Ct. 2174, 156 L.Ed.2d 197 (2003). There the Court held that the district court's pretrial order

affirming the magistrate judge's order requiring the defendant involuntarily to receive medication in order to render him competent to stand trial qualified as an appealable collateral order: "[T]he basic issue—whether Sell must undergo medication against his will—is 'completely separate from the merits of the action,' i.e. whether Sell is guilty or innocent of the crimes charged." 539 U.S. at 176, 123 S.Ct. at 2182. Moreover, the Court found, the issue was effectively unreviewable, because "[b]y the time of trial Sell will have undergone forced medication—the very harm that he seeks to avoid. He cannot undo that harm even if he is acquitted." Id. at 176–77; 123 S.Ct. at 2182. Justice Scalia, joined by Justices O'Connor and Thomas, dissented: "Today's narrow holding will allow criminal defendants to engage in opportunistic behavior. They can, for example, voluntarily take their medication until halfway through trial, then abruptly refuse and demand an interlocutory appeal from the order that medication continue on a compulsory basis." Id. at 191, 123 S.Ct. at 2190.

5. Consider the use of the collateral order doctrine to allow appeal in *Eisen v. Carlisle & Jacquelin*, 417 U.S. 156, 171–72, 94 S.Ct. 2140, 2149–50, 40 L.Ed.2d 732 (1974) (*"Eisen* IV"), concerning an appeal from the district court's order imposing 90% of the costs of notifying absent class members on the defendants. The Supreme Court, holding the order appealable from the district court to the court of appeals, held that the case was controlled by *Cohen*. It reasoned that the district court's order "conclusively rejected [defendants'] contention that they could not lawfully be required to bear the expense of notice to the members of [plaintiff's] proposed class. Moreover, it involved a collateral matter unrelated to the merits of [plaintiff's] claim. Like the order in *Cohen*, the district court's judgment on the allocation of notice costs was 'a final disposition of a claimed right which is not an ingredient of the cause of action and does not require consideration with it,' and it was similarly appealable as a 'final decision' under § 1291." Does this decision still stand following *Digital Equipment?*

6. In *Moses H. Cone,* supra p. 1024 n. 2, the Supreme Court held that a federal court's stay of its own proceedings in deference to parallel state proceedings was immediately appealable both as a final order and under the collateral order doctrine. The *second* prong of the collateral order doctrine— that the order resolved an important issue completely separate from the merits of the action—was obviously satisfied. The *third* prong—that it was effectively unreviewable on appeal from a final judgment—was deemed satisfied because "[o]nce the state court decided the issue of arbitrability, the federal court would be bound to honor that determination as res judicata."

As for the *first* prong—whether the order conclusively determined the disputed question—the Court contrasted two kinds of nonfinal orders: those that are "inherently tentative" (like the denial of class certification in *Coopers & Lybrand*) and those that, although technically amendable, are "made with the expectation that they will be the final word on the subject addressed." It found this stay order to be of the latter type; it "necessarily contemplates that the federal court will have nothing further to do in resolving any substantive part of the case" because the court should only enter a stay if it is confident that the parallel state proceeding will "be an adequate vehicle for the complete and prompt resolution of the issues between the parties." Justice Rehnquist, dissenting, termed the majority's finding that the matter was conclusively determined "nothing short of sheer speculation about the state of mind of the District Judge." Should determination of the conclusiveness prong depend on the particular circumstances of this judge's granting of a stay or on the general characteristic of the type of stay (here a *Colorado River* stay only invocable under "extraordinary circumstances")?

7. In Gulfstream Aerospace Corp. v. Mayacamas Corp., 485 U.S. 271, 108 S.Ct. 1133, 99 L.Ed.2d 296 (1988), the Supreme Court was confronted with the reverse of *Moses Cone*—a refusal (rather than a grant) of a federal court stay in deference to a pre-existing state action. Gulfstream sued Mayacamas in state court in Georgia for breach of contract regarding its failure to purchase aircraft as agreed upon. A month later, Mayacamas sued Gulfstream in federal district court in California, alleging breach of the same contract. Gulfstream moved for a stay or dismissal of the federal action, citing *Colorado River* and *Moses Cone*. The district court denied the stay, and the circuit court dismissed the appeal, finding no right to immediate appeal. The Supreme Court affirmed. It found that the first prong of the collateral order doctrine was not satisfied:

> The order fails to meet the initial requirement of a conclusive determination of the disputed question. A district court that denies a *Colorado River* motion does not "necessarily contemplate" that the decision will close the matter for all time. In denying such a motion, the district court may well have determined only that it should await further developments before concluding that the balance of factors to be considered under *Colorado River* warrants a dismissal or stay. The district court, for example, may wish to see whether the state-court proceeding becomes more comprehensive than the federal-court action or whether the former begins to proceed at a more rapid pace. Thus, whereas the granting of a *Colorado River* motion necessarily implies an expectation that the state court will resolve the dispute, the denial of such a motion may indicate nothing more than that the district court is not completely confident of the propriety of a stay or dismissal at that time. Indeed, given both the nature of the factors to be considered under *Colorado River* and the natural tendency of courts to attempt to eliminate matters that need not be decided from their dockets, a district court usually will expect to revisit and reassess an order denying a stay in light of events occurring in the normal course of litigation. Because an order denying a *Colorado River* motion is "inherently tentative" in this critical sense—because it is not "made with the expectation that it will be the final word on the subject addressed"—the order is not a conclusive determination within the meaning of the collateral-order doctrine and therefore is not appealable under § 1291.

The Court's ruling that the denial of the stay was also not appealable under § 1292(a) is discussed infra, p. 1069.

8. Note that one of the requirements of the collateral order doctrine, as that doctrine has developed, is that the order be "effectively unreviewable" after final judgment. Was that true of *Cohen* itself? Of *Eisen* IV?

In Firestone Tire & Rubber Co. v. Risjord, 449 U.S. 368, 101 S.Ct. 669, 66 L.Ed.2d 571 (1981), the Supreme Court relied on this factor in holding that the collateral order doctrine is inapplicable to an appeal from an order denying a motion to disqualify counsel. The Court reasoned:

> An order denying a disqualification motion meets the first part of the "collateral order" test. It "conclusively determine[s] the disputed question", because the only issue is whether challenged counsel will be permitted to continue his representation. In addition, we will assume, although we do not decide, that the disqualification question "resolve[s] an important issue completely separate from the merits of the action," the second part of the test. Nevertheless, petitioner is unable to demonstrate that an order denying disqualification is "effectively unreviewable on appeal form a final judgement" within the meaning of our cases.

* * *

> An order refusing to disqualify counsel plainly falls within the large class of orders that are indeed reviewable on appeal after final judgment, and not within the much smaller class of those that are not. The propriety of the district court's denial of a disqualification motion will often be difficult to assess until its impact on the underlying litigation may be evaluated, which is normally only after final judgment. The decision whether to disqualify an attorney ordinarily turns on the peculiar factual situation of the case then at hand, and the order embodying such a decision will rarely, if ever, represent a final rejection of a claim of fundamental right that cannot effectively be reviewed following judgment on the merits.

In Flanagan v. United States, 465 U.S. 259 (1984), the Court extended its *Firestone* holding concerning the unappealability of pretrial denials of disqualification motions in civil cases to criminal cases. It rejected the argument that disqualification orders were analogous to orders denying bail or refusing to dismiss on grounds of double jeopardy, reasoning that the disqualification order lacks "the essential characteristics" that make the other orders immediately appealable. Specifically, requests for bail reduction are in "danger of becoming moot upon conviction and sentence" and double jeopardy provides a right not to be tried, rather than merely not to be convicted, which could not be resurrected by post-trial review.

The Court expounded upon the "nonreviewability" requirement in Stringfellow v. Concerned Neighbors in Action, 480 U.S. 370, 107 S.Ct. 1177, 94 L.Ed.2d 389 (1987). There the United States and California filed suit against owners of a waste disposal site. Concerned Neighbors in Action (CNA), a group whose members lived near the dump site, moved to intervene pursuant to Rule 24 of the Federal Rules of Civil Procedure. The district court denied the motion to intervene as of right, but granted permissive intervention subject to restrictions CNA found onerous. CNA appealed both elements of the decision. The Supreme Court held that appeal to the court of appeals was improper because the district court's order would not be effectively unreviewable after final judgment. CNA argued that the right to effective review was irretrievably lost as a practical matter because the appellate court would be highly reluctant to vacate a judgment, reached after years of litigation, on grounds of an erroneous intervention order. The Court was not moved: "The difficulties of which CNA complains are the same as those faced by any party who is subject to an adverse pre-trial order." The Court acknowledged that a party completely denied intervention may appeal immediately, but asserted the reason for this rule was that the litigant denied intervention could not appeal after the trial, since it was not formally a party to the case. CNA, on the other hand, had been allowed to intervene, and the Court rejected CNA's argument that it had effectively been denied *all* participation because of the sweeping restrictions imposed on its intervention by the district court.

9. In Lauro Lines S.R.L. v. Chasser, 490 U.S. 495, 109 S.Ct. 1976, 104 L.Ed.2d 548 (1989), discussed in *Digital Equipment*, plaintiffs filed suit in the Southern District of New York against the shipping line to recover damages for injuries sustained as a result of the hijacking of the Achille Lauro and subsequent wrongful death, despite a forum-selection clause, printed on the passenger ticket, providing that any suit must be filed in Naples, Italy. The defendant sought to appeal the district court's denial of its motion to dismiss on the basis on the forum-selection clause, relying on the collateral order doctrine. The Supreme Court, in an opinion by Justice Brennan, rejected the defendant's argument:

> We recently reiterated the "general rule" that an order is "effectively unreviewable" only "where the order at issue involves 'an asserted right the legal and practical value of which would be destroyed if it were not vindicated before trial.'" Midland Asphalt Corp. v. United States, 489 U.S. [794, 798], 109 S.Ct. [1494,] 1498 [(1989)].
>
> Cost associated with unnecessary litigation is not enough to set aside the finality requirement. Instead, we have insisted that the right asserted be one that is essentially destroyed if its vindication must be postponed until trial is completed.

490 U.S. at 498–99, 109 S.Ct. at 1978. The Court distinguished the asserted right, under the forum-selection clause, not to be haled into a courtroom outside the selected forum, from a right not to be subjected to suit altogether: "[Defendant's] claim that it may be sued only in Naples, while not perfectly secured by appeal after final judgment, is adequately vindicable at that stage—surely as effectively vindicable as a claim that the trial court lacked personal jurisdiction over the defendant—and hence does not fall within the third prong of the collateral order doctrine." Id. at 501, 109 S.Ct. at 1979.

Justice Scalia, concurring, wrote (id. at 502, 109 S.Ct. at 1980):

> The reason we say that the right not to be sued elsewhere than in Naples is "adequately vindicable" * * * by merely reversing any judgment obtained in violation of it is, quite simply, that the law does not deem the right *important enough* to be vindicated by, as it were, an injunction against its violation obtained through interlocutory appeal. The importance of the right asserted has always been a significant part of our collateral order doctrine.

In Midland Asphalt Corp. v. United States, 489 U.S. 794, 109 S.Ct. 1494, 103 L.Ed.2d 879 (1989), cited in *Lauro Lines,* the Court rejected application of the collateral order doctrine to a criminal case, where the defendant had moved to dismiss an indictment partly on the grounds that prosecutors had publicly disclosed matters before the grand jury, in violation of a Federal Rule of Criminal Procedure. The defendant had argued that since violation of the rule would be deemed harmless error after conviction, the denial of its motion was effectively unreviewable later. The Court, however, indicated that in any event the ruling would be part and parcel of the merits, thus violating another prong of the collateral order doctrine. The Court also rejected the argument that the rule effectively gave the defendant a right not to be tried: "A right not to be tried in the sense relevant to the *Cohen* exception rests upon an explicit statutory or constitutional guarantee that trial will not occur * * *." 489 U.S. at 801, 109 S.Ct. at 1499. Neither the rule nor the Constitution, said the Court, "affords such a guarantee in the event of a violation of grand jury secrecy." Id.

10.   The Court held in Puerto Rico Aqueduct and Sewer Authority v. Metcalf & Eddy, Inc., 506 U.S. 139, 113 S.Ct. 684, 121 L.Ed.2d 605 (1993), that appeal is permitted under the collateral order doctrine from an order denying a claim of state sovereign immunity pursuant to the Eleventh Amendment:

> Once it is acknowledged that a State and its "arms" are, in effect, immune from federal–court suit under the [Eleventh] Amendment * * * it follows that the elements of the collateral order doctrine necessary to bring an order within *Cohen*'s "small class" * * * are satisfied. First, denials of Eleventh Amendment immunity claims purport to be conclusive determinations that States and their entities have no right not to be sued in federal court. Second, a motion to dismiss on Eleventh Amendment grounds involves a claim to a fundamental constitutional protection whose resolution generally will have no bearing on the merits of the underlying action. Third, the value to the States of their constitutional immunity—like the benefits conferred by qualified immunity to individual officials * * *—is for the most part lost as litigation proceeds past motion practice, such that the denial order will be effectively unreviewable on appeal from a final judgment.

Is this decision distinguishable from *Digital Equipment*?

11.   In Van Cauwenberghe v. Biard, 486 U.S. 517, 108 S.Ct. 1945, 100 L.Ed.2d 517 (1988), the Court indicated that a determination of forum non conveniens is not sufficiently separate from the merits to come within the *Cohen* doctrine. On the relationship of the collateral order doctrine to denials of motions to dismiss for lack of personal jurisdiction, see generally Comment, Immediate Appealability of Minimum Contact Defenses: How Far Does the *Cohen* Doctrine Extend?, 63 Tul. L. Rev. 913 (1989).

12.   In Swint v. Chambers County Comm'n, 514 U.S. 35, 115 S.Ct. 1203, 131 L.Ed.2d 60 (1995), the Court held that there is no pendent party jurisdiction that allows review of a related order involving another party because of its connection to an order that is appealable under the collateral order doctrine. The case was a suit against a city and various police officers for civil rights violations arising out of a raid on a nightclub. After defendants' motions for summary judgment were denied, they all appealed. For the individual defendants, this appeal was easy to justify because they relied on qualified immunity and the Supreme Court had authorized immediate

appeals. (See the discussion of Civil Rights Cases, below). The city and county commission also appealed on both collateral order and pendent party jurisdiction theories. The Court rejected both.

Denial of the municipalities' summary judgment motions did not qualify as a collateral order under *Cohen* because the ruling could be effectively reviewed after final judgment. The treatment of holders of qualified immunity is a special case of "an immunity from suit rather that a mere defense to liability," and the municipalities' claim that they were not responsible for what the officers did was not similar. Neither could there be pendent appellate jurisdiction, much as that might save time in this case. Saving time is the concept behind § 1292(b), but that was not satisfied in this case. Moreover, Congress had expanded the rule-making power of the Court to specify by rule when a decision becomes final, so that expanding the common law collateral order doctrine would not be warranted. Although there may be cases in which the otherwise unappealable orders are "inextricably intertwined" with the appealable ones so that it is proper to exercise such pendent jurisdiction, this was not such a case.

CIVIL RIGHTS CASES

The "effectively nonreviewable" rationale has been used to justify a significant extension of the collateral order doctrine in civil rights cases. In Harlow v. Fitzgerald, 457 U.S. 800, 102 S.Ct. 2727, 73 L.Ed.2d 396 (1982), the Supreme Court held that state officials are entitled to a defense of qualified immunity unless their conduct violates "clearly established statutory or constitutional rights of which a reasonable person would have known." Qualified immunity has become a standard defense in civil rights cases, with the defendant state official (for example, a policeman or prison guard charged with excessive use of force) moving for dismissal or summary judgment on the ground that he could not reasonably have known that his conduct violated clearly established constitutional rights. Normally, if the trial court denied the motion, the defendant would have to proceed with the case and could only appeal the denial if a final judgment were entered against him. However, in Mitchell v. Forsyth, 472 U.S. 511, 105 S.Ct. 2806, 86 L.Ed.2d 411 (1985), the Court held that a trial court's denial of summary judgment sought on the basis of qualified immunity is appealable under the collateral order doctrine.

Forsyth analogized qualified immunity to absolute immunity where, for example, a defendant who asserts that he is immune on double jeopardy grounds may immediately appeal a refusal to dismiss because "such a right cannot be effectively vindicated after the trial has occurred." See Abney v. United States, 431 U.S. 651, 97 S.Ct. 2034, 52 L.Ed.2d 651 (1977). The Court concluded that the essence of qualified immunity is "an entitlement not to stand trial under certain circumstances" and thus that a defendant should be entitled to immediate appellate review of his qualified immunity claim. Are the policy grounds justifying an immediate appeal when absolute immunity is raised (a small number of situations involving such matters as double jeopardy or official-conduct suits against judges or prosecutors) applicable to the much more frequent qualified immunity situation? In any event, is it accurate to conclude that such orders meet the requirements of the collateral order doctrine?

The immediate appeal doctrine was curtailed substantially by Johnson v. Jones, 515 U.S. 304, 115 S.Ct. 2151, 132 L.Ed.2d 238 (1995), which limited appeals on grounds of qualified immunity to those in which there is no dispute about the facts. Plaintiff there claimed that police had beaten him after they found him suffering an insulin seizure on a street, but the officers argued that he had no evidence they had done so. The district court denied their motion for summary judgment on the ground there was a genuine issue for trial, and the Supreme Court held that their appeal was properly dismissed for lack of jurisdiction. It explained its earlier decision that denial of summary judgment is immediately appealable in qualified immunity cases as premised on the assumption that there is no dispute regarding the facts. In *Forsyth*, the Court said that the appellate court "need not consider the correctness of plaintiff's version of the facts." 472 U.S. at 528. Where there is a dispute about the facts, an immediate appeal is not allowed.

In Behrens v. Pelletier, 516 U.S. 299, 116 S.Ct. 834, 133 L.Ed.2d 773 (1996), the Court held that defendants entitled to an immediate appeal of rejection of a qualified immunity defense may be allowed more than one such immediate appeal as a matter of right. After denial of a Rule 12(b)(6) motion, defendant appealed and lost. Then defendant moved for summary judgment, and when that was denied he appealed again. The Court held that he had a right to a second interlocutory appeal because "an order rejecting the defense of qualified immunity at either the dismissal stage or the summary-judgment stage is a 'final' judgment subject to immediate appeal." Id. at 839.

The effect of the *Forsyth* rule on the strategic positions of parties in civil rights suits is substantial. A defendant, no matter how weak his claim to qualified immunity, can bring the suit to a halt while a time-consuming and expensive appeal takes place on the issue of qualified immunity. This provides an opportunity for defendants (who are often represented by city or county attorneys or state attorney general offices) to raise the ante for continuing the case and thus to out-resource the plaintiff. Are there other situations in which an interlocutory appeal can also have this effect? Should that be a factor in applying the collateral order doctrine? Should defendants with weak claims of qualified immunity be sanctioned for taking an immediate appeal?

In Johnson v. Fankell, 520 U.S. 911, 117 S.Ct. 1800, 138 L.Ed.2d 108 (1997), the Court held that the federal doctrine of immediate appealability does not apply to § 1983 suits against state officials in state court. The ruling was based on the inapplicability of "converse *Erie*" reasoning to state court procedure. See supra p. 997. Consider how this ruling will affect the strategic positions of the parties in regard to removing to federal court.

In *Digital Equipment*, the Court rejected Digital's attempt to have its case brought within the scope of *Forsyth*. How persuasive is the Court's suggested distinction?

DISCOVERY ORDERS

Many discovery orders might appear at first glance to be suited to immediate appeal under the collateral order doctrine. They can conclusively determine a disputed question that is separate from the merits of the action, and often the order will be effectively unreviewable after final judgment. For example, a discovery order requiring the production of documents containing what a party deems trade secrets cannot effectively be reviewed after final judgment: once the secret information is revealed, the damage is done. Similar situations may arise in other discovery contexts. See, e.g., United States v. Fried, 386 F.2d 691 (2d Cir.1967) (witness sought review of an order requiring his presence for testimony, claiming that his attendance could seriously jeopardize his health); Gialde v. Time, Inc., 480 F.2d 1295 (8th Cir.1973) (attempted interlocutory appeal from pre-trial discovery order in a libel and invasion-of-privacy suit requiring newsmen to reveal secret sources).

Yet the federal courts have generally denied review of pretrial discovery orders. See, e.g., FDIC v. Ogden Corp., 202 F.3d 454, 458 n.2 (1st Cir. 2000); Simmons v. City of Racine, 37 F.3d 325 (7th Cir.1994). This is because "in the rare case when appeal after final judgment will not cure an erroneous discovery order, a party may defy the order, permit a contempt citation to be entered against him, and challenge the order on direct appeal of the contempt ruling." Firestone Tire & Rubber Co. v. Risjord, 449 U.S. 368, 377, 101 S.Ct. 669, 675, 66 L.Ed.2d 571 (1981). But see United States v. Philip Morris, Inc., 314 F.3d 612, 620 (D.C. Cir. 2003) ("At least some of the holdings [denying collateral order appeal for discovery orders] are based in part upon the assumption that disobedience may lead to a contempt citation that itself would be an appealable order. * * * In this circuit, however, it is settled that a civil contempt citation is not appealable as a collateral order.")

An illustration of the contempt theory is United States v. Ryan, 402 U.S. 530, 91 S.Ct. 1580, 29 L.Ed.2d 85 (1971). There the Court held that an order denying a motion to quash a grand jury subpoena duces tecum was not appealable. The Court indicated that if the subpoena were unlawful or unduly burdensome, the party "may refuse to comply and litigate those questions in the event that contempt or similar proceedings are brought against him. Should his contentions be rejected at that time by the trial court they will then be ripe for appellate review." As a practical matter, how viable is this "contempt" alternative likely to be? Put yourself in the position of the party who wishes to seek appellate review of a discovery order. If you were to take this "contempt" avenue, what are likely to be the consequences if you are wrong in your belief that the discovery order is improper?

The "contempt" approach endorsed in *Ryan* and *Firestone* presents another difficulty as well. Recall that generally a person who disobeys a court order is not allowed to attack the legality of that order when prosecuted for contempt under the collateral-bar rule. See supra p. 97 n. 4. Thus, in Walker v. City of Birmingham, 388 U.S. 307, 87 S.Ct. 1824, 18 L.Ed.2d 1210 (1967), the Court reasoned that this rule was necessary because "in the fair administration of justice no man can be judge in his own case, however exalted his station, however righteous his motives, and irrespective of his race, color, politics, or religion." The proper method to obtain appellate review, said the Court, was to seek it *prior* to violating the order. Is this doctrine inconsistent with the practice authorized in *Ryan*? In a footnote the Court in *Ryan* distinguished *Walker,* because "[o]ur holding that the claims there sought to be asserted were not open on review of petitioners' contempt convictions was based upon the availability of review of those claims at an earlier stage." 402 U.S. at 532, n.4. Does this logic beg the question about the applicability of the collateral order doctrine to appeal of discovery orders? Isn't the Court simply making it harder to get appellate review of discovery orders?

Note two important qualifications on the general reluctance to employ the collateral order doctrine for discovery appeals. First, the contempt alternative is of course not available when it is an order *denying* discovery from which appeal is sought. While normally such a denial may be appealed following a final judgment in the underlying suit, this option is not available when the denial of discovery takes place in an ancillary discovery proceeding in another court. In this situation, such an order has been deemed appealable as a collateral order. Nicholas v. Wyndham International, Inc., 373 F.3d 537 (4th Cir. 2004). Moreover, the collateral order doctrine may be employed when it is the party, rather than the witness, who seeks immediate appeal. In such a situation, the contempt alternative is of course unavailable. FDIC v. Ogden Corp., 202 F.3d 454 (1st Cir. 2000). See also Nguyen v. Excel Corp., 197 F.3d 200, 204 (5th Cir. 1999) ("When a subpoenaed third party does not have a direct and personal interest in suppression of the requested information...the third party is not likely to risk a contempt citation.")

In Cunningham v. Hamilton County, 527 U.S. 198, 119 S.Ct. 1915, 144 L.Ed.2d 184 (1999), the Court held that the discovery sanctions imposed on a lawyer under Rule 37 are not immediately appealable under 28 U.S.C.A. § 1391. The lawyer was ordered to pay nearly $4,000 in costs and fees in connection with discovery violations, and sought immediate review. Finding that an inquiry into the sanctions order "would differ only marginally from an inquiry into the merits," the Court concluded that review could not be justified under the collateral order doctrine. It also reasoned that "[t]o permit an immediate appeal from such a sanctions order would undermine the very purposes of Rule 37(a), which was designed to protect courts and opposing parties from delaying or harassing tactics during the discovery process." Thus, although it "candidly recognize[d] the hardship that a sanctions order may sometimes impose on an attorney," the Court held that the solution to these problems lay in new legislation or rulemaking, not interpretation of existing statutes and rules.

On occasion, review of discovery orders has been authorized via mandamus pursuant to the All Writs Act, 28 U.S.C.A. § 1651, discussed infra p. 1055.

b. *Appeal Under § 1292(b)*

CARDWELL v. CHESAPEAKE & OHIO RAILWAY CO.

United States Court of Appeals, Sixth Circuit, 1974.
504 F.2d 444.

Before EDWARDS, McCREE and MILLER, CIRCUIT JUDGES.

McCREE, CIRCUIT JUDGE.

This is an appeal from an order overruling a reserved motion for a directed verdict in a Federal Employer's Liability Act (FELA) action, 45 U.S.C. § 51 et seq., to recover damages for injury and for wrongful death. The jury awarded $10,500, adjusted for contributory negligence, on the claim for injury, but was unable to decide whether death was caused by the injury. This appeal requires us to decide whether there was sufficient competent evidence of the causal relationship between the injury and death for the submission of this claim to the jury. We determine that there was.

On August 14, 1969, Winfred M. Cardwell filed a complaint under the FELA alleging that he sustained a back injury while he was employed at defendant's Huntington, West Virginia Diesel Shops on June 27, 1969, when he attempted to close a locomotive cab door that had been left hanging on only its right upper hinge. After the answer was filed and some depositions were taken, a suggestion of plaintiff's death was filed and Cardwell's widow, who had been appointed administratrix of his estate, filed an amended complaint August 6, 1971, in which she alleged that Cardwell's death on January 25, 1971, was the result of the accident pleaded in the original complaint.

In a trial that extended over parts of four days, after decision on a motion for a directed verdict was reserved and defendant submitted its proofs, the case was submitted to the jury upon instructions requiring separate verdicts on the claim for injury and lost wages during Cardwell's lifetime and a verdict on the death claim. The jury found that the accident on June 22, 1969 resulted in part from the negligence of both Cardwell and the railroad and assessed damages at $10,500. It advised the court that it could not agree whether Cardwell's death resulted from defendant's negligence.

Appellant filed a motion for judgment notwithstanding the absence of a verdict on the wrongful death claim and a motion for judgment n.o.v. or for a new trial on the claim for injury. On May 25, 1973, the district court entered judgment on the verdict of $10,500 and overruled both motions, but certified, at defendant's request that "Whether or not there was sufficient medical evidence of the causal relationship between the accident claimed to have been sustained by the plaintiff's decedent and the death of the said decedent to warrant submission of such issue to the jury" involved "a controlling question of law as to which there is substantial ground for difference of opinion" and that an immediate appeal from the order overruling the motion for judgment notwithstanding the absence of a verdict "may materially advance the ultimate termination of this litigation."

Our Court, one judge dissenting, permitted the appeal to be taken * * *.

28 U.S.C. § 1292(b) provides:

> (b) When a district judge, in making in a civil action an order not otherwise appealable under this section, shall be of the opinion that such order involves a controlling question of law as to which there is substantial ground for difference of opinion and that an immediate appeal from the order may materially advance the ultimate termination of the litigation, he shall so state in writing in such order. The Court of Appeals may thereupon, in its discretion, permit an appeal to be taken from such order, if application is made to it within ten days after the entry of the order. . . .

This provision applies to interlocutory orders that are not otherwise appealable of right and requires the existence of four elements: (1) The question involved must be one of "law"; (2) it must be "controlling"; (3) there must be substantial ground for "difference of opinion" about it; and (4) an immediate appeal must "materially advance the ultimate termination of the litigation."

In considering an application from a defendant in a diversity automobile action [in Kraus v. Board of County Road Commissioners, 364 F.2d 919 (6th Cir.1966)], we were asked to review under 28 U.S.C. § 1292(b) the grant of summary judgment determining that a Michigan statute requiring notice within sixty days of injuries caused by defective roads does not apply to actions for wrongful death. We quoted with approval this statement from Milbert v. Bison Laboratories, 260 F.2d 431, 433 (3d Cir.1958):

> It is quite apparent from the legislative history of the Act of September 2, 1958 that Congress intended that section 1292(b) should be sparingly applied. It is to be used only in exceptional cases where an intermediate appeal may avoid protracted and expensive litigation and is not intended to open the floodgates to a vast number of appeals from interlocutory orders in ordinary litigation.

We observed further in denying the request to permit the appeal:

> "This statute was not intended to authorize interlocutory appeals in *ordinary suits for personal injuries or wrongful death that can be tried and disposed of on their merits in a few days.* Haraburda v. United States Steel Corp., 187 F.Supp. 79 (W.D.Mich. 1960) (emphasis supplied).

The granting of an interlocutory appeal in the present case would not 'materially advance the ultimate termination of the litigation.' Many months would be required before the case would be reached for argument on the congested docket of this court. If we grant the appeal and then should affirm the order of the district court * * * the case then would be remanded to the district court for trial on its merits.

On the other hand, it would appear that only a few days would be required for a jury trial and final disposition of the case in the district court. This procedure, which would avoid a piecemeal appeal, is preferable except in the extraordinary type of case contemplated by 1292(b)."

Kraus v. Board of County Road Commissioners, 364 F.2d 919, 922 (6th Cir.1966).

* * *

This appears to be precisely the kind of ordinary suit for personal injuries or wrongful death that can be tried and disposed of on its merits within a few days and that * * * should not be considered on interlocutory appeal.

Notes and Questions

1. 28 U.S.C.A. § 1292(b) was added by the Interlocutory Appeals Act of 1958. Its purpose was to "expedite the ultimate termination of litigation and thereby some unnecessary expense and delay" by allowing appeal of certain nonfinal orders. H.R.Rep.No. 1667, 85th Cong., 2d Sess. 1 (1958). See also Note, Section 1292(b): Eight Years of Undefined Discretion, 54 Geo.L.J. 940, 941 (1966): "The [final judgment] rule caused a manifest waste of time and money for both litigants and the court whenever the parties were forced to await final judgment in a lengthy trial only to have a ruling, made at the outset of the trial, reversed." Recall, however, that one of the primary purposes of the final judgment rule was to accomplish precisely the same goal. Could they both logically be designed to achieve the same end?

2. Professor Michael Solimine has noted that "[d]espite the [Supreme] Court's frequent reference to section 1292(b) commentators generally discount its effectiveness as a safety valve for interlocutory appeals, since it has been historically utilized infrequently." Solimine, Revitalizing Interlocutory Appeals in the Federal Courts, 58 Geo. Wash. L. Rev. 1165, 1193 (1990). He suggests that "[m]uch of the blame is attributable to the narrow construction given the statute by some courts, as well as the fear that relaxing the use of the statute will open the floodgates to appeals," and argues that "[t]hese fears have been greatly exaggerated." Id.

3. Note that § 1292(b) effectively requires dual certification, both by the district and appellate courts. Both are deemed to be wholly discretionary, in the appellate court explicitly by the terms of the law and in the district court by judicial practice. See, e.g., In re Convertible Rowing Exerciser Patent Litigation, 903 F.2d 822 (Fed.Cir.1990); D'Ippolito v. Cities Service Co., 374 F.2d 643, 649 (2d Cir.1967). The appellate court may deny the

appeal for any reason, including docket congestion. See Coopers & Lybrand v. Livesay, 437 U.S. 463, 475, 98 S.Ct. 2454, 57 L.Ed.2d 351 (1978). Not surprisingly, these certification requirements have limited use of the procedure. See Gellhorn & Larsen, Interlocutory Appeal Procedures in Administrative Hearings, 70 Mich.L.Rev. 109, 137 (1971): "District courts * * * have not been overly sympathetic to claims of error. Neither have they been persuaded that the order involves a 'controlling question of law' or that immediate appeal will speed the final determination." At least in part for this reason, the procedure over the years has had relatively little impact on the total number of appeals taken. See Carrington, Crowded Dockets and the Courts of Appeals: The Threat to the Function of Review and the National Law, 82 Harv.L.Rev. 542, 546–47 (1969); C. Wright & M. Kane, Law of Federal Courts 761 (6th ed. 2002) (§ 1292(b) generally reserved for the "exceptional" case).

4. Possibly another reason for the limited resort to § 1292(b) is the view, adopted in *Cardwell,* that the statute's use is appropriate only in the larger, more complex cases. This analysis, associated primarily with the Third Circuit's decision in *Bison Laboratories,* quoted in *Cardwell,* limits use of § 1292(b) to "the 'big' and expensive case where an unusual amount of time and money may be expended in the pre-trial phases of the case or where the trial itself is likely to be long and costly." Bobolakis v. Compania Panamena Maritima San Gerassimo, 168 F.Supp. 236, 239 (S.D.N.Y.1958). Is it wise to limit resort to § 1292(b) in this manner? See Note, Interlocutory Appeals in the Federal Courts Under 28 U.S.C. § 1292(b), 88 Harv.L.Rev. 607, 626–27 (1975): "[B]ecause the Act is premised on a notion that there should be a case-by-case evaluation of efficiency, any universal standard restricting certification seems out of place."

Not all federal courts have viewed § 1292(b) in so limited a manner. In fact, according to one commentator, "no uniform analysis of when it is proper to certify an order for appeal has emerged," with the result that "[d]ifferent circuits, and even different panels within a circuit, have taken opposing positions on the general framework of analysis for applying the Act to an individual case." Note, Interlocutory Appeals in the Federal Courts Under 28 U.S.C.A. § 1292(b), 88 Harv.L.Rev. 607, 608 & n.6. (1975).

5. How do the substantive factors mentioned in the statute interrelate? It has been argued that the listed criteria "are not to be read so broadly that the district court can allow appeal whenever it would promote the 'efficient administration of justice,' since the Judicial Conference draftsmen rejected this phraseology in favor of a more restricted wording." Note, Discretionary Appeals of District Court Interlocutory Orders: A Guided Tour Through Section 1292(b) of the Judicial Code, 69 Yale L.J. 333, 341 (1959).

6. Consider the requirement that immediate review of the order "materially advance" the litigation's termination. Should appeal be allowed where reversal of a nonfinal order would reduce expense to the litigants without advancing the ultimate termination of litigation? For example, could a court certify an appeal under § 1292(b) of a decision granting or denying a transfer under 28 U.S.C.A. § 1404(a)? It is hard to understand why immediate review would hasten the ultimate termination of the action, but it is also unlikely that after final judgment an appellate court would reverse an

otherwise correct judgment on the ground that the transfer issue should have been handled differently. Not surprisingly, the courts are split, some treating the conclusive issue to be whether the question raised is the trial court's power under the statute to transfer and others treating it as whether the trial court abused its discretion in exercising its conceded power. See 16 C. Wright, A. Miller & E. Cooper, Federal Practice & Procedure § 3931 at 175–76.

7. When does an order involve "a controlling issue of law"? Obviously, this requirement is intended to reach more than just rulings on the substantive law applicable to the case. Orders denying a motion to dismiss for lack of personal jurisdiction have been granted § 1292(b) interlocutory appeal. How can they be said to constitute controlling issues of law? See Witt v. Scully, 539 F.2d 950 (3d Cir.1976); Rebozo v. Washington Post Co., 515 F.2d 1208 (5th Cir.1975). Orders rejecting challenges to venue, subject matter jurisdiction, justiciability, and removal have also come under § 1292(b). 16 C. Wright, A. Miller, & E. Cooper & E. Gressman, Federal Practice & Procedure § 3931. Would an order to comply with a discovery request be "controlling"? Would an order denying discovery?

8. The Supreme Court clearly has assumed that the judge-made collateral order doctrine survived enactment of § 1292(b). Is this a valid assumption? See Redish, The Pragmatic Approach to Appealability in the Federal Courts, 75 Colum.L.Rev. 89, 126 (1975): "Although it is possible to fashion an argument which might reconcile [a judge-made] balancing approach with the dictates of section 1291, it is considerably harder to harmonize the approach with the more detailed scheme of appealability promulgated by Congress in section 1292(b). [A judge-made] balancing approach, when employed in situations to which section 1292(b) was intended to apply, effectively repeals the legislative compromise, which established the dual certification requirement * * *." Is this a valid criticism of the collateral order doctrine? Does your answer depend on whether that doctrine is deemed an *exception to,* rather than an *interpretation of,* the final judgment rule? In Gillespie v. United States Steel Corp., 379 U.S. 148, 85 S.Ct. 308, 13 L.Ed.2d 199 (1964) (supra p. 1026 n. 4), Justice Black noted that allowance of an interlocutory appeal in that case would implement "the same policy Congress sought to promote in § 1292(b)," notwithstanding the district court's unequivocal denial of a section 1292(b) certificate. Does this reasoning make sense?

9. In Yamaha Motor Corp. v. Calhoun, 516 U.S. 199, 116 S.Ct. 619, 133 L.Ed.2d 578 (1996), the Court held that an appellate court which accepts a certification under § 1292(b) can address a question different from the one certified by the district court so long as it is included within the order on which the appeal is based. Plaintiffs there sued after their daughter was killed in a jet ski accident. Defendant moved for partial summary judgment, arguing that federal maritime law displaced state law remedies. The district court agreed, but concluded also that maritime law permitted recovery for loss of society, and the district court certified the question whether such recoveries are allowed under maritime law to the court of appeals. Rather than answer this question, the court of appeals held that state law remedies remained available. In affirming, the Supreme Court said that "[t]he court of appeals may not reach beyond the certified order to address other orders

made in the case," but that it may address "any issue fairly included within the certified order" whether or not that was the question posed by the district judge.

c. *Mandamus*

WILL v. UNITED STATES

Supreme Court of the United States, 1967.
389 U.S. 90, 88 S.Ct. 269, 19 L.Ed.2d 305.

CHIEF JUSTICE WARREN delivered the opinion of the Court.

The question in this case is the propriety of a writ of mandamus issued by the Court of Appeals for the Seventh Circuit to compel the petitioner, a United States District Judge, to vacate a portion of a pretrial order in a criminal case.

Simmie Horwitz, the defendant in a criminal tax evasion case pending before petitioner in the Northern District of Illinois, filed a motion for a bill of particulars, which contained thirty requests for information. The Government resisted a number of the requests, and over the course of several hearings most of these objections were either withdrawn by the Government or satisfied by an appropriate narrowing of the scope of the bill of particulars by petitioner. Ultimately the dispute centered solely on defendant's request number 25. This request sought certain information concerning any oral statements of the defendant relied upon by the Government to support the charge in the indictment. It asked the names and addresses of the persons to whom such statements were made, the times and places at which they were made, whether the witnesses to the statements were government agents and whether any transcripts or memoranda of the statements had been prepared by the witnesses and given to the Government. After considerable discussion with counsel for both sides, petitioner ordered the Government to furnish the information. The United States Attorney declined to comply with the order on the grounds that request number 25 constituted a demand for a list of prosecution witnesses and that petitioner had no power under Rule 7(f) of the Federal Rules of Criminal Procedure to require the Government to produce such a list.

Petitioner indicated his intention to dismiss the indictments against Horwitz because of the Government's refusal to comply with his order for a bill of particulars. * * * The Court of Appeals * * * granted the Government leave to file a petition for a writ of mandamus and issued a rule to show cause why such a writ should not issue to compel petitioner to strike request number 25 from his bill of particulars order. * * * The Court of Appeals at first denied the writ. The Government petitioned for reconsideration, however, and the Court of Appeals * * * reversed itself and without opinion issued a writ of mandamus directing petitioner "to vacate his order directing the Government to answer question 25 in defendant's motion for bill of particulars." * * * We vacate the writ and remand the case to the Court of Appeals for further proceedings.

Both parties have devoted substantial argument in this Court to the propriety of petitioner's order. In our view of the case, however, it is unnecessary to reach this question. The peremptory writ of mandamus has traditionally been used in the federal courts only "to confine an inferior court to a lawful exercise of its prescribed jurisdiction or to compel it to exercise its authority when it is its duty to do so." Roche v. Evaporated Milk Assn., 319 U.S. 21, 26, 63 S.Ct. 938, 941 (1943). While the courts have never confined themselves to an arbitrary and technical definition of "jurisdiction," it is clear that only exceptional circumstances amounting to a judicial "usurpation of power" will justify the invocation of this extraordinary remedy. Thus the writ has been invoked where unwarranted judicial action threatened "to embarrass the executive arm of the government in conducting foreign relations," where it was the only means of forestalling intrusion by the federal judiciary on a delicate area of federal-state relations, where it was necessary to confine a lower court to the terms of an appellate tribunal's mandate, and where a district judge displayed a persistent disregard of the Rules of Civil Procedure promulgated by this Court. And the party seeking mandamus has "the burden of showing that its right to issuance of the writ is clear and indisputable." Bankers Life & Cas. Co. v. Holland, 346 U.S. 379, 384, 74 S.Ct. 145, 148, 98 L.Ed. 106 (1953).

We also approach this case with an awareness of additional considerations which flow from the fact that the underlying proceeding is a criminal prosecution. All our jurisprudence is strongly colored by the notion that appellate review should be postponed, except in certain narrowly defined circumstances, until after final judgment has been rendered by the trial court. This general policy against piecemeal appeals takes on added weight in criminal cases, where the defendant is entitled to a speedy resolution of the charges against him. Moreover, "in the federal jurisprudence, at least, appeals by the Government in criminal cases are something unusual, exceptional, not favored," Carroll v. United States, 354 U.S. 394, 400, 77 S.Ct. 1332, 1336, 1 L.Ed.2d 1442 (1957), at least in part because they always threaten to offend the policies behind the double-jeopardy prohibition. * * * Mandamus, of course, may never be employed as a substitute for appeal in derogation of these clear policies. * * * This is not to say that mandamus may never be used to review procedural orders in criminal cases. * * * We need not decide under what circumstances, if any, such a use of mandamus would be appropriate. It is enough to note that we approach the decision in this case with an awareness of the constitutional precepts that a man is entitled to a speedy trial and that he may not be placed twice in jeopardy for the same offense.

In light of these considerations and criteria, neither the record before us nor the cryptic order of the Court of Appeals justifies the invocation of the extraordinary writ in this case.

* * *

The Government seeks * * * to justify the employment of the writ in this instance on the ground that petitioner's conduct displays a "pattern of manifest noncompliance with the rules governing federal criminal trials." It argues that the federal rules place settled limitations upon pretrial discovery in criminal cases, and that a trial court may not, in the absence of compelling justification, order the Government to produce a list of its witnesses in advance of trial. * * * The Government concludes that since petitioner obviously had no power to adopt such a rule, mandamus will lie under this Court's decision in La Buy v. Howes Leather Co., 352 U.S. 249, 77 S.Ct. 309, 1 L.Ed.2d 290 (1957), to correct this studied disregard of the limitations placed upon the district courts by the federal rules.

The action of the Court of Appeals cannot, on the record before us, bear the weight of this justification. There is absolutely no foundation in this record for the Government's assertions concerning petitioner's practice. The legal proposition that mandamus will lie in appropriate cases to correct willful disobedience of the rules laid down by this Court is not controverted. But the position of the Government rests on two central factual premises: (1) that petitioner in effect ordered it to produce a list of witnesses in advance of trial; and (2) that petitioner took this action pursuant to a deliberately adopted policy in disregard of the rules of criminal procedure. Neither of these premises finds support in the record.

* * *

Even more important in our view, however, than these deficiencies in the record is the failure of the Court of Appeals to attempt to supply any reasoned justification of its action. Had the Government in fact shown that petitioner adopted a policy in deliberate disregard of the criminal discovery rules and that this policy had proved seriously disruptive of the efficient administration of criminal justice in the Northern District of Illinois, it would have raised serious questions under this Court's decision in La Buy v. Howes Leather Co.[14] In *La Buy*, however, we specifically relied upon evidence in the record which showed a pattern of improper references of cases to special masters by the District Judge. There is no evidence in this record concerning petitioner's practice in other cases, aside from his own remark that the Government was generally dissatisfied with it, and his statements do not reveal any intent to evade or disregard the rules. We do not know what he ordered the Government to reveal under what circumstances in other cases. This state of the record renders the silence of the Court of Appeals all the

---

14. The Government also places reliance on Schlagenhauf v. Holder, arguing that it reaffirmed *La Buy*. Insofar as it did so, the case does not help the Government here, since we have no quarrel with *La Buy*, which is simply inappropriate where there is no showing of a persistent disregard of the federal rules. And it cannot be contended that *Schlagenhauf* on its facts supports an invocation of mandamus in this case. The Court these did note that the various questions concerning the construction of Rule 35 were new and substantial, but it rested the existence of mandamus jurisdiction squarely on the fact that there was real doubt whether the District Court had any power at all to order a defendant to submit to a physical examination.

more critical. We recognized in *La Buy* that the familiarity of a court of appeals with the practice of the individual district courts within its circuit was relevant to an assessment of the need for mandamus as a corrective measure. But without an opinion from the Court of Appeals we do not know what role, if any, this factor played in the decision below. * * *

Due regard, not merely for the reviewing functions of this Court, but for the "drastic and extraordinary" nature of the mandamus remedy, and for the extremely awkward position in which it places the District Judge, demands that a court issuing the writ give a reasoned exposition of the basis for its action.

Mandamus is not a punitive remedy. The entire thrust of the Government's justification for mandamus in this case, moreover, is that the writ serves a vital corrective and didactic function. While these aims lay at the core of this Court's decisions in *La Buy* and Schlagenhauf v. Holder, 379 U.S. 104, 85 S.Ct. 234 (1964), we fail to see how they can be served here without findings of fact by the issuing court and some statement of the court's legal reasoning. A mandamus from the blue without rationale is tantamount to an abdication of the very expository and supervisory functions of an appellate court upon which the Government rests its attempt to justify the action below.

The peremptory common-law writs are among the most potent weapons in the judicial arsenal. "As extraordinary remedies, they are reserved for really extraordinary causes." Ex parte Fahey, 332 U.S. 258, 260, 67 S.Ct. 1558, 1559 (1947). There is nothing in the record here to demonstrate that this case falls into that category, and thus the judgment below cannot stand. What might be the proper decision upon a more complete record, supplemented by the findings and conclusions of the Court of Appeals, we cannot and do not say. Hence the writ is vacated and the cause is remanded to the Court of Appeals for the Seventh Circuit for further proceedings not inconsistent with this opinion.

Justice Marshall took no part in the consideration or decision of this case.

[The concurring opinion of Justice Black is omitted.]

Notes and Questions

1. The All Writs Act, 28 U.S.C.A. § 1651, authorizes federal courts "to issue all writs necessary or appropriate in aid of their respective jurisdiction and agreeable to the usage and principles of law." Pursuant to this provision, the circuit courts of appeals may issue writs of mandamus to the district courts, requiring those courts to take certain actions. Traditionally, such writs have been reserved for extraordinary situations. Recall In the Matter of Rhone–Poulenc Rorer, Inc., supra p. 309, in which the court used mandamus to review a class certification order.

2. Mandamus is traditionally employed as a means of protecting a right to jury trial claimed to have been improperly denied in the district court.

See, e.g., Dairy Queen, Inc. v. Wood, 369 U.S. 469, 82 S.Ct. 894, 8 L.Ed.2d 44 (1962), supra p. 539; Beacon Theatres, Inc. v. Westover, 359 U.S. 500, 79 S.Ct. 948, 3 L.Ed.2d 988 (1959), supra p. 531. Is there a rational way to distinguish this interlocutory ruling from any other?

In First National Bank of Waukesha v. Warren, 796 F.2d 999 (7th Cir.1986), Judge Easterbrook criticized this use of mandamus:

> Neither *Beacon Theatres* nor *Dairy Queen* answers the question: Why mandamus? * * * Surely the answer is not * * * that there is a constitutional right at stake. Much federal litigation involves constitutional rights, but the nature of the right does not dictate whether review comes in mid-course or at the end of the district court's proceedings. Jury trial is not the most essential of rights, either.

He suggested that *Will* has significantly confined the approval of mandamus in *Beacon Theatres* and *Dairy Queen*.

3. Prior to *Will*, the Court had utilized mandamus as a means of providing interlocutory review of a discovery order in a civil case, Schlagenhauf v. Holder, 379 U.S. 104, 85 S.Ct. 234, 13 L.Ed.2d 152 (1964). The case involved the validity and construction of Rule 35(a), providing for court-ordered mental and physical examinations of parties [see supra p. 350], as applied to a defendant in a negligence action. Rule 35 had generally been used only against plaintiffs—the individuals who undertook the action in the first place—even though by its terms Rule 35 is not so limited.

In response to the claim that use of mandamus was inappropriate to review the interlocutory discovery order, Justice Goldberg, speaking for the Court, stated:

> It is, of course, well settled, that the writ is not to be used as a substitute for appeal, even though hardship may result from delay and perhaps unnecessary trial. The writ is appropriately issued, however, when there is "usurpation of judicial power" or a clear abuse of discretion.

> Here petitioner's basic allegation was lack of power in a district court to order a mental and physical examination of a defendant. That this issue was substantial is underscored by the fact that the challenged order requiring examination of a defendant appears to be the first of its kind in any reported decision in the federal courts under Rule 35, and we have found only one such modern case in the state courts. The Court of Appeals recognized that it had the power to review on a petition for mandamus the basic, undecided question of whether a district court could order the mental or physical examination of a defendant. We agree that, under these unusual circumstances and in light of the authorities, the Court of Appeals had such power.

Does *Schlagenhauf*, on its face, provide a foundation for widespread use of mandamus as a basis for obtaining interlocutory review of discovery orders? What is left of it after *Will*? Recall the discussion concerning appeal of discovery orders following *Cohen* and *Digital Equipment Corp.* [supra p. 1030]. The Court has chosen not to use the collateral order doctrine in appeals from discovery orders, because of the availability of the "contempt" method sanctioned in United States v. Ryan [supra p. 1048]. It should be noted that the "contempt" avenue was unavailable in *Schlagenhauf,* because Rule 37 expressly exempts Rule 35 orders from enforcement by means of contempt.

According to a recent court of appeals' decision, mandamus may be available today where a discovery issue is of "extraordinary significance" or where there is an extreme need for reversal of the district court's mandate before the case goes to judgment. In re Security and Exchange Commission, 374 F.3d 184 (2d Cir. 2004). The court reasoned that under "unusual circumstances," the contempt avenue may not be adequate, and in such situations mandamus may be available.

4. Since *Will v. United States,* the Court has generally continued to emphasize the limited nature of mandamus review. In Will v. Calvert Fire Insurance Co., 437 U.S. 655, 98 S.Ct. 2552, 57 L.Ed.2d 504 (1978), for example, Justice Rehnquist, speaking for four justices in an opinion announcing the judgment of the Court, stated: "On direct appeal, a court of appeals has broad authority to 'modify, vacate, set aside or reverse' an order of a district court, and it may direct such further action on remand 'as may be just under the circumstances.' 28 U.S.C. § 2106. By contrast, under the All Writs Act, courts of appeals may issue a writ of mandamus only when 'necessary or appropriate in aid of their respective jurisdictions.' Whereas a simple showing of error may suffice to obtain a reversal on direct appeal, to issue a writ of mandamus under such circumstances 'would undermine the settled limitations on the power of an appellate court to review interlocutory orders.' Will v. United States."

In Kerr v. United States District Court, 426 U.S. 394, 96 S.Ct. 2119, 48 L.Ed.2d 725 (1976), the Court, relying on Will v. United States, stated:

> The remedy of mandamus is a drastic one, to be invoked only in extraordinary situations. * * * [M]andamus actions * * * "have the unfortunate consequence of making the [district court] judge a litigant, obliged to obtain personal counsel or to leave his defense to one of the litigants [appearing] before him" in the underlying case. Bankers Life & Cas. Co. v. Holland, 346 U.S., at 384–385. More importantly, particularly in an era of excessively crowded lower court dockets, it is in the interest of the fair and prompt administration of justice to discourage piecemeal litigation.

The Court in *Kerr* noted that "the party seeking issuance of the writ [must] have no other adequate means to attain the relief he desires" and must also satisfy the burden of showing that his right to issuance of the writ is "clear and indisputable."

The Court stated in Allied Chemical Corp. v. Daiflon, Inc., 449 U.S. 33, 101 S.Ct. 188, 66 L.Ed.2d 193 (1980) (per curiam): "[O]ur cases have answered the question as to the availability of mandamus * * * with the refrain: 'What never? Well, *hardly ever!*' " In that decision, mandamus had been sought to require the trial judge to reinstate a jury verdict. The Court concluded that

> [a] trial court's ordering of a new trial rarely, if ever, will justify the issuance of a writ of mandamus. On the contrary, such an order is not an uncommon feature of any trial which goes to verdict. A litigant is free to seek review of the propriety of such an order on direct appeal after a

final judgment has been entered. Consequently, it cannot be said that the litigant "has no other adequate means to seek the relief he desires." The authority to grant a new trial, moreover, is confided almost entirely to the exercise of discretion on the part of the trial court. Where a matter is committed to discretion, it cannot be said that a litigant's right to a particular result is "clear and indisputable."

One case in which the Supreme Court did, in fact, authorize mandamus is Mallard v. United States District Court for the Southern District of Iowa, 490 U.S. 296, 109 S.Ct. 1814, 104 L.Ed.2d 318 (1989). There the Court held that an attorney whose motion to withdraw from a mandatory appointment to represent an indigent civil litigant had been denied could obtain mandamus in the court of appeals. The Court noted that "[t]o ensure that mandamus remains an extraordinary remedy, petitioners must show that they lack adequate alternative means to obtain the relief they seek * * * and carry the burden of showing that [their] right to issuance of the writ is 'clear and indisputable' * * * ". The petitioner in *Mallard*, said the Court, "met this demanding standard," because "the District Court plainly acted beyond its 'jurisdiction' " under the relevant federal statute, and because petitioner "had no alternative remedy available to him." 490 U.S. at 308. The case may be of limited precedential value, however, because the Court also noted that, due to the unique procedural circumstances, "the principal reasons for our reluctance to condone use of the writ, the undesirability of making a district court judge a litigant and the inefficiency of piecemeal appellate litigation, Fare not present here. The District Court Judge never was made a party to this action, nor did Mallard's petition attempt to sever one element of the merits litigation from the rest." Id.

It is well established that "a writ of mandamus may be used to review the disqualification of counsel." This is "because the harm of such disqualification cannot be corrected with an ordinary appeal." Whether the writ will, in fact, be used in such cases depends upon a case-by-case synthesis of a variety of factors, including whether a direct appeal is available, uncorrectable damage is caused, the order is clear legal error or is oft-repeated, and whether the order raises new and important issue. Cole v. United States District Court for the District of Idaho, 366 F.3d 813, 816–17 (9th Cir. 2004).

  d. *Partial Final Judgment Under Rule 54(b)*

CURTISS–WRIGHT CORPORATION v.
GENERAL ELECTRIC COMPANY

Supreme Court of the United States, 1980.
446 U.S. 1, 100 S.Ct. 1460, 64 L.Ed.2d 1.

CHIEF JUSTICE BURGER delivered the opinion of the Court.

Federal Rule of Civil Procedure 54(b) allows a district court dealing with multiple claims or multiple parties to direct the entry of final judgment as to fewer than all of the claims or parties; to do so, the court must make an express determination that there is no just reason for delay.

I

From 1968 to 1972, respondent General Electric Co. entered into a series of 21 contracts with petitioner Curtiss–Wright Corp. for the manufacture of components designed for use in nuclear powered naval vessels. These contracts had a total value of $215 million.

In 1976, Curtiss–Wright brought a diversity action in the United States District Court for the District of New Jersey, seeking damages and reformation with regard to the 21 contracts. The complaint asserted claims based on alleged fraud, misrepresentation, and breach of contract by General Electric. It also sought $19 million from General Electric on the outstanding balance due on the contracts already performed.

General Electric counterclaimed for $1.9 million in costs allegedly incurred as the result of "extraordinary efforts" provided to Curtiss–Wright during performance of the contracts which enabled Curtiss–Wright to avoid a contract default. General Electric also sought, by way of counterclaim, to recover $52 million by which Curtiss–Wright was allegedly unjustly enriched as a result of these "extraordinary efforts."

The facts underlying most of these claims and counterclaims are in dispute. As to Curtiss–Wright's claims for the $19 million balance due, however, the sole dispute concerns the application of a release clause contained in each of the 21 agreements, which states that "Seller ... agree[s] as a condition precedent to final payment, that the Buyer and the Government ... are released from all liabilities, obligations and claims arising under or by virtue of this order." When Curtiss–Wright moved for summary judgment on the balance due, General Electric contended that so long as Curtiss–Wright's other claims remained pending, this provision constituted a bar to recovery of the undisputed balance.

The District Court rejected this contention and granted summary judgment for Curtiss–Wright on this otherwise undisputed claim. Applying New York law by which the parties had agreed to be bound, the District Court held that Curtiss–Wright was entitled to payment of the balance due notwithstanding the release clause. The court also ruled that Curtiss–Wright was entitled to prejudgment interest at the New York statutory rate of 6% per annum.

Curtiss–Wright then moved for a certification of the District Court's orders as final judgments under Federal Rule of Civil Procedure 54(b).
* * *

The court expressly directed entry of final judgment for Curtiss–Wright and made the determination that there was "no just reason for delay" pursuant to Rule 54(b).

The District Court also provided a written statement of reasons supporting its decision to certify the judgment as final. It acknowledged that Rule 54(b) certification was not to be granted as a matter of course, and that this remedy should be reserved for the infrequent harsh case because of the overload in appellate courts which would otherwise result from appeals of an interlocutory nature. The essential inquiry was stated to be "whether, after balancing the competing factors, finality of judgment should be ordered to advance the interests of sound judicial administration and justice to the litigants."

The District Court then went on to identify the relevant factors in the case before it. It found that certification would not result in unnecessary appellate review; that the claims finally adjudicated were separate, distinct, and independent of any of the other claims or counterclaims involved; that review of these adjudicated claims would not be mooted by any future developments in the case; and that the nature of the claims was such that no appellate court would have to decide the same issues more than once even if there were subsequent appeals.

Turning to considerations of justice to the litigants, the District Court found that Curtiss–Wright would suffer severe daily financial loss from nonpayment of the $19 million judgment because current interest rates were higher than the statutory prejudgment rate, a situation compounded by the large amount of money involved. The court observed that the complex nature of the remaining claims could, without certification, mean a delay that "would span many months, if not years."

The court found that solvency of the parties was not a significant factor, since each appeared to be financially sound. Although the presence of General Electric's counterclaims and the consequent possibility of a setoff recovery were factors which weighed against certification, the court, in balancing these factors, determined that they were outweighed by the other factors in the case. Accordingly, it granted Rule 54(b) certification. It also granted General Electric's motion for a stay without bond pending appeal.

A divided panel of the United States Court of Appeals for the Third Circuit held that the case was controlled by its decision in Allis–Chalmers Corp. v. Philadelphia Electric Co., 521 F.2d 360 (1975), where the court had stated:

> "In the absence of unusual or harsh circumstances, we believe that the presence of a counterclaim, which could result in a set-off against any amounts due and owing to the plaintiff, weighs heavily against the grant of 54(b) certification."

In *Allis-Chalmers,* the court defined unusual or harsh circumstances as those factors "involving considerations of solvency, economic duress, etc." In the Third Circuit's view, the question was which of the parties should have the benefit of the amount of the balance due pending final resolution of the litigation. * * * The Court of Appeals acknowledged that Curtiss–Wright's inability to have use of the money from the judgment might seem harsh, but noted that the same could be said for General Electric if it were forced to pay Curtiss–Wright now but later prevailed on its counterclaims.

The Court of Appeals concluded that the District Court had abused its discretion by granting Rule 54(b) certification in this situation and dismissed the case for want of an appealable order; it also directed the District Court to vacate its Rule 54(b) determination of finality. * * * We reverse.

II

Nearly a quarter of a century ago, in Sears, Roebuck & Co. v. Mackey, 351 U.S. 427, 76 S.Ct. 895, 100 L.Ed. 1297 (1956), this Court outlined the steps to be followed in making determinations under Rule 54(b). A district court must first determine that it is dealing with a "final judgment." It must be a "judgment" in the sense that it is a decision upon a cognizable claim for relief, and it must be "final" in the sense that it is "an ultimate disposition of an individual claim entered in the course of a multiple claims action."

Once having found finality, the district court must go on to determine whether there is any just reason for delay. Not all final judgments on individual claims should be immediately appealable, even if they are in some sense separable from the remaining unresolved claims. The function of the district court under the Rule is to act as a "dispatcher." It is left to the sound judicial discretion of the district court to determine the "appropriate time" when each final decision in a multiple claims action is ready for appeal. This discretion is to be exercised "in the interest of sound judicial administration."

Thus, in deciding whether there are no just reasons to delay the appeal of individual final judgments in a setting such as this, a district court must take into account judicial administrative interests as well as the equities involved. Consideration of the former is necessary to assure that application of the Rule effectively "preserves the historic federal policy against piecemeal appeals." It was therefore proper for the District Judge here to consider such factors as whether the claims under review were separable from the others remaining to be adjudicated and whether the nature of the claims already determined was such that no appellate court would have to decide the same issues more than once even if there were subsequent appeals.

Here the District Judge saw no sound reason to delay appellate resolution of the undisputed claims already adjudicated. The contrary conclusion of the Court of Appeals was strongly influenced by the existence of nonfrivolous counterclaims. The mere presence of such claims, however, does not render a Rule 54(b) certification inappropriate. If it did, Rule 54(b) would lose much of its utility. * * * Like other claims, their significance for Rule 54(b) purposes turns on their interrelationship with the claims on which certification is sought. Here, the District Judge determined that General Electric's counterclaims were severable from the claims which had been determined in terms of both the factual and the legal issues involved. The Court of Appeals did not conclude otherwise.

What the Court of Appeals found objectionable about the District Judge's exercise of discretion was the assessment of the equities involved. The Court of Appeals concluded that the possibility of a setoff required that the status quo be maintained unless petitioner could show harsh or unusual circumstances; it held that such a showing had not been made in the District Court.

This holding reflects a misinterpretation of the standard of review for Rule 54(b) certifications and a misperception of the appellate function in such cases. The Court of Appeals relied on a statement of the Advisory Committee on the Rules of Civil Procedure, and its error derives from reading a description in the commentary as a standard of construction. When Rule 54(b) was amended in 1946, the Notes of the Advisory Committee which accompanied the suggested amendment indicated that the entire lawsuit was generally the appropriate unit for appellate review, "and that this rule needed only the exercise of a discretionary power to afford a remedy in the infrequent harsh case to provide a simple, definite, workable rule." 5 F.R.D. 433, 473 (1946). However accurate it may be as a description of cases qualifying for Rule 54(b) treatment, the phrase "infrequent harsh case" in isolation is neither workable nor entirely reliable as a benchmark for appellate review. There is no indication it was ever intended by the drafters to function as such.

In *Sears*, the Court stated that the decision to certify was with good reason left to the sound judicial discretion of the district court. At the same time, the Court noted that "[w]ith equally good reason, any *abuse* of that discretion remains reviewable by the Court of Appeals." The Court indicated that the standard against which a district court's exercise of discretion is to be judged is the "interest of sound judicial administration." Admittedly this presents issues not always easily resolved, but the proper role of the court of appeals is not to reweigh the equities or reassess the facts but to make sure that the conclusions derived from those weighings and assessments are juridically sound and supported by the record.

There are thus two aspects to the proper function of a reviewing court in Rule 54(b) cases. The court of appeals must, of course, scrutinize the district court's evaluation of such factors as the interrelationship of the claims so as to prevent piecemeal appeals in cases which should be reviewed only as single units. But once such juridical concerns have been met, the discretionary judgment of the district court should be given substantial deference, for that court is "the one most likely to be familiar with the case and with any justifiable reasons for delay." The reviewing court should disturb the trial court's assessment of the equities only if it can say that the judge's conclusion was clearly unreasonable.

Plainly, sound judicial administration does not require that Rule 54(b) requests be granted routinely. That is implicit in commending them to the sound discretion of a district court. Because this discretion "is, with good reason, vested by the rule primarily" in the district courts, and because the number of possible situations is large, we are reluctant either to fix or sanction narrow guidelines for the district courts to follow. We are satisfied, however, that on the record here the District Court's assessment of the equities was reasonable.

One of the equities which the District Judge considered was the difference between the statutory and market rates of interest. Respondent correctly points out that adjustment of the statutory prejudgment interest rate is a matter within the province of the legislature, but that fact does not make the existing differential irrelevant for Rule 54(b) purposes. If the judgment is otherwise certifiable, the fact that a litigant who has successfully reduced his claim to judgment stands to lose money because of the difference in interest rates is surely not a "just reason for delay."

The difference between the prejudgment and market interest rates was not the only factor considered by the District Court. The court also noted that the debts in issue were liquidated and large, and that absent Rule 54(b) certification they would not be paid for "many months, if not years" because the rest of the litigation would be expected to continue for that period of time. The District Judge had noted earlier in his opinion on the merits of the release clause issue that respondent General Electric contested neither the amount of the debt nor the fact that it must eventually be paid. The only contest was over the effect of the release clause on the timing of the payment, an isolated and strictly legal issue on which summary judgment had been entered against respondent.

The question before the District Court thus came down to which of the parties should get the benefit of the difference between the prejudgment and market rates of interest on debts admittedly owing and adjudged to be due while unrelated claims were litigated. The central factor weighing in favor of General Electric was that its pending counterclaims created the possibility of a setoff against the amount it owed petitioner. This possibility was surely not an insignificant factor, especially since the counterclaims had survived a motion to dismiss for failure to state a claim. But the District Court took this into account when it determined that both litigants appeared to be in financially sound condition, and that Curtiss–Wright would be able to satisfy a judgment on the counterclaims should any be entered.

The question in cases such as this is likely to be close, but the task of weighing and balancing the contending factors is peculiarly one for the trial judge, who can explore all the facets of a case. As we have noted, that assessment merits substantial deference on review. Here, the District Court's assessment of the equities between the parties was based on an intimate knowledge of the case and is a reasonable one. The District Court having found no other reason justifying delay, we conclude that it did not abuse its discretion in granting petitioner's motion for certification under Rule 54(b).

Notes and Questions

1. Why is Rule 54(b) necessary? Why don't the other methods of obtaining appellate review adequately deal with the situation covered by

Rule 54(b)? Cf. Dickinson v. Petroleum Conversion Corp., 338 U.S. 507, 70 S.Ct. 322, 324, 94 L.Ed. 299 (1950): "The liberalization of our practice to allow more issues and parties to be joined in one action and to expand the privilege of intervention by those not originally parties has increased the danger of hardship and denial of justice through delay if each issue must await the determination of all issues as to all parties before a final judgment can be had."

2. Note that the Court in *Curtiss-Wright* emphasizes the importance of district court discretion in issuing certificates under Rule 54(b). See also Sussex Drug Products v. Kanasco, Ltd., 920 F.2d 1150 (3d Cir.1990). This discretion has no applicability to any other avenue of appeal from a final judgment. Why is it thought to be of special importance in the context of Rule 54(b) appeals?

While district court discretion in invoking Rule 54(b) is broad, it is not unlimited. In Gerardi v. Pelullo, 16 F.3d 1363 (3d Cir.1994), the court held that "the district court abused its discretion when it concluded that [the judgments] were ready for appeal" pursuant to Rule 54(b). The court expressed the view "that a district court should be conservative in invoking Rule 54(b) to certify a judgment as final because if an aggrieved party appeals following the certification, the district court effectively will be electing to control the docket of a court of appeals." Moreover, despite the broad discretion vested in district courts in issuing Rule 54(b) certifications, where the district court fails to provide reasons for its determination that there was no just reason for delay and the reason for certification is not apparent from the record, the court of appeals will not find jurisdiction. Cemar, Inc. v. Nissan Motor Corp., 897 F.2d 120 (3d Cir.1990). In addition, the district court's discretion extends only to the determination that there exists no just reason for delay. The district court's determination of the ruling's finality for purposes of Rule 54(b) is reviewed de novo. W. L. Gore & Associates, Inc. v. International Medical Prosthetics Research Associates, Inc., 975 F.2d 858 (Fed.Cir.1992); Ginett v. Computer Task Group, Inc., 962 F.2d 1085 (2d Cir.1992).

3. By its terms, Rule 54(b) applies only where either multiple claims for relief or multiple parties are involved. While the issue of whether multiple parties are present has caused no great problems, whether more than one claim is involved has often proven difficult to answer.

As originally adopted, Rule 54(b) referred to a "separate judgment", and therefore was construed to require that to be appealable, a claim must be "separate" from the other claims, a concept whose definition was not entirely clear. In Dickinson v. Petroleum Conversion Corp., 338 U.S. 507, 70 S.Ct. 322, 94 L.Ed. 299 (1950), the Court held that under this original version of the Rule, the claims should be entirely distinct, arising out of different occurrences or transactions that form the basis of separate units of judicial action. In 1948, however, the Rule was amended to remove the relevant language and to add the language concerning the district court's determination about delay. But it was by no means clear how "separate" the claims had to be under the amended Rule to authorize appeal of a decided claim.

The Supreme Court considered the issue in two cases decided the same day in 1956. In Sears, Roebuck and Co. v. Mackey, 351 U.S. 427, 76 S.Ct. 895, 100 L.Ed. 1297 (1956), the complaint contained four operative counts. Count I alleged conduct by Sears violating the Sherman Antitrust Act and causing injury to three of Mackey's commercial ventures. The remaining counts alleged common law violations for the conduct concerning each of the three separate ventures. The claims stated in counts I and II were dismissed in the district court. The issue was whether the court of appeals had jurisdiction to hear Mackey's appeal from that dismissal. The Supreme Court held that appeal could be taken under Rule 54(b):

> In the case before us, there is no doubt that each of the claims dismissed is a "claim for relief" within the meaning of Rule 54(b), or that their dismissal constitutes a "final decision" on individual claims. Also, it cannot well be argued that the claims stated in Counts I and II are so inherently inseparable from, or closely related to, those stated in Counts III and IV that the District Court has abused its discretion in certifying that there exists no just reason for delay.

The Supreme Court reached this conclusion, even though count I was obviously factually related to counts III and IV, and thus the counts were not totally independent.

In the other decision, Cold Metal Process Co. v. United Engineering & Foundry Co., 351 U.S. 445, 76 S.Ct. 904, 100 L.Ed. 1311 (1956), the Court held that Rule 54(b) allowed appeal from a judgment on plaintiff's claim, despite the fact that defendant's counterclaim, arising in part out of the same transaction as plaintiff's claim, remained undecided:

> [U]nder [original Rule 54(b)], it is likely that if [defendant's] counterclaim qualified as "permissive," rather than as "compulsory," the Court of Appeals would have had jurisdiction to entertain the appeal now before us. This conclusion follows from the fact that the test of appealability under the original rule was whether the adjudicated claims were separate from, and independent of the unadjudicated claims.

> However, * * * that test led to uncertainty, of which the present case might have been an example. The amended rule overcomes that difficulty and, under its terms, we need not decide whether [defendant's] counterclaim is compulsory or permissive. * * * [U]nder the amended rule, the relationship of the adjudicated claims to the unadjudicated claims is one of the factors the District Court can consider, in the exercise of its discretion. If the District Court certifies a final order on a claim which arises out of the same transaction and occurrence as pending claims, and the Court of Appeals is satisfied that there has been no abuse of discretion, the order is appealable.

In the words of one group of commentators, "[w]hen read together, these decisions repudiate the notion that a separate claim for purposes of Rule 54(b) is one that must be entirely distinct from all the other claims in the action and arise from a different occurrence or transaction." Of course, if the claims factually are separate and independent, then multiple claims clearly are present. "At the other extreme, the decided cases do not go so far as to treat every variation in legal theory as a separate 'claim.'" 10 C. Wright, A. Miller & M. Kane, Federal Practice and Procedure § 2657 at 63–64 (1983).

See generally Comment, Multiple Claims Under Rule 54(b): A Time for Reexamination, 1985 B.Y.U.L.Rev. 327.

4.   Note that Rule 54(b) requires "an express determination" by the district court "that there is no just reason for delay." It has been held that a court of appeals should "not require a mechanical recitation of the rule's requirements," but instead merely "that the district court manifest 'unmistakable intent' to make its judgment final." Swope v. Columbian Chemicals Co., 281 F.3d 185, 191, n. 5 (5th Cir. 2002).

5.   In Reiter v. Cooper, 507 U.S. 258, 113 S.Ct. 1213, 122 L.Ed.2d 604 (1993), the Supreme Court noted that while Rule 54(b) applies to counterclaims, it is inapplicable to separate disposition of a defense.

   e.   *Appeal of Interlocutory Injunctions*

GULFSTREAM AEROSPACE CORPORATION v. MAYACAMAS CORPORATION

Supreme Court of the United States, 1988.
485 U.S. 271, 108 S.Ct. 1133, 99 L.Ed.2d 296.

JUSTICE MARSHALL delivered the opinion of the Court.

[Gulfstream sued Mayacamas in state court in Georgia for breach of contract regarding its failure to purchase aircraft as agreed upon. Mayacamas, choosing not to remove the action to federal court, filed an answer and a counterclaim. A month after the commencement of the state suit, Mayacamas sued Gulfstream in federal district court in California, alleging breach of the same contract. Gulfstream moved for a stay or dismissal of the federal action, citing *Colorado River* and *Moses H. Cone* supra p. 1024 n. 2. The district court denied the stay, and the circuit court dismissed the appeal, finding no right to appeal under § 1291 or § 1292(a)(1) and declining to treat the notice of appeal as an application for mandamus on the ground the district court's order would not cause "serious hardship or prejudice."

The portion of this opinion dealing with appealability under the collateral order doctrine is discussed supra p. 1042 n. 7]

Petitioner argues in the alternative that the District Court's order in this case is immediately appealable under § 1292(a)(1), which gives the courts of appeals jurisdiction of appeals from interlocutory orders granting or denying injunctions. An order by a federal court that relates only to the conduct or progress of litigation before that court ordinarily is not considered an injunction and therefore is not appealable under § 1292(a)(1). Under the *Enelow-Ettelson* doctrine, however, certain orders that stay or refuse to stay judicial proceedings are considered injunctions and therefore are immediately appealable. Petitioner asserts that the order in this case, which denied a motion for a stay of a federal-court action pending the resolution of a concurrent state-court proceeding, is appealable under § 1292(a)(1) pursuant to the *Enelow-Ettelson* doctrine.

The line of cases we must examine to resolve this claim began some fifty years ago, when this Court decided Enelow v. New York Life Ins. Co., 293 U.S. 379 (1935). At the time of that decision, law and equity remained separate jurisprudential systems in the federal courts. The same judges administered both these systems, however, so that a federal district judge was both a chancellor in equity and a judge at law. In *Enelow*, the plaintiff sued at law to recover on a life insurance policy. The insurance company raised the affirmative defense that the policy had been obtained by fraud and moved the District Court to stay the trial of the law action pending resolution of this equitable defense. The District Court granted this motion, and the plaintiff appealed. This Court likened the stay to an injunction issued by an equity court to restrain an action at law. The Court stated:

> "[T]he grant or refusal of a stay by a court of equity of proceedings at law is a grant or refusal of an injunction within the meaning of [the statute]. And, in this aspect, it makes no difference that the two cases, the suit in equity for an injunction and the action at law in which proceedings are stayed, are both pending in the same court, in view of the established distinction between 'proceedings in equity in the national courts. . . .'

> "It is thus apparent that when an order or decree is made . . . requiring, or refusing to require, that an equitable defense shall first be tried, the court, exercising what is essentially an equitable jurisdiction, in effect grants or refuses an injunction restraining proceedings at law precisely as if the court had acted upon a bill of complaint in a separate suit for the same purpose."

The Court thus concluded that the District Court's order was appealable under § 1292(a)(1).

In Ettelson v. Metropolitan Life Ins. Co., 317 U.S. 188 (1942), the Court reaffirmed the rule of *Enelow*, notwithstanding that the Federal Rules of Civil Procedure had fully merged law and equity in the interim. The relevant facts of *Ettelson* were identical to those of *Enelow*, and the Court responded to them in the same fashion. In response to the argument that the fusion of law and equity had destroyed the analogy between the stay ordered in the action and an injunction issued by a chancellor of a separate proceeding at law, the Court stated only that the plaintiffs were "in no different position than if a state equity court had restrained them from proceeding in the law action." Thus, the order granting the stay was held to be immediately appealable as an injunction.

The historical analysis underlying the results in *Enelow* and *Ettelson* has bred a doctrine of curious contours. Under the *Enelow-Ettelson* rule, most recently restated in Baltimore Contractors, Inc. v. Bodinger, 348 U.S. 176 (1955), an order by a federal court staying or refusing to stay its own proceedings is appealable under § 1292(a)(1) as the grant or denial of an injunction if two conditions are met. First, the action in which the order is entered must be an action that, before the merger of law and equity, was by its nature an action at law. Second, the order must arise from or be based on some matter that would then have been considered an equitable defense or counterclaim. If both conditions are satisfied, the historical equivalent of the modern order would have been an injunction, issued by a separate equity court, to restrain proceedings in an action at law. If either condition is not met, however, the historical analogy fails. When the underlying suit is historically equitable and the stay is based on a defense or counterclaim that is historically legal, the analogy fails because a law judge had no power to issue an injunction restraining equitable proceedings. And when both the underlying suit and the defense or counterclaim on which the stay is based are historically equitable, or when both are historically legal, the analogy fails because when a chancellor or a law judge stayed an action in his own court, he was not issuing an injunction, but merely arranging matters on his docket. Thus, unless a stay order is made in a historically legal action on the basis of a historically equitable defense or counterclaim, the order cannot be analogized to a pre-merger injunction and therefore cannot be appealed under § 1292(a)(1) pursuant to the *Enelow-Ettelson* doctrine.

The parties in this case dispute whether the *Enelow-Ettelson* rule makes the District Court's decision to deny a stay immediately appealable under § 1292(a)(1). Both parties agree that an action for breach of contract was an action at law prior to the merger of law and equity. They vigorously contest, however, whether the stay of an action pending the resolution of similar proceedings in a state court is equitable in the requisite sense. Petitioner relies primarily on the decision of the United States Court of Appeals for the Seventh Circuit in Microsoftware Computer Systems, Inc. v. Ontel Corp., 686 F.2d 531 (1982). The court held that a stay issued under *Colorado River* is based on the policy of avoiding "the unnecessary and wasteful duplication of lawsuits," which is historically an equitable defense. Respondent, on the other hand, urges us to adopt the reasoning of the Ninth Circuit in this case. In its decision, the court below drew a distinction between motions that raised equitable "defenses" and motions that raised equitable "considerations." The court held that a motion for a stay pursuant to *Colorado River* was based only on equitable considerations and that the *Enelow-Ettelson* rule therefore did not apply.

We decline to address the issue of appealability in these terms; indeed, the sterility of the debate between the parties illustrates the need for a more fundamental consideration of the precedents in this area. This Court long has understood that the *Enelow-Ettelson* rule is deficient in utility and sense. In the two cases we have decided since *Ettelson* relating to the rule, we criticized its perpetuation of "outmoded procedural differentiations" and its consequent tendency to produce incongruous results. We refrained then from overruling the *Enelow* and *Ettelson* decisions, but today we take that step. A half century's experience has persuaded us, as it has persuaded an impressive array of judges and commentators, that the rule is unsound in theory, unworkable and arbitrary in practice, and unnecessary to achieve any legitimate goals.

As an initial matter, the *Enelow-Ettelson* doctrine is, in the modern world of litigation, a total fiction. Even when the rule was announced, it was artificial. Although at that time law and equity remained two separate systems, they were administered by the same judges. When a single official was both chancellor and law judge, a stay of an action at law on equitable grounds required nothing more than an order issued by the official regulating the progress of the litigation before him, and the decision to call this order an injunction just because it would have been an injunction in a system with separate law and equity judges had little justification. With the merger of law and equity, which was accomplished by the Federal Rules of Civil Procedure, the practice of describing these stays as injunctions lost all connection with the reality of the federal courts' procedural system. As Judge Charles Clark, the principal drafts-man of the Rules, wrote:

> [W]e lack any rationale to explain the concept of a judge joining himself when he merely decides upon the method he will follow in trying the case. The metamorphosis of a law judge into a hostile chancellor on the other "side" of the court could not have been overclear to the lay litigant under the divided procedure; but if now without even that fictitious sea change one judge in one form of action may split his judicial self at one instant into two mutually antagonistic parts, the litigant surely will think himself in Alice's Wonderland. Beaunit Mills, Inc. v. Eday Fabric Sales Corp., 124 F.2d 563, 565 (C.A.2 1942).

The *Enelow* rule had presupposed two different systems of justice administered by separate tribunals, even if these tribunals were no more than two "sides" to the same court; with the abandonment of that separation, the premise of the rule disappeared. The doctrine, and the distinctions it drew between equitable and legal actions and defenses, lost all moorings to the actual practice of the federal courts.

The artificiality of the *Enelow-Ettelson* doctrine is not merely an intellectual infelicity; the gulf between the historical procedures underlying the rule and the modern procedures of federal courts renders the rule hopelessly unworkable in operation. The decisions in *Enelow* and *Ettelson* treated as straightforward the questions whether the underlying suit, on the one hand, and the motion for a stay, on the other, would properly have been brought in a court of equity or in a court of law. Experience since the merger of law and equity, however, has shown that both questions are frequently difficult and sometimes insoluble. Suits that involve diverse claims and request diverse forms of relief often are not easily categorized as equitable or legal. As one Court of Appeals complained in handling such a suit, "*Enelow-Ettelson* is virtually impossible to apply to a complaint . . . in which the averments and prayers are a puree of legal and equitable theories and of claims that had no antecedents in the old bifurcated system." Danford v. Schwabacher, 488 F.2d 454, 456 (C.A.9 1973). Actions for declaratory judgments are neither legal nor equitable, and courts have therefore had to look to the kind of action that would have been brought had Congress not provided the declaratory judgment remedy. Thus, the rule has placed courts "in the unenviable position not only of solving modern procedural problems by the application of labels which have no currency, but also of considering the nature of law suits which were never brought." Diematic Manufacturing Corp. v. Packaging Industries, Inc., 516 F.2d 975, 978 (CA2), cert. denied, 423 U.S. 913 (1975). The task of characterizing stays as based in either law or equity has proved equally intractable. In an early case applying the doctrine, for example, this Court held that a stay of an action at law pending arbitration is appealable as an injunction because "the special defense setting up the arbitration agreement is an equitable defense." Shanferoke Coal & Supply Corp. v. Westchester Service Corp., 293 U.S. 449, 452 (1935). But as one Court of Appeals has noted, a chancellor could not have enforced an arbitration agreement and, correlatively, could not have stayed a suit at law pending arbitration. See Olson v. Paine, Webber, Jackson & Curtis, Inc., 806 F.2d 731, 735 (C.A.7 1986), citing, e.g., J. Story, Commentaries on Equity Pleadings § 804 (J. Gould 10th rev. ed. 1892). More recently, lower courts have differed as to whether a stay pending the completion of administrative proceedings is based on an equitable defense. The conflict regarding the proper characterization of *Colorado River* stays is just one more example of the confusion that results from requiring courts to assign obsolete labels to orders that may or may not have an analogue in the bifurcated system of equity and law.

Most important, the *Enelow-Ettelson* doctrine is "divorced from any rational or coherent appeals policy." Lee v. Ply Gem Industries, Inc., 193 U.S.App.D.C. 112, 115, 593 F.2d 1266, 1269, cert. denied, 441 U.S. 967 (1979). Under the rule, appellate jurisdiction of orders granting or denying stays depends upon a set of considerations that in no way reflects or relates to the need for interlocutory review. There is no reason to think that appeal of a stay order is more suitable in cases in which the underlying action is at law and the stay is based on equitable grounds than in cases in which one of these conditions is not satisfied. The rule's focus on historical distinctions thus produces arbitrary and anomalous results. See Baltimore Contractors, Inc. v. Bodinger, 348 U.S., at 184 (noting the "incongruity of taking jurisdiction from a stay in a law type [proceeding] and denying jurisdiction in an equity type proceeding"). Two orders may involve similar issues and produce similar consequences, and yet one will be appealable whereas the other will not.

For these reasons, the lower federal courts repeatedly have lambasted the *Enelow-Ettelson* doctrine. The rule has been called "a remnant from the jurisprudential attic," Danford v. Schwabacher, supra, at 455, "an anachronism wrapped up in an atavism," Hartford Financial Systems, Inc. v. Florida Software Services, Inc., 712 F.2d 724, 727 (C.A.1 1983), and a "Byzantine peculiarity," New England Power Co. v. Asiatic Petroleum Corp. 456 F.2d 183, 189 (C.A.1 1972). With the exception of the Federal Circuit, which apparently has not yet confronted an *Enelow-Ettelson* appeal, every Circuit is on record with criticism of the doctrine. One Circuit Judge has urged his court to reject the doctrine outright.

Mar–Len of Louisiana, Inc. v. Parsons–Gilbane, 732 F.2d 444, 445–47 (C.A.5 1984) (Rubin, J., dissenting). Although a majority of the panel declined to do so, it agreed that the *Enelow-Ettelson* rule was "artificial," "medieval," and "outmoded." Id., at 445, n. 1 (citations omitted). Another Circuit Judge, in a majority opinion, recently wrote an extensive and scholarly critique of the doctrine and concluded only with great reluctance that repudiating the doctrine would be improper. Olson v. Paine, Webber, Jackson & Curtis, Inc., supra, at 733–742 (Posner, J.).

Commentators have been no less scathing in their evaluations of the *Enelow-Ettelson* rule. Professor Moore and his collaborators have noted the difficulty of applying archaic labels to modern actions and defenses and expressed the wish that "the Supreme Court will accept the first opportunity offered to decide that the reason for the *Enelow-Ettelson* rule having ceased, the rule is no more." 9 J. Moore, B. Ward, & J. Lucas, Moore's Federal Practice ¶ 110.20[3], p. 245 (1987). Professor Wright and his collaborators have gone further, arguing that the extensive experience that the courts of appeals have had in attempting to rationalize and apply the rule would justify them in rejecting it. 16 C. Wright, A. Miller, E. Cooper, & E. Gressman, Federal Practice and Procedure § 3923, p. 65 (1977).

The case against perpetuation of this sterile and antiquated doctrine seems to us conclusive. We therefore overturn the cases establishing the *Enelow-Ettelson* rule and hold that orders granting or denying stays of "legal" proceedings on "equitable" grounds are not automatically appealable under § 1292(a)(1). This holding will not prevent interlocutory review of district court orders when such review is truly needed. Section 1292(a)(1) will, of course, continue to provide appellate jurisdiction over orders that grant or deny injunctions and orders that have the practical effect of granting or denying injunctions and have " 'serious, perhaps irreparable, consequence.' " Carson v. American Brands, Inc., 450 U.S. 79, 84 (1981), quoting Baltimore Contractors, Inc. v. Bodinger, supra, at 181. As for orders that were appealable under § 1292(a)(1) solely by virtue of the *Enelow-Ettelson* doctrine, they may, in appropriate circumstances, be reviewed under the collateral-order doctrine of § 1291, see Moses H. Cone Memorial Hospital v. Mercury Construction Corp., 460 U.S. 1 (1983), and the permissive appeal provision of § 1292(b), as well as by application for writ of mandamus. Our holding today merely prevents interlocutory review of district court orders on the basis of historical circumstances that have no relevance to modern litigation. Because we repudiate the *Enelow-Ettelson* doctrine, we reject petitioner's claim that the District Court's order in this case is appealable under § 1292(a)(1) pursuant to that doctrine.

Notes and Questions

1. Eight months after *Gulfstream*, Congress in 1988 amended § 16 of the Federal Arbitration Act, 9 U.S.C.A. § 16, allowing an immediate appeal of an order denying arbitration. In Microchip Technology, Inc. v. U.S. Philips Corp., 367 F.3d 1350 (Fed. Cir. 2004), the court concluded that § 16 removes

the barriers to appeal of a denial of arbitration that was suggested in *Gulfstream* for cases that lacked serious or irreparable consequences.

2.   Examine the language of § 1292(a)(1). Given the well-established policy against piecemeal appeals, why would Congress create this exception to the finality rule? According to Judge Friendly, "although the language is broader, * * * it seems rather plain that Congress was thinking primarily of the case where erroneous denial of a *temporary* injunction may cause injury quite as irreparable as an erroneous grant of one." Stewart–Warner Corp. v. Westinghouse Elec. Corp., 325 F.2d 822, 829–30 (2d Cir.1963), cert. denied, 376 U.S. 944, 84 S.Ct. 800, 11 L.Ed.2d 767 (1964) (Friendly, J., dissenting). What, if anything, does this logic say concerning the debate over the value of the right to appeal, discussed in section A of this chapter?

3.   In light of the judicial assumptions about congressional intent in § 1292(a)(1), should the Court limit applicability of the statute to interlocutory appeals from rulings on *preliminary* injunctions and not include appeals from interlocutory rulings on *permanent* injunctions? In Switzerland Cheese Association, Inc. v. E. Horne's Market, Inc., 385 U.S. 23, 87 S.Ct. 193, 17 L.Ed.2d 23 (1966), the district court had denied plaintiffs' motion for summary judgment granting a permanent injunction and damages, on the grounds that the court could not conclude that there was "no genuine issue as to any material fact." Plaintiffs appealed, claiming that the order denying its summary judgment motion was an "interlocutory" order "refusing" an injunction within the meaning of § 1292(a)(1).

In rejecting this argument, the Supreme Court stated that "we approach this statute somewhat gingerly lest a floodgate be opened that brings into the exception many pretrial orders." However, the Court refused to hold that denials of requests for permanent injunctive relief could *never* fall within the terms of § 1292(a)(1). It reached this view, "not because 'interlocutory' or preliminary orders may not at times embrace denials of permanent injunctions, but for the reason that the denial of a motion for a summary judgment because of unresolved issues of fact does not settle or even tentatively decide anything about the merits of the claim. It is strictly a pretrial order that decides only one thing, that the case should go to trial. Orders that in no way touch on the merits of the claim but only relate to pretrial procedures are not in our view 'interlocutory' within the meaning of § 1292(a)(1). We see no other way to protect the integrity of the congressional policy against piecemeal appeals."

Is the Court correct to conclude that a ruling on a summary judgment motion does not "even tentatively decide anything about the merits of the claim?" Does the fact that such a ruling does not "settle" the merits mean that it cannot fall within the terms of a statute authorizing review of *interlocutory* orders? In any event, is there anything in the text or apparent policy of § 1292(a)(1) that limits the statute's reach to rulings on the merits? Would the Court have been on sounder ground had it construed § 1292(a)(1) to have no applicability to permanent injunctions?

4.   It is universally held that § 1292(a)(1) has no applicability to appeal of rulings on motions seeking temporary restraining orders, as opposed to those seeking preliminary injunctions. See C. Wright, A. Miller, E. Cooper & E. Gressman, 16 Federal Practice and Procedure § 3922.1 (2d ed. 1996)

(referring to this practice as "[s]omewhat surprising)." These commentators suggest that "[o]n balance, it seems desirable to develop a principle that rulings with respect to temporary restraining orders are appealable on a sufficiently strong showing of potentially irreparable injury." Is this a good idea? Why not simply include *all* temporary restraining orders?

5. In Sherri A.D. v. Kirby, 975 F.2d 193, 203 (5th Cir.1992), the court held that for "[o]rders which explicitly grant or deny injunctive relief * * * no additional finding of a threat of immediate, irreparable injury is required." However, "[t]hose orders which * * * have the practical effect of denying an injunction, but do not do so in explicit terms, are immediately appealable if the order threatens 'serious, perhaps irreparable consequences' and can be effectively challenged only by immediate appeal." Id. (quoting Carson v. American Brands, Inc., 450 U.S. 79, 84, 101 S.Ct. 993, 996, 67 L.Ed.2d 59 (1981)).

3. *Supreme Court Appellate Jurisdiction*

Traditionally, the Supreme Court exercised two distinct forms of appellate jurisdiction: appeal and certiorari. Appeals could be taken from the courts of appeals by a party relying on a state statute held by the court to be repugnant to either the Constitution, treaties or laws of the United States and from the state's highest court where that court had ruled against the validity of a treaty or statute of the United States or where the state court has upheld a state statute which had been challenged on federal constitutional or statutory grounds. Certiorari was available from the courts of appeals "upon the petition of any party to any civil or criminal case, before or after rendition of judgment or decree" and from the state's highest court where that court had invalidated a state statute on federal constitutional or statutory grounds "or where any title, right, privilege or immunity is generally set up or claimed" under federal law.

Technically, the primary distinction between the two was that appeal, where applicable, was of right while certiorari lay purely within the Court's discretion. As a practical matter, however, the Court treated its appeal jurisdiction as if it were discretionary. In fact, the Court appeared to decide whether to hear a case falling within its mandatory appeal jurisdiction with virtually the same degree of minimal review given to cases in which a writ of certiorari was sought. The problem was that while a denial of certiorari in no way constituted a decision on the merits and therefore had absolutely no precedential impact, dismissal of an appeal, at least as a technical matter, did constitute a decision on the merits and therefore a precedent.

This situation gave rise to considerable confusion. See generally Kurland, Jurisdiction of the United States Supreme Court: Time for a Change?, 59 Cornell L.Rev. 616 (1974). In response, Congress enacted, and the President signed into law, Pub.L. 100–352, 102 Stat. 662 (1988). Under the Act, the relevant statutes [28 U.S.C. § 1254 and § 1257] were amended effectively to do away with the Court's mandatory jurisdiction.

Supreme Court jurisdiction is limited to issues of federal law. Thus, the Court may not review state court interpretations of state law, unless those interpretations somehow implicate issues of federal law. Moreover, pursuant to what is known as the "adequate state ground" doctrine, the Court will not even review state court interpretations of federal law, if the decision also rests on a ground of state law that would independently support the decision. Murdock v. City of Memphis, 87 U.S. (20 Wall.) 590, 22 L.Ed. 429 (1874). See generally Redish, Supreme Court Review of State Court "Federal" Decisions: A Study in Interactive Federalism, 19 Ga.L.Rev. 861 (1985).

Whether or not there is an independent state ground, the Court will not review a state court decision that is interlocutory even if subject to immediate appellate review under state law. In Jefferson v. City of Tarrant, 522 U.S. 75, 118 S.Ct. 481, 139 L.Ed.2d 433 (1997), the state trial court certified the question whether the Alabama wrongful death act controlled the recovery in a claim under 42 U.S.C.A. § 1983 for immediate appellate review pursuant to state procedure, and the Alabama Supreme Court decided it. Although the Supreme Court initially granted certiorari to decide this question, it determined that it lacked jurisdiction under 28 U.S.C. § 1257(a) because further proceedings in state court that could include a full trial were required. However, in Cox Broadcasting Corp. v. Cohn, 420 U.S. 469, 95 S.Ct. 1029, 43 L.Ed.2d 328 (1975), the Court recognized four categories of cases in which appeal could be allowed despite the absence of technical finality. The first two included cases in which the federal issue would not be mooted or otherwise affected by the proceedings yet to be had because those proceedings have little substance, their outcome is certain, or they are wholly unrelated to the federal question." In the third category were cases where, "if the party seeking interim review ultimately prevails on the merits, the federal issue will be mooted; if he were to lose on the merits, however, the governing state law would not permit him again to present his federal claim for review." The final category—considered the most controversial—included "those situations where the federal issue has been finally decided in the state courts with further proceedings pending in which the party seeking review ... might prevail on the merits on nonfederal grounds, thus rendering unnecessary review of the federal issue by this Court...." For a detailed analysis and critique of *Cohn*, see M. Redish, Federal Jurisdiction: Tensions in the Allocation of Judicial Power 247–60 (2d ed. 1990).

C. APPELLATE REVIEW OF JUDICIAL FINDINGS OF FACT

BOSE CORPORATION v. CONSUMERS UNION OF UNITED STATES, INC.

Supreme Court of the United States, 1984.
466 U.S. 485, 104 S.Ct. 1949, 80 L.Ed.2d 502.

JUSTICE STEVENS delivered the opinion of the Court.

[In the May 1970 issue of its magazine, "Consumer Reports," respondent published an article evaluating the quality of numerous brands of medium-priced loudspeakers. After describing the Bose 901 system and some of its virtues, the article made the following statement: "[I]ndividual instruments heard through the Bose system seemed to grow to gigantic proportions and tended to wander about the room. For instance, a violin appeared to be 10 feet wide and a piano stretched from wall to wall. With orchestral music, such effects seemed inconsequential. But we think they might become annoying when listening to soloists."

Petitioner took exception to certain statements contained in the article, and brought a product disparagement action in the District Court for the District of Massachusetts. Following a bench trial on the issue of liability, the trial court issued a detailed opinion in respondent's favor on most issues. Finding that petitioner was a "public figure" for purposes of the doctrine of New York Times Co. v. Sullivan, 376 U.S. 254 (1964), it held petitioner could recover only if it proved by clear and convincing evidence that respondent made a false disparaging statement with "actual malice," defined as knowledge of falsity or reckless disregard of the truth.

On three key points, however, the court agreed with petitioner: It found that one sentence in the article contained a "false" statement of "fact" concerning the tendency of the instrument to wander; it found that the statement was disparaging, and it concluded "on the basis of proof which it considers clear and convincing, that the plaintiff has sustained its burden of proving that the defendant published a false statement of material fact" with knowledge that it was false or with reckless disregard of the truth. The court rendered this conclusion because it found that at the time of the article's publication the researcher for Consumer Reports knew that the words "individual instruments ... tended to wander about the room" did not accurately describe the effects he had heard when testing the system. On this point, the trial court received testimony from Arnold Seligson, the engineer who supervised the testing of the product for respondent and wrote the report on which the article was based. As the Supreme Court concluded, "since there was no evidence that the editors were aware of the inaccuracy in the original report, the actual malice determination rests entirely on an evaluation of Seligson's state of mind when he wrote his initial report, or when he checked the article against that report."

On appeal, the First Circuit held that its review of the "actual malice" determination was not limited to the "clearly erroneous" standard of Rule 52(a), but rather that it "must perform a de novo review, independently examining the record to ensure that the district court has applied properly the governing constitutional law and that the plaintiff has indeed satisfied its burden of proof", though it acknowledged its inability to consider issues of witness credibility. On the basis of this standard, the court of appeals held that it was "unable to find clear and convincing evidence that CU published the statement that individual instruments tended to wander about the room with knowledge that it was false or with reckless disregard * * *."]

II

This is a case in which two well settled and respected rules of law point in opposite directions.

Petitioner correctly reminds us that Rule 52(a) provides:

> "Findings of fact shall not be set aside unless clearly erroneous, and due regard shall be given to the opportunity of the trial court to judge of the credibility of the witnesses."

We have repeatedly held that the rule means what it says. United States v. United States Gypsum Co., 333 U.S. 364, 394–396, 68 S.Ct. 525, 541–42, 92 L.Ed. 746 (1948). It surely does not stretch the language of the rule to characterize an inquiry into what a person knew at a given point in time as a question of "fact." In this case, since the trial judge expressly commented on Seligson's credibility, petitioner argues that the Court of Appeals plainly erred when it refused to uphold the District Court's actual malice "finding" under the clearly erroneous standard of Rule 52(a).

On the other hand, respondent correctly reminds us that in cases raising First Amendment issues we have repeatedly held that an appellate court has an obligation to "make an independent examination of the whole record" in order to make sure "that the judgment does not constitute a forbidden intrusion on the field of free expression." New York Times v. Sullivan, 376 U.S., at 284–286, 84 S.Ct., at 728–729. Although such statements have been made most frequently in cases to which Rule 52(a) does not apply because they arose in state courts, respondent argues that the constitutional principle is equally applicable to federal litigation. We quite agree; surely it would pervert the concept of federalism for this Court to lay claim to a broader power of review over state court judgments than it exercises in reviewing the judgments of intermediate federal courts.

Our standard of review must be faithful to both Rule 52(a) and the rule of independent review applied in New York Times v. Sullivan. The conflict between the two rules is in some respects more apparent than real. The *New York Times* rule emphasizes the need for an appellate court to make an independent examination of the entire record; Rule 52(a) never forbids such an examination, and indeed our seminal decision on the rule expressly contemplated a review of the entire record, stating that a "finding is 'clearly erroneous' when although there is evidence to support it, the reviewing court on the entire evidence is left with the definite and firm conviction that a mistake has been committed." United States v. Gypsum Co., supra, 333 U.S., at 395, 68 S.Ct., at 542. Moreover, Rule 52(a) commands that "due regard" shall be given to the trial judge's opportunity to observe the demeanor of the witnesses; the constitutionally-based rule of independent review permits this opportunity to be given its due. Indeed, as we previously observed, the Court of Appeals in this case expressly declined to second-guess the district judge on the credibility of the witnesses.

The requirement that special deference be given to a trial judge's credibility determinations is itself a recognition of the broader proposition that the presumption of correctness that attaches to factual findings is stronger in some cases than in others. The same "clearly erroneous" standard applies to findings based on documentary evidence as to those based entirely on oral testimony, but the presumption has lesser force in the former situation than in the latter. Similarly, the standard does not change as the trial becomes longer and more complex, but the likelihood that the appellate court will rely on the presumption tends to increase when trial judges have lived with the controversy for weeks or months instead of just a few hours. One might therefore assume that the cases in which the appellate courts have a duty to exercise independent review are merely those in which the presumption that the trial court's ruling is correct is particularly weak. The difference between the two rules, however, is much more than a mere matter of degree. For the rule of independent review assigns to judges a constitutional responsibility that cannot be delegated to the trier of fact, whether the factfinding function be performed in the particular case by a jury or by a trial judge.

Rule 52(a) applies to findings of fact, including those described as "ultimate facts" because they may determine the outcome of litigation. But Rule 52(a) does not inhibit an appellate court's power to correct errors of law, including those that may infect a so-called mixed finding of law and fact, or a finding of fact that is predicated on a misunderstanding of the governing rule of law. Nor does Rule 52(a) "furnish particular guidance with respect to distinguishing law from fact." Pullman–Standard v. Swint, 456 U.S., at 288, 102 S.Ct., at 1789. What we have characterized as "the vexing nature" of that distinction does not, however, diminish its importance, or the importance of the principles that require the distinction to be drawn in certain cases.

* * *

The First Amendment presupposes that the freedom to speak one's mind is not only an aspect of individual liberty—and thus a good unto itself * * * but also is essential to the common quest for truth and the vitality of society as a whole. * * * Nevertheless, there are categories of communication and certain special utterances to which the majestic protection of the First Amendment does not extend because they "are no essential part of any exposition of ideas, and are of such slight social value as a step to truth that any benefit that may be derived from them is clearly outweighed by the social interest in order and morality." Chaplinsky v. New Hampshire, 315 U.S. 568, 572, 62 S.Ct. 766, 86 L.Ed. 1031 (1942).

Libelous speech has been held to constitute one such category; others that have been held to be outside the scope of the freedom of speech are fighting words, incitement to riot, obscenity, and child pornography. In each of these areas, the limits of the unprotected category, as well as the unprotected character of particular communications, have been determined by the judicial evaluation of special facts that have been deemed to have constitutional significance. In such cases, the Court has regularly conducted an independent review of the record both to be sure that the speech in question actually falls within the unprotected category and to confine the perimeters of any unprotected category within acceptably narrow limits in an effort to ensure that protected expression will not be inhibited. Providing triers of fact with a general description of the type of communication whose content is unworthy of protection has not, in and of itself, served sufficiently to narrow the category, nor served to eliminate the danger that decisions by triers of fact may inhibit the expression of protected ideas. * * *

Hence, in New York Times v. Sullivan, after announcing the constitutional requirement for a finding of "actual malice" in certain types of defamation actions, it was only natural that we should conduct an independent review of the evidence on the dispositive constitutional issue. * * *

In Time, Inc. v. Pape, 401 U.S. 279, 91 S.Ct. 633, 28 L.Ed.2d 45 (1971), a case in which the federal District Court had entered a directed verdict, we again conducted an independent examination of the evidence on the question of actual malice, labeling our definition of "actual malice" as a "constitutional rule" and stating that the question before us was whether that rule had been correctly applied to the facts of the case. Again we stated that independent inquiries "of this kind are familiar under the settled principle that '[i]n cases in which there is a claim of denial of rights under the Federal Constitution, this Court is not bound by the conclusions of lower courts, but will re-examine the evidentiary basis on which those conclusions are founded,'" noting that "in cases involving the area of tension between the First and Fourteenth Amendments on the one hand and state defamation laws on the other, we have frequently had occasion to review 'the evidence in the ... record to determine whether it could constitutionally support a judgment' for the plaintiff."

The requirement of independent appellate review reiterated in New York Times v. Sullivan is a rule of federal constitutional law. It emerged from the exigency of deciding concrete cases; it is law in its purest form under our common law heritage. It reflects a deeply held conviction that judges, and particularly members of this Court, must exercise such review in order to preserve the precious liberties established and ordained by the Constitution. The question whether the evidence in the record in a defamation case is of the convincing clarity required to strip the utterance of First Amendment protection is not merely a question for the trier of fact. Judges, as expositors of the Constitution, must independently decide whether the evidence in the record is sufficient to cross the constitutional threshold that bars the entry of any judgment that is not supported by clear and convincing proof of "actual malice."

III

The Court of Appeals was correct in its conclusions (1) that there is a significant difference between proof of actual malice and mere proof of falsity, and (2) that such additional proof is lacking in this case.

THE CHIEF JUSTICE concurs in the judgment.

[The dissenting opinion of JUSTICE WHITE is omitted.]

JUSTICE REHNQUIST, with whom JUSTICE O'CONNOR joins, dissenting.

It is * * * ironic that, in the interest of protecting the First Amendment, the Court rejects the "clearly erroneous" standard of review mandated by Fed.Rule of Civ.Proc. 52(a) in favor of a "de novo" standard of review for the "constitutional facts" surrounding the "actual malice" determination.

But the facts dispositive of that determination, actual knowledge or subjective reckless disregard for truth, involve no more than findings about the mens rea of an author, findings which appellate courts are simply ill-prepared to make in any context, including the First Amendment context. Unless "actual malice" now means something different from the definition given to the term 20 years ago by this Court in *New York Times*, I do not think that the constitutional requirement of "actual malice" properly can bring into play any standard of factual review other than the "clearly erroneous" standard.

In this case the District Court concluded by what it found to be clear and convincing evidence that respondent's engineer Arnold Seligson had written the defamatory statement about Bose's product with actual knowledge that it was false. It reached that conclusion expressly relying on its determination about the credibility of Seligson's testimony. On appeal there was no issue as to whether the District Court had properly understood what findings were legally sufficient to establish "actual malice" nor was there any issue as to the necessary quantum of proof nor the proper allocation of the burden of proof of "actual malice." The issue on appeal thus was only the propriety of the District Court's factual conclusion that Bose had actually proven "actual malice" in this case. Yet the Court of Appeals never rebutted the District Court's conclusion that Seligson had actual knowledge that what he printed was false. Instead it concluded after de novo review that Seligson's language was merely "imprecise" and that as such, it would not "support an inference of actual malice."

It is unclear to me just what that determination by the Court of Appeals has to do with the mens rea conclusion necessary to the finding of "actual malice" and with the District Court's finding of actual knowledge here. In approving the Court of Appeals' de novo judgment on the "actual malice" question, for all the factual detail and rehearsal of testimony with which the majority's opinion is adorned, the Court never quite comes to grips with what factual finding it must focus on. * * *

In my view the problem results from the Court's attempt to treat what is here and in other contexts always has been, a pure question of fact, as something more than a fact—a so-called "constitutional fact." The Court correctly points out that independent appellate review of facts underlying constitutional claims has been sanctioned by previous decisions of this Court where "a conclusion of law as to a Federal right and a finding of fact are so intermingled as to make it necessary, in order to pass upon the Federal question, to analyze the facts." Fiske v. Kansas, 274 U.S. 380, 385–386, 47 S.Ct. 655, 656–657, 71 L.Ed. 1108. But in other contexts we have always felt perfectly at ease leaving state of mind determinations, such as the actual knowledge and recklessness determinations involved here, to triers of fact with only deferential appellate review—for example, in criminal cases where the burden of proving those facts is even greater than the "clear and convincing" standard applicable under *New York Times*.

Presumably any doctrine of "independent review" of facts exists, not so that an appellate court may inexorably place its thumb on the scales in favor of the party claiming the constitutional right, but so that perceived shortcomings of the trier of fact by way of bias or some other factor may be compensated for. But to me, the only shortcoming here is an appellate court's inability to make the determination which the Court mandates today the de novo determination about the state of mind of a particular author at a particular time. Although there well may be cases where the "actual malice" determination can be made on the basis of objectively reviewable facts in the record, it seems to me that just as often it is made, as here, on the basis of an evaluation of the credibility of the testimony of the author of the defamatory statement. I am at a loss to see how appellate courts can even begin to make such determinations. In any event, surely such determinations are best left to the trial judge.

It is of course true as the Court recognizes that "where particular speech falls close to the line separating the lawful and the unlawful, the possibility of mistaken fact-finding—inherent in all litigation—will create the danger that the legitimate utterance will be penalized." Speiser v. Randall, 357 U.S. 513, 526, 78 S.Ct. 1332, 1342, 2 L.Ed.2d 1460 (1958). But the *New York Times* rule adequately addresses the need to shield protected speech from the risk of erroneous fact-finding by placing the burden of proving "actual malice" on the party seeking to penalize expression. * * *

I think that the issues of "falsity" and "actual malice" in this case may be close questions, but I am convinced that the District Court, which heard the principal witness for the respondent testify for almost six days during the trial, fully understood both the applicable law and its role as a finder of fact. Because it is not clear to me that the de novo findings of appellate courts, with only bare records before them, are likely to be any more reliable than the findings reached by trial judges, I cannot join the majority's sanctioning of factual second guessing by appellate courts. I believe that the primary result of the Court's holding today will not be greater protection for First Amendment values, but rather only lessened confidence in the judgments of lower courts and more entirely factbound appeals.

I continue to adhere to the view expressed in Pullman–Standard v. Swint, 456 U.S. 273, 287, 102 S.Ct. 1781, 1789, 72 L.Ed.2d 66 (1982), that Rule 52(a) "does not make exceptions or purport to exclude certain categories of factual findings from the obligation of a court of appeals to accept a district court's findings unless clearly erroneous." There is no reason to depart from that rule here, and I would therefore reverse and remand this case to the Court of Appeals so that it may apply the "clearly erroneous" standard of review to the factual findings of the District Court.

Notes and Questions

1. Rule 52(a) commands that the trial judge, sitting as the finder of fact, "find the facts specially." This is different, of course, from the "general verdict" practice usually used in jury trials. What purposes are served by requiring the trial court to list factual findings specially? Would the same purposes be served by requiring a jury to make findings of fact? One reason for not requiring a jury to do so is the difficulty of getting a group of people to draw up detailed findings of fact. Special verdicts and interrogatories can serve as a substitute for findings of fact by a jury. But are there countervailing reasons for not requiring a jury to justify its verdict with specific fact-finding?

2. When judgment is entered on a jury verdict, the Rule 52(a) "clearly erroneous" standard obviously does not apply. Nevertheless, the *Bose* requirement that, in libel cases involving a public figure, the appellate court must make a *de novo* review to determine whether the record presents clear and convincing proof of actual malice also applies when the factfinder is a jury. Levine v. CMP Publications, Inc., 738 F.2d 660, 674 (5th Cir.1984). If the jury finds that actual malice was not proved, should the *Bose* standard apply on appeal? Bartimo v. Horsemen's Benevolent and Protective Ass'n, 771 F.2d 894, 897–98 (5th Cir.1985), suggests that it should. Does this make sense?

3. *Bose* viewed the de novo appellate review requirement as arising from the constitutional limitation imposed by the First Amendment on libel actions. A similar limitation has been imposed on libel actions arising out of labor disputes. The Court has held that the federal labor laws contemplate vigorous and even overblown and pejorative speech, and that, as a statutory matter, proof of actual malice is required in a libel action by a public figure

(which includes unions and companies) arising out of a labor dispute. Letter Carriers v. Austin, 418 U.S. 264, 272, 94 S.Ct. 2770, 2775, 41 L.Ed.2d 745 (1974); National Labor Relations Act § 8(c), 29 U.S.C.A. § 158(c). In such cases, must actual malice be proven by "clear and convincing evidence" rather than just a "preponderance of the evidence," and does the *Bose* requirement of *de novo* appellate review apply? National Ass'n of Government Employees v. National Federation of Fed. Employees, 844 F.2d 216 (5th Cir.1988), a libel action brought by a union against a rival union in a collective bargaining certification election, indicated in *dictum* that *Bose* should be so extended.

4. What does "clearly erroneous", as used in Rule 52(a), mean? In United States v. U.S. Gypsum Co., 333 U.S. 364, 395, 68 S.Ct. 525, 541, 92 L.Ed. 746 (1948), the Supreme Court stated that a finding is "clearly erroneous" when "although there is evidence to support it, the reviewing court on the entire evidence is left with the definite and firm conviction that a mistake has been committed." See also Ceraso v. Motiva Enterprises, 326 F.3d 303, 316 (2d Cir. 2003).("In reviewing findings for clear error, we are not allowed to second-guess either the trial court's credibility assessments or its choices between permissible competing inferences. * * * Even if the appellate court might have weighed the evidence differently, it may not over turn findings that are not clearly erroneous.... The weight of the evidence is not a ground for reversal on appeal. * * * and the fact that there may have been evidence to support an inference contrary to that drawn by the trial court does not mean that the findings are clearly erroneous").

5. In what way does the standard of Rule 52(a) for appellate review of a trial court's factual findings differ from the standard of review a trial court may employ in deciding whether to overturn a jury's verdict on a motion for judgment as a matter of law after trial? Why is this distinction drawn?

6. In what way does appellate review of a trial court's factual findings differ from the standard of review of a trial court's conclusions of law? What is the reason for this distinction?

7. Many decisions, including numerous procedural decisions, are not reviewed under either the clearly erroneous or the full plenary review standards. Instead, they are reversed only for an "abuse of discretion." What does this mean? It is difficult to be certain, although one should recognize that it is "a phrase which sounds worse than it really is." In re Josephson, 218 F.2d 174, 182 (1st Cir.1954). The abuse of discretion standard affords the appellate court a chance to change rulings it views as seriously wrong while allowing the trial court substantial latitude in a variety of areas such as discovery, amendment to pleadings, and mode of conducting the trial. For discussion, see Friendly, Indiscretion About Discretion, 31 Emory L.J. 747 (1982); Rosenberg, Judicial Discretion in the Trial Court, Viewed From Above, 22 Syracuse L.Rev. (1971).

8. In *Bose*, was the Court correct in requiring more searching appellate review on the question of actual malice? Was the Court creating a First Amendment exception to Rule 52(a), or was it merely characterizing the question of actual malice as a conclusion of law? If the former, is such an exception legitimate? Compare the Court's summary judgment decision in

Anderson v. Liberty Lobby, Inc., supra p. 463. If the latter, is this a legitimate characterization?

Contrast with *Bose* the decision in Pullman–Standard v. Swint, 456 U.S. 273, 102 S.Ct. 1781, 72 L.Ed.2d 66 (1982). Plaintiffs there, black workers at a Pullman–Standard plant, claimed that the seniority system at the plant violated Title VII because it had the effect of discriminating against them. Under the applicable employment discrimination law, to prevail plaintiffs had to prove that the seniority system was negotiated or maintained with actual intent to discriminate. The trial court entered findings that defendants did not have this intent, but the appellate court reversed, concluding that "[a]lthough discrimination vel non is essentially a question of fact it is, at the same time, the ultimate issue for resolution in this case, being expressly proscribed by [the statute]. As such, a finding of discrimination or non-discrimination is a finding of ultimate fact." Based on what the Supreme Court found to be an independent evaluation of the record, the court of appeals reversed.

The Supreme Court held that this review violated Rule 52(a). It reasoned that "[t]reating issues of intent as factual matters for the trier of fact is commonplace" and that the intent issue in the case "appears to us to be a pure question of fact." The appellate court's approach was therefore wrong:

> Rule 52(a) broadly requires that findings of fact not be set aside unless clearly erroneous. It does not make exceptions or purport to exclude certain categories of factual findings from the obligation of a court of appeals to accept a district court's findings unless clearly erroneous. It does not divide facts into categories; in particular, it does not divide findings of fact into those that deal with "ultimate" and those that deal with "subsidiary" facts.

> The Rule does not apply to conclusions of law. The Court of Appeals, therefore, was quite right in saying that if a district court's findings rest on an erroneous view of the law, they may be set aside on that basis. But here the District Court was not faulted for misunderstanding or applying an erroneous definition of intentional discrimination. It was reversed for arriving at what the Court of Appeals thought was an erroneous finding as to whether the differential impact of the seniority system reflected an intent to discriminate on account of race. That question, as we see it, is a pure question of fact, subject to Rule 52(a)'s clearly-erroneous standard. It is not a question of law and not a mixed question of law and fact.

456 U.S. at 287–88, 102 S.Ct. at 1789–90. Can this case be reconciled with *Bose*? If not, which expresses the proper rule for cases not involving the First Amendment?

Professor Louis discerned a general trend toward diminished appellate scrutiny of trial court decisions applying law to the facts of specific cases. He explained that "[t]he doctrine of constitutional fact is the only expanding exception to trial level hegemony over law application, but its expansion seems attributable principally to substantive constitutional considerations rather than to any general desire for appellate decisional authority." Louis, Allocating Adjudicative Decision Making Authority Between the Trial and

Appellate Levels: A Unified View of the Scope of Review, the Judge/Jury Question, and Procedural Discretion, 64 N.C.L.Rev. 993, 1005–06 (1986).

9. In 1985, Rule 52(a) was amended to add the words, "whether based on oral or documentary evidence," following the words, "Findings of fact". The Rule was amended, according to the Advisory Committee's Note, "(1) to avoid continued confusion and conflicts among the circuits as to the standard of appellate review of findings of fact by the court, (2) to eliminate the disparity between the standard of review as literally stated in Rule 52(a) and the practice of some courts of appeals, and (3) to promote nationwide uniformity."

What the Note refers to was a conflict in the lower courts over whether the deferential "clearly erroneous" standard of Rule 52(a) applied only to findings based on *oral* testimony, thereby leaving findings based on *written* evidence to be reviewed de novo, or whether the "clearly erroneous" standard applied to *all* lower court factual findings. The leading advocate of the dual standard interpretation of Rule 52(a) was Judge Jerome Frank. See Orvis v. Higgins, 180 F.2d 537, 539–40 (2d. Cir.), cert. denied, 340 U.S. 810, 71 S.Ct. 37, 95 L.Ed. 595 (1950). Most other lower courts, however, rejected it. The Advisory Committee expressed the view that the policy considerations in favor of the dual standard "are outweighed by the public interest in the stability and judicial economy that would be promoted by recognizing that the trial court, not the appellate tribunal, should be the finder of the facts. To permit courts of appeals to share more actively in the fact-finding function would tend to undermine the legitimacy of the district courts in the eyes of the litigants, multiply appeals by encouraging appellate retrial of some factual issues, and needlessly reallocate judicial authority." For a view similar to that of the Advisory Committee, see Wright, The Doubtful Omniscience of Appellate Courts, 41 Minn.L.Rev. 751 (1957). See also Cooper, Civil Rule 52(a): Rationing and Rationalizing the Resources of Appellate Review, 63 Notre Dame L.Rev. 645 (1988); Note, Rule 52(a): Appellate Review of Findings of Fact Based on Documentary or Undisputed Evidence, 49 Va.L.Rev. 506 (1963).

10. Who actually writes the findings? Suppose that the district judge, sitting as the factfinder, finds for the defendant, then asks defense counsel to prepare proposed findings of fact, and proceeds to adopt those findings as the findings of the court. Should this practice be deemed invalid? Consider Roberts v. Ross, 344 F.2d 747, 751–52 (3d Cir.1965): "The purpose of [Rule 52(a)] is to require the trial judge to formulate and articulate his findings of fact and conclusions of law in the course of his consideration and determination of the case and as a part of his decision making process, so that he himself may be satisfied that he has dealt fully and properly with all the issues in the case before he decides and so that the parties involved and this court on appeal may be fully informed as to the bases of his decision when it is made. Findings and conclusions prepared ex post facto by counsel, even though signed by the judge, do not serve adequately the function contemplated by the rule."

Suppose that the trial judge, *before* finding for either party, seeks and obtains proposed findings from *both* sides, and, after reaching his decision, adopts without change the proposed findings of the victorious party. Should this practice be deemed invalid? Is it less troublesome than the practice of having findings prepared by the side already identified as victorious? This practice has been described as especially valuable "in a case where the evidence is highly technical * * *." Heterochemical Corp. v. United States Rubber Co., 368 F.2d 169, 172 (7th Cir.1966). What would be your initial reaction when you saw that a district judge in a highly technical patent case had adopted in toto the proposed factual findings of the victorious party?

D. PROBLEMS OF APPELLATE PROCEDURE

STANDING ON APPEAL

In order to sue in federal court, the plaintiff must have standing. The requirement flows in part from the case-or-controversy requirement embodied in Article III of the Constitution and in part from judge-made prudential doctrines. That a party had standing to bring suit, however, does not automatically imply that an unsuccessful party will necessarily have standing to appeal. Illustrative is the decision in Bender v. Williamsport Area School District, 475 U.S. 534, 106 S.Ct. 1326, 89 L.Ed.2d 501 (1986). The issue before the Court was "[w]hether one member of a School Board has standing to appeal from a declaratory judgment against the Board." The Court concluded that "although the School Board itself had a sufficient stake in the outcome of the litigation to appeal, an individual Board member cannot invoke the Board's interest in the case to confer standing upon himself."

Students had filed suit in federal court against the Williamsport Area School District, the nine members of the School Board, the Superintendent of the District, and the high school principal. They alleged that that the defendants' refusal to recognize their religiously oriented group and to allow it to meet on the same basis as other student groups violated their First Amendment rights. The district court granted summary judgment for the plaintiff students, though no injunction was issued, and no other form of relief was granted against any defendant in his individual capacity. Although the School District did not challenge the judgment in any way, one member of the Board, John C. Youngman, Jr., did file a timely notice of appeal.

No one raised any question about Youngman's standing in the court of appeals. That court reversed on the merits of the First Amendment challenge. The Supreme Court, recognizing that only Youngman had challenged the district court's order, held that the court of appeals was without jurisdiction. "As a member of the School Board sued in his official capacity," the Court reasoned, "Mr. Youngman had no personal stake in the outcome of the litigation and therefore did not have standing to file the notice of appeal." His status as a school board member, the Court found, "does not permit him to 'step into the shoes of the Board' and invoke its right to appeal." As a general matter, "members of collegial bodies do not have standing to perfect an appeal the body itself has declined to take." Though Youngman claimed at oral argument that he was the parent of at least one student attending the high school and that as a matter of conscience he opposed prayer activities on school premises during regular school hours, the Court found nothing in the record about his status as a parent.

Chief Justice Burger, dissenting, found that Youngman did have standing to appeal: "Mr. Youngman is a parent of a student at Williamsport High School; as a matter of conscience he is opposed to prayer activities on school premises during school hours. As this Court has repeatedly held, parents have standing to challenge conditions in public schools that their children attend." While he agreed with the Court that a plaintiff has the burden to plead facts showing his standing, these burdens "need not be placed upon a properly named defendant, like Mr. Youngman, who seeks to invoke the jurisdiction of the Court of Appeals."

Dissent

Should it *ever* be deemed improper for a named party, who is on the losing side of a case in the trial court, to appeal? Would the policies underlying the requirement of standing have been undermined by allowing Youngman's appeal? In his dissent, the Chief Justice argued that standing rules, normally employed to determine whether a party may initiate an action, should be relaxed when the issue is whether an appeal may be taken. Do you agree? In Stringfellow v. Concerned Neighbors in Action, 480 U.S. 370, 107 S.Ct. 1177, 94 L.Ed.2d 389 (1987), the Court ruled that an intervenor could not appeal because he lacked standing. The intervenor had been aligned with the defendant state, seeking to uphold an anti-abortion statute. When the state decided not to appeal an adverse ruling by the court of appeals, the intervenor sought to do so, but the Supreme Court held that he lacked a sufficient interest even though he had been allowed to intervene. Compare Devlin v. Scardelletti, 536 U.S. 1, 122 S.Ct. 2005, 153 L.Ed.2d 27 (2002) (dissident class members who object to a settlement presented to the court for its approval under Rule 23(e) may appeal approval over their objections even though they do not intervene in the class action).

Intervenors lack standing

Should a party who *won* at trial ever be allowed to take an appeal? Consider the decision in Midland–Guardian of Pensacola, Inc. v. Carr, 425 F.2d 793 (5th Cir.1970). Midland, a creditor of Carr's, challenged their transfer of certain property as fraudulent. Midland won in the district court, but the effect of the district court's decision was simply to declare the alleged transfer of property void and to make the property subject to the claims of Carr's creditors. While the district court granted Midland the relief which it sought, Midland insisted on appeal that the district court should have nullified the sale only as to it. Midland made this objection because it was the last of Carr's creditors to reduce its claim to judgment and would rank last in its claim to the proceeds from the sale of the property. However, if the decree operated only in favor of the creditor bringing the action, Midland would have the right to execute against the property. Since defendants had no interest in this question, they did not oppose Midland's appeal.

Judge Rives, writing for the court, held that Midland could not appeal:

> Midland argues that it is an aggrieved party with a right to appeal from a judgment in its favor which denied it a part of the relief which it prayed. That much may be conceded arguendo, but the question goes much deeper. Under Article III, Section 2 of the Constitution of the United States, the judicial power extends only to actual cases or controversies. There is no case or controversy on this appeal between Midland and the Carrs. As between them the case has become moot.

> To constitute a case or controversy there must be adverse parties with real interests whose contentions are submitted to the court for adjudication.

> There are no such adverse parties on this appeal. * * *

Was the decision correct? Would the policies served by the "case or controversy" requirement have been undermined had Midland been allowed to appeal? Who might have been harmed by the allowance of such an appeal? Would those people have been any less harmed had the Carrs vigorously opposed Midland's appeal?

A related concept is the notion that even where the trial judge has committed an error, the losing party is entitled to reversal only when that error was harmful. See Rule 61. This determination should depend on a consideration of the entire case and all the evidence.

THE MECHANICS OF TAKING AN APPEAL

By now, you may be asking how one goes about appealing. Once an appealable order is entered, the objecting party must file a notice of appeal. This notice must be filed within the applicable time limits, 30 days in federal court unless the appealing party is the United States. See Fed.R.App.P. 4. The federal courts treat these timing requirements as essential to their subject matter jurisdiction, and dismiss appeals that do not comply with them. Does this make sense? See Hall, The Jurisdictional Nature of the Time to Appeal, 21 Ga.L.Rev. 399 (1986) (arguing that timing requirements should be subject to waiver). The notice of appeal need not say much about the appellant's arguments, however, since it should only specify the order or judgment appealed from and the parties to the appeal. See Fed.R.App.P. 3. Failure to comply with these requirements can, however, be fatal. See Torres v. Oakland Scavenger Co., 487 U.S. 312, 108 S.Ct. 2405, 101 L.Ed.2d 285 (1988) (where one plaintiff's name was omitted from notice of appeal due to clerical error, judgment became final as to him even though it was reversed as to the other 15 plaintiffs).

When one party has filed a notice of appeal, other litigants have 14 more days in which to file a notice of cross appeal. See Fed.R.App.P. 4(a)(3). Why should a litigant who didn't choose to appeal in the first instance decide to cross appeal after another litigant had noticed an appeal?

The filing of the appeal does not prevent the trial court's judgment from being enforced. Ordinarily, the appellant can ask the trial court to stay enforcement of the judgment, but the stay is often conditioned on the posting of a bond. See Fed.R.Civ.P. 62; cf. Pennzoil Co. v. Texaco, Inc., 481 U.S. 1, 107 S.Ct. 1519, 95 L.Ed.2d 1 (1987) (judgment debtor required to file $13 billion bond to forestall execution of judgment).

After the notices of appeal are filed, the parties prepare their written submissions to the appellate court. In some states, this includes the process of "designating" the record, in which the litigants indicate which portions of the trial court record should be included in the record on appeal. In federal court, the entire trial court record is viewed as the record on appeal, although the parties may submit an appendix containing the pertinent materials. See Fed.R.App.P. 10; 11; 30. In any event the appellate court's review is limited to matters that are properly in the record, so that something that was overlooked at the trial level cannot be added on appeal. The issues raised by the record are argued in the parties' briefs; usually the appellant files the first brief, after which the appellee files an opposing brief and the appellant may close with a reply brief. See Fed.R.App.P. 28; 31.

After the briefing is completed, there is customarily an oral argument before a panel of judges. See Fed.R.App.P. 34. In some cases this is preceded by a conference that resembles the pretrial conference in the trial court. See Fed.R.App.P. 33. The case is then submitted for decision, which is usually by written opinion mailed to the parties and filed with the clerk of the appellate court. A party unhappy with the decision may petition for a rehearing by the same panel (Fed.R.App.P. 40), request rehearing by the entire court of appeals en banc (Fed.R.App.P. 35), or appeal again if a further appeal is possible.

Chapter XIII

PRECLUSIVE EFFECTS
OF JUDGMENTS

Putting an end to litigation by according finality to judgments is a central objective of a modern system of civil procedure. But how to accomplish that without forfeiting the opportunity for parties to pursue in a later suit aspects of the matter that they could not reasonably have litigated (or that they had valid reasons for not litigating) in the first suit has long troubled courts.

At common law, the writ system dictated narrow principles of finality. The fact that a plaintiff might lose by selecting one writ and proving a right to relief under another implied that there would be a second chance to proceed under the correct writ. Thus, finality was limited to the writ selected. The 19th century approach, however, favored certainty over fairness. Formalistic rules were developed which viewed preclusion of relitigating claims and issues as an inherent right flowing from the nature of a judgment. "They were absolute in the sense of controlling results without regard to any competing elements of decision," and "mandatory in that their controlling effect was not subject to equitable dispensation or qualification on grounds of general notions of fairness or justice in particular cases." Holland, Modernizing Res Judicata: Reflections on the *Parklane* Doctrine, 55 Ind.L.J. 615, 616–17 (1980). One focus of this chapter will be the interplay of formalistic versus public policy considerations in the application of the modern counterparts of these preclusion doctrines.

RES JUDICATA AND COLLATERAL ESTOPPEL

The term res judicata is sometimes loosely used to refer to the totality of preclusion doctrines. However, it refers more appropriately to the prohibition on relitigating a claim which has already been litigated and gone to judgment. The Restatement (Second) of Judgments favors the term "claim preclusion," and this usage has been increasingly adopted by courts.

The central propositions of the doctrine of res judicata (or claim preclusion) are expressed in terms of "merger" and "bar." When a party obtains a final personal judgment in its favor, its claim is extinguished and "merged" in the judgment, thus precluding further litigation on the same claim. Likewise, when a party suffers a judgment against it, the claim is also extinguished and the party is "barred" by the judgment from relitigating the same claim. Merger and bar only apply when the second action is based on the same claim or cause of action, between the same parties or those in privity with them, and when the determination of the first action was "on the merits."

Collateral estoppel (or issue preclusion) is a doctrine applicable in situations that are not covered by res judicata because the second action is not based on the same claim or cause of action.[1] It forecloses the relitigation of issues that were actually litigated (that is, contested by the parties and submitted for determination by the court) and that were necessarily decided by the court.

One significant difference between res judicata and collateral estoppel is that the former operates to preclude relitigation of the claim without regard to what issues were litigated in the first suit, while the latter only precludes relitigation of those issues that were actually litigated and necessarily determined in the first suit. Justice Field described this difference in Cromwell v. County of Sac, 94 U.S. (4 Otto) 351, 352–53, 24 L.Ed. 195 (1876):

> In [an action on the same claim or cause of action], the judgment, if rendered upon the merits, constitutes an absolute bar to a subsequent action. It is a finality as to the claim or demand in controversy, concluding parties and those in privity with them, not only as to every matter which was offered and received to sustain or defeat the claim or demand, but as to any other admissible matter which might have been offered for that purpose. Thus, for example, a judgment rendered upon a promissory note is conclusive as to the validity of the instrument and the amount due upon it, although it be subsequently alleged that perfect defenses actually existed, of which no proof was offered, such as forgery, want of consideration, or payment. If such defenses were not presented in the action, and established by competent evidence, the subsequent allegation of their existence is of no legal consequence. * * * [T]hat a judgment estops not only as to every ground of recovery or defense actually presented in the action, but also as to every ground which might have been presented, is strictly accurate, when applied to the demand or claim in controversy. * * *

---

1.   When res judicata does not apply because, although the second suit is on the same claim or cause of action, the first suit was not decided on the merits, the doctrine of "direct estoppel" applies to preclude relitigation of the issues that were actually decided. For example, if the first action were dismissed for failure to join an indispensable party under Rule 12(b)(7), and plaintiff filed a second suit still not joining that party, he would be estopped from relitigating the issue determined in the first suit that the party was indispensable. "Direct estoppel," together with collateral estoppel, is subsumed under the broad term of "issue preclusion."

But where the second action between the same parties is upon a different claim or demand, the judgment in the prior action operates as an estoppel only as to those matters in issue or points controverted, upon the determination of which the finding or verdict was rendered. In all cases, therefore, where it is sought to apply the estoppel of a judgment rendered upon one cause of action to matters arising in a suit upon a different cause of action, the inquiry must always be as to the point or question actually litigated and determined in the original action, not what might have been thus litigated and determined.

The late 20th century witnessed significant changes in the preclusion doctrines. Courts moved to less absolute rules permitting a wider range of policy and fairness considerations, while at the same time extending the formal boundaries of res judicata and collateral estoppel. Thus, most courts have embraced a transactional test for defining "the same claim" requirement for res judicata and have recast the strict "mutuality" requirement for collateral estoppel. Judicial concern over crowded dockets and impatience with certain kinds of recurring litigation have encouraged this extension of the scope of preclusion. We shall examine whether these evolving rules satisfy the needs of a modern system of procedure and how the policies of finality and judicial economy are counterbalanced against those of flexibility and fairness.

FINAL JUDGMENTS

The doctrines of claim and issue preclusion only apply to "final" judgments. We have had occasion to consider what is a "final judgment" for purposes of direct appeal to a U.S. Circuit Court of Appeals. See Chapter XII. 28 U.S.C.A. § 1291 allows appeal of a "final judgment," which, although not specifically defined there, is a judgment that "terminates the litigation on the merits and leaves nothing to be done but to enforce by execution what has been determined." Asher v. Ruppa, 173 F.2d 10, 11 (7th Cir.1949). The policy underlying the finality requirement for purposes of preclusion resembles the policy justification for insisting on a final judgment as a prerequisite for the right to appeal. "Appeals would be wasteful, and preclusion would be folly, as to decisions that are merely tentative and contemplate further proceedings." 18 C. Wright, A. Miller, & E. Cooper, Federal Practice and Procedure § 4432 at 299. But the purpose of assuring effective appellate review and the purpose of assuring the finality and economy objectives of the preclusion doctrines are not always served by the same definition of "final judgment." For example, although a judgment on liability (but not damages) or a judgment as to some, but not all, claims or parties (Rule 54(b)) may be considered "final" for an appeal, it may be undesirable to accord it finality for purposes of precluding further litigation since other aspects of the matter are still to be settled. Id. at §§ 4432, 4434.

The status of a judgment which is on appeal raises distinctive finality issues obviously not addressed by the definition of "final judgment" for purposes of appeal. Curiously, there is no firm agreement among jurisdictions as to whether a judgment on appeal should be given preclusive effect. "On the one hand, it makes little sense to accord conclusive effect to a determination that itself may be nullified through reversal on appeal; on the other hand, it may be a waste of effort to retry an issue simply because an appeal is pending in the case where the issue was originally determined." F. James, G. Hazard & J. Leubsdorf, Civil Procedure 678 (5th ed.2001). Some courts simply postpone consideration of the preclusive effect of a judgment until the appeal has been completed, which appears consistent with the procedural effect of Rule 62 (allowing a losing party to obtain a stay of judgment pending appeal). But see Restatement (Second) of Judgments § 13, comment f (1980) ("The better view is that a judgment otherwise final remains so despite the taking of an appeal unless what is called an appeal actually consists of a trial de novo."). The federal courts adhere to the Restatement view. A judgment is not deprived of finality simply because there is still time to file a motion in the trial court for a new trial or because the time for appeal has not yet expired.

A. CLAIM PRECLUSION (RES JUDICATA)

1. *Same Claim or Cause of Action*

MANEGO v. ORLEANS BOARD OF TRADE

United States Court of Appeals, First Circuit, 1985.
773 F.2d 1.

Before COFFIN, RUBIN, and BOWNES, CIRCUIT JUDGES.

BOWNES, CIRCUIT JUDGE.[a]

* * *

In late 1978 and early 1979, Manego applied to the Orleans Board of Selectmen for entertainment and liquor licenses for a disco which he wanted to build on a vacant lot. The lot was located in a commercial district a few hundred feet from an ice skating rink. The rink at that time was primarily used by children for hockey and figure skating. During the winter there was also a "Disco on Ice" program for children under sixteen. As a result of a mortgage foreclosure, the Cape Cod Five Cents Savings Bank owned the rink from 1978 until July 1979. The vice-president of the bank, David Willard, served as general manager of the rink during this period. As owner of the rink, the bank was concerned about the close proximity of an establishment serving liquor to a recreational facility primarily patronized by children and the increased likelihood of automobile accidents involving inebriated drivers and children walking to and from the rink. The bank also had more general concerns about the presence of a disco in the area.

In January of 1979, there was a meeting of the Orleans Board of Trade, a private organization which functions as the chamber of com-

---

a. Minor changes in wording have been made throughout the opinion to excise confusing references to another earlier suit that has no bearing on this opinion.—Eds.

merce for the town. At that time, Willard was also the president of the Board of Trade. Membership in this organization is open to anyone who pays the $15.00 membership fee. Willard raised the issue of the proposed disco at the meeting and after some discussion the membership voted to oppose the disco.

On January 11, 1979, a public hearing on Manego's liquor license application was held by the Orleans Board of Selectmen. Two of the selectmen, Gaston Norgeot and Thomas Nickerson, were also members of the Board of Trade. Over 100 people attended the meeting and expressed concern over the increased traffic and noise which would result from the disco as well as the effect of an establishment serving liquor in close proximity to the skating rink and the general effect of a disco on the atmosphere of the Town of Orleans. The Board of Selectmen received a petition containing 369 signatures opposing the disco and eleven letters, only two of which favored Manego's proposal. At the hearing, Willard announced that the Board of Trade had voted to oppose granting a license for the disco.

On February 8, 1979, the Selectmen denied Manego's application for a liquor license and Manego appealed this decision to the Board of Appeals, which met on February 8 and 14. Willard wrote a letter to the Board of Appeals setting forth the bank's opposition to the disco and its concern for the safety of the youngsters using the skating rink. Local counsel for the bank attended the Board of Appeals hearings. In late February, the Board of Appeals denied Manego's appeal.

On February 13, 1979, the Orleans Board of Trade held its monthly meeting and, according to the minutes, mention was made of a hearing scheduled for the next day on Manego's amusement license application and of Manego's appeal of the denial of the liquor license application by the Selectmen. At the February 14 amusement license hearing, the Selectmen requested that the Town Traffic Safety Committee study the effects of the proposed disco. On February 22, 1979, the Selectmen turned down Manego's application for an amusement license.

In spite of these license denials, the Orleans Board of Appeals granted Manego a building permit in May of 1979. The bank then filed suit in Barnstable Superior Court challenging the issuance of this permit. In July of 1979, the bank sold the rink to Paul Thibert and sometime in August withdrew its superior court suit.

In March of 1979, the entertainment license of the rink expired; no renewal was sought until July of 1979, after Thibert purchased the rink. Because the license had lapsed, the application was treated as a new application and not a renewal and a public hearing was held. During that summer, a concrete floor had been poured at the rink to allow roller skating so the new application added roller skating to the proposed activities of the facility. In addition, the rink planned to offer a ballroom dancing program for adults featuring live music from the 1940's and refreshments in the nature of soft drinks. This, too, was an addition to the rink's activities. The rink's application was granted by the Selectmen. Among the reasons cited by the Selectmen for their approval were its unique status as the only skating facility on the Lower Cape, its use by young people as safe and "noncorrupting" entertainment and the lack of noise or traffic problems created by the facility.

* * *

Manego brought a lawsuit in federal district court, naming the Board of Selectmen, the Cape Cod Five Cents Savings Bank and Willard as defendants and claiming that they had conspired to deny him the licenses because of his race in violation of 42 U.S.C. §§ 1981, 1983, 1985, 1986, 1988, 2000e et seq., § 3605 of the Fair Housing Act, and Mass. Gen.Laws Ann. ch. 151B, § 4(3B). The claims under 42 U.S.C. §§ 2000e et seq., the Fair Housing Act, and the state law claims were all dismissed by the district court for failure to state a cause of action. As to the other claims, [the district court granted summary judgment for the defendants.] * * *

The district court found that despite being given an extra ninety days to produce some concrete, factual basis for his allegation of conspiracy, which defendants had affirmatively denied in their affidavits, Manego produced only the following: two personal affidavits explaining his theory and suggesting that direct evidence of the conspiracy would emerge under cross-examination and a third affidavit of a local building contractor employed by Manego reporting that he had heard that a lumber company had been told by the Bank not to supply Manego with materials and vaguely suggesting that his own relationship with the bank had been adversely affected by his association with Manego. The district court found that since Manego had not taken advantage of an "ample opportunity" to take depositions or conduct any other form of discovery, his promise of evidence arising out of cross-examination was pure speculation, and that, furthermore, the affidavit of the building contractor could not be given any weight because it consisted primarily of hearsay.

In our opinion affirming the district court's grant of summary judgment on this ground, we said:

> In this case, plaintiff sought to infer the existence of an illegal conspiracy from the fact that the Selectmen granted a license to someone who was white but not to plaintiff, who was black. His inference is supported only by affidavit evidence of a general racial animus in the community. The fact that a group of private citizens, organized as the Orleans Board of Trade, voted unanimously to oppose his license and that members of the Board of Selectmen may have attended the meeting established nothing about the motivation of those individuals in opposing his license. The defendants countered his inference with an explanation of the difference between his disco and the skating rink which was granted a license. . . .

In the face of this explanation, plaintiff's promise that circumstantial evidence would emerge at trial could not withstand the defendants' motions for summary judgment.

Despite the rebuff, Manego filed another lawsuit, this time against the bank, Willard, and the Orleans Board of Trade and its members. This lawsuit, which is the subject of this appeal, differed from [the earlier suit] in two respects: it dropped the Board of Selectmen as a defendant and added the Board of Trade; and it alleged a new legal theory, antitrust violations under the Sherman Antitrust Act, 15 U.S.C. § 1. As evidence of a conspiracy between the bank and the Board of Trade to prevent the proposed disco from competing with the rink, Manego offered depositions, answers to interrogatories, affidavits, and other documents which showed: that Willard was simultaneously an officer of the bank, general manager of the rink, and President of the Board of Trade; that various members of the Board present at the January and February meetings were also Selectmen; that the Selectmen denied the licenses after the Board of Trade voted to oppose their issuance; that the Selectmen subsequently granted an entertainment license to the rink which included live music, dancing and roller disco; and that the bank brought a lawsuit challenging a construction permit granted to Manego by the Orleans Board of Appeal but dropped the lawsuit after it sold the rink. According to Manego, the Board of Trade's interest in preventing the competition between the proposed disco and the rink was derived from the interest of its president, David Willard, who managed the rink for the bank.

Willard and the Bank moved for summary judgment on the grounds that these new claims were barred by the doctrine of *res judicata* and that, in any event, its conduct was protected by the first amendment under the *Noerr-Pennington* doctrine.[b] The Board of Trade also moved for summary judgment under the doctrine of *res judicata* and additionally argued that there was no genuine issue of fact concerning the alleged conspiracy.

DEFENDANTS CAPE COD FIVE CENTS SAVINGS BANK AND DAVID WILLARD

As to Willard and the bank, the district court found that this lawsuit was barred by the final judgment of the Court of Appeals in [the earlier suit] affirming the district court's grant of summary judgment to the Bank and Willard on civil rights claims. Applying a "transactional" approach to claim preclusion, the district court found that the facts forming the basis of Manego's claim of antitrust violations were the same as those which formed the basis of his earlier civil rights claims and that they were, therefore, barred by the final judgment against Manego on the civil rights claims. We agree.

b. "[T]his doctrine exempts, with certain exceptions, concerted attempts to influence the passage or enforcement of laws from the sweep of anti-trust legislation regardless of anticompetitive intent." Manego v. Orleans Board of Trade, 598 F.Supp. 231, 236 (D.Mass.1984).—Eds.

While most of our previous cases have involved the preclusive effect of a previous *state* judgment on the merits and have, therefore, been based upon state *res judicata* doctrine, we have indicated that the preclusive effect given to prior judgments by various states does not differ from the preclusive effect we would give to our own judgments. In Capraro v. Tilcon Gammino, Inc., 751 F.2d 56, 58 (1st Cir.1985), we stated that "Rhode Island state law . . . , so far as we are aware, does not in connection with the principles of res judicata differ from the Restatement (Second) of Judgments or the law of Massachusetts or federal law." We then turned, as we have in many previous cases, to § 24 of the Restatement (Second) of Judgments (1982) concerning the scope of claim preclusion. It thus appears that, *sub silentio*, we have come to view the Restatement rule as our own, even though we have never formally adopted it. We now officially embrace it.

Under the doctrine of *res judicata*, "a final judgment on the merits of an action precludes the parties or their privies from relitigating issues that were or could have been raised in that action." Allen v. McCurry, 449 U.S. 90, 94, 101 S.Ct. 411, 414, 66 L.Ed.2d 308 (1980). This bar is limited, however, to cases arising out of the same cause of action or claim. E.g., Cromwell v. County of Sac, 94 U.S. 351, 4 Otto 351, 24 L.Ed. 195 (1876). Our adoption of the Restatement (Second) approach commits us to a "transactional" definition of the underlying claim or cause of action:

(1) When a valid and final judgment rendered in an action extinguishes the plaintiff's claim pursuant to the rules of merger or bar . . . , the claim extinguished includes all rights of the plaintiff to remedies against the defendant with respect to all or any part of the transaction, or series of connected transactions, out of which the action arose.

(2) What factual grouping constitutes a "transaction," and what groupings constitute a "series," are to be determined pragmatically, giving weight to such considerations as whether the facts are related in time, space, origin, or motivation, whether they form a convenient trial unit, and whether their treatment as a unit conforms to the parties' expectations or business understanding or usage.

Restatement (Second) of Judgments § 24 (1982).

Manego has argued that [this case] does not involve the same transaction as that which formed the basis for [the earlier case] for three reasons: the nature of the conspiracy alleged is different; the parties to the conspiracy are different, although they do share common members; and there was no allegation in [the earlier case] that the rink and disco would be offering similar entertainment and thus competing for the same customers.

As the district court pointed out, however, the mere fact that different legal theories are presented in each case does not mean that the same transaction is not behind each. Thus, the fact that one suit alleges a conspiracy with a racial animus and the other alleges a conspiracy with anticompetitive animus does not demonstrate that separate transactions are involved. Nor does it matter in this case that the named defendants are not identical. Even though the Board of Trade was not a defendant in [the earlier case], the fact that it met under the leadership of Willard and voted to oppose the disco was brought out and no new facts concerning conduct of the bank and the Board of Trade have been alleged.

We next consider whether the absence from [the earlier case] of the allegation that the bank had plans to offer live music and dancing at the rink was sufficient to prevent the application of *res judicata*. The focus of the argument below was on whether Manego reasonably could have alleged this at the time of the racial discrimination suit. Manego claimed that he did not allege the "similar entertainment" facts in [the earlier case] because he did not know of them until too late—three days before summary judgment issued. While it is the law that, if information is not reasonably discoverable, *res judicata* will not apply, see Marrapese v. State of Rhode Island, 749 F.2d 934 (1st Cir.1984), the district court found that this exception was not available here because the "entertainment" facts could have been uncovered if Manego had been diligent in his discovery efforts. The court then went on to reason that because the legal theory which rested upon the "entertainment" facts *could have been* asserted during the prior suit, *res judicata* applied to bar its assertion in a later suit. We believe, however, that, once the reasonable discovery issue is resolved, the focus of a "transactional" analysis is not on whether a second claim could have been brought in a prior suit, but whether the underlying facts of both transactions were the same or substantially similar.

There will be situations where the factual bases for separate causes of action are different but intertwined and joining them together is both possible and convenient. A failure to do so, however, will not justify the application of *res judicata*. A good illustration of this can be found in Landrigan v. City of Warwick, 628 F.2d 736 (1st Cir.1980), where we held that a law suit charging the police with covering-up an alleged use of excessive force was not precluded by a prior lawsuit based on the actual use of excessive force. The plaintiff in *Landrigan* could have pursued both causes of action in the same lawsuit and it might have been very convenient to do so, since the alleged cover-up was intimately connected to the initial police misconduct. We found, however, that because the factual basis for the cover-up was distinct from the factual basis for the misconduct, the plaintiff was not required to do so. This is to be contrasted with a situation in which the factual basis for each claim is essentially the same, so that not only *could* both claims be joined in one lawsuit, but [they] *must* be joined or be barred by *res judicata*. A good example is again provided by *Landrigan,* where we held that a prior state court suit for assault and battery precluded a later federal suit under § 1983 for excessive use of force.

The question, therefore, is whether the absence from [the earlier suit] of an allegation that the bank had plans to offer live music and dancing at the rink creates a transactional difference precluding the application of *res judicata*. Manego now argues that because an allegation that the rink and disco were competitors was essential to provide a motive for a conspiracy to restrain trade, the factual basis for such a conspiracy is distinctly different from that needed to show racial discrimination and that the antitrust action cannot be considered to arise from the same transaction or series of transactions. The answer to this question depends upon whether the underlying facts are the same regardless of the different motives, i.e., racial discrimination and restraint of trade. Aside from motive, the conduct alleged is precisely the same, i.e., the actions of the bank and Willard vis-a-vis the proposed disco. Each alleged conspiracy had the same practical end—keeping Manego from operating the disco—and each used essentially the same means—denial of the licenses, intimidation of building suppliers, and an ultimately withdrawn lawsuit challenging a building permit. This is not a case like *Landrigan* where, although the events in question are closely connected in time and space, two relatively distinct sets of facts can be separated out as the bases for separate legal wrongs. We conclude, therefore, that the difference in motive for the conspiracy does not create a separate transaction. This means that once Manego chose to allege a conspiracy involving particular specified conspiratorial acts he was required to allege all possible motives for such a conspiracy and all facts necessary to support these allegations or lose the right to do so. Whether he took that risk by failure to discover the facts which diligent effort would have unearthed or by deliberate choice, the result is the same: the antitrust claim is barred by *res judicata* as to the bank and Willard.

Defendant Orleans Board of Trade

The Board of Trade moved for summary judgment on the grounds that the present suit was barred by the doctrine of *res judicata* and that there was no genuine issue of material fact which would allow Manego to fall under an exception to the *Noerr-Pennington* doctrine. The district court found that *res judicata* did not apply, but that Manego had not alleged facts sufficient to overcome the protection provided by *Noerr-Pennington,*[c] and granted summary judgment for the Board of Trade. The district court's treatment of both these issues was excellent and we see no point in gilding the lily. We affirm the grant of summary judgment to the Board of Trade and its members on the basis of the district court's opinion.

Notes and Questions

1. The Court of Appeals' opinion affirming summary judgment for defendants in Manego's first suit, 692 F.2d 174 (1st Cir.1982), recounted facts that put Manego in a more sympathetic light and indicate evidentiary

c. The plaintiff had contended that two exceptions to the *Noerr-Pennington* doctrine applied: the "sham" exception, which applies where a party seeks not to influence public officials but to bar its competitor from meaningful access to adjudicatory tribunals, and the "conspiracy" exception, which applies where government officials participate with private individuals in a scheme to restrain trade.—Eds.

support for both his civil rights and antitrust conspiracy claims. In February, 1979, arsonists set fire to a building he owned in the area. An affidavit from the building contractor he had hired to build his disco stated that the bank had pressured one of his suppliers not to supply Manego's project and that local persons had uttered racial slurs against the contractor because of his association with Manego. A license for a similar operation was granted to a white man a year and a half after Manego's application was denied. The court noted, however:

> We recognize that, to a lay person, aggregating all of the circumstances of plaintiff's case—the denial of his license, the granting—a half year later—of a license to a white man, the fact that someone set fire to his property, and rumors that unnamed persons had uttered racial slurs—might suggest the old adage that where there is smoke, there is fire. In this case, however, the district judge invited the plaintiff to lead him to at least some glowing embers and plaintiff failed to do so. The district court recognized, properly, that smoke alone is not enough to force the defendants to a trial to prove their actions were not discriminatory.

Id. at 177. Should this information affect the res judicata issue?

2. Why wasn't the Board of Trade entitled to assert the defense of res judicata in *Manego*?

3. How can it be said that the second suit in *Manego* (for violation of the antitrust act through a conspiracy among the bank, Willard, and the Board of Trade) was the same claim as the earlier suit (for violation of the civil rights statutes through a conspiracy among the bank, Willard, and the Board of Selectmen)? Since the elements of an antitrust cause of action are different from a civil rights cause of action, why aren't these different claims? Further, how can res judicata apply here when the parties are different?

4. Under the transactional test adopted in *Manego,* how does a court determine the "factual basis" of each suit? In *Manego,* the second suit alleged a number of facts not raised in the first suit. It gave a new account of the role of the Board of Selectmen and of the interrelationship between the bank and Willard. It also relied heavily on the claim that the bank had plans to offer live music and dancing at its rink. Wouldn't these allegations add significantly different facts to what was alleged in the first suit? How can these be called the same "factual basis" as the first suit? One court has described the transactional test as asking whether the claims derive from the "same nucleus of operative facts," with relevant factors being whether the facts are related in time, space, origin, or motivation; whether they form a convenient trial unit; and whether treating them as a unit conforms to the parties' expectations. Apparel Art Int'l, Inc. v. Amertex Enter., 48 F.3d 576, 584 (1st Cir.1995). Does *Manego* satisfy this test?

5. Are the tests for determining the "same transaction or occurrence" for purposes of a compulsory counterclaim in Rule 13(a), supra p. 207, or for purposes of relation back of amendments under Rule 15(c), supra p. 218, applicable to the transactional test for res judicata? Recall the language in Blair v. Durham (quoted in Swartz v. Gold Dust Casino, Inc., supra pp. 221–22 (allowing relation back of an amendment under the Rule 15(c) "same

transaction or occurrence" test because "the two acts alleged were but different invasions of appellee's primary right and different breaches of the same duty").

Compare Dillard v. Crenshaw County, 640 F.Supp. 1347 (M.D.Ala.1986). There an earlier judgment was entered against a class of African–American voters, who challenged the constitutionality of the at-large method of electing county officials, on the ground that they had not proven discriminatory intent. The court found that a second suit on behalf of the same class, based on a provision of the Voting Rights Act of 1965 that proscribed policies with a racially discriminatory intent, was barred by res judicata, stating:

> [T]he primary rights and duties are the same. Despite the nominal difference between the claim in [the first suit] and that raised here, the plaintiffs in both suits were asserting the same right—namely, the right to be free from intentional racial discrimination. Furthermore, the Eleventh Circuit has more recently explained that the bar of res judicata "extends not only to the precise legal theory presented in the previous litigation, but to all legal theories and claims arising out of the same 'operative nucleus of fact.' " Olmstead v. Amoco Oil Co., 725 F.2d 627, 629 (11th Cir.1984). Since the plaintiffs in both suits challenged the same election system in the same county it would appear that their claims did arise out of the identical "operative nucleus of fact." The principles of res judicata may therefore apply regardless of the fact that the plaintiffs in the first suit relied on the constitution, whereas the plaintiffs in the present suit rely on [the civil rights act].

6.   The plaintiff in *Manego* claimed that he learned of the bank's plans to offer live music and dancing only three days before summary judgment was entered. How could he have been expected to plead these facts in the first suit? How does the court determine what facts plaintiff should know when he files the first suit? Cf. Rule 11.

Would it have made a difference if Manego had based his second suit on events that *occurred* after his first suit was filed? In Pleming v. Universal–Rundle Corp., 142 F.3d 1354 (11th Cir.1998), plaintiff claimed that defendant employer discriminated against her when it refused her request to switch from her laborer job to a clerical job after she was injured at work. Defendant asserted that it had not discriminated based on its policy against allowing employees to transfer to lower paying jobs. During discovery, plaintiff found out that, while her suit was pending, defendant had filled two more clerical positions with other applicants, and she referred to these later events in her opposition to defendant's motion for summary judgment to show that defendant's purported policy was a pretext for discrimination. The district court eventually granted defendant's motion for summary judgment on the ground plaintiff had failed to prove that defendant's explanation for its decision was a pretext.

Plaintiff then filed a second suit, alleging that defendant discriminated against her in hiring others for the later two openings, and the district court held that res judicata barred the suit. Observing that res judicata "depends upon whether the primary right and duty are the same in both cases," the court of appeals ruled that res judicata did not apply because plaintiff never formally asserted claims for the later incidents in the first suit. It noted that

Rule 15(d) governs supplemental complaints and saw the issue as "whether the discussion of a related but distinct cause of action in briefs amounts to the *actual assertion* of that claim in the first proceeding." Because no supplemental complaint, amendment pursuant to Rule 15(b), or consideration of the claim in a pretrial order pursuant to Rule 16(e) had occurred, the court viewed the "isolated reference" to the later events in a decision in the first case as insufficient to show that the district court "actually adjudicated an unpled and unasserted claim."

7. In *Landrigan,* which is described in *Manego,* why was the factual basis for the first suit (based on assault and battery) considered different from that in the second suit (based on the police cover-up of the use of excessive force)? Are they really "two relatively distinct sets of facts," as the *Manego* court suggests in distinguishing the case? Is it significant that the first suit was based on a state-law claim in a state court while the second was based on a federal civil rights claim in a federal court?

8. Is a party bound by something like a "due diligence" or "should have known" standard regarding issues that could have been raised in the first suit? Consider McWilliams v. McWilliams, 804 F.2d 1400 (5th Cir.1986). Mrs. McWilliams filed suit in federal court alleging a § 1983 civil rights claim against the judge who presided over her divorce proceedings two years earlier. She alleged that the judge had ignored her constitutional rights in entering a divorce judgment, pursuant to a jury finding, appointing her husband managing conservator of their children. The judgment also forbade her from taking the children to the Endtime Evangelistic Pentecostal Church, a predominantly African–American church to which Mrs. McWilliams, a white, had regularly taken the children. The Fifth Circuit found the record was "replete with racial references manifestly intended to prejudice judge and jury against Mrs. McWilliams," but that her counsel made no objections at trial. Her second suit relied on the Supreme Court's decision in Palmore v. Sidoti, 466 U.S. 429, 104 S.Ct. 1879, 80 L.Ed.2d 421 (1984), rendered *after* her divorce decree, holding that racial biases of the community (there regarding a white mother cohabiting with an African–American) are not permissible considerations for denying child custody to a natural mother.

The Fifth Circuit found her civil rights suit barred by res judicata: "Looking at the plaintiff's federal claim for what it really is, it is one for the custody of the McWilliams children, a matter that was purportedly put to rest in appropriate proceedings in the appropriate forum, subject to review by the Texas appellate courts." 804 F.2d at 1402. Cf. Ankenbrandt v. Richards, supra p. 867 n. 11 (applying "domestic relations exception" to diversity jurisdiction for child custody disputes). It did not specifically discuss the fact that the *Palmore* decision was after the divorce suit, but seemed to assume that Mrs. McWilliams' counsel should have known that injection of the racial considerations was unconstitutional (see infra pp. 1151–58, concerning effect of change of law on claim and issue preclusion). It conceded that the parties in the two suits were not identical; the judge was not a party to the divorce suit, and her husband was not a proper party to the civil rights suit since he was not a state actor. Nevertheless, it found that Mr. and Mrs. McWilliams were the real parties in interest in both actions and that "[t]here is a difference in the two proceedings, but only because counsel for Mrs. McWilliams failed to present the constitutional issues in the state court." Is this a proper application of res judicata?

9.   Many older cases did not follow the transactional test endorsed by the Restatement (Second) of Judgments and adopted in *Manego*. It was often held that causes of action were different if they involved different "rights" and "wrongs." See Baltimore S.S. Co. v. Phillips, 274 U.S. 316, 47 S.Ct. 600, 71 L.Ed. 1069 (1927). For example, in Smith v. Kirkpatrick, 111 N.E.2d 209 (N.Y.1953), plaintiff sued his employer for money due him under a theory of quantum meruit, after having lost a previous suit for the same sum based on an oral contract because it did not comply with the Statute of Frauds. The court declined to find the second suit barred by res judicata, stating:

> The two actions involve different "rights" and "wrongs." The requisite elements of proof and hence the evidence necessary to sustain recovery vary materially. The causes of action are different and distinct and the rights and interests established by the previous adjudication will not be impaired by a recovery, if that be the outcome, in quantum meruit.

What did the *Smith* court mean by saying the suits involved "different rights and wrongs"? Is it because they involved different proof and evidence? Would that indicate that the theories raised in the two suits would not make a convenient trial package and therefore that res judicata should not be used to prevent splitting the cause of action? If that is so, wouldn't the same rationale be applicable in *Manego* where the antitrust claim would seem to require different evidence from the civil rights claim? Does the transactional test leave room for considering whether the claims would be a convenient trial package? Is the "right-wrong" distinction a more satisfactory test?

In *Smith,* the judge in the first case noted that the defendant had clearly overreached the plaintiff, but that plaintiff could not recover on the oral contract because of the Statute of Frauds and had not pleaded quantum meruit. Should sympathy for a plaintiff who had a good cause of action but lost the first time because of faulty lawyering be a factor in deciding whether to apply res judicata? Is there a better procedural response? Compare Rule 15(b).

10.   If the holder of a series of notes, all of which are due and in default, sues on only one, will the judgment constitute a merger or bar as to the others? The general answer is no, because each note is a separate liability arising out of a separate transaction. But what if all the notes were given as payment in a single commercial transaction? The traditional view is also that they are separate liabilities, and the plaintiff may choose to sue on them separately, although under the modern transactional approach this may not be so certain, depending on the facts. What if there is a common reason for the default that will require the same evidence in each suit on any of the notes—as that they are invalid for charging usurious interest, or that the holder defaulted on the consideration that was paid for them, or that an identical clause in each of them is the center of the dispute? Should they not be considered the same transaction for purposes of res judicata? See generally, F. James, G. Hazard & J. Leubsdorf, Civil Procedure § 11.11 (5th ed.2001).

Separate leases for different time periods on the same piece of property, or for different parcels of one piece of property, pose the same kind of separate liability issue. However, it is settled that claims for amounts due on running accounts, for installment payments such as rent under a lease, for royalties under a patent, for claims affecting realty such as a continuing trespass, or for claims in quantum meruit for occupancy of land must be brought for all amounts due at the time of filing. See Sutcliffe Storage & Warehouse Co. v. United States, 162 F.2d 849 (1st Cir.1947).

11. Under the Restatement's "transactional" test, a final judgment extinguishes all rights against the defendant with respect to "the transaction, *or series of connected transactions*, out of which the action arose." Restatement (Second) of Judgments § 24. What groupings constitute a "series" "are to be determined pragmatically" based on "such considerations as whether the facts are related in time, space, origin, or motivation, whether they form a convenient trial unit, and whether their treatment as a unit conforms to the parties' expectations or business understanding or usage." This issue can arise in employment discrimination cases where the employee, whose first suit went to judgment, files a second later suit alleging discriminatory acts of a somewhat different nature. In Havercombe v. Department of Education of the Commonwealth of Puerto Rico, 250 F.3d 1 (1st Cir. 2001), the plaintiff won a judgment based on allegations of race and age discrimination, and then filed a second suit alleging additional acts of discrimination. The court found the second suit precluded as part of a series of connected transactions based on similar allegations of discriminatory animus and of a hostile work environment "that does not turn on single acts but on an aggregation of acts over a period of time". It also found no basis for invoking the exceptions to claim-splitting in the Restatement—"where formal barriers existed against full presentation of claim in the first action or where the defendant has committed fraud on the plaintiff by concealing evidence of a part or phase of claim that the plaintiff failed to include in an earlier action." Restatement, supra, § 26.

12. Decisions of administrative agencies are entitled to preclusive effect when the agency acted in a judicial capacity. University of Tennessee v. Elliott, 478 U.S. 788 (1986). Restatement (Second) of Judgments, § 83(2) provides that an adjudicative determination by an administrative tribunal has preclusive effect only insofar as the proceeding entailed the essential elements of adjudication, including adequate notice to persons who are to be bound, right to present evidence and legal argument, formulation of issues of law and fact in terms of the application of rules to the specific transaction, a rule of finality, and such other procedural elements as may be necessary to conclusively determine the matter in question. See also Mack v. South Bay Beer Distributors, Inc., 798 F.2d 1279 (9th Cir.1986) (decision by state unemployment agency that plaintiff was discharged for misconduct was not accorded preclusive effect in federal-court suit for violation of Age Discrimination in Employment Act (ADEA) because there were no specific findings, and the record did not indicate the evidence as to the age discrimination claims).

13. The doctrine of "election of remedies" can have an effect somewhat similar to the prohibition on splitting a cause of action. The doctrine, now increasingly rejected or limited, views the pleading of an action for one remedy as an irrevocable election preventing the pleader from later seeking a different remedy. A contemporary example is Fischer v. Powers, 597

N.W.2d 774 (Wis.App.1999). There the purchaser of a house discovered that, contrary to the "condition report" signed by the seller, the house had carpenter ants. She sued for damages in small claims court, but later removed to the circuit court on an amended complaint seeking rescission. The court refused to find that she had made an irrevocable election, saying that the doctrine "should be confined to cases where the plaintiff may be unjustly enriched or the defendant has actually been misled by the plaintiff's conduct or the result is otherwise inequitable or res judicata can be applied." It noted that even when she filed her small claims suit plaintiff lacked knowledge of the pervasiveness of the ant problem and reasonably believed an extermination plan would be successful and damages would be adequate. Should such evidence be necessary to avoid election?

OTHER ACTION PENDING

Parties sometimes file two or more suits on the same cause of action in different courts which are pending at the same time (referred to as repetitive suits). Reasons for this include doubts as to jurisdiction in some of the fora, concern about missing the statute of limitations deadline if some of the suits are dismissed on non-merits grounds, desire to be able to forum-shop according to choice of law and other pre-trial determinations, and sometimes simply the urge to harass the other party.

A party subjected to repetitive suits need not wait until one goes to judgment and then raise it as a bar to prosecution of the other; the simultaneous defense of multiple suits is itself an onerous burden. It is possible instead to raise the defense of "other action pending," thus seeking a dismissal if there is another action on the same cause of action pending in the same state or federal district court. Where a repetitive suit is pending in a different state or federal district court, a defendant may seek to enjoin the opposing party from prosecuting the repetitive suit or seek an order from the other court staying the repetitive suit pending completion of the first suit. See 5A C. Wright & A. Miller, Federal Practice and Procedure § 1360 at 438–41. The suit that was first-in-time is usually given priority, but other considerations may alter that priority. See William Gluckin & Co. v. International Playtex Corp., 407 F.2d 177 (2d Cir.1969).

If a defendant faced with repetitive suits moves to dismiss or stay the second suit for "other action pending," the issue of their similarity would be resolved at that time and if the second suit were dismissed or stayed, that would not constitute a bar to the continued prosecution of the other. Thus a dismissal or stay for "other action pending" might be viewed as less harsh to the plaintiff than allowing one of the suits to go to final judgment and then bar the other under res judicata. Should a defendant be required to use remedies available under "other action pending" as a prerequisite to raising the defense of res judicata later?

APPLICATION OF RES JUDICATA TO DEFENDANTS

The policies underlying res judicata apply to the responses of a defendant to a lawsuit, but in a distinctive way. There is little problem with *defenses:* if a defendant fails to raise defenses available to it, it cannot as a general rule thereafter use them to attack the judgment. See Restatement (Second) of Judgments § 18(2).

The treatment of *counterclaims* is more involved. When a defendant actually raises a counterclaim, all aspects of it are subject to the rules of claim preclusion. The only exception is the rare case when the defendant cannot obtain full recovery on his counterclaim (as in a court of limited jurisdiction from which the defendant could not remove the case). Id., §§ 21, 23. In that case, merger should not apply to prevent a second suit for the amount not recoverable. Id., § 21(2).

When the defendant does not raise a counterclaim available to it, there are further considerations. The same facts may constitute a ground of defense to the plaintiff's claim and also a ground for a counterclaim. For example, in the case of a *compulsory counterclaim* (i.e., arising out of the same transaction or occurrence as the claim) that shares common facts with a defense raised by the defendant, economy concerns and the interest in consistent judgments favor requiring the defendant to raise the counterclaim or lose it. This result is accomplished by Federal Rule 13(a) and by the majority of states that have a compulsory counterclaim rule. The compulsory counterclaim rule is sometimes referred to as a codification of res judicata as applied to counterclaims. The "same transaction or occurrence" language in Rule 13(a) (see Wigglesworth v. Teamsters Local Union No. 592, supra p. 207) is quite close to the transactional analysis of modern res judicata. The compulsory counter-claim rule is stated in terms of waiver rather than of merger and bar, but the effect in this type of situation is similar.

When there is no compulsory counterclaim rule, can a defendant fail to raise a counterclaim and still sue on it later? Where the defendant alleges as a defense the same facts that would support a counterclaim, he is not precluded from maintaining a subsequent action on the counter-claim. Schwabe v. Chantilly, Inc., 226 N.W.2d 452 (Wis.1975); Restate-ment (Second) of Judgments § 22 and comments c & d. The rationale seems to be that where the jurisdiction chose not to make the counter-claim compulsory (in *Schwabe,* Wisconsin made all counterclaims per-missive), the defendant should have the freedom to select its own forum for its counterclaim. This rule obviously subordinates the benefits of requiring the defendant to litigate common issues in the same suit to the defendant's right to select the forum for his permissive counterclaim. (Note, however, that the defendant may be collaterally estopped from relitigating issues that were actually decided in the first suit, as in Little v. Blue Goose Motor Coach Co., infra p. 1142.)

There is an exception to the rule that the defendant is not precluded from a second suit on his counterclaim: preclusion does apply when "the relationship between the counterclaim and the plaintiff's claim is such that successful prosecution of the second action would nullify the initial judgment or would impair rights established in the initial action." Restatement (Second) of Judgments, § 22(1)(b). Consider Martino v.

McDonald's System, Inc., 598 F.2d 1079 (7th Cir.1979). There Martino entered into a franchise agreement to operate a McDonald's outlet. The agreement forbade Martino or any member of his family to acquire an interest in a competing fast food business. When Martino's son bought a Burger Chef franchise in a nearby town, McDonald's sued in federal court to terminate the franchise. Before Martino's answer was filed, the parties entered into settlement negotiations that resulted in a consent judgment declaring that Martino had breached the franchise agreement and that the breach justified termination. The judgment therefore directed that Martino sell his franchise back to McDonald's for a specified sum. Martino later filed a second suit, claiming that the noncompete provision of the franchise agreement violated the antitrust laws. McDonald's argued res judicata. The court held that the consent judgment in the first action foreclosed the second suit even though Rule 13(a)'s compulsory counterclaim rule never came into play because Martino never filed an answer in the first suit. The court relied on "long-standing principles of res judicata establish[ing] a narrowly defined class of 'common law compulsory counterclaims,' " explaining:

> It is impossible to interpret this [antitrust] count as anything but a direct challenge to the outcome of [McDonald's] 1973 lawsuit. The 1973 lawsuit concluded that termination [of the franchise contract] was justified. The plaintiff now contends that termination was not justified, because the federal antitrust laws forbade it. If Martino's antitrust theory had merit, it would have been a defense in 1973, changing the outcome of the litigation.

The appellate court conceded that the antitrust violation constituted a separate ground for recovery as well as a defense and therefore was a different "cause of action" for the purpose of res judicata. It thus recognized the general rule that in such a situation "the defendant's failure to allege these facts as a defense and a counterclaim 'does not preclude him from relying on those facts in an action subsequently brought by him against the plaintiff.' " It stated, however, that the rule was not absolute:

> Both precedent and policy require that res judicata bar a counterclaim when its prosecution would nullify rights established by the prior action. Judicial economy is not the only basis for the doctrine of res judicata. Res judicata also preserves the integrity of judgments and protects those who rely on them. McDonald's System [has] * * * terminated and repurchased Martino's franchise in reliance on the trial court's 1973 judgment telling them they were justified in doing so. Now Martino seeks to impose significant financial liability on the defendants for these actions. We cannot hold that the counterclaim exception to the res judicata rule, based merely on notions of convenience, permits the plaintiff to wage this direct attack on the rights established by the prior judgment.

Notes and Questions

1. Is the exception provided by *Martino* and Restatement (Second) § 22(1)(b), good policy? Should it apply to most cases where common facts

support both a defense and a counterclaim? Is the key to the test merely whether later recovery on the counterclaim would be inconsistent with the earlier judgment, or is something more required? Would it apply to the following situation (taken from Restatement (Second) of Judgments § 22, comment f)?

> *A* brings an action against *B* for failure to pay the contract price for goods sold and delivered and recovers judgment for default. After entry of final judgment and payment of the price, *B* brings an action against *A* to rescind the contract for mutual mistake, seeking restitution of the contract price and offering to return the goods.

2. Franchise agreements often contain arbitration clauses, and if the franchisor seeks relief in arbitration, the franchisee may prefer to raise its defenses in a court rather than the arbitration. In Rudell v. Comprehensive Accounting Corp., 802 F.2d 926 (7th Cir. 1986), the franchisor invoked arbitration claiming that its franchisee, the Rudells, had defaulted on contractual obligations. When the Rudells did not make an appearance, the arbitrator awarded the franchisor termination of the franchise and damages. The Rudells then sued in federal court alleging the franchise agreement was procured by fraud and seeking to void the arbitration clause and to obtain damages under RICO. The Second Circuit affirmed the lower court's finding that the suit was precluded. Although it viewed *Martino* as only establishing "a narrowly defined class of common law compulsory counterclaims," it found that precedent and policy would bar a suit on a claim that could have been filed as a defense or counterclaim "when its prosecution would nullify rights established by the prior action" (citing Restatement (Second) of Judgments § 22(2)(B)). Here, it found, the Rudells' suit would make the relief obtained by the franchisor in arbitration meaningless.

Should an arbitration award be given the same preclusive effect as a court judgment? 28 U.S.C.A. § 1738, which obliges federal courts to give the same preclusive effect to a state-court judgment as would the court of the rendering state, does not apply to arbitration awards because they are not "judicial proceedings." In *Rudell*, the arbitration award was confirmed by a federal district court judgment (see 9 U.S.C. § 9). See Flynn v. Gorton, 255 Cal.Rptr. 768 (Cal.App.1989) (judgment confirming arbitration award constitutes final judgment on the merits for purposes of collateral estoppel); Aufderhar v. Data Dispatch, Inc., 452 N.W.2d 648, 652 (Minn. 1990) (where claimant was afforded a full opportunity to litigate concerning personal injury in an arbitration, he may be estopped from relitigating the issues in a suit). In the absence of such a judgment, any preclusive effect given an arbitration award must arise from common law. Compare Flynn v. Gorton, 207 Cal.App.3d 1550 (1989) (arbitration award not accorded collateral estoppel effect because "in judicial arbitration, the low monetary amount in controversy and option of trial de novo can leave parties without a serious incentive to litigate") with Dorrance v. Lee, 976 P.2d 904 (Haw.S.Ct. 1999) (non-binding "court-annexed arbitration" award has collateral estoppel effect where state rules of civil procedure require the parties to participate and the consequences of failure to seek a trial de novo are made clear).

3. What if the defendant in *Martino* had not been able to file the antitrust counterclaim? See Lyons v. Westinghouse Elec. Corp., 222 F.2d 184 (2d Cir.), cert. denied, 350 U.S. 825, 76 S.Ct. 52, 100 L.Ed. 737 (1955), where defendant in a state court suit on a contract raised the defense that the contract violated the antitrust laws, but could not file an antitrust counter-claim because federal courts have exclusive jurisdiction over federal antitrust claims. Judgment was for the plaintiff. The appellate court denied collateral estoppel effect to the state court's rejection of the antitrust defense. (We will give further consideration to the effect of exclusive federal court jurisdiction on the application of res judicata to state-court judgments in Marrese v. American Academy of Orthopaedic Surgeons, infra p. 1125.)

2. *Exceptions to the Rule Against Splitting a Cause of Action*

Res judicata is often referred to as a rule for enforcing the prohibi-tion on "splitting a cause of action," that is, not suing on all the theories arising out of the matter being litigated and then attempting to raise them in a second suit. The prohibition against splitting a cause of action reflects not only the desirability of finality in litigation but also concern for the efficient use of judicial resources.

There may be occasions in which there are policy reasons for withholding some aspect of the claim for future litigation, or in which, due to procedural or substantive limitations, a party may be involuntari-ly forced to split his cause of action, or in which application of a strict rule against splitting a cause of action results in unfairness. Should there be exceptions for such situations? Consider the following case.

FEDERATED DEPARTMENT STORES, INC. v. MOITIE

Supreme Court of the United States, 1981.
452 U.S. 394, 101 S.Ct. 2424, 69 L.Ed.2d 103.

Justice Rehnquist delivered the opinion of the Court.

The only question presented in this case is whether the Court of Appeals for the Ninth Circuit validly created an exception to the doctrine of res judicata. The court held that res judicata does not bar relitigation of an unappealed adverse judgment where, as here, other plaintiffs in similar actions against common defendants successfully appealed the judgments against them. We disagree with the view taken by the Court of Appeals for the Ninth Circuit and reverse.

[In 1976, seven consumers (including Moitie and Brown) filed class actions against defendant department stores, charging them with illegal-ly fixing retail prices of women's clothing in Northern California. All the complaints tracked the allegations of an earlier antitrust suit by the United States. Moitie filed a class action in California state court and invoked only state antitrust law. There was apparently diversity of citizenship, and Moitie's claim was for the amount of any overcharges she had incurred due to the price fixing, which she asserted amounted to $5,000. Defendants removed Moitie's suit to federal court, citing federal question and diversity grounds, and it was consolidated with the other six, one of which had been brought by Brown. The district court then dismissed all seven suits "in their entirety" under the then-current view that retail purchasers of price-fixed goods could not sue because they had not suffered harm to their "business or property" within the meaning of the federal antitrust statute, 15 U.S.C.A. § 15. This dismissal is referred to as *Moitie I* and *Brown I*.

Five of the seven plaintiffs appealed and, after Reiter v. Sonotone Corp., 442 U.S. 330 (1979), held that consumers could sue under the federal antitrust laws, the Ninth Circuit reversed the judgments against them. Moitie and Brown did not appeal. Instead, they filed new suits in California state court relying solely on California state law (as Moitie had done originally). These suits were called *Moitie II* and *Brown II*. Defendants removed these cases to federal court, and the district court refused to remand because they were "in many respects identical" to the earlier complaints and therefore raised "essentially federal" claims. It then dismissed on res judicata grounds. The Ninth Circuit reversed, refusing on grounds of "public policy" and "simple justice" to apply res judicata.

Before turning to the res judicata question, the Supreme Court stated (in a footnote) that the removal of *Moitie II* and *Brown II* was proper. This conclusion was based on the finding by the district court that the claims were "in many respects identical" with the prior complaints removed to federal court in *Moitie I* and had been "artfully couched in terms of state law" in order to avoid removal. The Court has since narrowed the "artful pleading" doctrine. See supra p. 890 n.9.]

There is little to be added to the doctrine of res judicata as developed in the case law of this Court. A final judgment on the merits of an action precludes the parties or their privies from relitigating issues that were or could have been raised in that action. Nor are the res judicata consequences of a final, unappealed judgment on the merits altered by the fact that the judgment may have been wrong or rested on a legal principle subsequently overruled in another case. As this Court explained in Baltimore S.S. Co. v. Phillips, 274 U.S. 316, 325, 47 S.Ct. 600, 604, 71 L.Ed. 1069 (1927), an "erroneous conclusion" reached by the court in the first suit does not deprive the defendants in the second action "of their right to rely upon the plea of res judicata.... A judgment merely voidable because based upon an erroneous view of the law is not open to collateral attack, but can be corrected only by a direct review and not by bringing another action upon the same cause [of action]." We have observed that "[t]he indulgence of a contrary view would result in creating elements of uncertainty and confusion and in undermining the conclusive character of judgments, consequences which it was the very purpose of the doctrine of res judicata to avert." Reed v. Allen, 286 U.S. 191, 201, 52 S.Ct. 532, 534, 76 L.Ed. 1054 (1932).

* * *

In Reed v. Allen, supra, this Court addressed the issue presented here. The case involved a dispute over the rights to property left in a will. A won an interpleader action for rents derived from the property and, while an appeal was pending, brought an ejectment action against the rival claimant B. On the basis of the decree in the interpleader suit A won the ejectment action. B did not appeal this judgment, but prevailed on his earlier appeal from the interpleader decree and was awarded the rents which had been collected. When B sought to bring an ejectment action against A, the latter pleaded res judicata, based on his previous successful ejectment action. This Court held that res judicata was available as a defense and that the property belonged to A:

> "The judgment in the ejectment action was final and not open to assault collaterally, but subject to impeachment only through some form of direct attack. The appellate court was limited to a review of the [interpleader] decree; and it is hardly necessary to say that jurisdiction to review one judgment gives an appellate court no power to reverse or modify another and independent judgment. If respondent, in addition to appealing from the [interpleader] decree, had appealed from the [ejectment] judgment, the appellate court, having both cases before it, might have afforded a remedy.... But this course respondent neglected to follow." Id., at 198, 52 S.Ct., at 533.

This Court's rigorous application of res judicata in *Reed,* to the point of leaving one party in possession and the other party entitled to the rents, makes clear that this Court recognizes no general equitable doctrine, such as that suggested by the Court of Appeals, which countenances an exception to the finality of a party's failure to appeal merely because his rights are "closely interwoven" with those of another party. Indeed, this case presents even more compelling reasons to apply the doctrine of res judicata than did *Reed.* Respondents here seek to be the windfall beneficiaries of an appellate reversal procured by other independent parties, who have no interest in respondents' case, not a reversal in interrelated cases procured, as in *Reed,* by the same affected party. Moreover, in contrast to *Reed,* where it was unclear why no appeal was taken, it is apparent that respondents here made a calculated choice to forgo their appeals.

The Court of Appeals also rested its opinion in part on what it viewed as "simple justice." But we do not see the grave injustice which would be done by the application of accepted principles of res judicata. "Simple justice" is achieved when a complex body of law developed over a period of years is evenhandedly applied. The doctrine of res judicata serves vital public interests beyond any individual judge's ad hoc determination of the equities in a particular case. There is simply "no principle of law or equity which sanctions the rejection by a federal court of the salutary principle of res judicata." Heiser v. Woodruff, 327 U.S. 726, 733, 66 S.Ct. 853, 856, 90 L.Ed. 970 (1946). The Court of Appeals' reliance on "public policy" is similarly misplaced. This Court has long recognized that "[p]ublic policy dictates that there be an end of litigation; that those who have contested an issue shall be bound by the result of the contest, and that matters once tried shall be considered forever settled as between the parties." Baldwin v. Traveling Men's Assn., 283 U.S. 522, 525, 51 S.Ct. 517, 518, 75 L.Ed. 1244 (1931). We have stressed that "[the] doctrine of res judicata is not a mere matter of practice or procedure inherited from a more technical time than ours. It is a rule of fundamental and substantial justice, 'of public policy and of private peace,' which should be cordially regarded and enforced by the courts. . . . " Hart Steel Co. v. Railroad Supply Co., 244 U.S. 294, 299, 37 S.Ct. 506, 507, 61 L.Ed. 1148 (1917). The language used by this Court half a century ago is even more compelling in view of today's crowded dockets:

> "The predicament in which respondent finds himself is of his own making. . . . [W]e cannot be expected, for his sole relief, to upset the general and well-established doctrine of res judicata, conceived in the light of the maxim that the interest of the state requires that there be an end to litigation—a maxim which comports with common sense as well as public policy. And the mischief which would follow the establishment of precedent for so disregarding this salutary doctrine against prolonging strife would be greater than the benefit which would result from relieving some case of individual hardship." Reed v. Allen, 286 U.S., at 198–199, 52 S.Ct., at 533.

Respondents * * * argue that "the district court's dismissal on grounds of res judicata should be reversed, and the district court directed to grant respondent's motion to remand to the California state court." In their view, *Brown I* cannot be considered res judicata as to their state-law claims, since *Brown I* raised only federal-law claims and *Brown II* raised additional state-law claims not decided in *Brown I,* such as unfair competition, fraud, and restitution.

It is unnecessary for this Court to reach that issue. It is enough for our decision here that *Brown I* is res judicata as to respondents' federal-law claims. Accordingly, the judgment of the Court of Appeals is reversed, and the cause is remanded for proceedings consistent with this opinion.

JUSTICE BLACKMUN, with whom JUSTICE MARSHALL joins, concurring in the judgment.

* * * I, for one, would not close the door upon the possibility that there are cases in which the doctrine of res judicata must give way to what the Court of Appeals referred to as "overriding concerns of public policy and simple justice." 611 F.2d 1267, 1269 (C.A.9 1980). Professor Moore has noted: "Just as res judicata is occasionally qualified by an overriding, competing principle of public policy, so occasionally it needs an equitable tempering." 1B J. Moore & T. Currier, Moore's Federal Practice ¶ 0.405(12), p. 791 (1980). See also Reed v. Allen, 286 U.S. 191, 209, 52 S.Ct. 532, 537, 76 L.Ed. 1054 (1932) (Cardozo, J., joined by Brandeis and Stone, J., dissenting) ("A system of procedure is perverted from its proper function when it multiplies impediments to justice

without the warrant of clear necessity"). But this case is clearly not one in which equity requires that the doctrine give way. Unlike the nonappealing party in *Reed,* respondents were not "caught in a mesh of procedural complexities." Instead, they made a deliberate tactical decision not to appeal. Nor would public policy be served by making an exception to the doctrine in this case; to the contrary, there is a special need for strict application of res judicata in complex multiple party actions of this sort so as to discourage "break-away" litigation.

Finally, this is not a case "where the rights of appealing and nonappealing parties are so interwoven or dependent on each other as to require a reversal of the whole judgment when a part thereof is reversed." See Ford Motor Credit Co. v. Uresti, 581 S.W.2d 298, 300 (Tex.Civ.App.1979).

Second, and in contrast, I would flatly hold that *Brown I* is res judicata as to respondents' state-law claims. Like the District Court, the Court of Appeals found that those state-law claims were simply disguised federal claims; since respondents have not cross-petitioned from that judgment, their argument that this case should be remanded to state court should be itself barred by res judicata. More important, even if the state and federal claims are distinct, respondents' failure to allege the state claims in *Brown I* manifestly bars their allegation in *Brown II.* The dismissal of *Brown I* is res judicata not only as to all claims respondents actually raised, but also as to all claims that could have been raised. Since there is no reason to believe that it was clear at the outset of this litigation that the District Court would have declined to exercise pendent jurisdiction over state claims, respondents were obligated to plead those claims if they wished to preserve them. Because they did not do so, I would hold the claims barred.

JUSTICE BRENNAN, dissenting.

[Justice Brennan disputed the Court's conclusion that *Brown II* was properly removed, emphasizing the right of a plaintiff who may sue under either federal or state law to choose to limit its claim to state law. Since federal law did not preempt state law, much less provide the exclusive remedy (see supra pp. 889–90 nn. 8 & 9), he felt that the case should have been remanded.]

Notes and Questions

1. Before turning to the reasoning of the Court on res judicata, consider the jurisdictional rulings in the case:

(a) Was *Moitie I* properly removed? Recall that under Snyder v. Harris, supra p. 892, in class actions the amount in controversy requirement cannot be satisfied by aggregation of the claims of the class members. If the initial case was not properly removable, what should Moitie have done when her motion to remand was denied and judgment was entered against her?

(b) Having concluded that there was no valid federal antitrust claim in *Moitie I*, what should the district court have done with the state law claim? Recall 28 U.S.C. § 1367(c)(3) and Carnegie–Mellon University v. Cohill, supra p. 918. If the court should not have done what it did in *Moitie I,* what should Moitie have done about that?

(c) Is there any doubt that dismissal in *Brown I* operated as res judicata with regard to any state-law claims that Brown had, whether or not they were overtly asserted in that complaint? If there is no doubt, couldn't the federal court have enjoined prosecution of the state-law action after remand? See 28 U.S.C.A. § 2283 (permitting federal court to enjoin proceedings in state-court action to "effectuate its judgments").

2.   Do at least some "fairness" exceptions survive *Moitie?* Consider Adams v. Pearson, 104 N.E.2d 267 (Ill.1952), where a prior judgment, obtained by fraud, was not given res judicata effect. Compare Rule 60(b)(3).

3.   Should the strictness of *Moitie* apply even in a suit involving important constitutional rights? Consider Dillard v. Crenshaw County, 640 F.Supp. 1347 (M.D.Ala.1986) [also discussed supra p. 1103 n. 5], in which a class of African–American residents (who had lost their first challenge to county at-large voting procedures, based on a constitutional claim, because of a finding of no discriminatory intent) brought a second suit based on a claim of discriminatory intent in violation of the Voting Rights Act. The lower court acknowledged that "the rights at stake here are fundamental and are being denied to a large group of individuals." It also expressed concern that the finding in the first suit that there was no discriminatory intent was at odds with findings in other suits that there was discriminatory intent by the state concerning county at-large election procedures. Nevertheless, it ruled:

> Despite these concerns founded on both justice and public policy, the court concludes that it has little choice but to dismiss the intent claim against Pickens County on the grounds of res judicata. In Federated Department Stores, Inc. v. Moitie, 452 U.S. 394, 101 S.Ct. 2424, 69 L.Ed.2d 103 (1981), the Supreme Court held that res judicata bars relitigation of an unappealed adverse judgment even though other plaintiffs in similar actions against common defendants had actually prevailed on appeal. In reaching this conclusion, the Court explicitly rejected the argument that a court may refuse to apply the res judicata doctrine merely because it believes that injustice might result. According to the Court [in *Moitie*],
>
> > "Simple justice" is achieved when a complex body of law developed over a period of years is evenhandedly applied. The doctrine of res judicata serves vital public interests beyond any individual judge's ad hoc determination of the equities in a particular case. There is simply "no principle of law or equity which sanctions the rejection by a federal court of the salutary principle of res judicata."
>
> The mere fact that a suit involves a large number of plaintiffs claiming a deprivation of their rights also makes little difference. In Nevada v. United States, 463 U.S. 110, 103 S.Ct. 2906, 77 L.Ed.2d 509 (1983), the Supreme Court held that an entire Indian tribe was barred from litigating a water rights claim on the ground of res judicata. Furthermore, a judgment in a class action will generally bind all members of the class, even in civil rights cases; the size of the class apparently makes little difference. The fact that a plaintiff asserts a

fundamental constitutional right also does not affect the application of res judicata. See, e.g., Harmon v. Berry, 776 F.2d 259 (11th Cir.1985) (per curiam) (prisoner's claim of denial of access to court dismissed on grounds of res judicata); Jones v. Texas Tech University, 656 F.2d 1137 (5th Cir.1981) (due process claim dismissed on grounds of res judicata); Kemp v. Birmingham News Co., 608 F.2d 1049 (5th Cir.1979) (Title VII claim of race discrimination in employment practices dismissed on grounds of res judicata).

      The court is also barred from creating an exception to res judicata on the grounds of public policy. First, Federated Department Stores [Inc. v. Moitie] makes clear that res judicata is to be given weight as a public policy in its own right. * * * Furthermore, courts have frequently applied res judicata where policies equally important as those embodied in [the Voting Rights Act] were at stake.

    4. In Spilker v. Hankin, 188 F.2d 35 (D.C.Cir.1951), defendant paid plaintiff, her attorney, for services with seven notes which became due at three month intervals. She did not pay the second note, and the attorney filed suit on it. She pleaded duress based on a claim that the attorney had charged an exorbitant fee. She also claimed that the attorney had been overpaid and brought a counterclaim to void the remaining notes. After trial without a jury, the attorney was awarded judgment on the note and the counterclaim. Defendant did not appeal that judgment, and the attorney later brought suit to enforce the five remaining notes when they had become due. Defendant resisted that suit on grounds of misrepresentation. The lower court granted the attorney's motion for summary judgment on the ground the defense was precluded by res judicata. The D.C. Circuit reversed, stating:

> Fee contracts between attorney and client are a subject of special interest and concern to the courts. They are not to be enforced upon the same basis as ordinary commercial contracts. * * * Ordinarily the matter of a fee will be litigated but once, and the first determination will be conclusive. Were this merely a suit upon the original judgment we would, of course, consider res judicata to be applicable. But here we have a series of notes, one brought into litigation prior to the others. The original suit was for a much smaller amount, and some of the issues here in question were only indirectly involved in it. And it is the attorney who seeks further court aid with regard to his fee. The fee arrangement in question was reduced to promissory notes shortly before the termination of the litigation in which the attorney acted for the client, and appears to have been required by the attorney as a condition of his remaining in the case. While we do not mean to imply that an attorney can never protect himself with regard to his fee by making an arrangement of this sort, we consider that when under such circumstances the attorney twice brings the matter into court, the requirements of justice are better served by permitting reexamination of the merits than by treating the prior suit as foreclosing the matter.

Would *Spilker* have been decided the same way after *Moitie?* Is it a "fairness" exception or an exercise of courts' inherent regulatory authority over the attorney-client relationship? Did the court's concerns about overreaching by the attorney justify an alteration in the res judicata doctrine? Or is *Spilker* not really an exception to res judicata? What did the court mean that "the original suit was for a much smaller amount, and some of the issues here in question were only indirectly involved in it"? Would that justify not applying res judicata?

5. Should a change in the law ever give a litigant a second chance? Consider the following case: A California court entered a final divorce decree that made a division of property but did not mention the husband's matured military retirement pension. At that time, there was uncertainty as to whether federal military pensions could, consistent with federal law, be divided as community property under California law. Three years later the California Supreme Court held that they were properly subject to California community property law. The wife then filed suit to establish her community property interest in the pension.

Is she barred by res judicata? Note that a change in law in a later case would not help her; under *Moitie,* "the res judicata consequences of a final, unappealed judgment on the merits [are not] altered by the fact that the judgment may have been wrong or rested on a legal principle subsequently overruled in another case." But was the divorce decree a ruling that she had no right to the pension? The California Supreme Court said it was not, because, under California community property law, property which is not mentioned in the pleadings as community property is left unadjudicated by the divorce decree. Thus, under its interpretation of California law, the decree did not adjudicate the ownership of the pension, and she was allowed to litigate that issue in a later suit. See Henn v. Henn, 605 P.2d 10 (Cal.1980). But doesn't the rule of res judicata apply to whatever was part of the transaction raised in the suit and not merely to what was actually adjudicated? Is the court saying that the divorce court not only did not, but could not, have adjudicated the interest in the property? This case has been referred to as "manipulat[ing] the scope of the 'cause of action' to permit a renewed claim." James, Hazard & Leubsdorf, Civil Procedure 698 (5th ed. 2001). Do you agree? Is it justified as a fairness exception?

6. Reed v. Allen, discussed by the Court in *Moitie,* illustrates the problem that can result from treating a judgment subject to appeal as final for purposes of res judicata. In that case the first judgment was made the basis for the judgment against the loser in the second case even though the decision in the first case was on appeal, and the Supreme Court ultimately held that the unappealed second judgment was entitled to binding effect even though the first decision, on which it was based, was reversed. What could be done to avoid this situation? See Fed.R.Civ.P. 60(b)(5); Restatement (Second) of Judgments § 16.

Reed v. Allen suggests another problem that can arise in connection with res judicata where there are multiple lawsuits between the parties. Suppose res judicata is available as a defense to a second lawsuit but is not raised, or, if raised, is improperly rejected by the court in the second case. If the second case is decided the other way, so that there are two contradictory judgments, which is entitled to be given res judicata effect thereafter? On the one hand, the earlier decision might be preferred because that would take away the incentive to relitigate. On the other hand, res judicata is merely an affirmative defense, and it would be odd to allow a party who has failed to assert it to resurrect it later. The courts' answer has been to find the second judgment is controlling because it is last in time. See Treinies v. Sunshine Mining Co., 308 U.S. 66, 60 S.Ct. 44, 84 L.Ed. 85 (1939). What are the advantages and disadvantages of such a rule? See Ginsburg, Judgments in Search of Full Faith and Credit: The Last-in-Time Rule for Conflicting Judgments, 82 Harv.L.Rev. 798 (1969).

7. A "jurisdictional competence" exception to the rule against splitting a cause of action applies if the plaintiff was unable to assert a particular claim or theory in the original case "because of the limitations on the subject matter jurisdiction of the courts." Restatement (Second) of Judgments § 26(*l*)(c) (1982); see also Marrese v. American Academy of Orthopaedic Surgeons, infra p. 1125. This usually arises when the first suit is filed in a state court of limited jurisdiction in which it is not possible to bring the claim sued on in the second action.

The exception will not arise simply because the plaintiff failed to assert all bases for jurisdiction in the first suit. In Kale v. Combined Insurance Co. of America, 924 F.2d 1161 (1st Cir.1991), plaintiff filed suit in federal court under federal question jurisdiction alleging that his firing violated the Age Discrimination in Employment Act (ADEA), joining a pendent state-law claim for breach of an implied covenant of good faith and fair dealing. The judge granted summary judgment for the defendant on the ground that the statute of limitations had run on the ADEA claim and then dismissed the pendent state-law claims without prejudice.

Plaintiff then filed suit on the state-law claim in state court, no doubt confident that the dismissal of his first suit without prejudice entitled him to do so. Not so, said the First Circuit. Once there has been an adjudication on the merits, all claims that are part of the same cause of action are extinguished. It rejected plaintiff's reliance on the "jurisdictional competence" exception, finding that because the parties were from different states, he could have asserted diversity jurisdiction in the first suit. Judge Breyer wrote: "The existence of an alternate hook on which federal court jurisdiction could have been hung, permitting state-law claims to be freely litigated in a federal forum, rendered the competency exception inapplicable. After all, for it to pertain, the jurisdictional obstacle to joinder of all claims must be attributable to limitations on the first court's power to hear and decide a claim rather than to a party's contrivance." Id. at 1167. The opinion also found the first court's dismissal of the state-law claim without prejudice was not an express reservation of plaintiff's right to maintain it in the second action and that there was no basis for a *Moitie*-type exception to prevent unusual hardship.

8. The Supreme Court justified the removal of *Moitie II* and *Brown II* to federal court, despite the fact that the claims were based solely on state antitrust laws, on the fact that the claims were essentially the same as those that had been removed to federal court and dismissed in *Moitie I* and were "artfully couched in terms of state law." In Carpenter v. Wichita Falls Independent School Dist., 44 F.3d 362 (5th Cir.1995), a school administrator who was reassigned after objecting to a restructuring plan simultaneously filed suit in state court for breach of contract and violation of the state

constitutional right to free speech and in federal court under the First Amendment. The school district removed the state case to federal court based on federal question jurisdiction. Relying on the footnote in *Moitie* in which the Supreme Court addressed the "artful pleading doctrine," it argued that "by electing to pursue a parallel federal suit," the plaintiff had "endowed the state suit with a 'sufficient federal character' to support removal." Pointing to the well-pleaded complaint rule under which the plaintiff is the "master of his complaint" (recall Louisville & Nashville R.R. v. Mottley, supra p. 871), the federal court said that the *Moitie* decision could not have intended, "in a case for which the removal issue was neither presented nor briefed, to bring about a significant revision of removal jurisprudence." "If there was any federal character at all to the plaintiff's state-law claims in *Moitie*," the court said, "it must be the federal law of preclusion." It distinguished *Moitie* as a case in which the plaintiffs filed their state claim *after* the federal statutory claim had gone to federal-court judgment against them and had not appealed the federal-court judgment, thus seeking "to outflank the effect of the federal district court's judgment." It refused to permit removal in this case where both actions were filed simultaneously, there was no prior federal-court judgment, and therefore "no judgment to protect and no federal preclusion law to apply."

3. On the Merits

The traditional requirement of res judicata that the first judgment have been "on the merits" has gradually undergone change until today those words cannot be taken literally. The term once meant what it said. Judgments on the merits (for example after a trial or a motion for summary judgment) were accorded res judicata effect, but judgments on non-merits grounds (such as dismissal for lack of jurisdiction or failure to join an indispensable party) were not.

Dismissal on a common law demurrer (or a Rule 12(b)(6) motion for failure to state a claim upon which relief can be granted) was viewed as a non-merits determination because it only tested the sufficiency of the complaint. Many courts, as well as the first Restatement of Judgments § 50 (1942), held that if "new and additional facts are alleged that cure the defects in the original pleading, it is settled that the former judgment is not a bar to the subsequent action whether or not plaintiff had an opportunity to amend his complaint." Keidatz v. Albany, 249 P.2d 264 (Cal.1952). Some courts deviated to the extent of according res judicata effect if the plaintiff was granted leave to amend but failed to do so. Elfman v. Glaser, 47 N.E.2d 925 (Mass.1943). The conflicting policies concerning the res judicata effect of a dismissal for failure to state a claim were described by Justice Traynor in *Keidatz:* "[T]here are forceful arguments, in view of the liberal rules relating to amendments to the pleadings, for requiring the plaintiff to set forth in one action all the facts relating to his dispute. * * * On the other hand less prejudice is suffered by a defendant who has had only to attack the pleadings, than by one who has been forced to go to trial until a nonsuit is granted, and the hardship suffered by being forced to defend against a new action, instead of against an amended complaint, is not materially greater." 249 P.2d at 266. However, today the policies favoring requiring plaintiffs to plead all their claims, and thus not to take up judicial time with repetitive suits, have won out, and many courts and the Restatement (Second) of Judgments § 19, comment d (1982), apply res judicata to a dismissal for failure to state a claim.

RINEHART v. LOCKE

United States Court of Appeals, Seventh Circuit, 1971.
454 F.2d 313.

Before SWYGERT, CHIEF JUDGE, and FAIRCHILD and STEVENS, CIRCUIT JUDGES.

FAIRCHILD, CIRCUIT JUDGE.

On June 17, 1970, plaintiff filed a complaint seeking damages and claiming that an arrest on November 24, 1964 deprived him of rights secured by the Constitution. As one defense, defendants asserted that the matter was res judicata by virtue of dismissal on May 15, 1969 of a complaint based on the same arrest. The district court sustained the defense of res judicata and dismissed the action. Plaintiff appealed. Defendants also raised, in the district court and here, the defense that the period of limitations had expired. The two complaints are identical in substance except that an averment that the arrest was made without probable cause was included in the second, but not the first. The 1969 complaint may be summarized as follows: on November 24, 1964, three defendants, private detectives, observed plaintiff at an intersection talking to a man on a motorcycle and caused a false report to be made to the county police that plaintiff was falsely representing himself to be a police officer. As a result of the report, four other defendants, county police officers, arrested plaintiff for impersonating a government official. They also charged him falsely with unlawful use of weapons and resisting arrest. No warrant had been issued for the arrest. Plaintiff was imprisoned at the police station and later convicted of the charges, but in 1967 the conviction was reversed on appeal for insufficient evidence.

The district court entered an order dismissing the 1969 complaint for failure to state a claim. In an oral ruling on the motion to dismiss, the court based dismissal on the failure to allege the absence of probable cause, although the court made other comments which may shed light on its subsequent refusal to permit amendment.

Plaintiff sought leave to file an amended complaint in which he included an averment that defendants had no probable cause to suspect plaintiff of committing an offense. On June 13, 1969, leave was denied. The court stated no reason. Under Rule 15(a), F.R.Civ.P., "leave shall be freely given when justice so requires." Presumably the court felt justice did not so require in view of the court's earlier suggestion that the complaint itself showed that the arrest was based upon information given by three private detectives who said they had seen the offense and that the court thought plaintiff's failure to allege lack of probable cause was not inadvertent.

Plaintiff did not appeal from either 1969 order.

RES JUDICATA.

Plaintiff contends that the May, 1969 dismissal did not establish that defendants were not liable to him under § 1983 on account of the 1964 arrest, but established only that he had no cause of action unless he was able to plead and prove lack of probable cause.

The traditional general rule supports plaintiff's position: " . . . it is equally well settled, that, if the plaintiff fails on demurrer in his first action from the omission of an essential allegation in his declaration which is fully supplied in the second suit, the judgment in the first suit is no bar to the second, although the respective actions were instituted to enforce the same right; for the reason that the merits of the case, as disclosed in the second declaration, were not heard and decided in the first action." Gould v. Evansville and C.R.R. Co., 91 U.S. 526, 23 L.Ed. 416 (1875).

Comment c, § 50, Restatement, Judgments, supports the same proposition, illustrating as follows: "Thus, if in an action for breach of contract a demurrer to the complaint is sustained on the ground that the plaintiff failed to allege consideration, he is not precluded from bringing a new action in which the complaint contains an allegation of consideration. . . ."

Arguably Rule 41(b), F.R.C.P., may have changed this rule where the earlier judgment, as in this case, was entered in a federal court. The rule provides in part: "Unless the court in its order for dismissal otherwise specifies, a dismissal under this subdivision and any dismissal not provided for in this rule, other than a dismissal for lack of jurisdiction, for improper venue, or for failure to join a party under rule 19, operates as an adjudication upon the merits."

It has been held that the list in Rule 41(b) of types of dismissal which are not presumptively adjudications on the merits is not exclusive, and that the situations where dismissals not provided for in Rule 41 are to operate as [an] adjudication on the merits are those "in which the defendant must incur the inconvenience of preparing to meet the merits because there is no initial bar to the court's reaching them." [Costello v. United States, 365 U.S. 265, 286, 81 S.Ct. 534, 545, 5 L.Ed.2d 551 (1961).] The same decision indicates that a dismissal for failure to fulfill a "precondition" for consideration of the merits is not a decision on the merits.

With this gloss upon the rule, the question remains a close one, but we are persuaded that under the rule an order of a district court which dismisses a complaint for failure to state a claim, but which does not specify that the dismissal is without prejudice, is res judicata as to the then existing claim which it appears plaintiff was attempting to state.

This view places upon a plaintiff in a case like the 1969 case in this instance the burden of persuading the district court either to include a specification that the dismissal is without prejudice or to permit an amendment. If plaintiff is unsuccessful, his recourse is to appeal. We think this view is consistent with the expedient purpose of the rules.

Notes and Questions

1. The reliance in *Rinehart* on Rule 41(b), as opposed to preclusion doctrine, needs to be reexamined in light of the Supreme Court's 2001 decision in Semtek International, Inc. v. Lockheed Martin Corp., infra p. 1133. Note that in *Rinehart* the plaintiff's complaint was dismissed for failure to state a claim, and he filed a suit identical in substance in the *same federal district court*. The court's refusal to allow him to amend the first complaint to allege lack of probable cause for his arrest seems to have been based on the court's conclusion that there was probable cause and the failure to allege its absence was not inadvertent. Consider whether these facts warrant a different result as to the applicability of Rule 41(b) in *Semtek*. See Woolley, The Sources of Federal Preclusion Law After *Semtek*, 72 U.Cin. L.Rev. 527, 597 (2003): "Rule 41(b) * * * provides that a judgment entered on a Rule 12(b)(6) dismissal for failure to state a claim shall be treated as a judgment on the merits. The provision rejects the view of some jurisdictions that a judgment entered on a 12(b)(6) dismissal (or demurrer) need not be given claim-preclusive effect, insisting instead that a judgment entered on a 12(b)(6) dismissal is entitled to the same preclusive effect as a judgment entered after trial."

2. Should res judicata be used to prevent the plaintiff in *Rinehart* from redressing violations of his civil rights just because his lawyer failed to allege lack of probable cause in the initial complaint? Is the justification that judicial resources were wasted because the court in the earlier case had to rule on a Rule 12(b)(6) motion? Couldn't that be remedied by awarding the defendant his costs and attorneys' fees for having to respond to the first inadequate complaint?

3. The court in *Rinehart* relies on the Supreme Court's decision in Costello v. United States, 365 U.S. 265, 81 S.Ct. 534, 5 L.Ed.2d 551 (1961). *Costello* was an action by the United States to revoke an order granting the defendant, a naturalized citizen with reputed connections to the criminal underworld, American citizenship. An earlier proceeding brought by the government to accomplish the same goal had been dismissed for the government's failure to include an affidavit of good cause, although the order of dismissal had not expressly indicated whether or not the dismissal was with prejudice. The defendant contended that "the order dismissing the earlier complaint must be construed to be with prejudice because it did not specify that it was without prejudice, and the ground of dismissal was not within one of the exceptions under Rule 41(b) of the Federal Rules of Civil Procedure." 365 U.S. at 284, 81 S.Ct. at 544. However, the Court, in an opinion by Justice Brennan, held "that a dismissal for failure to file the affidavit of good cause is a dismissal 'for lack of jurisdiction' within the meaning of the exception under Rule 41(b)." Id. at 285, 81 S.Ct. at 544. The Court reasoned that the exception encompasses "those dismissals which are based on a plaintiff's failure to comply with a precondition requisite to the

Court's going forward to determine the merits of his claim. Failure to file the affidavit of good cause in a denaturalization proceeding falls within this category." Id. It added that

> [a]ll of the dismissals enumerated in Rule 41(b) which operate as adjudications on the merits * * * primarily involve situations in which the defendant must incur the inconvenience of preparing to meet the merits because there is no initial bar to the Court's reaching them. It is therefore logical that a dismissal on one of these grounds should, unless the Court otherwise specifies, bar a subsequent action. * * *

> In contrast, the failure of the Government to file the affidavit of good cause in a denaturalization proceeding does not present a situation calling for the application of the policy making dismissals operative as adjudications on the merits. The defendant is not put to the necessity of preparing a defense because the failure of the Government to file the affidavit with the complaint requires the dismissal of the proceeding.

Did the Court properly define the term, "jurisdiction" in Rule 41(b)? Did the court in *Rinehart* properly distinguish *Costello?*

4. What is the justification for applying res judicata even though the plaintiff sought leave to amend and was refused it? Is there any valid reason for denying leave to amend under circumstances such as these? What should plaintiff have done if leave to amend was erroneously denied?

5. The Restatement (Second) of Judgments § 20(1) provides three exceptions to a valid and final judgment having claim preclusive effect:

> (a) When the judgment is one of dismissal for lack of jurisdiction, for improper venue, or for nonjoinder or misjoinder of parties, or

> (b) When the plaintiff agrees to or elects a nonsuit (or voluntary dismissal) without prejudice or the court directs that the plaintiff be nonsuited (or that the action be otherwise dismissed) without prejudice, or

> (c) When by statute or rule of court the judgment does not operate as a bar to another action on the same claim, or does not so operate unless the court specifies, and no such specification is made.

6. Should preclusive effect be given to a judgment based on a ground that is not applicable to the claim raised in the second suit? In Williamson v. Columbia Gas & Electric Corp., 186 F.2d 464 (3d Cir.1950), one of two repetitive suits pending at the same time in the same court was dismissed on the ground of statute of limitations. Although the other suit was not barred by statute of limitations because it had a conspiracy count which prevented the statute of limitations from being tolled, the court found the second claim barred by res judicata.

In contrast, the Restatement (Second) of Judgments § 20(2) provides:

> A valid and final personal judgment for the defendant, which rests on the prematurity of the action or on the plaintiff's failure to satisfy a precondition to suit, does not bar another action by the plaintiff instituted after the claim has matured, or the precondition has been satisfied, unless a second action is precluded by the operation of the substantive law.

7. A default judgment is considered to be on the merits. Otherwise there would be no finality when a defendant failed to appear. A denial of a motion for leave to amend the complaint has also been held to be a final judgment on the merits. EFCO v. U.W. Marx, Inc., 124 F.3d 394, 399–400 (2d Cir.1997) ("Where a plaintiff's motion to amend its complaint in the first action is denied, and plaintiff fails to appeal the denial, res judicata applies to the claims sought to be added in the proposed amended complaint.").

8. In Watkins v. Resorts International Hotel and Casino, 591 A.2d 592 (N.J.1991), minority bus-line owners brought a civil rights suit in federal court alleging discrimination by casinos in Atlantic City. The federal court dismissed for insufficient service of process (failure to comply with Rule 4(m)'s requirement of service within 120 days) and lack of standing. The bus-line owners then sued in state court, and it concluded that the binding effect of the earlier judgment of dismissal should be determined by federal law. It found that the dismissal for insufficient service was without prejudice under the express terms of Rule 4(m). Standing is not listed in Rule 41(b) as a non-merits basis for dismissal, but non-merits dismissals under Rule 41(b) have been construed as including threshold determinations concerning the court's ability to proceed to the substantive merits. The court concluded that preclusion should not apply because standing is such a threshold issue that does not depend on or determine the merits of plaintiff's claim.

4. *Preclusion in State–Federal Court Adjudications*

MARRESE v. AMERICAN ACADEMY OF ORTHOPAEDIC SURGEONS

Supreme Court of the United States, 1985.
470 U.S. 373, 105 S.Ct. 1327, 84 L.Ed.2d 274.

JUSTICE O'CONNOR delivered the opinion of the Court.

[Two Illinois orthopedic surgeons who were denied membership in the Academy sued it in an Illinois state court, claiming that the denial of their applications without a hearing violated their common law associational rights under Illinois law. They did not assert claims under state antitrust law. The state court dismissed on the ground that they had failed to state a cause of action. They then sued in federal court, claiming that the denial of their membership applications constituted a boycott in violation of federal antitrust law. The Court of Appeals held that federal principles of claim preclusion barred the federal suit, noting that Illinois antitrust law was similar to federal antitrust law.]

The issue presented by this case is whether a state court judgment may have preclusive effect on a federal antitrust claim that could not have been raised in the state proceeding. Although federal antitrust claims are within the exclusive jurisdiction of the federal courts, the Court of Appeals ruled that the dismissal of petitioners' complaints in state court barred them from bringing a claim based on the same facts under the Sherman Act. The Court of Appeals erred by suggesting that in these circumstances a federal court should determine the preclusive effect of a state court judgment without regard to the law of the State in which judgment was rendered.

The preclusive effect of a state court judgment in a subsequent federal lawsuit generally is determined by the full faith and credit statute, which provides that state judicial proceedings "shall have the same full faith and credit in every court within the United States ... as they have by law or usage in the courts of such State ... from which they are taken." 28 U.S.C. § 1738.

This statute directs a federal court to refer to the preclusion law of the State in which judgment was rendered. "It has long been established that § 1738 does not allow federal courts to employ their own rules of res judicata in determining the effect of state judgments. Rather, it goes beyond the common law and commands a federal court to accept the rules chosen by the State from which the judgment is taken." Kremer v. Chemical Construction Corp., 456 U.S. 461, 481–482, 102 S.Ct. 1883, 1897, 72 L.Ed.2d 262 (1982). Section 1738 embodies concerns of comity and federalism that allow the States to determine, subject to the requirements of the statute and the Due Process Clause, the preclusive effect of judgments in their own courts.

The fact that petitioners' antitrust claim is within the exclusive jurisdiction of the federal courts does not necessarily make § 1738 inapplicable to this case. Our decisions indicate that a state court judgment may in some circumstances have preclusive effect in a subsequent action within the exclusive jurisdiction of the federal courts. Without discussing § 1738, this Court has held that the issue preclusive effect of a state court judgment barred a subsequent patent suit that could not have been brought in state court. Becher v. Contoure Laboratories, Inc., 279 U.S. 388, 49 S.Ct. 356, 73 L.Ed. 752 (1929). Moreover, *Kremer* held that § 1738 applies to a claim of employment discrimination under Title VII of the Civil Rights Act of 1964, 42 U.S.C. §§ 2000e et seq., although the Court expressly declined to decide whether Title VII claims can be brought only in federal courts. 456 U.S., at 479, n.20, 102 S.Ct., at 1896, n.20. *Kremer* implies that absent an exception to § 1738, state law determines at least the issue preclusive effect of a prior state judgment in a subsequent action involving a claim within the exclusive jurisdiction of the federal courts.

More generally, *Kremer* indicates that § 1738 requires a federal court to look first to state preclusion law in determining the preclusive effects of a state court judgment. The Court's analysis in *Kremer* began with the finding that state law would in fact bar relitigation of the discrimination issue decided in the earlier state proceedings. That finding implied that the plaintiff could not relitigate the same issue in federal court unless some exception to § 1738 applied. *Kremer* observed that "an exception to § 1738 will not be recognized unless a later statute contains an express or implied repeal." Title VII does not expressly repeal § 1738, and the Court concluded that the statutory provisions and legislative history do not support a finding of implied repeal. We conclude that the basic approach adopted in *Kremer* applies in a lawsuit involving a claim within the exclusive jurisdiction of the federal courts.

To be sure, a state court will not have occasion to address the specific question whether a state judgment has issue or claim preclusive effect in a later action that can be brought only in federal court. Nevertheless, a federal court may rely in the first instance on state preclusion principles to determine the extent to which an earlier state judgment bars subsequent litigation. *Kremer* illustrates that a federal court can apply state rules of issue preclusion to determine if a matter actually litigated in state court may be relitigated in a subsequent federal proceeding.

With respect to matters that were not decided in the state proceedings, we note that claim preclusion generally does not apply where "[t]he plaintiff was unable to rely on a certain theory of the case or to seek a certain remedy because of the limitations on the subject matter jurisdiction of the courts...." Restatement (Second) of Judgments § 26(1)(c) (1982). If state preclusion law includes this requirement of prior jurisdictional competency, which is generally true, a state judgment will not have claim preclusive effect on a cause of action within the exclusive jurisdiction of the federal courts.

Even in the event that a party asserting the affirmative defense of claim preclusion can show that state preclusion rules in some circumstances bar a claim outside the jurisdiction of the court that rendered the initial judgment, the federal court should first consider whether application of the state rules would bar the particular federal claim.[2]

Reference to state preclusion law may make it unnecessary to determine if the federal court, as an exception to § 1738, should refuse to give preclusive effect to a state court judgment. The issue whether there is an exception to § 1738 arises only if state law indicates that litigation of a particular claim or issue should be barred in the subsequent federal proceeding. To the extent that state preclusion law indicates that a judgment normally does not have claim preclusive effect as to matters that the court lacked jurisdiction to entertain, lower courts and commentators have correctly concluded that a state court judgment does not bar a subsequent federal antitrust claim. Unless application of Illinois preclusion law suggests, contrary to the usual view, that petition-

---

2. Our analysis does not necessarily suggest that the Court of Appeals for the Fourth Circuit erred in its holding in Nash County Board of Education v. Biltmore Co., 640 F.2d 484, cert. denied, 454 U.S. 878, 102 S.Ct. 359, 70 L.Ed.2d 188 (1981). The Court of Appeals there applied federal preclusion principles to conclude that a state judgment approving settlement of state antitrust claims barred a subsequent federal antitrust claim. Although our decision today indicates that the Court of Appeals should have looked in the first instance to state law to determine the preclusive effect of the state judgment, the same holding would result if application of state preclusion law suggests that the settlement bars the subsequent federal claim and if there is no exception to § 1738 in these circumstances. Cf. 640 F.2d, at 487, n.2 (noting that State law gives preclusive effect to consent judgment). We, of course, do not address those issues here.

ers' federal antitrust claim is somehow barred, there will be no need to decide in this case if there is an exception to § 1738. * * *

The Court of Appeals did not apply the approach to § 1738 that we have outlined.

* * *

If we had a single system of courts and our only concerns were efficiency and finality, it might be desirable to fashion claim preclusion rules that would require a plaintiff to bring suit initially in the forum of most general jurisdiction, thereby resolving as many issues as possible in one proceeding. See Restatement (Second) of Judgments § 24, Comment g (1982); C. Wright, A. Miller, & E. Cooper, [Federal Practice & Procedure] § 4407, p. 51; id. § 4412, p. 93. The decision of the Court of Appeals approximates such a rule inasmuch as it encourages plaintiffs to file suit initially in federal district court and to attempt to bring any state law claims pendent to their federal antitrust claims. Whether this result would reduce the overall burden of litigation is debatable, and we decline to base our interpretation of § 1738 on our opinion on this question.

More importantly, we have parallel systems of state and federal courts, and the concerns of comity reflected in § 1738 generally allow States to determine the preclusive scope of their own courts' judgments. These concerns certainly are not made less compelling because state courts lack jurisdiction over federal antitrust claims. We therefore reject a judicially created exception to § 1738 that effectively holds as a matter of federal law that a plaintiff can bring state law claims initially in state court only at the cost of forgoing subsequent federal antitrust claims. * * *

In this case the Court of Appeals should have first referred to Illinois law to determine the preclusive effect of the state judgment. Only if state law indicates that a particular claim or issue would be barred is it necessary to determine if an exception to § 1738 should apply. Although for purposes of this case, we need not decide if such an exception exists for federal antitrust claims, we observe that the more general question is whether the concerns underlying a particular grant of exclusive jurisdiction justify a finding of an implied partial repeal of § 1738. Resolution of this question will depend on the particular federal statute as well as the nature of the claim or issue involved in the subsequent federal action. Our previous decisions indicate that the primary consideration must be the intent of Congress.

CHIEF JUSTICE BURGER, concurring in the judgment.

[The Chief Justice agreed that § 1738 required that federal courts look first to state law, and that preclusion is forbidden if state law clearly would not bar a later federal action, but he criticized the Court's failure to address the possibility that Illinois law would not speak to this question.]

I cannot agree with the Court's interpretation of the jurisdictional competency requirement. If state law provides a cause of action that is virtually identical with a federal statutory cause of action, a plaintiff suing in state court is able to rely on the same theory of the case and obtain the same remedy as would be available in federal court, even when the plaintiff cannot expressly invoke the federal statute because it is within the exclusive jurisdiction of the federal courts. In this situation, the jurisdictional competency requirement is effectively satisfied. Therefore, the fact that state law recognizes the jurisdictional competency requirement does not necessarily imply that a state court judgment has no claim preclusive effect on a cause of action within exclusive federal jurisdiction.

* * *

[I]t is likely that the principles of Illinois claim preclusion law do not speak to the preclusive effect that petitioners' state court judgments should have on the present action. In this situation, it may be consistent with § 1738 for a federal court to formulate a federal rule to resolve the matter. If state law is simply indeterminate, the concerns of comity and federalism underlying § 1738 do not come into play. At the same time, the federal courts have direct interests in ensuring that their resources are used efficiently and not as a means of harassing defendants with repetitive lawsuits, as well as in ensuring that parties asserting federal rights have an adequate opportunity to litigate those rights. Given the insubstantiality of the state interests and the weight of the federal interests, a strong argument could be made that a federal rule would be more appropriate than a creative interpretation of ambiguous state law.[4]

A federal rule might be fashioned from the test, which this Court has applied in other contexts, that a party is precluded from asserting a claim that he had a "full and fair opportunity" to litigate in a prior action. Thus, if a state statute is identical in all material respects with a federal statute within exclusive federal jurisdiction, a party's ability to assert a claim under the state statute in a prior state court action might be said to have provided, in effect, a "full and fair opportunity" to litigate his rights under the federal statute. The Court will eventually have to face these questions; I would resolve them now.

Notes and Questions

1. How can it be said that the plaintiffs in *Marrese* split their cause of action by not raising in a state-court suit a federal claim that could not be sued on there because it is subject to exclusive federal jurisdiction? Is it a sufficient answer that the plaintiffs didn't have to file in the state court, but could instead have filed both state and federal claims in federal court? This, of course, would only be possible if the federal court were willing to exercise

---

4. By contrast, when a federal court construes substantive rights and obligations under state law in the context of a diversity action, the federal interest is insignificant and the state's interest is much more direct than it is in the present situation, even if the relevant state law is ambiguous.

its discretionary authority to grant supplemental jurisdiction over the state claims. Furthermore, must plaintiffs give up their right to a state forum for adjudication of their state claims under the threat of being barred from ever raising the exclusive federal jurisdiction claims?

In the Seventh Circuit opinion in *Marrese* that was reversed by the Supreme Court, Judge Posner responded to the contention that res judicata did not bar the federal antitrust claim because it could not have been raised in the state court as follows: "The plaintiffs could, however, have joined with their other state claims a claim under the Illinois Antitrust Act, and if that Act is materially identical to the Sherman Act their failure to do so bars this suit." 726 F.2d at 1153. Regarding § 1738, Judge Posner found plaintiffs' arguments that they would not be barred under Illinois preclusion law irrelevant. In his view, that statute was intended "to protect the authority of state courts, [so it] ought not prevent a federal court from giving a state court judgment *more* effect in a federal suit than the courts of the state would give it in state court." Id. at 1154.

2.   If the usual rule is that a state-court judgment does not preclude litigation of an exclusive federal jurisdiction claim, see Restatement (Second) of Judgments § 26(1)(c), what circumstances warrant deviation from that rule? Would those in *Marrese* satisfy? Do you find persuasive Chief Justice Burger's arguments for preclusion when a plaintiff sues in state court on a state-law claim that is virtually identical to a statutory exclusive federal jurisdiction claim?

In Matsushita Elec. Indus. Co. v. Epstein, 516 U.S. 367, 116 S.Ct. 873, 134 L.Ed.2d 6 (1996), the Supreme Court said that "*Marrese* provides the analytical framework" for resolving these problems. It emphasized that *Marrese* "made clear that where § 1738 is raised as a defense in a subsequent suit, the fact that an allegedly precluded claim is within the exclusive jurisdiction of the federal courts *does not necessarily make § 1738 inapplicable*." The appeal arose from competing class actions making claims about Matsushita's acquisition of MCA, Inc., through a tender offer. One suit, filed in Delaware state court, asserted claims of mismanagement and disloyalty under Delaware law. The other suit, filed in federal court, made claims under the Securities Exchange Act that were within exclusive federal jurisdiction. After defendants obtained summary judgment from the district court in the federal case, the Delaware court approved a settlement of the state-court class action for a very modest sum even though there had been an appeal from the summary judgment in federal court. Defendants then attempted to abort the federal appeal on the basis of the Delaware class action judgment, and the Court found that § 1738 required preclusion. There was a strong dissent contending that the lawyers for the Delaware plaintiffs had not properly represented the class.

3.   *Marrese* suggests that an exception to § 1738 might be found for exclusive federal jurisdiction claims depending on "whether the concerns underlying a particular grant of exclusive jurisdiction justify finding a partial repeal of § 1738," with the primary focus on the intent of Congress. What would one look for concerning congressional intent in an exclusive federal jurisdiction statute? In the antitrust context involved in *Marrese*, is it relevant that exclusive federal jurisdiction is not explicitly provided in the

statutes, but has been inferred by the courts? In *Matsushita*, supra note 2, the Supreme Court rejected the argument that the exclusive federal jurisdiction provisions of the Securities Exchange Act created an exception to § 1738. It said that there should be a "relatively stringent standard" for finding such repeals, and that they would depend on showing an "irreconcilable conflict" between § 1738 and the statute granting exclusive federal jurisdiction. The Court held there was no exception in this case because it found no congressional intent to afford plaintiffs more than one day in court to challenge the legality of a securities transaction, or to prevent litigants who assert related state-law claims in state court from effectively releasing their federal claims as part of a state-court settlement. Will there often be cases in which § 1738 can be overcome?

4. There may be occasions when the law of the state that entered the judgment does not control its enforcement elsewhere. In Baker v. General Motors Corp., 522 U.S. 222, 118 S.Ct. 657, 139 L.Ed.2d 580 (1998), the Court held that a Missouri district court should not forbid testimony by a witness even though a Michigan court consent judgment forbade his testifying in actions against General Motors, his former employer. The injunction resulted from litigation resulting from the witness's departure from his GM job. Although the witness had testified in several other cases thereafter, GM argued that he should not be allowed to do so in the Bakers' suit. The district court disagreed on the ground that Missouri had a policy in favor of presenting evidence at trial. The witness (a former GM engineer) testified that a safer design was available than the one GM had used. Plaintiffs recovered $11.3 million, and the court of appeals reversed on the ground that it was improper to allow the witness to testify.

The Supreme Court unanimously concluded that the court of appeals was wrong, although there were three explanations why. Writing for the Court, Justice Ginsburg first rejected the public policy justification for refusing to enforce the Michigan judgment and recognized that the Michigan decree was entitled to full faith and credit although it was an equity decree. But other states need not adopt the enforcement mechanisms of the entering state, and the Court regarded GM's argument as eroding the Missouri federal court's power to administer its own proceedings. "Michigan lacks authority to control courts elsewhere by precluding them in actions brought by strangers to the Michigan litigation, from determining for themselves what witnesses are competent to testify and what evidence is relevant and admissible in their search for the truth." Justice Scalia concurred in the judgment, finding it sufficient to say that full faith and credit did not compel Missouri to execute the Michigan injunction. Justice Kennedy, also concurring in the judgment, expressed uneasiness about the possible breadth of the majority's reasoning about interference with litigation pending in the forum.

Compare Bay Area Factors v. Calvert, 105 F.3d 315 (6th Cir.1997), in which the court held that a California default judgment precluded discharge of a debt in a federal bankruptcy proceeding because the claim asserted in state court was for fraud, which could not be discharged in bankruptcy. In pre-*Marrese* cases, the court had refused to accord collateral estoppel effect to a default judgment as a matter of federal common law, but it concluded that *Marrese* compelled application of California law, which does give default judgments such effect. It then concluded that there was no ground for an exception to the requirements of the full faith and credit statute.

5. Nash County Board of Education v. Biltmore Co., 640 F.2d 484 (4th Cir.1981), cited by the Court, involved similar questions. The first action there was brought by the state attorney general, under state antitrust law, on behalf of all public school systems in the state, alleging price fixing in the sale of milk to schools. After this suit was settled by a consent decree, Nash County brought its own suit. The appellate court held that the school board was in privity with the attorney general, and that res judicata applied although there was exclusive federal jurisdiction:

> The two suits allege the same wrongful act, the same illegal price fixing conspiracy. The state and federal statutes upon which the two actions are based are identical in language * * *. In both cases, the evidence will be identical and the damages recoverable and the relief available the same.

Is this a stronger case for preclusion than *Marrese?*

6. After *Marrese,* can the federal courts ever accord more preclusive effect to a state-court judgment than the state courts would?

7. Does the fact that federal interests may in some instances justify an exception to § 1738 suggest that preclusion law should be governed by the law that creates the claim that was decided?

8. What law should determine the preclusive effect of *federal* judgments? Note the resolution of this issue in *Manego,* supra p. 1095. and reconsider the issue in relation to Semtek International, Inc. v. Lockheed Martin Corp., infra p. 1133.

9. Preclusion law in interjurisdictional cases raises extremely difficult problems. For examination of these problems, see Erichson, Interjurisdictional Preclusion, 96 Mich. L. Rev. 945 (1998) (concluding that the second forum should apply the preclusion principles of the first one unless (1) there are grounds for an implied repeal of § 1738, or (2) the preclusion rules in question are explicitly linked to particular substantive rights of action). Reconsider these points in connection with Semtek International, Inc. v. Lockheed Martin Corp., infra p. 1133.

10. Although American courts generally accord res judicata effect to judgments of foreign countries, they have sometimes refused to do so for policy reasons. See Hilton v. Guyot, 159 U.S. 113, 202, 16 S.Ct. 139, 158, 40 L.Ed. 95 (1895) (merits of a foreign judgment should not be retried "where there has been opportunity for a full and fair trial abroad before a court of competent jurisdiction, conducting the trial upon regular proceedings, after due citation or voluntary appearance of the defendant, and under a system of jurisprudence likely to secure an impartial administration of justice between the citizens of its own country and those of other countries, and there is nothing to show either prejudice in the court, or in the system of laws under which it was sitting, or fraud in procuring the judgment."). What differences in procedures would warrant an American court not recognizing a foreign judgment? In *Hilton,* the American defendant objected that the plaintiff was permitted to testify not under oath and was not subjected to cross-examination, and that documents were admitted in evidence with which the defen-

dants had no connection. Are such procedures "likely to secure an impartial administration of justice"?

SEMTEK INTERNATIONAL, INC. v. LOCKHEED MARTIN CORP.

Supreme Court of the United States, 2001.
531 U.S. 497, 121 S.Ct. 1021, 149 L.Ed.2d 32.

Justice SCALIA delivered the opinion of the Court.

This case presents the question whether the claim-preclusive effect of a federal judgment dismissing a diversity action on statute-of-limitations grounds is determined by the law of the State in which the federal court sits.

I

Petitioner filed a complaint against respondent in California state court, alleging breach of contract and various business torts. Respondent removed the case to the United States District Court for the Central District of California on the basis of diversity of citizenship, see 28 U.S.C. §§ 1332, 1441, and successfully moved to dismiss petitioner's claims as barred by California's 2–year statute of limitations. In its order of dismissal, the District Court, adopting language suggested by respondent, dismissed petitioner's claims "in [their] entirety on the merits and with prejudice." Without contesting the District Court's designation of its dismissal as "on the merits," petitioner appealed to the Court of Appeals for the Ninth Circuit, which affirmed the District Court's order.

Petitioner also brought suit against respondent in the State Circuit Court for Baltimore City, Maryland, alleging the same causes of action, which were not time barred under Maryland's 3–year statute of limitations. Respondent sought injunctive relief against this action from the California federal court under the All Writs Act, 28 U.S.C. § 1651, and removed the action to the United States District Court for the District of Maryland on federal-question grounds (diversity grounds were not available because Lockheed "is a Maryland citizen," Semtek Int'l Inc. v. Lockheed Martin Corp., 988 F.Supp. 913, 914 (1997)). The California federal court denied the relief requested, and the Maryland federal court remanded the case to state court because the federal question arose only by way of defense. Following a hearing, the Maryland state court granted respondent's motion to dismiss on the ground of res judicata. Petitioner then returned to the California federal court and the Ninth Circuit, unsuccessfully moving both courts to amend the former's earlier order so as to indicate that the dismissal was not "on the merits." Petitioner also appealed the Maryland trial court's order of dismissal to the Maryland Court of Special Appeals. The Court of Special Appeals affirmed, holding that, regardless of whether California would have accorded claim-preclusive effect to a statute-of-limitations dismissal by one of its own courts, the dismissal by the California federal court barred the complaint filed in Maryland, since the res judicata effect of federal diversity judgments is prescribed by federal law, under which the earlier dismissal was on the merits and claim preclusive. After the Maryland Court of Appeals declined to review the case, we granted certiorari.

II

Petitioner contends that the outcome of this case is controlled by Dupasseur v. Rochereau, 21 Wall. 130, 135, 22 L.Ed. 588 (1875), which held that the res judicata effect of a federal diversity judgment "is such as would belong to judgments of the State courts rendered under similar circumstances," and may not be accorded any "higher sanctity or effect." Since, petitioner argues, the dismissal of an action on statute-of-limitations grounds by a California state court would not be claim preclusive, it follows that the similar dismissal of this diversity action by the California federal court cannot be claim preclusive. While we agree that this would be the result demanded by *Dupasseur*, the case is not dispositive because it was decided under the Conformity Act of 1872, 17 Stat. 196, which required federal courts to apply the procedural law of the forum State in nonequity cases. That arguably affected the outcome of the case. See Restatement (Second) of Judgments § 87, Comment a, p. 315 (1980) (hereinafter Restatement) ("Since procedural law largely determines the matters that may be adjudicated in an action, state law had to be considered in ascertaining the effect of a federal judgment").

Respondent, for its part, contends that the outcome of this case is controlled by Federal Rule of Civil Procedure 41(b), which provides as follows:

> "Involuntary Dismissal: Effect Thereof. For failure of the plaintiff to prosecute or to comply with these rules or any order of court, a defendant may move for dismissal of an action or of any claim against the defendant. Unless the court in its order for dismissal otherwise specifies, a dismissal under this subdivision and any dismissal not provided for in this rule, other than a dismissal for lack of jurisdiction, for improper venue, or for failure to join a party under Rule 19, operates as an adjudication upon the merits."

Since the dismissal here did not "otherwise specif[y]" (indeed, it specifically stated that it *was* "on the merits"), and did not pertain to the excepted subjects of jurisdiction, venue, or joinder, it follows, respondent contends, that the dismissal "is entitled to claim preclusive effect."

Implicit in this reasoning is the unstated minor premise that all judgments denominated "on the merits" are entitled to claim-preclusive effect. That premise is not necessarily valid. The original connotation of an "on the merits" adjudication is one that actually "pass[es] directly on the substance of [a particular] claim" before the court. Restatement § 19, Comment a, at 161. That connotation remains common to every jurisdiction of which we are aware. See ibid. ("The prototyp[ical] [judgment on the merits is] one in which the merits of [a party's] claim are in fact adjudicated [for or] against the [party] after trial of the substantive issues"). And it is, we think, the meaning intended in those many statements to the effect that a judgment "on the merits" triggers the doctrine of res judicata or claim preclusion.

But over the years the meaning of the term "judgment on the merits" "has gradually undergone change," R. Marcus, M. Redish, & E. Sherman, Civil Procedure: A Modern Approach 1140–1141 (3d ed.2000), and it has come to be applied to some judgments (such as the one involved here) that do not pass upon the substantive merits of a claim and hence do not (in many jurisdictions) entail claim-preclusive effect. That is why the Restatement of Judgments has abandoned the use of the term—"because of its possibly misleading connotations," Restatement § 19, Comment a, at 161.

In short, it is no longer true that a judgment "on the merits" is necessarily a judgment entitled to claim-preclusive effect; and there are a number of reasons for believing that the phrase "adjudication upon the merits" does not bear that meaning in Rule 41(b). To begin with, Rule 41(b) sets forth nothing more than a default rule for determining the import of a dismissal (a dismissal is "upon the merits," with the three stated exceptions, unless the court "otherwise specifies"). This would be a highly peculiar context in which to announce a federally prescribed rule on the complex question of claim preclusion, saying in effect, "All federal dismissals (with three specified exceptions) preclude suit elsewhere, unless the court otherwise specifies."

And even apart from the purely default character of Rule 41(b), it would be peculiar to find a rule governing the effect that must be accorded federal judgments by other courts ensconced in rules governing the internal procedures of the rendering court itself. Indeed, such a rule would arguably violate the jurisdictional limitation of the Rules Enabling Act: that the Rules "shall not abridge, enlarge or modify any substantive right," 28 U.S.C. § 2072(b). In the present case, for example, if California law left petitioner free to sue on this claim in Maryland even after the California statute of limitations had expired, the federal court's extinguishment of that right (through Rule 41(b)'s mandated claim-preclusive effect of its judgment) would seem to violate this limitation.

Moreover, as so interpreted, the Rule would in many cases violate the federalism principle of Erie R. Co. v. Tompkins, 304 U.S. 64, 78–80, 58 S.Ct. 817, 82 L.Ed. 1188 (1938), by engendering " 'substantial' variations [in outcomes] between state and federal litigation" which would "[l]ikely ... influence the choice of a forum," Hanna v. Plumer, 380 U.S. 460, 467–468, 85 S.Ct. 1136, 14 L.Ed.2d 8 (1965). See also Guaranty Trust Co. v. York, 326 U.S. 99, 108–110, 65 S.Ct. 1464, 89 L.Ed. 2079 (1945). Cf. Walker v. Armco Steel Corp., 446 U.S. 740, 748–753, 100 S.Ct. 1978, 64 L.Ed.2d 659 (1980). With regard to the claim-preclusion issue involved in the present case, for example, the traditional rule is that expiration of the applicable statute of limitations merely bars the remedy and does not extinguish the substantive right, so that dismissal on that ground does not have claim-preclusive effect in other jurisdictions with longer, unexpired limitation periods. Out-of-state defendants sued on stale claims in California and in other States adhering to this traditional rule would systematically remove state-law suits brought against them to federal court—where, unless otherwise specified, a statute-of-limitations dismissal would bar suit everywhere.[5]

Finally, if Rule 41(b) did mean what respondent suggests, we would surely have relied upon it in our cases recognizing the claim-preclusive effect of federal judgments in federal-question cases. Yet for over half a century since the promulgation of Rule 41(b), we have not once done so.

We think the key to a more reasonable interpretation of the meaning of "operates as an adjudication upon the merits" in Rule 41(b) is to be found in Rule 41(a), which, in discussing the effect of voluntary dismissal by the plaintiff, makes clear that an "adjudication upon the merits" is the opposite of a "dismissal without prejudice":

> "Unless otherwise stated in the notice of dismissal or stipulation, the dismissal is without prejudice, except that a notice of dismissal operates as an adjudication upon the merits when filed by a plaintiff who has once dismissed in any court of the United States or of any state an action based on or including the same claim."

See also 18 Wright & Miller, [Federal Practice & Procedure] § 4435, at 329, n. 4 ("Both parts of Rule 41 . . . use the phrase 'without prejudice' as a contrast to adjudication on the merits"); 9 id., § 2373, at 396, n. 4 (" '[W]ith prejudice' is an acceptable form of shorthand for 'an adjudication upon the merits' "). The primary meaning of "dismissal without prejudice," we think, is dismissal without barring the plaintiff from returning later, to the same court, with the same underlying claim. That will also ordinarily (though not always) have the consequence of not barring the claim from other courts, but its primary meaning relates to the dismissing court itself. Thus, Black's Law Dictionary (7th ed.1999) defines "dismissed without prejudice" as "removed from the court's docket in such a way that the plaintiff may refile the same suit on the same claim," and defines "dismissal without prejudice" as "[a] dismissal that does not bar the plaintiff from refiling the lawsuit within the applicable limitations period."

We think, then, that the effect of the "adjudication upon the merits" default provision of Rule 41(b)—and, presumably, of the explicit order in the present case that used the language of that default provision—is simply that, unlike a dismissal "without prejudice," the dismissal in the present case barred refiling of the same claim in the United States District Court for the Central District of California. That is undoubtedly

---

5. Rule 41(b), interpreted as a preclusion-establishing rule, would not have the two effects described in the preceding paragraphs—arguable violation of the Rules Enabling Act and incompatibility with Erie R. Co. v. Tompkins, 304 U.S. 64, 58 S.Ct. 817, 82 L.Ed. 1188 (1938)—if the court's failure to specify an other-than-on-the-merits dismissal were subject to reversal on appeal whenever it would alter the rule of claim preclusion applied by the State in which the federal court sits. No one suggests that this is the rule, and we are aware of no case that applies it.

a necessary condition, but it is not a sufficient one, for claim-preclusive effect in other courts.[6]

III

Having concluded that the claim-preclusive effect, in Maryland, of this California federal diversity judgment is dictated neither by Dupasseur v. Rochereau, as petitioner contends, nor by Rule 41(b), as respondent contends, we turn to consideration of what determines the issue. Neither the Full Faith and Credit Clause, U.S. Const., Art. IV, § 1, nor the full faith and credit statute, 28 U.S.C. § 1738, addresses the question. By their terms they govern the effects to be given only to state-court judgments (and, in the case of the statute, to judgments by courts of territories and possessions). And no other federal textual provision, neither of the Constitution nor of any statute, addresses the claim-preclusive effect of a judgment in a federal diversity action.

It is also true, however, that no federal textual provision addresses the claim-preclusive effect of a federal-court judgment in a federal-question case, yet we have long held that States cannot give those judgments merely whatever effect they would give their own judgments, but must accord them the effect that this Court prescribes. The reasoning of that line of cases suggests, moreover, that even when States are allowed to give federal judgments (notably, judgments in diversity cases) no more than the effect accorded to state judgments, that disposition is by direction of this Court, which has the last word on the claim-preclusive effect of all federal judgments:

> "It is true that for some purposes and within certain limits it is only required that the judgments of the courts of the United States shall be given the same force and effect as are given the judgments of the courts of the States wherein they are rendered; but it is equally true that whether a Federal judgment has been given due force and effect in the state court is a Federal question reviewable by this court, which will determine for itself whether such judgment has been given due weight or otherwise....

> "When is the state court obliged to give to Federal judgments only the force and effect it gives to state court judgments within its own jurisdiction? Such cases are distinctly pointed out in the opinion of Mr. Justice Bradley in Dupasseur v. Rochereau [which stated that the case was a diversity case, applying state law under state procedure]." Deposit Bank [v. Frankfort], 191 U.S. [499], at 514–515, 24 S.Ct. 154 [(1903)].

---

6. We do not decide whether, in a diversity case, a federal court's "dismissal upon the merits" (in the sense we have described), under circumstances where a state court would decree only a "dismissal without prejudice," abridges a "substantive right" and thus exceeds the authorization of the Rules Enabling Act. We think the situation will present itself more rarely than would the arguable violation of the Act that would ensue from interpreting Rule 41(b) as a rule of claim preclusion; and if it is a violation, can be more easily dealt with on direct appeal.

In other words, in *Dupasseur* the State was allowed (indeed, required) to give a federal diversity judgment no more effect than it would accord one of its own judgments only because reference to state law was *the federal rule that this Court deemed appropriate*. In short, federal common law governs the claim-preclusive effect of a dismissal by a federal court sitting in diversity. See generally R. Fallon, D. Meltzer, & D. Shapiro, Hart and Wechsler's The Federal Courts and the Federal System 1473 (4th ed.1996); Degnan, Federalized Res Judicata, 85 Yale L.J. 741 (1976).

It is left to us, then, to determine the appropriate federal rule. And despite the sea change that has occurred in the background law since *Dupasseur* was decided—not only repeal of the Conformity Act but also the watershed decision of this Court in *Erie*—we think the result decreed by *Dupasseur* continues to be correct for diversity cases. Since state, rather than federal, substantive law is at issue there is no need for a uniform federal rule. And indeed, nationwide uniformity in the substance of the matter is better served by having the same claim-preclusive rule (the state rule) apply whether the dismissal has been ordered by a state or a federal court. This is, it seems to us, a classic case for adopting, as the federally prescribed rule of decision, the law that would be applied by state courts in the State in which the federal diversity court sits. See Gasperini v. Center for Humanities, Inc., 518 U.S. 415, 429–431, 116 S.Ct. 2211, 135 L.Ed.2d 659 (1996); Walker v. Armco Steel Corp., 446 U.S., at 752–753, 100 S.Ct. 1978; Bernhardt v. Polygraphic Co. of America, 350 U.S. 198, 202–205, 76 S.Ct. 273, 100 L.Ed. 199 (1956). As we have alluded to above, any other rule would produce the sort of "forum-shopping ... and ... inequitable administration of the laws" that *Erie* seeks to avoid, Hanna, 380 U.S., at 468, 85 S.Ct. 1136, since filing in, or removing to, federal court would be encouraged by the divergent effects that the litigants would anticipate from likely grounds of dismissal. See Guaranty Trust Co. v. York, 326 U.S., at 109–110, 65 S.Ct. 1464.

This federal reference to state law will not obtain, of course, in situations in which the state law is incompatible with federal interests. If, for example, state law did not accord claim-preclusive effect to dismissals for willful violation of discovery orders, federal courts' interest in the integrity of their own processes might justify a contrary federal rule. No such conflict with potential federal interests exists in the present case. Dismissal of this state cause of action was decreed by the California federal court only because the California statute of limitations so required; and there is no conceivable federal interest in giving that time bar more effect in other courts than the California courts themselves would impose.

* * *

Because the claim-preclusive effect of the California federal court's dismissal "upon the merits" of petitioner's action on statute-of-limitations grounds is governed by a federal rule that in turn incorporates California's law of claim preclusion (the content of which we do not pass upon today), the Maryland Court of Special Appeals erred in holding that the dismissal necessarily precluded the bringing of this action in the Maryland courts. The judgment is reversed, and the case remanded for further proceedings not inconsistent with this opinion.

Notes and Questions

1. "It would be difficult for even the most adept spinner of law school hypotheticals to devise a case more challenging than *Semtek*." Burbank, *Semtek*, Forum Shopping, and Federal Common Law, 77 Notre Dame L.Rev. 1027, 1033–34 (2002). What are the parameters of *Semtek*'s statement that "it is no longer true that a judgment 'on the merits' is necessarily a judgment entitled to claim-preclusive effect" and that "the phrase 'adjudication upon the merits' does not bear that meaning in Rule 41(b)?" Is the ruling in Rinehart v. Locke, supra p. 1121, that under Rule 41(b) "an order of a district court which dismisses a complaint for failure to state a claim, but which does not specify that the dismissal is without prejudice, is res judicata as to the then existing claim which it appears plaintiff was attempting to state" still correct? Are the contrary positions in the cases based on the ground for dismissal, that is, failure to state a claim in *Rinehart* versus statute of limitations in *Semtek*?

Which is the stronger case for applying preclusion? Are the differing positions as to Rule 41(b) explainable by the fact that in *Rinehart* the suit was refiled in the same federal district court, as opposed to being filed in a state court in *Semtek*? In Styskal v. Weld County Board of County Commissioners, 365 F.3d 855 (10th Cir. 2004), the district court dismissed plaintiff's state-law claims "with prejudice" for lack of supplemental jurisdiction. The appellate court held that "the dismissal with prejudice by the district court in this case does not necessarily mean anything more than that Plaintiff cannot refile her claim in the United States District Court for the District of Colorado." Does Rule 41(b) have any further application beyond this situation? The court in *Syskal* explained as follows (id. at 859):

> For example, if the federal court's ruling is based on the substance of the claim (what has been termed "adjudication on the merits," see *Semtek*), the doctrine of claim preclusion would ordinarily prevent further proceedings on the claim in a later state action. But if the federal court's dismissal is based on a procedural ground, the federal ruling is unlikely to have any preclusive effect in state court, even though the dismissal may bar the plaintiff from returning to federal court.

Contrast Wagh v. Metris Direct, Inc., 363 F.3d 821 (9th Cir.2003), in which defendant removed a suit raising state-law claims and claims based on the federal Racketeer Influenced and Corrupt Practices Act (RICO), 18 U.S.C.A. § 1862, from a California state court. The federal court dismissed the RICO claims under Rule 12(b)(6) and, declining to exercise supplemental jurisdiction over the state-law claims, remanded the case to state court. On appeal, plaintiff argued that the federal court should not have dismissed the RICO claims with prejudice because that would preclude him from proceeding with those claims in state court, where he claimed that the pleading requirements were "less stringent than are those of the federal courts." The appellate court rejected plaintiff's argument: "The district court's Rule 12(b)(6) dismissal with prejudice operates as an adjudication on the merits of the claims under Fed.R.Civ.P. 41(b). Even though the state courts have concurrent jurisdiction over RICO actions, given the pleading flaws in this case, res judicata bars Waugh from reasserting his RICO claims in state court." Id. at 832.

2. Examine the text of Rule 41(b). At no point does the rule state explicitly that a dismissal for failure to comply with the statute of limitations constitutes a dismissal on the merits absent an express contrary statement by the court. How, then, can the rule be construed to dictate such a conclusion?

Once one reaches the conclusion that, under the terms of the rule, a dismissal for failure to comply with the statute of limitations is to be deemed a dismissal "on the merits," the next question naturally concerns the meaning of that phrase. The phrase may be construed on two levels: "applicational" (i.e., in what situations does it apply?), and "consequential" (i.e., what legal consequences flow from a finding that a dismissal was "on the merits"?). We have already discussed how Rule 41(b) interprets the phrase in the applicational sense. Because the rule by its terms fails to define the phrase "on the merits" in the consequential sense, however, one must draw upon preexisting constructions. Traditionally, what have been the legal consequences of a finding that a dismissal was on the merits? See supra, pp. 1134–35, indicating that, traditionally, dismissals on the merits "were accorded res judicata effect . . ."

How did the Supreme Court interpret the phrase, "on the merits," in *Semtek*? Is that construction consistent with the traditional understanding? How does the Court rely on the language of Rule 41(a) in construing "on the merits" in Rule 41(b)? Does the text of Rule 41(a) in reality support or undermine the Court's construction of Rule 41(b)? See Burbank, supra note 1, at 1042 (characterizing *Semtek* as a "transparently dubious interpretation" of Rule 41(b)).

To what extent do you think the Court's construction of the phrase, "on the merits," in Rule 41(b) was influenced by the federalism considerations embodied in the *Erie* doctrine? Cf. *Gasperini* (supra p. 975) and *Walker* (supra p. 972). Is the Court's use of that approach as legitimate here as it was in those decisions?

3. If Rule 41(b) did, in fact, dictate that a dismissal for failure to comply with the statute of limitations, absent a contrary statement by the court, is to have res judicata effect, would either the Constitution or the Rules Enabling Act be violated? How would the constitutional test fashioned in *Hanna* (supra p. 949) apply? As to the limits imposed by the Rules Enabling Act, consider the test developed by the Supreme Court in *Burlington Northern* (supra p. 965). How would such a federal rule fare under that standard? Is that conclusion consistent with the attitude reflected on the question in *Semtek*?

4. *Semtek* held that while federal law determines the preclusive effect of federal judgments on the merits of a case, the federal rule of decision in diversity cases generally should refer to the law of the state in which the rendering court sits. Is the Court's comment that there is no need for

nationwide uniformity persuasive? Is this similar to the policy justification given in *Erie* for federal courts being required to apply state substantive law? Should this ruling in *Semtek* apply in federal question cases? See Peia v. United States, 152 F.Supp.2d 226 (D.Conn. 2001): "The present case is distinguishable from *Semtek*, which dealt with state law claims under diversity jurisdiction. When claims are brought under diversity jurisdiction, the statute of limitations period may vary in districts located in different states. However, when claims are brought under RICO [as here] the statute of limitations period will not vary from district to district."

In Harper Macleod Solicitors v. Keaty & Keaty, 260 F.3d 389 (5th Cir. 2001), the defendants defaulted in a suit in a federal district court in Texas, which made jurisdictional findings that it had jurisdiction and defendants had been properly served. When the plaintiffs sought to register the default judgment in a federal court in Louisiana, that court upheld the defendants' challenge to the jurisdiction of the Texas federal court. The Fifth Circuit rejected the argument that the Louisiana federal court should have followed Texas law that limited jurisdictional challenges in collateral attacks on judgments. It noted that *Semtek* did not address the role of state law in determining the preclusive effect of jurisdictional findings of a federal court in a diversity suit, and found that applying the restrictive Texas rule would undermine federal jurisdictional law.

5. Consider whether the subsequent suit should be precluded in the following hypothetical cases:

a. A federal court in a diversity case dismisses plaintiff's complaint on the grounds that the substance of his complaint constituted a compulsory counterclaim in an earlier diversity suit in the same federal court pursuant to Federal Rule of Civil Procedure 13(a). Under the law of the state in which the federal court sits, all counterclaims are permissive.

b. A federal court in a diversity case dismisses as a sanction under Rule 37 because plaintiff disobeyed a discovery order. Under the law of the state, there is no parallel power to dismiss for discovery violations.

c. A federal court in a diversity case dismisses as a sanction for violation of Rule 11. State law does not permit dismissals as sanctions in analogous circumstances.

d. A federal court dismisses plaintiff's complaint on grounds of collateral estoppel, even though the defendant had not been a party to the first suit in which the fact in question had been decided, because under federal common law the doctrine of mutuality of estoppel (dictating that a party who could not be bound by a finding in an earlier case because he was not a party may not use a finding from the earlier case as collateral estoppel against a litigant who was a party in that action) is no longer applicable. However, under the law of the state in which the federal court sits, the doctrine of mutuality of estoppel still controls.

e. A federal court dismissed plaintiff's suit alleging violation of federal constitutional rights "with prejudice" under Rule 41(b) for violating a court order when he stated he would not attend the trial after being denied a continuance. Plaintiff then filed a nearly identical complaint in a state court which dismissed it as precluded. The Alaska Supreme Court concluded that federal common law would govern the preclusive effect of the judgment, which, after *Semtek*, would incorporate the state's preclusion law if not incompatible with federal interests. It found that "federal cases unequivocally treat a punitive dismissal like [plaintiff's]—a judgment that terminates a case for failing to follow court orders—as a judgment 'on the merits' that has claim-preclusive effect." DeNardo v. Barrans, 59 P.3d 266 (Alaska 2002).

B. ISSUE PRECLUSION (COLLATERAL ESTOPPEL)

1. *Same Issue Litigated*

LITTLE v. BLUE GOOSE MOTOR COACH CO.

Supreme Court of Illinois, 1931.
346 Ill. 266, 178 N.E. 496.

PER CURIAM.

* * *

Dr. Robert M. Little, the deceased, while driving his automobile in the city of East St. Louis, collided with a passenger bus, owned and operated by defendant in error [Blue Goose]. Defendant in error sued Dr. Little before a justice of the peace for damage to its bus caused by that collision. Evidence was heard and a judgment entered in favor of defendant in error against Dr. Little for $139.35. He appealed from that judgment to the county court. That appeal was later dismissed for want of prosecution, and a procedendo awarded. During the pendency of the case before the justice of the peace, Dr. Little filed a suit in the city court of East St. Louis to recover damages for personal injuries alleged to have been suffered by him in the collision.

[This suit was prosecuted by his executrix who was substituted as plaintiff upon Dr. Little's death. Her declaration alleged a general charge of negligence in the first count and willful negligence in the second count. Blue Goose raised the defense of estoppel by verdict and, in support, introduced evidence including the transcript of the judgment in the JP court and testimony by the JP that he had held a trial at which witnesses testified, had found in favor of Blue Goose, and had entered a judgment in its favor for $139.35. This defense was rejected and, after trial in the City Court of East St. Louis on the two counts of Dr. Little's executrix' declaration, judgment was entered for her in the amount of $5,000.]

On appeal from this judgment to the Appellate Court, that court reversed the same with the following finding of fact: "The court finds that appellant sued Dr. Robert M. Little, appellee's testate, before a justice of the peace for damages to its bus in the collision which occurred on November 1, 1925, and recovered a judgment therefor in the sum of $139.35; that in the rendition of said judgment it was necessarily determined that the collision and damages occasioned to the bus was due to the negligence of Dr. Little, and that immediately prior to his death he could not have maintained an action for personal injuries growing out of the same collision."

The first question arises on the ruling of the Appellate Court invoking against the claim of plaintiff in error the doctrine of estoppel by verdict. It is argued on behalf of plaintiff in error that, where a former adjudication is relied on as a bar to a subsequent action, it is essential that there be identity both of the subject-matter and of the parties, and that, in the instant case, the subject-matter is not the same, as this is the action for death by wrongful act for the benefit of the widow and next of kin, while the former suit was a claim for damages for injury to personal property. The issue on which this case is bottomed was the issue of fact which lay at the base of the judgment recovered before the justice of the peace. The allegation of the special plea is that the issue there raised was one of negligence on the part of Dr. Little on one hand and the defendant in error on the other, and that issue having been determined against Dr. Little, the fact is forever settled between these parties or their privies. Estoppel by verdict arises when a material fact in any litigation has been determined in a former suit between the same parties or between parties with whom the parties to the subsequent suit are in privity, where the fact was also material to the issue. The Appellate Court found as a matter of fact that the issue tried before the justice of the peace was an issue of negligence and was the same issue, arising on the same facts as those relied upon in the action for the wrongful death of Dr. Little, and that the issue of negligence was necessarily determined in the suit by the defendant in error against Dr. Little. That question of fact was tried before the city court in this case, and on the evidence there adduced the Appellate Court made its finding of fact. That issue of fact therefore is not open here, and we are to proceed to further consideration of the cause under the established fact that the issue of negligence, at least under the first count of the declaration, is the same issue tried before the justice of the peace.

While on appeal to the county court the trial, had there been one, would have been de novo; yet, when the appeal was dismissed and a procedendo was issued to the justice of the peace, the judgment of the justice of the peace became a final determination of that issue between the parties, and is conclusive not only upon the immediate parties to that suit, but also upon all persons in privity with them, and cannot be litigated again between the parties to that case or their privies in any subsequent action in the same or other court where that question arises, whether upon the same or a different cause of action or whatever may have been the nature or purpose of the action in which the judgment was rendered or of that in which the estoppel is set up. It follows that Dr. Little could not during his lifetime maintain the action filed by him against the defendant in error, and since plaintiff in error's right to recover damages under the Injuries Act depends upon Dr. Little's right, during his lifetime, to recover damages for injuries arising out of the same collision, plaintiff in error cannot recover here. In a suit under the Injuries Act, the cause of action is the wrongful act and not merely the death itself. Plaintiff in error therefore was not entitled to recover under the first count of her declaration, and the Appellate Court did not err in so holding.

It is contended, however, that as the second count of the declaration charges wanton and willful negligence on the part of defendant in error, contributory negligence on the part of Dr. Little is not a defense, and that the judgment of the city court was therefore right. Contributory negligence is not a defense to willful and wanton conduct, but it does not follow that the judgment of the city court was right because of that fact. In all cases charging willful and wanton negligence, it is necessary to make proof of such negligence, and, where there is no such proof, no recovery under such charge can be had. The finding of the Appellate Court that the collision was caused by the negligence of Dr. Little necessarily was a finding of fact on the willful negligence count as well as the general negligence count. Thus the rule that contributory negligence on the part of the plaintiff is not a defense to a charge of willful negligence does not apply. Whether Dr. Little or the bus driver was responsible for the accident was, as we have seen, settled. The judgment for $139.35 necessarily decided that the bus driver was not guilty of willful negligence.

* * *

[T]he Appellate Court was right in reversing the judgment without remanding it, and its judgment will be affirmed.

Notes and Questions

1. Dr. Little's executrix sued for "willful" or gross negligence. Contributory negligence is not a defense to gross negligence. Thus, even though Dr. Little was found negligent in the JP action, Blue Goose could not use his negligence as a defense if it were found in the second suit to have been grossly negligent. Why then did the issues determined by the JP judgment preclude the Executrix' gross negligence claim in the second suit? Would it be important to know that at the time this case was decided plaintiffs suing for negligence had to plead and prove freedom from contributory negligence?

2. Is it fair to Dr. Little's Executrix to accord issue preclusion to the judgment of a JP court which had limited jurisdiction, was not a court of record, was subject to *de novo* appeal, and in which the claim solely for property damage was so small that there was little incentive to litigate it?

3. If Dr. Little had won in the JP court, would his executrix have been able to preclude Blue Goose from relitigating the issues of each party's negligence in the second suit?

4. Is it likely that there will be uncertainty about what a judge found in resolving an earlier case? See Fed.R.Civ.P. 52 (requiring the court to make written findings of fact in cases tried to the court).

5. Courts are increasingly willing to accord collateral estoppel effect to decisions that result from processes different from full dress court trials. Thus, the decisions of administrative agencies are regularly treated as binding in court. See Perschbacher, Rethinking Collateral Estoppel: Limiting

the Preclusive Effect of Administrative Determinations in Judicial Proceedings, 35 U.Fla.L.Rev. 422 (1983). But the preclusive effect to be given to administrative determinations is fraught with uncertainty. In University of Tennessee v. Elliott, 478 U.S. 788, 106 S.Ct. 3220, 92 L.Ed.2d 635 (1986), the Supreme Court held that federal common law rules of preclusion incorporate state issue-preclusion rules in a federal suit brought after a state administrative adjudication arising from the same facts. Thus, where a state administrative-law judge ruled against an African–American state university employee challenging termination, the findings were given preclusive effect in a later § 1981 civil rights suit brought by him. However, preclusive effect was denied as to his Title VII claims because the Court found a congressional intent in that statute to allow a trial de novo from administrative remedies. Should this conclusion be reconsidered under Semtek v. Lockheed Martin Corp., supra p. 1133?

In Frazier v. King, 873 F.2d 820 (5th Cir.), cert. denied 493 U.S. 977, 110 S.Ct. 502, 107 L.Ed.2d 504 (1989), a nurse at a state facility appealed her termination to the state civil-service commission which ordered her reinstated with back pay. She then filed a civil rights suit under § 1983. The Fifth Circuit held that there was no *claim preclusion* effect barring her from suing. It also held that, in applying the state law of issue preclusion pursuant to *Elliott*, no *issue-preclusive* effect should be given to the commission's finding that she was discharged in violation of her First Amendment rights.

6. The ever-increasing use of arbitration makes the question of applying collateral estoppel to arbitrators' decisions of considerable importance. The general rule is that if a party had a full opportunity to present its case in an arbitration, an arbitration award will be treated as a final judgment for purposes of res judicata and collateral estoppel. See Taylor v. Peoples Gas Light & Coke Co., 656 N.E.2d 134, 139 (Ill.App.1995) (where the same issues were determined in an arbitration held pursuant to an employee grievance program, "as a general rule, arbitration awards have the same res judicata and collateral estoppel effect as court judgments"); Aufderhar v. Data Dispatch, Inc., 452 N.W.2d 648, 652 (Minn.1990) (where personal injury damages were determined in an arbitration required by an insurance policy, the claimant was estopped from relitigating the issues in a later action against a different defendant). See also Shell, Res Judicata and Collateral Estoppel Effects of Commercial Arbitration, 35 U.C.L.A.L. Rev. 623 (1988).

A further question arises when the arbitration award arises from a "court annexed arbitration" program that permits either party to appeal for a trial de novo (see pp. 486–90 supra). When there was no appeal, courts will generally accord collateral estoppel effect to the arbitration. For example, in Dorrance v. Lee, 976 P.2d 904 (Hawaii 1999), the parties in a mandatory "court-annexed arbitration" did not appeal the arbitrator's determination of who was negligent (and in what percentages) in an automobile accident. Summary judgment was then granted in a suit that had been filed by one of the parties prior to the issuance of the arbitration award on the ground that the findings of the arbitrator could not be relitigated. However, Flynn v. Gorton, 255 Cal.Rptr. 768 (Cal.App.1989), refused to accord such a "court-annexed arbitration" award collateral estoppel effect because it found that the low amount in controversy and option of a trial de novo did not provide the parties a serious incentive to litigate.

28 U.S.C.A. § 1738, which requires federal courts to give the same preclusive effect to a state-court judgment as would the court of the state rendering the judgment, does not apply to arbitration awards because they are not "judicial proceedings." Therefore preclusion rules applicable to arbitration must be judicially fashioned.

A further question is whether an earlier arbitration award should be given preclusive effect in a later arbitration. In Gonce v. Veterans Administration, 872 F.2d 995 (Fed.Cir.1989), the cases of certain co-workers discharged for alleged abuse of patients recorded on videotape reached arbitration first, and the arbitrators found their grievances arbitrable despite a 17–month delay. Other co-workers argued in their subsequent arbitrations that collateral estoppel effect must be given to the earlier arbitral awards on that point. In Kroeger v. United States Postal Service, 865 F.2d 235 (Fed.Cir. 1988), the Federal Circuit had accorded collateral estoppel effect to labor arbitration decisions where the issue was identical. However, the *Gonce* court refused to follow that case, finding that the actions taken against the employees were based on separate instances of misconduct, and there were no transcripts of the proceedings, making it impossible to tell whether mitigating circumstances distinguished the cases. It commented that, pursuant to Supreme Court precedents, the preclusive effect to be given to prior arbitration awards is "for individual resolution, absent a provision in the governing contract that requires earlier awards to bind subsequent arbitrators." Id. at 997.

HARDY v. JOHNS–MANVILLE
SALES CORPORATION

United States Court of Appeals, Fifth Circuit, 1982.
681 F.2d 334.

Before GEE and JOHNSON, CIRCUIT JUDGES, and VAN PELT, DISTRICT JUDGE.

GEE, CIRCUIT JUDGE.

[Persons exposed to asbestos suffering from asbestos-related diseases—insulators, pipefitters, carpenters, factory workers—sued various manufacturers, sellers, and distributors of asbestos, asserting causes of action including negligence, breach of implied warranty, and strict liability. The district court entered a collateral estoppel order that certain issues had been determined in plaintiffs' favor by a judgment for unrelated plaintiffs against six manufacturers of asbestos in Borel v. Fibreboard Paper Products Corp., 493 F.2d 1076 (5th Cir.1973), cert. denied, 419 U.S. 869, 95 S.Ct. 127, 42 L.Ed.2d 107 (1974). It construed *Borel* as establishing as a matter of law and/or fact that: (1) insulation products containing asbestos as a generic ingredient are "unavoidably unsafe products," (2) asbestos is a competent producing cause of mesothelioma and asbestosis, (3) no warnings were issued by any asbestos insulation manufacturers prior to 1964, and (4) the "warning standard" was not met by the *Borel* defendants in the period from 1964 through 1969.]

Appellants argue that *Borel* did not necessarily decide that asbestos-containing insulation products were unreasonably dangerous because of failure to warn. According to appellants, the general *Borel* verdict, based on general instructions and special interrogatories, permitted the jury to ground strict liability on the bases of failures to test, of unsafeness for intended use, of failures to inspect, or of unsafeness of the product. Strict liability on the basis of failure to warn, although argued to the jury by trial counsel for the plaintiff in *Borel,* was, in the view of the appellants, never formally presented in the jury instructions and therefore was not essential to the *Borel* jury verdict.

Appellants' view has some plausibility. The special interrogatories answered by the *Borel* jury were general and not specifically directed to failure to warn. Indeed, as we discussed at length in our review of the *Borel* judgment, the jury was instructed in terms of "breach of warranty." 493 F.2d at 1091. Although the jury was accurately instructed as to "strict liability in tort" as defined in section 402A of the Restatement (Second) of Torts, that phrase was never specifically mentioned in the jury's interrogatories. It is also true that the general instructions to the *Borel* jury on the plaintiff's causes of action did not charge on failure to warn, except in connection with negligence. Yet appellants' argument in its broadest form must ultimately fail. We concluded in *Borel:*

> The jury found that the unreasonably dangerous condition of the defendants' products was the proximate cause of Borel's injury. This necessarily included a finding that, had adequate warnings been provided, Borel would have chosen to avoid the danger.

As the appellants at times concede in their briefs, "if *Borel* stands for any rule at all, it is that defendants have a duty to warn the users of their products of the long-term dangers attendant upon its use, including the danger of an occupational disease." Indeed, the first sentence in our *Borel* opinion states that that case involved "the scope of an asbestos manufacturer's duty to warn industrial insulation workers of dangers associated with the use of asbestos." Id. at 1081. Our conclusion in *Borel* was grounded in that trial court's jury instructions concerning proximate cause and defective product * * *. Close reading of these instructions convinced our panel in *Borel* that a failure to warn was necessarily implicit in the jury's verdict. While the parties invite us to reconsider our holding in *Borel* that failure to warn grounded the jury's strict liability finding in that case, we cannot, even if we were so inclined, displace a prior decision of this court absent reconsideration en banc. Further, there is authority for the proposition that once an appellate court has disposed of a case on the basis of one of several alternative issues that may have grounded a trial court's judgment, the issue decided on appeal is conclusively established for purposes of issue preclusion. Nonetheless, we must ultimately conclude that the judgment in *Borel* cannot estop even the *Borel* defendants in this case for three interrelated reasons.

First, after review of the issues decided in *Borel,* we conclude that *Borel,* while conclusive as to the general matter of a duty to warn on the part of manufacturers of asbestos-containing insulation products, is ultimately ambiguous as to certain key issues. As the authors of the Restatement (Second) of Judgments § 29, comment g (1982), have noted, collateral estoppel is inappropriate where the prior judgment is ambivalent. * * * The *Borel* jury decided that Borel, an industrial insulation worker who was exposed to fibers from his employer's insulation products over a 33–year period (from 1936 to 1969), was entitled to have been given fair warning that asbestos dust may lead to asbestosis, mesothelioma, and other cancers. The jury dismissed the argument that the danger was obvious and regarded as conclusive the fact that Borel testified that he did not know that inhaling asbestos dust could cause serious injuries until his doctor so advised him in 1969. The jury necessarily found "that, had adequate warning been provided, Borel would have chosen to avoid the danger." In *Borel,* the evidence was that the industry as a whole issued no warnings at all concerning its insulation products prior to 1964, that Johns–Manville placed a warnings label on packages of its products in 1964, and that Fibreboard and Rubberoid placed warnings on their products in 1966.

Given these facts, it is impossible to determine what the *Borel* jury decided about *when* a duty to warn attached. Did the jury find the defendants liable because their warnings after 1966, when they acknowledge that they knew the dangers of asbestosis, were insufficiently explicit as to the grave risks involved? If so, as appellants here point out, the jury may have accepted the state of the art arguments provided by the defendants in *Borel,*—i.e., that the defendants were not aware of the danger of asbestosis until the 1960's. Even under this view, there is a second ambiguity: was strict liability grounded on the fact that the warnings issued, while otherwise sufficient, never reached the insulator in the field? If so, perhaps the warnings, while insufficient as to insulation workers like Borel, were sufficient to alert workers further down the production line who may have seen the warnings—such as the carpenters and pipefitters in this case. Alternatively, even if the *Borel* jury decided that failure to warn before 1966 grounded strict liability, did the duty attach in the 1930's when the "hazard of asbestosis as a pneumoconiotic dust was universally accepted," or in 1965, when documentary evidence was presented of the hazard of asbestos insulation products to the installers of these products?

As we noted in *Borel,* strict liability because of failure to warn is based on a determination of the manufacturer's reasonable knowledge. * * * Thus, the trial judge in *Borel* instructed the jury that the danger "must have been reasonably foreseen by the manufacturer." As both this instruction and the ambiguities in the *Borel* verdict demonstrate, a determination that a particular product is so unreasonably hazardous as to require a warning of its dangers is not an absolute. Such a determination is necessarily relative to the scientific knowledge generally known or available to the manufacturer at the time the product in question was sold or otherwise placed in the stream of commerce.

Not all the plaintiffs in this case were exposed to asbestos-containing insulation products over the same 30–year period as plaintiff Borel. Not all plaintiffs here are insulation workers isolated from the warning issued by some of the defendants in 1964 and 1966. Some of the products may be different from those involved in *Borel*. Our opinion in *Borel*, "limited to determining whether there [was] a conflict in substantial evidence sufficient to create a jury question," did not resolve that as a matter of fact all manufacturers of asbestos-containing insulation products had a duty to warn as of 1936, and all failed to warn adequately after 1964. Although we determined that the jury must have found a violation of the manufacturers' duty to warn, we held only that the jury could have grounded strict liability on the absence of a warning prior to 1964 or "could have concluded that the [post–1964 and post–1966] 'cautions' were not warnings in the sense that they adequately communicated to Borel and other insulation workers knowledge of the dangers to which they were exposed so as to give them a choice of working or not working with a dangerous product." * * * [O]ur opinion in *Borel* merely approved of the various ways the jury could have come to a conclusion concerning strict liability for failure to warn. We did not say that any of the specific alternatives that the jury had before it were necessary or essential to its verdict. * * * Like *stare decisis,* collateral estoppel applies only to issues of fact or law necessarily decided by a prior court. Since we cannot say that *Borel* necessarily decided, as a matter of fact, that all manufacturers of asbestos-containing insulation products knew or should have known of the dangers of their particular products at all relevant times, we cannot justify the trial court's collaterally estopping the defendants from presenting evidence as to the state of the art.

Notes and Questions

1.   Would more detailed "special verdicts" or "general verdicts accompanied by answer to interrogatories" (as provided for in Rule 49) have accomplished a more precise record of what the jury found in *Borel* on which issue preclusion could have been based? Are there any reasons in such a situation not to use special verdicts or interrogatories?

2.   It may be of interest to you to learn something more about the way in which the *Borel* jury reached its verdict. Consider the following:

> [T]he twelve members of the jury had been evenly split when they took their first vote, and had subsequently divided eleven to one in favor of the plaintiff. The lone holdout was a man who felt deeply that workers were lucky to have jobs and that no company which provided them should be judged too harshly for its actions, whatever they may be. Finally, after the other jurors had tried vainly to get him to change his mind, a face-saving deal was struck in which, in return for their finding Borel guilty of contributory negligence, he agreed to find that four of the

defendants were negligent, and all six of them liable to Borel under the doctrine of strict liability.

P. Brodeur, Outrageous Misconduct 64 (1985). Should a "face-saving deal" be the basis for broad collateral estoppel effects? Although the jury processes are not usually known, when they are should they be taken into account in determining the preclusive effect of a judgment?

Should a post-trial inquiry generally be employed to determine what the earlier jury decided (and perhaps whether it acted in a responsible manner)? Would use of juror affidavits violate Fed.R.Evid. 606(b)? For an example of attempts to obtain juror information for use in connection with a collateral estoppel determination, see Milks v. Eli Lilly & Co., 97 F.R.D. 467 (S.D.N.Y. 1983). If former jurors disagree about what occurred, will the court have to hold a trial to determine who is correct?

3.   In *Hardy* the court had no reports about the actual deliberations of the *Borel* jury except the information in the record of that case. It found that the interrogatories the jury answered were not specifically directed to failure to warn. How could the appellate court in *Borel* have concluded that the jury did find a failure to warn? Why wouldn't the *Hardy* court reconsider that ruling?

4.   Different plaintiffs always have different characteristics, and obviously complete identity is not necessary for plaintiffs in a subsequent suit to obtain the benefit of issues decided against the common defendant in an earlier suit by other plaintiffs. Which characteristics of the plaintiff in *Borel* were so distinctive as to prevent issue preclusion as to the plaintiffs in *Hardy*? Which issues did those characteristics relate to?

5.   Should differences in the circumstances of individual plaintiffs prevent the use of offensive collateral estoppel in environmental, drug, and mass-injury cases? For example, in the Bendectin cases (see Lynch v. Merrell–National Laboratories, 646 F.Supp. 856 (D.Mass.1986)), in which thousands of women claimed injuries based on taking the same drug, should a prior case in which the plaintiff used the drug during her third trimester of pregnancy be given preclusive effect on causation for a plaintiff who used it in her second trimester? What would we need to know to answer that? Should special weight be given to the economy of not relitigating basic issues affecting thousands of plaintiffs in claims against the same defendant? Recall that similar issues arose in connection with mass-tort class actions in Chp. III, supra pp. 309–28.

6.   Does *Borel* have any effect at all in *Hardy*? Recall the doctrine of stare decisis. To what extent does the decision in *Borel* foreclose the opportunity of defendants to defend in *Hardy*? Is this effect limited to "legal" issues decided in *Borel*? For discussion of the "preclusive" effect of stare decisis, see Barrett, Stare Decisis and Due Process, 74 U.Colo.L.Rev. 1011 (2003) (arguing that there are due process limits to applying stare decisis).

COMMISSIONER OF INTERNAL REVENUE v. SUNNEN

Supreme Court of the United States, 1948.
333 U.S. 591, 68 S.Ct. 715, 92 L.Ed. 898.

JUSTICE MURPHY delivered the opinion of the Court.

[Sunnen was an inventor-patentee who assigned a 1928 patent license contract to his wife. In 1935, the Board of Tax Appeals held that payments made to the wife during 1929–31 under this contract were not taxable to Sunnen. The Commissioner thereafter brought a second suit claiming that payments to the wife in later years under the same 1928 contract and under other contracts modeled on the 1928 contract were taxable to Sunnen. The Tax Court, relying on a series of 1940 decisions by the Supreme Court, held that the payments made under the other contracts were income to Sunnen. But as to payments under the 1928 contract, it concluded that it was bound by res judicata to follow the 1935 decision that they were not income of Sunnen.]

[The concepts of collateral estoppel] are applicable in the federal income tax field. Income taxes are levied on an annual basis. Each year is the origin of a new liability and of a separate cause of action. Thus if a claim of liability or non-liability relating to a particular tax year is litigated, a judgment on the merits is res judicata as to any subsequent proceeding involving the same claim and the same tax year. But if the later proceeding is concerned with a similar or unlike claim relating to a different tax year, the prior judgment acts as a collateral estoppel only as to those matters in the second proceeding which were actually presented and determined in the first suit. Collateral estoppel operates, in other words, to relieve the government and the taxpayer of "redundant litigation of the identical question of the statute's application to the taxpayer's status." Tait v. Western Md. R. Co., 289 U.S. 620, 624, 53 S.Ct. 706, 707, 77 L.Ed. 1405.

But collateral estoppel is a doctrine capable of being applied so as to avoid an undue disparity in the impact of income tax liability. A taxpayer may secure a judicial determination of a particular tax matter, a matter which may recur without substantial variation for some years thereafter. But a subsequent modification of the significant facts or a change or development in the controlling legal principles may make that determination obsolete or erroneous, at least for future purposes. If such a determination is then perpetuated each succeeding year as to the taxpayer involved in the original litigation, he is accorded a tax treatment different from that given to other taxpayers of the same class. As a result, there are inequalities in the administration of the revenue laws, discriminatory distinctions in tax liability, and a fertile basis for litigious confusion. Such consequences, however, are neither necessitated nor justified by the principle of collateral estoppel. That principle is designed to prevent repetitious lawsuits over matters which have once been decided and which have remained substantially static, factually and legally. It is not meant to create vested rights in decisions that have become obsolete or erroneous with time, thereby causing inequities among taxpayers.

And so where two cases involve income taxes in different taxable years, collateral estoppel must be used with its limitations carefully in mind so as to avoid injustice. It must be confined to situations where the matter raised in the second suit is identical in all respects with that decided in the first proceeding and where the controlling facts and applicable legal rules remain unchanged. If the legal matters determined in the earlier case differ from those raised in the second case, collateral estoppel has no bearing on the situation. And where the situation is vitally altered between the time of the first judgment and the second, the prior determination is not conclusive. * * *

It is readily apparent in this case that the royalty payments growing out of the license contracts which were not involved in the earlier action before the Board of Tax Appeals and which concerned different tax years are free from the effects of the collateral estoppel doctrine. That is true even though those contracts are identical in all important respects with the 1928 contract, the only one that was before the Board, and even though the issue as to those contracts is the same as that raised by the 1928 contract. For income tax purposes, what is decided as to one contract is not conclusive as to any other contract which is not then in issue, however similar or identical it may be. In this respect, the instant case thus differs vitally from Tait v. Western Md. R. Co., supra, where the two proceedings involved the same instruments and the same surrounding facts.

A more difficult problem is posed as to the $4,881.35 in royalties paid to the taxpayer's wife in 1937 under the 1928 contract. Here there is complete identity of facts, issues and parties as between the earlier Board proceeding and the instant one. The Commissioner claims, however, that legal principles developed in various intervening decisions of this Court have made plain the error of the Board's conclusion in the earlier proceeding. * * * This change in the legal picture is said to have been brought about by such cases as Helvering v. Clifford, 309 U.S. 331 (1940), [and] Helvering v. Horst, 311 U.S. 112 (1940). These cases all imposed income tax liability on transferors who had assigned or transferred various forms of income to others within their family groups, although none specifically related to the assignment of patent license contracts between members of the same family. It must therefore be determined whether this *Clifford-Horst* line of cases represents an intervening legal development which is pertinent to the problem raised by the assignment of the 1928 agreement and which makes manifest the error of the result reached in 1935 by the Board. If that is the situation, the doctrine of collateral estoppel becomes inapplicable. A different result is then permissible as to the royalties paid in 1937 under the agreement in question.

* * *

[T]he clarification and growth of these principles through the *Clifford-Horst* line of cases constitute, in our opinion, a sufficient change in the legal climate to render inapplicable in the instant proceeding, the doctrine of collateral estoppel relative to the assignment of the 1928 contract. True, these cases did not originate the concept that an assignor is taxable if he retains control over the assigned property or power to defeat the receipt of income by the assignee. But they gave much added emphasis and substance to that concept, making it more suited to meet the "attenuated subtleties" created by taxpayers. So substantial was the amplification of this concept as to justify a reconsideration of earlier Tax Court decisions reached without the benefit of the expanded notions, decisions which are now sought to be perpetuated regardless of their present correctness. Thus in the earlier litigation in 1935, the Board of Tax Appeals was unable to bring to bear on the assignment of the 1928 contract the full breadth of the ideas enunciated in the *Clifford-Horst* series of cases. And, as we shall see, a proper application of the principles as there developed might well have produced a different result, such as was reached by the Tax Court in this case in regard to the assignments of the other contracts. Under those circumstances collateral estoppel should not have been used by the Tax Court in the instant proceeding to perpetuate the 1935 viewpoint of the assignment.

Notes and Questions

1. Collateral estoppel is said to apply only to issues of fact and not of law. "Ordinarily, the refusal to apply the rule of issue preclusion to an issue of law makes sense. There seems no reason why a party who has litigated an issue of law should be under greater disability to invite a court to depart from precedent than a party who has not litigated the issue. The law, whatever the content of its rules, governs all litigants alike and generally speaking should be applied to all." F. James, G. Hazard & J. Leubsdorf, Civil Procedure § 11.21 (5th ed. 2001). On the other hand, is there reason to grant more preclusive effect to legal rulings than to factual findings? Consider Professor Hazard's arguments:

> The epistemological grounds for preclusion as to issues of law are stronger than those for preclusion as to issues of fact. In resolving issues of fact, the court endeavors to portray for itself a historical transaction in the outside world of events. Its method is to infer an image of reality—a scenario—from conflicting evidence. (If the evidence were not in conflict, there would not be an issue to decide.) In deciding fact questions the court necessarily works through the medium of extrajudicial resources, for example, evidence from witnesses. That dependency on outside resources entails a possible discrepancy between what the court believes was the fact and what actually was the fact. By contrast, in the resolution of issues of law the court constructs a verbal formulation from materials of which the court has direct knowledge. These materials include the relevant legal documentary sources, such as precedents and statutes. They also include the general view of reality in which those verbal materials take on meaning. Epistemologically, that general view of reality can be considered an envelope of judicially

noticed legislative facts. That reality is seen and understood through direct judicial perception, not by perception through the medium of informants, which is how a court apprehends the facts of a case. Of course, different judges have different world views, which is why they often disagree on what the law is. But these differences are necessarily dissolved or composed in deciding an issue of law.

When a court retries an issue of fact, it makes the new determination on a different evidentiary predicate. When it retries an issue of law, however, it proceeds on the same verbal and circumstantial predicates that were involved in the first instance. Purely epistemological considerations offer considerable justification for a judicial change of mind regarding the decision of an issue of fact. They offer none regarding the decision of an issue of law. Moreover, institutional considerations militate more strongly against a judicial change of mind about the law as compared to a change of mind about the facts. In redeciding an issue of fact, the court can say that its previous decision had been ill-informed. In redeciding an issue of law, the court must say that its previous decision had been ill-considered. Yet paradoxically, once determined, an issue of law may be more easily reopened than an issue of fact.

Hazard, Preclusion as to Issues of Law: The Legal System's Interest, 70 Iowa L.Rev. 81, 88–89 (1984).

2.   Collateral estoppel can, however, apply to mixed issues of law and fact where general legal principles are applied in specific factual circumstances, as established in United States v. Moser, 266 U.S. 236, 45 S.Ct. 66, 69 L.Ed. 262 (1924). When Moser retired as a captain in the U.S. Navy in 1904, he sued in the Court of Claims for the retirement pay of a rear admiral under a statute providing that officers who had served in the Civil War would be retired with the benefits of the next higher rank. The issue was whether the statute applied to someone like Moser whose only Civil War service was as a cadet at the Naval Academy. The Court of Claims decided in his favor. In a later suit by another claimant, the Court of Claims discovered another statute which it found warranted denial of the benefits. However, in three later suits by Moser for further installments of his retirement pay, the court relied on its original judgment as to Moser and granted him the benefits. The government appealed the third suit to the Supreme Court, contending that collateral estoppel should not apply to an issue of law that had been wrongly decided in the first suit. The Court held that although collateral estoppel does not apply to "unmixed questions of law," it does apply to mixed law and fact questions:

> Where, for example, a court in deciding a case has enunciated a rule of law, the parties in a subsequent action upon a different demand are not estopped from insisting that the law is otherwise, merely because the parties are the same in both cases. But a *fact, question* or *right* distinctly adjudged in the original action cannot be disputed in a subsequent action, even though the determination was reached upon an erroneous view or by an erroneous application of the law.

Because the Court found that Moser's case involved a fact question that had been adjudged in his first suit, it held that the government was estopped by the decision in the first suit. Can *Moser* be distinguished from *Sunnen*?

The problem after *Moser* became how to draw the line between an unmixed question of law and mixed issues of law and fact. This proved to be a difficult distinction. What a judge or jury usually finds are mixed questions of law and fact. When a rule of law has been determined in the context of a particular set of facts, there seems to be no reason to allow that issue to be relitigated. Modern cases and the Restatement (Second) of Judgments §§ 27–28 allow preclusion as to issues of law as well as fact except when (1) the result would place the party who won in a favored position in the general administration of the law, as in *Sunnen*, (2) the first determination was not fully appealed as it was in the second suit (thus trying to avoid allowing "repeat players" like the government from making every case a "test case"), id. at § 29, comment i, (3) the two actions involve claims that are substantially unrelated, id. at § 28(2)(a), (4) a new determination is warranted in order to take account of an intervening change in the applicable legal context or otherwise to avoid inequitable administration of the laws, id., or (5) the party against whom preclusion is sought had a significantly heavier burden of persuasion on the issue in the first suit than in the second, id. at § 28(4).

3. The *Sunnen* "separable facts" doctrine—"if the relevant facts in the two cases are separable, even though they be similar or identical, collateral estoppel does not govern the legal issues which recur in the second case"—has increasingly been questioned. Montana v. United States, 440 U.S. 147, 99 S.Ct. 970, 59 L.Ed.2d 210 (1979), limited *Sunnen* to cases where there has been a significant "change in the legal climate." Two circuits concluded that the "separable facts" doctrine is not good law after *Montana*. American Medical Int'l, Inc. v. Secretary of Health, Education and Welfare, 677 F.2d 118, 120 (D.C.Cir.1981) (per curiam); Hicks v. Quaker Oats Co., 662 F.2d 1158, 1167 (5th Cir.1981). The Ninth Circuit stated that it would not follow *Sunnen* "on the question of similarity of facts" but that its principles "are especially important in the context of agency relitigation of legal issues with substantial public policy implications." Western Oil & Gas Assoc. v. United States Environmental Protection Agency, 633 F.2d 803, 809 (9th Cir.1980); Peck v. C.I.R., 904 F.2d 525, 527 (9th Cir.1990).

4. New Hampshire sued Maine claiming a different boundary than had been confirmed in litigation in the 1970s over the states' lobster fishing rights. In New Hampshire v. Maine, 532 U.S. 742, 121 S.Ct. 1808, 1811–1812, 149 L.Ed.2d 968 (2001), the Supreme Court held New Hampshire was judicially estopped:

> [U]navailing is New Hampshire's reliance on this Court's recognition that the doctrine of estoppel or that part of it which precludes inconsistent positions in judicial proceedings is ordinarily not applied to States, Illinois ex rel. Gordon v. Campbell, 329 U.S. 362, 369, 67 S.Ct. 340, 91 L.Ed. 348. This is not a case where estoppel would compromise a governmental interest in enforcing the law. Cf. Heckler v. Community Health Services of Crawford Cty, Inc., 467 U.S. 51, 60, 104 S.Ct. 2218, 81 L.Ed.2d 42. Nor is this a case where the shift in the government's position results from a change in public policy, cf. Commissioner v. Sunnen, or a change in the facts essential to the prior judgment, cf. Montana v. United States, 440 U.S. 147, 159, 99 S.Ct. 970, 59 L.Ed.2d 210 (1979). Instead, it is a case between two States, in which each owes the other a full measure of respect. The Court is unable to discern any

substantial public policy interest allowing New Hampshire to construe "Middle of the River" differently today than it did 25 years ago.

5. The Court in *Sunnen* noted that since the earlier suit, the 1940 *Clifford-Horst* line of cases had resulted in a change in the "legal climate." Had it not been for that change in the law, presumably Sunnen would have been entitled to collateral estoppel as to the question of law as to taxability of the payments. The Court's concern was that if collateral estoppel applied even after a change in the law, it would result in favoritism to some taxpayers by "creat[ing] vested rights in decisions that have become obsolete or erroneous with time."

6. Can *Sunnen* rationally be confined to tax and customs cases? The rule is sometimes stated that "changes in the law after a final judgment do not prevent the application of res judicata and collateral estoppel, even though the grounds on which the decision was based are subsequently overruled." Precision Air Parts, Inc. v. Avco Corp., 736 F.2d 1499, 1503 (11th Cir.1984), cert. denied, 469 U.S. 1191, 105 S.Ct. 966, 83 L.Ed.2d 970 (1985). The Fifth Circuit has recognized an exception in constitutional law cases: "Faced with changing law, courts hearing questions of constitutional rights cannot be limited by res judicata. If they were, the Constitution would be applied differently in different locations." Parnell v. Rapides Parish School Bd., 563 F.2d 180, 185 (5th Cir.1977), cert. denied, 438 U.S. 915, 98 S.Ct. 3144, 57 L.Ed.2d 1160 (1978).

Is this a legitimate exception? Doesn't the problem of conflict among lower and circuit courts, resulting in different applications of the law, also exist in non-constitutional cases? Why shouldn't that rationale justify a general "change of law" exception to res judicata? On the other hand, why should one federal court have to accept the resolution by a co-equal federal court of an issue of federal law? See Marcus, Conflicts Among Circuits and Transfers Within the Federal Judicial System, 93 Yale L.J. 677, 702 (1984) ("If a federal court accepts the interpretation of another circuit without addressing the merits, it is not doing its job."). Isn't the need to resolve conflicts between circuits one of the circumstances favoring a grant of certiorari by the Supreme Court, thus providing a better solution without requiring an exception to the res judicata rule?

7. In United States v. Stauffer Chemical Co., 464 U.S. 165, 104 S.Ct. 575, 78 L.Ed.2d 388 (1984), the Supreme Court significantly cut back on *Sunnen*'s insistence that preclusion be limited to cases that are "identical in all respects." The issue there was whether the Environmental Protection Agency could use private contractors to perform inspections of Stauffer's plants under the federal Clean Air Act. The EPA had been rebuffed when it tried to do so at Stauffer plants in Wyoming and Tennessee, and in each case litigation ensued. After the federal court in Wyoming decided that the EPA could not use private contractors, the EPA sought to relitigate that question in the Tennessee case. It argued that estoppel should be limited to "the very same facts or transaction," which was not present because two different plants were involved. Characterizing the two cases as involving "virtually identical facts," the Court rejected the limitation, observing that "[w]hatever applicability that interpretation may have in the tax context, see Commissioner v. Sunnen, we reject its general applicability outside that context."

Note, however, that *Stauffer Chemical* may be limited to litigation between the same parties. With regard to preclusion against the government in litigation against different parties, see United States v. Mendoza, infra p. 1199.

In Burlington Northern R.R. v. Hyundai Merchant Marine Co., 63 F.3d 1227 (3d Cir.1995), the court ruled that, in the wake of *Stauffer Chemical Co.*, nonmutual collateral estoppel could be used as to an unmixed question of law. Plaintiff filed a declaratory judgment action seeking to avoid having to indemnify defendant for liability it incurred due to damages to cargo done by the railroad before it was delivered to the defendant shipping company in Seattle for eventual transport to South Korea. The railroad's position was that it was too late to make such a claim under the railroad's contract of carriage. The problem for the railroad was that the district court in Seattle had rejected this argument in a suit by another shipping company in 1992, reasoning that an indemnity claim does not mature until the primary liability is imposed, and that the time to present the claim cannot begin to run until then. Fearing probable suit in Seattle, the railroad filed a declaratory judgment action in New Jersey, and the district court refused to follow the Seattle decision and granted the railroad summary judgment.

The court of appeals reversed, relying on Restatement of Judgments § 28, which authorizes estoppel unless the two claims are "substantially unrelated" or a new determination is warranted to take account of an intervening change in the law. Although the contractual provision had a different time period and referred to the presentation of "claims" rather than "suits," as in the provision involved in the earlier litigation, the court found that "these distinctions are of no legal significance." Instead, the "substantial relationship" prong looks to "whether the two cases involve the same application of law," and the question whether the time period starts running before the claimant is required to make a payment is "identical" in application in the two cases. There was no intervening change in the law; to the contrary it appears only that the railroad took this case on the road to engage in forum shopping and avoid the certain loss on this point in the Ninth Circuit. Under these circumstances, the court saw no ground for avoiding collateral estoppel as to this pure issue of law, and directed the district court to grant preclusive effect to the earlier resolution of this legal issue.

8. The Supreme Court in Richards v. Jefferson County, Alabama, 517 U.S. 793, 116 S.Ct. 1761, 135 L.Ed.2d 76 (1996), distinguished between two types of actions brought by taxpayers. The first category encompasses cases in which the taxpayer is using that status to complain of an alleged misuse of funds, e.g., Massachusetts v. Mellon, 262 U.S. 447 (1923), or about other public action that has only an indirect impact on his interests, e.g., Stromberg v. Board of Ed. Of Bratenahl, 64 Ohio St.2d 98, 413 N.E.2d 1184 (1980). As to these cases, states have wide latitude to establish procedures to limit the number of judicial proceedings through such means as application of res judicata. The second category involves a federal constitutional challenge to a state's attempt to levy personal funds. While states may determine the applicable adjective law, the taxpayer must be accorded due process and the tax will be struck down if there is a denial of "any practicable opportunity to contest a tax on federal constitutional grounds," see Brinkerhoff–Faris Trust

& Sav. Co. v. Hill, 281 U.S. 673, 50 S.Ct. 451, 74 L.Ed. 1107 (1930). In this case, the Court refused to bind the taxpayers by res judicata under a prior state court action (that had been brought by the city and three county taxpayers) as to which they had received neither notice nor sufficient representation.

2. *Alternative Grounds for Decision*

HALPERN v. SCHWARTZ

United States Court of Appeals, Second Circuit, 1970.
426 F.2d 102.

Before MEDINA, WATERMAN and SMITH, CIRCUIT JUDGES.

J. JOSEPH SMITH, CIRCUIT JUDGE.

[Creditors filed an involuntary petition of bankruptcy against Evelyn Halpern, alleging three "acts of bankruptcy": (1) transfer of a bond and mortgage to her son with intent to hinder and delay creditors, (2) transfer by an insolvent without fair consideration, and (3) preference-payment of an antecedent debt. She contested the petition against her, and, after trial, District Judge Rosling found she had committed all three acts and adjudged her a bankrupt. The judgment was affirmed on appeal. The matter was then referred to the trustee in bankruptcy.]

Trustee Schwartz opposed Evelyn's discharge from bankruptcy under section 14 of the Act, 11 U.S.C. § 32, by filing specification of objection number 3 to her discharge. That specification charged:

> "3. On or about April 8, 1963, . . . she transferred and removed a valuable bond and mortgage owned in part by her on realty in Suffolk County, to her son I. David Halpern, with intent to hinder, delay, or defraud her creditors."

Section 14c(4) of the Act, 11 U.S.C. § 32(c)(4) provides that:

> "The court shall grant the discharge unless satisfied that the bankrupt has . . . (4) . . . transferred, removed, destroyed, or concealed . . . any of his property, with intent to hinder, delay, or defraud his creditors. . . . "

The trustee then moved, pursuant to Rule 56 of the Federal Rules of Civil Procedure, for summary judgment denying Evelyn a discharge on the ground there was no defense to specification number 3 because the issue had been concluded in the bankruptcy adjudication and was now res judicata. [The referee granted summary judgment for the trustee denying a discharge to Evelyn, which was affirmed on petition to the district court for review.]

In order to deny discharge to a bankrupt under section 14c(4) of the Act, 11 U.S.C. § 32(c)(4), the court must find that the transfer or removal of property in question was effected with actual intent to hinder, delay, or defraud creditors. Therefore, one prerequisite to sustaining the summary denial of Evelyn's discharge on the ground of collateral estoppel is that in the prior adjudication of bankruptcy Judge

Rosling found actual intent to hinder, delay or defraud creditors. Only one of Judge Rosling's three legal bases for finding an act of bankruptcy necessarily involved a finding of actual intent. Thus, his finding that the assignment was a preferential transfer under section 3a(2) of the Act as defined in section 60, required no inquiry into the bankrupt's intent since the effect of the transfer is the sole criterion of whether it is preferential. Nor did his finding that the assignment was a transfer of property "fraudulent within the intent of § 3a(1) under the provisions of § 67" of the Act, 11 U.S.C. §§ 21(a)(1), 107, entail a finding of any actual fraudulent intent. The requisite intent for finding an act of bankruptcy based on a fraudulent transfer is set out in sections 67 and 70 of the Act, 11 U.S.C. § 107, § 110. Section 67d(2) provides that a transfer is fraudulent without regard to the bankrupt's actual intent, if made while insolvent and without fair consideration. And section 70e(1) refers to the state law applicable to the transfer. New York Debtor and Creditor Law, McKinney's Consol.Laws, c. 12, 273 (McKinney 1945) provides that a conveyance by an insolvent without fair consideration "is fraudulent as to creditors without regard to his actual intent."

Therefore only one of Judge Rosling's three grounds for adjudication necessarily entailed a finding of actual intent, namely his conclusion that the assignment was "a removal of a part of the property of the said assignors with intent to hinder and delay the creditors of the said bankrupt" within the meaning of section 3a(1) of the Act, 11 U.S.C. § 21(a)(1).

It was with great care that the court below affirmed the denial of a discharge to Evelyn on the ground that this one finding by Judge Rosling concluded the issue of actual intent alleged in the specification of objection number 3 under section 14c(4), 11 U.S.C. § 32(c)(4).

This case presents a unique issue in the law of collateral estoppel which has not been analyzed exhaustively by any court. When the prior judgment rested on several (here three) independent, alternative grounds, is that judgment conclusive as to the facts which were necessarily found in order to establish only one separate ground? We conclude that on the facts before us it is not.

It is well established that although an issue was fully litigated and a finding on the issue was made in the prior litigation, the prior judgment will not foreclose reconsideration of the same issue if that issue was not necessary to the rendering of the prior judgment, and hence was incidental, collateral, or immaterial to that judgment. The reason for this rule is twofold. First, the decision on an issue not essential to the prior judgment may not have been afforded the careful deliberation and analysis normally applied to essential issues, since a different disposition of the inessential issue would not affect the judgment.

Second, the decision on an inessential issue in the prior judgment was not subject to the important safeguard as to its correctness, to wit: a contested review on appeal. An appeal from the prior judgment by the losing litigant, asserting error in the determination of an issue not central to the judgment, probably would be deemed frivolous by the appellate court, which would affirm without considering the merits of the claim of alleged error. Moreover, the losing litigant, unless he foresaw a potential collateral effect, would have little motivation to take an appeal from an alleged error which had no effect on the judgment. Finally, even if the losing litigant were to take an appeal, the winning litigant might not diligently oppose the claim of error on the merits, since he could demur, in effect, and rely solely on the argument that the claimed error was not essential to the judgment.

The same two considerations are present in the case (as here) of the conclusiveness of a prior judgment which is based on more than one alternative, independent ground. First, if the court in the prior case were sure as to one of the alternative grounds and this ground by itself was sufficient to support the judgment, then it may not feel as constrained to give rigorous consideration to the alternative grounds. In the present case, a finding of a transfer while insolvent was sufficient without inquiry into Evelyn's intent under sections 3a(1) and 67 to establish the act of bankruptcy which supported the adjudication. Also, the finding that the transfer had the effect of preferring creditors, was sufficient under section 3a(2) to establish the act of bankruptcy. Therefore Judge Rosling may have made the determination as to Evelyn's intent in connection with the alternative ground of removal of property with confidence that nothing turned on the decision.[1]

Second, since there are alternative grounds which could independently support the prior judgment, vigorous review of an asserted error as to one ground probably would not occur. The losing litigant would have little motivation to appeal from an alleged erroneous finding in connection with one of several independent alternative grounds, since even if his claim of error were sustained, the judgment would be affirmed on one of the other grounds. This in fact happened in Evelyn's appeal from the involuntary adjudication: she claimed on appeal that there was no assignment at all (which, if correct, would invalidate all three alternative grounds) but made no attack on the finding as to her intent.

It would be unwise to require a losing litigant in bankruptcy to take an appeal from alleged errors in one alternative ground simply to ward off the conclusive effect of collateral estoppel on a later discharge proceeding, when on appeal the court could affirm on one of the other alternative grounds. This seems particularly so in bankruptcy litigation, when debtors particularly are often handicapped in financing litigation in the predischarge stages of the proceeding. The losing litigant may not have the foresight to see that the allegedly erroneous ground may have unwanted collateral effects in the future, and hence if not clairvoyant, he may fall into a trap. Second, the winning litigant would not vigorously

---

1. It may be noted that Evelyn did not testify, and that the determination as to intent in her adjudication echoes that in Joseph's case, based in part on his demeanor on the stand, while it is not at all clear that her interest in the bond and mortgage was substantial, if any, while Joseph's was at least a far greater interest.

oppose the merits of the appeal as to one ground since he would simply stress the existence of alternative grounds on which to affirm. So, if the appellate court were to consider the merits of the claim of error, it might not have the benefit of adversary argument on the merits. And if the appellate court were to choose to avoid the merits of the claim of error on one ground, and affirm solely on the basis of one or several of the other alternative grounds, some courts have held that the lower court judgment is conclusive as to the allegedly erroneous ground despite the appellate court's unwillingness to rely on it. Even if the appellate court's affirmance on narrower grounds removes the conclusive effect as to grounds not relied on in the affirmance, the requirement of taking an appeal to protect issues in future collateral suits would not serve one important purpose of the doctrine of collateral estoppel, to minimize litigation and bring it to an end. Such a requirement would, in effect, require cautionary appeals litigating issues on appeal for their possible effect on future indeterminate collateral litigation, which neither party can be sure will occur. The rule at best would preclude some future trial litigation at the expense of currently creating extra appellate litigation.

We therefore hold that when a prior judgment adjudicating one a bankrupt rests on two or more independent alternative grounds, it is not conclusive as to issues in trial of objections to discharge which issues were necessarily found in order to establish only one of those grounds.[3] * * *

We do not reach appellant's contention that privity is necessarily lacking here, but feel that the application of the doctrine is error under the circumstances. The trap for the unwary created by the diverse requirements for adjudication and discharge makes it altogether too likely that error may be frozen or made permanent without a genuine adversary presentation and review of the essential issue of actual fraud. It is true that a contrary position in some comparable situations is apparently taken by the Restatement of Judgments and various commentators. Restatement of the Law of Judgments § 68 Comment n. However, these apparently contrary authorities either do not attempt to justify their position, or else they state the proposition that a judgment based on alternative grounds either precludes necessary issues decided in each or precludes no issues necessary to only one ground, apparently content that the statement of the proposition compels acceptance of the former alternative. While we agree with the proposition as stated, in the present circumstances we choose the latter alternative for the reasons expressed above. Nor is this situation controlled by the cases holding that decisions resting on alternative independent grounds are stare decisis as to each independent ground. In stare decisis, the questions of law decided in each of the alternative grounds may be reconsidered when

3. If the prior judgment rests on the finding of a fact necessary to establish all alternative grounds, then the judgment is conclusive as to this fact. The initial determination of this fact was essential to the judgment on whatever ground it might be rested. And on appeal, a claim of error as to this finding, if sustained, would require reversal.

the issues again arise, and the rules thereby established can be modified or overturned if there are compelling reasons. In the case of collateral estoppel, the prior judgment precludes any reconsideration of the issues concluded (with certain narrow exceptions).

Since Judge Rosling's finding of Evelyn's actual intent to hinder and delay her creditors was necessarily found in connection with only one of the three independent grounds establishing an act of bankruptcy, this finding cannot be given conclusive effect in the present litigation as to her application for a discharge.

Notes and Questions

1. Is *Halpern* correct that a trial court "may not feel as constrained to give rigorous consideration to the alternative grounds" if it is sure as to one of the alternative grounds? Why would the court have added alternative grounds if that were the case?

2. Is the effect of the *Halpern* rule to deny issue preclusion to any judgment that is based upon alternative holdings?

3. In the early 20th century, it was generally accepted that, in Judge Learned Hand's words, "if a court decides a case on two grounds, each is a good estoppel." Irving National Bank v. Law, 10 F.2d 721 (2d Cir.1926). A number of courts still take a position contrary to *Halpern*, holding that when there are alternative holdings, each of which independently would support the judgment, issue preclusion applies to both. See In re Westgate–California Corp., 642 F.2d 1174, 1176–77 (9th Cir.1981); Winters v. Lavine, 574 F.2d 46, 67 (2d Cir.1978). However, Restatement (Second) of Judgments § 27, comment i (1982) follows the approach in *Halpern* (except that, if a judgment has been appealed and the appellate court upholds both holdings as sufficient, the judgment is conclusive as to both, id., comment o). For a critical assessment of the problem, see Lucas, The Direct and Collateral Estoppel Effects of Alternative Holdings, 50 U.Chi.L.Rev. 701 (1983).

4. The concern expressed in *Halpern* that "it would be unwise to require a losing litigant in bankruptcy to take an appeal from alleged errors in one alternative ground simply to ward off the conclusive effect of collateral estoppel on a later discharge proceeding, when on appeal the court could affirm on one of the other alternative grounds" was echoed in efficiency terms in Stebbins v. Keystone Insurance Co., 481 F.2d 501 (D.C.Cir.1973). There, judgment was entered against a plaintiff who alleged racially discriminatory denial of job opportunities on the grounds that he (1) had not applied for a job with the defendant and (2) was not employable in that industry. He then applied for a job and, upon being refused, filed a second suit. The court refused to apply collateral estoppel on the issue of whether he was employable, citing *Halpern*. Plaintiff might not have appealed, it said, because the ruling that he had not applied for a job was of no crucial significance to him since he could, as he did, readily remedy that deficiency. It concluded that to require a party to fully litigate each and every issue solely for the purpose of avoiding collateral estoppel would compel expensive and unnecessary litigation in both the trial and appellate courts.

5. Related to the question of the preclusive effect of alternative hold-ings is the determination whether a decided issue was sufficiently important in the first action that it was foreseeable that it might be subject to subsequent litigation and therefore to preclusion. Judge Hand sought to answer this question in The Evergreens v. Nunan, 141 F.2d 927 (2d Cir.1944), by drawing a distinction between "ultimate facts" on the one hand and "evidentiary facts" or "mediate data" on the other. Ultimate facts would be precluded, but evidentiary facts would not. Ultimate facts were those "upon which combined occurrence the law raises the duty, or the right, in question" and "which the law makes the occasion for imposing its sanctions." Mediate data were those "from whose existence may be rational-ly inferred the existence of one of the facts upon whose combined occurrence the law raises the duty, or the right." Id. at 928.

Restatement of Judgments § 68, comment p (1948) adopted this analy-sis, but the distinction has been criticized as difficult to administer. "[T]he real danger in according preclusive effect to subsidiary findings are (1) that such effect will be given to determinations of issues that were not seriously contested and may have been barely relevant and (2) that determinations may have wholly unforeseeable consequences." Restatement (Second) of Judgments § 27, Reporter's Note, p. 271. The Restatement (Second) of Judgments § 27, comment j (1982) felt that these dangers could be better avoided by abandoning the prior analysis and focusing instead on "whether the issue was actually recognized by the parties as important and by the trier as necessary to the first judgment."

6. In *Halpern* the court says that alternate findings are not likely to be reviewed carefully on appeal. Is this argument persuasive? Consider Aetna Casualty & Surety Co. v. Cunningham, 224 F.2d 478 (5th Cir.1955). Plaintiff there sought recovery of the same sum alternatively for breach of contract and fraud. The trial court awarded judgment in the sum sought for breach of contract but found no fraud. Plaintiff appealed, contending that it had a stake in proving fraud as well in order to defeat efforts to obtain a discharge in bankruptcy. Defendant argued that plaintiff was not entitled to review of this decision because the relief it had obtained on the contract claim—a judgment for the sum demanded—was all it could obtain for fraud. The appellate court held that plaintiff could nevertheless appeal the fraud claim because the rejection of that claim affected the "quality of the judgment" since "amount is not the sole measure of the relief to which a party may be entitled. The judgment may have different qualities and legal consequences dependent on the claim on which it is based." Is this a more sensible way of approaching the problem presented in *Halpern*?

7. There is a split in the circuits as to what preclusive effect to give alternative findings. A number of circuits (Third, Fourth, Eighth, and Tenth) follow the Restatement (Second) of Judgments § 27 comment i (1980): "If a judgment of a court of first instance is based on determination of two issues, either of which standing independently would be sufficient to support the result, the judgment is not conclusive with respect to either issue standing alone." The Second, Seventh, Ninth, and D.C. Circuits hold that "plaintiff is precluded from relitigating an issue actually decided against it in a prior case, even if the court in the prior case rested its judgment on alternative grounds." National Satellite Sports, Inc. v. Eliadis, Inc., 253 F.3d

900, 909 (6th Cir. 2001). The Sixth Circuit in *Eliadis* declined to resolve the issue holding, however, "that where one ground for the decision is clearly primary and the other secondary, the secondary ground is not 'necessary to the outcome' for the purposes of issue preclusion." Id. at 910.

C. PERSONS BOUND BY JUDGMENT

1. *Parties and Persons in Privity*

The traditional view of res judicata and collateral estoppel is that a judgment only binds parties and those in privity with them. The term "privity" is one of those conclusory words that provides little insight into the underlying policies. "The legal definition of a person in privity with another, is a person so identified with another that he represents the same legal right." Searle Brothers v. Searle, 588 P.2d 689, 691 (Utah 1978). Restatement (Second) of Judgments (1982) eschews use of the term "privity," instead describing the various kinds of nonparties who are deemed to have a sufficient relationship to a party to be bound by the judgment. See id., §§ 39–41. The concept of privity is rooted in due process, as a non-party should not be bound by a judgment unless he had an opportunity to be heard or was so identified with a party that his interests were represented.

BENSON AND FORD, INC. v. WANDA PETROLEUM CO.

United States Court of Appeals, Fifth Circuit, 1987.
833 F.2d 1172.

Before SNEED, REAVLEY and JOHNSON, CIRCUIT JUDGES.

REAVLEY, CIRCUIT JUDGE.

The district court dismissed defendants on the ground that plaintiff Benson and Ford's claims were precluded by a prior judgment in a case in which Benson and Ford was not a party. We reverse for the reason that privity did not exist between Benson and Ford and the plaintiff in the prior case.

The prior case was brought by Shelby L.P. Gas Co. against Wanda Petroleum Co. and others alleging various antitrust claims. Shelby alleged that the defendants retaliated against it because it refused to join a price fixing conspiracy in western Louisiana. The defendants split into two groups: the Enterprise group (Wanda Petroleum Company, d/b/a Gas TEC, Enterprise Products Co., Holicer Gas Co., Joe Havens, and Dan Duncan) and the Petrolane group (Petrolane Inc., and Petrolane Gas Services). The Petrolane group settled with Shelby but the Enterprise group elected to go to trial.

During the pendency of the *Shelby* litigation, Benson and Ford filed a separate suit against the Enterprise and Petrolane defendants alleging the same antitrust violations.

The Enterprise group won a jury verdict in the *Shelby* case. David Ford of Benson and Ford voluntarily appeared to testify as a witness for Shelby. The jury found against Shelby on all of its theories—price fixing, monopolization, attempt to monopolize, conspiracy to monopolize and tortious interference.

After the *Shelby* judgment, Enterprise moved for summary judgment against Ford. Enterprise argued that Ford, who had voluntarily testified, had the same lawyer and asserted the same claims arising from the same facts, was barred from relitigating the issues. The district court granted the motion and issued a Fed.R.Civ.P. 54(b) certificate.

A litigant has a due process right to a "full and fair opportunity to litigate an issue." Hardy v. Johns–Manville Sales Corp., 681 F.2d 334, 338 (5th Cir.1982). Therefore, the conclusive effect of a prior judgment may only be invoked against a party or a privy. The concept of "privity" is a legal conclusion, not a "judgmental process." A nonparty will be considered in privity, or sufficiently close to a party in the prior suit so as to justify preclusion, in three situations:

> First, a nonparty who has succeeded to a party's interest in property is bound by any prior judgments against that party.... Second, a nonparty who controlled the original suit will be bound by the resulting judgment.... Third, federal courts will bind a nonparty whose interests were represented adequately by a party in the original suit....

Freeman v. Lester Coggins Trucking, Inc., 771 F.2d 860, 864 (5th Cir.1985). Enterprise argues that Ford is precluded by either the second or third situation.

A

"To have control of litigation requires that a person have effective choice as to the legal theories and proofs to be advanced in behalf of the party to the action. He must also have control over the opportunity to obtain review." Hardy, 681 F.2d at 339 (quoting Restatement (Second) of Judgments § 39, comment c (1982)). Examples of the "control" necessary to preclude a nonparty are: the president and sole shareholder controls his company; a parent corporation controls its subsidiary; a liability insurer assumes control of a defense; and the indemnitor defends an action against an indemnitee. However, "[l]esser measures of participation without control do not suffice. Thus it is not enough the nonparty supplied an attorney or is represented by the same law firm; helped to finance the litigation; appeared as an amicus curiae; testified as a witness; participated in consolidated pretrial proceedings; undertook some limited presentations to the court; or otherwise participated in a limited way. Even a nonparty who was 'heavily involved' may remain free from preclusion." [18 C. Wright, A. Miller & E. Cooper, Federal Practice and Procedure § 4451] at 432–33. It is essential that the nonparty have actual control.

There is no evidence that Ford had control of the *Shelby* litigation. Enterprise argues that Ford had the same attorney, and urges the same facts on the same issues, that Ford was a witness at the *Shelby* trial and that there were meetings about their common interest which Ford and Shelby's president attended. That evidence, however, would not warrant a finding that Ford had actual control over the *Shelby* case. Absent evidence that Ford directly exercised some actual control over Shelby's cause of action, compare Montana v. United States, 440 U.S. 147, 155, 99 S.Ct. 970, 59 L.Ed.2d 210 (1979), the control theory cannot apply. We reject Enterprise's argument that because Ford's attorney was the same attorney who "controlled" the *Shelby* litigation, Ford controlled that case. A plaintiff cannot be precluded from bringing his own suit because he chose an attorney who participated in a prior suit.

B

Enterprise also argues that Ford's suit is barred by reason of "adequate representation." The adequate representation concept does not pertain to the competence of the previous litigation. Instead, "it refers to the concept of virtual representation, by which a nonparty may be bound because the party to the first suit 'is so closely aligned with his [the nonparty's] interests as to be his virtual representative.' " *Freeman*, 771 F.2d at 864. For a nonparty to be so "closely aligned . . . requires more than a showing of parallel interest or, even, a use of the same attorney in both suits." *Freeman*, 771 F.2d at 864. The question of virtual representation is one of fact and is to be kept within "strict confines." As explained in Pollard [v. Cockrell], 578 F.2d [1002] at 1008 [(5th Cir.1978)]:

> Virtual representation demands the existence of an express or implied legal relationship in which parties to the first suit are accountable to non-parties who file a subsequent suit raising identical issues.

Freeman provides a good example of how narrowly the virtual representation theory is applied. In that case, the plaintiff was injured and his daughter killed in a car crash. Freeman brought suit in state court for his own personal injury but lost on a finding of no defendant negligence. He then brought suit in federal court, on behalf of himself and as representative of his wife and three other minor children, for the wrongful death of his daughter from the same accident. We affirmed the use of collateral estoppel for Freeman's own claim but reversed for his wife's and children's claims. We held that, despite his own personal role in both cases, his use of the same attorney to pursue the same claims of negligence arising out of the same accident, Freeman was not the virtual representative to preclude the other family members' claims. The holding was based on the ground that other family members had their own personal claims for wrongful death and were due their day in court.

The same legal reasoning, that the virtual representation concept demands the existence of an express or implied legal relationship, determined that a federal challenge to a massage parlor ordinance was not foreclosed by a prior unsuccessful state court challenge. *Pollard,* 578 F.2d at 1008. Despite the presence of the same attorneys and the same claims decided by state court, because the federal plaintiffs had no legal relationship to the state plaintiffs, there was no preclusion.

Freeman and *Pollard* control the decision in this case. Despite having the same attorney and the same claim from the same set of facts, there is no indication that Ford and Shelby had any expressed or implied legal relationship. The meetings which Ford and Shelby attended were simply discussions of the subject by the dealers in the area. There was no implication that Shelby was in any way accountable to Ford. Virtual representation does not apply.

Enterprise argues that two cases, Southwest Airlines [Co. v. Texas International Airlines], 546 F.2d 84 (5th Cir.1977), and Cauefield v. Fidelity and Casualty Co. of New York, 378 F.2d 876 (5th Cir.), support preclusion. Both cases are distinguishable. *Southwest Airlines* concerned the airline's attempt to remain at Dallas's Love Field. The City of Dallas had previously lost a federal suit to oust the airline from Love Field, which suit had been predicated on a Dallas city ordinance. Other private carriers then filed suit in state court, using the same ordinance, to again attempt to oust Southwest. We held that the district court properly enjoined that state suit. The only legal interest the private airlines had was the Dallas ordinance. Our holding rested on the proposition that private parties cannot relitigate to enforce an ordinance after the public body fails in its attempt to enforce the same ordinance. By contrast, Ford does not seek to relitigate Shelby's rights. Although the alleged conspiracy was directed toward Shelby, Ford pursues only its own cause of action to which it has a legal right.

Cauefield was a Louisiana grave desecration case. The federal court action was stayed while a Louisiana state court case went forward. The plaintiffs lost in state court and we held that the district court properly dismissed the federal suit. Although the facts were similar to this case— same cause of action, same facts, same attorney, and use of federal plaintiffs—we see one crucial difference. The court pointed out that the federal case had been continued indefinitely until the state case could be resolved, and concluded that "[i]t thus appears that the [state court] case tacitly was intended to resolve all the numerous identical claims that the cemetery had been desecrated." That tacit agreement was the implied legal relationship that is not present in this case.

C

Enterprise then argues its equities. It argues that Ford should have been required to join in the *Shelby* litigation; failing to do so, Ford should be barred from relitigating the issues. However, the general rule is "that a nonparty is not obliged to seize an available opportunity to intervene in pending litigation that presents [a] question affecting the nonparty...." 18 C. Wright, A. Miller & E. Cooper, Federal Practice and

Procedure § 4452, at 446 (1981). Ford was not obligated to join the *Shelby* case.

Enterprise says it would be unfair for Ford not to be precluded in this case, because Ford would have been entitled to use offensive collateral estoppel against Enterprise if Shelby had won the first suit. Even if we were free to modify our precedents, which we may not do, the fairness argument is not a strong one. First, Ford has a due process right to be heard. Enterprise, on the other hand, already has had an opportunity to fully litigate the issues. Because the due process rights are not the same, the two situations are not parallel. Second, we are not at all certain that Ford could have used a favorable *Shelby* verdict. The Supreme Court has said that offensive collateral estoppel should not be used "where a plaintiff could easily have joined in the earlier action...." Parklane Hosiery Co., Inc. v. Shore, 439 U.S. 322, 331, 99 S.Ct. 645, 652, 58 L.Ed.2d 552 (1979) [infra p. 1174]. This circuit followed that restriction on offensive collateral estoppel in Hauser v. Krupp Steel Producers, Inc., 761 F.2d 204, 207 (5th Cir.1985). Finally, in this case Enterprise might have avoided the two trials by moving to consolidate Ford's claim with Shelby's under Fed.R.Civ.P. 42.

Ford is not precluded from relitigating the same issues that were decided in the *Shelby* case.

Notes and Questions

1. Restatement (Second) of Judgments § 39 provides that anyone who "controls or substantially participates in the control of the presentation on behalf of a party" is bound by the outcome. Montana v. United States, 440 U.S. 147, 99 S.Ct. 970, 59 L.Ed.2d 210 (1979), referred to in *Benson and Ford*, is an example of sufficient control to warrant a finding of privity. There the contractor on a federal dam project brought suit in state court against the Montana State Board of Equalization, contending that the state's gross receipts tax upon contractors for public, but not private, construction projects was unconstitutional. The Montana Supreme Court found the tax constitutional. The United States then sued Montana in federal court, challenging the constitutionality of the tax as it affected it in its dealings with contractors. The Court held that the U.S. was bound by the state judgment because it had required that the suit be filed; reviewed and approved the complaint; paid the attorneys' fees and costs; directed the appeal; and submitted an amicus brief on appeal.

Why should it be critical that the nonparty control the conduct of the case? To what extent does a party control the actual conduct of a case? Isn't it usually more directly in the control of the lawyer? Cf. Wainwright v. Sykes, 433 U.S. 72, 93, 97 S.Ct. 2497, 2509, 53 L.Ed.2d 594 (1977) (Burger, C.J., concurring) (in a criminal case, "[o]nce counsel is appointed, the day-to-day conduct of the defense rests with the attorney. * * * Not only do these decisions rest with the attorney, but such decisions must, as a practical matter, be made without consulting the client. The trial process simply does not permit the type of frequent and protracted interruptions which would be necessary if it were required that clients give knowing and intelligent approval to each of the myriad tactical decisions as a trial proceeds."). Ford had the same lawyer as Shelby; if that lawyer proposed to put on the exact same case would there be any reason to force defendant to go to trial against that case again? Is it likely that the lawyer planned to rely on the exact same evidence a second time?

2.   When should the law bind a nonparty who does not control the conduct of the case? As set out in Restatement (Second) of Judgments § 41, a nonparty is bound when "represented" by a party because that party is "(a) the trustee of an estate or interest of which the person is a beneficiary; or (b) invested by the person with authority to represent him in an action; or (c) the executor, administrator, guardian, conservator, or similar fiduciary manager of an interest of which the person is a beneficiary; or (d) an official or agency invested by law with authority to represent the person's interests; or (e) the representative of a class of persons similarly situated, designated as such with the approval of the court, of which the person is a member." Would any of these situations apply in *Benson and Ford?*

3.   Class members are bound by a judgment in a class action because the class representative has been designated by the court to represent them. But what if class members exercise their right to opt out? In Becherer v. Merrill Lynch, Pierce, Fenner & Smith, Inc., 193 F.3d 415 (6th Cir. 1999), a group of investors in a condominium opted out of a settlement class action that had been brought on behalf of all investors, and later filed identical claims in a separate suit. They, or at least some of them, had previously retained the same lawyer to represent them, contributed money to the class-action expense fund, and worked closely with the Association of Unit Owners which financed and controlled the class action. The district court found them bound by the judgment, noting that they had "improperly maneuvered in order to avoid the potential effects of res judicata" by having their counsel argue inconsistently in earlier proceedings concerning the effect of a class judgment. Citing *Benson and Ford*, the court of appeals found that such financing and involvement in the class action was not sufficient to demonstrate "control" and that there was no evidence that they could have held the class representatives or the Association legally "accountable" for the result. A dissent said this was "an unduly narrow rule of virtual representation"—that a class member "may be bound by the judgment only if a party to the action is legally accountable to the opt-out plaintiff." Id. at 429 The majority "also found that 'acquiescence cannot be shown in a class action case where the nonparties opt out of the class and there is no other court approval of representation by a party.' " Id. at 427.

4.   Beyond the above situations, courts sometimes, as in *Benson and Ford,* refer to the concept of "virtual representation," which is said to mean that "a person may be bound by a judgment even though not a party if one of the parties to the suit is so closely aligned with his interests as to be his virtual representative." Aerojet–General Corp. v. Askew, 511 F.2d 710, 719 (5th Cir.1975). This amorphous doctrine has been used in cases like *Aerojet-General* to bind subordinate governmental entities by the litigation results of higher governmental entities. In Southwest Airlines Co. v. Texas International Airlines, 546 F.2d 84 (5th Cir.1977), the court applied it to private airlines seeking to enforce a regulation after the public authority that promulgated it had tried and failed to enforce it. Was this argument forceful in *Benson* and *Ford,* where both suits deal with the application of the federal

antitrust laws to the same conduct of defendants? Would it matter that the federal antitrust laws grant a claim to anyone injured by a violation of the act?

The "virtual representation" idea may be quite limited. For example, in Pollard v. Cockrell, 578 F.2d 1002 (5th Cir.1978), plaintiffs sued in federal court challenging the constitutionality of ordinances regulating massage parlors. Defendants claimed that they were bound by the earlier decision of a state court rejecting the same challenges in a suit brought by other massage parlors represented by the same lawyers. The court refused to bind the federal plaintiffs because there was no showing of any other relationship between the two groups of plaintiffs. "Virtual representation demands the existence of an express or implied legal relationship in which parties to the first suit are accountable to non-parties who file a subsequent suit raising identical issues." Id. at 1008.

Contrast Terrell v. DeConna, 877 F.2d 1267 (5th Cir.1989), where the court held that a spouse seeking to recover for loss of consortium is barred by collateral estoppel from relitigating defendant's liability for an accident if the injured spouse has earlier failed in an action against this defendant. The court rejected a virtual representation argument, but found the case different from Freeman v. Lester Coggins Trucking Inc. (discussed in *Benson and Ford*): "Although close family relationships will not alone suffice to establish privity between successive parties for purposes of issue or claim preclusion, the relevant considerations are different when, as in this case but unlike in *Freeman,* the successor plaintiff's claims are also derivative from the first plaintiff's claims." The court also cited commentary suggesting that a claim for loss of consortium should be barred, whatever the outcome of the injured spouse's litigation, unless pursued as part of that litigation. See 18 C. Wright, A. Miller & E. Cooper, Federal Practice & Procedure § 4459 at 525–26.

5. Tyus v. Schoemehl, 93 F.3d 449 (8th Cir. 1996), reflects a broad view of virtual representation. There African–American officials filed suit challenging the districting of the city as violating the Voting Rights Act. When disagreements arose among plaintiffs, some attempted to withdraw from the case and these dissidents, along with others, filed a second case. In the original case, defendants moved for summary judgment, and the remaining plaintiffs filed only limited materials in opposition to that motion. The dissidents were denied leave to file supplemental materials opposing summary judgment, and the court later granted defendants' motion for summary judgment and denied the request by the dissidents to withdraw from the first case.

The preclusion problems then arose in the new suit. Plaintiffs there sought to drop the plaintiffs who had participated in the first suit, although they had the same lawyer as plaintiffs in the first suit. The district court granted summary judgment for defendants on issue preclusion grounds, and the court of appeals affirmed under the virtual representation theory. Characterizing the Fifth Circuit's view of virtual representation as limited to cases of an express or implied legal relationship, the court opted for "wider use of virtual representation." It said that this approach depends upon a "special relationship between the parties justifying preclusion," but acknowledged that "there is no clear test for determining the applicability of the doctrine." Identity of interest between the current and former parties is necessary, but other factors such as participation in the earlier litigation, apparent acquiescence, or deliberate attempts to avoid the effect of the prior litigation are needed as well. The court found the doctrine particularly appropriate in public law cases, where a plaintiff victory is likely to benefit the nonparties without their participation, thereby deterring intervention. Given the history of the first case and the identity of interest of the nonparties and the original plaintiffs (all elected African–American officials), the court was satisfied these circumstances were satisfied. The later plaintiffs objected to the lackluster opposition to defendants' summary judgment motion and raised due process concerns, but the court said that it would look only to whether there was an incentive to litigate rather than actual performance.

For a narrower view of virtual representation, see Tice v. American Airlines, Inc., 162 F.3d 966 (7th Cir.1998) (refusing to apply virtual representation in suit challenging airline's policy regarding rights of older pilots that had been upheld in earlier litigation brought by other pilots); see also Bone, Rethinking the "Day in Court" Ideal and Nonparty Preclusion, 67 N.Y.U.L.Rev. 193 (1992) (examining historical background and policy bases for binding nonparties).

6. Ultimately, due process limits binding nonparties through virtual representation. In Richards v. Jefferson County, Alabama, 517 U.S. 793, 116 S.Ct. 1761, 135 L.Ed.2d 76 (1996), the Supreme Court therefore held that state-law preclusion principles could not foreclose a second suit challenging the constitutionality of a tax on the basis that other litigants had asserted similar challenges in an earlier suit. In South Central Bell Tel. Co. v. Alabama, 526 U.S. 160, 119 S.Ct. 1180, 143 L.Ed.2d 258 (1999), the Court reaffirmed that ruling even though the later litigants were represented by the same lawyer. Despite that shared representation by counsel, it reasoned, there was "no special relationship between the earlier and later plaintiffs." It added that "[t]he two relevant cases involve different plaintiffs and different tax years. Neither is a class action, and no one claims that there is 'privity' or some other special relationship between the two sets of plaintiffs; hence, the Case Two plaintiffs are strangers to Case One, and * * * they cannot be bound by the earlier judgment."

7. Virtual representation may have negative implications for the right to intervene. In People Who Care v. Rockford Board of Education, 68 F.3d 172 (7th Cir.1995), an individual who had previously filed a number of state-court suits challenging taxes that were levied to fund remedial educational programs sought to intervene in a federal-court suit challenging the Board's reorganization plan that was related to the remedial programs. He claimed he would be prejudiced if not allowed to intervene because his interests were so closely aligned with those of the plaintiff organization that he would be bound by res judicata under virtual representation. The court upheld denial of intervention, commenting that "if he is so closely aligned with * * * the parties that they are his virtual representatives, then his concerns have certainly received adequate representation."

8. What is the justification for binding "represented" persons? Consider McCoid, A Single Package for Multiparty Disputes, 28 Stan.L.Rev. 707, 716–17 (1976):

> I believe that consent and/or necessity are the principal supports of all res judicata privity categories based on representation, a concept that covers a number of quite different relationships. * * * Several relationships, such as trustee-beneficiary and agent-principal, are contractual, and the role of one party is understood to include representation in litigation. Even where there is no prearrangement there may be a subsequent assent, such as accepting the representation of a personal representative, which amounts to the same thing. In these cases representation is supported by consent. In still other cases representation flows from necessity. This factor itself is a broad one covering a variety of exigencies such as incompetency (guardian-ward), need for marketable title (unborn remaindermen), and need for unified estate administration (administrator-estate beneficiary). The common element is the need to go forward with litigation which will be effective.

9. Beyond representational grounds for binding nonparties, the law prescribes special rules of preclusion in a number of substantive contexts. The most common example binds successors in interest by judgments concerning interests in property. Recall Hansberry v. Lee, supra p. 291; see Restatement (Second) of Judgments §§ 43; 44. Similarly, where an injured person sues and recovers for his injuries, but later dies from them, special rules apply concerning preclusion in survival and wrongful death actions. Restatement (Second) of Judgments §§ 46; 47. Where one is obligated to indemnify another against the claim asserted in a suit, there are special rules on preclusion if the indemnitor is notified of the suit and given an opportunity to participate. See id., §§ 57; 58. Finally, actions by partners on behalf of a partnership usually bind the other partners. Id. § 60.

10. In *Benson and Ford,* Enterprise argued that Ford should have been required to join the first suit and, having failed to do so, was bound by the result. Cf. Provident Tradesmens Bank & Trust Co. v. Patterson, 390 U.S. 102, 114, 88 S.Ct. 733, 740, 19 L.Ed.2d 936 (1968) (nonparty who "purposefully bypassed an adequate opportunity to intervene" might be foreclosed by the outcome reached in his absence). Is this consistent with Rule 19 (governing "necessary parties")? Would it mean that all who have a right to intervene are necessary parties?

In Martin v. Wilks, 490 U.S. 755, 109 S.Ct. 2180, 104 L.Ed.2d 835 (1989), the Court rejected arguments for a rule of mandatory intervention. Plaintiffs there were white firefighters who challenged preferences in promotion for African–American firefighters given pursuant to the decree in an earlier employment discrimination case in which these whites were not parties. The defendant city argued that plaintiffs could not attack the provisions of the earlier decree collaterally because they should have intervened. The Supreme Court held that they could not be required to intervene to protect their rights, and therefore that they could proceed with their suit.

The Civil Rights Act of 1991 contained provisions aimed at overturning certain aspects of Martin v. Wilks. It insulated employment practices implementing a litigated or consent judgment against later attack by a person who had, prior to the entry of judgment, actual notice of the proposed judgment and its possible adverse effect and a "reasonable opportunity to present objections to such judgment." It further insulated such employment practices against later attack by a person without notice or an opportunity to present objections if that person's interests "were adequately represented by another person who had previously challenged the judgment or order on the same legal grounds and with a similar factual situation." 42 U.S.C.A. § 2000e–2(n)(1). Did this clarify what constitutes a "purposeful bypass" of an opportunity to intervene?

Assume that the objector is allowed to intervene. Should the intervenor be bound by a judgment if not given the full rights of a party? Increasingly courts grant intervention on condition that the intervenor not file separate pleadings, or not call separate witnesses, or only communicate with the court through the counsel of the side on which it has intervened. How should a court decide whether these limitations are so incapacitating as to prevent preclusion? Note the relationship between intervention and preclusion. For intervention of right, one must demonstrate that "the disposition of the action may as a practical matter impair or impede 'his ability to protect his interest relating to the property or transaction that is the subject of the action.' " Rule 24(a). See People Who Care v. Rockford Board of Education, 68 F.3d 172, 179 (7th Cir. 1995) (finding a would-be intervenor had no risk of preclusion and "if his interests are so similar to those of the parties in this case that his concerns were fully represented, then he has no right to intervene").

11.   Enterprise also argued that it is unfair that although it might be foreclosed from relitigating had it lost the *Shelby* case, it must relitigate against Ford although it won. Is there equitable appeal to this argument? We turn now to the doctrine of mutuality, which, until recently, prevented such uneven application of estoppel.

2.   *Mutuality of Estoppel*

The traditional view of collateral estoppel accepted the principle that estoppel must be mutual, which is referred to as the doctrine of "mutuality of estoppel." It rested on the principle that a person should not benefit from collateral estoppel unless he would also have been bound by the prior judgment. This approach was followed in the Restatement of Judgments § 99 (1942). The requirement of mutuality was viewed an as elementary aspect of fairness under due process, as well as a necessary limitation of the scope of an in personam judgment.

An exception to the mutuality doctrine arose in the area of indemnity. Assume that a person involved in an accident with the master's car, which was driven by a servant, sued the servant and lost and then sued the master. The master was not a party to the action, nor in privity with the servant, and since the master couldn't be bound by the judgment if the servant had lost, the mutuality rule would prohibit the master from benefitting from it. Nevertheless, courts allowed the master to use the judgment in favor of the servant to prevent the plaintiff from relitigating the issues of negligence decided against him in the first suit. This was viewed as a limited exception to protect the master's right of indemnity where the third-party had chosen the structure of the first suit and had full opportunity to litigate the issues. Good Health Dairy Products Corp. v. Emery, 275 N.Y. 14, 9 N.E.2d 758 (1937); Restatement of Judgments § 96 (1942).

Among the earliest, and most influential, opinions to reject the mutuality requirement was Bernhard v. Bank of America, 19 Cal.2d 807, 122 P.2d 892 (1942). There Mrs. Bernhard sued the executor of an estate of which she was a beneficiary, claiming he had converted to his own use money from the deceased's bank account. Judgment was for the executor on a finding that the money was a gift to him from the deceased. Mrs. Bernhard then sued the bank for allowing the executor to withdraw the money. The critical issue was whether the executor had a right to the money. Under the mutuality doctrine, the bank was not a party to the first suit and since it would not have been bound had the executor lost, it could not take advantage of the favorable judgment in the executor's favor. Nevertheless the court allowed the bank to collaterally estop Mrs. Bernhard from relitigating the issue of the ownership of the money taken by the executor.

Justice Traynor found that while "due process of law forbids the assertion of a plea of res judicata *against* a party" unless he was a party or in privity with a party, there is no compelling reason "for requiring that the party *asserting* the plea of res judicata must have been a party, or in privity with a party, to the earlier litigation." He thus shifted the inquiry away from whether the person asserting the preclusion would have been bound by the judgment to whether the party against whom it was asserted had a full and fair opportunity to litigate the issue in the first suit.

In Blonder–Tongue Laboratories, Inc. v. University of Illinois Foundation, 402 U.S. 313, 91 S.Ct. 1434, 28 L.Ed.2d 788 (1971), the Supreme Court abandoned mutuality as a matter of federal law, at least to the extent of permitting the "defensive use" of issue preclusion by a person not a party to the first suit against a plaintiff who was a party to the first suit. The Court questioned "whether it is any longer tenable to afford a litigant more than one full and fair opportunity for judicial resolution of the same issue." Id. at 328. It stated, however, that a judgment would not preclude a losing party from relitigating an issue if he could demonstrate that the first action failed to allow him a "fair opportunity procedurally, substantively, and evidentially to pursue his claim." Id. at 333.

PARKLANE HOSIERY CO. v. SHORE

Supreme Court of the United States, 1979.
439 U.S. 322, 99 S.Ct. 645, 58 L.Ed.2d 552.

JUSTICE STEWART delivered the opinion of the Court.

This case presents the question whether a party who has had issues of fact adjudicated adversely to it in an equitable action may be collaterally estopped from relitigating the same issues before a jury in a subsequent legal action brought against it by a new party.

The respondent brought this stockholder's class action against the petitioners in a Federal District Court. The complaint alleged that the petitioners, Parklane Hosiery Co., Inc. (Parklane), and 13 of its officers, directors, and stockholders, had issued a materially false and misleading proxy statement in connection with a merger. The proxy statement, according to the complaint, had violated [federal securities laws and regulations]. The complaint sought damages, rescission of the merger, and recovery of costs.

Before this action came to trial, the SEC filed suit against the same defendants in the Federal District Court, alleging that the proxy statement that had been issued by Parklane was materially false and misleading in essentially the same respects as those that had been alleged in the respondent's complaint. Injunctive relief was requested. After a 4–day trial, the District Court found that the proxy statement was materially false and misleading in the respects alleged. The Court of Appeals for the Second Circuit affirmed this judgment.

The respondent in the present case then moved for partial summary judgment against the petitioners, asserting that the petitioners were collaterally estopped from relitigating the issues that had been resolved against them in the action brought by the SEC.[2] The District Court denied the motion on the ground that such an application of collateral estoppel would deny the petitioners their Seventh Amendment right to a jury trial. The Court of Appeals for the Second Circuit reversed, holding that a party who has had issues of fact determined against him after a full and fair opportunity to litigate in a nonjury trial is collaterally estopped from obtaining a subsequent jury trial of these same issues of fact. The appellate court concluded that "the Seventh Amendment preserves the right to jury trial only with respect to issues of fact, [and] once those issues have been fully and fairly adjudicated in a prior proceeding, nothing remains for trial, either with or without a jury."
* * *

I

The threshold question to be considered is whether, quite apart from the right to a jury trial under the Seventh Amendment, the petitioners can be precluded from relitigating facts resolved adversely to them in a prior equitable proceeding with another party under the general law of collateral estoppel. Specifically, we must determine whether a litigant who was not a party to a prior judgment may nevertheless

---

2. A private plaintiff in an action under the proxy rules is not entitled to relief simply by demonstrating that the proxy solicitation was materially false and misleading. The plaintiff must also show that he was injured and prove damages. Since the SEC action was limited to a determination of whether the proxy statement contained materially false and misleading information, the respondent conceded that he would still have to prove these other elements of his prima facie case in the private action. The petitioners' right to a jury trial on those remaining issues is not contested.

use that judgment "offensively" to prevent a defendant from relitigating issues resolved in the earlier proceeding.

A

Collateral estoppel, like the related doctrine of res judicata, has the dual purpose of protecting litigants from the burden of relitigating an identical issue with the same party or his privy and of promoting judicial economy by preventing needless litigation. Blonder–Tongue Laboratories, Inc. v. University of Illinois Foundation, 402 U.S. 313, 328–329, 91 S.Ct. 1434, 1442–1443, 28 L.Ed.2d 788. Until relatively recently, however, the scope of collateral estoppel was limited by the doctrine of mutuality of parties. Under this mutuality doctrine, neither party could use a prior judgment as an estoppel against the other unless both parties were bound by the judgment. Based on the premise that it is somehow unfair to allow a party to use a prior judgment when he himself would not be so bound,[7] the mutuality requirement provided a party who had litigated and lost in a previous action an opportunity to relitigate identical issues with new parties.

By failing to recognize the obvious difference in position between a party who has never litigated an issue and one who has fully litigated and lost, the mutuality requirement was criticized almost from its inception. Recognizing the validity of this criticism, the Court in Blonder–Tongue Laboratories, Inc. v. University of Illinois Foundation, supra, abandoned the mutuality requirement, at least in cases where a patentee seeks to relitigate the validity of a patent after a federal court in a previous lawsuit has already declared it invalid. The "broader question" before the Court, however, was "whether it is any longer tenable to afford a litigant more than one full and fair opportunity for judicial resolution of the same issue." 402 U.S., at 328, 91 S.Ct., at 1442. The Court strongly suggested a negative answer to that question:

"In any lawsuit where a defendant, because of the mutuality principle, is forced to present a complete defense on the merits to a claim which the plaintiff has fully litigated and lost in a prior action, there is an arguable misallocation of resources. To the extent the defendant in the second suit may not win by asserting, without contradiction, that the plaintiff had fully and fairly, but unsuccessfully, litigated the same claim in the prior suit, the defendant's time and money are diverted from alternative uses—productive or otherwise—to relitigation of a decided issue. And, still assuming that the issue was resolved correctly in the first suit, there is reason to be concerned about the plaintiff's allocation of resources. Permitting repeated litigation of the same issue as long as the supply of unrelated defendants holds out reflects either the aura of the gaming table or 'a lack of discipline and of disinterestedness on the part of the lower courts, hardly a worthy or wise basis for fashioning

---

7. It is a violation of due process for a judgment to be binding on a litigant who was not a party or a privy and therefore has never had an opportunity to be heard. Hansberry v. Lee, 311 U.S. 32, 40.

rules of procedure.' Kerotest Mfg. Co. v. C–O–Two Co., 342 U.S. 180, 185, 72 S.Ct. 219, 222, 96 L.Ed. 200 (1952). Although neither judges, the parties, nor the adversary system performs perfectly in all cases, the requirement of determining whether the party against whom an estoppel is asserted had a full and fair opportunity to litigate is a most significant safeguard." Id., at 329, 91 S.Ct., at 1443.

B

The *Blonder-Tongue* case involved defensive use of collateral estoppel—a plaintiff was estopped from asserting a claim that the plaintiff had previously litigated and lost against another defendant. The present case, by contrast, involves offensive use of collateral estoppel—a plaintiff is seeking to estop a defendant from relitigating the issues which the defendant previously litigated and lost against another plaintiff. In both the offensive and defensive use situations, the party against whom estoppel is asserted has litigated and lost in an earlier action. Nevertheless, several reasons have been advanced why the two situations should be treated differently.

First, offensive use of collateral estoppel does not promote judicial economy in the same manner as defensive use does. Defensive use of collateral estoppel precludes a plaintiff from relitigating identical issues by merely "switching adversaries." Bernhard v. Bank of America Nat. Trust & Savings Assn., 19 Cal.2d, at 813, 122 P.2d, at 895. Thus defensive collateral estoppel gives a plaintiff a strong incentive to join all potential defendants in the first action if possible. Offensive use of collateral estoppel, on the other hand, creates precisely the opposite incentive. Since a plaintiff will be able to rely on a previous judgment against a defendant but will not be bound by that judgment if the defendant wins, the plaintiff has every incentive to adopt a "wait and see" attitude, in the hope that the first action by another plaintiff will result in a favorable judgment. Thus offensive use of collateral estoppel will likely increase rather than decrease the total amount of litigation, since potential plaintiffs will have everything to gain and nothing to lose by not intervening in the first action.[13]

A second argument against offensive use of collateral estoppel is that it may be unfair to a defendant. If a defendant in the first action is sued for small or nominal damages, he may have little incentive to defend vigorously, particularly if future suits are not foreseeable. Cf. Berner v. British Commonwealth Pac. Airlines, 346 F.2d 532 (CA2) (application of offensive collateral estoppel denied where defendant did not appeal an adverse judgment awarding $35,000 and defendant was later sued for over $7 million). Allowing offensive collateral estoppel may also be unfair to a defendant if the judgment relied upon as a basis for the estoppel is itself inconsistent with one or more previous judgments in favor of the

---

13. The Restatement (Second) of Judgments (Tent. Draft No. 2, 1975) § 88(3) provides that application of collateral estoppel may be denied if the party asserting it "could have effected joinder in the first action between himself and his present adversary."

defendant.[14] Still another situation where it might be unfair to apply offensive estoppel is where the second action affords the defendant procedural opportunities unavailable in the first action that could readily cause a different result.[15]

We have concluded that the preferable approach for dealing with these problems in the federal courts is not to preclude the use of offensive collateral estoppel, but to grant trial courts broad discretion to determine when it should be applied. The general rule should be that in cases where a plaintiff could easily have joined in the earlier action or where, either for the reasons discussed above or for other reasons, the application of offensive estoppel would be unfair to a defendant, a trial judge should not allow the use of offensive collateral estoppel.

In the present case, however, none of the circumstances that might justify reluctance to allow the offensive use of collateral estoppel is present. The application of offensive collateral estoppel will not here reward a private plaintiff who could have joined in the previous action, since the respondent probably could not have joined in the injunctive action brought by the SEC even had he so desired.[17] Similarly, there is no unfairness to the petitioners in applying offensive collateral estoppel in this case. First, in light of the serious allegations made in the SEC's complaint against the petitioners, as well as the foreseeability of subsequent private suits that typically follow a successful Government judgment, the petitioners had every incentive to litigate the SEC lawsuit fully and vigorously. Second, the judgment in the SEC action was not inconsistent with any previous decision. Finally, there will in the respondent's action be no procedural opportunities available to the petitioners that were unavailable in the first action of a kind that might be likely to cause a different result.[19]

14. In Professor Currie's familiar example, a railroad collision injures 50 passengers all of whom bring separate actions against the railroad. After the railroad wins the first 25 suits, a plaintiff wins in suit 26. Professor Currie argues that offensive use of collateral estoppel should not be applied so as to allow plaintiffs 27 through 50 automatically to recover. Currie, [Mutuality of Estoppel: Limits of the *Bernhard* Doctrine, 9 Stanford L.Rev. 281 (1957)], at 304.

15. If, for example, the defendant in the first action was forced to defend in an inconvenient forum and therefore was unable to engage in full scale discovery or call witnesses, application of offensive collateral estoppel may be unwarranted. Indeed, differences in available procedures may sometimes justify not allowing a prior judgment to have estoppel effect in a subsequent action even between the same parties, or where defensive estoppel is asserted against a plaintiff who has litigated and lost. The problem of unfairness is particularly acute in cases of offensive estoppel, however, because the defendant against whom estoppel is asserted typically will not have chosen the forum in the first action.

17. SEC v. Everest Management Corp., 475 F.2d 1236, 1240 (CA2) ("[T]he complicating effect of the additional issues and the additional parties outweighs any advantages of a single disposition of the common issues"). Moreover, consolidation of a private action with one brought by the SEC without its consent is prohibited by statute. 15 U.S.C. § 78u(g).

19. It is true, of course, that the petitioners in the present action would be entitled to a jury trial of the issues bearing on whether the proxy statement was materially false and misleading had the SEC action never been brought—a matter to be discussed in Part II of this opinion. But the presence or absence of a jury as fact finder is basically neutral, quite unlike, for example, the necessity of defending the first lawsuit in an inconvenient forum.

We conclude, therefore, that none of the considerations that would justify a refusal to allow the use of offensive collateral estoppel is present in this case. Since the petitioners received a "full and fair" opportunity to litigate their claims in the SEC action, the contemporary law of collateral estoppel leads inescapably to the conclusion that the petitioners are collaterally estopped from relitigating the question of whether the proxy statement was materially false and misleading.

II

The question that remains is whether, notwithstanding the law of collateral estoppel, the use of offensive collateral estoppel in this case would violate the petitioners' Seventh Amendment right to a jury trial.

[The court observed that its jury-trial decisions in *Beacon Theatres* [supra p. 531] and *Katchen* [supra pp. 544–45] assumed that relitigation of issues common to both legal and equitable claims could be foreclosed by res judicata or collateral estoppel. It found no persuasive reason why the meaning of the Seventh Amendment should depend on whether mutuality of parties is present and thus rejected the argument that non-mutual estoppel violates the Seventh Amendment.]

The judgment of the Court of Appeals is affirmed.

JUSTICE REHNQUIST, dissenting.

* * *

I think it is clear that petitioners were denied their Seventh Amendment right to a jury trial in this case. Neither respondent nor the Court doubts that at common law as it existed in 1791, petitioners would have been entitled in the private action to have a jury determine whether the proxy statement was false and misleading in the respects alleged. The reason is that at common law in 1791, collateral estoppel was permitted only where the parties in the first action were identical to, or in privity with, the parties to the subsequent action. It was not until 1971 that the doctrine of mutuality was abrogated by this Court in certain limited circumstances. Blonder–Tongue Laboratories, Inc. v. University of Illinois Foundation, 402 U.S. 313, 91 S.Ct. 1434, 28 L.Ed.2d 788. But developments in the judge-made doctrine of collateral estoppel, however salutary, cannot, consistent with the Seventh Amendment, contract in any material fashion the right to a jury trial that a defendant would have enjoyed in 1791. In the instant case, resort to the doctrine of collateral estoppel does more than merely contract the right to a jury trial: It eliminates the right entirely and therefore contravenes the Seventh Amendment.

The Court responds, however, that at common law "a litigant was not entitled to have a jury (in a subsequent action at law between the same parties) determine issues that had been previously adjudicated by a chancellor in equity," and that "petitioners have advanced no persuasive reason ... why the meaning of the Seventh Amendment should depend on whether or not mutuality of parties is present." But that is tantamount to saying that since a party would not be entitled to a jury trial if he brought an equitable action, there is no persuasive reason why he should receive a jury trial on virtually the same issues if instead he chooses to bring his lawsuit in the nature of a legal action. The persuasive reason is that the Seventh Amendment requires that a party's right to jury trial which existed at common law be "preserved" from incursions by the government or the judiciary. Whether this Court believes that use of a jury trial in a particular instance is necessary, or fair or repetitive is simply irrelevant. If that view is "rigid," it is the Constitution which commands that rigidity. To hold otherwise is to rewrite the Seventh Amendment so that a party is guaranteed a jury trial in civil cases unless this Court thinks that a jury trial would be inappropriate.

* * *

Relying on Galloway v. United States, 319 U.S. 372, 63 S.Ct. 1077, 87 L.Ed. 1458 (1943) [supra p. 607], Champlin Refining Co., [283 U.S. 494, 51 S.Ct. 513, 75 L.Ed. 1188 (1931)], and Fidelity & Deposit Co. v. United States, 187 U.S. 315, 23 S.Ct. 120, 47 L.Ed. 194 (1902), the Court seems to suggest that the offensive use of collateral estoppel in this case is permissible under the limited principle that a mere procedural change that does not invade the province of the jury and a defendant's right thereto to a greater extent than authorized by the common law is permissible. But the Court's actions today constitute a far greater infringement of the defendant's rights than it ever before has sanctioned. In *Galloway,* the Court upheld the modern form of directed verdict against a Seventh Amendment challenge, but it is clear that a similar form of directed verdict existed at common law in 1791. The modern form did not materially alter the function of the jury. Similarly, the modern device of summary judgment was found not to violate the Seventh Amendment because in 1791 a demurrer to the evidence, a procedural device substantially similar to summary judgment, was a common practice. The procedural devices of summary judgment and directed verdict are direct descendants of their common-law antecedents. They accomplish nothing more than could have been done at common law, albeit by a more cumbersome procedure. * * *

By contrast, the development of nonmutual estoppel is a substantial departure from the common law and its use in this case completely deprives petitioners of their right to have a jury determine contested issues of fact. * * *

Even accepting, arguendo, the majority's position that there is no violation of the Seventh Amendment here, I nonetheless would not sanction the use of collateral estoppel in this case. * * * In my view, it is "unfair" to apply offensive collateral estoppel where the party who is sought to be estopped has not had an opportunity to have the facts of his case determined by a jury. Since in this case petitioners were not entitled to a jury trial in the Securities and Exchange Commission (SEC) lawsuit, I would not estop them from relitigating the issues determined in the

SEC suit before a jury in the private action. I believe that several factors militate in favor of this result.

First, the use of offensive collateral estoppel in this case runs counter to the strong federal policy favoring jury trials, even if it does not, as the majority holds, violate the Seventh Amendment. * * *

Second, I believe that the opportunity for a jury trial in the second action could easily lead to a different result from that obtained in the first action before the court and therefore that it is unfair to estop petitioners from relitigating the issues before a jury. This is the position adopted in the Restatement (Second) of Judgments, which disapproves of the application of offensive collateral estoppel where the defendant has an opportunity for a jury trial in the second lawsuit that was not available in the first action.[22] The Court accepts the proposition that it is unfair to apply offensive collateral estoppel "where the second action affords the defendant procedural opportunities unavailable in the first action that could readily cause a different result." Differences in discovery opportunities between the two actions are cited as examples of situations where it would be unfair to permit offensive collateral estoppel. But in the Court's view, the fact that petitioners would have been entitled to a jury trial in the present action is not such a "procedural opportunit[y]" because "the presence or absence of a jury as factfinder is basically *neutral,* quite unlike, for example, the necessity of defending the first lawsuit in an inconvenient forum." Ante, n.19 (emphasis added).

* * *

Contrary to the majority's supposition, juries can make a difference, and our cases have, before today at least, recognized this obvious fact. * * * Jurors bring to a case their common sense and community values; their "very inexperience is an asset because it secures a fresh perception of each trial, avoiding the stereotypes said to infect the judicial eye." H. Kalven & H. Zeisel, The American Jury 8 (1966).

The ultimate irony of today's decision is that its potential for significantly conserving the resources of either the litigants or the judiciary is doubtful at best. That being the case, I see absolutely no reason to frustrate so cavalierly the important federal policy favoring jury decisions of disputed fact questions. The instant case is an apt example of the minimal savings that will be accomplished by the Court's decision. As the Court admits, even if petitioners are collaterally estopped from relitigating whether the proxy was materially false and misleading, they are still entitled to have a jury determine whether respondent was injured by the alleged misstatements and the amount of damages, if any, sustained by respondent. Thus, a jury must be impan-

---

22. Restatement (Second) of Judgments § 88(2), comment d (Tent. Draft No. 2, Apr. 15, 1975). * * * [T]he Reporter's note states: "The differences between the procedures available in the first and second actions, while not sufficient to deny issue preclusion between the same parties, may warrant a refusal to carry over preclusion to an action involving another party."

eled in this case in any event. The time saved by not trying the issue of whether the proxy was materially false and misleading before the jury is likely to be insubstantial. It is just as probable that today's decision will have the result of coercing defendants to agree to consent orders or settlements in agency enforcement actions in order to preserve their right to jury trial in the private actions. In that event, the Court, for no compelling reason, will have simply added a powerful club to the administrative agencies' arsenals that even Congress was unwilling to provide them.

Notes and Questions

1. For a plaintiff to be denied use of offensive collateral estoppel (arising from an earlier judgment in which he was not a party) because he could have joined the first suit, should the cost and inconvenience of joining the earlier suit be considered? Is a person required to go to another state to join a suit there in order not to be labelled a "wait and see" plaintiff who is excluded from the benefits of the judgment? Must he do so even if the other state's law is less favorable to him? Should his financial ability or legal sophistication be taken into account?

2. Must a plaintiff who filed suit first join a later suit in order to take advantage of a judgment arising out of it? In Polk v. Montgomery County, Maryland, 782 F.2d 1196 (4th Cir.1986), Polk was arrested at her home for failure to obtain a Maryland drivers' license and related minor offenses. She was forced to disrobe and submit to a strip search by a jail matron in the presence of another female detainee. She sued the county for violation of her civil rights, and later a second plaintiff filed a similar suit that was certified as a class action. The class action came to trial first, and the county lost. Should Ms. Polk be able to use the judgment offensively?

3. Consider the following cases concerning the "wait and see" plaintiff problem:

(a) In Hauser v. Krupp Steel Producers, Inc., 761 F.2d 204 (5th Cir. 1985), plaintiff was the wife of a truck driver injured in a highway accident. Her husband recovered for his injuries against the owner of the other vehicle in a suit in which she did not join. She then sued for loss of consortium. The court found she was not entitled to offensive use of collateral estoppel on the finding that the other vehicle was responsible for the accident because she failed to present a valid reason for not joining her husband's earlier action. What would be a valid reason?

(b) Defendant's oil well exploded, killing two workers and injuring a third. The families of the deceased workers brought a joint wrongful death action and obtained a judgment. The injured worker then filed his own suit and invoked collateral estoppel to preclude relitigation of the liability issue. There was no procedural bar to his joining the first action. Nations v. Sun Oil Co., 695 F.2d 933 (5th Cir.1983), held he was entitled to wait until the consequences of his injuries were clear and so was not a "wait and see" plaintiff denied the preclusive effect of the judgment.

(c) Despite cases like *Nations*, the *Parklane* concern with "wait and see" parties continues to have resonance. In Dana v. E.S. Originals, Inc., 342

F.3d 1320 (Fed.Cir.2003), plaintiff sued for infringement of his patent for "flashing Discoshoes" by defendants' marketing footwear with flashing lights. He moved for summary judgment as to liability on the ground that defendants had previously been sued in a California court by a company that had purchased the patent from him. After the California court found the patent was enforceable, the parties entered a consent decree that enjoined the defendants from marketing infringing footwear, but stated that it would have not collateral estoppel effect in favor of any party. Plaintiff in the federal suit then sued for infringement that took place *before* he had assigned the patent to the plaintiff in the California suit. The district court allowed collateral estoppel because defendants were aware that plaintiff might be "a potential adversary in a future action and attempted to preclude future litigation by private agreement in lieu of joining the assignor." The Federal Circuit found this was not the right inquiry and remanded for the lower court to determine whether plaintiff "could easily have joined the earlier action." Plaintiff argued that he had not joined the California suit "for reasons of expense or because he had no right to join that action." Should failure to join because of expense protect him from being considered a "wait and see" party not entitled to invoke collateral estoppel? Would a finding that the plaintiff in the California suit was not willing to join him as a plaintiff, and that he would therefore have to intervene, protect him from being a "wait and see" party?

4. When will "tactical" considerations justify not joining the earlier suit? In Starker v. United States, 602 F.2d 1341 (9th Cir.1979), the son sued the IRS and won a $37,000 tax refund, and his father then sued for a $300,000 tax refund arising out of the same transaction. The court "decline[d] to speculate on motivation," finding there were valid tactical reasons for the father's not joining the first suit. In contrast, Richardson Oil Co. v. Cook, 617 F.Supp. 669 (W.D.Ark.1985), involved an accident between an oil company truck and another truck in which the oil company's driver was killed. The oil company sued the driver of the other truck in federal court for property damage, and its driver's widow sued the same defendant in state court for wrongful death. The widow's case went to trial first, and she received a judgment with findings that the defendant was negligent. The federal court refused to apply collateral estoppel, finding there was no reason that the oil company could not have joined the widow's suit and so, as a "wait and see" plaintiff, it was not entitled to use the earlier judgment. Is this consistent with *Starker*? What tactical reasons might the oil company have had in not joining the widow's suit?

5. What criteria should be used to judge if a party had a sufficient "incentive to litigate" the issues sought to be precluded? In Benjamin v. Coughlin, 643 F.Supp. 351 (S.D.N.Y.1986), a class of Rastafarians sought to enjoin the N.Y. Department of Corrections from shaving their hair, alleging violation of their religious beliefs. In two prior actions by single Rastafarian plaintiffs, N.Y. state courts held that shaving violated their religious beliefs. Did the state have sufficient incentive to litigate those actions? The court allowed the plaintiffs to use the preclusive effect of the judgment.

6. How much "inconsistency of prior judgments" will preclude offensive use of collateral estoppel? Is one prior inconsistent suit sufficient? Sometimes a number of similar suits will go to judgment before a plaintiff

attempts to take advantage of one of the favorable judgments. In Hardy v. Johns–Manville Sales Co., supra p. 1146, the court, noting that of 70 prior cases defendants had won 35, refused to accord preclusive effect. Should the court have looked to the nature of the cases, including whether they were hotly contested? Even in a group of 70 prior cases, could a court determine that one was regarded by the parties, and particularly by the common defendant, as a "test case" and therefore accord it preclusive effect?

Note that Justice Rehnquist argues in his dissent in *Parklane* that a second trial could "easily" have led to a different result. Similarly, the court in Hardy v. Johns–Manville found the existence of prior defense verdicts important because "[o]ne jury's determination should not * * * bind another jury's determination of an issue over which there are equally reasonable resolutions of doubt." 681 F.2d at 346. How can a court know whether there are "equally reasonable" resolutions of the case? Recall the standard for taking the case from the jury on a motion for judgment as a matter of law. Does that standard mean that the case should not go to the jury unless it could reasonably decide either way? If so, does this mean that in any case that should go to the jury, the jury's verdict should not have collateral estoppel effect when invoked by nonparties?

7. The court in State Farm Fire & Casualty Co. v. Century Home Components, Inc., 550 P.2d 1185 (Ore.1976), was faced with the problem of inconsistent judgments. Approximately 50 suits were filed on behalf of persons whose goods were damaged in a fire alleged to have been caused by defendant's negligence. The first case tried resulted in a judgment for the defendant, but plaintiff appealed on the ground defendant failed to produce certain critical evidence. While that appeal was pending, the second and third cases were tried; defendant won the second and lost the third. Then the initial decision in the first case was reversed and, on retrial, defendant lost. All the other plaintiffs then conformed their complaints to those in the successful suits and asserted collateral estoppel as to liability. The court refused to apply offensive collateral estoppel because, due to defendant's victory in the second case, "we are not free to disregard incongruous results when they are looking us in the face." It noted, however, that "[w]e do not mean to say that one favorable determination can never be overcome and estoppel never applied despite the number of subsequent determinations to the contrary."

Plaintiffs in *Century Home* argued that the results were not incongruous because the cases were tried differently, but the court disagreed:

> We do not give much weight to variations in the wording of the pleadings, however, where essentially the same acts and omissions are alleged. To concentrate on slight discrepancies in the allegations of negligence would put defendant at a distinct disadvantage, for claimants could modify the wording after each judgment for defendant until one claimant prevailed, after which all remaining claimants could conform their complaints to that of the prevailing claimant and could then successfully claim that the prior judgments for defendant were based upon different issues.
>
> The thrust of plaintiff's argument must be that the jury in [the third case] and the court in [the retrial of the first case] adjudicated

defendant negligent in respects which were not considered by the jury in [the second case]. The records of the cases, however, do not permit such a conclusion. Since the jury in [the third case] returned a general verdict, we do not know in which respects it found defendant negligent and, given the substantial similarity of some of the allegations and the basic thrust of the negligence alleged, we are unable to conclude that it found defendant negligent on the basis of conduct not submitted to the jury in [the second case]. * * * Allegations of essentially the same conduct were submitted to the jury in [the second case] under proper instructions by the court, and the jury obviously found that defendant was not negligent in the respects specified by the court in [the retrial of the first case].

* * *

Plaintiffs maintain, however, that the circumstances of the [retrial of the first case] clearly indicate that it was the better tried of all the cases. They assert that the issues were more clearly defined, there was substantially more money at stake than in [the second case], defendant brought in additional experts to testify at considerable expense, the evidence regarding the fire, and particularly its origin, was more fully developed, and defendant was aware that the outcome might have a significant effect on the cases waiting in the wings.

The only relevant implication of plaintiffs' position is that, since [the retrial of the first case] was more fully tried, the result must be substantially better than the jury verdict in [the second case]. We decline the invitation to decide which case was the better tried, in which case the evidence more truly presented the facts, and which "full and fair opportunity" by defendant resulted in the "correct" decision. The existence of conflicting determinations of similar issues demonstrates that different bodies can legitimately draw different conclusions.

8. Courts are generally reluctant to deny issue preclusion on grounds of "inadequate procedural opportunity" when there was a reasonable opportunity for discovery and trial in the prior forum. In United States v. $100,000 in United States Currency, 602 F.Supp. 712 (S.D.N.Y.1985), an earlier bail hearing was found not to be a full and fair proceeding so as to preclude relitigation of issues determined there.

9. If a losing defendant, fearing the use of the judgment against him in other cases, enters into a generous settlement in exchange for an order vacating the judgment, should a later plaintiff be allowed to assert the vacated judgment as collateral estoppel? For an argument in favor of honoring such agreements, see Note, Avoiding Issue Preclusion by Settlement Conditioned Upon the Vacatur of Entered Judgments, 96 Yale L.J. 860 (1987). In Chemetron Corp. v. Business Funds, Inc., 682 F.2d 1149 (5th Cir.1982), the court held that where the final judgment entered in a prior securities fraud case was withdrawn after a settlement agreement, it would still be applied offensively against the defendant as to issues of fact adjudicated in the prior case where such application was determined not to be unfair. See also U.S. Bancorp Mortgage Co. v. Bonner Mall Partnership, 513 U.S. 18, 115 S.Ct. 386, 130 L.Ed.2d 233 (1994) (refusing to vacate lower court's judgment in case that settled on appeal because this "refined form of

collateral attack would * * * disturb the orderly operation of the federal judicial system").

10. Prior criminal case judgments may be given preclusive effect. In *Allen v. McCurry*, 449 U.S. 90, 101 S.Ct. 411, 66 L.Ed.2d 308 (1980), the plaintiff in a civil rights action, alleging violation of his Fourth Amendment rights by seizure of evidence, had earlier been convicted in a state court prosecution in which his motion to suppress the evidence on Fourth Amendment grounds was denied. The Supreme Court upheld a finding that the Fourth Amendment issue was precluded. Preclusive effect has been accorded to guilty pleas. *Rodriguez v. Schweiger*, 796 F.2d 930 (7th Cir.1986).

11. *Parklane* found that the judgment resulting from a judge trial in a solely equitable action would collaterally estop relitigation of the same issues in a subsequent legal action despite the right to trial by jury. What if both equitable and legal claims are brought in the same action, but the legal claims are erroneously dismissed? That was the situation in *Lytle v. Household Mfg., Inc.*, 494 U.S. 545, 110 S.Ct. 1331, 108 L.Ed.2d 504 (1990). A fired employee sued his employer for damages and injunctive relief, alleging race discrimination under both Title VII of the Civil Rights of 1964 (which is treated as an equitable claim for purposes of trial by jury, see pp. 555–57 supra) and 42 U.S.C.A. § 1981. The district court dismissed the § 1981 claims on the ground that Title VII provided the exclusive remedy. Then the court conducted a bench trial on the Title VII claims and entered judgment for the defendant. The Court of Appeals found the dismissal of the § 1981 claims was erroneous because the two remedies were distinct. However, it ruled that the court's findings on the Title VII claims collaterally estopped plaintiff from relitigating the same issues in relation to his § 1981 claims.

The Supreme Court reversed, rejecting that analogy to *Parklane* and invoking right-to-jury-trial cases:

> Only the district Court's erroneous dismissal of the § 1981 claims enabled that court to resolve issues common to both claims, issues that otherwise would have been resolved by a jury. But for that erroneous ruling this case would be indistinguishable from Beacon Theatres [v. Westover, supra p. 531] and Dairy Queen [v. Wood, supra p. 539]. It would be anomalous to hold that a district court may not deprive a litigant of his right to a jury trial by resolving an equitable claim before a jury hears a legal claim raising common issues, but that a court may accomplish the same result by erroneously dismissing the legal claim.

The Court also commented that "the purposes served by collateral estoppel do not justify applying the doctrine to this case." Collateral estoppel was unnecessary, it said, to prevent multiple lawsuits because the case involved only one suit and there would be no dissipation of judicial resources in "needless litigation." But wouldn't a new trial be required? Yes, said the Court, but "relitigation of factual issues before a jury is no more 'needless' in this context than in cases in which a trial court erroneously concludes that a claim is equitable rather than legal, see, e.g., *Dairy Queen*, or that the resolution of an equitable claim can precede resolution of a legal claim, see, e.g., *Beacon Theatres*."

Is *Lytle* consistent with *Parklane*? *Ritter v. Mount St. Mary's College*, 814 F.2d 986 (4th Cir.1987), reached a different conclusion: "The effect of this error, just like the 'effect' of the prior suit in *Parklane*, is the same. Issues on which the plaintiff had a right to a jury determination were tried to the court. What the appellant in this case is in reality concerned about is not the error of the district court, which was rectified, but rather the 'harm' of the denial of jury trial, which resulted from the error." Does *Lytle* just reflect the Court's unwillingness to go that far in favoring finality over the right to jury trial?

12. The concerns over fairness and a conflict with the traditional purposes of collateral estoppel expressed in *Lytle* persuaded the Texas Supreme Court not to apply the doctrine in Sysco Food Services, Inc. v. Benjamin Trapnell, 890 S.W.2d 796 (Tex.1994). That suit resulted from the death of a woman from consuming sulfites at a Navy officers club buffet. The sulfites could have come from three foods she ate—potato whitener on the fruit salad, pie filling, or hash browns. The manufacturers of the three foods were sued in state court, and the Navy was sued in federal court under the Federal Tort Claims Act for negligence in using sulfites and failing to warn. This bifurcation was necessary because federal courts have exclusive jurisdiction over suits brought under the Federal Tort Claims Act, and at this time prior to the passage in 1990 of 28 U.S.C.A. § 1367, there was no supplemental jurisdiction over the additional parties (see supra p. 892). The federal court granted summary judgment for the Navy based on its finding that no potato whitener had been added to the fruit salad. The manufacturer of the potato whitener then moved for summary judgment in the state court on the ground that the plaintiffs were collaterally estopped from relitigating the finding that potato whitener was not added to the salad.

The Texas Supreme Court held that collateral estoppel was properly refused because doing so would not promote the goals served by the doctrine, citing *Lytle*. It would not conserve judicial resources because the two other manufacturers, who were not parties to the federal suit, could still relitigate whether there was potato whitener in the salad and therefore that the whitener, and not their products, caused the death. Likewise, the goal of protecting defendants from multiple suits would not be achieved by applying collateral estoppel here because the manufacturers were the only parties to the state-court suit. Could this reasoning prevent the application of collateral estoppel wherever the parties are not identical in the two suits?

13. Only a small number of states presently continue to adhere to the mutuality of parties requirement. *See* 1B J. Moore & J. Lucas, Moore's Federal Practice ¶ 0.441[3.2] (1995). Tennessee, one of these, permits mutual offensive collateral estoppel—that is, the plaintiff can foreclose a defendant from relitigating an issue that the defendant had previously litigated unsuccessfully in another action against the *same plaintiff*. A Tennessee court commented that this "use of mutual offensive collateral estoppel seems to provide all the benefits of the issue preclusion doctrine without any of the perceived undesirable consequences of nonmutual offensive collateral estoppel" since it "will not increase the total amount of litigation, and it will not necessarily be unfair to the defendant." Beaty v. McGraw, 15 S.W.3d 819, 826 (Tenn.Ct.App. 1998). However, it noted, "the trial court must take special care to ensure that the offensive application of the doctrine does not work a hardship on the party against whom the estoppel is asserted. See Remington Rand Corp. v. Amsterdam–Rotterdam Bank, N.V., 68 F.3d 1478,

1486 (2d Cir. 1995); Raytech Corp. v. White, 54 F.3d 187, 190 (3d Cir. 1995). In exercising its discretion, the trial court may consider (1) whether the plaintiff could have joined the former suit but decided instead to adopt a 'wait and see' attitude, (2) whether the defendant had an incentive to defend the former suit vigorously, and (3) whether the judgment on which the plaintiff seeks to rely is itself inconsistent with previous judgments against the defendant." Id.

3. *Collateral Attack on Class Action Judgments*

STEPHENSON v. DOW CHEMICAL CO.

United States Court of Appeals, Second Circuit, 2001.
273 F.3d 249, aff'd, 539 U.S. 111, 123 S.Ct. 2161 (2003).

Before: CARDAMONE and F.I. PARKER, Circuit Judges, and SPATT, District Judge.

PARKER, Circuit Judge.

This appeal requires us to determine the effect of the Supreme Court's landmark class action decisions in Amchem Products, Inc. v. Windsor, 521 U.S. 591, 117 S.Ct. 2231, 138 L.Ed.2d 689 (1997), and Ortiz v. Fibreboard Corp., 527 U.S. 815, 119 S.Ct. 2295, 144 L.Ed.2d 715 (1999), on a previously settled class action concerning exposure to Agent Orange during the Vietnam War.

* * *

I. BACKGROUND

* * *

The first Agent Orange litigation began in the late 1970s, when individual veterans and their families filed class action suits in the Northern District of Illinois and Southern and Eastern Districts of New York, alleging that exposure to Agent Orange caused them injury. In re "Agent Orange" Prod. Liab. Litig., 635 F.2d 987, 988 (2d Cir.1980) ("Agent Orange I"). By order of the MDL Panel, these actions were transferred to the Eastern District of New York and consolidated for pretrial purposes. Plaintiffs asserted claims of negligent manufacture, strict liability, breach of warranty, intentional tort and nuisance. In re "Agent Orange" Prod. Liab. Litig., 597 F.Supp. 740, 750 (E.D.N.Y.1984) ("Agent Orange III"); aff'd 818 F.2d 145 (2d Cir.1987).

In 1983, the district court certified the following class under Federal Rule of Civil Procedure 23(b)(3):

> those persons who were in the United States, New Zealand or Australian Armed Forces at any time from 1961 to 1972 who were injured while in or near Vietnam by exposure to Agent Orange or other phenoxy herbicides, including those composed in whole or in part of 2, 4, 5–trichlorophenoxyacetic acid or containing some amount of 2, 3, 7, 8–tetrachlorodibenzo-p-dioxin. The class also includes spouses, parents, and children of the veterans born before

January 1, 1984, directly or derivatively injured as a result of the exposure.

* * * The court also ordered notice by mail, print media, radio and television to be provided to class members, providing in part that persons who wished to opt out must do so by May 1, 1984.

Trial of the class claims was to begin on May 7, 1984. On the eve of trial, the parties reached a settlement. The settlement provided that defendants would pay $180 million into a settlement fund, $10 million of which would indemnify defendants against future state court actions alleging the same claims. The settlement provided that "[t]he Class specifically includes persons who have not yet manifested injury." Additionally, the settlement specifically stated that the district court would "retain jurisdiction over the Fund pending its final disposition."

The district court held fairness hearings throughout the country, and approved the settlement as fair, reasonable and adequate. The court rejected the motion to certify a subclass of those class members who objected to terms of the settlement. The court concluded that "[n]o purpose would have been served by appointing counsel for a subclass of disappointed claimants except to increase expenses to the class and delay proceedings."

Seventy-five percent of the $180 million was to be distributed directly " 'to exposed veterans who suffer from long-term total disabilities and to the surviving spouses or children of exposed veterans who have died.' " "A claimant would qualify for compensation by establishing exposure to Agent Orange and death or disability not 'predominately' caused by trauma...." Payments were to be made for ten years, beginning January 1, 1985 and ending December 31, 1994:

> No payment will be made for death or disability occurring after December 31, 1994. Payment will be made for compensable deaths occurring both before and after January 1, 1985. Payments will be made for compensable disability to the extent that the period of disability falls within the ten years of the program's operation.

"Most of the remaining [25%] of the settlement fund established the Agent Orange Class Assistance Program, ... which made grants to agencies serving Vietnam veterans and their families." Explaining the creation of this kind of fund, Judge Weinstein stated that it was "[t]he most practicable and equitable method of distributing benefits to" those claimants who did not meet eligibility criteria for cash payments.

We affirmed class certification, settlement approval and much of the distribution plan. We rejected challenges to class certification, concluding that "class certification was justified under Rule 23(b)(3) due to the centrality of the military contractor defense." We specifically rejected an attack based on adequacy of representation, again based on the military contractor defense which, we reasoned, "would have precluded recovery by all plaintiffs, irrespective of the strengths, weaknesses, or idiosyncrasies of their claims." We additionally concluded that the notice scheme devised by Judge Weinstein was the "best notice practicable" under Federal Rule of Civil Procedure 23(c)(2). Finally, we affirmed the settlement as fair, reasonable and adequate, given the serious weaknesses of the plaintiffs' claims.

In 1989 and 1990, two purported class actions, Ivy v. Diamond Shamrock Chemicals Co. and Hartman v. Diamond Shamrock Chemicals Co., were filed in Texas state courts. These suits, on behalf of Vietnam veterans exposed to Agent Orange,[3] sought compensatory and punitive damages against the same companies as in the settled suit. The plaintiffs alleged that their injuries manifested only after the May 7, 1984 settlement. Additionally, the *Ivy/Hartman* plaintiffs expressly disclaimed any reliance on federal law, asserting only state law claims. Nonetheless, the defendants removed the actions to federal court on the grounds that these claims had already been asserted and litigated in federal court. The MDL Panel transferred the actions to Judge Weinstein in the Eastern District of New York.

* * *

[Plaintiffs argued] that it was unfair to bind them to the settlement when their injuries were not manifested until after the settlement had been reached. The district court rejected this argument, based on the following reasoning:

> All of the courts which considered the Agent Orange Settlement were fully cognizant of the conflict arguments now hypothesized by the plaintiffs and took steps to minimize the problem in the way they arranged for long-term administration of the Settlement Fund.

> In many cases the conflict between the interests of present and future claimants is more imagined than real. In the instant case, for example, the injustice wrought upon the plaintiffs is nonexistent. *These plaintiffs, like all class members who suffer death or disability before the end of 1994, are eligible for compensation from the Agent Orange Payment Fund.* The relevant latency periods and the age of the veterans ensure that almost all valid claims will be revealed before that time.

> Even when it is proper and necessary for the courts to be solicitous of the interests of future claimants, the courts cannot ignore the interests of presently injured plaintiffs as well as defendants in achieving a settlement. Class action settlements simply will not occur if the parties cannot set definitive limits on defendants' liability. Making settlement of Rule 23 suits too difficult will work harms upon plaintiffs, defendants, the courts, and the general public.

The district court therefore dismissed the *Ivy/Hartman* litigation.

3. Two plaintiffs in the *Ivy* litigation alleged injuries stemming from Agent Orange exposure while acting in a civilian capacity, and thus were not members of the class bound by the 1984 settlement. Their claims were severed from the claims of the other plaintiffs.

We affirmed the district court's dismissal. *Ivy/Hartman II*, 996 F.2d 1425, 1439 [(2d Cir.1993)]. * * *

We * * * addressed plaintiffs' argument that they were not members of the prior class, because they were not "injured" as the term was used in the class definition. We concluded that, for the purposes of the Agent Orange litigation, "injury occurs when a deleterious substance enters a person's body, even though its adverse effects are not immediately apparent." We emphasized that the plaintiffs in the original suit had sought to include such "at-risk" plaintiffs, over defendants' objections, and that we had already affirmed the inclusion of these plaintiffs in the class.

We likewise rejected plaintiffs' argument that their due process rights were violated because they were denied adequate representation and adequate notice in the prior action. We reasoned that "providing individual notice and opt-out rights to persons who are unaware of an injury would probably do little good." We concluded that the plaintiffs were adequately represented in the prior action, and that a subclass of future claimants was unnecessary " 'because of the way [the settlement] was structured to cover future claimants.' "

Shortly before our decision in *Ivy/Hartman II*, the $10 million set aside for indemnification from state court Agent Orange judgments was transferred to the Class Assistance Program, because the district court deemed such a fund unnecessary. The distribution activities had begun in 1988, and concluded in June 1997. During the ten year period of the settlement, $196.5 million was distributed as cash payments to approximately 52,000 class members. The program paid approximately $52 million to "after-manifested" claimants, whose deaths or disabilities occurred after May 7, 1984. Approximately $71.3 million of the fund was distributed through the Class Assistance Program.

[In August, 1998, Joe Isaacson sued the chemical manufacturers who produced Agent Orange in New Jersey state court. Isaacson had served in Vietnam in 1968–69 in the Air Force, working on planes that sprayed Agent Orange. In 1996, he was diagnosed with non-Hodkins Lymphoma, and in his suit he alleged state-law claims that defendants were liable for his condition. In February, 1999, Daniel Stephenson sued the same defendants in federal court in Louisiana. He had served in Vietnam from 1965 to 1970 as a helicopter pilot, and was in regular contact with Agent Orange during that time. In February, 1998, he was diagnosed with multiple myeloma, a bone marrow cancer.

Defendants removed Isaacson's suit to federal court, and the federal court denied his motion to remand. The MDL Panel transferred both Stephenson's and Isaacson's suits to Judge Weinstein, who consolidated them.]

Defendants moved to dismiss under Federal Rule of Civil Procedure 12(b)(6), asserting that plaintiffs' claims were barred by the 1984 class action settlement and subsequent final judgment. Judge Weinstein granted this motion from the bench following argument, rejecting plaintiffs' argument that they were inadequately represented and concluding that plaintiffs' suit was an impermissible collateral attack on the prior settlement.

Because we disagree with this conclusion, based on the Supreme Court's holdings in *Amchem* and *Ortiz*, we must vacate the district court's dismissal and remand for further proceedings.

II. DISCUSSION

* * *

Collateral Attack

The parties devote much energy to debating the permissibility of a collateral attack in this case. Plaintiffs assert that, since the Supreme Court's decision in Hansberry v. Lee, 311 U.S. 32, 61 S.Ct. 115, 85 L.Ed. 22 (1940) [*supra* p. 291], courts have allowed collateral attacks on class action judgments based upon due process concerns. Defendants strenuously disagree and contend that to allow plaintiffs' suit to go forward, in the face of the 1984 global settlement, would "violate defendants' right to due process of law." Defendants likewise strenuously argue that the district court's injunction against future litigation prevents these appellants from maintaining their actions. While it is true that "[a]n injunction must be obeyed until modified or dissolved, and its unconstitutionality is no defense to disobedience," defendants' injunction-based argument misses the point. The injunction was part and parcel of the judgment that plaintiffs contend failed to afford them adequate representation. If plaintiffs' inadequate representation allegations prevail, as we so conclude, the judgment, which includes the injunction on which defendants rely, is not binding as to these plaintiffs.

Defendants contend that Supreme Court precedent permits a collateral attack on a class action judgment "only where there has been no prior determination of absent class members' due process rights." According to defendants, because the "due process rights of absent class members have been extensively litigated in the Agent Orange litigation," these plaintiffs cannot now attack those prior determinations. We reject defendants' arguments and conclude that plaintiffs' collateral attack, which seeks only to prevent the prior settlement from operating as res judicata to their claims, is permissible.

First, even if, as defendants contend, collateral attack is only permitted where there has been no prior determination of the absent class members' rights, plaintiffs' collateral attack is allowed. It is true that, on direct appeal and in the *Ivy/Hartman* litigation, we previously concluded that there was adequate representation of all class members in the original Agent Orange settlement. However, neither this Court nor the district court has addressed specifically the adequacy of representation for those members of the class whose injuries manifested after depletion of the settlements funds. See *Ivy/Hartman II*, 996 F.2d at 1436 (creating a subclass of future claimants was unnecessary because the settlement covered such claimants); *Ivy/Hartman I*, 781 F.Supp. at 919 ("These plaintiffs, like all class members *who suffer death or disability before the end of 1994*, are eligible for compensation from the Agent Orange Payment Fund." (emphasis added.)) Therefore, even accepting defendants' argument, plaintiffs' suit can go forward because there has been no prior adequacy of representation determination with respect to individuals whose claims arise after the depletion of the settlement fund.[6]

Second, the propriety of a collateral attack such as this is amply supported by precedent. In Hansberry v. Lee, 311 U.S. 32, 61 S.Ct. 115, 85 L.Ed. 22 (1940), the Supreme Court entertained a collateral attack on an Illinois state court class action judgment that purported to bind the plaintiffs. The Court held that class action judgments can only bind absent class members where "the interests of those not joined are of the same class as the interests of those who are, and where it is considered that the latter fairly represent the former in the prosecution of the litigation." Additionally, we have previously stated that a "[j]udgment in a class action is not secure from collateral attack unless the absentees were adequately and vigorously represented."

Allowing plaintiffs' suit would be consistent with many other circuit decisions recognizing the ability of later plaintiffs to attack the adequacy of representation in an earlier class action. For example, the Fifth Circuit holds:

> To answer the question whether the class representative adequately represented the class so that the judgment in the class suit will bind the absent members of the class requires a two-pronged inquiry: (1) Did the trial court in the first suit correctly determine, initially, that the representative would adequately represent the class? and (2) Does it appear, after the termination of the suit, that the class representative adequately protected the interest of the class? The first question involves us in a collateral review of the ... [trial] court's determination to permit the suit to proceed as a class action with [the named plaintiff] as the representative, while the second involves a review of the class representative's conduct of the entire suit—an inquiry which is not required to be made by the trial court but which is appropriate in a collateral attack on the judgment....

---

6. Defendants rely heavily on a recent Ninth Circuit decision, Epstein v. MCA, Inc., 179 F.3d 641 (9th Cir.1999), in support of their limited collateral review theory. *Epstein* held that a collateral attack is available only "to consider whether the procedures in the prior litigation afforded the party against whom the earlier judgment is asserted a 'full and fair opportunity' to litigate the claim or issue." According to the Ninth Circuit,

> Due process requires that an absent class member's right to adequate representation be protected by the adoption of the

appropriate procedures by the certifying court and by the courts that review its determinations; due process does not require collateral second-guessing of those determinations and that review.

Here, neither the district court nor this Court has determined the adequacy of representation with respect to these plaintiffs whose injuries did not arise until after the settlement expired. Without adopting the Ninth Circuit's decision in *Epstein*, we conclude that plaintiffs' collateral attack is proper even under its standard.

Gonzales v. Cassidy, 474 F.2d 67, 72 (5th Cir.1973).

Defendants' citation to Federated Department Stores, Inc. v. Moitie, 452 U.S. 394, 101 S.Ct. 2424, 69 L.Ed.2d 103 (1981) [supra p. 1111], is unavailing. According to that case, a "judgment merely voidable because based upon an erroneous view of the law is not open to collateral attack, but can be corrected only by a direct review and not by bringing another action upon the same cause [of action]." Defendants' reliance on this case misperceives plaintiffs' argument. Plaintiffs do not attack the merits or finality of the settlement itself, but instead argue that they were not proper parties to that judgment. If plaintiffs were not proper parties to that judgment, as we conclude below, res judicata cannot defeat their claims. Further, such collateral review would not, as defendants maintain, violate defendants' due process rights by exposing them to double liability. Exposure to liability here is not duplicative if plaintiffs were never proper parties to the prior judgment in the first place.

We therefore hold that a collateral attack to contest the application of res judicata is available. We turn next to the merits of this attack.

Due Process Considerations and Res Judicata

The doctrine of res judicata dictates that "a final judgment on the merits of an action precludes the parties or their privies from relitigating issues that were or could have been raised in that action." Res judicata ordinarily applies "if the earlier decision was (1) a final judgment on the merits, (2) by a court of competent jurisdiction, (3) in a case involving the same parties or their privies, and (4) involving the same cause of action."

Plaintiffs' argument focuses on element number three in the res judicata analysis: whether they are parties bound by the settlement. Plaintiffs rely primarily on the United States Supreme Court's decisions in Amchem Products, Inc. v. Windsor, 521 U.S. 591, 117 S.Ct. 2231, 138 L.Ed.2d 689 (1997), and Ortiz v. Fibreboard Corp., 527 U.S. 815, 119 S.Ct. 2295, 144 L.Ed.2d 715 (1999).

In *Amchem*, the Supreme Court confronted, on direct appeal, a challenge to class certification for settlement purposes in an asbestos litigation. The class defined in the complaint included both individuals who were presently injured as well as individuals who had only been exposed to asbestos. The Supreme Court held that this "sprawling" class was improperly certified under Federal Rules of Civil Procedure 23(a) and (b). Specifically, the Court held that Rule 23(a)(4)'s requirement that the named parties " 'will fairly and adequately protect the interests of the class' " had not been satisfied. The Court reasoned that

> named parties with diverse medical conditions sought to act on behalf of a single giant class rather than on behalf of discrete subclasses. In significant respects, the interests of those within the single class are not aligned. Most saliently, for the currently injured, the critical goal is generous immediate payments. That goal tugs

against the interest of exposure-only plaintiffs in ensuring an ample, inflation-protected fund for the future.

Amchem also implied, but did not decide, that the notice provided to exposure-only class members was likewise inadequate. The Court stated that, because many exposure-only individuals, may not be aware of their exposure or realize the ramifications of exposure, "those without current afflictions may not have the information or foresight needed to decide, intelligently, whether to stay in or opt out."

In *Ortiz*, the Supreme Court again addressed a settlement-only class action in the asbestos litigation context. *Ortiz*, however, involved a settlement-only limited fund class under Rule 23(b)(1)(B). The Supreme Court ultimately held that the class could not be maintained under Rule 23(b)(1)(B), because "the limit of the fund was determined by treating the settlement agreement as dispositive, an error magnified" by conflicted counsel. In so holding, *Ortiz* noted that "it is obvious after Amchem that a class divided between holders of present and future claims (some of the latter involving no physical injury and attributable to claimants not yet born) requires division into homogeneous subclasses under Rule 23(c)(4)(B), with separate representation to eliminate conflicting interests of counsel."

Res judicata generally applies to bind absent class members except where to do so would violate due process. Due process requires adequate representation "at all times" throughout the litigation, notice "reasonably calculated ... to apprise interested parties of the pendency of the action," and an opportunity to opt out. Shutts, 472 U.S. at 811–12, 105 S.Ct. 2965.

Both Stephenson and Isaacson fall within the class definition of the prior litigation: they served in the United States military, stationed in Vietnam, between 1961 and 1972, and were allegedly injured by exposure to Agent Orange. However, they both learned of their allegedly Agent Orange-related injuries only after the 1984 settlement fund had expired in 1994. Because the prior litigation purported to settle all future claims, but only provided for recovery for those whose death or disability was discovered prior to 1994, the conflict between Stephenson and Isaacson and the class representatives becomes apparent. No provision was made for post–1994 claimants, and the settlement fund was permitted to terminate in 1994. *Amchem* and *Ortiz* suggest that Stephenson and Isaacson were not adequately represented in the prior Agent Orange litigation.[8] Those cases indicate that a class which purports to represent both present and future claimants may encounter internal conflicts.

8. We also note that plaintiffs likely received inadequate notice. [Phillips Petroleum v.] Shutts [472 U.S. 797, 105 S.Ct. 2965, 86 L.Ed.2d 628 (1985)], provides that adequate notice is necessary to bind absent class members. As described earlier, Amchem indicates that effective notice could likely not ever be given to exposure-only class members. Because we have already concluded that these plaintiffs were inadequately represented, and thus were not proper parties to the prior litigation, we need not definitively decide whether notice was adequate.

Defendants contend that there was, in fact, no conflict because all class members' claims were equally meritless and would have been defeated by the "military contractor" defense. This argument misses the mark. At this stage, we are only addressing whether plaintiffs' claims should be barred by res judicata. We are therefore concerned only with whether they were afforded due process in the earlier litigation. Part of the due process inquiry (and part of the Rule 23(a) class certification requirements) involves assessing adequacy of representation and intra-class conflicts. The ultimate merits of the claims have no bearing on whether the class previously certified adequately represented these plaintiffs.

Because these plaintiffs were inadequately represented in the prior litigation, they were not proper parties and cannot be bound by the settlement. We therefore must vacate the district court's dismissal and remand for further proceedings. We, of course, express no opinion as to the ultimate merits of plaintiffs' claims.

Notes and Questions

1. The Supreme Court granted certiorari in *Stephenson*, but ultimately issued a per curiam decision, affirming the judgment of the Second Circuit on Stephenson's suit by an equally divided court, Justice Stevens not participating. Counsel for plaintiffs characterized this result as a "fabulous total victory" because it did not vacate the Second Circuit's decision regarding Stephenson's suit, but counsel for Dow pointed out that the Supreme Court's decision had no precedential value. See Mauro, High Court Affirms 2nd Circuit in Agent Orange Case, S.F. Recorder, June 10, 2003, at 3.

2. As an alternative to relying on state courts to give effect to res judicata, federal courts that enter class action judgments can enjoin subsequent litigation filed by class members that is covered by the preclusive effect of the judgment if they retain jurisdiction over the action for purposes of enforcing their decrees. See In the Matter of VMS Securities Litig., 103 F.3d 1317, 1324 (7th Cir.1996) ("in the context of complex class action litigation, a federal district court may appropriately use the All Writs Act to * * * enjoin the prosecution of subsequent state court claims in order to enforce its ongoing orders against relitigation and to guard the integrity of its prior rulings over which it had expressly retained jurisdiction"); compare Grimes v. Vitalink Communications Corp., 17 F.3d 1553 (3d Cir.1994) (questioning whether failure to opt out would suffice to provide personal jurisdiction for such an injunction, at least if entered by a state court).

3. Does *Stephenson* allow collateral attacks so liberally that the finality of class action judgments is threatened? That should not be the case if the *Stephenson* holding is limited to its facts. The finding that the class representatives were inadequate flowed directly from Amchem Products, Inc. v. Windsor, 521 U.S. 591 (1997), which overturned the certification of a settlement class action on behalf of persons exposed to asbestos (including both those who presently manifested injury and "futures plaintiffs" who have not). The court found an inherent conflict between the interests of these two groups since each would want a larger share of the settlement. The impact of *Amchem* was that "futures plaintiffs" should not be combined

in a class action with persons who have manifested injury (unless possibly by subclasses and represented by different attorneys). Thus the combining of both groups in the Agent Orange class action could simply not stand after *Amchem*. This situation in which a clear bright-line precedent now demonstrates inadequacy of representation in an earlier class action judgment is not likely to occur in many cases. See Hoffman, Syngenta, Stephenson and the Federal Judicial Injunctive Power, 37 Akron L. Rev. 605 (2004).

In Hospital Management Associates, Inc. v. Shell Oil Co., 591 S.E.2d 611 (S.Car.S.Ct.2004), the court upheld summary judgment according full faith and credit to two nationwide class action settlements in other state courts despite the assertion of opt-out class members that they were collaterally entitled to attack the judgments. Noting the inconclusive Supreme Court handling of *Stephenson*, the court commented:

> In our opinion, there are important policy considerations favoring both limited and broad collateral review. Certainly, in the specialized context of class action litigation, the significant interest in efficiency and finality favor limited review. If the due process issues are fully and fairly litigated and necessarily decided by the rendering court, then the strong interest in finality militates in favor of an extremely limited collateral review. Without limited review, a nationwide class action could be vulnerable to collateral actions in the 49 other states in which it was not litigated initially. It would seem to be a waste of judicial resources to require reviewing courts to conduct an extensive substantive review when one has already been undertaken in a sister state. As the Ohio court stated in Fine v. America Online: "To allow substantive collateral attacks would be counter intuitive to [the] procedural relief that a class-action suit is intended to afford our judicial system nationwide." 743 N.E.2d at 421–22.

> On the other hand, there is a fundamental interest in not allowing constitutionally infirm judgments to be enforced. It would be troublesome to enforce a class action settlement against parties over whom the rendering court did not have personal jurisdiction. We note, however * * * that direct appellate review of a class action is the appropriate vehicle to correct whatever errors may have been made at the trial court level.

> We hold that in a case such as this one, only a limited collateral review is appropriate. It would run counter to the class action goals of efficiency and finality to allow successive reviews of issues that were, in fact, fully and fairly litigated in the rendering court. Moreover, second-guessing the fully litigated decisions of our sister courts would violated the spirit of full faith and credit.

> * * * [W]hat this limited review entails is "an examination of *procedural* due process and nothing more." Fine v. America Online, 743 N.E.2d at 421. More specifically, we must determine: (1) whether there were safeguards in place to guarantee sufficient notice and adequate representation; and (2) whether such safeguards were, in fact applied.

The court then proceeded to examine the notice given (an extensive multimedia campaign which the court found to be constitutionally sufficient) and the adequacy of representation. On that score, it found that the courts, in contrast to *Amchem*, had procedures in place to ensure adequate representation and that they were implemented throughout the litigations. It therefore found that full faith and credit should be accorded the two class action settlement judgments.

3. In *Stephenson* the court says that the original class action provided inadequate representation for those whose injuries manifested themselves after 1994. What solution could there be to such a problem? What should the original class action have provided to overcome this difficulty? Compare the way in which the settlement regimes in *Amchem* and *Ortiz* addressed the question of future claims. Keep in mind that, at the time the class-action settlement was arranged, no class member would know whether he would become sick before 1994, and some might consider the coverage for another decade reasonable protection. Consider the analysis in Nagareda, Administering Adequacy in Class Representation, 82 Texas L. Rev. 287, 322 (2003);

> The ten-year term for cash benefits under the Agent Orange class settlement appears far from arbitrary, however, when one considers that any veteran would have had an exceedingly weak scientific case on the causation element, at least as of 1984, and that the ten-year term for cash benefits extended to more than two decades after the last alleged exposure of class members.

4. The court in *Stephenson* also says in footnote 8 that notice may have been inadequate in the original Agent Orange litigation with regard to these plaintiffs. But it had earlier held that notice in that suit was adequate in the *Ivy/Hartman* litigation (996 F.2d at 1435):

> In the instant case, society's interest in the efficient and fair resolution of large-scale litigation outweighs the gains from individual notice and opt-out rights, whose benefits here are conjectural at best. As appellants correctly note, providing individual notice and opt-out rights to persons who are unaware of an injury would probably do little good.

Why should the *Stephenson* plaintiffs be treated differently for purposes of notice?

5. The Class Action Fairness Act of 2005 requires defendants to give notice of proposed settlements to state and federal officials, and provides that if this notice is not given, class members may choose not to be bound. 28 U.S.C.A. § 1715(e)(1). Would this solve the due process problem?

6. Besides notice and the right to opt out of the class action, is there any other way in which to protect the interests of class members? Read Rule 23(e). It requires court approval of any class action settlement, and calls for careful examination of the proposed settlement. Would such review by the court strengthen the case for binding class members?

In Matsushita Elec. Indus. Co. v. Epstein, 516 U.S. 367, 116 S.Ct. 873, 134 L.Ed.2d 6 (1996), two class actions were filed on behalf of shareholders claiming improprieties in relation to a merger of the company. One was in federal court, and asserted claims that were subject to exclusive federal jurisdiction. The other, in a Delaware state court, asserted state-law claims. The Supreme Court ruled that a judgment entered in the Delaware state court based on a court-approved settlement of that case was entitled to enforcement under 28 U.S.C.A. § 1738 in the federal-court class action. In reaching this result, the Court noted that the Delaware Supreme Court had held in another case that courts called upon to approve class-action settlements had to ensure that the class members were adequately represented, and that the state-court judge had reviewed the proposed settlement before approving it. Should that review suffice? Compare Kahan & Silberman, Matsushita and Beyond: The Role of State Courts in Class Actions Involving Exclusive Federal Claims, 1996 Sup.Ct.Rev. 219 (arguing that when class members have an opportunity to object to a proposed settlement they should not be permitted to attack it in a collateral proceeding) with Woolley, The Availability of Collateral Attack for Inadequate Representation in Class Suits, 79 Tex.L.Rev. 383 (2000) (arguing that there must be a constitutional right to litigate adequacy of representation in a later proceeding).

4. *Collateral Estoppel Against the Government*

UNITED STATES v. MENDOZA

Supreme Court of the United States, 1984.
464 U.S. 154, 104 S.Ct. 568, 78 L.Ed.2d 379.

Justice Rehnquist delivered the opinion of the Court.

[A Filipino national residing in the U.S. petitioned in 1978 for naturalization under a World War II statute that granted foreigners who served honorably in the U.S. military during the war the right to apply for and receive U.S. citizenship. The act was repealed after the war, and only applicants applying for citizenship prior to December 31, 1946 were entitled to naturalization. The U.S. immigration office in the Philippines was closed between October 1945 and August 1946. Mendoza argued that this fact excused his delay in petitioning. He relied on a 1975 decision of a district court holding that 68 Filipino war veterans were entitled to naturalization despite delay due to the closure of the immigration office in the Philippines, which it found to violate their rights to due process. The court of appeals held that the government was estopped to relitigate this issue. The Supreme Court reversed.]

We have long recognized that "the Government is not in a position identical to that of a private litigant," INS v. Hibi, 414 U.S. 5, 8, 94 S.Ct. 19, 21, 38 L.Ed.2d 7 (1973) (per curiam), both because of the geographic breadth of government litigation and also, most importantly, because of the nature of the issues the government litigates. It is not open to serious dispute that the government is a party to a far greater number of cases on a nationwide basis than even the most litigious private entity; in 1982, the United States was a party to more than 75,000 of the 206,193 filings in the United States District Courts. In the same year the United States was a party to just under 30% of the civil cases appealed from the District Courts to the Court of Appeals. Government litigation frequently involves legal questions of substantial public importance; indeed, because the proscriptions of the United States Constitution are so generally directed at governmental action, many constitutional questions can arise only in the context of litigation to which the government is a party. Because of those facts the government is more likely than any private party to be involved in lawsuits against different parties which nonetheless involve the same legal issues.

A rule allowing nonmutual collateral estoppel against the government in such cases would substantially thwart the development of important questions of law by freezing the first final decision rendered on a particular legal issue. Allowing only one final adjudication would deprive this Court of the benefit it receives from permitting several courts of appeals to explore a difficult question before this Court grants certiorari. Indeed, if nonmutual estoppel were routinely applied against the government, this Court would have to revise its practice of waiting for a conflict to develop before granting the government's petitions for certiorari.

The Solicitor General's policy for determining when to appeal an adverse decision would also require substantial revision. The Court of Appeals faulted the government in this case for failing to appeal a decision that it now contends is erroneous. But the government's litigation conduct in a case is apt to differ from that of a private litigant. Unlike a private litigant who generally does not forego an appeal if he believes that he can prevail, the Solicitor General considers a variety of factors, such as the limited resources of the government and the crowded dockets of the courts, before authorizing an appeal. The application of nonmutual estoppel against the government would force the Solicitor General to abandon those prudential concerns and to appeal every adverse decision in order to avoid foreclosing further review.

In addition to those institutional concerns traditionally considered by the Solicitor General, the panoply of important public issues raised in governmental litigation may quite properly lead successive Administrations of the Executive Branch to take differing positions with respect to the resolution of a particular issue. While the Executive Branch must of course defer to the Judicial Branch for final resolution of questions of constitutional law, the former nonetheless controls the progress of governmental litigation through the federal courts.

* * *

The Court of Appeals did not endorse a routine application of nonmutual collateral estoppel against the government, because it recognized that the government does litigate issues of far-reaching national significance which in some cases, it concluded, might warrant relitigation. But in this case it found no "record evidence" indicating that there was a "crucial need" in the administration of the immigration laws for a redetermination of the due process question. * * * The Court of Appeals did not make clear what sort of "record evidence" would have satisfied it that there *was* a "crucial need" for redetermination of the question in this case, but we pretermit further discussion of that approach; we believe that the standard announced by the Court of Appeals for determining when relitigation of a legal issue is to be permitted is so wholly subjective that it affords no guidance to the courts or to the government. Such a standard leaves the government at sea because it can not possibly anticipate, in determining whether or not to appeal an adverse decision, whether a court will bar relitigation of the issue in a later case. * * *

We hold, therefore, that nonmutual offensive collateral estoppel simply does not apply against the government in such a way as to preclude relitigation of issues such as those involved in this case.[7] The conduct of government litigation in the courts of the United States is sufficiently different from the conduct of private civil litigation in those courts so that what might otherwise be economy interests underlying a broad application of collateral estoppel are outweighed by the constraints which peculiarly affect the government. We think that our conclusion will better allow thorough development of legal doctrine by allowing litigation in multiple forums. Indeed, a contrary result might disserve the economy interests in whose name estoppel is advanced by requiring the government to abandon virtually any exercise of discretion in seeking to review judgments unfavorable to it. The doctrine of res judicata, of course, prevents the government from relitigating the same cause of action against the parties to a prior decision,[8] but beyond that point principles of nonmutual collateral estoppel give way to the policies just stated.

Our holding in this case is consistent with each of our prior holdings to which the parties have called our attention, and which we reaffirm. Today in a companion case we hold that the government may be estopped under certain circumstances from relitigating a question when the parties to the two lawsuits are the same. United States v. Stauffer Chemical Co., 464 U.S. 165, 104 S.Ct. 575, 78 L.Ed.2d 388 (1984); see also Montana v. United States, [440 U.S. 147, 99 S.Ct. 970, 59 L.Ed.2d 210 (1979)]; United States v. Moser, 266 U.S. 236, 45 S.Ct. 66, 69 L.Ed. 262 (1924) [supra p. 1154 n.2]. None of those cases, however, involve the effort of a party to estop the government in the absence of mutuality.

The concerns underlying our disapproval of collateral estoppel against the government are for the most part inapplicable where mutuality is present, as in *Stauffer Chemical, Montana,*[9] and *Moser.* The application of an estoppel when the government is litigating the same issue with the same party avoids the problem of freezing the develop-

---

7. The government does not base its argument on the exception to the doctrine of collateral estoppel for "unmixed questions of law" arising in "successive cases involving unrelated subject matter." Montana v. United States, supra, 440 U.S., at 162, 99 S.Ct., at 978. Our holding in no way depends on that exception.

8. In Nevada v. United States, 463 U.S. 110, 103 S.Ct. 2906, 77 L.Ed.2d 509 (1983), we applied principles of res judicata against the United States as to one class of claimants who had not been parties to an earlier adjudication, but we recognized that this result obtained in the unique context of "a comprehensive adjudication of water rights intended to settle once and for all the ques-

tion of how much of the Truckee River each of the litigants was entitled to."

9. In *Montana* an individual contractor brought an initial action to challenge Montana's gross receipts tax in state court, and the federal government brought a second action in federal court raising the same challenge. The government totally controlled and financed the state-court action; thus for all practical purposes there was mutuality of parties in the two cases. "The United States had a sufficient 'laboring oar' in the conduct of the state-court litigation," Montana v. United States, 440 U.S. at 155, 99 S.Ct. at 974, to be constituted a "party" in all but a technical sense.

ment of the law because the government is still free to litigate that issue in the future with some other party. And, where the parties are the same, estopping the government spares a party that has already prevailed once from having to relitigate—a function it would not serve in the present circumstances. We accordingly hold that the Court of Appeals was wrong in applying nonmutual collateral estoppel against the government in this case.

Notes and Questions

1. In a companion case to *Mendoza*, United States v. Stauffer Chemical Co., 464 U.S. 165, 104 S.Ct. 575, 78 L.Ed.2d 388 (1984) (supra p. 1156 n. 6), the Court held that "the doctrine of mutual defensive collateral estoppel is applicable against the government to preclude relitigation of the same issue already litigated against the same party in another case involving virtually identical facts." The issue was whether the Environmental Protection Agency could use private contractors to inspect private plants for compliance with its regulations. The government argued that collateral estoppel should not apply to this "unmixed question of law," but the Court disagreed: "we think that applying an exception to the doctrine of mutual defensive estoppel in this case would substantially frustrate the doctrine's purpose of protecting litigants from burdensome relitigation and of promoting judicial economy." Note, Nonmutual Issue Preclusion Against States, 109 Harv.L.Rev. 792 (1996), critiques *Mendoza* for its "blunt approach" and urges a presumption against, rather than a categorical ban on, estoppel against state governments. The Note chronicles the problems that *Mendoza* has wrought in the federal courts in the form of relitigation of matters thought settled in a given circuit, and the ways in which state courts have reacted to the doctrine. Concluding that since the likelihood of divergent lower court interpretations is less, and that the burden on states of allowing estoppel would also be less, the Note concludes that a flat ban is too strong.

2. The opinion refers to issues "such as those involved in this case," in denying collateral estoppel. Is there any situation in which *Mendoza* might permit offensive collateral estoppel against the U.S.?

3. Why shouldn't *Mendoza* apply to any defendant subject to multiple litigation on the same issues, for example, automobile manufacturers? How different is the government from other litigants? Recall Hardy v. Johns–Manville Sales Corp., supra p. 1146. That case involved problems of nonmutual collateral estoppel in the context of asbestos claims which have run into the tens of thousands. Are issues of foreseeability, or other problems of fairness, so different in holding these repeat litigants to be bound by the outcomes of earlier cases?

4. The Eighth Circuit in United States v. Gurley, 43 F.3d 1188, 1198 n. 2 (8th Cir. 1994), viewed the government exception as an "unsettled issue of law" in light of the different results in *Mendoza* and *Stauffer Chemical Co.* It did not reach the issue, resolving the appeal on other grounds. Some courts have refused to follow the government exception. See, e.g., U.S. v. Butner, 2000 WL 1842410, *3 (W.D.Mo. 2000) (finding the government estopped from prosecuting defendant for testifying falsely in another case in which it had taken the contradictory position that his testimony was not

material). State of Alaska v. United Cook Inlet Drift Association, 895 F.2d 947 (Alaska S.Ct. 1995), a case challenging regulations of the state board of fisheries, rejected the exception to preclude offensive use of collateral estoppel in all cases against the state. It distinguished state from federal litigation since the state attorney general litigates in a single jurisdiction and is faced with a smaller volume of litigation, and here the state had a wide variety of options even if it were collaterally estopped.

5. Can it legitimately be argued that the government should be *more* subject to preclusion with regard to legal issues than private parties? For an argument that due to its size and power, the government should be required to adhere to decisions about the legality of its conduct, see Note, Collateral Estoppel and Nonacquiescence: Precluding Government Relitigation in the Pursuit of Litigant Equality, 99 Harv.L.Rev. 847 (1986). As this note points out, the government currently makes conscious choices to refuse to follow judicial decisions holding its conduct illegal except with respect to a litigant who has successfully challenged its actions in court. This practice is called "nonacquiescence." After *Mendoza,* does the government have a license to pursue such a strategy? Should it?

In some instances, the lack of connection between government agencies would make preclusion a questionable policy. Where one agency litigates and loses an issue, it may be inappropriate to bind another independent agency. For an argument that, where agencies have overlapping authority, privity between them should be found, see Comment, Interagency Privity and Claim Preclusion, 57 U.Chi.L.Rev. 195 (1990).

Index

References are to Pages

References are to Pages

†

0–314–15613–5

90000

9 780314 156136